Organizational Behavior

ISBN: 978-1-947172-71-5

OpenStax
Rice University
6100 Main Street MS-375
Houston, Texas 77005

To learn more about OpenStax, visit https://openstax.org.
Individual print copies and bulk orders can be purchased through our website.

HARDCOVER BOOK ISBN-10	**1-947172-71-9**
HARDCOVER BOOK ISBN-13	**978-1-947172-71-5**
PAPERBACK BOOK ISBN-10	**1-947172-73-5**
PAPERBACK BOOK ISBN-13	**978-1-947172-73-9**
PDF VERSION ISBN-10	**1-947172-72-7**
PDF VERSION ISBN-13	**978-1-947172-72-2**

10 9 8 7 6 5 4 3 2 1

Printed by
XanEdu
17177 Laurel Park Dr., Suite 233
Livonia, MI 48152
800-562-2147
www.xanedu.com

OpenStax

OpenStax provides free, peer-reviewed, openly licensed textbooks for introductory college and Advanced Placement® courses and low-cost, personalized courseware that helps students learn. A nonprofit ed tech initiative based at Rice University, we're committed to helping students access the tools they need to complete their courses and meet their educational goals.

Rice University

OpenStax, OpenStax CNX, and OpenStax Tutor are initiatives of Rice University. As a leading research university with a distinctive commitment to undergraduate education, Rice University aspires to path-breaking research, unsurpassed teaching, and contributions to the betterment of our world. It seeks to fulfill this mission by cultivating a diverse community of learning and discovery that produces leaders across the spectrum of human endeavor.

Philanthropic Support

OpenStax is grateful for our generous philanthropic partners, who support our vision to improve educational opportunities for all learners.

Laura and John Arnold Foundation

Arthur and Carlyse Ciocca Charitable Foundation

Ann and John Doerr

Bill & Melinda Gates Foundation

Girard Foundation

Google Inc.

The William and Flora Hewlett Foundation

Rusty and John Jaggers

The Calvin K. Kazanjian Economics Foundation

Charles Koch Foundation

Leon Lowenstein Foundation, Inc.

The Maxfield Foundation

Burt and Deedee McMurtry

Michelson 20MM Foundation

National Science Foundation

The Open Society Foundations

Jumee Yhu and David E. Park III

Brian D. Patterson USA-International Foundation

The Bill and Stephanie Sick Fund

Robin and Sandy Stuart Foundation

The Stuart Family Foundation

Tammy and Guillermo Treviño

TABLE OF CONTENTS

Preface

Welcome to *Organizational Behavior*, an OpenStax resource. This textbook was written to increase student access to high-quality learning materials, maintaining the highest standards of academic rigor at little to no cost.

About OpenStax

OpenStax is a nonprofit based at Rice University, and it's our mission to improve student access to education. Our first openly licensed college textbook was published in 2012, and our library has since scaled to over 30 books for college and AP® courses used by hundreds of thousands of students. OpenStax Tutor, our low-cost personalized learning tool, is being used in college courses throughout the country. Through our partnerships with philanthropic foundations and our alliance with other educational resource organizations, OpenStax is breaking down the most common barriers to learning and empowering students and instructors to succeed.

About OpenStax Resources

Customization

Organizational Behavior is licensed under a Creative Commons Attribution 4.0 International (CC BY) license, which means that you can distribute, remix, and build upon the content, as long as you provide attribution to OpenStax and its content contributors.

Because our books are openly licensed, you are free to use the entire book or pick and choose the sections that are most relevant to the needs of your course. Feel free to remix the content by assigning your students certain chapters and sections in your syllabus, in the order that you prefer. You can even provide a direct link in your syllabus to the sections in the web view of your book.

Instructors also have the option of creating a customized version of their OpenStax book. The custom version can be made available to students in low-cost print or digital form through their campus bookstore. Visit the Instructor Resources section of your book page on openstax.org for more information.

Art Attribution

In *Organizational Behavior,* most art contains attribution to its title, creator, or rights holder, host platform, and license within the caption. Because the art is openly licensed, anyone may reuse the art as long as they provide the same attribution to its original source.

Errata

All OpenStax textbooks undergo a rigorous review process. However, like any professional-grade textbook, errors sometimes occur. Since our books are web based, we can make updates periodically when deemed pedagogically necessary. If you have a correction to suggest, submit it through the link on your book page on openstax.org. Subject matter experts review all errata suggestions. OpenStax is committed to remaining transparent about all updates, so you will also find a list of past errata changes on your book page on openstax.org.

Format

You can access this textbook for free in web view or PDF through openstax.org, and for a low cost in print.

About *Organizational Behavior*

The field of management and organizational behavior exists today in a constant state of evolution and change. Casual readers of publications like the New York Times, The Economist and the Wall Street Journal will learn about the dynamic nature of organizations in today's ever-changing business environment. *Organizational Behavior* is designed to meet the scope and sequence requirements of the introductory course on Organizational Behavior. This is a traditional approach to organizational behavior. The table of contents of this book was designed to address two main themes. What are the variables that affect how, when, where, and why managers perform their jobs? What theories and techniques are used by successful managers at a variety of organizational levels to achieve and exceed objectives effectively and efficiently throughout their careers? Management is a broad business discipline, and the Organizational Behavior course covers many areas such as individual and group behavior at work, as well as organizational processes such as communication in the workplace and managing conflict and negotiation. No one individual can be an expert in all areas of management, so an additional benefit of this text is that specialists in a variety of areas have authored individual chapters. Finally, we all made an effort to present a balanced approach to gender and diversity throughout the text in the examples used, the photographs selected, and the use of both male and female in alternating chapters when referring to generic managers or employees.

Pedagogical Foundation

We have taken a structured approach in the writing of the chapters that reduces inconsistencies throughout and makes selecting topics to match the course syllabus easier for faculty.

Exploring Managerial Careers. Each chapter starts with a profile that describes a manager and illustrates how the content of the chapter is vital for a successful managerial career.

Consistent, integrated learning. Targeted learning outcomes are listed at the beginning of each chapter and then repeated throughout the chapter. The learning outcomes connect to the text and the additional resources that accompany *Organizational Behavior.* After reading each section, students can test their retention by answering the questions in the Concept Checks. Every learning goal is further reinforced by a summary at the end of the chapter.

Hundreds of business examples to bring concepts to life. This book is designed to speak to the typical student. We have done a lot of research about student needs, abilities, experiences, and interests, and then we have shaped the text around them. We have used experiences both inside and outside the classroom to create a book that is both readable and enjoyable. We believe that the real applications found throughout every chapter set the standard for readability and understanding of key concepts.

Learning business terminology, made easy. As students begin to study management, they will explore new words and concepts. To help them learn this language, we define each new term in the chapter, display the terms in bold, and offer a complete glossary at the end of the book.

Applied Features

Rather than provide a dry recitation of facts, we illustrate concepts with contemporary examples. In addition to the in-text examples, we have several boxed features that provide more extensive examples in areas of importance in today's business environment. Each of the boxed features described below includes a series of critical thinking questions to prompt the student to consider the implications of each business strategy.

Ethics in Practice. Ethics in Practice features demonstrate how businesses are responsible not only to the bottom line, but to providing goods and services in a responsible manner.

Managing Change. The turbulent business climate requires companies to adapt their business strategies in response to a variety of economic, social, competitive, and technological forces. The Managing Change feature highlights how businesses have altered their business strategies in response to these forces.

Catching the Entrepreneurial Spirit. This feature highlights the challenges and opportunities available in small businesses and other entrepreneurial ventures.

Managerial Leadership. It is generally agreed that in a turbulent business climate leadership is an important function of management that helps to maximize efficiency and to achieve organizational goals. Leaders initiate action, motivate organizations, provide guidance, build morale, and create a sense of confidence within the organization and to outside stakeholders.

Sustainability and Responsible Management. This feature highlights the knowledge, skills, tools, and self-awareness that are needed to become responsible managers. While the area of corporate social responsibility and sustainability has gained wide general support and commentary, these featured boxed items should provide the reader with insights of how managers can embed responsible practices in their careers.

Activities and Cases That Put Knowledge to Work

Organizational Behavior helps students develop a solid grounding in the skills that they can apply throughout their managerial careers. These skill-building activities and resources help build and polish competencies that future employers will value.

Chapter Review Questions. These questions provide a broad set of challenging questions that students can use to assure themselves that they have mastered the chapter concepts.

Management Skills Application Exercises. These activities at the end of each chapter present real-world challenges and provide assignment material for students to hone their business skills.

Managerial Decision Exercises. These activities provide assignment material that challenge students' decision-making processes. There are a variety of exercises for individual or team assignments.

Critical Thinking Case. The Critical Thinking case in each chapter invites students to explore business strategies of various companies, analyze business decisions, and prepare comments.

Additional Resources

Student and Instructor Resources

We've compiled additional resources for both students and instructors, including Getting Started Guides. Instructor resources require a verified instructor account, which you can apply for when you log in or create your account on openstax.org.

Instructor and student resources are typically available within a few months after the book's initial publication. Take advantage of these resources to supplement your OpenStax book.

Comprehensive instructor's manual. Each component of the instructor's manual is designed to provide maximum guidance for delivering the content in an interesting and dynamic manner. The instructor's manual includes an in-depth lecture outline, which is interspersed with lecture "tidbits" that allow instructors to add timely and interesting enhancements to their lectures.

Test bank. With nearly 1,000 true/false, multiple-choice, fill-in-the-blank, and short-answer questions in our test bank, instructors can customize tests to support a variety of course objectives. The test bank is available in Word format.

PowerPoint lecture slides. The PowerPoint slides provide images and descriptions as a starting place for instructors to build their lectures.

Community Hubs

OpenStax partners with the Institute for the Study of Knowledge Management in Education (ISKME) to offer Community Hubs on OER Commons—a platform for instructors to share community-created resources that support OpenStax books, free of charge. Through our Community Hubs, instructors can upload their own materials or download resources to use in their own courses, including additional ancillaries, teaching material, multimedia, and relevant course content. We encourage instructors to join the hubs for the subjects most relevant to your teaching and research as an opportunity both to enrich your courses and to engage with other faculty.

To reach the Community Hubs, visit **www.oercommons.org/hubs/OpenStax**.

Technology Partners

As allies in making high-quality learning materials accessible, our technology partners offer optional low-cost tools that are integrated with OpenStax books. To access the technology options for your text, visit your book page on openstax.org.

Contributing Authors

J. Stewart Black, INSEAD
David S. Bright, Wright State University
Donald G. Gardner, University of Colorado-Colorado Springs
Eva Hartmann, University of Richmond
Jason Lambert, Texas Woman's University
Laura M. Leduc, James Madison University
Joy Leopold, Webster University
James S. O'Rourke, University of Notre Dame
Jon L. Pierce, University of Minnesota-Duluth
Richard M. Steers, University of Oregon
Siri Terjesen, American University
Joseph Weiss, Bentley University

Reviewers

Susan Adams, Bentley University
Shane Bowyer, Minnesota State University
Kim S. Cameron, University of Michigan
Stephen J. Carroll, University of Maryland
Daniel R. Cillis, Molloy College
Linda Davenport, Klamath Community College
Diana L. Deadrick, Old Dominion University
James J. Freiburger, Southern New Hampshire University
Robert A. Giacalone, John Carroll University
Gregory O. Ginn, Embry-Riddle Aeronautical University
John Goldberg, University of California-Davis

Brian Graham-Moore, University of Texas
Regina Greenwood, Nova University
William F. Grossnickle, East Carolina University
Nell Tabor Hartley, Robert Morris University
Nai H. Lamb, University of Tennessee at Chattanooga
Kristie J. Loescher, University of Texas
Marcia Marriott, Monroe Community College
Therese Madden, Notre Dame de Namur University
Eleonor Moore, Kirtland Community College
Bonnie L. McNeely, Murray State University
Robert McNulty, Bentley University
Jeffrey Muldoon, Emporia State University
Karli Peterson, Colorado State University
Raymond Pfang, Tarrant Community College
Jodell Raymond, Monroe Community College
Richard Savior, SUNY Empire State
Amit Shah, Frostburg State University
Paul L. Starkey, Pennsylvania College of Technology
Carolyn Stevenson, Kaplan University
Dianna L. Stone, University of New Mexico
Maria Vitale, Chaffey College
Valerie Wallingford, Bemidji State University

1

Management and Organizational Behavior

Exhibit 1.1 (leyla.a/ flickr/ Attribution 2.0 Generic (CC BY 2.0))

Introduction

Learning Outcomes

After reading this chapter, you should be able to answer these questions:

1. What is the meaning of work in a societal context?
2. How do recognize and meet the challenges facing managers in the new millennium?
3. What is expected of a manager?
4. What is the role of the behavioral sciences in management and organizations?

EXPLORING MANAGERIAL CAREERS

The Management Challenge at Apple and Google

When Apple was developing iOS 10, a group of 600 engineers was able to debug, develop, and deploy the new programming within two years. Contrarily, Microsoft engineers were able to develop and execute the programming on Vista, but it took considerably longer and was a bigger undertaking, with almost 6,000 engineers at hand. What was the difference?

According to the study conducted by leadership consulting firm Bain & Company, companies like Apple, Google, and Netflix are 40 percent more productive than the average company. Some may think that this is a product of the hiring pool; big companies generally attract a more talented group of recruits. With unique benefits and prowess in the industry, this must be the case. Wrong. Google and Apple have found a way to answer the most fundamental question in management: How do you balance productivity while maintaining employee satisfaction and commitment?

Companies such as Google have approximately the same percentage of "star players" as other companies, but instead of spreading out the talent, they group them dynamically to achieve more throughout the day. This grouping focuses on grouping key players in the most business-critical roles, and is the key to success for the overall company. You've heard the saying "You're only as strong as your weakest link," and in the case of Apple, there were no weak links, making their productivity extremely high overall. To make matters more complicated, the fast-paced workplace and technology changes, including the diversity of employees and the global marketplace, takes a considerable toll on employee expectations, as do the overall stresses of the business performance. Apple is just one example of a company that figured out one of the pieces to this puzzle, but it is illustrative of what is happening in the workplace all around the globe.

Contemporary managers are witnessing changes in technologies, markets, competition, workforce demographics, employee expectations, and ethical standards. At the heart of these changes is the issue of how to manage people effectively. To attain corporate objectives, each manager must discover how to develop and maintain a workforce that can meet today's needs while getting ready for tomorrow's challenges. As a result, managers are asking questions such as:

How can we meet the international competition?
How can we make this organization more effective?
How can we better utilize our human resources?
How can we create a more satisfying and rewarding work environment for all employees?
How can we improve the quality of our products?
How can we improve communication and decision-making processes at work?
How should we evaluate and reward performance?
How can we develop the company leaders of tomorrow?

Questions such as these point to the issue of effective management. That is, what can managers do to improve both organizational and employee performance? Effective management requires an in-depth knowledge of financial management, marketing research and consumer behavior, accounting and control practices, manufacturing and production techniques, and quantitative methods. In addition, however, effective management requires "people skills." That is, a good manager must be able to motivate his employees, to lead skillfully, to make appropriate and timely decisions, to communicate effectively, to organize work, to deal with organizational politics, and to work to develop both employees and the organization as a whole. These issues constitute the subject of this course. We shall examine principles of the behavioral sciences that can help managers improve both their own skills and abilities and those of their subordinates in order to enhance organizational performance and effectiveness.

As a prelude to this analysis, we begin with a brief look at the natures of work and of management. Contemporary challenges are discussed. Next, we consider a model of organizational behavior that will serve as a guide throughout the study of management and organizational behavior. We begin with an examination of work.

1.1 The Nature of Work

1. What is the meaning of work in a societal context?

The Meaning of Work

What is work, and how do people feel about the work they do? These questions may be answered from several perspectives. Perhaps one of the best ways to understand how people feel about their jobs is simply to ask them. A number of years ago Chicago writer Studs Terkel did exactly that. How did the people he interviewed feel about their jobs? Here are some excerpts from his book *Working*.[1]

> I'm a dying breed. . . . A laborer. Strictly muscle work . . . pick it up, put it down, pick it up, put it down . . . you can't take pride any more. You remember when a guy could point to a house he built, how many logs he stacked. He built it and he was proud of it.
>
> **—Steelworker [p. 1]**

> I changed my opinion of receptionists because now I'm one. It wasn't the dumb broad at the front desk who took telephone messages. She had to be something else because I thought I was something else. I was fine until there was a press party. We were having a fairly intelligent conversation. Then they asked me what I did. When I told them, they turned around to find other people with name tags. I wasn't worth bothering with. I wasn't being rejected because of what I said or the way I talked, but simply because of my function.
>
> **—Receptionist [p. 57]**

> People ask me what I do, I say, "I drive a garbage truck for the city." . . . I have nothing to be ashamed of. I put in my eight hours. We make a pretty good salary. I feel I earn my money. . . . My wife's happy; this is the big thing. She doesn't look down at me. I think that's more important than the white-collar guy looking down at me.
>
> **—Sanitation Truck Driver [p. 149]**

> I'm human. I make mistakes like everybody else. If you want a robot, build machines. If you want human beings, that's what I am.
>
> **—Policeman [p. 186]**

> I usually say I'm an accountant. Most people think it's somebody who sits there with a green eyeshade and his sleeves rolled up with a garter, poring over books, adding things—with glasses. I suppose a certified public accountant has status. It doesn't mean much to me. Do I like the job or don't I? That's important.
>
> **—Accountant [p. 351]**

> The boss . . . lost his secretary. She got promoted. So they told this old timekeeper she's to be his secretary-assistant. Oh, she's in her glory. No more money or anything and she's doing two jobs all day long. She's rushin' and runnin' all the time, all day. She's a nervous wreck. And when she asked him to write her up for an award, he refused. That's her reward for being so faithful, obedient.
>
> **—Process Clerk [p. 461]**

Examples such as these—and there are many, many more—show how some employees view their jobs and the work they perform. Obviously, some jobs are more meaningful than others, and some individuals are more easily satisfied than others. Some people live to work, while others simply work to live. In any case, people clearly have strong feelings about what they do on the job and about the people with whom they work. In our study of behavior in organizations, we shall examine what people do, what causes them to do it, and how they feel about what they do. As a prelude to this analysis, however, we should first consider the basic unit of analysis in this study: work itself. What is work, and what functions does it serve in today's society?

Work has a variety of meanings in contemporary society. Often we think of work as paid employment—the exchange of services for money. Although this definition may suffice in a technical sense, it does not adequately describe why work is necessary. Perhaps **work** could be more meaningfully defined as an activity that produces something of value for other people. This definition broadens the scope of work and emphasizes the social context in which the wage-effort bargain transpires. It clearly recognizes that work has purpose—it is productive. Of course, this is not to say that work is necessarily interesting or rewarding or satisfying. On the contrary, we know that many jobs are dull, repetitive, and stressful. Even so, the activities performed do have utility for society at large. One of the challenges of **management** is to discover ways of transforming necessary yet distasteful jobs into more meaningful situations that are more satisfying and rewarding for individuals and that still contribute to organizational productivity and effectiveness.

Functions of Work

We know why work activities are important from an organization's viewpoint. Without work there is no product or service to provide. But why is work important to individuals? What functions does it serve?

First, work serves a rather obvious economic function. In exchange for labor, individuals receive necessary income with which to support themselves and their families. But people work for many reasons beyond simple economic necessity.

Second, work also serves several social functions. The workplace provides opportunities for meeting new people and developing friendships. Many people spend more time at work with their co-workers than they spend at home with their own families.

Third, work also provides a source of social status in the community. One's occupation is a clue to how one is regarded on the basis of standards of importance prescribed by the community. For instance, in the United States a corporate president is generally accorded greater status than a janitor in the same corporation. In China, on the other hand, great status is ascribed to peasants and people from the working class, whereas managers are not so significantly differentiated from those they manage. In Japan, status is first a function of the company you work for and how well-known it is, and then the position you hold. It is important to note here that the status associated with the work we perform often transcends the boundaries of our organization. A corporate president or a university president may have a great deal of status in the community at large because of his position in the organization. Hence, the work we do can simultaneously represent a source of social differentiation and a source of social integration.

Fourth, work can be an important source of identity and self-esteem and, for some, a means for self-actualization. It provides a sense of purpose for individuals and clarifies their value or contribution to society. As Freud noted long ago, "Work has a greater effect than any other technique of living in binding the individual more closely to reality; in his work he is at least securely attached to a part of reality, the human community."[2] Work contributes to self-esteem in at least two ways. First, it provides individuals with an opportunity to demonstrate competence or mastery over themselves and their environment. Individuals discover that they can actually *do* something. Second, work reassures individuals that they are carrying out activities that produce something of value to others—that they have something significant to offer. Without this, the individual feels that he has little to contribute and is thus of little value to society.

We clearly can see that work serves several useful purposes from an individual's standpoint. It provides a degree of economic self-sufficiency, social interchange, social status, self-esteem, and identity. Without this, individuals often experience sensations of powerlessness, meaninglessness, and normlessness—a condition called **alienation**. In work, individuals have the possibility of finding some meaning in their day-to-day activities—if, of course, their work is sufficiently challenging. When employees are not involved in their jobs because the work is not challenging enough, they usually see no reason to apply themselves, which, of course, jeopardizes productivity and organizational effectiveness. This self-evident truth has given rise to a general concern among managers about declining productivity and work values. In fact, concern about this situation has caused many managers to take a renewed interest in how the behavioral sciences can help them solve many of the problems of people at work.

CONCEPT CHECK 

1. Define work.
2. What functions does work serve in modern society?

1.2 The Changing Workplace

2. How do recognize and meet the challenges facing managers in the new millennium?

It has often been said that the only constant in life is change, and nowhere is this truer than in the workplace. As one recent study concluded, "The United States is a competitive location to the extent that firms operating in the U.S. are able to compete successfully in the global economy while supporting high and rising living standards for the average American. Although the U.S. retains profound competitive strengths—for instance, in higher education and entrepreneurship—those strengths are increasingly threatened by weaknesses in areas such as the tax code, basic education, macroeconomic policies, and regulation."[3] Companies face a variety of changes and challenges that will have a profound impact on organizational dynamics and performance. In fact, in many ways these changes and challenges will determine who will survive and prosper into the next century and who will not. Among these challenges are the following:

The Challenge of International Competition

Until the 1980s, many American firms had little in the way of serious international competition. As a result, there was little incentive to innovate and remain efficient and competitive. Many companies became lazy and lost touch with their customers. This situation changed abruptly as companies in Asia and Western Europe developed more sophisticated products and marketing systems and gained significant market shares in home electronics, automobiles, medical equipment, telecommunications, and shipbuilding, to name a few areas. As a result, American companies lost considerable clout—and profitability. In the 1990s and into the new millennium, the lowering of trade barriers and acceptance of trade agreements like NAFTA led corporations to seek less expensive labor overseas. This led to lower costs and the ability to offer products at more competitive prices, but also led to a drop in manufacturing in industries like steel production, a drop in manufacturing of products like iPhones, and the relocation of call centers from the U.S. to India.

If we examine corporate behavior during the early decades of the new millennium, it is not difficult to see some of the reasons for the demise. In short, many North American firms lost their **industrial competitiveness**; that is, they lost their capacity to compete effectively in global markets, or they chose to locate in foreign countries as a way to broaden their reach and become more competitive. Consider the following examples:[4]

During the last year reported, India experienced a 7.5 percent *annual growth rate in real GDP* while China recorded an increase of 6.7 percent. This is a measure of how economies are progressing. Great Britain, France, and Italy all had close to 2 percent increases. At the same time, however, the United States recorded a 3.8 percent annual increase (and Canada had a 3 percent increase), a larger increase after a lethargic recovery from the 2009 financial crisis.

While traditional jobs have shifted to developing countries, countries like the United States and Canada have transformed their economies by incorporating more **technology** and automation as well as having a greater proportion of the workforce in the service sectors. It is anticipated that the coming decades will continue to bring disruption to traditional workplace skills that will result in challenging workers to continually evolve their skills.

Finally, the number of products that were *invented in the United States* but are now primarily *manufactured overseas* has increased dramatically—advances in technology are helping the United States regain the top spot in world manufacturing. There had been a significant decline in our manufacturing sector as less expensive labor in markets like India and China led companies to locate factories there. Since 2010, however, the United States has risen from fourth place to second and is expected to claim the spot as the leading nation by 2020. The major reasons for this are: advanced manufacturing capabilities require fewer "line workers," and having products produced near their major markets reduces transport and time to market.

Considering several indicators of the relative competitiveness of economies using seven metrics, the U.S. performs quite well. The seven metrics are institutions, infrastructure, macroeconomic environment, health and primary education, higher education and training, goods market efficiency, and labor market efficiency. When taking all of these factors into consideration (see **Table 1.1**), the United States ranks very well and has an environment of stable growth. One challenge is that workers will need to be nimble and evolve as new skills arise and will need to embrace continuous education and training as a way of managing their careers.

Global Competitive Index			
Rank	Country/Economy	Score	Distance from Best
1	Switzerland	**5.9**	0.00% from best
2	United States	**5.9**	0.09% from best
3	Singapore	**5.7**	2.60% from best
4	Netherlands	**5.7**	3.34% from best
5	Germany	**5.7**	3.46% from best
6	Hong Kong SAR	**5.5**	5.56% from best

Table 1.1 (Attribution: Copyright Rice University, OpenStax, under CC BY-NC-SA 4.0 license)

Global Competitive Index			
Rank	Country/Economy	Score	Distance from Best
7	Sweden	5.5	5.78% from best
8	United Kingdom	5.5	5.99% from best
9	Japan	5.5	6.19% from best
10	Finland	5.5	6.29% from best
Source: Adapted from World Economic Forum, "Global Competitiveness Index," http://reports.weforum.org/global-competitiveness-index-2017-2018/competitiveness-rankings/#series=GCI, accessed July 19, 2018.			

Table 1.1 (Attribution: Copyright Rice University, OpenStax, under CC BY-NC-SA 4.0 license)

In terms of organizational survival, herein lies what is perhaps management's biggest challenge: how to become more competitive. Greater competitiveness requires an understanding of individuals, groups, and entire organizational systems. Throughout this course, we shall see numerous examples of how companies from around the world are meeting the challenges of global competition. Particular emphasis will be placed on management practices in other countries as a point of comparison.

The Challenge of New Technologies

Although it is common to think of "high tech" as applying only to the aerospace and telecommunications industries, advanced technologies can be found throughout most industries. For example, most of us are familiar with the explosive growth in computing. Both hardware and software change so rapidly that it is difficult for many companies to keep up. Personal computers are being replaced by cell phones that are now faster and more powerful than their predecessors. Cloud computing and access to big data and applications transform data into useful information that is increasingly complex and increasingly user friendly. In November of 1971 Intel launched the first microchip. Today, a modern Intel Skylake processor contains around 1.75 billion transistors—half a million of them would fit on a single transistor from the 4004—and collectively they deliver about 400,000 times as much computing muscle.[5] More and more companies are using computer-based systems and equipment—such as e-mail, real-time messaging and file sharing, PDAs, and cell phones—for communications. As a result, the way in which employees and managers communicate and make decisions is changing dramatically, and the importance of educated and knowledgeable workers is increasing rapidly.

Technological changes also can be seen in the increased use of robotics, expert systems, and computer-integrated manufacturing systems, which have changed the way many products are manufactured today. Such changes affect not only production efficiency and product quality but also the nature of jobs. In many industries, the first-line supervisors are disappearing and being replaced by self-managing work teams who assume responsibility for production scheduling, quality control, and even performance appraisals. All of these technological changes require managers who are capable of effectively implementing technological change in the workplace—managers who can adapt to the technological imperative while still maintaining and developing the organization's human resources. We will examine the role of technology as it relates to organization structure, job design, communication, decision-making, and work-related stress. We will see how some companies successfully adapted to technological change in a way that benefited all parties concerned.

MANAGING CHANGE

Siri Struggles to Keep Up with the Competition

Many executives struggle in the ongoing competitive landscape of technology. With fast-paced changes, staying one step ahead as well as being able to pivot quickly to respond to action are two critical elements to successful leadership.

Apple Inc. has made its third change in the past year to the leadership of the artificial intelligence voice-assistance system Siri. Due to many factors, including being outperformed by the competition such as Google Assistant and Amazon Inc.'s Alexa, the company decided to pivot and make the change.

These two systems have seen incredible growth in 2018, with the Amazon Echo and Google Home claiming each 34 percent of the market. Now John Giannandrea, formerly Google's head of search and AI, has joined the Apple team and is tasked with getting on the rival's level from which he came (Verge 2018).

He will be challenged not only by having a new culture and company to fit into, but also by finding a good balance on how to innovate in his new role, as well as taking the best practices that he has from his previous role and applying it to boost the success of the Apple artificial intelligence. Keys to his success will be how quickly he can adapt to the new role, learning, adapting, and making changes along the way to bring Apple back to the playing field of artificial intelligence.

Question 1: What other challenges would a new executive have coming from a competing company?

Question 2: How much change is too much? What cautions should Apple be concerned about with all of the turnover for this position?

Sources: Nick Statt, "Apple's New AI Chief Now Oversees Siri, Core ML, and Machine Learning Teams," *The Verge*, July 10, 2018, https://www.theverge.com/2018/7/10/17555652/apple-siri-ai-john-giannandrea-machine-learning-core-ml-teams; Stephen Nellis, "Apple Shifts Responsibility For Siri to Operating System Chief," *Reuters*, September 1, 2017, https://www.reuters.com/article/us-apple-siri/apple-shifts-responsibility-for-siri-to-operating-system-chief-idUSKCN1BC65B; Tripp Mickle, Apple Hands Siri Responsibility to Executive Poached from Google," *The Wall Street Journal*, July 10, 2018, https://www.wsj.com/articles/apple-hands-siri-responsibilities-to-executive-poached-from-google-1531261759.

The Challenge of Increased Quality

The challenge of industrial competitiveness incorporates several interrelated factors, including an appropriate product mix, manufacturing efficiency, effective cost controls, investment in research and development, and so forth. Not to be ignored in this pursuit is the quest for increased quality control of the products and services offered in the marketplace. Total Quality Management (TQM) is a term often used to describe comprehensive efforts to monitor and improve all aspects of quality within a firm. BMW established and continues to maintain its reputation in part because customers have come to respect its high level of quality. Quality is also a major reason for the success of many Japanese products in North America. Simply put, if companies are going to compete, renewed efforts must be devoted to enhanced quality assurance. This, too, is a management challenge. How can managers get employees to care about the products they produce or the services they offer? In this book, we will consider both the issue of quality control (what is it?) and mechanisms of ensuring improved product quality (how do we get it?).

Moreover, quality control includes several organizational issues. For instance, how can managers get parties who are traditionally independently associated with a product to work together to build a better product? That is, how can they get the design staff, manufacturing engineers, workers, suppliers—and potential customers—to come together and cooperate in developing and manufacturing a superior product? Later in the book we will examine several instances in which such teamwork played a major role in quality improvement.

The Challenge of Employee Motivation and Commitment

A major hurdle in the pursuit of industrial competitiveness is the traditional adversarial relationship between management and workers. Whether a company is unionized or not, we see situations in which the average employee simply sees no reason to increase output or to improve the quality of existing outputs. Frequently, the company's reward system restricts, rather than increases, performance. At other times, rewards encourage employees to increase quantity at the expense of quality. Furthermore, North American companies often view their workforce as a variable expense (in contrast to Japan, where the workforce is viewed as a fixed expense) and lay workers off when they are not needed for short-run activities. As a result, returning the favor, employees see little reason to be committed or loyal to their employers. Turnover and absenteeism rates are often unreasonably high, further eroding performance efficiency and effectiveness.

If companies are to succeed in an increasingly turbulent environment, managers must discover better ways to develop and motivate employees. A company's human resources often represent its biggest single asset, and failing to properly nurture this asset leads to suboptimal return on an organization's resources. Part of solving this problem involves knowing and understanding today's employees. **Exhibit 1.2** illustrates the various characteristics employees consider important in their employers. Overall, employees seem to have a fairly positive outlook on their employers. As illustrated in **Exhibit 1.3**, however, many millennials do not see their tenure lasting for a long period and expect to have another job soon.

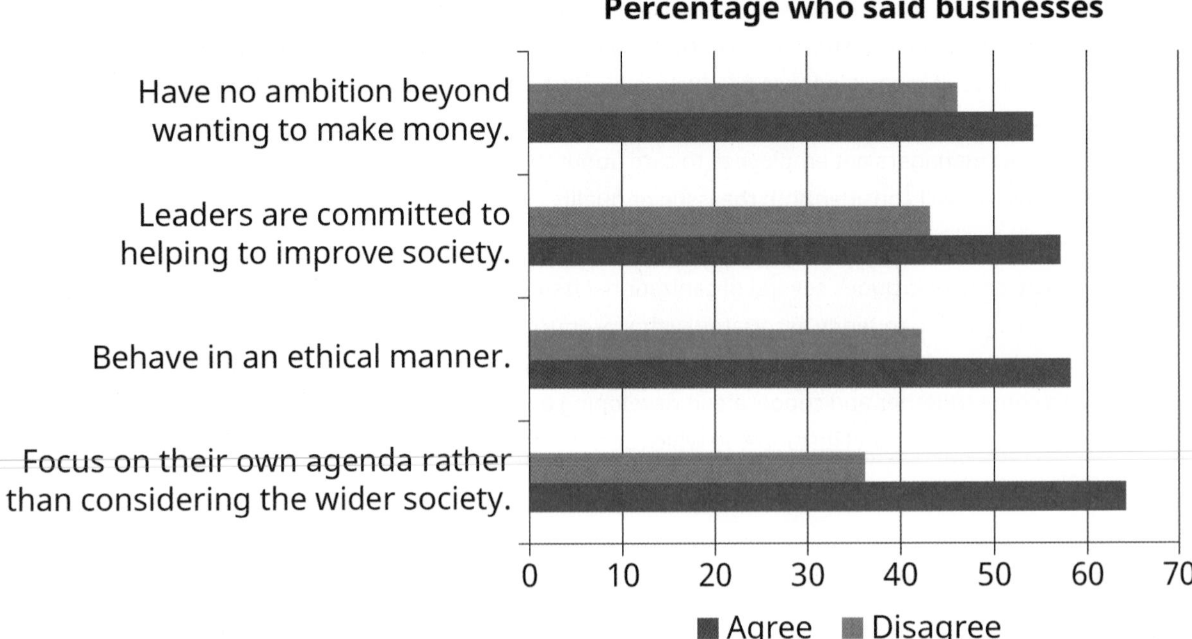

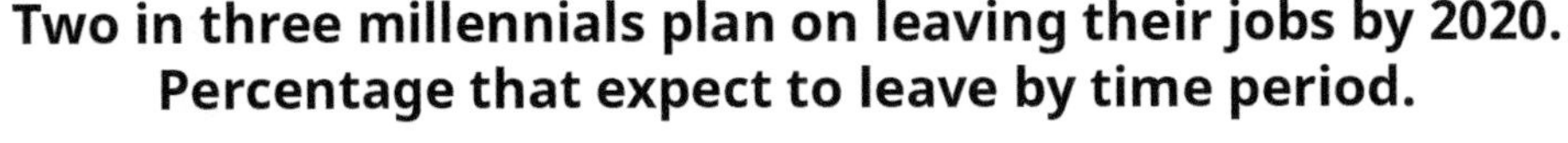

Exhibit 1.2 How Employees View Their Employers Source: Adapted from Deloitte, "2016 Deloitte Millennial Survey," accessed July 18, 2018, https://www2.deloitte.com/content/dam/Deloitte/global/Documents/About-Deloitte/gx-millenial-survey-2016-exec-summary.pdf. (Attribution: Copyright Rice University, OpenStax, under CC BY-NC-SA 4.0 license)

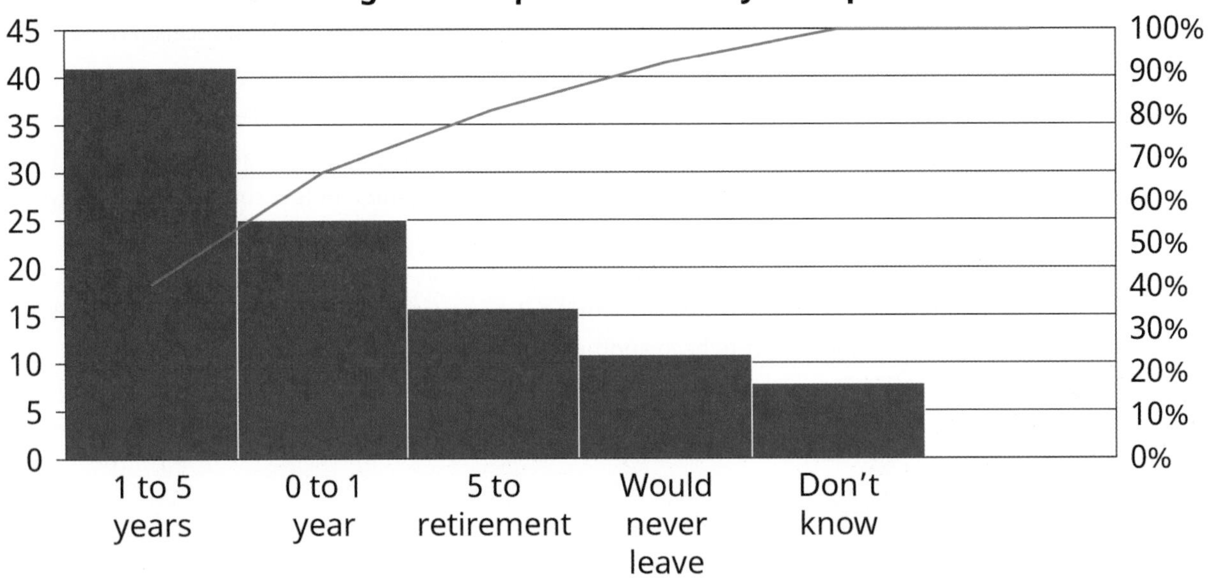

Exhibit 1.3 Millennials and the Workplace Source: Adapted from Deloitte, "2016 Deloitte Millennial Survey," accessed July 18, 2018, https://www2.deloitte.com/content/dam/Deloitte/global/Documents/About-Deloitte/gx-millenial-survey-2016-exec-summary.pdf. (Attribution: Copyright Rice University, OpenStax, under CC BY-NC-SA 4.0 license)

This problem is made all the more difficult by the changing nature of occupations. As shown in **Table 1.2**, we are seeing a sharp increase in the number of technicians, service workers, and sales workers. Growth also can be expected in engineering and managerial positions. These changes require a new look at how such employees are motivated. For example, do we motive an engineer the same way we motivate a sales representative? How do we motivate senior executives as opposed to junior managers? In this book, we shall touch on these issues when we examine approaches to employee motivation. Managers have at their disposal several ways in which to increase employee motivation and performance, and an effective manager learns how and when to use each approach.

The Fastest-Growing Occupations		
Occupation	Growth Rate 2016–2026	2017 Median Pay
Solar photovoltaic installers	105%	$39,490
Wind turbine service technicians	96%	$53,580
Home health aides	47%	$23,210
Personal care aids	39%	$23,110
Physician assistants	37%	$104,860
Nurse practitioner	36%	$103,880
Statistician	34%	$84,060
Physical therapist assistant	31%	$57,440
Software developers, applications	31%	$101,790
Mathematicians	30%	$103,010
Physical therapist aides	29%	$25,730
Bicycle repairs	29%	$28,390
Medical assistants	29%	$32,480
Source: "Fastest Growing Occupations," Occupational Outlook Handbook, Bureau of Labor Statistics, https://www.bls.gov/ooh/fastest-growing.htm, accessed July 18, 2018.		

Table 1.2

The Challenge of Managing a Diverse Workforce

Historically, the American economy has been dominated by white males. They have filled the vast majority of managerial positions and many of the more important blue-collar jobs, becoming skilled craftsmen. Traditionally, women filled lower-paying clerical positions and often left the workforce to raise their families. Minorities of both genders found considerable barriers to entering the labor market at the higher (and higher-paying) levels. Now, things are changing, and the pace of this change is accelerating. Among other changes, the twenty-first century will also bring major changes in terms of workforce demographics. We will see changes in gender, race, and age.

Exhibit 1.4 Kaisee Permanente The winner of the E Pluribus Unum Corporate Leadership Award, Kaiser Permanente focuses on the elimination of racial and ethnic health care disparities and has been in the vanguard of efforts to create innovative, scalable approaches that address the cultural and linguistic needs of patients, and thereby improve overall health care quality and outcomes. Its industry-leading training, testing, and certification process for multilingual staff who serve as health care interpreters, as well as for the physicians who speak with patients in languages other than English, helps to improve the quality of patient care while also capitalizing on the organization's diverse workforce. (Credit: Ted Eytan/ flickr/ Attribution-ShareAlike 2.0 Generic (CC BY-SA 2.0))

For example, we are seeing a drop in the percentage of white American-born male workers in the workplace. Only 15 percent of new entrants into the workforce will be white males.[6] The percentages for nonwhites and immigrants of both genders will increase (see **Exhibit 1.5**). In general, there are more women in positions of responsibility in both the public and private sectors and more opportunities for minorities. Some predict that the coming labor shortage will cause many companies to try to retain older workers for longer periods of time, beyond the traditional retirement age. Additionally, the belief that mentally or physically challenged individuals can play productive roles at work is increasing. Such changes bring opportunities for companies but also potential problems of adjustment if not managed intelligently. We will examine several of these issues when we discuss careers and employee development.

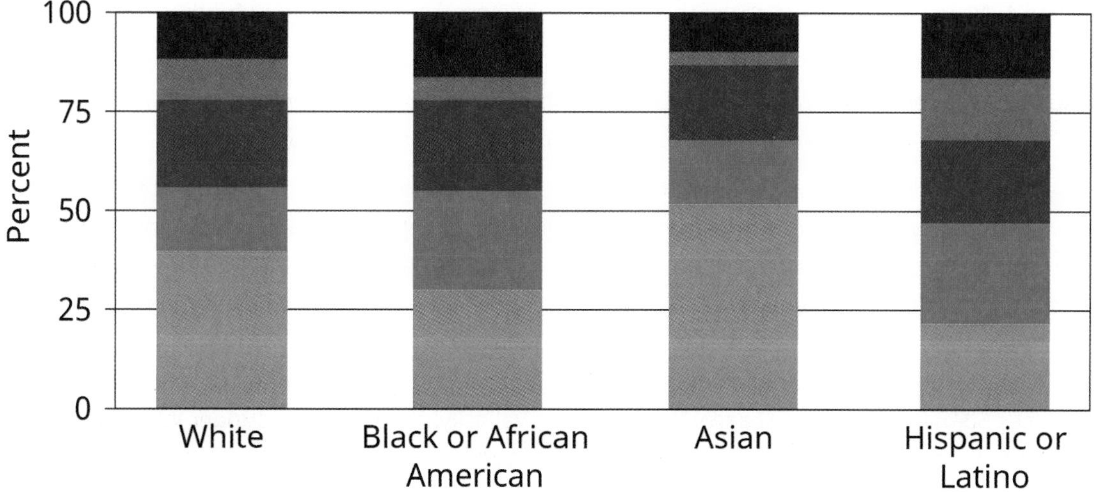

Exhibit 1.5 Employed People by Race and Latino or Hispanic Ethnicity, 2016 Note: People whose ethnicity is identified as Hispanic or Latino may be of any race. Data may not sum to 100 percent because of rounding. Source: U.S. Bureau of Labor Statistics, Current Population Survey (CPS). (Attribution: Copyright Rice University, OpenStax, under CC BY-NC-SA 4.0 license)

The Challenge of Ethical Behavior

Finally, the future will bring a renewed concern with maintaining high standards of ethical behavior in business transactions and in the workplace. Many executives and social scientists see unethical behavior as a cancer working on the fabric of society both in business and beyond. Many are concerned that we face a crisis of ethics in the West that is undermining our competitive strength. This crisis involves business, government, customers, and employees. Especially worrisome is unethical behavior among employees at all levels of the organization. For example, recent reports found that employees and vendors accounted for a higher percentage of thefts than did retail customers.[7]

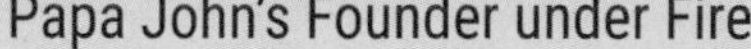

ETHICS IN PRACTICE

Papa John's Founder under Fire

As a manager, and leader, the words and actions you take are incredibly important. John Schnatter, founder and chairman of Papa John's Pizza, found this out the hard way. During a media training conference call, Schnatter used derogatory comments and racial slurs. This call, although intended to be a role-playing exercise, quickly turned into a bad dream for Schnatter. In response to this action, and having admitted the fault, Schnatter was forced to resign as chairman after the local NAACP branch called for his resignation. In addition, the board of directors decided that he would be removed from all marketing, publicity, and pizza boxes, and they took the stance that "Papa John's is not an individual.

Papa John's is a pizza company with 120,000 corporate and franchise team members around the world" (Forbes 2018). Shares of stock for Papa John's soared after the announcement of his resignation, adding $50 million to Schnatter's total net worth (CNN Money 2018). The values of the company prevailed through the actions of Schnatter, showcasing that despite making a mistake, the commitment to maintaining an ethical standard is still an important value to Schnatter as well as the company overall.

Question 1: Do you think the actions of the board of directors were enough to uphold Papa John's reputation?

Question 2: What other actions or types of training should Papa John's take with their employees in light of the current state of ethical defamation of the company and founder?

Sources: Julie Jargon, "Papa John's Stock Soars After Chairman's resignation," *The Wall Street Journal*, July 12, 2018, https://www.wsj.com/articles/papa-johns-directors-accept-chairmans-resignation-1531404524; Megan Friedman, "John Schnatter Will No longer Be the Face of Papa John's," *Delish*, July 16, 2018, https://www.delish.com/food-news/a22162275/papa-johns-john-schnatter-removed-marketing/; Noah Kirsch, "Papa John's Founder Resigns, Gains $50 Million in a Day," Forbes, July 13, 2018, https://www.forbes.com/sites/noahkirsch/2018/07/13/papa-johns-founder-john-schnatter-resigns-net-worth-rises-50-million-in-a-day/#6aaf997f7123; Jordan Valinsky, "Papa John's Founder John Schnatter Kicked Out of His Office," *CNN Money*, July 16, 2018, https://money.cnn.com/2018/07/16/news/companies/papa-johns-office/index.html

In addition, we hear about illegal and unethical behavior on Wall Street—pension scandals in which disreputable executives gamble on risky business ventures with employee retirement funds, companies that expose their workers to hazardous working conditions, and blatant favoritism in hiring and promotion practices. Although such practices occur throughout the world, their presence nonetheless serves to remind us of the challenges we face.

This challenge is especially difficult because standards for what constitutes ethical behavior lie in a "gray zone" where clear-cut right-or-wrong answers may not always exist. For example, if you were a sales representative for an American company abroad and your foreign competitors used bribes to get business, what would you do? In the United States such behavior is illegal, yet it is perfectly acceptable in other countries. What is ethical here? Similarly, in many countries women are systematically discriminated against in the workplace; it is felt that their place is in the home. In the United States, again, this practice is illegal. If you ran an American company in one of these countries, would you hire women in important positions? If you did, your company might be isolated in the larger business community, and you might lose business. If you did not, you might be violating what most Americans believe to be fair business practices.

Effective managers must know how to deal with ethical issues in their everyday work lives; therefore, we will devote parts of this course to the role of **ethics** in decision-making, the exercise of power, performance appraisals and reward systems, and so forth.

CONCEPT CHECK

1. Describe the extent and nature of the challenges facing the workplace in the next decade.

2. What can be done about these challenges?

1.3 The Nature of Management

3. What is expected of a manager?

If organizations are to be successful in meeting these challenges, management must lead the way. With effective management, contemporary companies can accomplish a great deal toward becoming more competitive in the global environment. On the other hand, ineffective management dooms the organization to mediocrity and sometimes outright failure. Because of this, we turn now to a look at the nature of management. However, we want to point out that even though our focus is on managers, what we discuss is also relevant to the actions of nonmanagers. On the basis of this examination, we should be ready to begin our analysis of what managers can learn from the behavioral sciences to improve their effectiveness in a competitive environment.

What Is Management?

Many years ago, Mary Parker Follett defined management as "the art of getting things done through people." A manager coordinates and oversees the work of others to accomplish ends he could not attain alone. Today this definition has been broadened. **Management** is generally defined as the process of planning, organizing, directing, and controlling the activities of employees in combination with other resources to accomplish organizational objectives. In a broad sense, then, the task of management is to facilitate the organization's effectiveness and long-term goal attainment by coordinating and efficiently utilizing available resources. Based on this definition, it is clear that the topics of effectively managing individuals, groups, or organizational systems is relevant to anyone who must work with others to accomplish organizational objectives.

Management exists in virtually all goal-seeking organizations, whether they are public or private, large or small, profit-making or not-for-profit, socialist or capitalist. For many, the mark of an excellent company or organization is the quality of its managers.

Managerial Responsibilities

An important question often raised about managers is: What responsibilities do managers have in organizations? According to our definition, managers are involved in planning, organizing, directing, and controlling. Managers have described their responsibilities that can be aggregated into nine major types of activities. These include:

1. *Long-range planning*. Managers occupying executive positions are frequently involved in strategic planning and development.
2. *Controlling*. Managers evaluate and take corrective action concerning the allocation and use of human, financial, and material resources.
3. *Environmental scanning*. Managers must continually watch for changes in the business environment and monitor business indicators such as returns on equity or investment, economic indicators, business cycles, and so forth.
4. *Supervision*. Managers continually oversee the work of their subordinates.
5. *Coordinating*. Managers often must coordinate the work of others both inside the work unit and out.

6. *Customer relations and marketing*. Certain managers are involved in direct contact with customers and potential customers.
7. *Community relations*. Contact must be maintained and nurtured with representatives from various constituencies outside the company, including state and federal agencies, local civic groups, and suppliers.
8. *Internal consulting.* Some managers make use of their technical expertise to solve internal problems, acting as inside consultants for organizational change and development.
9. *Monitoring products and services*. Managers get involved in planning, scheduling, and monitoring the design, development, production, and delivery of the organization's products and services.

As we shall see, not every manager engages in all of these activities. Rather, different managers serve different roles and carry different responsibilities, depending upon where they are in the organizational hierarchy. We will begin by looking at several of the variations in managerial work.

Variations in Managerial Work

Although each manager may have a diverse set of responsibilities, including those mentioned above, the amount of time spent on each activity and the importance of that activity will vary considerably. The two most salient perceptions of a manager are (1) the manager's level in the organizational hierarchy and (2) the type of department or function for which he is responsible. Let us briefly consider each of these.

Management by Level. We can distinguish three general levels of management: executives, **middle management**, and **first-line management** (see **Exhibit 1.6**). **Executive managers** are at the top of the hierarchy and are responsible for the entire organization, especially its strategic direction. Middle managers, who are at the middle of the hierarchy, are responsible for major departments and may supervise other lower-level managers. Finally, first-line managers supervise rank-and-file employees and carry out day-to-day activities within departments.

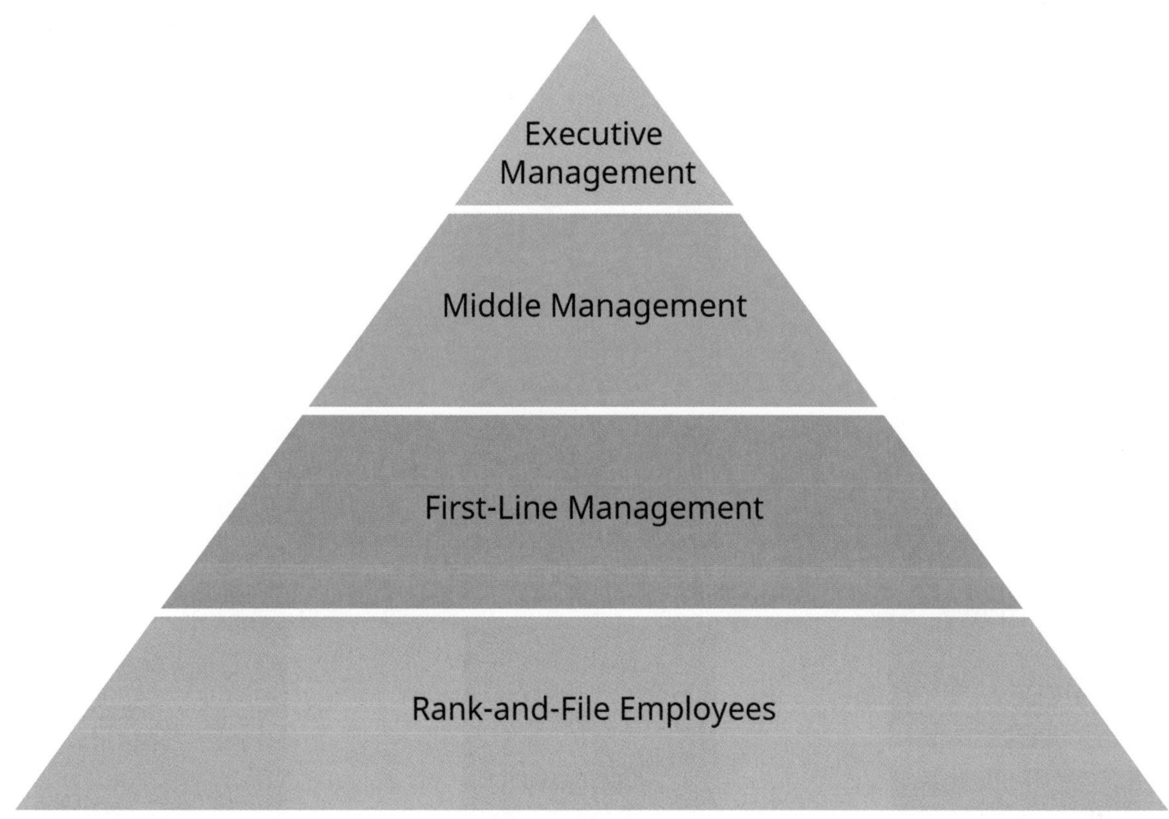

Exhibit 1.6 Levels in the Management Hierarchy (Attribution: Copyright Rice University, OpenStax, under CC BY-NC-SA 4.0 license)

Exhibit 1.7 shows differences in managerial activities by hierarchical level. Senior executives will devote more of their time to conceptual issues, while first-line managers will concentrate their efforts on technical issues. For example, top managers rate high on such activities as **long-range planning**, monitoring business indicators, coordinating, and internal consulting. Lower-level managers, by contrast, rate high on supervising because their responsibility is to accomplish tasks through rank-and-file employees. Middle managers rate near the middle for all activities. We can distinguish three types of managerial skills:[8]

1. *Technical skills*. Managers must have the ability to use the tools, procedures, and techniques of their special areas. An accountant must have expertise in accounting principles, whereas a production manager must know operations management. These skills are the mechanics of the job.
2. *Human relations skills*. Human relations skills involve the ability to work with people and understand employee motivation and group processes. These skills allow the manager to become involved with and lead his or her group.
3. *Conceptual skills*. These skills represent a manager's ability to organize and analyze information in order to improve organizational performance. They include the ability to see the organization as a whole and to understand how various parts fit together to work as an integrated unit. These skills are required to coordinate the departments and divisions successfully so that the entire organization can pull together.

As shown in **Exhibit 1.7**, different levels of these skills are required at different stages of the managerial hierarchy. That is, success in executive positions requires far more conceptual skill and less use of technical skills in most (but not all) situations, whereas first-line managers generally require more technical skills and fewer conceptual skills. Note, however, that human or people skills remain important for success at all three levels in the hierarchy.

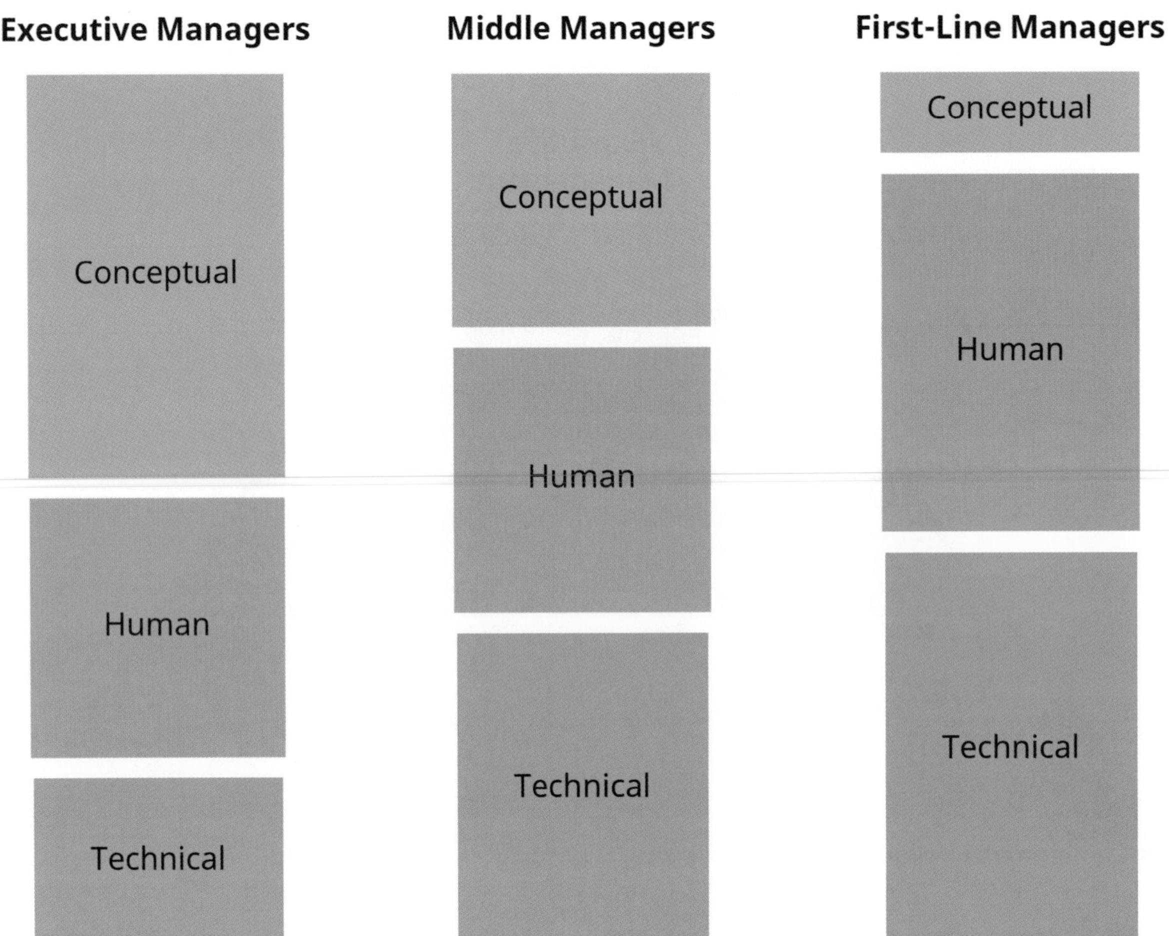

Exhibit 1.7 Difference in Skills Required for Successful Management According to Level in the Hierarchy (Attribution: Copyright Rice University, OpenStax, under CC BY-NC-SA 4.0 license)

Management by Department or Function. In addition to level in the hierarchy, managerial responsibilities also differ with respect to the type of department or function. There are differences found for quality assurance, manufacturing, marketing, accounting and finance, and human resource management departments. For instance, manufacturing department managers will concentrate their efforts on products and services, controlling, and supervising. Marketing managers, in comparison, focus less on planning, coordinating, and consulting but more on customer relations and external contact. Managers in both accounting and human resource management departments rate high on long-range planning, but will spend less time on the organization's products and service offerings. Managers in accounting and finance are also concerned with controlling and with monitoring performance indicators, while human resource managers provide consulting expertise, coordination, and external contacts. The emphasis on and intensity of managerial activities varies considerably by the department the manager is assigned to.

At a personal level, knowing that the mix of conceptual, human, and technical skills changes over time and that different functional areas require different levels of specific management activities can serve at least two important functions. First, if you choose to become a manager, knowing that the mix of skills changes over time can help you avoid a common complaint that often young employees want to think and act like a CEO before they have mastered being a first-line supervisor. Second, knowing the different mix of management activities by functional area can facilitate your selection of an area or areas that best match your skills and interests.

In many firms, managers are rotated through departments as they move up in the hierarchy. In this way they obtain a well-rounded perspective on the responsibilities of the various departments. In their day-to-day tasks they must emphasize the right activities for their departments and their managerial levels. Knowing what types of activity to emphasize is the core of the manager's job. In any event, we shall return to this issue when we address the nature of individual differences in the next chapter.

The Twenty-First Century Manager

We discussed above many of the changes and challenges facing organizations in the twenty-first century. Because of changes such as these, the managers and executives of tomorrow will have to change their approaches to their jobs if they are to succeed in meeting the new challenges. In fact, their profiles may even look somewhat different than they often do today. Consider the five skills that *Fast Company* predicts that successful future managers, compared to the senior manager in the year 2000, will need. The five skills are: the ability to think of new solutions, being comfortable with chaos, an understanding of technology, high emotional intelligence, and the ability to work with people and technology together.

For the past several decades, executive profiles have typically looked like this: He started out in finance with an undergraduate degree in accounting. He methodically worked his way up through the company from the controller's office in a division, to running that division, to the top job. His military background shows. He is used to giving orders—and to having them obeyed. As head of the philanthropic efforts, he is a big man in his community. However, the first time he traveled overseas on business was as chief executive. Computers, which became ubiquitous during his career, make him nervous.[9]

Now compare this with predictions about what a twenty-first-century executive will look like:

Her [or his] undergraduate degree might be in French literature, but she also has a joint MBA/engineering degree. She started in research and was quickly picked out as a potential CEO. She is able to think creatively and thrives in a chaotic environment. She zigzagged from research to marketing to finance. She is comfortable with technology and people, with a high degree of emotional intelligence. She proved valuable in Brazil by turning around a failing joint venture. She speaks multiple languages and is on a first-name basis with commerce ministers in half a dozen countries. Unlike her predecessor's predecessor, she isn't a drill sergeant. She is first among equals in a five-person office of the chief executive.

Clearly, the future holds considerable excitement and promise for future managers and executives who are properly prepared to meet the challenges. How do we prepare them? One study suggested that the manager of the future must be able to fill at least the following four roles:[10]

Global strategist. Executives of the future must understand world markets and think internationally. They must have a capacity to identify unique business opportunities and then move quickly to exploit them.

Master of technology. Executives and managers of the future must be able to get the most out of emerging technologies, whether these technologies are in manufacturing, communications, marketing, or other areas.

Leadership that embraces vulnerability. The successful executive of the future will understand how to cut through red tape to get a job done, how to build bridges with key people from highly divergent backgrounds and points of view, and how to make coalitions and joint ventures work.

Follow-from-the-front motivator. Finally, the executive of tomorrow must understand group dynamics and how to counsel, coach, and command work teams and individuals so they perform at their best. Future organizations will place greater emphasis on teams and coordinated efforts, requiring managers to understand participative management techniques.

Great communicator. To this list of four, we would add that managers of the future must be great communicators. They must be able to communicate effectively with an increasingly diverse set of employees as well as customers, suppliers, and community and government leaders.

Whether these predictions are completely accurate is difficult to know. Suffice it to say that most futurists agree that the organizational world of the twenty-first century will likely resemble, to some extent, the portrait described here. The task for future managers, then, is to attempt to develop these requisite skills to the extent possible so they will be ready for the challenges of the next decade.

CONCEPT CHECK

1. Define management.
2. How does the nature of management change according to one's level and function in the organization?

1.4 A Model of Organizational Behavior and Management

4. What is the role of the behavioral sciences in management and organizations?

A major responsibility—perhaps *the* major responsibility—of managers is to make organizations operate effectively. Bringing about effective performance, however, is no easy task. As Nadler and Tushman note:

Understanding one individual's behavior is challenging in and of itself; understanding a group that's made up of different individuals and comprehending the many relationships among those individuals is even more complex. Imagine, then, the mind-boggling complexity of a large organization made up of thousands of individuals and hundreds of groups with myriad relationships among these individuals and groups.[11]

Despite this difficulty, however, organizations must be managed. Nadler and Tushman continue:

Ultimately the organization's work gets done through people, individually or collectively, on their own or in collaboration with technology. Therefore, the management of **organizational behavior** is central to the management task—a task that involves the capacity to *understand* the behavior patterns of individuals, groups, and organizations, to *predict* what behavioral responses will be elicited by various managerial actions, and finally to use this understanding and these predictions to achieve *control*.[12]

The work of society is accomplished largely through organizations, and the role of management is to see to it that organizations perform this work. Without it, the wheels of society would soon grind to a halt.

What Is Organizational Behavior?

The study of the behavior of people in organizations is typically referred to as *organizational behavior*. Here, the focus is on applying what we can learn from the social and behavioral sciences so we can better understand and predict human behavior at work. We examine such behavior on three levels—the individual, the group, and the organization as a whole. In all three cases, we seek to learn more about what causes people—individually or collectively—to behave as they do in organizational settings. What motivates people? What makes some employees leaders and others not? Why do groups often work in opposition to their employer? How do organizations respond to changes in their external environments? How do people communicate and make decisions? Questions such as these constitute the domain of organizational behavior and are the focus of this course.

To a large extent, we can apply what has been learned from psychology, sociology, and cultural anthropology. In addition, we can learn from economics and political science. All of these disciplines have something to say about life in organizations. However, what sets organizational behavior apart is its particular focus on the organization (not the discipline) in organizational analysis (see **Exhibit 1.8**). Thus, if we wish to examine a problem of employee motivation, for example, we can draw upon economic theories of wage structures in the workplace. At the same time, we can also draw on the psychological theories of motivation and incentives as they relate to work. We can bring in sociological treatments of social forces on behavior, and we can make use of anthropological studies of cultural influences on individual performance. It is this conceptual richness that establishes organizational behavior as a unique applied discipline. And throughout our analyses, we are continually concerned with the implications of what we learn for the quality of working life and organizational performance. We always look for management implications so the managers of the future can develop more humane and more competitive organizations for the future.

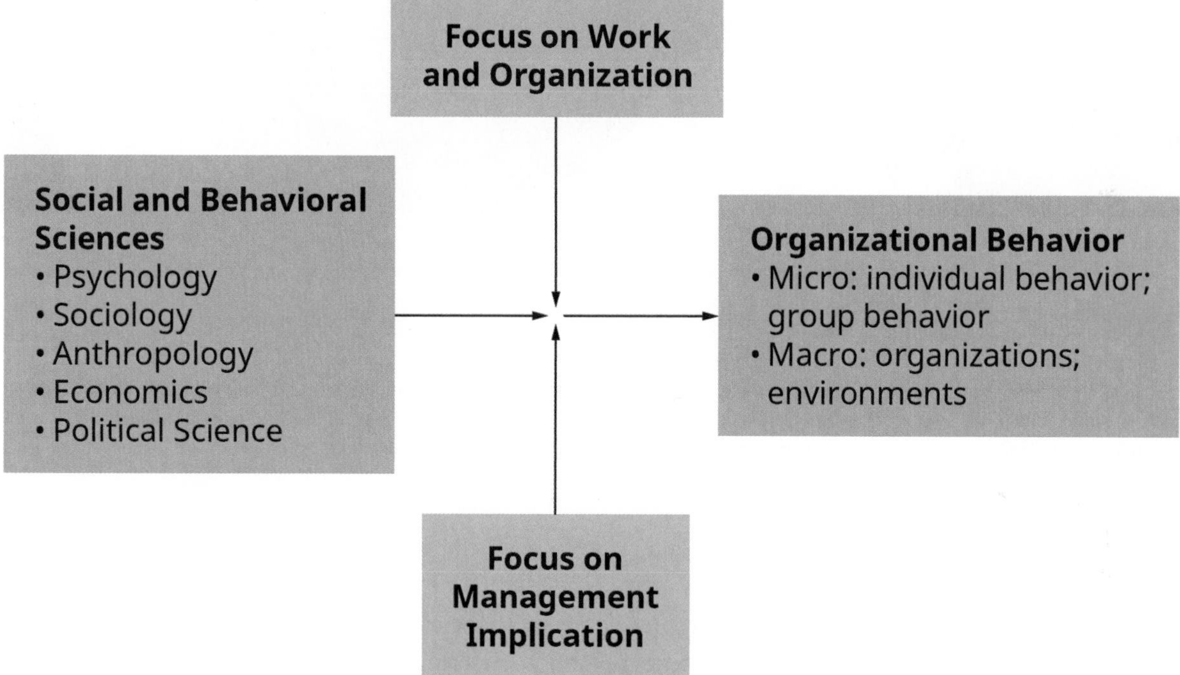

Exhibit 1.8 Origins of Organizational Behavior (Attribution: Copyright Rice University, OpenStax, under CC BY-NC-SA 4.0 license)

For convenience, we often differentiate between micro- and macro-organizational behavior. **Micro-organizational behavior** is primarily concerned with the behavior of individuals and groups, while **macro-organizational behavior** (also referred to as **organization theory**) is concerned with organization-wide issues, such as organization design and the relations between an organization and its environment. Although there are times when this distinction is helpful, it is always important to remember that in most instances we learn the most when we take a comprehensive view of organizational behavior and integrate these two perspectives. That is, issues such as organization structure can influence employee motivation. Hence, by keeping these two realms separate we lose valuable information that can help us better understand how to manage organizations.

Exhibit 1.9 Invo new Hire Xinyu Liu was hired as the studio as a designer at Invo, a Massachusetts-based firm. Prior to joining Invo, she was a user experience researcher at Samsung, where she investigated how to apply future technologies in everyday living. Changing behavior for good was a key component of the R&D work, leveraging invisible sensing tech, devising emotional effects, and crafting just-in-time graphic communication. Her wide-ranging skills, from analyzing social behavior to 3D modeling to electronics to UI design, are well-suited for the multi-domain projects at Invo. As part of the employee selection process, the hiring managers at Invo needed to recognize that their employees come from various backgrounds and have varying abilities and skills, differing motivational levels, and different ambitions. Within the organizational context, they needed to consider how Xinyu would fit on the team in the areas of communication, decision-making, and leadership, and how she would handle power and organizational politics as she carried out her responsibilities. (Credit: Juhan Sonin/ flickr/ Attribution 2.0 Generic (CC BY 2.0))

Building Blocks of Organizations

Understanding the behavior of people at work is fundamental to the effective management of an organization. Obviously, a number of factors come together to determine this behavior and its organizational consequences. In order to understand the origins and characteristics of these factors, it is necessary to have a model that organizes and simplifies the variables involved. We offer such a model here in the hope that it will bring some order to the study of this subject. The model can be considered in two parts (see **Exhibit 1.10**).

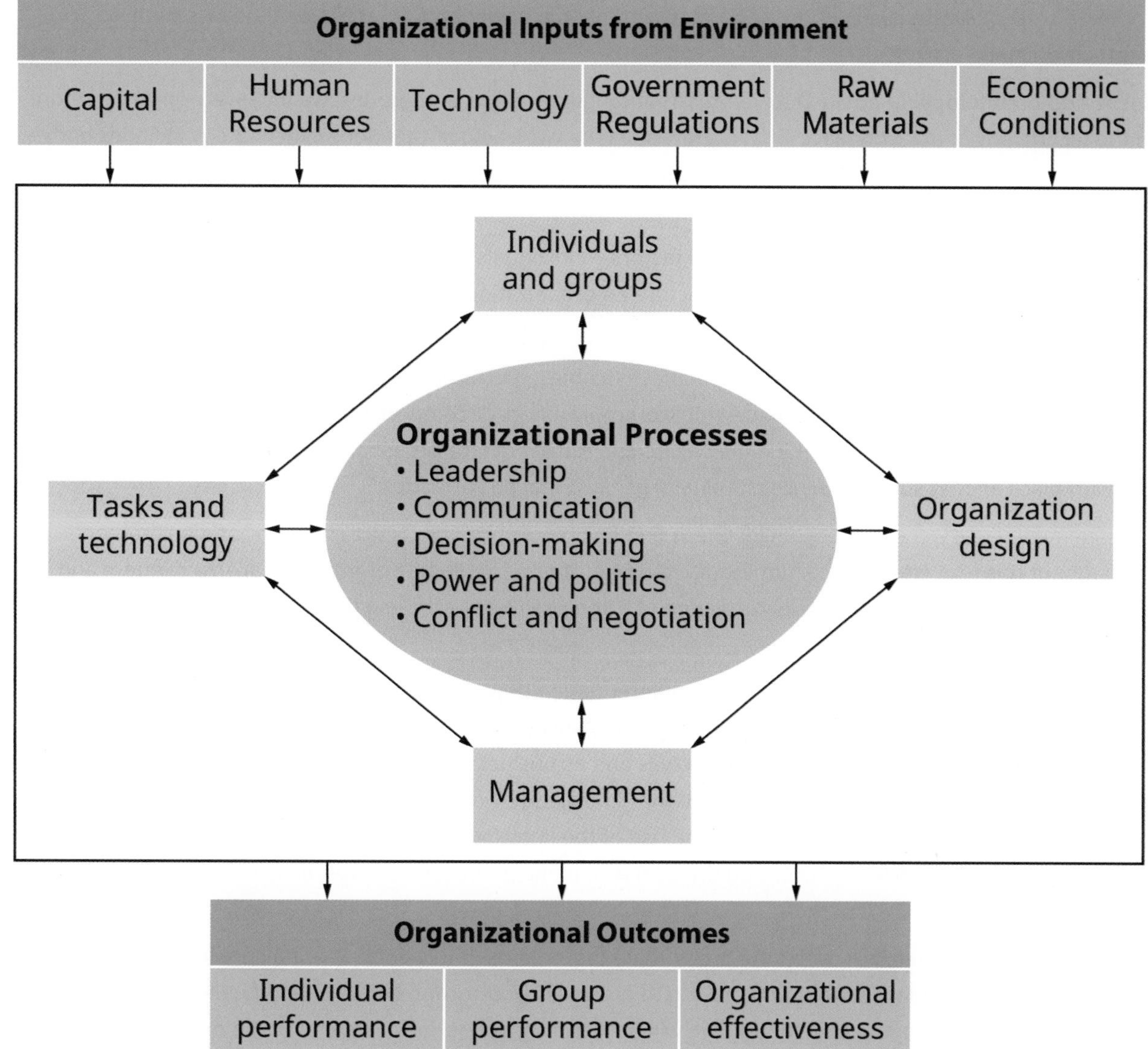

Exhibit 1.10 A Model of Management and Organizational Behavior (Attribution: Copyright Rice University, OpenStax, under CC BY-NC-SA 4.0 license)

The first part of the model is the simple recognition of organizational inputs and outcomes. That is, organizations receive inputs from the external environment in the form of capital, raw materials, labor, community or government support, and so forth. In addition, organizations experience or produce certain outcomes, including (1) organizational goal attainment, (2) group performance and effectiveness, and (3) individual performance and effectiveness. Thus, organizations and the people in them exist in a constant state of flux, receiving and transforming inputs from the environment and returning those transformed inputs in the form of finished goods and services, return on stockholders' equity, salaries that are paid to employees, and so forth. It is, in short, a dynamic system.

The second aspect of the model is the organization itself and all of its parts. One way to understand the complexity of organizations is to think of them simply as a set of building blocks, including:

Individuals and groups. Organizations are collectives of individuals and groups working to pursue common objectives. Their members come from various backgrounds and have varying abilities and skills, differing motivational levels, and different ambitions. Within the organizational context, these people must communicate, make decisions, show leadership, and handle power and organizational politics as they carry out their assigned activities.

Tasks and technology. In addition to variations among individuals and groups, we must recognize variations in the technology of the workplace. That is, how does the work actually get done? Technology includes both the actual design of jobs and the tools and techniques used in manufacture (e.g., robotics and expert systems).

Organization design. Putting together these factors—individuals and groups and tasks—is the subject of **organization design**. That is, how do we structure an organization so it effectively coordinates and controls employee behavior to facilitate performance?

Organizational processes. In addition to people, machines, and structure, we must recognize a series of **organizational processes**, such as leadership, communication, decision-making, power and politics, and so forth. The processes largely determine the nature and quality of interpersonal and intergroup relations within the workplace and, as such, influence ultimate organizational performance.

Management. Finally, the glue that holds these building blocks together is the character of management. Throughout this text, we shall see numerous examples of how the degree of managerial effectiveness and prowess have determined the success or failure of a venture. We shall take a managerial view throughout our survey of organizational behavior.

There have been many attempts to provide a differentiation between leadership and management over time. While they are not the same thing, they are necessarily linked, and complementary. Any effort to separate the two is likely to cause more problems than it solves and as business evolved the content of leadership and management has changed. The emergence of the "knowledge worker," and the profound differences that this causes the way business is organized. With the rise of the knowledge worker, one does not 'manage' people, and instead the task is to lead people and the goal is to make productive the specific strengths and knowledge of every individual.

These five variables, then, will constitute the primary ingredients of this book. We shall proceed sequentially, beginning with individual behavior and moving to group and intergroup behavior and finally to organization design and structure. On the basis of this, we will turn to a consideration of several of the more important organizational processes. Finally, we will look to the future and examine ways that organizations can continue to develop and improve their workforces and the organization as a whole. Throughout, the roles of technology and management will be considered. Also, throughout, we will blend **theory** with research and practice.

CONCEPT CHECK

1. Discuss the role of management in the larger societal context.
2. What do you think the managers of the future will be like?
3. Identify what you think are the critical issues facing contemporary management. Explain.

Key Terms

Alienation The experience of being isolated from a group or an activity to which one should belong, or in which one should be involved.

Ethics Moral principles that govern a person's behavior or the conducting of an activity.

Executive managers Generally, a team of individuals at the highest level of management of an organization.

First-line management The level of management directly managing nonmanagerial employees.

Industrial competitiveness The ability to provide products and services more effectively and efficiently than competitors.

Long-range planning A process of setting goals that outlines the path for the company's future.

Macro-organizational behavior Macro-organizational behavioral research steps back and looks at an organization as a whole.

Management The process of planning, organizing, directing, and controlling the activities of employees in combination with other resources to accomplish organizational objectives.

Micro-organizational behavior Micro-organizational behavioral studies focus on individual and group dynamics within an organization.

Middle management The managers in an organization at a level just below that of senior executives.

Organization theory The study of organization designs and organization structures, relationship of organizations with their external environment, and the behavior of managers and workers within organizations.

Organizational behavior The study of the actions and attitudes of individuals and groups toward one another and toward the organization as a whole.

Organizational design A formal methodology that identifies dysfunctional aspects of workflow, procedures, structures and systems, and then realigns them to fit current business goals and develops plans to implement change.

Organizational processes The activities that establish the business goals of the organization and develop **processes**, product and resource assets that when used will help to achieve business goals.

Technology The application of scientific knowledge for practical purposes.

Theory A set of principles on which the practice of an activity is based.

Work All activity involving mental or physical effort done in order to achieve a purpose or result.

Summary of Learning Outcomes

1.1 The Nature of Work

1. What is the meaning of work in a societal context?

Work will almost inevitably be a large part of your life. An understanding of organizational behavior will aid you in making that part of life more productive and enjoyable for yourself as well those you are in a position to influence. In this course, our objective is to provide sound and relevant insights concerning individuals, groups, and overall organizational systems that will be helpful to you not just as an executive or CEO but also when you are starting your career as an individual contributor or subordinate.

1.2 The Changing Workplace

2. How do recognize and meet the challenges facing managers in the new millennium?

The fundamental challenge facing managers is how to achieve performance goals while simultaneously providing for employee welfare and satisfaction. Work may be defined as an activity that produces something of value for other people. Work serves several functions, including economic, social, status, self-esteem, and self-actualization. As managers in today's environment, several challenges arise, including international competition, new technologies, the need for increased quality, employee motivation and commitment, a diverse workforce, and ethical behavior. These challenges must be met by managers concerned about survival and competitiveness in the future.

1.3 The Nature of Management

3. What is expected of a manager?

Management is the process of planning, organizing, directing, and controlling the activities of employees in combination with other resources to accomplish organizational goals. Managerial responsibilities include long-range planning, controlling, environmental scanning, supervision, coordination, customer relations, community relations, internal consulting, and monitoring of products and services. These responsibilities differ by level in the organizational hierarchy and by department or function. The twenty-first-century manager will differ from most current managers in four ways. In essence, he or she will be a global strategist, a master of technology, a good politician, and a premier leader-motivator.

1.4 A Model of Organizational Behavior and Management

4. What is the role of the behavioral sciences in management and organizations?

Organizational behavior is the study of people in organizations. It can be studied on a micro level, which focuses on individual or group behavior, or on a macro level, which focuses on organization-wide actions and events. A model of organizational behavior is presented, consisting of five building blocks: individuals and groups, tasks and technology, organization design, organizational processes, and management.

Chapter Review Questions

1. Define *work*.
2. What functions does work serve in modern society?
3. Describe the extent and nature of the challenges facing the workplace in the next decade.
4. What can be done about these challenges?
5. Define *management*.
6. How does the nature of management change according to one's level and function in the organization?
7. Discuss the role of management in the larger societal context. What do you think the managers of the future will be like?
8. Identify what you think are the critical issues facing contemporary management. Explain.

Critical Thinking Case

New Management Challenges for the New Age

Today's news is littered with scandals, new allegations of sexual assault, and tragedy. Since 2017 and the #metoo movement, stemming from the Harvey Weinstein scandal, more and more public figures have been put into the spotlight to defend themselves against allegations from women around the globe.

Not only publicly, but privately in companies around the world, there have been firings and investigations into misconduct from coworkers, managers, and CEOs. It is a relevant topic that is getting long-overdue publicity and encouraging more men and women to come forward to discuss openly rather than hide the events and injustices of the past. Other events showcase the tumultuous and on-edge society we are living in, such as the Charlottesville, VA, attack that left one dead and 19 injured when a person drove a car through a crowd of protestors during a white nationalist gathering.

With unanticipated events on a daily business, it is important for companies to take a stand against racial hatred and harassment of any kind, and to have firm policies when such events occur. Take Netflix, for example, who in July 2018 fired their chief communications officer for saying the "N-word" in full form. This event occurred during an internal meeting in which the speaker was not directing the slur at anyone specific, but claimed it was being made as an emphatic point about offensive words in comedy programming. The "Netflix way," the culture that is built around radical candor and transparency, was put to the test during this occurrence.

The offender, Jonathan Friedland, attempted to apologize for his misdeed, hoping it would fade away and his apology would be accepted. However, it didn't work that way; instead, the anger was palpable between coworkers and eventually led to the firing of Friedland after a few months of inaction.

Netflixers are given a high level of freedom and responsibility within their "Netflix way" culture. Blunt feedback is encouraged, and trust and discretion are the ultimate gatekeeper, as employees have access to sensitive information and are ultimately trusted for how they expense items and take vacation time.

In the insanely fast-paced streaming-services industry, it is hard to keep this culture at a premium, but it is imperative for the success of the company overall. "As you scale a company to become bigger and bigger, how do you scale that kind of culture?" said Colin Estep, a former senior engineer who left voluntarily in 2016. "I don't know that we ever had a good answer."

In order to keep up, sometimes the company is seen as harsh in their tactics to keep the best of the best. "I think we're transparent to a fault in our culture and that can come across as cutthroat," said Walta Nemariam, an employee in talent acquisition at Netflix.

Netflix has stayed true to their cultural values despite the pressures and sometimes negative connotations associated with this "cutthroat" environment. Their ability to remain agile, while displaying no tolerance for societal injustices, puts them at the forefront of new-age companies. It is a difficult pace to stay in line with, but it seems that they are keeping in stride and remaining true to who they are, for now.

Questions:

1. How has the current cultural environment of our country shaped the way that companies are looking at their own corporate cultural standards?
2. What are the potential downfalls and positive influences of the "Netflix way"?
3. How does Netflix's internal culture negatively or positively affect their ability to stay competitive and deliver cutting-edge content?

Sources: B. Stelter, "The Weinstein Effect: Harvey Weinstein scandal sparks movements in Hollywood and beyond," CNN Business, October 20, 2017, https://money.cnn.com/2017/10/20/media/weinstein-effect-harvey-weinstein/; L. Hertzler, "Talking #MeToo, one year after bombshell Weinstein allegations," Penn Today, October 30, 2018, https://penntoday.upenn.edu/news/talking-me-too-one-year-later; S. Ramachandaran and J. Flint, "At Netflix, Radical Transparency and Blunt Firings Unsettle the Ranks," Wall Street Journal, October 25, 2018, https://www.wsj.com/articles/at-netflix-radical-transparency-and-blunt-firings-unsettle-the-ranks-1540497174.

2 Individual and Cultural Differences

Exhibit 2.1 (Credit: US Army Africa/ flickr/ Attribution 2.0 Generic (CC BY 2.0))

Introduction

Learning Outcomes

After reading this chapter, you should be able to answer these questions:

1. How do managers and organizations appropriately select individuals for particular jobs?
2. How do people with different abilities, skills, and personalities build effective work teams?
3. How do managers and employees deal effectively with individual differences in the workplace?
4. How can organizations foster a work environment that allows employees an opportunity to develop and grow?
5. How do managers know how to get the best from each employee?
6. What is the role of ethical behavior in managerial actions?
7. How do you manage and do business with people from different cultures?

EXPLORING MANAGERIAL CAREERS

Building Back Trust on the Back End

One institution that has been around for generations is banking. However, many individuals have lost faith in the banking system, and who's to blame them? Big banks have let the general consumer down with security breaches and countless stories of scandals. One glaring example is Wells Fargo & Co., who are still recovering their brand from their admission of creating nearly two million accounts for customers without their permission. But this problem is not new. The approach to bolstering this trust factor is, however, taking on a new perspective with some quick adaptation and managerial foresight.

One CEO, Cathie Mahon, chief executive officer of the National Federation of Community Development Credit Unions, is not taking the disparities between credit unions and big banks lying down. Credit unions have always operated differently from big banks, and one key factor is that they are nonprofit while their big-bank counterparts are for-profit enterprises. This also can mean that they offer higher interest rates on deposits due to their size. Mahon has begun a keen undertaking to educate and empower low-income residents about financial resources. Her most recent endeavor is to provide a platform called CU Impact that keeps customers more informed about their balances, creates more trustworthy auto-pay features, more information delivered at ATMs as well. The improvements to the back-end reliability within the credit union system sustain the small, community feel of the credit union, while providing powerful, trustworthy systems that restore faith in their business. Her willingness to embrace technology and embrace differences of customers, employees, and the company structure overall made her the key to success for the future of their business.

Sources: Cohen, Arianne, "The CEO Who's Leveling the Playing Field Between Credit Unions and Big Banks," *Bloomberg Businessweek*, July 9, 2018, https://www.bloomberg.com/news/articles/2018-07-09/the-ceo-who-s-leveling-the-playing-field-between-credit-unions-and-big-banks; Koren, James Rufus, "It's been a year since the Wells Fargo scandal broke—and new problems are still surfacing," *Los Angeles Times*, September 8, 2017, http://www.latimes.com/business/la-fi-wells-fargo-one-year-20170908-story.html.

2.1 Individual and Cultural Factors in Employee Performance

1. How do managers and organizations appropriately select individuals for particular jobs?

As we can see in the example of Cathie Mahon, our unique personal characteristics can have a dramatic influence on both individual behavior and the behavior of those around us. To succeed in any managerial position, it is necessary to have the appropriate skills and abilities for the situation. Moreover, when selecting subordinates, managers have similar concerns. In short, individual differences can play a major role in how well someone performs on the job. They can even influence whether someone gets the job in the first place. Because of this, we begin this section with a look at individual differences in the workplace.

Several factors can be identified that influence employee behavior and performance. One early model of job performance argued simply that performance was largely a function of *ability* and *motivation*.[1] Using this simple model as a guide, we can divide our discussion of individual factors in performance into two categories: those that influence our *capacity to respond* and those that influence our will or *desire to respond*. The first category includes such factors as mental and physical abilities, personality traits, perceptual capabilities, and stress-tolerance levels. The second category includes those variables dealing with employee motivation. Both of these sets of factors are discussed in this part of the book as a prelude to more complex analyses of overall organizational performance.

Specifically, we begin our analysis in this chapter with a look at individual differences, including employee abilities and skills, personality variables, and work values. We will also examine the nature of culture and cultural diversity as it affects behavior in organizations both at home and abroad. Later we look at perception and job attitudes, and we review basic learning and reinforcement techniques. The basic theories of employee motivation are then introduced, including the concept of employee needs. More complex cognitive models of motivation will be examined, and finally, we review contemporary approaches to performance appraisals and reward systems in organizations. All told, this coverage aims to introduce the reader to the more salient aspects of individual behavior as they relate to organizational behavior and effectiveness.

CONCEPT CHECK 

1. What are the various abilities and skills that should be considered when hiring employees?
2. How should the personality differences and work values be taken into account when selecting employees?
3. What is the role of cultural diversity in selecting employees?

2.2 Employee Abilities and Skills

2. How do people with different abilities, skills, and personalities build effective work teams?

We begin with a look at *employee abilities and skills*. Abilities and skills generally represent those physical and intellectual characteristics that are relatively stable over time and that help determine an employee's capability to respond. Recognizing them is important in understanding organizational behavior, because they often bound an employee's ability to do the job. For example, if a clerk-typist simply does not have the manual dexterity to master the fundamentals of typing or keyboard entry, her performance will likely suffer. Similarly, a sales representative who has a hard time with simple numerical calculations will probably not do well on the job.

Mental Abilities

It is possible to divide our discussion of abilities and skills into two sections: mental abilities and physical abilities. **Mental abilities** are an individual's intellectual capabilities and are closely linked to how a person makes decisions and processes information. Included here are such factors as verbal comprehension, inductive reasoning, and memory. A summary is shown in **Table 2.1**.

Dimensions of Mental Abilities
• *Verbal comprehension*. The ability to understand the meanings of words and their relations to each other. • *Word fluency*. The ability to name objects or use words to form sentences that express an idea. • *Number aptitude*. The ability to make numerical calculations speedily and accurately. • *Inductive reasoning*. The ability to discover a rule or principle and apply it to the solution of a problem. • *Memory*. The ability to remember lists of words and numbers and other associations. • *Spatial aptitude*. The ability to perceive fixed geometric figures and their relations with other geometric figures. • *Perceptual speed*. The ability to perceive visual details quickly and accurately.

Table 2.1

From a managerial standpoint, a key aspect of mental ability is cognitive complexity. **Cognitive complexity** represents a person's capacity to acquire and sort through various pieces of information from the environment and organize them in such a way that they make sense. People with high cognitive complexity tend to use more information—and to see the relationships between aspects of this information—than people with low cognitive complexity. For example, if a manager was assigned a particular problem, would she have the capacity to break the problem down into its various facets and understand how these various facets relate to one another? A manager with low cognitive complexity would tend to see only one or two salient aspects of the problem, whereas a manager with higher cognitive complexity would understand more of the nuances and subtleties of the problem as they relate to each other and to other problems.

People with *low* cognitive complexity typically exhibit the following characteristics:[2]

They tend to be categorical and stereotypical. Cognitive structures that depend upon simple fixed rules of integration tend to reduce the possibility of thinking in terms of degrees.

Internal conflict appears to be minimized with simple structures. Since few alternative relationships are generated, closure is quick.

Behavior is apparently anchored in external conditions. There is less personal contribution in simple structures.

Fewer rules cover a wider range of phenomena. There is less distinction between separate situations.

On the other hand, people with *high* levels of cognitive complexity are typically characterized by the following:[3]

Their cognitive system is less deterministic. Numerous alternative relationships are generated and considered.

The environment is tracked in numerous ways. There is less compartmentalization of the environment.

The individual utilizes more internal processes. The self as an individual operates on the process.

Research on cognitive complexity has focused on two important areas from a managerial standpoint: leadership style and decision-making. In the area of leadership, it has been found that managers rated high on cognitive complexity are better able to handle complex situations, such as rapid changes in the external environment. Moreover, such managers also tend to use more resources and information when solving a problem and tend to be somewhat more considerate and consultative in their approach to managing their subordinates.[4] In the area of decision-making, fairly consistent findings show that individuals with high cognitive complexity (1) seek out more information for a decision, (2) actually process or use more information, (3) are better able to integrate discrepant information, (4) consider a greater number of possible solutions to the problem, and (5) employ more complex decision strategies than individuals with low cognitive complexity.[5]

Physical Abilities

The second set of variables relates to someone's **physical abilities**. Included here are both basic physical abilities (for example, strength) and **psychomotor abilities** (such as manual dexterity, eye-hand coordination, and manipulation skills). These factors are summarized in **Table 2.2**.[6] Considering both mental and physical abilities helps one understand the behavior of people at work and how they can be better managed. The recognition of such abilities—and the recognition that people have *different* abilities—has clear implications for employee recruitment and selection decisions; it brings into focus the importance of matching people to jobs. For example, Florida Power has a 16-hour selection process that involves 12 performance tests. Over the test period of a couple of years, 640 individuals applied for "lineperson" jobs. Of these, 259 were hired. As a consequence of the new performance tests and selection process, turnover went from 43 percent to 4.5 percent, and the program saved net $1 million.[7] In addition to selection, knowledge of job requirements and individual differences is also useful in evaluating training and development needs. Because human resources are important to management, it is imperative that managers become more familiar with the basic characteristics of their people.

Dimensions of Physical Abilities
Physical Abilities
• *Dynamic strength*. The ability to exert muscular force repeatedly or continuously for a period of time. • *Trunk strength*. The ability to exert muscular strength using the back and abdominal muscles. • *Static strength*. The amount of continuous force one is capable of exerting against an external object. • *Explosive strength*. The amount of force one is capable of exerting in one or a series of explosive acts. • *Extent flexibility*. The ability to move the trunk and back muscles as far as possible. • *Dynamic flexibility*. The ability to make rapid and repeated flexing movements. • *Gross body coordination*. The ability to coordinate the simultaneous actions of different parts of the body. • *Equilibrium*. The ability to maintain balance and equilibrium in spite of disruptive external forces. • *Stamina*. The ability to continue maximum effort requiring prolonged effort over time; the degree of cardiovascular conditioning.
Psychomotor Abilities
• *Control precision.* The ability to make fine, highly controlled muscular movements needed to adjust a control mechanism. • *Multilimb coordination*. The ability to coordinate the simultaneous movement of hands and feet. • *Response orientation*. The ability to make an appropriate response to a visual signal indicating a direction. • *Rate control*. The ability to make continuous anticipatory motor adjustments in speed and direction to follow a continuously moving target. • *Manual dexterity*. The ability to make skillful and well-directed arm-hand movements in manipulating large objects quickly. • *Finger dexterity*. The ability to make skillful and controlled manipulations of small objects. • *Arm-hand steadiness*. The ability to make precise arm-hand movements where steadiness is extremely important, and speed and strength are relatively unimportant. • *Reaction time.* How quickly a person can respond to a single stimulus with a simple response. • *Aiming.* The ability to make highly accurate, restricted hand movements requiring precise eye-hand coordination.

Table 2.2 (Attribution: Copyright Rice University, OpenStax, under CC BY-NC-SA 4.0 license)

CONCEPT CHECK 

1. Why should abilities and skills be taken into account when selecting employees?

2. Describe the components of mental abilities, cognitive complexity, physical ability, and psychomotor abilities.

2.3 Personality: An Introduction

3. How do managers and employees deal effectively with individual differences in the workplace?

The second individual difference variable deals with the concept of personality. We often hear people use and misuse the term **personality**. For example, we hear that someone has a "nice" personality. For our purposes, we will examine the term from a psychological standpoint as it relates to behavior and performance in the workplace. To do this, let us start with a more precise definition of the concept.

Definition of Personality

Personality can be defined in many ways. Perhaps one of the more useful definitions for purposes of organizational analysis is offered by Salvatore Maddi, who defines *personality* as follows:

". . . a stable set of characteristics and tendencies that determine those communalities and differences in the psychological behavior (thoughts, feelings, and actions) of people that have continuity in time and that may not be easily understood as the sole result of the social and biological pressures of the moment."[8]

Several aspects of this definition should be noted. First, personality is best understood as a constellation of interacting characteristics; it is necessary to look at the whole person when attempting to understand the phenomenon and its effects on subsequent behavior. Second, various dimensions of personality are relatively stable across time. Although changes—especially evolutionary ones—can occur, seldom do we see major changes in the personality of a normal individual. And third, the study of personality emphasizes both similarities and differences across people. This is important for managers to recognize as they attempt to formulate actions designed to enhance performance and employee well-being.

Influences on Personality Development

Early research on personality development focused on the issue of whether heredity or environment determined an individual's personality. Although a few researchers are still concerned with this issue, most contemporary psychologists now feel this debate is fruitless. As noted long ago by Kluckhohn and Murray:

"The two sets of determinants can rarely be completely disentangled once the environment has begun to operate. The pertinent questions are: (1) which of the various genetic potentialities will be actualized as a consequence of a particular series of life-events in a given physical, social, and cultural environment? and (2) what limits to the development of this personality are set by genetic constitution?"[9]

In other words, if the individual is viewed from the whole-person perspective, the search for the determinants of personal traits focuses on both heredity and environment as well as the interaction between the two over time. In this regard, five major categories of determinants of personal traits may be identified: physiological, cultural, family and social group, role, and situational determinants.

Physiological Determinants. Physiological determinants include factors such as stature, health, and sex that often act as constraints on personal growth and development. For instance, tall people often tend to become more domineering and self-confident than shorter people. Traditional sex-role stereotyping has served to channel males and females into different developmental patterns. For example, males have been trained to be more assertive and females more passive.

Cultural Determinants. Because of the central role of culture in the survival of a society, there is great emphasis on instilling cultural norms and values in children growing up. For instance, in capitalist societies, where individual responsibility is highly prized, emphasis is placed on developing achievement-oriented, independent, self-reliant people, whereas in socialistic societies, emphasis is placed on developing cooperative, group-oriented individuals who place the welfare of the whole society ahead of individual needs. Cultural determinants affect personal traits. As Mussen notes, "The child's cultural group defines the range of experiments and situations he is likely to encounter and the values and personality characteristics that will be reinforced and hence learned."[10] Consider, for example, how Japanese society develops its world-renowned work ethic.

Family and Social Group Determinants. Perhaps the most important influences on personal development are family and social group determinants. For instance, it has been found that children who grow up in democratic homes tend to be more stable, less argumentative, more socially successful, and more sensitive to praise or blame than those who grow up in authoritarian homes.[11] One's immediate family and peers contribute significantly to the socialization process, influencing how individuals think and behave through an intricate system of rewards and penalties.

Role Determinants. People are assigned various roles very early in life because of factors such as sex, socioeconomic background, and race. As one grows older, other factors, such as age and occupation, influence the roles we are expected to play. Such role determinants often limit our personal growth and development as individuals and significantly control acceptable behavior patterns.

Situational Determinants. Finally, personal development can be influenced by situational determinants. These are factors that are often unpredictable, such as a divorce or death in the family. For instance, James Abegglen studied 20 successful male executives who had risen from lower-class childhoods and discovered that in three-fourths of the cases these executives had experienced some form of severe separation trauma from their fathers. Their fathers (and role models) had either died, been seriously ill, or had serious financial setbacks. Abegglen hypothesized that the sons' negative identification with their fathers' plights represented a major motivational force for achievement and success.[12]

CONCEPT CHECK 

1. What is the role of personality and personality development in the workplace?

2.4 Personality and Work Behavior

4. How can organizations foster a work environment that allows employees an opportunity to develop and grow?

Personality theories that utilize the trait approach have proven popular among investigators of employee behavior in organizations. There are several reasons for this. To begin with, trait theories focus largely on the normal, healthy adult, in contrast to psychoanalytic and other personality theories that focus largely on abnormal behavior. Trait theories identify several characteristics that describe people. Allport insisted that our understanding of individual behavior could progress only by breaking behavior patterns down into a series of elements (traits).[13] "The only thing you can do about a *total* personality is to send flowers to it," he once said. Hence, in the study of people at work, we may discuss an employee's dependability, emotional stability, or cognitive complexity. These traits, when taken together, form a large mosaic that provides insight into individuals. A third reason for the popularity of trait theories in the study of organizational behavior is that the traits that are identified are measurable and tend to remain relatively stable over time. It is much easier to make comparisons among employees using these tangible qualities rather than the somewhat mystical psychoanalytic theories or the highly abstract and volatile self theories.

The number of traits people are believed to exhibit varies according to which theory we employ. In an exhaustive search, over 17,000 can be identified. Obviously, this number is so large as to make any reasonable analysis of the effects of personality in the workplace impossible. In order for us to make any sense out of this, it is necessary for us to concentrate on a small number of personality variables that have a direct impact on work behavior. If we do this, we can identify six traits that seem to be relatively important for our purposes here. It will be noted that some of these traits (for example, self-esteem or locus of control) have to do with how we see ourselves, whereas other traits (for example, introversion-extroversion or dependability) have to do with how we interact with others. Moreover, these traits are largely influenced by one's personality development and, in turn, influence actual attitudes and behaviors at work, as shown in **Exhibit 2.2**.

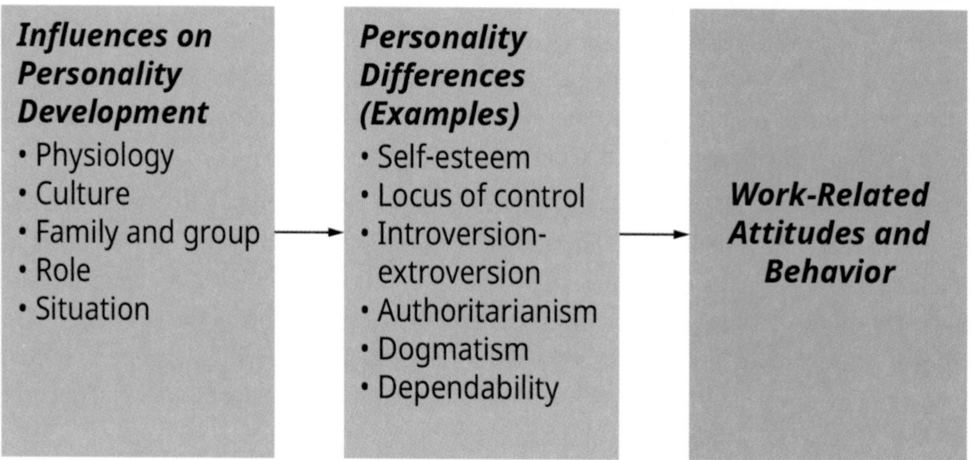

Exhibit 2.2 Relation of Personality to Attitudes and Behavior (Attribution: Copyright Rice University, OpenStax, under CC BY-NC-SA 4.0 license)

Self-Esteem

One trait that has emerged recently as a key variable in determining work behavior and effectiveness is an employee's self-esteem. **Self-esteem** can be defined as one's opinion or belief about one's self and self-worth. It is how we see ourselves as individuals. Do we have confidence in ourselves? Do we think we are successful? Attractive? Worthy of others' respect or friendship?

Research has shown that high self-esteem in school-age children enhances assertiveness, independence, and creativity. People with high self-esteem often find it easier to give and receive affection, set higher goals for personal achievement, and exert energy to try to attain goals set for them. Moreover, individuals with high self-esteem will be more likely to seek higher-status occupations and will take more risks in the job search. For example, one study found that students possessing higher self-esteem were more highly rated by college recruiters, received more job offers, and were more satisfied with their job search than students with low self-esteem.[14] Hence, personality traits such as this one can affect your job and career even before you begin work!

Locus of Control

Locus of control refers to the tendency among individuals to attribute the events affecting their lives either to their own actions or to external forces; it is a measure of how much you think you control your own destiny. Two types of individual are identified. People with an *internal* locus of control tend to attribute their successes—and failures—to their own abilities and efforts. Hence, a student would give herself credit for passing an examination; likewise, she would accept blame for failing.

In contrast, people with an *external* locus of control tend to attribute things that happen to them as being caused by someone or something else. They give themselves neither credit nor blame. Hence, passing an exam may be dismissed by saying it was "too easy," whereas failing may be excused by convincing one's self that the exam was "unfair."

If you want to determine your own locus of control, fill out the self-assessment in the end-of-chapter assignments. This is an abbreviated and adapted version of the scale originally developed by Rotter. When you have finished, refer to that reference for scoring procedures.

Recent research on locus of control suggests that people with an internal locus of control (1) exhibit greater work motivation, (2) have stronger expectations that effort will lead to actual high job performance, (3) perform better on tasks requiring learning or problem-solving, (4) typically receive higher salaries and salary increases, and (5) exhibit less job-related anxiety than externals.[15] Locus of control has numerous implications for management. For example, consider what would happen if you placed an "internal" under tight supervision or an "external" under loose supervision. The results probably would not be very positive. Or what would happen if you placed both internals and externals on a merit-based compensation plan? Who would likely perform better? Who might perform better under a piece-rate system?

Introversion-Extroversion

The third personality dimension we should consider focuses on the extent to which people tend to be shy and retiring or socially gregarious. *Introverts* (**introversion**) tend to focus their energies inwardly and have a greater sensitivity to abstract feelings, whereas *extroverts* (**extroversion**) direct more of their attention to other people, objects, and events. Research evidence suggests that both types of people have a role to play in organizations.[16] Extroverts more often succeed in first-line management roles, where only superficial "people skills" are required; they also do better in field assignments—for example, as sales representatives. Introverts, on the other hand, tend to succeed in positions requiring more reflection, analysis, and sensitivity to people's inner feelings and qualities. Such positions are included in a variety of departments within organizations, such as accounting, personnel, and computer operations. In view of the complex nature of modern organizations, both types of individual are clearly needed.

Authoritarianism and Dogmatism

Authoritarianism refers to an individual's orientation toward authority. More specifically, an authoritarian orientation is generally characterized by an overriding conviction that it is right and proper for there to be clear status and power differences among people.[17] According to T. W. Adorno, a high authoritarian is typically (1) demanding, directive, and controlling of her subordinates; (2) submissive and deferential toward superiors;

(3) intellectually rigid; (4) fearful of social change; (5) highly judgmental and categorical in reactions to others; (6) distrustful; and (7) hostile in response to restraint. Nonauthoritarians, on the other hand, generally believe that power and status differences should be minimized, that social change can be constructive, and that people should be more accepting and less judgmental of others.

In the workplace, the consequences of these differences can be tremendous. Research has shown, for example, that employees who are high in authoritarianism often perform better under rigid supervisory control, whereas those rated lower on this characteristic perform better under more participative supervision.[18] Can you think of other consequences that might result from these differences?

Related to this authoritarianism is the trait of dogmatism. **Dogmatism** refers to a particular cognitive style that is characterized by closed-mindedness and inflexibility.[19] This dimension has particularly profound implications for managerial decision-making; it is found that dogmatic managers tend to make decisions quickly, based on only limited information and with a high degree of confidence in the correctness of their decisions.[20] Do you know managers (or professors) who tend to be dogmatic? How does this behavior affect those around them?

Dependability

Finally, people can be differentiated with respect to their behavioral consistency, or **dependability**. Individuals who are seen as self-reliant, responsible, consistent, and dependable are typically considered to be desirable colleagues or group members who will cooperate and work steadfastly toward group goals.[21] Personnel managers often seek a wide array of information concerning dependability before hiring job applicants. Even so, contemporary managers often complain that many of today's workers simply lack the feeling of personal responsibility necessary for efficient operations. Whether this is a result of the personal failings of the individuals or a lack of proper motivation by superiors remains to be determined.

Obviously, personality factors such as those discussed here can play a major role in determining work behavior both on the shop floor and in the executive suite. A good example of this can be seen in the events leading up to the demise of one of America's largest and oldest architectural firms. Observe the role of personality in the events that follow.

MANAGING CHANGE

Personality Clash: Design vs. Default

Philip Johnson, at age 86, was considered the dean of American architecture and was known for such landmarks as the AT&T building in New York and the Pennzoil Center in Houston, but he was also forced out of the firm that he built, only to watch it fall into default and bankruptcy.

In 1969, Johnson invited John Burgee, who was just 35, to become his sole partner to handle the management side of the business and thereby allow him to focus on the creative side. "I picked John Burgee as my righthand man. Every design architect needs a Burgee. The more leadership he took, the happier I was," Johnson said. Burgee's personality was perfectly suited to the nuts-and-bolts tasks of managing the firm and overseeing the projects through construction.

For all his management effort, Burgee felt that only Johnson's name ever appeared in the press. "It was always difficult for me, being a younger man and less flamboyant," commented Burgee. Eventually, Burgee was able to get Johnson to change the name of the firm, first to Philip Johnson & John Burgee Architects, then to Johnson/Burgee Architects, and finally to John Burgee Architects, with Philip Johnson. Although Burgee wanted to be involved in all aspects of the business, Johnson was unwilling to relinquish control over design to Burgee.

In 1988, Burgee sent a four-page memo to Johnson in which he listed each of the firm's 24 projects and outlined the ones for which Johnson could initiate designs, initiate contact with clients, or work on independently at home. Burgee also instructed Johnson not to involve himself with the younger architects or advise them on their drawings.

The clash of the creative personality of Johnson and the controlling personality of Burgee came to a climax when Burgee asked Johnson to leave the firm. Unfortunately, Burgee underestimated the reaction of clients and lost many key contracts. Eventually, Burgee had to file for bankruptcy, and Johnson continued working on his own, including a project for Estée Lauder.

Source: Michelle Pacelle, "Design Flaw." *Wall Street Journal,* September 2, 1992, p. A1, A5.

CONCEPT CHECK

1. What are the things that managers can do to foster an environment where employees can gain personal development and grow?

2.5 Personality and Organization: A Basic Conflict?

5. How do managers know how to get the best from each employee?

Most theories of personality stress that an individual's personality becomes complete only when the individual interacts with other people; growth and development do not occur in a vacuum. Human personalities are the individual expressions of our culture, and our culture and social order are the group expressions of individual personalities. This being the case, it is important to understand how work organizations influence the growth and development of the adult employee.

A model of person-organization relationships has been proposed by Chris Argyris.[22] This model, called the **basic incongruity thesis**, consists of three parts: what individuals want from organizations, what organizations want from individuals, and how these two potentially conflicting sets of desires are harmonized.

Argyris begins by examining how healthy individuals change as they mature. On the basis of previous work, Argyris suggests that as people grow to maturity, seven basic changes in needs and interests occur:

1. People develop from a state of passivity as infants to a state of increasing activity as adults.
2. People develop from a state of dependence upon others to a state of relative independence.
3. People develop from having only a few ways of behaving to having many diverse ways of behaving.
4. People develop from having shallow, casual, and erratic interests to having fewer, but deeper, interests.
5. People develop from having a short time perspective (i.e., behavior is determined by present events) to having a longer time perspective (behavior is determined by a combination of past, present, and future

events).

6. People develop from subordinate to superordinate positions (from child to parent or from trainee to manager).
7. People develop from a low understanding or awareness of themselves to a greater understanding of and control over themselves as adults.

Although Argyris acknowledges that these developments may differ among individuals, the general tendencies from childhood to adulthood are believed to be fairly common.

Next, Argyris turns his attention to the defining characteristics of traditional work organizations. In particular, he argues that in the pursuit of efficiency and effectiveness, organizations create work situations aimed more at getting the job done than at satisfying employees' personal goals. Examples include increased task specialization, unity of command, a rules orientation, and other things aimed at turning out a standardized product with standardized people. In the pursuit of this standardization, Argyris argues, organizations often create work situations with the following characteristics:

1. Employees are allowed minimal control over their work; control is often shifted to machines.
2. They are expected to be passive, dependent, and subordinate.
3. They are allowed only a short-term horizon in their work.
4. They are placed on repetitive jobs that require only minimal skills and abilities.
5. On the basis of the first four items, people are expected to produce under conditions leading to psychological failure.

Hence, Argyris argues persuasively that many jobs in our technological society are structured in such a way that they conflict with the basic growth needs of a healthy personality. This conflict is represented in **Exhibit 2.3**. The magnitude of this conflict between personality and organization is a function of several factors. The strongest conflict can be expected under conditions where employees are very mature, organization are highly structured and rules and procedures are formalized, and jobs are fragmented and mechanized. Hence, we would expect the strongest conflict to be at the lower levels of the organization, among blue-collar and clerical workers. Managers tend to have jobs that are less mechanized and tend to be less subject to formalized rules and procedures.

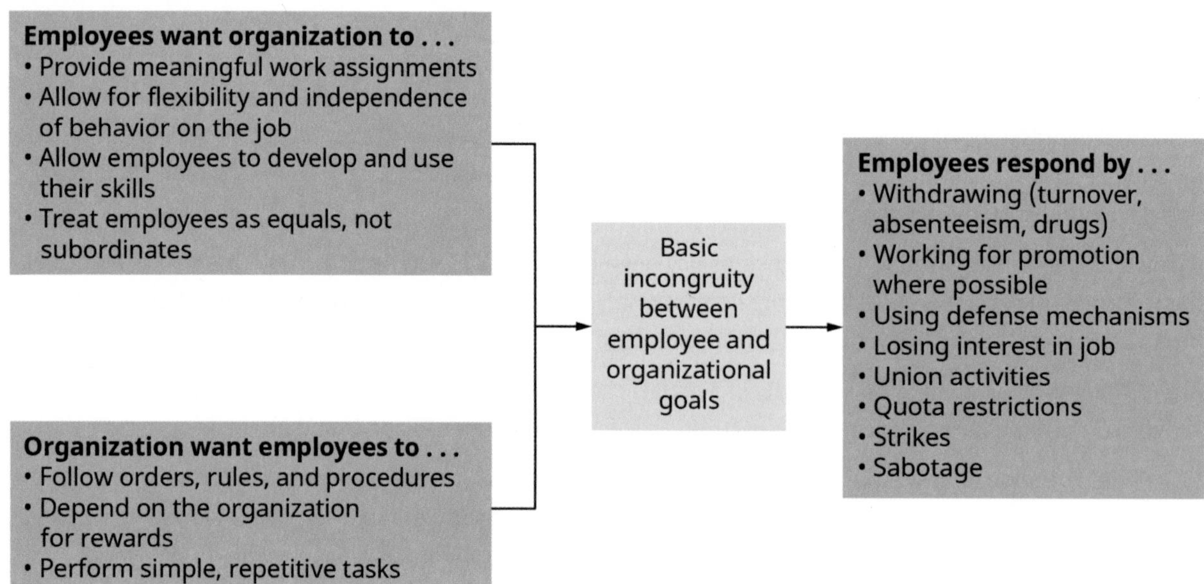

Exhibit 2.3 Basic Conflict Between Employees and Organizations (Attribution: Copyright Rice University, OpenStax, under CC BY-NC-SA 4.0 license)

Where strong conflicts between personalities and organizations exist, or, more precisely, where strong conflicts exist between what employees and organizations want from each other, employees are faced with difficult choices. They may choose to leave the organization or to work hard to climb the ladder into the upper echelons of management. They may defend their self-concepts and adapt through the use of defense mechanisms. Disassociating themselves psychologically from the organization (e.g., losing interest in their work, lowering their work standards, etc.) and concentrating instead on the material rewards available from the organization is another possible response. Or they may find allies in their fellow workers and, in concert, may further adapt *as a group* by such activities as quota restrictions, unionizing efforts, strikes, and sabotage.

Unfortunately, although such activities may help employees feel that they are getting back at the organization, they do not alleviate the basic situation that is causing the problem. To do this, one has to examine the nature of the job and the work climate. Personality represents a powerful force in the determination of work behavior and must be recognized before meaningful change can be implemented by managers to improve the effectiveness of their organizations.

MANAGING CHANGE

Integrating Employee and Organizational Goals at Kayak

In many ways the above scenario paints a bleak portrait of the relationship of many workers to their employers. However, it should be noted that many companies are trying to change this relationship and create a partnership between employees and company in which the goals of both are realized. In doing so, however, these companies are careful to select and hire only those employees who have the potential to fit in with the company's unique culture. A case in point is Kayak, an Internet-based travel company in Stamford, Connecticut. The company strives to create customer satisfaction, starting with their own culture and employees within the walls of their building. Cofounder and former CTO Paul English's goal was to bring a constant stream of "new-new ideas" and surround himself with "childlike creative people" to liven up the space and be able to promote inspiration.

Kayak doesn't hire based on technical skills; their philosophy is to hire an employee on the basis of being the smartest person that somebody knows. Employees are constantly pushed to put their ideas to the test, and the company emphasizes a work-life balance that puts their employees first, which in turn makes for a productive work environment.

Kayak's ability to make fast-paced decisions comes from the empowerment of their employees to try out their ideas. Current CTO Giorgos Zacharia takes pride in the way they are able to keep order and drive deadlines. "Anyone on any team can come up with the idea, prototype it, and then we see what the user thinks about it. If it works, great! But there's no grand design; it's very organic and we see that as a strength," says Zacharia.

By encouraging and rewarding risk-taking, Kayak is able to make fast decisions, fail fast, and then turn around and come up with something more innovative that will be better than the last idea. Overall, the company hopes to offer its employees a work environment that allows for considerable personal growth and need-satisfaction. In short, the company aims to reduce the possibility of a basic incongruity developing between employee and organizational goals.

Sources: Hawkes, Jocelyn, "KAYAK on Creating a Culture of Innovation," *Fast Company*, April 4, 2012. (https://www.fastcompany.com/1827003/kayak-creating-culture-innovation); Hickey, Matt, "How KAYAK

Converts Employee Well-Being Into Customer satisfaction," *Forbes*, October 4, 2015. https://www.forbes.com/sites/matthickey/2015/10/07/how-kayak-converts-employee-well-being-into-customer-satisfaction/#6c97f519b7a4.

Personality and Employee Selection

Recent years have seen an increased interest in the use of preemployment screening tests. Several key assumptions underlie the use of personality tests as one method of selecting potential employees: (1) individuals have different personalities and traits, (2) these differences affect their behavior and performance, and (3) different job have different requirements. Consequently, tests can be used to select individuals who match the overall company as well as match particular types of people to specific jobs. However, managers must be careful in their use of these selection instruments. Legally all selection tests must meet the guidelines for nondiscrimination set forth in the Equal Employment Opportunity Commission's Uniform Guidelines on Employee Selection Procedures. Specifically, in 1971 the Supreme Court ruled (Griggs v. Duke Power Company) that "good intent or the absence of discriminatory intent does not redeem . . . testing mechanisms that operate as built-in 'head-winds' for minority groups and are unrelated to measuring job capability." This ruling led to two important cases in which discrimination might apply to selection practices. First, "disparate treatment" involves the intentional discrimination against an individual based on race, color, gender, religion, or national origin. Second, "disparate impact" involves the adverse effect of selection practices (as well as other practices) on minorities regardless of whether these practices were intended to have an adverse impact or not. Consequently, although personality tests can be an important means of selecting potential employees as well as matching them to appropriate jobs, care must be taken to demonstrate that the characteristics measured actually predict job performance.

CONCEPT CHECK

1. What are some things that managers can do to foster organizational harmony where they get the best results from all employees?

2.6 Personal Values and Ethics

6. What is the role of ethical behavior in managerial actions?

A factor that has surprised many business leaders is the alarming rise in accusations of unethical or disreputable behavior in today's companies. We hear with increasing regularity of stock market manipulations, disregard of environmental hazards, bribes, and kickbacks. To understand these behaviors, we must examine the role of values and personal ethics in the workplace. We begin with the concept of values.

A *value* may be defined as "an enduring belief that a specific mode of conduct or end-state of existence is personally or socially preferable to an opposite or converse mode of conduct or end-state of existence."[23] In other words, a value represents a judgment by an individual that certain things are "good" or "bad," "important" or "unimportant," and so forth. As such, values serve a useful function in providing guidelines or standards for choosing one's own behavior and for evaluating the behavior of others.

Characteristics of Values

The values people have tend to be relatively stable over time. The reason for this lies in the manner in which values are acquired in the first place. That is, when we first learn a value (usually at a young age), we are taught that such-and-such behavior is *always* good or *always* bad. For instance, we may be taught that lying or stealing is always unacceptable. Few people are taught that such behavior is acceptable in some circumstances but not in others. Hence, this definitive quality of learned values tends to secure them firmly in our belief systems. This is not to say that values do not change over time. As we grow, we are increasingly confronted with new and often conflicting situations. Often, it is necessary for us to weigh the relative merits of each and choose a course of action. Consider, for example, the worker who has a strong belief in hard work but who is pressured by her colleagues not to outperform the group. What would you do in this situation?

Rokeach has identified two fundamental types of values: instrumental and terminal.[24] **Instrumental values** represent those values concerning the way we approach end-states. That is, do we believe in ambition, cleanliness, honesty, or obedience? What factors guide your everyday behavior? **Terminal values**, on the other hand, are those end-state goals that we prize. Included here are such things as a comfortable life, a sense of accomplishment, equality among all people, and so forth. Both sets of values have significant influence on everyday behavior at work.

You can assess your own instrumental and terminal values by completing the self-assessment in the end-of-chapter assignments. Simply rank-order the two lists of values, and then refer to the reference for scoring procedures.

Role of Values and Ethics in Organizations

Personal values represent an important force in organizational behavior for several reasons. In fact, at least three purposes are served by the existence of personal values in organizations: (1) values serve as standards of behavior for determining a correct course of action; (2) values serve as guidelines for decision-making and conflict resolution; and (3) values serve as an influence on employee motivation. Let us consider each of these functions.

Standards of Behavior. First, values help us determine appropriate standards of behavior. They place limits on our behavior both inside and outside the organization. In such situations, we are referring to what is called *ethical behavior*, or **ethics**. Employees at all levels of the organization have to make decisions concerning what to them is right or wrong, proper or improper. For example, would you conceal information about a hazardous product made by your company, or would you feel obliged to tell someone? How would you respond to petty theft on the part of a supervisor or coworker in the office? To some extent, ethical behavior is influenced by societal values. Societal norms tell us it is wrong to engage in certain behaviors. In addition, however, individuals must often determine for themselves what is proper and what is not. This is particularly true when people find themselves in "gray zones"—situations where ethical standards are ambiguous or unclear. In many situations, a particular act may not be illegal. Moreover, one's colleagues and friends may disagree about what is proper. In such circumstances, people have to determine their own standards of behavior.

EXPANDING AROUND THE GLOBE

Two Cultures' Perspectives of Straight Talk

Yukiko Tanabe, a foreign exchange student from Tokyo, Japan, was both eager and anxious about making new friends during her one-year study abroad in the United States. After a month-long intensive course in English over the summer, she began her studies at the University of California. Yukiko was in the same psychology class as Jane McWilliams. Despite Yukiko's somewhat shy personality, it did not take long before she and Jane were talking before and after class and studying together.

Part of the way through the term, the professor asked for volunteers to be part of an experiment on personalities and problem-solving. The professor also offered extra credit for participation in the experiment and asked interested students to stay after class to discuss the project in more detail.

When class was over, Jane asked Yukiko if she wanted to stay after and learn more about the project and the extra credit. Yukiko hesitated and then said that she was not sure. Jane replied that it would only take a few minutes to listen to the explanation, and so the two young women went up to the front of the class, along with about 20 other students, to hear the details.

The project would simply involve completing a personality questionnaire and then attempting to solve three short case problems. In total, it would take about one hour of time and would be worth 5 percent extra credit. Jane though it was a great idea and asked Yukiko if she wanted to participate. Yukiko replied that she was not sure. Jane responded that they could go together, that it would be fun, and that 5 percent extra credit was a nice bonus. To this Yukiko made no reply, so Jane signed both of them up for the project and suggested that they meet at the quad about 10 minutes before the scheduled beginning of the experiment.

On the day of the experiment, however, Yukiko did not show up. Jane found out later from Yukiko that she did not want to participate in the experiment. "Then why didn't you just say so?" asked Jane. "Because I did not want to embarrass you in front of all your other friends by saying no," explained Yukiko.

Source: Personal communication by the author. Names have been disguised.

Guidelines for Decision-Making and Conflict Resolution. In addition, values serve as guidelines for making decisions and for attempting to resolve conflicts. Managers who value personal integrity are less likely to make decisions they know to be injurious to someone else. Relatedly, values can influence how someone approaches a conflict. For example, if your boss asks your opinion about a report she wrote that you don't like, do you express your opinion candidly or be polite and flatter her?

An interesting development in the area of values and decision-making involves integrity or honesty tests. These tests are designed to measure an individual's level of integrity or honesty based on the notion that honest or dishonest behavior and decisions flow from a person's underlying values. Today over 5,000 firms use these tests, some of which use direct questions and some of which use camouflaged questions. Although the reliability of the most common tests seem good, their validity (i.e., the extent to which they can accurately predict dishonest behavior) is more open to question.[25] Nevertheless, because they do not cost much and are less intrusive than drug or polygraph testing, integrity tests are increasingly used to screen potential employees.

Influence on Motivation. Values affect employee motivation by determining what rewards or outcomes are sought. Employees are often offered overtime work and the opportunity to make more money at the expense of free time and time with their families. Which would you choose? Would you work harder to get a promotion to a perhaps more stressful job or "lay back" and accept a slower and possibly less rewarding career path? Value questions such as these confront employees and managers every day.

Prominent among work-related values is the concept of the **work ethic**. Simply put, the work ethic refers to the strength of one's commitment and dedication to hard work, both as an end in itself and as a means to future rewards. Much has been written lately concerning the relative state of the work ethic in North America. It has been repeatedly pointed out that one reason for our trouble in international competition lies in our rather mediocre work ethic. This is not to say that many Americans do not work hard; rather, it is to say that others (most notably those in East Asia) simply work harder.

There are many ways to assess these differences, but perhaps the simplest way is to look at actual hours worked on average in different countries both in Asia and Western Europe. Looking at **Table 2.3**, you may be surprised to discover that although the average American works 1,789 hours (and takes an average of 19.5 vacation days) per year, the average South Korean works 2,070 hours per year (and takes only 4.5 days of vacation)![26] The typical Japanese worker works 1,742 hours per year and takes 9.6 days of vacation. Meanwhile, Western Europeans work fewer hours and take more vacation days. Thus, although Americans may work longer hours than many Europeans, they fall far behind many in East Asia.

Average Hours Worked and Vacation Taken per Worker		
Country	Average Hours Worked per Year	Vacation Days Actually Taken
South Korea	2,070	4.5
United States	1,789	19.5
OECD Average	1,763	
Japan	1,742	9.6
United Kingdom	1,676	22.5
Germany	1,288	30.2
France	1,472	25.0
Source: Adapted from OECD.Stat, "Average annual hours actually worked per worker," accessed July 20, 2018, https://stats.oecd.org/Index.aspx?DataSetCode=ANHRS; and Richard M. Steers, Yoo Keun Shin, and Gerardo R. Ungson, *The Chaebol: Korea's New Industrial Might* (Philadelphia: Ballinger, 1989).		

Table 2.3 (Attribution: Copyright Rice University, OpenStax, under CC BY-NC-SA 4.0 license)

Example: A Country Tries to Reduce Its Workweek

What does a country do when its people are overmotivated? Consider the case of Japan. On the basis of Japan's newfound affluence and success in the international marketplace, many companies—and the government—are beginning to be concerned that perhaps Japanese employees work too hard and should slow down. They may be too motivated for their own good. As a result, the Japanese Department of Labor has initiated a drive to shorten the workweek and encourage more Japanese employees to take longer holidays. The effort is focusing on middle-aged and older employees, because their physical stamina may be less than that of their more junior colleagues. Many companies are following this lead and are beginning to reduce the workweek. This is no easy task in a land where such behavior may be seen by employees as showing disloyalty toward the company. It requires a fundamental change in employee attitudes.

At the same time, among younger employees, cracks are beginning to appear in the fabled Japanese work ethic. Younger workers are beginning to express increased frustration with dull jobs and routine assignments, and job satisfaction appears to be at an all-time low. Young Japanese are beginning to take longer lunch periods and look forward to Friday and the coming weekend. Whether this is attributable to increasing affluence in a changing society or simply the emergence of a new generation, things are changing—however slowly—in the East.[27]

CONCEPT CHECK 

1. What role do managers undertake to ensure an environment where ethics and values are followed?

2.7 Cultural Differences

7. How do you manage and do business with people from different cultures?

The final topic we will discuss in this chapter is the role of culture and cultural diversity in organizational behavior. Cultural diversity can be analyzed in many ways. For instance, we can compare cultural diversity *within* one country or company, or we can compare cultures *across* units. That is, we can look inside a particular North American firm and see employees who are Asian, black, Latino, American Indian, white, and so forth. Clearly, these individuals have different cultural backgrounds, frames of reference, traditions, and so forth. Or we can look more globally and compare a typical American firm with a typical Mexican, Italian, or Chinese firm and again see significant differences in culture.

We can also analyze cultural diversity by looking at different patterns of behavior. For instance, Americans often wonder why Japanese or Korean businesspeople always bow when they meet; this seems strange to some. Likewise, many Asians wonder why Americans always shake hands, a similarly strange behavior. Americans often complain that Japanese executives say "yes" when they actually mean something else, while Japanese executives claim many Americans promise things they know they cannot deliver. Many of these differences result from a lack of understanding concerning the various cultures and how they affect behavior both inside and outside the workplace. As the marketplace and economies of the world merge ever closer, it is increasingly important that we come to understand more about cultural variations as they affect our world.

What Is Culture?

Simply put, **culture** may be defined as "the collective programming of the mind which distinguishes the members of one human group from another; the interactive aggregate of common characteristics that influences a human group's response to its environment."[28] More to the point, culture is the "collective mental programming of a people."[29] It is the unique characteristics of a people. As such, culture is:

- Something that is shared by all or most of the members of a society
- Something that older members of a society attempt to pass along to younger members
- Something that shapes our view of the world

The concept of culture represents an easy way to understand a people, albeit on a superficial level. Thus, we refer to the Chinese culture or the American culture. This is not to say that every member within a culture behaves in exactly the same way. On the contrary, every culture has diversity, but members of a certain culture tend to exhibit similar behavioral patterns that reflect where and how they grew up. A knowledge of a culture's patterns should help us deal with its members.

Culture affects the workplace because it affects what we do and how we behave. As shown in **Exhibit 2.4**, cultural variations influence our values, which in turn affect attitudes and, ultimately, behaviors. For instance, a culture that is characterized by hard work (e.g., the Korean culture discussed above) would exhibit a value or ethic of hard work. This work ethic would be reflected in positive attitudes toward work and the workplace; people would feel that hard work is satisfying and beneficial—they might feel committed to their employer and they might feel shame if they do not work long hours. This, in turn, would lead to actual high levels of work. This behavior, then, would serve to reinforce the culture and its value, and so on.

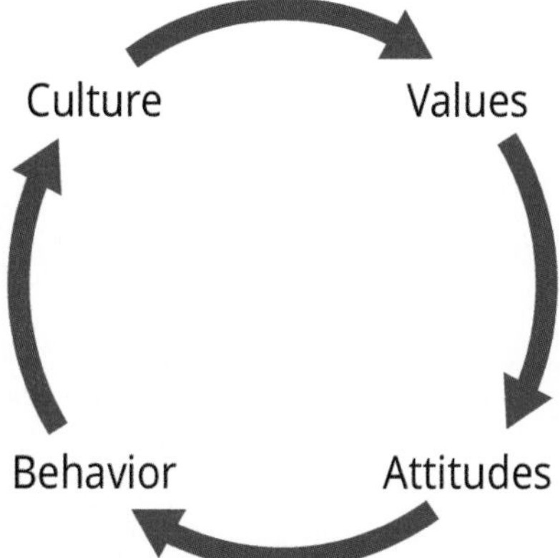

Exhibit 2.4 Relationship of Culture to Values, Attitudes, and Behavior (Attribution: Copyright Rice University, OpenStax, under CC BY-NC-SA 4.0 license)

To see how this works, consider the results of a survey of managerial behavior by French researcher Andre Laurent.[30] He asked managers how important it was for managers to have precise answers when asked a question by subordinates. The results, shown in **Exhibit 2.5**, clearly show how culture can influence very specific managerial behavior. In some countries, it is imperative for the manager to "know" the answer (even when she really doesn't), whereas in other countries it made little difference. Thus, if we want to understand why someone does something in the workplace, at least part of the behavior may be influenced by her cultural background.

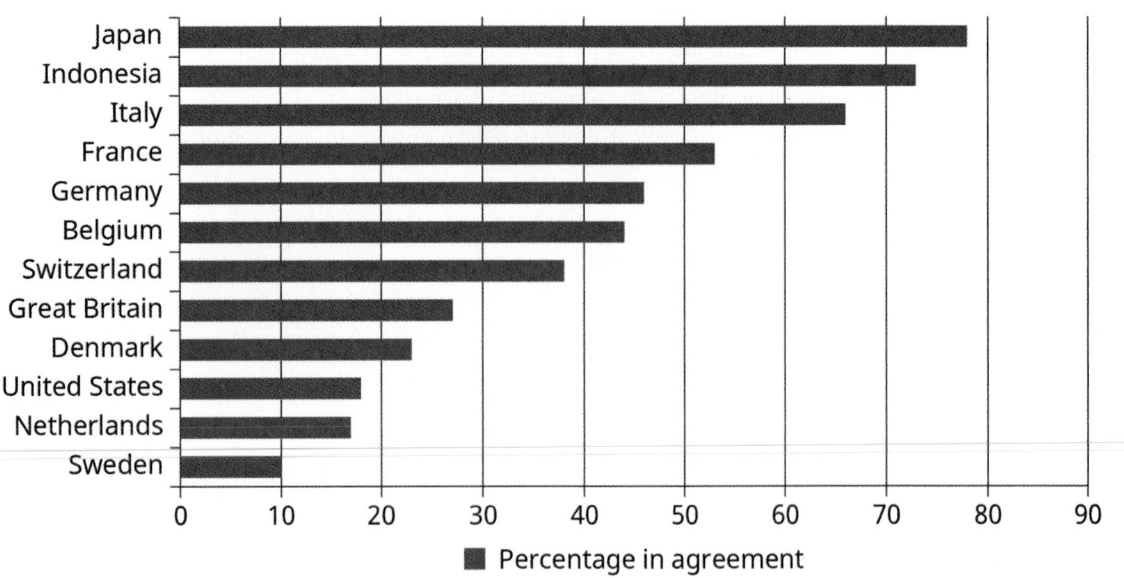

Exhibit 2.5 Appropriate Managerial Behavior in Different Countries (Attribution: Copyright Rice University, OpenStax, under CC BY-NC-SA 4.0 license)

Dimensions of Culture

There are several ways to distinguish different cultures from one another. Kluckhohn and Strodtbeck have identified six dimensions that are helpful in understanding such differences.[31] These are as follows:

1. *How people view humanity*. Are people basically good, or are they evil? Can most people be trusted or not? Are most people honest? What is the true nature of humankind?
2. *How people see nature*. What is the proper relationship between people and the environment? Should people be in harmony with nature, or should they attempt to control or harness nature?
3. *How people approach interpersonal relationships*. Should one stress individualism or membership in a group? Is the person more or less important than the group? What is the "pecking order" in a society? Is it based on seniority or on wealth and power?
4. *How people view activity and achievement*. Which is a more worthy goal: activity (getting somewhere) or simply being (staying where one is)?
5. *How people view time*. Should one focus on the past, the present, or the future? Some cultures are said to be living in the past, whereas others are looking to the future.
6. *How people view space*. How should physical space be used in our lives? Should we live communally or separately? Should important people be physically separated from others? Should important meetings be held privately or in public?

To see how this works, examine **Exhibit 2.7**, which differentiates four countries (Mexico, Germany, Japan, and the United States) along these six dimensions. Although the actual place of each country on these scales may be argued, the exhibit does serve to highlight several trends that managers should be aware of as they approach their work. For example, although managers in all four countries may share similar views on the nature of people (good versus bad), significant differences are noted on such dimensions as people's relation to nature and interpersonal relations. This, in turn, can affect how managers in these countries approach contract negotiations, the acquisition of new technologies, and the management of employees.

Exhibit 2.6 Japanese train station Kluckhohn and Strodtbeck identified six dimensions that are helpful in understanding such differences. Japan is a populous country that requires workers to take public transportation to and from work. *How does the Japanese geography affect Japanese culture?* (Credit: elminium/ flickr/ Attribution 2.0 Generic (CC BY 2.0))

Dimensions such as these help us frame any discussion about how people differ. We can say, for example, that most Americans are individualistic, activity-oriented, and present/future-oriented. We can further say that they value privacy and want to control their environment. In another culture, perhaps the mode is past-oriented, reflective, group-oriented, and unconcerned with achievement. In Japan we hear that "the nail that sticks out gets hammered down"—a comment reflecting a belief in homogeneity within the culture and the importance of the group. In the United States, by contrast, we hear "Look out for Number One" and "A man's home is his castle"—comments reflecting a belief in the supremacy of the individual over the group. Neither culture is "right" or "better." Instead, each culture must be recognized as a force within individuals that motivates their behaviors within the workplace. However, even within the U.S. workforce, we must keep in mind that there are subcultures that can influence behavior. For example, recent work has shown that the Hispanic culture within the United States places a high value on groups compared to individuals and as a consequence takes a more collective approach to decision-making.[32] As we progress through this discussion, we shall continually build upon these differences as we attempt to understand behavior in the workplace.

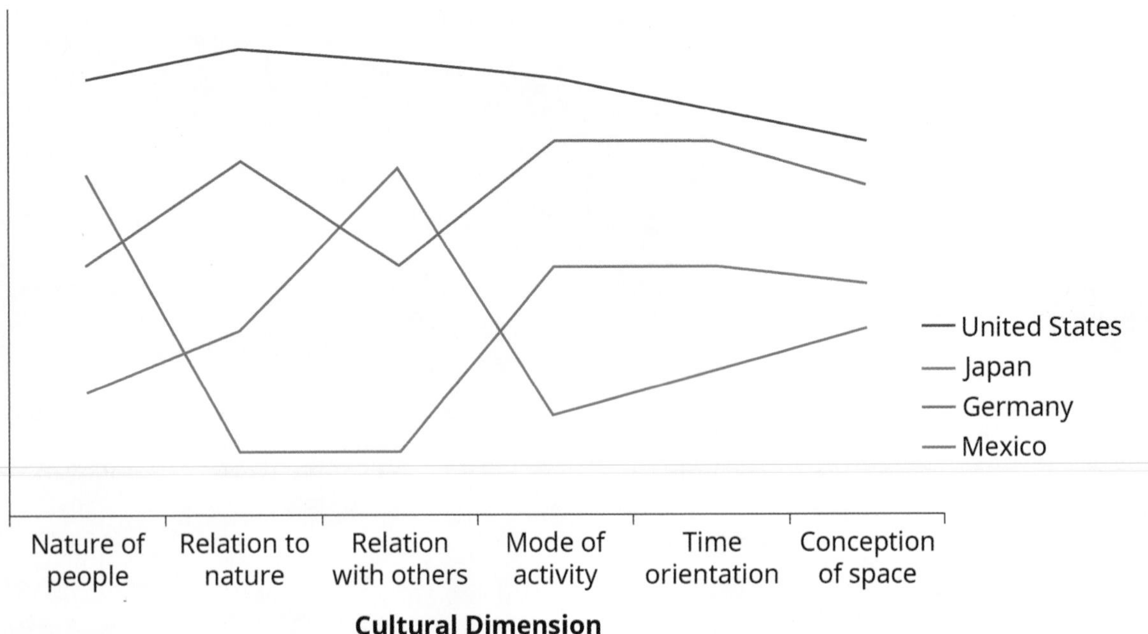

Exhibit 2.7 Cultural Differences among Managers in Four Countries (Attribution: Copyright Rice University, OpenStax, under CC BY-NC-SA 4.0 license)

CONCEPT CHECK

1. What role do managers play to ensure that the culture of individuals are valued and appreciated and contribute to a successful work environment?

Key Terms

Authoritarianism Refers to an individual's orientation toward authority.

Basic incongruity thesis Consists of three parts: what individuals want from organizations, what organizations want from individuals, and how these two potentially conflicting sets of desires are harmonized.

Cognitive complexity Represents a person's capacity to acquire and sort through various pieces of information from the environment and organize them in such a way that they make sense.

Culture The collective programming of the mind that distinguishes the members of one human group from another; the interactive aggregate of common characteristics that influences a human group's response to its environment.

Dependability Individuals who are seen as self-reliant, responsible, and consistent, are viewed as dependable.

Dogmatism Refers to a particular cognitive style that is characterized by closed-mindedness and inflexibility.

Ethics Values that help us determine appropriate standards of behavior and place limits on our behavior both inside and outside the organization.

Extroversion Refers to people who direct more of their attention to other people, objects, and events.

Instrumental values Represent those values concerning the way we approach end-states and whether individuals believe in ambition, cleanliness, honesty, or obedience.

Introversion Refers to people who focus their energies inwardly and have a greater sensitivity to abstract feelings.

Locus of control Refers to the tendency among individuals to attribute the events affecting their lives either to their own actions or to external forces; it is a measure of how much you think you control your own destiny.

Mental abilities An individual's intellectual capabilities and are closely linked to how a person makes decisions and processes information. Included here are such factors as verbal comprehension, inductive reasoning, and memory.

Personal values Represent an important force in organizational behavior for several reasons.

Personality A stable set of characteristics and tendencies that determine those communalities and differences in the psychological behavior (thoughts, feelings, and actions) of people that have continuity in time and that may not be easily understood as the sole result of the social and biological pressures of the moment.

Physical abilities Basic functional abilities such as strength, and psychomotor abilities such as manual dexterity, eye-hand coordination, and manipulation skills.

Psychomotor abilities Examples are manual dexterity, eye-hand coordination, and manipulation skills.

Self-esteem One's opinion or belief about one's self and self-worth.

Terminal values End-state goals that we prize.

Work ethic Refers to the strength of one's commitment and dedication to hard work, both as an end in itself and as a means to future rewards.

Summary of Learning Outcomes

2.1 Individual and Cultural Factors in Employee Performance

1. How do managers and organizations appropriately select individuals for particular jobs?

Because people enter organizations with preset dispositions, it is important to be able to analyze important individual characteristics, effectively select individuals, and appropriately match them to their jobs. However, this must be done carefully in light of both ethical and legal issues that face managers today.

2.2 Employee Abilities and Skills

2. How do people with different abilities, skills, and personalities build effective work teams?

Ability refers to one's capacity to respond, whereas motivation refers to one's desire to respond. Abilities can be divided into mental abilities and physical abilities. Personality represents a stable set of characteristics and tendencies that determines the psychological behavior of people.

Personality development is influenced by several factors, including physiological, cultural, family and group, role, and situational determinants.

2.3 Personality: An Introduction

3. How do managers and employees deal effectively with individual differences in the workplace?

Self-esteem represents opinions and beliefs concerning one's self and one's self-worth.

Locus of control is a tendency for people to attribute the events affecting their lives either to their own actions (referred to as internal locus of control) or to external forces (referred to as external locus of control).

2.4 Personality and Work Behavior

4. How can organizations foster a work environment that allows employees an opportunity to develop and grow?

Authoritarianism represents an individual's orientation toward authority and is characterized by an overriding conviction that it is appropriate for there to be clear status and power differences between people.

2.5 Personality and Organization: A Basic Conflict?

5. How do managers know how to get the best from each employee?

Dogmatism refers to a cognitive style characterized by closed-mindedness and inflexibility.

The basic incongruity thesis asserts that individuals and organizations exist in a constant state of conflict because each has different goals and expectations from the other. Employees want organizations to provide more autonomy and meaningful work, while organizations want employees to be more predictable, stable, and dependable.

2.6 Personal Values and Ethics

6. What is the role of ethical behavior in managerial actions?

A value is an enduring belief that one specific mode of conduct or end-state is preferable to others. Instrumental values are beliefs concerning the most appropriate ways to pursue end-states, whereas terminal values are beliefs concerning the most desirable end-states themselves.

Ethics are important to individuals because they serve as (1) standards of behavior for determining a correct course of action, (2) guidelines for decision-making and conflict resolution, and (3) influences on employee motivation. The work ethic refers to someone's belief that hard work and commitment to a task are both ends in themselves and means to future rewards.

2.7 Cultural Differences

7. How do you manage and do business with people from different cultures?

Culture refers to the collective mental programming of a group or people that distinguishes them from others. Culture (1) is shared by the members of the group, (2) is passed on from older members to younger members, and (3) shapes our view of the world. Six dimensions of culture can be identified: (1) how people see themselves, (2) how people see nature, (3) how people approach interpersonal relationships, (4) how people view activity and achievement, (5) how people view time, and (6) how people view space.

Chapter Review Questions

1. Why is it important for managers to understand individual differences at work?
2. Which employee abilities seem to be most important in determining job performance? Explain.
3. Define *personality*. Which personality traits are most relevant to understanding organizational behavior? Why?
4. Explain how the concept of *locus of control* works. Provide an example.
5. Describe the basic incongruity thesis. Do you agree with this thesis? Under what circumstances might the thesis be most likely to be true? Least likely to be true? Explain.
6. Why is it important for managers to understand ethical standards in the workplace? How do ethics affect our behavior at work?
7. How should managers handle the "gray zones" that are common to ethical dilemmas in organizations? Explain.
8. Define *culture*. How do culture and cultural variations affect work behavior and job performance? Provide examples to show why a knowledge of such differences is important for managers.

Management Skills Application Exercises

1. What Is Your Locus of Control?

Instructions: This instrument lists several pairs of statements concerning the possible causes of behavior. For each pair, select the letter (*A* or *B*) that better describes your own beliefs. Remember: there are no right or wrong answers. To view the scoring key, go to **Appendix B**.

1. A. In the long run, the bad things that happen to us are balanced by the good ones.
   B. Most misfortunes are the result of lack of ability, ignorance, laziness, or all three.
2. A. I have often found that what is going to happen will happen.
   B. Trusting to fate has never turned out as well for me as making a decision to take a definite course of action.
3. A. Many of the unhappy things in people's lives are partly due to bad luck.
   B. People's misfortunes result from the mistakes they make.
4. A. Without the right breaks, one cannot be an effective leader.
   B. Capable people who fail to become leaders have not taken advantage of their opportunities.
5. A. Many times, I feel I have little influence over the things that happen to me.
   B. It is impossible for me to believe that chance or luck plays an important role in my life.
6. A. Most people don't realize the extent to which their lives are controlled by accidental happenings.
   B. There really is no such thing as "luck."
7. A. Unfortunately, an individual's worth often passes unrecognized no matter how hard she tries.
   B. In the long run, people get the respect they deserve.

Source: Adapted from Julian B. Rotter, "Generalized Expectancies for Internal Versus External Control of Reinforcement." *Psychological Monographs, 80* (Whole No. 609, 1966), pp. 11–12.

2. Which Values Are Most Important to You?

Instructions: People are influenced by a wide variety of personal values. In fact, it has been argued that values represent a major influence on how we process information, how we feel about issues, and how we behave. In this exercise, you are given an opportunity to consider your own personal values. Below are listed two sets of statements. The first list presents several instrumental values, while the second list presents several terminal values. For each list you are asked to rank the statements according to how important each is to you personally. In the list of instrumental values, place a “1” next to the value that is most important to you, a “2” next to the second most important, and so forth. Clearly, you will have to make some difficult decisions concerning your priorities. When you have completed the list for instrumental values, follow the same procedure for the terminal values. Please remember that this is not a test—there are no right or wrong answers—so be completely honest with yourself. To view the scoring key, go to **Appendix B**.

Instrumental Values

____ Assertiveness; standing up for yourself
____ Being helpful or caring toward others
____ Dependability; being counted upon by others
____ Education and intellectual pursuits
____ Hard work and achievement
____ Obedience; following the wishes of others
____ Open-mindedness; receptivity to new ideas
____ Self-sufficiency; independence
____ Truthfulness; honesty
____ Being well-mannered and courteous toward others

Terminal Values

____ Happiness; satisfaction in life
____ Knowledge and wisdom
____ Peace and harmony in the world
____ Pride in accomplishment
____ Prosperity; wealth
____ Lasting friendships
____ Recognition from peers
____ Salvation; finding eternal life
____ Security; freedom from threat
____ Self-esteem; self-respect

Managerial Decision Exercises

1. You work for a large multinational corporation with offices around the globe. One of your colleagues has been offered an assignment overseas to either the Japanese, South Korean, or German offices for a long-term assignment (three to seven years). She has asked your advice on the opportunity because she is concerned about the failure some others have encountered. Often, they want to return home before their assignment is complete, or they decide to quit. She is also concerned about building relationships as a manager with the local employees. Your friend is very skilled technically and you know that she could be successful in the positions being offered. You wonder whether her apprehension has to do with her personality, and whether that might have an impact on her success for this role.

   a. Identify the personality traits you think might be relevant to being successful in a global assignment in either Japan, South Korea, or Germany.
   b. Develop a personality test aimed at measuring these dimensions.
   c. Do you think that your friend will fill out this questionnaire honestly? If not, how would you ensure that the results you get would be honest and truly reflect her personality?
   d. How would you validate such a test? Describe the steps you would take.
2. It's your final semester in college and you're going through several interviews with recruiters on campus. Among the opportunities that you are interviewing for is an entry-level position as a data analyst with a large accounting firm. You have been told during the initial interview that the firm uses a personality assessment as part of their selection process. You feel that this job requires someone who is very high in introversion since it involves a lot of individual work involving analysis of data on the one hand, but that in potential future roles on an audit team, one would need a high level of extroversion dealing with colleagues on the team and with clients. You have a high level of technical ability and can concentrate on tasks for long periods and also feel that you are sociable, but perhaps not as much as some other students in other disciplines. The opportunity is terrific, it is a great stepping-stone to career advancement, and your faculty adviser is very supportive. Refer to the personality test in the Managerial Skills Application Exercises question 2 as an example of the personality test that will be given. How are you going to respond when completing the personality test? Are you going to answer the questions truthfully?
   a. What are the advantages and disadvantages of completing the questions honestly?
   b. What are the advantages and disadvantages of completing the questions in a way you think the company is looking for?

Critical Thinking Case

Making a Diverse Workplace the Top Priority

Johnson & Johnson is a leader in multinational medical devices as well as pharmaceutical and consumer packaged goods. Founded in 1886, the company has been through generations of cultural differences and is consistently listed among the Fortune 500. Johnson & Johnson is a household name for millions with many of their products lining the shelves of medicine cabinets around the globe. In 2017, Johnson & Johnson took the number two spot on the Thomson Reuters Diversity & Inclusion Index.

At such a multinational company, with over 130,000 employees worldwide, the forefront of the focus on their internal workforce is diversity. At the forefront of their mission statement, this is clearly stated: "Make diversity and inclusion how we work every day." Having a mission statement is wonderful, but how does Johnson & Johnson live up to these standards day in and day out?

Chief Diversity & Inclusion Officer Wanda Bryant Hope works tirelessly to inject the company with the very founding principles that built the company 130 years ago. She is one of 46 percent of employees worldwide that are women, and is delivering solutions that serve all of the patients and companies that work with Johnson & Johnson.

One initiative that sets Johnson & Johnson apart in the diversity category is their programs and initiatives such as the Scientist Mentoring and Diversity Program (SMDP), which is a yearlong mentorship program pairing ethnically diverse students with industry leaders.

Additionally, the company commits to alignment with Human Rights Campaign Equality Index benchmarks, as well as supporting the armed forces and wounded soldiers. These benefits include transgender-inclusive health insurance coverage and paid time off after military leave for soldiers to acclimate back to life at home.

These commitments make Johnson & Johnson one of the best cases for a company that is making great strides in a tough cultural climate to bridge the gaps and make all of their employees, customers, and clients feel included and a part of the bigger whole.

Questions:

1. What diversity challenges do you think Johnson & Johnson management and employees face due to their presence as worldwide organization?
2. What other considerations should the company take in order to increase their impact of diversity and inclusion in the workplace?
3. Johnson & Johnson prides themselves on bridging the gender equality gap. What are some challenges or concerns to consider in the future with their hiring practices?

Sources: Johnson & Johnson website accessed August 1, 2018, https://www.jnj.com/about-jnj/diversity; Johnson & Johnson website accessed August 1, 2018, http://www.careers.jnj.com/careers/what-makes-johnson-johnson-a-global-leader-in-diversity-inclusion.

3 Perception and Job Attitudes

Exhibit 3.1 (Credit: Quinn Dombroski/ flickr/ Attribution-ShareAlike 2.0 Generic (CC BY-SA 2.0)

Introduction

Learning Outcomes

After reading this chapter, you should be able to answer these questions:

1. How do differences in perception affect employee behavior and performance?
2. How can managers and organizations minimize the negative impact of stereotypes and other barriers to accurate social perception in interpersonal relations?
3. How do people attribute credit and blame for organizational events?
4. How can a work environment characterized by positive work attitudes be created and maintained?
5. How can managers and organizations develop a committed workforce?

EXPLORING MANAGERIAL CAREERS

Personal Perceptions Affect Workplace Harmony

Conflict was a feeling that James and Chaz were familiar with in their workplace. It was just a matter of time before their differences bubbled up to form a real hardship on themselves as well as their management teams.

Chaz is anxious to get ahead, really focused on how fast he can accelerate his career. In order to showcase his tenacity, he stays extra hours and often takes on extra assignments from upper management and doesn't seem to mind. James, on the other hand, is content in his position and believes that if he does his regular job, he will be seen a stable part of the team and will be rewarded for his everyday efforts. James views Chaz's behavior as "kissing up" and resents Chaz for his extra efforts because it may make his own work look bad. James doesn't give a thought to the personal reasons why Chaz may be acting that way, and instead ends up treating Chaz poorly, with a short temper every time they have to work together.

Chaz talks to his manager, Jerry, about the way that he is being treated by James. He explains that he has been having some personal troubles at home, his wife is expecting, and they are trying to save for the new addition to their family. Chaz is feeling pressure to work hard and showcase his talents in order to get a raise. He also expresses his feelings against James, mainly that he shouldn't be scrutinized for going above and beyond when his colleagues may just decide to do the minimum requirements. Jerry understands, and he appreciates Chaz coming to him with his concerns. They talk about ways to measure Chaz's extra efforts and plan a conversation during their annual review period to discuss his raise again. Jerry also suggests that Chaz talk with James to alleviate some of the negative behavior he is experiencing. He feels that if James understood the reasons behind Chaz's actions, he may be less jealous and feel less threatened by him.

Questions:

1. How can an individual's perceptions be a challenge in the workplace?
2. What can James do in the future to address Chaz in a different manner and better understand his actions?
3. What do you think Jerry could have done differently to help his employees overcome their differences and work more efficiently together?

3.1 The Perceptual Process

1. How do differences in perception affect employee behavior and performance?

By **perception**, we mean the process by which one screens, selects, organizes, and interprets stimuli to give them meaning.[1] It is a process of making sense out of the environment in order to make an appropriate behavioral response. Perception does not necessarily lead to an accurate portrait of the environment, but rather to a unique portrait, influenced by the needs, desires, values, and disposition of the perceiver. As described by Kretch and associates,[2] an individual's perception of a given situation is not a photographic representation of the physical world; it is a partial, personal construction in which certain objects, selected by the individual for a major role, are perceived in an individual manner. Every perceiver is, as it were, to some degree a nonrepresentational artist, painting a picture of the world that expresses an individual view of reality.

The multitude of objects that vie for attention are first selected or screened by individuals. This process is called **perceptual selectivity**. Certain of these objects catch our attention, while others do not. Once individuals notice a particular object, they then attempt to make sense out of it by organizing or categorizing it according to their unique frame of reference and their needs. This second process is termed **perceptual organization**. When meaning has been attached to an object, individuals are in a position to determine an appropriate response or reaction to it. Hence, if we clearly recognize and understand we are in danger from a falling rock or a car, we can quickly move out of the way.

Because of the importance of perceptual selectivity for understanding the perception of work situations, we will examine this concept in some detail before considering the topic of social perception.

Perceptual Selectivity: Seeing What We See

As noted above, **perceptual selectivity** refers to the process by which individuals select objects in the environment for attention. Without this ability to focus on one or a few stimuli instead of the hundreds constantly surrounding us, we would be unable to process all the information necessary to initiate behavior. In essence, perceptual selectivity works as follows (see **Exhibit 3.2**). The individual is first exposed to an object or stimulus—a loud noise, a new car, a tall building, another person, and so on. Next, the individual focuses attention on this one object or stimulus, as opposed to others, and concentrates his efforts on understanding or comprehending the stimulus. For example, while conducting a factory tour, two managers came across a piece of machinery. One manager's attention focused on the stopped machine; the other manager focused on the worker who was trying to fix it. Both managers simultaneously asked the worker a question. The first manager asked why the machine was stopped, and the second manager asked if the employee thought that he could fix it. Both managers were presented with the same situation, but they noticed different aspects. This example illustrates that once attention has been directed, individuals are more likely to retain an image of the object or stimulus in their memory and to select an appropriate response to the stimulus. These various influences on selective attention can be divided into external influences and internal (personal) influences (see **Exhibit 3.3**).

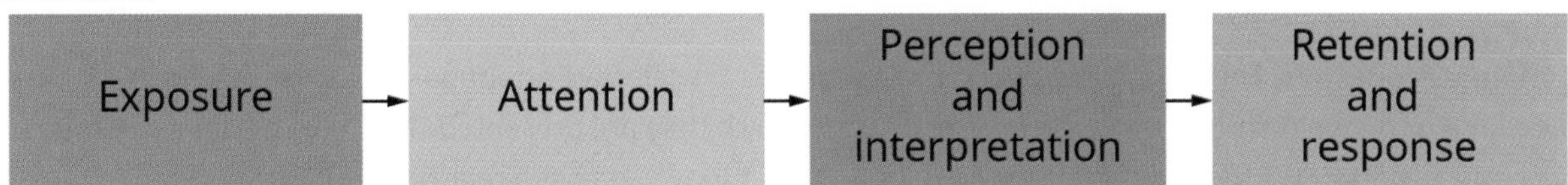

Exhibit 3.2 The Process of Perceptual Selectivity (Attribution: Copyright Rice University, OpenStax, under CC BY-NC-SA 4.0 license)

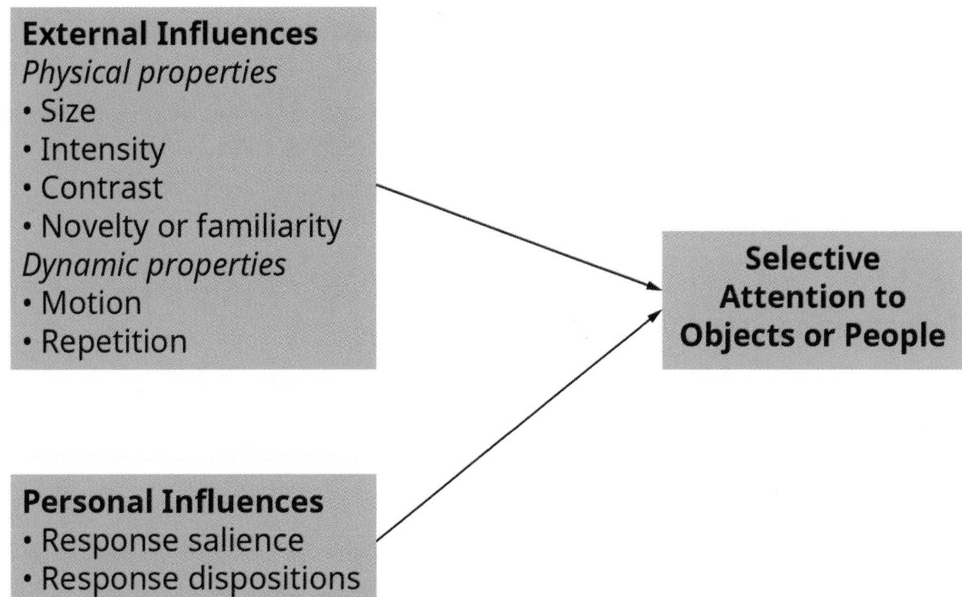

Exhibit 3.3 Major Influences on Selective Attention (Attribution: Copyright Rice University, OpenStax, under CC BY-NC-SA 4.0 license)

External Influences on Selective Attention

External influences consist of the characteristics of the observed object or person that activate the senses. Most external influences affect selective attention because of either their physical properties or their dynamic properties.

Physical Properties. The physical properties of the objects themselves often affect which objects receive attention by the perceiver. Emphasis here is on the unique, different, and out of the ordinary. A particularly important physical property is *size*. Generally, larger objects receive more attention than smaller ones. Advertising companies use the largest signs and billboards allowed to capture the perceiver's attention. However, when most of the surrounding objects are large, a small object against a field of large objects may receive more attention. In either case, size represents an important variable in perception. Moreover, brighter, louder, and more colorful objects tend to attract more attention than objects of less *intensity*. For example, when a factory foreman yells an order at his subordinates, it will probably receive more notice (although it may not receive the desired response) from workers. It must be remembered here, however, that intensity heightens attention only when compared to other comparable stimuli. If the foreman always yells, employees may stop paying much attention to the yelling. Objects that *contrast* strongly with the background against which they are observed tend to receive more attention than less-contrasting objects. An example of the contrast principle can be seen in the use of plant and highway safety signs. A terse message such as "Danger" is lettered in black against a yellow or orange background. A final physical characteristic that can heighten perceptual awareness is the *novelty* or *unfamiliarity* of the object. Specifically, the unique or unexpected seen in a familiar setting (an executive of a conservative company who comes to work in Bermuda shorts) or the familiar seen in an incongruous setting (someone in church holding a can of beer) will receive attention.

Dynamic Properties. The second set of external influences on selective attention are those that either change over time or derive their uniqueness from the order in which they are presented. The most obvious dynamic property is *motion*. We tend to pay attention to objects that move against a relatively static background. This principle has long been recognized by advertisers, who often use signs with moving lights or moving objects to attract attention. In an organizational setting, a clear example is a rate-buster, who shows up his colleagues by working substantially faster, attracting more attention.

Another principle basic to advertising is *repetition* of a message or image. Work instructions that are repeated tend to be received better, particularly when they concern a dull or boring task on which it is difficult to concentrate. This process is particularly effective in the area of plant safety. Most industrial accidents occur because of careless mistakes during monotonous activities. Repeating safety rules and procedures can often help keep workers alert to the possibilities of accidents.

Personal Influences on Selective Attention

In addition to a variety of external factors, several important personal factors are also capable of influencing the extent to which an individual pays attention to a particular stimulus or object in the environment. The two most important personal influences on perceptual readiness are **response salience** and **response disposition**.

Response Salience. This is a tendency to focus on objects that relate to our *immediate* needs or wants. Response salience in the work environment is easily identified. A worker who is tired from many hours of work may be acutely sensitive to the number of hours or minutes until quitting time. Employees negotiating a new contract may know to the penny the hourly wage of workers doing similar jobs across town. Managers with a high need to achieve may be sensitive to opportunities for work achievement, success, and promotion. Finally, female managers may be more sensitive than many male managers to condescending male attitudes toward women. Response salience, in turn, can distort our view of our surroundings. For example, as Ruch notes:

"Time spent on monotonous work is usually overestimated. Time spent in interesting work is usually underestimated. . . . Judgment of time is related to feelings of success or failure. Subjects who are experiencing failure judge a given interval as longer than do subjects who are experiencing success. A given interval of time is also estimated as longer by subjects trying to get through a task in order to reach a desired goal than by subjects working without such motivation."[3]

Response Disposition. Whereas response salience deals with immediate needs and concerns, **response disposition** is the tendency to recognize familiar objects more quickly than unfamiliar ones. The notion of response disposition carries with it a clear recognition of the importance of past learning on what we perceive in the present. For instance, in one study, a group of individuals was presented with a set of playing cards with the colors and symbols reversed—that is, hearts and diamonds were printed in black, and spades and clubs in red. Surprisingly, when subjects were presented with these cards for brief time periods, individuals consistently described the cards as they expected them to be (red hearts and diamonds, black spades and clubs) instead of as they really were. They were predisposed to see things as they always had been in the past.[4]

Thus, the basic perceptual process is in reality a fairly complicated one. Several factors, including our own personal makeup and the environment, influence how we interpret and respond to the events we focus on. Although the process itself may seem somewhat complicated, it in fact represents a shorthand to guide us in our everyday behavior. That is, without perceptual selectivity we would be immobilized by the millions of stimuli competing for our attention and action. The perceptual process allows us to focus our attention on the more salient events or objects and, in addition, allows us to categorize such events or objects so that they fit into our own conceptual map of the environment.

EXPANDING AROUND THE GLOBE

Which Car Would You Buy?

When General Motors teamed up with Toyota to form California-based New United Motor Manufacturing Inc. (NUMMI), they had a great idea. NUMMI would manufacture not only the popular Toyota Corolla but would also make a GM car called the Geo Prizm. Both cars would be essentially identical except for minor styling differences. Economies of scale and high quality would benefit the sales of both cars. Unfortunately, General Motors forgot one thing. The North American consumer holds a higher opinion of Japanese-built cars than American-made ones. As a result, from the start of the joint venture, Corollas have sold rapidly, while sales of Geo Prizms have languished.

With hindsight, it is easy to explain what happened in terms of perceptual differences. That is, the typical consumer simply perceived the Corolla to be of higher quality (and perhaps higher status) and bought accordingly. Not only was the Prizm seen more skeptically by consumers, but General Motors' insistence on a whole new name for the product left many buyers unfamiliar with just what they were buying. Perception was that main reason for lagging sales; however, the paint job on the Prizm was viewed as being among the worst ever. As a result, General Motors lost $80 million on the Prizm in its first year of sales. Meanwhile, demand for the Corolla exceeded supply.

The final irony here is that no two cars could be any more alike than the Prizm and the Corolla. They are built on the same assembly line by the same workers to the same design specifications. They are, in fact, the same car. The only difference is in how the consumers perceive the two cars—and these perceptions obviously are radically different.

Over time, however, perceptions did change. While there was nothing unique about the Prizm, the vehicle managed to sell pretty well for the automaker and carried on well into the 2000s. The Prizm was also the base for the Pontiac Vibe, which was based on the Corolla platform as well, and this is one of the few collaborations that worked really well.

Sources: C. Eitreim, "10 Odd Automotive Brand Collaborations (And 15 That Worked)," *Car Culture*, January 19, 2019; R. Hof, "This Team-Up Has It All—Except Sales," *Business Week,* August 14, 1989, p. 35; C. Eitreim, "15 GM Cars With The Worst Factory Paint Jobs (And 5 That'll Last Forever)," *Motor Hub*, November 8, 2018.

Social Perception in Organizations

Up to this point, we have focused on an examination of basic perceptual processes—how we see objects or attend to stimuli. Based on this discussion, we are now ready to examine a special case of the perceptual process—**social perception** as it relates to the workplace. Social perception consists of those processes by which we perceive other people.[5] Particular emphasis in the study of social perception is placed on how we interpret other people, how we categorize them, and how we form impressions of them.

Clearly, social perception is far more complex than the perception of inanimate objects such as tables, chairs, signs, and buildings. This is true for at least two reasons. First, people are obviously far more complex and dynamic than tables and chairs. More-careful attention must be paid in perceiving them so as not to miss important details. Second, an accurate perception of others is usually far more important to us personally than are our perceptions of inanimate objects. The consequences of misperceiving people are great. Failure to accurately perceive the location of a desk in a large room may mean we bump into it by mistake. Failure to perceive accurately the hierarchical status of someone and how the person cares about this status difference might lead you to inappropriately address the person by their first name or use slang in their presence and thereby significantly hurt your chances for promotion if that person is involved in such decisions. Consequently, social perception in the work situation deserves special attention.

We will concentrate now on the three major influences on social perception: the characteristics of (1) the person being perceived, (2) the particular situation, and (3) the perceiver. When taken together, these influences are the dimensions of the environment in which we view other people. It is important for students of management to understand the way in which they interact (see **Exhibit 3.4**).

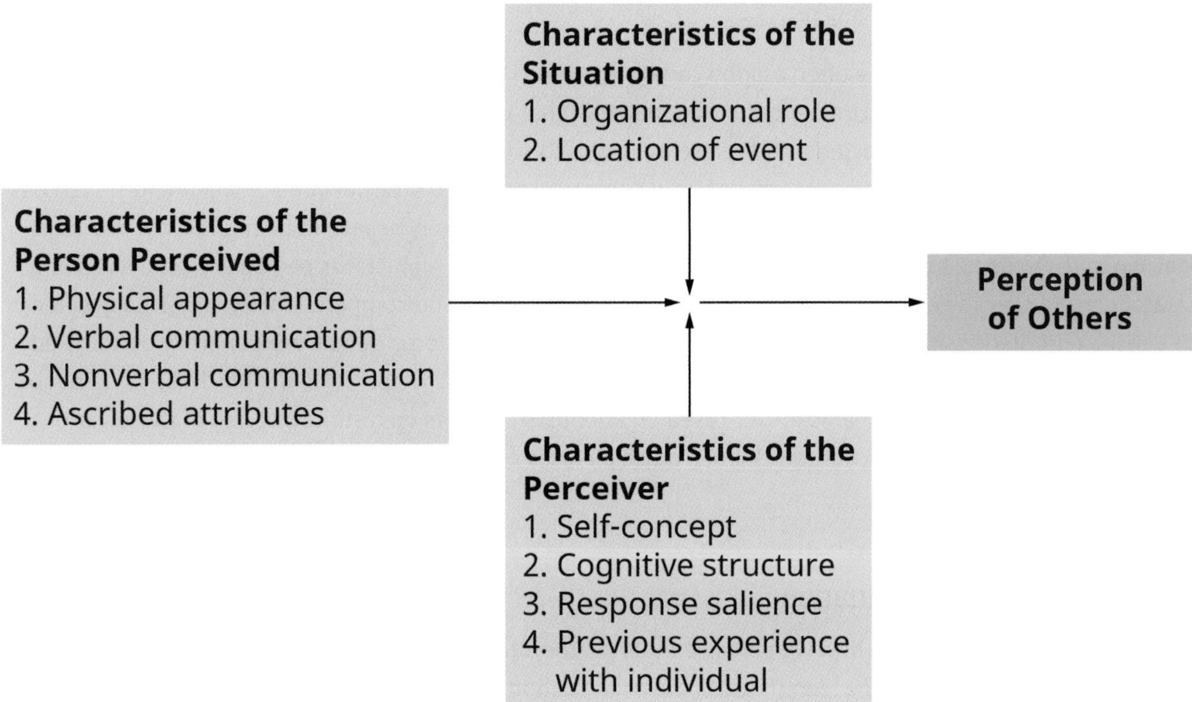

Exhibit 3.4 Major Influences on Social Perception in Organizations (Attribution: Copyright Rice University, OpenStax, under CC BY-NC-SA 4.0 license)

The way in which we are evaluated in social situations is greatly influenced by our own unique sets of personal characteristics. That is, our dress, talk, and gestures determine the kind of impressions people form of us. In particular, four categories of personal characteristics can be identified: (1) physical appearance, (2) verbal communication, (3) nonverbal communication, and (4) ascribed attributes.

Physical Appearance. A variety of physical attributes influence our overall image. These include many of the obvious demographic characteristics such as age, sex, race, height, and weight. A study by Mason found that most people agree on the physical attributes of a leader (i.e., what leaders *should* look like), even though these attributes were not found to be consistently held by actual leaders. However, when we see a person who appears to be assertive, goal-oriented, confident, and articulate, we infer that this person is a natural leader.[6] Another example of the powerful influence of physical appearance on perception is clothing. People dressed in business suits are generally thought to be professionals, whereas people dressed in work clothes are assumed to be lower-level employees.

Verbal and Nonverbal Communication. What we say to others—as well as how we say it—can influence the impressions others form of us. Several aspects of verbal communication can be noted. First, the *precision* with which one uses language can influence impressions about cultural sophistication or education. An *accent* provides clues about a person's geographic and social background. The *tone of voice* used provides clues about a speaker's state of mind. Finally, the *topics* people choose to converse about provide clues about them.

Impressions are also influenced by nonverbal communication—how people behave. For instance, facial expressions often serve as clues in forming impressions of others. People who consistently smile are often thought to have positive attitudes.[7] A whole field of study that has recently emerged is **body language**, the way in which people express their inner feelings subconsciously through physical actions: sitting up straight versus being relaxed, looking people straight in the eye versus looking away from people. These forms of expressive behavior provide information to the perceiver concerning how approachable others are, how self-confident they are, or how sociable they are.

Ascribed Attributes. Finally, we often ascribe certain attributes to a person before or at the beginning of an encounter; these attributes can influence how we perceive that person. Three ascribed attributes are status, occupation, and personal characteristics. We ascribe *status* to someone when we are told that he or she is an executive, holds the greatest sales record, or has in some way achieved unusual fame or wealth. Research has consistently shown that people attribute different motives to people they believe to be high or low in status, even when these people behave in an identical fashion.[8] For instance, high-status people are seen as having greater control over their behavior and as being more self-confident and competent; they are given greater influence in group decisions than low-status people. Moreover, high-status people are generally better liked than low-status people. *Occupations* also play an important part in how we perceive people. Describing people as salespersons, accountants, teamsters, or research scientists conjures up distinct pictures of these various people before any firsthand encounters. In fact, these pictures may even determine whether there can be an encounter.

Characteristics of the Situation

The second major influence on how we perceive others is the situation in which the perceptual process occurs. Two situational influences can be identified: (1) the organization and the employee's place in it, and (2) the location of the event.

Organizational Role. An employee's place in the organizational hierarchy can also influence his perceptions. A classic study of managers by Dearborn and Simon emphasizes this point. In this study, executives from various departments (accounting, sales, production) were asked to read a detailed and factual case about a steel company.[9] Next, each executive was asked to identify the major problem a new president of the company should address. The findings showed clearly that the executives' perceptions of the most important problems in the company were influenced by the departments in which they worked. Sales executives saw sales as the biggest problem, whereas production executives cited production issues. Industrial relations and public relations executives identified human relations as the primary problem in need of attention.

In addition to perceptual differences emerging horizontally across departments, such differences can also be found when we move vertically up or down the hierarchy. The most obvious difference here is seen between managers and unions, where the former see profits, production, and sales as vital areas of concern for the company whereas the latter place much greater emphasis on wages, working conditions, and job security. Indeed, our views of managers and workers are clearly influenced by the group to which we belong. The positions we occupy in organizations can easily color how we view our work world and those in it. Consider the results of a classic study of perceptual differences between superiors and subordinates.[10] Both groups were asked how often the supervisor gave various forms of feedback to the employees. The results, shown in **Table 3.1**, demonstrate striking differences based on one's location in the organizational hierarchy.

Differences in Perception between Supervisors and Subordinates		
	Frequency with Which Supervisors Give Various Types of Recognition for Good Performance	
Types of Recognition	As Seen by Supervisors	As Seen by Subordinates
Gives privileges	**52%**	**14%**
Gives more responsibility	**48**	**10**
Gives a pat on the back	**82**	**13**
Gives sincere and thorough praise	**80**	**14**
Trains for better jobs	**64**	**9**
Gives more interesting work	**51**	**5**
Source: Adapted from R. Likert, New Patterns in Management (New York: McGraw Hill, 1961), p. 91.		

Table 3.1 (Attribution: Copyright Rice University, OpenStax, under CC BY-NC-SA 4.0 license)

Location of Event. Finally, how we interpret events is also influenced by where the event occurs. Behaviors that may be appropriate at home, such as taking off one's shoes, may be inappropriate in the office. Acceptable customs vary from country to country. For instance, assertiveness may be a desirable trait for a sales representative in the United States, but it may be seen as being brash or coarse in Japan or China. Hence, the context in which the perceptual activity takes place is important.

Characteristics of the Perceiver

The third major influence on social perception is the personality and viewpoint of the perceiver. Several characteristics unique to our personalities can affect how we see others. These include (1) self-concept, (2) cognitive structure, (3) response salience, and (4) previous experience with the individual.[11]

Self-Concept. Our self-concept represents a major influence on how we perceive others. This influence is manifested in several ways. First, when we understand ourselves (i.e., can accurately describe our own personal characteristics), we are better able to perceive others accurately. Second, when we accept ourselves (i.e., have a positive self-image), we are more likely to see favorable characteristics in others. Studies have shown that if we accept ourselves as we are, we broaden our view of others and are more likely to view people uncritically. Conversely, less secure people often find faults in others. Third, our own personal characteristics influence the characteristics we notice in others. For instance, people with authoritarian tendencies tend to view others in terms of power, whereas secure people tend to see others as warm rather than cold.[12] From a management standpoint, these findings emphasize how important it is for administrators to understand themselves; they also provide justification for the human relations training programs that are popular in many organizations today.

Cognitive Structure. Our cognitive structures also influence how we view people. People describe each other differently. Some use physical characteristics such as tall or short, whereas others use central descriptions such as deceitful, forceful, or meek. Still others have more complex cognitive structures and use multiple traits in their descriptions of others; hence, a person may be described as being aggressive, honest, friendly, *and* hardworking. (See the discussion in Individual and Cultural Differences on cognitive complexity.) Ostensibly, the greater our cognitive complexity—our ability to differentiate between people using multiple criteria—the more accurate our perception of others. People who tend to make more complex assessments of others also tend to be more positive in their appraisals.[13] Research in this area highlights the importance of selecting managers who exhibit high degrees of cognitive complexity. These individuals should form more accurate perceptions of the strengths and weaknesses of their subordinates and should be able to capitalize on their strengths while ignoring or working to overcome their weaknesses.

Response Salience. This refers to our sensitivity to objects in the environment as influenced by our particular needs or desires. Response salience can play an important role in social perception because we tend to see what we *want* to see. A company personnel manager who has a bias against women, minorities, or handicapped persons would tend to be adversely sensitive to them during an employment interview. This focus may cause the manager to look for other potentially negative traits in the candidate to confirm his biases. The influence of positive arbitrary biases is called the **halo effect**, whereas the influence of negative biases is often called the *horn effect*. Another personnel manager without these biases would be much less inclined to be influenced by these characteristics when viewing prospective job candidates.

Previous Experience with the Individual. Our previous experiences with others often will influence the way in which we view their current behavior. When an employee has consistently received poor performance evaluations, a marked improvement in performance may go unnoticed because the supervisor continues to think of the individual as a poor performer. Similarly, employees who begin their careers with several successes develop a reputation as fast-track individuals and may continue to rise in the organization long after their performance has leveled off or even declined. The impact of previous experience on present perceptions should be respected and studied by students of management. For instance, when a previously poor performer earnestly tries to perform better, it is important for this improvement to be recognized early and properly rewarded. Otherwise, employees may give up, feeling that nothing they do will make any difference.

Together, these factors determine the impressions we form of others (see **Exhibit 3.4**). With these impressions, we make conscious and unconscious decisions about how we intend to behave toward people. Our behavior toward others, in turn, influences the way they regard us. Consequently, the importance of understanding the perceptual process, as well as factors that contribute to it, is apparent for managers. A better understanding of ourselves and careful attention to others leads to more accurate perceptions and more appropriate actions.

CONCEPT CHECK

1. How can you understand what makes up an individual's personality?
2. How does the content of the situation affect the perception of the perceiver?
3. What are the characteristics that the perceiver can have on interpreting personality?

3.2 Barriers to Accurate Social Perception

2. How can managers and organizations minimize the negative impact of stereotypes and other barriers to accurate social perception in interpersonal relations?

In the perceptual process, several barriers can be identified that inhibit the accuracy of our perception. These barriers are (1) stereotyping, (2) selective perception, and (3) perceptual defense. Each of these will be briefly considered as it relates to social perception in work situations (see **Table 3.2**).

Barriers to Accurate Perception of Others	
Barrier	**Definition**
Stereotyping	A tendency to assign attributes to people solely on the basis of their class or category
Selective perception	A process by which we systematically screen out or discredit information we don't wish to hear and focus instead on more salient information
Perceptual defense	A tendency to distort or ignore information that is either personally threatening or culturally unacceptable

Table 3.2 (Attribution: Copyright Rice University, OpenStax, under CC BY-NC-SA 4.0 license)

Stereotyping

One of the most common barriers in perceiving others at work is **stereotyping**. A stereotype is a widely held generalization about a group of people. Stereotyping is a process in which attributes are assigned to people solely on the basis of their class or category. It is particularly likely to occur when one meets new people, since very little is known about them at that time. On the basis of a few prominent characteristics such as sex, race, or age, we tend to place people into a few general categories. We ascribe a series of traits to them based upon the attributes of the category in which we have put them. We assume that older people are old-fashioned, conservative, obstinate, and perhaps senile. We view professors as absentminded, impractical, idealistic, or eccentric.

One explanation for the existence of stereotypes has been suggested by Jain, Triandis, and Weick.[14] They argue that stereotypes may be to some extent based upon fact. People tend to compare other groups with their own group, accentuating minor differences between groups to form a stereotype. For example, older people as a group may indeed be more conservative or more old-fashioned. These traits then become emphasized and attributed to particular older individuals.

At least three types of stereotype can be found in organizations: those dealing with age, race, and gender. Age stereotypes can be found throughout organizations. A recent study by[15] found that there are still clear stereotypes of older employees. They are thought to be (1) more resistant to organizational change, (2) less creative, (3) less likely to take calculated risks, (4) lower in physical capacity, (5) less interested in learning new techniques, and (6) less capable of learning new techniques. When asked to make personnel decisions concerning older people, the business students generally followed several trends. First, they gave older people lower consideration in promotion decisions. Older people also received less attention and fewer resources for training and development. Finally, older people tended to be transferred to other departments instead of confronted by their superiors when a problem with their performance emerged.

Similar problems arise for people from different racial or cultural backgrounds and for gender. A particular problem in many companies today is that of attitudes toward women as managers or executives. Although succeeding in a managerial position is always difficult, the job is all the harder if your coworkers, superiors, or subordinates are not supportive.

EXPANDING AROUND THE GLOBE

To See Ourselves as Others See Us

In considering stereotyping in organizations, it may be interesting to examine how people in different countries and cultures see others around the world. Specifically, we should note that "foreigners" often hold certain stereotypes of what a "typical" American looks and acts like. Look, for example, at Table 3.3. This table shows how people in seven countries around the globe view the typical American. Note the sizable differences in perceptions.

Foreign Observations of Americans
The following are quotations from foreign visitors to the United States:
India: "Americans seem to be in a perpetual hurry. Just watch the way they walk down the street. They never allow themselves the leisure to enjoy life; there are too many things to do."
Kenya: "Americans appear to us rather distant. They are not really as close to other people—even fellow Americans—as Americans overseas tend to portray. It's almost as if an American says, 'I won't let you get too close to me.' It's like building a wall."
Turkey: "Once we were out in a rural area in the middle of nowhere and saw an American come to a stop sign. Though he could see in both directions for miles and no traffic was coming, he still stopped!"
Colombia: "The tendency in the United States to think that life is only work hits you in the face. Work seems to be the one type of motivation."
Indonesia: "In the United States everything has to be talked about and analyzed. Even the littlest thing has to be 'Why, Why, Why?' I get a headache from such persistent questions."
Ethiopia: "The American is very explicit; he wants a 'yes' or 'no.' If someone tries to speak figuratively, the American is confused."
Iran: "The first time . . . my [American] professor told me, 'I don't know the answer, I will have to look it up,' I was shocked. I asked myself, 'Why is he teaching me?' In my country a professor would give the wrong answer rather than admit ignorance."

Table 3.3 (Attribution: Copyright Rice University, OpenStax, under CC BY-NC-SA 4.0 license)

Foreign Observations of Americans
Source: J. Feig and G. Blair, *There Is a Difference,* 2nd ed. (Washington: Meridian House International). Meridian House International is an organization that conducts intercultural training for visitors to the United States and for Americans going abroad.

Table 3.3

When examining these comments, consider the extent to which you think these perceptions and stereotypes are accurate or inaccurate. Why do people in different countries form such divergent opinions of our country? How do their perceptions color the behavior and effectiveness of American managers working abroad? On the basis of this assessment, you might want to reassess your own stereotypes of people in different countries. How accurate do you think your own stereotypes have been?

Selective Perception

Selective perception is the process by which we systematically screen out information we don't wish to hear, focusing instead on more salient information. Saliency here is obviously a function of our own experiences, needs, and orientations. The example of the Dearborn and Simon[16] study of managers described earlier provides an excellent glimpse of selective perception. Production managers focused on production problems to the exclusion of other problems. Accountants, personnel specialists, and sales managers were similarly exclusive. Everyone saw his own specialty as more important in the company than other specialties.

Another example of selective perception in groups and organizations is provided by Miner.[17] Miner summarizes a series of experiments dealing with groups competing on problem-solving exercises. Consistently, the groups tended to evaluate their own solutions as better than the solutions proposed by others. Such findings resemble a syndrome found in many research organizations. There is a frequent tendency for scientists to view ideas or products originating outside their organization or department as inferior and to judge other researchers as less competent and creative than themselves. This is often referred to as the "Not-Invented-Here" syndrome. Similar patterns of behavior can be found among managers, service workers, and secretaries.

Perceptual Defense

A final barrier to social perception is **perceptual defense.**[18] Perceptual defense is founded on three related principles:

1. Emotionally disturbing or threatening stimuli have a higher recognition threshold than neutral stimuli.
2. Such stimuli are likely to elicit substitute perceptions that are radically altered so as to prevent recognition of the presented stimuli.
3. These critical stimuli arouse emotional reactions even though the stimuli are not recognized.

In other words, through perceptual defense we tend to distort or ignore information that is either personally threatening or culturally unacceptable. Because emotionally disturbing stimuli have a higher recognition threshold, people are less likely to fully confront or acknowledge the threat. Instead, they may see entirely different or even erroneous stimuli that are safer. Even so, the presence of the critical stimulus often leads to heightened emotions despite the lack of recognition. For instance, suppose that during a contract negotiation for an assembly plant, word leaked out that because of declining profits, the plant might have to close down permanently. Anxious workers might ignore this message and instead choose to believe the company management is only starting false rumors to increase their leverage during wage negotiations. Even if the leverage claim is accepted by the workers as truth, strong emotional reactions against the company can be expected.

One effect of perceptual defense is to save us from squarely facing events that we either do not wish to handle or may be incapable of handling. We dissipate our emotions by directing our attention to other (substitute) objects and hope the original event that distressed us will eventually disappear.

Perceptual defense is especially pronounced when people are presented with a situation that contradicts their long-held beliefs and attitudes. In a classic study of perceptual defense among college students, Haire and Grunes presented the students with descriptions of factory workers. Included in these descriptions was the word *intelligent*. Because the word was contrary to the students' beliefs concerning factory workers, they chose to reject the description by using perceptual defenses.[19] Four such defense mechanisms can be identified:[20]

1. *Denial*. A few of the subjects denied the existence of intelligence in factory workers.
2. *Modification and distortion*. This was one of the most frequent forms of defense. The pattern was to explain away the perceptual conflict by joining intelligence with some other characteristics—for instance, "He is intelligent but doesn't possess initiative to rise above his group."
3. *Change in perception*. Many students changed their perception of the worker because of the intelligence characteristic. Most of the change, however, was very subtle—for example, "cracks jokes" became "witty."
4. *Recognition, but refusal to change*. A very few students explicitly recognized the conflict between their perception of the worker and the characteristic that was confronting them. For example, one subject stated, "The trait seems to be conflicting . . . most factory workers I have heard about aren't too intelligent."

Perceptual defense makes any situation in which conflict is likely to be present more difficult. It creates blind spots, causing us to fail to hear and see events as they really are. The challenge for managers is to reduce or minimize the perception of threat in a situation so these defenses are not immediately called into play. This can be accomplished by reassuring people that things that are important to them will not be tampered with, or by accentuating the positive.

CONCEPT CHECK

1. What are the barriers that can inhibit the accuracy of our perception?
2. What are the cultural factors that can influence perception?
3. What is perceptual defense, and what are examples of the mechanisms that can be identified?

3.3 Attributions: Interpreting the Causes of Behavior

3. How do people attribute credit and blame for organizational events?

A major influence on how people behave is the way they interpret the events around them. People who feel they have control over what happens to them are more likely to accept responsibility for their actions than those who feel control of events is out of their hands. The cognitive process by which people interpret the reasons or causes for their behavior is described by **attribution theory**.[21] Specifically, "attribution theory concerns the process by which an individual interprets events as being caused by a particular part of a relatively stable environment."[22]

Attribution theory is based largely on the work of Fritz Heider. Heider argues that behavior is determined by a combination of internal forces (e.g., abilities or effort) and external forces (e.g., task difficulty or luck). Following the cognitive approach of Lewin and Tolman, he emphasizes that it is *perceived* determinants, rather than actual ones, that influence behavior. Hence, if employees perceive that their success is a function of their own abilities and efforts, they can be expected to behave differently than they would if they believed job success was due to chance.

The Attribution Process

The underlying assumption of attribution theory is that people are motivated to understand their environment and the causes of particular events. If individuals can understand these causes, they will then be in a better position to influence or control the sequence of future events. This process is diagrammed in **Exhibit 3.5**. Specifically, attribution theory suggests that particular behavioral events (e.g., the receipt of a promotion) are analyzed by individuals to determine their causes. This process may lead to the conclusion that the promotion resulted from the individual's own effort or, alternatively, from some other cause, such as luck. Based on such cognitive interpretations of events, individuals revise their cognitive structures and rethink their assumptions about causal relationships. For instance, an individual may infer that performance does indeed lead to promotion. Based on this new structure, the individual makes choices about future behavior. In some cases, the individual may decide to continue exerting high levels of effort in the hope that it will lead to further promotions. On the other hand, if an individual concludes that the promotion resulted primarily from chance and was largely unrelated to performance, a different cognitive structure might be created, and there might be little reason to continue exerting high levels of effort. In other words, the way in which we perceive and interpret events around us significantly affects our future behaviors.

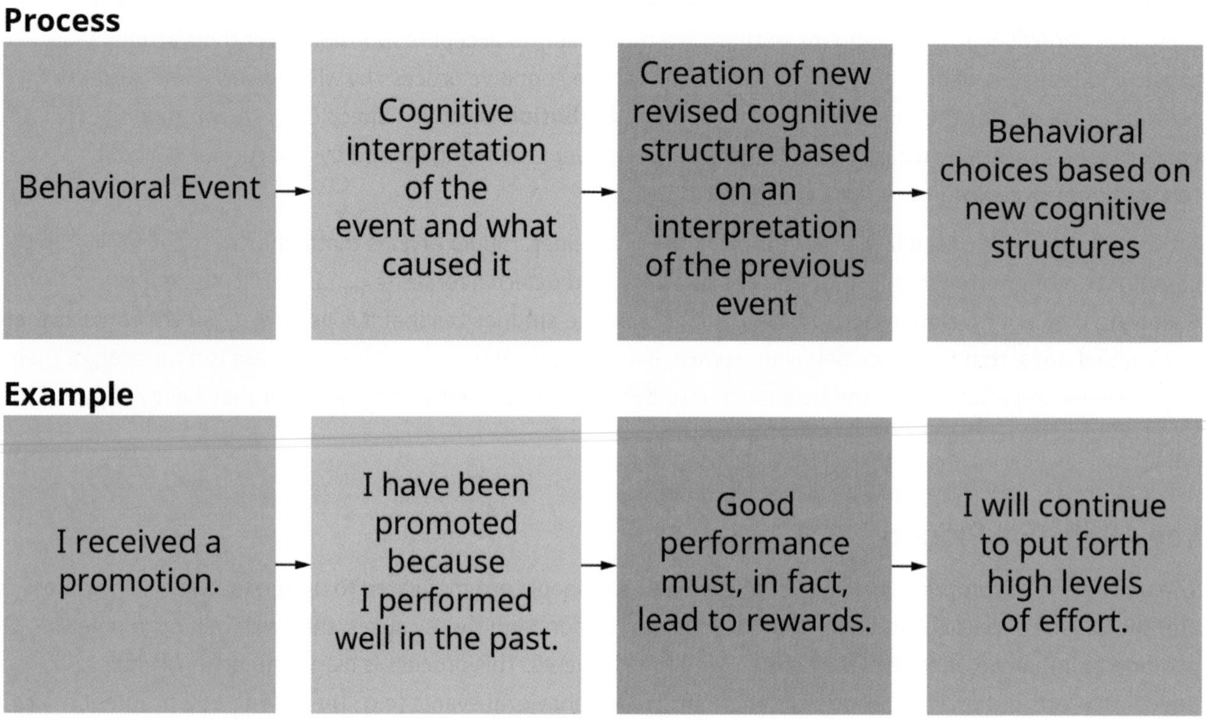

Process

Behavioral Event → Cognitive interpretation of the event and what caused it → Creation of new revised cognitive structure based on an interpretation of the previous event → Behavioral choices based on new cognitive structures

Example

I received a promotion. → I have been promoted because I performed well in the past. → Good performance must, in fact, lead to rewards. → I will continue to put forth high levels of effort.

Exhibit 3.5 **The General Attribution Process** (Attribution: Copyright Rice University, OpenStax, under CC BY-NC-SA 4.0 license)

Internal and External Causes of Behavior

Building upon the work of Heider, Harold Kelley attempted to identify the major antecedents of internal and external attributions.[23] He examined how people determine—or, rather, how they actually perceive—whether the behavior of another person results from internal or external causes. Internal causes include ability and effort, whereas external causes include luck and task ease or difficulty.[24] Kelley's conclusion, illustrated in **Exhibit 3.6**, is that people actually focus on three factors when making causal attributions:

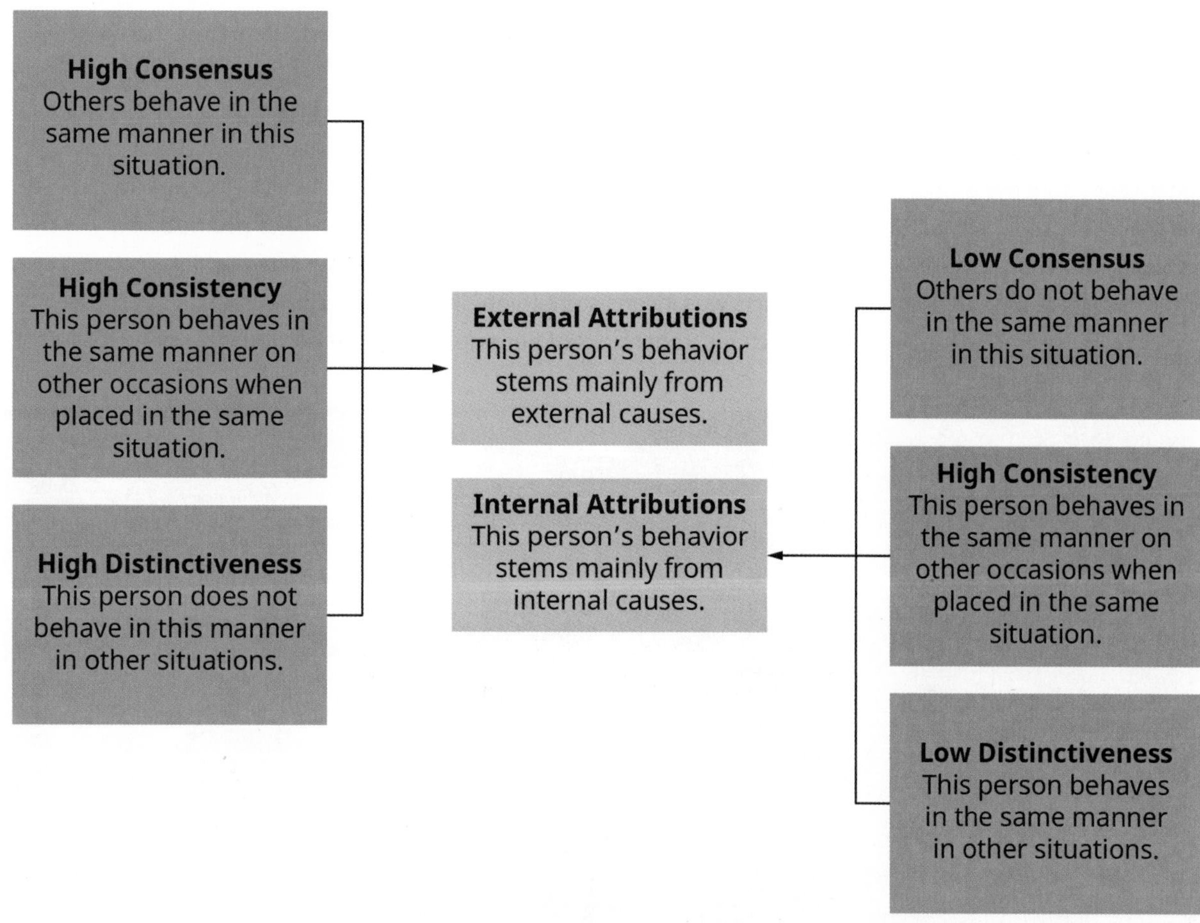

Exhibit 3.6 Causes of Internal and External Attributions Adapted from Nyla Branscombe and Robert A. Baron. *Social Psychology*. Fourteenth Edition, 2016, Pearson.

1. *Consensus*. The extent to which you believe that the person being observed is behaving in a manner that is consistent with the behavior of his or her peers. High consensus exists when the person's actions reflect or are similar to the actions of the group; low consensus exists when the person's actions do not.
2. *Consistency*. The extent to which you believe that the person being observed behaves consistently—in a similar fashion—when confronted on other occasions with the same or similar situations. High consistency exists when the person repeatedly acts in the same way when faced with similar stimuli.
3. *Distinctiveness.* The extent to which you believe that the person being observed would behave consistently when faced with different situations. Low distinctiveness exists when the person acts in a similar manner in response to different stimuli; high distinctiveness exists when the person varies his or her response to different situations.

How do these three factors interact to influence whether one's attributions are internal or external? According to the exhibit, under conditions of high consensus, high consistency, and high distinctiveness, we would expect the observer to make external attributions about the causes of behavior. That is, the person would attribute the behavior of the observed (say, winning a golf tournament) to good fortune or some other external event. On the other hand, when consensus is low, consistency is high, and distinctiveness is low, we would expect the observer to attribute the observed behavior (winning the golf tournament) to internal causes (the winner's skill).

In other words, we tend to attribute the reasons behind the success or failure of others to either internal or external causes according to how we interpret the underlying forces associated with the others' behavior. Consider the example of the first female sales manager in a firm to be promoted to an executive rank. How do you explain her promotion—luck and connections or ability and performance? To find out, follow the model. If she, as a sales representative, had sold more than her (male) counterparts (low consensus in behavior), consistently sold the primary product line in different sales territories (high consistency), and was also able to sell different product lines (low distinctiveness), we would more than likely attribute her promotion to her own abilities. On the other hand, if her male counterparts were also good sales representatives (high consensus) and her sales record on secondary products was inconsistent (high distinctiveness), people would probably attribute her promotion to luck or connections, regardless of her sales performance on the primary product line (high consistency).

Exhibit 3.7 Golf What internal and external attributions can you make about this golfer who is celebrating a hole in one? (Notice the untied shoe.) (Credit: John Fink/ flickr/ Attribution 2.0 Generic (CC BY 2.0))

Attributional Bias

One final point should be made with respect to the attributional process. In making attributions concerning the causes of behavior, people tend to make certain errors of interpretation. Two such errors, or **attribution biases**, should be noted here. The first is called the **fundamental attribution error**. This error is a tendency to *underestimate* the effects of external or situational causes of behavior and to *overestimate* the effects of internal or personal causes. Hence, when a major problem occurs within a certain department, we tend to blame people rather than events or situations.

The second error in attribution processes is generally called the **self-serving bias**. There is a tendency, not surprisingly, for individuals to attribute success on an event or project to their own actions while attributing failure to others. Hence, we often hear sales representatives saying, "*I* made the sale," but "*They* stole the sale from me" rather than "I lost it." These two biases in interpreting how we see the events around us help us understand why employees looking at the same event often see substantially different things.

CONCEPT CHECK 

1. What is attribution theory? Describe the attribution process.
2. What are the internal and external causes of attribution?

3.4 Attitudes and Behavior

4. How can a work environment characterized by positive work attitudes be created and maintained?

Closely related to the topic of perception and attribution—indeed, largely influenced by it—is the issue of attitudes. An **attitude** can be defined as a predisposition to respond in a favorable or unfavorable way to objects or persons in one's environment.[25] When we like or dislike something, we are, in effect, expressing our attitude toward the person or object.

Three important aspects of this definition should be noted. First, an attitude is a hypothetical construct; that is, although its consequences can be observed, the attitude itself cannot. Second, an attitude is a unidimensional concept: An attitude toward a particular person or object ranges on a continuum from very favorable to very unfavorable. We like something or we dislike something (or we are neutral). Something is pleasurable or unpleasurable. In all cases, the attitude can be evaluated along a single evaluative continuum. And third, attitudes are believed to be related to subsequent behavior. We will return to this point later in the discussion.

An attitude can be thought of as composed of three highly interrelated components: (1) a *cognitive* component, dealing with the beliefs and ideas a person has about a person or object; (2) an *affective* component (**affect**), dealing with a person's feelings toward the person or object; and (3) an *intentional* component, dealing with the behavioral intentions a person has with respect to the person or object.[26]

Now that we know what an attitude is, let us consider how attitudes are formed and how they influence behavior. A general model of the relationship between attitudes and behavior is shown in **Exhibit 3.8**. As can be seen, attitudes lead to behavioral intentions, which, in turn, lead to actual behavior. Following behavior, we can often identify efforts by the individual to justify his behavior. Let us examine each of these components of the model separately, beginning with the process of attitude formation.

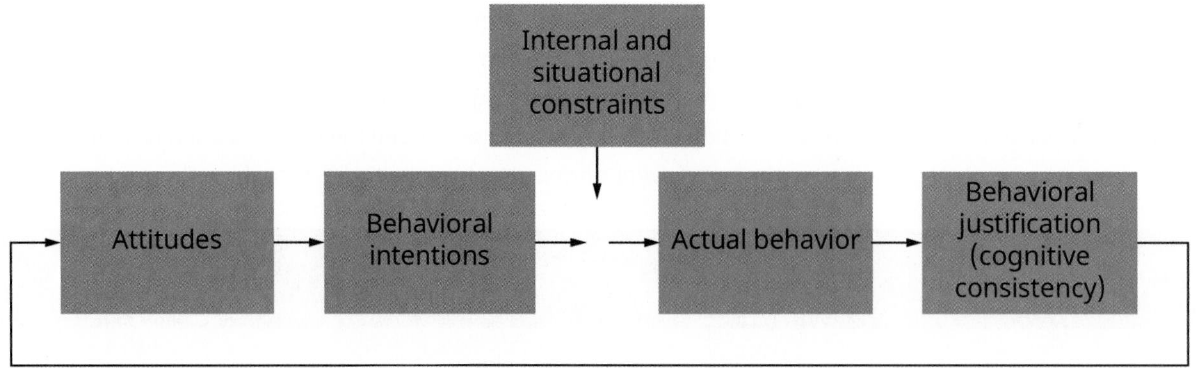

Exhibit 3.8 Relationship between Attitudes and Behavior (Attribution: Copyright Rice University, OpenStax, under CC BY-NC-SA 4.0 license)

How Are Attitudes Formed?

There is considerable disagreement about this question. One view offered by psychologist Barry Staw and others is the **dispositional approach**,[27] which argues that attitudes represent relatively stable predispositions to respond to people or situations around them. That is, attitudes are viewed almost as personality traits. Thus, some people would have a tendency—a predisposition—to be happy on the job, almost regardless of the nature of the work itself. Others may have an internal tendency to be unhappy, again almost regardless of the actual nature of the work. Evidence in support of this approach can be found in a series of studies that found that attitudes change very little among people before and after they make a job change. To the extent that these findings are correct, managers may have little influence over improving job attitudes short of trying to select and hire only those with appropriate dispositions.

A second approach to attitude formation is called the **situational approach**. This approach argues that attitudes emerge as a result of the uniqueness of a given situation. They are situationally determined and can vary in response to changing work conditions. Thus, as a result of experiences at work (a boring or unrewarding job, a bad supervisor, etc.), people react by developing appropriate attitudes. Several variations on this approach can be identified. Some researchers suggest that attitudes result largely from the nature of the job experience itself. That is, an employee might reason: "I don't get along well with my supervisor; therefore, I become dissatisfied with my job." To the extent that this accurately describes how attitudes are formed, it also implies that attitudes can be changed relatively easily. For example, if employees are dissatisfied with their job because of conflicts with supervisors, either changing supervisors or changing the supervisors' behavior may be viable means of improving employee job attitudes. In other words, if attitudes are largely a function of the situation, then attitudes can be changed by altering the situation.

Other advocates of the situational approach suggest a somewhat more complicated process of attitude formation—namely, the **social-information-processing approach**. This view, developed by Pfeffer and Salancik, asserts that attitudes result from "socially constructed realities" as perceived by the individual (see **Exhibit 3.9**).[28] That is, the social context in which the individual is placed shapes his perceptions of the situation and hence his attitudes.

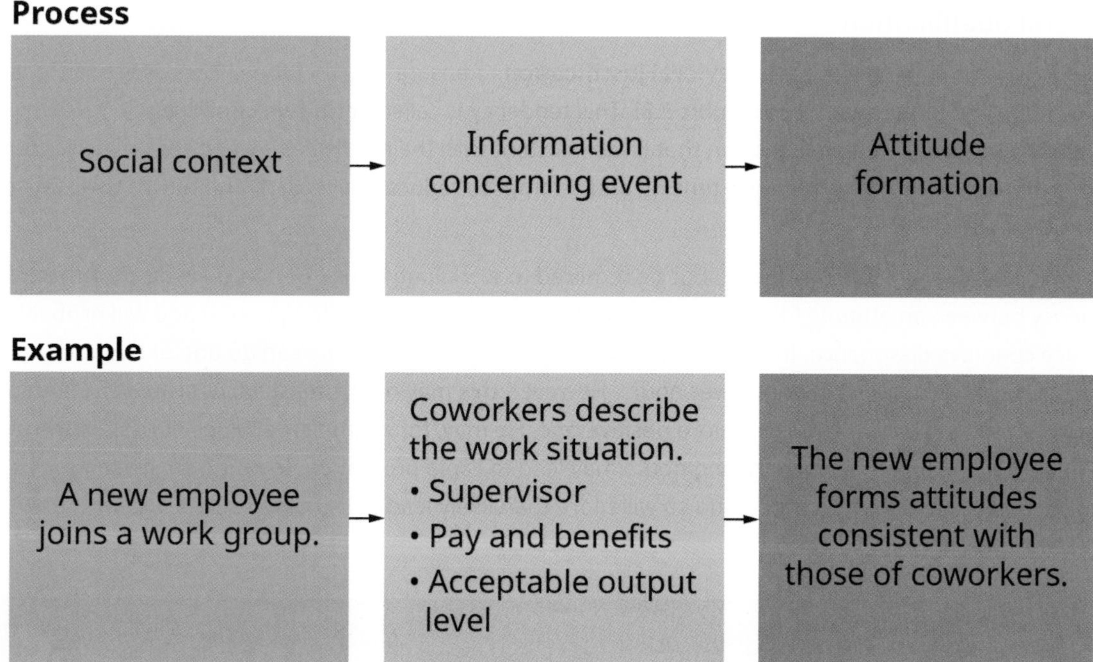

Exhibit 3.9 A Social-Information-Processing View of Attitudes (Attribution: Copyright Rice University, OpenStax, under CC BY-NC-SA 4.0 license)

Here is how it works. Suppose a new employee joins a work group consisting of people who have worked together for some time. The existing group already has opinions and feelings about the fairness of the supervisor, the quality of the workplace, the adequacy of the compensation, and so forth. Upon arriving, the new worker is fed socially acceptable cues from co-workers about acceptable attitudes toward various aspects of the work and company. Thus, due in part to social forces, the new employee begins to form attitudes based on externally provided bits of information from the group instead of objective attributes of the workplace. If the social-information-processing perspective is correct, changing the attitudes of one person will be difficult unless the individual is moved to a different group of coworkers or unless the attitudes of the current coworkers are changed.

Which approach is correct? In point of fact, research indicates that both the dispositional and the social-information-processing views have merit, and it is probably wise to recognize that socially constructed realities and dispositions interact to form the basis for an individual's attitudes at work. The implication of this combined perspective for changing attitudes is that efforts should not assume that minor alterations in the situation will have significant impacts on individual attitudes, but that systematic efforts focusing on groups and interconnected social systems are likely required for successful changes in attitudes.

Behavioral Intentions and Actual Behavior

Regardless of how the attitudes are formed (either through the dispositional or social-information-processing approach), the next problem we face is understanding how resulting behavioral intentions guide actual behavior (return to **Exhibit 3.8**). Clearly, this relationship is not a perfect one. Despite one's intentions, various internal and external constraints often serve to modify an intended course of action. Hence, even though you decide to join the union, you may be prevented from doing so for a variety of reasons. Similarly, a person may have every intention of coming to work but may get the flu. Regardless of intent, other factors that also determine actual behavior often enter the picture.

Behavioral Justification

Finally, people often feel a need for **behavioral justification** to ensure that their behaviors are consistent with their attitudes toward the event (see Exhibit 3.8). This tendency is called **cognitive consistency**.[29] When people find themselves acting in a fashion that is inconsistent with their attitudes—when they experience **cognitive dissonance**—they experience tension and attempt to reduce this tension and return to a state of cognitive consistency.

For example, a manager may hate his job but be required to work long hours. Hence, he is faced with a clear discrepancy between an attitude (dislike of the job) and a behavior (working long hours) and will probably experience cognitive dissonance. In order to become cognitively consistent, he can do one of two things. First, he can change his behavior and work fewer hours. However, this may not be feasible. Alternatively, he can change his attitude toward the job to a more positive one. He may, for example, convince himself that the job is really not that bad and that working long hours may lead to rapid promotion. In doing so, he achieves a state of cognitive consistency. Failure to do so will more than likely lead to increased stress and withdrawal from the job situation.

CONCEPT CHECK 

1. What is attitude, and how does it impact the work environment?
2. What is behavioral justification?

3.5 Work-Related Attitudes

5. How can managers and organizations develop a committed workforce?

When we apply the concept of attitudes to work settings, we have to specify which attitude we are concerned with. Although a variety of work-related attitudes can be identified, the one receiving the most attention is job satisfaction. As this is one of the most widely studied concepts in organizational behavior, we will examine it here in some detail.

Job Involvement and Organizational Commitment

First, however, we should introduce two job attitudes that should also be recognized: job involvement and organizational commitment. **Job involvement** refers to the extent to which a person is interested in and committed to assigned tasks. This is not to say that the person is "happy" (or satisfied) with the job, only that he feels a certain responsibility toward ensuring that the job itself is done correctly and with a high standard of competence. Here the focus of the attitude is the job itself.[30]

Organizational commitment, on the other hand, represents the relative strength of an individual's identification with and involvement in an organization.[31] Commitment can be characterized by three factors: (1) a strong belief in and acceptance of the organization's goals and values, (2) a willingness to exert considerable effort on behalf of the organization, and (3) a strong desire to maintain membership in the organization. When viewed this way, commitment represents something beyond mere passive loyalty to the company. Instead, it involves an active relationship with the organization in which individuals are willing to give something of themselves in order to help the company succeed and prosper. A careful reading of the research on keys to the success of many Japanese firms will highlight the importance played by a committed work force. Now we turn to the third work attitude of job satisfaction.

Job Satisfaction

Job satisfaction may be defined as "a pleasurable or positive emotional state resulting from the appraisal of one's job or job experience."[32] It results from the perception that an employee's job actually provides what he values in the work situation.

Several characteristics of the concept of job satisfaction follow from this definition. First, satisfaction is an emotional response to a job situation. It can be fully understood only by introspection. As with any attitude, we cannot observe satisfaction; we must infer its existence and quality either from an employee's behavior or verbal statements.

Second, job satisfaction is perhaps best understood in terms of discrepancy. Several writers have pointed to the concept of job satisfaction as being a result of how much a person wants or expects from the job compared to how much he actually receives.[33] People come to work with varying levels of job expectations. These expectations may vary not only in quality (different people may value different things in a job), but also in intensity. On the basis of work experiences, people receive outcomes (rewards) from the job. These include not only extrinsic rewards, such as pay and promotion, but also a variety of intrinsic rewards, such as satisfying coworker relations and meaningful work. To the extent that the outcomes received by an employee meet or exceed expectations, we would expect the employee to be satisfied with the job and wish to remain. On those occasions when outcomes actually surpass expectations, we would expect employees to reevaluate their expectations and probably raise them to meet available outcomes. However, when outcomes do not meet expectations, employees are dissatisfied and may prefer to seek alternative sources of satisfaction, either by changing jobs or by placing greater value on other life activities, such as outside recreation.

Dimensions of Job Satisfaction. It has been argued that job satisfaction actually represents several related attitudes. So, when we speak of satisfaction, we must specify "satisfaction with what?" Research has suggested that five job dimensions represent the most salient characteristics of a job about which people have affective responses. These five are:

1. *Work itself*. The extent to which tasks performed by employees are interesting and provide opportunities for learning and for accepting responsibility.
2. *Pay*. The amount of pay received, the perceived equity of the pay, and the method of payment.
3. *Promotional opportunities*. The availability of realistic opportunities for advancement.
4. *Supervision*. The technical and managerial abilities of supervisors; the extent to which supervisors demonstrate consideration for and interest in employees.
5. *Coworkers*. The extent to which coworkers are friendly, technically competent, and supportive.

Although other dimensions of job satisfaction have been identified, these five dimensions are used most often when assessing various aspects of job attitudes in organizations.

Measurement of Job Satisfaction. Probably the most common attitude surveys in organizations today focus on job satisfaction. Satisfaction is considered by many managers to be an important indicator of organizational effectiveness, and therefore it is regularly monitored to assess employee feelings toward the organization. By far the most common means of assessing satisfaction is the rating scale. Rating scales represent direct verbal self-reports concerning employee feelings; they have been widely used in companies since the 1930s. Several job satisfaction scales exist. One of the most popular is the Minnesota Satisfaction Questionnaire (MSQ). This instrument uses a Likert-response format to generate satisfaction scores on 26 scales, including satisfaction with compensation, promotion opportunities, coworkers, recognition, and so forth. You can assess your scoring on a short version of this instrument in the assessment section of this chapter.

The MSQ and similar rating scales have several advantages for evaluating levels of job satisfaction. First, they are relatively short and simple and can be completed by large numbers of employees quickly. Second, because of the generalized wording of the various terms, the instruments can be administered to a wide range of employees in various jobs. It is not necessary to alter the questionnaire for each job classification. Finally, extensive normative data (or norms) are available. These norms include summaries of the scores of thousands of people who have completed the instruments. Hence, it is possible for employers in other organizations to determine relative standings.

However, although rating scales have many virtues compared to other techniques, at least two drawbacks must be recognized. First, as with any self-report inventory, it is assumed that respondents are both willing and able to describe their feelings accurately. As noted by several researchers,[34] people often consciously or unconsciously distort information that they feel is damaging and enhance information that they feel is beneficial. For example, it is possible that employees who think their supervisors may see the results of their questionnaire may report overly favorable job attitudes.

A second problem with rating scales is the underlying assumption that questionnaire items mean the same thing to all people. There may, in fact, not be a common interpretation across individuals. Even so, rating scales have proved to be helpful in assessing satisfaction in various aspects of the job situation. Managers can use the results to identify potential problem areas and to generate discussions and action plans of how to correct aspects of jobs or the organization that are causing unacceptable levels of dissatisfaction.

CUSTOMER SATISFACTION AND QUALITY

How Satisfied Are Employees?

If you've ever flown on Southwest Airlines, you can tell something is different just from the first interaction with their employees. From the flight attendants, to the pilot's announcements, and even to their customer service representatives, they have a cheerful disposition, and contrary to popular belief, this isn't an act.

In 2017, Southwest Airlines announced that it would be sharing their $586 million in profits with its 54,000 employees, given them a bonus of approximately 13.2 percent on average. This doesn't account for the extra $351 million that they contributed to the employee's 401(k) plans either. This is just one of the many ways that Southwest has given back to their employees in a day and age when minimum wage for even qualified candidates seems like a fight.

Southwest CEO Gary Kelly reflects that "Our people-first approach, which has guided our company since it was founded, means our company does well, our people do really, really well. Our people work incredibly hard and deserve to share in Southwest's success." With this attitude, it is no wonder the employees on and off your flight are showing their satisfaction in their everyday attitudes. The year 2017 was the 43rd year that Southwest shared its profits with their people. While compensation ranks among one of the most attributed traits of a company to help with employee satisfaction, it goes much deeper than that to keep motivation high.

At Southwest, they rank employees first and customers second. They create a culture of fun and inclusive core values that help to give their employees a sense of community and belonging. When their employees are motivated and take pride in what they do, they are able to give their best to their customers every day, which accounts for their highly ranked customer satisfaction results on surveys each year.

Sources: Dahl, Darren, "Why do Southwest Employees Always Seem so Happy," *Forbes*, July, 28, 2017, https://www.forbes.com/sites/darrendahl/2017/07/28/why-do-southwest-airlines-employees-always-seem-so-happy/#3cba8dbc59b0; Martin, Emmie, "A major airline says there's something it values more than its customers, and there's a good reason why," *Business Insider*, July 29, 2015, https://www.businessinsider.com/southwest-airlines-puts-employees-first-2015-7; Ramdas, Shreesha, "The Southwest Way to Employee Satisfaction: Flying High Like the High Flier," *Customer Think*, May 12, 2018, (http://customerthink.com/the-southwest-way-to-employee-satisfaction-flying-high-like-the-high-flier/.

Questions:

1. Oftentimes it is hard to stay at the top. What considerations should Southwest take to maintain their employee satisfaction and keep improving?
2. Not all companies can share profits. What would you suggest to a new company that is just starting off to help gain high employee satisfaction?

CONCEPT CHECK

1. How can organizations foster positive job involvement and instill positive attitudes in their employees?
2. What are the dimensions of job satisfaction?

Key Terms

Affect Dealing with a person's feelings toward the person or object.

Attitude A predisposition to respond in a favorable or unfavorable way to objects or persons in one's environment.

Attribution biases Covers both the fundamental attribution error and the self-serving bias.

Attribution theory Concerns the process by which an individual interprets events as being caused by a particular part of a relatively stable environment.

Behavioral justification The need to ensure that one's behaviors are consistent with their attitudes toward the event.

Body language The manner in which people express their inner feelings subconsciously through physical actions such as sitting up straight versus being relaxed or looking people straight in the eye versus looking away from people.

Cognitive consistency The need for behavioral justification to ensure that a person's behaviors are consistent with their attitudes toward an event.

Cognitive dissonance Finding one's self acting in a fashion that is inconsistent with their attitudes and experiencing tension and attempting to reduce this tension and return to a state of cognitive consistency.

Dispositional approach Argues that attitudes represent relatively stable predispositions to respond to people or situations around them.

Fundamental attribution error The tendency to *underestimate* the effects of external or situational causes of behavior and to *overestimate* the effects of internal or personal causes.

Halo effect The influence of positive arbitrary biases.

Job involvement Refers to the extent to which a person is interested in and committed to assigned tasks.

Job satisfaction A pleasurable or positive emotional state resulting from the appraisal of one's job or job experience.

Organizational commitment Represents the relative strength of an individual's identification with and involvement in an organization.

Perception The process by which one screens, selects, organizes, and interprets stimuli to give them meaning.

Perceptual defense A defense that perceives emotionally disturbing or threatening stimuli as having a higher recognition threshold than neutral stimuli. Such stimuli are likely to elicit substitute perceptions that are radically altered so as to prevent recognition of the presented stimuli that arouse emotional reactions even though the stimuli are not recognized.

Perceptual organization When meaning has been attached to an object, individuals are in a position to determine an appropriate response or reaction to it.

Perceptual selectivity Refers to the process by which individuals select objects in the environment for attention.

Response disposition The tendency to recognize familiar objects more quickly than unfamiliar ones.

Response salience The tendency to focus on objects that relate to our *immediate* needs or wants.

Selective perception The process by which we systematically screen out information we don't wish to hear, focusing instead on more salient information.

Self-serving bias The tendency for individuals to attribute success on an event or project to their own actions while attributing failure to others.

Situational approach This approach argues that attitudes emerge as a result of the uniqueness of a given situation.

Social perception Consists of those processes by which we perceive other people.

Social-information-processing approach Asserts that attitudes result from "socially constructed realities" as perceived by the individual.

Stereotyping A tendency to assign attributes to people solely on the basis of their class or category.

 Summary of Learning Outcomes

3.1 The Perceptual Process

1. How do differences in perception affect employee behavior and performance?

One of the key determinants of people's behavior in organizations is how they see and interpret situations and people around them. It is vital for anyone (manager or subordinate) who desires to be more effective to understand the critical aspects of context, object, and perceiver that influence perceptions and interpretations and the relationship between these and subsequent attitudes, intentions, and behaviors. This understanding will not only facilitate the ability to correctly understand and anticipate behaviors, but it will also enhance the ability to change or influence that behavior. Perception is the process by which individuals screen, select, organize, and interpret stimuli in order to give them meaning. Perceptual selectivity is the process by which individuals select certain stimuli for attention instead of others. Selective attention is influenced by both external factors (e.g., physical or dynamic properties of the object) and personal factors (e.g., response salience). Social perception is the process by which we perceive other people. It is influenced by the characteristics of the person perceived, the perceiver, and the situation.

3.2 Barriers to Accurate Social Perception

2. How can managers and organizations minimize the negative impact of stereotypes and other barriers to accurate social perception in interpersonal relations?

Stereotyping is a tendency to assign attributes to people solely on the basis of their class or category. Selective perception is a process by which we systematically screen or discredit information we don't wish to hear and instead focus on more salient information. Perceptual defense is a tendency to distort or ignore information that is either personally threatening or culturally unacceptable.

3.3 Attributions: Interpreting the Causes of Behavior

3. How do people attribute credit and blame for organizational events?

Attribution theory concerns the process by which individuals attempt to make sense of the cause-effect relationships in their life space. Events are seen as being either internally caused (that is, by the individual) or externally caused (that is, by other factors in the environment). In making causal attributions, people tend to focus on three factors: consensus, consistency, and distinctiveness. The fundamental attribution error is a tendency to underestimate the effects of external or situational causes of behavior and overestimate the effects of personal causes.

The self-serving bias is a tendency for people to attribute success on a project to themselves while attributing failure to others.

3.4 Attitudes and Behavior

4. How can a work environment characterized by positive work attitudes be created and maintained?

An attitude can be defined as a predisposition to respond in a favorable or unfavorable way to objects or persons in one's environment. There are two theories concerning the manner in which attitudes are formed. The first, called the dispositional approach, asserts that attitudes are fairly stable tendencies to respond to events in certain ways, much like personality traits. Thus, some people may be happy on almost any job regardless of the nature of the job. The second, called the situational approach, asserts that attitudes result largely from the particular situation in which the individual finds himself. Thus, some jobs may lead to more favorable attitudes than others. The social-information-processing approach to attitudes is a situational model that suggests that attitudes are strongly influenced by the opinions and assessments of coworkers. Cognitive consistency is a tendency to think and act in a predictable manner. Cognitive dissonance occurs when our actions and our attitudes are in conflict. This dissonance will motivate us to attempt to return to a state of cognitive consistency, where attitudes and behaviors are congruent.

3.5 Work-Related Attitudes

5. How can managers and organizations develop a committed workforce?

Job involvement refers to the extent to which an individual is interested in his or her assigned tasks. Organizational commitment refers to the relative strength of an individual's identification with and involvement in a particular organization. Job satisfaction is a pleasurable or positive emotional state resulting from the appraisal of one's job or job experience.

Chapter Review Questions

1. Describe how the basic perceptual process works. Why should managers understand this process?
2. How can variations in social perception affect everyday work behavior? Provide an example to illustrate.
3. What can managers do to reduce the incidences of stereotyping in the workplace?
4. How does the attributional process work? Provide an example to show why this process is so important in understanding organizational behavior.
5. How do attributional biases work? What can managers do to reduce such biases?
6. What are the differences between job involvement, organizational commitment, and job satisfaction? Are all three influenced by the same factors?
7. What are the major reasons for job satisfaction? What are the primary consequences of dissatisfaction? Explain.

Management Skills Application Exercises

1. In order to understand how response salience works, you may want to complete this self-assessment. Read the passage, and rate it on its comprehensibility. Does it make sense to you? Next, look at the appropriate frame of reference given in **Appendix B**. Now read the passage again, and rate it for its comprehensibility. Does it make more sense now that you have a specific frame of reference?

   Can You Understand This Passage?

   Instructions: The procedure is actually quite simple. First you arrange things into different groups. Of course, one pile may be sufficient depending on how much there is to do. If you have to go somewhere else due to lack of facilities that is the next step, otherwise you are pretty well set. It is important not to overdo things. That is, it is better to do too few things at once than too many. In the short run this may not seem important, but complications can easily arise. A mistake can be expensive as well. At first the whole procedure will seem complicated. Soon, however, it will become just another facet of life. It is difficult to foresee any end to the necessity for this task in the immediate future, but then one never can tell. After the procedure is completed one arranges the materials into different groups again. Then they can be put into their appropriate places. Eventually they will be used once more and the whole cycle will then have to be repeated. However, that is part of life.

Comprehensive Scale				
Very incomprehensive		Neutral	Very comprehensive	
1	2	3	4	5
Adapted from "Contextual Prerequisites for Understanding: Some Investigations of Comprehension and Recall" by John D. Bransford and Marcia K. Johnson, in *Journal of Verbal Learning and Verbal Behavior,* December 1972, p. 722.				

2. **How Do You Feel About Women Executives?**
   Instructions: This instrument focuses on your attitudes toward women in executive positions. For each item, circle the number that best represents your feelings concerning women executives in organizations. Be completely honest with yourself in responding. For a scoring key, refer to **Appendix B**.

	Strongly Disagree			Strongly Agree	
1. It is high time we had more women in executive positions.	1	2	3	4	5
2. Women make just as good managers as men.	1	2	3	4	5
3. Women often fail to have the same level of technical competence as men.	1	2	3	4	5
4. Women executives should receive the same respect and trust as their male counterparts.	1	2	3	4	5
5. Men tend to be better suited for managerial positions than women.	1	2	3	4	5
6. Women are too emotional to succeed in top-level management.	1	2	3	4	5
7. Women have a hard time supervising the work of male subordinates.	1	2	3	4	5
8. I would prefer not to work for a female manager.	1	2	3	4	5
9. Success as an executive has nothing to do with one's gender.	1	2	3	4	5
10. Many women executives get to the top either because of affirmative action pressure or connections.	1	2	3	4	5

3. Examples of the MSQ for two scales (compensation and recognition) can be seen in this self-assessment. If you wish to complete this sample questionnaire, simply refer to a (paid or unpaid) job that you have had and answer the questionnaire. To score the instrument, refer to **Appendix B**.

Are You Satisfied with Your Job?

Instructions: Answer each of the ten questions by circling the numbers that best describe how satisfied or dissatisfied you are with the particular item. Then sum your results for questions 1–5 and 6–10 separately.

	Very Dissatisfied			**Very Satisfied**	
1. The way I am noticed when I do a good job	1	2	3	4	5
2. The way I get full credit for the work I do	1	2	3	4	5
3. The recognition I get for the work I do	1	2	3	4	5
4. The way they usually tell me when I do my job well	1	2	3	4	5
5. The praise I get for doing a good job	1	2	3	4	5
6. The amount of pay for the work I do	1	2	3	4	5
7. The chance to make as much money as my friends	1	2	3	4	5
8. How my pay compares with that for similar jobs in other companies	1	2	3	4	5
9. My pay and the amount of work I do	1	2	3	4	5
10. How my pay compares with that of other workers	1	2	3	4	5
Adapted from David J. Weiss, Rene V. Dawis, George W. England, and Lloyd H. Lofquist, *Manual for the Minnesota Satisfaction Questionnaire* (Minneapolis: Industrial Relations Center, University of Minnesota).					

Managerial Decision Exercises

1. You remember from your Organizational Behavior class that several assessments to increase one's self-awareness, like the Minnesota Multiphasic Personality Inventory that you read about in this chapter and is profiled in the Managerial Skill Application Exercises of this chapter, were very beneficial for you as an understanding of your emotional intelligence, values, cognitive style, and ability to cope with change. You have been assigned to a team that will interview both internal and external candidates for a new sales manager position for the California region, which is a position at the same level organizationally as your present position. During the initial orientation meeting, one of the team members—the manager of a distribution center for the organization—says, "I like to use the results of the Myers-Briggs Types Indicator assessment to screen applicants for this position, and since sales managers should be extroverts and should possess sensing, thinking, and judging skills, we should only consider ESTJ types." Your boss, the national sales manager, asks you to write a report on whether the selection process should only consider ESTJ types and to provide it to the team for discussion. Write a report and share it for discussion with a team of students in this class who will assume the role of the hiring interview team.
2. Recall a meeting that you recently had, such as a team presentation of a case analysis. What were your impressions of what happened in the planning of the presentation and how things like the assignment of roles and timetables for subsequent meetings and deliverables unfolded. What were the behaviors of the others at the meeting, and why do you think they acted as they did? Finally, how do you think that others

perceived your behavior at the meeting? After you have recorded these recollections, meet with another attendee of that meeting. Ask them these questions, and record what they say happened at that meeting and what they thought of the behavior of the participants, including you. Let them know that this is for your class and you want them to be as honest as possible. As they are answering, record their recollections and do not interrupt or offer possible corrections. Finally, compare your recollections and notes with those of the interviewee and use the knowledge from this chapter to assess the differences and similarities in perception and attribution.

3. As a way to measure job satisfaction, ask someone at a local business the following questions:
    a. What is your job title, and what do you do in your own words? How do these match up to tasks, duties, and responsibilities in your job description?
    b. Are you satisfied with the work that you do?
    c. How satisfied are you with the training and supervision that you receive?
    d. How satisfied are you with the people that you work with?
    e. Are you happy with your salary?
    f. Are you happy with the benefits that are offered as part of the job?
    g. Do you see any possibilities for advancement in the organization?
    h. What are your general feelings about your employer?
    i. Do you have any additional comments regarding how you feel about your job?

    Write an assessment of this individual's job satisfaction and what a supervisor and organization could do to improve the lever of job satisfaction for their employees.

Critical Thinking Case

Stereotypes at Pitney Bowes

Many times, we think of stereotypes or discrimination only being an issue when it comes to things like gender, race, or religion. However, at Pitney Bowes Inc., the toughest stereotype to overcome is age.

Brigitte Van Den Houte starts her day in the normal way; however, she has taken a keen focus on persuading employees in their 20s that they have a future at Pitney Bowes.

For almost 100 years, Pitney Bowes, founded in 1920, has been all about commerce. But as the world turned to technology, the definition of what that meant for the traditional postage-meter equipment company had to change as well.

One of the biggest challenges of this ever-changing technological world is how the generations of employees can step aside from their stereotypes and understand one another to better work effectively.

At Pitney Bowes, their proactive approach puts younger colleagues with older colleagues in a mentoring situation. This is not the typical older mentor to younger mentor setup, however. Every few months, Houte arranges for the younger employees to spend the day with a seasoned executive with the plan of sharing experiences and ideas and offering advice. Houte states, "the old way of working no longer works," and she's right.

With over one-third of the workforce aging to 50 or older and millennials (young people aged 22–37) being the largest workforce group, it is imperative to put stereotypes aside and learn to work together. One big mistake for a manager would be to focus on the age difference rather than on what skills each person individually can bring to the table.

Stereotypes such as "older individuals don't know about technology" or "millennials are constantly job hopping and feel entitled" are put aside at Pitney Bowes in order to get the job done. With a more proactive approach, the range of variables within each generation can be utilized in the most effective way possible for an organization.

Sources: Hymowitz, Carol, "The Tricky Task of Managing the New, Multigenerational Workplace," *The Wall Street Journal*, August 12, 2018, https://www.wsj.com/articles/the-tricky-task-of-managing-the-new-multigenerational-workplace-1534126021?mod=searchresults&page=1&pos=9; Ault, Nicole, " Don't Trust Anyone Over 21," *The Wall Street Journal*, August 22, 2018, https://www.wsj.com/articles/dont-trust-anyone-over-21-1534977740?mod=searchresults&page=1&pos=1.

Questions:

1. What are other ways that a company can utilize a multigenerational team to their advantage?
2. What challenges does a multigenerational team pose for management?
3. What should the company and management team consider when attracting new employees of all generations?

4 Learning and Reinforcement

Exhibit 4.1 (JD Kirk/ flickr/ Attribution 2.0 Generic (CC BY 2.0))

Introduction

Learning Outcomes

After reading this chapter, you should be able to answer these questions:

1. How do organizations offer appropriate rewards in a timely fashion?
2. What are the best practices that organizations utilize to train employees in new job skills?
3. How do managers and organizations reduce undesirable employee behavior while reinforcing desirable behavior?
4. How can employees be trained to assume more responsibility for self-improvement and job performance with the goal of creating a work environment characterized by continual self-learning and employee development?

EXPLORING MANAGERIAL CAREERS

The Google Way to a Culture of Continued Learning

Google is great at many things—attracting top talent, maintaining employee satisfaction, and encouraging creativity, to name a few.

According to the Association of Training and Development (ATD), companies that offer comprehensive training programs have 218 percent higher income per employee than companies without formalized training. Not only that, but companies that have required programs for their employees see a much higher profit margin than those that don't. Investing in people and promoting a self-learning environment is the right plan for companies that are looking to keep employees' behavior in check, train for new skills, and increase employee development.

Spending millions of dollars is not necessary to create a culture that promotes learning.

Google follows the simple principles that gives their employees purpose and a career path. They provide information that is relevant and important to their employees. They know that in order to get this information to stick, it must be pertinent and presented at the right time, and in the right format. They also archive important information, which empowers employees to access this information at any and all times. Instead of providing gateways that impede learning, they open the doors.

Secondly, they share "dumb questions." This may seem like a silly tactic, but encouraging employees to share their questions and opinions allows for sharing of information and learning on all levels. Google also employs the values of celebrated failure, which allows for the teams to learn from their mistakes and their failures. Then they can move on to the next project with newly found valuable information to get better each time.

Lastly, formalized plans for continued learning are employed for "informal and continuous learning" to occur. Examples of these events can be allowing employees to pursue their own interests, utilizing coaching and support tools, and then training being requested at various times. With these tactics, the cultivation of learning can be expressed throughout the company. Google is at the forefront of this pursuit, but other companies can learn from their methods to get ahead and get their employees on track as well.

Sources: Ault, Nicole, "Don't Trust Anyone Over 21," *The Wall Street Journal*, August 22, 2018, https://www.wsj.com/articles/dont-trust-anyone-over-21-1534977740?mod=searchresults&page=1&pos=1; and Gutierrez, Karla, "Mind-blowing Statistics that Prove the Value of Employee Training and Development, Shift, August 22, 2017, https://www.shiftelearning.com/blog/statistics-value-of-employee-training-and-development.

Questions:

1. What considerations should Google take into account when creating formalized training for their employees?
2. Name three reasons why training and continued learning can be important for a company's success.
3. Why is encouraging and celebrating failure an important thing for a company to promote?

A major responsibility of managers is to evaluate and reward their subordinates. If managers are to maximize the impact of available (and often limited) rewards, a thorough knowledge of reinforcement techniques is essential. We shall devote this chapter to developing a detailed understanding of learning processes in organizations. We begin by looking at basic models of learning.

4.1 Basic Models of Learning

1. How do organizations offer appropriate rewards in a timely fashion?

Learning may be defined, for our purposes, as a relatively permanent change in behavior that occurs as a result of experience. That is, a person is said to have learned something when she consistently exhibits a new behavior over time. Several aspects of this definition are noteworthy.[1] First, learning involves a change in an attitude or behavior. This change does not necessarily have to be an improvement, however, and can include such things as learning bad habits or forming prejudices. In order for learning to occur, the change that takes place must be relatively permanent. So changes in behavior that result from fatigue or temporary adaptation to a unique situation would not be considered examples of learning. Next, learning typically involves some form of practice or experience. For example, the change that results from physical maturation, as when a baby develops the physical strength to walk, is in itself not considered learning. Third, this practice or experience must be reinforced over time for learning to take place. Where reinforcement does not follow practice or experience, the behavior will eventually diminish and disappear ("extinction"). Finally, learning is an inferred process; we cannot observe learning directly. Instead, we must infer the existence of learning from observing changes in overt behavior.

We can best understand the learning process by looking at four stages in the development of research on learning (see **Exhibit 4.2**). Scientific interest in learning dates from the early experiments of Pavlov and others around the turn of the century. The focus of this research was on stimulus-response relationships and the environmental determinants of observable behaviors. This was followed by the discovery of the law of effect, experiments in operant conditioning, and, finally, the formulation of social learning theory.

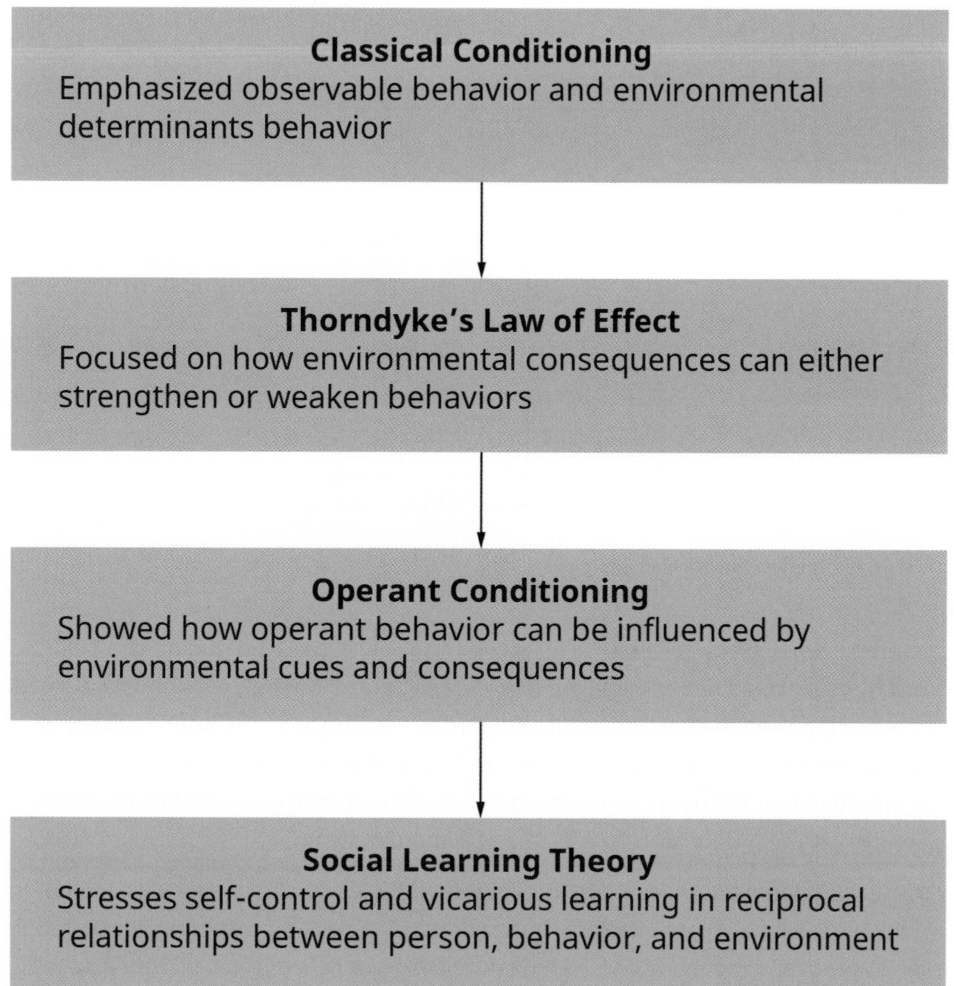

Exhibit 4.2 The Development of Modern Behavioral Learning Theory (Attribution: Copyright Rice University, OpenStax, under CC BY-NC-SA 4.0 license)

Classical Conditioning

Classical conditioning is the process whereby a stimulus-response (S-R) bond is developed between a conditioned stimulus and a **conditioned response** through the repeated linking of a conditioned stimulus with an unconditioned stimulus. This process is shown in **Exhibit 4.3**. The classic example of Pavlov's experiments illustrates the process. Pavlov was initially interested in the digestive processes of dogs but noticed that the dogs started to salivate at the first signal of approaching food. On the basis of this discovery, he shifted his attention to the question of whether animals could be trained to draw a causal relationship between previously unconnected factors. Specifically, using the dogs as subjects, he examined the extent to which the dogs could learn to associate the ringing of a bell with the act of salivation. The experiment began with unlearned, or *unconditioned*, stimulus-response relationships. When a dog was presented with meat (unconditioned stimulus), the dog salivated (unconditioned response). No learning was necessary here, as this relationship represented a natural physiological process.

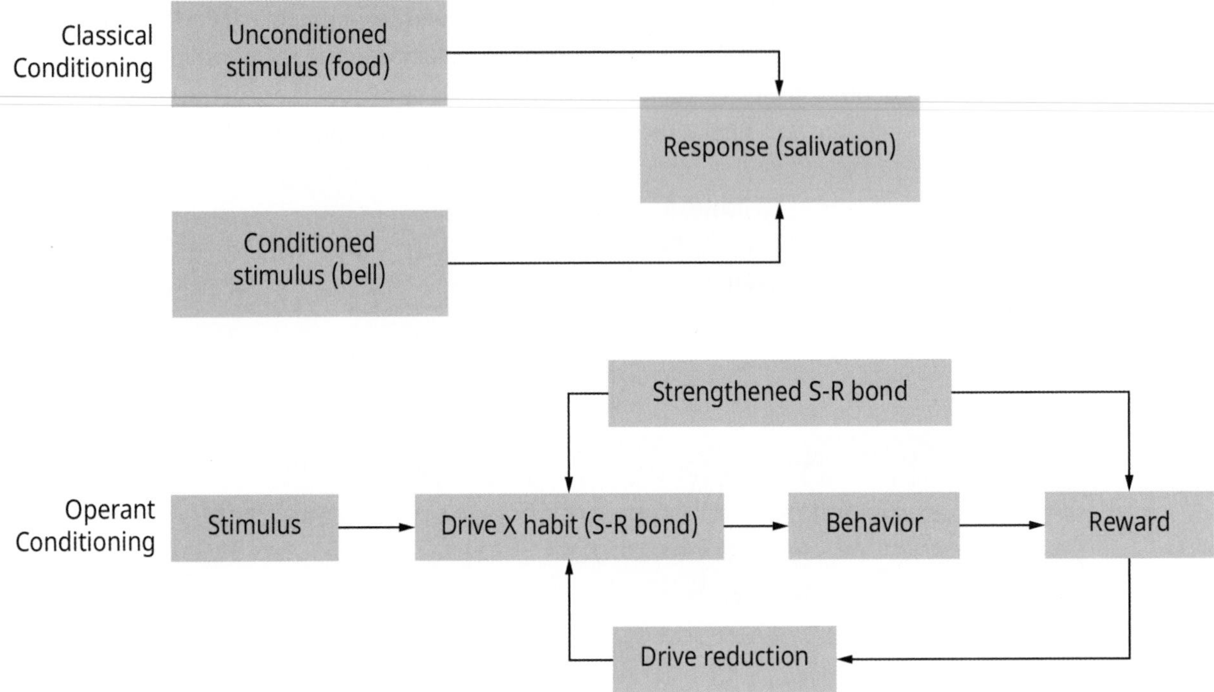

Exhibit 4.3 Classical versus Operant Conditioning (Attribution: Copyright Rice University, OpenStax, under CC BY-NC-SA 4.0 license)

Next, Pavlov paired the unconditioned stimulus (meat) with a neutral one (the ringing of a bell). Normally, the ringing of the bell by itself would not be expected to elicit salivation. However, over time, a learned linkage developed for the dog between the bell and meat, ultimately resulting in an S-R bond between the conditioned stimulus (the bell) and the response (salivation) without the presence of the unconditioned stimulus (the meat). Evidence emerged that learning had occurred and that this learning resulted from conditioning the dogs to associate two normally unrelated objects, the bell and the meat.

Although Pavlov's experiments are widely cited as evidence of the existence of classical conditioning, it is necessary from the perspective of organizational behavior to ask how this process relates to people at work. Ivancevich, Szilagyi, and Wallace provide one such work-related example of classical conditioning:

An illustration of classical conditioning in a work setting would be an airplane pilot learning how to use a newly installed warning system. In this case the behavior to be learned is to respond to a warning light that indicates that the plane has dropped below a critical altitude on an assigned glide path. The proper response is to increase the plane's altitude. The pilot already knows how to appropriately respond to the trainer's warning to increase altitude (in this case we would say the trainer's warning is an unconditioned stimulus and the corrective action of increasing altitude is an **unconditioned response**). The training session consists of the trainer warning the pilot to increase altitude every time the warning light goes on. Through repeated pairings of the warning light with the trainer's warning, the pilot eventually learns to adjust the plane's altitude in response to the warning light even though the trainer is not present. Again, the unit of learning is a new S-R connection, or habit.[2]

Although classical conditioning clearly has applications to work situations, particularly in the area of training and development, it has been criticized as explaining only a limited part of total human learning. Psychologist B. F. Skinner argues that classical conditioning focuses on respondent, or reflexive, behaviors; that is, it concentrates on explaining largely involuntary responses that result from stimuli.[3] More complex learning cannot be explained solely by classical conditioning. As an alternative explanation, Skinner and others have proposed the operant conditioning model of learning.

Operant Conditioning

The major focus of **operant conditioning** is on the effects of reinforcements, or rewards, on desired behaviors. One of the first psychologists to examine such processes was J. B. Watson, a contemporary of Pavlov, who argued that behavior is largely influenced by the rewards one receives as a result of actions.[4] This notion is best summarized in Thorndike's **law of effect**. This law states that of several responses made to the same situation, those that are accompanied or closely followed by satisfaction (reinforcement) will be more likely to occur; those that are accompanied or closely followed by discomfort (punishment) will be less likely to occur.[5]

In other words, it posits that behavior that leads to positive or pleasurable outcomes tends to be repeated, whereas behavior that leads to negative outcomes or punishment tends to be avoided. In this manner, individuals learn appropriate, acceptable responses to their environment. If we repeatedly dock the pay of an employee who is habitually tardy, we would expect that employee to learn to arrive early enough to receive a full day's pay.

A basic operant model of learning is presented in **Exhibit 4.2**. There are three important concepts of this model:

Drive. A **drive** is an internal state of disequilibrium; it is a felt need. It is generally believed that drive increases with the strength of deprivation. A drive, or desire, to learn must be present for learning to take place. For example, not currently being able to afford the house you want is likely to lead to a drive for more money to buy your desired house. Living in a run-down shack is likely to increase this drive compared to living in a nice apartment.

Habit. A **habit** is the experienced bond or connection between stimulus and response. For example, if a person learns over time that eating satisfies hunger, a strong stimulus-response (hunger-eating) bond will develop. Habits thus determine the behaviors, or courses of action, we choose.

Reinforcement or reward. This represents the feedback individuals receive as a result of action. For example, if as a salesperson you are given a bonus for greater sales and plan to use the money to buy the house you have always wanted, this will reinforce the behaviors that you believed led to greater sales, such as smiling at customers, repeating their name during the presentation, and so on.

A stimulus activates an individual's motivation through its impact on drive and habit. The stronger the drive and habit (S-R bond), the stronger the motivation to behave in a certain way. As a result of this behavior, two things happen. First, the individual receives feedback that reduces the original drive. Second, the individual strengthens his or her belief in the veracity of the S-R bond to the extent that it proved successful. That is, if one's response to the stimulus satisfied one's drive or need, the individual would come to believe more strongly in the appropriateness of the particular S-R connection and would respond in the same way under similar circumstances.

An example will clarify this point. Several recent attempts to train chronically unemployed workers have used a daily pay system instead of weekly or monthly systems. The primary reason for this is that the workers, who do not have a history of working, can more quickly see the relationship between coming to work and receiving pay. An S-R bond develops more quickly because of the frequency of the reinforcement, or reward.

Operant versus Classical Conditioning

Operant conditioning can be distinguished from classical conditioning in at least two ways.[6] First, the two approaches differ in what is believed to cause changes in behavior. In classical conditioning, changes in behavior are thought to arise through changes in stimuli—that is, a transfer from an unconditioned stimulus to a conditioned stimulus. In operant conditioning, on the other hand, changes in behavior are thought to result from the *consequences* of previous behavior. When behavior has not been rewarded or has been punished, we would not expect it to be repeated.

Second, the two approaches differ in the role and frequency of rewards. In classical conditioning, the unconditioned stimulus, acting as a sort of reward, is administered during every trial. In contrast, in operant conditioning the reward results only when individuals choose the correct response. That is, in operant conditioning, individuals must correctly operate on their environment before a reward is received. The response is instrumental in obtaining the desired reward.

Social Learning Theory

The last model of learning we should examine is noted psychologist Albert Bandura's social learning theory. **Social learning theory** is defined as the process of molding behavior through the reciprocal interaction of a person's cognitions, behavior, and environment.[7] This is done through a process that Bandura calls **reciprocal determinism**. This concept implies that people control their own environment (for example, by quitting one's job) as much as the environment controls people (for example, being laid off). Thus, learning is seen as a more active, interactive process in which the learner has at least some control.

Social learning theory shares many of the same roots as operant conditioning. Like Skinner, Bandura argues that behavior is at least in part controlled by environmental cues and consequences, and Bandura uses observable behavior (as opposed to attitudes, feelings, etc.) as the primary unit of analysis. However, unlike operant conditioning, social learning theory posits that cognitive or mental processes affect our response to the environmental cues.

Social learning theory has four central elements: attention, retention, reproduction, and incentives. Before someone can learn something, they must notice or pay attention to the thing that is to be learned. For example, you probably would not learn much as a student in any class unless you paid attention to information conveyed by the text or instructor. Retention is the process by which what you have noticed is encoded into your memory. Reproduction involves the translation of what was recorded in your mind into overt actions or behaviors. Obviously, the higher the level of attention and the greater the retention, the better the reproduction of what was learned. Finally, incentives can influence all three processes. For example, if you are rewarded (say, praised) for paying attention, you will pay more attention. If you are rewarded for remembering what you studied (say, good grades), you will retain more. If you are rewarded for reproducing what you learned (say, a promotion for effectively motivating your subordinates), you will produce that behavior more.

Central to this theory is the concept of vicarious learning. **Vicarious learning** is learning that takes place through the imitation of other role models. That is, we observe and analyze what another person does and the resulting consequences. As a result, we learn without having to experience the phenomenon firsthand. Thus, if we see a fellow employee being disciplined or fired for being disruptive in the workplace, we might learn not to be disruptive ourselves. If we see that gifts are usually given with the right hand in the Middle East, we might give gifts in that manner ourselves.

A model of social learning processes is shown in **Exhibit 4.4**. As can be seen, three factors—the person, the environment, and the behavior—interact through such processes as vicarious learning, symbolic representations, and self-control to cause actual learned behaviors.

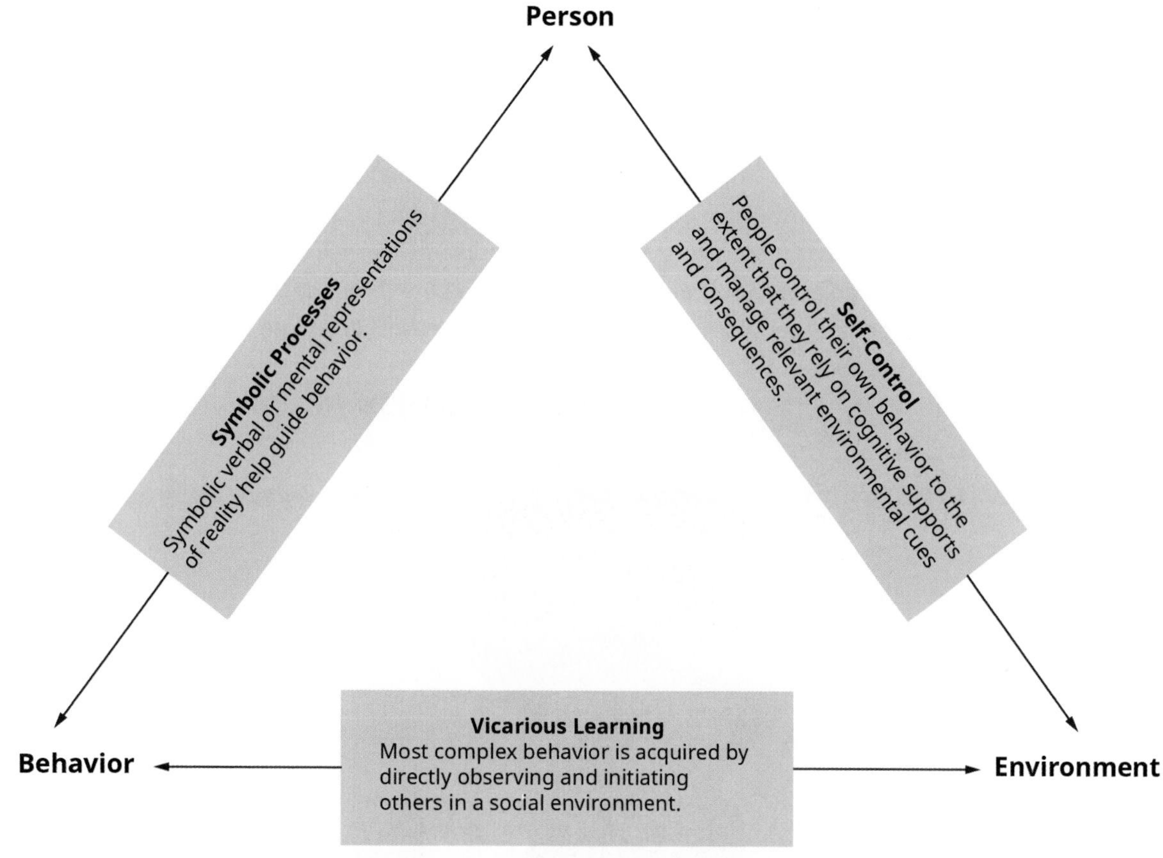

Exhibit 4.4 A Basic Model of Social Learning *Source:* Adapted from "A Social Learning Approach to Behavioral Management: Radical Behaviorists 'Mellowing Out,' " by Robert Kreitner et al. *Organizational Dynamics.* (Attribution: Copyright Rice University, OpenStax, under CC BY-NC-SA 4.0 license)

Major Influences on Learning. On the basis of this work, it is possible by way of summary to identify several general factors that can enhance our learning processes. An individual's desire to learn, background knowledge of a subject, and the length of the learning period are some of the components of a learning environment. Filley, House, and Kerr identify five major influences on learning effectiveness.[8]

Drawn largely from behavioral science and psychology literature, substantial research indicates that learning effectiveness is increased considerably when individuals have high *motivation to learn*. We sometimes encounter students who work day and night to complete a term paper that is of interest to them, whereas writing an uninteresting term paper may be postponed until the last possible minute. Maximum transfer of knowledge is achieved when a student or employee is motivated to learn by a high need to know.

Considerable evidence also demonstrates that we can facilitate learning by providing individuals with feedback on their performance. A *knowledge of results* serves a gyroscopic function, showing individuals where they are correct or incorrect and furnishing them with the perspective to improve. Feedback also serves as an important positive reinforcer that can enhance an individual's willingness or desire to learn. Students who are told by their professor how they performed on an exam and what they could do to improve next time are likely to study harder.

In many cases, *prior learning* can increase the ability to learn new materials or tasks by providing needed background or foundation materials. In math, multiplication is easier to learn if addition has been mastered. These beneficial effects of prior learning on present learning tend to be greatest when the prior tasks and the present tasks exhibit similar stimulus-response connections. For instance, most of the astronauts selected for the space program have had years of previous experience flying airplanes. It is assumed that their prior experience and developed skill will facilitate learning to fly the highly technical, though somewhat similar, vehicles.

Another influence on learning concerns whether the materials to be learned are presented in their entirety or in parts—*whole versus part learning*.[9] Available evidence suggests that when a task consists of several distinct and unrelated duties, part learning is more effective. Each task should be learned separately. However, when a task consists of several integrated and related parts (such as learning the components of a small machine), whole learning is more appropriate, because it ensures that major relationship among parts, as well as proper sequencing of parts, is not overlooked or underemphasized.

Exhibit 4.5 Stop sign in Quebec Would your prior learning lead you to come to a full stop while driving in Quebec, just north of New York State? (Credit: Joe Schlabotnik/ flickr/ Attribution 2.0 Generic (CC BY 2.0))

The final major influence on learning highlights the advantages and disadvantages of concentrated as opposed to distributed training sessions. Research suggests that *distribution of practice*—short learning periods at set intervals—is more effective for learning motor skills than for learning verbal or cognitive skills.[10] Distributed practice also seems to facilitate learning of very difficult, voluminous, or tedious material. It should be noted, however, that concentrated practice appears to work well where insight is required for task completion. Apparently, concentrated effort over short durations provides a move synergistic approach to problem-solving.

Although there is general agreement that these influences are important (and are under the control of management in many cases), they cannot substitute for the lack of an adequate reinforcement system. In fact, reinforcement is widely recognized as the key to effective learning. If managers are concerned with eliciting desired behaviors from their subordinates, a knowledge of reinforcement techniques is essential.

EXPANDING AROUND THE GLOBE

Learning to Be Effective Overseas

General Motors has learned by experience that it pays not to have managers learn only by experience how to function effectively while working in foreign countries. Managing expatriate assignments in difficult locations was brought to life by the experiences of Richard Pennington, General Motors' head of global mobility for the EMEA (Europe, Middle East, and Africa) region. He knows from experience some of the things that tend to go well, as well as some of those that don't, and has learned lessons from moving employees to places like Uzbekistan. This became important when the company took on a new engine manufacturing operation in the capital, Tashkent, as well as an existing manufacturing plant in Andijan. The objectives were the same as for most global mobility projects: to get the right people to the right place at the right time for the right cost. The general approach was Action—Plan—Do—Check. Pennington urged potential relocation candidates not to be overreliant on the Internet and, if possible, to go and see for themselves. "Nothing beats going to a location—particularly a harsh location—yourself," he says. Pennington also emphasizes the importance of selecting suppliers on the ground carefully, even if you already have a network of existing suppliers. Strong relationships in the host location are of paramount importance. In difficult locations, it is particularly important that the local HR, finance, and legal staff work with you proactively, as making payments at the right time can be critical. Equally, cultural training and language providers are essential.

These training programs involve a wide variety of teaching methods. Factual information may be conveyed through lectures or printed material. More subtle information is learned through role plays, case studies, and simulations.

The research on cross-cultural training suggests that the more involved participants are in the training, the more they learn, and that the more they practice or simulate new behaviors that they need to master in the foreign environment, the more effective they will be in actual situations.

The results for GM have been impressive. Most companies that do not provide cross-cultural training for their employees sent on international assignments experience failure rates of about 25 percent, and each failure or early return costs the company on average $150,000. GM has a failure rate of less than 1 percent. Also, in GM's case, the training has been extended to the manager's family and has helped reluctant spouses and children more readily accept, if not embrace, the foreign assignment.

Sources: F. Furnie, "International assignments: Managing change and complexity," *Relocate Global*, September 23, 2015, https://www.relocatemagazine.com/articles/4697international-assignments-managing-change-and-complexity; J. Lublin. "Companies Use Cross-Cultural Training to Help Their Employees Adjust Abroad." *Wall Street Journal*, August 4, 2004 p. B1.

CONCEPT CHECK 

1. How can learning theory be used to change behaviors?
2. Define classical conditioning, and differentiate it from operant conditioning.
3. What is social learning theory?

4.2 Reinforcement and Behavioral Change

2. What are the best practices that organizations utilize to train employees in new job skills?

A central feature of most approaches to learning is the concept of reinforcement. This concept dates from Thorndike's law of effect, which, as mentioned earlier, states that behavior that is positively reinforced tends to be repeated, whereas behavior that is not reinforced will tend not to be repeated. Hence, **reinforcement** can be defined as anything that causes a certain behavior to be repeated or inhibited.

Reinforcement versus Motivation

It is important to differentiate reinforcement from the concept of employee motivation. Motivation, as described in the next chapter, represents a primary psychological process that is largely cognitive in nature. Thus, motivation is largely internal—it is *experienced* by the employee, and we can see only subsequent manifestations of it in actual behavior. Reinforcement, on the other hand, is typically observable and most often externally administered. A supervisor may reinforce what he or she considers desirable behavior without knowing anything about the underlying motives that prompted it. For example, a supervisor who has a habit of saying "That's interesting" whenever she is presented with a new idea may be reinforcing innovation on the part of the subordinates without the supervisor really knowing why this result is achieved. The distinction between theories of motivation and reinforcement should be kept in mind when we examine behavior modification and behavioral self-management later in this chapter.

Strategies for Behavioral Change

From a managerial standpoint, several strategies for behavioral change are available to facilitate learning in organizational settings. At least four different types should be noted: (1) positive reinforcement; (2) avoidance learning, or negative reinforcement; (3) extinction; and (4) punishment. Each type plays a different role in both the manner in which and extent to which learning occurs. Each will be considered separately here.

Positive Reinforcement. Positive reinforcement consists of presenting someone with an attractive outcome following a desired behavior. As noted by Skinner, "A positive reinforcer is a stimulus which, when added to a situation, strengthens the probability of an operant response."[11] A simple example of positive reinforcement is supervisory praise for subordinates when they perform well in a certain situation. That is, a supervisor may praise an employee for being on time consistently (see **Exhibit 4.6**). This behavior-praise pattern may encourage the subordinate to be on time in the future in the hope of receiving additional praise.

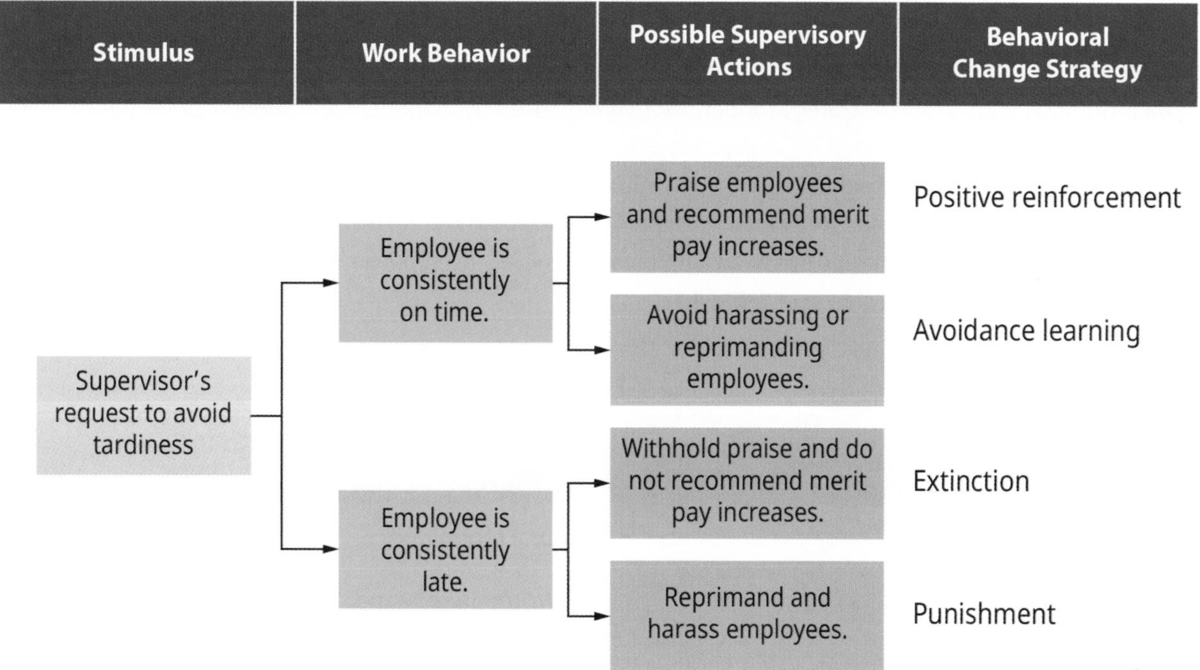

Exhibit 4.6 Strategies for Behavioral Change (Attribution: Copyright Rice University, OpenStax, under CC BY-NC-SA 4.0 license)

In order for a positive reinforcement to be effective in facilitating the repetition of desired behavior, several conditions must be met. First, the reinforcer itself (praise) must be valued by the employee. It would prove ineffective in shaping behavior if employees were indifferent to it. Second, the reinforcer must be strongly tied to the desired behavior. Receipt of the reinforcer by the employee must be directly contingent upon performing the desired behavior. "Rewards must result from performance, and the greater the degree of performance by an employee, the greater should be his reward."[12] It is important to keep in mind here that "desired behavior" represents behavior defined by the supervisor, not the employee. Thus, for praise to be a reinforcer, not only must it be valued by the employee, but it must directly follow the desired behavior and should be more intense as the behavior is closer to the ideal the supervisor has in mind. Praise thrown out at random is unlikely to reinforce the desired behavior. Third, there must be ample occasion for the reinforcer to be administered following desired behavior. If the reinforcer is tied to certain behavior that seldom occurs, then individuals will seldom be reinforced and will probably not associate this behavior with a reward. For example, if praise is only provided for truly exceptional performance, then it is unlikely to have a powerful impact on the desired behavior. It is important that the performance-reward contingencies be structured so that they are easily attainable.

Avoidance Learning. A second method of reinforcement is **avoidance learning**, or negative reinforcement. Avoidance learning refers to seeking to avoid an unpleasant condition or outcome by following a desired behavior. Employees learn to avoid unpleasant situations by behaving in certain ways. If an employee correctly performs a task or is continually prompt in coming to work (see **Exhibit 4.6**), the supervisor may refrain from harassing, reprimanding, or otherwise embarrassing the employee. Presumably, the employee learns over time that engaging in correct behavior diminishes admonition from the supervisor. In order to maintain this condition, the employee continues to behave as desired.

Extinction. The principle of **extinction** suggests that undesired behavior will decline as a result of a lack of positive reinforcement. If the perpetually tardy employee in the example in **Exhibit 4.6** consistently fails to receive supervisory praise and is not recommended for a pay raise, we would expect this nonreinforcement to lead to an "extinction" of the tardiness. The employee may realize, albeit subtly, that being late is not leading to desired outcomes, and she may try coming to work on time.

Punishment. Finally, a fourth strategy for behavior change used by managers and supervisors is punishment. **Punishment** is the administration of unpleasant or adverse outcomes as a result of undesired behavior. An example of the application of punishment is for a supervisor to publicly reprimand or fine an employee who is habitually tardy (see **Exhibit 4.6**). Presumably, the employee would refrain from being tardy in the future in order to avoid such an undesirable outcome. The most frequently used punishments (along with the most frequently used rewards) are shown in **Table 4.1**.

Frequently Used Rewards and Punishments	
Rewards	Punishments
Pay raise	Oral reprimands
Bonus	Written reprimands
Promotion	Ostracism
Praise and recognition	Criticism from superiors
Awards	Suspension
Self-recognition	Demotion
Sense of accomplishment	Reduced authority
Increased responsibility	Undesired transfer
Time off	Termination

Table 4.1 (Attribution: Copyright Rice University, OpenStax, under CC BY-NC-SA 4.0 license)

The use of punishment is indeed one of the most controversial issues of behavior change strategies. Although punishment can have positive work outcomes—especially if it is administered in an impersonal way and as soon as possible after the transgression—negative repercussions can also result when employees either resent the action or feel they are being treated unfairly. These negative outcomes from punishment are shown in **Exhibit 4.7**. Thus, although punishment represents a potent force in corrective learning, its use must be carefully considered and implemented. In general, for punishment to be effective the punishment should "fit the crime" in severity, should be given in private, and should be explained to the employee.

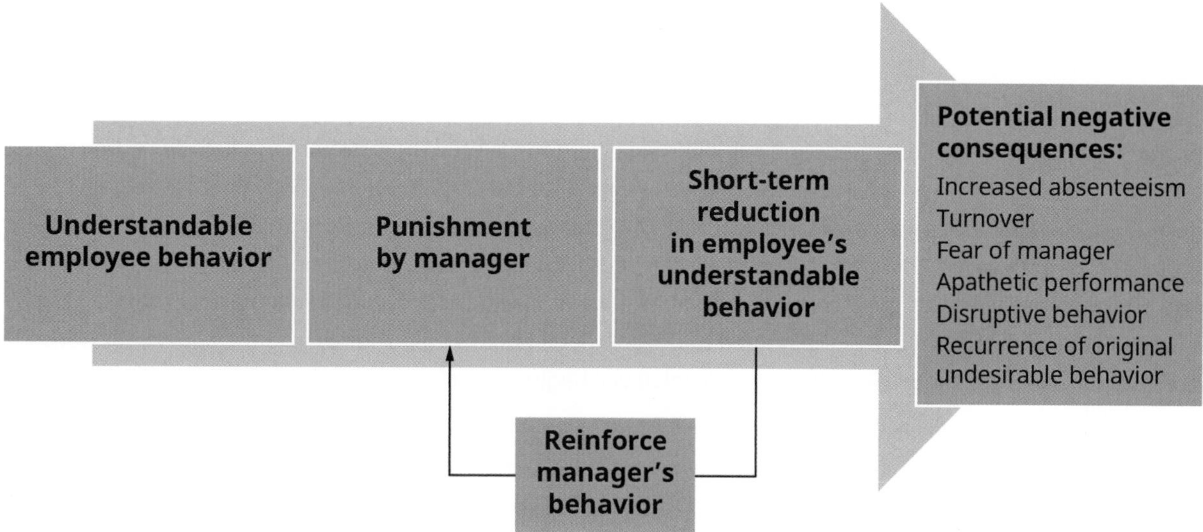

Exhibit 4.7 Potential Negative Consequences of Punishment (Attribution: Copyright Rice University, OpenStax, under CC BY-NC-SA 4.0 license)

ETHICS IN PRACTICE

Detracting a Workplace Bully

Studies showcase that nearly 50 percent of employees in the U.S. workforce face bullying at one point in time. All types of bullying, not just discrimination or harassment, are important to consider.

Angela Anderson was working for a law school administration council and experienced bullying firsthand. Often her manager would yell at her in front of other coworkers, and it was clear to Angela that she was not well-liked. Unfortunately it was not just Angela who felt the wrath of this manager, who often handled interactions with other employees the same way. Many of the employees, including Angela, attempted to appease their bullying manager, but nothing would help. One day Angela was threatened by her manager, and before Angela could reach the HR department, she was fired. This example is an extreme case, but being able to take recourse against unwanted and disruptive employee behavior is an important action for any workplace manager.

Questions:

1. What steps can you take to ensure that your company can detract from employees' bullying behavior?
2. What actions should an employee take if they are experiencing unwanted behaviors from another employee or manager?
3. What other departments should be involved when developing a plan and policies for how to handle unacceptable workplace behavior?

Sources: Acceptable and Unacceptable Behaviours, *University of Cambridge* website, accessed January 15, 2019, https://www.hr.admin.cam.ac.uk/policies-procedures/dignity-work-policy/guidance-managers-and-staff/guidance-managers/acceptable-and; Hedges, Kristi, How to Change Your Employee's Behavior," *Forbes*, March, 4, 2015, https://www.forbes.com/sites/work-in-progress/2015/03/04/how-to-change-your-employees-behavior/#c32ad4b6732a; and Kane, Sally, Workplace Bullying: True Stories, Statistics and Tips, *The Balance Careers*, January 29, 2019, https://www.thebalancecareers.com/bullying-stories-2164317.

In summary, positive reinforcement and avoidance learning focus on bringing about the *desired* response from the employee. With positive reinforcement the employee behaves in a certain way in order to gain desired rewards, whereas with avoidance learning the employee behaves in order to avoid certain unpleasant outcomes. In both cases, however, the behavior desired by the supervisor is enhanced. In contrast, extinction and punishment focus on supervisory attempts to reduce the incidence of *undesired* behavior. That is, extinction and punishment are typically used to get someone to stop doing something the supervisor doesn't like. It does not necessarily follow that the individual will begin acting in the most desired, or correct, manner.

Often students have difficulty seeing the distinction between avoidance and extinction or in understanding how either could have a significant impact on behavior. Two factors are important to keep in mind. The first we will simply call the "history effect." Not being harassed could reinforce an employee's prompt arrival at work if in the past the employee had been harassed for being late. Arriving on time and thereby avoiding the past harassment would reinforce arriving on time. This same dynamic would hold true for extinction. If the employee had been praised in the past for arriving on time, then arrived late and was not praised, this would serve to weaken the tendency to arrive late. The second factor we will call the "social effect." For example, if you see others harassed when they arrive late and then you are not harassed when you arrive on time, this could reinforce your arriving at work on time. Again, this same dynamic would hold true for extinction. If you had observed others being praised for arriving on time, then not receiving praise when you arrived late would serve to weaken the tendency to arrive late.

From a managerial perspective, questions arise about which strategy of behavioral change is most effective. Advocates of behavioral change strategies, such as Skinner, answer that positive reinforcement combined with extinction is the most suitable way to bring about desired behavior. There are several reasons for this focus on the positive approach to reinforcement. First, although punishment can inhibit or eliminate undesired behavior, it often does not provide information to the individual about how or in which direction to change. Also, the application of punishment may cause the individual to become alienated from the work situation, thereby reducing the chances that useful change can be effected. Similarly, avoidance learning tends to emphasize the negative; that is, people are taught to stay clear of certain behaviors, such as tardiness, for fear of repercussions. In contrast, it is felt that combining positive reinforcement with the use of extinction has the fewest undesirable side effects and allows individuals to receive the rewards they desire. A positive approach to reinforcement is believed by some to be the most effective tool management has to bring about favorable changes in organizations.

Schedules of Reinforcement

Having examined four distinct strategies for behavioral change, we now turn to an examination of the various ways, or *schedules*, of administering these techniques. As noted by Costello and Zalkind, "The speed with which learning takes place and also how lasting its effects will be is determined by the timing of reinforcement."[13] Thus, a knowledge of the types of schedules of reinforcement is essential to managers if they are to know how to choose rewards that will have maximum impact on employee performance. Although there are a variety of ways in which rewards can be administered, most approaches can be categorized into two groups: continuous and partial (or intermittent) reinforcement schedules. A **continuous reinforcement** schedule rewards desired behavior every time it occurs. For example, a manager could praise (or pay) employees every time they perform properly. With the time and resource constraints most managers work under, this is often difficult, if not impossible. So, most managerial reward strategies operate on a partial schedule. A **partial reinforcement** schedule rewards desired behavior at specific intervals, not every time desired behavior is exhibited. Compared to continuous schedules, partial reinforcement schedules lead to slower learning but stronger retention. Thus, learning is generally more permanent. Four kinds of partial reinforcement schedules can be identified: (1) fixed interval, (2) fixed ratio, (3) variable interval, and (4) variable ratio (see **Table 4.2**).

Schedules of Partial Reinforcement				
Schedule of Reinforcement	Nature of Reinforcement	Effects on Behavior When Applied	Effects on Behavior When Terminated	Example
Fixed interval	Reward on fixed time basis	Leads to average and irregular performance	Quick extinction of behavior	Weekly paycheck
Fixed ratio	Reward consistently tied to output	Leads quickly to very high and stable performance	Quick extinction of behavior	Piece-rate pay system
Variable interval	Reward given at variable intervals around some average time	Leads to moderately high and stable performance	Slow extinction of behavior	Monthly performance appraisal and reward at random times each month
Variable ratio	Reward given at variable output levels around some average output	Leads to very high performance	Slow extinction of behavior	Sales bonus tied to selling *X* accounts, but *X* constantly changes around some mean

Table 4.2

Fixed-Interval Schedule. A fixed-interval reinforcement schedule rewards individuals at specified intervals for their performance, as with a biweekly paycheck. If employees perform even minimally, they are paid. This technique generally does not result in high or sustained levels of performance because employees know that marginal performance usually leads to the same level of reward as high performance. Thus, there is little incentive for high effort and performance. Also, when rewards are withheld or suspended, extinction of desired behavior occurs quickly. Many of the recent job redesign efforts in organizations were prompted by recognition of the need for alternate strategies of motivation rather than paying people on fixed-interval schedules.

Fixed-Ratio Schedule. The second fixed schedule is the fixed-ratio schedule. Here the reward is administered only upon the completion of a given number of desired responses. In other words, rewards are tied to performance in a ratio of rewards to results. A common example of the fixed-ratio schedule is a piece-rate pay system, whereby employees are paid for each unit of output they produce. Under this system, performance rapidly reaches high levels. In fact, according to Hamner, "The response level here is significantly higher than that obtained under any of the interval (time-based) schedules."[14] On the negative side, however, performance declines sharply when the rewards are withheld, as with fixed-interval schedules.

Variable-Interval Schedule. Using variable reinforcement schedules, both variable-interval and variable-ratio reinforcements are administered at random times that cannot be predicted by the employee. The employee is generally not aware of when the next evaluation and reward period will be. Under a variable-interval schedule, rewards are administered at intervals of time that are based on an average. For example, an employee may know that *on the average* her performance is evaluated and rewarded about once a month, but she does not know when this event will occur. She does know, however, that it will occur sometime during the interval of a month. Under this schedule, effort and performance will generally be high and fairly stable over time because employees never know when the evaluation will take place.

Variable-Ratio Schedule. Finally, a variable-ratio schedule is one in which rewards are administered only after an employee has performed the desired behavior a number of times, with the number changing from the administration of one reward to the next but averaging over time to a certain *ratio* of number of performances to rewards. For example, a manager may determine that a salesperson will receive a bonus for every 15th new account sold. However, instead of administering the bonus every 15th sale (as in a fixed-interval schedule), the manager may vary the number of sales that is necessary for the bonus, from perhaps 10 sales for the first bonus to 20 for the second. On the average, however, the 15:1 ratio prevails. If the employee understands the parameters, then the "safe" level of sales, or the level of sales most likely to result in a bonus, is in excess of 15. Consequently, the variable-ratio schedule typically leads to high and stable performance. Moreover, extinction of desired behavior is slow.

Which of these four schedules of reinforcement is superior? In a review of several studies comparing the various techniques, Hamner concludes:

The necessity for arranging appropriate reinforcement contingencies is dramatically illustrated by several studies in which rewards were shifted from a response-contingent (ratio) to a time-contingent (interval) basis. During the period in which rewards were made conditional upon occurrence of the desired behavior, the appropriate response patterns were exhibited at a consistently high level. When the same rewards were given based on time and independent of the worker's behavior, there was a marked drop in the desired behavior. The reinstatements of the performance-contingent reward schedule promptly restored the high level of responsiveness.

In other words, the performance-contingent (or ratio) reward schedules generally lead to better performance than the time-contingent (or interval) schedules, regardless of whether such schedules are fixed or variable. We will return to this point in a subsequent chapter on performance appraisal and reward systems.

Two additional approaches to learning are found in the work of David Kolb and Mel Silberman. Kolb's experiential learning style theory is typically represented by a four-stage learning cycle in which the learner 'touches all the bases'. The Four stages are achieved when a person progresses through a cycle of four stages: of (1) having a concrete experience followed by (2) observation of and reflection on that experience which leads to (3) the formation of abstract concepts (analysis) and generalizations (conclusions) which are then (4) used to test hypothesis in future situations, resulting in new experiences. Silberman in his book *Active Training*, identified eight qualities of an effective and active learning experience. The eight qualities are: a moderate level of content; a balance between affective, behavioral, and cognitive learning, a variety of learning approaches, opportunities for group participation, encouraging participants to share their expertise, recycling concepts and skills learned earlier, advocating real-life problem solving, and allowing time for re-entry.[15]

MANAGERIAL LEADERSHIP

Shaping a Salesperson's Behavior

Sharon Johnson worked for a publishing company based in Nashville, Tennessee, that sold a line of children's books directly to the public through a door-to-door sales force. Sharon had been a very successful salesperson and was promoted first to district and then to regional sales manager after just four years with the company. Sales bonuses were fixed, and a fixed-dollar bonus was tied to every $1,000 in sales over a specific minimum quota. However, there was a wide variety of rewards, from praise to gift certificates, that were left to Sharon's discretion.

Sharon knew from her organizational behavior class that giving out praise to those who liked it and gifts to those who preferred them was an important means of reinforcing desired behavior, and she had been quite successful in implementing this principle. She also knew that if you reinforced a behavior that was "on the right track" to the ideal behavior you wanted out of a salesperson, eventually you could shape their behavior, almost without their realizing it.

Sharon had one particular salesperson, Lyle, that she thought had great potential, yet his weekly sales were somewhat inconsistent and often lower than she thought possible. When Lyle was questioned about his performance, he indicated that sometimes he felt that the families he approached could not afford the books he was selling and so he did not think it was right to push the sale too hard. Although Sharon argued that it was not Lyle's place to decide for others what they could or could not afford, Lyle still felt uncomfortable about utilizing his normal sales approach with these families.

Sharon believed that through subtle reinforcement of certain behaviors she could shape Lyle's behavior and that over time he would increasingly use his typical sales approach with the families he thought could not afford the books. For example, she knew that in the cases of families Lyle thought could not afford the books, he spent only 3.5 minutes in the house compared to 12.7 minutes in homes of families he judged able to afford the books. Sharon believed that if she praised Lyle when the average time he spent in each family's home was quite similar that Lyle would increase the time he spent in the homes of families he judged unable to afford the books. She believed that the longer he spent in these homes, the more likely Lyle was to utilize his typical sales approach. This was just one of several ways Sharon thought she could shape Lyle's behavior without trying to change his mind about pushing books onto people he thought could not afford them.

Sharon saw no ethical issues in this case until she told a friend about it and the friend questioned whether it was ethical to utilize learning and reinforcement techniques to change people's behavior "against their will" even if they did not realize that this was happening.

Source: This ethical challenge is based on a true but disguised case observed by author J. Stewart Black.

CONCEPT CHECK 

1. What is reinforcement, and how can it be applied to motivation?
2. What are the four strategies to use for behavioral change?
3. What is the significance of schedules in changing behavior?

4.3 Behavior Modification in Organizations

3. How do managers and organizations reduce undesirable employee behavior while reinforcing desirable behavior?

When the above principles and techniques are applied to the workplace, we generally see one of two approaches: **behavior modification** or **behavioral self-management**. Both approaches rest firmly on the principles of learning described above. Because both of these techniques have wide followings in corporations, we shall review them here. First, we look at the positive and negative sides of behavior modification.

Behavior modification is the use of operant conditioning principles to shape human behavior to conform to desired standards defined by superiors. In recent years, behavior modification has been applied in a wide variety of organizations. In most cases, positive results are claimed. There is interest in the technique as a management tool to improve performance and reduce costs.

Because of its emphasis on shaping behavior, it is more appropriate to think of behavior modification as a technique for motivating employees rather than as a theory of work motivation. It does not attempt to provide a comprehensive model of the various personal and job-related variables that contribute to motivation. Instead, its managerial thrust is how to motivate, and it is probably this emphasis that has led to its current popularity among some managers. Even so, we should be cautioned against the unquestioned acceptance of any technique until we understand the assumptions underlying the model. If the underlying assumptions of a model appear to be uncertain or inappropriate in a particular situation or organization, its use is clearly questionable.

EXPANDING AROUND THE GLOBE 

In Japan's Hell Camp

There is a saying in Japan that "the nail that sticks up gets hammered down." This means that in corporate Japan employees are supposed to act together and move in unison. Individuality is not encouraged. Although Japanese companies use many techniques to train their employees to work hard and overcome adversity as a group, one rather notable approach that is used by many companies is known as Hell Camp.

The purpose of Hell Camp is to develop employees so they can "concentrate under difficulty."

Representing something of a blend of Outward Bound and assertiveness training, Hell Camp is designed to toughen employees by putting them through numerous humiliating exercises (e.g., making them shout their company song outside the local train station). If they pass each exercise (for example, if they shout loud enough and with sufficient emotion), they are allowed to remove one of several "badges of shame." Criteria for removing a badge are left vague, so, in essence, the program uses a variable-ratio reinforcement system. The employee never quite knows when the trainer will say she has succeeded; therefore, the most likely level of performance that will result in the removal of shame badges is that at the higher end of the spectrum of performance. If the employee succeeds during the week-long program in removing all of the badges and shows her sincerity and commitment, she graduates. If not, she must repeat the program.

Far from the trust-building exercises and fun runs of modern corporate retreats, Japan's executive Hell Camps were run with the discipline and intensity of military basic training. The goal was to whip into shape underperforming middle-management types, as well as give them the assertiveness the Japanese felt they lacked in dealing with Western competitors.

It is estimated that over 50,000 Japanese managers have gone through the program. Companies like it because they see it as a way to keep managers from getting soft. As one executive notes, "Companies have been getting very soft, very weak in their way of demanding excellence." It is thought that the harassment received during Hell Camp and the reinforcement following satisfactory task accomplishment instill character, and Japanese companies show no sign of losing interest in the program.

Sources: Richarz, Allan, " The Intense Corporate 'Hell Camps' of 1980s Japan," Atlas Obscura, May 30, 2017, https://www.atlasobscura.com/articles/hell-camp-japan-80s; Phallon, R., "Hell Camp," Forbes, June 18, 1984; Neill, Michael and Lustig, David, " A 13-Day Japanese Boot Camp Shows U.S. Executives How to Succeed in Business Through Suffering," People, May 30, 1988, https://people.com/archive/a-13-day-japanese-boot-camp-shows-u-s-executives-how-to-succeed-in-business-through-suffering-vol-29-no-21/.

Assumptions of Behavior Modification

The foundation of behavior modification as a technique of management rests on three ideas.[16] First, advocates of behavior modification believe that individuals are basically passive and reactive (instead of proactive). They tend to respond to stimuli in their environment rather than assuming personal responsibility in initiating behavior. This assertion is in direct contrast to cognitive theories of motivation (such as expectancy/valence theory), which hold that individuals make conscious decisions about their present and future behaviors and take an active role in shaping their environment.

Second, advocates of behavior modification focus on observable and measurable behavior instead of on unobservable needs, attitudes, goals, or motivational levels. In contrast, cognitive theories focus on both observable and unobservable factors as they relate to motivation. Social learning theory, in particular, argues that individuals can change their behavior simply by observing others and noticing the punishments or rewards that the observed behaviors produce.

Third, behavior modification stresses that permanent changes can be brought about only as a result of reinforcement. Behaviors that are positively reinforced will be repeated (that is, learned), whereas behaviors not so reinforced will diminish (according to the law of effect, discussed earlier).

Designing a Behavior Modification Program

If behavior modification techniques are to work, their application must be well-designed and systematically applied. Systematic attempts to implement these programs typically go through five phases (see **Exhibit 4.8**).

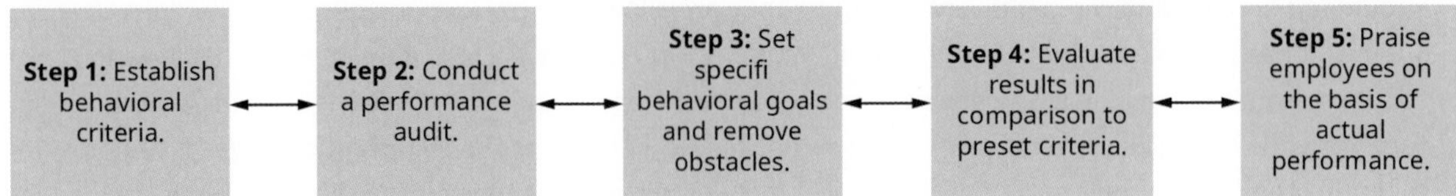

Exhibit 4.8 Steps in Implementing a Behavior Modification Program (Attribution: Copyright Rice University, OpenStax, under CC BY-NC-SA 4.0 license)

Establishing Clear Behavioral Criteria. First, management attempts to define and clearly specify the behavioral aspects of acceptable performance. Management must be able to designate what constitutes acceptable behavior in terms that employees can understand, and this specification must be in objective, measurable terms. Examples of **behavioral criteria** include good attendance, promptness in arriving for work, and completing tasks on schedule. Sometimes it is difficult to determine suitable objective indicators of successful performance. For instance, as a training director of a major airline asked, "How do you quantify what a flight attendant does?" Even so, there are many situations and work behaviors that do lend themselves to clear specification.

Conducting a Performance Audit. Once acceptable behavioral criteria have been specified, a **performance audit** can be done. Because management is concerned about the extent to which employees are successfully meeting the behavioral criteria, the audit is aimed at pinpointing trouble spots where desired behaviors are not being carried out. For instance, a review of attendance records of various department may reveal a department in which absenteeism or tardiness is unusually high. Action can then be taken to focus on the problem area. In short, the performance audit aims to identify discrepancies between what management sees as desired or acceptable behavior and actual behavior.

Setting Specific Behavioral Goals. Third, specific behavioral goals must be set for each employee. Failure to specify concrete behavioral goals is a primary reason for the failure of many behavior modification programs. Examples of such goals are decreasing absenteeism or tardiness, reducing product defects on an assembly line, and meeting production schedules. The goals should be both realistic (that is, reasonably achievable by the employees) and acceptable to the employee. Otherwise, the goals lack relevance, and resulting effort will diminish.

Evaluating Results. Next, employees and supervisors keep track of the employee's performance record as compared to the preset behavioral criteria and goals. Discrepancies are noted and discussed. For example, the record could provide employees with continuous feedback concerning the extent to which they are on target in meeting their defect reduction goals.

Administering Feedback and Rewards. Finally, on the basis of the assessment of the employee's performance record, the supervisor administers feedback and, where warranted, praise. For example, praise could strengthen the employees' efforts to reduce defects (positive reinforcement). The withholding of praise for defect levels deemed less than adequate or below established goals could cause employees to stop behavior that was contributing to defects or work harder to reduce defects (extinction).

Central to this phase of the process is the notion of **shaping**. Shaping is the process of improving performance incrementally, step by step. Suppose that an employee is absent 30 percent of the time during one month. To improve attendance, we would set a goal of being absent only 5 percent of the time. After implementing the above procedure, we find that absenteeism falls to 20 percent in the second month. Although this is not at goal level, it is clearly an improvement and, as such, is rewarded. The next month, absenteeism falls to 15 percent, and, again, we reward the incremental improvement. Hence, by this incremental approach, the employee gets ever closer to the desired level of behavior. In other words, we have "shaped" her behavior.

Behavior Modification in Practice

There are many ways to see how the principles of behavior modification can be applied in organizational settings. Perhaps one of the best examples can be found in a classic study carried out by Luthans and Kreitner.[17] These researchers carried out a field experiment in a medium-sized light manufacturing plant. Two separate groups of supervisors were used in the study. In one group (the experimental group—see **Appendix A**), the supervisors were trained in the techniques of behavior modification. This program was called "behavioral contingency management," or BCM. Included here were ten 90-minute lectures conducted over 10 weeks on behavioral change strategies. The second group of supervisors (the control group) received no such training. Following this, the trained supervisors were asked to implement what they had learned among their groups; obviously, the control group supervisors were given no such instructions.

After 10 weeks, group performance was examined for all groups. Two types of data were collected. First, the researchers were interested in any possible behavioral changes among the various workers in the experimental groups (compared to the control groups) as a result of the behavior modification efforts. Significantly, the following changes were noted for these groups in areas that were targeted for change: (1) the frequency of complaints among group members declined, (2) the scrap rates declined, (3) group quality indicators increased, and (4) the frequency of individual performance problems declined. No such changes were recorded for the control groups not exposed to behavior modification. The second measure taken focused on the overall performance rates for the various groups. This was calculated as a measure of direct labor effectiveness for each group. Again, overall group performance—that is, labor effectiveness ratings—improved significantly in the experimental groups but remained unchanged in the control groups. This can be seen in **Exhibit 4.9**. The researchers concluded that the introduction of the behavioral modification program led to substantive improvements in factory performance.

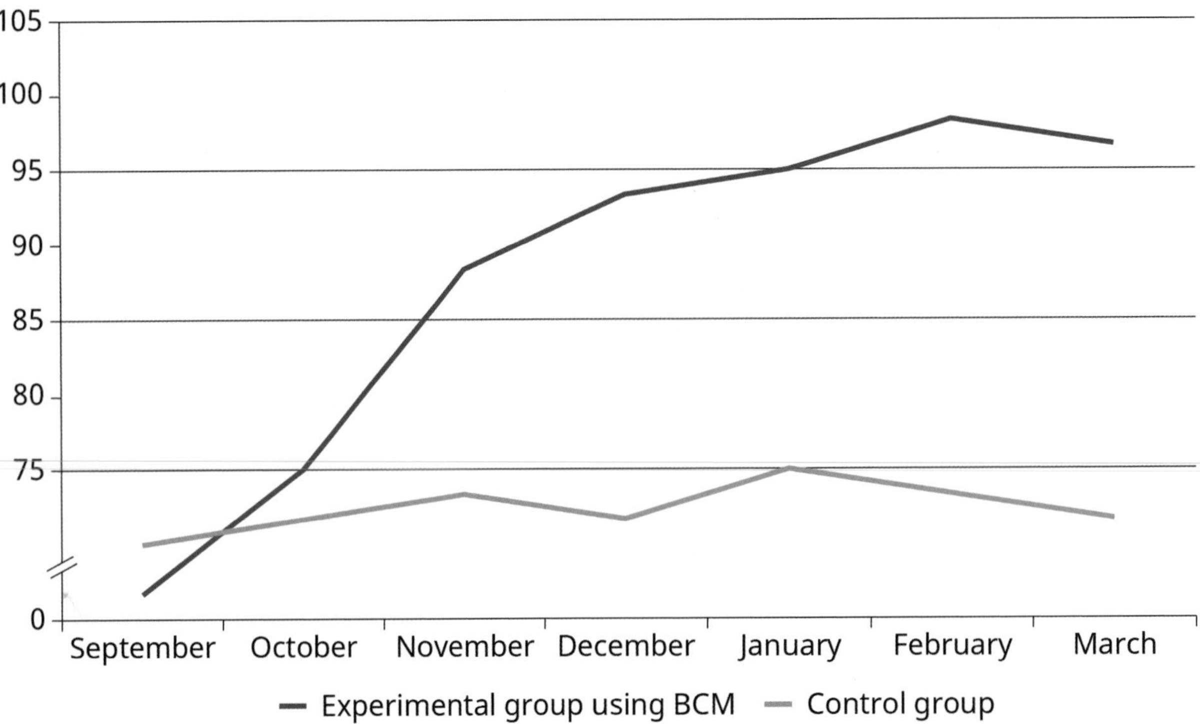

Exhibit 4.9 Intergroup Comparison of Performance using BCM (Attribution: Copyright Rice University, OpenStax, under CC BY-NC-SA 4.0 license)

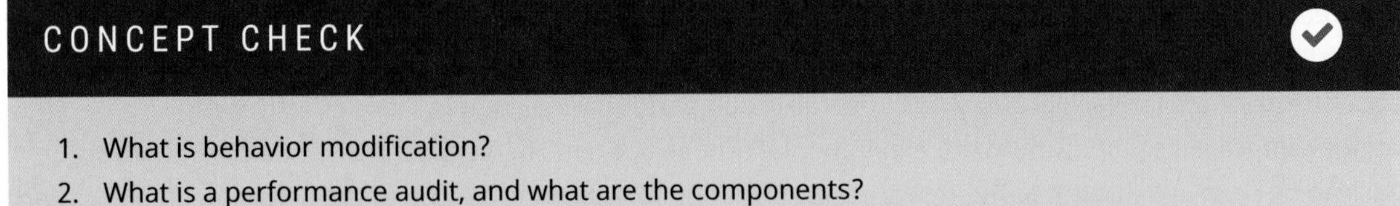

CONCEPT CHECK

1. What is behavior modification?
2. What is a performance audit, and what are the components?

4.4 Behavioral Self-Management

4. How can employees be trained to assume more responsibility for self-improvement and job performance with the goal of creating a work environment characterized by continual self-learning and employee development?

The second managerial technique for shaping learned behavior in the workplace is *behavioral self-management* (or BSM). Behavioral self-management is the process of modifying one's own behavior by systematically managing cues, cognitive processes, and contingent consequences.[18] BSM is an approach to learning and behavioral change that relies on the individual to take the initiative in controlling the change process. The emphasis here is on "behavior" (because our focus is on changing behaviors), not attitudes, values, or personality. Although similar to behavior modification, BSM differs in one important respect: there is a heavy emphasis on cognitive processes, reflecting the influence of Bandura's social learning theory.

The Self-Regulation Process

Underlying BSM is a firm belief that individuals are capable of self-control; if they want to change their behavior (whether it is to come to work on time, quit smoking, lose weight, etc.), it is possible through a process called **self-regulation**, as depicted in **Exhibit 4.10**.[19] According to the model, people tend to go about their day's activities fairly routinely until something unusual or unexpected occurs. At this point, the individual initiates the self-regulation process by entering into **self-monitoring** (Stage 1). In this stage, the individual tries to identify the problem. For example, if your supervisor told you that your choice of clothing was unsuitable for the office, you would more than likely focus your attention on your clothes.

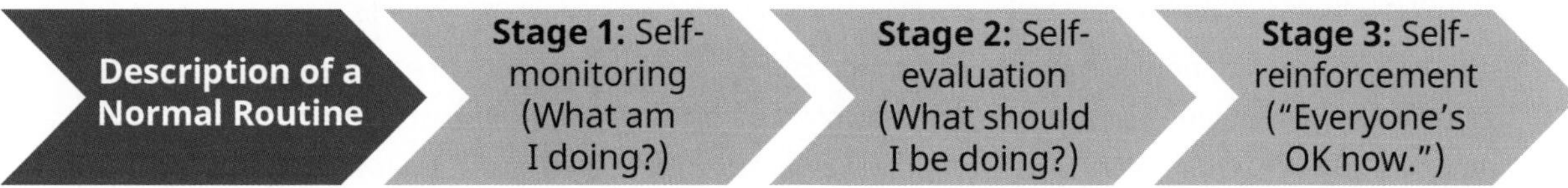

Exhibit 4.10 Kanfer's Model of Self-Regulation (Attribution: Copyright Rice University, OpenStax, under CC BY-NC-SA 4.0 license)

Next, in Stage 2, or *self-evaluation*, you would consider what you should be wearing. Here, you would compare what you have on to acceptable standards that you learned from colleagues, other relevant role models, and advertising, for example. Finally, after evaluating the situation and taking corrective action if necessary, you would assure yourself that the disruptive influence had passed and everything was now fine. This phase (Stage 3) is called **self-reinforcement**. You are now able to return to your normal routine. This self-regulation process forms the foundation for BSM.

Self-Management in Practice

When we combine the above self-regulation model with social learning theory (discussed earlier), we can see how the self-management process works. As shown in **Exhibit 4.11**, four interactive factors must be considered. These are *situational cues, the person, behaviors,* and *consequences*.[20] (Note that the arrows in this diagram go in both directions to reflect the two-way process among these four factors.)

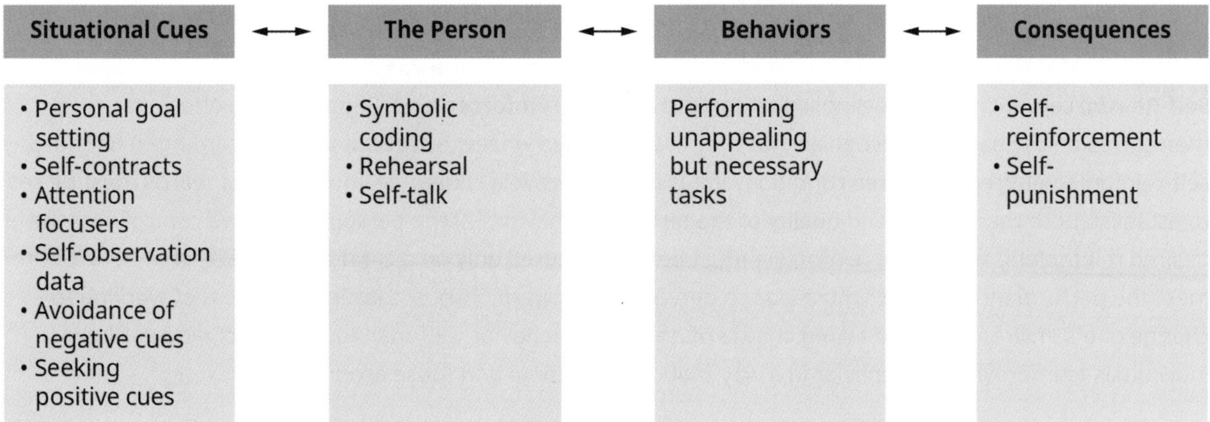

Exhibit 4.11 A Social Learning Theory Model of Self-Management (Attribution: Copyright Rice University, OpenStax, under CC BY-NC-SA 4.0 license)

Situational Cues. In attempting to change any behavior, people respond to the cues surrounding them. One reason it is so hard for some people to give up smoking is the constant barrage of advertisements on billboards, in magazines, and so forth. There are too many cues reminding people to smoke. However, situational cues can be turned to our advantage when using BSM. That is, through the use of six kinds of cue (shown in **Exhibit 4.11**, column 1), people can set forth a series of positive reminders and goals concerning the desired behaviors. These reminders serve to focus our attention on what we are trying to accomplish. Hence, a person who is trying to quit smoking would (1) avoid any contact with smokers or smoking ads, (2) seek information on the hazards of smoking, (3) set a personal goal of quitting, and (4) keep track of cigarette consumption. These activities are aimed at providing the right situational cues to guide behavior.

Cognitive Supports. Next, the person makes use of three types of cognitive support to assist with the self-management process. Cognitive supports represent psychological (as opposed to environmental) cues. Three such supports can be identified:

1. *Symbolic Coding*. First, people may use **symbolic coding**, whereby they try to associate verbal or visual stimuli with the problem. For example, we may create a picture in our mind of a smoker who is coughing and obviously sick. Thus, every time we think of cigarettes, we would associate it with illness.
2. *Rehearsal*. Second, people may mentally rehearse the solution to the problem. For example, we may imagine how we would behave in a social situation without cigarettes. By doing so, we develop a self-image of how it would be under the desired condition.
3. *Self-Talk*. Finally, people can give themselves "pep talks" to continue their positive behavior. We know from behavioral research that people who take a negative view of things ("I can't do this") tend to fail more than people who take a more positive view ("Yes, I can do this"). Thus, through **self-talk**, we can help convince ourselves that the desired outcome is indeed possible.

Behavioral Dilemmas. Obviously, self-management is used almost exclusively to get people to do things that may be unappealing; we need little incentive to do things that are fun. Hence, we use self-management to get individuals to stop procrastinating on a job, attend to a job that may lack challenge, assert themselves, and so forth. These are the "**behavioral dilemmas**" referred to in the model (**Exhibit 4.11**). In short, the challenge is to get people to substitute what have been called low-probability behaviors (e.g., adhering to a schedule or forgoing the immediate gratification from one cigarette) for high-probability behaviors (e.g., procrastinating or contracting lung cancer). In the long run, it is better for the individual—and her career—to shift behaviors, because failure to do so may lead to punishment or worse. As a result, people often use self-management to change their short-term dysfunctional behaviors into long-range beneficial ones. This short-term versus long-term conflict is referred to as a behavioral dilemma.

Self-Reinforcement. Finally, the individual can provide **self-reinforcement**. People can, in effect, pat themselves on the back and recognize that they accomplished what they set out to do. According to Bandura, self-reinforcement requires three conditions if it is to be effective: (1) clear performance standards must be set to establish both the quantity and quality of the targeted behavior, (2) the person must have control over the desired reinforcers, and (3) the reinforcers must be administered only on a conditional basis—that is, failure to meet the performance standard must lead to denial of the reward.[21] Thus, through a process of working to change one's environment and taking charge of one's own behavior, self-management techniques allow individuals to improve their behavior in a way that can help them and those around them.

Reducing Absenteeism through Self-Management

In a recent study, efforts were made to reduce employee absenteeism using some of the techniques found in behavioral self-management. The employees were unionized state government workers with a history of absenteeism. Self-management training was given to these workers. Training was carried out over eight one-hour sessions for each group, along with eight 30-minute one-on-one sessions with each participant.

Included in these sessions were efforts to (1) teach the participants how to describe problem behaviors (e.g., disagreements with coworkers) that led to absences, (2) identify the causes creating and maintaining the behaviors, and (3) develop coping strategies. Participants set both short-term and long-term goals with respect to modifying their behaviors. In addition, they were shown how to record their own absences in reports including their frequency and the reasons for and consequences of them. Finally, participants identified potential reinforcers and punishments that could be self-administered contingent upon goal attainment or failure.

When, after nine months, the study was concluded, results showed that the self-management approach had led to a significant reduction in absences (compared to a control group). The researchers concluded that such an approach has important applications to a wide array of behavioral problems in the workplace.[22]

CONCEPT CHECK

1. Understand Kanfer's behavioral self-management process.
2. What are things you can do to instill self-management techniques for yourself?
3. What behavioral self-management techniques can you use as a manager?

Key Terms

Avoidance learning Refers to seeking to avoid an unpleasant condition or outcome by following a desired behavior.

Behavior modification The use of operant conditioning principles to shape human behavior to conform to desired standards defined by superiors.

Behavioral criteria Defining what constitutes acceptable behavior in terms that employees can understand in objective, measurable terms.

Behavioral dilemmas The process of getting people to substitute what have been called low-probability behaviors for high-probability behaviors.

Behavioral self-management The use of operant conditioning principles to shape your own behavior to conform to desired standards defined by superiors.

Classical conditioning The process whereby a stimulus-response bond is developed between a conditioned stimulus and a conditioned response through the repeated linking of a conditioned stimulus with an unconditioned stimulus.

Conditioned response The process of conditioning through the repeated linking of a conditioned stimulus with an unconditioned stimulus.

Continuous reinforcement Rewards desired behavior every time it occurs.

Drive An internal state of disequilibrium; it is a felt need. It is generally believed that drive increases with the strength of deprivation.

Extinction The principle that suggests that undesired behavior will decline as a result of a lack of positive reinforcement.

Habit The experienced bond or connection between stimulus and response.

Law of effect States that of several responses made to the same situation, those that are accompanied or closely followed by satisfaction (reinforcement) will be more likely to occur; those that are accompanied or closely followed by discomfort (punishment) will be less likely to occur.

Operant conditioning Measures the effects of reinforcements, or rewards, on desired behaviors.

Partial reinforcement Rewards desired behavior at specific intervals, not every time desired behavior is exhibited.

Performance audit Aims to identify discrepancies between what management sees as desired or acceptable behavior and actual behavior.

Positive reinforcement Consists of presenting someone with an attractive outcome following a desired behavior.

Punishment The administration of unpleasant or adverse outcomes as a result of undesired behavior.

Reciprocal determinism This concept implies that people control their own environment as much as the environment controls people.

Reinforcement Anything that causes a certain behavior to be repeated or inhibited.

Self-regulation The belief that individuals are capable of self-control if they want to change their behavior.

Self-reinforcement The stage in Kanfer's model where, by evaluating the situation and taking corrective action if necessary, one would assure themselves that the disruptive influence had passed and everything was now fine.

Self-talk The process of convincing ourselves that the desired outcome is indeed possible.

Shaping The process of improving performance incrementally, step by step.

Social learning theory The process of molding behavior through the reciprocal interaction of a person's cognitions, behavior, and environment.

Symbolic coding When people try to associate verbal or visual stimuli with the problem.

Unconditioned response From classical conditioning, a response to an unconditioned stimulus that is naturally evoked by that stimulus.

Vicarious learning Learning that takes place through the imitation of other role models.

 Summary of Learning Outcomes

4.1 Basic Models of Learning

1. How do organizations offer appropriate rewards in a timely fashion?

People learn through both direct experience and vicarious experience. What is retained and produced as behavior is a function of the positive and negative consequences either directly experience by individuals or observed as the result of the actions of others. Often, managers and trainers underestimate the power of vicarious learning. Also, keep in mind that reinforcement that has some variability in its application (variable ratio or interval) has the strongest and longest-lasting impact on desired learned behaviors.

Learning is a relatively permanent change in behavior that occurs as a result of experience.

Thorndike's law of effect notes that behavior that is rewarded is likely to be repeated, whereas behavior that is punished is unlikely to be repeated. Operant conditioning can be distinguished from classical conditioning in two ways: (1) it asserts that changes in behavior result from the consequences of previous behaviors instead of changes in stimuli, and (2) it asserts that desired behaviors result only when rewards are tied to correct responses instead of when unconditioned stimuli are administered after every trial.

Social learning is the process of altering behavior through the reciprocal interaction of a person's cognitions, previous behavior, and environment. This is done through a process of reciprocal determinism.

Vicarious learning is learning that takes place through observation and imitation of others.

Learning is influenced by (1) a motivation to learn, (2) knowledge of results, (3) prior learning, (4) the extent to which the task to be learned is presented as a whole or in parts, and (5) distribution of practice.

4.2 Reinforcement and Behavioral Change

2. What are the best practices that organizations utilize to train employees in new job skills?

Reinforcement causes a certain behavior to be repeated or inhibited. Positive reinforcement is the practice of presenting someone with an attractive outcome following a desired behavior.

Avoidance learning occurs when someone attempts to avoid an unpleasant condition or outcome by behaving in a way desired by others.

Punishment is the administration of an unpleasant or adverse outcome following an undesired behavior. Reinforcement schedules may be continuous or partial. Among the partial reinforcement schedules are (1) fixed interval, (2) fixed ratio, (3) variable interval, and (4) variable ratio.

4.3 Behavior Modification in Organizations

3. How do managers and organizations reduce undesirable employee behavior while reinforcing desirable behavior?

Behavior modification is the use of operant principles to shape human behavior to conform to desired standards as defined by superiors. A behavior modification program follows five steps: (1) establish clear objectives, (2) conduct a performance audit, (3) set specific goals and remove obstacles, (4) evaluate results against preset criteria, and (5) administer feedback and praise where warranted.

4.4 Behavioral Self-Management

4. How can employees be trained to assume more responsibility for self-improvement and job performance with the goal of creating a work environment characterized by continual self-learning and employee development?

Behavioral self-management is the process of modifying one's own behavior by systematically managing cues, cognitions, and contingent consequences. BSM makes use of the self-regulation process.

Chapter Review Questions

1. Define learning. Why is an understanding of learning important for managers?
2. Compare and contrast operant conditioning with classical conditioning. Provide examples of each.
3. What is social learning theory? Describe how this process works.
4. What implications of social learning theory for management can you identify?
5. Identify four strategies for reinforcement, and provide an example of each.
6. Describe the four different schedules of reinforcement, and show how their use by managers can vary.
7. How might you design a simple behavior modification program for a group of employees? Explain.
8. What are some problems in trying to implement a behavioral self-management program? How can managers attempt to overcome these problems?

Management Skills Application Exercises

1. In order to better understand how behavioral self-management programs operate, you might want to complete this self-assessment and design your own self-management program. This exercise allows you to see firsthand how these programs can be applied to a wide array of problems. It also highlights the advantages and drawbacks of such programs. Refer to **Appendix B** when you are finished in order to evaluate your results.

Designing Your Own Behavioral Self-Management Program

Instructions: Think of a personal problem that you would like to overcome. This problem could be to stop smoking, improve your grades, stop a certain habit, and so forth. With this problem in mind, design your own behavioral self-management program using the procedures and principles previously outlined in this chapter. After you have designed and started the program, monitor your performance over time and see how effective you are both in following the program and in meeting your objectives. In light of your experience, how do you feel about the potential of behavioral self-management programs in the industrial setting? (See **Appendix B**.)

Managerial Decision Exercises

1. You manage the human resources department for a mid-sized retailer. Part of the operations consists of a call center with 100 employees spread over three shifts operating 24 hours a day, seven days a week. There is a main group with 20 people reporting to a shift supervisor on the main daytime shift from 8 a.m. to 4 p.m. There are regularly scheduled times for breaks and lunch. Recently senior management reported to you that they were concerned regarding tardiness of some employees. While the customer

relationship management reports signal that there are no service issues, senior managers are concerned that they are overstaffed. You feel that the daytime shift is the most experienced group, and you do not want to lose some of the best employees through termination. You also do not have any budget money to use for incentive payments aimed at reducing tardiness. What ideas from operant conditioning, behavior modification, and social learning theory would you use to reduce the problems of tardiness?

2. Organizations are facing changes in their business environment because of globalization of markets and competition, growth of immediate digital information and communications, growth of the service-based economy, and changes in rules affecting corporate governance and trade relationships. Assume the role of a CEO who needs to change their corporate culture and their standards of operation. The organizational structures in your industry have trended from tall, hierarchical bureaucracies to flat, decentralized operations that encourage innovation. Changes like this do not happen automatically. What theories and techniques would you use to change your organization's culture?

Critical Thinking Case

Walt Disney World

When it comes to presenting world-class customer experiences, Walt Disney World is at the top of the list. It's literally called the Most Magical Place on Earth. However, it isn't just their customers who are receiving rewards for visiting—their cast members and crew are getting rewarded big-time as well.

Incentives go above and beyond a 401(k) program, and they can go a long way in retaining employees and increasing employee satisfaction as well. Disney has over 180 employee recognition programs to give their employees a sense of accomplishment, recognition, and appreciation.

There are over 70,000 cast members at Walt Disney World, each of whom receive extensive training to make sure that they make the customer experience a world-class enjoyment. According to Mike Fox, author of *Hidden Secrets & Stories of Walt Disney World*, "it always impresses me, especially at the cast member level, the training that goes into helping these folks to provide a superior experience and to see it on stage and see it executed."

Walt Disney exemplifies many ways of recognition, lots of them being physical in-park recognitions. These include names in windows on Main Street tributes, featuring Disney's best "imagineers" that helped create some of the park's greatest rides and innovations. One of the most unique is the Lifetime Fred award, which recognizes employees who exhibit the core company values of friendliness and dependability. It is these varying types of recognition that make Walt Disney's rewards program so robust and versatile and keep employees engaged and willing to work hard to achieve more.

Questions:

1. What key factors are important to consider when creating a rewards program?
2. Why is timing a key component to a rewards program?
3. What can be problematic about the wrong type of reward or the wrong frequency of the reward for employees?

Sources: Rhatigan, Chris, "These 4 Companies Totally Get Employee Recognition," *TINY pulse*, July 21, 2015, https://www.tinypulse.com/blog/these-4-companies-totally-get-employee-recognition; "Rewarding Your Employees: 15 Examples of Successful Incentives in The Corporate World," *Robinson Resource Group*, June 30, 2013, http://www.rrgexec.com/rewarding-your-employees-15-examples-of-successful-incentives-in-the-corporate-world/; Kober, Jeff, "Reward & Recognition at Walt Disney World," World Class Benchmarking,

October 17, 2016, http://worldclassbenchmarking.com/reward-recognition-at-the-walt-disney-world-resort/; Cain, Áine, "15 insider facts about working at Walt Disney World only cast members know," *Business Insider*, May 1, 2018, https://www.businessinsider.com/walt-disney-world-cast-member-secrets-2018-2#if-the-guests-can-see-you-youre-technically-onstage-5.

5 Diversity in Organizations

Exhibit 5.1 (Credit: rawpixel/ Pixabay/ (CC BY 0))

Introduction

Learning Outcomes

After reading this chapter, you should be able to answer these questions:

1. What is diversity?
2. How diverse is the workforce?
3. How does diversity impact companies and the workforce?
4. What is workplace discrimination, and how does it affect different social identity groups?
5. What key theories help managers understand the benefits and challenges of managing the diverse workforce?
6. How can managers reap benefits from diversity and mitigate its challenges?
7. What can organizations do to ensure applicants, employees, and customers from all backgrounds are valued?

EXPLORING MANAGERIAL CAREERS

Dr. Tamara A. Johnson, Assistant Chancellor for Equity, Diversity, and Inclusion at University of Wisconsin-Eau Claire

Dr. Tamara Johnson's role as assistant chancellor for equity, diversity, and inclusion at the University of Wisconsin-Eau Claire involves supervising and collaborating with various campus entities to ensure their operations continue to support the university's initiatives to foster diversity and equity within the university community. Dr. Johnson oversees the Affirmative Action, Blugold Beginnings (pre-college program), Gender and Sexuality Resource Center, Office of Multicultural Affairs, Ronald E. McNair Program, Services for Students with Disabilities, Student Support Services, University Police, and Upward Bound units and leads campus-wide initiatives to educate and train faculty, students, and staff about cultural awareness, diversity, and institutional equity.

Dr. Johnson's journey to her current role began more than 20 years ago when she worked as a counselor for the Office of Multicultural Student Affairs at the University of Illinois. Her role in this office launched her on a path through university service—Dr. Johnson went on to work as the associate director for University Career Services at Illinois State University, the director for multicultural student affairs at Northwestern University, and the director for faculty diversity initiatives at the University of Chicago. As faculty at the Chicago School of Professional Psychology, Argosy University, and Northwestern University, Dr. Johnson taught counseling courses at the undergraduate, master's, and doctorate levels.

Dr. Johnson's work at the University of Wisconsin-Eau Claire involves developing a program and protocols to ensure all faculty and staff across the institution receive baseline diversity training. In addition, one of her goals is to include criteria related to diversity factors in the evaluations of all faculty/staff. A primary issue that she seeks to address is to increase the awareness of the challenges experienced by underrepresented students. This includes individuals who may come from backgrounds of low income, students of color, first-generation students, and other marginalized groups such as lesbian, gay, bisexual, and transgender students. Dr. Johnson understands the importance of creating initiatives to support individuals in those groups so their specific concerns may be addressed in multiple ways. As you will learn in this chapter, when leaders proactively create an inclusive and supportive climate that values diversity, benefits are produced that result in in positive outcomes for organizations.

5.1 An Introduction to Workplace Diversity

1. What is diversity?

Diversity refers to identity-based differences among and between two or more people[1] that affect their lives as applicants, employees, and customers. These identity-based differences include such things as race and ethnicity, gender, sexual orientation, and age. Groups in society based on these individual differences are referred to as **identity groups**. These differences are related to discrimination and disparities between groups in areas such as education, housing, healthcare, and employment. The term **managing diversity** is commonly used to refer to ways in which organizations seek to ensure that members of diverse groups are valued and treated fairly within organizations[2] in all areas including hiring, compensation, performance evaluation, and customer service activities. The term *valuing diversity* is often used to reflect ways in which organizations show appreciation for diversity among job applicants, employees, and customers.[3] **Inclusion**, which represents the degree to which employees are accepted and treated fairly by their organization,[4] is one way in which companies demonstrate how they value diversity. In the context of today's rapidly changing organizational environment, it is more important than ever to understand diversity in organizational contexts and make progressive strides toward a more inclusive, equitable, and representative workforce.

Three kinds of diversity exist in the workplace (see **Table 5.1**). **Surface-level diversity** represents an individual's visible characteristics, including, but not limited to, age, body size, visible disabilities, race, or sex.[5] A collective of individuals who share these characteristics is known as an identity group. **Deep-level diversity** includes traits that are nonobservable such as attitudes, values, and beliefs.[6] **Hidden diversity** includes traits that are deep-level but may be concealed or revealed at the discretion of individuals who possess them.[7]

These hidden traits are called **invisible social identities**[8] and may include sexual orientation, a hidden disability (such as a mental illness or chronic disease), mixed racial heritage,[9] or socioeconomic status. Researchers investigate these different types of diversity in order to understand how diversity may benefit or hinder organizational outcomes.

Diversity presents challenges that may include managing dysfunctional conflict that can arise from inappropriate interactions between individuals from different groups. Diversity also presents advantages such as broader perspectives and viewpoints. Knowledge about how to manage diversity helps managers mitigate some of its challenges and reap some of its benefits.

Types of Diversity	
Surface-level diversity	Diversity in the form of characteristics of individuals that are readily visible including, but not limited to, age, body size, visible disabilities, race or sex.
Deep-level diversity	Diversity in characteristics that are nonobservable such as attitudes, values, and beliefs, such as religion.
Hidden diversity	Diversity in characteristics that are deep-level but may be concealed or revealed at discretion by individuals who possess them, such as sexual orientation.

Table 5.1

CONCEPT CHECK 

1. What is diversity?
2. What are the three types of diversity encountered in the workplace?

5.2 Diversity and the Workforce

2. How diverse is the workforce?

In 1997, researchers estimated that by the year 2020, 14% of the workforce would be Latino, 11% Black, and 6% Asian.[10] Because of an increase in the number of racial minorities entering the workforce over the past 20 years, most of those projections have been surpassed as of 2016, with a workforce composition of 17% Hispanic or Latino of any race, followed by 12% Black and 6% Asian (see **Exhibit 5.2**). American Indians, Alaska Natives, Native Hawaiians, and Other Pacific Islanders together made up a little over 1% of the labor force, while people of two or more races made up about 2% of the labor force.[11] Women constitute approximately 47% of the workforce compared to approximately 53% for men,[12] and the average age of individuals participating in the labor force has also increased because more employees retire at a later age.[13] Although Whites still predominantly make up the workforce with a 78% share,[14] the U.S. workforce is becoming increasingly more diverse, a trend that presents both opportunities and challenges. These demographic shifts in the labor market affect the workforce in a number of ways due to an increasing variety of workers who differ by sex, race, age, sexual orientation, disability status, and immigrant status.

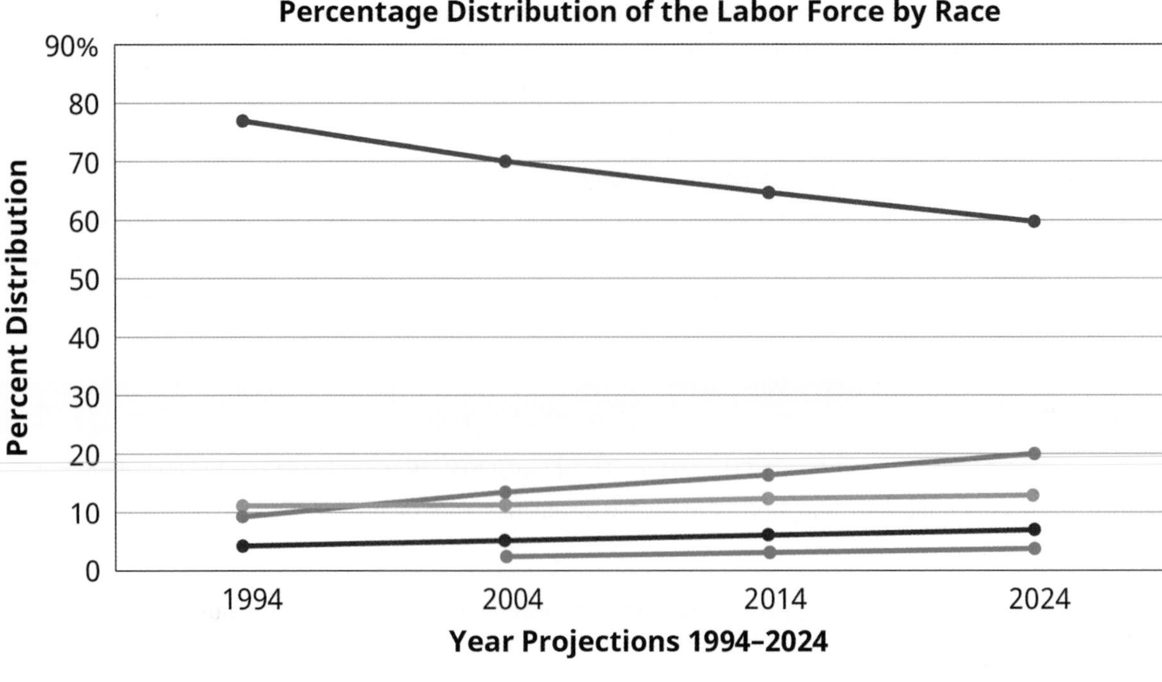

Exhibit 5.2 Percentage distribution of the labor force by race (Attribution: Copyright Rice University, OpenStax, under CC-BY 4.0 license)

Gender

Increasingly more women are entering the workforce.[15] Compared to 59% in 1977, the labor force participation rate for men is now approximately 53% and is expected to decrease through 2024 to 52%.[16] As the labor force participation rate decreases for men, the labor force growth rate for women will be faster. Their percentage of the workforce has steadily risen, as can be seen in **Exhibit 5.3**, which compares the percentage of the workforce by gender in 1977 to 2017.[17]

Although more women are entering the labor force and earning bachelor's degrees at a higher rate than men,[18] women still face a number of challenges at work. The lack of advancement opportunities awarded to qualified women is an example of a major challenge that women face called the **glass ceiling**,[19] which is an invisible barrier based on the prejudicial beliefs that underlie organizational decisions that prevent women from moving beyond certain levels within a company. Additionally, in organizations in which the upper-level managers and decision makers are predominantly men, women are less likely to find mentors, which are instrumental for networking and learning about career opportunities. Organizations can mitigate this challenge by providing mentors for all new employees. Such a policy would help create a more equal playing field for all employees as they learn to orient themselves and navigate within the organization.

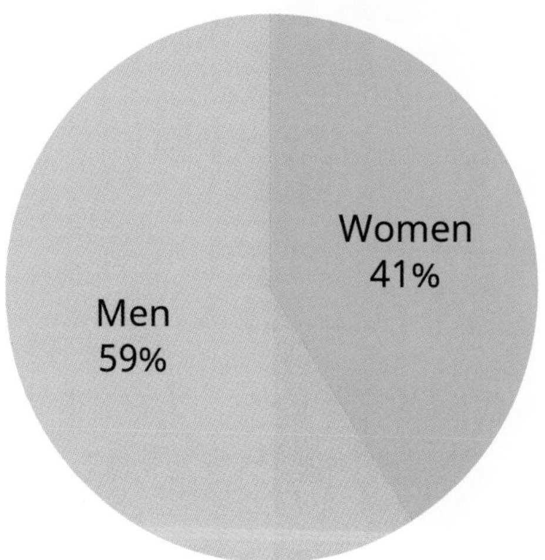

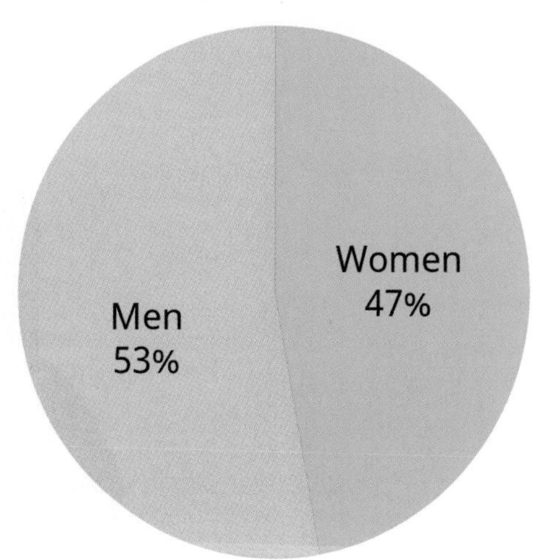

Exhibit 5.3 Percentage Distribution of the Labor Force by Sex (Attribution: Copyright Rice University, OpenStax, under CC-BY 4.0 license)

One factor that greatly affects women in organizations is **sexual harassment**. Sexual harassment is illegal, and workers are protected from it by federal legislation.[20] Two forms of sexual harassment that can occur at work are quid pro quo and hostile environment.[21] Quid pro quo harassment refers to the exchange of rewards for sexual favors or punishments for refusal to grant sexual favors. Harassment that creates a hostile environment refers to behaviors that create an abusive work climate. If employees are penalized (for example by being demoted or transferred to another department) for refusing to respond to repeated sexual advances, quid pro quo sexual harassment has taken place. The telling of lewd jokes, the posting of pornographic material at work, or making offensive comments about women in general are actions that are considered to create a hostile work environment. According to the Equal Employment Opportunity Commission, sexual harassment is defined as the "unwelcome sexual advances, requests for sexual favors, and other verbal or physical harassment of a sexual nature. Harassment can also include offensive remarks about a person's sex."[22] Although both men and women can be sexually harassed, women are sexually harassed at work more often.[23] In addition, Black and other minority women are especially likely to be subjected to sexual discrimination and harassment.[24]

Exhibit 5.4 Tamara Johnson The treatment of women in business has become a hot topic in corporate boardrooms, human resources departments, and investment committees. Tamara Johnson, who is profiled in the opening feature to this chapter, moves beyond simply acknowledging widespread discrimination to focusing on solutions. Also on the agenda: the need to improve diversity and inclusion across the board and breaking through the glass ceiling. (Credit: Tamara Johnson/ Attribution 2.0 Generic (CC BY 2.0))

Because employees who experience sexual harassment are more likely to quit their jobs and experience emotional distress that can negatively impact their performance,[25] it is in the organization's best interest to prevent sexual harassment at work from occurring. Ways to do this include companies providing ongoing (e.g., annual) training so that employees are able to recognize sexual harassment. Employees should know what constitutes acceptable and unacceptable behavior and what channels and protocols are in place for reporting unacceptable behaviors. Managers should understand their role and responsibilities regarding harassment prevention, and a clear and understandable policy should be communicated throughout the organization.

Race

Another important demographic shift in workforce diversity is the distribution of race. (Note that we are using categories defined by the U.S. Census Bureau. It uses the term "Black (African-American)" to categorize U.S. residents. In this chapter, we use the term "Black.")

While the White non-Hispanic share of the workforce continues to shrink, the share of racial and ethnic minority groups will continue to grow.[26] Specifically, Hispanics and Asians will grow at a faster rate than other racial minorities, and Hispanics are projected to make up almost one-fifth of the labor force by 2024.[27] The projected changes in labor force composition between 2014 and 2024 are as follows:

White non-Hispanic participation in the labor force will decline by 3%. Other groups' share of the labor force is expected to increase: Black (10.1%), Hispanic (28%), Asian (23.2%), and Other groups (i.e., multiracial, American Indian, Alaska Native, Native Hawaiian, and Other Pacific Islanders) labor force share is expected to increase by 22.2%.[28] With the workforce changing, managers will need to be mindful of issues employees encounter that are uniquely tied to their experiences based on race and ethnicity, including harassment, discrimination, stereotyping, and differential treatment by coworkers and decision makers in organizations.

Discrimination Against Black Employees

Race is one of the most frequent grounds for discrimination.[29] Although Blacks do not make up the largest share of the workforce for racial minorities, research studies show they face discrimination more often than other racial minorities. As a matter of fact, some experts believe that hiring discrimination against Blacks has not declined over the past 25 years while workplace discrimination against other racial minority groups has declined.[30]

ETHICS IN PRACTICE

Discrimination in the Sharing Economy—#AirbnbWhileBlack

Airbnb, a popular home-sharing website founded in San Francisco in 2008, offers millions of homes for short-term rental in more than 190 countries. This company has revolutionized the sharing economy in the same way that ride-sharing services such as Uber and Lyft have, and according to the company, the site's drive to connect hosts and potential renters has been able to contribute to the quality of life of both homeowners and travelers. According to Airbnb's press releases and information campaigns, their services can reduce housing costs for travelers on a budget and can provide unique experiences for adventurous travelers who wish to have the flexibility to experience a city like a local. The organization also claims that most of its users are homeowners looking to supplement their incomes by renting out rooms in their homes or by occasionally renting out their whole homes. According to a statement, most of the listings on the site are rented out fewer than 50 nights per year.

Despite the carefully crafted messages Airbnb has presented to the public, in 2016 the company came under intense scrutiny when independent analyses by researchers and journalists revealed something startling: While some Airbnb hosts did in fact use the services only occasionally, a significant number of hosts were using the services as though they were hotels. These hosts purchased a large number of properties and continuously rented them, a practice that affected the availability of affordable housing in cities and, because these hosts were not officially registered as hoteliers, made it possible for Airbnb hosts to avoid paying the taxes and abiding by the laws that hotels are subject to.

Title II of the Civil Rights Act of 1964 mandates that hotels and other public accommodations must not discriminate based on race, national origin, sex, or religion, and Title VIII of the Civil Rights Act of 1968 (also known as the Fair Housing Act [FHA]) prohibits discrimination specifically in housing. However, Airbnb's unique structure allows it to circumvent those laws. The company also claims that while it encourages hosts to comply with local and federal laws, it is absolved from responsibility if any of its hosts break these laws. In 2017, researcher Ben Edelman conducted a field experiment and found that Airbnb users looking to rent homes were 16% less likely to have their requests to book accepted if they had traditionally African American sounding names like Tamika, Darnell, and Rasheed.

These findings, coupled with a viral social media campaign, #AirbnbWhileBlack, in which users claimed they were denied housing requests based on their race, prompted the state of California's Department of Fair Employment and Housing (DFEH) to file a complaint against the company. In an effort to resolve the complaint, Airbnb reported banning any hosts who were found to have engaged in discriminatory practices, and they hired former U.S. Attorney General Eric Holder and former ACLU official Laura Murphy to investigate any claims of discrimination within the company.[31] In 2016, Airbnb released a statement outlining changes to company practices and policies to combat discrimination, and while they initially resisted demands by the DFEH to conduct an audit of their practices, the company eventually agreed to an audit of roughly 6,000 of the hosts in California who have the highest volume of properties listed on the site.

Sources: AirBnB Press Room, accessed December 24, 2018, https://press.atairbnb.com/about-us/; "Airbnb's data shows that Airbnb helps the middle class. But does it?", *The Guardian*, accessed December 23, 2018, https://www.theguardian.com/technology/2016/jul/27/airbnb-panel-democratic-national-convention-survey ; and Quittner, Jeremy, "Airbnb and Discrimination: Why It's All So Confusing", *Fortune*, June 23, 2016, http://fortune.com/2016/06/23/airbnb-discrimination-laws/.

Discussion Questions

1. What are some efforts companies in the sharing economy can take before problems of discrimination threaten to disrupt operations?
2. Should Airbnb be held responsible for discriminatory actions of its hosts?

Currently, White men have higher participation rates in the workforce than do Black men,[32] and Black women have slightly higher participation rates than White women.[33] Despite growth and gains in both Black education and Black employment, a Black person is considerably more likely to be unemployed than a White person, even when the White person has a lower level of education[34] or a criminal record.[35]

Blacks frequently experience discrimination in the workplace in spite of extensive legislation in place to prohibit such discrimination. Research has shown that stereotypes and prejudices about Blacks can cause them to be denied the opportunity for employment when compared to equally qualified Whites.[36] It is estimated that about 25% of businesses have no minority workers and another 25% have less than 10% minority workers.[37] In terms of employed Blacks, research has shown that, regardless of managers' race, managers tended to give significantly higher performance ratings to employees who were racially similar to them. Because Whites are much more likely to be managers than Blacks, this similarity effect tends to advantage White employees over Black employees.[38] Blacks are also significantly more likely to be hired in positions that require low skills, offer little to no room for growth, and pay less. These negative employment experiences affect both the mental and physical health of Black employees.[39]

Hispanics

Hispanics are the second-fastest-growing minority group in the United States behind Asians,[40] and they make up 17% of the labor force.[41] Despite this and the fact that Hispanics have the highest labor participation rate of all the minority groups, they still face discrimination and harassment in similar ways to other minority groups.

Hispanics can be of any race.[42] As a matter of fact, increasingly more Hispanics are identifying racially as White. In 2004 almost half of Hispanics identified themselves racially as White, while just under half identified themselves as "some other race."[43] More than 10 years later, approximately 66% of Hispanics now identify themselves racially as White while only 26% identify themselves as "some other race."[44] The remaining Hispanic population, totaling approximately 7%, identify as either Black, American Indian, Asian, Alaskan

Native, Pacific Islander, or Native Hawaiian.[45]

Why would a minority identity group identify racially as White? A Pew study found that the longer Hispanic families lived in the United States, the more likely they were to claim White as their race even if they had not done so in the past.[46] This suggests that upward mobility in America may be perceived by some Hispanics to be equated with "Whiteness."[47] Consequently, Hispanics who self-identify racially as White experience higher rates of education and salary, and lower rates of unemployment.[48] Additionally, only 29% of Hispanics polled by the Pew Hispanic Center believe they share a common culture.[49] According to the Pew Research Center, this finding may be due to the fact that the Hispanic ethnic group in the United States is made up of at least 14 Hispanic origin groups (such as Puerto Rican, Cuban, Spanish, Mexican, Dominican, and Guatemalan, among many others).[50] Each of these groups has its own culture with different customs, values, and norms.

These cultural differences among the various Hispanic groups, combined with different self-perceptions of race, may also affect attitudes toward their workplace environment. For example, one study found that the absenteeism rate among Blacks was related to the level of diversity policies and activities visible in the organization, while the absenteeism rate among Hispanics was similar to that of Whites and not related to those diversity cues.[51] Results from this study suggest that managers need to be aware of how diversity impacts their workplace, namely addressing the relationship between Hispanic job seekers or workers and organizational outcomes concerning diversity policies as it may differ from that of other racial minorities.

Asians

Asians are the fastest-growing ethnic group in the United States, growing 72% between 2000 and 2015.[52] Compared to the rest of the U.S. population overall, households headed by Asian Americans earn more money and are more likely to have household members who hold a bachelor's degree.[53] However, there is a wide range of income levels among the Asian population that differs between the more than 19 groups of Asian origin in the United States.[54]

Similar to other racial and ethnic minority groups, Asians are stereotyped and face discrimination at work. Society through media often stereotypes Asian men as having limited English-speaking skills and as being highly educated, affluent, analytical, and good at math and science.[55] Asian women are often portrayed as weak and docile.[56] For Asian women, and other minority women as well, social stereotypes depicting them as exotic contribute to reports of sexual harassment from women minority groups.[57]

The **model minority myth**[58] is a reflection of perceptions targeting Asians and Asian Americans that contrast the stereotypes of "conformity" and "success" of Asian men with stereotypes of "rebelliousness" and "laziness" of other minority men. It also contrasts the stereotyped "exotic" and "obedient" nature of Asian women against the stereotypical beliefs that White women are "independent" and "pure."[59] These perceptions are used not only to invalidate injustice that occurs among other racial minorities, but also to create barriers for Asians seeking leadership opportunities as they are steered toward "behind the scenes" positions that require less engagement with others. These stereotypes also relegate Asian women into submissive roles in organizations, making it challenging for Asian men and women to advance in rank at the same rate as White male employees.[60]

Multiracial

Although the U.S. Census Bureau estimates that approximately 2% of the U.S. population describes themselves as belonging to more than one race, the Pew Research Center estimates that number should be higher, with around 7% of the U.S. population considered multiracial.[61] This is due to the fact that some individuals may claim one race for themselves even though they have parents from different racial backgrounds. To complicate matters even more, when collecting data from multiracial group members, racial identity for individuals in this group may change over time because race is a social construct that is not necessarily based on a shared culture or country of origin in the same way as ethnicity. As a result, multiracial individuals (and Hispanics) have admitted to changing their racial identity over the course of their life and even based on the situation. Approximately 30% of multiracial individuals polled by the Pew Research Center say that they have varied between viewing themselves as belonging to one race or belonging to multiple races. Within the group polled, the order in which they first racially identified as belonging to one racial group versus belonging to more than one group varied.[62]

Despite the fact that multiracial births have risen tenfold between 1970 and 2013,[63] their participation in the labor force is only around 2%.[64] Additionally, multiracial individuals with a White racial background are still considered a racial minority unless they identify themselves solely as White, and approximately 56% of them on average say they have been subjected to racial jokes and slurs.[65] Discrimination also varies when multiracial groups are broken down further, with Black–American Indians having the highest percentage of individuals reporting discrimination and White–Asians having the lowest percentage.[66]

At work, multiracial employees are sometimes mistaken for races other than their own. If their racial minority background is visible to others, they may experience negative differential treatment. Sometimes they are not identified as having a racial or ethnic minority background and are privy to disparaging comments from unsuspecting coworkers about their own race, which can be demoralizing and can lead to lower organizational attachment and emotional strain related to concealing their identity.[67]

Other Groups

Approximately 1% of the labor force identifies as American Indian, Alaska Native, Native Hawaiian or Pacific Islander, or some other race.[68]

Age

The age distribution of an organization's workforce is an important dimension of workplace diversity as the working population gets older. Some primary factors contributing to an older population include the aging of the large Baby Boomer generation (people born between 1946 and 1964), lower birth rates, and longer life expectancies[69] due to advances in medical technology and access to health care. As a result, many individuals work past the traditional age of retirement (65 years old) and work more years than previous generations in order to maintain their cost of living.

Exhibit 5.5 compares the percentage of the population over the age of 65 to those under the age of 18 between 2010 and 2016. The number of older individuals has increased and is projected to reach 20.6% by the year 2030 while the number of younger individuals has steadily decreased within that time period. These numbers imply that organizations will increasingly have employees across a wide range of ages, and cross-generational interaction can be difficult manage. Although older workers are viewed as agreeable and comfortable to work with, they are also stereotyped by some employees as incompetent[70] and less interested in learning new tasks at work compared to younger workers.[71] Studies have found support for the proposition that age negatively relates to cognitive functioning.[72] However, if managers offer less opportunity to older workers solely because of declining cognitive functioning, it can be detrimental to organizational performance because older workers outperform younger workers on a number of other job performance measures. Compared to younger workers, older workers are more likely to perform above their job expectations and follow safety protocols. They are also less likely to be tardy, absent, or abuse drugs or alcohol at work compared to their younger counterparts.

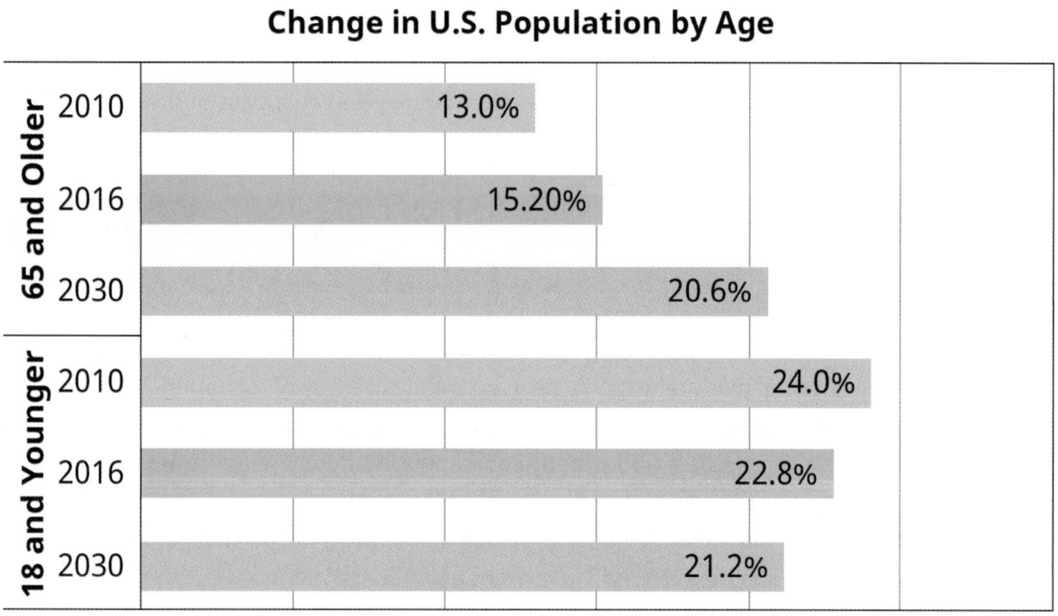

Change in U.S. Population by Age

65 and Older
2010 13.0%
2016 15.20%
2030 20.6%

18 and Younger
2010 24.0%
2016 22.8%
2030 21.2%

Exhibit 5.5 Change in U.S. population by age (Attribution: Copyright Rice University, OpenStax, under CC-BY 4.0 license)

Sexual Orientation

Sexual orientation diversity is increasing in the workforce.[73] However, only 21 states and Washington D.C. prohibit discrimination based on sexual orientation.[74] Without federal protection, individuals who do not live in these states could be overlooked for employment or fired for their sexual orientation unless their employer has policies to protect them.[75] Many employers are beginning to understand that being perceived as inclusive will make them more attractive to a larger pool of job applicants.[76] So although the Civil Rights Act does not explicitly provide federal protection to lesbian, gay, bisexual, and transgender (LGBT) employees, more than half of the Fortune 500 companies have corporate policies that protect sexual minorities from discrimination at work and offer domestic-partner benefits.[77]

Unfortunately, the percentage of hate crimes relating to sexual orientation discrimination has increased.[78] Indeed, LGBT employees are stigmatized so much that in a recent study, researchers found that straight-identifying participants were more attracted to employers with no job security to offer them compared to gay-friendly employers.[79] In other words, individuals would waive job security to avoid working with sexual minorities. Also, compared to heterosexuals, sexual minorities have higher education levels[80] but still face hiring and treatment discrimination frequently.[81]

LGBT employees are often faced with the decision of whether or not to be truthful about their sexual orientation at work for fear of being stigmatized and treated unfairly. The decision to not disclose is called **passing**, and for some it involves a great risk of emotional strain that can affect performance.[82] Individuals who pass may distance themselves from coworkers or clients to avoid disclosure about their personal life. This behavior can also result in decreased networking and mentoring opportunities, which over time can limit advancement opportunities. The decision to be transparent about sexual orientation is called **revealing**.[83] Just like passing, revealing has its own set of risks including being ostracized, stigmatized, and subjected to other forms of discrimination at work. However, compared to passing, the benefits of building relationships at work and using their identity as a catalyst for tolerance and progressive organizational change may outweigh the risks when LGBT employees decide to reveal.

Research shows that when local or state laws are passed to prevent sexual orientation discrimination, incidents of workplace discrimination decrease.[84] This same effect occurs when firms adopt policies that protect the rights of sexual minority employees.[85] By creating a safe and inclusive work environment for LGBT employees, companies can create a culture of tolerance for all employees regardless of their sexual orientation or gender identity.

MANAGING CHANGE

Blind Recruiting

An increasing number of companies are testing a new and innovative way of recruiting. *Blind recruiting* is a process by which firms remove any identifying information about applicants during the recruitment process. An example of this may include anonymous applications that omit fields requesting information such as an applicant's name or age. Using computer application technology, some companies like Google administer surveys to their anonymous applicants that measure the abilities required for the job before they are considered in the next step of the recruitment process. Alternatively, companies may request that applicants remove identifying information such as names and address from their resumes before applying for positions. As resumes are received, hiring managers can assign a temporary identification number.

Although more companies are using this method of recruiting, the idea is not new for symphony orchestras, many of which have been using blind auditioning since the 1970s. In some instances musicians audition behind screens so they are evaluated only by their music. This process removes bias associated with race and gender because the performer cannot be seen and only heard. A study investigating this practice examined 11 symphony orchestras that varied on the use of blind auditions. Researchers found that blind auditions increased the likelihood that a woman would be hired by between 25 and 46%. A recruitment process like this can help organizations attract more candidates, hire the best talent, increase their workplace diversity, and avoid discrimination liability.

Sources: Grothaus, M. (Mar 14 2016). How "blind" recruitment works and why you should consider it. Fast Company. Retrieved from https://www.fastcompany.com/3057631/how-blind-recruitment-works-and-why-you-should-consider; and MIller, C.C. (Feb 25 2016). Is blind hiring the best hiring? The New York Times Magazine. Retrieved from https://www.nytimes.com/2016/02/28/magazine/is-blind-hiring-the-best-hiring.html.

Discussion Questions

1. Should all companies use blind recruiting in place of traditional recruiting, or are there exceptions that must be considered?
2. If blind recruiting helps eliminate bias during the recruitment process, then what does that say about social media platforms such as Linked In that are commonly used for recruiting applicants? Will using those platforms expose companies to greater liability compared to using more traditional means of recruiting?
3. How does blind recruiting help organizations? How may it hinder organizations?

Immigrant Workers

Every year a new record is set for the time it takes to reach the U.S. cap of H-1B visas granted to employers.[86] H- 1B visas are a type of **work visa**, a temporary documented status that authorizes individuals to permanently or temporarily live and work in the United States.[87] As a result of the demand for work visas by employers, the number of immigrant workers in the U.S. workforce has steadily grown within the last decade from 15% in 2005 to 17% in 2016.[88] Compared to those born in the United States, the immigrant population in America is growing significantly faster.[89] This is partly because of the U.S. demand for workers who are proficient in math and science[90] and wish to work in America.

Although a huge demand for immigrant labor exists in the United States, immigrant labor exploitation occurs, with immigrant employees receiving lower wages and working longer hours compared to American workers.[91] Foreign-born job seekers are attracted to companies that emphasize work visa sponsorship for international employees, yet they are still mindful of their vulnerability to unethical employers who may try to exploit them. For example, Lambert and colleagues found that some of the job-seeking MBA students from the Philippines in their study believed that companies perceived to value international diversity and sponsor H-1B visas signaled a company wishing to exploit workers.[92] Others believed that those types of companies might yield diminishing returns to each Filipino in the company because their token value becomes limited. In news stories, companies have been accused of drastically shortchanging foreign student interns on their weekly wages.[93] In another case, Infosys, a technology consulting company, paid $34 million to settle allegations of visa fraud due to suspicion of underpaying foreign workers to increase profits.[94]

Other Forms of Diversity at Work

Workers with disabilities are projected to experience a 10% increase in job growth through the year 2022.[95] This means that more public and corporate policies will be revised to allow greater access to training for workers with disabilities and employers.[96] Also, more companies will use technology and emphasize educating employees about physical and mental disabilities as workplace accommodations are used more often.

In the past, the United States has traditionally been a country with citizens who predominantly practice the Christian faith. However, over the past almost 30 years the percentage of Americans who identify as Christian has significantly decreased—by approximately 12%. Over that same time period, affiliation with other religions overall increased by approximately 25%.[97] The increase in immigrant workers from Asian and Middle Eastern countries means that employers must be prepared to accommodate religious beliefs other than Christianity. Although federal legislation protects employees from discrimination on the basis of race, religion, and disability status, many employers have put in place policies of their own to deal with the variety of diversity that is increasingly entering the workforce.

CONCEPT CHECK

1. How is diversity defined in relation to the workplace?
2. What are the components that make up a diverse workplace and workforce?

5.3 Diversity and Its Impact on Companies

3. How does diversity impact companies and the workforce?

Due to trends in globalization and increasing ethnic and gender diversity, it is imperative that employers learn how to manage cultural differences and individual work attitudes. As the labor force becomes more diverse there are both opportunities and challenges to managing employees in a diverse work climate. Opportunities include gaining a competitive edge by embracing change in the marketplace and the labor force. Challenges include effectively managing employees with different attitudes, values, and beliefs, in addition to avoiding liability when leadership handles various work situations improperly.

Reaping the Advantages of Diversity

The business case for diversity introduced by Taylor Cox and Stacy Blake outlines how companies may obtain a competitive advantage by embracing workplace diversity.[98] Six opportunities that companies may receive when pursuing a strategy that values diversity include cost advantages, improved resource acquisition, greater marketing ability, system flexibility, and enhanced creativity and better problem solving (see **Exhibit 5.6**).

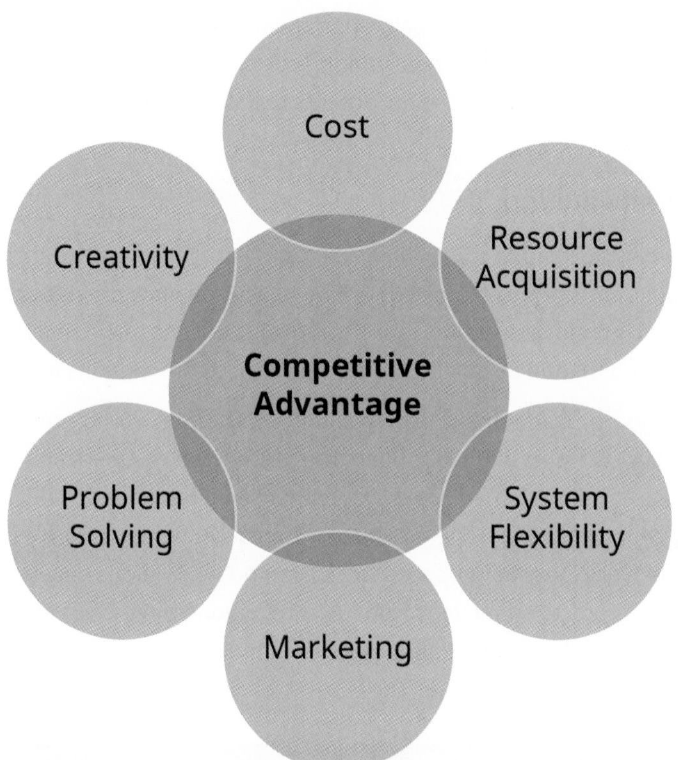

Exhibit 5.6 Managing Cultural Diversity (Attribution: Copyright Rice University, OpenStax, under CC-BY 4.0 license)

Cost Advantages

Traits such as race, gender, age, and religion are protected by federal legislation against various forms of discrimination (covered later in this chapter). Organizations that have policies and procedures in place that encourage tolerance for a work climate of diversity and protect female and minority employees and applicants from discrimination may reduce their likelihood of being sued due to workplace discrimination. Cox and Blake identify this decreased liability as an opportunity for organizations to reduce potential expenses in lawsuit damages compared to other organizations that do not have such policies in place.

Additionally, organizations with a more visible climate of diversity experience lower turnover among women and minorities compared to companies that are perceived to not value diversity.[99] Turnover costs can be substantial for companies over time, and diverse companies may ameliorate turnover by retaining their female and minority employees. Although there is also research showing that organizations that value diversity experience a higher turnover of White employees and male employees compared to companies that are less diverse,[100] some experts believe this is due to a lack of understanding of how to effectively manage diversity. Also, some research shows that Whites with a strong ethnic identity are attracted to diverse organizations similarly to non-Whites.[101]

Resource Acquisition

Human capital is an important resource of organizations, and it is acquired through the knowledge, skills, and abilities of employees. Organizations perceived to value diversity attract more women and minority job applicants to hire as employees. Studies show that women and minorities have greater job-pursuit intentions and higher attraction toward organizations that promote workplace diversity in their recruitment materials compared to organizations that do not.[102] When employers attract minority applicants, their labor pool increases in size compared to organizations that are not attractive to them. As organizations attract more job candidates, the chances of hiring quality employees increases, especially for jobs that demand highly skilled labor. In summary, organizations gain a competitive advantage by enlarging their labor pool by attracting women and minorities.

Marketing

When organizations employ individuals from different backgrounds, they gain broad perspectives regarding consumer preferences of different cultures. Organizations can gain insightful knowledge and feedback from demographic markets about the products and services they provide. Additionally, organizations that value diversity enhance their reputation with the market they serve, thereby attracting new customers.

System Flexibility

When employees are placed in a culturally diverse work environment, they learn to interact effectively with individuals who possess different attitudes, values, and beliefs. Cox and Blake contend that the ability to effectively interact with individuals who differ from oneself builds *cognitive flexibility*, the ability to think about things differently and adapt one's perspective. When employees possess cognitive flexibility, system flexibility develops at the organizational level. Employees learn from each other how to tolerate differences in opinions and ideas, which allows communication to flow more freely and group interaction to be more effective.

Creativity and Problem Solving

Teams from diverse backgrounds produce multiple points of view, which can lead to innovative ideas. Different perspectives lead to a greater number of choices to select from when addressing a problem or issue.

Life experience varies from person to person, sometimes based on race, age, or sex. Creativity has the opportunity to flourish when those experiences are shared. Diverse teams not only produce more alternatives, but generate a broader range of perspectives to address tasks and problems. One way in which diverse teams enhance problem-solving ability is by preventing **groupthink**,[103] a dysfunction in decision-making that occurs in homogeneous groups as a result of group pressures and group members' desire for conformity and consensus. Diverse group membership prevents groupthink because individuals from varied backgrounds with different values, attitudes, and beliefs can test the assumptions and reasoning of group members' ideas.

Aligning Diversity Programs with an Organization's Mission and Strategic Goals

Diversity helps organizations perform best when it is aligned with a specific business strategy. For example, when companies use heterogeneous management teams that are directed by an entrepreneurial strategy focusing on innovation, the companies' productivity increases.

When an entrepreneurial strategy is not present, however, team diversity has little effect on productivity.[104] An entrepreneurial strategy includes innovation that reflects a company's commitment to being creative, supporting new ideas, and supporting experimentation as a way to gain a competitive advantage. In other words, managers may properly utilize the multiple perspectives that emerge from heterogeneous teams by integrating them as a resource for pursuing the overall strategy of the organization.

Using Human Resources Tools Strategically

To effectively align diversity with an organization's strategy, the human resources function must be able to engage employees at dynamic levels. Using a strategic human resources management approach to an organization can successfully integrate diversity with the organization's goals and objectives.[105] **Strategic human resources management (SHRM)** is a system of activities arranged to engage employees in a manner that assists the organization in achieving a sustainable competitive advantage. SHRM practices vertically integrate with the mission and strategy of the organization while horizontally integrating human resources activities across its functional areas. By doing so, a unique set of resources can be made available to specific to the needs of the organization. Furthermore, when human resources becomes a part of the strategic planning process instead of just providing ancillary services, improved communication, knowledge sharing, and greater synergy between decision makers can occur within the organization to improve organizational functioning.

The **resource-based view** of the firm has been used to support the argument for diversity because it demonstrates how a diverse workforce can create a sustainable competitive advantage for organizations. Based on the resource-based view of the firm, when companies possess resources that are rare, valuable, difficult to imitate, and non-substitutable, a sustained competitive advantage can be attained.[106] The SHRM approach assumes that human capital—the current and potential knowledge, skills, and abilities of employees—is instrumental to every organization's success and sustainability and longevity.

If a diverse composition of employees within organizations is rare, employing minorities in positions of leadership is even rarer. One exception is Northern Trust, an investment management firm that was recently listed on Forbes magazine's 2018 Best Employers for Diversity list.[107] Thirty-eight percent of Northern Trust's top executives are women, which is impressive because it matches the average percentage of women in full-time one-year MBA programs over the past five years.[108] The average for S&P 500 companies is just 27%. In addition, African Americans make up 23% of Northern Trust's board, which also demonstrates the commitment Northern Trust has to diversity. This rare degree of diversity helps Northern Trust become an employer of choice for minorities and women. In turn, attracting minority applicants increases the labor pool available to Northern Trust and increases its ability to find good talent.

Exhibit 5.7 Bank staff watching presentation The Disability Awareness Players present to the staff at Northern Trust. (Credit: JJ's List/ flickr/ Attribution 2.0 Generic (CC BY 2.0))

Diverse companies may capitalize on the multiple perspectives that employees from different backgrounds contribute to problem solving and idea generation. In group settings, members from collectivist cultures from Asia and South America, for example, engage with others on tasks differently than members from North America. Similarly, Asians, Blacks, and Hispanics usually act more collectively and engage more interdependently than Whites, who are generally more individualistic. More harmonious working interactions benefit group cohesion and team performance,[109] and employees can grasp better ways of doing things when there is a diverse population to learn from.

For a company to attain a sustained competitive advantage, its human resource practices must be difficult to copy or imitate. As we will see later in the chapter, companies may hold one of three perspectives on workplace diversity. The integration and learning perspective results in the best outcomes for employees and the organization. However, it is not easy to become an employer that can effectively manage diversity and avoid the challenges we learned about earlier in this chapter. Historical conditions and often-complex interplay between various organizational units over time can contribute to a company's ability to perform effectively as a diverse organization. Best practices for targeting diverse applicants or resolving conflicts based on cultural differences between employees may occur organically and later become codified into the organizational culture. Sometimes, however, the origin of diversity practices is unknown because they arose from cooperation among different functional areas (e.g., marketing and human resources working strategically with leadership to develop recruitment ideas) that occurred so long ago that not even the company itself, let alone other companies, could replicate the process.

Diversity and Organizational Performance

Research indicates that having diversity in an organization produces mixed results for its success. Some studies show a positive relationship, some show a negative relationship, and others show no relationship between diversity and performance. Some researchers believe that although findings regarding a direct relationship between diversity and success in the marketplace may be inconsistent, the relationship may be due to other variables not taken into account.

Taking the resource-based view perspective, Richard and colleagues demonstrated that racially diverse banking institutions focused on innovation experienced greater performance than did racially diverse banks with a low focus on innovation.[110] These findings suggest that for the potential of racial diversity to be fully realized, companies should properly manage the system flexibility, creativity, and problem-solving abilities used in an innovative strategy. Other studies show that when top management includes female leadership, firm performance improves when organizations are innovation driven.[111]

CONCEPT CHECK

1. What are the challenges and opportunities that diversity provides to companies?
2. What are the responsibilities of human resources regarding diversity?
3. Can diversity be a strategic advantage to organizations?

5.4 Challenges of Diversity

4. What is workplace discrimination, and how does it affect different social identity groups?

Although diversity has it benefits, there are also challenges that managers must face that can only be addressed with proper leadership. Some of the most common challenges observed in organizations and studied in research include lower organizational attachment and misunderstanding work diversity initiatives and programs.

Lower Organizational Attachment

Although diversity programs attract and retain women and minorities, they may have the opposite effect on other, nonminority employees. When diversity is not managed effectively, White and male employees can feel alienated from or targeted by the organization as diversity programs are put in place. A study that examined 151 work groups across three large organizations investigated whether the proportion of group membership based on race or sex affected the group members' absentee rates, psychological attachment to their work group, and turnover intentions,[112] three factors that play significant roles in an employee's attachment to their organization. Results showed a positive relationship between group heterogeneity and lower organizational attachment, higher turnover intentions, and greater frequency of absences for men and for White group members. In other words, as work group diversity increased, White employees and male employees felt less attached to the organization and were more likely to quit. Because heterogeneous groups improve creativity and judgement, managers should not avoid using them because they may be challenging to manage. Instead, employers need to make sure they understand the communication structure and decision-making styles of their work groups and seek feedback from employees to learn how dominant group members may adjust to diversity.

Legal Challenges and Diversity

The legal system is used to combat discrimination. Among the ways that we will cover here are reverse discrimination, workplace discrimination, harassment, age discrimination, disability discrimination, national origin discrimination, pregnancy discrimination, race/color discrimination, religious discrimination, sex-based discrimination and other forms of discrimination.

Reverse Discrimination

As research shows, workplace discrimination against women and racial or ethnic minorities is common. **Reverse discrimination** is a term that has been used to describe a situation in which dominant group members perceive that they are experiencing discrimination based on their race or sex. This type of discrimination is uncommon, but is usually claimed when the dominant group perceives that members of a protected (diverse) class of citizens are given preference in workplace or educational opportunities based not on their merit or talents, but on a prescribed preferential treatment awarded only on the basis of race or sex.

Research conducted in the 1990s shows that only six federal cases of reverse discrimination were upheld over a four-year period (1990–1994), and only 100 of the 3,000 cases for discrimination over that same four-year period were claims of reverse discrimination.[113] Interestingly, a recent poll administered by the Robert Wood Johnson Foundation and the Harvard T.H. Chan School of Public Health found that a little more than half of White Americans believe that White people face discrimination overall, and 19% believe they have experienced hiring discrimination due to the color of their skin.[114] This misperception stems in part from the recalibration of the labor force as it become more balanced due to increased equal employment opportunities for everyone. Members of dominant identity groups, Whites and men, perceive fewer opportunities for themselves when they observe the workforce becoming more diverse. In reality, the workforce of a majority of companies is still predominantly White and male employees. The only difference is that legislation protecting employees from discrimination and improvements in equal access to education have created opportunities for minority group members when before there were none.

Workplace Discrimination

Workplace discrimination occurs when an employee or an applicant is treated unfairly at work or in the job-hiring process due to an identity group, condition, or personal characteristic such as the ones mentioned above. Discrimination can occur through marital status, for example when a person experiences workplace discrimination because of the characteristics of a person to whom they are married. Discrimination can also occur when the offender is of the same protected status of the victim, for example when someone discriminates against someone based on a national origin that they both share.

The **Equal Employment Opportunity Commission** (EEOC) was created by Title VII of the Civil Rights Act of 1964 with the primary goal of making it illegal to discriminate against someone in the workplace due to their race, national origin, sex, disability, religion, or pregnancy status.[115] The EEOC enforces laws and issues guidelines for employment-related treatment. It also has the authority to investigate charges of workplace discrimination, attempt to settle the charges, and, if necessary, file lawsuits when the law has been broken.

All types of workplace discrimination are prohibited under different laws enacted and enforced by the EEOC, which also considers workplace harassment and sexual harassment forms of workplace discrimination and mandates that men and women must be given the same pay for equal work.[116]

The provision for equal pay is covered under the **Equal Pay Act of 1963**, which was an amendment to the Fair Labor Standards Act of 1938. Virtually all employers are subject to the provisions of the act, which was an attempt to address pay inequities between men and women. More than 50 years later, however, women still earn about 80 cents to every dollar that men earn, even while performing the same or similar jobs.[117]

Harassment

Harassment is any unwelcome conduct that is based on characteristics such as age, race, national origin, disability, sex, or pregnancy status. Harassment is a form of workplace discrimination that violates Title VII of the Civil Rights Act of 1964, the Age Discrimination in Employment Act of 1967, and the Americans with Disabilities Act of 1990.[118]

Sexual harassment specifically refers to harassment based on a person's sex, and it can (but does not have to) include unwanted sexual advances, requests for sexual favors, or physical and verbal acts of a sexual nature. Though members of any sex can be the victim of sexual harassment, women are the primary targets of this type of harassment.[119]

Age Discrimination

Age discrimination consists of treating an employee or applicant less favorably due to their age. The **Age Discrimination in Employment Act (ADEA)** forbids discrimination against individuals who are age 40 and above. The act prohibits harassment because of age, which can include offensive or derogatory remarks that create a hostile work environment.[120]

Disability Discrimination

A person with a disability is a person who has a physical or mental impairment that limits one or more of the person's life actions. **Disability discrimination** occurs when an employee or applicant who is covered by the **Americans with Disabilities Act (ADA)** is treated unfavorably due to their physical or mental disability. The ADA is a civil rights law that prohibits discrimination in employment, public services, public accommodations, and telecommunications against people with disabilities.[121] To be covered under the ADA, individuals must be able to perform the essential functions of their job with or without reasonable accommodations. Research has shown that reasonable accommodations are typically of no or low cost (less than $100) to employers.[122]

National Origin Discrimination

National origin discrimination involves treating someone unfavorably because of their country of origin, accent, ethnicity, or appearance. EEOC regulations make it illegal to implement an employment practice or policy that applies to everyone if it has a negative impact on people of a certain national origin. For example, employers cannot institute an "English-only" language policy unless speaking English at all times is essential to ensure the safe and efficient operation of the business. Employers also cannot mandate employees be fluent in English unless fluency in English is essential to satisfactory job performance. The EEOC also prohibits businesses from hiring only U.S. citizens or lawful residents unless the business is required by law to do so.[123]

Pregnancy Discrimination

Pregnancy discrimination involves treating an employee or applicant unfairly because of pregnancy status, childbirth, or medical conditions related to pregnancy or childbirth. The **Pregnancy Discrimination Act (PDA)** prohibits any discrimination as it relates to pregnancy in any of the following areas: hiring, firing, compensation, training, job assignment, insurance, or any other employment conditions. Further, certain conditions that result from pregnancy may be protected under the ADA, which means employers may need to make reasonable accommodations for any employee with disabilities related to pregnancy.

Under the **Family and Medical Leave Act (FMLA)**, new parents, including adoptive and foster parents, may be eligible for 12 weeks of unpaid leave (or paid leave only if earned by the employee) to care for the new child. Also, nursing mothers have the right to express milk on workplace premises.[124]

Race/Color Discrimination

Race/color discrimination involves treating employees or applicants unfairly because of their race or because of physical characteristics typically associated with race such as skin color, hair color, hair texture, or certain facial features.

As with national origin discrimination, certain workplace policies that apply to all employees may be unlawful if they unfairly disadvantage employees of a certain race. Policies that specify that certain hairstyles must or must not be worn, for example, may unfairly impact African American employees, and such policies are prohibited unless their enforcement is necessary to the operations of the business.[125]

Religious Discrimination

Religious discrimination occurs when employees or applicants are treated unfairly because of their religious beliefs. The laws protect those who belong to traditional organized religions and those who do not belong to organized religions but hold strong religious, ethical, or moral beliefs of some kind. Employers must make reasonable accommodations for employees' religious beliefs, which may include flexible scheduling or modifications to workplace practices. Employees are also permitted accommodation when it comes to religious dress and grooming practices, unless such accommodations will place an undue burden on the employer. Employees are also protected from having to participate (or not participate) in certain religious practices as terms of their employment.[126]

Sex-Based Discrimination

Sex-based discrimination occurs when employees or applicants are treated unfairly because of their sex. This form of discrimination includes unfair treatment due to gender, transgender status, and sexual orientation. Harassment and policies that unfairly impact certain groups protected under sex discrimination laws are prohibited under EEOC legislation.[127]

The key diversity-related federal laws are summarized in **Table 5.2**.

Key Diversity Related Legislation	
Title VII of the Civil Rights Act of 1964	Created the Equal Employment Opportunity Commission with the primary role of making it illegal to discriminate against someone in the workplace due to their race, national origin, sex, disability, religion, or pregnancy status.
Equal Pay Act of 1963	Mandates that men and women must be given the same pay for equal work
Age Discrimination in Employment Act (ADEA)	Forbids discrimination against individuals who are age 40 and above.
Americans with Disabilities Act (ADA)	Prohibits discrimination against people with disabilities in employment, public services, public accommodations, and in telecommunications
Pregnancy Discrimination Act (PDA)	Prohibits any discrimination as it relates to pregnancy, including hiring, firing, compensation, training, job assignment, insurance, or any other employment conditions.
Family and Medical Leave Act (FMLA)	Grants new parents up to 12 weeks of paid or unpaid leave to care for the new child, and gives nursing mothers the right to express milk on workplace premises.

Table 5.2 (Attribution: Copyright Rice University, OpenStax, under CC-BY 4.0 license)

Other Types of Discrimination

Beyond the key types of discrimination outlined by the EEOC, diversity and management scholars have identified other types of discrimination that frequently impact certain identity groups more than others. **Access discrimination** is a catchall term that describes when people are denied employment opportunities because of their identity group or personal characteristics such as sex, race, age, or other factors. **Treatment discrimination** describes a situation in which people are employed but are treated differently while employed, mainly by receiving different and unequal job-related opportunities or rewards.[128] Scholars have also identified a form of discrimination called **interpersonal** or **covert discrimination** that involves discrimination that manifests itself in ways that are not visible or readily identifiable, yet is serious because it can impact interpersonal interactions between employees, employees and customers, and other important workplace relationships.

This type of discrimination poses unique challenges because it is difficult to identify. For example, one study examining customer service and discrimination found that obese customers were more likely to experience interpersonal discrimination than average-weight customers. Salespersons spent less time interacting with obese customers than average-weight customers, and average-weight customers reported more positive interactions with salespeople when asked about standard customer service metrics such as being smiled at, receiving eye contact, and perceived friendliness.[129]

CONCEPT CHECK 

1. What is the role of the EEOC?
2. What are the types of discrimination encountered in the workplace?

5.5 Key Diversity Theories

5. What key theories help managers understand the benefits and challenges of managing the diverse workforce?

Many theories relevant to managing the diverse workforce center on an individual's reactions (such as categorization and assessment of the characteristics of others) to people who are different from the individual. Competing viewpoints attempt to explain how diversity is either harmful or beneficial to organizational outcomes.

- The **cognitive diversity hypothesis** suggests that multiple perspectives stemming from the cultural differences between group or organizational members result in creative problem solving and innovation.
- The **similarity-attraction paradigm** and **social identity theory** hold that individuals' preferences for interacting with others like themselves can result in diversity having a negative effect on group and organizational outcomes.
- The **justification-suppression model** explains under what conditions individuals act on their prejudices.

Cognitive Diversity Hypothesis

Some research shows that diversity has no relationship to group performance, and some shows that there is a relationship. Of the latter research, some shows a negative relationship (greater diversity means poorer group performance, less diversity means better group performance) and some shows a positive relationship.

These various findings may be due to the difference in how diversity can affect group members. **Cognitive diversity** refers to differences between team members in characteristics such as expertise, experiences, and perspectives.[130] Many researchers contend that physical diversity characteristics such as race, age, or sex (also known as bio-demographic diversity) positively influence performance because team members contribute unique cognitive attributes based on their experiences stemming from their demographic background.[131]

There is research that supports the relationship between group performance and task-related diversity as reflected in characteristics not readily detectable such as ability, occupational expertise, or education. However, the relationship between bio-demographic diversity and group performance has produced mixed results.[132] For example, Watson and colleagues studied the comparison of group performance between culturally homogeneous and culturally heterogeneous groups. Groups were assigned business cases to analyze, and their group performance was measured over time based on four factors: the range of perspectives generated, the number of problems identified in the case, the number of alternatives produced, and the quality of the solution. Overall performance was also calculated as the average of all the factors. The factors were measured at four intervals: Interval 1 (at 5 weeks), Interval 2 (at 9 weeks), Interval 3 (at 13 weeks), and Interval 4 (at 17 weeks).

For Intervals 1 and 2, the overall performance of homogeneous groups was higher than heterogeneous groups. However, by Intervals 3 and 4, there were no significant differences in overall performance between the groups, but the heterogeneous group outperformed the homogeneous group in generating a greater range of perspectives and producing a greater number of alternatives.

This research suggests that although homogeneous groups may initially outperform culturally diverse groups, over time diverse groups benefit from a wider range of ideas to choose from when solving a problem. Based on the cognitive diversity hypothesis, these benefits stem from the multiple perspectives generated by the cultural diversity of group members. On the other hand, it takes time for members of diverse groups to work together effectively due to their unfamiliarity with one another, which explains why homogeneous groups outperform heterogeneous groups in the early stages of group functioning. (This is related to the similarity-attraction paradigm, discussed in the next section.) Other studies have shown that ethnically diverse groups cooperate better than homogeneous groups at tasks that require decision-making and are more creative and innovative. While homogeneous groups may be more efficient, heterogeneous groups sacrifice efficiency for effectiveness in other areas.

Similarity-Attraction Paradigm

The cognitive diversity hypothesis explains how diversity benefits organizational outcomes. The similarity-attraction paradigm explains how diversity can have negative outcomes for an organization.

Some research has shown that members who belong to diverse work units may become less attached, are absent from work more often, and are more likely to quit.[133] There is also evidence that diversity may produce conflict and higher employee turnover. Similarity-attraction theory is one of the foundational theories that attempts to explain why this occurs; it posits that individuals are attracted to others with whom they share attitude similarity.[134]

Attitudes and beliefs are common antecedents to interpersonal attraction. However, other traits such as race, age, sex, and socioeconomic status can serve as signals to reveal deep-level traits about ourselves. For example, numerous studies investigating job-seeker behaviors have shown that individuals are more attracted to companies whose recruitment literature includes statements and images that reflect their own identity group. One study showed that companies perceived to value diversity based on their recruitment literature are more attractive to racial minorities and women compared to Whites.[135] Another study showed that when organizations use recruitment materials that target sexual minorities, the attraction of study participants weakened among heterosexuals.[136] Even foreign-born potential job candidates are more attracted to organizations that depict international employees in their job ads.[137]

Social Cognitive Theory

Social cognitive theory is another theory that seeks to explain how diversity can result in negative outcomes in a group or organization. Social cognitive theory suggests that people use categorization to simplify and cope with large amounts of information. These categories allow us to quickly and easily compartmentalize data, and people are often categorized by their visible characteristics, such as race, sex, and age. Thus, when someone sees a person of a particular race, automatic processing occurs and beliefs about this particular race are activated. Even when the person is not visible, he or she can be subject to this automatic categorization. For example, when sorting through resumes a hiring manager might engage in sex categorization because the person's name provides information about the person's sex or racial categorization because the person's name provides information about their race.[138] **Stereotypes** are related to this categorization, and refer to the overgeneralization of characteristics about large groups. Stereotypes are the basis for prejudice and discrimination. In a job-related context, using categorization and stereotyping in employment decision-making is often illegal. Whether illegal or not, this approach is inconsistent with a valuing-diversity approach.

Social Identity Theory

Social identity theory is another explanation of why diversity may have a negative outcome. Social identity theory suggests that when we first come into contact with others, we categorize them as belonging to an in-group (i.e., the same group as us) or an out-group (not belonging to our group).[139] We tend to see members of our in-group as heterogeneous but out-group members as homogeneous. That is, we perceive out-group members as having similar attitudes, behaviors, and characteristics (i.e., fitting stereotypes).

Researchers posit that this perspective may occur because of the breadth of interactions we have with people from our in-group as opposed to out-groups. There is often strong in-group favoritism and, sometimes, derogation of out-group members. In some cases, however, minority group members do not favor members of their own group.[140] This may happen because of being continually exposed to widespread beliefs about the positive attributes of Whites or men and to common negative beliefs about some minorities and women. When in-group favoritism does occur, majority-group members will be hired, promoted, and rewarded at the expense of minority-group members, often in violation of various laws.

Schema Theory

Schema theory explains how individuals encode information about others based on their demographic characteristics.[141] Units of information and knowledge experienced by individuals are stored as having patterns and interrelationships, thus creating schemas that can be used to evaluate one's self or others. As a result of the prior perceived knowledge or beliefs embodied in such schemas, individuals categorize people, events, and objects. They then use these categories to evaluate newly encountered people and make decisions regarding their interaction with them.

Based on schema theory, employees develop schemas about coworkers based on race, gender, and other diversity traits. They also form schemas about organizational policies, leadership, and work climates. Schemas formed can be positive or negative and will affect the attitudes and behaviors employees have toward one another.

Justification-Suppression Model

The **justification-suppression model** explains the circumstances in which prejudiced people might act on their prejudices. The process by which people experience their prejudice is characterized as a "two-step" process in which people are prejudiced against a certain group or individual but experience conflicting emotions in regard to that prejudice and are motivated to suppress their prejudice rather than act upon it.[142] Theory about prejudice suggests that all people have prejudices of some sort, that they learn their prejudices from an early age, and that they have a hard time departing from them as they grow older. Prejudices are often reinforced by intimate others, and individuals use different methods to justify those prejudices.

Most people will attempt to suppress any outward manifestations of their prejudices. This suppression can come from internal factors like empathy, compassion, or personal beliefs regarding proper treatment of others. Suppression can also come from societal pressures; overt displays of prejudice are no longer socially acceptable, and in some cases are illegal.

At times, however, prejudiced individuals will look for reasons to justify acting on their prejudiced beliefs. Research has shown people are more likely to act in prejudiced ways when they are physically or emotionally tired, when they can do so and remain anonymous, or when social norms are weak enough that their prejudiced behavior will not be received negatively.

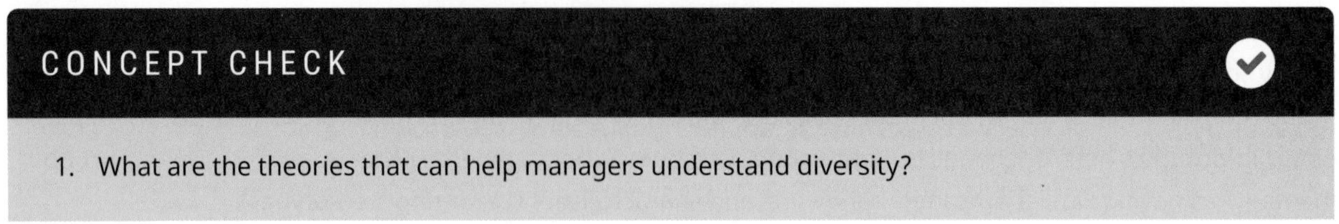

1. What are the theories that can help managers understand diversity?

5.6 Benefits and Challenges of Workplace Diversity

6. How can managers reap benefits from diversity and mitigate its challenges?

Much theoretical work has espoused the benefits of workplace diversity, but empirical studies have often had conflicting results, which have shown researchers that certain conditions can affect how successful initiatives to increase and enhance workplace diversity are. Managers can work to make sure that the efforts and initiatives they enact to increase diversity in the workplace come from a perspective that ensures and strives for equity and fairness, and not simply from the perspective of only benefitting the company's bottom line. By approaching diversity and diversity issues in a thoughtful, purposeful way, managers can mitigate the challenges posed by a diverse workforce and enhance the benefits a diverse workforce can offer.

Three Perspectives on Workplace Diversity

Ely and Thomas's work on cultural diversity was designed to theoretically and empirically support some of the hypothesized relationships between diversity and workplace outcomes. Their research yielded a paradigm that identifies three perspectives regarding workplace diversity:[143] integration and learning, access and legitimacy, and discrimination and fairness.

The Integration-and-Learning Perspective

The **integration-and-learning perspective** posits that the different life experiences, skills, and perspectives that members of diverse cultural identity groups possess can be a valuable resource in the context of work groups. Under this perspective, the members of a culturally diverse workgroup can use their collective differences to think critically about work issues, strategies, products, and practices in a way that will allow the group to be successful in its business operations. The assumption under this perspective is that members of different cultural identity groups can learn from each other and work together to best achieve shared goals. This perspective values cultural identity and strongly links diversity of the group to the success of the firm.

Downfalls of the integration-and-learning perspective can be that White members of the work group can feel marginalized when they are not asked to join in on diversity-related projects or discussions. Similarly, workforce members of color might experience burnout if they are always expected to work on those projects and discussions that specifically deal with diversity issues.

The Access-and-Legitimacy Perspective

The **access-and-legitimacy perspective** focuses on the benefit that a diverse workforce can bring to a business that wishes to operate within a diverse set of markets or with culturally diverse clients. Work groups that operate under this perspective are doing so in order to gain access to diverse markets and because their diversity affords them some level of legitimacy when attempting to gain access to diverse markets. This type of workplace diversity is more of a functional type of diversity that does not attempt to integrate or value diversity at the business's core. The danger of this diversity perspective is that it can limit the roles of certain minority groups by valuing members of these groups only because they can increase the access to diverse markets and clients and not because they can make other potentially valuable contributions.[144]

The Discrimination-and-Fairness Perspective

The **discrimination-and-fairness perspective** stems from a belief that a culturally diverse workforce is a moral duty that must be maintained in order to create a just and fair society. This perspective is characterized by a commitment to equal opportunities in hiring and promotions, and does not directly link a work group's productivity or success with diversity. Many times firms operating under this perspective will have a spoken or unspoken assumption that assimilation into the dominant (White) culture should take place by the members of other cultural identity groups. One drawback of this perspective is that because it measures progress by the recruitment and retention of diverse people, employees of traditionally underrepresented groups can feel devalued. Often, assimilation is pushed on diverse employees under the guise of reducing conflict or in an effort to demonstrate that differences between cultural identity groups are unimportant.[145]

Exhibit 5.8 shows the degrees of effectiveness and benefits for each perspective.

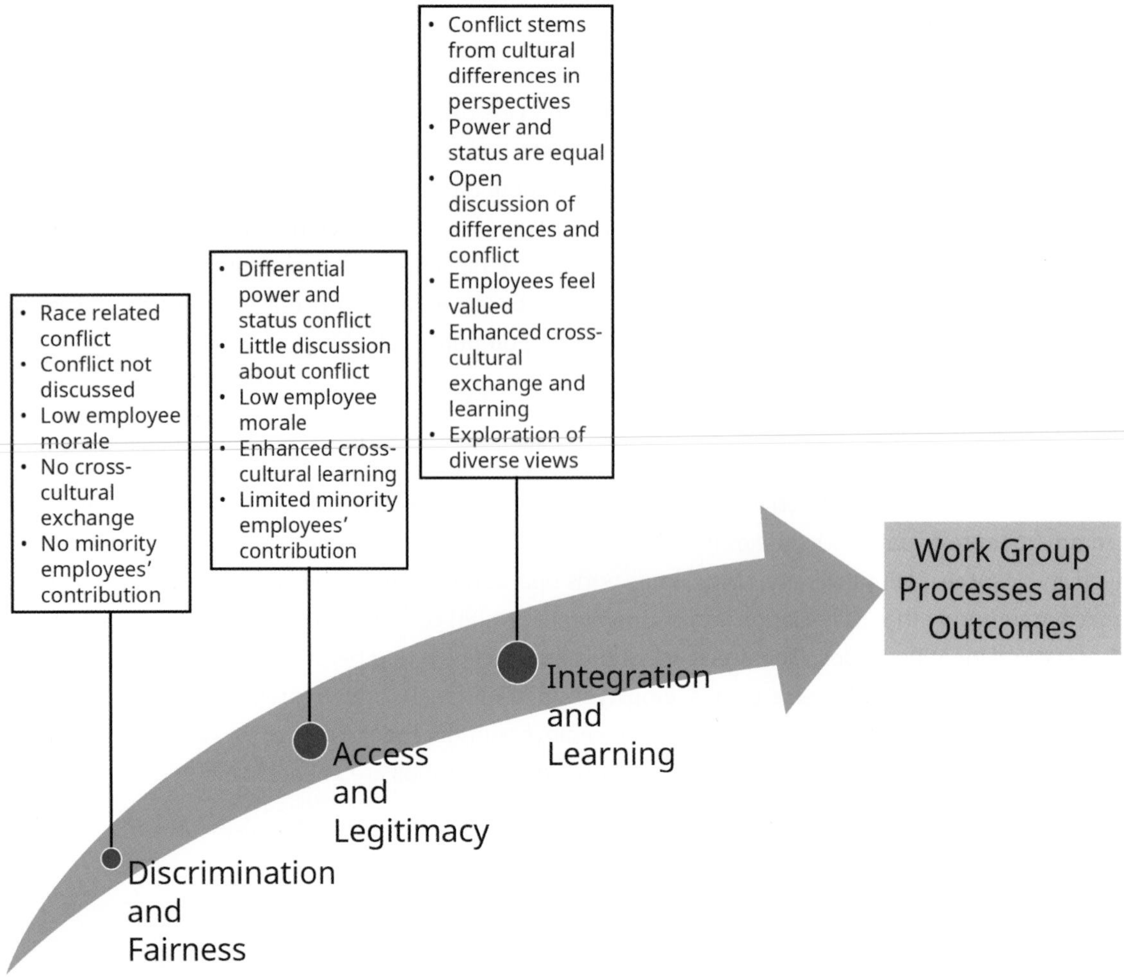

- Race related conflict
- Conflict not discussed
- Low employee morale
- No cross-cultural exchange
- No minority employees' contribution

Discrimination and Fairness

- Differential power and status conflict
- Little discussion about conflict
- Low employee morale
- Enhanced cross-cultural learning
- Limited minority employees' contribution

Access and Legitimacy

- Conflict stems from cultural differences in perspectives
- Power and status are equal
- Open discussion of differences and conflict
- Employees feel valued
- Enhanced cross-cultural exchange and learning
- Exploration of diverse views

Integration and Learning

Work Group Processes and Outcomes

Exhibit 5.8 Cultural Diversity Perspectives at Work Source: Adapted from Ely, Robin J., and David A. Thomas. "Cultural diversity at work: The effects of diversity perspectives on work group processes and outcomes." Administrative science quarterly. 46.2 (2001): 229-273.

CONCEPT CHECK 

1. How can managers reap the benefits of diversity?
2. How can managers mitigate the challenges of diversity?
3. What is the access-and-legitimacy perspective? Differentiate it from the discrimination-and-fairness perspective.

5.7 Recommendations for Managing Diversity

7. What can organizations do to ensure applicants, employees, and customers from all backgrounds are valued?

Organizations that are committed to equality and inclusion must take steps to combat the examples of discrimination and harassment that have been covered in this chapter. And they must take steps to make diversity a goal in the pre-employment stages as well as in the post-employment stages. Anyone with managerial or supervisory responsibilities should pay careful attention to hiring and performance-rewarding practices, and make sure to rely on relevant information for making decisions and ignore race-based stereotypes. The following are examples of what leaders and organizations can do make sure employees feel valued.

Interview Selection Process

To ensure fairness for all applicants, organizations should use **highly structured interviews** during the selection process to avoid bias based on race or gender.[146] Highly structured interviews consists of the following 15 characteristics: "(1) job analysis, (2) same questions, (3) limited prompting, (4) better questions, (5) longer interviews, (6) control of ancillary information, (7) limited questions from candidates, (8) multiple rating scales, (9) anchored rating scales, (10) detailed notes, (11) multiple interviewers, (12) consistent interviewers, (13) no discussion between interviews, (14) training, and (15) statistical prediction."[147] Similarity bias can occur when interviewers prefer interviewees with whom they share similar traits. Organizations can mitigate this challenge if all 15 characteristics of a structured interview are used consistently with each job applicant.

Diversified Mentoring Relationships

Thanks to the rapid growth of international travel and globalization, managers are often called upon to manage a workforce that is increasingly diverse. Research has shown that racially and ethnically diverse firms have better financial performance than more homogeneous firms, because, as mentioned, employees from different backgrounds and with different experiences can give the firm a competitive advantage in various ways. It is necessary, however, that managers and those in positions of power are adequately equipped to manage diverse workforces in ways that are beneficial to all. **Diversified mentoring relationships** are relationships in which the mentor and the mentee differ in terms of their status within the company and within larger society. The differences could be in terms of race, gender, class, disability, sexual orientation, or other status. Research has found that these types of relationships are mutually beneficial and that the mentor and the mentee both have positive outcomes in terms of knowledge, empathy, and skills related to interactions with people from different power groups.[148]

MANAGERIAL LEADERSHIP

Diversity Training Programs

As the workforce becomes increasingly more diverse, managers will face a major challenge in understanding how to manage diversity. One of many decisions to be made is whether an organization should offer diversity training and, if so, what topics and issues should be addressed based on the organizational goals.

There has been a debate over the effectiveness of corporate diversity training since the Civil Rights Act of 1964 helped prompt corporate diversity training with the organizational goal of simply being compliant with the law. Prior research shows that it can be effective, ineffective, or even detrimental for employees, but as diversity training has evolved through the years, it has become an important factor in helping employers manage diversity.

In the 1980s through the late 1990s, diversity training evolved from focusing solely on compliance to addressing the needs of women and minorities as they entered the workforce at a faster rate. Unfortunately, this type of training was perceived by Whites and men as singling them out as the problem; sometimes such training was even formatted as "confession" sessions for White employees to express their complicity in institutional racism. Not unexpectedly, this type of training would often backfire and would further separate employees from each other, the exact opposite of its intention.

Recently, diversity training has evolved to focus on (1) building cultural competencies regarding fellow employees, (2) valuing differences, and (3) learning how diversity helps make better business decisions. This perspective toward diversity training is more effective than simply focusing on causes of a lack of diversity and the historical roots of discrimination. Understanding how to comply with the law is still important, but training has a greater effect when the other factors are also included.

A recent study investigated various diversity-training methods, including having participants engage in activities on perspective taking and goal setting. For perspective-taking activities, participants were asked to write a few sentences about the challenges they believed minority group members might experience. Goal-setting activities involved writing specific and measurable goals related to workplace diversity such as crafting future policies or engaging in future behaviors. Researchers found that when these activities were used as a diversity-training method, pro-diversity attitudes and behavioral intentions persisted months later.

Issues regarding employee sexual orientation have also been introduced into corporate diversity training in recent years. Because employees' religious beliefs are protected by Title VII of the Civil Rights Act, employers should be sensitive to balancing the rights of lesbian, gay, and bisexual employees and employees' religious rights. Attempting to protect the rights of one group and not be perceived to disrespect another is a difficult situation for managers. In order to mitigate any backlash from some employees, employers should seek feedback from all groups to learn the best ways to accommodate them, and should assess the organizational climate. Additionally, managers should explain how diversity based on sexual orientation aligns with the company's strategic objectives and explain the company's legal position with supportive reasoning. Lastly, based on their organizational climate and how it reshapes itself over time, some companies may wish to address diversity training on sexual orientation in a voluntary training separate from other diversity issues.

Sources: Young, Cheri A., Badiah Haffejee, and David L. Corsun. "Developing Cultural Intelligence and Empathy Through Diversified Mentoring Relationships." *Journal of Management Education* (2017): 1052562917710687; Bezrukova, K., Jehn, K.A., & Spell, C.S. (2012). Reviewing diversity training: Where we have been and where we should go. *Academy of Management Learning & Education*, 11 (2): 207-227; Anand, R., & Winters, M. (2008). A retrospective view of corporate diversity training from 1964 to the present. *Academy of Management Learning & Education*, 7 (3): 356-372; Lindsey, A., King, E., Membere, A., & Cheung, H.K. (July 28, 2017). Two types of diversity training that really work. *Harvard Business Review*.

Discussion Questions

1. Why do you believe diversity training is resisted by some employees?
2. Do you believe there will always be a need for workplace diversity training?
3. How would you determine what types of diversity training are needed at your company?

Visible Leadership

Another key to ensure that employees are treated fairly is utilizing appropriate leadership strategies.[149] Leadership must sincerely value variety of opinions, and organizational culture must encourage openness and make workers feel valued. Organizations must also have a well-articulated and widely understood mission and a relatively egalitarian, nonbureaucratic structure. Having such a work environment will ensure that the attitudes and values of employees are aligned with those of the organization. In this way culture serves as a control mechanism for shaping behaviors.

Strategies for Employees

Individuals can increase positive employment outcomes by obtaining high levels of education, because for all groups education is a predictor of employment and increased earnings. Individuals can also seek employment in larger firms, which are more likely to have formal hiring programs and specific diversity provisions in place. Individuals of any race or ethnic background can also take steps to eliminate discrimination by being aware of their own personal stereotypes or biases and taking steps to challenge and address them.

CONCEPT CHECK

1. How can managers ensure fairness in the interviewing and selection process regarding diversity?
2. What is the role of leadership regarding diversity?

Key Terms

access discrimination A catchall term that describes when people are denied employment opportunities because of their identity group or personal characteristics such as sex, race, or age.

access-and-legitimacy perspective Focuses on the benefits that a diverse workforce can bring to a business that wishes to operate within a diverse set of markets or with culturally diverse clients.

age discrimination Treating an employee or applicant less favorably due to their age.

Age Discrimination in Employment Act (ADEA) Forbids discrimination against individuals who are age 40 and above, including offensive or derogatory remarks that create a hostile work environment.

Americans with Disabilities Act (ADA) Prohibits discrimination in employment, public services, public accommodations, and telecommunications against people with disabilities.

cognitive diversity Differences between team members regarding characteristics such as expertise, experiences, and perspectives.

cognitive diversity hypothesis Multiple perspectives stemming from the cultural differences between group or organizational members result in creative problem-solving and innovation.

covert discrimination (interpersonal) An interpersonal form of discrimination that manifests in ways that are not visible or readily identifiable.

deep-level diversity Diversity in characteristics that are nonobservable such as attitudes, values, and beliefs, such as religion.

disability discrimination Occurs when an employee or applicant is treated unfavorably due to their physical or mental disability.

discrimination-and-fairness perspective A culturally diverse workforce is a moral duty that must be maintained in order to create a just and fair society.

diversified mentoring relationships Relationships in which the mentor and the mentee differ in terms of their status within the company and within larger society.

diversity Identity-based differences among and between people that affect their lives as applicants, employees, and customers.

Equal Employment Opportunity Commission An organization that enforces laws and issues guidelines for employment-related treatment according to Title VII of the Civil Rights Act of 1964.

Equal Pay Act of 1963 An amendment to the Fair Labor Standards Act of 1938.

Family and Medical Leave Act (FMLA) Provides new parents, including adoptive and foster parents, with 12 weeks of unpaid leave (or paid leave only if earned by the employee) to care for the new child and requires that nursing mothers have the right to express milk on workplace premises.

glass ceiling An invisible barrier based on the prejudicial beliefs of organizational decision makers that prevents women from moving beyond certain levels within a company.

groupthink A dysfunction in decision-making that is common in homogeneous groups due to group pressures and group members' desire for conformity and consensus.

harassment Any unwelcome conduct that is based on characteristics such as age, race, national origin, disability, sex, or pregnancy status.

hidden diversity Differences in traits that are deep-level and may be concealed or revealed at discretion by individuals who possess them.

highly structured interviews Interviews that are be structured objectively to remove bias from the selection process.

identity group A collective of individuals who share the same demographic characteristics such as race, sex, or age.

inclusion The degree to which employees are accepted and treated fairly by their organization.

integration-and-learning perspective Posits that the different life experiences, skills, and perspectives that members of diverse cultural identity groups possess can be a valuable resource in the context of work groups.

invisible social identities Membership in an identity group based on hidden diversity traits such as sexual orientation or a nonobservable disability that may be concealed or revealed.

justification-suppression model Explains the circumstances in which prejudiced people might act on their prejudices.

justification-suppression model Explains under what conditions individuals act on their prejudices.

managing diversity Ways in which organizations seek to ensure that members of diverse groups are valued and treated fairly within organizations.

model minority myth A stereotype that portrays Asian men and women as obedient and successful and is often used to justify socioeconomic disparities between other racial minority groups.

national origin discrimination Treating someone unfavorably because of their country of origin, accent, ethnicity, or appearance.

passing The decision to not disclose one's invisible social identity.

pregnancy discrimination Treating an employee or applicant unfairly because of pregnancy status, childbirth, or medical conditions related to pregnancy or childbirth.

Pregnancy Discrimination Act (PDA) Prohibits any discrimination as it relates to pregnancy in hiring, firing, compensation, training, job assignment, insurance, or any other employment conditions.

race/color discrimination Treating employees or applicants unfairly because of their race or because of physical characteristics typically associated with race such as skin color, hair color, hair texture, or certain facial features.

religious discrimination When employees or applicants are treated unfairly because of their religious beliefs.

resource-based view Demonstrates how a diverse workforce can create a sustainable competitive advantage for organizations.

revealing The decision to disclose one's invisible social identity.

reverse discrimination Describes a situation in which dominant group members perceive that they are experiencing discrimination based on their race or sex.

schema theory Explains how individuals encode information about others based on their demographic characteristics.

sex-based discrimination When employees or applicants are treated unfairly because of their sex, including unfair treatment due to gender, transgender status, or sexual orientation.

sexual harassment Harassment based on a person's sex, and can (but does not have to) include unwanted sexual advances, requests for sexual favors, or physical and verbal acts of a sexual nature.

sexual harassment Harassment based on a person's sex; it can (but does not have to) include unwanted sexual advances, requests for sexual favors, or physical and verbal acts of a sexual nature.

similarity-attraction paradigm Individuals' preferences for interacting with others like themselves can result in diversity having a negative effect on group and organizational outcomes.

social identity theory Self-concept based on an individual's physical, social, and mental characteristics.

stereotypes Overgeneralization of characteristics about groups that are the basis for prejudice and discrimination.

strategic human resources management (SHRM) System of activities arranged to engage employees in a manner that assists the organization in achieving a sustainable competitive advantage.

surface-level diversity Diversity in the form of characteristics of individuals that are readily visible, including, but not limited to, age, body size, visible disabilities, race, or sex.

treatment discrimination A situation in which people are employed but are treated differently while employed, mainly by receiving different and unequal job-related opportunities or rewards.

work visa A temporary documented status that authorizes individuals from other countries to permanently or temporarily live and work in the United States.

workplace discrimination Unfair treatment in the job hiring process or at work that is based on the identity group, physical or mental condition, or personal characteristic of an applicant or employee.

Summary of Learning Outcomes

5.1 An Introduction to Workplace Diversity

1. What is diversity?

Diversity refers to identity-based differences among and between people that affect their lives as applicants, employees, and customers. Surface-level diversity represents characteristics of individuals that are readily visible, including, but not limited to, age, body size, visible disabilities, race, or sex. Deep-level diversity includes traits that are nonobservable such as attitudes, values, and beliefs. Finally, hidden diversity includes traits that are deep-level but may be concealed or revealed at the discretion of individuals who possess them.

5.2 Diversity and the Workforce

2. How diverse is the workforce?

In analyzing the diversity of the workforce, several measures can be used. Demographic measures such as gender and race can be used to measure group sizes. Measures of such things as discrimination toward specific groups can be analyzed to gauge the diversity of the workforce. Other measures of diversity in the workforce can include examination of differences in age and sexual orientation.

5.3 Diversity and Its Impact on Companies

3. How does diversity impact companies and the workforce?

The demography of the labor force is changing in many ways as it becomes racially diverse and older and includes more women and individuals with disabilities. Diversity affects how organizations understand that employing people who hold multiple perspectives increases the need to mitigate conflict between workers from different identity groups, enhances creativity and problem solving in teams, and serves as a resource to create a competitive advantage for the organization.

5.4 Challenges of Diversity

4. What is workplace discrimination, and how does it affect different social identity groups?

Workplace discrimination occurs when an employee or an applicant is treated unfairly at work or in the job-hiring process due to an identity group, condition, or personal characteristic such as age, race, national origin, sex, disability, religion, or pregnancy status. The Equal Employment Opportunity Commission enforces laws and legislation related to individuals with those protected statuses.

Harassment is any unwelcome conduct that is based on the protected characteristics listed above. Sexual harassment refers specifically to harassment based on a person’s sex, and it can (but does not have to) include unwanted sexual advances, requests for sexual favors, or physical and verbal acts of a sexual nature.

5.5 Key Diversity Theories

5. What key theories help managers understand the benefits and challenges of managing the diverse workforce?

The cognitive-diversity hypothesis suggests that multiple perspectives stemming from the cultural differences between groups or organizational members result in creative problem solving and innovation. The similarity-attraction paradigm and social identity theory explain how, because individuals prefer to interact with others like themselves, diversity may have a negative effect on group and organizational outcomes. The justification-suppression model explains under what conditions individuals act on their prejudice.

5.6 Benefits and Challenges of Workplace Diversity

6. How can managers reap benefits from diversity and mitigate its challenges?

By approaching diversity and diversity issues in a thoughtful, purposeful way, managers can mitigate the challenges posed by a diverse workforce and enhance the benefits a diverse workforce can offer.

Managers can work to make sure that the efforts and initiatives they enact to increase diversity in the workplace come from a perspective that ensures and strives for equity and fairness, not simply one that will benefit the company's bottom line.

Using an integration-and-learning perspective strongly links diversity to the work and success of the firm by viewing cultural identity, different life experiences, skills, and perspectives from members of diverse cultural identity groups as a valuable resource.

5.7 Recommendations for Managing Diversity

7. What can organizations do to ensure applicants, employees, and customers from all backgrounds are valued?

Organizations should use objective and fair recruitment and selection tools and policies.

Leadership should make employees feel valued, be open to varied perspectives, and encourage a culture of open dialogue. Women and racial minorities can increase positive employment outcomes by pursuing higher levels of education and seeking employment in larger organizations. All individuals should be willing to listen, empathize with others, and seek to better understand sensitive issues that affect different identity groups.

Chapter Review Questions

1. Define the three types of diversity and compare them using examples for each type.
2. How are demographics of the workforce changing?
3. What are some major challenges that women face in organizations?
4. What is the model minority myth? How does it compare to how Blacks and Hispanics are stereotyped?
5. What are some benefits of hiring older workers?
6. Why would an employee "pass" or "reveal" at work? What are the positive and negative consequences of doing so?
7. Explain the six benefits of workplace diversity described by Cox and Blake's business case for diversity.
8. Compare how the cognitive diversity hypothesis and the similarity-attraction paradigm relate to diversity outcomes.
9. Based on the justification-suppression model, explain why individuals act on their prejudicial beliefs.
10. Describe challenges that managers must face when managing diversity.
11. How can employees ensure they are compliant with the laws and legislation enforced by the EEOC?
12. What are some recommendations for managing diversity?

Management Skills Application Exercises

1. Do you agree that diversity can be a source of greater benefit than harm to organizations? Why or why not?
2. Have you ever worked in a diverse team setting before? If so, did you encounter any attitudes or behaviors that could potentially cause conflict? If not, how would you manage conflict stemming from diversity?
3. List three organizational goals you would implement to create an organizational culture of diversity and inclusion.
4. Have you or has someone you know experienced discrimination? How did that affect you or that person emotionally, physically, or financially?
5. Pick an identity group (e.g., gay, Black, or woman) other than your own. Imagine and list the negative experiences and interactions you believe you might encounter at work. What policies or strategies could an organization implement to prevent those negative experiences from occurring?
6. Provide a concrete example of how different perspectives stemming from diversity can positively impact an organization or work group. You may use a real-life personal example or make one up.

Managerial Decision Exercises

1. As a manager for a hospital, you oversee a staff of marketing associates. Their job is to find doctors and persuade them to refer their patients to your hospital. Associates have a very flexible work schedule and manage their own time. They report to you weekly concerning their activities in the field. Trusting them is very important, and it is impossible to track and confirm all of their activities. Your assistant, Nancy, manages the support staff for the associates, works very closely with them, and often serves as your eyes and ears to keep you informed as to how well they are performing.
   One day, Nancy comes into your office crying and tells you that your top-performing associate, Susan, has for the past few weeks repeatedly asked her out to dinner and she has repeatedly refused. Susan is a lesbian and Nancy is not. Today, when she refused, Susan patted her on the bottom and said, "I know, you are just playing hard to get."
   After Nancy calms down, you tell her that you will fill out the paperwork to report a sexual harassment case. Nancy says that she does not want to report it because it would be too embarrassing if word of the incident got out. To impress upon you how strongly she feels, she tells you that she will consider resigning if you report the incident. Nancy is essential to the effective operation of your group, and you dread how difficult it would be to get things done without her assisting you.
   What do you do? Do you report the case, lose Nancy's trust, and jeopardize losing a high-performing employee? Or do you not report it, thereby protecting what Nancy believes to be her right to privacy?
2. Recently your company has begun to promote its diversity efforts, including same-sex (and heterosexual) partner benefits and a nonharassment policy that includes sexual orientation, among other things. Your department now has new posters on the walls with photos of employees who represent different aspects of diversity (e.g., Black, Hispanic, gay). One of your employees is upset about the diversity initiative and has begun posting religious scriptures condemning homosexuality on his cubicle in large type for everyone to see. When asked to remove them, your employee tells you that the posters promoting diversity offend Christian and Muslim employees. What should you do?
3. You are a recently hired supervisor at a paper mill factory. During your second week on the job, you learn about a White employee who has been using a racial slur during lunch breaks when discussing some of her Black coworkers with others. You ask the person who reported it to you about the woman and learn that she is an older woman, around 67 years old, and has worked at the factory for more than 40 years.

You talk to your boss about it, and he tells you that she means no harm by it, she is just from another era and that is just her personality. What would you do in this situation?

4. You are a nurse manager who oversees the triage for the emergency room, and today is a slow day with very few patients. During the downtime, one of your subordinates is talking with another coworker about her new boyfriend. You observe her showing her coworkers explicit images of him that he emailed her on her phone. Everyone is joking and laughing about the ordeal. Even though it appears no one is offended, should you address it? What would you say?
5. You work for a company that has primarily Black and Hispanic customers. Although you employ many racial minorities and women, you notice that all of your leaders are White men. This does not necessarily mean that your organization engages in discriminatory practices, but how would you know if your organization was managing diversity well? What information would you need to determine this, and how would you collect it?
6. Your company's founder believes that younger workers are more energetic and serve better in sales positions. Before posting a new job ad for your sales division, he recommends that you list an age requirement of the position for applicants between ages 18 and 25. Is his recommendation a good one? Why or why not?
7. You work for a real estate broker who recently hired two gay realtors, Steven and Shauna, to be a part of the team. During a staff meeting, your boss mentions an article she read about gay clients feeling ostracized in the real estate market. She tells the new employees she hired them to help facilitate the home-buying process for gay buyers and sellers. She specifically instructs them to focus on recruiting gay clients, even telling them that they should pass along any straight customers to one of the straight realtors on the team. A few weeks later, Shauna reports that she has made her first sale to a straight couple that is expecting a baby. During the next staff meeting, your boss congratulates Shauna on her sale, but again reiterates that Shauna and Steven should pass along straight clients to another realtor so they can focus on recruiting gay clients. After the meeting, Shauna tells you that she thinks it is unfair that she should have to focus on gay clients and that she is thinking of filing a discrimination complaint with HR. Do you think that Shauna is correct in her assessment of the situation? Is there merit to your boss's desire to have the gay realtors focus on recruiting gay clients? What might be a better solution to help gay clients feel more comfortable in the home-buying and -selling process?

Critical Thinking Case

Uber Pays the Price

Nine years ago, Uber revolutionized the taxi industry and the way people commute. With the simple mission "to bring transportation—for everyone, everywhere," today Uber has reached a valuation of around $70 billion and claimed a market share high of almost 90% in 2015. However, in June 2017 Uber experienced a series of bad press regarding an alleged culture of sexual harassment, which is what most experts believe caused their market share to fall to 75%.

In February of 2017 a former software engineer, Susan Fowler, wrote a lengthy post on her website regarding her experience of being harassed by a manager who was not disciplined by human resources for his behavior. In her post, Fowler wrote that Uber's HR department and members of upper management told her that because it was the man's first offense, they would only give him a warning. During her meeting with HR about the incident, Fowler was also advised that she should transfer to another department within the organization. According to Fowler, she was ultimately left no choice but to transfer to another department, despite having specific expertise in the department in which she had originally been working.

As her time at the company went on, she began meeting other women who worked for the company who relayed their own stories of harassment. To her surprise, many of the women reported being harassed by the same person who had harassed her. As she noted in her blog, "It became obvious that both HR and management had been lying about this being his 'first offense.'" Fowler also reported a number of other instances that she identified as sexist and inappropriate within the organization and claims that she was disciplined severely for continuing to speak out. Fowler eventually left Uber after about two years of working for the company, noting that during her time at Uber the percentage of women working there had dropped to 6% of the workforce, down from 25% when she first started.

Following the fallout from Fowler's lengthy description of the workplace on her website, Uber's chief executive Travis Kalanick publicly condemned the behavior described by Fowler, calling it "abhorrent and against everything Uber stands for and believes in." But later in March, Uber board member Arianna Huffington claimed that she believed "sexual harassment was not a systemic problem at the company." Amid pressure from bad media attention and the company's falling market share, Uber made some changes after an independent investigation resulted in 215 complaints. As a result, 20 employees were fired for reasons ranging from sexual harassment to bullying to retaliation to discrimination, and Kalanick announced that he would hire a chief operating officer to help manage the company. In an effort to provide the leadership team with more diversity, two senior female executives were hired to fill the positions of chief brand officer and senior vice president for leadership and strategy.

Critical Thinking Questions

1. Based on Cox's business case for diversity, what are some positive outcomes that may result in changes to Uber's leadership team?
2. Under what form of federal legislation was Fowler protected?
3. What strategies should have been put in place to help prevent sexual harassment incidents like this from happening in the first place?

Sources: Uber corporate Website, https://www.uber.com/newsroom/company-info/ (February, 2017); Marco della Cava, "Uber has lost market share to Lyft during crisis," *USA Today*, June 13, 2017, https://www.usatoday.com/story/tech/news/2017/06/13/uber-market-share-customer-image-hit-string-scandals/102795024/; Tracey Lien, "Uber fires 20 workers after harassment investigation," *Los Angeles Times*, Jun 6, 2017, http://www.latimes.com/business/la-fi-tn-uber-sexual-harassment-20170606-story.html; Susan Fowler, "Reflecting On One Very, Very Strange Year At Uber," February 19, 2017, https://www.susanjfowler.com/blog/2017/2/19/reflecting-on-one-very-strange-year-at-uber.

6 Perception and Managerial Decision Making

Exhibit 6.1 (i_yudai/ flickr/ Attribution 2.0 Generic (CC BY 2.0))

Introduction

Learning Outcomes

After reading this chapter, you should be able to answer these questions:

1. What are the basic characteristics of managerial decision-making?
2. What are the two systems of decision-making in the brain?
3. What is the difference between programmed and nonprogrammed decisions?
4. What barriers exist that make effective decision-making difficult?
5. How can a manager improve the quality of her individual decision-making?
6. What are the advantages and disadvantages of group decision-making, and how can a manager improve the quality of group decision-making?

EXPLORING MANAGERIAL CAREERS

Up, Up, and Away: How Stephanie Korey and Jen Rubio founded their luggage company

Jen Rubio and Stephanie Korey faced a number of important decisions in starting their luggage company, Away—beginning with the decision to start a business! That decision came about after Rubio's luggage broke on a trip. She found it frustrating that all the luggage options were either inexpensive ($100 or less) but low quality, or high quality but incredibly expensive ($400 and above). There was no midrange option. So in 2015 Rubio and her friend Stephanie Korey began researching the luggage industry. They found that much of the reason for the high prices on quality luggage was because of how it was distributed and sold, through specialty retail shops and department stores. If they opted instead for a model in which they sold directly to consumers, they could provide high-quality luggage at more of a midrange ($200-$300) price. After considerable research, the two were convinced that they had an idea worth pursuing. Rubio and Korey settled on the company name "Away," which is intended to invoke the pleasure that comes from travelling.

Both of the founders had prior experience working for a start-up in the e-commerce space (Warby Parker), which helped them with making sound choices. Rubio's background was more in branding and marketing, while Korey's was in operations and supply chain management—so each was able to bring great expertise to various aspects of the business. They raised money initially from friends and family, but within a few months they sought venture capital funding to ensure that they had enough money to get off to a successful start.

A big decision that Rubio and Korey had to make fairly early in the process of establishing their business was to settle on an initial design for the product. This decision required extensive marketing and consumer research to understand customer needs and wants. They asked hundreds of people what they liked about their existing luggage, and what they found most irritating about their existing luggage. They also contracted with a two-person design team to help create the first prototype. This research and development ultimately led to the design of an attractive hard case that is surprisingly lightweight. It also boasts extremely high-quality wheels (four of them, not two) and high-quality zippers. As a bonus, the carry-on includes a built-in battery for charging phones and other devices.

The two founders also had to choose a partner to manufacture their product. Because their product had a hard, polycarbonate shell, Rubio and Korey discovered that manufacturing in the United States was not a viable option—the vast majority of luggage manufacturers using a polycarbonate shell were based in Asia. They researched a number of possible business partners and asked lots of questions. In addition, they eventually visited all of the factories on their list of options to see what they were actually like. This was an important piece of research, because the companies that looked best on paper didn't always turn out to be the best when they visited in person. Rubio and Korey ended up working with a manufacturing partner in China that also produces luggage for many high-end brands, and they have been extremely pleased with the partnership. They continue to devote time to building and maintaining that relationship, which helps to avoid issues and problems that might otherwise come up.

By the end of 2015, Rubio and Korey had developed their first product. Because the luggage was not going to be available in time for the holiday shopping season, they decided to allow customers to preorder the luggage. To drum up interest, the duo engaged in a unique storytelling effort. They interviewed 40 well-respected members of the creative community about their travel experiences and created a hardcover book of travel memoirs called *The Places We Return To*. Not only was the book interesting and engaging, it also made lots of people in the creative community aware of Away luggage. Starting in November 2015, the travel memoir book was available for free with the purchase of a gift card that could be redeemed in February 2016 for luggage. The book project generated tremendous advance interest in the product, and the 1,200 printed copies sold out. Away generated $12 million in first-year sales.

Stephanie Corey and Jen Rubio faced many important and novel decisions in initially developing and building their business. They have been successful in part because they made those decisions wisely—by relying on shared knowledge, expertise, and lots of research before reaching a decision. They will continue to face many decisions, big and small. They have expanded their product line from one piece of luggage to four, with more luggage—and other travel accessories—in the works for the future. Their company, which is based in New York, has grown to over 60 employees in the first two years. These employees include the two design-team members who were contracted to help create their first prototype; Rubio and Korey appreciated working with them so much, they offered them full-time positions with Away. Each new hire represents new decisions—decisions about what additional work needs to be done and who they should hire to do it. Each new product also brings additional decisions—but it seems Rubio and Korey have positioned themselves (and their business) well for future successes.

Sources: Kendall Baker, "An Interview With the Co-Founder of Away," *The Hustle*, December 5, 2016, https://thehustle.co/episodes; Bond Street Blog, "Up and Away," *Bond Street*, https://bondstreet.com/blog/jen-rubio-interview/; Josh Constine, "Away nears 100k stylish suitcases sold as it raises $20M," *TechCrunch*, May 19, 2017, https://techcrunch.com/; Adeline Duff, " The T&L Carry-On: Away Travel Co-Founders Jen Rubio and Stephanie Korey," Travel & Leisure, March 9, 2017, http://www.travelandleisure.com/; Burt Helm, "How This Company Launched With Zero Products –and Hit $12 Million in First-Year Sales," *Inc.com*, July/August 2017, https://www.inc.com/; Veronique Hyland, "The Duo Trying to Make Travel More Glamorous," *The Cut*, December 22, 2015, https://www.thecut.com/.

Managers and business owners—like Jen Rubio and Stephanie Korey—make decisions on a daily basis. Some are big, like the decision to start a new business, but most are smaller decisions that go into the regular running of the company and are crucial to its long-term success. Some decisions are predictable, and some are unexpected. In this chapter we look at important information about decision-making that can help you make better decisions and, ultimately, be a better manager.

6.1 Overview of Managerial Decision-Making

1. What are the basic characteristics of managerial decision-making?

Decision-making is the action or process of thinking through possible options and selecting one.

It is important to recognize that managers are continually making decisions, and that the quality of their decision-making has an impact—sometimes quite significant—on the effectiveness of the organization and its **stakeholders**. Stakeholders are all the individuals or groups that are affected by an organization (such as customers, employees, shareholders, etc.).

Members of the top management team regularly make decisions that affect the future of the organization and all its stakeholders, such as deciding whether to pursue a new technology or product line. A good decision can enable the organization to thrive and survive long-term, while a poor decision can lead a business into bankruptcy. Managers at lower levels of the organization generally have a smaller impact on the organization's survival, but can still have a tremendous impact on their department and its workers. Consider, for example, a first-line supervisor who is charged with scheduling workers and ordering raw materials for her department. Poor decision-making by lower-level managers is unlikely to drive the entire firm out of existence, but it can lead to many adverse outcomes such as:

- reduced productivity if there are too few workers or insufficient supplies,
- increased expenses if there are too many workers or too many supplies, particularly if the supplies have a limited shelf life or are costly to store, and
- frustration among employees, reduced morale, and increased turnover (which can be costly for the organization) if the decisions involve managing and training workers.

Deciding When to Decide

While some decisions are simple, a manager's decisions are often complex ones that involve a range of options and uncertain outcomes. When deciding among various options and uncertain outcomes, managers need to gather information, which leads them to another necessary decision: how much information is needed to make a good decision? Managers frequently make decisions without complete information; indeed, one of the hallmarks of an effective leader is the ability to determine when to hold off on a decision and gather more information, and when to make a decision with the information at hand. Waiting too long to make a decision can be as harmful for the organization as reaching a decision too quickly. Failing to react quickly enough can lead to missed opportunities, yet acting too quickly can lead to organizational resources being poorly allocated to projects with no chance of success. Effective managers must decide when they have gathered enough information and must be prepared to change course if additional information becomes available that makes it clear that the original decision was a poor one. For individuals with fragile egos, changing course can be challenging because admitting to a mistake can be harder than forging ahead with a bad plan. Effective managers recognize that given the complexity of many tasks, some failures are inevitable. They also realize that it's better to minimize a bad decision's impact on the organization and its stakeholders by recognizing it quickly and correcting it.

What's the Right (Correct) Answer?

It's also worth noting that making decisions as a manager is not at all like taking a multiple-choice test: with a multiple-choice test there is always one right answer. This is rarely the case with management decisions. Sometimes a manager is choosing between multiple good options, and it's not clear which will be the best. Other times there are multiple bad options, and the task is to minimize harm. Often there are individuals in the organization with competing interests, and the manager must make decisions knowing that someone will be upset no matter what decision is reached.

What's the Right (Ethical) Answer?

Sometimes managers are asked to make decisions that go beyond just upsetting someone—they may be asked to make decisions in which harm could be caused to others. These decisions have ethical or moral implications. Ethics and morals refer to our beliefs about what is right vs. wrong, good vs. evil, virtuous vs. corrupt. Implicitly, ethics and morals relate to our interactions with and impact on others—if we never had to interact with another creature, we would not have to think about how our behaviors affected other individuals or groups. All managers, however, make decisions that impact others. It is therefore important to be mindful about whether our decisions have a positive or a negative impact. "Maximizing shareholder wealth" is often used as a rationalization for placing the importance of short-term profits over the needs of others who will be affected by a decision—such as employees, customers, or local citizens (who might be affected, for example, by environmental decisions). Maximizing shareholder wealth is often a short-sighted decision, however, because it can harm the organization's financial viability in the future.[1] Bad publicity, customers boycotting the organization, and government fines are all possible long-term outcomes when managers make choices that cause harm in order to maximize shareholder wealth. More importantly, increasing the wealth of shareholders is not an acceptable reason for causing harm to others.

As you can see from these brief examples, management is not for the faint of heart! It can, however, be incredibly rewarding to be in a position to make decisions that have a positive impact on an organization and its stakeholders. We see a great example of this in the *Sustainability and Responsible Management* box.

SUSTAINABILITY AND RESPONSIBLE MANAGEMENT

Brewing Sustainable Success

The focus of a manager or a business owner is often primarily on doing well (making a profit). Sometimes, though, organizational leaders choose to pursue two big goals at once: doing well, and simultaneously doing good (benefiting society in some way). Why? Generally because they think it's an important thing to do. The business provides an opportunity to pursue another goal that the founders, owners, or managers are also passionate about. In the case of New Belgium Brewing, the company's cofounders, Jeff Lebesch and Kim Jordan, were passionate about two things: making great beer and environmental stewardship. So it should come as no surprise that their brewery is dedicated to reducing its environmental footprint. The brewery has created a culture that fosters sustainability in a wide range of ways, such as by giving employees a bicycle on their one-year anniversary as a way to encourage them to ride bicycles to work. The organization is also active in advocacy efforts, such as the "Save the Colorado" (river) campaign, and it works hard to promote responsible decision-making when it comes to environmental issues. In fact, in 1999, following an employee vote, the brewery began to purchase all of its electricity from wind power, even though it was more expensive than electricity from coal-burning power plants (which meant reduced profitability and less money for employee bonuses).

While the brewery still relies primarily on wind power, it also now generates a portion of its electricity onsite—some from rooftop solar panels, and even more from biogas, the methane gas byproduct that is created by microbes in the brewery's water treatment plant. The company cleans the wastewater generated from beer production, and in doing so it generates the biogas, which is captured and used for energy to help run the brewery.

Brewing is water intensive, so New Belgium works hard to reduce water consumption and to recycle the water that it does use. The company also reduces other types of waste by selling used grain, hops, and yeast to local ranchers for cattle feed. The company, which has been employee owned since 2013, also works with the local utility through a Smart Meter program to reduce their energy consumption at peak times.

All of these efforts at doing good must come at a cost, right? Actually, research shows that companies that are committed to sustainability have superior financial performance, on average, relative to those that are not. In coming up with creative ways to reduce, reuse, and recycle, employees often also find ways to save money (like using biogas). In addition, organizations that strive to do good are often considered attractive and desirable places to work (especially by people who have similar values) and are also valued by the surrounding communities. As a result, employees in those organizations tend to be extremely committed to them, with high levels of engagement, motivation, and productivity. Indeed, it seems clear that the employees at the New Belgium Brewery are passionate about where they work and what they do. This passion generates value for the organization and proves that it is, in fact, possible to do well while having also made the decision to do good. And in the case of New Belgium Brewery, that means working to protect the environment while also making delicious beer.

Discussion Questions

1. What challenges does New Belgium Brewery face in pursuing environmental goals?
2. Can you think of any other examples of companies that try to "do good" while also doing well?
3. Would you like to work for an organization that is committed to something more than just

profitability, even if it meant your salary or bonus would be smaller?

Sources: Karen Crofton, "How New Belgium Brewery leads Colorado's craft brewers in energy," *GreenBiz*, August 1, 2014, https://www.greenbiz.com/. Darren Dahl, "How New Belgium Brewing Has Found Sustainable Success," *Forbes*, February 8, 2016, https://www.forbes.com/. Jenny Foust, "New Belgium Brewing Once Again Named Platinum-Level Bicycle Friendly Business by the League of American Bicyclists," Craft Beer.com, February 18, 2016. Robert G. Eccles, Ioannis Ioannou, & George Serafeim, "The Impact of Corporate Sustainability on Organizational Processes and Performance," *Management Science*, 60, 2014, https://doi.org/10.1287/mnsc.2014.1984. New Belgium Brewery Sustainability web page, http://www.newbelgium.com/sustainability, accessed September 18, 2017.

CONCEPT CHECK 

1. What are some positive outcomes of decision-making for an organization? What are some possible negative outcomes?
2. How is managerial decision-making different from a multiple-choice test?
3. In addition to the owners of a business, who are some of the other stakeholders that managers should consider when making decisions?

6.2 How the Brain Processes Information to Make Decisions: Reflective and Reactive Systems

2. What are the two systems of decision-making in the brain?

The human brain processes information for decision-making using one of two routes: a reflective system and a reactive (or reflexive) system.[2,3] The **reflective system** is logical, analytical, deliberate, and methodical, while the **reactive system** is quick, impulsive, and intuitive, relying on emotions or habits to provide cues for what to do next. Research in neuropsychology suggests that the brain can only use one system at a time for processing information [Darlow & Sloman] and that the two systems are directed by different parts of the brain. The prefrontal cortex is more involved in the reflective system, and the basal ganglia and amygdala (more primitive parts of the brain, from an evolutionary perspective) are more involved in the reactive system.[4]

Reactive Decision-Making

We tend to assume that the logical, analytical route leads to superior decisions, but whether this is accurate depends on the situation. The quick, intuitive route can be lifesaving; when we suddenly feel intense fear, a fight-or-flight response kicks in that leads to immediate action without methodically weighing all possible options and their consequences. Additionally, experienced managers can often make decisions very quickly because experience or expertise has taught them what to do in a given situation. These managers might not be able to explain the logic behind their decision, and will instead say they just went with their "gut," or did what "felt" right. Because the manager has faced a similar situation in the past and has figured out how to deal with it, the brain shifts immediately to the quick, intuitive decision-making system.[5]

Reflective Decision-Making

The quick route is not always the best decision-making path to take, however. When faced with novel and complex situations, it is better to process available information logically, analytically, and methodically. As a manager, you need to think about whether a situation requires not a fast, "gut" reaction, but some serious thought prior to making a decision. It is especially important to pay attention to your emotions, because strong emotions can make it difficult to process information rationally. Successful managers recognize the effects of emotions and know to wait and address a volatile situation after their emotions have calmed down. Intense emotions—whether positive or negative—tend to pull us toward the quick, reactive route of decision-making. Have you ever made a large "impulse" purchase that you were excited about, only to regret it later? This speaks to the power our emotions exert on our decision-making. Big decisions should generally not be made impulsively, but reflectively.

The Role of Emotions

Being aware of the role emotions play in decision-making does not mean that we should ignore them. Emotions can serve as powerful signals about what we should do, especially in situations with ethical implications. You can read more about this particular type of decision-making in the *Ethics in Practice* box later in this chapter. Thinking through how we feel about the possible options, and why we feel that way, can greatly enhance our decision-making.[6] Effective decision-making, then, relies on both logic *and* emotions. For this reason, the concept of emotional intelligence has become popular as a characteristic of effective managers. **Emotional intelligence** is the ability to recognize, understand, pay attention to, and manage one's own emotions and the emotions of others. It involves self-awareness and self-regulation—essentially, this is a toggling back and forth between emotions and logic so that we analyze and understand our own emotions and then exert the necessary control to manage them as appropriate for the situation. Emotional intelligence also involves empathy—the ability to understand other peoples' emotions (and an interest in doing so). Finally, emotional intelligence involves social skills to manage the emotional aspects of relationships with others. Managers who are aware of their own emotions can think through what their emotions mean in a given situation and use that information to guide their decision-making. Managers who are aware of the emotions of others can also utilize that information to help groups function more effectively and engage in better group decision-making. While emotional intelligence seems to come easily to some people, it is something that we can develop and improve on with practice. A model of emotional intelligence is presented in **Exhibit 6.2**.

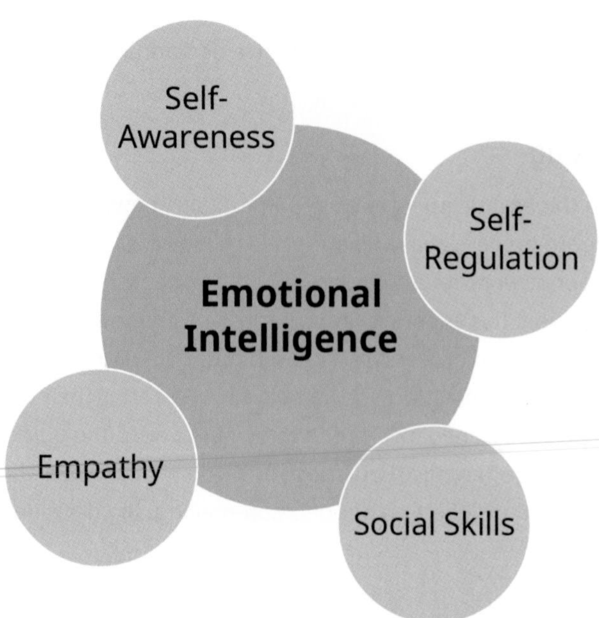

Exhibit 6.2 Emotional Intelligence (Attribution: Copyright Rice University, OpenStax, under CC-BY 4.0 license)

CONCEPT CHECK

1. Explain the two systems used by the brain in decision-making.
2. What is emotional intelligence, and why is it important for decision-making?

6.3 Programmed and Nonprogrammed Decisions

3. What is the difference between programmed and nonprogrammed decisions?

Because managers have limited time and must use that time wisely to be effective, it is important for them to distinguish between decisions that can have structure and routine applied to them (called programmed decisions) and decisions that are novel and require thought and attention (nonprogrammed decisions).

Programmed Decisions

Programmed decisions are those that are repeated over time and for which an existing set of rules can be developed to guide the process. These decisions might simple, or they could be fairly complex, but the criteria that go into making the decision are all known or can at least be estimated with a reasonable degree of accuracy. For example, deciding how many raw materials to order should be a programmed decision based on anticipated production, existing stock, and anticipated length of time for the delivery of the final product. As another example, consider a retail store manager developing the weekly work schedule for part-time employees. The manager must consider how busy the store is likely to be, taking into account seasonal fluctuations in business. Then, she must consider the availability of the workers by taking into account requests for vacation and for other obligations that employees might have (such as school). Establishing the schedule might be complex, but it is still a programmed decision: it is made on a regular basis based on well-understood criteria, so structure can be applied to the process. For programmed decisions, managers often develop **heuristics**, or mental shortcuts, to help reach a decision. For example, the retail store manager may not know how busy the store will be the week of a big sale, but might routinely increase staff by 30% every time there is a big sale (because this has been fairly effective in the past). Heuristics are efficient—they save time for the decision maker by generating an adequate solution quickly. Heuristics don't necessarily yield the optimal solution—deeper cognitive processing may be required for that. However, they generally yield a good solution. Heuristics are often used for programmed decisions, because experience in making the decision over and over helps the decision maker know what to expect and how to react. Programmed decision-making can also be taught fairly easily to another person. The rules and criteria, and how they relate to outcomes, can be clearly laid out so that a good decision can be reached by the new decision maker. Programmed decisions are also sometimes referred to as *routine* or *low-involvement* decisions because they don't require in-depth mental processing to reach a decision. High- and low-involvement decisions are illustrated in **Exhibit 6.3**.

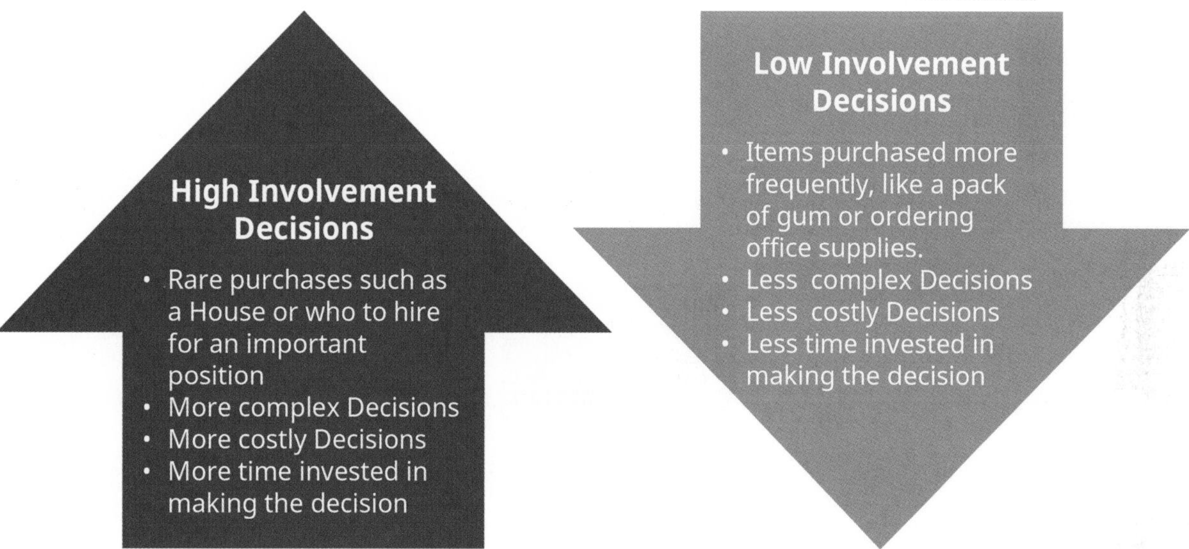

Exhibit 6.3 High-Involvement and Low-Involvement Decisions. (Attribution: Copyright Rice University, OpenStax, under CC-BY 4.0 license)

Nonprogrammed Decisions

In contrast, **nonprogrammed decisions** are novel, unstructured decisions that are generally based on criteria that are not well-defined. With nonprogrammed decisions, information is more likely to be ambiguous or incomplete, and the decision maker may need to exercise some thoughtful judgment and creative thinking to reach a good solution. These are also sometimes referred to as *nonroutine* decisions or as *high-involvement* decisions because they require greater involvement and thought on the part of the decision maker. For example, consider a manager trying to decide whether or not to adopt a new technology. There will always be unknowns in situations of this nature. Will the new technology really be better than the existing technology? Will it become widely accepted over time, or will some other technology become the standard? The best the manager can do in this situation is to gather as much relevant information as possible and make an educated guess as to whether the new technology will be worthwhile. Clearly, nonprogrammed decisions present the greater challenge.

The Decision-Making Process

While decisions makers can use mental shortcuts with programmed decisions, they should use a systematic process with nonprogrammed decisions. The decision-making process is illustrated in **Exhibit 6.4** and can be broken down into a series of six steps, as follows:

1. Recognize that a decision needs to be made.
2. Generate multiple alternatives.
3. Analyze the alternatives.
4. Select an alternative.
5. Implement the selected alternative.
6. Evaluate its effectiveness.

While these steps may seem straightforward, individuals often skip steps or spend too little time on some steps. In fact, sometimes people will refuse to acknowledge a problem (Step 1) because they aren't sure how to address it. We'll discuss the steps more later in the chapter, when we review ways to improve the quality of decision-making.

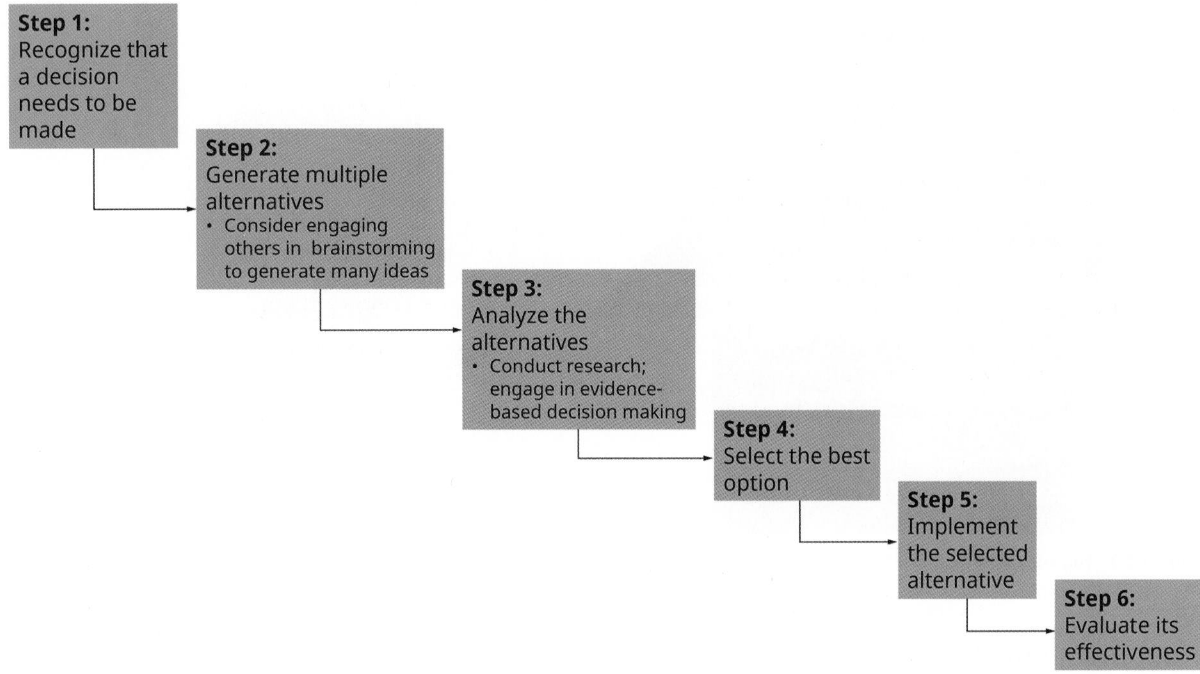

Exhibit 6.4 The Decision-Making Process.

You may notice similarities between the two systems of decision-making in our brains and the two types of decisions (programmed and nonprogrammed). Nonprogrammed decisions will generally need to be processed via the reflective system in our brains in order for us to reach a good decision. But with programmed decisions, heuristics can allow decision makers to switch to the quick, reactive system and then move along quickly to other issues.

CONCEPT CHECK 

1. Give an example of a programmed decision that a manager might face.
2. Give an example of a nonprogrammed decision.
3. What are heuristics, and when are they helpful?
4. How are programmed and nonprogrammed decisions connected to the reflective and reactive systems in the brain?

6.4 Barriers to Effective Decision-Making

4. What barriers exist that make effective decision-making difficult?

There are a number of barriers to effective decision-making. Effective managers are aware of these potential barriers and try to overcome them as much as possible.

Bounded Rationality

While we might like to think that we can make completely rational decisions, this is often unrealistic given the complex issues faced by managers. Nonrational decision-making is common, especially with nonprogrammed decisions. Since we haven't faced a particular situation previously, we don't always know what questions to ask or what information to gather. Even when we have gathered all the possible information, we may not be able to make rational sense of all of it, or to accurately forecast or predict the outcomes of our choice. **Bounded rationality** is the idea that for complex issues we cannot be completely rational because we cannot fully grasp all the possible alternatives, nor can we understand all the implications of every possible alternative. Our brains have limitations in terms of the amount of information they can process. Similarly, as was alluded to earlier in the chapter, even when managers have the cognitive ability to process all the relevant information, they often must make decisions without first having time to collect all the relevant data—their information is incomplete.

Escalation of Commitment

Given the lack of complete information, managers don't always make the right decision initially, and it may not be clear that a decision was a bad one until after some time has passed. For example, consider a manager who had to choose between two competing software packages that her organization will use on a daily basis to enhance efficiency. She initially chooses the product that was developed by the larger, more well-established company, reasoning that they will have greater financial resources to invest in ensuring that the technology is good. However, after some time it becomes clear that the competing software package is going to be far superior. While the smaller company's product could be integrated into the organization's existing systems at little additional expense, the larger company's product will require a much greater initial investment, as well as substantial ongoing costs for maintaining it. At this point, however, let's assume that the manager has already paid for the larger company's (inferior) software. Will she abandon the path that she's on, accept the loss on the money that's been invested so far, and switch to the better software? Or will she continue to invest time and money into trying to make the first product work? **Escalation of commitment** is the tendency of decision makers to remain committed to poor decision, even when doing so leads to increasingly negative outcomes. Once we commit to a decision, we may find it difficult to reevaluate that decision rationally. It can seem easier to "stay the course" than to admit (or to recognize) that a decision was poor. It's important to acknowledge that not all decisions are going to be good ones, in spite of our best efforts. Effective managers recognize that progress down the wrong path isn't really progress, and they are willing to reevaluate decisions and change direction when appropriate.

Time Constraints

Managers often face time constraints that can make effective decision-making a challenge. When there is little time available to collect information and to rationally process it, we are much less likely to make a good nonprogrammed decision. Time pressures can cause us to rely on heuristics rather than engage in deep processing. While heuristics save time, however, they don't necessarily lead to the best possible solution. The best managers are constantly assessing the risks associated with acting too quickly against those associated with not acting quickly enough.

Uncertainty

In addition, managers frequently make decisions under conditions of uncertainty—they cannot know the outcome of each alternative until they've actually chosen that alternative. Consider, for example, a manager who is trying to decide between one of two possible marketing campaigns. The first is more conservative but is consistent with what the organization has done in the past. The second is more modern and edgier, and might bring much better results . . . or it might be a spectacular failure. The manager making the decision will ultimately have to choose one campaign and see what happens, without ever knowing what the results would have been with the alternate campaign. That uncertainty can make it difficult for some managers to make decisions, because committing to one option means forgoing other options.

Personal Biases

Our decision-making is also limited by our own biases. We tend to be more comfortable with ideas, concepts, things, and people that are familiar to us or similar to us. We tend to be less comfortable with that which is unfamiliar, new, and different. One of the most common biases that we have, as humans, is the tendency to like other people who we think are similar to us (because we like ourselves).[7] While these similarities can be observable (based on demographic characteristics such as race, gender, and age), they can also be a result of shared experiences (such as attending the same university) or shared interests (such as being in a book club together). This "similar to me" bias and preference for the familiar can lead to a variety of problems for managers: hiring less-qualified applicants because they are similar to the manager in some way, paying more attention to some employees' opinions and ignoring or discounting others, choosing a familiar technology over a new one that is superior, sticking with a supplier that is known over one that has better quality, and so on.

It can be incredibly difficult to overcome our biases because of the way our brains work. The brain excels at organizing information into categories, and it doesn't like to expend the effort to re-arrange once the categories are established. As a result, we tend to pay more attention to information that confirms our existing beliefs and less attention to information that is contrary to our beliefs, a shortcoming that is referred to as **confirmation bias**.[8]

In fact, we don't like our existing beliefs to be challenged. Such challenges feel like a threat, which tends to push our brains towards the reactive system and prevent us from being able to logically process the new information via the reflective system. It is hard to change people's minds about something if they are already confident in their convictions. So, for example, when a manager hires a new employee who she really likes and is convinced is going to be excellent, she will tend to pay attention to examples of excellent performance and ignore examples of poor performance (or attribute those events to things outside the employee's control). The manager will also tend to trust that employee and therefore accept their explanations for poor performance without verifying the truth or accuracy of those statements. The opposite is also true; if we dislike someone, we will pay attention to their negatives and ignore or discount their positives. We are less likely to trust them or believe what they say at face value. This is why politics tend to become very polarized and antagonistic within a two-party system. It can be very difficult to have accurate perceptions of those we like and those we dislike. The effective manager will try to evaluate situations from multiple perspectives and gather multiple opinions to offset this bias when making decisions.

Conflict

Finally, effective decision-making can be difficult because of conflict. Most individuals dislike conflict and will avoid it when possible. However, the best decision might be one that is going to involve some conflict. Consider a manager who has a subordinate who is often late to work, causing others to have to step away from their responsibilities in order to cover for the late employee. The manager needs to have a conversation with that employee to correct the behavior, but the employee is not going to like the conversation and may react in a negative way. Both of them are going to be uncomfortable. The situation is likely to involve conflict, which most people find stressful. Yet, the correct decision is still to have the conversation even if (or especially if) the employee otherwise is an asset to the department.

Exhibit 6.5 Dante Disparte Dante Disparte is the founder and CEO of Risk Cooperative and also coauthor of *Global Risk Agility and Decision Making*. He suggests that unforeseen and unanticipated risks are becoming more frequent and less predictable and are having a greater impact on more people at one time. Credit (New America/ flickr/ Attribution 2.0 Generic (CC BY 2.0))

If the bad behavior is not corrected, it will continue, which is going to cause more problems in the workplace in the long run. Other employees may recognize that this behavior is allowed, and they may also start coming to work late or engaging in other negative behaviors. Eventually, some employees may become sufficiently frustrated that they look for another place to work. It's worth noting that in this situation, the best employees will find new jobs the most quickly. It's important for managers to recognize that while conflict can be uncomfortable (especially in the short-term), there are times when it is necessary for the group, department, or organization to function effectively in the long run.

It is also helpful to think about conflict in terms of process conflict or relationship conflict.[9] **Process conflict,** conflict about the best way to do something, can actually lead to improved performance, as individuals explore various options together in order to identify superior solutions. **Relationship conflict** is conflict between individuals that is more personal and involves attacks on a person rather than an idea. This kind of conflict is generally harmful and should be quelled when possible. The harm from relationship conflict arises at least in part because feeling personally attacked will cause an individual to revert to the reactive system of the brain.

Effective managers should be particularly aware of the possibility of relationship conflict when giving feedback and should keep feedback focused on behaviors and activities (how things are done) rather than on the individual. Being aware of and dealing with relationship conflict points to why emotional intelligence and empathy are beneficial in organizational leaders. Such leaders are more likely to be attentive to the harmful consequences of relationship conflict. The "Managerial Leadership" segment shows how one CEO encourages empathetic collaboration and how that effort is proving beneficial.

MANAGERIAL LEADERSHIP

Satya Nadella's Transformation of Microsoft

When Satya Nadella became the CEO of Microsoft in 2014, he set in motion a major transformation of the organization's culture. He wanted it to shift from a culture that valued "know-it-alls" to one that values "learn-it-all." Instead of employees feeling the need to prove that they were the smartest person in the room, he wanted them to become curious and effective listeners, learners, and communicators. Only through continual learning and collaboration with one another, and with customers, would Microsoft remain able to develop and provide great technology solutions.

One of Nadella's first mandates as CEO was to ask all the members of the top management team to read the book *Nonviolent Communication* by Marshall Rosenberg. The primary focus of the book is on empathetic communication—a kinder, gentler approach than Microsoft employees were accustomed to. Nadella believes that developing empathy leads to a heightened understanding of consumer needs and wants and an enhanced ability to develop better products and services through collaboration.

Nadella has also embraced diversity and inclusion initiatives, though he readily acknowledges that there is more to be done. This is, in part, an extension of his focus on empathy. However, it's also good business, because increasing the diversity of perspectives can help to drive innovation.

This cultural shift is reflected in Microsoft's new mission statement: "To empower every person and every organization on the planet to achieve more." Empowering every person includes Microsoft's own employees. Achieving diversity is particularly a challenge in an industry that is male dominated, and Nadella admits that he has made mistakes based on his own biases. At a Women in Computing conference early in his tenure as CEO, Nadella suggested that women did not need to ask for raises when they deserved them; the system, he said, would work it out. He later admitted that he was wrong and used the mistake as a platform for making greater strides in this arena.

Senior management team meetings at Microsoft have apparently changed dramatically as a result of the culture change driven by Nadella. Previously, members felt the need to constantly prove that they knew all the right answers at team meetings. Nadella has established different norms; he seeks out honest opinions from team members and gives positive feedback on a regular basis. By moving the focus away from always being right and toward a focus of continual learning, the culture at Microsoft has become more collaborative, and employees are more willing to take risks to create something amazing. The culture shift seems to be paying off: Microsoft's products are being described as "cool" and "exciting," its cloud-computing platform is outperforming the competition, and its financial performance has improved dramatically. Transforming the culture of an organization is a massive undertaking, but Nadella's leadership of Microsoft clearly shows that it's a decision that can pay off.

Discussion Questions

1. Do you think a culture focused on learning makes sense for Microsoft? Why or why not?
2. What are the advantages of a culture that emphasizes empathetic communication? Can you think of any disadvantages?
3. The job of CEO means making big decisions that impact the entire organization—like deciding to change the culture. How do you think you prepare for that job?

Sources: Kendall Baker, "Confirmed: Microsoft is a legit threat to Apple," *The Hustle*, March 16, 2017. Bob Evans, "10 Powerful examples of Microsoft CEO Satya Nadella's Transformative Vision," Forbes, July 26, 2017. Harry McCraken, "Satya Nadella Rewrites Microsoft's Code," *Fast Company*, September 18, 2017, https://www.fastcompany.com/40457458/satya-nadella-rewrites-microsofts-code. Annie Palmer, "Microsoft has been reborn under CEO Satya Nadella," *The Street*, September 20, 2017.

CONCEPT CHECK

1. Explain the concept of confirmation bias.
2. List and describe at least three barriers to effective decision-making.
3. When is conflict beneficial, and when is it harmful? Why?

6.5 Improving the Quality of Decision-Making

5. How can a manager improve the quality of her individual decision-making?

Managers can use a variety of techniques to improve their decision-making by making better-quality decisions or making decisions more quickly. **Table 6.1** summarizes some of these tactics.

Summary of Techniques That May Improve Individual Decision-Making		
Type of Decision	Technique	Benefit
Programmed decisions	Heuristics (mental shortcuts)	Saves time
	Satisficing (choosing first acceptable solution)	Saves time
Nonprogrammed decisions	Systematically go through the six steps of the decision-making process.	Improves quality
	Talk to other people.	Improves quality: generates more options, reduces bias
	Be creative.	Improves quality: generates more options
	Conduct research; engage in evidence-based decision-making.	Improves quality
	Engage in critical thinking.	Improves quality
	Think about the long-term implications.	Improves quality
	Consider the ethical implications.	Improves quality

Table 6.1 (Attribution: Copyright Rice University, OpenStax, under CC-BY 4.0 license)

The Importance of Experience

An often overlooked factor in effective decision-making is experience. Managers with more experience have generally learned more and developed greater expertise that they can draw on when making decisions. Experience helps managers develop methods and heuristics to quickly deal with programmed decisions and helps them know what additional information to seek out before making a nonprogrammed decision.

Techniques for Making Better Programmed Decisions

In addition, experience enables managers to recognize when to minimize the time spent making decisions on issues that are not particularly important but must still be addressed. As discussed previously, heuristics are mental shortcuts that managers take when making programmed (routine, low-involvement) decisions. Another technique that managers use with these types of decisions is satisficing. When **satisficing**, a decision maker selects the first *acceptable* solution without engaging in additional effort to identify the *best* solution. We all engage in satisficing every day. For example, suppose you are shopping for groceries and you don't want to overspend. If you have plenty of time, you might compare prices and figure out the price by weight (or volume) to ensure that every item you select is the cheapest option. But if you are in a hurry, you might just select generic products, knowing that they are cheap enough. This allows you to finish the task quickly at a reasonably low cost.

Techniques for Making Better Nonprogrammed Decisions

For situations in which the quality of the decision is more critical than the time spent on the decision, decision makers can use several tactics. As stated previously, nonprogrammed decisions should be addressed using a systematic process. We therefore discuss these tactics within the context of the decision-making steps. To review, the steps include the following:

1. Recognize that a decision needs to be made.
2. Generate multiple alternatives.
3. Analyze the alternatives.
4. Select an alternative.
5. Implement the selected alternative.
6. Evaluate its effectiveness.

Step 1: Recognizing That a Decision Needs to Be Made

Ineffective managers will sometimes ignore problems because they aren't sure how to address them. However, this tends to lead to more and bigger problems over time. Effective managers will be attentive to problems and to opportunities and will not shy away from making decisions that could make their team, department, or organization more effective and more successful.

Step 2: Generating Multiple Alternatives

Often a manager only spends enough time on Step 2 to generate two alternatives and then quickly moves to Step 3 in order to make a quick decision. A better solution may have been available, but it wasn't even considered. It's important to remember that for nonprogrammed decisions, you don't want to rush the process. Generating many possible options will increase the likelihood of reaching a good decision. Some tactics to help with generating more options include talking to other people (to get their ideas) and thinking creatively about the problem.

Talk to other people

Managers can often improve the quality of their decision-making by involving others in the process, especially when generating alternatives. Other people tend to view problems from different perspectives because they have had different life experiences. This can help generate alternatives that you might not otherwise have considered. Talking through big decisions with a mentor can also be beneficial, especially for new managers who are still learning and developing their expertise; someone with more experience will often be able to suggest more options.

Be creative

We don't always associate management with creativity, but creativity can be quite beneficial in some situations. In decision-making, creativity can be particularly helpful when generating alternatives. **Creativity** is the generation of new or original ideas; it requires the use of imagination and the ability to step back from traditional ways of doing things and seeing the world. While some people seem to be naturally creative, it is a skill that you can develop. Being creative requires letting your mind wander and combining existing knowledge from past experiences in novel ways. Creative inspiration may come when we least expect it (in the shower, for example) because we aren't intensely focused on the problem—we've allowed our minds to wander. Managers who strive to be creative will take the time to view a problem from multiple perspectives, try to combine information in news ways, search for overarching patterns, and use their imaginations to generate new solutions to existing problems. We'll review creativity in more detail in **Improving the Quality of Decision-Making**.

Step 3: Analyzing Alternatives

When implementing Step 3, it is important to take many factors into consideration. Some alternatives might be more expensive than others, for example, and that information is often essential when analyzing options. Effective managers will ensure that they have collected sufficient information to assess the quality of the various options. They will also utilize the tactics described below: engaging in evidence-based decision-making, thinking critically, talking to other people, and considering long-term and ethical implications.

Do you have the best-quality data and evidence?

Evidence-based decision-making is an approach to decision-making that states that managers should systematically collect the best evidence available to help them make effective decisions. The evidence that is collected might include the decision maker's own expertise, but it is also likely to include external evidence, such as a consideration of other stakeholders, contextual factors relevant to the organization, potential costs and benefits, and other relevant information. With evidence-based decision-making, managers are encouraged to rely on data and information rather than their intuition. This can be particularly beneficial for new managers or for experienced managers who are starting something new. (Consider all the research that Rubio and Korey conducted while starting Away).

Talk to other people

As mentioned previously, it can be worthwhile to get help from others when generating options. Another good time to talk to other people is while analyzing those options; other individuals in the organization may help you assess the quality of your choices. Seeking out the opinions and preferences of others is also a great way to maintain perspective, so getting others involved can help you to be less biased in your decision-making (provided you talk to people whose biases are different from your own).

Are you thinking critically about the options?

Our skill at assessing alternatives can also be improved by a focus on **critical thinking**. Critical thinking is a disciplined process of evaluating the quality of information, especially data collected from other sources and arguments made by other people, to determine whether the source should be trusted or whether the argument is valid.

An important factor in critical thinking is the recognition that a person's analysis of the available information may be flawed by a number of *logical fallacies* that they may use when they are arguing their point or defending their perspective. Learning what those fallacies are and being able to recognize them when they occur can help improve decision-making quality. See **Table 6.2** for several examples of common logical fallacies.

Common Logical Fallacies			
Name	Description	Examples	Ways to Combat This Logical Fallacy
Non sequitur (does not follow)	The conclusion that is presented isn't a logical conclusion or isn't the only logical conclusion based on the argument(s).	Our biggest competitor is spending more on marketing than we are. They have a larger share of the market. Therefore, we should spend more on marketing. *The unspoken assumption:* They have a larger share of the market BECAUSE they spend more on marketing.	• Examine all the arguments. Are they reasonable? • Look for any assumptions that are being made in the argument sequence. Are they reasonable? • Try to gather evidence that supports or refutes the arguments and/or assumptions. *In this example, you should ask:* Are there any other reasons, besides their spending on marketing, why our competitor has a larger share of the market?
False cause	Assuming that because two things are related, one caused the other	"Our employees get sick more when we close for holidays. So we should stop closing for holidays."	This is similar to non sequitur; it makes an assumption in the argument sequence. • Ask yourself whether the first thing really causes the second, or if something else may be the cause. In this case, most holidays for which businesses close are in the late fall and winter (Thanksgiving, Christmas), and there are more illnesses at this time of year because of the weather, not because of the business being closed.

Table 6.2

Common Logical Fallacies			
Name	Description	Examples	Ways to Combat This Logical Fallacy
Ad hominem (attack the man)	Redirects from the argument itself to attack the person making the argument	"You aren't really going to take John seriously, are you? I heard his biggest client just dropped him for another vendor because he's all talk and no substance." *The goal:* if you stop trusting the person, you'll discount their argument.	• Does the second person have something to gain, a hidden agenda, in trying to make you distrust the first person? • If the first person's argument came from someone else, would it be persuasive?
Genetic fallacy	You can't trust something because of its origins.	"This was made in China, so it must be low quality." "He is a lawyer, so you can't trust anything he says."	This fallacy is based on stereotypes. Stereotypes are generalizations; some are grossly inaccurate, and even those that are accurate in SOME cases are never accurate in ALL cases. Recognize this for what it is—an attempt to prey on existing biases.
Appeal to tradition	If we have always done it one particular way, that must be the right or best way.	"We've always done it this way." "We shouldn't change this; it works fine the way it is."	• Consider whether the situation has changed, calling for a change in the way things are being done. • Consider whether new information suggests that the traditional viewpoint is incorrect. Remember, we used to think that the earth was flat.

Table 6.2

Common Logical Fallacies			
Name	Description	Examples	Ways to Combat This Logical Fallacy
Bandwagon approach	If the majority of people are doing it, it must be good.	"Everybody does it." "Our customers don't want to be served by people like that."	• Remember that the majority is sometimes wrong, and what is popular isn't always what is right. • Ask yourself whether "following the pack" is going to get you where you want to be. • Remember that organizations are usually successful by being better than their competitors at something . . . so following the crowd might not be the best approach to success.
Appeal to emotion	Redirects the argument from logic to emotion	"We should do it for [recently deceased] Steve; it's what he would have wanted."	• Develop your awareness of your own emotions, and recognize when someone is trying to use them. • Ask yourself whether the argument stands on its own without the appeal to your emotions.

Table 6.2

Have you considered the long-term implications?

A focus on immediate, short-term outcomes—with little consideration for the future—can cause problems. For example, imagine that a manager must decide whether to issue dividends to investors or put that money into research and development to maintain a pipeline of innovative products. It's tempting to just focus on the short-term: providing dividends to investors tends to be good for stock prices. But failing to invest in research and development might mean that in five years the company is unable to compete effectively in the marketplace, and as a result the business closes. Paying attention to the possible long-term outcomes is a crucial part of analyzing alternatives.

Are there ethical implications?

It's important to think about whether the various alternatives available to you are better or worse from an ethical perspective, as well. Sometimes managers make unethical choices because they haven't considered the ethical implications of their actions. In the 1970s, Ford manufactured the Pinto, which had an unfortunate flaw: the car would easily burst into flames when rear-ended. The company did not initially recall the vehicle because they viewed the problem from a financial perspective, without considering the ethical implications.[10] People died as a result of the company's inaction. Unfortunately, these unethical decisions continue to occur—and cause harm—on a regular basis in our society. Effective managers strive to avoid these situations by thinking through the possible ethical implications of their decisions. The decision tree in **Exhibit 6.6** is a great example of a way to make managerial decisions while also taking ethical issues into account.

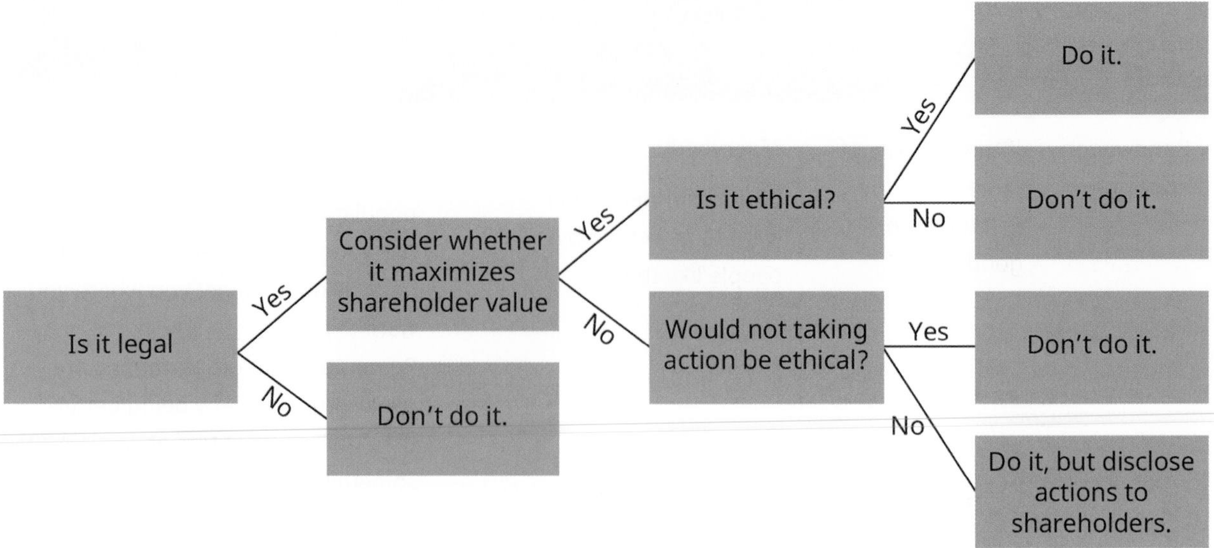

Exhibit 6.6 Ethical Decision Tree (Attribution: Copyright Rice University, OpenStax, under CC-BY 4.0 license)

Thinking through the steps of ethical decision-making may also be helpful as you strive to make good decisions. James Rest's ethical decision-making model[11] identifies four components to ethical decision-making:

1. Moral sensitivity—recognizing that the issue has a moral component;
2. Moral judgment—determining which actions are right vs. wrong;
3. Moral motivation/intention—deciding to do the right thing; and
4. Moral character/action—actually doing what is right.

Note that a failure at any point in the chain can lead to unethical actions! Taking the time to identify possible ethical implications will help you develop moral sensitivity, which is a critical first step to ensuring that you are making ethical decisions.

Once you have determined that a decision has ethical implications, you must consider whether your various alternatives are right or wrong—whether or not they will cause harm, and if so, how much and to whom. This is the moral judgment component. If you aren't sure about whether something is right or wrong, think about how you would feel if that decision ended up on the front page of a major newspaper. If you would feel guilty or ashamed, don't do it! Pay attention to those emotional cues—they are providing important information about the option that you are contemplating.

The third step in the ethical decision-making model involves making a decision to do what is right, and the fourth step involves following through on that decision. These may sound, but consider a situation in which your boss tells you to do something that you know to be wrong. When you push back, your boss makes it clear that you will lose your job if you don't do what you've been told to do. Now, consider that you have family at home who rely on your income. Making the decision to do what you know is right could come at a substantial cost to you personally. In these situations, your best course of action is to find a way to persuade your boss that the unethical action will cause greater harm to the organization in the long-term.

Step 4: Selecting an Alternative

Once alternative options have been generated and analyzed, the decision maker must select one of the options. Sometimes this is easy—one option is clearly superior to the others. Often, however, this is a challenge because there is not a clear "winner" in terms of the best alternative. As mentioned earlier in the chapter, there may be multiple good options, and which one will be best is unclear even after gathering all available evidence. There may not be a single option that doesn't upset some stakeholder group, so you will make someone unhappy no matter what you choose. A weak decision maker may become paralyzed in this situation, unable to select among the various alternatives for lack of a clearly "best" option. They may decide to keep gathering additional information in hopes of making their decision easier. As a manager, it's important to think about whether the benefit of gathering additional information will outweigh the cost of waiting. If there are time pressures, waiting may not be possible.

Recognize that perfection is unattainable

Effective managers recognize that they will not always make optimal (best possible) decisions because they don't have complete information and/or don't have the time or resources to gather and process all the possible information. They accept that their decision-making will not be perfect and strive to make good decisions overall. Recognizing that perfection is impossible will also help managers to adjust and change if they realize later on that the selected alternative was not the best option.

Talk to other people

This is another point in the process at which talking to others can be helpful. Selecting one of the alternatives will ultimately be your responsibility, but when faced with a difficult decision, talking through your choice with someone else may help you clarify that you are indeed making the best possible decision from among the available options. Sharing information verbally also causes our brains to process that information differently, which can provide new insights and bring greater clarity to our decision-making.

Step 5: Implementing the Selected Alternative

After selecting an alternative, you must implement it. This may seem too obvious to even mention, but implementation can sometimes be a challenge, particularly if the decision is going to create conflict or dissatisfaction among some stakeholders. Sometimes we know what we need to do but still try to avoid actually doing it because we know others in the organization will be upset—even if it's the best solution. Follow-through is a necessity, however, to be effective as a manager. If you are not willing to implement a decision, it's a good idea to engage in some self-reflection to understand why. If you know that the decision is going to create conflict, try to think about how you'll address that conflict in a productive way. It's also possible that we feel that there is no good alternative, or we are feeling pressured to make a decision that we know deep down is not right from an ethical perspective. These can be among the most difficult of decisions. You should always strive to make decisions that you feel good about—which means doing the right thing, even in the face of pressures to do wrong.

Step 6: Evaluating the Effectiveness of Your Decision

Managers sometimes skip the last step in the decision-making process because evaluating the effectiveness of a decision takes time, and managers, who are generally busy, may have already moved on to other projects. Yet evaluating effectiveness is important. When we fail to evaluate our own performance and the outcomes of our decisions, we cannot learn from the experience in a way that enables us to improve the quality of our future decisions.

Attending fully to each step in the decision-making process improves the quality of decision-making and, as we've seen, managers can engage in a number of tactics to help them make good decisions. Take a look at the *Ethics in Practice* box to see an example of how one particular manager puts these techniques into practice to make good decisions.

ETHICS IN PRACTICE

Rob Ault, Project Manager, Bayside Community Church

Bradenton, Florida

When it comes to decision-making, ethical dilemmas require particular care. Because managers make many decisions, it should not be surprising that some of those decisions will have ethical implications. With multiple stakeholders to consider, sometimes what is best for one group of stakeholders is not what is best for others. I talked to Rob Ault about his experiences with ethical dilemmas over the course of his career. Rob has been in managerial roles for over 25 years, since he was 19 years old. He told me that he had experienced a number of ethical dilemmas in that time.

Rob has spent most of his career working for for-profit organizations, and for about half of that time he has worked in a union environment. What he has found most frustrating, regardless of environment, was when it was clear to him what was right, but what was right conflicted with what his boss was telling him to do. This included a situation in which he felt an employee should be fired for misbehavior (but wasn't), as well as situation in which he was asked to fire someone undeservedly. What we mostly talked about, though, was his process. How did he go about making decisions in these challenging situations?

Rob clearly stated that his approach to these situations has changed with experience. What he did early in his career is not necessarily what he would do now. He said that it takes experience and some maturity to recognize that, as a leader, the decisions you make affect other people's lives. He also explained that a starting point for the decision-making process is always a recognition of the fact that you have been hired to generate a benefit for your company. So a manager's decisions need to come from the perspective of what is going to be in the best long-term interest of the organization (in addition to what is morally right). This isn't always easy, because short-term consequences are much easier to observe and predict.

I asked Rob who he talked to prior to making decisions in situations with an ethical component. Rob told me that he felt one of the most important things you should do as a leader is to intentionally create and build relationships with people you trust in the organization. That way you have people you know you can talk to when difficult situations come up. He was very clear that you should always talk to your boss, who will tend to have a broader understanding of what is going on in the context of the larger organization. He also told me that he liked to talk to his father, who happened to work in human resource management for a large Fortune 500 organization. His father was always helpful in providing the perspective of how things were likely to play out long-term if one person was allowed to bend the rules. Rob realized eventually that the long-term consequences of this were almost always negative: once one person is allowed to misbehave, others find out about it and realize that they can do the same thing without repercussions. Rob also seeks out the opinions of other individuals in the organization before reaching decisions with an ethical component; he told me that when he worked in a union environment, he tried to make sure he had a good relationship with the union steward, because it was helpful to get the perspective of someone who was committed to the side of the employee.

The biggest ethical dilemma Rob faced was one that he actually couldn't talk to me about. He disagreed with what he was being asked to do, and when it was clear that he had no other choice in the matter, he quit his job rather than do something he felt wasn't right. He accepted a severance package in exchange for signing a nondisclosure agreement, which is why he can't share any details . . . but it was clear from our conversation that he feels he made the right choice. That particular ethical dilemma makes it clear how challenging managerial decision-making can sometimes be.

Discussion Questions

1. If you were faced with an ethical dilemma, from whom would you seek advice?
2. Describe some decisions that might be good for an organization's profitability in the short-term, but bad for the organization in the long-term.
3. What factors would you take into consideration if you were thinking about leaving your job rather than do something unethical?

CONCEPT CHECK 

1. Explain what satisficing is and when it may be a good strategy.
2. What are the six steps in the decision-making process?
3. What are the four steps involved in ethical decision-making?

6.6 Group Decision-Making

6. What are the advantages and disadvantages of group decision-making, and how can a manager improve the quality of group decision-making?

Involving more people in the decision-making process can greatly improve the quality of a manager's decisions and outcomes. However, involving more people can also increase conflict and generate other challenges. We turn now to the advantages and disadvantages of group decision-making.

Advantages of Group Decisions

An advantage to involving groups in decision-making is that you can incorporate different perspectives and ideas. For this advantage to be realized, however, you need a diverse group. In a diverse group, the different group members will each tend to have different preferences, opinions, biases, and stereotypes. Because a variety of viewpoints must be negotiated and worked through, group decision-making creates additional work for a manager, but (provided the group members reflect different perspectives) it also tends to reduce the effects of bias on the outcome. For example, a hiring committee made up of all men might end up hiring a larger proportion of male applicants (simply because they tend to prefer people who are more similar to themselves). But with a hiring committee made up of an equal number of men and women, the bias should be cancelled out, resulting in more applicants being hired based on their qualifications rather than their physical attributes.

Having more people involved in decision-making is also beneficial because each individual brings unique information or knowledge to the group, as well as different perspectives on the problem. Additionally, having the participation of multiple people will often lead to more options being generated and to greater intellectual stimulation as group members discuss the available options. **Brainstorming** is a process of generating as many solutions or options as possible and is a popular technique associated with group decision-making.

All of these factors can lead to superior outcomes when groups are involved in decision-making. Furthermore, involving people who will be affected by a decision in the decision-making process will allow those individuals to have a greater understanding of the issues or problems and a greater commitment to the solutions.

Disadvantages of Group Decisions

Group decision-making is not without challenges. Some groups get bogged down by conflict, while others go to the opposite extreme and push for agreement at the expense of quality discussions. **Groupthink** occurs when group members choose not to voice their concerns or objections because they would rather keep the peace and not annoy or antagonize others. Sometimes groupthink occurs because the group has a positive team spirit and camaraderie, and individual group members don't want that to change by introducing conflict. It can also occur because past successes have made the team complacent.

Often, one individual in the group has more power or exerts more influence than others and discourages those with differing opinions from speaking up (**suppression of dissent**) to ensure that only their own ideas are implemented. If members of the group are not really contributing their ideas and perspectives, however, then the group is not getting the benefits of group decision-making.

How to Form a Quality Group

Effective managers will try to ensure quality group decision-making by forming groups with diverse members so that a variety of perspectives will contribute to the process. They will also encourage everyone to speak up and voice their opinions and thoughts prior to the group reaching a decision. Sometimes groups will also assign a member to play the **devil's advocate** in order to reduce groupthink. The devil's advocate intentionally takes on the role of critic. Their job is to point out flawed logic, to challenge the group's evaluations of various alternatives, and to identify weaknesses in proposed solutions. This pushes the other group members to think more deeply about the advantages and disadvantages of proposed solutions before reaching a decision and implementing it.

Exhibit 6.7 The Devils Advocate At a meeting of McDonald's franchise owners, attorney Brian Schnell was placed in the audience as a devil's advocate and often would strongly disagree with franchisee attorney Bob Zarco that the National Labor Relations Board (NLRB)'s joint-employer ruling on McDonald's is a boon for franchisees. He would raise his hand often and vehemently, which Zarco had asked him to do before the meeting. In that way, the franchisors' articulate arguments could be heard by all franchisee leaders in attendance, and rebutted. Credit (Mr. Blue MauMau/ flickr/ Attribution 2.0 Generic (CC BY 2.0))

The methods we've just described can all help ensure that groups reach good decisions, but what can a manager do when there is too much conflict within a group? In this situation, managers need to help group members reduce conflict by finding some common ground—areas in which they can agree, such as common interests, values, beliefs, experiences, or goals. Keeping a group focused on a common goal can be a very worthwhile tactic to keep group members working with rather than against one another. **Table 6.3** summarizes the techniques to improve group decision-making.

Summary of Techniques That May Improve Group Decision-Making		
Type of Decision	Technique	Benefit
Group decisions	Have diverse members in the group.	Improves quality: generates more options, reduces bias
	Assign a devil's advocate.	Improves quality: reduces groupthink

Table 6.3

Summary of Techniques That May Improve Group Decision-Making		
Type of Decision	Technique	Benefit
	Encourage everyone to speak up and contribute.	Improves quality: generates more options, prevents suppression of dissent
	Help group members find common ground.	Improves quality: reduces personality conflict

Table 6.3 (Attribution: Copyright Rice University, OpenStax, under CC-BY 4.0 license)

Conclusion

Decision-making is a crucial daily activity for managers. Decisions range from small and simple, with straightforward answers, to big and complex, with little clarity about what the best choice will be. Being an effective manager requires learning how to successfully navigate all kinds of decisions. Expertise, which develops gradually through learning and experience, generally improves managerial decision-making, but managers rarely rely solely on their own expertise. They also conduct research and collect information from others; they pay attention to their own biases and to ethical implications; and they think critically about the information that they have received to make decisions that will benefit the organization and its stakeholders.

CONCEPT CHECK

1. Explain why group decision-making can be more effective than individual decision-making.
2. What are some things that can prevent groups from making good decisions?
3. As a manager, what can you do to enhance the quality of group decision-making?

Key Terms

Bounded rationality The concept that when we make decisions, we cannot be fully rational because we don't have all the possible information or the cognitive processing ability to make fully informed, completely rational decisions.

Brainstorming A process of generating as many ideas or alternatives as possible, often in groups.

Confirmation bias The tendency to pay attention to information that confirms our existing beliefs and to ignore or discount information that conflicts with our existing beliefs.

Creativity The generation of new or original ideas.

Critical thinking A disciplined process of evaluating the quality of information, especially by identifying logical fallacies in arguments.

Decision-making The action or process of thinking through possible options and selecting one.

Devil's advocate A group member who intentionally takes on the role of being critical of the group's ideas in order to discourage groupthink and encourage deep thought and discussion about issues prior to making decisions.

Emotional intelligence The ability to understand and manage emotions in oneself and in others.

Escalation of commitment The tendency of decision makers to remain committed to poor decision, even when doing so leads to increasingly negative outcomes.

Evidence-based decision-making A process of collecting the best available evidence prior to making a decision.

Groupthink The tendency of a group to reach agreement very quickly and without substantive discussion.

Heuristics Mental shortcuts that allow a decision maker to reach a good decision quickly. They are strategies that develop based on prior experience.

Nonprogrammed decisions Decisions that are novel and not based on well-defined or known criteria.

Process conflict Conflict about the best way to do something; conflict that is task-oriented and constructive, and not focused on the individuals involved.

Programmed decisions Decisions that are repeated over time and for which an existing set of rules can be developed.

Reactive system System of decision-making in the brain that is quick and intuitive.

Reflective system System of decision-making in the brain that is logical, analytical, and methodical.

Relationship conflict Conflict between individuals that is based on personal (or personality) differences; this type of conflict tends to be destructive rather than constructive.

Satisficing Choosing the first acceptable solution to minimize time spent on a decision.

Stakeholders Individuals or groups who are impacted by the organization. These include owners, employees, customers, suppliers, and members of the community in which the organization is located.

Suppression of dissent When a group member exerts his or her power to prevent others from voicing their thoughts or opinions.

Summary of Learning Outcomes

6.1 Overview of Managerial Decision-Making

1. What are the basic characteristics of managerial decision-making?

Managers are constantly making decisions, and those decisions often have significant impacts and implications for both the organization and its stakeholders. Managerial decision-making is often characterized by complexity, incomplete information, and time constraints, and there is rarely one right answer. Sometimes there are multiple good options (or multiple bad options), and the manager must try to decide which will generate the most positive outcomes (or the fewest negative outcomes). Managers must weigh the possible consequences of each decision and recognize that there are often multiple stakeholders with conflicting needs and preferences so that it often will be impossible to satisfy everyone. Finally, managerial decision-making can sometimes have ethical implications, and these should be contemplated before reaching a final decision.

6.2 How the Brain Processes Information to Make Decisions: Reflective and Reactive Systems

2. What are the two systems of decision-making in the brain?

The brain processes information to make decisions using one of two systems: either the logical, rational (reflective) system or the quick, reactive system. The reflective system is better for significant and important decisions; these generally should not be rushed. However, the reactive system can be lifesaving when time is of the essence, and it can be much more efficient when based on developed experience and expertise.

6.3 Programmed and Nonprogrammed Decisions

3. What is the difference between programmed and nonprogrammed decisions?

Programmed decisions are those that are based on criteria that are well understood, while nonprogrammed decisions are novel and lack clear guidelines for reaching a solution. Managers can establish rules and guidelines for programmed decisions based on known fact, which enables them to reach decisions quickly. Nonprogrammed decisions require more time to resolve; the decision maker may need to conduct research, collect additional information, gather opinions and ideas from other people, and so on.

6.4 Barriers to Effective Decision-Making

4. What barriers exist that make effective decision-making difficult?

There are numerous barriers to effective decision-making. Managers are limited in their ability to collect comprehensive information, and they are limited in their ability to cognitively process all the information that is available. Managers cannot always know all the possible outcomes of all the possible options, and they often face time constraints that limit their ability to collect all the information that they would like to have. In addition, managers, like all humans, have biases that influence their decision-making, and that can make it difficult for them to make good decisions. One of the most common biases that can confound decision-making is confirmation bias, the tendency for a person to pay attention to information that confirms her existing beliefs and ignore information that conflicts with these existing beliefs. Finally, conflict between individuals in organizations can make it challenging to reach a good decision.

6.5 Improving the Quality of Decision-Making

5. How can a manager improve the quality of her individual decision-making?

Managers tend to get better at decision-making with time and experience, which helps them build expertise. Heuristics and satisficing can also be useful techniques for making programmed decisions quickly. For nonprogrammed decisions, a manager can improve the quality of her decision-making by utilizing a variety of other techniques. Managers should also be careful to not skip steps in the decision-making process, to involve others in the process at various points, and to be creative in generating alternatives. They should also engage in evidence-based decision-making: doing research and collecting data and information on which to base the decision. Effective managers also think critically about the quality of the evidence that they collect, and they carefully consider long-term outcomes and ethical implications prior to making a decision.

6.6 Group Decision-Making

6. What are the advantages and disadvantages of group decision-making, and how can a manager improve the quality of group decision-making?

Groups can make better decisions than individuals because group members can contribute more knowledge and a diversity of perspectives. Groups will tend to generate more options as well, which can lead to better solutions. Also, having people involved in making decisions that will affect them can improve their attitudes about the decision that is made. However, groups sometimes fail to generate added value in the decision-making process as a result of groupthink, conflict, or suppression of dissent.

Managers can improve the quality of group decision-making in a number of ways. First, when forming the group, the manager should ensure that the individual group members are diverse in terms of knowledge and perspectives. The manager may also want to assign a devil's advocate to discourage groupthink. Managers should also encourage all group members to contribute their ideas and opinions, and they should not allow a single voice to dominate. Finally, they should not allow personality conflicts to derail group processes.

Chapter Review Questions

1. What are some of the factors that enabled to Jen Rubio and Stephanie Korey to make good decisions when they established their luggage company, Away?
2. What are the two systems that the brain uses in decision-making? How are they related to programmed and nonprogrammed decisions?
3. What is a heuristic, and when would it be appropriate to use a heuristic for decision-making?
4. What is confirmation bias? Explain how it can be a barrier to effective decision-making.
5. What is a logical fallacy?
6. What are the two types of conflict? Which one is constructive, and which is destructive?
7. What are the steps in the decision-making process? Which ones do people tend to skip or spend insufficient time on?
8. What can individuals do to improve the quality of their decision-making?
9. What can groups or group leaders do to improve the quality of group decision-making?
10. What are the benefits of decision-making in a group, instead of individually?

Management Skills Application Exercises

1. If you wanted to buy a new car, what research would you do first to increase the likelihood of making a good decision? As a manager, do you think you would engage in more research or less research than that prior to making big decisions for the organization?
2. Think about a big decision that you have made. What impact did your emotions have on that decision? Did they help or hinder your decision-making? Would you make the same decision again?
3. If you were faced with an ethical dilemma at work, who would you want to talk to for advice prior to reaching a decision?
4. Which would be better to involve a group with, a programmed or a nonprogrammed decision? Why?
5. If you were manager of a group with a lot of personality conflict, what would you do?

Managerial Decision Exercises

1. Imagine that you are a manager and that two of your employees are blaming one another for a recent project not going well. What factors would you consider in deciding whom to believe? Who else would you

talk to before making a decision? What would you do to try to reduce the likelihood of this happening again?
2. You have been asked whether your organization should expand from selling its products only in North America to selling its products in Europe as well. What information would you want to collect? Who would you want to discuss the idea with before making a decision?
3. You have a colleague who decided the organization should pursue a new technology. Nine months into the project of transitioning to the new technology, based on new information you are convinced that the new technology is not going to work out as anticipated. In fact, you expect it to be a colossal failure. However, when you try to talk to your colleague about the issue, she won't listen to your arguments. She is adamant that this new technology is the correct direction for your organization. Why do you think she is so resistant to seeing reason? Given what you learned in this chapter, what could you do to persuade her?
4. Your manager has asked you to take the lead on a new and creative project. She has encouraged you to create your own team (from existing employees) to work with you on the project. What factors would you want to consider in deciding who should join your project team? What would you want to do as the team leader to increase the likelihood that the group will be successful?
5. Identify the logical flaw(s) in this argument:
    - We want to have effective leaders in this organization.
    - Taller individuals tend to be perceived as more leader-like.
    - Men are usually taller than women.
    - So, we should only hire men to be managers in our organization.

Critical Thinking Case

Vinyl Records Make a Comeback

The music industry has seen a series of innovations that have improved audio quality—vinyl records sales were eventually surpassed by compact discs in the 1980s, which were then eclipsed by digital music in the early 2000s. Both of the newer technologies boast superior sound quality to vinyl records. Vinyl should be dead . . . yet it's not. Some say this is simply a result of nostalgia—people love to harken back to older times. However, some audiophiles say that vinyl records produce a "warm" sound that can't be reproduced in any other format. In addition, a vinyl record is a tangible product (you can feel it, touch it, and see it when you own the physical record) and is more attractive, from an aesthetic perspective, than a CD. It is also a format that encourages listening to an entire album at once, rather than just listening to individual tracks, which can change the listening experience.

Whatever the reasons, vinyl is making an impressive comeback. Sales growth has been in the double digits for the last several years (over 50% in 2015 and again in 2016) and is expected to exceed $5 billion in 2017. Sony, which hasn't produced a vinyl record since 1989, recently announced that it is back in the vinyl business.

One of the biggest challenges to making vinyl records is that most of the presses are 40+ years old. In the record-making process, vinyl bits are heated to 170 degrees, and then a specialized machine exerts 150 tons of pressure to press the vinyl into the shape of the record. About a dozen new vinyl record manufacturers have sprung up in the last decade in the United States. Independent Record Pressing, a company based in New Jersey, began producing vinyl records in 2015 using old, existing presses. Their goal upon starting up was to produce over a million records a year. Even at that level of production, though, demand far outstrips the company's capacity to produce because of the limited number of presses available. They could run their machines nonstop, 24 hours a day, and not catch up with demand.

The big question is what the future holds for this industry. Will this just be a passing fad? Will the vinyl record industry remain a small niche market? Or is this the renaissance, the rebirth of a product that can withstand the test of time and alternative technologies? If it's a rebirth, then we should see demand continue to grow at its recent rapid pace . . . and if demand remains strong, then investing in new presses may well be worthwhile. If this is just a short-lived nostalgic return to an outdated media, however, then the large capital investment required to purchase new presses will never be recouped. Even with the recent growth, vinyl records still accounted for only 7% of overall music industry sales in 2015. That may be enough to get old presses running again, but so far it hasn't been enough to promote a lot of investment in new machines. The cost of a new press? Almost half a million dollars.

At least one manufacturer is optimistic about the future of vinyl. GZ Media, based in Czechoslovakia, is currently the world's largest producer of vinyl records. President and owner Zdenek Pelc kept his record factory going during the lean years when vinyl sales bottomed out. He admits that the decision was not wholly logical; he continued in part because of an emotional attachment to the media. After demand for vinyl records practically disappeared, Pelc kept just a few of the presses running to meet the demand that remained. His intention was to be the last remaining manufacturer of vinyl records. Pelc's emotional attachment to vinyl records seems to have served him well, and it's a great example of why basing decisions on pure logic doesn't always lead to the best results. Consumers make purchasing decisions in part based on the emotional appeal of the product, so it shouldn't be surprising that consumers also feel an emotional attachment to vinyl records, as Pelc did.

When demand for vinyl records was low, Pelc stored the company's presses that were no longer in use so that they could be cannibalized for parts as needed. When sales began to grow again in 2005, he started pulling old machines out of storage and even invested in a few new ones. This has made GZ Media not only the largest vinyl record producer in the world, but also one of the only ones with new factory equipment. GZ Media produces over 20 million vinyl records a year, and Pelc is excited to continue that trend and to remain a major manufacturer in what is currently still considered a niche market.

Critical Thinking Questions

1. Why do you think vinyl records are appealing to customers?
2. Do you think the sales growth will continue to be strong for vinyl sales? Why or why not?
3. What research would you want to conduct prior to making a decision to invest in new presses?

Sources: Lee Barron, "Back on record – the reasons behind vinyl's unlikely comeback," *The Conversation*, April 17, 2015, https://theconversation.com/back-on-record-the-reasons-behind-vinyls-unlikely-comeback-39964. Hannah Ellis-Peterson, "Record sales: vinyl hits 25-year high," The Guardian, January 3, 2017, https://www.theguardian.com/music/2017/jan/03/record-sales-vinyl-hits-25-year-high-and-outstrips-streaming. Allan Kozinn, "Weaned on CDs, They're Reaching for Vinyl," *The New York Times*, June 9, 2013. Rick Lyman, "Czech company, pressing hits for years on vinyl, finds it has become one," The New York Times, August 6, 2015. Alec Macfarlane and Chie Kobayashi, "Vinyl comeback: Sony to produce records again after 28-year break," *CNN Money*, June 30, 2017, http://money.cnn.com/2017/06/30/news/sony-music-brings-back-vinyl-records/index.html. Kate Rogers, "Why millennials are buying more vinyl records," CNBC.com, November 6, 2015. https://www.cnbc.com/2015/11/06/why-millennials-are-buying-more-vinyl-records.html. Robert Tait, "In the groove: Czech firm tops list of world's vinyl record producers," *The Guardian*, August 18, 2016.

7 Work Motivation for Performance

Exhibit 7.1 (Credit: mohamed_hassan/ Pixabay/ (CC BY 0))

Introduction

Learning Outcomes

After reading this chapter, you should be able to answer these questions:

1. Define motivation, and distinguish direction and intensity of motivation.
2. Describe a content theory of motivation, and compare and contrast the main content theories of motivation: manifest needs theory, learned needs theory, Maslow's hierarchy of needs, Alderfer's ERG theory, Herzberg's motivator-hygiene theory, and self-determination theory.
3. Describe the process theories of motivation, and compare and contrast the main process theories of motivation: operant conditioning theory, equity theory, goal theory, and expectancy theory.
4. Describe the modern advancements in the study of human motivation.

EXPLORING MANAGERIAL CAREERS

Bridget Anderson

Bridget Anderson thought life would be perfect out in the "real world." After earning her degree in computer science, she landed a well-paying job as a programmer for a large nonprofit organization whose mission she strongly believed in. And—initially—she was happy with her job.

Lately however, Bridget gets a sick feeling in her stomach every morning when her alarm goes off. Why this feeling of misery? After all, she's working in her chosen field in an environment that matches her values. What else could she want? She's more puzzled than anyone.

It's the end of her second year with the organization, and Bridget apprehensively schedules her annual performance evaluation. She knows she's a competent programmer, but she also knows that lately she's been motivated to do only the minimum required to get by. Her heart is just not in her work with this organization. Not exactly how she thought things would turn out, that's for sure.

Bridget's manager Kyle Jacobs surprises her when he begins the evaluation by inquiring about her professional goals. She admits that she hasn't thought much about her future. Kyle asks if she's content in her current position and if she feels that anything is missing. Suddenly, Bridget realizes that she *does* want more professionally.

Question: Are Bridget's motivational problems intrinsic or extrinsic? Which of her needs are currently not being met? What steps should she and her manager take to improve her motivation and ultimately her performance?

Outcome: Once Bridget admits that she's unhappy with her position as a computer programmer, she's ready to explore other possibilities. She and Kyle brainstorm for tasks that will motivate her and bring her greater job satisfaction. Bridget tells Kyle that while she enjoys programming, she feels isolated and misses interacting with other groups in the organization. She also realizes that once she had mastered the initial learning curve, she felt bored. Bridget is ready for a challenge.

Kyle recommends that Bridget move to an information systems team as their technical representative. The team can use Bridget's knowledge of programming, and Bridget will be able to collaborate more frequently with others in the organization.

Bridget and Kyle set specific goals to satisfy her needs to achieve and to work collaboratively. One of Bridget's goals is to take graduate classes in management and information systems. She hopes that this will lead to an MBA and, eventually, to a position as a team leader. Suddenly the prospect of going to work doesn't seem so grim—and lately, Bridget's been beating her alarm!

If you've ever worked with a group of people, and we all have, you have no doubt noticed differences in their performance. Researchers have pondered these differences for many years. Indeed, John B. Watson first studied this issue in the early 1900s. Performance is, of course, an extremely important issue to employers because organizations with high-performing employees will almost always be more effective.

To better understand why people perform at different levels, researchers consider the major determinants of performance: ability, effort (motivation), accurate role perceptions, and environmental factors (see **Exhibit 7.2**). Each performance determinant is important, and a deficit in one can seriously affect the others. People who don't understand what is expected of them will be constrained by their own inaccurate role perceptions, even if they have strong abilities and motivation and the necessary resources to perform their job. None of the performance determinants can compensate for a deficiency in any of the other determinants. Thus, a manager cannot compensate for an employee's lack of skills and ability by strengthening their motivation.

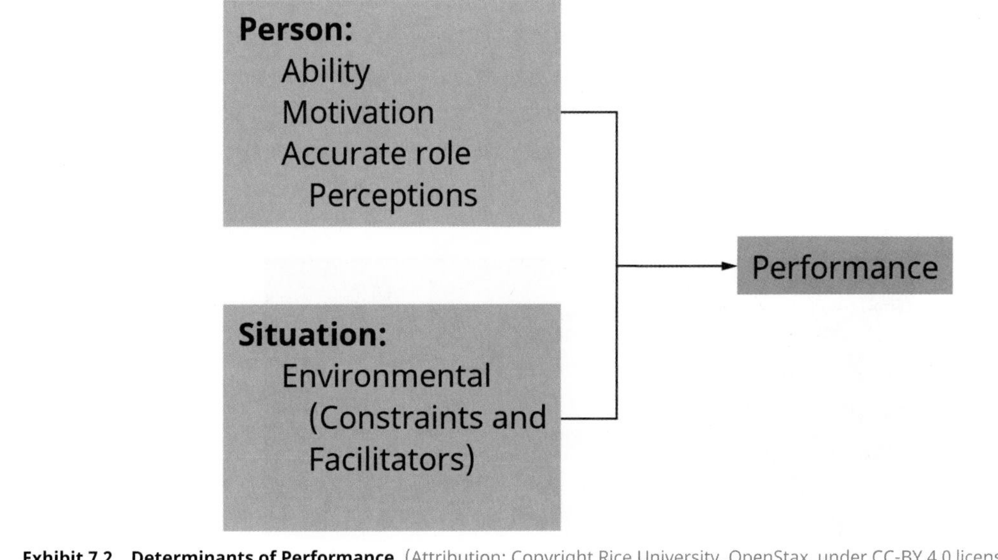

Exhibit 7.2 Determinants of Performance (Attribution: Copyright Rice University, OpenStax, under CC-BY 4.0 license)

7.1 Motivation: Direction and Intensity

1. Define motivation and distinguish direction and intensity of motivation.

Ability refers to the knowledge, skills, and receptiveness to learning that a person brings to a task or job. Knowledge is what a person knows. Skill is their capacity to perform some particular activity (like welding or accounting), including knowing what is expected of them (called accurate role perceptions). Receptiveness to learning is a function of how quickly a person acquires new knowledge. Some people have more ability than others, and high-ability people generally perform better than low-ability people (although we will see that this is not always the case).[1]

Accurate **role perceptions** refer to how well an individual understands their organizational role. This includes the goals (outcomes) the person is expected to achieve and the process by which the goals will be achieved. An employee who has accurate role perceptions knows both their expected outcomes *and* how to go about making those outcomes a reality. Incomplete or inaccurate role perceptions limit employees' capacity to meet expectations, regardless of their abilities and motivation.

The **performance environment** refers to those factors that impact employees' performance but are essentially out of their control. Many environmental factors influence performance. Some factors facilitate performance, while others constrain it. A word processor who has to work with a defective personal computer is certainly not going to perform at peak levels, regardless of ability or desire. Students who are working full time and carrying a full load of classes may not do as well on an exam as they would if they could cut back on their work hours, despite the fact that they have high ability and high motivation.

Motivation is the fourth major factor that determines whether a person will perform a task well. **Motivation** is a force within or outside of the body that energizes, directs, and sustains human behavior. Within the body, examples might be needs, personal values, and goals, while an incentive might be seen as a force outside of the body. The word stems from its Latin root *movere*, which means "to move." Generally speaking, motivation arises as a consequence of a person's desire to (1) fulfill unmet needs or (2) resolve conflicting thoughts that produce anxiety (an unpleasant experience). There are many ways in which we describe and categorize human needs, as we will see later in this chapter. Certain needs are fundamental to our existence, like the need for food and water. When we are hungry, we are energized to satisfy that need by securing and ingesting food.

Our other needs operate in a similar manner. When a need is unfulfilled, we are motivated to engage in behaviors that will satisfy it. The same is true for situations in which we experience conflicting thoughts. When we find ourselves in situations inconsistent with our beliefs, values, or expectations, we endeavor to eliminate the inconsistency. We either change the situation, or we change our perception of it. In both cases, motivation arises out of our interaction with and perception of a particular situation. We perceive the situation as satisfying our needs, or not. Motivation is thus a result of our interacting with situations to satisfy unmet needs or to resolve cognitive dissonance.

Exhibit 7.3 Tom Brady At the University of Michigan, Tom Brady was always a backup to high-potential quarterbacks and was a sixth-round draft pick after his college career. He commented, "A lot of people don't believe in you. It's obvious by now, six other quarterbacks taken and 198 other picks. And I always thought 'you know what, once I get my shot, I'm gonna be ready. I'm gonna really take advantage of that.'" Rather than give up, he hired a sports psychologist to help him deal with constant frustrations. Brady would eventually become an elite quarterback and is now considered one of the greatest players ever. "I guess in a sense I've always had a chip on my shoulder. If you were the 199th pick, you were the 199th pick for a reason: because someone didn't think you were good enough." His passion and motivation helped him achieve that status. (Credit: Brook Ward/ flickr/ Attribution 2.0 Generic (CC BY 2.0))

Simply stated, **work motivation** is the amount of effort a person exerts to achieve a certain level of job performance. Some people try very hard to perform their jobs well. They work long hours, even if it interferes with their family life. Highly motivated people go the "extra mile." High scorers on an exam make sure they know the examination material to the best of their ability, no matter how much midnight oil they have to burn. Other students who don't do as well may just want to get by—football games and parties are a lot more fun, after all.

Motivation is of great interest to employers: *All* employers want their people to perform to the best of their abilities. They take great pains to screen applicants to make sure they have the necessary abilities and motivation to perform well. They endeavor to supply all the necessary resources and a good work environment. Yet motivation remains a difficult factor to manage. As a result, it receives the most attention from organizations and researchers alike, who ask the perennial question "What motivates people to perform well?"

In this chapter we look at current answers to this question. What work conditions foster motivation? How can theories of motivation help us understand the general principles that guide organizational behavior? Rather than analyze why a particular student studies hard for a test, we'll look at the underlying principles of our general behavior in a variety of situations (including test taking). We also discuss the major theories of motivation, along with their implications for management and organizational behavior. By the end of this chapter you should have a better understanding of why some people are more motivated than others. Successful employees know what they want to achieve (direction), and they persist until they achieve their goals (intensity).

Our discussion thus far implies that motivation is a matter of effort. This is only partially true. Motivation has two major components: direction and intensity. **Direction** is *what* a person wants to achieve, what they intend to do. It implies a target that motivated people try to "hit." That target may be to do well on a test. Or it may be to perform better than anyone else in a work group. **Intensity** is *how hard* people try to achieve their targets. Intensity is what we think of as effort. It represents the energy we expend to accomplish something. If our efforts are getting nowhere, will we try different strategies to succeed? (High-intensity-motivated people are persistent!)

It is important to distinguish the direction and intensity aspects of motivation. If *either* is lacking, performance will suffer. A person who knows what they want to accomplish (direction) but doesn't exert much effort (intensity) will not succeed. (Scoring 100 percent on an exam—your target—won't happen unless you study!) Conversely, people who don't have a direction (what they want to accomplish) probably won't succeed either. (At some point you have to decide on a major if you want to graduate, even if you do have straight As.)

Employees' targets don't always match with what their employers want. Absenteeism (some employees call this "calling in well") is a major example.[2] Pursuing your favorite hobby (your target) on a workday (your employer's target) is a conflict in direction; below, we'll examine some theories about why this conflict occurs.

There is another reason why employees' targets are sometimes contrary to their employers'—sometimes employers do not ensure that employees understand what the employer wants. Employees can have great intensity but poor direction. It is management's job to provide direction: Should we stress quality as well as quantity? Work independently or as a team? Meet deadlines at the expense of costs? Employees flounder without direction. Clarifying direction results in accurate *role perceptions,* the behaviors employees think they are expected to perform as members of an organization. Employees with accurate role perceptions understand their purpose in the organization and how the performance of their job duties contributes to organizational objectives. Some motivation theorists assume that employees know the correct direction for their jobs. Others do not. These differences are highlighted in the discussion of motivation theories below.

At this point, as we begin our discussion of the various motivation theories, it is reasonable to ask "Why isn't there just one motivation theory?" The answer is that the different theories are driven by different philosophies of motivation. Some theorists assume that humans are propelled more by needs and instincts than by reasoned actions. Their **content motivation theories** focus on *the content of what* motivates people. Other theorists focus on the process by which people are motivated. **Process motivation theories** address *how* people become motivated—that is, how people perceive and think about a situation. Content and process theories endeavor to predict motivation in a variety of situations. However, none of these theories can predict what will motivate an individual in a given situation 100 percent of the time. Given the complexity of human behavior, a "grand theory" of motivation will probably never be developed.

A second reasonable question at this point is "Which theory is best?" If that question could be easily answered, this chapter would be quite short. The simple answer is that there is no "one best theory." All have been supported by organizational behavior research. All have strengths and weaknesses. However, understanding something about each theory is a major step toward effective management practices.

CONCEPT CHECK 

1. Explain the two drivers of motivation: direction and intensity.
2. What are the differences between content and process theories of motivation?
3. Will there ever be a grand theory of motivation?

7.2 Content Theories of Motivation

2. Describe a content theory of motivation.

The theories presented in this section focus on the importance of human needs. A common thread through all of them is that people have a variety of needs. A **need** is a human condition that becomes "energized" when people feel deficient in some respect. When we are hungry, for example, our need for food has been energized. Two features of needs are key to understanding motivation. First, when a need has been energized, we are motivated to satisfy it. We strive to make the need disappear. **Hedonism,** one of the first motivation theories, assumes that people are motivated to satisfy mainly their own needs (seek pleasure, avoid pain). Long since displaced by more refined theories, hedonism clarifies the idea that needs provide direction for motivation. Second, once we have satisfied a need, it ceases to motivate us. When we've eaten to satiation, we are no longer motivated to eat. Other needs take over and we endeavor to satisfy them. A **manifest need** is whatever need is motivating us at a given time. Manifest needs dominate our other needs.

Instincts are our natural, fundamental needs, basic to our survival. Our needs for food and water are instinctive. Many needs are learned. We are not born with a high (or low) need for achievement—we learn to need success (or failure). The distinction between instinctive and learned needs sometimes blurs; for example, is our need to socialize with other people instinctive or learned?

Manifest Needs Theory

One major problem with the need approach to motivation is that we can make up a need for every human behavior. Do we "need" to talk or be silent? The possibilities are endless. In fact, around the 1920s, some 6,000 human needs had been identified by behavioral scientists!

Henry A. Murray recognized this problem and condensed the list into a few instinctive and learned needs.[3] Instincts, which Murray called **primary needs**, include physiological needs for food, water, sex (procreation), urination, and so on. Learned needs, which Murray called **secondary needs**, are learned throughout one's life and are basically psychological in nature. They include such needs as the need for achievement, for love, and for affiliation (see **Table 7.1**).[4]

Sample Items from Murray's List of Needs	
Social Motive	Brief Definition
Abasement	To submit passively to external force. To accept injury, blame, criticism, punishment. To surrender.
Achievement	To accomplish something difficult. To master, manipulate, or organize physical objects, human beings, or ideas.
Affiliation	To draw near and enjoyably cooperate or reciprocate with an allied other (an other who resembles the subject or who likes the subject). To please and win affection of a coveted object. To adhere and remain loyal to a friend.
Aggression	To overcome opposition forcefully. To fight. To revenge an injury. To attack, injure, or kill another. To oppose forcefully or punish another.
Autonomy	To get free, shake off restraint, break out of confinement.
Counteraction	To master or make up for a failure by restriving.
Defendance	To defend the self against assault, criticism, and blame. To conceal or justify a misdeed, failure, or humiliation. To vindicate the ego.
Deference	To admire and support a superior. To praise, honor, or eulogize.
Dominance	To control one's human environment. To influence or direct the behavior of others by suggestion, seduction, persuasion, or command.
Exhibition	To make an impression. To be seen and heard. To excite, amaze, fascinate, entertain, shock, intrigue, amuse, or entice others.
Harm avoidance	To avoid pain, physical injury, illness, and death. To escape from a dangerous situation. To take precautionary measures.
Infavoidance	To avoid humiliation. To quit embarrassing situations or to avoid conditions that may lead to belittlement or the scorn or indifference of others.
Nurturance	To give sympathy and gratify the needs of a helpless object: an infant or any object that is weak, disabled, tired, inexperienced, infirm, defeated, humiliated, lonely, dejected, sick, or mentally confused. To assist an object in danger. To feed, help, support, console, protect, comfort, nurse, heal.
Order	To put things in order. To achieve cleanliness, arrangement, organization, balance, neatness, tidiness, and precision.

Table 7.1

Sample Items from Murray's List of Needs	
Social Motive	Brief Definition
Play	To act for "fun" without further purpose. To like to laugh and make jokes. To seek enjoyable relaxation from stress.
Rejection	To separate oneself from a negatively valued object. To exclude, abandon, expel, or remain indifferent to an inferior object. To snub or jilt an object.
Sentience	To seek and enjoy sensuous impressions.
Sex	To form and further an erotic relationship. To have sexual intercourse.
Succorance	To have one's needs gratified by the sympathetic aid of an allied object.
Understanding	To ask or answer general questions. To be interested in theory. To speculate, formulate, analyze, and generalize.
Source: Adapted from C. S. Hall and G. Lindzey, *Theories of Personality.* Sample items from Murray's List of Needs. Copyright 1957 by John Wiley & Sons, New York.	

Table 7.1

Murray's main premise was that people have a variety of needs, but only a few are expressed at a given time. When a person is behaving in a way that satisfies some need, Murray called the need manifest. **Manifest needs theory** assumes that human behavior is driven by the desire to satisfy needs. Lucretia's chattiness probably indicates her need for affiliation. This is a manifest need. But what if Lucretia also has a need to dominate others? Could we detect that need from her current behavior? If not, Murray calls this a latent need. A **latent need** cannot be inferred from a person's behavior at a given time, yet the person may still possess that need. The person may not have had the opportunity to express the need. Or she may not be in the proper environment to solicit behaviors to satisfy the need. Lucretia's need to dominate may not be motivating her current behavior because she is with friends instead of coworkers.

Manifest needs theory laid the groundwork for later theories, most notably McClelland's learned needs theory, that have greatly influenced the study of organizational behavior. The major implication for management is that some employee needs are latent. Managers often assume that employees do not have certain needs because the employees never try to satisfy them at work. Such needs may exist (latent needs); the work environment is simply not conducive to their manifestation (manifest needs). A reclusive accountant may not have been given the opportunity to demonstrate his need for achievement because he never received challenging assignments.

Learned Needs Theory

David C. McClelland and his associates (especially John W. Atkinson) built on the work of Murray for over 50 years. Murray studied many different needs, but very few in any detail. McClelland's research differs from Murray's in that McClelland studied three needs in depth: the need for achievement, the need for affiliation, and the need for power (often abbreviated, in turn, as nAch, nAff, and nPow).[5] McClelland believes that these three needs are learned, primarily in childhood. But he also believes that each need can be taught, especially nAch. McClelland's research is important because much of current thinking about organizational behavior is based on it.

Need for Achievement

The **need for achievement (nAch)** is how much people are motivated to excel at the tasks they are performing, especially tasks that are difficult. Of the three needs studied by McClelland, nAch has the greatest impact. The need for achievement varies in intensity across individuals. This makes nAch a personality trait as well as a statement about motivation. When nAch is being expressed, making it a manifest need, people try hard to succeed at whatever task they're doing. We say these people have a high achievement motive. A **motive** is a source of motivation; it is the need that a person is attempting to satisfy. Achievement needs become manifest when individuals experience certain types of situations.

To better understand the nAch motive, it's helpful to describe high-nAch people. You probably know a few of them. They're constantly trying to accomplish something. One of your authors has a father-in-law who would much rather spend his weekends digging holes (for various home projects) than going fishing. Why? Because when he digs a hole, he gets results. In contrast, he can exert a lot of effort and still not catch a fish. A lot of fishing, no fish, and no results equal failure!

McClelland describes three major characteristics of high-nAch people:

1. They feel personally responsible for completing whatever tasks they are assigned. They accept credit for success and blame for failure.
2. They like situations where the probability of success is moderate. High-nAch people are not motivated by tasks that are too easy or extremely difficult. Instead, they prefer situations where the outcome is uncertain, but in which they believe they can succeed if they exert enough effort. They avoid both simple and impossible situations.
3. They have very strong desires for feedback about how well they are doing. They actively seek out performance feedback. It doesn't matter whether the information implies success or failure. They want to know whether they have achieved or not. They constantly ask how they are doing, sometimes to the point of being a nuisance.

Why is nAch important to organizational behavior? The answer is, the success of many organizations is dependent on the nAch levels of their employees.[6] This is especially true for jobs that require self-motivation and managing others. Employees who continuously have to be told how to do their jobs require an overly large management team, and too many layers of management spell trouble in the current marketplace. Today's flexible, cost-conscious organizations have no room for top-heavy structures; their high-nAch employees perform their jobs well with minimal supervision.

Many organizations manage the achievement needs of their employees poorly. A common perception about people who perform unskilled jobs is that they are unmotivated and content doing what they are doing. But, if they have achievement needs, the job itself creates little motivation to perform. It is too easy. There are not enough workers who feel personal satisfaction for having the cleanest floors in a building. Designing jobs that are neither too challenging nor too boring is key to managing motivation. Job enrichment is one effective strategy; this frequently entails training and rotating employees through different jobs, or adding new challenges.

Exhibit 7.4 New York Metro workers carrying a sign The New York City Metropolitan Transit Authority undertook a new approach to how they perform critical inspection and maintenance of subway components that are necessary to providing reliable service. Rather than schedule these inspections during regular hours, they consulted with the maintenance workers, who suggested doing the inspections while sections of the subway were closed to trains for seven consecutive hours. This process was adopted and provided a safer and more efficient way to maintain and clean New York City's sprawling subway. With no trains running, MTA employees are able to inspect signals, replace rails and crossties, scrape track floors, clean stations, and paint areas that are not reachable during normal train operation. Workers also took the opportunity to clean lighting fixtures, change bulbs, and repair platform edges while performing high-intensity station cleaning. (Credit: Patrick Cashin/ flickr/ Attribution 2.0 Generic (CC BY 2.0))

Need for Affiliation

This need is the second of McClelland's learned needs. The **need for affiliation (nAff)** reflects a desire to establish and maintain warm and friendly relationships with other people. As with nAch, nAff varies in intensity across individuals. As you would expect, high-nAff people are very sociable. They're more likely to go bowling with friends after work than to go home and watch television. Other people have lower affiliation needs. This doesn't mean that they avoid other people, or that they dislike others. They simply don't exert as much effort in this area as high-nAff people do.

The nAff has important implications for organizational behavior. High-nAff people like to be around other people, including other people at work. As a result, they perform better in jobs that require teamwork. Maintaining good relationships with their coworkers is important to them, so they go to great lengths to make the work group succeed because they fear rejection. So, high-nAff employees will be especially motivated to perform well if others depend on them. In contrast, if high-nAff people perform jobs in isolation from other people, they will be less motivated to perform well. Performing well on this job won't satisfy their need to be around other people.

Effective managers carefully assess the degree to which people have high or low nAff. Employees high in nAff should be placed in jobs that require or allow interactions with other employees. Jobs that are best performed alone are more appropriate for low-nAff employees, who are less likely to be frustrated.

Need for Power

The third of McClelland's learned needs, the **need for power (nPow)**, is the need to control things, especially other people. It reflects a motivation to influence and be responsible for other people. An employee who is often talkative, gives orders, and argues a lot is motivated by the need for power over others.

Employees with high nPow can be beneficial to organizations. High-nPow people do have effective employee behaviors, but at times they're disruptive. A high-nPow person may try to convince others to do things that are detrimental to the organization. So, when is this need good, and when is it bad? Again, there are no easy answers. McClelland calls this the "two faces of power."[7] A *personal power seeker* endeavors to control others mostly for the sake of dominating them. They want others to respond to their wishes whether or not it is good for the organization. They "build empires," and they protect them.

McClelland's other power seeker is the *social power seeker.* A high social power seeker satisfies needs for power by influencing others, like the personal power seeker. They differ in that they feel best when they have influenced a work group to achieve the group's goals, and not some personal agenda. High social power seekers are concerned with goals that a work group has set for itself, and they are motivated to influence others to achieve the goal. This need is oriented toward fulfilling responsibilities to the employer, not to the self.

McClelland has argued that the high need for social power is the most important motivator for successful managers. Successful managers tend to be high in this type of nPow. High need for achievement can also be important, but it sometimes results in too much concern for personal success and not enough for the employer's success. The need for affiliation contributes to managerial success only in those situations where the maintenance of warm group relations is as important as getting others to work toward group goals.

The implication of McClelland's research is that organizations should try to place people with high needs for social power in managerial jobs. It is critical, however, that those managerial jobs allow the employee to satisfy the nPow through social power acquisition. Otherwise, a manager high in nPow may satisfy this need through acquisition of personal power, to the detriment of the organization.

ETHICS IN PRACTICE

Corporate Social Responsibility as a Motivating Force

Whatever their perspective, most people have a cause that they are passionate about. Bitcoin or net neutrality, sea levels or factory farming—social causes bind us to a larger context or assume a higher purpose for living better.

So what motivates employees to give their all, work creatively, and be fully engaged? According to CB Bhattacharya, the Pietro Ferrero Chair in Sustainability at ESMT European School of Management and Technology in Berlin, Germany, employment engagement, or how positive employees feel about their current job, was at an all-time low globally in 2016: 13 percent. But not all companies battle such low engagement rates. Unilever employees more than 170,000 workers globally and has an employ engagement level around 80 percent. How? Bhattacharya credits the success of Unilever, and other companies with similar engagement levels, to an emphasis on a "sustainable business model." He outlines eight steps that companies take to move sustainability and social responsibility from buzzwords to a company mission capable of motivating employees (Knowledge @ Wharton 2016).

According to Bhattacharya, a company needs to first define what it does and its long-term purpose, and then reconcile its sustainability goals with its economic goals. With its purpose and goals defined, it can then educate the workforce on sustainable methods to create knowledge and competence. Champions for the effort must be found throughout the organization, not just at the top. Competition should be encouraged among employees to find and embrace new goals. Sustainability should be visible both within and outside the company. Sustainability should be tied to a higher purpose and foster a sense of unity not simply among employees, but even with competition at a societal level (Knowledge @ Wharton 2016).

Other companies have made social responsibility an everyday part of what they do. Launched in 2013, Bombas is the brain child of Randy Goldberg and David Heath. Goldberg and Heath discovered that socks are the most-requested clothing at homeless shelters. In response, the two entrepreneurs launched a line of socks that not only "reinvents" the sock (they claim), but also helps those in need. For each pair of socks purchased, the company donates a pair of socks to someone in need (Mulvey 2017). According to the company website, "Bombas exists to help solve this problem, to support the homeless community, and to bring awareness to an under-publicized problem in the United States" (n.p.). Although the New York–based company is still growing, as of October 2017 Bombas had donated more than four million pairs of socks (Bombas 2017).

In 2016, the Royal Bank of Scotland (RBS) launched a pilot program called Jump in which employees participated in challenges on ways to save water and electricity, as well as other sustainability issues. At the end of the pilot, 95 percent of the employees reported that they felt the program had contributed to employee engagement, team building, and environmental stability. Given the success of the program, in 2017 it was expanded to all RBS sites and a smartphone app was added to help employees participate in the challenges (Barton 2017).

Placing a *company* in a larger context and adding a second, higher purpose than the established company goals motivates employees to police the company itself to be a better global citizen. Companies benefit from reduced waste and increased employee engagement. Many companies are successfully motivating their staff, and working toward more sustainable practices, while improving lives directly.

Sources:

Barton, Tynan. 2017. "RBS boosts employee motivation and engagement through its CSR approach." *employee benefits.* https://www.employeebenefits.co.uk/issues/april-2017/rbs-boosts-employee-motivation-engagement-csr-approach/

Bombas. 2017. "Giving Back." https://bombas.com/pages/giving-back

Knowledge @ Wharton. 2016. "How Companies Can Tap Sustainability to Motivate Staff." http://knowledge.wharton.upenn.edu/article/how-companies-tap-sustainability-to-motivate-staff/

Mulvey, Kelsey. 2017. "This company spent two years perfecting gym socks, and it paid off." *Business*

Insider. http://www.businessinsider.com/bombas-athletic-sock-review-2017-1

1. Do you think social responsibility to promote sustainable practices? Why or why not?
2. Do you think most companies' CSR programs are essentially PR gimmicks? Why or why not? Give examples.

Maslow's Hierarchy of Needs

Any discussion of needs that motivate performance would be incomplete without considering Abraham Maslow.[8] Thousands of managers in the 1960s were exposed to Maslow's theory through the popular writings of Douglas McGregor.[9] Today, many of them still talk about employee motivation in terms of Maslow's theory.

Maslow was a psychologist who, based on his early research with primates (monkeys), observations of patients, and discussions with employees in organizations, theorized that human needs are arranged hierarchically. That is, before one type of need can manifest itself, other needs must be satisfied. For example, our need for water takes precedence over our need for social interaction (this is also called *prepotency*). We will always satisfy our need for water before we satisfy our social needs; water needs have prepotency over social needs. Maslow's theory differs from others that preceded it because of this hierarchical, prepotency concept.

Maslow went on to propose five basic types of human needs. This is in contrast to the thousands of needs that earlier researchers had identified, and also fewer than Murray identified in his theory. Maslow condensed human needs into a manageable set. Those five human needs, in the order of prepotency in which they direct human behavior, are:

1. *Physiological and survival needs.* These are the most basic of human needs, and include the needs for water, food, sex, sleep, activity, stimulation, and oxygen.
2. *Safety and security needs.* These needs invoke behaviors that assure freedom from danger. This set of needs involves meeting threats to our existence, including extremes in environmental conditions (heat, dust, and so on), assault from other humans, tyranny, and murder. In other words, satisfaction of these needs prevents fear and anxiety while adding stability and predictability to life.
3. *Social needs.* These needs reflect human desires to be the target of affection and love from others. They are especially satisfied by the presence of spouses, children, parents, friends, relatives, and others to whom we feel close. Feelings of loneliness and rejection are symptoms that this need has not been satisfied.
4. *Ego and esteem.* Esteem needs go beyond social needs. They reflect our need to be respected by others, and to have esteem for ourselves. It is one thing to be liked by others. It is another thing to be respected for our talents and abilities. Ego and esteem needs have internal (self) and external (others) focuses. An internal focus includes desires for achievement, strength, competence, confidence, and independence. An external focus includes desires to have prestige, recognition, appreciation, attention, and respect from others. Satisfaction of external esteem needs can lead to satisfaction of internal esteem needs.
5. *Self-actualization.* Self-actualization needs are the most difficult to describe. Unlike the other needs, the need for self-actualization is never completely satisfied. Self-actualization involves a desire for self-fulfillment, "to become more and more what one is, to become everything that one is capable of becoming."[10] Because people are so different in their strengths and weaknesses, in capacities and limitations, the meaning of self-actualization varies greatly. Satisfying self-actualization needs means developing all of our special abilities to their fullest degree.

Exhibit 7.5 Seattle protester with sign (Credit: Adrenalin Tim /flickr/ Attribution 2.0 Generic (CC BY 2.0))

Exhibit 7.5 A protester at an anti-war demonstration in Seattle held up this sign. Where would you place that on Maslow's hierarchy of needs?

Exhibit 7.6 illustrates Maslow's proposed hierarchy of needs. According to his theory, people first direct their attention to satisfying their lower-order needs. Those are the needs at the bottom of the pyramid (physiological, safety, and security). Once those needs have been satisfied, the next level, social needs, become energized. Once satisfied, we focus on our ego and esteem needs. Maslow believed that most people become fixated at this level. That is, most people spend much of their lives developing self-esteem and the esteem of others. But, once those esteem needs are satisfied, Maslow predicted that self-actualization needs would dominate. There are no higher levels in the pyramid, because self-actualization needs can never be fully satisfied. They represent a continuing process of self-development and self-improvement that, once satisfied on one dimension (painting), create motivation to continue on other dimensions (sculpting). One wonders if athletes like Tim Tebow are self-actualizing when they participate in multiple sporting endeavors at the professional level.

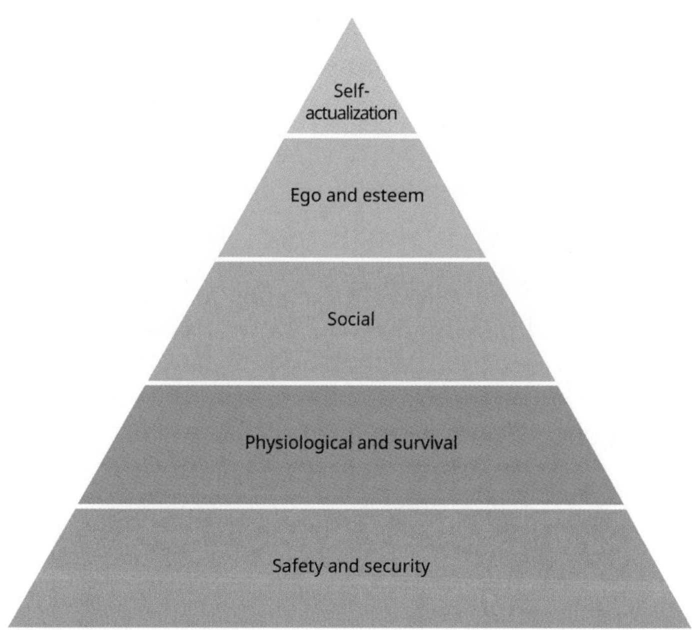

Exhibit 7.6 Maslow's Hierarchy of Needs *Source:* Based on A. H. Maslow. 1943. A theory of human motivation. *Psychological Bulletin* 50:370–396.

An overriding principle in this theory is that a person's attention (direction) and energy (intensity) will focus on satisfying the lowest-level need that is not currently satisfied. Needs can also be satisfied at some point but become active (dissatisfied) again. Needs must be "maintained" (we must continue to eat occasionally). According to Maslow, when lower-level needs are reactivated, we once again concentrate on that need. That is, we lose interest in the higher-level needs when lower-order needs are energized.

The implications of Maslow's theory for organizational behavior are as much conceptual as they are practical. The theory posits that to maximize employee motivation, employers must try to guide workers to the upper parts of the hierarchy. That means that the employer should help employees satisfy lower-order needs like safety and security and social needs. Once satisfied, employees will be motivated to build esteem and respect through their work achievements. **Exhibit 7.6** shows how Maslow's theory relates to factors that organizations can influence. For example, by providing adequate pay, safe working conditions, and cohesive work groups, employers help employees satisfy their lower-order needs. Once satisfied, challenging jobs, additional responsibilities, and prestigious job titles can help employees satisfy higher-order esteem needs.

Maslow's theory is still popular among practicing managers. Organizational behavior researchers, however, are not as enamored with it because research results don't support Maslow's hierarchical notion. Apparently, people don't go through the five levels in a fixed fashion. On the other hand, there is some evidence that people satisfy the lower-order needs before they attempt to satisfy higher-order needs. Refinements of Maslow's theory in recent years reflect this more limited hierarchy.[11] The self-assessment below will allow you to evaluate the strength of your five needs.

Alderfer's ERG Theory

Clayton Alderfer observed that very few attempts had been made to test Maslow's full theory. Further, the evidence accumulated provided only partial support. During the process of refining and extending Maslow's theory, Alderfer provided another need-based theory and a somewhat more useful perspective on motivation.[12] Alderfer's **ERG theory** compresses Maslow's five need categories into three: existence, relatedness, and growth.[13] In addition, ERG theory details the dynamics of an individual's movement between the need categories in a somewhat more detailed fashion than typically characterizes interpretations of Maslow's work.

As shown in **Exhibit 7.7**, the ERG model addresses the same needs as those identified in Maslow's work:

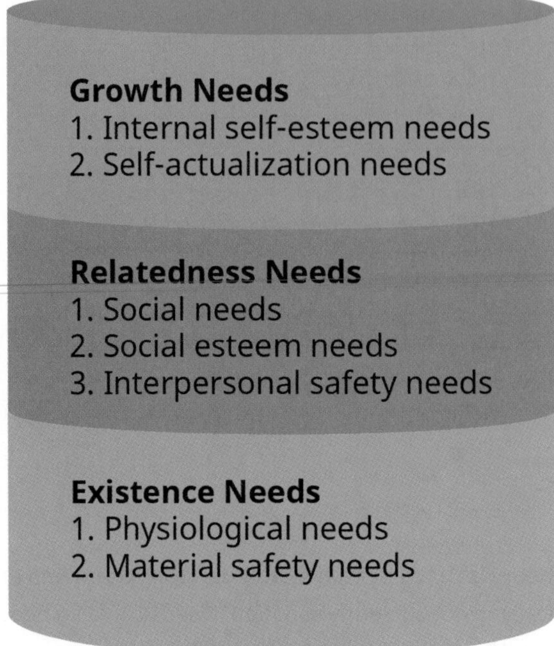

Exhibit 7.7 Alderfer's ERG Theory (Attribution: Copyright Rice University, OpenStax, under CC-BY 4.0 license)

- *Existence needs* include physiological and material safety needs. These needs are satisfied by material conditions and not through interpersonal relations or personal involvement in the work setting.
- *Relatedness needs* include all of Maslow's social needs, plus social safety and social esteem needs. These needs are satisfied through the exchange of thoughts and feelings with other people.
- *Growth needs* include self-esteem and self-actualization needs. These needs tend to be satisfied through one's full involvement in work and the work setting.

Exhibit 7.8 identifies a number of ways in which organizations can help their members satisfy these three needs.

Growth Opportunities

- Challenging job
- Creativity
- Organizational advancement
- Responsibility
- Autonomy
- Interesting work
- Achievement
- Participation

Relatedness Opportunities

- Friendship
- Interpersonal security
- Athletic teams
- Social recognition
- Quality supervision
- Work teams
- Social events
- Merit pay

Existence Opportunities

- Heat
- Lighting
- Base salary
- Insurance
- Retirement
- Air conditioning
- Restrooms
- Cafeteria
- Job security
- Health programs
- Clean air
- Drinking water
- Safe conditions
- No layoffs
- Time off

Exhibit 7.8 Satisfying Existence, Relatedness, and Growth Needs (Attribution: Copyright Rice University, OpenStax, under CC-BY 4.0 license)

Four components—satisfaction progression, frustration, frustration regression, and aspiration—are key to understanding Alderfer's ERG theory. The first of these, *satisfaction progression,* is in basic agreement with Maslow's process of moving through the needs. As we increasingly satisfy our existence needs, we direct energy toward relatedness needs. As these needs are satisfied, our growth needs become more active. The second component, *frustration,* occurs when we attempt but fail to satisfy a particular need. The resulting frustration may make satisfying the unmet need even more important to us—unless we repeatedly fail to satisfy that need. In this case, Alderfer's third component, *frustration regression,* can cause us to shift our attention to a previously satisfied, more concrete, and verifiable need. Lastly, the *aspiration* component of the ERG model notes that, by its very nature, growth is intrinsically satisfying. The more we grow, the more we want to grow. Therefore, the more we satisfy our growth need, the more important it becomes and the more strongly we are motivated to satisfy it.

Exhibit 7.9 Jamie Dimon Jamie Dimon, CEO at JP Morgan Chase, is reported to make $27 million dollars per year, and as CEO has an interesting and intrinsically rewarding job. Starting tellers at a Chase Bank make a reported $36,100 per year and are in a position that has repeated tasks and may not be the most rewarding from a motivational point of view. How does this pay structure relate to self-determination theory (SDT)? (Credit: Stefan Chow/ flickr/ Attribution 2.0 Generic (CC BY 2.0))

Alderfer's model is potentially more useful than Maslow's in that it doesn't create false motivational categories. For example, it is difficult for researchers to ascertain when interaction with others satisfies our need for acceptance and when it satisfies our need for recognition. ERG also focuses attention explicitly on movement through the set of needs in both directions. Further, evidence in support of the three need categories and their order tends to be stronger than evidence for Maslow's five need categories and their relative order.

Herzberg's Motivator-Hygiene Theory

Clearly one of the most influential motivation theories throughout the 1950s and 1960s was Frederick Herzberg's motivator-hygiene theory.[14] This theory is a further refinement of Maslow's theory. Herzberg argued that there are two sets of needs, instead of the five sets theorized by Maslow. He called the first set "motivators" (or growth needs). **Motivators**, which relate to the jobs we perform and our ability to feel a sense of achievement as a result of performing them, are rooted in our need to experience growth and self-actualization. The second set of needs he termed "hygienes." **Hygienes** relate to the work environment and are based in the basic human need to "avoid pain." According to Herzberg, growth needs motivate us to perform well and, when these needs are met, lead to the experience of satisfaction. Hygiene needs, on the other hand, must be met to avoid dissatisfaction (but do not necessarily provide satisfaction or motivation).[15]

Hygiene factors are not directly related to the work itself (job content). Rather, hygienes refer to job context factors (pay, working conditions, supervision, and security). Herzberg also refers to these factors as "dissatisfiers" because they are frequently associated with dissatisfied employees. These factors are so frequently associated with dissatisfaction that Herzberg claims they never really provide satisfaction. When they're present in sufficient quantities, we avoid dissatisfaction, but they do not contribute to satisfaction. Furthermore, since meeting these needs does not provide satisfaction, Herzberg concludes that they do not motivate workers.

Motivator factors involve our long-term need to pursue psychological growth (much like Maslow's esteem and self-actualization needs). Motivators relate to *job content.* Job content is what we actually *do* when we perform our job duties. Herzberg considered job duties that lead to feelings of achievement and recognition to be motivators. He refers to these factors as "satisfiers" to reflect their ability to provide satisfying experiences. When these needs are met, we experience satisfaction. Because meeting these needs provides satisfaction, they motivate workers. More specifically, Herzberg believes these motivators lead to high performance (achievement), and the high performance itself leads to satisfaction.

The unique feature of Herzberg's theory is that job conditions that prevent dissatisfaction do not cause satisfaction. Satisfaction and dissatisfaction are on different "scales" in his view. Hygienes can cause dissatisfaction if they are not present in sufficient levels. Thus, an employee can be dissatisfied with low pay. But paying him more will not cause long-term satisfaction *unless* motivators are present. Good pay *by itself* will only make the employee neutral toward work; to attain satisfaction, employees need challenging job duties that result in a sense of achievement. Employees can be dissatisfied, neutral, or satisfied with their jobs, depending on their levels of hygienes and motivators. Herzberg's theory even allows for the possibility that an employee can be satisfied and dissatisfied at the same time—the "I love my job but I hate the pay" situation!

Herzberg's theory has made lasting contributions to organizational research and managerial practice. Researchers have used it to identify the wide range of factors that influence worker reactions. Previously, most organizations attended primarily to hygiene factors. Because of Herzberg's work, organizations today realize the potential of motivators. Job enrichment programs are among the many direct results of his research.

Herzberg's work suggests a two-stage process for managing employee motivation and satisfaction. First, managers should address the hygiene factors. Intense forms of dissatisfaction distract employees from important work-related activities and tend to be demotivating.[16] Thus, managers should make sure that such basic needs as adequate pay, safe and clean working conditions, and opportunities for social interaction are met. They should then address the much more powerful motivator needs, in which workers experience recognition, responsibility, achievement, and growth. If motivator needs are ignored, neither long-term satisfaction nor high motivation is likely. When motivator needs are met, however, employees feel satisfied and are motivated to perform well.

Self-Determination Theory

One major implication of Herzberg's motivator-hygiene theory is the somewhat counterintuitive idea that managers should focus more on motivators than on hygienes. (After all, doesn't everyone want to be paid well? Organizations have held this out as a chief motivator for decades!) Why might concentrating on motivators give better results? To answer this question, we must examine *types* of motivation. Organizational behavior researchers often classify motivation in terms of what stimulates it. In the case of **extrinsic motivation**, we endeavor to acquire something that satisfies a lower-order need. Jobs that pay well and that are performed in safe, clean working conditions with adequate supervision and resources directly or indirectly satisfy these lower-order needs. These "outside the person" factors are *extrinsic rewards.*

Factors "inside" the person that cause people to perform tasks, **intrinsic motivation**, arise out of performing a task in and of itself, because it is interesting or "fun" to do. The task is enjoyable, so we continue to do it *even in the absence* of extrinsic rewards. That is, we are motivated by *intrinsic rewards,* rewards that we more or less give ourselves. Intrinsic rewards satisfy higher-order needs like relatedness and growth in ERG theory. When we sense that we are valuable contributors, are achieving something important, or are getting better at some skill, we like this feeling and strive to maintain it.

Self-determination theory (SDT) seeks to explain not only what causes motivation, but also how extrinsic rewards affect intrinsic motivation.[17] In SDT, extrinsic motivation refers to the performance of an activity in order to attain some valued outcome, while intrinsic motivation refers to performing an activity for the inherent satisfaction of the activity itself. SDT specifies when an activity will be intrinsically motivating and when it will not. Considerable numbers of studies have demonstrated that tasks are intrinsically motivating when they satisfy at least one of three higher-order needs: competence, autonomy, and relatedness. These precepts from SDT are entirely consistent with earlier discussions of theories by McClelland, Maslow, Alderfer, and Herzberg.

SDT takes the concepts of extrinsic rewards and intrinsic motivation further than the other need theories. SDT researchers have consistently found that as the level of extrinsic rewards increases, the amount of intrinsic motivation *decreases.* That is, SDT posits that extrinsic rewards not only do not provide intrinsic motivation, they diminish it. Think of this in terms of hobbies. Some people like to knit, others like to carve wood. They do it because it is intrinsically motivating; the hobby satisfies needs for competence, autonomy, and relatedness. But what happens if these hobbyists start getting paid well for their sweaters and carvings? Over time the hobby becomes less fun and is done in order to receive extrinsic rewards (money). Extrinsic motivation increases as intrinsic motivation decreases! When extrinsic rewards are present, people do not feel like what they do builds competence, is self-determined, or enhances relationships with others.

SDT theory has interesting implications for the management of organizational behavior. Some jobs are by their very nature uninteresting and unlikely to be made interesting. Automation has eliminated many such jobs, but they are still numerous. SDT would suggest that the primary way to motivate high performance for such jobs is to make performance contingent on extrinsic rewards. Relatively high pay is necessary to sustain performance on certain low-skill jobs. On the other hand, SDT would suggest that to enhance intrinsic motivation on jobs that are interesting, don't focus only on increasing extrinsic rewards (like large pay bonuses). Instead, create even more opportunities for employees to satisfy their needs for competence, autonomy, and relatedness. That means giving them opportunities to learn new skills, to perform their jobs without interference, and to develop meaningful relationships with other customers and employees in other departments. Such actions enhance intrinsic rewards.

You may have noticed that content theories are somewhat quiet about what determines the intensity of motivation. For example, some people steal to satisfy their lower-order needs (they have high intensity). But most of us don't steal. Why is this? Process theories of motivation attempt to explain this aspect of motivation by focusing on the intensity of motivation as well as its direction. According to self-determination theory, skilled workers who are given a chance to hone their skills and the freedom to practice their craft will be intrinsically motivated.

CONCEPT CHECK 

1. Understand the content theories of motivation.
2. Understand the contributions that Murray, McClelland, Maslow, Alderfer, and Herzberg made toward an understanding of human motivation.

7.3 Process Theories of Motivation

3. Describe the process theories of motivation, and compare and contrast the main process theories of motivation: operant conditioning theory, equity theory, goal theory, and expectancy theory.

Process theories of motivation try to explain *why* behaviors are initiated. These theories focus on the mechanism by which we choose a target, and the effort that we exert to "hit" the target. There are four major process theories: (1) operant conditioning, (2) equity, (3) goal, and (4) expectancy.

Operant Conditioning Theory

Operant conditioning theory is the simplest of the motivation theories. It basically states that people will do those things for which they are rewarded and will avoid doing things for which they are punished. This premise is sometimes called the "law of effect." However, if this were the sum total of conditioning theory, we would not be discussing it here. Operant conditioning theory does offer greater insights than "reward what you want and punish what you don't," and knowledge of its principles can lead to effective management practices.

Operant conditioning focuses on the learning of voluntary behaviors.[18] The term **operant conditioning** indicates that learning results from our "operating on" the environment. After we "operate on the environment" (that is, behave in a certain fashion), consequences result. These consequences determine the likelihood of similar behavior in the future. Learning occurs because we do something to the environment. The environment then reacts to our action, and our subsequent behavior is influenced by this reaction.

The Basic Operant Model

According to **operant conditioning theory**, we learn to behave in a particular fashion because of consequences that resulted from our past behaviors.[19] The learning process involves three distinct steps (see **Table 7.2**). The first step involves a *stimulus* (S). The stimulus is any situation or event we perceive that we then respond to. A homework assignment is a stimulus. The second step involves a *response* (R), that is, any behavior or action we take in reaction to the stimulus. Staying up late to get your homework assignment in on time is a response. (We use the words response and behavior interchangeably here.) Finally, a *consequence* (C) is any event that follows our response and that makes the response more or less likely to occur in the future. If Colleen Sullivan receives praise from her superior for working hard, and if getting that praise is a pleasurable event, then it is likely that Colleen will work hard again in the future. If, on the other hand, the superior ignores or criticizes Colleen's response (working hard), this consequence is likely to make Colleen avoid working hard in the future. It is the experienced consequence (positive or negative) that influences whether a response will be repeated the next time the stimulus is presented.

Process Theories of Motivation	
General Operant Model: S → R → C	
Ways to Strengthen the S → R Link	
1. S → R → C+	(Positive Reinforcement)
2. S → R → C-	(Negative Reinforcement)
3. S → R → (no C-)	(Avoidance Learning)
Ways to Weaken the S → R Link	
1. S → R → (no C)	(Nonreinforcement)
2. S → R → C-	(Punishment)

Table 7.2 (Attribution: Copyright Rice University, OpenStax, under CC-BY 4.0 license)

Reinforcement occurs when a consequence makes it more likely the response/behavior will be repeated in the future. In the previous example, praise from Colleen's superior is a reinforcer. **Extinction** occurs when a consequence makes it less likely the response/behavior will be repeated in the future. Criticism from Colleen's supervisor could cause her to stop working hard on any assignment.

There are three ways to make a response more likely to recur: positive reinforcement, negative reinforcement, and avoidance learning. In addition, there are two ways to make the response less likely to recur: nonreinforcement and punishment.

Making a Response More Likely

According to reinforcement theorists, managers can encourage employees to repeat a behavior if they provide a desirable consequence, or reward, after the behavior is performed. A **positive reinforcement** is a desirable consequence that satisfies an active need or that removes a barrier to need satisfaction. It can be as simple as a kind word or as major as a promotion. Companies that provide "dinners for two" as awards to those employees who go the extra mile are utilizing positive reinforcement. It is important to note that there are wide variations in what people consider to be a positive reinforcer. Praise from a supervisor may be a powerful reinforcer for some workers (like high-nAch individuals) but not others.

Another technique for making a desired response more likely to be repeated is known as **negative reinforcement**. When a behavior causes something undesirable to be taken away, the behavior is more likely to be repeated in the future. Managers use negative reinforcement when they remove something unpleasant from an employee's work environment in the hope that this will encourage the desired behavior. Ted doesn't like being continually reminded by Philip to work faster (Ted thinks Philip is nagging him), so he works faster at stocking shelves to avoid being criticized. Philip's reminders are a negative reinforcement for Ted.

Approach using negative reinforcement with extreme caution. Negative reinforcement is often confused with punishment. Punishment, unlike reinforcement (negative or positive), is intended to make a particular behavior go away (not be repeated). Negative reinforcement, like positive reinforcement, is intended to make a behavior more likely to be repeated in the future. In the previous example, Philip's reminders simultaneously punished one behavior (slow stocking) and reinforced another (faster stocking). The difference is often a fine one, but it becomes clearer when we identify the behaviors we are trying to encourage (reinforcement) or discourage (punishment).

Exhibit 7.10 Workers stacking eggs A worker stacks eggs on the shelves at a supermarket. Consider the interchange between Ted and Philip regarding speeding up the shelf restocking process. What could go wrong? (Credit: Alex Barth/ flickr/ Attribution 2.0 Generic (CC BY 2.0))

A third method of making a response more likely to occur involves a process known as avoidance learning. **Avoidance learning** occurs when we learn to behave in a certain way to avoid encountering an undesired or unpleasant consequence. We may learn to wake up a minute or so before our alarm clock rings so we can turn it off and not hear the irritating buzzer. Some workers learn to get to work on time to avoid the harsh words or punitive actions of their supervisors. Many organizational discipline systems rely heavily on avoidance learning by using the threat of negative consequences to encourage desired behavior. When managers warn an employee not to be late again, when they threaten to fire a careless worker, or when they transfer someone to an undesirable position, they are relying on the power of avoidance learning.

Making a Response Less Likely

At times it is necessary to discourage a worker from repeating an undesirable behavior. The techniques managers use to make a behavior less likely to occur involve doing something that frustrates the individual's need satisfaction or that removes a currently satisfying circumstance. **Punishment** is an aversive consequence that follows a behavior and makes it less likely to reoccur.

Note that managers have another alternative, known as **nonreinforcement**, in which they provide no consequence at all following a worker's response. Nonreinforcement eventually reduces the likelihood of that response reoccurring, which means that managers who fail to reinforce a worker's desirable behavior are also likely to see that desirable behavior less often. If Philip never rewards Ted when he finishes stocking on time, for instance, Ted will probably stop trying to beat the clock. Nonreinforcement can also reduce the likelihood that employees will repeat undesirable behaviors, although it doesn't produce results as quickly as punishment does. Furthermore, if other reinforcing consequences are present, nonreinforcement is unlikely to be effective.

While punishment clearly works more quickly than does nonreinforcement, it has some potentially undesirable side effects. Although punishment effectively tells a person what *not* to do and stops the undesired behavior, it does not tell them what they *should* do. In addition, even when punishment works as intended, the worker being punished often develops negative feelings toward the person who does the punishing. Although sometimes it is very difficult for managers to avoid using punishment, it works best when reinforcement is also used. An experiment conducted by two researchers at the University of Kansas found that using nonmonetary reinforcement in addition to punitive disciplinary measures was an effective way to decrease absenteeism in an industrial setting.[20]

Schedules of Reinforcement

When a person is learning a new behavior, like how to perform a new job, it is desirable to reinforce effective behaviors every time they are demonstrated (this is called *shaping*). But in organizations it is not usually possible to reinforce desired behaviors every time they are performed, for obvious reasons. Moreover, research indicates that constantly reinforcing desired behaviors, termed *continuous reinforcement,* can be detrimental in the long run. Behaviors that are learned under continuous reinforcement are quickly extinguished (cease to be demonstrated). This is because people will expect a reward (the reinforcement) every time they display the behavior. When they don't receive it after just a few times, they quickly presume that the behavior will no longer be rewarded, and they quit doing it. Any employer can change employees' behavior by simply not paying them!

If behaviors cannot (and should not) be reinforced every time they are exhibited, how often should they be reinforced? This is a question about **schedules of reinforcement**, or the frequency at which effective employee behaviors should be reinforced. Much of the early research on operant conditioning focused on the best way to maintain the performance of desired behaviors. That is, it attempted to determine how frequently behaviors need to be rewarded so that they are not extinguished. Research zeroed in on four types of reinforcement schedules:

Fixed Ratio. With this schedule, a fixed number of responses (let's say five) must be exhibited before any of the responses are reinforced. If the desired response is coming to work on time, then giving employees a $25 bonus for being punctual every day from Monday through Friday would be a fixed ratio of reinforcement.

Variable Ratio. A variable-ratio schedule reinforces behaviors, *on average,* a fixed number of times (again let's say five). Sometimes the tenth behavior is reinforced, other times the first, but on average every fifth response is reinforced. People who perform under such variable-ratio schedules like this don't know *when* they will be rewarded, but they do know that they *will* be rewarded.

Fixed Interval. In a fixed-interval schedule, a certain amount of time must pass before a behavior is reinforced. With a one-hour fixed-interval schedule, for example, a supervisor visits an employee's workstation and reinforces the first desired behavior she sees. She returns one hour later and reinforces the next desirable behavior. This schedule doesn't imply that reinforcement will be received automatically after the passage of the time period. The time must pass *and* an appropriate response must be made.

Variable Interval. The variable interval differs from fixed-interval schedules in that the specified time interval passes *on average* before another appropriate response is reinforced. Sometimes the time period is shorter than the average; sometimes it is longer.

Which type of reinforcement schedule is best? In general, continuous reinforcement is best while employees are learning their jobs or new duties. After that, variable-ratio reinforcement schedules are superior. In most situations the fixed-interval schedule produces the least effective results, with fixed ratio and variable interval falling in between the two extremes. But remember that effective behaviors must be reinforced with some type of schedule, or they may become extinguished.

Equity Theory

Suppose you have worked for a company for several years. Your performance has been excellent, you have received regular pay increases, and you get along with your boss and coworkers. One day you come to work to find that a new person has been hired to work at the same job that you do. You are pleased to have the extra help. Then, you find out the new person is making $100 more per week than you, despite your longer service and greater experience. How do you feel? If you're like most of us, you're quite unhappy. Your satisfaction has just evaporated. Nothing about your job has changed—you receive the same pay, do the same job, and work for the same supervisor. Yet, the addition of one new employee has transformed you from a happy to an unhappy employee. This feeling of unfairness is the basis for equity theory.

Equity theory states that motivation is affected by the outcomes we receive for our inputs compared to the outcomes and inputs of other people.[21] This theory is concerned with the reactions people have to outcomes they receive as part of a "social exchange." According to equity theory, our reactions to the outcomes we receive from others (an employer) depend both on how we value those outcomes in an absolute sense *and* on the circumstances surrounding their receipt. Equity theory suggests that our reactions will be influenced by our perceptions of the "inputs" provided in order to receive these outcomes ("Did I get as much out of this as I put into it?"). Even more important is our comparison of our inputs to what we believe others received for their inputs ("Did I get as much for my inputs as my coworkers got for theirs?").

The Basic Equity Model

The fundamental premise of equity theory is that we continuously monitor the degree to which our work environment is "fair." In determining the degree of fairness, we consider two sets of factors, inputs and outcomes (see **Exhibit 7.11**). **Inputs** are any factors we contribute to the organization that we feel have value and are relevant to the organization. Note that the value attached to an input is based on *our* perception of its relevance and value. Whether or not anyone else agrees that the input is relevant or valuable is unimportant to us. Common inputs in organizations include time, effort, performance level, education level, skill levels, and bypassed opportunities. Since any factor we consider relevant is included in our evaluation of equity, it is not uncommon for factors to be included that the organization (or even the law) might argue are inappropriate (such as age, sex, ethnic background, or social status).

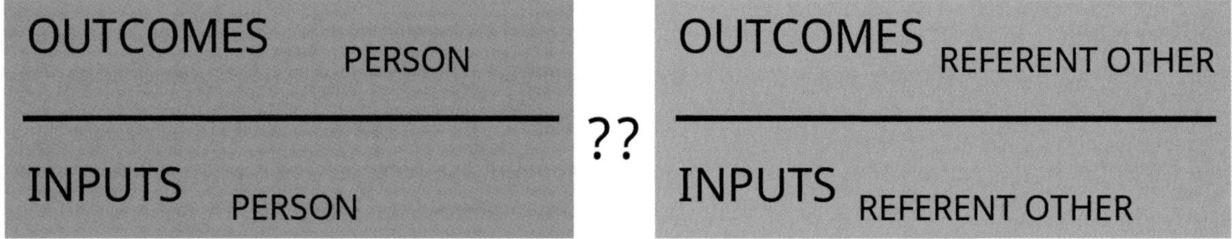

Exhibit 7.11 The Equity Theory Comparison (Attribution: Copyright Rice University, OpenStax, under CC-BY 4.0 license)

Outcomes are anything we perceive as getting back from the organization in exchange for our inputs. Again, the value attached to an outcome is based on our perceptions and not necessarily on objective reality. Common outcomes from organizations include pay, working conditions, job status, feelings of achievement, and friendship opportunities. Both positive and negative outcomes influence our evaluation of equity. Stress, headaches, and fatigue are also potential outcomes. Since any outcome we consider relevant to the exchange influences our equity perception, we frequently include unintended factors (peer disapproval, family reactions).

Equity theory predicts that we will compare our outcomes to our inputs in the form of a ratio. On the basis of this ratio we make an initial determination of whether or not the situation is equitable. If we perceive that the outcomes we receive are commensurate with our inputs, we are satisfied. If we believe that the outcomes are not commensurate with our inputs, we are dissatisfied. This dissatisfaction can lead to ineffective behaviors for the organization if they continue. The key feature of equity theory is that it predicts that we will compare our ratios to the ratios of other people. It is this comparison of the two ratios that has the strongest effect on our equity perceptions. These other people are called referent others because we “refer to” them when we judge equity. Usually, referent others are people we work with who perform work of a similar nature. That is, **referent others** perform jobs that are similar in difficulty and complexity to the employee making the equity determination (see **Exhibit 7.11**).

Three conditions can result from this comparison. Our outcome-to-input ratio could equal the referent other’s. This is a **state of equity**. A second result could be that our ratio is greater than the referent other’s. This is a state of **overreward inequity**. The third result could be that we perceive our ratio to be less than that of the referent other. This is a state of **underreward inequity**.

Equity theory has a lot to say about basic human tendencies. The motivation to compare our situation to that of others is strong. For example, what is the first thing you do when you get an exam back in class? Probably look at your score and make an initial judgment as to its fairness. For a lot of people, the very next thing they do is look at the scores received by fellow students who sit close to them. A 75 percent score doesn’t look so bad if everyone else scored lower! This is equity theory in action.

Most workers in the United States are at least partially dissatisfied with their pay.[22] Equity theory helps explain this. Two human tendencies create feelings of inequity that are not based in reality. One is that we tend to overrate our performance levels. For example, one study conducted by your authors asked more than 600 employees to anonymously rate their performance on a 7-point scale (1 = poor, 7 = excellent). The average was 6.2, meaning the *average* employee rated his or her performance as *very good to excellent.* This implies that the average employee also expects excellent pay increases, a policy most employers cannot afford if they are to remain competitive. Another study found that the average employee (one whose performance is better than half of the other employees and worse than the other half) rated her performance at the 80th percentile (better than 80 percent of the other employees, worse than 20 percent).[23] Again it would be impossible for most organizations to reward the average employee at the 80th percentile. In other words, most employees inaccurately overrate the inputs they provide to an organization. This leads to perceptions of inequity that are not justified.

The second human tendency that leads to unwarranted perceptions of inequity is our tendency to *overrate* the outcomes of others.[24] Many employers keep the pay levels of employees a "secret." Still other employers actually forbid employees to talk about their pay. This means that many employees don't know for certain how much their colleagues are paid. And, because most of us overestimate the pay of others, we tend to think that they're paid more than they actually are, and the unjustified perceptions of inequity are perpetuated.

The bottom line for employers is that they need to be sensitive to employees' need for equity. Employers need to do everything they can to prevent feelings of inequity because employees engage in effective behaviors when they perceive equity and ineffective behaviors when they perceive inequity.

Perceived Overreward Inequity

When we perceive that overreward inequity exists (that is, we unfairly make more than others), it is rare that we are so dissatisfied, guilty, or sufficiently motivated that we make changes to produce a state of perceived equity (or we leave the situation). Indeed, feelings of overreward, when they occur, are quite transient. Very few of us go to our employers and complain that we're overpaid! Most people are less sensitive to overreward inequities than they are to underreward inequities.[25] However infrequently they are used for overreward, the same types of actions are available for dealing with both types of inequity.

Perceived Underreward Inequity

When we perceive that underreward inequity exists (that is, others unfairly make more than we do), we will likely be dissatisfied, angered, and motivated to change the situation (or escape the situation) in order to produce a state of perceived equity. As we discuss shortly, people can take many actions to deal with underreward inequity.

Reducing Underreward Inequity

A simple situation helps explain the consequences of inequity. Two automobile workers in Detroit, John and Mary, fasten lug nuts to wheels on cars as they come down the assembly line, John on the left side and Mary on the right. Their inputs are equal (both fasten the same number of lug nuts at the same pace), but John makes $500 per week and Mary makes $600. Their equity ratios are thus:

$500	$600
John:	<Mary:
10 lug nuts/car	10 lug nuts/car

As you can see, their ratios are not equal; that is, Mary receives greater outcome for equal input. Who is experiencing inequity? According to equity theory, both John *and* Mary—underreward inequity for John, and overreward inequity for Mary. Mary's inequity won't last long (in real organizations), but in our hypothetical example, what might John do to resolve this?

Adams identified a number of things people do to reduce the tension produced by a perceived state of inequity. They change their own outcomes or inputs, *or* they change those of the referent other. They distort their own perceptions of the outcomes or inputs of either party by using a different referent other, or they leave the situation in which the inequity is occurring.

1. Alter inputs of the person. The perceived state of equity can be altered by changing our own inputs, that is, by decreasing the quantity or quality of our performance. John can effect his own mini slowdown and install only nine lug nuts on each car as it comes down the production line. This, of course, might cause him to lose his job, so he probably won't choose this alternative.
2. Alter outcomes of the person. We could attempt to increase outcomes to achieve a state of equity, like ask for a raise, a nicer office, a promotion, or other positively valued outcomes. So John will likely ask for a raise. Unfortunately, many people enhance their outcomes by stealing from their employers.
3. Alter inputs of the referent other. When underrewarded, we may try to achieve a state of perceived equity by encouraging the referent other to increase their inputs. We may demand, for example, that the referent other "start pulling their weight," or perhaps help the referent other to become a better performer. It doesn't matter that the referent other is already pulling their weight—remember, this is all about perception. In our example, John could ask Mary to put on two of his ten lug nuts as each car comes down the assembly line. This would not likely happen, however, so John would be motivated to try another alternative to reduce his inequity.
4. Alter outcomes of the referent other. We can "correct" a state of underreward by directly or indirectly reducing the value of the other's outcomes. In our example, John could try to get Mary's pay lowered to reduce his inequity. This too would probably not occur in the situation described.
5. Distort perceptions of inputs or outcomes. It *is* possible to reduce a perceived state of inequity without changing input or outcome. We simply distort our own perceptions of our inputs or outcomes, *or* we distort our perception of those of the referent other. Thus, John may tell himself that "Mary does better work than I thought" or "she enjoys her work much less than I do" or "she gets paid less than I realized."
6. Choose a different referent other. We can also deal with both over- and underreward inequities by changing the referent other ("my situation is really more like Ahmed's"). This is the simplest and most powerful way to deal with perceived inequity: it requires neither actual nor perceptual changes in anybody's input or outcome, and it causes us to look around and assess our situation more carefully. For example, John might choose as a referent other Bill, who installs dashboards but makes less money than John.
7. Leave the situation. A final technique for dealing with a perceived state of inequity involves removing ourselves from the situation. We can choose to accomplish this through absenteeism, transfer, or termination. This approach is usually not selected unless the perceived inequity is quite high or other attempts at achieving equity are not readily available. Most automobile workers are paid quite well for their work. John is unlikely to find an equivalent job, so it is also unlikely that he will choose this option.

Implications of Equity Theory

Equity theory is widely used, and its implications are clear. In the vast majority of cases, employees experience (or perceive) underreward inequity rather than overreward. As discussed above, few of the behaviors that result from underreward inequity are good for employers. Thus, employers try to prevent unnecessary perceptions of inequity. They do this in a number of ways. They try to be as fair as possible in allocating pay. That is, they measure performance levels as accurately as possible, then give the highest performers the highest pay increases. Second, most employers are no longer secretive about their pay schedules. People are naturally curious about how much they are paid relative to others in the organization. This doesn't mean that employers don't practice discretion—they usually don't reveal specific employees' exact pay. But they do tell employees the minimum and maximum pay levels for their jobs and the pay scales for the jobs of others in the organization. Such practices give employees a factual basis for judging equity.

Supervisors play a key role in creating perceptions of equity. "Playing favorites" ensures perceptions of inequity. Employees want to be rewarded on their merits, not the whims of their supervisors. In addition, supervisors need to recognize differences in employees in their reactions to inequity. Some employees are highly sensitive to inequity, and a supervisor needs to be especially cautious around them.[26] Everyone is sensitive to reward allocation.[27] But "equity sensitives" are even more sensitive. A major principle for supervisors, then, is simply to implement fairness. Never base punishment or reward on whether or not you like an employee. Reward behaviors that contribute to the organization, and discipline those that do not. Make sure employees understand what is expected of them, and praise them when they do it. These practices make everyone happier and your job easier.

Goal Theory

No theory is perfect. If it was, it wouldn't be a theory. It would be a set of facts. Theories are sets of propositions that are right more often than they are wrong, but they are not infallible. However, the basic propositions of goal theory* come close to being infallible. Indeed, it is one of the strongest theories in organizational behavior.

The Basic Goal-Setting Model

Goal theory states that people will perform better if they have difficult, specific, accepted performance goals or objectives.[28],[29] The first and most basic premise of goal theory is that people will attempt to achieve those goals that they *intend* to achieve. Thus, if we intend to do something (like get an A on an exam), we will exert effort to accomplish it. Without such goals, our effort at the task (studying) required to achieve the goal is less. Students whose goals are to get As study harder than students who don't have this goal—we all know this. This doesn't mean that people without goals are unmotivated. It simply means that people with goals are more motivated. The intensity of their motivation is greater, and they are more directed.

The second basic premise is that *difficult* goals result in better performance than easy goals. This does not mean that difficult goals are always achieved, but our performance will usually be better when we intend to achieve harder goals. Your goal of an A in Classical Mechanics at Cal Tech may not get you your A, but it may earn you a B+, which you wouldn't have gotten otherwise. Difficult goals cause us to exert more effort, and this almost always results in better performance.

Another premise of goal theory is that *specific* goals are better than vague goals. We often wonder what we need to do to be successful. Have you ever asked a professor "What do I need to do to get an A in this course?" If she responded "Do well on the exams," you weren't much better off for having asked. This is a vague response. Goal theory says that we perform better when we have specific goals. Had your professor told you the key thrust of the course, to turn in *all* the problem sets, to pay close attention to the essay questions on exams, and to aim for scores in the 90s, you would have something concrete on which to build a strategy.

A key premise of goal theory is that people must *accept* the goal. Usually we set our own goals. But sometimes others set goals for us. Your professor telling you your goal is to "score at least a 90 percent on your exams" doesn't mean that you'll accept this goal. Maybe you don't feel you can achieve scores in the 90s. Or, you've heard that 90 isn't good enough for an A in this class. This happens in work organizations quite often. Supervisors give orders that something must be done by a certain time. The employees may fully understand what is wanted, yet if they feel the order is unreasonable or impossible, they may not exert much effort to accomplish it. Thus, it is important for people to accept the goal. They need to feel that it is also their goal. If they do not, goal theory predicts that they won't try as hard to achieve it.

Goal theory also states that people need to *commit* to a goal in addition to accepting it. **Goal commitment** is the degree to which we dedicate ourselves to achieving a goal. Goal commitment is about setting priorities. We can accept many goals (go to all classes, stay awake during classes, take lecture notes), but we often end up doing only some of them. In other words, some goals are more important than others. And we exert more effort for certain goals. This also happens frequently at work. A software analyst's major goal may be to write a new program. Her minor goal may be to maintain previously written programs. It is minor because maintaining old programs is boring, while writing new ones is fun. Goal theory predicts that her commitment, and thus her intensity, to the major goal will be greater.

Allowing people to participate in the goal-setting process often results in higher goal commitment. This has to do with ownership. And when people participate in the process, they tend to incorporate factors they think will make the goal more interesting, challenging, and attainable. Thus, it is advisable to allow people some input into the goal-setting process. Imposing goals on them from the outside usually results in less commitment (and acceptance).

The basic goal-setting model is shown in **Exhibit 7.12**. The process starts with our values. Values are our beliefs about how the world should be or act, and often include words like "should" or "ought." We compare our present conditions against these values. For example, Randi holds the value that everyone should be a hard worker. After measuring her current work against this value, Randi concludes that she doesn't measure up to her own value. Following this, her goal-setting process begins. Randi will set a goal that affirms her status as a hard worker. **Exhibit 7.12** lists the four types of goals. Some goals are self-set. (Randi decides to word process at least 70 pages per day.) Participative goals are jointly set. (Randi goes to her supervisor, and together they set some appropriate goals for her.) In still other cases, goals are assigned. (Her boss tells her that she must word process at least 60 pages per day.) The fourth type of goal, which can be self-set, jointly determined, or assigned, is a "do your best" goal. But note this goal is vague, so it usually doesn't result in the best performance.

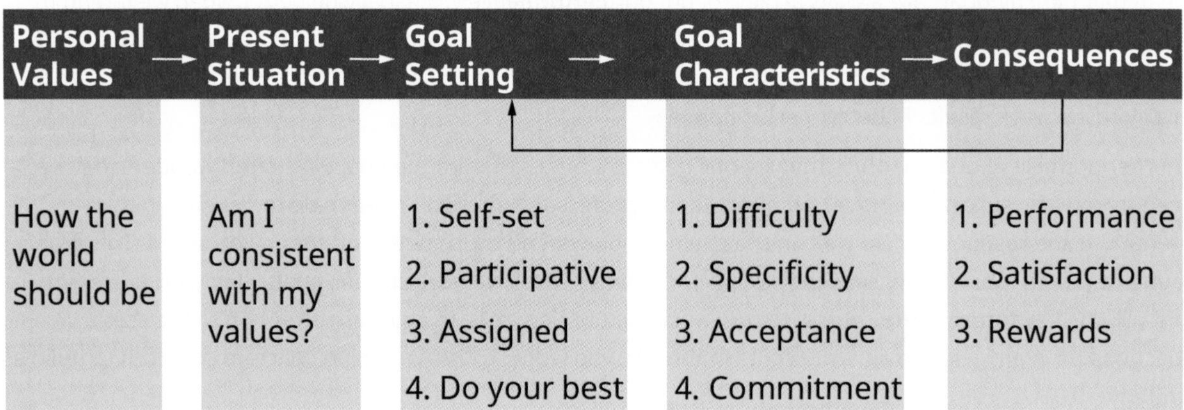

Exhibit 7.12 The Goal-Setting Process (Attribution: Copyright Rice University, OpenStax, under CC-BY 4.0 license)

Depending on the characteristics of Randi's goals, she may or may not exert a lot of effort. For maximum effort to result, her goals should be difficult, specific, accepted, and committed to. Then, if she has sufficient ability and lack of constraints, maximum performance should occur. Examples of constraints could be that her old computer frequently breaks down or her supervisor constantly interferes.

The consequence of endeavoring to reach her goal will be that Randi will be satisfied with herself. Her behavior is consistent with her values. She'll be even more satisfied if her supervisor praises her performance and gives her a pay increase!

In Randi's case, her goal achievement resulted in several benefits. However, this doesn't always happen. If goals are not achieved, people may be unhappy with themselves, and their employer may be dissatisfied as well. Such an experience can make a person reluctant to accept goals in the future. Thus, setting difficult yet attainable goals cannot be stressed enough.

Goal theory can be a tremendous motivational tool. In fact, many organizations practice effective management by using a technique called "management by objectives" (MBO). MBO is based on goal theory and is quite effective when implemented consistently with goal theory's basic premises.

Despite its many strengths, several cautions about goal theory are appropriate. Locke has identified most of them.[30] First, setting goals in one area can lead people to neglect other areas. (Randi may word process 70 pages per day, but neglect her proofreading responsibilities.) It is important that goals be set for most major duties. Second, goal setting sometimes has unintended consequences. For example, employees set easy goals so that they look good when they achieve them. Or it causes unhealthy competition between employees. Or an employee sabotages the work of others so that only she has goal achievement.

Some managers use goal setting in unethical ways. They may manipulate employees by setting impossible goals. This enables them to criticize employees even when the employees are doing superior work and, of course, causes much stress. Goal setting should never be abused. Perhaps the key caution about goal setting is that it often results in too much focus on quantified measures of performance. Qualitative aspects of a job or task may be neglected because they aren't easily measured. Managers must keep employees focused on the qualitative aspects of their jobs as well as the quantitative ones. Finally, setting individual goals in a teamwork environment can be counterproductive.[31] Where possible, it is preferable to have group goals in situations where employees depend on one another in the performance of their jobs.

The cautions noted here are not intended to deter you from using goal theory. We note them so that you can avoid the pitfalls. Remember, employees have a right to reasonable performance expectations and the rewards that result from performance, and organizations have a right to expect high performance levels from employees. Goal theory should be used to optimize the employment relationship. Goal theory holds that people will exert effort to accomplish goals if those goals are difficult to achieve, accepted by the individual, and specific in nature.

Expectancy Theory

Expectancy theory posits that we will exert much effort to perform at high levels so that we can obtain valued outcomes. It is the motivation theory that many organizational behavior researchers find most intriguing, in no small part because it is currently also the most comprehensive theory. Expectancy theory ties together many of the concepts and hypotheses from the theories discussed earlier in this chapter. In addition, it points to factors that other theories miss. Expectancy theory has much to offer the student of management and organizational behavior.

Expectancy theory is sufficiently general that it is useful in a wide variety of situations. Choices between job offers, between working hard or not so hard, between going to work or not—virtually any set of possibilities can be addressed by expectancy theory. Basically, the theory focuses on two related issues:

1. When faced with two or more alternatives, which will we select?
2. Once an alternative is chosen, how motivated will we be to pursue that choice?

Expectancy theory thus focuses on the two major aspects of motivation, *direction* (which alternative?) and *intensity* (how much effort to implement the alternative?). The attractiveness of an alternative is determined by our "expectations" of what is likely to happen if we choose it. The more we believe that the alternative chosen will lead to positively valued outcomes, the greater its attractiveness to us.

Expectancy theory states that, when faced with two or more alternatives, we will select the most attractive one. And, the greater the attractiveness of the chosen alternative, the more motivated we will be to pursue it. Our natural hedonism, discussed earlier in this chapter, plays a role in this process. We are motivated to maximize desirable outcomes (a pay raise) and minimize undesirable ones (discipline). Expectancy theory goes on to state that we are also logical in our decisions about alternatives. It considers people to be *rational.* People evaluate alternatives in terms of their "pros and cons," and then choose the one with the most "pros" and fewest "cons."

The Basic Expectancy Model

The three major components of expectancy theory reflect its assumptions of hedonism and rationality: effort-performance expectancy, performance-outcome expectancy, and valences.

The **effort-performance expectancy**, abbreviated E1, is the perceived probability that effort will lead to performance (or E ➡ P). Performance here means anything from doing well on an exam to assembling 100 toasters a day at work. Sometimes people believe that no matter how much effort they exert, they won't perform at a high level. They have weak E1s. Other people have strong E1s and believe the opposite—that is, that they can perform at a high level if they exert high effort. You all know students with different E1s—those who believe that if they study hard they'll do well, and those who believe that no matter how much they study they'll do poorly. People develop these perceptions from prior experiences with the task at hand, and from self-perceptions of their abilities. The core of the E1 concept is that people don't always perceive a direct relationship between effort level and performance level.

The **performance-outcome expectancy**, E2, is the perceived relationship between performance and outcomes (or P ➡ O).[1] Many things in life happen as a function of how well we perform various tasks. E2 addresses the question "What will happen if I perform well?" Let's say you get an A in your Classical Mechanics course at Cal Tech. You'll be elated, your classmates may envy you, and you are now assured of that plum job at NASA. But let's say you got a D. Whoops, that was the last straw for the dean. Now you've flunked out, and you're reduced to going home to live with your parents (perish the thought!). Likewise, E2 perceptions develop in organizations, although hopefully not as drastically as your beleaguered career at Cal Tech. People with strong E2s believe that if they perform their jobs well, they'll receive desirable outcomes—good pay increases, praise from their supervisor, and a feeling that they're really contributing. In the same situation, people with weak E2s will have the opposite perceptions—that high performance levels don't result in desirable outcomes and that it doesn't really matter how well they perform their jobs as long as they don't get fired.

---

1 Sometimes E2s are called *instrumentalities,* because they are the perception that performance is instrumental in getting some desired outcome.

Valences are the easiest of the expectancy theory concepts to describe. Valences are simply the degree to which we perceive an outcome as desirable, neutral, or undesirable. Highly desirable outcomes (a 25 percent pay increase) are positively valent. Undesirable outcomes (being disciplined) are negatively valent. Outcomes that we're indifferent to (where you must park your car) have neutral valences. Positively and negatively valent outcomes abound in the workplace—pay increases and freezes, praise and criticism, recognition and rejection, promotions and demotions. And as you would expect, people differ dramatically in how they value these outcomes. Our needs, values, goals, and life situations affect what valence we give an outcome. Equity is another consideration we use in assigning valences. We may consider a 10 percent pay increase desirable until we find out that it was the lowest raise given in our work group.

Exhibit 7.13 summarizes the three core concepts of expectancy theory. The theory states that our perceptions about our surroundings are essentially predictions about "what leads to what." We perceive that certain effort levels result in certain performance levels. We perceive that certain performance levels result in certain outcomes. Outcomes can be **extrinsic**, in that others (our supervisor) determine whether we receive them, or **intrinsic**, in that we determine if they are received (our sense of achievement). Each outcome has an associated valence (outcome A's valence is V_a). Expectancy theory predicts that we will exert effort that results in the maximum amount of positive-valence outcomes.[2] If our E1 or E2 is weak, or if the outcomes are not sufficiently desirable, our motivation to exert effort will be low. Stated differently, an individual will be motivated to try to achieve the level of performance that results in the most rewards.

2
It can also be expressed as an equation:

$$\begin{matrix}\textit{Force}\text{ to} \\ \text{Choose} \\ \text{A level of Effort}\end{matrix} = E1 \times \sum (E2_o \times V_o)$$

Where V_o is the valence of a given outcome (o), and $E2_o$ is the perceived probability that a certain level of performance (e.g., Excellent, average, poor) will result in that outcome. So, for multiple outcomes, and different performance levels, the valence of the outcome and its associated performance→outcome expectancy (E2) are multiplied and added to the analogous value for the other outcomes. Combined with the E1 (the amount of effort required to produce a level of performance), the effort level with the greatest *force* associated with it will be chosen by the individual.

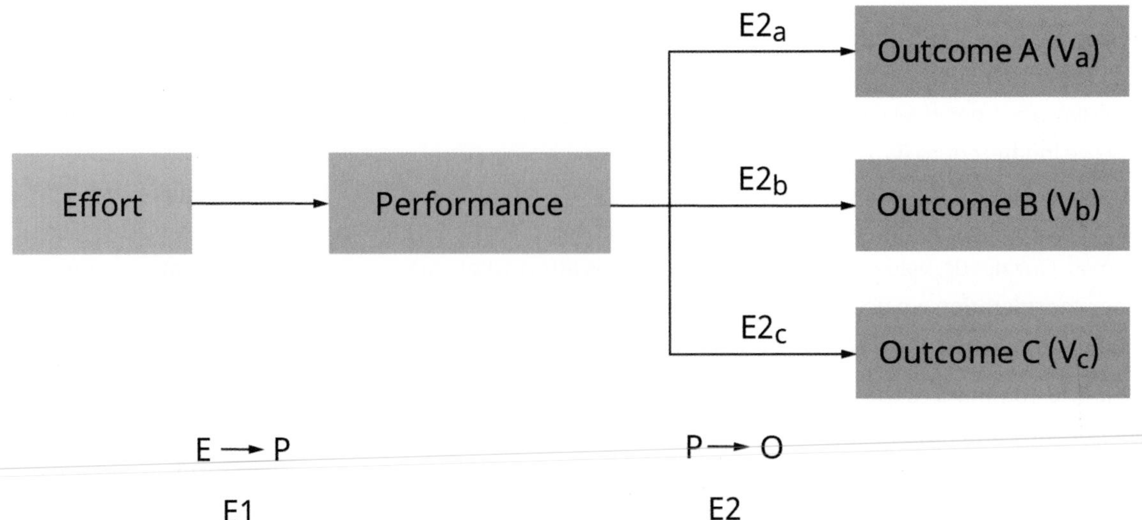

1. Effort ⟶ Performance expectancy (E ⟶ P; E1)
2. Performance ⟶ Outcome expectancy (P ⟶ O; E2)
3. Valences (V) of Outcomes (V_o)

Exhibit 7.13 The Expectancy Theory of Motivation (Attribution: Copyright Rice University, OpenStax, under CC-BY 4.0 license)

V_o is the valence of the outcome. The effort level with the greatest force associated with it will be chosen by the individual.

Implications of Expectancy Theory

Expectancy theory has major implications for the workplace. Basically, expectancy theory predicts that employees will be motivated to perform well on their jobs under two conditions. The first is when employees believe that a reasonable amount of effort will result in good performance. The second is when good performance is associated with positive outcomes and low performance is associated with negative outcomes. If neither of these conditions exists in the perceptions of employees, their motivation to perform will be low.

Why might an employee perceive that positive outcomes are not associated with high performance? Or that negative outcomes are not associated with low performance? That is, why would employees develop weak E2s? This happens for a number of reasons. The main one is that many organizations subscribe too strongly to a principle of equality (not to be confused with equity). They give all of their employees equal salaries for equal work, equal pay increases every year (these are known as across-the-board pay raises), and equal treatment wherever possible. Equality-focused organizations reason that some employees "getting more" than others leads to disruptive competition and feelings of inequity.

In time employees in equality-focused organizations develop weak E2s because no distinctions are made for differential outcomes. If the best and the worst salespeople are paid the same, in time they will both decide that it isn't worth the extra effort to be a high performer. Needless to say, this is not the goal of competitive organizations and can cause the demise of the organization as it competes with other firms in today's global marketplace.

Expectancy theory states that to maximize motivation, organizations must make outcomes contingent on performance. This is the main contribution of expectancy theory: it makes us think about *how* organizations should distribute outcomes. If an organization, or a supervisor, believes that treating everyone "the same" will result in satisfied and motivated employees, they will be wrong more times than not. From equity theory we know that some employees, usually the better-performing ones, will experience underreward inequity. From expectancy theory we know that employees will see no difference in outcomes for good and poor performance, so they will not have as much incentive to be good performers. Effective organizations need to actively encourage the perception that good performance leads to positive outcomes (bonuses, promotions) and that poor performance leads to negative ones (discipline, termination). Remember, there is a big difference between treating employees equally and treating them equitably.

What if an organization ties positive outcomes to high performance and negative outcomes to low performance? Employees will develop strong E2s. But will this result in highly motivated employees? The answer is maybe. We have yet to address employees' E1s. If employees have weak E1s, they will perceive that high (or low) effort does *not* result in high performance and thus will not exert much effort. It is important for managers to understand that this can happen despite rewards for high performance.

Task-related abilities are probably the single biggest reason why some employees have weak E1s. **Self-efficacy** is our belief about whether we can successfully execute some future action or task, or achieve some result. High self-efficacy employees believe that they are likely to succeed at most or all of their job duties and responsibilities. And as you would expect, low self-efficacy employees believe the opposite. Specific self-efficacy reflects our belief in our capability to perform a specific task at a specific level of performance. If we believe that the probability of our selling $30,000 of jackrabbit slippers in one month is .90, our self-efficacy for this task is high. Specific self-efficacy is our judgment about the likelihood of successful task performance measured immediately before we expend effort on the task. As a result, specific self-efficacy is much more variable than more enduring notions of personality. Still, there is little doubt that our state-based beliefs are some of the most powerful motivators of behavior. Our efficacy expectations at a given point in time determine not only our initial decision to perform (or not) a task, but also the amount of effort we will expend and whether we will persist in the face of adversity.[32] Self-efficacy has a strong impact on the E1 factor. As a result, self-efficacy is one of the strongest determinants of performance in any particular task situation.[33]

Employees develop weak E1s for two reasons. First, they don't have sufficient resources to perform their jobs. Resources can be internal or external. Internal resources include what employees bring to the job (such as prior training, work experience, education, ability, and aptitude) and their understanding of what they need to do to be considered good performers. The second resource is called role perceptions—how employees believe their jobs are done and how they fit into the broader organization. If employees don't know *how* to become good performers, they will have weak E1s. External resources include the tools, equipment, and labor necessary to perform a job. The lack of good external resources can also cause E1s to be weak.

The second reason for weak E1s is an organization's failure to measure performance accurately. That is, performance *ratings* don't correlate well with actual performance *levels.* How does this happen? Have you ever gotten a grade that you felt didn't reflect how much you learned? This also happens in organizations. Why are ratings sometimes inaccurate? Supervisors, who typically give out ratings, well, they're human. Perhaps they're operating under the mistaken notion that similar ratings for everyone will keep the team happy. Perhaps they're unconsciously playing favorites. Perhaps they don't know what good and poor performance levels are. Perhaps the measurements they're expected to use don't fit their product/team/people. Choose one or all of these. Rating people is rarely easy.

Whatever the cause of rating errors, some employees may come to believe that no matter what they do they will never receive a high performance rating. They may in fact believe that they are excellent performers but that the performance rating system is flawed. Expectancy theory differs from most motivation theories because it highlights the need for accurate performance measurement. Organizations cannot motivate employees to perform at a high level if they cannot identify high performers.

Organizations exert tremendous influence over employee choices in their performance levels and how much effort to exert on their jobs. That is, organizations can have a major impact on the direction and intensity of employees' motivation levels. Practical applications of expectancy theory include:

1. Strengthening the effort ➡ performance expectancy by selecting employees who have the necessary abilities, providing proper training, providing experiences of success, clarifying job responsibilities, etc.
2. Strengthening the performance ➡ outcome expectancy with policies that specify that desirable behavior leads to desirable outcomes and undesirable behavior leads to neutral or undesirable outcomes. Consistent enforcement of these policies is key—workers must believe in the contingencies.
3. Systematically evaluating which outcomes employees value. The greater the valence of outcomes offered for a behavior, the more likely employees will commit to that alternative. By recognizing that different employees have different values and that values change over time, organizations can provide the most highly valued outcomes.
4. Ensuring that effort actually translates into performance by clarifying what actions lead to performance and by appropriate training.
5. Ensuring appropriate worker outcomes for performance through reward schedules (extrinsic outcomes) and appropriate job design (so the work experience itself provides intrinsic outcomes).
6. Examining the level of outcomes provided to workers. Are they equitable, given the worker's inputs? Are they equitable in comparison to the way other workers are treated?
7. Measuring performance levels as accurately as possible, making sure that workers are capable of being high performers.

MANAGING CHANGE

Differences in Motivation across Cultures

The disgruntled employee is hardly a culturally isolated feature of business, and quitting before leaving takes the same forms, regardless of country. Cross-cultural signaling, social norms, and simple language barriers can make the task of motivation for the global manager confusing and counterintuitive. Communicating a passion for a common vision, coaching employees to see themselves as accountable and as owning their work, or attempting to create a "motivational ecosystem" can all fall flat with simple missed cues, bad translations, or tone-deaf approaches to a thousand-year-old culture.

Keeping employees motivated by making them feel valued and appreciated is not just a "Western" idea. The Ghanaian blog site Starrfmonline emphasizes that employee motivation and associated work quality improve when employees feel "valued, trusted, challenged, and supported in their work." Conversely, when employees feel like a tool rather than a person, or feel unengaged with their work, then productivity suffers. A vicious cycle can then begin when the manager treats an employee as unmotivated and incapable, which then demotivates the employee and elicits the predicted response.

The blogger cites an example from Eastern Europe where a manager sidelined an employee as inefficient and incompetent. After management coaching, the manager revisited his assessment and began working with the employee. As he worked to facilitate the employee's efficiency and motivation, the employee went from being the lowest performer to a valuable team player. In the end, the blog says, "The very phrase 'human resources' frames employees as material to be deployed for organizational objectives. While the essential nature of employment contracts involves trading labour for remuneration, if we fail to see and appreciate our employees as whole people, efforts to motivate them will meet with limited success" (Starrfmonline 2017 n.p.)

Pavel Vosk, a business and management consultant based in Puyallup, Washington, says that too often, overachieving employees turn into unmotivated ones. In looking for the answer, he found that the most common source was a lack of recognition for the employee's effort or exceptional performance. In fact, Vosk found that most employees go the extra mile only three times before they give up. Vosk's advice is to show gratitude for employees' effort, especially when it goes above and beyond. He says the recognition doesn't have to be over the top, just anything that the employees will perceive as gratitude, from a catered lunch for a team working extra hours to fulfill a deadline to a simple face-to-face thank you (Huhman 2017).

Richard Frazao, president of Quaketek, based in Montreal, Quebec, stresses talking to the employees and making certain they are engaged in their jobs, citing boredom with one's job as a major demotivating factor (Huhman 2017).

But motivating employees is not "one size fits all" globally. Rewarding and recognizing individuals and their achievements works fine in Western cultures but is undesirable in Asian cultures, which value teamwork and the collective over the individual. Whether to reward effort with a pay raise or with a job title or larger office is influenced by culture. Demoting an employee for poor performance is an effective motivator in Asian countries but is likely to result in losing an employee altogether in Western cultures. According to Matthew MacLachlan at Communicaid, "Making the assumption that your international workforce will be motivated by the same incentives can be dangerous and have a real impact on talent retention" (2016 n.p.).

Huhman, Heather R. 2017. "Employee Motivation Has to Be More Than 'a Pat on the Back.'" *Entrepreneur.* https://www.entrepreneur.com/article/287770

MacLachlan, Matthew. 2016. "Management Tips: How To Motivate Your International Workforce." *Communicaid.* https://www.communicaid.com/cross-cultural-training/blog/motivating-international-workforce/

Starrfmonline. 2017. "HR Today: Motivating People Starts With Right Attitude."

http://starrfmonline.com/2017/03/30/hr-today-motivating-people-starts-with-right-attitude/#

1. As a Western manager working in the Middle East or sub-Saharan Africa, what motivational issues might you face?
2. What problems would you expect a manager from a Confucian culture to encounter managing employees in America? In Europe?
3. What regional, cultural, or ethnic issues do you think managers have to navigate within the United States?

Expectancy Theory: An Integrative Theory of Motivation

More so than any other motivation theory, expectancy theory can be tied into most concepts of what and how people become motivated. Consider the following examples.

1. *Need theories* state that we are motivated to satisfy our needs. We positively value outcomes that satisfy unmet needs, negatively value outcomes that thwart the satisfaction of unmet needs, and assign neutral values to outcomes that do neither. In effect, the need theories explain how valences are formed.
2. *Operant conditioning theories* state that we will probably repeat a response (behavior) in the future that was reinforced in the past (that is, followed by a positively valued consequence or the removal of a negatively valued consequence). This is the basic process involved in forming performance ➡ outcome expectancies. Both operant theories and expectancy theory argue that our interactions with our environment influence our future behavior. The primary difference is that expectancy theory explains this process in cognitive (rational) terms.
3. *Equity theories* state that our satisfaction with a set of outcomes depends not only on how we value them but also on the circumstances surrounding their receipt. Equity theory, therefore, explains part of the process shown in **Exhibit 7.11**. If we don't feel that the outcomes we receive are equitable compared to a referent other, we will associate a lower or even negative valence with those outcomes.
4. *Goal theory* can be integrated with the expanded expectancy model in several ways. Locke has noted that expectancy theory explains how we go about choosing a particular goal.[34] A reexamination of **Exhibit 7.11** reveals other similarities between goal theory and expectancy theory. Locke's use of the term "goal acceptance" to identify the personal adoption of a goal is similar to the "choice of an alternative" in the expectancy model. Locke's "goal commitment," the degree to which we commit to reaching our accepted (chosen) goal, is very much like the expectancy description of choice of effort level. Locke argues that the difficulty and specificity of a goal are major determinants of the level of performance attempted (goal-directed effort), and expectancy theory appears to be consistent with this argument (even though expectancy theory is not as explicit on this point). We can reasonably conclude that the major underlying processes explored by the two models are very similar and will seldom lead to inconsistent recommendations.

CONCEPT CHECK 

1. Understand the process theories of motivation: operant conditioning, equity, goal, and expectancy theories.
2. Describe the managerial factors managers must consider when applying motivational approaches.

7.4 Recent Research on Motivation Theories

4. Describe the modern advancements in the study of human motivation.

Employee motivation continues to be a major focus in organizational behavior.[35] We briefly summarize current motivation research here.

Content Theories

There is some interest in testing content theories (including Herzberg's two-factor theory), especially in international research. Need theories are still generally supported, with most people identifying such workplace factors as recognition, advancement, and opportunities to learn as the chief motivators for them. This is consistent with need satisfaction theories. However, most of this research does not include actual measures of employee performance. Thus, questions remain about whether the factors that employees *say* motivate them to perform actually do.

Operant Conditioning Theory

There is considerable interest in operant conditioning theory, especially within the context of what has been called organizational behavior modification. Oddly enough, there has not been much research using operant conditioning theory in designing reward systems, even though there are obvious applications. Instead, much of the recent research on operant conditioning focuses on punishment and extinction. These studies seek to determine how to use punishment appropriately. Recent results still confirm that punishment should be used sparingly, should be used only after extinction does not work, and should not be excessive or destructive.

Equity Theory

Equity theory continues to receive strong research support. The major criticism of equity theory, that the inputs and outcomes people use to evaluate equity are ill-defined, still holds. Because each person defines inputs and outcomes, researchers are not in a position to know them all. Nevertheless, for the major inputs (performance) and outcomes (pay), the theory is a strong one. Major applications of equity theory in recent years incorporate and extend the theory into the area called *organizational justice.* When employees receive rewards (or punishments), they evaluate them in terms of their fairness (as discussed earlier). This is *distributive justice.* Employees also assess rewards in terms of how fair the processes used to distribute them are. This is *procedural justice.* Thus during organizational downsizing, when employees lose their jobs, people ask whether the loss of work is fair (distributive justice). But they also assess the fairness of the process used to decide *who* is laid off (procedural justice). For example, layoffs based on seniority may be perceived as more fair than layoffs based on supervisors' opinions.

Goal Theory

It remains true that difficult, specific goals result in better performance than easy and vague goals, assuming they are accepted. Recent research highlights the positive effects of performance feedback and goal commitment in the goal-setting process. Monetary incentives enhance motivation when they are tied to goal achievement, by increasing the level of goal commitment. There are negative sides to goal theory as well. If goals conflict, employees may sacrifice performance on important job duties. For example, if both quantitative and qualitative goals are set for performance, employees may emphasize quantity because this goal achievement is more visible.

Expectancy Theory

The original formulation of expectancy theory specifies that the motivational force for choosing a level of effort is a function of the multiplication of expectancies and valences. Recent research demonstrates that the individual components predict performance just as well, without being multiplied. This does not diminish the value of expectancy theory. Recent research also suggests that high performance results not only when the valence is high, but also when employees set difficult goals for themselves.

One last comment on motivation: As the world of work changes, so will the methods organizations use to motivate employees. New rewards—time off instead of bonuses; stock options; on-site gyms, cleaners, and dental services; opportunities to telecommute; and others—will need to be created in order to motivate employees in the future. One useful path that modern researchers can undertake is to analyze the previous studies and aggregate the findings into more conclusive understanding of the topic through meta-analysis studies.[36]

CATCHING THE ENTREPRENEURIAL SPIRIT

Entrepreneurs and Motivation

Motivation can be difficult to elicit in employees. So what drives entrepreneurs, who by definition have to motivate themselves as well as others? While everyone from Greek philosophers to football coaches warn about undirected passion, a lack of passion will likely kill any start-up. An argument could be made that motivation is simply *part* of the discipline, or the *outcome* of remaining fixed on a purpose to mentally remind yourself of why you get up in the morning.

Working from her home in Egypt, at age 30 Yasmine El-Mehairy launched Supermama.me, a start-up aimed at providing information to mothers throughout the Arab world. When the company began, El-Mehairy worked full time at her day job and 60 hours a week after that getting the site established. She left her full-time job to manage the site full time in January 2011, and the site went live that October. El-Mehairy is motivated to keep moving forward, saying that if she stops, she might not get going again (Knowledge @ Wharton 2012).

For El-Mehairy, the motivation didn't come from a desire to work for a big company or travel the world and secure a master's degree from abroad. She had already done that. Rather, she said she was motivated to "do something that is useful and I want to do something on my own" (Knowledge @ Wharton 2012 n.p.).

Lauren Lipcon, who founded a company called Injury Funds Now, attributes her ability to stay motivated to three factors: purpose, giving back, and having fun outside of work. Lipcon believes that most entrepreneurs are not motivated by money, but by a sense of purpose. Personally, she left a job with Arthur Andersen to begin her own firm out of a desire to help people. She also thinks it is important for people to give back to their communities because the change the entrepreneur sees in the community loops back, increasing motivation and making the business more successful. Lipcon believes that having a life outside of work helps keep the entrepreneur motivated. She particularly advocates for physical activity, which not only helps the body physically, but also helps keep the mind sharp and able to focus (Rashid 2017).

But do all entrepreneurs agree on what motivates them? A July 17, 2017 survey on the hearpreneur blog site asked 23 different entrepreneurs what motivated them. Seven of the 23 referred to some sense of purpose in what they were doing as a motivating factor, with one response stressing the importance of discovering one's "personal why." Of the remaining entrepreneurs, answers varied from keeping a positive attitude (three responses) and finding external sources (three responses) to meditation and prayer (two responses). One entrepreneur said his greatest motivator was fear: the fear of being in the same place financially one year in the future "causes me to take action and also alleviates my fear of risk" (Hear from Entrepreneurs 2017 n.p.). Only one of the 23 actually cited money and material success as a motivating factor to keep working.

However it is described, entrepreneurs seem to agree that passion and determination are key factors that carry them through the grind of the day-to-day.

Sources:

Hear from Entrepreneurs. 2017. "23 Entrepreneurs Explain Their Motivation or if 'Motivation is Garbage.'" https://hear.ceoblognation.com/2017/07/17/23-entrepreneurs-explain-motivation-motivation-garbage/

Knowledge @ Wharton. 2012. "The Super-motivated Entrepreneur Behind Egypt's SuperMama." http://knowledge.wharton.upenn.edu/article/the-super-motivated-entrepreneur-behind-egypts-supermama/

Rashid, Brian. 2017. "How This Entrepreneur Sustains High Levels of Energy and Motivation." *Forbes.* https://www.forbes.com/sites/brianrashid/2017/05/26/how-this-entrepreneur-sustains-high-levels-of-energy-and-motivation/2/#2a8ec5591111

Questions:

1. In the article from Hear from Entrepreneurs, one respondent called motivation "garbage"? Would you agree or disagree, and why?
2. How is staying motivated as an entrepreneur similar to being motivated to pursue a college degree? Do you think the two are related? How?
3. How would you expect motivation to vary across cultures?[/BOX]

CONCEPT CHECK

1. Understand the modern approaches to motivation theory.

Key Terms

ability The knowledge, skills, and receptiveness to learning that an individual brings to a task or job.

avoidance learning Occurs when people learn to behave in a certain way to avoid encountering an undesired or unpleasant consequence.

content motivation theories Theories that focus on what motivates people.

direction What a person is motivated to achieve.

effort-performance expectancy E1, the perceived probability that effort will lead to performance (or E ➡ P).

equity theory States that human motivation is affected by the outcomes people receive for their inputs, compared to the outcomes and inputs of other people.

ERG theory Compresses Maslow's five need categories into three: existence, relatedness, and growth.

expectancy theory Posits that people will exert high effort levels to perform at high levels so that they can obtain valued outcomes.

extinction Occurs when a consequence or lack of a consequence makes it less likely that a behavior will be repeated in the future.

extrinsic motivation Occurs when a person performs a given behavior to acquire something that will satisfy a lower-order need.

extrinsic outcomes Are awarded or given by other people (like a supervisor).

goal commitment The degree to which people dedicate themselves to achieving a goal.

goal theory States that people will perform better if they have difficult, specific, accepted performance goals or objectives.

hedonism Assumes that people are motivated to satisfy mainly their own needs (seek pleasure, avoid pain).

hygienes Factors in the work environment that are based on the basic human need to "avoid pain."

input Any personal qualities that a person views as having value and that are relevant to the organization.

instincts Our natural, fundamental needs, basic to our survival.

intensity (1) The degree to which people try to achieve their targets; (2) the forcefulness that enhances the likelihood that a stimulus will be selected for perceptual processing.

intrinsic motivation Arises out of performing a behavior in and of itself, because it is interesting or "fun" to do.

intrinsic outcomes Are awarded or given by people to themselves (such as a sense of achievement).

latent needs Cannot be inferred from a person's behavior at a given time, yet the person may still possess those needs.

manifest needs Are needs motivating a person at a given time.

manifest needs theory Assumes that human behavior is driven by the desire to satisfy needs.

motivation A force within or outside of the body that energizes, directs, and sustains human behavior. Within the body, examples might be needs, personal values, and goals, while an incentive might be seen as a force outside of the body. The word stems from its Latin root *movere*, which means "to move."

motivators Relate to the jobs that people perform and people's ability to feel a sense of achievement as a result of performing them.

motive A source of motivation; the need that a person is attempting to satisfy.

need A human condition that becomes energized when people feel deficient in some respect.

need for achievement (nAch) The need to excel at tasks, especially tasks that are difficult.

need for affiliation (nAff) The need to establish and maintain warm and friendly relationships with other people.

need for power (nPow) The need to control things, especially other people; reflects a motivation to influence and be responsible for other people.

negative reinforcement Occurs when a behavior causes something undesirable to be removed, increasing the likelihood of the behavior reoccurring.

nonreinforcement Occurs when no consequence follows a worker's behavior.

operant conditioning A learning process based on the results produced by a person "operating on" the environment.

operant conditioning theory Posits that people learn to behave in a particular fashion as a result of the consequences that followed their past behaviors.

outcome Anything a person perceives as getting back from an organization in exchange for the person's inputs.

overreward inequity Occurs when people perceive their outcome/input ratio to be greater than that of their referent other.

performance environment Refers to those factors that impact employees' performance but are essentially out of their control.

performance-outcome expectancy E2, the perceived relationship between performance and outcomes (or P ➡ O).

positive reinforcement Occurs when a desirable consequence that satisfies an active need or removes a barrier to need satisfaction increases the likelihood of a behavior reoccurring.

primary needs Are instinctual in nature and include physiological needs for food, water, and sex (procreation).

process motivation theories Theories that focus on the how and why of motivation.

punishment An aversive consequence that follows a behavior and makes it less likely to reoccur.

referent others Workers that a person uses to compare inputs and outcomes, and who perform jobs similar in difficulty and complexity to the employee making an equity determination.

reinforcement Occurs when a consequence makes it more likely a behavior will be repeated in the future.

role perceptions The set of behaviors employees think they are expected to perform as members of an organization.

schedules of reinforcement The frequency at which effective employee behaviors are reinforced.

secondary needs Are learned throughout one's life span and are psychological in nature.

self-determination theory (SDT) Seeks to explain not only what causes motivation, but also the effects of extrinsic rewards on intrinsic motivation.

self-efficacy A belief about the probability that one can successfully execute some future action or task, or achieve some result.

state of equity Occurs when people perceive their outcome/input ratio to be equal to that of their referent other.

underreward inequity Occurs when people perceive their outcome/input ratio to be less than that of their referent other.

valences The degree to which a person perceives an outcome as being desirable, neutral, or undesirable.

work motivation The amount of effort a person exerts to achieve a level of job performance

Summary of Learning Outcomes

7.1 Motivation: Direction and Intensity

1. Define motivation, and distinguish direction and intensity of motivation.

This chapter has covered the major motivation theories in organizational behavior. Motivation theories endeavor to explain how people become motivated. Motivation has two major components: direction and intensity. Direction is what a person is trying to achieve. Intensity is the degree of effort a person expends to achieve the target. All motivation theories address the ways in which people develop direction and intensity.

7.2 Content Theories of Motivation

2. Describe a content theory of motivation, and compare and contrast the main content theories of motivation: manifest needs theory, learned needs theory, Maslow's hierarchy of needs, Alderfer's ERG theory, Herzberg's motivator-hygiene theory, and self-determination theory.

Motivation theories are classified as either content or process theories. Content theories focus on what motivates behavior. The basic premise of content theories is that humans have needs. When these needs are not satisfied, humans are motivated to satisfy the need. The need provides direction for motivation. Murray's manifest needs theory, McClelland's learned needs theory, Maslow's hierarchy of needs, and Herzberg's motivator-hygiene theory are all content theories. Each has something to say about the needs that motivate humans in the workplace.

7.3 Process Theories of Motivation

3. Describe the process theories of motivation, and compare and contrast the main process theories of motivation: operant conditioning theory, equity theory, goal theory, and expectancy theory.

Process theories focus on how people become motivated. Operant conditioning theory states that people will be motivated to engage in behaviors for which they have been reinforced (rewarded). It also states that people will avoid behaviors that are punished. The rate at which behaviors are rewarded also affects how often they will be displayed. Equity theory's main premise is that people compare their situations to those of other people. If a person feels that they are being treated unfairly relative to a referent other, the person may engage in behaviors that are counterproductive for the organization. Employers should try to develop feelings of fairness in employees. Goal theory is a strong theory. It states that difficult, specific goals will result in high performance if employees accept the goals and are committed to achieving them.

7.4 Recent Research on Motivation Theories

4. Describe the modern advancements in the study of human motivation.

Expectancy theory is a process theory. It also is the broadest of the motivation theories. Expectancy theory predicts that employees will be motivated to be high performers if they perceive that high performance leads to valued outcomes. Employees will be motivated to avoid being low performers if they perceive that it leads to negative outcomes. Employees must perceive that they are capable of achieving high performance, and they must have the appropriate abilities and high self-efficacy. Organizations need to provide adequate resources and to measure performance accurately. Inaccurate performance ratings discourage high performance. Overall, expectancy theory draws attention to how organizations structure the work environment and distribute rewards.

Chapter Review Questions

1. Discuss the benefits that accrue when an organization has a good understanding of employee needs.
2. How might Maslow explain why organizational rewards that motivate workers today may not motivate the same workers in 5 or 10 years?
3. Describe the process by which needs motivate workers.
4. Discuss the importance of Herzberg's motivators and hygienes.
5. Describe a work situation in which it would be appropriate to use a continuous reinforcement schedule.

6. Discuss the potential effectiveness and limitations of punishment in organizations.
7. How can equity theory explain why a person who receives a high salary might be dissatisfied with their pay?
8. Equity theory specifies a number of possible alternatives for reducing perceived inequity. How could an organization influence which of these alternatives a person will pursue?
9. What goals would be most likely to improve your learning and performance in an organizational behavior class?
10. Identify two reasons why a formal goal-setting program might be dysfunctional for an organization.
11. What steps can an organization take to increase the motivational force for high levels of performance?
12. Discuss how supervisors sometimes unintentionally weaken employees $E \rightarrow P$ and $P \rightarrow O$ expectancies.
13. How can an employee attach high valence to high levels of performance, yet not be motivated to be a high performer?
14. Is there "one best" motivation theory? Explain your answer.

Management Skills Application Exercises

1. Many companies strive to design jobs that are intrinsically motivating. Visit several small and large company websites and search their career section. What job features related to motivation are highlighted? What type of employees do you think the companies will attract with these jobs?
2. You will be paired with another student in this class. Each of you will take one side of the issue and debate:
   a. Student A: All members of the organization should be given the same specific, difficult-to-achieve goals.
   b. Student B: Specific, difficult-to-achieve goals should only be given to certain members of the organization.
3. Assume the role of sales manager, and write a memo to two of your reports that have the following situations and job performance.
   a. Employee 1: Shawn is a onetime stellar performer. They were twice the top performing salesperson in the company in the past decade. In the past year, Shawn has missed goal by 4 percent. Shawn recently became the parent to twins and says that the reason for missing goal this year was due to the territory being saturated with product from previous years.
   b. Employee 2: Soo Kim is an energetic salesperson who is putting in long hours and producing detailed sales reports, but their performance on the sales side has not met expectations. When you examine the customer feedback page on your website, you notice that they have five times as many positive reviews and glowing comments about Soo Kim.

Managerial Decision Exercises

1. You are a manager and it's performance appraisal time, which is a yearly exercise to provide feedback to your direct reports that is often stressful for both the employee and the manager. You feel that the feedback process should be more of an ongoing process than the yearly formal process. What are the benefits of this yearly process, and what, if any, are the drawbacks of providing both positive and remediation feedback to your direct reports?
2. You have been told by a worker on another team that one of your direct reports made an inappropriate

comment to a coworker. What do you do to investigate the matter, and what actions would you take with your report, the person that the comment was directed to, and other people in the organization?

3. You learn that an employee who doesn't report to you has made an inappropriate comment to one of your direct reports. What do you do to investigate the matter, and what actions would you take with your report, the person that made the comment, their manager, and other people in the organization?
4. Your company is considering implementing a 360° appraisal system where up to 10 people in the organization provide feedback on every employee as part of the annual performance appraisal process. This feedback will come from subordinates, peers, and senior managers as well as individuals in other departments. You have been asked to prepare a memo to the director of human resources about the positive and negative effects this could have on the motivation of employees. Note that not all of the employees are on a bonus plan that will be impacted by this feedback.

Critical Thinking Case

Motivating Employees at JCPenney, Walmart, and Amazon in the Age of Online Shopping

In the 1980s, Walmart had killed (or was killing) the mom-and-pop store. "Buy local" signs were seen, urging consumers to buy from their local retailers rather than from the low-cost behemoth. Markets have continued to shift and the "buy local" signs are still around, but now the battleground has shifted with the disruptive growth of e-commerce. Even mighty Walmart is feeling some growing pains.

Census Bureau data for 2017 shows that e-commerce, or online shopping, accounted for 8.9 percent of all retail sales in the United States, accounting for $111.5 billion (U.S. Census Bureau 2017). Feeling the pinch, many malls across the country are closing their doors, and their empty retail spaces are being repurposed. Credit Suisse predicts that due to competition from online shopping, 20 to 25 percent of American malls will close within the next five years (Dying Malls Make Room for New Condos Apartment 2017). Furthermore, according to a 2017 study, 23 percent of Americans already purchase their groceries online (Embrace the Internet, Skip the Checkout 2017).

Whether face-to-face with customers or filling orders in a warehouse, motivated employees are essential to business success. And company culture helps drive that motivation. As a 2015 *Harvard Business Review* article put it, "Why we work determines how well we work" (McGregor & Doshi 2015). Adapting earlier research for the modern workplace, the study found six reasons that people work: play, purpose, potential, emotional pressure, economic pressure, and inertia. The first three are positive motives while that later three are negative. The researchers found that role design, more than any other factor, had the highest impact on employee motivation.

Anecdotally, using role design to motivate employees can be seen across industries. Toyota allows factory workers to innovate new processes on the factory floor. Southwest Airlines encourages a sense of "play" among crewmembers who interact directly with passengers (which has resulted in some humorous viral videos). A sense of the organization's identity (and a desire to be part of it) and how the career ladder within the company is perceived are second and third in their impact on employee motivation. Unhealthy competition for advancement can do more harm than good to employee motivation, and as a result many large companies are restructuring their performance review and advancement systems (McGregor & Doshi 2015). Conversely, costs from unmotivated employees can be high. In August 2017, retailer JCPenney had an employee arrested who had allegedly cost the company more than $10,000 in stolen cash and under-rung merchandise at a mall store. Another employee had stolen more than $1,000 of clothes from the store less than a month earlier.

Brick-and-mortar retail outlets from Macy's to Walmart have come under pressure by increased online shopping, particularly at Amazon.com. Walmart has responded by both trying to improve the shopping experience in its stores and creating an online presence of its own. A recent study funded by Walmart found that 60 percent of retails workers lack proficiency in reading and 70 percent have difficulty with math (Class is in session at Walmart Academy 2017). Increasing math and team skills for the employees would increase efficiency and certainly help improve employee self-image and motivation. With this in mind, Walmart has created one of the largest employer training programs in the country, Walmart Academy (McGregor & Doshi 2015). The company expects to graduate more than 225,000 of its supervisors and managers from a program that covers topics such as merchandising and employee motivation. In another program, Pathways, Walmart has created a course that covers topics such as merchandising, communication, and retail math (Walmart 2016 Global Responsibility Report 2016). The Pathways program was expected to see 500,000 entry-level workers take part in 2016 (Walmart 2016). All employees who complete the course receive a dollar an hour pay increase. Educating employees pays off by recognizing that the effort put in pays off with better-motivated and better-educated employees. In the case of Walmart, "upskilling" has become a priority.

Walmart has gone beyond education to motivate or empower employees. In 2016, pay raises for 1.2 million employees took effect as part of a new minimum-wage policy, and it streamlined its paid time off program that same year (Schmid 2017). In its 2016 Global Responsibility Report, Walmart points out that over the course of two years, the company has invested $2.7 billion in wages, benefits, and training in the United States (Staley 2017).

Sources:

Ciubotariu, Nick. 2015. "An Amazonian's response to "Inside Amazon: Wrestling Big Ideas in a Bruising Workplace." *LinkedIn.* https://www.linkedin.com/pulse/amazonians-response-inside-amazon-wrestling-big-ideas-nick-ciubotariu/?redirectFromSplash=true

Class is in session at Walmart Academy. 2017. Bend Bulletin. http://www.bendbulletin.com/home/5507742-151/class-is-in-session-at-walmart-academy

Cook, John. 2015. "Full memo: Jeff Bezos responds to brutal NYT story, says it doesn't represent the Amazon he leads." *GeekWire.* https://www.geekwire.com/2015/full-memo-jeff-bezos-responds-to-cutting-nyt-expose-says-tolerance-for-lack-of-empathy-needs-to-be-zero/

"Dying Malls Make Room for New Condos Apartment." 2017. Bend Bulletin. http://www.bendbulletin.com/business/5654908-151/dying-malls-make-room-for-new-condos-apartments

"Embrace the Internet, Skip the Checkout." 2017. Bend Bulletin. http://www.bendbulletin.com/business/5635713-151/embrace-the-internet-skip-the-checkout

McGregor, Lindsay and Doshi, Neel. 2015. "How Company Culture Shapes Employee Motivation." Boston, MA: Harvard Business Review. https://hbr.org/2015/11/how-company-culture-shapes-employee-motivation

Schmid, Emily. 2017. "Work That Matters: Looking Back on 2 Years of Investing in People." *Walmart Today.* Bentonville, AR: Walmart Digital Communications. https://blog.walmart.com/opportunity/20170223/work-that-matters-looking-back-on-2-years-of-investing-in-people

Staley, Oliver. 2017. " Walmart—yes, Walmart—is making changes that could help solve America's wealth inequality problem." *Yahoo! Finance.* https://finance.yahoo.com/news/walmart-yes-walmart-making-changes-100102778.html

U.S. Census Bureau. 2017. *Quarterly Retail E-Commerce Sales, 2nd Quarter 2017.* Washington, DC: U.S. Department of Commerce. https://www.census.gov/retail/mrts/www/data/pdf/ec_current.pdf

WalMart 2016 Global Responsibility Report. 2016. Bentonville, AR: Walmart. https://corporate.walmart.com/2016grr

Walmart. 2016. “Pathways program infographic. Bentonville, AR: Walmart. https://corporate.walmart.com/photos/pathways-program-infographic

Questions:

1. A 2015 *New York Times* article described Amazon as “a soulless, dystopian workplace where no fun is had and no laughter heard” (Cook 2015 n.p.). Employees themselves came to the company’s defense (Ciubotariu 2015). Does this reputation continue to haunt Amazon, or has it been addressed?
2. How do employees differ between a Walmart retail location and an Amazon order fulfillment center? How many white-collar or skilled jobs does Amazon have compared to Walmart?
3. With Amazon moving into the retail market with the purchase of Whole Foods, and with Walmart expanding its e-commerce, how are employee motivation challenges going to shift?

8 Performance Appraisal and Rewards

Exhibit 8.1 (Credit: home thods/ flickr/ Attribution 2.0 Generic (CC BY 2.0))

Introduction

Learning Outcomes

After reading this chapter, you should be able to answer these questions:

1. How do organizations effectively use performance appraisals to improve individual job performance, and what are the limitations inherent in the use of various appraisal systems?
2. What practices are used in the performance appraisal process?
3. How do managers give effective feedback to subordinates?
4. How do organizations choose the best appraisal system for their organization?
5. How do managers and organizations use incentives and rewards effectively to secure the best possible performance from employees?

EXPLORING MANAGERIAL CAREERS

Two Performance Appraisal Interviews

"Janet, thanks for coming in. As you know, it's that time of year again. I've been going over this performance appraisal form and have written in my evaluation. I'd like you to look it over and then sign it."

Janet looked over her ratings, which were nearly all in the "satisfactory" range. Even the category of dependability was marked "satisfactory"; yet, it was Janet who came in on three different occasions to cover for workers in her group who were absent for one reason or another. Janet mentioned this issue to her boss, Ken.

"Well, Janet, you're right and that's exactly what I expect of my employees. You know this is your first year here and you can't expect to reach the top in one jump. But I like your style and if you keep it up, who knows how far you'll go."

Twenty-four minutes after the interview began, Janet left, bewildered and disappointed. She had worked hard during her first year; in fact, she had gone the extra mile on a few occasions, and now she was more confused than ever about what was expected of her and what constituted good performance. "Maybe it just doesn't pay to work hard."

Two weeks before their scheduled interview, Mary asked Ron to review his goals and accomplishments for the last six months and to note any major changes in his job that had taken place during that period. In the meantime, Mary pulled out the file in which she had periodically recorded both positive and negative specific incidents over the last six months concerning Ron's performance. She also reviewed the goals they had jointly set at the end of the last review and thought carefully about not only the possible goals for the next six months but longer-term development needs and goals that might be appropriate for Ron.

On the day of the interview, both Mary and Ron came well prepared to review the past six months as well as to think about and plan for the next performance period and beyond. The interview took nearly two hours. After candidly discussing Ron's past performance and the extent to which both sides felt he had or had not accomplished the goals for that period, they began to focus on what should be accomplished in the future. The discussion caused both sides to make changes in their original evaluations and ideas about targets for the future. When it was over, Ron left more motivated than before and confident that even though he had areas in which he could improve, he had a bright future ahead of him if he continued to be motivated and work hard.

8.1 Performance Appraisal Systems

1. How do organizations effectively use performance appraisals to improve individual job performance, and what are the limitations inherent in the use of various appraisal systems?

Performance appraisals are one of the most important and often one of the most mishandled aspects of management. Typically, we think of performance appraisals as involving a boss evaluating a subordinate. However, performance appraisals increasingly involve subordinates appraising bosses through a feedback process known as 360 feedback,[1] customers appraising providers, and peers evaluating coworkers.

Whether appraisals are done by subordinates, peers, customers, or superiors, the process itself is vital to the lifeblood of the organization. Performance appraisal systems provide a means of systematically evaluating employees across various performance dimensions to ensure that organizations are getting what they pay for. They provide valuable feedback to employees and managers, and they assist in identifying promotable people as well as problems. However, such appraisals are meaningless unless they are accompanied by an effective feedback system that ensures that the employee gets the right messages concerning performance.

Reward systems represent a powerful motivational force in organizations, but this is true only when the system is fair and tied to performance. Because a variety of approaches to appraising performance exists, managers should be aware of the advantages and disadvantages of each. In turn, an understanding of reward systems will help managers select the system best suited to the needs and goals of the organization.

Performance appraisal systems serve a variety of functions of central importance to employees. Appraisal techniques practiced today are not without problems, though. Managers should keep abreast of recent developments in compensation and reward systems so they can modify existing systems when more appropriate alternatives become available.

A key management responsibility has always been to oversee and develop subordinates. In fact, it has been said that every manager is a human resource manager. Nowhere is this truer than with regard to evaluating and rewarding subordinates. Managers are consistently involved with employee training and development, monitoring employee performance, providing job-related feedback, and administering rewards.

In this chapter, we examine three interrelated aspects of the performance appraisal and reward process. As **Exhibit 8.2** shows, this process moves from evaluating employee performance to providing adequate and constructive feedback to determining discretionary rewards. Where effort and performance are properly evaluated and rewarded, we would expect to see more stable and consistent job performance. On the other hand, where such performance is only evaluated intermittently or where the appraisal and review process is poorly done, we would generally see less consistent performance. We begin our discussion with a look at the nature of appraisals.

We begin by examining three aspects of performance appraisal systems: (1) the uses of performance appraisals, (2) problems found in performance appraisals, and (3) methods for reducing errors in the appraisal system. This overview will provide a foundation for studying specific techniques of performance appraisal. Those interested in more detailed information on performance appraisal systems may wish to consult books on personnel administration or compensation.

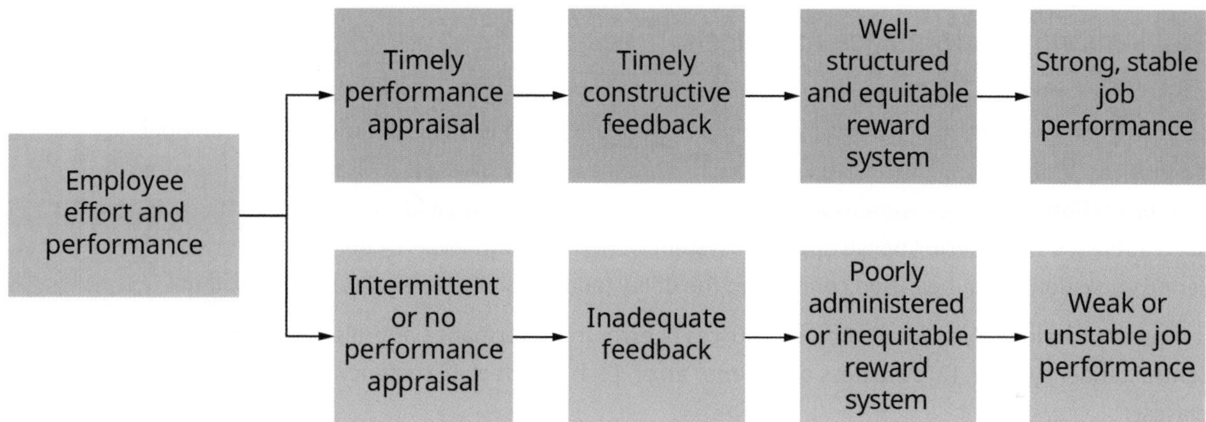

Exhibit 8.2 The Performance Appraisal and Reward Process (Attribution: Copyright Rice University, OpenStax, under CC BY-NC-SA 4.0 license)

Uses of Performance Appraisals

In most work organizations, performance appraisals are used for a variety of reasons. These reasons range from improving employee productivity to developing the employees themselves. This diversity of uses is well documented in a study of why companies use performance appraisals.[2] Traditionally, compensation and performance feedback have been the most prominent reasons organizations use performance appraisals.

Feedback to employees. Performance appraisals provide feedback to employees about quantity and quality of job performance. Without this information, employees have little knowledge of how well they are doing their jobs and how they might improve their work.

Self-development. Performance appraisals can also serve as an aid to employee self-development. Individuals learn about their strengths and weaknesses as seen by others and can initiate self-improvement programs (see discussion on behavioral self-management programs).

Reward systems. In addition, appraisals may form the bases of organizational reward systems—particularly merit-based compensation plans.

Personnel decisions. Performance appraisals serve personnel-related functions as well. In making personnel decisions, such as those relating to promotions, transfers, and terminations, they can be quite useful. Employers can make choices on the basis of information about individual talents and shortcomings. In addition, appraisal systems help management evaluate the effectiveness of its selection and placement functions. If newly hired employees generally perform poorly, managers should consider whether the right kind of people are being hired in the first place.

Training and development. Finally, appraisals can help managers identify areas in which employees lack critical skills for either immediate or future performance. In these situations, new or revised training programs can be established to further develop the company's human resources.

It is apparent that performance appraisal systems serve a variety of functions in organizations. In light of the importance of these functions, it is imperative that the accuracy and fairness of the appraisal be paramount considerations in the evaluation of a system. Many performance appraisal systems exist. It is the manager's job to select the technique or combination of techniques that best serves the particular needs (and constraints) of the organization. Before considering these various techniques, let us look at some of the more prominent problems and sources of error that are common to several of them.

Problems with Performance Appraisals

A number of problems can be identified that pose a threat to the value of appraisal techniques. Most of these problems deal with the related issues of the validity and reliability of the instruments or techniques themselves. **Validity** is the extent to which an instrument actually measures what it intends to measure, whereas **reliability** is the extent to which the instrument consistently yields the same results each time it is used. Ideally, a good performance appraisal system will exhibit high levels of both validity and reliability. If not, serious questions must be raised concerning the utility (and possibly the legality) of the system.

It is possible to identify several common sources of error in performance appraisal systems. These include: (1) central tendency error, (2) strictness or leniency error, (3) halo effect, (4) recency error, and (5) personal biases.

Central Tendency Error. It has often been found that supervisors rate most of their employees within a narrow range. Regardless of how people actually perform, the rater fails to distinguish significant differences among group members and lumps everyone together in an "average" category. This is called **central tendency error** and is shown in **Exhibit 8.3**. In short, the central tendency error is the failure to recognize either very good or very poor performers.

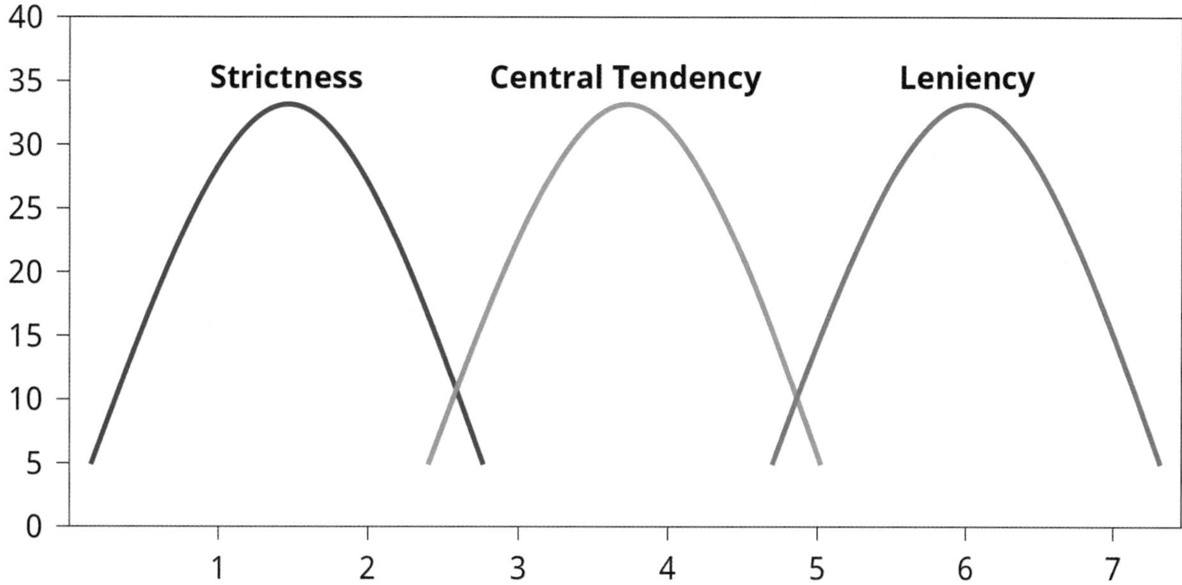

Exhibit 8.3 Examples of Strictness, Central Tendency, and Leniency Errors (Attribution: Copyright Rice University, OpenStax, under CC BY-NC-SA 4.0 license)

Strictness or Leniency Error. A related rating problem exists when a supervisor is overly strict or overly lenient in evaluations (see **Exhibit 8.3**). In college classrooms, we hear of professors who are "tough graders" or, conversely, "easy A's." Similar situations exist in the workplace, where some supervisors see most subordinates as not measuring up to their high standards, whereas other supervisors see most subordinates as deserving of a high rating. As with central tendency error, **strictness error** and **leniency error** fail to distinguish adequately between good and bad performers and instead relegate almost everyone to the same or related categories.

Halo Effect. The **halo effect** exists where a supervisor assigns the same rating to each factor being evaluated for an individual. For example, an employee rated above average on quantity of performance may also be rated above average on quality of performance, interpersonal competence, attendance, and promotion readiness. In other words, the supervisor cannot effectively differentiate between relatively discrete categories and instead gives a global rating.

These types of bias are based on our perceptions of others. The halo effect occurs when managers have an overly positive view of a particular employee. This can impact the objectivity of reviews, with managers consistently giving an employee high ratings and failing to recognize areas for improvement.

Whether positive or negative, we also have a natural tendency to confirm our preconceived beliefs about people in the way we interpret or recall performance, which is known as confirmatory bias.

For example, a manager may have a preconception that her male report is more assertive. This could cause her to recall instances more easily in which her report asserted his position during a meeting. On the other hand, she may perceive her female report to be less assertive, predisposing her to forget when the report suggested an effective strategy or was successful in a tough negotiation.

The halo effect is often a consequence of people having a similarity bias for certain types of people. We naturally tend to favor and trust people who are similar to us. Whether it's people who also have a penchant for golf or people who remind us of a younger version of ourselves, favoritism that results from a similarity bias can give certain employees an unfair advantage over others. This can impact a team to the point that those employees may receive more coaching, better reviews and, as a result, more opportunities for advancement.[3]

Recency Error. Oftentimes evaluators focus on an employee's most recent behavior in the evaluation process. This is known as the **recency error**. That is, in an annual evaluation, a supervisor may give undue emphasis to performance during the past months—or even weeks—and ignore performance levels prior to this. This practice, if known to employees, leads to a situation where employees may "float" for the initial months of the evaluation period and then overexert themselves in the last few months or weeks prior to evaluation. This practice leads to uneven performance and contributes to the attitude of "playing the game."

Personal Biases. Finally, it is not uncommon to find situations in which supervisors allow their own personal biases to influence their appraisals. Such biases include like or dislike for someone, as well as racial and sexual biases. Personal biases can interfere with the fairness and accuracy of an evaluation and are illegal in many situations.

Reducing Errors in Performance Appraisals

A number of suggestions have been advanced recently to minimize the effects of various biases and errors on the performance appraisal process.[4] When errors are reduced, more accurate information is available for personnel decisions and personal development. These methods for reducing error include

- ensuring that each dimension or factor on a performance appraisal form represents a single job activity instead of a group of job activities.
- avoiding terms such as *average*, because different evaluators define the term differently.
- ensuring that raters observe subordinates on a regular basis throughout the evaluation period. It is even helpful if the rater takes notes for future reference.
- keeping the number of persons evaluated by one rater to a reasonable number. When one person must evaluate many subordinates, it becomes difficult to discriminate. Rating fatigue increases with the number of ratees.
- ensuring that the dimensions used are clearly stated, meaningful, and relevant to good job performance.
- training raters so they can recognize various sources of error and understand the rationale underlying the evaluation process.

Using mechanisms like these, better employee ratings that can have greater meaning both for the individual employee and the organization will result.

CONCEPT CHECK

1. What are performance appraisals, and how are they used in organizations?
2. How are performance appraisals used as a reward system, and what problems can they cause?

8.2 Techniques of Performance Appraisal

2. What practices are used in the performance appraisal process?

Organizations use numerous methods to evaluate personnel. We will summarize several popular techniques.

Although countless variations on these themes can be found, the basic methods presented provide a good summary of the commonly available techniques. Following this review, we will consider the various strengths and weaknesses of each technique. Six techniques are reviewed here: (1) graphic rating scales, (2) critical incident technique, (3) behaviorally anchored rating scales, (4) behavioral observation scales, (5) management by objectives, and (6) assessment centers.

Graphic Rating Scales

Certainly, the most popular method of evaluation used in organizations today is the **graphic rating scale**. One study found that 57 percent of the organizations surveyed used rating scales, and another study found the figure to be 65 percent.[5] Although this method appears in many formats, the supervisor or rater is typically presented with a printed or online form that contains both the employee's name and several evaluation dimensions (quantity of work, quality of work, knowledge of job, attendance). The rater is then asked to rate the employee by assigning a number or rating on each of the dimensions. An example of a graphic rating scale is shown in **Table 8.1**.

A Sample of a Typical Graphic Rating Scale					
Name ____________ **Dept.** ____________ **Date** ____________					
Quantity of work	**Outstanding**	**Good**	**Satisfactory**	**Fair**	**Unsatisfactory**
Volume of acceptable work under normal conditions					
Comments:					
Quality of work	**Outstanding**	**Good**	**Satisfactory**	**Fair**	**Unsatisfactory**
Thoroughness, neatness, and accuracy of work					
Comments:					
Knowledge of job	**Outstanding**	**Good**	**Satisfactory**	**Fair**	**Unsatisfactory**
Clear understanding of the facts or factors pertinent to the job					
Comments:					
Personal qualities	**Outstanding**	**Good**	**Satisfactory**	**Fair**	**Unsatisfactory**
Personality, appearance, sociability, leadership, integrity					
Comments:					

Table 8.1 (Attribution: Copyright Rice University, OpenStax, under CC BY-NC-SA 4.0 license)

A Sample of a Typical Graphic Rating Scale					
Name ___________ **Dept.** ___________ **Date** ___________					
Cooperation	**Outstanding**	**Good**	**Satisfactory**	**Fair**	**Unsatisfactory**
Ability and willingness to work with associates, supervisors, and subordinates toward common goal					
Comments:					
Dependability	**Outstanding**	**Good**	**Satisfactory**	**Fair**	**Unsatisfactory**
Conscientious, thorough, accurate, reliable with respect to attendance, lunch periods, reliefs, etc.					
Comments:					
Initiative	**Outstanding**	**Good**	**Satisfactory**	**Fair**	**Unsatisfactory**
Earnestness in seeking increased responsibilities Self-starting, unafraid to proceed alone					
Comments:					

Table 8.1 (Attribution: Copyright Rice University, OpenStax, under CC BY-NC-SA 4.0 license)

By using this method, if we assume that evaluator biases can be minimized, it is possible to compare employees objectively. It is also possible to examine the relative strengths and weaknesses of a single employee by comparing scores on the various dimensions.

However, one of the most serious drawbacks of this technique is its openness to central tendency, strictness, and leniency errors. It is possible to rate almost everyone in the middle of the scale or, conversely, at one end of the scale. In order to control for this, some companies have assigned required percentage distributions to the various scale points. Supervisors may be allowed to rate only 10 percent of their people outstanding and are required to rate 10 percent unsatisfactory, perhaps assigning 20 percent, 40 percent, and 20 percent to the remaining middle categories. By doing this, a distribution is forced within each department. However, this procedure may penalize a group of truly outstanding performers or reward a group of poor ones.

Critical Incident Technique

With the **critical incident technique** of performance appraisal, supervisors record incidents, or examples, of each subordinate's behavior that led to either unusual success or unusual failure on some aspect of the job. These incidents are recorded in a daily or weekly log under predesignated categories (planning, decision-making, interpersonal relations, report writing). The final performance rating consists of a series of descriptive paragraphs or notes about various aspects of an employee's performance (see **Table 8.2**).

An Example of Critical Incident Evaluation

The following performance areas are designed to assist you in preparing this appraisal and in discussing an individual's performance with her. It is suggested that areas of performance that you feel are significantly good or poor be documented below with specific examples or actions. The points listed are suggested as typical and are by no means all-inclusive. Examples related to these points may be viewed from either a positive or negative standpoint.

1. Performance on Technology of the Job
   A. *Safety Effectiveness*—possible considerations:
      1. sets an excellent safety example for others in the department by words and action
      2. trains people well in safety areas
      3. gains the cooperation and participation of people in safety
      4. insists that safety be designed into procedure and processes
      5. is instrumental in initiating departmental safety program
      6. accepts safety as a fundamental job responsibility

Item	Related Examples

   B. *Job Knowledge*—Technical and/or Specialized—possible considerations:
      1. shows exceptional knowledge in methods, materials, and techniques; applies in a resourceful and practical manner
      2. stays abreast of development(s) in field and applies to job
      3. "keeps up" on latest material in her special field
      4. participates in professional or technical organizations pertinent to her activities

Item	Related Examples

2. Performance on Human Relations
   A. *Ability to Communicate*—possible considerations:

Table 8.2 (Attribution: Copyright Rice University, OpenStax, under CC BY-NC-SA 4.0 license)

An Example of Critical Incident Evaluation

1. gives logical, clear-cut, understandable instructions on complex problems
2. uses clear and direct language in written and oral reporting
3. organizes presentations in logical order and in order of importance
4. provides supervisor and subordinates with pertinent and adequate information
5. tailors communications approach to group or individual
6. keeps informed on how subordinates think and feel about things

Item	Related Examples

B. *Results Achieved through Others*—possible considerations:
   1. develops enthusiasm in others that gets the job done
   2. has respect and confidence of others
   3. recognizes and credits skills of others
   4. coordinates well with other involved groups to get the job done

Item	Related Examples

Source: Adapted from R. Daft and R. Steers, *Organizations: A Micro/Macro Approach* (Glenview, III.: Scott, Foresman and Company, 1986), p. 129.

Table 8.2

The critical incident method provides useful information for appraisal interviews, and managers and subordinates can discuss specific incidents. Good qualitative information is generated. However, because little quantitative data emerge, it is difficult to use this technique for promotion or salary decisions. The qualitative output here has led some companies to combine the critical incident technique with one of the quantitative techniques, such as the rating scale, to provide different kinds of feedback to the employees.

Behaviorally Anchored Rating Scales

An appraisal system that has received increasing attention in recent years is the **behaviorally anchored rating scale** (BARS). This system requires considerable work prior to evaluation but, if the work is carefully done, can lead to highly accurate ratings with high inter-rater reliability. Specifically, the BARS technique begins by selecting a job that can be described in observable behaviors. Managers and personnel specialists then identify these behaviors as they relate to superior or inferior performance.

An example of this is shown in **Exhibit 8.4**, where the BARS technique has been applied to the job of college professor. As shown, as one moves from extremely poor performance to extremely good performance, the performance descriptions, or behavioral anchors, increase. Oftentimes, six to ten scales are used to describe performance on the job. **Exhibit 8.4** evaluates the professor's organizational skills. Other scales could relate to the professor's teaching effectiveness, knowledge of the material, availability to students, and fairness in grading. Once these scales are determined, the evaluator has only to check the category that describes what she observes on the job, and the employee's rating is simultaneously determined. The BARS technique has several purported advantages. In particular, many of the sources of error discussed earlier (central tendency, leniency, halo) should be significantly reduced because raters are considering verbal descriptions of specific behaviors instead of general categories of behaviors, such as those used in graphic rating scales. In addition, the technique focuses on job-related behaviors and ignores less relevant issues such as the subordinate's personality, race, or gender. This technique should also lead to employees being less defensive during performance appraisals, because the focus of the discussion would be actual measured behaviors, not the person. Finally, BARS can aid in employee training and development by identifying those domains needing most attention.

Organizational skills: A good constructional order of material slides smoothly from one topic to another; design of course optimizes interest; students can easily follow organizational strategy; course outline is followed.

Follows course syllabus; presents lectures in a logical order; ties each lecture into the previous one

Prepares a course syllabus but follows it only occasionally; presents lectures in no particular order, lthough does tie them together

Makes no use of a course syllabus; lectures on topics randomly with no logical order

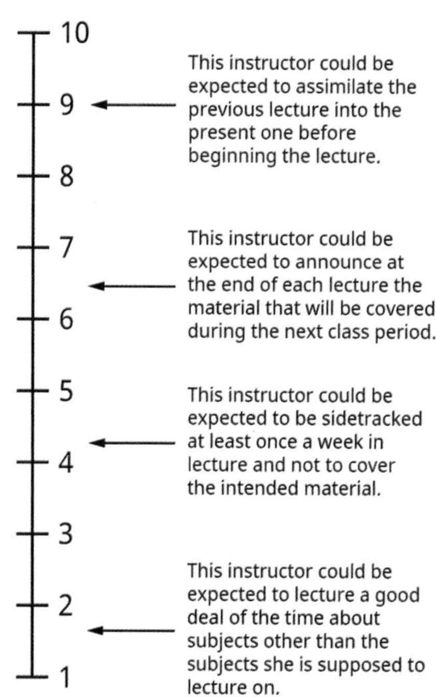

Exhibit 8.4 A Behaviorally Anchored Scale for Rating College Professors *Source:* Reprinted by permission of H. John Bernardin. (Attribution: Copyright Rice University, OpenStax, under CC BY-NC-SA 4.0 license)

On the negative side, as noted above, considerable time and effort in designing the forms are required before the actual rating. Because a separate BARS is required for each distinct job, it is only cost-efficient for common jobs. Finally, because the technique relies on observable behaviors, it may have little applicability for such jobs in such areas as research science (and sometimes management), where much of the work is mental and relevant observable behaviors are difficult to obtain.

Behavioral Observation Scales

The **behavioral observation scale** (BOS) is similar to BARS in that both focus on identifying observable behaviors as they relate to performance. It is, however, less demanding of the evaluator. Typically, the evaluator is asked to rate each behavior on a scale from 1 to 5 to indicate the frequency with which the employee exhibits the behavior. Evaluation of an employee's performance on a particular dimension is derived by summing the frequency ratings for the behaviors in each dimension.

For example, in **Table 8.3** we can see an example of a form to evaluate a manager's ability to overcome resistance to change. The rater simply has to circle the appropriate numbers describing observed behaviors and get a summary rating by adding the results. The BOS technique is easier to construct than the BARS and makes the evaluator's job somewhat simpler. Even so, this is a relatively new technique that is only now receiving some support in industry.

Example of a Behavioral Observation Scale for Managers: Overcoming Resistance to Change					
	Almost Never				**Almost Always**
1. Describes the details of the change to subordinates	**1**	**2**	**3**	**4**	**5**
2. Explains why the change is necessary	**1**	**2**	**3**	**4**	**5**
3. Discusses how the change will affect the employee	**1**	**2**	**3**	**4**	**5**
4. Listens to the employee's concerns	**1**	**2**	**3**	**4**	**5**
5. Asks the employee for help in making the change work	**1**	**2**	**3**	**4**	**5**
6. If necessary, specifies the date for a follow-up meeting to respond to employee's concerns	1	2	3	4	5
Total:	6–10	11–15	16–20	21–25	26–30
	Below adequate	Adequate	Full	Excellent	Superior
Source: Adapted from K. Wexley and G. Latham, *Increasing Productivity Through Performance Appraisal,* 3rd ed. Englewood Cliffs, NJ: Prentice Hall, 2001.					

Table 8.3 (Attribution: Copyright Rice University, OpenStax, under CC BY-NC-SA 4.0 license)

Management by Objectives

A popular technique for evaluating employees who are involved in jobs that have clear quantitative output is **management by objectives** (MBO). Although the concept of MBO encompasses much more than just the appraisal process (incorporating an organization-wide motivation, performance, and control system), we will focus here on its narrower application to evaluating employee performance. MBO is closely related to the goal-setting theory of motivation.

Under MBO, individual employees work with their supervisor to establish goals and objectives for which they will be responsible during the coming year. These goals are stated in clear language and relate to tasks that are within the domain of the employee. An example of these goals for a sales representative is shown in **Table 8.4**. Following a specified period of time, the employee's performance is compared to the preset goals to determine the extent to which the goals have been met or exceeded.

MBO Evaluation Report for Sales Representative			
Goals Categories	**Goal**	**Actual Performance**	**Variance**
1. Number of sales calls	40	38	95%
2. Number of new customers contacted	10	10	100%
3. Number of customer complaints	5	10	50%
4. Sales of product #1	10,000 units	11,000 units	110%
5. Sales of product #2	15,000 units	14,000 units	93%
6. Sales of product #3	25,000 units	30,000 units	120%

Table 8.4 (Attribution: Copyright Rice University, OpenStax, under CC BY-NC-SA 4.0 license)

Several advantages of MBO have been observed. These include the ability to do better planning; improved motivation, because of knowledge of results; fairer evaluations, done on the basis of results rather than personality; improved commitment through participation; and improved supervisory skills in such areas as listening, counseling, and evaluating. On the negative side, however, MBO has been criticized because it emphasizes quantitative goals at the expense of qualitative goals and often creates too much paperwork. It is difficult to compare performance levels among employees because most are responsible for different goals. Sometimes the implementation of MBO goals are autocratic and therefore ineffective or even counterproductive. As discussed in the study of motivation, goals must be accepted to be effective. Finally, in order to be successful, MBO implementation must have constant attention and support from top management; MBO does not run itself. In the absence of this support, the technique loses legitimacy and often falls into disrepair.

Assessment Centers

A relatively new method of evaluation is the **assessment center**. Assessment centers are unique among appraisal techniques in that they focus more on evaluating an employee's long-range potential to an organization than on her performance over the past year. They are also unique in that they are used almost exclusively among managerial personnel.

An assessment center consists of a series of standardized evaluations of behavior based on multiple inputs. Over a two- or three-day period (away from the job), trained observers make judgments on managers' behavior in response to specially developed exercises. These exercises may consist of in-basket exercises, role-playing, and case analyses, as well as personal interviews and psychological tests. An example of an assessment center program is shown in **Table 8.5**.

Example of Two-Day Assessment Center Schedule			
Day #1		**Day #2**	
8:00–9:00 A.M.	Orientation session	8:00–10:30 A.M.	In-basket exercise
9:00 –10:30 A.M.	Psychological testing	10:30–10:45 A.M.	Coffee break
10:30–10:45 A.M.	Coffee break	10:45–12:30 P.M.	Role-playing exercise
10:45–12:30 P.M.	Management simulation game	12:30–1:30 P.M.	Lunch
12:30–1:30 P.M.	Lunch	1:30–3:15 P.M.	Group problem-solving exercise
1:30–3:15 P.M.	Individual decision-making exercise	3:15–3:30 P.M.	Coffee break
3:15–3:30 P.M.	Coffee break	3:30–4:30 P.M.	Debriefing by raters
3:30–4:30 P.M.	Interview with raters		

Table 8.5 (Attribution: Copyright Rice University, OpenStax, under CC BY-NC-SA 4.0 license)

On the basis of these exercises, the trained observers make judgments on employees' potential for future managerial assignments in the organization. More specifically, information is obtained concerning employees' interpersonal skills, communication ability, creativity, problem-solving skills, tolerance for stress and ambiguity, and planning ability. This technique has been used successfully by some of the largest corporations in the United States, including AT&T, IBM, and General Electric.

Results from a series of assessment center programs appear promising, and the technique is growing in popularity as a means of identifying future managerial potential. For example, Coca-Cola USA experimented with using assessment centers to select its managerial personnel. After a detailed study, the company found that those selected in this way were only one-third as likely to leave the company or be fired than those selected in the traditional way. Although the assessment center approach added about 6 percent to the cost of hiring, the lower turnover rate led to large overall savings.[6]

Some problems with the technique have been noted. In particular, because of the highly stressful environment created in assessment centers, many otherwise good managers may simply not perform to their potential. Moreover, the results of a poor evaluation in an assessment center may be far-reaching; individuals may receive a "loser" image that will follow them for a long time. And, finally, there is some question concerning exactly how valid and reliable assessment centers really are in predicting future managerial success.[7] Despite these problems, assessment centers remain a popular vehicle in some companies for developing and appraising managerial potential.

ETHICS IN PRACTICE

Tesla's Performance Review

At Tesla, the automotive giant, the standards are set extremely high for their employees. In 2017, Tesla conducted its annual performance reviews as it does each year. Due to the review process, the company sees both voluntary and involuntary departures. During the review process, the managers discuss "results that were achieved, as well as how those results were achieved" with their employees.* Tesla also has a performance recognition and compensation program that includes equity rewards as well as promotions in some cases, along with the constructive feedback.

The departure of employees during the review period is not unique to Tesla; however, in 2017 there was a large exodus of approximately 700 employees following their employee reviews. Elon Musk, who recently has stepped down from the role of chairman and has been under scrutiny for his behavior,* saw the media coverage of this news as "ridiculous."

"You have two boxes of equal ability, and one's much smaller, the big guy's going to crush the little guy, obviously," states Musk. "So, the little guy better have a heck of a lot more skill or he's going to get clobbered. So that is why our standards are high . . . if they're not high, we will die."

Overall, approximately 17 percent of their employees were promoted, almost half in manufacturing. As Tesla continues to grow and develop new vehicles, it is consistently pushing the boundaries and pushing its employees to new limits. Performance reviews are of the highest importance for Tesla's business to succeed; the company needs the best people with the best skills. It is constantly growing and attempting to "suck the labor pool dry" to fill positions at many of its locations and factories.

Questions:

1. What factors do you feel could have changed in Tesla's approach to its performance reviews?
2. How can a high-pressure environment affect an employee's performance? What factors should be considered to combat these issues?

Sources: K. Korosec. "Tesla Fires Hundreds of Workers After Their Annual Performance Review." *Fortune*, October 14, 2017, http://fortune.com/2017/10/13/tesla-fires-employees/; D. Muoio. "Tesla fired 700 employees after performance reviews in the third quarter." *Business Insider*, November 1, 2017, https://www.businessinsider.com/tesla-fired-700-employees-performance-reviews-2017-11; J. Wattles. "Elon Musk agrees to pay $20 million and quit as Tesla chairman in deal with SEC." *Money*, September 30, 2018, https://money.cnn.com/2018/09/29/technology/business/elon-musk-tesla-sec-settlement/index.html.

Comparison of Appraisal Techniques

It is important to consider which appraisal technique or set of techniques may be most appropriate for a given situation. Although there is no simple answer to this question, we can consider the various strengths and weaknesses of each technique. This is done in Table 8.6. It is important to keep in mind that the appropriateness of a particular appraisal technique is in part a function of the purpose for the appraisal. For example, if the purpose of the appraisal is to identify high potential executives, then assessment centers are more appropriate than rating scales.

Major Strengths and Weaknesses of Appraisal Techniques						
	Rating Scales	Critical Incidents	BARS	BOS	MBO	Assessment Centers
Meaningful dimensions	Sometimes	Sometimes	Usually	Usually	Usually	Usually
Amount of time required	Low	Medium	High	Medium	High	High
Development costs	Low	Low	High	Medium	Medium	High
Potential for rating errors	High	Medium	Low	Low	Low	Low
Acceptability to subordinates	Low	Medium	High	High	High	High
Acceptability to superiors	Low	Medium	High	High	High	High
Usefulness for allocating rewards	Poor	Fair	Good	Good	Good	Fair
Usefulness for employee counseling	Poor	Fair	Good	Good	Good	Good
Usefulness for identifying promotion potential	Poor	Fair	Fair	Fair	Fair	Good

Table 8.6 (Attribution: Copyright Rice University, OpenStax, under CC BY-NC-SA 4.0 license)

As would be expected, the easiest and least expensive techniques are also the least accurate. They are also the least useful for purposes of personnel decisions and employee development. Once again, it appears that managers and organizations get what they pay for. If performance appraisals represent an important aspect of organizational life, clearly the more sophisticated—and more time-consuming—techniques are preferable. If, on the other hand, it is necessary to evaluate employees quickly and with few resources, techniques such as the graphic rating scale may be more appropriate. Managers must make cost-benefit decisions about the price (in time and money) they are willing to pay for a quality performance appraisal system.

CONCEPT CHECK 

1. What are the techniques and scales used in performance appraisals?
2. What are MBOs, and how do they relate to performance appraisals?
3. What are assessment centers?

8.3 Feedback

3. How do managers give effective feedback to subordinates?

As previously noted, feedback represents a critical variable in determining the success or failure of the goal-setting process. The same applies to the performance appraisal process. Without effective knowledge of results, the motivational impact of the appraisal process is lost. To better understand how feedback in work settings affects employee behavior, consider the model shown in **Exhibit 8.5**.[8]

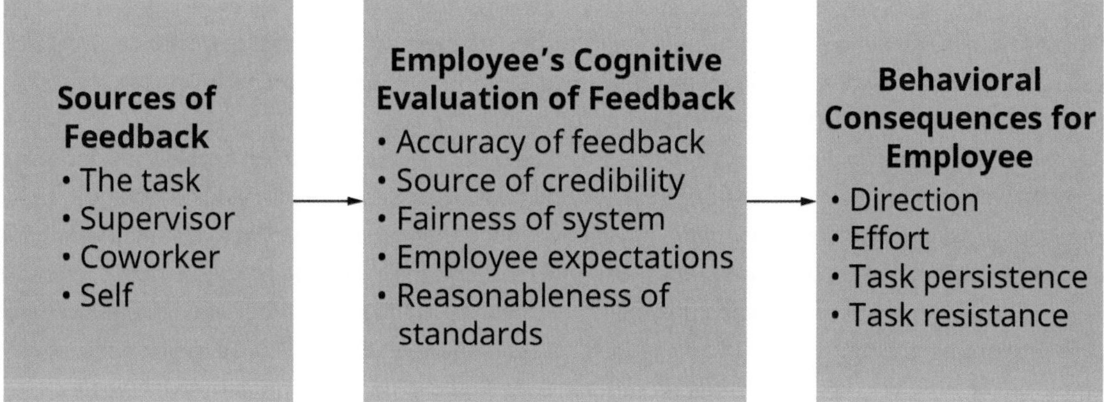

Exhibit 8.5 Effects of Feedback on Job Performance (Attribution: Copyright Rice University, OpenStax, under CC BY-NC-SA 4.0 license)

Feedback comes from many sources, including the task at hand, the supervisor, coworkers, and oneself. This input is then cognitively evaluated by the employee, who considers such factors as the perceived *accuracy* of the feedback (e.g., does the employee consider the information to be correct?); the *credibility of the source* of the feedback (e.g., does the employee trust the supervisor's opinion?); the employee's opinion concerning the *fairness* of the evaluation-process; the extent to which the feedback met the employee's *expectations* (e.g., does the employee think she could have done better?); and the *reasonableness* of the performance standards.

If one or more of these evaluations prove negative (for example, the employee believes she is being unfairly evaluated), the credibility of the feedback is dismissed, and the employee may increase her resistance to task effort. On the other hand, where the feedback is accepted, it reinforces the employee's direction, effort on the task, and persistence on the task. Thus, although feedback is essential, it is the nature and quality of the feedback that ultimately determines employee response.

CONCEPT CHECK 

1. What types of feedback do performance appraisals provide to all organization members?

8.4 Reward Systems in Organizations

4. How do organizations choose the best appraisal system for their organization?

After a company has designed and implemented a systematic performance appraisal system and provided adequate feedback to employees, the next step is to consider how to tie available corporate rewards to the outcomes of the appraisal. Behavioral research consistently demonstrates that performance levels are highest when rewards are contingent upon performance. Thus, in this section, we will examine five aspects of reward systems in organizations: (1) functions served by reward systems, (2) bases for reward distribution, (3) intrinsic versus extrinsic rewards, (4) the relationship between money and motivation and, finally, (5) pay secrecy.

Functions of Reward Systems

Reward systems in organizations are used for a variety of reasons. It is generally agreed that reward systems influence the following:

- *Job effort and performance.* Following expectancy theory, employees' effort and performance would be expected to increase when they felt that rewards were contingent upon good performance. Hence, reward systems serve a very basic motivational function.
- *Attendance and retention.* Reward systems have also been shown to influence an employee's decision to come to work or to remain with the organization. This was discussed in the previous chapter.
- *Employee commitment to the organization.* It has been found that reward systems in no small way influence employee commitment to the organization, primarily through the exchange process.[9] That is, employees develop ties with organizations when they perceive that the organization is interested in their welfare and willing to protect their interests. This exchange process is shown in **Exhibit 8.6**. To the extent that employee needs and goals are met by the company, we would expect commitment to increase.
- *Job satisfaction*. Job satisfaction has also been shown to be related to rewards, as discussed in the previous chapter. Edward E. Lawler, a well-known researcher on employee compensation, has identified four conclusions concerning the relationship between rewards and satisfaction: (1) satisfaction with a reward is a function of both how much is received and how much the individual feels should have been received; (2) satisfaction is influenced by comparisons with what happens to others, especially one's coworkers; (3) people differ with respect to the rewards they value; and (4) some rewards are satisfying because they lead to other rewards.[10]
- *Occupational and organizational choice.* Finally, the selection of an occupation by an individual, as well as the decision to join a particular organization within that occupation, are influenced by the rewards that are thought to be available in the occupation or organization. To prove this, simply look at the classified section of your local newspaper and notice how many jobs highlight beginning salaries.

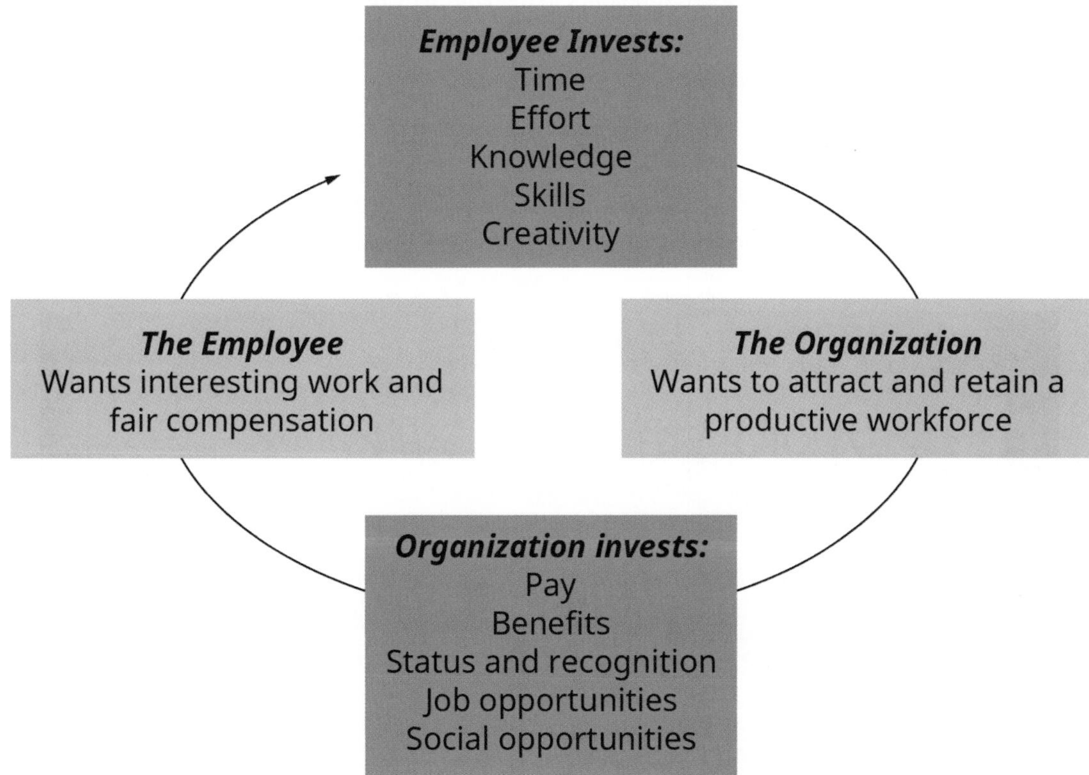

Exhibit 8.6 The Exchange Process Between Employee and Organization (Attribution: Copyright Rice University, OpenStax, under CC BY-NC-SA 4.0 license)

Reward systems in organizations have far-reaching consequences for both individual satisfaction and organizational effectiveness. Unfortunately, cases can easily be cited where reward systems have been distorted to punish good performance or inhibit creativity. Consider, for example, the Greyhound Bus Company driver who was suspended for 10 days without pay for breaking a company rule against using a CB radio on his bus. The bus driver had used the radio to alert police that his bus, with 32 passengers on board, was being hijacked by an armed man. The police arrested the hijacker, and the bus driver was suspended for breaking company rules.[11] Such incidents hardly encourage employees to focus their efforts on responsible performance.

Bases for Reward Distribution

A common reality in many contemporary work organizations is the inequity that exists in the distribution of available rewards. One often sees little correlation between those who perform well and those who receive the greatest rewards. At the extreme, it is hard to understand how a company could pay its president $10 to $20 million per year (as many large corporations do) while it pays its secretaries and clerks less than $15,000. Each works approximately 40 hours per week, and both are important for organizational performance. Is it really possible that the president is 1,000 times more important than the secretary, as the salary differential suggests?

How do organizations decide on the distribution of available rewards? At least four mechanisms can be identified. In more cases than we choose to admit, rewards go to those with the greatest *power* (either market power or personal power). In many of the corporations whose presidents earn eight-figure incomes, we find that these same people are either major shareholders in the company or have certain abilities, connections, or status that the company wants. Indeed, a threat of resignation from an important or high-performing executive often leads to increased rewards.

A second possible basis for reward distribution is *equality*. Here, all individuals within one job classification would receive the same, or at least similar, rewards. The most common example here can be found among unionized workers, where pay rates are established and standardized with little or no reference to actual performance level. Instead of ability or performance, these systems usually recognize seniority as the key factor in pay raises or promotions.

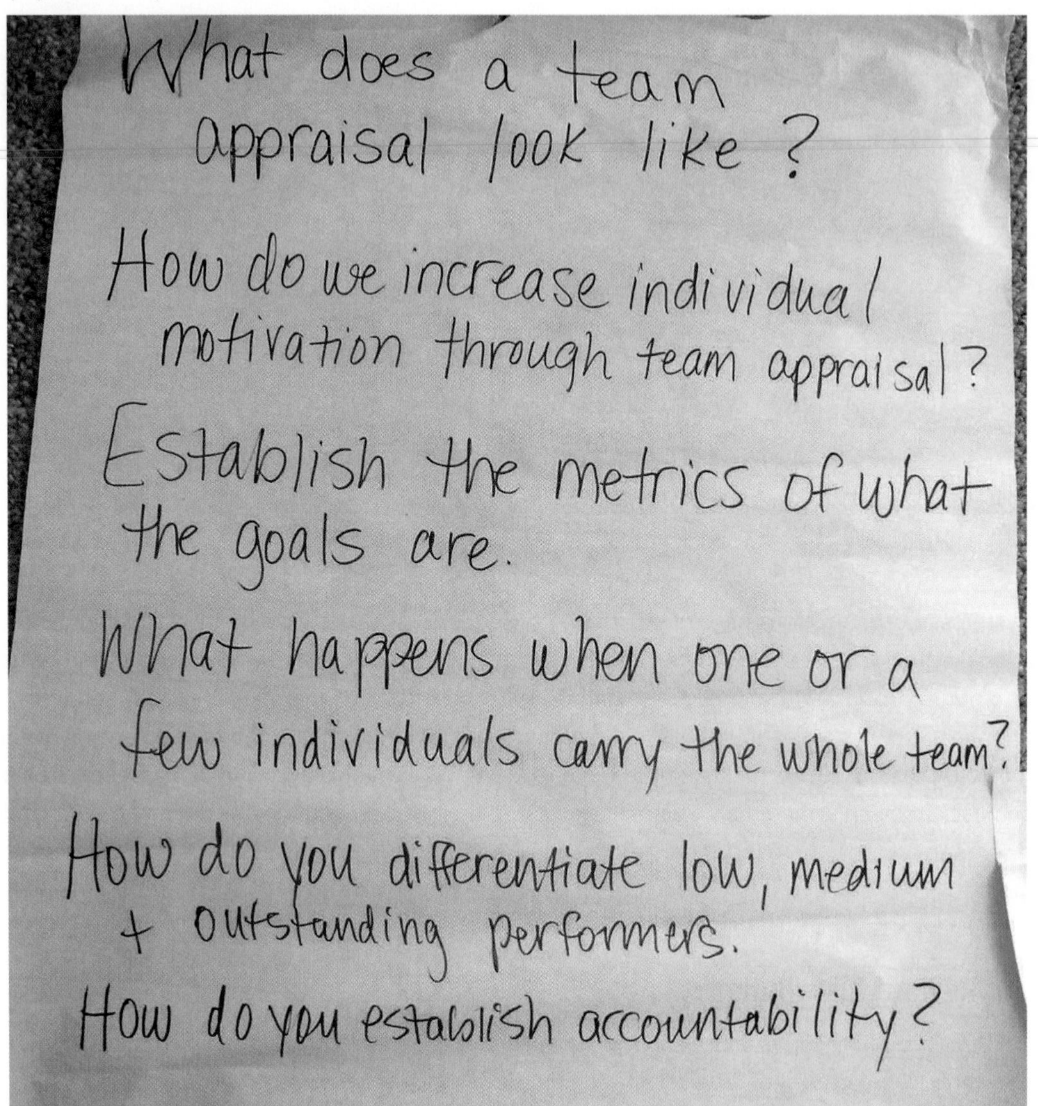

Exhibit 8.7 Team Based Rewards Performance appraisals, whether team or individual, provide feedback to workers or organizational teams. Traditionally, performance evaluations provide information to help improve individual performance, increase efficiency and define management's expectations. Performance appraisals compare work performed against measurable objectives that the employee and supervisor agreed to at the beginning of the appraisal period. As work has become more team oriented, performance appraisals now measure how a team of workers perform rather than just how an individual performs his job. (Attribution; Deb Nystrom/ flickr/ Attribution 2.0 Generic (CC BY 2.0))

The basis for the social welfare reward system in this country is need. In large part, the greater the need, the greater the level of support. It is not uncommon to see situations in business firms where need is taken into account in layoff situations—where an employee is not laid off because she is the sole support of a family.

A fourth mechanism used by organizations in allocating rewards is **distributive justice**. Under this approach, employees receive (at least a portion of) their rewards as a function of their level of contribution to the organization. The greater the contribution (such as performance), the greater the reward. This mechanism is most prominent in merit-based incentive programs, where pay and bonuses are determined by performance levels.

Extrinsic and Intrinsic Rewards

The variety of rewards that employees can receive in exchange for their contributions of time and effort can be classified as either *extrinsic* or *intrinsic* rewards. **Extrinsic rewards** are external to the work itself. They are administered externally—that is, by someone else (usually management). Examples of extrinsic rewards include wages and salary, fringe benefits, promotions, and recognition and praise from others.

On the other hand, **intrinsic rewards** represent those rewards that are related directly to performing the job. In this sense, they are often described as "self-administered" rewards, because engaging in the task itself leads to their receipt. Examples of intrinsic rewards include feelings of task accomplishment, autonomy, and personal growth and development that come from the job.

In the literature on employee motivation, there is considerable controversy concerning the possible interrelationship of these two kinds of reward. It has been argued (with some research support) that extrinsic rewards tend to drive out the positive effects of some intrinsic rewards and can lead to unethical behavior.[12] Consider, for example, the child next door who begs you to let her help you wash your car. For a young child, this task can carry considerable excitement (and intrinsic motivation). Now, consider what happens on a Saturday afternoon when you need your car washed but the child has other options. What do you do? You offer to pay her this time to help wash your car. What do you think will happen the next time you ask the neighbor to help you wash the car for free? In other words, when extrinsic rewards such as pay are tied closely to performance (called performance-reward contingency), **intrinsic motivation**—the desire to do a task because you enjoy it—can decrease.

Also, it is important to keep in mind that because extrinsic rewards are administered by sources external to the individual, their effectiveness rests on accurate and fair monitoring, evaluating, and administration. Implementation can be expensive, and the timing of performance and rewards may not always be close. For example, you may perform well on a task, but unless there is a way for that to be noticed, evaluated, recorded, and rewarded within a reasonable time frame, an extrinsic reward may not have a significant impact. Intrinsic rewards are a function of self-monitoring, evaluation, and administration; consequently, these rewards often are less costly and more effectively administered. For example, even if no one else notices or rewards you for superior performance on a task, you can still reward yourself with a mental pat on the back for a job well done or a sense of satisfaction for overcoming a challenge. The implications of this finding will become apparent when exploring efforts to enrich employees' jobs.

Money and Motivation: A Closer Look

A recurring debate among managers focuses on the issue of whether money is a primary motivator. Some argue that most behavior in organizational settings is motivated by money (or at least monetary factors), whereas others argue that money is only one of many factors that motivate performance. Whichever group is correct, we must recognize that money can have important motivational consequences for many people in many situations. In fact, money serves several important functions in work settings.[13] These include serving as (1) a goal or incentive, (2) a source of satisfaction, (3) an instrument for gaining other desired outcomes, (4) a standard of comparison for determining relative standing or worth, and (5) a conditional reinforcer where its receipt is contingent upon a certain level of performance. Even so, experience tells us that the effectiveness of pay as a motivator varies considerably. Sometimes there seems to be an almost direct relationship between pay and effort, whereas at other times no such relationship is found. Why? Lawler suggests that certain conditions must be present in order for pay to act as a strong motivator:[14]

- Trust levels between managers and subordinates must be high.
- Individual performance must be able to be accurately measured.
- Pay rewards to high performers must be substantially higher than those to poor performers.
- Few, if any, negative consequences for good performance must be perceived.

Under these conditions, a climate or culture is created in which employees have reason to believe that significant performance-reward contingencies truly exist. Given this perception (and assuming the reward is valued), we would expect performance to be increased.[15]

Pay Secrecy

Secrecy about pay rates seems to be a widely accepted practice in work organizations, particularly among managerial personnel. It is argued that salary is a personal matter and we should not invade another's privacy. Available evidence, however, suggests that pay secrecy may have several negative side effects. To begin, it has been consistently found that in the absence of actual knowledge, people have a tendency to *over*estimate the pay of coworkers and those above them in the hierarchy. As a result, much of the motivational potential of a differential reward system is lost.[16] Even if an employee receives a relatively sizable salary increase, she may still perceive an inequity compared to what others are receiving. This problem is highlighted in the results of a study by Lawler. In considering the effects of pay secrecy on motivation, Lawler noted:

Almost regardless of how well the individual manager was performing, he felt he was getting less than the average raise. This problem was particularly severe among high performers, since they believed that they were doing well yet received minimal reward. They did not believe that pay was in fact based upon merit. This was ironic, since their pay did reflect performance. . . . Thus, even though pay was tied to performance, these managers were not motivated because they could not see the connection.[17]

Pay secrecy also affects motivation via feedback. Several studies have shown the value of feedback in motivating performance (see previous discussion). The problem is that for managers, money represents one of the most meaningful forms of feedback. Pay secrecy eliminates the feedback.

When salary information is open (or at least when the range of percentage increases within a job classification are made known to the people in that group), employees are generally provided with more recognition for satisfactory performance and are often more motivated to perform on subsequent tasks. It is easier to establish feelings of pay equity and trust in the salary administration system. On the other hand, publicizing pay rates and pay raises can cause jealousy among employees and create pressures on managers to reduce perceived inequities in the system. There is no correct position concerning whether pay rates should be secret or open. The point is that managers should not assume a priori that pay secrecy—or pay openness—is a good thing. Instead, careful consideration should be given to the possible consequences of either approach in view of the particular situation in the organization at the time.

CONCEPT CHECK 

1. What is the best appraisal system for organizations to adopt?
2. How are rewards tied to performance appraisals?

8.5 Individual and Group Incentive Plans

5. How do managers and organizations use incentives and rewards effectively to secure the best possible performance from employees?

We now turn to an examination of various employee incentive programs used by organizations. First, we consider the relative merits of individuals versus group incentive programs. Next, we focus on several relatively new approaches to motivation and compensation. Finally, we suggest several guidelines for effective incentive systems.

Individual versus Group Incentives

Companies usually have choices among various compensation plans and must make decisions about which is most effective for its situation. Incentive systems in organizations are usually divided into two categories on the basis of whether the unit of analysis—and the recipient of the reward—is the individual or a group. Among individual incentive plans, several approaches can be identified, including merit-based compensation (commonly known as merit compensation), piece-rate incentive programs (where people are paid according to the quantity of output), bonus systems of various sorts, and commissions. In each case, rewards are tied fairly directly to the performance level of the individual.

Although individual incentive systems often lead to improved performance, some reservations have been noted. In particular, these programs may at times lead to employees competing with one another, with undesirable results. For instance, department store salespeople on commission may fight over customers, thereby chasing the customers away. After all, customers don't care who they deal with, only that the service is good. Second, these plans typically are resisted by unions, which prefer compensation to be based on seniority or job classification. Third, where quality control systems are lax, individual incentives such as piece rates may lead employees to maximize units of output while sacrificing quality. And, finally, in order for these programs to be successful, an atmosphere of trust and cooperation is necessary.

In order to overcome some of these shortcomings, many companies have turned to group or organizational incentive plans. Group incentive programs base at least some of an employee's rewards on group or organization performance. Hence, employees are encouraged to cooperate with one another and with the corporation so that all employees can benefit. Programs such as profit-sharing or gain-sharing plans (discussed below) are designed to tie the employees' future rewards and prosperity to that of the company and reduce the age-old antagonism between the two. The results are often dramatic.

Creative Pay Practices

Recently, we have seen several innovations in the way corporations approach reward systems. These efforts are designed to facilitate the integration of employee and company interests in a way that maximizes both productivity and quality of working life. Five such creative pay practices should be noted: (1) gain-sharing plans, (2) skills-based incentives, (3) lump-sum pay increases, (4) participative pay decisions, and (5) flexible benefits programs. These approaches, along with their major advantages and drawbacks, are summarized in **Table 8.7**.

Advantages and Disadvantages of New Pay Practices		
Pay Practice	Advantages	Disadvantages
Gain sharing	Ties pay to performance; encourages group cooperation	Plans that focus exclusively on productivity may lead employees to ignore other important objectives, such as quality.
Skills-based incentives	More flexible and skilled workforce; increased satisfaction	Higher training and salary costs
Lump-sum increase	Greater visibility of pay increases; increased pay satisfaction	Cost of administration
Participative pay decisions	Increased trust in a satisfaction with pay decisions; better pay decisions	Time-consuming
Flexible benefits	Increased satisfaction with pay and benefits	Cost of administration

Table 8.7 (Attribution: Copyright Rice University, OpenStax, under CC BY-NC-SA 4.0 license)

Gain-Sharing Plans. Giving executives and senior managers bonuses to reflect their contributions to organizational effectiveness is commonplace. In fact, in some companies executive bonuses are often larger than salaries. Recently, companies have increasingly applied this same principle to all employees in the form of **gain-sharing** (profit-sharing) plans. Here, employees are given a chance to share in corporate productivity gains through increased earnings. The greater the productivity gains, the greater the earnings. Several variations on this theme can be found, including the Scanlon Plan, IMPROSHARE, the Ruker Plan, and the Lincoln Electric Plan. Regardless of the title, the basic plan is similar.

For example, under the Scanlon Plan (probably the oldest such program), three operating guidelines are used: (1) each department or division is treated as a business unit for purposes of performance measurement, (2) specific cost measures associated with the production process are identified and agreed to by all parties, and (3) bonuses are paid to all employees according to a predetermined formula tying the amount of the bonus to the actual cost savings realized during the time period. Under such a plan, it is clearly in the employees' best interest to contribute to cost savings, thereby increasing their own incomes.

EXPANDING AROUND THE GLOBE

Providing Feedback in Different Countries

Global workplaces are increasing within the world businesses, and it has become a trend to have managers from one country, most likely the country in which the headquarters arise, manage employees abroad. An important consideration when managing globally is how cultural differences can have a profound effect on performance evaluations, negotiations, and criticisms.

For example, oftentimes in the United States, a method of critical feedback in the "hamburger method" (Step 1: Identify tasks. As a group, identify technical steps that would be involved in implementing. Step 2: Identify options for tasks. Split the team into several small groups. Step 3: Combine results.) is acceptable, while other countries give their feedback with just the meal alone. This strategy in the Netherlands and Germany can be off-putting to other cultures, and when you read into another culture's technique with your own lens of reference, it can feel wrong.

Managing globally means that you need to do your research on which approach for feedback is best received for the employee's cultural differences. For example, being direct is key when communicating with a Dutch person. In contrast, in England or the United States, criticism is not delivered directly, but with positive pieces wrapped around the negative. In Asian countries, feedback is often avoided or the message is blurred in order to "save face." With all of these complications and considerations, it is ever more important to acutely understand the culture, the cultural understandings of employees who are direct reports, and also the lens through which feedback is being viewed as well.

Questions:

1. How can a new manager that is working with international employees ensure she is providing reviews in an appropriate manner?
2. What methods can a manager employ in her preparation for the review to be successful when providing feedback to employees of different cultures?

Sources: C. Solbach. "Feedback through cultural looking glass." *Krauthammer*, September 16, 2015, https://www.krauthammer.com/en/publications/personal-development/2017/04/12/12/07/feedback-through-cultural-looking-glass; M. Abadi. "The exact same sentence from your boss can mean 'yes,' 'no,' or 'maybe' depending on the country where you work." *Business Insider*, December 7, 2017, https://www.businessinsider.com/direct-feedback-work-depends-on-culture-2017-12; J. Windust. "An International Approach to 360-Degree Feedback." *Cognology*, July 26, 2016, https://www.cognology.com.au/international-approach-360-degree-feedback/; "Giving Employee Feedback To A Culturally Diverse Workforce." *Impraise Blog*, accessed January 26, 2019, https://blog.impraise.com/360-feedback/how-to-handle-cultural-differences-between-branchescountries-in-feedback-behavior-performance-review.

Skills-Based Incentives. Typical compensation programs are tied to job evaluations. In these, jobs are analyzed to assess their characteristics, and then salary levels are assigned to each job on the basis of factors such as job difficulty and labor market scarcity. In other words, pay levels are set on the basis of the job, not the individual. This approach fails to encourage employees to improve their skills on the job, because there is no reward for the improvement. This thinking also keeps all employees in their places and minimizes the possibility of inter-job transfers.

Under the **skills-based incentive** program, employees are paid according to their skills level (that is, the *number* of jobs they can perform), regardless of the actual tasks they are allowed to perform. This approach has proved successful in organizations such as Procter & Gamble and General Foods. Employees are encouraged to learn additional skills and are appropriately rewarded. The organization is provided with a more highly trained and more flexible workforce. However, training and compensation costs are necessarily increased, so the program is appropriate only in some situations. The technique is most often seen as part of a larger quality-of-working-life program, where it is associated with job redesign efforts.

Lump-Sum Pay Increases. Another technique that has received some attention is to allow employees to decide how (that is, in what amounts) they wish to receive their pay raises for the coming year. Under the traditional program, pay raises are paid in equal amounts in each paycheck over the year. Under the alternate plan, employees can elect to receive equal amounts during the year, or they can choose to take the entire raise in one **lump-sum pay increase**. This plan allows employees greater discretion over their own financial matters. If an employee wants to use the entire pay raise for a vacation, it can be paid in a lump sum in June. Then, if the employee quits before the end of the year, the unearned part of the pay raise is subtracted from the final paycheck. This plan increases the visibility of the reward to the employee. The employee receives, for example, a $600 pay raise (a rather sizable amount) instead of twelve $50 monthly pay raises. As with the flexible rewards system discussed below, however, the administration costs of the lump-sum plan are greater than those of the traditional method.

Participative Pay Decisions. In addition, of concern to many managers is the extent to which employees should be involved in decisions over pay raises. This is the issue of **participative pay decisions**. Recently, several organizations have been experimenting with involving employees in pay raise decisions, and the results seem to be quite positive. By allowing employees to participate either in the design of the reward system or in actual pay raise decisions (perhaps through a committee), it is argued that decisions of higher quality are made on the basis of greater information. Also, employees then have greater reason to place confidence in the fairness of the decisions. On the negative side, this approach requires considerably more time for both the manager and the participating subordinates. Costs must be weighed against benefits to determine which approach is most suitable for the particular organization and its goals.

Flexible Benefits Systems. A typical fringe benefit package provides the same benefits—and the same number of benefits—to all employees. As a result, individual differences or preferences are largely ignored. Studies by Lawler indicate variations in benefit preferences.[18] For instance, young unmarried men prefer more vacation time, whereas young married men prefer to give up vacation time for higher pay. Older employees want more retirement benefits, whereas younger employees prefer greater income. Through a **flexible benefits program** (also called a "cafeteria benefits program"), employees are allowed some discretion in the determination of their own packages and can make trade-offs, within certain limits. Organizations such as PepsiCo, TRW, and the Educational Testing Service already use such programs. Although certain problems of administration exist with the programs, efforts in this direction can lead to increased need satisfaction among employees.

We have seen a number of different creative solutions to the compensation dilemma. Which approaches are most effective in motivating employees? This is obviously a difficult question to answer. However, one way to get relevant information on this question is to see what corporations actually use. One such study asked major employers which of a variety of approaches had been used with a high success level. The results are shown in Table 8.8. As can be seen, skills-based compensation, earned time off, and **gain sharing** all received high marks from personnel executives, although other programs are also widely supported. It would appear from these results that many approaches can be useful; the choice of which one to use would depend upon the circumstances and goals of a particular organization.

Guidelines for Effective Incentive Programs

Whatever incentive plan is selected, care must be taken to ensure that the plan is appropriate for the particular organization and workforce. In fact, a simple test of the effectiveness of an incentive plan would be as follows:[19]

- *Does the plan capture attention?* Do employees discuss the plan and take pride in their early successes?
- *Do employees understand the plan?* Can employees explain how the plan works, and do they understand what they must do to earn the incentive?
- *Does the plan improve communication?* As a result of the plan, do employees understand more about corporate mission, goals, and objectives?
- *Does the plan pay out when it should?* Are incentives being paid for desired results, and are they withheld for undesirable results?
- *Is the company performing better as a result of the plan?* Are profits or market share up or down? Have any gains resulted in part from the incentive plan?

Companies Successfully Using Creative Incentive Plans	
Type of Incentive	Percent of Companies Reporting Success
Skills-based compensation	89%
Earned time off	85
Gain-sharing plans	81
Small-group incentives	75
Individual incentives	73
All-salaried workforce	67
Lump-sum bonus	66
Source: Data adapted from J. Horn, *Psychology Today,* July 1987, pp. 54–57.	

Table 8.8 (Attribution: Copyright Rice University, OpenStax, under CC BY-NC-SA 4.0 license)

If a new (or existing) pay plan can meet these tests, it is probably fairly effective in motivating employee performance and should be retained by the organization. If not, perhaps some other approach should be tried. On the basis of such a test, several specific guidelines can be identified to increase the effectiveness of the programs. These include the following:[20]

- Any reward system or incentive plan should be as *closely tied to actual job performance* as possible. This point was discussed earlier in this chapter.
- If possible, incentive programs should *allow for individual differences*. They should recognize that different people want different outcomes from a job. Flexible benefits programs such as the ones discussed here make an effort to accomplish this.

- Incentive programs should *reflect the type of work that is done* and the structure of the organization. This simply means that the program should be tailored to the particular needs, goals, and structures of a given organization. Individual incentive programs, for example, would probably be less successful among unionized personnel than would group programs such as the Scanlon plan. This point has been clearly demonstrated in research by Lawler, which points out that organizations with traditional management and those with more participative management might approach reward systems quite differently in order to be effective.[21] As shown in **Table 8.9**, both types of company can be effective as long as their reward systems are congruent with their overall approach to management.
- The incentive program should *be consistent with the culture* and constraints of the organization. Where trust levels are low, for example, it may take considerable effort to get any program to work. In an industry already characterized by high levels of efficiency, basing an incentive system on increasing efficiency even further may have little effect, because employees may see the task as nearly impossible.
- Finally, incentive programs should *be carefully monitored over time* to ensure that they are being fairly administered and that they accurately reflect current technological and organizational conditions. For instance, it may be appropriate to offer sales clerks in a department store an incentive to sell outdated merchandise because current fashion items sell themselves. Responsibility falls on managers not to select the incentive program that is in vogue or used "next door," but rather to consider the unique situations and needs of their own organizations. Then, with this understanding, a program can be developed and implemented that will facilitate goal-oriented performance.

Matching Reward Systems to Management Style		
Reward System	Traditional	Participative
Fringe benefits	Vary according to organizational level	Cafeteria—same for all levels
Promotion	All decisions made by top management	Open posting for all jobs; peer group involvement in decision process
Status symbols	A great many, carefully allocated on the basis of job position	Few present, low emphasis on organization level
Pay type	Hourly and salary	All salary
Base rate	Based on job performed; high enough to attract job applicants	Based on skills; high enough to provide security and attract applicants
Incentive plan	Piece rate	Group and organization-wide bonus, lump-sum increase
Communication policy	Very restricted distribution of information	Individual rates, salary survey data, all other information made public
Decision-making locus	Top management	Close to location of person whose pay is being set
Source: Adapted from E. E. Lawler, *The Design of Effective Reward Systems,* Technical Report (Los Angeles:		

Table 8.9 (Attribution: Copyright Rice University, OpenStax, under CC BY-NC-SA 4.0 license)

Matching Reward Systems to Management Style		
Reward System	Traditional	Participative
University of Southern California, 1983), p. 52.		

Table 8.9 (Attribution: Copyright Rice University, OpenStax, under CC BY-NC-SA 4.0 license)

CONCEPT CHECK

1. What are the differences between individual and group incentives?
2. What is the variety of reward incentives available to organizations?

Key Terms

Assessment center Consists of a series of standardized evaluations of behavior based on multiple inputs.

Behavioral observation scale Identifies observable behaviors as they relate to performance and is less demanding of the evaluator.

Behaviorally anchored rating scale A system that requires considerable work prior to evaluation but, if the work is carefully done, can lead to highly accurate ratings with high inter-rater reliability.

Central tendency error The failure to recognize either very good or very poor performers.

Critical incident technique A technique where supervisors record incidents, or examples, of each subordinate's behavior that led to either unusual success or unusual failure on some aspect of the job.

Distributive justice Where employees receive (at least a portion of) their rewards as a function of their level of contribution to the organization.

Extrinsic rewards Rewards that are external to the work itself.

Flexible benefits system A rewards program where employees are allowed some discretion in the determination of their own packages and can make trade-offs, within certain limits.

Gain sharing An incentive plan in which employees or customers receive benefits directly as a result of cost-saving measures that they initiate or participate in.

Graphic rating scale A performance appraisal technique where the supervisor or rater is typically presented with a printed or online form that contains both the employee's name and several evaluation dimensions (quantity of work, quality of work, knowledge of job, attendance). The rater is then asked to rate the employee by assigning a number or rating on each of the dimensions.

Halo effect Results in a supervisor assigning the same rating to each factor being evaluated for an individual.

Intrinsic motivation The desire to do a task because you enjoy it.

Intrinsic rewards Rewards that are external to the work itself.

Leniency error Fails to distinguish adequately between good and bad performers and instead relegates almost everyone to the same or related categories.

Lump-sum pay increase A technique that allows employees to decide how (that is, in what amounts) they wish to receive their pay raises for the coming year.

Management by objectives Closely related to the goal-setting theory of motivation.

Participative pay decisions Involving employees in pay raise decisions.

Performance appraisals A system that provides a means of systematically evaluating employees across various performance dimensions to ensure that organizations are getting what they pay for.

Recency error Occurs when, in an evaluation, a supervisor may give undue emphasis to performance during the past months—or even weeks—and ignore performance levels prior to this.

Reliability The extent to which the instrument consistently yields the same results each time it is used.

Skills-based incentives Rewards employees on the basis of the skills they possess and not just the skills they are allowed to use at work.

Strictness error Fails to distinguish adequately between good and bad performers and instead relegates almost everyone to the same or related categories.

Validity The extent to which an instrument actually measures what it intends to measure.

Summary of Learning Outcomes

8.1 Performance Appraisal Systems

1. How do organizations effectively use performance appraisals to improve individual job performance, and what are the limitations inherent in the use of various appraisal systems?

If performance is to be changed or improved, it must be rewarded. To be rewarded, it must be measured. However, great care must be taken to (1) measure important behaviors and outcomes (individual, group, or organizational) and not just those that are easy to measure, (2) measure them with the appropriate technique(s), and (3) tie appropriate rewards to the desired behaviors and outcomes.

Organizations use performance appraisals for several reasons: (1) to provide feedback to employees, (2) to allow for employee self-development, (3) to allocate rewards, (4) to gather information for personnel decisions, and (5) to guide them in developing training and development efforts.

8.2 Techniques of Performance Appraisal

2. What practices are used in the performance appraisal process?

Performance appraisals are subject to several problems, including central tendency error, strictness or leniency error, halo effect, recency error, and personal biases.

8.3 Feedback

3. How do managers give effective feedback to subordinates?

Among the most common appraisal systems are graphic rating scales, critical incident technique, behaviorally anchored rating scales, behavioral observation scales, management by objectives, and assessment centers. Assessment centers represent a special case of evaluations in that they focus on assessing an employee's long-term potential to an organization.

8.4 Reward Systems in Organizations

4. How do organizations choose the best appraisal system for their organization?

Rewards serve several functions, including (1) stimulating job effort and performance, (2) reducing absenteeism and turnover, (3) enhancing employee commitment, (4) facilitating job satisfaction, and (5) facilitating occupational and organizational choice.

Rewards may be distributed on the basis of power, equality, need, or distributive justice. Distributive justice rests on the principle of allocating rewards in proportion to employee contribution. Intrinsic rewards represent those outcomes that are administered by the employee (e.g., a sense of task accomplishment), whereas extrinsic rewards are administered by others (e.g., wages).

Gain-sharing incentive plans base some of the employees' pay on corporate profits or productivity. As a result, employees are generally more interested in facilitating corporate performance. **Skills-based incentives** reward employees on the basis of the skills they possess, not the skills they are allowed to use at work. As a result, employees are encouraged to continually upgrade their skill levels.

A lump-sum salary increase simply provides employees with their pay raises at one time (possibly shortly before summer vacation or a major holiday).

Participative pay decisions allow employees some input in determining their pay raises.

8.5 Individual and Group Incentive Plans

5. How do managers and organizations use incentives and rewards effectively to secure the best possible performance from employees?

Flexible benefits allow employees to choose the fringe benefits that best suit their needs.

A good reward system (1) is closely tied to performance, (2) allows for individual differences, (3) reflects the type of work that is being done, (4) is consistent with the corporate culture, and (5) is carefully monitored over time.

Chapter Review Questions

1. Identify the various functions of performance appraisals. How are appraisals used in most work organizations?
2. What are some problems associated with performance appraisals?
3. Define *validity* and *reliability*. Why are these two concepts important from a managerial standpoint?
4. How can errors in appraisals be reduced?
5. Critically evaluate the advantages and disadvantages of the various techniques of performance appraisal.
6. Discuss the role of feedback in employee performance.
7. What is the difference between intrinsic and extrinsic rewards?
8. Identify the major bases of reward distribution.
9. How does money influence employee motivation?
10. Discuss the relative merits of individual and group incentive programs.
11. Describe the benefits and drawbacks of several of the new approaches to reward systems. Which ones do you feel would be most effective in work organizations?

Management Skills Application Exercises

How Would You Rate Your Supervisor?

Instructions: Think of your current supervisor or one for any job you have held, and evaluate her on the following dimensions. Give a "1" for very poor, a "3" for average, a "5" for outstanding, etc.

	Very Poor		**Average**	**Outstanding**	
1. Your boss's knowledge of the job	1	2	3	4	5
2. Your boss's leadership skills	1	2	3	4	5
3. Your boss's communication skills	1	2	3	4	5
4. Your boss's ability to motivate subordinates	1	2	3	4	5
5. Your boss's attendance and promptness	1	2	3	4	5
6. Your boss's commitment to the organization	1	2	3	4	5
7. Your boss's long-term potential for promotion	1	2	3	4	5
8. What is your overall assessment of your supervisor?	1	2	3	4	5

Think of a current or previous job, and evaluate the source and quality of the feedback you received from your supervisor. When you are through, refer to **Appendix B** for scoring procedures.

How Much Feedback Are You Getting from Your Job?

Instructions: Think of a current or previous job. With this in mind, answer the following questions as accurately as possible.

1. My boss lets me know when I make a mistake.

Strongly Disagree				Strongly Agree		
1	2	3	4	5	6	7

2. My coworkers help me improve on the job.

Strongly Disagree				Strongly Agree		
1	2	3	4	5	6	7

3. I receive formal evaluations from the company on my job.

Strongly Disagree				Strongly Agree		
1	2	3	4	5	6	7

4. My boss always tells me when I do a good job.

Strongly Disagree				Strongly Agree		
1	2	3	4	5	6	7

5. This company really appreciates good performance.

Strongly Disagree				Strongly Agree		
1	2	3	4	5	6	7

6. When I do something especially well, I receive a “thanks” from my boss.

Strongly Disagree				Strongly Agree		
1	2	3	4	5	6	7

7. My coworkers are very appreciative when I do a good job.

Strongly Disagree				Strongly Agree		
1	2	3	4	5	6	7

8. My coworkers compliment me on the quality of my work.

Strongly Disagree				Strongly Agree		
1	2	3	4	5	6	7

9. My coworkers are very supportive of my efforts.

Strongly Disagree				Strongly Agree		
1	2	3	4	5	6	7

10. I know when I have done a good job.

Strongly Disagree				Strongly Agree		
1	2	3	4	5	6	7

11. My job provides me with solid feedback on my performance.

Strongly Disagree				Strongly Agree		
1	2	3	4	5	6	7

12. I can see the results when I learn to do something better.

Strongly Disagree				Strongly Agree		
1	2	3	4	5	6	7

Managerial Decision Exercises

1. You are the general manager of a floral supplies distributor that provides independent florists with things that they need for their business, such as vases, ribbons, and balloons. You have read that many organizations use incentive pay plans that reward employees when the organization does well. You have 6 drivers, 12 warehouse workers, 3 inside salespeople, and an assistant that reports to you. What types of incentive plan would you propose for an organization like yours?
2. You are the HR manager at a midsized auto parts manufacturer. What are the pros and cons of establishing a 360-degree performance appraisal system in your organizations? Write a memo to the CEO outlining what you think should be done.

Critical Thinking Case

HubSpot Focus on Flexible Benefits

What would your manager say to you if you came up with the idea of traveling with Justin Timberlake on tour for an entire year? This would not just be a work from home agreement but an actual out of office plan for one full-year sabbatical. That is exactly what happened at HubSpot when Rosalia Cefalu had a crazy idea that actually got approved.

HubSpot, a global inbound marketing company, has approximately 19,000 customers in over 90 countries and 1,960 employees, stretching from Cambridge, MA, to Sydney, Australia.

"We don't think that culture is about free beer and ping-pong and dogs in the office, it's about what you believe, why you do what you do, and who you choose to work with," states CTO and cofounder Dharmesh Shah. Although HubSpot has plenty of free snacks on hand for their employees to enjoy, other flexible benefits HubSpotters enjoy are unlimited vacation time, tuition reimbursement, flexible hours, and an overall environment that balances freedom with accountability.

At HubSpot it goes deeper than just the perks. The focus from the top down instills pride and passion within its employees, which then translates into happy customers.

Although flexible benefits are a big perk of working at the third-best tech company to work for, according to Glassdoor's annual Employee Choice awards, the culture isn't for everyone. The company practices a sense of understanding, knowing that employees will move on and do not need to stay to be loyal and that sometimes someone is no longer needed—either because of performance, or changes in the company's needs. This isn't taken personally, and HubSpot is able to grow and continue to grow because it objectively sees the performance of its employees and what is best for the company and employee.

Questions:

1. How does HubSpot's focus on culture affect employee performance?

2. What concerns would you have regarding giving employees countless flexible benefits such as HubSpot does; for example, a yearly sabbatical?

Sources: S. Leibowitz. "What it's like to work at HubSpot, one of the best workplaces of 2018." *Business Insider*, January 21, 2018, https://www.businessinsider.com/hubspot-best-workplaces-united-states-2018-1; K. M. Newman. "Inside the Company Culture of Hubspot." *Tech.co*, April 5, 2013, https://tech.co/company-culture-of-hubspot-2013-04; InHerSight. "Company Profile: Hubspot." *The Motley Fool*, October 5, 2016, https://www.fool.com/investing/2016/10/05/company-spotlight-hubspot.aspx.

9 Group and Intergroup Relations

Exhibit 9.1 (Credit: Neil McIntosh/ flickr/ Attribution 2.0 Generic (CC BY 2.0))

Introduction

Learning Outcomes

After reading this chapter, you should be able to answer these questions:

1. How do you manage group and intergroup processes effectively?
2. How do group norms, roles, and status systems affect employee behavior and performance?
3. How do managers develop group cohesiveness, which facilitates organizational goal attainment?
4. What are barriers to intergroup cooperation, and how do you take action to minimize such impediments and understand how to get the most out of the collective actions of groups in organizations in order to enhance industrial competitiveness?

EXPLORING MANAGERIAL CAREERS

EA Engineering, Science, and Technology, Inc.

In the modern workplace, it is more common that an employee is not assigned to just one team in their role. More currently, individuals are being tasked with multiple roles that allow them to work within many teams on many projects. Research done estimates that 81 to 95 percent of employees around the world serve on multiple teams simultaneously. In some cases, this alone can have a negative effect on the way that employees are able to focus on the impact on their stress levels. Leadership plays a big role in combating the negative effects of multiple team memberships, or MTM.

EA Engineering, Science, and Technology, Inc. employees the MTM structure on a daily basis, with its employees working on up to six different projects concurrently. The environmental consulting company based in Baltimore, MD, has to collaborate often and work in a team-based environment to balance stakeholder management and profits.

Juggling six different projects at one given time can be stressful to any employee, but structuring the work within different teams gives employees a sense of autonomy so that they know specifically what piece of the project to focus on and contribute their skills to the overall group. Leaders naturally form within groups and take ownership of different tasks, which also is very helpful to both the overall success of the team and individual satisfaction of the employee. Research done with this group and others has shown that when leaders showcase empowering qualities to their employees, subsequently the employees are more proactive. Despite the fact that these individuals worked on many teams under a variety of leaders, the individuals often carried over the empowerment qualities of one leader to their other team even when the other leader was less empowering.

Being a part of many teams can help employees with job satisfaction and give them exposure to many leadership types within your organization. It is important to understand the basic dynamics such as those showcased within EA Engineering, Science, and Technology, Inc. to best approach tasks and, in this case, multiple team memberships is a highly positive strategy to help bring the best outcome to its business.

Based on our earlier analysis of individual behavior, we are now in a position to consider what happens when individuals are placed in work units to perform their tasks. We do this in the next four chapters. The nature of groups and intergroup relations is discussed in this chapter. The topics of job design and organization design as well as effectiveness and productivity may be discussed later in this course. Taken together, these topics provide a solid understanding of organizational *structure*—that is, how people and work units are put together for purposes of task accomplishment.

9.1 Work Groups: Basic Considerations

1. How do you manage group and intergroup processes effectively?

Available research on group dynamics demonstrates rather conclusively that individual behavior is highly influenced by coworkers in a work group. For instance, we see many examples of individuals who, when working in groups, intentionally set limits on their own incomes so they earn no more than the other group members. We see other situations where individuals choose to remain in an undesirable job because of their friends in the plant, even though preferable jobs are available elsewhere. In summarizing much research on the topic, Hackman and Morris concluded the following:

There is substantial agreement among researchers and observers of small task groups that something important happens in group interaction which can affect performance outcomes. There is little agreement about just what that "something" is—whether it is more likely to enhance or depress group effectiveness, and how it can be monitored, analyzed, and altered.[1]

In order to gain a clearer understanding of this "something," we must first consider in detail what we mean by a **group**, how groups are formed, and how various groups differ.

What Is a Group?

The literature of group dynamics is a very rich field of study and includes many definitions of work groups. For example, we might conceive of a group in terms of *perceptions*; that is, if individuals see themselves as a group, then a group exists. Or, we can view a group in *structural* terms. For instance, McDavid and Harari define a group as "an organized system of two or more individuals who are interrelated so that the system performs some function, has a standard set of role relationships among its members, and has a set of **norms** that regulate the function of the group and each of its members."[2] Groups can also be defined in *motivational* terms as "a collection of individuals whose existence as a collection is rewarding to the individuals."[3] Finally, a group can be viewed with regard to *interpersonal interactions*—the degree to which members communicate and interact with one another over time.[4]

By integrating these various approaches to defining groups, we may conclude for our purpose here that a *group* is a collection of individuals who share a common set of norms, generally have differentiated roles among themselves, and interact with one another toward the joint pursuit of common goals. (The definitions of roles and norms is provided later in this chapter.) This definition assumes a dynamic perspective and leads us to focus on two major aspects of groups: group structure and group processes. Group structure is the topic of this chapter, and group processes will be discussed in later chapters.

Types of Groups

There are two primary types of groups: formal and informal. Moreover, within these two types, groups can be further differentiated on the basis of their relative degree of permanence. The resulting four types are shown in **Table 9.1**.

Types of Groups		
	Relatively Permanent	Relatively Temporary
Formal	Command group	Task group
Informal	Friendship group	Interest group

Table 9.1 (Attribution: Copyright Rice University, OpenStax, under CC BY-NC-SA 4.0 license)

Formal Groups. Formal groups are work units that are prescribed by the organization. Examples of formal groups include sections of departments (such as the accounts receivable section of the accounting department), committees, or special project task forces. These groups are set up by management on either a temporary or permanent basis to accomplish prescribed tasks. When the group is permanent, it is usually called a **command group** or *functional group*. An example would be the sales department in a company. When the group is less permanent, it is usually referred to as a **task group**. An example here would be a corporate-sponsored task force on improving affirmative action efforts. In both cases, the groups are formal in that they are both officially established by the company to carry out some aspect of the business.

Informal Groups. In addition to formal groups, all organizations have a myriad of **informal groups**. These groups evolve naturally out of individual and collective self-interest among the members of an organization and are not the result of deliberate organizational design. People join informal groups because of common interests, social needs, or simply friendship. Informal groups typically develop their own norms and roles and establish unwritten rules for their members. Studies in social psychology have clearly documented the important role of these informal groups in facilitating (or inhibiting) performance and organizational effectiveness. Again, on the basis of their relative degree of permanence, informal groups can be divided into **friendship groups** (people you like to be around) and **interest groups** (e.g., a network of working women or minority managers). Friendship groups tend to be long-lasting, whereas interest groups often dissolve as people's interests change.

One of the more interesting aspects of group processes in organizations is the interaction between informal and formal groups. Both groups establish norms and roles and goals and objectives, and both demand loyalty from their members. When an individual is a member of many groups—both formal and informal—a wide array of potentially conflicting situations emerges that has an impact upon behavior in organizations. We will focus on this interplay throughout the next few chapters.

Reasons for Joining Groups

People join groups for many reasons. Often, joining a group serves several purposes at once. In general, at least six reasons can be identified for joining groups:

1. *Security.* Most people have a basic need for protection from external threats, real or imagined. These threats include the possibility of being fired or intimidated by the boss, the possibility of being embarrassed in a new situation, or simply the anxiety of being alone. Groups can be a primary source of *security* against such threats. We have often heard that there is "safety in numbers."
2. *Social Needs*. In addition, as discussed in previous chapters, basic theories of personality and motivation emphasize that most individuals have relatively strong *social needs*. They need to interact with other people and develop meaningful relationships. People are clearly social creatures. Groups provide structured environments in which individuals can pursue friendships.
3. *Self-Esteem*. Similarly, membership in groups can assist individuals in developing self-esteem. People often take pride in being associated with prestigious groups; note such examples as professors elected to membership in the National Academy of Sciences or salespeople who qualify for a million dollar club as a reward for sales performance.
4. *Economic Self-Interest*. People often associate with groups to pursue their own *economic self-interest*. Labor unions are a prime example of this phenomenon, as are various professional and accrediting agencies, such as the American Bar Association. These organizations often attempt to limit the supply of tradespeople or professionals in order to maintain employment and salaries.
5. *Mutual Interest*. Some groups are formed to pursue goals that are of *mutual interest* to group members. Included here are bridge clubs, company-sponsored baseball teams, and literary clubs. By joining together, individuals can pursue group goals that are typically not feasible alone.
6. *Physical Proximity*. Finally, many groups form simply because people are located in close *physical proximity* to one another. In fact, office architecture and layout can have considerable influence over the development of social networks and groups. Consider, for example, two floors in the same building. On the first floor, all the managers have private offices arranged in a long row, with their assistants arranged in a similar row in front of them. This horizontal pattern of offices does not allow for frequent interaction between either the managers or the secretaries, and as a result group formation may be slowed. On the second floor, however, suppose all the managers' offices are arranged in a cluster surrounding a similar cluster of assistants. The result would be more frequent social interaction among employees. This is not to say that one arrangement is superior to the other; rather, it is simply to point out how variations in office arrangements can have an impact on group formation.

Stages in Group Development

Before we begin a comprehensive examination of the structure of groups, consider briefly the stages of group development. How do groups grow and develop over time? Tuckman has proposed one model of group development that consists of four stages through which groups generally proceed.[5] These four stages are referred to by the deceptively simple titles *forming, storming, norming,* and *performing* (see **Exhibit 9.2**).

1. *Forming*. In the first stage of development, when group members first come together, emphasis is usually placed on making acquaintances, sharing information, testing one another, and so forth. This stage is referred to as forming. Group members attempt to discover which interpersonal behaviors are acceptable or unacceptable in the group. In this process of sensing out the environment, a new member is heavily dependent upon others for providing cues to acceptable behavior.
2. *Storming*. In the second stage of group development, a high degree of intergroup conflict (storming) can usually be expected as group members attempt to develop a place for themselves and to influence the development of group norms and roles. Issues are discussed more openly, and efforts are made to clarify group goals.
3. *Norming*. Over time, the group begins to develop a sense of oneness. Here, group norms emerge (norming) to guide individual behavior. Group members come to accept fellow members and develop a unity of purpose that binds them.
4. *Performing*. Once group members agree on basic purposes, they set about developing separate roles for the various members. In this final stage, role differentiation emerges to take advantage of task specialization in order to facilitate goal attainment. The group focuses its attention on the task (performing). As we consider this simple model, it should be emphasized that Tuckman does not claim that all groups proceed through this sequence of stages. Rather, this model provides a generalized conceptual scheme to help us understand the processes by which groups form and develop over time.

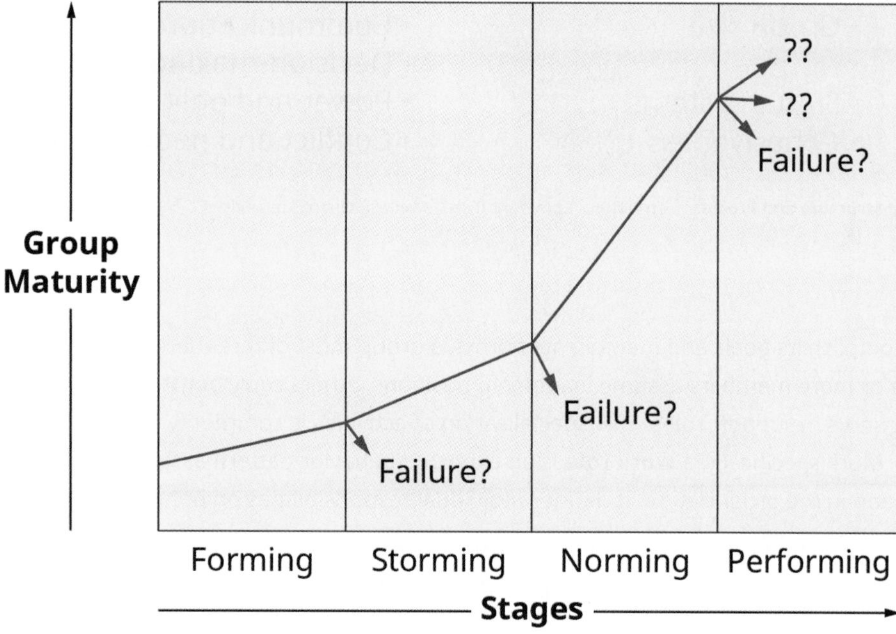

Exhibit 9.2 Stages in Group Development (Attribution: Copyright Rice University, OpenStax, under CC BY-NC-SA 4.0 license)

CONCEPT CHECK 

1. What are the reasons for joining a group?
2. What are the development stages groups often go through?
3. At the storming stage, what differences might you expect between groups formed for economic self-interest and groups formed for mutual self-interest?

9.2 Work Group Structure

2. How do group norms, roles, and status systems affect employee behavior and performance?

Work group structure can be characterized in many different ways. We examine several characteristics that are useful in describing and understanding what makes one group different from another. This matrix of variables will, when taken together, paint a portrait of work groups in terms of relatively enduring group properties. The aspects of group structure to be considered are (1) work roles, (2) work group size, (3) work group norms, (4) status relationships, and (5) work group cohesiveness. Each of these factors has been shown to influence group processes, as shown in **Exhibit 9.3**. Thus, the material presented here will be important when we focus on group processes later in the text.

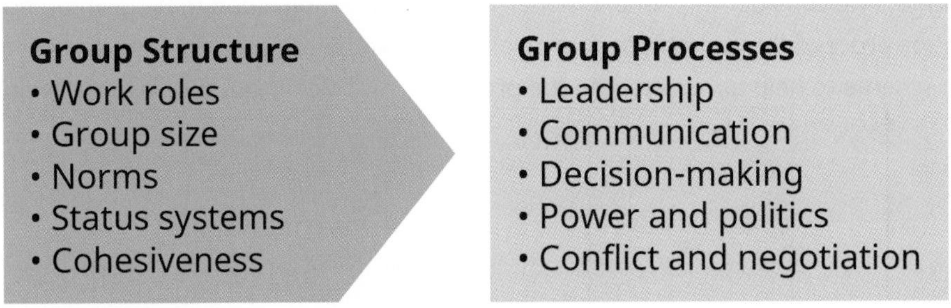

Exhibit 9.3 Group Structure and Process (Attribution: Copyright Rice University, OpenStax, under CC BY-NC-SA 4.0 license)

Work Roles

In order to accomplish its goals and maintain its norms, a group must differentiate the work activities of its members. One or more members assume leadership positions, others carry out the major work of the group, and still others serve in support roles. This specialization of activities is commonly referred to as role differentiation. More specifically, a **work role** is an expected behavior pattern assigned or attributed to a particular position in the organization. It defines individual responsibilities on behalf of the group.

It has been suggested that within organizational settings, work roles can be divided into three types on the basis of the nature of the activities that encompass the role.[6] These are:

1. *Task-oriented roles*. These roles focus on task-related activities aimed at achieving group performance goals.
2. *Relations-oriented roles*. These roles emphasize the further development of the group, including building group cohesiveness and consensus, preserving group harmony, looking after group member welfare, and so forth.
3. *Self-oriented roles*. These roles emphasize the specific needs and goals of individual members, often at the

expense of the group.

As we might expect, individual group members often perform several of these roles simultaneously. A group leader, for example, must focus group attention on task performance while at the same time preserving group harmony and cohesiveness. To see how this works, consider your own experience. You may be able to recognize the roles you have played in groups you have been a member of. In your experience, have you played multiple roles or single roles?

Perhaps the best way to understand the nature of work roles is to examine a **role episode**. A role episode is an attempt to explain how a particular role is learned and acted upon. As can be seen in **Exhibit 9.4**, a role episode begins with members' expectations about what one person should be doing in a particular position (Stage 1). These expectations are then communicated to the individual (Stage 2), causing the individual to perceive the expectations about the expected role (Stage 3). Finally, the individual decides to act upon the role in terms of actual role-related behavior (Stage 4). In other words, Stages 1 and 2 deal with the *expected* role, whereas Stage 3 focuses on the *perceived* role and Stage 4 focuses on the *enacted* role.

Consider the following simple example. A group may determine that its newest member is responsible for getting coffee for group members during breaks (Stage 1). This role is then explained to the incoming member (Stage 2), who becomes aware of his or her expected role (Stage 3). On the basis of these perceptions (and probably reinforced by group norms), the individual then would probably carry out the assigned behavior (Stage 4).

Several aspects of this model of a role episode should be noted. First, Stages 1 and 2 are initiated by the group and directed at the individual. Stages 3 and 4, on the other hand, represent thoughts and actions of the individual receiving the stimuli. In addition, Stages 1 and 3 represent cognitive and perceptual evaluations, whereas Stages 2 and 4 represent actual behaviors. The sum total of all the roles assigned to one individual is called the **role set**.

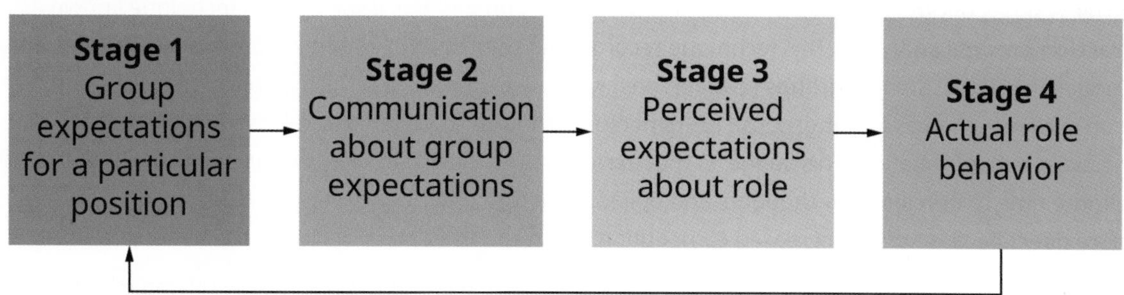

Exhibit 9.4 A Simplified Model of a Role Episode Source: Adapted from D. G. Myers and J. M. Twenge, *Social Psychology* 13th edition, (New York: McGraw Hill), 2018. (Attribution: Copyright Rice University, OpenStax, under CC BY-NC-SA 4.0 license)

Although the role episode presented here seems straightforward, in reality we know that it is far more complicated. For instance, individuals typically receive multiple and sometimes conflicting messages from various groups, all attempting to assign them a particular role. This can easily lead to **role conflict**. Messages sent to an individual may sometimes be unclear, leading to **role ambiguity**. Finally, individuals may simply receive too many role-related messages, contributing to **role overload**. Discussion of these topics is reserved for later study, where examination of several important aspects of psychological adjustment to work.

Work Group Size

Obviously, work groups can be found in various sizes. Early management theorists spent considerable time and effort to no avail attempting to identify the right size for the various types of work groups. There is simply no right number of people for most group activities. They did, however, discover a great deal about what happens as group size increases.[7] A number of relevant size-outcome relationships are summarized in **Table 9.2**.

Effects of Group Size on Group Dynamics		
Factor	Size of Group	
	Small	Large
Group interaction	Increased	Decreased
Group cohesiveness	Higher	Lower
Job satisfaction	Higher	Lower
Absenteeism	Lower	Higher
Turnover	Lower	Higher
Social loafing	Lower	Higher
Productivity	No clear relation	No clear relation

Table 9.2

Group Interaction Patterns. First, we will consider the effects of variations in group size on group interaction patterns. A series of classic studies by Bales and Borgatta examined this issue using a technique known as **interaction process analysis.**[8] This technique records who says what to whom; through using it, Bales and his colleagues found that smaller groups (2–4 persons) typically exhibited greater tension, agreement, and opinion seeking, whereas larger groups (13–16 persons) showed more tension release and giving of suggestions and information. This suggests that harmony is crucial in smaller groups and that people in them have more time to develop their thoughts and opinions. On the other hand, individuals in larger groups must be more direct because of the increased competition for attention.

Job Attitudes. Increases in work group size are fairly consistently found to be inversely related to satisfaction, although the relationship is not overly strong.[9] That is, people working in smaller work units or departments report higher levels of satisfaction than those in larger units. This finding is not surprising in view of the greater attention one receives in smaller groups and the greater importance group members typically experience in such things as their role set.

Absenteeism and Turnover. Available research indicates that increases in work group size and absenteeism are moderately related among blue-collar workers, although no such relationship exists for white-collar workers.[10] One explanation for these findings is that increased work group size leads to lower group cohesiveness, higher task specialization, and poorer communication. As a result, it becomes more difficult to satisfy higher-order needs on the job, and job attendance becomes less appealing. This explanation may be more relevant in the case of blue-collar workers, who typically have little job autonomy and control. White-collar workers typically have more avenues available to them for need satisfaction. Similar findings exist for employee turnover. Turnover rates are higher in larger groups.[11] It again can be hypothesized that because larger groups make need satisfaction more difficult, there is less reason for individuals to remain with the organization.

Productivity. No clear relationship has been found between group size and productivity.[12] There is probably a good reason for this. Unless we take into consideration the type of task that is being performed, we really cannot expect a clear or direct relationship. Mitchell explains it as follows:

Think of a task where each new member adds a new independent amount of productivity (certain piece-rate jobs might fit here). If we add more people, we will add more productivity. . . . On the other hand, there are tasks where everyone works together and pools their resources. With each new person the added increment of new skills or knowledge decreases. After a while increases in size will fail to add much to the group except coordination and motivation problems. Large groups will perform less well than small groups. The relationship between group size and productivity will therefore depend on the type of task that needs to be done.[13]

However, when we look at productivity and group size, it is important to recognize the existence of a unique factor called **social loafing**,[14] a tendency for individual group members to reduce their effort on a group task. This phenomenon occurs when (1) people see their task as being unimportant or simple, (2) group members think their individual output is not identifiable, and (3) group members expect their fellow workers to loaf. Social loafing is more prevalent in larger groups than in smaller groups, presumably because the above three factors are accentuated. From a managerial standpoint, this problem can be reduced by providing workers with greater responsibility for task accomplishment and more challenging assignments. This issue is addressed in the following chapter on job design.

Work Group Norms

The concept of work group norms represents a complex topic with a history of social psychological research dating back several decades. In this section, we will highlight several of the essential aspects of norms and how they relate to people at work. We will consider the characteristics and functions of work group norms as well as conformity with and deviance from them.

Characteristics of Work Group Norms. A *work group norm* may be defined as a standard that is shared by group members and regulates member behavior within an organization. An example can be seen in a typical classroom situation when students develop a norm against speaking up in class too often. It is believed that students who are highly visible improve their grades at the expense of others. Hence, a norm is created that attempts to govern acceptable classroom behavior. We see similar examples in the workplace. There may be a norm against producing too much or too little, against getting too close to the supervisor, against being late for work, and so forth.

Work group norms may be characterized by at least five factors:[15]

1. Norms summarize and simplify group influence processes. They denote the processes by which groups regulate and regularize member behavior.
2. Norms apply only to behavior, not to private thoughts and feelings. Although norms may be based on thoughts and feelings, they cannot govern them. That is, private acceptance of group norms is unnecessary—only public compliance is needed.
3. Norms are generally developed only for behaviors that are viewed as important by most group members.
4. Norms usually develop gradually, but the process can be quickened if members wish. Norms usually are developed by group members as the need arises, such as when a situation occurs that requires new ground rules for members in order to protect group integrity.
5. All norms do not apply to all members. Some norms, for example, apply only to young initiates (such as getting the coffee), whereas others are based on seniority, sex, race, or economic class.

Functions of Work Group Norms. Most all groups have norms, although some may be more extensive than others. To see this, examine the norms that exist in the various groups to which you belong. Which groups have more fully developed norms? Why? What functions do these norms serve? Several efforts have been made to answer this question. In general, work group norms serve four functions in organizational settings:[16]

1. *Norms facilitate group survival*. When a group is under threat, norms provide a basis for ensuring goal-directed behavior and rejecting deviant behavior that is not purposeful to the group. This is essentially a "circle the wagons" phenomenon.
2. *Norms simplify expected behaviors.* Norms tell group members what is expected of them—what is acceptable and unacceptable—and allow members to anticipate the behaviors of their fellow group members and to anticipate the positive or negative consequences of their own behavior.
3. *Norms help avoid embarrassing situations*. By identifying acceptable and unacceptable behaviors, norms tell group members when a behavior or topic is damaging to another member. For example, a norm against swearing signals group members that such action would be hurtful to someone in the group and should be avoided.
4. *Norms help identify the group and express its central values to others.* Norms concerning clothes, language, mannerisms, and so forth help tell others who belongs to the group and, in some cases, what the group stands for. Norms often serve as rallying points for group members.

Conformity and Deviance. Managers often wonder why employees comply with the norms and dictates of their work group even when they seemingly work against their best interests. This concern is particularly strong when workers intentionally withhold productivity that could lead to higher incomes. The answer to this question lies in the concept of conformity to group norms. Situations arise when the individual is swept along by the group and acts in ways that he would prefer not to.

To see how this works, consider the results of a classic study of individual conformity to group pressures that was carried out by Solomon Asch.[17] Asch conducted a laboratory experiment in which a native subject was placed in a room with several confederates. Each person in the room was asked to match the length of a given line (*X*) with that of one of three unequal lines (*A, B,* and *C*). This is shown in **Exhibit 9.5**. Confederates, who spoke first, were all instructed prior to the experiment to identify line *C* as the line most like *X,* even though *A* was clearly the answer. The results were startling. In over one-third of the trials in the experiment, the naive subject denied the evidence of his own senses and agreed with the answers given by the unknown confederates. In other words, when confronted by a unanimous answer from others in the group, a large percentage of individuals chose to go along with the group rather than express a conflicting opinion, even though these individuals were confident their own answers were correct.

What causes such conformity to group norms? And, under what conditions will an individual deviate from these norms? Conformity to group norms is believed to be caused by at least three factors.[18] First, personality plays a major role. For instance, negative correlations have been found between conformity and intelligence, tolerance, and ego strength, whereas authoritarianism was found to be positively related. Essentially, people who have a strong self-identity are more likely to stick to their own norms and deviate from those of the group when a conflict between the two exists. Second, the initial stimulus that evokes responses can influence conformity. The more ambiguous the stimulus (e.g., a new and confusing order from top management), the greater the propensity to conform to group norms ("I'm not sure what the new order from management really means, so I'll just go along with what others think it means"). In this sense, conformity provides a sense of protection and security in a new and perhaps threatening situation. Finally, group characteristics themselves can influence conformity to group norms. Factors such as the extent of pressure exerted on group members to conform, the extent to which a member identifies with the group, and the extent to which the group has been successful in achieving previous goals can influence conformity.

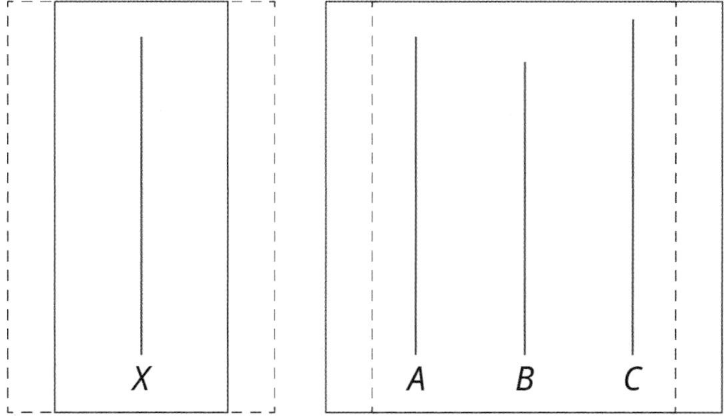

Exhibit 9.5 Asch's Experiment in Group Pressure and Individual Judgment (Attribution: Copyright Rice University, OpenStax, under CC BY-NC-SA 4.0 license)

What happens when someone deviates from group norms? Research indicates that groups often respond by increasing the amount of communication directed toward the deviant member.[19] This communication is aimed at bringing the deviant into the acceptable bounds set by the group. A good example of this process can be seen in Janis's classic study of the group processes leading up to the abortive Bay of Pigs invasion in Cuba.[20] At one meeting, Arthur Schlesinger, an adviser to President Kennedy, expressed opposition to the plan even though no one else expressed similar doubts. After listening to his opposition for a while, Robert Kennedy took Schlesinger aside and said, "You may be right or you may be wrong, but the President has his mind made up. Don't push it any further. Now is the time for everyone to help him all they can." Janis elaborated on this group decision-making process and termed it "groupthink."

When a deviant member refuses to heed the message and persists in breaking group norms, group members often respond by rejecting or isolating the deviant. They tell the deviant, in essence, that they will no longer tolerate such behavior and prefer to reconstitute the group. If the deviant is not expelled, the group must continually confront behavior that conflicts with what it holds to be true. Rather than question or reexamine its beliefs, the group finds it simpler—and safer—to rid itself of dangerous influences.

Status Systems

A fourth characteristic, or structural property, of work groups is the status system. **Status systems** serve to differentiate individuals on the basis of some criterion or set of criteria. There are five general bases on which status differentiations are made: birth, personal characteristics, achievement, possessions, and formal authority. All five bases can be seen as establishing status in work groups. For example, an employee may achieve high status because he is the boss's son (birth), the brightest or strongest member of the group (personal characteristics), the best performer (achievement), the richest or highest paid (possessions), or the foreman or supervisor (formal authority).

Reasons for Status Systems. Status systems can be seen throughout most organizations. We differentiate between blue-collar and white-collar employees (and even pink and gold collar), skilled tradespersons and unskilled workers, senior and junior managers, high achievers and low achievers, and popular and unpopular employees. Why do we do this? In essence, status differentiation in organizations (and their related status symbols) serves four purposes:[21]

Motivation. We ascribe status to persons as rewards or incentives for performance and achievement. If high achievement is recognized as positive behavior by an organization, individuals are more willing to exert effort.

Identification. Status and status symbols provide useful cues to acceptable behavior in new situations. In the military, for example, badges of rank quickly tell members who has authority and who is to be obeyed. Similarly, in business, titles serve the same purpose.

Dignification. People are often ascribed status as a means of signifying respect that is due them. A clergyman's attire, for instance, identifies a representative of the church.

Stabilization. Finally, status systems and symbols facilitate stabilization in an otherwise turbulent environment by providing a force for continuity. Authority patterns, role relationships, and interpersonal interactions are all affected and, indeed, defined by the status system in effect. As a result, much ambiguity in the work situation is reduced.

Status can be conferred on an individual in many different ways. One way common in organizations is through the assignment and decoration of offices. John Dean, counsel to former President Nixon, provides the following account concerning status in the White House:

Everyone [on the White House Staff] jockeyed for a position close to the President's ear, and even an unseasoned observer could sense minute changes in status. Success and failure could be seen in the size, decor, and location of offices. Anyone who moved into a smaller office was on the way down. If a carpenter, cabinetmaker, or wallpaper hanger was busy in someone's office, this was the sure sign he was on the rise. Every day, workmen crawled over the White House complex like ants. Movers busied themselves with the continuous shuffling of furniture from one office to another as people moved in, up, down, or out. We learned to read office changes as an index of the internal bureaucratic power struggles. The expense was irrelevant to Haldeman. . . . He once retorted when we discussed whether we should reveal such expense, "This place is a national monument, and I can't help it if the last three Presidents let it go to hell." Actually, the costs had less to do with the fitness of the White House than with the need of its occupants to see tangible evidence of their prestige.[22]

Modern businesses looking to attract top talent do not have office spaces that have a group of workers siloed in their own walled-off offices with doors 20 years old.[23]

One Orlando business, for instance, spent about $330,000 on the design and build-out of its space.

Status Incongruence. An interesting aspect of status systems in organizations is the notion of **status incongruence**. This situation exists when a person is high on certain valued dimensions but low on others, or when a person's characteristics seem inappropriate for a particular job. Examples of status incongruence include the college student who takes a janitorial job during the summer (usually referred to as the "college kid" by the other janitors), the president's son who works his way up through the organizational hierarchy (at an accelerated rate, needless to say), or the young fast-track manager who is promoted to a level typically held by older employees.

Status incongruence presents problems for everyone involved. The individual may become the target of hostility and jealousy from coworkers who feel the individual has risen above his station. The coworkers, on the other hand, may be forced to acknowledge their own lack of success or achievement. One might ask, for example, "Why has this youngster been promoted over me when I have more seniority?" At least two remedies for this conflict are available to managers. An organization can (1) select or promote only those individuals whose characteristics are congruent with the job and work group, and (2) attempt to change the values of the group. Neither of these possibilities seems realistic or fair. Hence, dynamic organizations that truly reward high achievement (instead of seniority) must accept some level of conflict resulting from status incongruence.

EXPANDING AROUND THE GLOBE

Status Systems in Japanese Business

In Japan, etiquette is not simply a prescription for appropriate social responses, it is a complete guide to conducting oneself in all social interactions. At the root of this system of social interaction is one's status within the organization and society.

The effects of status in Japan can be seen in many ways. For example, when two businesspeople meet for the first time, they exchange business cards—before they even say hello to each other. After carefully reading the cards, each knows precisely the other's rank (and status) in the organizational hierarchy and, thus, how to respond. The person with the lower status must bow lower than the person with the higher status.

Moreover, when four managers get into a car, status determines where each will sit. This is shown in **Exhibit 9.6**, where it can be seen that the most important (highest-status) manager will sit in the back seat, directly behind the driver. Similarly, when four managers enter an elevator, the least senior stands in front of the elevator controls, with the most senior behind. In a meeting room or in a restaurant, the most honored seat is farthest from the door, whereas the least honored is nearest the door. Even within the meeting room itself, a sofa is considered higher in rank than armchairs.

Automobile

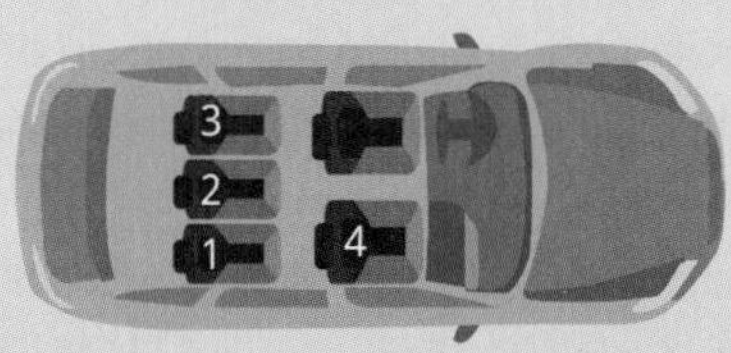

Elevator

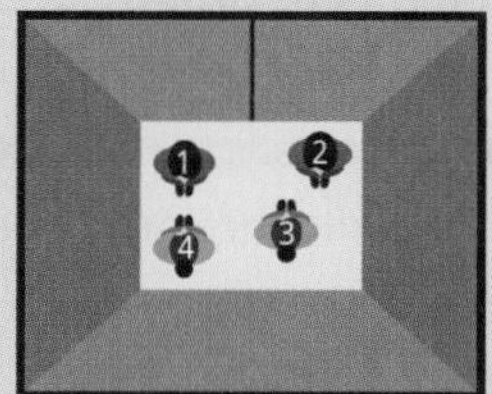

The numbers indicate the proper place to sit or stand according to one's status, with 1 being the most honored and 4 or 5 being the least honored. Note that in Japan, the driver is on the right-hand side as illustrated here.

Meeting Room

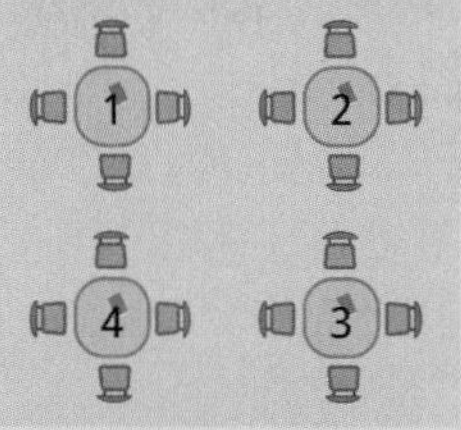

Restaurant

Exhibit 9.6 The Place of Honor in Japan (Attribution: Copyright Rice University, OpenStax, under CC BY-NC-SA 4.0 license)

Clearly, status plays an important role in Japanese (and several other East Asian) societies. Status recognizes age (an important cultural variable in these societies) and tells everyone involved how to behave. Though such prescriptive practices may seem strange to many Westerners, it is quite natural in Japan. In fact, many Japanese feel such guidelines are helpful and convenient in defining social relationships, avoiding awkward situations, and making business transactions more comfortable and productive. Whether or not this perception is accurate, status systems are a fact of life that must be recognized by Western managers attempting to do business in Asia. Failure to understand such social patterns puts the Western manager at a distinct disadvantage.

Sources: Allison, "Useful Japanese Business Manners to Impress a Client or Guest," *Fast Japan*, October 21, 2016; M. Yazinuma and R. Kennedy, "Life Is So Simple When You Know Your Place," *Intersect,* May 1986, pp. 35–39.

Group Cohesiveness

A fifth characteristic of work groups is group cohesiveness. We have all come in contact with groups whose members feel a high degree of camaraderie, group spirit, and unity. In these groups, individuals seem to be concerned about the welfare of other group members as well as that of the group as a whole. There is a feeling of "us against them" that creates a closeness among them. This phenomenon is called group cohesiveness. More specifically, **group cohesiveness** may be defined as the extent to which individual members of a group are motivated to remain in the group. According to Shaw, "Members of highly cohesive groups are more energetic in group activities, they are less likely to be absent from group meetings, they are happy when the group succeeds and sad when it fails, etc., whereas members of less cohesive groups are less concerned about the group's activities."[24]

We shall consider two primary aspects of work group cohesiveness. First, we look at major causes of cohesiveness. Following this, we examine its consequences.

Determinants of Group Cohesiveness. Why do some work groups develop a high degree of group cohesiveness while others do not? To answer this question, we have to examine both the composition of the group and several situational variables that play a role in determining the extent of cohesiveness. The major factors that influence group cohesiveness are shown in **Exhibit 9.7**.[25] These include the following:

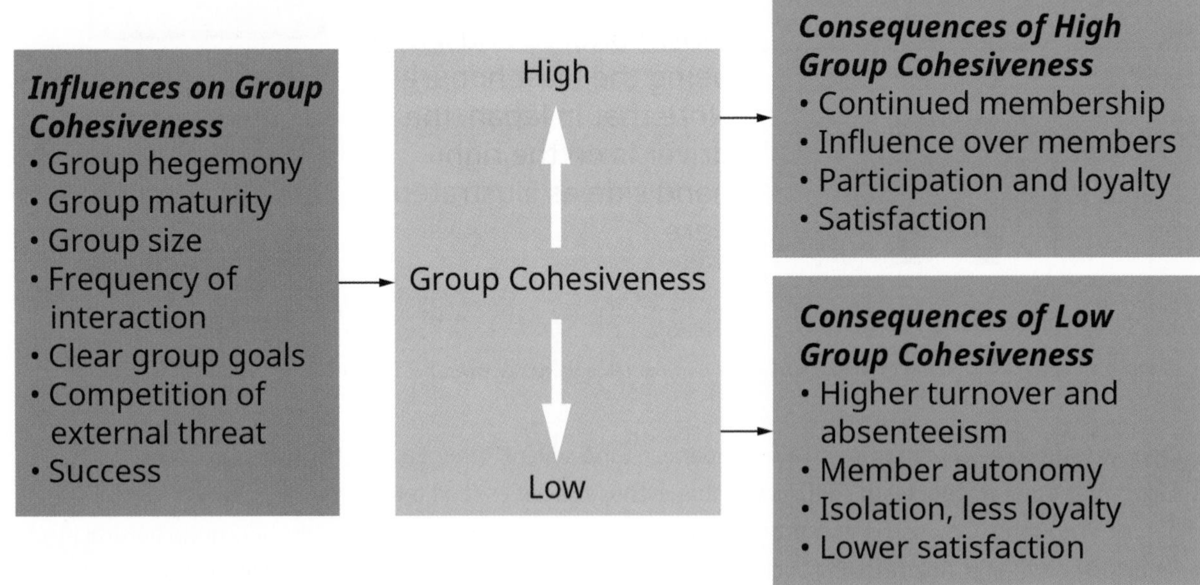

Exhibit 9.7 Determinants and Consequences of Group Cohesiveness (Attribution: Copyright Rice University, OpenStax, under CC BY-NC-SA 4.0 license)

- *Group homogeneity*. The more homogeneous the group—that is, the more members share similar characteristics and backgrounds—the greater the cohesiveness.
- *Group maturity*. Groups tend to become more cohesive simply as a result of the passage of time. Continued interaction over long periods of time helps members develop a closeness born of shared experiences.
- *Group size*. Smaller groups have an easier time developing cohesiveness, possibly because of the less complex interpersonal interaction patterns.
- *Frequency of interaction*. Groups that have greater opportunities to interact on a regular or frequent basis tend to become more cohesive than groups that meet less frequently or whose members are more isolated.
- *Clear group goals*. Groups that know exactly what they are trying to accomplish develop greater cohesiveness, in part because of a shared sense of mission and the absence of conflict over mission.
- *Competition or external threat*. When groups sense external threat or hostility, they tend to band together more closely. There is, indeed, "safety in numbers."
- *Success*. Group success on a previous task often facilitates increased cohesiveness and a sense of "we did it together."

In other words, a wide variety of factors can influence work group cohesiveness. The precise manner in which these processes occur is not known. Even so, managers must recognize the existence of certain forces of group cohesiveness if they are to understand the nature of group dynamics in organizations. The second aspect of group cohesiveness that must be understood by managers relates to their consequences.

Consequences of Group Cohesiveness. As shown in **Exhibit 9.7**, several consequences of group cohesiveness can also be identified. The first and most obvious consequence is *maintenance of membership*. If the attractiveness of the group is sufficiently stronger than the attractiveness of alternative groups, then we would expect the individual to remain in the group. Hence, turnover rates should be low.

In addition, high group cohesiveness typically provides the group with considerable *power over group members*. The power of a group over members depends upon the level of outcomes members expect to receive from the group compared to what they could receive through alternate means. When the group is seen as being highly instrumental to achieving personal goals, individuals will typically submit to the will of the group.

Third, members of highly cohesive groups tend to exhibit greater *participation and loyalty*. Several studies have shown that as cohesiveness increases, there is more frequent communication among members, a greater degree of participation in group activities, and less absenteeism. Moreover, members of highly cohesive groups tend to be more cooperative and friendly and generally behave in ways designed to promote integration among members.

Fourth, members of highly cohesive groups generally report high levels of *satisfaction*. In fact, the concept of group cohesiveness almost demands all this be the case, because it is unlikely that members will feel like remaining with a group with which they are dissatisfied.

Finally, what is the effect of group cohesiveness on *productivity*? No clear relationship exists here. Instead, research shows that the extent to which cohesiveness and productivity are related is moderated by the extent to which group members accept organizational goals. This is shown in **Exhibit 9.8**. Specifically, when cohesiveness and acceptance of organizational goals are high, performance will probably be high. When acceptance is high but cohesiveness is low, group performance will typically be moderate. Finally, performance will generally be low when goal acceptance is low regardless of the extent of group cohesiveness. In other words, high performance is most likely to result when highly cohesive teams accept the goals of the organization. At this time, both forces for performance are congruent.

		Agreement with Organizational Goals	
		High	Low
Degree of Group Cohesiveness	High	High performance	Low performance
	Low	Moderate performance	Low performance

Exhibit 9.8 Group Cohesiveness, Goal Agreement, and Performance (Attribution: Copyright Rice University, OpenStax, under CC BY-NC-SA 4.0 license)

MANAGING CHANGE

Group Cohesiveness

In the fast-moving innovative car industry, it is always important to be thinking about improving and staying ahead of the competition. For Ford and Chevrolet however, they have such popular vehicles—the F-150 and the hybrid Volt, respectively—that finding ways to improve them without taking away the qualities that make them popular is key.

With the F-150, Ford had one of the best-selling vehicles for more than 30 years, but improving upon their most popular vehicle came with its challenges. In 2015, the team wanted to introduce an economically six-cylinder EcoBoost engine, and an all-aluminum body. The team was worried about the marketplace and hoped that the customers would accept the change to their beloved truck.

The planning started 18 months before, working in parallel work teams on various parts of the project. Each team was responsible for a piece of the overall project, and they frequently came together to make sure that they were working cohesively to create a viable vehicle. The most successful piece of the dynamic for Ford was teams' ability to share feedback. Pete Reyes expresses the teamwork mentality: "Everybody crosses boundaries, and they came back with all of the feedback that shaped what we are going to do."

Having team cohesiveness was ultimately what brought Ford to the finish line. With over 1,000 members of the overall team, employees were able to accomplish a truly viable vehicle that weighed 700 pounds less, as well as countless other innovations that gave the truck 29 percent more fuel economy.

"We stuck to common goals . . . I don't think I'll ever work on a team that tight again," stated Reyes about his team of developmental managers. As a result of their close teamwork, Ford announced third-quarter earnings of 1.9 billion, an increase of 1.1 billion from 2014.

Sources: J. Motivalli, " 5 Inspiring Companies That Rely on Teamwork to Be Successful," *Success*, February 16, 2016, https://www.success.com/5-inspiring-companies-that-rely-on-teamwork-to-be-successful/; "All-

New 2015 F-150 Most Patented Truck in Ford History – New Innovations Bolster Next-Generation Light-Duty Pickup," *Ford Media Center*, May 23, 2014, https://media.ford.com/content/fordmedia/fna/us/en/news/2014/05/23/all-new-2015-f-150-most-patented-truck-in-ford-history--new-inno.html; P. Friedman, "Body of Work," Ford Corporate Website, accessed, December 13, 2018, https://corporate.ford.com/innovation/f-150-body-of-work.html.

Questions:

1. What challenges does a large project like Ford's F-150 project have to take into account for success?
2. What kind of work teams did Ford employ throughout its project to get the best results?
3. Can Ford's successes be translated into other smaller teams? How would you apply its best practices to a work environment of your own?

CONCEPT CHECK 

1. Explain what work roles are.
2. What role does group size play in the interactions of group members?
3. What are group norms and what role do they play toward group cohesiveness?

9.3 Managing Effective Work Groups

3. How do managers develop group cohesiveness, which facilitates organizational goal attainment?

We have examined in detail the nature and structure of work groups, noting that work groups differ along such dimensions as size, norms, and roles. Some groups are more cohesive than others. In view of these differences, it is interesting to ask how managers can facilitate increased work group effectiveness. To answer this question, we will make use of Hackman's model of group effectiveness.[26] According to this model, illustrated in **Exhibit 9.9**, the effectiveness of a work group is influenced by environmental factors, design factors, and task-related interpersonal processes. These three factors combine to influence what are called intermediate criteria, which, in turn, combine with the nature of the work technology to determine ultimate group effectiveness.

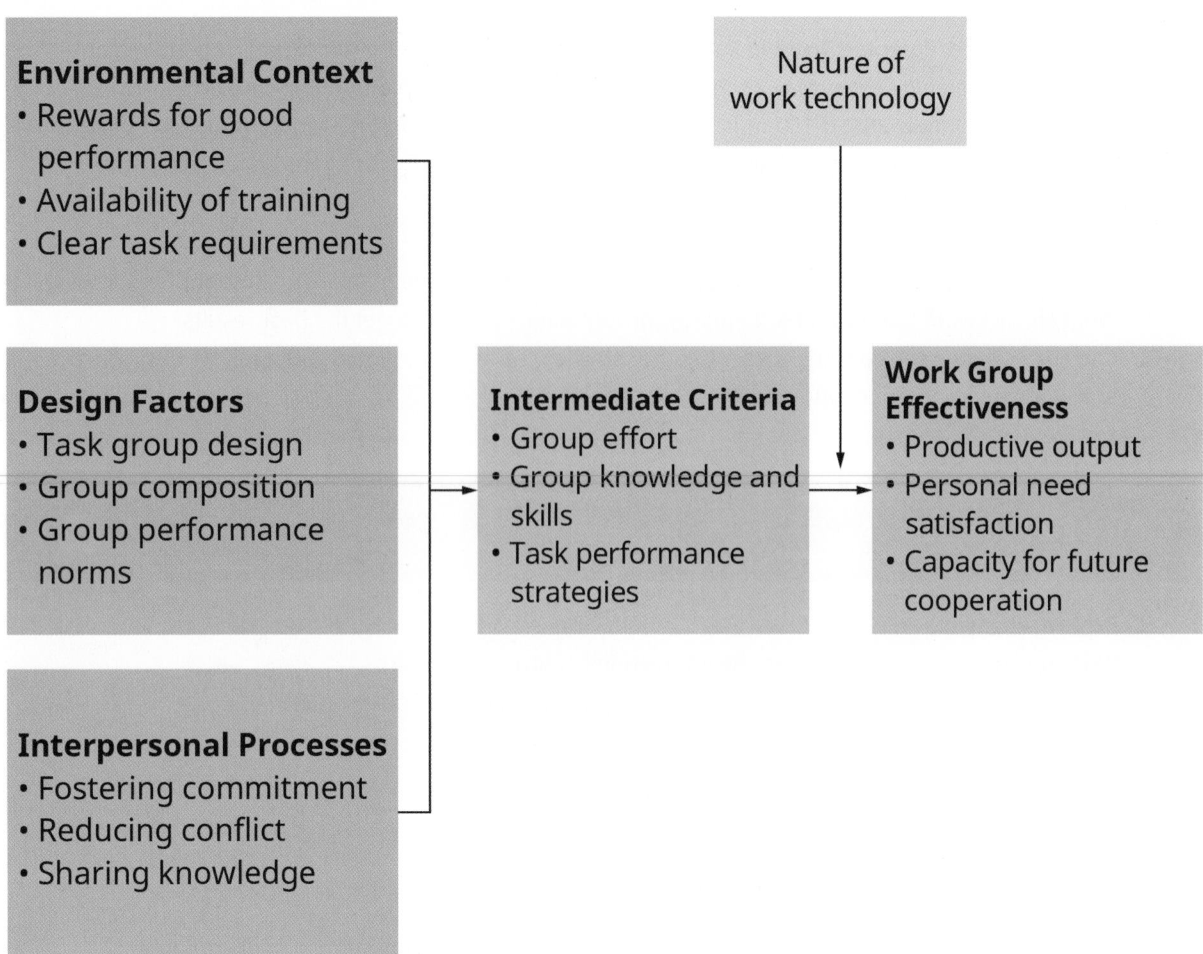

Exhibit 9.9 Determination of Work Group Effectiveness

What Is Work Group Effectiveness?

The first question to raise concerning work group effectiveness is what we mean by the concept itself. According to Hackman's model, effectiveness is defined in terms of three criteria:

1. *Productive output*. The productive output of the group must meet or exceed the quantitative and qualitative standards defined by the organization.
2. *Personal need satisfaction*. Groups are effective if membership facilitates employee need satisfaction.
3. *Capacity for future cooperation*. Effective groups employ social processes that maintain or enhance the capacity of their members to work together on subsequent tasks. Destructive social processes are avoided so members can develop long-term cohesiveness and effectiveness.

Determinants of Work-Group Effectiveness

Group effectiveness is largely determined by three factors that have been called *intermediate criteria*. These factors are as follows:

1. *Group effort*. The amount of effort group members exert toward task accomplishment.
2. *Group knowledge and skill*. The amount of knowledge and skills possessed by group members that are available for group effort and performance.
3. *Task performance strategies*. The extent to which the group's strategies for task performance (that is, how

it analyzes and attempts to solve problems) are appropriate.

Although the relative importance of each of these three intermediate factors may vary, all three are important. Without considerable group effort, appropriate skills and knowledge, and a clear strategy for task completion, groups are unlikely to be effective.

An important influence on the relative importance of these three variables is the nature of **work technology**. This includes the equipment and materials used in manufacture, the prescribed work procedures, and the physical layout of the work site. For example, if jobs are highly routinized, individual skills and knowledge may be somewhat less important than simple effort. On more complex tasks, however, such as research and development, effort alone will be of little help without concomitant skills and knowledge. Hence, although the relative importance of these three variables may vary with the job technology, all should be considered in any effort to understand determinants of work group effectiveness in a particular situation.

Finally, it must be recognized that these determinants of effectiveness are themselves influenced by three sets of factors (shown at the left-hand side of **Exhibit 9.9**). First, we must recognize a series of *environmental context* factors, such as the company's reward system, training programs, job descriptions, and so forth. Second are several *design factors,* including group structure, member composition, and performance norms. Finally, the role of *interpersonal processes*—such as efforts among group members and management to reduce conflict, foster commitment, and share knowledge—must be recognized. These three sets of factors, then, are largely responsible for determining the so-called intermediate criteria that, in turn, combine with appropriate job technologies to determine work group effectiveness.

Implications for Group Management

On the basis of this analysis of group processes in work organizations, we can identify several actions managers can take in order to help groups to be more effective.

Increased Managerial Awareness. To begin, managers can make themselves more aware of the nature of groups and the functions groups perform for individuals. By learning why individuals join groups, for example, managers should be able to better understand the motivational implications of group dynamics. Is high group cohesiveness in a particular group a result of high commitment to the organization and its goals, or is it a result of alienation from the organization?

Sensitivity to Group Norms. Managers can be sensitive to group norms and the extent to which they facilitate or inhibit group and organizational performance. The potency of group norms has been clearly established. It has also been shown that company actions can increase or decrease the likelihood that norms will work to the benefit of the organization. Much of the thrust of current organizational development efforts is to use process consultation techniques to develop group norms that are compatible with company goals.

Understanding Pressures for Conformity. Much has been said in the research literature about the effects of groups on individual conformity and deviance. Groups often place significant pressures on individuals to conform, and they punish deviants by such means as ostracism. From a managerial standpoint, conformity can represent a mixed blessing. On one hand, there are many work situations in which managers typically want workers to conform to standard operating procedures (this is called *dependable role performance*). On the other hand, employees must be sufficiently free to take advantage of what they believe to be unique or important opportunities on behalf of the organization (*innovative and spontaneous behavior*). If pressures toward conformity are too strong, this spontaneity may be lost, along with unique opportunities for the organization.

Harnessing Group Cohesiveness. Where it is desirable to develop highly cohesive groups, managers can show employees how group members can help one another by working together. It is important to note, however, that group cohesiveness by itself does not guarantee increased group effectiveness. Instead, managers must take the lead in showing group members why they benefit from working toward organizational goals. One way to accomplish this is through the reward systems used by the organization.

In short, there are several lessons for managers here concerning the effects of group dynamics on performance and effectiveness. The lesson is clear: managers must be sensitive to and deal with group processes in the workplace. Without doing so, the manager and the company are destined at best to achieve mediocre results.

CONCEPT CHECK 

1. Why must managers be sensitive to and deal with group processes in the workplace

9.4 Intergroup Behavior and Performance

4. What are barriers to intergroup cooperation, and how do you take action to minimize such impediments and understand how to get the most out of the collective actions of groups in organizations in order to enhance industrial competitiveness?

We are now ready to move on to an examination of intergroup behavior. That is, what happens when one group in an organization must interact with another? Clearly, in any corporation, a high degree of intergroup interaction is vital to organizational success. Even in small companies, the production group must interact with the sales group, and both must accommodate the finance and accounting groups. Without smooth intergroup relations, organizational effectiveness and industrial competitiveness are virtually impossible.

Determinants of Intergroup Performance

To understand how groups interact with one another, it is important to identify the primary variables that characterize intergroup behavior.[27] We can do this by suggesting a model of intergroup performance. This model is outlined in **Exhibit 9.10**. As shown, intergroup behavior occurs when two groups intersect. Each group has its own characteristics and uniqueness, but both operate within the larger confines of organizational policies, culture, reward systems, and so forth. Within this context, performance is largely influenced by three types of *interaction requirements:* interdependence requirements, information flow requirements, and integration requirements. The quality of intergroup performance is affected by the extent to which all parties to the interaction can meet these requirements.

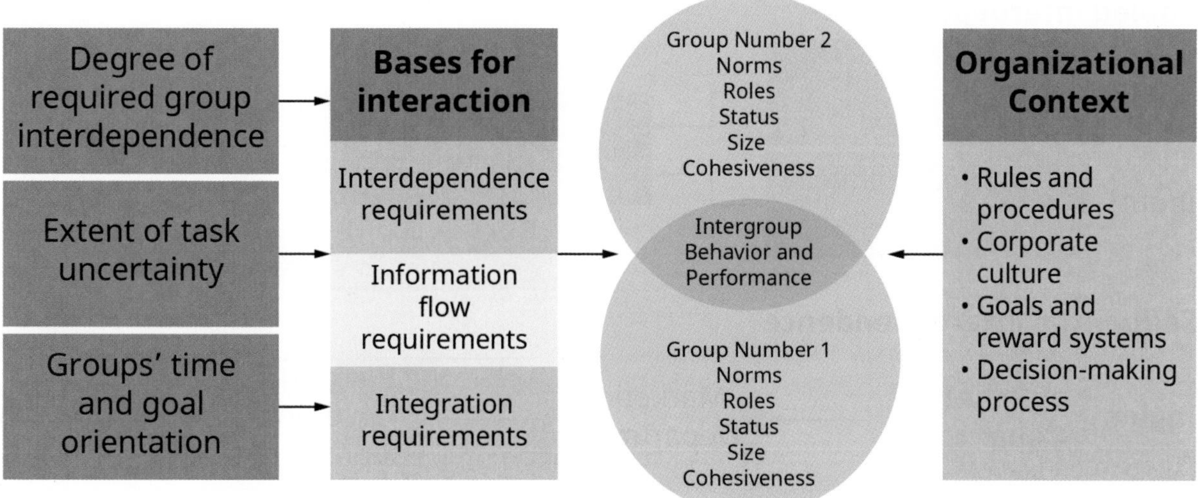

Exhibit 9.10 A Model of Intergroup Behavior and Performance (Attribution: Copyright Rice University, OpenStax, under CC BY-NC-SA 4.0 license)

Interdependence Requirements. *Interdependence requirements* relate to the frequency and quality of interactions among groups; high-quality interaction is required for successful task accomplishment. To successfully achieve corporate objectives, organizations must achieve enough intergroup interaction to coordinate resource allocation and utilization. The amount of interaction required is determined by the extent and nature of the groups' interdependence. Group interdependence takes three primary forms (see **Exhibit 9.11**):

Pooled interdependence

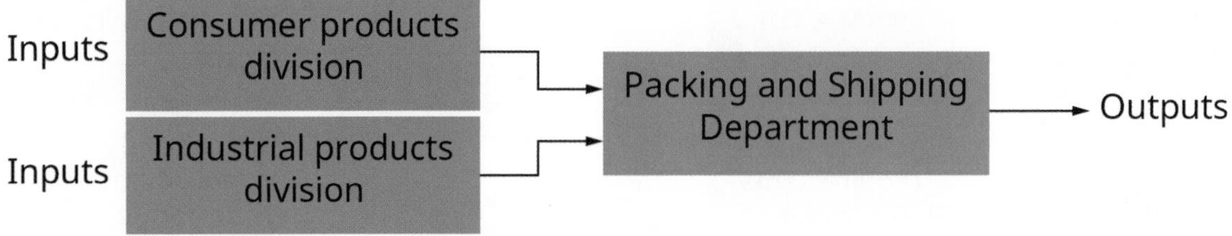

Sequential interdependence

Reciprocal interdependence

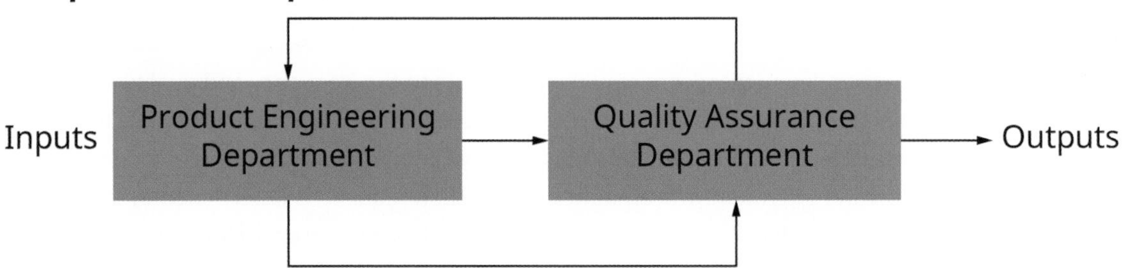

Exhibit 9.11 Three Types of Group Interdependence (Attribution: Copyright Rice University, OpenStax, under CC BY-NC-SA 4.0 license)

1. *Pooled interdependence*. **Pooled interdependence** occurs when various groups are largely independent of one another, even though each contributes to and is supported by the larger organization. For example, although the physics and music departments may not interact frequently, both contribute to the larger goals of the university, and both use university resources. In a factory setting, pooled interdependence can be seen in a company with two distinct manufacturing divisions; e.g., one for consumer products and one for industrial products. Although produced separately, both kinds of products come together in the shipping department, and both represent products of the same company.
2. *Sequential interdependence*. **Sequential interdependence** exists when the outputs of one unit or group become the inputs for another. For example, the manufacturing department in a company is clearly dependent on the purchasing department for the success of its own operation, whereas the purchasing department is much less dependent on manufacturing.
3. *Reciprocal interdependence*. **Reciprocal interdependence** occurs when two or more groups depend on one another for inputs. For example, without product engineering, the marketing department would have nothing to sell. On the other hand, without consumer information from marketing, product engineering might not know what to manufacture. The two units are highly dependent on each other, thereby requiring a high degree of interaction.

In summary, the type of interdependence determines in large part the degree of interrelationship that develops among two or more groups. High interdependence typically requires high intergroup interaction, whereas low interdependence typically requires relatively low intergroup interaction.

Information Flow Requirements. The second requirement for successful intergroup performance is optimal

information flow. To be successful, groups need the appropriate amount of information. Information flow is influenced to a large degree by the extent of **task uncertainty**. When groups are working on highly uncertain tasks (e.g., a new product, an experiment, or an old product in a new environment), the need for communication increases. When task uncertainty is low, less information is typically needed.

Task uncertainty, in turn, is influenced by two factors. The first, *task clarity*, is the extent to which the requirements and responsibilities of the group are clearly understood. The use of standard operating procedures in organizations is an example of a group requirement. The other consideration is *task environment*, those factors inside and outside the organization that can affect the group's performance. The task environment has two aspects: the number of groups that must be dealt with and the relative stability of the environment. Obviously, the more groups that must interact and the more dynamic the environment, the greater the task uncertainty. In a dynamic environment, groups tend to expand their information-gathering efforts to detect and cope with environmental changes. Hence, the greater the task uncertainty, the greater the need for comprehensive information flow systems.

Integration Requirements. The final requirement for successful intergroup performance is integration. *Integration requirements* focus on the extent of collaboration, cooperation, or structural relationships among groups needed to ensure success. Typically, various departments within an organization have different goals and time orientations. A technical research department, for example, often sees its goals in scientific terms and has a long-term perspective. A marketing department in the same company, focusing its goals on market considerations on the other hand, would typically have a short-term orientation. The production department, concerned with technical goals, would probably attempt to maintain a moderate time orientation in order to take advantage of the economies of scale associated with longer production runs.

A successful organization finds ways to integrate groups so that they coordinate their efforts on behalf of corporate objectives. The trick is to achieve some commonly acceptable coordinating mechanism—not a state in which all units have the same goals and time orientations. It would prove disastrous, for example, if the research unit looked for short-term results or the marketing department ignored short-term shifts in the marketplace. Through integration, various units can accommodate one another's needs while maintaining their individuality. In this way, the strengths of all groups are used in addressing organizational problems.

When we put these various requirements and their antecedents together, we can see why achieving intergroup coordination and performance is no easy task. **Table 9.3** shows the defining characteristics of four typical units of an organization: research, development, sales, and manufacturing. The interdependence, task uncertainty, and time and goal orientation of each unit are shown. Consider the complexities managers face in attempting to lead such an organization efficiently and effectively. Indeed, business magazines are filled with examples of corporate failures that can be traced to poor coordination of such units. These examples point to an endless array of potential sources of conflict that can reduce the capacity of a company to compete successfully in an ever-changing environment.

Intergroup Characteristics in Four Units of One Company			
Group	Interdependence Examples	Task Uncertainty	Time and Goal Orientation
Research	*Reciprocal* with development *Sequential* with market research *Pooled* with shipping	High	*Time:* Long term *Goal:* Science
Development	*Reciprocal* with market research *Sequential* with manufacturing *Pooled* with shipping	Moderate to high	*Time:* Long term *Goal:* Science and technoeconomic
Sales	*Reciprocal* with market research *Sequential* with manufacturing *Pooled* with personnel	Moderate	*Time:* Moderate term *Goal:* Market
Manufacturing	*Reciprocal* with accounting *Sequential* with shipping *Pooled* with research	Low	*Time:* Short term *Goal:* Technoeconomic
Source: Adapted from A. Szilagyi and M. Wallace, *Organizational Behavior and Performance,* 5th ed. (New York: HarperCollins, 1991), p. 272.			

Table 9.3 (Attribution: Copyright Rice University, OpenStax, under CC BY-NC-SA 4.0 license)

Managing Intergroup Behavior and Performance

When we analyze the challenge of managing intergroup behavior and performance, the key issue facing managers is the issue of coordination. In most situations, various units or departments in the organization all have talent needed to ensure task accomplishment. Yet, each unit has its own culture, goals, norms, and so forth. Hence, the challenge for managers is harnessing and coordinating this talent in such a way that group harmony is maintained while organizational objectives are achieved.

There are several techniques for managing intergroup relations and performance. These techniques include using rules and procedures, member exchange, linking roles, task forces, and decoupling. Let us briefly consider each as it relates to intergroup coordination and performance.

Rules and Procedures. A common way to manage intergroup relations is for senior management to establish rules and procedures governing the interactions of two or more departments or units. For example, if units consistently fail to communicate with one another, which leads to poor coordination, the company may institute a new policy requiring all groups to post certain types of information at regular time intervals or to inform other department heads of proposed new activities or changes. By simply increasing communication flow, group coordination should increase.

Member Exchange. In some circumstances, it is desirable for the organization to temporarily transfer a member from one group to another. Such exchanges offer the employee an opportunity to better understand the problems and procedures of the other group. Upon returning to his original group, the employee can share information about the other group. In addition, the transferred employee often develops better interpersonal contacts with the other department, thereby enhancing communication and coordination. An example of this can be seen when a company transfers a production engineer into the quality assurance department. As a result, the employee sees firsthand the problems of the quality control group and can take the knowledge back to production engineering.

Linking Roles. A **linking role** is a position or unit within the organization that is charged with overseeing and coordinating the activities of two or more groups. A good example is a product manager who is responsible for coordinating manufacturing, sales, quality control, and product research for a certain product line (see **Exhibit 9.12**). In essence, these linking role positions are designed to enhance communication among the various functional units and ensure that the right products are designed, manufactured, and marketed. We will say more about the product manager's role in Understanding and Managing Work Teams.

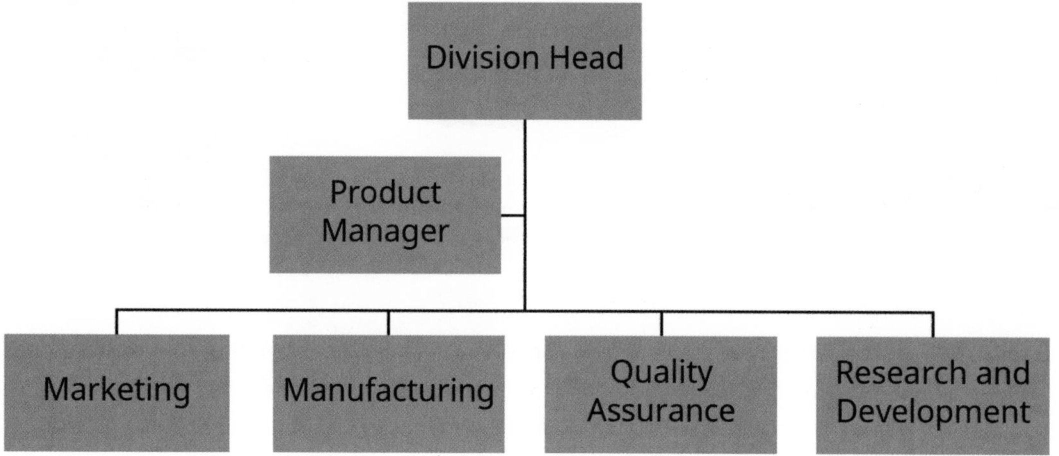

Exhibit 9.12 The Product Manager as a Linking Role (Attribution: Copyright Rice University, OpenStax, under CC BY-NC-SA 4.0 license)

Exhibit 9.13 Sales team The sales team at Dynamic Signal meets for reviewing goals. What can you say about the diversity of this team? (Credit: Jim Larisson/ flickr/ Attribution 2.0 Generic (CC BY 2.0))

Task Forces. A **task force** serves much the same purpose as a linking role except that the role is temporary instead of permanent. In a task force, individuals from several units are brought together to solve a specific problem, usually in a short period of time. It is felt that each unit has expertise to contribute and that by coordinating these efforts, a better solution can be achieved. A typical task force arrangement can be seen in **Exhibit 9.14**. For instance, a company facing a major financial cutback may create a task force consisting of members from across the company to identify ways to resolve the crisis. Or a company may create a task force to consider a joint venture offer from a foreign company. In both cases, the problem is that immediate and diverse skills are required to reach an optimal solution.

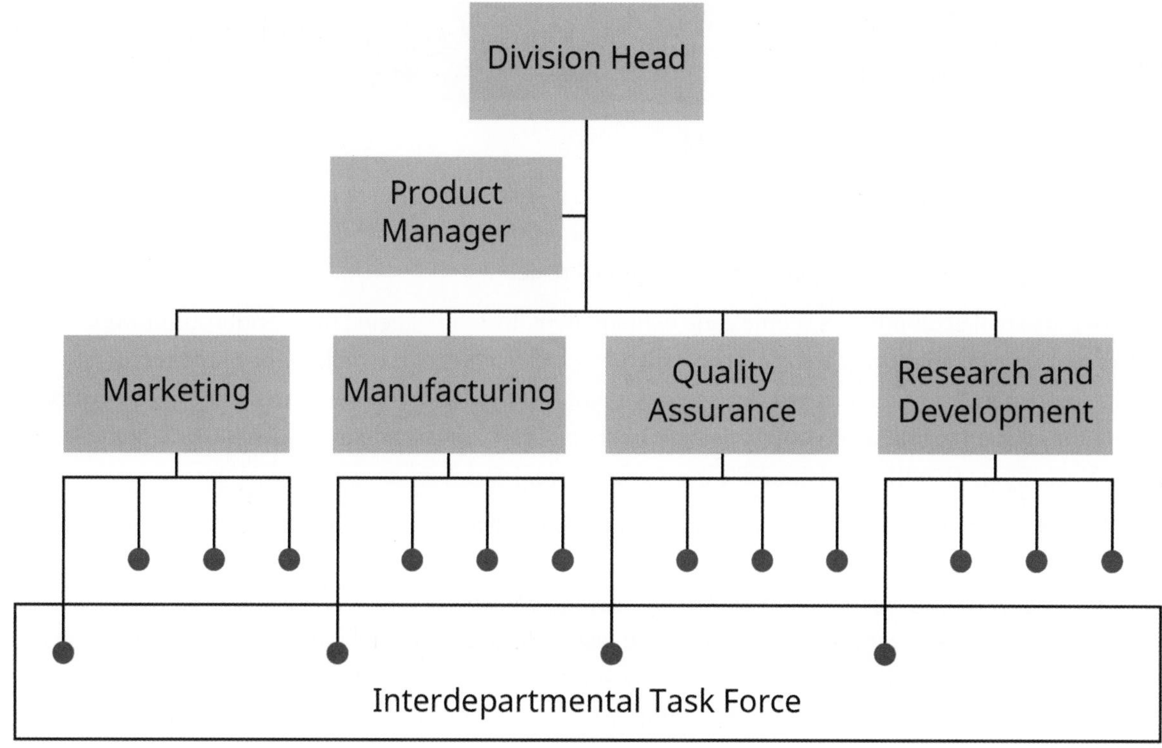

Exhibit 9.14 An Example of a Typical Task Force (Attribution: Copyright Rice University, OpenStax, under CC BY-NC-SA 4.0 license)

Decoupling. Finally, there are situations in which two or more closely related groups simply don't work together effectively. In such cases, **decoupling** may be the answer.[28] Decoupling involves separating two groups—physically or administratively—in such a way that the required tasks of the organization are fulfilled while the interaction between the two groups is minimized. For instance, hardware and software engineers ideally should work closely together on the design of a new computing system. Yet sometimes these people see problems and solutions quite differently, which may lead to overt hostility and uncooperative behavior. One solution would be to separate the two groups physically and then have one group (e.g., the hardware engineers) outline product specifications. Software engineers then could work more on their own to design software to meet these specifications. Obviously, some coordination would be required. Even so, such an approach could retain the services of two valued groups of engineers who see problems quite differently— a wise compromise strategy for the high-tech company.

In essence, several strategies are available to assist managers in coordinating the diverse talents of interdependent groups in ways that help achieve organizational goals. The choice of an appropriate technique depends upon the unique situation facing the manager. One such approach to managing intergroup coordination was practiced at General Motors Company as it approached the design and manufacture of the Saturn.

EXPANDING AROUND THE GLOBE

Engagement on Global Work Teams: IBM

Since 2008, IBM has increased its focus on becoming a globally integrated enterprise. Employing over 200,000 people from different countries and backgrounds, there are major challenges that IBM faces when managing its work teams on such a large global scale.

One of those main components is time zone management. Instead of being highly rigorous in work hours and causing employees to be available on teams at all hours of the night or day, IBM decided they would implement a results-oriented work environment (ROWE). This strategy allows employees to work where they live on virtual teams and base their hours on their own schedules. ROWE allows employees to work at the hours that they feel naturally most productive.

Another key component to managing a global work team is clear communication. IBM structures its leadership of the work teams with leaders that consist of four or five senior executives from multiple geographies. They must work side by side to understand one another's cultural differences, as well as provide input on their overall team objectives that enable business growth in that country. They are able to accommodate local differences, learn from one another's differences, and come to common objectives because of their remote location differences for a better outcome. Additionally, these leaders are better equipped to understand local nuances because of their deeper understanding of the global and cultural nuances of their team members.

IBM continues to focus on growing "global IBMers" by offering opportunities for global leadership experiences as well as offering opportunities to acquire new skills. The company focuses on three key actions:

1. Grow locally and globally via a consistent methodology. Align business strategies with national priorities and societal goals, build local expertise, and expand market relevance.
2. Develop leadership. Provide more employees with opportunities to enhance their skills, and offer more varied global experiences early in careers.
3. Enable the global integrated enterprise (GIE) vision. Accelerate enterprise-wide collaboration and an organizational culture based on shared values.

These key actions are clearly communicated by IBM and are demonstrated by leadership to help engage employees behind the methods. Utilizing the best technology to improve collaboration can garner the most productivity and empower employees. If leadership is engaged, employees will also engage with their work and workplace, which helps drive team cohesiveness overall.

Questions:

1. What challenges does IBM face due to the size and global reach of its employee base?
2. Name at least three strategies that managers and leaders can employ to help keep employees engaged, even when working in remote work teams.

Sources: K. White, "Enabling Growth through Global Enablement Teams," *IBM Thought Leadership*, accessed January 3, 2019, https://ibm.com/services/us/gbs/thoughtleadership/ibv-global-leaders.html; "Enabling Growth through Global Enablement teams," *IBM Thought Leadership*, accessed January 3, 2019, https://ibm.com/services/us/gbs/bus/html/gbs-integrated-enterprise-workforce.html; T. Neely, "Global

Teams that Work," *Harvard Business Review*, October 2015, https://hbr.org/2015/10/global-teams-that-work; D. DeRosa, "3 Companies With High-Performing Teams," *Onpoint Consulting*, October 3, 2017, https://www.onpointconsultingllc.com/blog/3-companies-with-high-performing-virtual-teams.

CONCEPT CHECK

1. Are well-functioning teams or groups in complex tasks more productive and leave workers more satisfied than in traditional arrangements?
2. What is the importance of the ability to effectively manage both the task requirements and the process or maintenance aspects of the group for them to function well?

Key Terms

Command group A group that is permanent.

Decoupling Involves separating two groups—physically or administratively—in such a way that the required tasks of the organization are fulfilled while the interaction between the two groups is minimized.

Formal group Work units that are prescribed by the organization.

Friendship group Friendship groups tend to be long lasting.

Group An organized system of two or more individuals who are interrelated so that the system performs some function, has a standard set of role relationships among its members, and has a set of norms that regulate the function of the group and each of its members.

Group cohesiveness The extent to which individual members of a group are motivated to remain in the group.

Informal group Groups that evolve naturally out of individual and collective self-interest among the members of an organization and are not the result of deliberate organizational design.

Information flow To be successful, groups need the appropriate amount of information.

Interaction process analysis A technique that records who says what to whom, and through using it illustrates that smaller groups typically exhibit greater tension, agreement, and opinion seeking, whereas larger groups show more tension release and giving of suggestions and information.

Interest group A network that forms due to mutual interests such as working women or minority managers.

Linking role A position or unit within the organization that is charged with overseeing and coordinating the activities of two or more groups.

Norms These regulate the function of the group and each of its members.

Pooled interdependence Occurs when various groups are largely independent of each other, even though each contributes to and is supported by the larger organization.

Reciprocal interdependence Occurs when two or more groups depend on one another for inputs.

Role ambiguity A condition that arises when messages sent to an individual may be unclear.

Role conflict A condition that can arise when individuals receive multiple and sometimes conflicting messages from various groups, all attempting to assign them a particular role.

Role episode An attempt to explain how a particular role is learned and acted upon.

Role overload A condition where individuals may simply receive too many role-related messages.

Role set The sum total of all the roles assigned to one individual.

Sequential interdependence Exists when the outputs of one unit or group become the inputs for another.

Social loafing A tendency for individual group members to reduce their effort on a group task.

Status incongruence A situation that exists when a person is high on certain valued dimensions but low on others, or when a person's characteristics seem inappropriate for a particular job.

Status system Serves to differentiate individuals on the basis of some criterion or set of criteria.

Task force Serves the same purpose as a linking role except that the role is temporary instead of permanent.

Task group Serves the same purpose as a command role except that the role is temporary instead of permanent.

Task uncertainty When groups are working on highly uncertain tasks, the need for communication increases. When task uncertainty is low, less information is typically needed.

Work role An expected behavior pattern assigned or attributed to a particular position in the organization.

Work technology Includes the equipment and materials used in manufacture, the prescribed work procedures, and the physical layout of the work site.

Summary of Learning Outcomes

9.1 Work Groups: Basic Considerations

1. How do you manage group and intergroup processes effectively?

A group is a collection of individuals who share a common set of norms, who generally have differentiated roles among themselves, and who interact with one another in the joint pursuit of common goals. Groups may be divided into permanent and temporary groups and formal and informal groups. Formal groups include command and task groups, whereas informal groups include friendship and interest groups.

9.2 Work Group Structure

2. How do group norms, roles, and status systems affect employee behavior and performance?

People join groups because they offer security, meet social needs, enhance self-esteem, fulfill economic interests, introduce them to people with mutual interests, and, sometimes, because they are in close physical proximity. Groups typically develop through several distinct stages, including forming, storming, norming, and performing. A role may be defined as an expected behavior pattern assigned or attributed to a particular position in the organization. Roles may be oriented toward the task, social relations, or the self.

9.3 Managing Effective Work Groups

3. How do managers develop group cohesiveness, which facilitates organizational goal attainment?

Social loafing is a tendency for individual members of a group to reduce their task effort in the belief that other members will cover for them. A norm is a standard that is shared by group members and that regulates member behavior within an organization. Norms facilitate group survival, simplify expected behaviors, help members avoid embarrassing situations, and help identify group members. Asch's experiment in group pressure and individual judgment demonstrated that individuals will discount their own perceptions of a situation and follow the will of a group. Status systems serve to differentiate individuals on the basis of some criterion or set of criteria. Status incongruence occurs when one individual holds a position in the status hierarchy that is inconsistent with the conventional criteria for that position. Group cohesiveness is the extent to which individual members of a group are motivated to remain in the group. Work group effectiveness is defined by three criteria: group productivity, personal need satisfaction of the members, and the group's capacity for future cooperation.

9.4 Intergroup Behavior and Performance

4. What are barriers to intergroup cooperation, and how do you take action to minimize such impediments and understand how to get the most out of the collective actions of groups in organizations in order to enhance industrial competitiveness?

Intergroup performance is influenced by three interaction requirements. These include the requirements for interdependence, information, and integration. A linking role is a position or unit within the organization that is charged with overseeing and coordinating the activities of two or more groups. A task force consists of members from several departments or units who are brought together on a temporary basis to solve a specific and immediate problem. Decoupling refers to the practice of physically or administratively separating groups that are not able to work together effectively.

Chapter Review Questions

1. What are the various types of groups often found in work situations?
2. Why do people join groups?
3. Describe the stages of group development.
4. How does work group size influence individual and group behavior?
5. Discuss the role of work group norms in the work situation.
6. Consider how groups influence conformity and deviance in work situations.
7. What is the major conclusion of Asch's experiment on group pressure and individual judgment?
8. Define a *role episode*.
9. Why is knowledge of role relationships important for managers?
10. What purposes are served by status differentiations in work organizations? What problems emerge from these differentiations?
11. What determines group cohesiveness, and what impact does it have on group behavior?
12. Discuss how managers can improve intergroup relations and performance. Provide examples from your own experience to defend your arguments.

Management Skills Application Exercises

1. To assist in your analysis, you may wish to complete this self-assessment. Simply think of a group you have belonged to, and answer each question as honestly as possible. When you are through, refer to **Appendix B** for interpretation.

How Do You Behave in a Group?

Instructions: Think of a typical group situation in which you often find yourself (e.g., a club, study group, small work group), and answer the following items as accurately as possible.

	Never	Seldom	Fairly Often	Frequently
In a group, how often do you:				
1. Keep the group focused on the task at hand?	1	2	3	4
2. Help the group clarify the issues?	1	2	3	4
3. Pull various ideas together?	1	2	3	4
4. Push the group to make a decision or complete a task?	1	2	3	4
5. Support and encourage other groups members?	1	2	3	4
6. Try to reduce interpersonal conflicts?	1	2	3	4
7. Help the group reach a compromise?	1	2	3	4
8. Assist in maintaining group harmony?	1	2	3	4
9. Seek personal recognition from other group members?	1	2	3	4
10. Try to dominate group activities?	1	2	3	4
11. Avoid unpleasant or undesirable group activities?	1	2	3	4
12. Express your impatience or hostility with the group?	1	2	3	4

2. To see how group effectiveness works, try this self-assessment. Choose a work group (or groups) to which you belong (or did belong in the past). Once you have selected a group, simply answer the items on the questionnaire by checking either "mostly yes" or "mostly no." When you have finished, refer to **Appendix B** for scoring.

How Effective Is Your Work Group?

Instructions: Select a group to which you belong, and use this group to answer the following questions. Check "mostly yes" or "mostly no" to answer each question.

	Mostly Yes	Mostly No
1. The atmosphere is relaxed and comfortable.	____	____
2. Group discussion is frequent, and it is usually pertinent to the task at hand.	____	____

3. Group members understand what they are trying to accomplish.	____	____
4. People listen to each other's suggestions and ideas.	____	____
5. Disagreements are tolerated, and an attempt is made to resolve them.	____	____
6. There is general agreement on most courses of action taken.	____	____
7. The group welcomes frank criticism from inside and outside sources.	____	____
8. When the group takes action, clear assignments are made and accepted.	____	____
9. There is a well-established, relaxed working relationship among the members.	____	____
10. There is a high degree of trust and confidence among the leader and subordinates.	____	____
11. The group members strive hard to help the group achieve its goal.	____	____
12. Suggestions and criticisms are offered and received with a helpful spirit.	____	____
13. There is a cooperative rather than a competitive relationship among group members.	____	____
14. The group goals are set high but not so high as to create anxieties or fear of failure.	____	____
15. The leaders and members hold a high opinion of the group's capabilities.	____	____
16. Creativity is stimulated within the group.	____	____
17. There is ample communication within the group of topics relevant to getting the work accomplished.	____	____
18. Group members feel confident in making decisions.	____	____
19. People are kept busy but not overloaded.	____	____
20. The leader of the group is well suited for the job.	____	____
Source: Adapted from A. J. DuBrin from *The Human Side of Enterprise* (New York: McGraw-Hill, 1960).		

Managerial Decision Exercises

1. Assume that you are the CEO of a major producer of potato chips. You have four plants and discover that one of the plants is more productive than the other three; specifically, the midnight to 8 a.m. shift is 22 percent more productive than every other shift. Since one of the things that makes chips more appealing to customers is freshness, increasing productivity and getting the product on the shelves is of enormous importance.

You decide to visit the plant based in San Antonio, Texas, and observe the 4 p.m. to midnight shift and then the midnight to 8 a.m. shift. During your visit, you are impressed with the effectiveness of the first shift and discuss the production process with the supervisor, which involves boiling the chips in hot oil, seasoning them in three varieties of salted seasoning, and having the chips go through a tube to fill the bags that are then placed in boxes for shipment to retailers. Everything seems to have been done efficiently, and you eagerly anticipate seeing what the midnight shift is doing to produce extraordinary results.

The new crew starts its shift by cleaning the production line and begins production. For the first hour, everything they do mirrors what the previous shift was doing. Then the shift supervisor calls out that it is time to clean the tubes, and for two minutes the team cleans the tubes that feed the bags with chips to remove the oil that has accumulated in the tubes. This process is repeated seven times throughout the night, with the final cleaning preparing the line for the morning shift. At the end of the night, the production report shows that this shift produced 23 percent more chips than the previous shifts. When you meet with the supervisor and workers, you ask them about their practice of cleaning the tubes. They report that they discovered that oil buildup in the tubes slowed the flow of chips, which caused everything before that step in the process to slow down. You thank them and consider what to do next. You obviously need to implement this practice across all shifts in the company and are considering how to roll this out. You also want to reward the shift supervisor, Manuel Santos, and the workers on the shift for their ingenuity. What are your next steps? Write the memo that you would send to all shift supervisors, or alternatively, write a memo to the general managers of the four plants to implement this. What are the benefits of each approach? Finally, decide on the rewards for Manuel Santos and the midnight shift workers, and write a letter that would be sent to them commending them. How might this incident be used to improve the performance of all work groups in the organization?

Critical Thinking Case

OECollaboration

At OECollaboration, a technology company that develops virtual collaboration software for new companies, Mike Jones is a new manager. One of the biggest challenges he has faced is that the team that he is managing is well established and because he is an outsider, the team members haven't yet developed trust in him.

Two weeks into his new employment, Mike held a meeting and discussed all of the changes to the remote work agreements as well as implementing new meeting requirements for each employee to have a biweekly meeting scheduled with him to discuss their projects. The team was outraged, they were not excited, and the following days he wasn't greeted in a friendly way; in addition, his team seemed less engaged when asked to participate in team functions.

Tracy James is also a new manager at OECollaboration who started at the same time as Mike, in a similar situation where she is a new manager of an existing team. Tracy was able to hold a meeting the first day on the job to listen to her team and get to know them. During this meeting she also told the team about herself and her past experiences. Additionally, she held one-on-one meetings to listen to each of her team members to discuss what they were working on and their career goals. After observation and discussion with upper management, she aligned her own team goals closely with the skills and experiences of her new team. She met with the whole team to make changes to a few policies, explaining why they were being changed, and set the strategy for the team moving forward.

Because she got her team involved and learned about them before implementing her new strategy, this was well received. Her team still had questions and concerns, but they felt like they could trust her and that they were included in the changes that were being made.

Questions:

1. What challenges can a new manager encounter when starting to manage an existing team?
2. What strategies can a new manager implement to ensure that his new team is engaged with him and builds relationships to succeed in his new role?

Sources: J. Morris, "How Smart Manager's Win over New teams Without Bringing in Free Food," *The Muse*, accessed January 4, 2019, https://www.themuse.com/advice/how-smart-managers-win-over-new-teams-without-bringing-in-free-food; B. Tulgan, "The Challenge of Taking Over Leadership of an Existing Team," *Association for Talent Development*, January 5, 2015, https://www.td.org/insights/the-challenge-of-taking-over-leadership-of-an-existing-team;

10 Understanding and Managing Work Teams

Exhibit 10.1 (Credit: MabelAmber/ Pixabay/ (CC BY 0))

Introduction

Learning Outcomes

After reading this chapter, you should be able to answer these questions:

1. What is the benefit of working in teams, and what makes teams effective?
2. How do teams develop over time?
3. What are some key considerations in managing teams?
4. What are the benefits of conflict for a team?
5. How does team diversity enhance decision-making and problem-solving?
6. What are some challenges and best practices for managing and working with multicultural teams?

EXPLORING MANAGERIAL CAREERS

Eva Hartmann, Trellis LLC

Eva Hartmann has nearly 20 years of experience as a strategic, results-driven, innovative leader with significant expertise in human resources strategy, talent and leadership development, and organizational effectiveness. She has worked in a variety of industries, from manufacturing to Fortune 500 consulting. Eva is a transformational change agent who has developed and led strategic human capital programs and talent initiatives in multiple challenging environments globally. Eva is passionate about enhancing both individual and organizational performance.

Eva began her career in one of the large “Big 6” management consulting firms at the time, and she happily returned several years ago to consulting. She is the founder and president of Trellis LLC, a human capital consulting and staffing firm in Richmond, Virginia.

Prior to Trellis, Eva was the global human resources leader for a large global manufacturer of plastic film products and was responsible for the HR strategy and operations of a $600 million global division. In this role, Eva led a global team of HR managers in North and South America, Europe, and Asia to support global HR initiatives to drive business results and build human capital and performance across the division.

Eva has also held a variety of leadership and managerial roles in both human resources and quality functions at several nationally and globally recognized companies, including Wachovia Securities, Genworth Financial, Sun Microsystems, and Andersen Consulting (now Accenture).

Eva holds an MBA from the College of William and Mary in Williamsburg, Virginia, and a BA in anthropology from the University of Virginia in Charlottesville, Virginia. She is also an adjunct faculty member with the University of Richmond Robins School of Business. Eva currently serves on the board of the Society of Human Resource Management (SHRM) of Richmond, Virginia.

Much of the work that is performed today in organizations requires a focus on teamwork. The ability to work successfully as a team member, as well as the ability to lead teams, is an ultimate advantage within the workforce. Teams themselves must be managed, in addition to managing just the individuals, to be successful. We've all heard the quote originally coined by Aristotle that states that "the whole is greater than the sum of its parts." This captures the nature of the team perfectly—there is such a synergy that comes from a team that the individuals alone are not able to create. This chapter details the importance of and benefits that you may derive from working as a team, as well as some of the ways we can make our teams more successful.

10.1 Teamwork in the Workplace

1. What is a team, and what makes a team effective?

Teamwork has never been more important in organizations than it is today. Whether you work in a manufacturing environment and utilize self-directed work teams, or if you work in the "**knowledge economy**" and derive benefits from collaboration within a team structure, you are harnessing the power of a team.

A team, according to Katzenbach and Smith in their *Harvard Business Review* (HBR) article "The Discipline of Teams," is defined as "people organized to function cooperatively as a group".[1] The five elements that make teams function are:

- Common commitment and purpose
- Specific performance goals
- Complementary skills
- Commitment to how the work gets done
- Mutual accountability

A team has a specific purpose that it delivers on, has shared leadership roles, and has both individual and mutual accountabilities. Teams discuss, make decisions, and perform real work together, and they measure their performance by assessing their collective work products. Wisdom of Teams reference. This is very different from the classic **working group** in an organization (usually organized by functional area) in which there is a focused leader, individual accountabilities and work products, and a group purpose that is the same as the broader organizational mission. Think of the finance organization or a particular business unit in your company—these are, in effect, larger working groups that take on a piece of the broader organizational mission. They are organized under a leader, and their effectiveness is measured by its influence on others within the business (e.g., financial performance of the business.)

Exhibit 10.2 Finance Working Group Smart managers understand that not all of a company's influential relationships appear as part of the organization chart. Consider a publishing company that might have a lead finance head for each group, such as adult fiction, nonfiction, young adult, and children's book divisions. A finance team working group would help spread best practices and lead to more cohesive operations for the entire organization. (Credit: thetaxhaven /flickr / Attribution 2.0 Generic (CC BY 2.0))

So, what makes a team truly effective? According to Katzenbach and Smith's "Discipline of Teams," there are several practices that the authors have observed in successful teams. These practices include:

Establish urgency, demanding performance standards, and direction. Teams work best when they have a compelling reason for being, and it is thus more likely that the teams will be successful and live up to performance expectations. We've all seen the teams that are brought together to address an "important initiative" for the company, but without clear direction and a truly compelling reason to exist, the team will lose momentum and wither.

Select members for their skill and skill potential, not for their personality. This is not always as easy as it sounds for several reasons. First, most people would prefer to have those with good personalities and positive attitudes on their team in order to promote a pleasant work environment. This is fine, but make sure that those individuals have the skill sets needed (or the potential to acquire/learn) for their piece of the project. The second caveat here is that you don't always know what skills you need on a project until you really dig in and see what's going on. Spend some time up front thinking about the purpose of the project and the anticipated deliverables you will be producing, and think through the specific types of skills you'll need on the team.

Pay particular attention to first meetings and actions. This is one way of saying that first impressions mean a lot—and it is just as important for teams as for individuals. Teams will interact with everyone from functional subject-matter experts all the way to senior leadership, and the team must look competent and be perceived as competent. Keeping an eye on your team's level of **emotional intelligence** is very important and will enhance your team's reputation and ability to navigate stakeholders within the organization.

Set some clear rules of behavior. I have been through many meetings and team situations in which we have rushed through "**ground rules**" because it felt like they were obvious—and everyone always came up with the same list. It is so critical that the team takes the time up front to capture their own rules of the road in order to keep the team in check. Rules that address areas such as attendance, discussion, confidentiality, project approach, and conflict are key to keeping team members aligned and engaged appropriately.

Set and seize upon a few immediate performance-oriented tasks and goals. What does this mean? Have some quick wins that make the team feel that they're really accomplishing something and working together well. This is very important to the team's confidence, as well as just getting into the practices of working as a team. Success in the larger tasks will come soon enough, as the larger tasks are really just a group of smaller tasks that fit together to produce a larger deliverable.

Challenge the group regularly with fresh facts and information. That is, continue to research and gather information to confirm or challenge what you know about your project. Don't assume that all the facts are static and that you received them at the beginning of the project. Often, you don't know what you don't know until you dig in. I think that the pace of change is so great in the world today that new information is always presenting itself and must be considered in the overall context of the project.

Spend lots of time together. Here's an obvious one that is often overlooked. People are so busy that they forget that an important part of the team process is to spend time together, think together, and bond. Time in person, time on the phone, time in meetings—all of it counts and helps to build camaraderie and trust.

Exploit the power of positive feedback, recognition, and reward. Positive reinforcement is a motivator that will help the members of the team feel more comfortable contributing. It will also reinforce the behaviors and expectations that you're driving within the team. Although there are many extrinsic rewards that can serve as motivators, a successful team begins to feel that its own success and performance is the most rewarding.

Collaboration is another key concept and method by which teams can work together very successfully. Bringing together a team of experts from across the business would seem to be a best practice in any situation. However, Gratton and Erickson, in their article Eight Ways to Build Collaborative Teams, found that collaboration seems to decrease sharply when a team is working on complex project initiatives. In their study, they examined 55 larger teams and identified those with strong collaboration skills, despite the level of complexity. There were eight success factors for having strong collaboration skills:

- "Signature" relationship practices
- Role models of collaboration among executives
- Establishment of "gift" culture, in which managers mentor employees
- Training in relationship skills
- A sense of community
- Ambidextrous leaders—good at task and people leadership
- Good use of heritage relationships
- Role clarity and talk ambiguity[2]

As teams grow in size and complexity, the standard practices that worked well with small teams don't work anymore. Organizations need to think about how to make collaboration work, and they should leverage the above best practices to build relationships and trust.

CONCEPT CHECK 

1. What is the definition of a team?
2. Name some practices that can make a team more successful.

10.2 Team Development Over Time

2. How do teams develop over time?

If you have been a part of a team—as most of us have—then you intuitively have felt that there are different "stages" of team development. Teams and team members often start from a position of friendliness and excitement about a project or endeavor, but the mood can sour and the team dynamics can go south very quickly once the real work begins. In 1965, educational psychologist Bruce Tuckman at Ohio State University developed a four-stage model to explain the complexities that he had witnessed in team development. The original model was called Tuckman's Stages of Group Development, and he added the fifth stage of "Adjourning" in 1977 to explain the disbanding of a team at the end of a project. The four stages of the Tuckman model are:[3]

- Forming
- Storming
- Norming
- Performing
- Adjourning

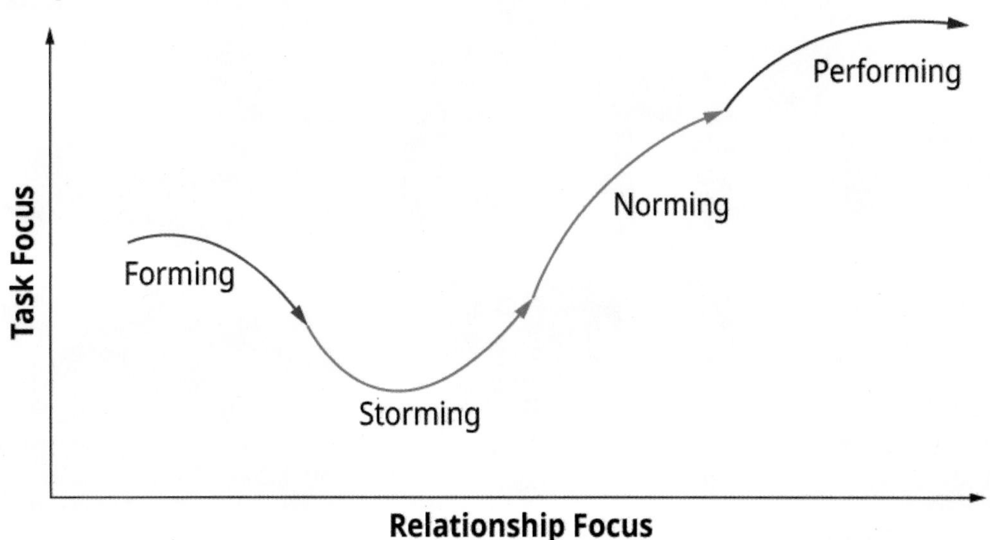

Exhibit 10.3 Tuckman's Model of Team Development Attribution: Copyright Rice University, OpenStax, under CC BY-NC-SA 4.0 license

The **Forming** stage begins with the introduction of team members. This is known as the "polite stage" in which the team is mainly focused on similarities and the group looks to the leader for structure and direction. The team members at this point are enthusiastic, and issues are still being discussed on a global, ambiguous level. This is when the informal pecking order begins to develop, but the team is still friendly.

The **Storming** stage begins as team members begin vying for leadership and testing the group processes. This is known as the "win-lose" stage, as members clash for control of the group and people begin to choose sides. The attitude about the team and the project begins to shift to negative, and there is frustration around goals, tasks, and progress.

Exhibit 10.4 The Storming Stage In the storming stage, protracted competition vying for leadership of the group can hinder progress. You are likely to encounter this in your coursework when a group assignment requires forming a team. (Credit: Gerald R. Ford School of Public Policy/ flickr/ Attribution 2.0 Generic (CC BY 2.0))

After what can be a very long and painful Storming process for the team, slowly the **Norming** stage may start to take root. During Norming, the team is starting to work well together, and buy-in to group goals occurs. The team is establishing and maintaining ground rules and boundaries, and there is willingness to share responsibility and control. At this point in the team formation, members begin to value and respect each other and their contributions.

Finally, as the team builds momentum and starts to get results, it is entering the **Performing** stage. The team is completely self-directed and requires little management direction. The team has confidence, pride, and enthusiasm, and there is a congruence of vision, team, and self. As the team continues to perform, it may even succeed in becoming a high-performing team. High-performing teams have optimized both task and people relationships—they are maximizing performance and team effectiveness. Katzenberg and Smith, in their study of teams, have created a "team performance curve" that graphs the journey of a team from a working group to a high-performing team. The team performance curve is illustrated in **Exhibit 10.5**.

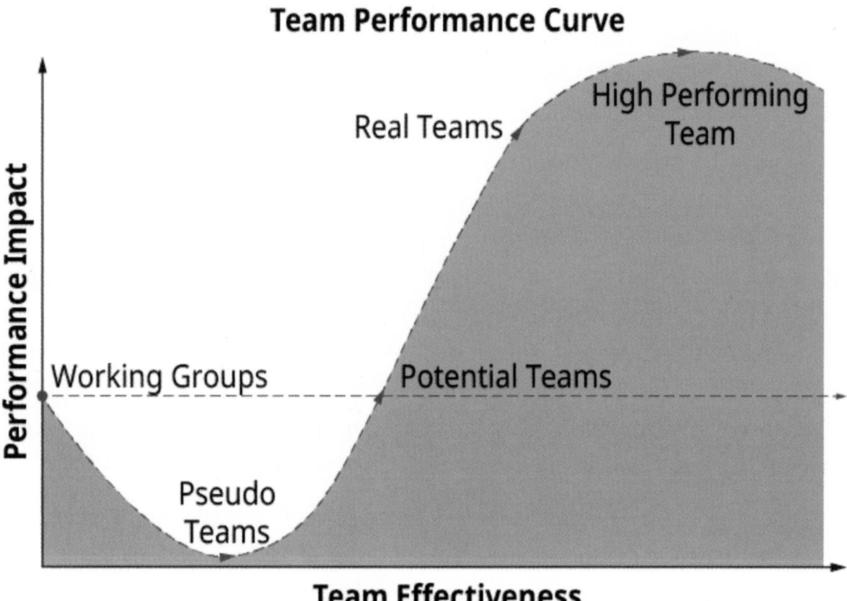

Exhibit 10.5 Team Performance Curve (Attribution: Copyright Rice University, OpenStax, under CC-BY 4.0 license)

The process of becoming a high-performance team is not a linear process. Similarly, the four stages of team development in the Tuckman model are not linear, and there are also factors that may cause the team to regress to an earlier stage of development. When a team member is added to the group, this may change the dynamic enough and be disruptive enough to cause a backwards slide to an earlier stage. Similarly, if a new project task is introduced that causes confusion or anxiety for the group, then this may also cause a backwards slide to an earlier stage of development. Think of your own experiences with project teams and the backslide that the group may have taken when another team member was introduced. You may have personally found the same to be true when a leader or project sponsor changes the scope or adds a new project task. The team has to re-group and will likely re-Storm and re-Form before getting back to Performing as a team.

CATCHING THE ENTREPRENEURIAL SPIRIT

Starting the Startup Team

Nothing is more exciting than a startup business. The enthusiasm is high, and people are excited about the new venture and the prospects that await. Depending on the situation, there may be funding that the startup has received from investors, or the startup could be growing and powering itself organically. Either way, the startup faces many different questions in the beginning, which will have a tremendous impact on its growth potential and performance down the road. One of the most critical questions that faces a startup —or any business for that matter—is the question of who should be on the team. Human capital is the greatest asset that any company can have, and it is an especially critical decision in a startup environment when you have limited resources and those resources will be responsible for building the company from ground up.

In Noam Wasserman's January 2012 HBSP article "Assembling the Startup Team," Wasserman asserts:

"*Nothing can bedevil a high-potential startup more than its people problems. In research on startup performance, venture capitalists attributed 65% of portfolio company failures to problems within the startup's management team. Another study asked investors to identify problems that might occur at their portfolio companies; 61% of the problems involved team issues. These problems typically result from choices that founders make as they add team members…"*

These statistics are based on people problems in startups, and it isn't quite clear what percent of larger company failures could be directly or indirectly attributed to people and team issues. I would imagine that the percentage is also significant. The impact of people problems and team issues in a startup organization that is just getting its footing and trying to make the right connections and decisions can be very significant. If you know anyone who has a company in startup mode, you may have noticed that some of the early team members who are selected to join the team are trusted family members, friends, or former colleagues. Once a startup company grows to a certain level, then it may acquire an experienced CEO to take the helm. In any case, the startup is faced early on with important questions on how to build the team in a way that will maximize the chance of success.

In "Assembling the Startup Team," the author refers to the three Rs: relationships, roles, and rewards as being key elements that must be managed effectively in order to avoid problems in the long term. Relationships refers to the actual team members that are chosen, and there are several caveats to keep in mind. Hiring relatives or close friends because they are trusted may seem like the right idea in the beginning, but the long-term hazards (per current research) outweigh the benefits. Family and friends may think too similarly, and the team misses the benefit of other perspectives and connections. Roles are important because you have to think about the division of labor and skills, as well as who is in the right roles for decision-making. The startup team needs to think through the implications of assigning people to specific roles, as that may dictate their decision power and status. Finally, defining the rewards can be difficult for the startup team because it essentially means that they are splitting the pie—i.e., both short-term and long-term compensation. For startup founders, this can be a very difficult decision when they have to weigh the balance of giving something away versus gaining human capital that may ultimately help the business to succeed. Thinking through the tradeoffs and keeping alignment between the "three Rs" is important because it challenges the startup team to think of the long-term consequences of some of their early decisions. It is easy to bring family and friends into the startup equation due to trust factors, but a careful analysis of the "three Rs" will help a startup leadership team make decisions that will pay off in the long term.

Discussion Questions

1. Why might it be a bad decision to hire someone for a key startup role based only on the fact that the person is close family or a friend? What are the potential tradeoffs to the business?
2. What does it mean for the "three Rs" to be in alignment? What is the potential risk of these not being in alignment? What could go wrong?

CONCEPT CHECK 

1. What are the four stages of team development?
2. What can cause a team to regress in its development?

10.3 Things to Consider When Managing Teams

3. What are some key considerations in managing teams?

For those of us who have had the pleasure of managing or leading a team, we know that it can feel like a dubious distinction. Leading a team is fulfilling—especially if the task or organizational mandate at hand is so critical to the organization that people are happy to be a part of the team that drives things forward. It can also be an exercise in frustration, as the charge is to lead a group composed of various individuals, which at various times will act both like a group and like a bunch of individuals. Managing teams is no small feat, and the most experience managers truly understand that success ultimately depends on their ability to build a strong and well-functioning team. In J.J. Gabarro's *The Dynamics of Taking Charge* (HBS Press, 1987, pp. 85–87), he quotes a manager who had successfully worked to turn around a number of organizations:[4]

"People have to want to work together; they have to see how to do it. There has to be an environment for it and that takes time. It's my highest priority right now but I don't write it down anywhere because it's not like other priorities. If I told corporate that building a team was my prime goal they'd tell me, so what? They'd expect that as part of making things better."

I love this quotation because it's so indicative of the state of most organizations today. The focus is on corporate goals and priorities—very task-driven and outcome-driven—but it is the people dynamics and how people work together in the company and in TEAMS that can make a real difference to the goals and outcome.

MANAGERIAL LEADERSHIP

Who Am I Managing?

Making the jump from individual contributor to manager is never easy, and it doesn't take long for a new manager to realize that what got him there is much different than what is needed to be successful in the future. Individual contributors that have been recently promoted would probably say that they have strong technical skills in their area, and that they were very good at doing what they were doing. In a more savvy organization that recognizes leadership competencies, individual contributors would probably say that they have strong technical skills AND that they showed some behaviors and potential to lead others. When new managers enter their new roles, they expect that they will be managing people—that is, the people on their teams. Few new managers fully realize that the challenge ahead is not just in managing their people, but in managing all the other stakeholders and constituencies that want to and need to weigh in.

One of the key challenges that faces new managers is figuring out to balance all of the multiple demands from both the team and the stakeholders and constituencies external to the team. Linda A. Hill, the Wallace Brett Donham Professor of Business Administration at Harvard Business School, states that "among all the challenges facing new managers, the need to reconcile different constituencies' expectations and interests is probably the most difficult." She asserts that the demands that the new manager's direct reports, his peers, his boss, and the company's customers place on the new manager will cause conflict at times. Having teams of their own, new managers may think that managing their direct reports is the most important role to play, even at the exclusion of managing other stakeholders. This is incorrect. A new manager needs to "manage his other consistencies just as carefully." ("Helping New Managers Succeed," Lauren Keller Johnson, *HBR* 2008).

Whenever I started a new role, I always created a quick stakeholder checklist for myself. This document is essentially a list of all the stakeholders (beyond the team I am managing) with whom I need to build a relationship in order to be successful. I listed the names of my boss, my boss's boss, my peers, and any other key influencers or internal customers from the business. This is a quick checklist of the people that

I need to immediately have a "meet and greet" with and then possibly even set up a regular meeting with at a certain cadence. I have learned over the years that each of these stakeholders will have some input and impact on my success, and the quicker and more effectively I engage them in the work my team is performing, the better the chance of my team's success. Some of the questions I will ask myself when figuring out my stakeholder list include:

- Whose support will I need?
- Who needs my support? What do they need from me or my team?
- Who can keep me and my team from being successful?
- What is my ongoing influencing strategy?

Some new managers will feel that these strategies for building stakeholder support are too "political" and they don't feel right. Trust me when I tell you that this is a necessary part of the new manager role, because now the role and the work call for greater interdependence and relation building in order to be successful. It is no longer just about individual technical skills, but more about building and managing relationships with people who will support you and your team to get your work done. So, if you are a new manager asking "Who am I managing?" ... the answer is EVERYONE.

Discussion Questions

1. Do you agree with the statement that "what got you there isn't what will make you successful in the future"? Why or why not?
2. Who would be on your stakeholder checklist? Which stakeholders are you already engaging and building relationships with?

In Linda A. Hill's *Harvard Business Review* article "Managing Your Team"[5] (HBR 1995), she discusses that managing a team means managing paradox. **Paradox** exists in the fact that teams have both individual and collective identities and goals. Each individual has goals and ideas as to what he wants to accomplish—on the project, in one's career, and in life. The team itself, of course, has goals and success metrics that it needs to meet in order to be successful. Sometimes these can be in conflict with each other. Competition may arise among team members, and a win-loss attitude may take place over a collaborative and problem-solving team dynamic. The team manager may need to step in to help integrate all of the individual differences to enable them to productively pursue the team goal. Therein lies the primary paradox—balancing individual differences and goals AND the collective identity and goals. Other paradoxes include:

- Fostering support AND confrontation among team members
- Focusing on performance AND learning and development
- Balancing managerial authority AND team member discretion and autonomy
- Balancing the Triangle of Relationships—manager, team, and individual

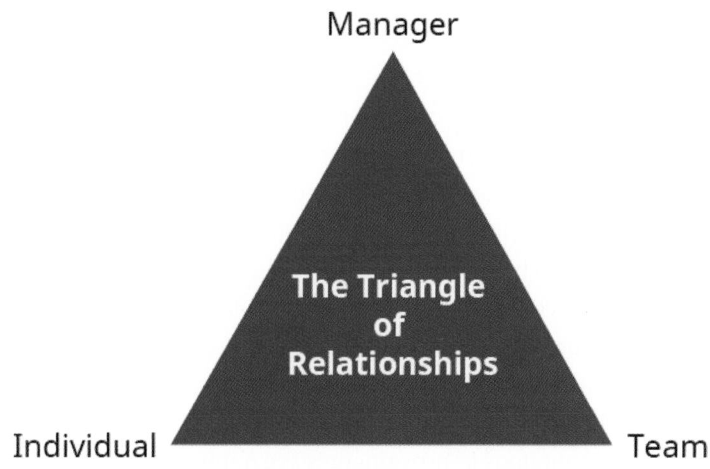

Exhibit 10.6 The Triangle of Relationships (Attribution: Copyright Rice University, OpenStax, under CC-BY 4.0 license)

Managing a team also means managing its boundaries. Managing the team's **boundaries**—or space between the team and its external forces, stakeholders, and pressures—is a delicate balance of strategy, stakeholder management, and organizational behavior. The team manager must serve, in part, as a buffer to these external factors so that they don't derail or distract the team from its goals. However, the manager must also understand enough about the external environment and have enough emotional intelligence to understand which forces, players, or situations must be synthesized within the team for its own benefit. Think about any medium or large-scale change initiative that you have been a part of in your career. Ideally, there is generally a vision for change and a level of sponsorship at the senior levels of the organization that is supposed to pave the way for that change to take root. The project team is officially "blessed" to kick off the team, create a charter, and identify the needed actions to drive the initiative to successful completion.

The dynamic that ensues after the kickoff is really what will determine the success of the team. There are numerous stakeholders in any organization, and many will be pro–change initiative, but others may be against the initiative—either due to lack of understanding or concerns about losing power, territory, etc. The external environment and business strategy may not be particularly well suited for a change initiative to take place, and so there may be the feeling of forces opposing the project team efforts. A strong team manager needs manage these "boundaries" with the organization to help the team navigate through and with the organizational complexities, goals, nuances, and egos that are a part of any organization. In Linda A. Hill's *Harvard Business Review* article "Exercising Influence," she states that "managers also need to manage relationships with those who are outside their team but inside their organizations.[6] To do so, they must understand the power dynamics of the larger organization and invest time and energy in building and maintaining relationship with those on who the team is dependent." It is also, in her view, "the manager's job, at a minimum, to educate other about organizational structures, systems, or politics that interfere with the team's performance." With all of the potential external influences on a team, managing a team's boundaries can truly mean the difference between success and failure.

The final element of managing a team is to manage the team itself—both the people elements and the process elements, or task at hand. The process-focused elements include managing the work plan to reach the overall goal, as well as the incremental meetings and milestones that are a part of the team's journey to reach the longer-term goal. Keeping the team focused on its objectives—beginning with setting agendas all the way to managing project tasks and celebrating milestones—assures that the team will stay on track. Projects and initiatives vary in size, scope, and complexity, and so the project management tools shouldn't be prescribed in a general sense. The important takeaway here is to choose an approach and a tool that works for the culture of the team and the organization, and that helps the team understand where they are, where they need to go, and what resources are a part of that process.

In managing the team members and interpersonal dynamics, there is the important element of selecting the right team members, shaping the team's norms and culture (how are decisions made, what are our rules, how do we manage conflict, etc.), and coaching the team. Defining the right skill sets, functions, perspectives, and expertise of the members will ensure a solid foundation. Helping the team to identify and formalize the ground rules for team engagement will help manage in the face of adversity or team conflict in the future. Finally, playing a role as a supportive coach will help both the individual team members and the group entity think through issues and make progress towards goals. A coach doesn't solve the individual/team problem, but helps the team think through a solution and move forward. Teams may need guidance on how to work things out within the team, and the manager must provide feedback and hold team members accountable for their behavior and contribution. Continuous improvement is the name of the game. A team may not start out as high performing, but they can certainly achieve that goal if everyone is focused on incremental improvements to communication, collaboration, and performance.

CONCEPT CHECK

1. Discuss the paradox(es) of a team.
2. How can a leader manage team boundaries?

10.4 Opportunities and Challenges to Team Building

4. What are the benefits of conflict for a team?

There are many sources of **conflict** for a team, whether it is due to a communication breakdown, competing views or goals, power struggles, or conflicts between different personalities. The perception is that conflict is generally bad for a team and that it will inevitably bring the team down and cause them to spiral out of control and off track. Conflict does have some potential costs. If handled poorly, it can create distrust within a group, it can be disruptive to group progress and moral, and it could be detrimental to building lasting relationships. It is generally seen as a negative, even though constructive conflicts and constructive responses to conflicts can be an important developmental milestone for a team. Some potential benefits of conflict are that it encourages a greater diversity of ideas and perspectives and helps people to better understand opposing points of view. It can also enhance a team's problem-solving capability and can highlight critical points of discussion and contention that need to be given more thought.

Another key benefit or outcome of conflict is that a team that trusts each other—its members and members' intentions—will arise from conflict being a stronger and higher-performing team. Patrick Lencioni, in his bestselling book *The Five Dysfunctions of a Team* (2002, p. 188), writes:[7]

"The first dysfunction is an absence of trust among team members. Essentially, this stems from their unwillingness to be vulnerable within the group. Team members who are not genuinely open with one another about their mistakes and weaknesses make it impossible to build a foundation for trust. This failure to build trust is damaging because it sets the tone for the second dysfunction: fear of conflict. Teams that lack trust are incapable of engaging in unfiltered and passionate debate of ideas. Instead, they resort to veiled discussions and guarded comments."

Lencioni also asserts that if a team doesn't work through its conflict and air its opinions through debate, team members will never really be able to buy in and commit to decisions. (This lack of commitment is Lencioni's third dysfunction.) Teams often have a fear of conflict so as not to hurt any team members' feelings. The downside of this avoidance is that conflicts still exist under the surface and may resurface in more insidious and back-channel ways that can derail a team. How can a team overcome its fear of conflict and move the team forward? Lencioni names a few strategies that teams can use to make conflict more common and productive. **Mining** is a technique that can be used in teams that tend to avoid conflict. This technique requires that one team member "assume the role of a 'miner of conflict'—someone who extracts buried disagreements within the team and sheds the light of day on them. They must have the courage and confidence to call out sensitive issues and force team members to work through them." **Real-time permission** is another technique to "recognize when the people engaged in conflict are becoming uncomfortable with the level of discord, and then interrupt to remind them that what they are doing is necessary." This technique can help the group to focus on the points of conflict by coaching the team not to sweep things under the rug.

The team leader plays a very important role in the team's ability to address and navigate successfully through conflicts. Sometime a leader will have the attitude that conflict is a derailer and will try to stymie it at any cost. This ultimately leads to a team culture in which conflict is avoided and the underlying feelings are allowed to accumulate below the surface of the discussion. The leader should, by contrast, model the appropriate behavior by constructively addressing conflict and bringing issues to the surface to be addressed and resolved by the team. This is key to building a successful and effective team.

There are a variety of individual responses to conflict that you may see as a team member. Some people take the constructive and thoughtful path when conflicts arise, while others may jump immediately to destructive behaviors. In *Managing Conflict Dynamics: A Practical Approach*, Capobianco, Davis, and Kraus (2005) recognized that there are both constructive and destructive responses to conflict, as well as active and passive responses that we need to recognize. In the event of team conflict, the goal is to have a constructive response in order to encourage dialogue, learning, and resolution.[8] Responses such as perspective taking, creating solutions, expressing emotions, and reaching out are considered active and constructive responses to conflict. Reflective thinking, delay responding, and adapting are considered passive and constructive responses to conflict. See **Exhibit 10.7** for a visual of the constructive responses, as well as the destructive responses, to conflict.

	Constructive	Destructive
Active	• Perspective taking • Creating solutions • Expressing emotions • Reaching out	• Winning • Displaying anger • Demeaning others • Retaliating
Passive	• Reflective thinking • Delay responding • Adapting	• Avoiding • Yielding • Hiding emotions • Self-criticizing

Exhibit 10.7 Responses to Conflict (Attribution: Copyright Rice University, OpenStax, under CC-BY 4.0 license)

In summary, conflict is never easy for an individual or a team to navigate through, but it can and should be done. Illuminating the team about areas of conflict and differing perspectives can have a very positive impact on the growth and future performance of the team, and it should be managed constructively.

CONCEPT CHECK 

1. What are some techniques to make conflict more productive?
2. What are some destructive responses to conflict?

10.5 Team Diversity

5. How does team diversity enhance decision-making and problem-solving?

Decision-making and problem-solving can be much more dynamic and successful when performed in a diverse team environment. The multiple diverse perspectives can enhance both the understanding of the problem and the quality of the solution. As I reflect on some of the leadership development work that I have done in my career, I can say from experience that the team activities and projects that intentionally brought diverse individuals together created the best environments for problem-solving. Diverse leaders from a variety of functions, from across the globe, at varying stages of their careers and experiences with and outside of the company had the most robust discussions and perspectives. **Diversity** is a word that is very commonly used today, but the importance of diversity and building diverse teams can sometimes get lost in the normal processes of doing business. Let's discuss why we need to keep these principles front of mind.

In the *Harvard Business Review* article "Why Diverse Teams are Smarter" (Nov. 2016), David Rock and Heidi Grant support the idea that increasing workplace diversity is a good business decision.[9] A 2015 McKinsey report on 366 public companies found that those in the top quartile for ethnic and racial diversity in management were 35% more likely to have financial returns above their industry mean, and those in the top quartile for gender diversity were 15% more likely to have returns above the industry mean. Similarly, in a global analysis conducted by Credit Suisse, organizations with at least one female board member yielded a higher return on equity and higher net income growth than those that did not have any women on the board.

Exhibit 10.8 The Benefits of Diversity for Teams Teams made up of diverse members tend to perform better than teams of similar backgrounds. Here, the Women of Color in Technology work on a project. The tech industry has been criticized for the lack of diversity among its ranks, and groups like the Women of Color in Technology are looking to change that. (Credit: WOCin Tech Chat/ flickr/ Attribution 2.0 Generic (CC BY 2.0))

Additional research on diversity has shown that diverse teams are better at decision-making and problem-solving because they tend to focus more on facts, per the Rock and Grant article.[10] A study published in the *Journal of Personality and Social Psychology* showed that people from diverse backgrounds "might actually alter the behavior of a group's social majority in ways that lead to improved and more accurate group thinking." It turned out that in the study, the diverse panels raised more facts related to the case than homogenous panels and made fewer factual errors while discussing available evidence. Another study noted in the article showed that diverse teams are "more likely to constantly reexamine facts and remain objective. They may also encourage greater scrutiny of each member's actions, keeping their joint cognitive resources sharp and vigilant. By breaking up workforce homogeneity, you can allow your employees to become more aware of their own potential biases—entrenched ways of thinking that can otherwise blind them to key information and even lead them to make errors in decision-making processes." In other words, when people are among homogeneous and like-minded (nondiverse) teammates, the team is susceptible to groupthink and may be reticent to think about opposing viewpoints since all team members are in alignment. In a more diverse team with a variety of backgrounds and experiences, the opposing viewpoints are more likely to come out and the team members feel obligated to research and address the questions that have been raised. Again, this enables a richer discussion and a more in-depth fact-finding and exploration of opposing ideas and viewpoints in order to solve problems.

Diversity in teams also leads to greater innovation. A Boston Consulting Group article entitled "The Mix that Matters: Innovation through Diversity" explains a study in which BCG and the Technical University of Munich conducted an empirical analysis to understand the relationship between diversity in managers (all management levels) and innovation. The key findings of this study show that:[11]

- The positive relationship between management diversity and innovation is statistically significant—and thus companies with higher levels of diversity derive more revenue from new products and services.
- The innovation boost isn't limited to a single type of diversity. The presence of managers who are either female or are from other countries, industries, or companies can cause an increase in innovation.
- Management diversity seems to have a particularly positive effect on innovation at complex companies—those that have multiple product lines or that operate in multiple industry segments.
- To reach its potential, gender diversity needs to go beyond tokenism. In the study, innovation performance only increased significantly when the workforce included more than 20% women in management positions. Having a high percentage of female employees doesn't increase innovation if only a small number of women are managers.
- At companies with diverse management teams, openness to contributions from lower-level workers and an environment in which employees feel free to speak their minds are crucial for fostering innovation.

When you consider the impact that diverse teams have on decision-making and problem-solving—through the discussion and incorporation of new perspectives, ideas, and data—it is no wonder that the BCG study shows greater innovation. Team leaders need to reflect upon these findings during the early stages of team selection so that they can reap the benefits of having diverse voices and backgrounds.

CONCEPT CHECK

1. Why do diverse teams focus more on data than homogeneous teams?
2. How are diversity and innovation related?

10.6 Multicultural Teams

6. What are some challenges and best practices for managing and working with multicultural teams?

As globalization has increased over the last decades, workplaces have felt the impact of working within multicultural teams. The earlier section on team diversity outlined some of the highlights and benefits of working on diverse teams, and a multicultural group certainly qualifies as diverse. However, there are some key practices that are recommended to those who are leading multicultural teams so that they can parlay the diversity into an advantage and not be derailed by it.

People may assume that communication is the key factor that can derail multicultural teams, as participants may have different languages and communication styles. In the *Harvard Business Review* article "Managing Multicultural Teams," the authors point out four key cultural differences that can cause destructive conflicts in a team.[12] The first difference is *direct versus indirect communication*. Some cultures are very direct and explicit in their communication, while others are more indirect and ask questions rather than pointing our problems. This difference can cause conflict because, at the extreme, the direct style may be considered offensive by some, while the indirect style may be perceived as unproductive and passive-aggressive in team interactions.

The second difference that multicultural teams may face is *trouble with accents and fluency*. When team members don't speak the same language, there may be one language that dominates the group interaction—and those who don't speak it may feel left out. The speakers of the primary language may feel that those members don't contribute as much or are less competent. The next challenge is when there are *differing attitudes toward hierarchy*. Some cultures are very respectful of the hierarchy and will treat team members based on that hierarchy. Other cultures are more egalitarian and don't observe hierarchical differences to the same degree. This may lead to clashes if some people feel that they are being disrespected and not treated according to their status. The final difference that may challenge multicultural teams is *conflicting decision-making norms*. Different cultures make decisions differently, and some will apply a great deal of analysis and preparation beforehand. Those cultures that make decisions more quickly (and need just enough information to make a decision) may be frustrated with the slow response and relatively longer thought process.

These cultural differences are good examples of how everyday team activities (decision-making, communication, interaction among team members) may become points of contention for a multicultural team if there isn't adequate understanding of everyone's culture. The authors propose that there are several potential interventions to try if these conflicts arise. One simple intervention is **adaptation**, which is working with or around differences. This is best used when team members are willing to acknowledge the cultural differences and learn how to work with them. The next intervention technique is **structural intervention**, or reorganizing to reduce friction on the team. This technique is best used if there are unproductive subgroups or cliques within the team that need to be moved around. **Managerial intervention** is the technique of making decisions by management and without team involvement. This technique is one that should be used sparingly, as it essentially shows that the team needs guidance and can't move forward without management getting involved. Finally, **exit** is an intervention of last resort, and is the voluntary or involuntary removal of a team member. If the differences and challenges have proven to be so great that an individual on the team can no longer work with the team productively, then it may be necessary to remove the team member in question.

There are some people who seem to be innately aware of and able to work with cultural differences on teams and in their organizations. These individuals might be said to have **cultural intelligence**. Cultural intelligence is a competency and a skill that enables individuals to function effectively in cross-cultural environments. It develops as people become more aware of the influence of culture and more capable of adapting their behavior to the norms of other cultures. In the *IESE Insight* article entitled "Cultural Competence: Why It Matters and How You Can Acquire It" (Lee and Liao, 2015), the authors assert that "multicultural leaders may relate better to team members from different cultures and resolve conflicts more easily.[13] Their multiple talents can also be put to good use in international negotiations." Multicultural leaders don't have a lot of "baggage" from any one culture, and so are sometimes perceived as being culturally neutral. They are very good at handling diversity, which gives them a great advantage in their relationships with teammates.

In order to help employees become better team members in a world that is increasingly multicultural, there are a few best practices that the authors recommend for honing cross-cultural skills. The first is to "broaden your mind"—expand your own cultural channels (travel, movies, books) and surround yourself with people from other cultures. This helps to raise your own awareness of the cultural differences and norms that you may encounter. Another best practice is to "develop your cross-cultural skills through practice" and experiential learning. You may have the opportunity to work or travel abroad—but if you don't, then getting to know some of your company's cross-cultural colleagues or foreign visitors will help you to practice your skills. Serving on a cross-cultural project team and taking the time to get to know and bond with your global colleagues is an excellent way to develop skills. In my own "past life," I led a global human resources organization, and my team included employees from China, India, Brazil, Hungary, the Netherlands, and the United States. We would have annual meetings as a global HR team, and it was so rewarding to share and learn about each other's cultures. We would initiate the week with a gift exchange in a "show and tell" format from our various countries, so that everyone would learn a little bit more about the cultures in which our fellow colleagues were working. This type of interaction within a global team is a great way to facilitate cross-cultural understanding and communication, and to sharpen everyone's cultural intelligence.

MANAGING CHANGE

Understanding Our Global Colleagues

If you are a part of a global team, there are so many challenges that confront you even before you talk about people dynamics and cultural differences. You first may have to juggle time zone differences to find an adequate meeting time that suits all team members. (I used to have a team call with my Chinese colleagues at 8 p.m. my time, so that I could catch them at 8 a.m. in China the next day!) Language challenges can also pose a problem. In many countries, people are beginning to learn English as one of the main business languages. However, as I have experienced, people don't always speak their language the same way that you might learn their language in a book. There are colloquialisms, terms, and abbreviations of words that you can't learn in a classroom—you need to experience how people speak in their native countries.

You also need to be open-minded and look at situations from the perspective of your colleagues' cultures, just as you hope they will be open-minded about yours. This is referred to as cultural intelligence. Whenever I would travel globally to visit my colleagues in other countries, I would see foods, traditions, situations, and behaviors that were very "foreign" to me. Although my first response to experiencing these might be to think "wow, that's strange," I would try to think about what some of my global colleagues find "foreign" when they come to visit me in the United States. For example, my travel to China would put me in contact with chicken feet, a very popular food in China and one that I dislike immensely. Whenever I was offered chicken feet, I would turn them down in the most polite way possible and would take another food that was offered instead. I started to wonder about what my Chinese colleagues thought about the food when they'd come to visit me in the United States. Every year, I would host a global HR meeting in the United States, and a bit part of that meeting was the camaraderie and the sharing of various meals together. When I asked my Chinese colleagues what foods they thought were unpleasant, they mentioned cheese and meat. I was surprised about the meat, and when I asked, they said that it wasn't the meat itself necessarily, but it was the giant portions of meat that Americans will eat that, to them, is pretty unappetizing. Again, it is so important to check yourself and your own culture every so often, and to think about those elements that we take for granted (e.g., gigantic meat portions) and try to look at them from the eyes of another culture. It really makes us smarter and better partners to our global colleagues around the world.

In the *HBR* article "Getting Cross-Cultural Teamwork Right," the author states that three key factors—mutual learning, mutual understanding, and mutual teaching—build trust with cross-cultural colleagues as you try to bridge cultural gaps. With mutual learning, global colleagues learn from each other and absorb the new culture and behaviors through listening and observation. In mutual understanding, you try to understand the logic and cultural behaviors of the new culture to understand why people are doing what they do. This, of course, requires suspending judgment and trying to understand and embrace the differences. Finally, mutual teaching involves instructing and facilitating. This means trying to bridge the gap between the two cultures and helping yourself and others see where different cultures are coming from in order to resolve misunderstandings.

Understanding and finding common ground with your global colleagues isn't easy, and it takes patience and continuous improvement. In the end, however, I think that you will find it one of the most rewarding and enlightening things you can do. The more we work to close the multicultural "gap" and make it a multicultural advantage, the better off we will be as professionals and as people.

Discussion Questions

1. What are some multicultural experiences that you've had in which you feel that there was a very wide gap between you and an individual from another culture? How did you handle it?
2. Has economic globalization helped people to bridge these cultural gaps? Why or why not?

Once you have a sense of the different cultures and have started to work on developing your cross-cultural skills, another good practice is to "boost your cultural metacognition" and monitor your own behavior in multicultural situations. When you are in a situation in which you are interacting with multicultural individuals, you should test yourself and be aware of how you act and feel. Observe both your positive and negative interactions with people, and learn from them. Developing "**cognitive complexity**" is the final best practice for boosting multicultural skills. This is the most advanced, and it requires being able to view situations from more than one cultural framework. In order to see things from another perspective, you need to have a strong sense of emotional intelligence, empathy, and sympathy, and be willing to engage in honest communications.

In the *Harvard Business Review* article "Cultural Intelligence," the authors describe three sources of cultural intelligence that teams should consider if they are serious about becoming more adept in their cross-cultural skills and understanding. These sources, very simply, are **head, body,** and **heart**. One first learns about the beliefs, customs, and taboos of foreign cultures via the **head**. Training programs are based on providing this type of overview information—which is helpful, but obviously isn't experiential. This is the cognitive component of cultural intelligence. The second source, the **body**, involves more commitment and experimentation with the new culture. It is this physical component (demeanor, eye contact, posture, accent) that shows a deeper level of understanding of the new culture and its physical manifestations. The final source, the **heart**, deals with a person's own confidence in their ability to adapt to and deal well with cultures outside of their own. Heart really speaks to one's own level of emotional commitment and motivation to understand the new culture.

The authors have created a quick assessment to diagnose cultural intelligence, based on these cognitive, physical, and emotional/motivational measures (i.e., head, body, heart).

Please refer to **Table 10.1** for a short diagnostic that allows you to assess your cultural intelligence.

Assessing Your Cultural Intelligence	
Give your responses using a 1 to 5 scale where 1 means that you strongly disagree and 5 means that you strongly agree with the statement.	
	Before I interact with people from a new culture, I wonder to myself what I hope to achieve.
	If I encounter something unexpected while working in a new culture, I use that experience to build new ways to approach other cultures in the future.
	I plan on how I am going to relate to people from a different culture before I meet with them.
	When I come into a new cultural situation, I can immediately sense whether things are going well or if things are going wrong.
	Add your total from the four questions above.

Table 10.1

Assessing Your Cultural Intelligence	
	Divide the total by 4. This is your ***Cognitive Cultural Quotient***.
	It is easy for me to change my body language (posture or facial expression) to suit people from a different culture.
	I can alter my expressions when a cultural encounter requires it.
	I can modify my speech style by changing my accent or pitch of voice to suit people from different cultures.
	I can easily change the way I act when a cross-cultural encounter seems to require it.
	Add your total from the four questions above.
	Divide the total by 4. This is your ***Cognitive Physical Quotient***.
	I have confidence in my ability to deal well with people from different cultures than mine.
	I am certain that I can befriend people of different cultural backgrounds than mine.
	I can adapt to the lifestyle of a different culture with relative ease.
	I am confident in my ability to deal with an unfamiliar cultural situation or encounter.
	Add your total from the four questions above.
	Divide the total by 4. This is your ***Emotional/Motivational Cognitive Quotient***.
Generally, scoring below 3 in any one of the three measures signals an area requiring improvement. Averaging over 4 displays strength in cultural intelligence.	
Adapted from “Cultural Intelligence,” Earley and Mosakowski, *Harvard Business Review*, October 2004	

Table 10.1

Cultural intelligence is an extension of emotional intelligence. An individual must have a level of awareness and understanding of the new culture so that he can adapt to the style, pace, language, nonverbal communication, etc. and work together successfully with the new culture. A multicultural team can only find success if its members take the time to understand each other and ensure that everyone feels included. Multiculturalism and cultural intelligence are traits that are taking on increasing importance in the business world today.[14] By following best practices and avoiding the challenges and pitfalls that can derail a multicultural team, a team can find great success and personal fulfillment well beyond the boundaries of the project or work engagement.

CONCEPT CHECK

1. What are some of the challenges of a multicultural team?
2. Explain the cultural intelligence techniques of head, body, and heart.

Key Terms

adaptation Technique of working with or around differences
boundaries Lines that make the limits of an area; team boundaries separate the team from its external stakeholders
cognitive complexity The ability to view situations from more than one cultural framework
collaboration The action of working with someone to produce or create something
cultural intelligence A skill that enables individuals to function effectively in cross-cultural environments
emotional intelligence The capability of individuals to recognize their own emotions and others' emotions
exit Technique of last resort—removal of a team member
Forming The first stage of team development—the positive and polite stage
ground rules Basic rules or principles of conduct that govern a situation or endeavor
head, body, and heart Techniques for becoming more adept in cross-cultural skills—learning about cultures (head), physical manifestations of culture (body), and emotional commitment to new culture (heart)
knowledge economy The information society, using knowledge to generate tangible and intangible values
managerial intervention Technique of making decisions by management and without team involvement
mining To delve in to extract something of value; a technique for generating discussion instead of burying it
Norming The third stage of team development—when team resolves its differences and begins making progress
paradox A self-contradictory statement or situation
Performing The fourth stage of team development—when hard work leads to the achievement of the team's goal
real-time permission A technique for recognizing when conflict is uncomfortable, and giving permission to continue
Storming The second stage of team development—when people are pushing against the boundaries
structural intervention Technique of reorganizing to reduce friction on a team
working group Group of experts working together to achieve specific goals; performance is made up of the individual results of all members

Summary of Learning Outcomes

10.1 Teamwork in the Workplace

1. What is a team, and what makes teams effective?

A team is defined as "people organized to function cooperatively as a group." Some of the characteristics of a team are that it has a common commitment and purpose, specific performance goals, complementary skills, commitment to how the work gets done, and mutual accountability.

Some of the practices that make a team effective are that they have a sense of urgency and direction; they set clear rules of behavior; they spend lots of time together; and they utilize feedback, recognition, and reward.

10.2 Team Development Over Time

2. How do teams develop over time?

Teams go through different stages of team development, which were coined in 1977 as Tuckman's Stages of Group Development by educational psychologist Bruce Tuckman. Tuckman's model includes these four stages: Forming, Storming, Norming, and Performing. A fifth stage, Adjourning, was added later to explain the disbanding and closure of a team at the end of a project.

Forming begins with team members being happy and polite as they get to know each other and understand the work they'll do together. Storming starts once the work is underway and the team is getting to know each other, and conflicts and project stress begins to seep in. During Norming, the team starts to set rules of the road and define how they want to work together. Performing means that the team is underway and is having some successes and gaining traction. This is definitely not a linear process. Teams can regress to earlier stages if there are changes in team members or work orders that cause disruption and loss of momentum and clarity.

10.3 Things to Consider When Managing Teams

3. What are some key considerations in managing teams?

Managing a team is often more complex than people would admit. Although a team and the team leader may be focused on the task or project work, it is actually the people dynamics and how the team works together that will make a real difference to the goals and outcomes. Managers need to remember that most of their time will be spent managing the people dynamics—not the tasks.

Managing teams also means a certain amount of paradox. A team has both individual and collective goals that need to be managed effectively. A manager needs to foster both team supportiveness and the ability to engage in conflict and confrontation. A team manager also needs to help the team with its boundaries and act as a buffer, a stakeholder manager, or a strategist when the situation calls for each. Exercising influence with key stakeholder groups external to the project group is one of the most critical functions in managing a team.

10.4 Opportunities and Challenges to Team Building

4. What are the benefits of conflict for a team?

Conflict during team interactions can feel like it derails progress, but it is one of the most important experiences that a team can have together. A team that can productively work through conflict will end up stronger, building more trust and being more open to sharing opinions. Team members will feel safe buying in and committing to decision-making as a team.

One of the other key benefits of conflict is that it encourages a greater diversity of ideas and perspectives, and it helps people to better understand opposing points of view. If a team doesn't work through conflict well and doesn't feel comfortable with the sharing and debating of ideas, it loses the opportunity to effectively vet ideas and potential solutions. The result is that the decision or solution will be limited, as team members haven't fully shared their concerns and perspectives.

10.5 Team Diversity

5. How does team diversity enhance team decision-making and problem-solving?

Decision-making and problem-solving is so much more dynamic and successful when performed in a diverse team environment. Much like the benefits of conflict, diversity can bring forward opposing points of view and different perspectives and information that might not have been considered if the team were more homogeneous. Diverse teams are thus made "smarter" by bringing together an array of information, sources, and experiences for decision-making.

Other research on diversity indicates that diverse teams excel at decision-making and problem-solving because they tend to focus more on facts. Studies indicate that diverse team members may actually sway the team's behavior to focus more on proven data—possibly because of the prospect of having to explain and back up one's perspectives if a conflict should erupt on the team. In a more homogenous team, there is more risk of "groupthink" and the lack of challenging of ideas.

10.6 Multicultural Teams

6. What are some challenges and best practices for managing and working with multicultural teams?

With the increase in globalization over the years, teams have seen the addition of multicultural individuals on their teams, who bring with them their own diverse backgrounds and perspectives. There are very positive aspects that result from the added diversity, as discussed in the previous questions. There are also challenges that we need to be aware of when we are managing these teams.

Challenges can arise from communication styles and accents, but can also appear in the form of decision-making norms and attitudes toward hierarchy. There are some team manager interventions that are best practices for addressing these challenges. There are also some best practices for building the cultural intelligence that will make the team more adept at understanding and dealing with differences among cultures.

Chapter Review Questions

1. What are the key differences between a team and a working group?
2. At what stage of team development does the team finally start to see results?
3. What can cause a team to digress to an earlier stage of team development?
4. What can a team leader do to manage the team's boundaries?
5. How does managing conflict help a team learn and grow?
6. What are some strategies to make conflict more productive?
7. Why are diverse teams better at decision-making and problem-solving?
8. Why do diverse teams utilize data more often than homogeneous teams?
9. What are some of the challenges that multicultural teams face?
10. What are the key sources of cultural intelligence?

Management Skills Application Exercises

1. Do you agree with Katzenbach and Smith's key practices that make teams effective? Why or why not? Which of these practices have you personally experienced? Are there any additional practices that you would add?
2. Have you ever been part of a team that made it through all four stages of team development? In which stage did the team remain the longest? In which stage did the team remain the shortest amount of time? What did you learn?
3. Why do you think it is so important to manage a team's boundaries? How can external stakeholders impact the function and performance of the team? Why is emotional intelligence such an important skill to have when managing a team?
4. In your experience, have you ever been in a situation in which conflict became a negative thing for a team? How was the conflict handled? How can a team manager ensure that conflict is handled constructively?
5. What is the difference between cultural intelligence and emotional intelligence? How can the cultural intelligence of a team improve performance? Have you ever been on a multicultural team that was high on cultural intelligence? How about a team that was low on cultural intelligence? What were the impacts?

Managerial Decision Exercises

1. You are a manager of a team that is taking a long time to move through the Storming stage. There are two individuals on the team that seem to be unproductive when dealing with conflict and are holding the team back. What would you do to help the team move through conflict management and begin Norming and Performing?
2. One of your direct reports on your team is very focused on his own personal development. He is a strong employee individually, but hasn't had as much experience working in a team environment on a project. He wants to do well, but isn't exactly sure how to work within this context. How would you instruct him?
3. You are leading a team responsible for a very important strategic initiative at your company. You have launched the project, and your team is very motivated and excited to move forward. You have the sense, however, that your sponsor and some other stakeholders are not fully engaged. What do you do to engage them?
4. You are the project manager of a cross-functional team project that was just approved. You have been given several good team members who are from different functions, but many of them think similarly and are unlikely to question each other on team decisions. You have the choice of keeping a homogeneous team that will probably have few team issues or building a diverse team that may well engage in conflict and take much longer to come to decisions. What choice would you make? What other information would you want to know to make the decision?
5. You are the director of a multicultural team with employees across the globe. Your team rarely has the opportunity to meet in person, but you have been given the budget to bring everyone together for a week-long global team meeting and team building. How would you structure the time together? What are some of the activities you would suggest to build stronger relationships among team members?

Critical Thinking Case

Diverse Teams Hold Court

Diverse teams have been proven to be better at problem-solving and decision-making for a number of reasons. First, they bring many different perspectives to the table. Second, they rely more on facts and use those facts to substantiate their positions. What is even more interesting is that, according to the *Scientific American* article "How Diversity Makes Us Smarter," simply "being around people who are different from us makes more creative, diligent, and harder-working."

One case in point is the example of jury decision-making, where fact-finding and logical decision-making are of utmost importance. A 2006 study of jury decision-making, led by social psychologist Samuel Sommers of Tufts University, showed that racially diverse groups exchanged a wider range of information during deliberation of a case than all-white groups did. The researcher also conducted mock jury trials with a group of real jurors to show the impact of diversity on jury decision-making.

Interestingly enough, it was the mere presence of diversity on the jury that made jurors consider the facts more, and they had fewer errors recalling the relevant information. The groups even became more willing to discuss the role of race case, when they hadn't before with an all-white jury. This wasn't the case because the diverse jury members brought new information to the group—it happened because, according to the author, the mere presence of diversity made people more open-minded and diligent. Given what we discussed on the benefits of diversity, it makes sense. People are more likely to be prepared, to be diligent, and to think logically about something if they know that they will be pushed or tested on it. And who else would push you or test you on something, if not someone who is different from you in perspective, experience, or thinking. "Diversity jolts us into cognitive action in ways that homogeneity simply does not."

So, the next time you are called for jury duty, or to serve on a board committee, or to make an important decision as part of a team, remember that one way to generate a great discussion and come up with a strong solution is to pull together a diverse team.

Critical Thinking Questions

1. If you don't have a diverse group of people on your team, how can you ensure that you will have robust discussions and decision-making? What techniques can you use to generate conversations from different perspectives?
2. Evaluate your own team at work. Is it a diverse team? How would you rate the quality of decisions generated from that group?

Sources: Adapted from Katherine W. Phillips, "How Diversity Makes Us Smarter," *Scientific American*, October 2014, p. 7–8.

11 Communication

Exhibit 11.1 (Credit: UC Davis College of Engineering/ flickr/ Attribution 2.0 Generic (CC BY 2.0))

Introduction

Learning Outcomes

After reading this chapter, you should be able to answer these questions:

1. Understand and describe the communication process.
2. Know the types of communications that occur in organizations.
3. Understand how power, status, purpose, and interpersonal skills affect communications in organizations.
4. Describe how corporate reputations are defined by how an organization communicates to all of its stakeholders.
5. Know why talking, listening, reading, and writing are vital to managing effectively.

EXPLORING MANAGERIAL CAREERS

John Legere, T-Mobile

The chief executive officer is often the face of the company. He or she is often the North Star of the company, providing guidance and direction for the entire organization. With other stakeholders, such as shareholders, suppliers, regulatory agencies, and customers, CEOs often take more reserved and structured approaches. One CEO who definitely stands out is John Legere, the CEO of T-Mobile. The unconventional CEO of the self-proclaimed “un-carrier” hosts a Sunday morning podcast called “Slow Cooker Sunday” on Facebook Live, and where most CEOs appear on television interviews in standard business attire, Legere appears with shoulder-length hair dressed in a magenta T-shirt, black jacket, and pink sneakers. Whereas most CEOs use well-scripted language to address business issues and competitors, Legere refers to T-Mobile's largest competitors, AT&T and Verizon, as "dumb and dumber."

In the mobile phone market, T-Mobile is the number-three player competing with giants AT&T and Verizon and recently came to an agreement to merge with Sprint. Of all the consolidation sweeping through the media and telecommunications arena, T-Mobile and Sprint are the most direct of competitors. Their merger would reduce the number of national wireless carriers from four to three, a move the Federal Communications Commission has firmly opposed in the past. Then again, the wireless market looks a bit different now, as does the administration in power.

John Legere and other CEOs such as Mark Cuban, Elon Musk, and Richard Branson have a more public profile than executives at other companies that keep a lower profile and are more guarded in their public comments, often restricting their public statements to quarterly investor and analyst meetings. It is likely that the personality and communication style that the executives reveal in public is also the way that they relate to their employees. The outgoing personality of someone such as John Legere will motivate some employees, but he might be seen as too much of a cheerleader by other employees.

Sometimes the unscripted comments and colorful language that Legere uses can cause issues with employees and the public. For instance, some T-Mobile employees in their call center admonished Legere for comments at a press event where he said Verizon and AT&T were "raping" customers for every penny they have. Legere's comments caused lengthy discussions in online forums such as Reddit about his choice of words. Legere is known for speaking his mind in public and often uses profanity, but many thought this comment crossed the line. While frank, open communication is often appreciated and leads to a clarity of message, senders of communication, be it in a public forum, an internal memo, or even a text message, should always think through the consequences of their words.

Sources: Tara Lachapelle, "T-Mobile's Argument for Sprint Deal is as Loud as CEO John Legere's Style," *The Seattle Times*, July 9, 2018, https://www.seattletimes.com/business/t-mobiles-argument-for-sprint-deal-is-as-loud-as-ceo-john-legeres-style/; Janko Roettgers, "T-Mobile CEO John Legere Pokes Fun at Verizon's Go90 Closure," *Variety*, June 29, 2018, https://variety.com/2018/digital/news/john-legere-go90-1202862397/; Rachel Lerman, "T-Mobile's Loud, Outspoken John Legere is Not Your Typical CEO," *The Chicago Tribune*, April 30, 2018, www.chicagotribune.com/business/sns-tns-bc-tmobile-legere-20180430-story.html; Steve Kovach, T-Mobile Employees Speak Out and Call CEO's Recent Rape Comments "Violent" and "Traumatizing"," *Business Insider*, June 27, 2014, https://www.businessinsider.com/t-mobile-employees-speak-out-legere-rape-comment-2014-6; Brian X. Chen, One on One: John Legere, the Hip New Chief of T-Mobile USA," *New York Times*, January 9, 2013, https://bits.blogs.nytimes.com/2013/01/09/one-on-one-john-legere-the-hip-new-chief-of-t-mobile-usa/.

We will distinguish between communication between two individuals and communication amongst several individuals (groups) and communication outside the organization. We will show that managers spend a majority of their time in communication with others. We will examine the reasons for communication and discuss the basic model of interpersonal communication, the types of interpersonal communication, and major influences on the communication process. We will also discuss how organizational reputation is defined by communication with stakeholders.

11.1 The Process of Managerial Communication

1. Understand and describe the communication process.

Interpersonal communication is an important part of being an effective manager:

- It influences the opinions, attitude, motivation, and behaviors of others.
- It expresses our feelings, emotions, and intentions to others.
- It is the vehicle for providing, receiving, and exchanging information regarding events or issues that concern us.
- It reinforces the formal structure of the organization by such means as making use of formal channels of communication.

Interpersonal communication allows employees at all levels of an organization to interact with others, to secure desired results, to request or extend assistance, and to make use of and reinforce the formal design of the organization. These purposes serve not only the individuals involved, but the larger goal of improving the quality of organizational effectiveness.

The model that we present here is an oversimplification of what really happens in communication, but this model will be useful in creating a diagram to be used to discuss the topic. Exhibit 11.2 illustrates a simple communication episode where a **communicator** encodes a message and a **receiver** decodes the message.[1]

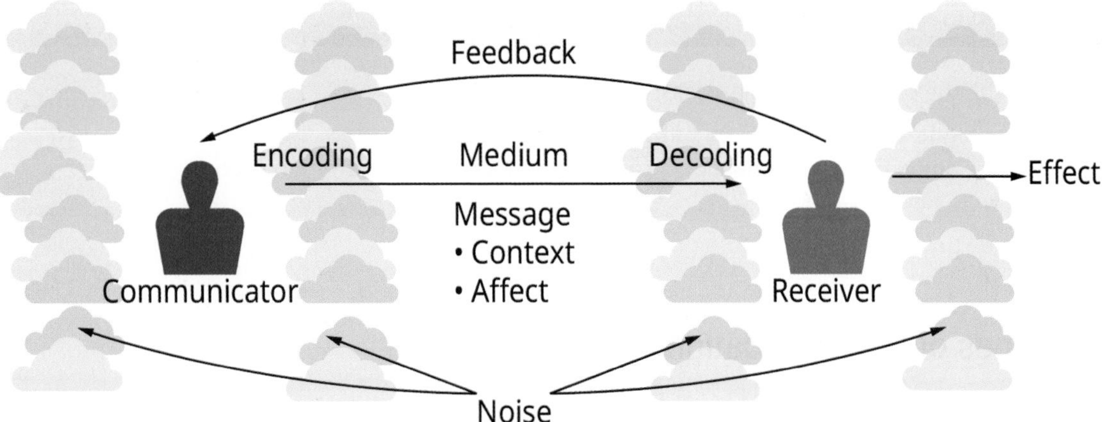

Exhibit 11.2 The Basic Communication Model (Attribution: Copyright Rice University, OpenStax, under CC-BY 4.0 license)

Encoding and Decoding

Two important aspects of this model are **encoding** and **decoding**. Encoding is the process by which individuals initiating the communication translate their ideas into a systematic set of symbols (language), either written or spoken. Encoding is influenced by the sender's previous experiences with the topic or issue, her emotional state at the time of the message, the importance of the message, and the people involved. Decoding is the process by which the recipient of the message interprets it. The receiver attaches meaning to the message and tries to uncover its underlying intent. Decoding is also influenced by the receiver's previous experiences and frame of reference at the time of receiving the message.

Feedback

Several types of feedback can occur after a message is sent from the communicator to the receiver. Feedback can be viewed as the last step in completing a communication episode and may take several forms, such as a verbal response, a nod of the head, a response asking for more information, or no response at all. As with the initial message, the response also involves encoding, medium, and decoding.

There are three basic types of feedback that occur in communication.[2] These are informational, corrective, and reinforcing. In informational feedback, the receiver provides nonevaluative information to the communicator. An example is the level of inventory at the end of the month. In corrective feedback, the receiver responds by challenging the original message. The receiver might respond that it is not her responsibility to monitor inventory. In reinforcing feedback, the receiver communicated that she has clearly received the message and its intentions. For instance, the grade that you receive on a term paper (either positive or negative) is reinforcing feedback on your term paper (your original communication).

Noise

There is, however, a variety of ways that the intended message can get distorted. Factors that distort message clarity are **noise**. Noise can occur at any point along the model shown in **Exhibit 11.2**, including the decoding process. For example, a manager might be under pressure and issue a directive, "I want this job completed today, and I don't care what it costs," when the manager does care what it costs.

CONCEPT CHECK 

1. Describe the communication process.
2. Why is feedback a critical part of the communication process?
3. What are some things that managers can do to reduce noise in communication?

11.2 Types of Communications in Organizations

2. Know the types of communications that occur in organizations.

In the communication model described above, three types of communication can be used by either the communicator in the initial transmission phase or the receiver in the feedback phase. These three types are discussed next.

Oral Communication

This consists of all messages or exchanges of information that are spoken, and it's the most prevalent type of communication.

Written Communication

This includes e-mail, texts, letters, reports, manuals, and annotations on sticky notes. Although managers prefer oral communication for its efficiency and immediacy, the increase in electronic communication is undeniable. As well, some managers prefer written communication for important messages, such as a change in a company policy, where precision of language and documentation of the message are important.

MANAGERIAL LEADERSHIP

Dealing with Information Overload

One of the challenges in many organizations is dealing with a deluge of emails, texts, voicemails, and other communication. Organizations have become flatter, outsourced many functions, and layered technology to speed communication with an integrated communication programs such as Slack, which allows users to manage all their communication and access shared resources in one place. This can lead to information overload, and crucial messages may be drowned out by the volume in your inbox.

Add the practice of "reply to all," which can add to the volume of communication, that many coworkers use, and that means that you may get five or six versions of an initial e-mail and need to understand all of the responses as well as the initial communication before responding or deciding that the issue is resolved and no response is needed. Here are suggestions to dealing with e-mail overload upward, horizontally, and downward within your organization and externally to stakeholders and customers.

One way to reduce the volume and the time you spend on e-mail is to turn off the spigot of incoming messages. There are obvious practices that help, such as unsubscribing to e-newsletters or turning off notifications from social media accounts such as Facebook and Twitter. Also consider whether your colleagues or direct reports are copying you on too many emails as an FYI. If yes, explain that you only need to be updated at certain times or when a final decision is made.

You will also want to set up a system that will organize your inbox into "folders" that will allow you to manage the flow of messages into groups that will allow you to address them appropriately. Your system might look something like this:

1. **Inbox**: Treat this as a holding pen. E-mails shouldn't stay here any longer than it takes for you to file them into another folder. The exception is when you respond immediately and are waiting for an immediate response.
2. **Today**: This is for items that need a response today.
3. **This week**: This is for messages that require a response before the end of the week.
4. **This month/quarter**: This is for everything that needs a longer-term response. Depending on your role, you may need a monthly or quarterly folder.
5. **FYI**: This is for any items that are for information only and that you may want to refer back to in the future.

This system prioritizes e-mails based on timescales rather than the e-mails' senders, enabling you to better schedule work and set deadlines.

Another thing to consider is your outgoing e-mail. If your outgoing messages are not specific, too long, unclear, or are copied too widely, your colleagues are likely to follow the same practice when communicating with you. Keep your communication clear and to the point, and managing your outbox will help make your inbound e-mails manageable.

Critical Thinking Questions

1. How are you managing your e-mails now? Are you mixing personal and school and work-related e-mails in the same account?
2. How would you communicate to a colleague that is sending too many FYI e-mails, sending too may unclear e-mails, or copying too many people on her messages?

Sources: Amy Gallo, Stop Email Overload, *Harvard Business Review*, February 21, 2012, https://hbr.org/2012/02/stop-email-overload-1; Barry Chingel, "How to beat email Overload in 2018", *CIPHER*, January 16, 2018, https://www.ciphr.com/advice/email-overload/; Monica Seely, "At the Mercy of Your Inbox? How to Cope With Email Overload", *The Guardian*, November 6, 2017, https://www.theguardian.com/small-business-network/2017/nov/06/at-the-mercy-of-your-inbox-how-to-cope-with-email-overload.

Nonverbal Communication

There is also the transformation of information without speaking or writing. Some examples of this are things such as traffic lights and sirens as well as things such as office size and placement, which connote something or someone of importance. As well, things such as body language and facial expression can convey either conscious or unconscious messages to others.

Exhibit 11.3 Body Language at a Meeting Your body language can send messages during a meeting. (Credit: Amtec Photos/ Flickr/ Attribution 2.0 Generic (CC BY 2.0))

Major Influences on Interpersonal Communication

Regardless of the type of communication involved, the nature, direction, and quality of interpersonal communication processes can be influenced by several factors.[3]

Social Influences

Communication is a social process, as it takes at least two people to have a communication episode. There is a variety of social influences that can affect the accuracy of the intended message. For examples, status barriers between employees at different levels of the organization can influence things such as addressing a colleague as at a director level as "Ms. Jones" or a coworker at the same level as "Mike." Prevailing norms and roles can dictate who speaks to whom and how someone responds. **Exhibit 11.4** illustrates a variety of communications that illustrate social influences in the workplace.

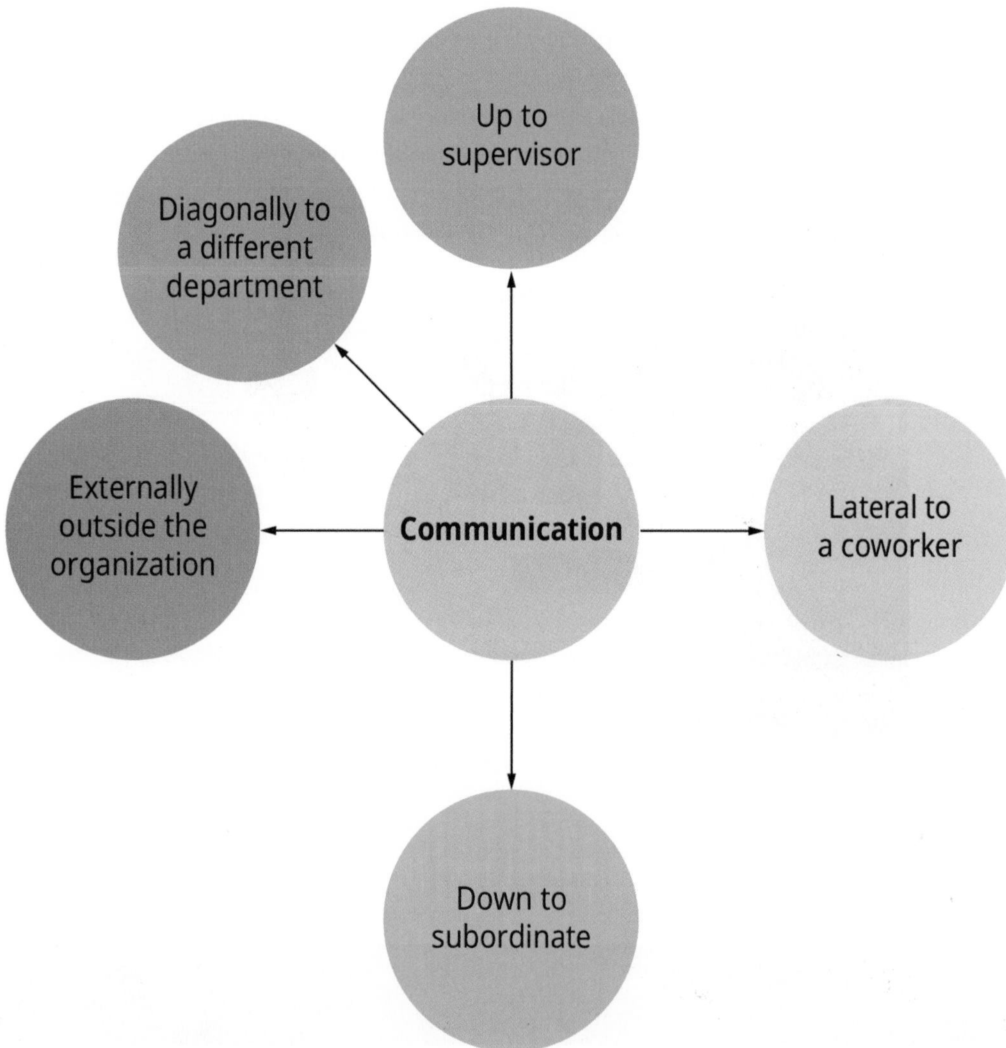

Exhibit 11.4 Patterns of Managerial Communication (Attribution: Copyright Rice University, OpenStax, under CC-BY 4.0 license)

Perception

In addition, the communication process is heavily influenced by perceptual processes. The extent to which an employee accurately receives job instructions from a manager may be influences by her perception of the manager, especially if the job instructions conflict with her interest in the job or if they are controversial. If an employee has stereotyped the manager as incompetent, chances are that little that the manager says will be taken seriously. If the boss is well regarded or seen as influential in the company, everything that she says may be interpreted as important.

Interaction Involvement

Communication effectiveness can be influenced by the extent to which one or both parties are involved in conversation. This attentiveness is called **interaction attentiveness** or **interaction involvement**.[4] If the intended receiver of the message is preoccupied with other issues, the effectiveness of the message may be diminished. Interaction involvement consists of three interrelated dimensions: responsiveness, perceptiveness, and attentiveness.

Organizational Design

The communication process can also be influenced by the design of the organization. It has often been argued to decentralize an organization because that will lead to a more participative structure and lead to improved communication in the organization. When messages must travel through multiple levels of an organization, the possibility of distortion can also occur, which would be diminished with more face-to-face communication.

Exhibit 11.5 Informal Communication in Organizations Smart managers understand that not all of a company's influential relationships appear as part of the organization chart. A web of informal, personal connections exists between workers, and vital information and knowledge pass through this web constantly. Using social media analysis software and other tracking tools, managers can map and quantify the normally invisible relationships that form between employees at all levels of an organization. How might identifying a company's informal organization help managers foster teamwork, motivate employees, and boost productivity? (Credit: Exeter/ flickr/ Attribution 2.0 Generic (CC BY 2.0))

CONCEPT CHECK 

1. What are the three major types of communication?
2. How can you manage the inflow of electronic communication?
3. What are the major influences on organizational communication, and how can organizational design affect communication?

11.3 Factors Affecting Communications and the Roles of Managers

3. Understand how power, status, purpose, and interpersonal skills affect communications in organizations.

The Roles Managers Play

In Mintzberg's seminal study of managers and their jobs, he found the majority of them clustered around three core management roles.[5]

Interpersonal Roles

Managers are required to interact with a substantial number of people during a workweek. They host receptions; take clients and customers to dinner; meet with business prospects and partners; conduct hiring and performance interviews; and form alliances, friendships, and personal relationships with many others. Numerous studies have shown that such relationships are the richest source of information for managers because of their immediate and personal nature.[6]

Three of a manager's roles arise directly from formal authority and involve basic interpersonal relationships. First is the **figurehead role**. As the head of an organizational unit, every manager must perform some ceremonial duties. In Mintzberg's study, chief executives spent 12% of their contact time on ceremonial duties; 17% of their incoming mail dealt with acknowledgments and requests related to their status. One example is a company president who requested free merchandise for a handicapped schoolchild.[7]

Managers are also responsible for the work of the people in their unit, and their actions in this regard are directly related to their role as a leader. The influence of managers is most clearly seen, according to Mintzberg, in the leader role. Formal authority vests them with great potential power. Leadership determines, in large part, how much power they will realize.

Does the leader's role matter? Ask the employees of Chrysler Corporation (now Fiat Chrysler). When Sergio Marchionne, who passed away in 2018, took over the company in the wake of the financial crisis, the once-great auto manufacturer was in bankruptcy, teetering on the verge of extinction. He formed new relationships with the United Auto Workers, reorganized the senior management of the company, and—perhaps, most importantly—convinced the U.S. federal government to guarantee a series of bank loans that would make the company solvent again. The loan guarantees, the union response, and the reaction of the marketplace, especially for the Jeep brand, were due in large measure to Marchionne's leadership style and personal charisma. More recent examples include the return of Starbucks founder Howard Schultz to reenergize and steer his company and Amazon CEO Jeff Bezos and his ability to innovate during a downturn in the economy.[8]

Popular management literature has had little to say about the liaison role until recently. This role, in which managers establish and maintain contacts outside the vertical chain of command, becomes especially important in view of the finding of virtually every study of managerial work that managers spend as much time with peers and other people outside of their units as they do with their own subordinates. Surprisingly, they spend little time with their own superiors. In Rosemary Stewart's (1967) study, 160 British middle and top managers spent 47% of their time with peers, 41% of their time with people inside their unit, and only 12% of their time with superiors. Guest's (1956) study of U.S. manufacturing supervisors revealed similar findings.

Informational Roles

Managers are required to gather, collate, analyze, store, and disseminate many kinds of information. In doing so, they become information resource centers, often storing huge amounts of information in their own heads, moving quickly from the role of gatherer to the role of disseminator in minutes. Although many business organizations install large, expensive management information systems to perform many of those functions, nothing can match the speed and intuitive power of a well-trained manager's brain for information processing. Not surprisingly, most managers prefer it that way.

As monitors, managers are constantly scanning the environment for information, talking with liaison contacts and subordinates, and receiving unsolicited information, much of it because of their network of personal contacts. A good portion of this information arrives in verbal form, often as gossip, hearsay, and speculation.[9]

In the disseminator role, managers pass privileged information directly to subordinates, who might otherwise have no access to it. Managers must decide not only who should receive such information, but how much of it, how often, and in what form. Increasingly, managers are being asked to decide whether subordinates, peers, customers, business partners, and others should have direct access to information 24 hours a day without having to contact the manager directly.[10]

In the spokesperson role, managers send information to people outside of their organizations: an executive makes a speech to lobby for an organizational cause, or a supervisor suggests a product modification to a supplier. Increasingly, managers are also being asked to deal with representatives of the news media, providing both factual and opinion-based responses that will be printed or broadcast to vast unseen audiences, often directly or with little editing. The risks in such circumstances are enormous, but so too are the potential rewards in terms of brand recognition, public image, and organizational visibility.[11]

Decisional Roles

Ultimately, managers are charged with the responsibility of making decisions on behalf of both the organization and the stakeholders with an interest in it. Such decisions are often made under circumstances of high ambiguity and with inadequate information. Often, the other two managerial roles—interpersonal and informational—will assist a manager in making difficult decisions in which outcomes are not clear and interests are often conflicting.

In the role of entrepreneur, managers seek to improve their businesses, adapt to changing market conditions, and react to opportunities as they present themselves. Managers who take a longer-term view of their responsibilities are among the first to realize that they will need to reinvent themselves, their product and service lines, their marketing strategies, and their ways of doing business as older methods become obsolete and competitors gain advantage.

While the entrepreneur role describes managers who initiate change, the disturbance or crisis handler role depicts managers who must involuntarily react to conditions. Crises can arise because bad managers let circumstances deteriorate or spin out of control, but just as often good managers find themselves in the midst of a crisis that they could not have anticipated but must react to just the same.[12]

The third decisional role of resource allocator involves managers making decisions about who gets what, how much, when, and why. Resources, including funding, equipment, human labor, office or production space, and even the boss's time, are all limited, and demand inevitably outstrips supply. Managers must make sensible decisions about such matters while still retaining, motivating, and developing the best of their employees.

The final decisional role is that of negotiator. Managers spend considerable amounts of time in negotiations: over budget allocations, labor and collective bargaining agreements, and other formal dispute resolutions. During a week, managers will often make dozens of decisions that are the result of brief but important negotiations between and among employees, customers and clients, suppliers, and others with whom managers must deal.[13]

CONCEPT CHECK 

1. What are the major roles that managers play in communicating with employees?
2. Why are negotiations often brought in to communications by managers?

11.4 Managerial Communication and Corporate Reputation

4. Describe how corporate reputations are defined by how an organization communicates to its stakeholders.

Management communication is a central discipline in the study of communication and corporate reputation. An understanding of language and its inherent powers, combined with the skill to speak, write, listen, and form interpersonal relationships, will determine whether companies succeed or fail and whether they are rewarded or penalized for their reputations.

At the midpoint of the twentieth century, Peter Drucker wrote, "Managers have to learn to know language, to understand what words are and what they mean. Perhaps most important, they have to acquire respect for language as [our] most precious gift and heritage. The manager must understand the meaning of the old definition of rhetoric as 'the art which draws men's hearts to the love of true knowledge.'"[14]

Later, Eccles and Nohria reframed Drucker's view to offer a perspective of management that few others have seen: "To see management in its proper light, managers need first to take language seriously."[15] In particular, they argue, a coherent view of management must focus on three issues: the use of rhetoric to achieve a manager's goals, the shaping of a managerial identity, and taking action to achieve the goals of the organizations that employ us. Above all, they say, "the essence of what management is all about [is] the effective use of language to get things done."[16] One of the things managers get done is the creation, management, and monitoring of corporate reputation.

The job of becoming a competent, effective manager thus becomes one of understanding language and action. It also involves finding ways to shape how others see and think of *you* in *your* role as a manager. Many noted researchers have examined the important relationship between communication and action within large and complex organizations and conclude that the two are inseparable. Without the right words, used in the right way, it is unlikely that the right reputations develop. "Words do matter," write Eccles and Nohria. "They matter very much. Without words we have no way of expressing strategic concepts, structural forms, or designs for performance measurement systems." Language, they conclude, "is too important to managers to be taken for granted or, even worse, abused."[17]

So, if language is a manager's key to corporate reputation management, the next question is obvious: How good are managers at using language? Managers' ability to act—to hire a talented workforce, to change an organization's reputation, to launch a new product line—depends entirely on how effectively they use management communication, both as a speaker and as a listener. Managers' effectiveness as a speaker and writer will determine how well they are able to manage the firm's reputation. And their effectiveness as listeners will determine how well they understand and respond to others and can change the organization in response to their feedback.

We will now examine the role management communication plays in corporate reputation formation, management, and change and the position occupied by rhetoric in the life of business organizations. Though, this chapter will focus on the skills, abilities, and competencies for using language, attempting to influence others, and responding to the requirements of peers, superiors, stakeholders, and the organization in which managers and employees work.

Management communication is about the movement of information and the skills that facilitate it—speaking, writing, listening, and processes of critical thinking. It's also about understanding who your organization is (identity), who others think your organization is (reputation), and the contributions individuals can make to the success of their business considering their organization's existing reputation. It is also about confidence—the knowledge that one can speak and write well, listen with great skill as others speak, and both seek out and provide the feedback essential to creating, managing, or changing their organization's reputation.

At the heart of this chapter, though, is the notion that communication, in many ways, is the work of managers. We will now examine the roles of writing and speaking in the role of management, as well as other specific applications and challenges managers face as they play their role in the creation, maintenance, and change of corporate reputation.

CONCEPT CHECK 

1. How are corporate reputations affected by the communication of managers and public statements?
2. Why is corporate reputation important?

11.5 The Major Channels of Management Communication Are Talking, Listening, Reading, and Writing

5. Know why talking, listening, reading, and writing are vital to managing effectively.

The major channels of managerial communication displayed in **Exhibit 11.6** are talking, listening, reading, and writing. Among these, talking is the predominant method of communicating, but as e-mail and texting increase, reading and writing are increasing. Managers across industries, according to Deirdre Borden, spend about 75% of their time in verbal interaction. Those daily interactions include the following.

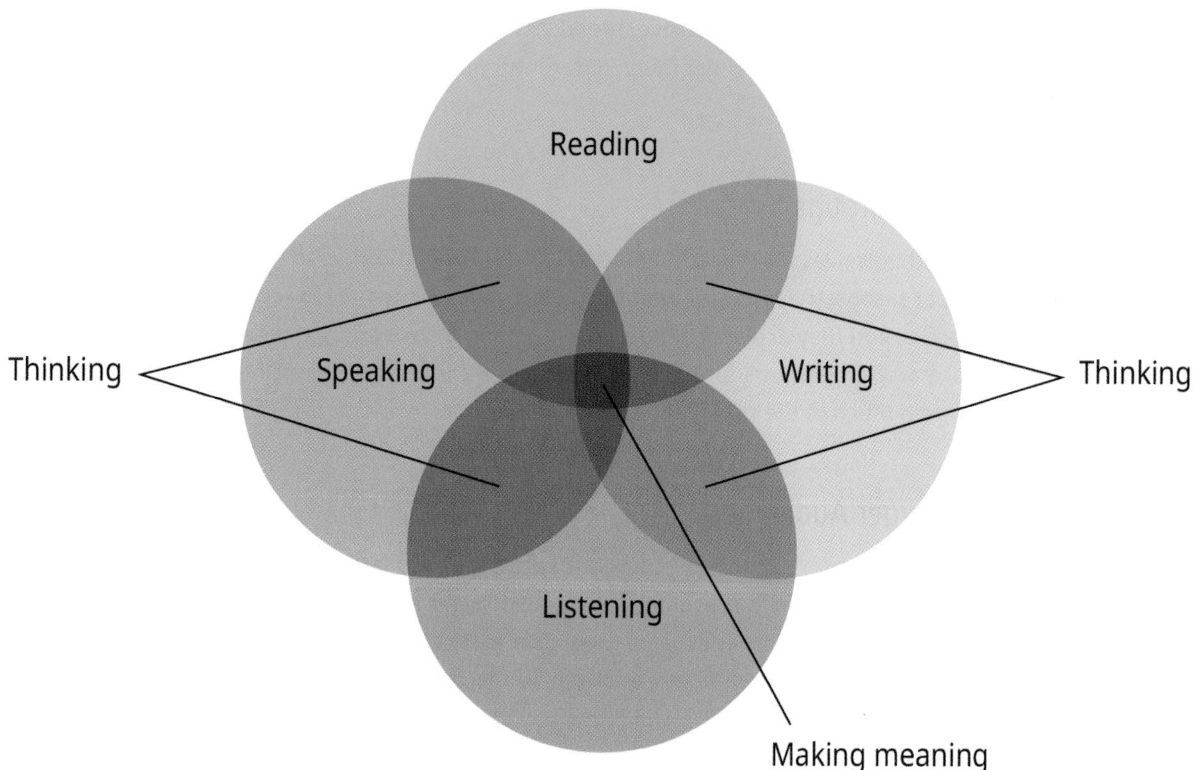

Exhibit 11.6 Reading, Writing, Speaking, and Listening: How They Help in Creating Meaning (Attribution: Copyright Rice University, OpenStax, under CC-BY 4.0 license)

One-on-One Conversations

Increasingly, managers find that information is passed orally, often face-to-face in offices, hallways, conference rooms, cafeterias, restrooms, athletic facilities, parking lots, and literally dozens of other venues. An enormous amount of information is exchanged, validated, confirmed, and passed back and forth under highly informal circumstances.

Telephone Conversations

Managers spend an astounding amount of time on the telephone these days. Curiously, the amount of time per telephone call is decreasing, but the number of calls per day is increasing. With the nearly universal availability of cellular and satellite telephone service, very few people are out of reach of the office for very long. The decision to switch off a cellular telephone, in fact, is now considered a decision in favor of work-life balance.

Video Teleconferencing

Bridging time zones as well as cultures, videoconferencing facilities make direct conversations with employees, colleagues, customers, and business partners across the nation or around the world a simple matter. Carrier Corporation, the air-conditioning manufacturer, is now typical of firms using desktop videoconferencing to conduct everything from staff meetings to technical training. Engineers at Carrier's Farmington, Connecticut, headquarters can hook up with service managers in branch offices thousands of miles away to explain new product developments, demonstrate repair techniques, and update field staff on matters that would, just recently, have required extensive travel or expensive, broadcast-quality television programming. Their exchanges are informal, conversational, and not much different than they would be if the people were in the same room.[18]

Presentations to Small Groups

Managers frequently find themselves making presentations, formal and informal, to groups of three to eight people for many different reasons: they pass along information given to them by executives, they review the status of projects in process, and they explain changes in everything from working schedules to organizational goals. Such presentations are sometimes supported by overhead transparencies or printed outlines, but they are oral in nature and retain much of the conversational character of one-to-one conversations.

Public Speaking to Larger Audiences

Most managers are unable to escape the periodic requirement to speak to larger audiences of several dozen or, perhaps, several hundred people. Such presentations are usually more formal in structure and are often supported by PowerPoint or Prezi software that can deliver data from text files, graphics, photos, and even motion clips from streaming video. Despite the more formal atmosphere and sophisticated audio-visual support systems, such presentations still involve one manager talking to others, framing, shaping, and passing information to an audience.

A series of scientific studies, beginning with Rankin, Nichols and Stevens, and Wolvin and Coakley, confirm: most managers spend the largest portion of their day talking and listening.[19] Werner's thesis, in fact, found that North American adults spend more than 78% of their communication time either talking or listening to others who are talking.

According to Werner and others who study the communication habits of postmodern business organizations, managers are involved in more than just speeches and presentations from the dais or teleconference podium. They spend their days in meetings, on the telephone, conducting interviews, giving tours, supervising informal visits to their facilities, and at a wide variety of social events.[20]

Exhibit 11.7 Public speaking Public speaking is often a terrifying but crucial skill for managers. (Credit: Mike Mozart/ flickr/ Attribution 2.0 Generic (CC BY 2.0))

Each of these activities may look to some managers like an obligation imposed by the job. Shrewd managers see them as opportunities to hear what others are thinking, to gather information informally from the grapevine, to listen in on office gossip, to pass along viewpoints that haven't yet made their way to the more formal channels of communication, or to catch up with a colleague or friend in a more relaxed setting. No matter what the intention of each manager who engages in these activities, the information they produce and the insight that follows from them can be put to work the same day to achieve organizational and personal objectives. "To understand why effective managers behave as they do," writes Kotter, "it is essential first to recognize two fundamental challenges and dilemmas found in most of their jobs." Managers must first figure out what to do, despite an enormous amount of potentially relevant information (along with much that is not), and then they must get things done "through a large and diverse group of people despite having little direct control over most of them."[21]

The Role of Writing

Writing plays an important role in the life of any organization. In some organizations, it becomes more important than in others. At Procter & Gamble, for example, brand managers cannot raise a work-related issue in a team meeting unless the ideas are first circulated in writing. For P&G managers, this approach means explaining their ideas in explicit detail in a standard one-to-three-page memo, complete with background, financial discussion, implementation details, and justification for the ideas proposed.

Other organizations are more oral in their traditions—3M Canada is a "spoken" organization—but the fact remains: the most important projects, decisions, and ideas end up in writing. Writing also provides analysis, justification, documentation, and analytic discipline, particularly as managers approach important decisions that will affect the profitability and strategic direction of the company.

Writing is a career sifter. If managers demonstrate their inability to put ideas on paper in a clear, unambiguous fashion, they're not likely to last. Stories of bad writers who've been shown the door early in their careers are legion. Managers' principal objective, at least during the first few years of their career, is to keep their name out of such stories. Remember: those who are most likely to notice the quality and skill in managers' written documents are the very people most likely to matter to managers' future.

Managers do most of their own writing and editing. The days when managers could lean back and thoughtfully dictate a letter or memo to a skilled secretarial assistant are mostly gone. Some senior executives know how efficient dictation can be, especially with a top-notch administrative assistant taking shorthand, but how many managers have that advantage today? Very few, mostly because buying a computer and printer is substantially cheaper than hiring another employee. Managers at all levels of most organizations draft, review, edit, and dispatch their own correspondence, reports, and proposals.

Documents take on lives of their own. Once it's gone from the manager's desk, it isn't theirs anymore. When they sign a letter and put it in the mail, it's no longer their letter—it's the property of the person or organization it was sent to. As a result, the recipient is free to do as she sees fit with the writing, including using it against the sender. If the ideas are ill-considered or not well expressed, others in the organization who are not especially sympathetic to the manager's views may head for the copy machine with the manager's work in hand. The advice for managers is simple: do not mail the first draft, and do not ever sign your name to a document you are not proud of.

Communication Is Invention

Without question, communication is a process of invention. Managers literally create meaning through communication. A company, for example, is not in default until a team of auditors sits down to examine the books and review the matter. Only after extended discussion do the accountants conclude that the company is, in fact, in default. It is their discussion that creates the outcome. Until that point, default was simply one of many possibilities.

The fact is managers create meaning through communication. It is largely through discussion and verbal exchange—often heated and passionate—that managers decide who they wish to be: market leaders, takeover artists, innovators, or defenders of the economy. It is only through communication that meaning is created for shareholders, employees, customers, and others. Those long, detailed, and intense discussions determine how much the company will declare in dividends this year, whether the company is willing to risk a strike or labor action, and how soon to roll out the new product line customers are asking for. Additionally, it is important to note that managers usually figure things out by talking about them as much as they talk about the things they have already figured out. Talk serves as a wonderful palliative: justifying, analyzing, dissecting, reassuring, and analyzing the events that confront managers each day.

Information Is Socially Constructed

If we are to understand just how important human discourse is in the life of a business, several points seem especially important.

Information is created, shared, and interpreted by people. Meaning is a truly human phenomenon. An issue is only important if people think it is. Facts are facts only if we can agree upon their definition. Perceptions and assumptions are as important as truth itself in a discussion about what a manager should do next.[22] Information never speaks for itself. It is not uncommon for a manager to rise to address a group of her colleagues and say, "The numbers speak for themselves." Frankly, the numbers never speak for themselves. They almost always require some sort of interpretation, some sort of explanation or context. Do not assume that others see the facts in the same way managers do, and never assume that what is seen is the truth. Others may see the same set of facts or evidence but may not reach the same conclusions. Few things in life are self-explanatory.

Context always drives meaning. The backdrop to a message is always of paramount importance to the listener, viewer, or reader in reaching a reasonable, rational conclusion about what she sees and hears. What's in the news these days as we take up this subject? What moment in history do we occupy? What related or relevant information is under consideration as this new message arrives? We cannot possibly derive meaning from one message without considering everything else that surrounds it.

A messenger always accompanies a message. It is difficult to separate a message from its messenger. We often want to react more to the source of the information than we do to the information itself. That's natural and entirely normal. People speak for a reason, and we often judge their reasons for speaking before analyzing what they have to say. Keep in mind that, in every organization, message recipients will judge the value, power, purpose, intent, and outcomes of the messages they receive by the source of those messages as much as by the content and intent of the messages themselves. If the messages managers send are to have the impact hoped for, they must come from a source the receiver knows, respects, and understands.

Managers' Greatest Challenge

Every manager knows communication is vital, but every manager also seems to "know" that she is great at it. Managers' greatest challenge is to admit to flaws in their skill set and work tirelessly to improve them. First, managers must admit to the flaws.

Larkin and Larkin write, "Deep down, managers believe they are communicating effectively. In ten years of management consulting, we have never had a manager say to us that he or she was a poor communicator. They admit to the occasional screw-up, but overall, everyone, without exception, believes he or she is basically a good communicator."[23]

Managers' Task as Professionals

As a professional manager, the first task is to recognize and understand one's strengths and weaknesses as a communicator. Until these communication tasks at which one is most and least skilled are identified, there will be little opportunity for improvement and advancement.

Foremost among managers' goals should be to improve existing skills. Improve one's ability to do what is done best. Be alert to opportunities, however, to develop new skills. Managers should add to their inventory of abilities to keep themselves employable and promotable.

Two other suggestions come to mind for improving managers' professional standing. First, acquire a knowledge base that will work for the years ahead. That means speaking with and listening to other professionals in their company, industry, and community. They should be alert to trends that could affect their company's products and services, as well as their own future.

It also means reading. Managers should read at least one national newspaper each day, including the *Wall Street Journal*, the *New York Times*, or the *Financial Times*, as well as a local newspaper. Their reading should include weekly news magazines, such as *U.S. News & World Report, Bloomberg's Business Week*, and the *Economist*. Subscribe to monthly magazines such as *Fast Company* and *Fortune*. And they should read at least one new hardcover title a month. A dozen books each year is the bare minimum on which one should depend for new ideas, insights, and managerial guidance.

Managers' final challenge is to develop the confidence needed to succeed as a manager, particularly under conditions of uncertainty, change, and challenge.

ETHICS IN PRACTICE

Disney and H-1B Visas

On January 30, 2015, The Walt Disney Company laid off 250 of its IT workers. In a letter to the laid-off workers, Disney outlined the conditions for receipt of a "stay bonus," which would entitle each worker to a lump-sum payment of 10% of her annual salary.

Of course, there was a catch. Only those workers who trained their replacements over a 90-day period would receive the bonus. One American worker in his 40s who agreed to Disney's severance terms explained how it worked in action:

> "The first 30 days was all capturing what I did. The next 30 days, they worked side by side with me, and the last 30 days, they took over my job completely. I had to make sure they were doing my job correctly."

To outside observers, this added insult to injury. It was bad enough to replace U.S. workers with cheaper, foreign labor. But to ask, let alone strong-arm, the laid-off workers into training their replacements seemed a bit much.

However unfortunate, layoffs are commonplace. But this was different. From the timing to the apparent neglect of employee pride, the sequence of events struck a nerve. For many, the issue was simple, and Disney's actions seemed wrong at a visceral level. As criticism mounted, it became clear that this story would develop legs. Disney had a problem.

For David Powers and Leo Perrero, each a 10-year information technology (IT) veteran at Disney, the invitation came from a vice president of the company. It had to be good news, the men thought. After all, they were not far removed from strong performance reviews—perhaps they would be awarded performance bonuses. Well, not exactly. Leo Perrero, one of the summoned workers, explains what happened next.

"I'm in the room with about two-dozen people, and very shortly thereafter an executive delivers the news that all of our jobs are ending in 90 days, and that we have 90 days to train our replacements or we won't get a bonus that we've been offered."

Powers explained the deflating effect of the news: "When a guillotine falls down on you, in that moment you're dead . . . and I was dead."

These layoffs and the hiring of foreign workers under the H-1B program lay at the center of this issue. Initially introduced by the Immigration and Nationality Act of 1965, subsequent modifications produced the current iteration of the H-1B visa program in 1990. Importantly, at that time, the United States faced a shortage of skilled workers necessary to fill highly technical jobs. Enter the H-1B visa program as the solution. This program permits U.S. employers to temporarily employ foreign workers in highly specialized occupations. "Specialty occupations" are defined as those in the fields of architecture, engineering, mathematics, science, medicine, and others that require technical and skilled expertise.

Congress limited the number of H-1B visas issued to 85,000 per year. That total is divided into two subcategories: "65,000 new H-1B visas issued for overseas workers in professional or specialty occupation positions, and an additional 20,000 visas available for those with an advanced degree from a U.S. academic institution." Further, foreign workers are not able to apply for an H-1B visa. Instead, a U.S. employer must petition on their behalf no earlier than six months before the starting date of employment.

In order to be eligible for an employer to apply a foreign worker for an H-1B visa, the worker needed to meet certain requirements, such as an employee-employer relationship with the petitioning U.S. employer and a position in a specialty occupation related to the employee's field of study, where the employee must meet one of the following criteria: a bachelor's degree or the foreign equivalent of a bachelor's degree, a degree that is standard for the position, or previous qualified experience within the specialty occupation.

If approved, the initial term of the visa is three years, which may be extended an additional three years. While residing in the United States on an H-1B visa, a worker may apply to become a permanent resident and receive a green card, which would entitle the worker to remain indefinitely.

U.S. employers are required to file a Labor Condition Application (LCA) on behalf of each foreign worker they seek to employ. That application must be approved by the U.S. Department of Labor. The LCA requires the employer to assure that the foreign worker will be paid a wage and be provided working conditions and benefits that meet or exceed the local prevailing market and to assure that the foreign worker will not displace a U.S. worker in the employer's workforce.

Given these representations, U.S. employers have increasingly been criticized for abuse of the H-1B program. Most significantly, there is rising sentiment that U.S. employers are displacing domestic workers in favor of cheaper foreign labor. Research indicates that a U.S. worker's salary for these specialty occupations often exceeds $100,000, while that of a foreign worker is roughly $62,000 for the very same job. The latter figure is telling, since $60,000 is the threshold below which a salary would trigger a penalty.

Disney faced huge backlash and negative press because of the layoffs and hiring of foreign workers. Because of this, Disney had communication challenges, both internally and externally.

Disney executives framed the layoffs as part of a larger plan of reorganization intended to enable its IT division to focus on driving innovation. Walt Disney World spokesperson Jacquee Wahler gave the following explanation:

> "We have restructured our global technology organization *to significantly increase our cast member focus on future innovation and new capabilities*, and are continuing to work with leading technical firms to maintain our existing systems as needed." (Italics added for emphasis.)

That statement is consistent with a leaked memo drafted by Disney Parks and Resort CIO Tilak Mandadi, which he sent to select employees on November 10, 2014 (not including those who would be laid off), to explain the rationale for the impending layoffs. The memo read, in part, as follows:

> "To enable a majority of our team to *shift focus to new capabilities*, we have executed five new managed services agreements to support testing services and application maintenance. Last week, we began working with both our internal subject matter experts and the suppliers to

> start transition planning for these agreements. We expect knowledge transfer to start later this month and last through January. Those Cast Members who are involved will be contacted in the next several weeks."

Responding to the critical *New York Times* article, Disney represented that when all was said and done, the company had in fact produced a net jobs increase. According to Disney spokesperson Kim Prunty:

> "Disney has created almost 30,000 new jobs in the U.S. over the past decade, and the recent changes to our parks' IT team resulted in a larger organization with 70 additional in-house positions in the U.S. External support firms are responsible for complying with all applicable employment laws for their employees."

New jobs were promised due to the restructuring, Disney officials said, and employees targeted for termination were pushed to apply for those positions. According to a confidential Disney source, of the approximately 250 laid-off employees, 120 found new jobs within Disney, 40 took early retirement, and 90 were unable to secure new jobs with Disney.

On June 11, 2015, Senator Richard Durbin of Illinois and Senator Jeffrey Sessions of Alabama released a statement regarding a bipartisan letter issued to the attorney general, the Department Homeland Security, and the Department of Labor.

> "A number of U.S. employers, including some large, well-known, publicly-traded corporations, have laid off thousands of American workers and replaced them with H-1B visa holders . . . . To add insult to injury, many of the replaced American employees report that they have been forced to train the foreign workers who are taking their jobs. That's just plain wrong and we'll continue to press the Administration to help solve this problem."

On July 7, 2015, *The Daily Caller* reported that the Department of Labor had commenced investigations of Disney after having received several formal complaints from laid-off workers. According to the report, Department of Labor personnel reached out to the former Disney workers to conduct phone interviews regarding names of displaced employees as well as typical salaries for the positions. Disney declined to comment on the report.

In response to request for comment on the communications issues raised by the Disney layoffs and aftermath, *New York Times* columnist Julia Preston shared the following exclusive analysis:

> "I would say Disney's handling of those lay-offs is a case study in how not to do things. But in the end it's not about the communications, it's about the company. Those layoffs showed a company that was not living up to its core vaunted family values and no amount of shouting by their communications folks could change the facts of what happened."

Questions for Discussion

1. Is it ethical for U.S. companies to lay off workers and hire foreign workers under the H-1B program? Should foreign countries restrict the hiring of foreign workers that meet their workforce requirements?
2. Discuss the internal and external communications that Disney employed in this situation. The examples here are of the formal written communications. What should Disney have been

communicating verbally to their employees and externally?

Sources: Preston, Julia, *Pink Slips at Disney. But First, Training Foreign Replacements*, The New York Times June 3, 2015, http://www.nytimes.com/2015/06/04/us/last-task-after-layoff-at-disney-train-foreign-replacements.html; Vargas, Rebecca, *EXCLUSIVE: Former Employees Speak Out About Disney's Outsourcing of High-Tech Jobs*, WWSB ABC 7 (Oct. 28, 2015), http://www.mysuncoast.com/news/local/exclusive-former-employees-speak-out-about-disney-s-outsourcing-of/article_d8867148-7d8c-11e5-ae40-fb05081380c1.html; Boyle, Mathew, *Ahead of GOP Debate, Two Ex-Disney Workers Displaced by H1B Foreigners Speak Out for First Time,* Breitbart.com, October 28, 2015, http://www.breitbart.com/big-government/2015/10/28/ahead-of-gop-debate-two-ex-disney-workers-displaced-by-h1b-foreigners-speak-out-for-first-time; Sandra Pedicini, *Tech Workers File Lawsuits Against Disney Over H-1B Visas*, *Orlando Sentinel*, published January 25, 2016, accessed February 6, 2016, available at http://www.orlandosentinel.com/business/os-disney-h1b-visa-lawsuit-20160125-story.html; U.S. Citizenship and Immigration Services, Understanding H-1B Requirements, accessed February 6, 2016, available at https://www.uscis.gov/eir/visa-guide/h-1b-specialty-occupation/understanding-h-1b-requirements; May, Caroline, Sessions, Durbin: Department Of Labor Has Launched Investigation Into H-1B Abuses, Breitbart.com (June 11, 2015), http://www.breitbart.com/big-government/2015/06/11/sessions-durbin-department-of-labor-has-launched-investigation-into-h-1b-abuses/; Stoltzfoos, Rachel, Feds Investigate Disney, HCL America Over January Layoffs, The Daily Caller (July 7, 2015), http://dailycaller.com/2015/07/07/feds-investigate-disney-hcl-america-over-january-layoffs/#ixzz41DY4x8Dy; Email from Julia Preston, National Immigration Correspondent, The New York Times, to Bryan Shannon, co-author of this case study, dated February 10, 2016.

CONCEPT CHECK

1. What are the four components of communication discussed in this section?
2. Why is it important to understand your limitations in communicating to others and in larger groups?
3. Why should managers always strive to improve their skills?

Key Terms

communicator The individual, group, or organization that needs or wants to share information with another individual, group, or organization.

decoding Interpreting and understanding and making sense of a message.

encoding Translating a message into symbols or language that a receiver can understand.

figurehead role A necessary **role** for a manager who wants to inspire people within the organization to feel connected to each other and to the institution, to support the policies and decisions made on behalf of the organization, and to work harder for the good of the institution.

interaction attentiveness/ interaction involvement A measure of how the receiver of a message is paying close attention and is alert or observant.

noise Anything that interferes with the communication process.

receiver The individual, group, or organization for which information is intended.

Summary of Learning Outcomes

11.1 The Process of Managerial Communication

1. Understand and describe the communication process.

The basic model of interpersonal communication consists of an encoded message, a decoded message, feedback, and noise. Noise refers to the distortions that inhibit message clarity.

11.2 Types of Communications in Organizations

2. Know the types of communications that occur in organizations.

Interpersonal communication can be oral, written, or nonverbal. Body language refers to conveying messages to others through such techniques as facial expressions, posture, and eye movements.

11.3 Factors Affecting Communications and the Roles of Managers

3. Understand how power, status, purpose, and interpersonal skills affect communications in organizations.

Interpersonal communication is influenced by social situations, perception, interaction involvement, and organizational design. Organizational communication can travel upward, downward, or horizontally. Each direction of information flow has specific challenges.

11.4 Managerial Communication and Corporate Reputation

4. Describe how corporate reputations are defined by how an organization communicates to all of its stakeholders.

It is important for managers to understand what your organization stands for (identity), what others think your organization is (reputation), and the contributions individuals can make to the success of the business considering their organization's existing reputation. It is also about confidence—the knowledge that one can speak and write well, listen with great skill as others speak, and both seek out and provide the feedback essential to creating, managing, or changing their organization's reputation.

11.5 The Major Channels of Management Communication Are Talking, Listening, Reading, and Writing

5. Describe the roles that managers perform in organizations.

There are special communication roles that can be identified. Managers may serve as gatekeepers, liaisons, or opinion leaders. They can also assume some combination of these roles. It is important to recognize that communication processes involve people in different functions and that all functions need to operate effectively to achieve organizational objectives.

Chapter Review Questions

1. Describe the communication process.
2. Why is feedback a critical part of the communication process?
3. What are some things that managers can do to reduce noise in communication?
4. Compare and contrast the three primary forms of interpersonal communication.
5. Describe the various individual communication roles in organizations.
6. How can managers better manage their effectiveness by managing e-mail communication?
7. Which communication roles are most important in facilitating managerial effectiveness?
8. Identify barriers to effective communication.
9. How can barriers to effective communication be overcome by managers?

Management Skills Application Exercises

1. The e-mails below are not written as clearly or concisely as they could be. In addition, they may have problems in organization or tone or mechanical errors. Rewrite them so they are appropriate for the audience and their purpose. Correct grammatical and mechanical errors. Finally, add a subject line to each.

   E-Mail 1

   To: Employees of The Enormously Successful Corporation

   From: CEO of The Enormously Successful Corporation

   Subject:

   Stop bringing bottled soft drinks, juices and plastic straws to work. Its an environment problem that increases our waste and the quality of our water is great. People don't realize how much wasted energy goes into shipping all that stuff around, and plastic bottles, aluminum cans and straws are ruining our oceans and filling land fills. Have you seen the floating island of waste in the Pacific Ocean? Some of this stuff comes from other countries like Canada Dry I think is from canada and we are taking there water and Canadians will be thirsty. Fancy drinks isn't as good as the water we have and tastes better anyway.

   E-Mail 2

   To: All Employees

   From: Management

   Subject:

   Our Committee to Improve Inter-Office Communication has decided that there needs to be an update and revision of our policy on emailing messages to and from those who work with us as employees of this company. The following are the results of the committee's decisions, and constitute recommendations for the improvement of every aspect of email communication.

   1. Too much wordiness means people have to read the same thing over and over repeatedly, time after time. Eliminating unnecessary words, emails can be made to be shorter and more to the point, making them concise and taking less time to read.
   2. You are only allowed to send and receive messages between 8:30AM east coat time and 4:30PM east coast time. You are also not allowed to read e-mails outside of these times. We know that for those of you on the west coast or travelling internationally it will reduce the time that you are allowed to attend to e-mail, but we need this to get it under control.
   3. You are only allowed to have up to 3 recipients on each e-mail. If more people need to be informed it is up to the people to inform them.

2. Write a self-evaluation that focuses specifically on your class participation in this course. Making comments during class allows you to improve your ability to speak extemporaneously, which is exactly what you will have to do in all kinds of business situations (e.g., meetings, asking questions at presentations, one-on-one conversations). Thus, write a short memo (two or three paragraphs) in which you describe the frequency with which you make comments in class, the nature of those comments, and what is easy and difficult for you when it comes to speaking up in class.
   If you have made few (or no) comments during class, this is a time for us to come up with a plan to help you overcome your shyness. Our experience is that as soon as a person talks in front of a group once or twice, it becomes much easier—so we need to come up with a way to help you break the ice.
   Finally, please comment on what you see as the strengths and weaknesses of your discussions and presentations in this class.
3. Refer to the photo in **Exhibit 11.3**. Comment on the body language exhibited by each person at the meeting and how engaged they are in the communication.
4. In the movie *The Martian*, astronaut Mark Watney (played by Matt Damon) is stranded on Mars with limited ability to communicate with mission control. Watney holds up questions to a camera that can transmit photographs of his questions, and mission control could respond by pointing the camera at a "yes" or "no" card with the camera. Eventually, they are able to exchange "text" messages but no voice exchanges. Also, there is a significant time delay between the sending and receipt of the messages. Which part of the communication process would have to be addressed to ensure that the encoding of the messages, the decoding of the messages, and that noise is minimized by Watney and mission control?

Managerial Decision Exercises

1. Ginni Rometty is the CEO of IBM. Shortly after taking on the role of CEO and being frustrated by the progress and sales performance, Rometty released a five-minute video to all 400,000 plus IBM employees criticizing the lack of securing deals to competitors and lashed out at the sales organization for poor sales in the preceding quarter. Six months later, Rometty sent another critical message, this time via e-mail. How effective will the video and e-mail be in communicating with employees? How should she follow up to these messages?
2. Social media, such as Facebook, is now widespread. Place yourself as a manager that has just received a "friend" request from one of your direct reports. Do you accept, reject, or ignore the request? Why, and what additional communication would you have regarding this with the employee?
3. During a cross-functional meeting, one of the attendees who reports to a manager who is also at the meeting accuses one of your reports of not being fit for the position she is in. You disagree and feel that your report is a good fit for her role. How do you handle this?

Critical Thinking Case

Facebook, Inc.

Facebook has been in the news with criticism of its privacy policies, sharing customer information with Fusion GPS, and criticism regarding the attempts to influence the 2016 election. In March 2014, Facebook released a study entitled "Experimental evidence of massive-scale emotional contagion through social networks." It was published in the *Proceedings of the National Academy of Sciences (PNAS)*, a prestigious, peer-reviewed scientific journal. The paper explains how social media can readily transfer emotional states from person to person through Facebook's News Feed platform. Facebook conducted an experiment on members to see how people would respond to changes in a percentage of both positive and negative posts. The results suggest that emotional contagion does occur online and that users' positive expressions can generate positive reaction, while, in turn, negative expression can generate negative reaction.

Facebook has two separate value propositions aimed at two different markets with entirely different goals.

Originally, Facebook's main market was its end users—people looking to connect with family and friends. At first, it was aimed only at college students at a handful of elite schools. The site is now open to anyone with an Internet connection. Users can share status updates and photographs with friends and family. And all of this comes at no cost to the users.

Facebook's other major market is advertisers, who buy information about Facebook's users. The company regularly gathers data about page views and browsing behavior of users in order to display targeted advertisements to users for the benefit of its advertising partners.

The value proposition of the Facebook News Feed experiment was to determine whether emotional manipulation would be possible through the use of social networks. This clearly could be of great value to one of Facebook's target audiences—its advertisers.

The results suggest that the emotions of friends on social networks influence our own emotions, thereby demonstrating emotional contagion via social networks. Emotional contagion is the tendency to feel and express emotions similar to and influenced by those of others. Originally, it was studied by psychologists as the transference of emotions between two people.

According to Sandra Collins, a social psychologist and University of Notre Dame professor of management, it is clearly unethical to conduct psychological experiments without the informed consent of the test subjects. While tests do not always measure what the people conducting the tests claim, the subjects need to at least know that they are, indeed, part of a test. The subjects of this test on Facebook were not explicitly informed that they were participating in an emotional contagion experiment. Facebook did not obtain informed consent as it is generally defined by researchers, nor did it allow participants to opt out.

When information about the experiment was released, the media response was overwhelmingly critical. Tech blogs, newspapers, and media reports reacted quickly.

Josh Constine of TechCrunch wrote:

> " . . . there is some material danger to experiments that depress people. Some people who are at risk of depression were almost surely part of Facebook's study group that were shown a more depressing feed, which could be considered dangerous. Facebook will endure a whole new level of backlash if any of those participants were found to have committed suicide or had other depression-related outcomes after the study."

The *New York Times* quoted Brian Blau, a technology analyst with the research firm Gartner, "Facebook didn't do anything illegal, but they didn't do right by their customers. Doing psychological testing on people crosses the line." Facebook should have informed its users, he said. "They keep on pushing the boundaries, and this is one of the reasons people are upset."

While some of the researchers have since expressed some regret about the experiment, Facebook as a company was unapologetic about the experiment. The company maintained that it received consent from its users through its terms of service. A Facebook spokesperson defended the research, saying, "We do research to improve our services and make the content people see on Facebook as relevant and engaging as possible. . . . We carefully consider what research we do and have a strong internal review process."

With the more recent events, Facebook is changing the privacy settings but still collects an enormous amount of information about its users and can use that information to manipulate what users see. Additionally, these items are not listed on Facebook's main terms of service page. Users must click on a link inside a different set of terms to arrive at the data policy page, making these terms onerous to find. This positioning raises questions about how Facebook will employ its users' behaviors in the future.

Critical Thinking Questions

1. How should Facebook respond to the 2014 research situation? How could an earlier response have helped the company avoid the 2018 controversies and keep the trust of its users?
2. Should the company promise to never again conduct a survey of this sort? Should it go even further and explicitly ban research intended to manipulate the responses of its users?
3. How can Facebook balance the concerns of its users with the necessity of generating revenue through advertising?
4. What processes or structures should Facebook establish to make sure it does not encounter these issues again?
5. Respond in writing to the issues presented in this case by preparing two documents: a communication strategy memo and a professional business letter to advertisers.

Sources: Kramer, Adam; Guillory, Jamie; and Hancock, Jeffrey, "Experimental evidence of massive scale emotional contagion through social networks," *PNAS (Proceedings of the National Academy of Sciences of the United States of America*). March 25, 2014 http://www.pnas.org/content/111/24/8788.full; Laja, Peep. "Useful Value Proposition Examples (and How to Create a Good One), *ConversionXL*, 2015 http://conversionxl.com/value-proposition-examples-how-to-create/; Yadav, Sid. "Facebook - The Complete Biography," Mashable, Aug. 25, 2006. http://mashable.com/2006/08/25/facebook-profile/#orb9TmeYHiqK; Felix, Samantha, "This Is How Facebook Is Tracking Your Internet Activity," *Business Insider*, Sept. 9, 2012 http://www.businessinsider.com/this-is-how-facebook-is-tracking-your-internet-activity-2012-9;

12

Leadership

Exhibit 12.1 (Credit: Tambako the Jaguar/ flickr/ Attribution 2.0 Generic (CC BY 2.0))

Introduction

Learning Outcomes

After reading this chapter, you should be able to answer these questions:

1. What is the nature of leadership and the leadership process?
2. What are the processes associated with people coming to leadership positions?
3. How do leaders influence and move their followers to action?
4. What are the trait perspectives on leadership?
5. What are the behavioral perspectives on leadership?
6. What are the situational perspectives on leadership?
7. What does the concept "substitute for leadership" mean?
8. What are the characteristics of transactional, transformational, and charismatic leadership?
9. How do different approaches and styles of leadership impact what is needed now?

EXPLORING MANAGERIAL CAREERS

John Arroyo: Springfield Sea Lions

John Arroyo is thrilled with his new position as general manager of the Springfield Sea Lions, a minor league baseball team in. Arroyo has been a baseball fan all of his life, and now his diligent work and his degree in sports management are paying off.

Arroyo knew he had a hard act to follow. The general manager whom John replaced, "T.J." Grevin, was a much-loved old-timer who had been with the Sea Lions since their inception 14 years ago. John knew it would be difficult for whoever followed T.J., but he didn't realize how ostracized and powerless he would feel. He tried a pep talk: "I'm the general manager—the CEO of this ball club! In time, the staff *will* respect me." [Not a very good pep talk!]

After his first season ends, Arroyo is discouraged. Ticket and concession sales are down, and some long-time employees are rumored to be thinking about leaving. If John doesn't turn things around, he knows his tenure with the Sea Lions will be short.

Questions: Is John correct in assuming that the staff will learn to respect him in time? What can John do to earn the loyalty of his staff and improve the ball club's performance?

Outcomes: During the winter, John thinks long and hard about how he can earn the respect of the Sea Lions staff. Before the next season opener, John announces his plan: "So I can better understand what your day is like, I'm going to spend one day in each of your shoes. I'm trading places with each of you. I will be a ticket taker, a roving hot dog vendor, and a janitor. And I will be a marketer, and an accountant—for a day. You in turn will have the day off so you can enjoy the game from the general manager's box." The staff laughs and whistles appreciatively. Then the Springfield mascot, Sparky the Sea Lion, speaks up: "Hey Mr. Arroyo, are you going to spend a day in my flippers?" "You bet!" says John, laughing. The entire staff cheers.

John continues. "At the close of the season, we will honor a staff member with the T.J. Grevin Award for outstanding contributions to the Sea Lions organization. T.J. was such a great guy, it's only right that we honor him." The meeting ends, but John's staff linger to tell him how excited they are about his ideas. Amidst the handshakes, he hopes that this year may be the best year yet for the Sea Lions.

Sarah Elizabeth Roisland is the manager of a district claims office for a large insurance company. Fourteen people work for her. The results of a recent attitude survey indicate that her employees have extremely high job satisfaction and motivation. Conflict is rare in Sarah's office. Furthermore, productivity measures place her group among the most productive in the entire company. Her success has brought the company's vice president of human resources to her office in an attempt to discover the secret to her success. Sarah's peers, superiors, and workers all give the same answer: she is more than a good manager—she is an outstanding leader. She continually gets high performance from her employees and does so in such a way that they enjoy working for her.

There is no magic formula for becoming a good leader. There are, however, many identifiable reasons why some people are better and more effective leaders. Leaders, especially effective leaders, are not created by simply attending a one-day leadership workshop. Yet effective leadership skills are not something most people are born with. You can become an effective leader if you are willing to invest the time and energy to develop all of the "right stuff."

According to Louise Axon, director of content strategy, and her colleagues at Harvard Business Publishing, in seeking management talent, *leadership* is an urgently needed quality in all managerial roles.[1] Good leaders and good leadership are rare. Harvard management professor John P. Kotter notes that "there is a leadership crisis in the U.S. today,"[2] and the late USC Professor Warren Bennis states that many of our organizations are overmanaged and underled.[3]

12.1 The Nature of Leadership

1. What is the nature of leadership and the leadership process?

The many definitions of leadership each have a different emphasis. Some definitions consider leadership an act or behavior, such as initiating structure so group members know how to complete a task. Others consider a leader to be the center or nucleus of group activity, an instrument of goal achievement who has a certain personality, a form of persuasion and power, and the art of inducing compliance.[4] Some look at leadership in terms of the management of group processes. In this view, a good leader develops a vision for the group, communicates that vision,[5] orchestrates the group's energy and activity toward goal attainment, "[turns] a group of individuals into a team," and "[transforms] good intentions into positive actions."[6]

Leadership is frequently defined as a social (interpersonal) influence relationship between two or more persons who depend on each other to attain certain mutual goals in a group situation.[7] Effective leadership helps individuals and groups achieve their goals by focusing on the group's *maintenance needs* (the need for individuals to fit and work together by having, for example, shared norms) and *task needs* (the need for the group to make progress toward attaining the goal that brought them together).

Exhibit 12.2 Joe Madden at pitcher mound Joe Maddon, manager of the Chicago Cubs baseball team, is lauded for both his managerial and leadership skills. Maddon is a role model for managers competing in the business world. Managers can learn and profit from the Cubs skipper's philosophy of instilling an upbeat attitude with the team, staying loose but staying productive, and avoiding being the center of attention.

Leader versus Manager

The two dual concepts, leader and manager, leadership and management, are not interchangeable, nor are they redundant. The differences between the two can, however, be confusing. In many instances, to be a good manager one needs to be an effective leader. Many CEOs have been hired in the hope that their leadership skills, their ability to formulate a vision and get others to "buy into" that vision, will propel the organization forward. In addition, effective leadership often necessitates the ability to manage—to set goals; plan, devise, and implement strategy; make decisions and solve problems; and organize and control. For our purposes, the two sets of concepts can be contrasted in several ways.

First, we define the two concepts differently. In Management and Organizational Behavior, we defined management as a process consisting of planning, organizing, directing, and controlling. Here we define leadership as a social (interpersonal) influence relationship between two or more people who are dependent on each another for goal attainment.

Second, managers and leaders are commonly differentiated in terms of the processes through which they initially come to their position. Managers are generally appointed to their role. Even though many organizations appoint people to positions of leadership, leadership per se is a relationship that revolves around the followers' acceptance or rejection of the leader.[8] Thus, leaders often emerge out of events that unfold among members of a group.

Third, managers and leaders often differ in terms of the types and sources of the power they exercise. Managers commonly derive their power from the larger organization. Virtually all organizations legitimize the use of certain "carrots and sticks" (rewards and punishments) as ways of securing the compliance of their employees. In other words, by virtue of the position that a manager occupies (president, vice president, department head, supervisor), certain "rights to act" (schedule production, contract to sell a product, hire and fire) accompany the position and its place within the hierarchy of authority. Leaders can also secure power and the ability to exercise influence using carrots and sticks; however, it is much more common for leaders to derive power from followers' perception of their knowledge (expertise), their personality and attractiveness, and the working relationship that has developed between leaders and followers.

From the perspective of those who are under the leader's and manager's influence, the motivation to comply often has a different base. The subordinate to a manager frequently complies because of the role authority of the manager, and because of the carrots and sticks that managers have at their disposal. The followers of a leader comply because they want to. Thus, leaders motivate primarily through intrinsic processes, while managers motivate primarily through extrinsic processes.

Finally, it is important to note that while managers may be successful in directing and supervising their subordinates, they often succeed or fail because of their ability or inability to lead.[9] As noted above, effective leadership often calls for the ability to manage, and effective management often requires leadership.

CONCEPT CHECK

1. What is the nature of leadership and the leadership process?

12.2 The Leadership Process

2. What are the processes associated with people coming to leadership positions?

Leadership is a process, a complex and dynamic exchange relationship built over time between leader and follower and between leader and the group of followers who depend on each other to attain a mutually desired goal.[10] There are several key components to this "working relationship": the leader, the followers, the context (situation), the leadership process per se, and the consequences (outcomes) (see **Exhibit 12.3**).[11] Across time, each component interacts with and influences the other components, and whatever consequences (such as leader-follower trust) are created influence future interactions. As any one of the components changes, so too will leadership.[12]

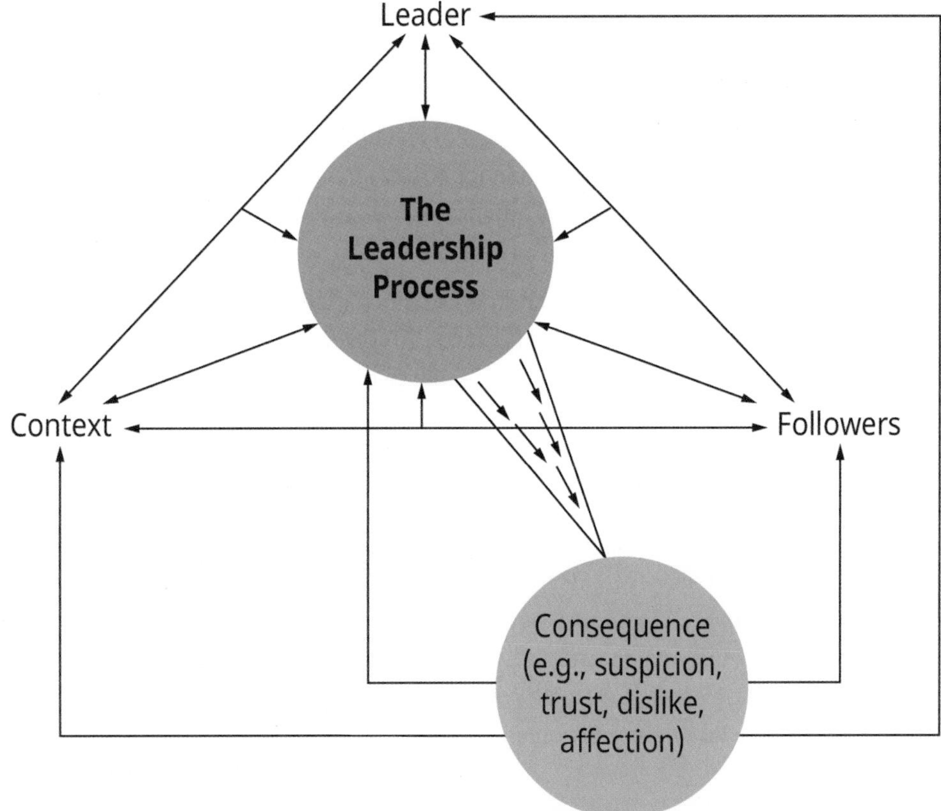

Exhibit 12.3 The Leadership Process (Attribution: Copyright Rice University, OpenStax, under CC-BY 4.0 license)

The Leader

Leaders are people who take charge of or guide the activities of others. They are often seen as the focus or orchestrater of group activity, the people who set the tone of the group so that it can move forward to attain its goals. Leaders provide the group with what is required to fulfill its maintenance and task-related needs. (Later in the chapter, we will return to the "leader as a person" as part of our discussion of the trait approach to leadership.)

Exhibit 12.4 New York Philharmonic @ UN The New York Philharmonic, conducted by Music Director Alan Gilbert, paid special tribute in the General Assembly Hall to UN Secretary-General Ban Ki-moon as a tribute to his 10-year term. Gilbert is the formal leader of the New York Philharmonic.

The Follower

The follower is not a passive player in the leadership process. Edwin Hollander, after many years of studying leadership, suggested that the follower is the most critical factor in any leadership event.[13] It is, after all, the follower who perceives the situation and comes to define the needs that the leader must fulfill. In addition, it is the follower who either rejects leadership or accepts acts of leadership by surrendering his power to the leader to diminish task uncertainty, to define and manage the meaning of the situation to the follower, and to orchestrate the follower's action in pursuit of goal attainment.

The follower's personality and readiness to follow determine the style of leadership that will be most effective. For example, individuals with an internal locus of control are much more responsive to participative styles of leadership than individuals with an external locus of control.[14] Individuals with an authoritarian personality are highly receptive to the effectiveness of directive acts of leadership.[15] It is the followers' expectations, as well as their performance-based needs, that determine what a leader must do in order to be effective.

The strength of the follower's self-concept has also been linked to the leadership process. High-self-esteem individuals tend to have a strong sense of self-efficacy, that is, a generalized belief they can be successful in difficult situations. They therefore tend to be strongly motivated to perform and persist in the face of adversity.[16] The high-self-esteem follower tends to be responsive to participative styles of leadership. Low-self-esteem individuals, who doubt their competence and worthiness and their ability to succeed in difficult situations, function better with supportive forms of leadership. This helps them deal with the stress, frustration, and anxiety that often emerge with difficult tasks. Followers without a readiness to follow, limited by their inability to perform and lack of motivation and commitment, usually need more directive forms of leadership.[17]

Follower behavior plays a major role in determining what behaviors leaders engage in. For example, followers who perform at high levels tend to cause their leaders to be considerate in their treatment and to play a less directive role. Followers who are poor performers, on the other hand, tend to cause their leaders to be less warm toward them and to be more directive and controlling in their leadership style.[18]

The Context

Situations make demands on a group and its members, and not all situations are the same. Context refers to the situation that surrounds the leader and the followers. Situations are multidimensional. We discuss the context as it pertains to leadership in greater detail later in this chapter, but for now let's look at it in terms of the task and task environment that confront the group. Is the task structured or unstructured? Are the goals of the group clear or ambiguous? Is there agreement or disagreement about goals? Is there a body of knowledge that can guide task performance? Is the task boring? Frustrating? Intrinsically satisfying? Is the environment complex or simple, stable or unstable? These factors create different contexts within which leadership unfolds, and each factor places a different set of needs and demands on the leader and on the followers.

The Process

The process of leadership is separate and distinct from the leader (the person who occupies a central role in the group). The process is a complex, interactive, and dynamic working relationship between leader and followers. This working relationship, built over time, is directed toward fulfilling the group's maintenance and task needs. Part of the process consists of an exchange relationship between the leader and follower. The leader provides a resource directed toward fulfilling the group's needs, and the group gives compliance, recognition, and esteem to the leader. To the extent that leadership is the exercise of influence, part of the leadership process is captured by the surrender of power by the followers and the exercise of influence over the followers by the leader.[19] Thus, the leader influences the followers and the followers influence the leader, the context influences the leader and the followers, and both leader and followers influence the context.

The Consequences

A number of outcomes or consequences of the leadership process unfold between leader, follower, and situation. At the group level, two outcomes are important:

- Have the group's maintenance needs been fulfilled? That is, do members of the group like and get along with one another, do they have a shared set of norms and values, and have they developed a good working relationship? Have individuals' needs been fulfilled as reflected in attendance, motivation, performance, satisfaction, citizenship, trust, and maintenance of the group membership?
- Have the group's task needs been met? That is, there are also important consequences of the leadership process for individuals: attendance, motivation, performance, satisfaction, citizenship, trust, and maintenance of their group membership.

The leader-member exchange (LMX) theory of the leadership process focuses attention on consequences associated with the leadership process. The theory views leadership as consisting of a number of dyadic relationships linking the leader with a follower. A leader-follower relationship tends to develop quickly and remains relatively stable over time. The quality of the relationship is reflected by the degree of mutual trust, loyalty, support, respect, and obligation. High- and low-quality relationships between a leader and each of his followers produce in and out groups among the followers. Members of the in group come to be key players, and high-quality exchange relationships tend to be associated with higher levels of performance, commitment, and satisfaction than are low-quality exchange relationships.[20] Attitudinal similarity and extroversion appear to be associated with a high-quality leader-member relationship.[21]

The nature of the leadership process varies substantially depending on the leader, the followers, and the situation and context. Thus, leadership is the function of an interaction between the leader, the follower, and the context.

The leadership context for the leader of a group of assembly line production workers differs from the context for the leader of a self-managing production team and from the context confronted by the lead scientists in a research laboratory. The leadership tactics that work in the first context might fail miserably in the latter two.

CATCHING THE ENTREPRENEURIAL SPIRIT

How a Start-Up Finds the Right Leader

Start-ups, by their very nature, require innovation to bring new products and services to market. Along with establishing a new brand or product, the leader has to develop the relationships and processes that make a company succeed, or risk its early demise. While leading an established firm has its challenges, a start-up requires even more from a leader.

How critical is leadership to a start-up? Ask the four cofounders of the now-defunct PYP (Pretty Young

Professionals), a website founded as a source of information for young professional women. What began as four young professional women working on a new start-up ended with hurt feelings and threats of legal action. In 2010, Kathryn Minshew, Amanda Pouchot, Caroline Ghosn, and Alex Cavoulacos decided to create the website and Minshew was named CEO (Cohan 2011a). Lines blurred about Minshew's authority and the ultimate look, feel, and direction of the website. Ideals about shared leadership, where the company was going, and how it was going to get there ultimately got lost in the power shuffle. By June 2011, passwords were changed and legal actions began, and in August Minshew and Cavoulacos left altogether (Cohan 2011b).

When the legal haggling from PYP was over, Alex Cavoulacos and Kathryn Minshew, joined by Melissa McCreery, tried again. But this time, rather than hoping for the best, they put a leadership plan in place. Minshew was named CEO of the new start-up, The Daily Muse, with Cavoulacos as chief operating officer and McCreery as editor in chief. Rather than trusting to luck, the three cofounders based their team positions on strengths and personalities. Cavoulacos and McCreery agreed that Minshew's outgoing personality and confidence made her the proper choice as CEO (Casserly 2013).

No single trait will guarantee that a person can lead a start-up from idea to greatness, but a survey of successful entrepreneurs does show some common traits. According to David Barbash, a partner at Boston-based law firm Posternak Blankstein & Lund LLP, personality is paramount: "You can have great technology but if you're not a great communicator it may die in the lab" (Casserly 2013 n.p.). A start-up needs a leader who is confident and willing, if not eager, to face the future. According to Michelle Randall, a principal of Enriching Leadership International, start-up CEOs have to be willing to fundraise and not be too proud to beg (Casserly 2013). Peter Shankman, an entrepreneur and angel investor, says leaders have to be willing to make the hard decisions, even risking being the bad guy (Casserly 2013).

Gary Vaynerchuk credits his success to six factors. Angel investor, social media marketer, and early social media adopter, Vaynerchuk leveraged YouTube in its early years to market wine from the family's liquor store, eventually increasing sales from $3 million to $60 million a year (Clifford 2017). Gary believes good leaders recognize that they don't dictate to the market, but rather respond to where it is going. They have respect for and believe in other people, and have a strong work ethic, what Vaynerchuk called a "lunch pail work ethic": they are willing to put in long hours because they love the work, not the perks. He also stresses that he loves technology and doesn't fear it, is obsessed with the youth of today, and is optimistic about people and the future of humanity (Vaynerchuk 2017).

Leading a startup requires more than simple management. It requires the right leader for the right company at the right time, which means matching the right management skills with the proper flexibility and drive to keep it all together and moving in the right direction.

Sources:

Casserly, Meghan. 2013. "Rocks, Paper, CEO: Finding The Best Leader For Your Startup." *Forbes.* https://www.forbes.com/sites/meghancasserly/2013/01/15/rocks-paper-ceo-finding-the-best-leader-for-your-startup/#16b520cd20a5

Clifford, Catherine. 2017. "Self-made millionaire Gary Vaynerchuk: This is the real secret to success." CNBC. https://www.cnbc.com/2017/03/13/self-made-millionaire-gary-vaynerchuk-shares-real-secret-to-success.html

Cohan, Peter. 2011a. "A Cautionary Tale: Friendship, Business Ethics, and Bad Breakups (Acts I and II). *Forbes.* August 9, 2011. https://www.forbes.com/sites/petercohan/2011/08/09/a-cautionary-tale-

friendship-business-ethics-and-bad-breakups-acts-i-and-ii/#256d318b2735
Cohan, Peter. 2011b. "A Cautionary Tale: Friendship, Business Ethics, and Bad Breakups (Acts III and IV). *Forbes.* August 9, 2011. https://www.forbes.com/sites/petercohan/2011/08/09/a-cautionary-tale-friendship-business-ethics-and-bad-breakups-acts-iii-and-iv/3/#66b22dd4a4f6
Vaynerchuk, Gary. 2017. "What Makes Me a Great CEO." https://www.garyvaynerchuk.com/makes-great-ceo/

1. Why would start-up leaders need different leadership qualities than someone managing an established firm?
2. Vaynerchuk has been quoted as saying that if you live for Friday, get a different job. How does this apply to successful entrepreneurs?

CONCEPT CHECK 

1. What are the processes associated with people coming to leadership positions?

12.3 Leader Emergence

3. How do leaders influence and move their followers to action?

Leaders hold a unique position in their groups, exercising influence and providing direction. Leonard Bernstein was part of the symphony, but his role as the New York Philharmonic conductor differed dramatically from that of the other symphony members. Besides conducting the orchestra, he created a vision for the symphony. In this capacity, leadership can be seen as a differentiated role and the nucleus of group activity.

Organizations have two kinds of leaders: formal and informal. A **formal leader** is that individual who is recognized by those outside the group as the official leader of the group. Often, the formal leader is appointed by the organization to serve in a formal capacity as an agent of the organization. Jack Welch was the formal leader of General Electric, and Leonard Bernstein was the formal leader of the symphony. Practically all managers act as formal leaders as part of their assigned role. Organizations that use self-managed work teams allow members of the team to select the individual who will serve as their team leader. When this person's role is sanctioned by the formal organization, these team leaders become formal leaders. Increasingly, leaders in organizations will be those who "best sell" their ideas on how to complete a project—persuasiveness and inspiration are important ingredients in the leadership equation, especially in high-involvement organizations.[22]

Informal leaders, by contrast, are not assigned by the organization. The **informal leader** is that individual whom members of the group acknowledge as their leader. Athletic teams often have informal leaders, individuals who exert considerable influence on team members even though they hold no official, formal leadership position. In fact, most work groups contain at least one informal leader. Just like formal leaders, informal leaders can benefit or harm an organization depending on whether their influence encourages group members to behave consistently with organizational goals.

As we have noted, the terms *leader* and *manager* are not synonymous. Grace Hopper, retired U.S. Navy admiral, draws a distinction between leading and managing: "You don't manage people, you manage *things*. You lead *people*."[23] Informal leaders often have considerable leverage over their colleagues. Traditionally, the roles of informal leaders have not included the total set of management responsibilities because an informal leader does not always exercise the functions of planning, organizing, directing, and controlling. However, high-involvement organizations frequently encourage their formal and informal leaders to exercise the full set of management roles. Many consider such actions necessary for self-managing work teams to succeed. Informal leaders are acknowledged by the group, and the group willingly responds to their leadership.

Paths to Leadership

People come to leadership positions through two dynamics. In many instances, people are put into positions of leadership by forces outside the group. University-based ROTC programs and military academies (like West Point) formally groom people to be leaders. We refer to this person as the **designated leader** (in this instance the designated and formal leader are the same person). **Emergent leaders**, on the other hand, arise from the dynamics and processes that unfold within and among a group of individuals as they endeavor to achieve a collective goal.

A variety of processes help us understand how leaders emerge. Gerald Salancik and Jeffrey Pfeffer observe that power to influence others flows to those individuals who possess the critical and scarce resources (often knowledge and expertise) that a group needs to overcome a major problem.[24] They note that the dominant coalition and leadership in American corporations during the 1950s was among engineers, because organizations were engaged in competition based on product design. The power base in many organizations shifted to marketing as competition became a game of advertising aimed at differentiating products in the consumer's mind. About 10–15 years ago, power and leadership once again shifted, this time to people with finance and legal backgrounds, because the critical contingencies facing many organizations were mergers, acquisitions, hostile takeovers, and creative financing. Thus, Salancik and Pfeffer reason that power and thus leadership flow to those individuals who have the ability to help an organization or group [overcome its critical contingencies]. As the challenges facing a group change, so too may the flow of power and leadership.

Many leaders emerge out of the needs of the situation. Different situations call for different configurations of knowledge, skills, and abilities. A group often turns to the member who possesses the knowledge, skills, and abilities that the group requires to achieve its goals.[25] People surrender their power to individuals whom they believe will make meaningful contributions to attaining group goals.[26] The individual to whom power is surrendered is often a member of the group who is in good standing. As a result of this member's contributions to the group's goals, he has accumulated *idiosyncrasy credits* (a form of competency-based status). These credits give the individual a status that allows him to influence the direction that the group takes as it works to achieve its goals.[27]

It is important to recognize that the traits possessed by certain individuals contribute significantly to their emergence as leaders. Research indicates that people are unlikely to follow individuals who, for example, do not display drive, self-confidence, knowledge of the situation, honesty, and integrity.

Leadership as an Exercise of Influence

As we have noted, leadership is the exercise of influence over those who depend on one another for attaining a mutual goal in a group setting. But *how* do leaders effectively exercise this influence? *Social or (interpersonal) influence* is one's ability to effect a change in the motivation, attitudes, and/or behaviors of others. *Power*, then, essentially answers the "how" question: How do leaders influence their followers? The answer often is that a leader's social influence is the source of his power.

French and Raven provide us with a useful typology that identifies the sources and types of power that may be at the disposal of leaders:

- *Reward power*—the power a person has because people believe that he can bestow rewards or outcomes, such as money or recognition that others desire
- *Coercive power*—the power a person has because people believe that he can punish them by inflicting pain or by withholding or taking away something that they value
- *Referent power*—the power a person has because others want to associate with or be accepted by him
- *Expert power*—the power a person has because others believe that he has and is willing to share expert knowledge that they need (The concept of *resource power* extends the idea of expert power to include the power that a person has because others believe that he possesses and is willing to share resources, such as information, time, or materials that are needed.)
- *Legitimate power*—the power a person has because others believe that he possesses the "right" to influence them and that they ought to obey. This right can originate in tradition; in the charisma or appeal of the person; and in laws, institutional roles within society, moralistic appeal, and rationality (that is, logical arguments, factual evidence, reason, and internally consistent positions).[28]

Not all forms of power are equally effective (see **Exhibit 12.5**), nor is a leader's total power base the simple sum of the powers at his disposal. Different types of power elicit different forms of compliance: Leaders who rely on coercive power often alienate followers who resist their influence attempts. Leaders who rely on reward power develop followers who are very measured in their responses to [what?]; the use of rewards often leads people to think in terms of "How much am I getting?" or "How much should I give?" or "Am I breaking even?" The use of referent power produces identification with the leader and his cause. The use of rationality, expert power, and/or moralistic appeal generally elicits commitment and the internalization of the leader's goals.[29]

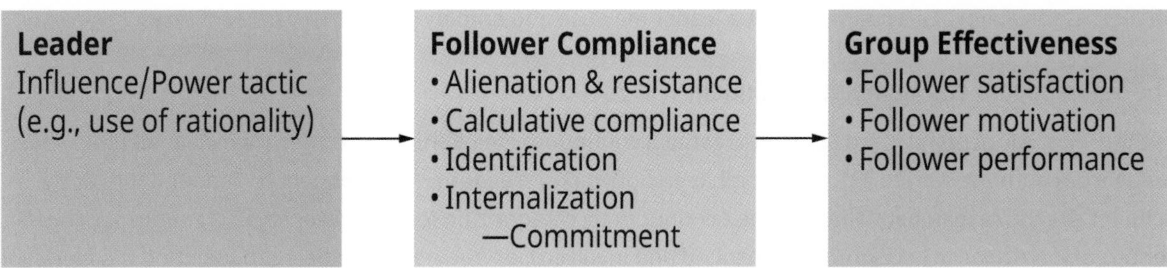

Exhibit 12.5 The Leader-Follower Power Relationship

Leaders who use referent and expert power commonly experience a favorable response in terms of follower satisfaction and performance. Research suggests that rationality is the most effective influence tactic in terms of its impact on follower commitment, motivation, performance, satisfaction, and group effectiveness.[30]

Reward and legitimate power (that is, relying on one's position to influence others) produce inconsistent results. Sometimes these powers lead to follower performance and satisfaction, yet they also sometimes fail. Coercive power can result in favorable performance, yet follower and resistance dissatisfaction are not uncommon.

Good leaders, whether formal or informal, develop many sources of power. Leaders who rely solely on their legitimate power and authority seldom generate the influence necessary to help their organization and its members succeed. In the process of building their power base, effective leaders have discovered that the use of coercive power tends to dilute the effectiveness of other powers, while the development and use of referent power tends to magnify the effectiveness of other forms of power. A compliment or reward from a person we like generally has greater value than one from someone we dislike, and punishment from someone we love (such as "tough love" from a parent) is less offensive than the pain inflicted by someone we dislike.[31]

In sum, one key to effective leadership, especially as it pertains to the exercise of social and interpersonal influence, relates to the type of power employed by the leader. Overall leader effectiveness will be higher when people follow because they want to follow. This is much more likely to happen when the leader's influence flows out of intrinsic such as rationality, expertise, moralistic appeal, and/or referent power.

Leadership is also about having a vision and communicating that vision to others in such a way that it provides meaning for the follower.[32] Language, ritual, drama, myths, symbolic constructions, and stories are some of the tools leaders use to capture the attention of their "followers to be" to evoke emotion and to manage the meaning "of the task (challenges) facing the group."[33] These tools help the leader influence the attitudes, motivation, and behavior of their followers.

Influence-Based Leadership Styles

Many writers and researchers have explored how leaders can use power to address the needs of various situations. One view holds that in traditional organizations members expect to be told what to do and are willing to follow highly structured directions. Individuals attracted to high-involvement organizations, however, want to make their own decisions, expect their leaders to allow them to do so, and are willing to accept and act on this responsibility. This suggests that a leader may use and employ power in a variety of ways.

The Tannenbaum and Schmidt Continuum

In the 1950s, Tannenbaum and Schmidt created a continuum (see **Exhibit 12.6**) along which leadership styles range from authoritarian to extremely high levels of worker freedom.[34] Subsequent to Tannenbaum and Schmidt's work, researchers adapted the continuum by categorizing leader power styles as *autocratic* (boss-centered), *participative* (workers are consulted and involved), or *free-rein* (members are assigned the work and decide on their own how to do it; the leader relinquishes the active assumption of the role of leadership).[35]

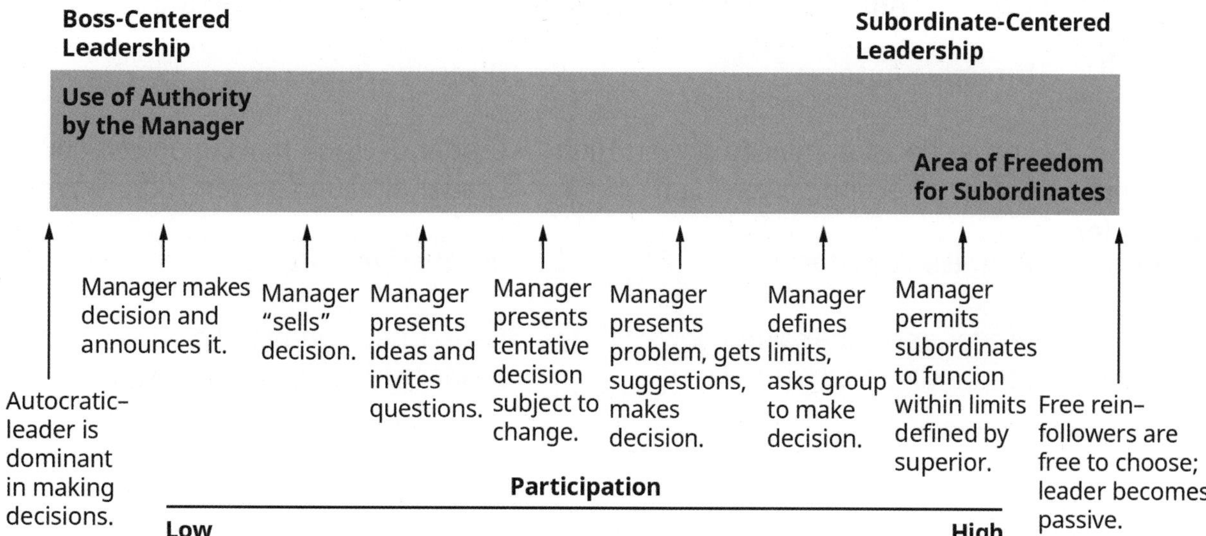

Exhibit 12.6 Tannenbaum and Schmidt's Leadership Continuum *Source:* Modified from R. Tannenbaum and W. H. Schmidt. May—June 1971. How to choose a leadership pattern. *Harvard Business Review*, 167.

Theory X and Theory Y Leaders

McGregor's Theory X and Theory Y posits two different sets of attitudes about the individual as an organizational member.[36] Theory X and Y thinking gives rise to two different styles of leadership. The *Theory X leader* assumes that the average individual dislikes work and is incapable of exercising adequate self-direction and self-control. As a consequence, they exert a highly controlling leadership style. In contrast, *Theory Y leaders* believe that people have creative capacities, as well as both the ability and desire to exercise self-direction and self-control. They typically allow organizational members significant amounts of discretion in their jobs and encourage them to participate in departmental and organizational decision-making. Theory Y leaders are much more likely to adopt involvement-oriented approaches to leadership and organically designed organizations for their leadership group.

Theory X and Theory Y thinking and leadership are not strictly an American phenomenon. Evidence suggests that managers from different parts of the global community commonly hold the same view. A study of 3,600 managers from 14 countries reveals that most of them held assumptions about human nature that could best be classified as Theory X.[37] Even though managers might publicly endorse the merits of participatory management, most of them doubted their workers' capacities to exercise self-direction and self-control and to contribute creatively.[38]

Directive/Permissive Leadership Styles

Contemplating the central role of problem-solving in management and leadership, Jan P. Muczyk and Bernard C. Reimann of Cleveland State University offer an interesting perspective on four different leadership styles (see **Exhibit 12.7**) that revolve around decision-making and implementation processes.[39]

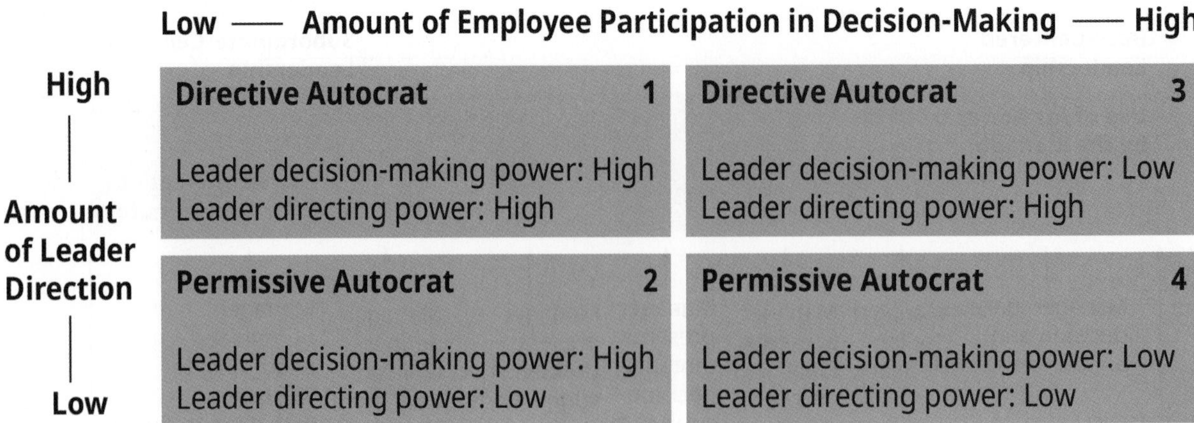

Exhibit 12.7 Leadership Behavior and the Uses of Power ***Source:*** Modified from J. P. Muczyk and B. C. Reimann. 1987. The case for directive leadership. *Academy of Management Executive*, 1:304.

A *directive autocrat* retains power, makes unilateral decisions, and closely supervises workers' activities. This style of leadership is seen as appropriate when circumstances require quick decisions and organizational members are new, inexperienced, or underqualified. A doctor in charge of a hastily constructed shelter for victims of a tornado may use this style to command nonmedical volunteers.

The *permissive autocrat* mixes his or her use of power by retaining decision-making power but permitting organizational members to exercise discretion when executing those decisions. This leader behavior is recommended when decision-making time is limited, when tasks are routine, or when organizational members have sufficient expertise to determine appropriate role behaviors.

Also sharing power is the *directive democrat,* who encourages participative decision-making but retains the power to direct team members in the execution of their roles. This style is appropriate when followers have valuable opinions and ideas, but one person needs to coordinate the execution of the ideas. A surgeon might allow the entire surgical team to participate in developing a plan for a surgical procedure. Once surgery begins, however, the surgeon is completely in charge.

Finally, the *permissive democrat* shares power with group members, soliciting involvement in both decision-making and execution. This style is appropriate when participation has both informational and motivational value, when time permits group decision-making, when group members are capable of improving decision quality, and when followers are capable of exercising self-management in their performance of work.

The permissive democratic approach to leadership is characteristic of leadership in high-involvement organizations. Here, leaders act as facilitators, process consultants, network builders, conflict managers, inspirationalists, coaches, teachers/mentors, and cheerleaders.[40] Such is the role of Ralph Stayer, founder, owner, and CEO of Johnsonville Foods. He defines himself as his company's philosopher. At Quad/Graphics, president Harry V. Quadracci is a permissive democrat because he encourages all Quad employees to play a major role in decision-making and execution as they manage their teams as independent profit centers.

Exhibit 12.8 Jeff Bezos Jeff Bezos, founder and CEO of Amazon, used to bring an empty chair to meetings to signal and remind participants of the most important people that did not have a seat at the table: the customers. He has now replaced the empty chair with Amazon employees with the job title Customer Experience Bar Raisers.

CONCEPT CHECK

1. What is the role of the leader and follower in the leadership process?
2. How do the theories of Tannenbaum and Schmidt's leadership continuum and McGregor's Theory X and Theory Y attempt to define leadership?

12.4 The Trait Approach to Leadership

4. What are the trait perspectives on leadership?

Ancient Greek, Roman, Egyptian, and Chinese scholars were keenly interested in leaders and leadership. Their writings portray leaders as heroes. Homer, in his poem *The Odyssey*, portrays Odysseus during and after the Trojan War as a great leader who had vision and self-confidence. His son Telemachus, under the tutelage of Mentor, developed his father's courage and leadership skills.[41] Out of such stories there emerged the "great man" theory of leadership, and a starting point for the contemporary study of leadership.

The **great man theory of leadership** states that some people are born with the necessary attributes to be great leaders. Alexander the Great, Julius Caesar, Joan of Arc, Catherine the Great, Napoleon, and Mahatma Gandhi are cited as naturally great leaders, born with a set of personal qualities that made them effective leaders. Even today, the belief that truly great leaders are born is common. For example, Kenneth Labich, writer for *Fortune* magazine, commented that "the best leaders seem to possess a God-given spark."[42]

During the early 1900s, scholars endeavored to understand leaders and leadership. They wanted to know, from an organizational perspective, what characteristics leaders hold in common in the hope that people with these characteristics could be identified, recruited, and placed in key organizational positions. This gave rise to early research efforts and to what is referred to as the *trait approach to leadership.* Prompted by the great man theory of leadership and the emerging interest in understanding what leadership is, researchers focused on the leader—Who is a leader? What are the distinguishing characteristics of the great and effective leaders? The great man theory of leadership holds that some people are born with a set of personal qualities that make truly great leaders. Mahatma Gandhi is often cited as a naturally great leader.

Leader Trait Research

Ralph Stogdill, while on the faculty at The Ohio State University, pioneered our modern (late 20th century) study of leadership.[43] Scholars taking the trait approach attempted to identify physiological (appearance, height, and weight), demographic (age, education, and socioeconomic background), personality (dominance, self-confidence, and aggressiveness), intellective (intelligence, decisiveness, judgment, and knowledge), task-related (achievement drive, initiative, and persistence), and social characteristics (sociability and cooperativeness) with leader emergence and leader effectiveness. After reviewing several hundred studies of leader traits, Stogdill in 1974 described the successful leader this way:

The [successful] leader is characterized by a strong drive for responsibility and task completion, vigor and persistence in pursuit of goals, venturesomeness and originality in problem solving, drive to exercise initiative in social situations, self-confidence and sense of personal identity, willingness to accept consequences of decision and action, readiness to absorb interpersonal stress, willingness to tolerate frustration and delay, ability to influence other person's behavior, and capacity to structure social interaction systems to the purpose at hand.[44]

The last three decades of the 20th century witnessed continued exploration of the relationship between traits and both leader emergence and leader effectiveness. Edwin Locke from the University of Maryland and a number of his research associates, in their recent review of the trait research, observed that successful leaders possess a set of core characteristics that are different from those of other people.[45] Although these core traits do not solely determine whether a person will be a leader—or a successful leader—they are seen as preconditions that endow people with leadership potential. Among the core traits identified are:

- *Drive*—a high level of effort, including a strong desire for achievement as well as high levels of ambition, energy, tenacity, and initiative
- *Leadership motivation*—an intense desire to lead others
- *Honesty and integrity*—a commitment to the truth (nondeceit), where word and deed correspond
- *Self-confidence*—an assurance in one's self, one's ideas, and one's ability
- *Cognitive ability*—conceptually skilled, capable of exercising good judgment, having strong analytical abilities, possessing the capacity to think strategically and multidimensionally
- *Knowledge of the business*—a high degree of understanding of the company, industry, and technical matters
- *Other traits*—charisma, creativity/originality, and flexibility/adaptiveness[46]

While leaders may be "people with the right stuff," effective leadership requires more than simply possessing the correct set of motives and traits. Knowledge, skills, ability, vision, strategy, and effective vision implementation are all necessary for the person who has the "right stuff" to realize their leadership potential.[47] According to Locke, people endowed with these traits engage in behaviors that are associated with leadership. As followers, people are attracted to and inclined to follow individuals who display, for example, honesty and integrity, self-confidence, and the motivation to lead.

Personality psychologists remind us that behavior is a result of an interaction between the person and the situation—that is, Behavior = *f* [(Person) (Situation)]. To this, psychologist Walter Mischel adds the important observation that personality tends to get expressed through an individual's behavior in "weak" situations and to be suppressed in "strong" situations.[48] A strong situation is one with strong behavioral norms and rules, strong incentives, clear expectations, and rewards for a particular behavior. Our characterization of the mechanistic organization with its well-defined hierarchy of authority, jobs, and standard operating procedures exemplifies a strong situation. The organic social system exemplifies a weak situation. From a leadership perspective, a person's traits play a stronger role in their leader behavior and ultimately leader effectiveness when the situation permits the expression of their disposition. Thus, personality traits prominently shape leader behavior in weak situations.

Finally, about the validity of the "great person approach to leadership": Evidence accumulated to date does not provide a strong base of support for the notion that leaders are born. Yet, the study of twins at the University of Minnesota leaves open the possibility that part of the answer might be found in our genes. Many personality traits and vocational interests (which might be related to one's interest in assuming responsibility for others and the motivation to lead) have been found to be related to our "genetic dispositions" as well as to our life experiences.[49] Each core trait recently identified by Locke and his associates traces a significant part of its existence to life experiences. Thus, a person is not born with self-confidence. Self-confidence is developed, honesty and integrity are a matter of personal choice, motivation to lead comes from within the individual and is within his control, and knowledge of the business can be acquired. While cognitive ability does in part find its origin in the genes, it still needs to be developed. Finally, drive, as a dispositional trait, may also have a genetic component, but it too can be self- and other-encouraged. It goes without saying that none of these ingredients are acquired overnight.

Other Leader Traits

Sex and gender, disposition, and self-monitoring also play an important role in leader emergence and leader style.

Sex and Gender Role

Much research has gone into understanding the role of sex and gender in leadership.[50] Two major avenues have been explored: sex and gender roles in relation to leader emergence, and whether style differences exist across the sexes.

Evidence supports the observation that men emerge as leaders more frequently than women.[51] Throughout history, few women have been in positions where they could develop or exercise leadership behaviors. In contemporary society, being perceived as experts appears to play an important role in the emergence of women as leaders. Yet, gender role is more predictive than sex. Individuals with "masculine" (for example, assertive, aggressive, competitive, willing to take a stand) as opposed to "feminine" (cheerful, affectionate, sympathetic, gentle) characteristics are more likely to emerge in leadership roles.[52] In our society males are frequently socialized to possess the masculine characteristics, while females are more frequently socialized to possess the feminine characteristics.

Recent evidence, however, suggests that individuals who are androgynous (that is, who simultaneously possess both masculine and feminine characteristics) are as likely to emerge in leadership roles as individuals with only masculine characteristics. This suggests that possessing feminine qualities does not distract from the attractiveness of the individual as a leader.[53]

With regard to leadership style, researchers have looked to see if male-female differences exist in task and interpersonal styles, and whether or not differences exist in how autocratic or democratic men and women are. The answer is, when it comes to interpersonal versus task orientation, differences between men and women appear to be marginal. Women are somewhat more concerned with meeting the group's interpersonal needs, while men are somewhat more concerned with meeting the group's task needs. Big differences emerge in terms of democratic versus autocratic leadership styles. Men tend to be more autocratic or directive, while women are more likely to adopt a more democratic/participative leadership style.[54] In fact, it may be because men are more directive that they are seen as key to goal attainment and they are turned to more often as leaders.[55]

Dispositional Trait

Psychologists often use the terms *disposition* and *mood* to describe and differentiate people. Individuals characterized by a positive affective state exhibit a mood that is active, strong, excited, enthusiastic, peppy, and elated. A leader with this mood state exudes an air of confidence and optimism and is seen as enjoying work-related activities.

Recent work conducted at the University of California-Berkeley demonstrates that leaders (managers) with positive affectivity (a positive mood state) tend to be more competent interpersonally, to contribute more to group activities, and to be able to function more effectively in their leadership role.[56] Their enthusiasm and high energy levels appear to be infectious, transferring from leader to followers. Thus, such leaders promote group cohesiveness and productivity. This mood state is also associated with low levels of group turnover and is positively associated with followers who engage in acts of good group citizenship.[57]

Self-Monitoring

Self-monitoring as a personality trait refers to the strength of an individual's ability and willingness to read verbal and nonverbal cues and to alter one's behavior so as to manage the presentation of the self and the images that others form of the individual. "High self-monitors" are particularly astute at reading social cues and regulating their self-presentation to fit a particular situation. "Low self-monitors" are less sensitive to social cues; they may either lack motivation or lack the ability to manage how they come across to others.

Some evidence supports the position that high self-monitors emerge more often as leaders. In addition, they appear to exert more influence on group decisions and initiate more structure than low self-monitors. Perhaps high self-monitors emerge as leaders because in group interaction they are the individuals who attempt to organize the group and provide it with the structure needed to move the group toward goal attainment.[58]

CONCEPT CHECK

1. What are the trait perspectives on leadership?

12.5 Behavioral Approaches to Leadership

5. What are the behavioral perspectives on leadership?

The nearly four decades of research that focused on identifying the personal traits associated with the emergence of leaders and leader effectiveness resulted in two observations. First, leader traits are important—people who are endowed with the "right stuff" (drive, self-confidence, honesty, and integrity) are more likely to emerge as leaders and to be effective leaders than individuals who do not possess these characteristics. Second, traits are only a part of the story. Traits only account for part of why someone becomes a leader and why they are (or are not) effective leaders.

Still under the influence of the great man theory of leadership, researchers continued to focus on the leader in an effort to understand leadership—who emerges and what constitutes effective leadership. Researchers then began to reason that maybe the rest of the story could be understood by looking at what it is that leaders *do*. Thus, we now turn our attention to leader behaviors and the behavioral approaches to leadership.

It is now common to think of effective leadership in terms of what leaders do. CEOs and management consultants agree that effective leaders display trust in their employees, develop a vision, keep their cool, encourage risk, bring expertise into the work setting, invite dissent, and focus everyone's attention on that which is important.[59] William Arruda, in a *Fortune* article, noted that "organizations with strong coaching cultures report their revenue to be above average, compared to their peer group." Sixty-five percent of employees "from strong coaching cultures rated themselves as highly engaged," compared to 13 percent of employees worldwide."[60] Jonathan Anthony calls himself an intrapreneur and corporate disorganizer, because same-old, same-old comms practices are dying in front of our eyes.[61] Apple founder Steve Jobs believed that the best leaders are coaches and team cheerleaders. Similar views have been frequently echoed by management consultant Tom Peters.

During the late 1940s, two major research programs—The Ohio State University and the University of Michigan leadership studies—were launched to explore leadership from a behavioral perspective.

The Ohio State University Studies

A group of Ohio State University researchers, under the direction of Ralph Stogdill, began an extensive and systematic series of studies to identify leader behaviors associated with effective group performance. Their results identified two major sets of leader behaviors: consideration and initiating structure.

Consideration is the "relationship-oriented" behavior of a leader. It is instrumental in creating and maintaining good relationships (that is, addressing the group's maintenance needs) with organizational members. Consideration behaviors include being supportive and friendly, representing people's interests, communicating openly with group members, recognizing them, respecting their ideas, and sharing concern for their feelings.

Initiating structure involves "task-oriented" leader behaviors. It is instrumental in the efficient use of resources to attain organizational goals, thereby addressing the group's task needs. Initiating structure behaviors include scheduling work, deciding what is to be done (and how and when to do it), providing direction to organizational members, planning, coordinating, problem-solving, maintaining standards of performance, and encouraging the use of uniform procedures.

After consideration and initiating structure behaviors were first identified, many leaders believed that they had to behave one way or the other. If they initiated structure, they could not be considerate, and vice versa. It did not take long, however, to recognize that leaders can simultaneously display any combination of both behaviors.

The Ohio State studies are important because they identified two critical categories of behavior that distinguish one leader from another. Both consideration and initiating structure behavior can significantly impact work attitudes and behaviors. Unfortunately, the effects of consideration and initiating structure are not consistent from situation to situation.[62] In some of the organizations studied, for example, high levels of initiating structure increased performance. In other organizations, the amount of initiating structure seemed to make little difference. Although most organizational members reported greater satisfaction when leaders acted considerately, consideration behavior appeared to have no clear effect on performance.

Initially, these mixed findings were disappointing to researchers and managers alike. It had been hoped that a profile of the most effective leader behaviors could be identified so that leaders could be trained in the best ways to behave. Research made clear, however, that there is no one best style of leader behavior for all situations.

The University of Michigan Studies

At about the same time that the Ohio State studies were underway, researchers at the University of Michigan also began to investigate leader behaviors. As at Ohio State, the Michigan researchers attempted to identify behavioral elements that differentiated effective from ineffective leaders.[63]

The two types of leader behavior that stand out in these studies are job centered and organizational member centered. *Job-centered behaviors* are devoted to supervisory functions, such as planning, scheduling, coordinating work activities, and providing the resources needed for task performance. *Employee-member-centered* behaviors include consideration and support for organizational members. These dimensions of behavior, of course, correspond closely to the dimensions of initiating structure and consideration identified at Ohio State. The similarity of the findings from two independent groups of researchers added to their credibility. As the Ohio State researchers had done, the Michigan researchers also found that any combination of the two behaviors was possible.

The studies at Michigan are significant because they reinforce the importance of leader behavior. They also provide the basis for later theories that identify specific, effective matches of work situations and leader behaviors. Subsequent research at Michigan and elsewhere has found additional behaviors associated with effective leadership: support, work facilitation, goal emphasis, and interaction facilitation.[64]

These four behaviors are important to the successful functioning of the group in that support and interaction facilitation contribute to the group's maintenance needs, and goal emphasis and work facilitation contribute to the group's task needs. The Michigan researchers also found that these four behaviors do not need to be brought to the group by the leader. In essence, the leader's real job is to set the tone and create the climate that ensure these critical behaviors are present.[65]

The Leadership Grid®

Much of the credit for disseminating knowledge about important leader behaviors must go to Robert R. Blake and Jane S. Mouton, who developed a method for classifying styles of leadership compatible with many of the ideas from the Ohio State and Michigan studies.[66] In their classification scheme, *concern for results* (production) emphasizes output, cost effectiveness, and (in for-profit organizations) a concern for profits. *Concern for people* involves promoting working relationships and paying attention to issues of importance to group members. As shown in **Exhibit 12.9**, the Leadership Grid® demonstrates that any combination of these two leader concerns is possible, and five styles of leadership are highlighted here.

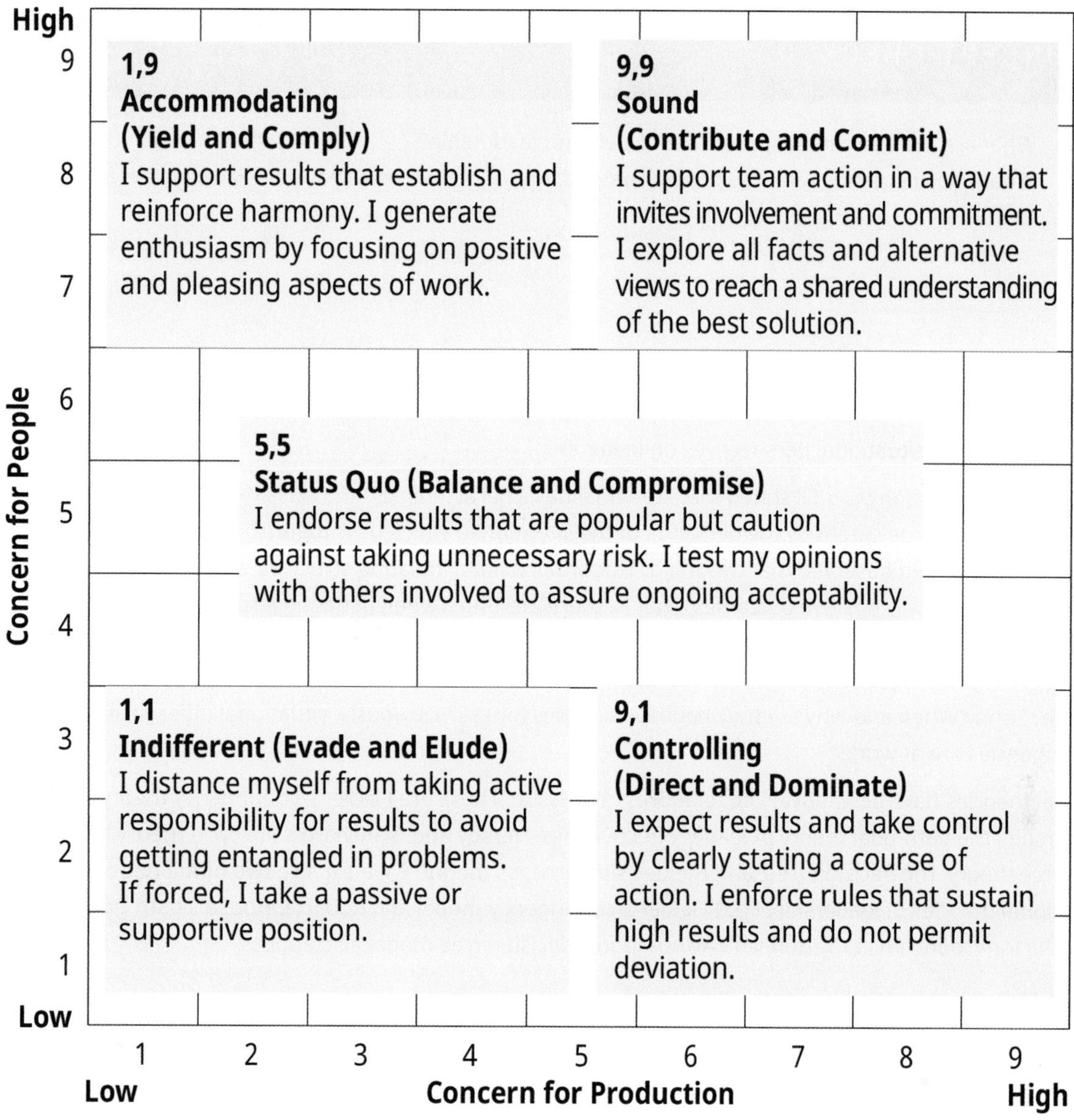

Exhibit 12.9 Blake and Mouton's Managerial Grid® ***Source:*** Adapted from R. McKee and B. Carlson. 1999. *The Power to Change*, p.16.

Blake and Mouton contend that the sound (contribute and commit) leader (a high concern for results and people, or 9,9) style is universally the most effective.[67] While the Leadership Grid® is appealing and well structured, research to date suggests that there is no universally effective style of leadership (9,9 or otherwise).[68] There are, however, well-identified situations in which a 9,9 style is unlikely to be effective. Organizational members of high-involvement organizations who have mastered their job duties require little production-oriented leader behavior. Likewise, there is little time for people-oriented behavior during an emergency. Finally, evidence suggests that the "high-high" style may be effective when the situation calls for high levels of initiating structure. Under these conditions, the initiation of structure is more acceptable, favorably affecting follower satisfaction and performance, when the leader is also experienced as warm, supportive, and considerate.[69]

CONCEPT CHECK 

1. What are the behavioral approaches to defining leadership?
2. What roles do gender and the popular perceptions of gender roles have on views of leadership traits?

12.6 Situational (Contingency) Approaches to Leadership

6. What are the situational perspectives on leadership?

As early as 1948, Ralph Stogdill stated that "the qualities, characteristics, and skills required in a leader are determined to a large extent by the demands of the situation in which he is to function as a leader."[70] In addition, it had been observed that two major leader behaviors, initiating structure and consideration, didn't always lead to equally positive outcomes. That is, there are times when initiating structure results in performance increases and follower satisfaction, and there are times when the results are just the opposite. Contradictory findings such as this lead researchers to ask "Under what conditions are the results positive in nature?" and "When and why are they negative at other times?" Obviously, situational differences and key contingencies are at work.

Several theories have been advanced to address this issue. These are Fiedler's contingency theory of leadership, the path-goal theory of leader effectiveness, Hersey and Blanchard's life cycle theory, cognitive resource theory, the decision tree, and the decision process theory.[71] We explore two of the better-known situational theories of leadership, Fred Fiedler's contingency model and Robert J. House's path-goal theory, here. Victor Vroom, Phillip Yetton, and Arthur Jago's decision tree model also applies.

Fiedler's Contingency Model

One of the earliest, best-known, and most controversial situation-contingent leadership theories was set forth by Fred E. Fiedler from the University of Washington.[72] This theory is known as the **contingency theory of leadership.** According to Fiedler, organizations attempting to achieve group effectiveness through leadership must assess the leader according to an underlying trait, assess the situation faced by the leader, and construct a proper match between the two.

The Leader's Trait

Leaders are asked about their **least-preferred coworker (LPC),** the person with whom they *least* like to work. The most popular interpretation of the LPC score is that it reflects a leader's underlying disposition toward others—for example: pleasant/unpleasant, cold/warm, friendly/unfriendly, and untrustworthy/trustworthy. (You can examine your own LPC score by completing the LPC self-assessment on the following page.)

Fiedler states that leaders with high LPC scores are *relationship oriented*—they need to develop and maintain close interpersonal relationships. They tend to evaluate their least-preferred coworkers in fairly favorable terms. Task accomplishment is a secondary need to this type of leader and becomes important only after the need for relationships is reasonably well satisfied. In contrast, leaders with low LPC scores tend to evaluate the individuals with whom they least like to work fairly negatively. They are *task-oriented* people, and only after tasks have been accomplished are low-LPC leaders likely to work on establishing good social and interpersonal relations.

The Situational Factor

Some situations favor leaders more than others do. To Fiedler, *situational favorableness* is the degree to which leaders have control and influence and therefore feel that they can determine the outcomes of a group interaction.[73] Several years later, Fiedler changed his situational factor from situational favorability to situational control—where situational control essentially refers to the degree to which a leader can influence the group process.[74] Three factors work together to determine how favorable a situation is to a leader. In order of importance, they are (1) *leader-member relations*—the degree of the group's acceptance of the leader, their ability to work well together, and members' level of loyalty to the leader; (2) *task structure*—the degree to which the task specifies a detailed, unambiguous goal and how to achieve it; and (3) *position power*—a leader's direct ability to influence group members. The situation is most favorable for a leader when the relationship between the leader and group members is good, when the task is highly structured, and when the leader's position power is strong (cell 1 in **Exhibit 12.10**). The least-favorable situation occurs under poor leader-member relations, an unstructured task, and weak position power (cell 8).

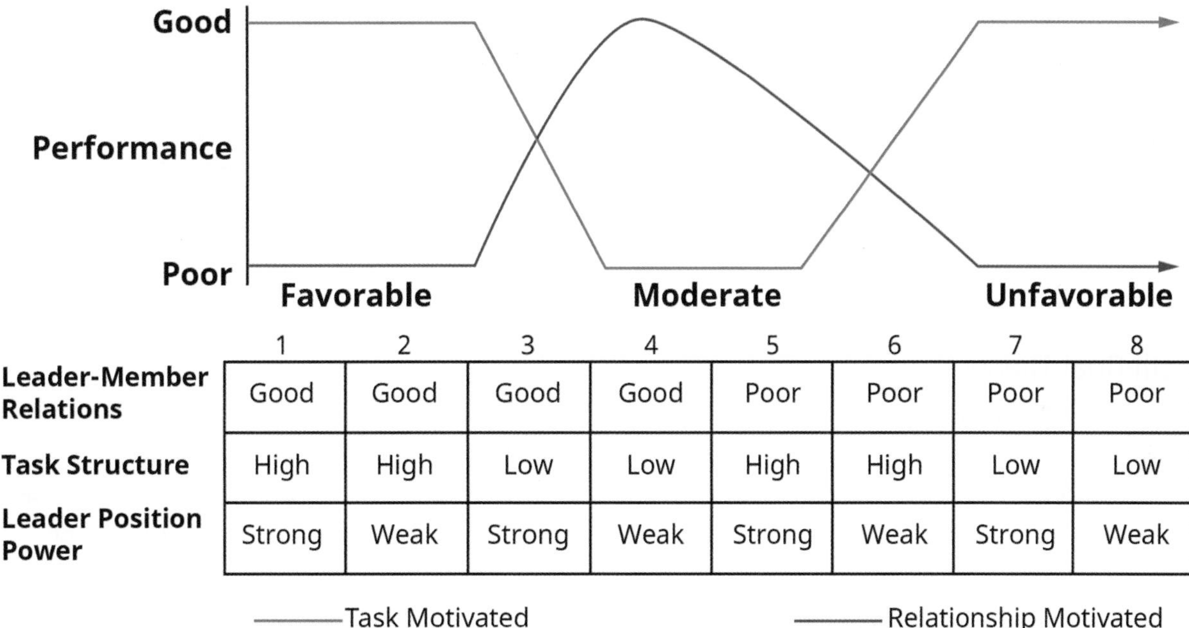

	1	2	3	4	5	6	7	8
Leader-Member Relations	Good	Good	Good	Good	Poor	Poor	Poor	Poor
Task Structure	High	High	Low	Low	High	High	Low	Low
Leader Position Power	Strong	Weak	Strong	Weak	Strong	Weak	Strong	Weak

Exhibit 12.10 Fiedler's Contingency Model of Leader-Situation Matches ***Source:*** Adapted from F. E. Fiedler and M. M. Chemers. 1974. *Leadership and effective management*. Glenview, IL: Scott, Foresman.

Leader-Situation Matches

Some combinations of leaders and situations work well; others do not. In search of the best combinations, Fiedler examined a large number of leadership situations. He argued that most leaders have a relatively unchangeable or dominant style, so organizations need to design job situations to fit the leader.[75]

While the model has not been fully tested and tests have often produced mixed or contradictory findings,[76] Fiedler's research indicates that relationship-oriented (high-LPC) leaders are much more effective under conditions of intermediate favorability than under either highly favorable or highly unfavorable situations. Fiedler attributes the success of relationship-oriented leaders in situations with intermediate favorability to the leader's nondirective, permissive attitude; a more directive attitude could lead to anxiety in followers, conflict in the group, and a lack of cooperation.

For highly favorable and unfavorable situations, task-oriented leaders (those with a low LPC) are very effective. As tasks are accomplished, a task-oriented leader allows the group to perform its highly structured tasks without imposing more task-directed behavior. The job gets done without the need for the leader's direction. Under unfavorable conditions, task-oriented behaviors, such as setting goals, detailing work methods, and guiding and controlling work behaviors, move the group toward task accomplishment.

As might be expected, leaders with mid-range LPC scores can be more effective in a wider range of situations than high- or low-LPC leaders.[77] Under conditions of low favorability, for example, a middle-LPC leader can be task oriented to achieve performance, but show consideration for and allow organizational members to proceed on their own under conditions of high situational favorability.

Controversy over the Theory

Although Fiedler's theory often identifies appropriate leader-situation matches and has received broad support, it is not without critics. Some note that it characterizes leaders through reference to their attitudes or personality traits (LPC) while it explains the leader's effectiveness through their behaviors—those with a particular trait will behave in a particular fashion. The theory fails to make the connection between the least-preferred coworker attitude and subsequent behaviors. In addition, some tests of the model have produced mixed or contradictory findings.[78] Finally, what is the true meaning of the LPC score—exactly what is being revealed by a person who sees their least-preferred coworker in positive or negative terms? Robert J. House and Ram N. Aditya recently noted that, in spite of the criticisms, there has been substantial support for Fiedler's theory.[79]

Path-Goal Theory

Robert J. House and Martin Evans, while on the faculty at the University of Toronto, developed a useful leadership theory. Like Fiedler's, it asserts that the type of leadership needed to enhance organizational effectiveness depends on the situation in which the leader is placed. Unlike Fiedler, however, House and Evans focus on the leader's observable behavior. Thus, managers can either match the situation to the leader or modify the leader's behavior to fit the situation.

The model of leadership advanced by House and Evans is called the **path-goal theory of leadership** because it suggests that an effective leader provides organizational members with a *path* to a valued *goal.* According to House, the motivational function of the leader consists of increasing personal payoffs to organizational members for work-goal attainment, and making the path to these payoffs easier to travel by clarifying it, reducing roadblocks and pitfalls, and increasing the opportunities for personal satisfaction en route.[80]

Effective leaders therefore provide rewards that are valued by organizational members. These rewards may be pay, recognition, promotions, or any other item that gives members an incentive to work hard to achieve goals. Effective leaders also give clear instructions so that ambiguities about work are reduced and followers understand how to do their jobs effectively. They provide coaching, guidance, and training so that followers can perform the task expected of them. They also remove barriers to task accomplishment, correcting shortages of materials, inoperative machinery, or interfering policies.

An Appropriate Match

According to the path-goal theory, the challenge facing leaders is basically twofold. First, they must analyze situations and identify the most appropriate leadership style. For example, experienced employees who work on a highly structured assembly line don't need a leader to spend much time telling them how to do their jobs—they already know this. The leader of an archeological expedition, though, may need to spend a great deal of time telling inexperienced laborers how to excavate and care for the relics they uncover.

Second, leaders must be flexible enough to use different leadership styles as appropriate. To be effective, leaders must engage in a wide variety of behaviors. Without an extensive repertoire of behaviors at their disposal, a leader's effectiveness is limited.[81] All team members will not, for example, have the same need for autonomy. The leadership style that motivates organizational members with strong needs for autonomy (participative leadership) is different from that which motivates and satisfies members with weaker autonomy needs (directive leadership). The degree to which leadership behavior matches situational factors will determine members' motivation, satisfaction, and performance (see **Exhibit 12.11**).[82]

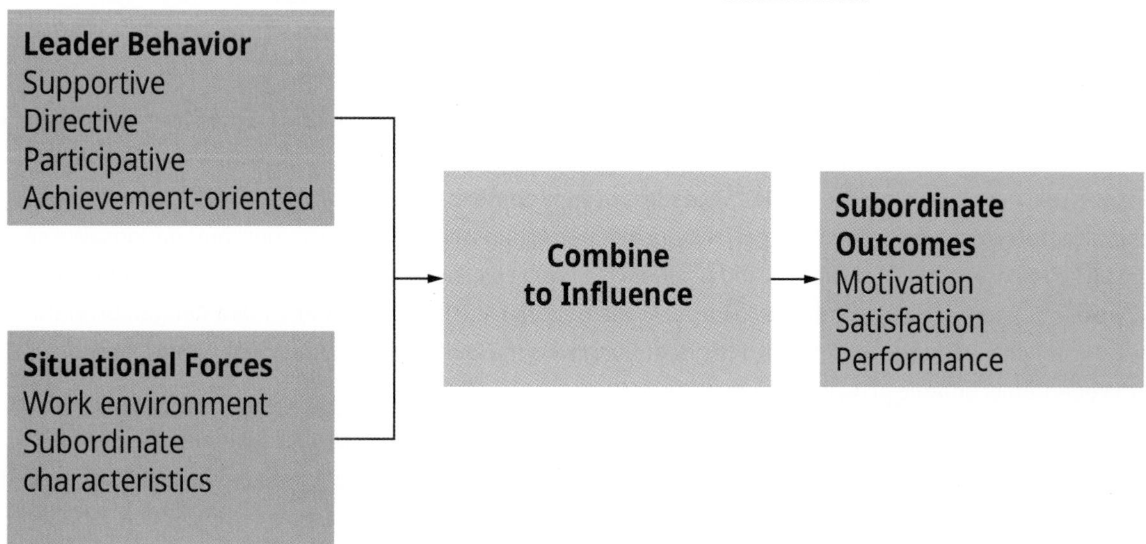

Exhibit 12.11 The Path-Goal Leadership Model

Behavior Dimensions

According to path-goal theory, there are four important dimensions of leader behavior, each of which is suited to a particular set of situational demands.[83]

- *Supportive leadership*—At times, effective leaders demonstrate concern for the well-being and personal needs of organizational members. Supportive leaders are friendly, approachable, and considerate to individuals in the workplace. Supportive leadership is especially effective when an organizational member is performing a boring, stressful, frustrating, tedious, or unpleasant task. If a task is difficult and a group member has low self-esteem, supportive leadership can reduce some of the person's anxiety, increase his confidence, and increase satisfaction and determination as well.
- *Directive leadership*—At times, effective leaders set goals and performance expectations, let organizational members know what is expected, provide guidance, establish rules and procedures to guide work, and schedule and coordinate the activities of members. Directive leadership is called for when role ambiguity is high. Removing uncertainty and providing needed guidance can increase members' effort, job satisfaction, and job performance.

- *Participative leadership*—At times, effective leaders consult with group members about job-related activities and consider their opinions and suggestions when making decisions. Participative leadership is effective when tasks are unstructured. Participative leadership is used to great effect when leaders need help in identifying work procedures and where followers have the expertise to provide this help.
- *Achievement-oriented leadership*—At times, effective leaders set challenging goals, seek improvement in performance, emphasize excellence, and demonstrate confidence in organizational members' ability to attain high standards. Achievement-oriented leaders thus capitalize on members' needs for achievement and use goal-setting theory to great advantage.

Cross-Cultural Context

Gabriel Bristol, the CEO of Intelifluence Live, a full-service customer contact center offering affordable inbound customer service, outbound sales, lead generation and consulting services for small to mid-sized businesses, notes "diversity breeds innovation, which helps businesses achieve goals and tackle new challenges."[84] *Multiculturalism* is a new reality as today's society and workforce become increasingly diverse. This naturally leads to the question "Is there a need for a new and different style of leadership?"

The vast majority of the contemporary scholarship directed toward understanding leaders and the leadership process has been conducted in North America and Western Europe. Westerners have "developed a highly romanticized, heroic view of leadership."[85] Leaders occupy center stage in organizational life. We use leaders in our attempts to make sense of the performance of our groups, clubs, organizations, and nations. We see them as key to organizational success and profitability, we credit them with organizational competitiveness, and we blame them for organizational failures. At the national level, recall that President Reagan brought down Communism and the Berlin Wall, President Bush won the Gulf War, and President Clinton brought unprecedented economic prosperity to the United States during the 1990s.

This larger-than-life role ascribed to leaders and the Western romance with successful leaders raise the question "How representative is our understanding of leaders and leadership across cultures?" That is, do the results that we have examined in this chapter generalize to other cultures?

Geert Hofstede points out that significant value differences (individualism-collectivism, power distance, uncertainty avoidance, masculinity-femininity, and time orientation) cut across societies. Thus, leaders of culturally diverse groups will encounter belief and value differences among their followers, as well as in their own leader-member exchanges.

There appears to be consensus that a universal approach to leadership and leader effectiveness does not exist. Cultural differences work to enhance and diminish the impact of leadership styles on group effectiveness. For example, when leaders empower their followers, the effect for job satisfaction in India has been found to be negative, while in the United States, Poland, and Mexico, the effect is positive.[86] The existing evidence suggests similarities as well as differences in such areas as the effects of leadership styles, the acceptability of influence attempts, and the closeness and formality of relationships. The distinction between task and relationship-oriented leader behavior, however, does appear to be meaningful across cultures.[87] Leaders whose behaviors reflect support, kindness, and concern for their followers are valued and effective in Western and Asian cultures. Yet it is also clear that democratic, participative, directive, and contingent-based rewards and punishment do not produce the same results across cultures. The United States is very different from Brazil, Korea, New Zealand, and Nigeria. The effective practice of leadership necessitates a careful look at, and understanding of, the individual differences brought to the leader-follower relationship by cross-cultural contexts.[88]

CONCEPT CHECK

1. Identify and describe the variables presented in Fiedler's theory of leadership.
2. What are the leadership behaviors in the path-goal theory of leadership?
3. What role does culture have in how leadership is viewed?
4. What are the differences between the trait, behavioral, and situational approaches to defining leadership?

12.7 Substitutes for and Neutralizers of Leadership

7. What does the concept "substitute for leadership" mean?

Several factors have been discovered that can substitute for or neutralize the effects of leader behavior (see **Table 12.1**).[89] *Substitutes* for leadership behavior can clarify role expectations, motivate organizational members, or satisfy members (making it unnecessary for the leader to attempt to do so). In some cases, these substitutes supplement the behavior of a leader. Sometimes it is a group member's characteristics that make leadership less necessary, as when a master craftsperson or highly skilled worker performs up to his or her own high standards without needing outside prompting. Sometimes the task's characteristics take over, as when the work itself—solving an interesting problem or working on a familiar job—is intrinsically satisfying. Sometimes the characteristics of the organization make leadership less necessary, as when work rules are so clear and specific that workers know exactly what they must do without help from the leader (see *An Inside Look* at flat management structure and the orchestra with no leader).

Substitutes for and Neutralizers of Leader Behavior

Supportive or Neutralizer	Leader Behavior Influenced	
	Substitute Leadership	Instrumental Leadership
A. Subordinate Characteristics:		
1. Experience, ability, training		Substitute
2. "Professional" orientation	Substitute	Substitute
3. Indifference toward rewards offered by organization	Neutralizer	Neutralizer
B. Task Characteristics:		
1. Structured, routine, unambiguous task		Substitute
2. Feedback provided by task		Substitute
3. Intrinsically satisfying task	Substitute	

Table 12.1

Substitutes for and Neutralizers of Leader Behavior		
	Leader Behavior Influenced	
Supportive or Neutralizer	Substitute Leadership	Instrumental Leadership
C. Organization Characteristics:		
1. Cohesive work group	Substitute	Substitute
2. Low position power (leader lacks control over organizational rewards)	Neutralizer	Neutralizer
3. Formalization (explicit plans, goals, areas of responsibility)		Substitute
4. Inflexibility (rigid, unyielding rules and procedures)		Neutralizer
5. Leader located apart from subordinates with only limited communication possible	Neutralizer	Neutralizer
Source: Adapted from *Leadership in organizations* by G. A. Yukl.		

Table 12.1

Neutralizers of leadership, on the other hand, are not helpful; they prevent leaders from acting as they wish. A computer-paced assembly line, for example, prevents a leader from using initiating structure behavior to pace the line. A union contract that specifies that workers be paid according to seniority prevents a leader from dispensing merit-based pay. Sometimes, of course, neutralizers can be beneficial. Union contracts, for example, clarify disciplinary proceedings and identify the responsibilities of both management and labor. Leaders must be aware of the presence of neutralizers and their effects so that they can eliminate troublesome neutralizers or take advantage of any potential benefits that accompany them (such as the clarity of responsibilities provided by a union contract). If a leader's effectiveness is being neutralized by a poor communication system, for example, the leader might try to remove the neutralizer by developing (or convincing the organization to develop) a more effective system.

Followers differ considerably in their *focus of attention* while at work, thereby affecting the effectiveness of the act of leadership. Focus of attention is an employee's cognitive orientation while at work. It reflects what and how strongly an individual thinks about various objects, events, or phenomena while physically present at work. Focus of attention reflects an individual difference in that not all individuals have the same cognitive orientation while at work—some think a great deal about their job, their coworkers, their leader, or off-the-job factors, while others daydream.[90] An employee's focus of attention has both "trait" and "state" qualities. For example, there is a significant amount of minute-by-minute variation in an employee's focus of attention (the "state" component), and there is reasonable consistency in the categories of events that employees think about while they are at work (the "trait" component).

Research suggests that the more followers focus on off-job (nonleader) factors, the less they will react to the leader's behaviors. Thus, a strong focus on one's life "away from work" (for example, time with family and friends) tends to neutralize the motivational, attitudinal, and/or behavioral effects associated with any particular leader behavior. It has also been observed, however, that a strong focus on the leader, either positive or negative, enhances the impact that the leader's behaviors have on followers.[91]

MANAGERIAL LEADERSHIP

You Are Now the Leader

Leading and managing are two very different things. Being a manager means something more than gaining authority or charge over former colleagues. With the title does come the power to affect company outcomes, but it also comes with something more: the power to shape the careers and personal growth of subordinates.

According to Steve Keating, a senior manager at the Toro Company, it is important not to assume that being made a manager automatically makes you a leader. Rather, being a manager means having the *opportunity* to lead. Enterprises need managers to guide processes, but the employees—the people—need a leader. Keating believes that leaders need a mindset that emphasizes people, and the leader's job is to help the people in the organization to be successful. According to Keating, "If you don't care for people, you can't lead them" (Hakim 2017 n.p.).

For someone who has been promoted over his peers, ground rules are essential. "Promotion doesn't mean the end of friendship but it does change it," according to Keating. If a *peer* has been promoted, rather than grouse and give in to envy, it is important to step back and look at the new manager; take a hard look at why the peer was promoted and what skill or characteristic made you a less appealing fit for the position (Hakim 2017).

Carol Walker, president of Prepared to Lead, a management consulting firm, advises new managers to develop a job philosophy. She urges new managers to develop a core philosophy that provides a guide to the day-to-day job of leading. She urges managers to build up the people they are leading and work as a "servant leader." The manager's perspective should be on employee growth and success. Leaders must bear in mind that employees don't work for the manager; they work for the organization—and for themselves. Managers coordinate this relationship; they are not the center of it. Work should not be assigned haphazardly, but with the employee's skills and growth in mind. "An employee who understands why she has been asked to do something is far more likely to assume true ownership for the assignment," Walker says (Yakowicz 2015 n.p.). A leader's agenda should be on employee success, not personal glory. Employees are more receptive when they recognize that their leader is working not for their own success, but for the employee's success.

A survey from HighGround revealed one important item that most new managers and even many seasoned managers overlook: asking for feedback. Everyone has room for growth, even managers. Traditional management dictates a top-down style in which managers review subordinates. But many companies have found it beneficial to turn things around and ask employees, "How can I be a better manager?" Of course, this upward review only works if employees believe that their opinion will be heard. Managers need to carefully cultivate a rapport where employees don't fear reprisals for negative feedback. Listening to criticism from those you are leading builds trust and helps ensure that as a manager, you are providing the sort of leadership that employees need to be successful (Kauflin 2017). Showing respect and caring for employees by asking this simple question is *inspiring*—an important aspect of leadership itself. Whether asking for feedback or focusing on an employee's fit with a particular job description, a leader helps guide employees through the day-to-day, builds a positive culture, and helps employees improve their skills.

Sources

Hakim, Amy C. 2017. “When a Manager Becomes a Leader.” *Psychology Today.* https://www.psychologytoday.com/blog/working-difficult-people/201706/when-manager-becomes-leader
Yakowicz, Will. 2015. “How to Help a New Manager Become a Great Leader.” *Inc.* https://www.inc.com/will-yakowicz/how-new-managers-become-great-leaders.html
Kauflin, Jeff. 2017. “Every Manager Can Become A Better Leader By Asking This One Question.” *Forbes.* https://www.forbes.com/sites/jeffkauflin/2017/04/21/every-manager-can-become-a-better-leader-by-asking-this-one-question/#3ca1eaff4ac1

Questions

1. What do you think are the most important qualities in a leader? In a manager? Are your two lists mutually exclusive? Why?
2. How do you think a leader can use feedback to model the growth process for employees?

CONCEPT CHECK 

1. Identify and describe substitutes of leadership.

12.8 Transformational, Visionary, and Charismatic Leadership

8. What are the characteristics of transactional, transformational, and charismatic leadership?

Many organizations struggling with the need to manage chaos, to undergo a culture change, to empower organizational members, and to restructure have looked for answers in “hiring the right leader.” Many have come to believe that the transformational, visionary, and charismatic leader represents the style of leadership needed to move organizations through chaos.

The Transformational and Visionary Leader

Leaders who subscribe to the notion that “if it ain’t broke, don’t fix it” are often described as *transactional leaders.* They are extremely task oriented and instrumental in their approach, frequently looking for incentives that will induce their followers into a desired course of action.[92] These reciprocal exchanges take place in the context of a mutually interdependent relationship between the leader and the follower, frequently resulting in interpersonal bonding.[93] The transactional leader moves a group toward task accomplishment by initiating structure and by offering an incentive in exchange for desired behaviors. The **transformational leader**, on the other hand, moves and changes (fixes) things “in a big way”! Unlike transactional leaders, they don’t cause change by offering inducements. Instead, they inspire others to action through their personal values, vision, passion, and belief in and commitment to the mission.[94] Through charisma (idealized influence), individualized consideration (a focus on the development of the follower), intellectual stimulation (questioning assumptions and challenging the status quo), and/or inspirational motivation (articulating an appealing vision), transformational leaders move others to follow.

The transformational leader is also referred to as a visionary leader. **Visionary leaders** are those who influence others through an emotional and/or intellectual attraction to the leader’s dreams of what “can be.” Vision links a present and future state, energizes and generates commitment, provides meaning for action, and serves as a standard against which to assess performance.[95] Evidence indicates that vision is positively related to follower attitudes and performance.[96] As pointed out by Warren Bennis, a vision is effective only to the extent that the leader can communicate it in such a way that others come to internalize it as their own.[97]

As people, transformational leaders are engaging. They are characterized by extroversion, agreeableness, and openness to experience.[98] They energize others. They increase followers' awareness of the importance of the designated outcome.[99] They motivate individuals to transcend their own self-interest for the benefit of the team and inspire organizational members to self-manage (become self-leaders).[100] Transformational leaders move people to focus on higher-order needs (self-esteem and self-actualization). When organizations face a turbulent environment, intense competition, products that may die early, and the need to move fast, managers cannot rely solely on organizational structure to guide organizational activity. In these situations, transformational leadership can motivate followers to be fully engaged and inspired, to internalize the goals and values of the organization, and to move forward with dogged determination!

Transformational leadership is positively related to follower satisfaction, performance, and acts of citizenship. These effects result from the fact that transformational leader behaviors elicit trust and perceptions of procedural justice, which in turn favorably impact follower satisfaction and performance.[101] As R. Pillai, C. Schriesheim, and E. Williams note, "when followers perceive that they can influence the outcomes of decisions that are important to them and that they are participants in an equitable relationship with their leader, their perceptions of procedural justice [and trust] are likely to be enhanced."[102] Trust and experiences of organizational justice promote leader effectiveness, follower satisfaction, motivation, performance, and citizenship behaviors.

Charismatic Leadership

Ronald Reagan, Jesse Jackson, and Queen Elizabeth I have something in common with Martin Luther King Jr., Indira Gandhi, and Winston Churchill. The effectiveness of these leaders originates in part in their **charisma**, a special magnetic charm and appeal that arouses loyalty and enthusiasm. Each exerted considerable personal influence to bring about major events.

It is difficult to differentiate the charismatic and the transformational leader. True transformational leaders may achieve their results through the magnetism of their personality. In this case, the two types of leaders are essentially one and the same, yet it is important to note that not all transformational leaders have a personal "aura."

Sociologist Max Weber evidenced an interest in charismatic leadership in the 1920s, calling **charismatic leaders** people who possess legitimate power that arises from "exceptional sanctity, heroism, or exemplary character."[103] Charismatic leaders "single-handedly" effect changes even in very large organizations. Their personality is a powerful force, and the relationship that they forge with their followers is extremely strong.

Exhibit 12.12 Travis Kalanick Travis Kalanick was a praised CEO of Uber who managed to increase the value of the company to over $60 billion. He was forced to resign after taking a leave of absence and having several key executives resign due to allegations of creating a hostile and unethical workplace.

The charismatic leadership phenomenon involves a complex interplay between the attributes of the leader and followers' needs, values, beliefs, and perceptions.[104] At its extreme, leader-follower relationships are characterized by followers' unquestioning acceptance; trust in the leader's beliefs; affection; willing obedience to, emulation of, and identification with the leader; emotional involvement with his mission; and feelings of self-efficacy directed toward the leader's mission.[105] This can work to better the welfare of individuals, such as when Lee Iacocca saved thousands of jobs through his dramatic turnaround of a failing corporate giant, the Chrysler Corporation. It also can be disastrous, as when David Koresh led dozens and dozens of men, women, and children to their fiery death in Waco, Texas. Individuals working for charismatic leaders often have higher task performance, greater task satisfaction, and lower levels of role conflict than those working for leaders with considerate or structuring behaviors.[106] What are the characteristics of these people who can exert such a strong influence over their followers? Charismatic leaders have a strong need for power and the tendency to rely heavily on referent power as their primary power base.[107] Charismatic leaders also are extremely self-confident and convinced of the rightness of their own beliefs and ideals. This self-confidence and strength of conviction make people trust the charismatic leader's judgment, unconditionally following the leader's mission and directives for action.[108] The result is a strong bond between leader and followers, a bond built primarily around the leader's personality.

Although there have been many effective charismatic leaders, those who succeed the most have coupled their charismatic capabilities with behaviors consistent with the same leadership principles followed by other effective leaders. Those who do not add these other dimensions still attract followers but do not meet organizational goals as effectively as they could. They are (at least for a time) the pied pipers of the business world, with lots of followers but no constructive direction.

ETHICS IN PRACTICE

Uber's Need for an Ethical Leader

Almost since its initial founding in 2009 as a luxury car service for the San Francisco area, controversy has followed Uber. Many complaints are against the tactics employed by the company's founder and former CEO, Travis Kalanick, but the effects are found throughout the business and its operations.

In 2009, UberBlack was a "black car" service, a high-end driving service that cost more than a taxi but less than hiring a private driver for the night. It wasn't until 2012 that the company launched UberX, the taxi-esque service most people think of today when they say "Uber." The UberX service contracted with private drivers who provided rides in their personal vehicles. A customer would use Uber's smartphone app to request the ride, and a private driver would show up. Originally launched in San Francisco, the service spread quickly, and by 2017, Uber was in 633 cities. The service was hailed by many as innovative and the free market's answer to high-priced and sometimes unreliable taxi services. But Uber has not been without its critics, both inside and outside of the company.

In 2013, as the UberX service spread, some UberBlack drivers protested at the company's headquarters complaining about poor company benefits and pay. They also claimed that competition from the newly launched UberX service was cutting into their sales and undermining job security. Kalanick rebuffed the protests, basically calling the complaints sour grapes: most of the protestors had been laid off earlier for poor service (Lawler 2013). Controversy also arose over the use of contract drivers rather than full-time employees. Contractors complained about a lack of benefits and low wages. Competitors, especially taxi services, complained that they were being unfairly undercut because Uber didn't have to abide by the same screening process and costs that traditional yellow taxi companies did. Some municipalities agreed, arguing further than Uber's lack of or insufficient screening of drivers put passengers at risk.

Uber quickly generated a reputation as a bully and Kalanick as an unethical leader (Ann 2016). The company has been accused of covering up cases of sexual assault, and Kalanick himself has been quoted as calling the service "Boob-er," a reference to using the service to pick up women (Ann 2016). Uber has been criticized for its recruiting practices; in particular, it has been accused of bribing drivers working for competitors to switch over and drive for Uber (Ann 2016).The company was also caught making false driver requests for competing companies and then canceling the order. The effect was to waste the other driver's time and make it more difficult for customers to secure rides on the competing service (D'Orazio 2014). Susan J. Fowler, former site reliability engineer at Uber, went public with cases of outright sexual harassment within Uber (Fowler 2017). Former employees described Uber's corporate culture as an "a**hole culture" and a "'Hobbesian jungle' where you can never get ahead unless someone else dies." (Wong 2017) One employee described a leadership that encouraged a company practice of developing incomplete solutions for the purpose of beating the competitor to market. Fowler went so far as to compare the experience to Game of Thrones, and other former employees even consider "making it" at Uber a black mark on a resume (Wong 2017).

In terms of social acrimony and PR disasters, arguably caused or even encouraged by leadership, Uber's rise to notoriety has arguably been more bad than good. In June 2017, Kalanick made one too many headlines and agreed to step down as the company's CEO.

Sources

Ann, Carrie. 2016. "Uber Is In Dire Need of Ethical Leadership." Industry Leaders. https://www.industryleadersmagazine.com/uber-dire-need-ethical-leadership/

D'Orazio, Dante. 2014. "Uber employees spammed competing car service with fake orders." *The Verge.* https://www.theverge.com/2014/1/24/5342582/uber-employees-spammed-competing-car-service-with-fake-orders

Fowler, Susan J. 2017. "Reflecting on One Very, Very Strange Year at Uber." https://www.susanjfowler.com/blog/2017/2/19/reflecting-on-one-very-strange-year-at-uber

Lawler, Ryan. 2013. "See, Uber — This Is What Happens When You Cannibalize Yourself." TechCruch.com. https://techcrunch.com/2013/03/15/see-uber-this-is-what-happens-when-you-cannibalize-yourself/

Wong, Julia. 2017. "Uber's 'hustle-oriented' culture becomes a black mark on employees' résumés" *The Guardian.* https://www.theguardian.com/technology/2017/mar/07/uber-work-culture-travis-kalanick-susan-fowler-controversy

Questions

1. In the summer of 2017, Transport of London (TfL) began proceedings to revoke Uber's permit to operate in London. How do think Uber's poor corporate reputation may have been a factor in TfL's thinking?
2. What steps do you think Uber's new CEO, Dara Khosrowshahi, needs to take to repair Uber's reputation?
3. Despite Uber's apparent success in launching in multiple markets, it continues to post quarterly losses in the millions and shareholders effectively subsidize 59 percent of every ride (https://www.reuters.com/article/us-uber-profitability/true-price-of-an-uber-ride-in-question-as-investors-assess-firms-value-idUSKCN1B3103). How is this an outworking of Uber's overall corporate culture?

CONCEPT CHECK 

1. What are the defining characteristics of transformational and charismatic leaders?

12.9 Leadership Needs in the 21st Century

9. How do different approaches and styles of leadership impact what is needed now?

Frequent headlines in popular business magazines like *Fortune* and *Business Week* call our attention to a major movement going on in the world of business. Organizations are being reengineered and restructured, and network, virtual, and modular corporations are emerging. People talk about the transnational organization, the boundaryless company, the post-hierarchical organization. By the end of the decade, the organizations that we will be living in, working with, and competing against are likely to be vastly different from what we know today.

The transition will not be easy; uncertainty tends to breed resistance. We are driven by linear and rational thinking, which leads us to believe that "we can get there from here" by making some incremental changes in who we are and what we are currently doing. Existing paradigms frame our perceptions and guide our thinking. Throwing away paradigms that have served us well in the past does not come easily.

A look back tells most observers that the past decade has been characterized by rapid change, intense competition, an explosion of new technologies, chaos, turbulence, and high levels of uncertainty. A quick scan of today's business landscape suggests that this trend is not going away anytime soon. According to Professor Jay A. Conger from Canada's McGill University, "In times of great transition, leadership becomes critically important. Leaders, in essence, offer us a pathway of confidence and direction as we move through seeming chaos. The magnitude of today's changes will demand not only *more* leadership, but *newer forms* of leadership."[109]

According to Conger, two major forces are defining for us the genius of the next generation of leaders. The first force is the organization's external environment. Global competitiveness is creating some unique leadership demands. The second force is the growing diversity in organizations' internal environments. Diversity will significantly change the relationship between organizational members, work, and the organization in challenging, difficult, and also very positive ways.

What will the leaders of tomorrow be like? Professor Conger suggests that the effective leaders of the 21st century will have to be many things.[110] They will have to be *strategic opportunists;* only organizational visionaries will find strategic opportunities before competitors. They will have to be *globally aware*; with 80 percent of today's organizations facing significant foreign competition, knowledge of foreign markets, global economics, and geopolitics is crucial. They will have to be *capable of managing a highly decentralized organization*; movement toward the high-involvement organization will accelerate as the environmental demands for organizational speed, flexibility, learning, and leanness increase. They will have be *sensitive to diversity*; during the first few years of the 21st century, fewer than 10 percent of those entering the workforce in North America will be white, Anglo-Saxon males, and the incoming women, minorities, and immigrants will bring with them a very different set of needs and concerns. They will have to be *interpersonally competent*; a highly diverse workforce will necessitate a leader who is extremely aware of and sensitive to multicultural expectations and needs. They will have to be *builders of an organizational community*; work and organizations will serve as a major source of need fulfillment, and in the process leaders will be called on to help build this community in such a way that organizational members develop a sense of ownership for the organization and its mission.

Finally, it is important to note that leadership theory construction and empirical inquiry are an ongoing endeavor. While the study of traits, behavior, and contingency models of leadership provide us with a great deal of insight into leadership, the mosaic is far from complete. During the past 15 years, several new theories of leadership have emerged; among them are leader-member exchange theory, implicit leadership theory, neocharismatic theory, value-based theory of leadership, and visionary leadership,[111] each of which over time will add to our bank of knowledge about leaders and the leadership process.

Leaders of the 21st-century organization have a monumental challenge awaiting them and a wealth of self-enriching and fulfilling opportunities. The challenge and rewards awaiting effective leaders are awesome!

CONCEPT CHECK

1. What is the role of leadership in the 21st century?

Key Terms

charisma A special personal magnetic charm or appeal that arouses loyalty and enthusiasm in a leader-follower relationship.

charismatic leader A person who possesses legitimate power that arises from "exceptional sanctity, heroism, or exemplary character."

consideration A "relationship-oriented" leader behavior that is supportive, friendly, and focused on personal needs and interpersonal relationships.

contingency theory of leadership A theory advanced by Dr. Fred E. Fiedler that suggests that different leadership styles are effective as a function of the favorableness of the leadership situation least preferred.

designated leader The person placed in the leadership position by forces outside the group.

emergent leader The person who becomes a group's leader by virtue of processes and dynamics internal to the group.

formal leader That individual who is recognized by those outside the group as the official leader of the group.

great man theory of leadership The belief that some people are born to be leaders and others are not.

informal leader That individual whom members of the group acknowledge as their leader.

initiating structure A "task-oriented" leader behavior that is focused on goal attainment, organizing and scheduling work, solving problems, and maintaining work processes.

leadership A social (interpersonal) influence relationship between two or more persons who depend on each other to attain certain mutual goals in a group situation.

Least-preferred coworker (LPC) The person with whom the leader least likes to work.

path-goal theory of leadership A theory that posits that leadership is path- and goal-oriented, suggesting that different leadership styles are effective as a function of the task confronting the group.

transformational leader A leader who moves and changes things "in a big way" by inspiring others to perform the extraordinary.

visionary leader A leader who influences others through an emotional and/or intellectual attraction to the leader's dreams of what "can be."

Summary of Learning Outcomes

12.1 The Nature of Leadership

1. What is the nature of leadership and the leadership process?

Leadership is a primary vehicle for fulfilling the directing function of management. Because of its importance, theorists, researchers, and practitioners have devoted a tremendous amount of attention and energy to unlocking the secrets of effective leadership. They have kept at this search for perhaps a greater period of time than for any other single issue related to management.

12.2 The Leadership Process

2. What are the processes associated with people coming to leadership positions?

Organizations typically have both formal and informal leaders. Their leadership is effective for virtually identical reasons. Leadership and management are not the same. Although effective leadership is a necessary part of effective management, the overall management role is much larger than leadership alone. Managers plan, organize, direct, and control. As leaders, they are engaged primarily in the directing function.

12.3 Leader Emergence

3. How do leaders influence and move their followers to action?

There are many diverse perspectives on leadership. Some managers treat leadership primarily as an exercise of power. Others believe that a particular belief and attitude structure makes for effective leaders. Still others believe it is possible to identify a collection of leader traits that produces a leader who should be universally effective in any leadership situation. Even today, many believe that a profile of behaviors can universally guarantee successful leadership. Unfortunately, such simple solutions fall short of the reality.

12.4 The Trait Approach to Leadership

4. What are the trait perspectives on leadership?

12.5 Behavioral Approaches to Leadership

5. What are the behavioral perspectives on leadership?

It is clear that effective leaders are endowed with the "right stuff," yet this "stuff" is only a precondition to effective leadership. Leaders need to connect with their followers and bring the right configuration of knowledge, skills, ability, vision, and strategy to the situational demands confronting the group.

12.6 Situational (Contingency) Approaches to Leadership

6. What are the situational perspectives on leadership?

We now know that there is no one best way to be an effective leader in all circumstances. Leaders need to recognize that how they choose to lead will affect the nature of their followers' compliance with their influence tactics, and ultimately impacts motivation, satisfaction, performance, and group effectiveness. In addition, the nature of the situation—contextual demands and characteristics of the follower—dictates the type of leadership that is likely to be effective. Fiedler focuses on leader traits and argues that the favorableness of the leadership situation dictates the type of leadership approach needed. He recommends selecting leaders to match the situation or changing the situation to match the leader. Path-goal theory focuses on leader behavior that can be adapted to the demands of a particular work environment and organizational members' characteristics. Path-goal theorists believe both that leaders can be matched with the situation and that the situation can be changed to match leaders. Together, these theories make clear that leadership is effective when the characteristics and behavior of the leader match the demands of the situation.

12.7 Substitutes for and Neutralizers of Leadership

7. What does the concept of "substitute for leadership" mean?

Characteristics of followers, tasks, and organizations can substitute for or neutralize many leader behaviors. Leaders must remain aware of these factors, no matter which perspective on leadership they adopt. Such awareness allows managers to use substitutes for, and neutralizers of, leadership to their benefit, rather than be stymied by their presence.

12.8 Transformational, Visionary, and Charismatic Leadership

8. What are the characteristics of transactional, transformational, and charismatic leadership?

In recent years, there has been a renewed interest in key leader traits and behaviors. As organizations face increasing amounts of chaos in their external environments, searches for "the right leader" who can bring about major organizational transformations has intensified. This search once again focuses our attention on a set of "key" motives, knowledge, skills, and personality attributes. Emerging from this search has been the identification of the charismatic and transformational leader.

12.9 Leadership Needs in the 21st Century

9. How do different approaches and styles of leadership impact what is needed now?

Leadership in the high-involvement organization differs dramatically from that in the traditional and control-oriented organization. Leaders external to the team have as one of their primary roles empowering group members and the teams themselves to self-lead and self-manage. Leaders internal to the team are peers; they work alongside and simultaneously facilitate planning, organizing, directing, controlling, and the execution of the team's work.

Although we know a great deal about the determinants of effective leadership, we have much to learn. Each theory presented in this chapter is put into practice by managers every day. None provides the complete answer to what makes leaders effective, but each has something important to offer.

Finally, our understanding of leadership has many shortcomings and limitations. The existing literature is largely based on observations from a Western industrialized context. The extent to which our theories of leadership are bound by our culture, limiting generalization to other cultures, is largely unknown. Cross-cultural leadership research will no doubt intensify as the global economy becomes an ever more dominant force in the world.

Chapter Review Questions

1. Define leadership and distinguish between leadership and management.
2. Discuss the processes associated with people coming to positions of leadership.
3. Discuss the different forms of power available to leaders and the effects associated with each.
4. It has been observed that effective leaders have the "right stuff." What traits are commonly associated with leader emergence and effective leaders?
5. Both the Ohio State University and University of Michigan leadership studies identified central leader behaviors. What are these behaviors, and how are they different from one another?
6. Blake and Mouton's work with the Leadership Grid® identified several leadership types. What are they, and how does this leadership model look from the perspective of situation theories of leadership?
7. Identify and describe the three situational variables presented in Fiedler's contingency theory of leadership.
8. What are the four leadership behaviors in the path-goal theory of leadership?
9. Discuss the differences between the internal and external leadership roles surrounding self-managed work teams.
10. What are substitutes for leadership? What are neutralizers? Give an example of each.
11. What are the distinguishing features of the transformational and the charismatic leader?

Management Skills Application Exercises

1. Identify a charismatic leader and a leader with little charisma. What are the traits and skills that allow them to succeed in their roles? How can you incorporate the traits that allow them to be successful in their roles into the skills you will need to have in a leadership position?
2. You have just taken a leadership position where 40 percent of the workforce telecommutes. You want to encourage teamwork and want to ensure that telecommuting is not hurting teamwork. What is your plan to discover how things are working and how to communicate your desire to have effective teamwork?
3. You are at a meeting, and during the meeting someone on the team addresses their manager and points out a crucial mistake that could doom the project. The person says that their manager should have

caught it and because of that should resign. As a leader of the group, how would you deal with the subordinate, the manager, and communication with the entire team?

Managerial Decision Exercises

1. You are the newly appointed commissioner of a major sports league that is currently in a very public game three of a best-of-seven-game playoff. After an emotional opening ceremony that recognizes a tragic event in the community that is widely praised, you settle in to enjoy the game. Early in the game, a player on one team is seen celebrating a scoring play by acting out a racially insensitive behavior after the play. How would you act in a leadership position? Read the ESPN article [**http://www.espn.com/mlb/story/_/id/21199462/rob-manfred-leadership-was-tested-yuli-gurriel-racially-insensitive-behavior-passed**] and comment on how this commissioner acted in this instance.
2. One of the challenges for a new manager in a leadership position is managing stress. Reflect on a time in your life where you have taken a leadership role in a summer job, as a member of a team, or in a study group for this or another course. Develop a stress management plan that includes how you can recognize stress, how you will notice the stress, how you will manage changes to address stress, and how you will seek outside counsel and help, including a mentor to help you manage stress.
3. Few people would want to hire a skilled manager with no leadership skills, and you would not want to hire an inspirational leader who can't manage planning, delegating, or keeping things organized. Draw two "T accounts" with positive attributes on the left and negative attributes on the right for managerial skills and leadership skills that you would look for as a hiring manager for a crucial managerial and leadership position in your organization.

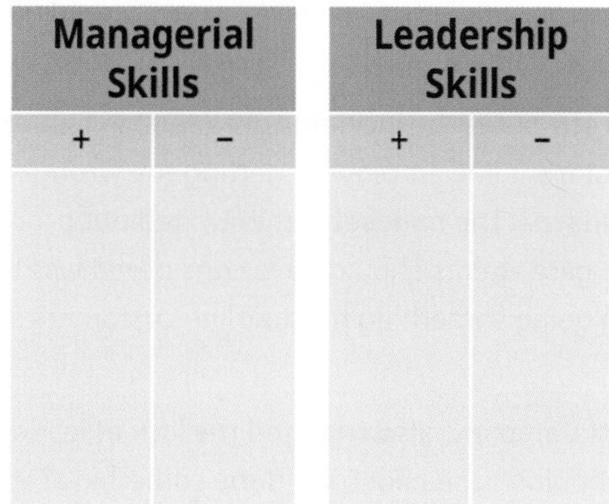

Exhibit 12.13

Critical Thinking Case

The Leadership Challenge at United

Anyone who has traveled even a little has at least one airline horror story: being stranded at an airport, obnoxious passengers, missed connections, flight delays, or just bad in-flight food. Even the most seasoned travelers would be hard-pressed to match Dr. David Dao's experience of being forcibly removed, kicking and screaming, from a United Airlines flight. Most airline horror stories don't end in a concussion, missing teeth, and a broken nose.

United Airlines CEO Oscar Munoz's strangely detached response only made things worse. The incident was caught on video, and that video went viral almost immediately. Munoz issued a response that mischaracterized what plainly happened in the video and termed the violent assault as a passenger "re-accommodation" (Taylor 2017). Social media erupted with condemnation, which was echoed by late-night monologues. United was left with a damaged reputation, and its management was left wondering why their processes failed, what to do to mitigate the damage, and how to both restore their reputation and ensure that company values are followed in the future.

William Taylor (2017), in a commentary in *Fortune*, attributes United's "re-accommodation" disaster as the product of company policy, airport security procedures, pilot protocols, and the "wisdom of crowds." At each step, the gate agent, pilot, airport security, and the passengers themselves could have intervened but didn't.

Brian Fielkow, business leader, author, and keynote speaker, writing at Entrepreneur.com, outlined some points that apply to Munoz's response and the first reactions by United. Citing United's core values, Fielkow points to Munoz's failure to address the incident in light of the company's values, take the blame, or even accurately describe what happened on the plane. Any *one* of these lapses in leadership would have caused confusion or stymied the recovery process. As a leader, Munoz was setting the tone for thousands of people. Seemingly abandoning United's core values likely caused a rift in trust or just simple confusion company-wide. Miscasting the situation in a world of smartphones and social media reach only multiplied the effect. As a leader, Munoz was duty-bound to take responsibility for what literally the entire world saw—a breach of social ethics, let alone United's core values. Failing to do this immediately created a problem larger than poorly planned company policy or just a perfect storm of contributing outside factors. Fielkow is keen to point out another crucial part of a company response— "You can't walk it back" (2017 n.p.). Before responding, leadership should take time to gather the facts and thoroughly consider the possibilities of how the message will be received. Again, Munoz's response failed at several key points, leading to the perception that Munoz's second statement was "an attempt at damage control" (Fielkow 2017 n.p.).

Al Bolea, a leadership trainer, also attributes the incident to leadership failure. In a piece written for *Applied Leadership*, Bolea writes, "It's about front line employees getting the wrong messages from the most senior levels of the company." He contends that the mindset within United put procedures above context in the minds of the employees. What the gate agents should have considered was the company's reputation, which should have prevented them from doing something most airline customers see as "profoundly immoral" (Bolea 2017 n.p.)

William C. Taylor, cofounder of Fast Company, also criticized the lack of leadership across United. As the presumptive leader of the flight, shouldn't the pilot have done something? Why didn't the gate agent think outside the box to solve the problem of getting the crew members from Chicago to Louisville, Kentucky? Why didn't—or couldn't—the gate agent use what Taylor refers to as a "common sense and a little bit of creativity" and prevent a highly embarrassing (and ultimately expensive) fiasco? Taylor muses that he would like to think he would have done more than shoot video, but the passengers on the flight remained quiet and submissive, expressing no group outrage. Finally, Taylor questions the weak initial response from United's CEO, Oscar Munoz, writing, "If CEO Oscar Munoz's goal was to make a disastrous situation even worse, well, he gets credit as a leader for succeeding at that" (2017 n.p.). And of the board, he questions their response, and says that response will be a "make or break test" of the company's character (Taylor 2017).

So what will it take to lead United out of such a public mistake?

According to Brian Fielkow, the incident flew in the face of United's core values, values which should never be sacrificed. United should have acknowledged this and addressed that failure. United should have held itself accountable for the incident rather than try to deflect blame. Fielkow contends that Munoz's first response was to blame the passenger when Munoz should have accepted responsibility instead. Further, Fielkow writes that companies should anticipate what "can" go wrong, something the gate agents at United failed to do. Increasing passenger compensation to even three times the normal ticket price would have been cheaper than the PR nightmare (and stock price drop) that followed. After Munoz's tepid response failed to quell general complaints about United's handling of the passenger, he tried to issue a second "more appropriate" statement, but by then the damage had been done. Fielkow recommends waiting before issuing a response if need be. It's better to prepared and issue a suitable response than to try to walk back a bad response. Above all, Fielkow recommends leaders "be human." The first response Munoz gave had little empathy and made him, and United, appear insensitive and callous. A company's first response should be to empathize with the customer, even if the customer is wrong. He writes, "When triaging a difficult problem, above all recognize the human factor" (Fielkow 2017 n.p.).

Writing in *Forbes*, Glenn Llopis emphasizes that how managers react to failure shapes their futures as leaders. Not only how leaders respond, but what is learned from a failure, will affect how future decisions are approached. Remember, you have to be doing something to fail, and if you never fail, then you aren't stretching yourself. Venturing into the unknown and unfamiliar always risks failure (Llopis 2012).

Sources:

Fielkow, Brian. 2017. "5 Leadership Failures that Contributed to the United Fiasco." *Entrepreneur.* https://www.entrepreneur.com/article/292820

Bolea, Al. 2017. "United Airlines: A System Failure?" *Applied Leadership.* http://appliedleadership.co/leadership/united-airlines-system-failure/

Taylor, William C. 2017. "Where was the Pilot on That United Airlines Flight?" *Fortune.* http://fortune.com/2017/04/11/united-airlines-video/

Llopis, Glenn. 2012. "5 Things Failure Teaches You About Leadership." *Forbes.* https://www.forbes.com/sites/glennllopis/2012/08/20/5-things-failure-teaches-you-about-leadership/2/#2f44c3873e70

Questions:

1. How have other airlines handled similar situations?
2. How much was in United Airlines's control, and how much was actually outside their control? What social or company factors caused a seemingly common practice to escalate to this level?
3. How did the other airlines or the industry respond to the United Airlines incident?

13 Organizational Power and Politics

Exhibit 13.1 (Credit: United States Mission Geneva/ flickr/ Attribution 2.0 Generic (CC BY 2.0))

Introduction

Learning Outcomes

After reading this chapter, you should be able to answer these questions:

1. How do power bases work in organizational life?
2. How do you recognize and account for the exercise of counterpower and make appropriate use of strategic contingencies in interunit or interorganizational relations?
3. How do managers cope effectively with organizational politics?
4. How do you recognize and limit inappropriate or unethical political behavior where it occurs?

EXPLORING MANAGERIAL CAREERS

Power Play at General Electric

For years, General Electric has been the pillar of manufacturing standards and stood as an icon for the American economy. Despite its strong history, CEO woes and a power struggle from within during the past few years have started to unravel the company's control.

Jeff Immelt, long-time CEO, was respected and revered for his discipline. However, this mentality took its toll and led to declines and complacency. The struggling company wanted change and desperately needed growth; it appointed John Flannery. Shortly after the appointment of Flannery, the new CEO pulled a change of his own as well—firing half of the company's board.

This type of move was almost unheard of, and the purge as presented was planning to cut dividends and slash less profitable business lines. The pressure from investors was felt immediately by Flannery, and this move was a desperate attempt to regain some footing and remain atop the industry standard.

Fast forward to 2018: after only one year on the job, the board decided it was done waiting for the turnaround and took drastic action, ousting Flannery and absorbing $23 billion in loss from the process.

The tumultuous and fast-paced changing tech-dominated economy of the 21st century showcases the harsh realities in this GE change of power. "The market didn't even give the company the benefit of the doubt that things would work," said Ivan Feinseth, chief investment officer at Tigress Financial Partners. "Flannery's plan hasn't worked." The market favors tech companies such as Google and Amazon rather than traditional manufacturers. And the new CEO, Lawrence Culp, will have an uphill battle to take over all of the woes of GE. As the first outsider to take over leadership, he has a lot to prove as well. His successes at Danaher preceded him and the company's stock has soared since the change occurred, already showing a positive impact.

Sources: O. Staley, " GE is firing half its board as a new CEO cleans house," *Quartz at Work*, November 20, 2017, https://qz.com/work/1133787/ge-is-firing-half-its-board-as-new-ceo-john-flannery-cleans-house/; T. Heath and J. McGregor, "General Electric, fallen icon of corporate stability, names first outsider as CEO," *Washington Post*, October 2, 2018, https://www.washingtonpost.com/business/2018/10/01/general-electric-replaces-new-chief-executive-announces-massive-billion-charge-amid-struggles/?utm_term=.0111eb2c36ea; M. Sheetz, "GE shares soar after company suddenly dumps John Flannery as CEO," *CNBC*, October 1, 2018, https://www.cnbc.com/2018/10/01/ge-removes-flannery-as-ceo-takes-23-billion-non-cash-charge-for-power-business-problems-and-withdraws-guidance.html; T. Rivas, "GE's New CEO Inherits a Troubled Kingdom. Here's What He Has to Do Now," *Barons*, October 2, 2018, https://www.barrons.com/articles/ges-new-ceo-inherits-a-troubled-kingdom-heres-what-he-has-to-do-now-1538495223.

Although the circumstances of the changes in leadership at GE may be unique, the exercise of power and political behavior in organizations is certainly not. Power and politics are the lifeblood of most organizations, and, as a result, informed managers need to understand power dynamics. In fact, organizations are composed of coalitions and alliances of different parties that continually compete for available resources. As such, a major influence on how decisions are made is the distribution of power among the decision makers. Unequal distribution of power in organizations can have a critical impact on many aspects of work life, including employee motivation, job satisfaction, absenteeism and turnover, and stress. Hence, an awareness of the nature and pervasiveness of power and politics is essential for a better understanding of these other behavioral processes.

The concept of power is closely related to the concepts of authority and leadership. It is important to understand when one method of influence ceases and another begins. For example, when does a manager stop using legitimate authority in a work situation and start using unauthorized power?

Finally, on an individual level, many people attempt to exercise influence in organizations by using power tactics. An awareness of such tactics helps managers to recognize them and to take appropriate actions. Keep in mind that attempts by others to exercise power do not have to be successful. A number of mechanisms are available to countermand or neutralize influence attempts. Knowledge of these strategies gives a manager greater latitude in his response to power plays by others.

In short, power and political processes in organizations represent a topic of central importance to students of organizational behavior. Along with other group processes, such as communication and decision-making, power and politics can considerably influence both the behavior and the attitudes of employees at various levels of the organization. In addition, they can further influence the extent to which various units within the organization secure the necessary resources for task accomplishment and ultimate organizational success. In short, General Electric is not alone.

13.1 Power in Interpersonal Relations

1. How do power bases work in organizational life?

In this chapter, we will examine various aspects of power and politics in organizations, beginning with the topic of power in interpersonal relations. Here, power is defined and distinguished from the related concepts of authority and leadership, and several bases of power and aspects of power dependency are discussed. Although these aspects of power also relate to group situations, they are more germane to interpersonal relations.

What Is Power?

Numerous definitions of power abound in the literature on organizations. One of the earliest was suggested by Max Weber, the noted German sociologist, who defined **power** as "the probability that one actor within a social relationship will be in a position to carry out his own will despite resistance."[1] Similarly, Emerson wrote, "The power of actor A over actor B is the amount of resistance on the part of B which can be potentially overcome by A."[2] Following these and other definitions, we will define *power* for our purposes as an interpersonal relationship in which one individual (or group) has the ability to cause another individual (or group) to take an action that would not be taken otherwise.

In other words, power involves one person changing the behavior of another. It is important to note that in most organizational situations, we are talking about *implied* force to comply, not necessarily actual force. That is, person *A* has power over person *B* if person *B* believes that person *A* can, in fact, force person *B* to comply.

Power, Authority, and Leadership

Clearly, the concept of power is closely related to the concepts of authority and leadership (see **Exhibit 13.2**). In fact, power has been referred to by some as "informal authority," whereas authority has been called "legitimate power." However, these three concepts are not the same, and important differences among the three should be noted.[3]

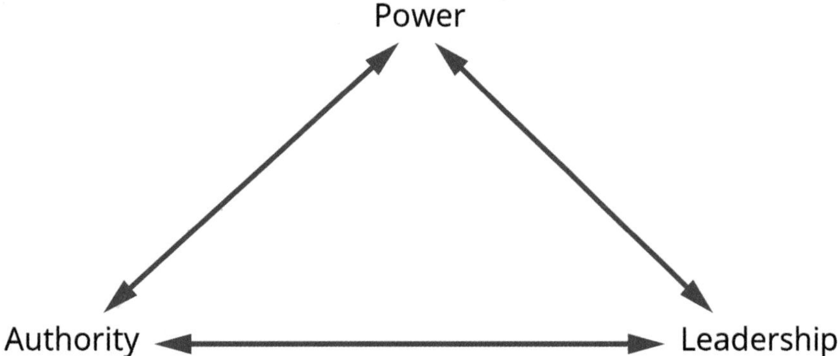

Exhibit 13.2 Three Major Types of Influence (Attribution: Copyright Rice University, OpenStax, under CC BY-NC-SA 4.0 license)

As stated previously, power represents the capacity of one person or group to secure compliance from another person or group. Nothing is said here about the *right* to secure compliance—only the ability. In contrast, **authority** represents the right to seek compliance by others; the exercise of authority is backed by legitimacy. If a manager instructs a secretary to type certain letters, he presumably has the authority to make such a request. However, if the same manager asked the secretary to run personal errands, this would be outside the bounds of the legitimate exercise of authority. Although the secretary may still act on this request, the secretary's compliance would be based on power or influence considerations, not authority.

Hence, the exercise of authority is based on group acceptance of someone's right to exercise legitimate control. As Grimes notes, "What legitimates authority is the promotion or pursuit of collective goals that are associated with group consensus. The polar opposite, power, is the pursuit of individual or particularistic goals associated with group compliance."[4]

Finally, **leadership** is the ability of one individual to elicit responses from another person that go beyond required or mechanical compliance. It is this voluntary aspect of leadership that sets it apart from power and authority. Hence, we often differentiate between headship and leadership. A department head may have the right to require certain actions, whereas a leader has the ability to inspire certain actions. Although both functions may be served by the same individual, such is clearly not always the case.

Types of Power

If power is the ability to secure compliance by others, how is such power exercised? On what is it based? At least two efforts have been made to identify the bases of power. One model has been proposed by Etzioni, identifying three types of power.[5] In fact, it is argued that organizations can be classified according to which of the three types of power is most prevalent. **Coercive power** involves forcing someone to comply with one's wishes. A prison organization is an example of a coercive organization. **Utilitarian power** is power based on performance-reward contingencies; for example, a person will comply with a supervisor in order to receive a pay raise or promotion. Business organizations are thought to be essentially utilitarian organizations. Finally, **normative power** rests on the beliefs of the members in the right of the organization to govern their behavior. An example here would be a religious organization.

Bases of Power

Although useful for comparative analysis of divergent organizations, this model may have limited applicability, because most business and public organizations rest largely on utilitarian power. Instead, a second model, developed by French and Raven, of the **bases of power** may be more helpful.[6] French and Raven identified five primary ways in which power can be exerted in social situations.

Referent Power. In some cases, person *B* looks up to or admires person *A,* and, as a result, *B* follows *A* largely because of *A*'s personal qualities, characteristics, or reputation. In this case, *A* can use **referent power** to influence *B*. Referent power has also been called *charismatic power,* because allegiance is based on interpersonal attraction of one individual for another. Examples of referent power can be seen in advertising, where companies use celebrities to recommend their products; it is hoped that the star appeal of the person will rub off on the products. In work environments, junior managers often emulate senior managers and assume unnecessarily subservient roles more because of personal admiration than because of respect for authority.

Expert Power. Expert power is demonstrated when person *A* gains power because *A* has knowledge or expertise relevant to *B*. For instance, professors presumably have power in the classroom because of their mastery of a particular subject matter. Other examples of expert power can be seen in staff specialists in organizations (e.g., accountants, labor relations managers, management consultants, and corporate attorneys). In each case, the individual has credibility in a particular—and narrow—area as a result of experience and expertise, and this gives the individual power in that domain.

Legitimate Power. Legitimate power exists when person *B* submits to person *A* because *B* feels that *A* has a right to exert power in a certain domain.[7] Legitimate power is really another name for authority, as explained earlier. A supervisor has a right, for instance, to assign work. Legitimate power differs from reward and coercive power in that it depends on the official position a person holds, and not on his or her relationship with others.

Legitimate power derives from three sources. First, prevailing cultural values can assign power to some group. In Japan and Korea, for instance, older employees derive power simply because of their age. Second, legitimate power can be attained as a result of the accepted social structure. For example, many Western European countries, as well as Japan, have royal families that serve as a cornerstone to their societies. Third, legitimate power may be designated, as in the case of a board of directors choosing a new company president or a person being promoted into a managerial position. Whatever the reason, people exercise legitimate power because subordinates assume they have a right to exercise it. A principal reason given for the downfall of the shah of Iran is that the people came to first question and then denounce his right to legitimate power.

Reward Power. Reward power exists when person *A* has power over person *B* because *A* controls rewards that *B* wants. These rewards can cover a wide array of possibilities, including pay raises, promotions, desirable job assignments, more responsibility, new equipment, and so forth. Research has indicated that reward power often leads to increased job performance as employees see a strong performance-reward contingency.[8] However, in many organizations, supervisors and managers really do not control very many rewards. For example, salary and promotion among most blue-collar workers is based on a labor contract, not a performance appraisal.

Coercive Power. *Coercive power* is based primarily on fear. Here, person *A* has power over person *B* because *A* can administer some form of punishment to *B*. Thus, this kind of power is also referred to as punishment power. As Kipnis points out, coercive power does not have to rest on the threat of violence. "Individuals exercise coercive power through a reliance upon physical strength, verbal facility, or the ability to grant or withhold emotional support from others. These bases provide the individual with the means to physically harm, bully, humiliate, or deny love to others."[9] Examples of coercive power in organizations include the ability (actual or implied) to fire or demote people, transfer them to undesirable jobs or locations, or strip them of valued perquisites. Indeed, it has been suggested that a good deal of organizational behavior (such as prompt attendance, looking busy, avoiding whistle-blowing) can be attributed to coercive, not reward, power. As Kipnis explains, "Of all the bases of power available to man, the power to hurt others is possibly the most often used, most often condemned and most difficult to control."[10]

Behavioral Consequences of Power

We have seen, then, that at least five bases of power can be identified. In each case, the power of the individual rests on a particular attribute of the power holder, the follower, or their relationship. In some cases (e.g., reward power), power rests in the superior; in others (e.g., referent power), power is given to the superior by the subordinate. In all cases, the exercise of power involves subtle and sometimes threatening interpersonal consequences for the parties involved. In fact, when power is exercised, employees have several ways in which to respond. These are shown in **Exhibit 13.3**.

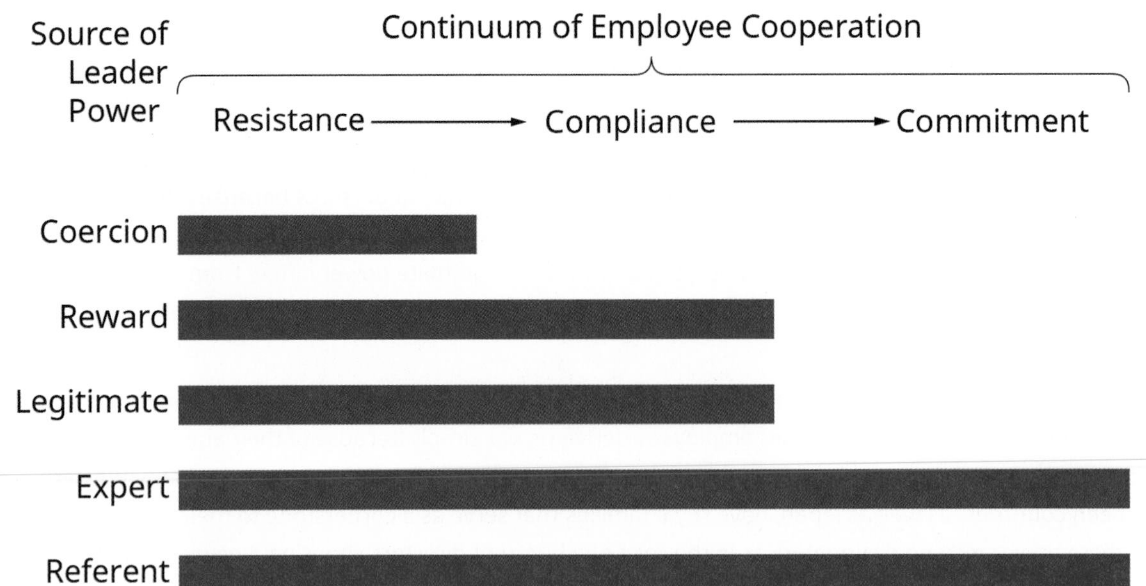

Exhibit 13.3 Employee Reactions to Bases of Power (Attribution: Copyright Rice University, OpenStax, under CC BY-NC-SA 4.0 license)

If the subordinate accepts and identifies with the leader, his behavioral response will probably be one of *commitment.* That is, the subordinate will be motivated to follow the wishes of the leader. This is most likely to happen when the person in charge uses referent or expert power. Under these circumstances, the follower believes in the leader's cause and will exert considerable energies to help the leader succeed.

A second possible response is *compliance.* This occurs most frequently when the subordinate feels the leader has either legitimate power or reward power. Under such circumstances, the follower will comply, either because it is perceived as a duty or because a reward is expected; but commitment or enthusiasm for the project is lacking. Finally, under conditions of coercive power, subordinates will more than likely use *resistance*. Here, the subordinate sees little reason—either altruistic or material—for cooperating and will often engage in a series of tactics to defeat the leader's efforts.

Power Dependencies

In any situation involving power, at least two persons (or groups) can be identified: the person attempting to influence others and the target or targets of that influence. Until recently, attention focused almost exclusively on how people tried to influence others. Only recently has attention been given to how people try to nullify or moderate such influence attempts. In particular, we now recognize that the extent to which influence attempts are successful is determined in large part by the **power dependencies** of those on the receiving end of the influence attempts. In other words, all people are not subject to (or dependent upon) the same bases of power. What causes some people to be more submissive or vulnerable to power attempts? At least three factors have been identified.[11]

Subordinate's Values. To begin, person *B*'s values can influence his susceptibility to influence. For example, if the outcomes that *A* can influence are important to *B*, then *B* is more likely to be open to influence than if the outcomes were unimportant. Hence, if an employee places a high value on money and believes the supervisor actually controls pay raises, we would expect the employee to be highly susceptible to the supervisor's influence. We hear comments about how young people don't really want to work hard anymore. Perhaps a reason for this phenomenon is that some young people don't place a high value on those things (for example, money) that traditionally have been used to influence behavior. In other words, such complaints may really be saying that young people are more difficult to influence than they used to be.

Nature of Relationship Between *A* and *B*. In addition, the nature of the relationship between *A* and *B* can be a factor in power dependence. Are *A* and *B* peers or superior and subordinate? Is the job permanent or temporary? A person on a temporary job, for example, may feel less need to acquiesce, because he won't be holding the position for long. Moreover, if *A* and *B* are peers or good friends, the influence process is likely to be more delicate than if they are superior and subordinate.

Counterpower. Finally, a third factor to consider in power dependences is **counterpower**. The concept of counterpower focuses on the extent to which *B* has other sources of power to buffer the effects of *A*'s power. For example, if *B* is unionized, the union's power may serve to negate *A*'s influence attempts. The use of counterpower can be clearly seen in a variety of situations where various coalitions attempt to bargain with one another and check the power of their opponents.

Exhibit 13.4 presents a rudimentary model that combines the concepts of bases of power with the notion of power dependencies. As can be seen, *A*'s bases of power interact with *B*'s extent of power dependency to determine *B*'s response to *A*'s influence attempt. If *A* has significant power and *B* is highly dependent, we would expect *B* to comply with *A*'s wishes.

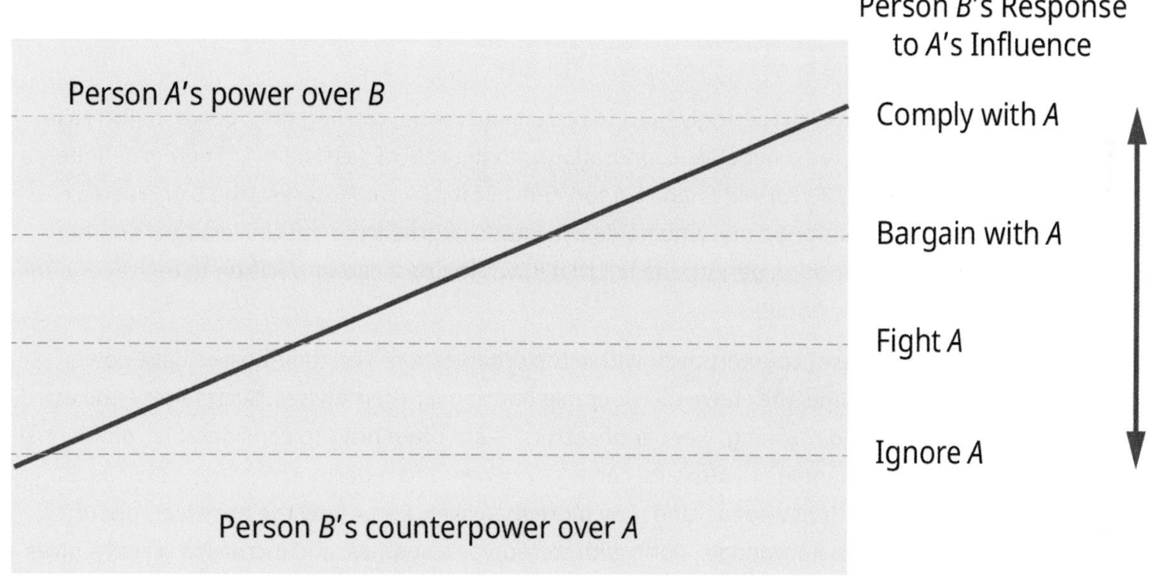

Exhibit 13.4 Typical Response Patterns in Dyadic Power Relationships (Attribution: Copyright Rice University, OpenStax, under CC BY-NC-SA 4.0 license)

If *A* has more modest power over *B,* but *B* is still largely power dependent, *B* may try to bargain with *A*. Despite the fact that *B* would be bargaining from a point of weakness, this strategy may serve to protect *B*'s interests better than outright compliance. For instance, if your boss asked you to work overtime, you might attempt to strike a deal whereby you would get compensatory time off at a later date. If successful, although you would not have decreased your working hours, at least you would not have increased them. Where power distribution is more evenly divided, *B* may attempt to develop a cooperative working relationship with *A* in which both parties gain from the exchange. An example of this position is a labor contract negotiation where labor-management relations are characterized by a balance of power and a good working relationship.

If *B* has more power than *A, B* will more than likely reject *A*'s influence attempt. *B* may even become the aggressor and attempt to influence *A*. Finally, when *B* is not certain of the power relationships, he may simply try to ignore *A*'s efforts. In doing so, *B* will discover either that *A* does indeed have more power or that *A* cannot muster the power to be successful. A good illustration of this last strategy can be seen in some companies' responses to early governmental efforts to secure equal opportunities for minorities and women. These companies simply ignored governmental efforts until new regulations forced compliance.

MANAGERIAL LEADERSHIP

Administrative Assistants: The Power Behind the Throne

It is relatively easy to see the power of managers. They often have the ability to hire and fire, make important decisions, sign contracts, spend money, and so forth. They are, in fact, powerful entities within a corporation. What may be less apparent, however, is the power that managers' executive or administrative assistants (EA) often have. In fact, if you want to discover just how powerful secretaries are, think of what would happen if they were not there. Most paperwork would not get done, many important decisions would not be made, and the organization would eventually grind to a halt.

The EA is intertwined with a very important piece of privileged information and requires the person to be highly detail oriented and have incredible soft skills and to be more than just technologically savvy. Many tech companies are paying top dollar to procure the right person for the job. Base salaries for executive assistants in the Bay area have been reportedly starting at $80–100K base.

Highly skilled EAs have become increasingly hard to recruit and retain, causing their power to increase. Despite the salary, there is often a negative connotation with the role of "assistant." "There's definitely a stigma" about the title, says 32-year-old Shana Larson, one of four EAs at Pinterest, the San Francisco visual discovery company. But for Shana, who holds a master's degree from the University of Southern California, after the initial transition period, she felt that it was the best career decision to make—a long-term career with growth opportunities.

EAs represent a true example of counterpower within the organization. Yes, their bosses have power over them; but at the same time, they have considerable power over their bosses. Secretaries—the word is derived from the Latin word meaning "keeper of secrets"—are often privy to considerable confidential information. They routinely handle private calls, correspondence, and reports. They often serve as the manager's sounding board for new ideas, and they more than likely know how the boss feels about coworkers and superiors. This knowledge, along with stereotypes, stigmas, and increased scarcity, gives high-quality EAs considerable leverage in dealing with their bosses and their organizations.

Questions:

1. As a new manager who receives an assistant, what are important considerations to consider when starting in the role?
2. What other stigmas or stereotypes can occur with support roles in the workplace? How does this affect your personal feelings about taking a support role for a company in the future?
3. Why is it important for CEOs and other organizational powers to understand the innate power of an administrative assistant as part of the holistic picture to understand the company environment as a whole?

Sources: *Linkedin* website accessed November 12, 2018, https://www.linkedin.com/salary/senior-executive-assistant-salaries-in-san-francisco-bay-area-at-hitachi-data-systems; S. Sathian, "Executive assistant is the new power job," *USA Today*, October 14, 2014, https://www.usatoday.com/story/money/business/2014/10/14/ozy-executive-assistant-power-job/17244533/; M. Lawn, "The Real Power of the Executive Assistant," *Executive Secretary Magazine*, July 27, 2013, http://executivesecretary.com/the-real-power-of-the-executive-assistant/; N. Price, "The Evolving Role of the Company Secretary in Today's Corporate World," *Board Effect Blog*, June 12, 2017, https://www.boardeffect.com/blog/evolving-role-company-secretary-todays-corporate-world/.

CONCEPT CHECK 

1. Define what Power is.
2. What are the components that constitute power in organizations?

13.2 Uses of Power

2. How do you recognize and account for the exercise of counterpower and make appropriate use of strategic contingencies in interunit or interorganizational relations?

As we look around organizations, it is easy to see the manifestations of power almost anywhere. In fact, there are a wide variety of power-based methods used to influence others. Here, we will examine three aspects of the use of power: commonly used power tactics in organizations, symbols of managerial power, and the ethical use of power.

Common Power Tactics in Organizations

As noted above, many power tactics are available for use by managers. However, as we will see, some are more ethical than others. Here, we look at some of the more commonly used power tactics found in both business and public organizations.[12]

Controlling Access to Information. Most decisions rest on the availability of relevant information, so persons *controlling access to information* play a major role in decisions made. A good example of this is the common corporate practice of pay secrecy. Only the personnel department and senior managers typically have salary information—and power—for personnel decisions.

Controlling Access to Persons. Another related power tactic is the practice of *controlling access to persons.* A well-known factor contributing to President Nixon's downfall was his isolation from others. His two senior advisers had complete control over who saw the president. Similar criticisms were leveled against President Reagan.

Selective Use of Objective Criteria. Very few organizational questions have one correct answer; instead, decisions must be made concerning the most appropriate criteria for evaluating results. As such, significant power can be exercised by those who can practice *selective use of objective criteria* that will lead to a decision favorable to themselves. According to Herbert Simon, if an individual is permitted to select decision criteria, he needn't care who actually makes the decision. Attempts to control objective decision criteria can be seen in faculty debates in a university or college over who gets hired or promoted. One group tends to emphasize teaching and will attempt to set criteria for employment dealing with teacher competence, subject area, interpersonal relations, and so on. Another group may emphasize research and will try to set criteria related to number of publications, reputation in the field, and so on.

Controlling the Agenda. One of the simplest ways to influence a decision is to ensure that it never comes up for consideration in the first place. There are a variety of strategies used for *controlling the agenda.* Efforts may be made to order the topics at a meeting in such a way that the undesired topic is last on the list. Failing this, opponents may raise a number of objections or points of information concerning the topic that cannot be easily answered, thereby tabling the topic until another day.

Using Outside Experts. Still another means to gain an advantage is *using outside experts.* The unit wishing to exercise power may take the initiative and bring in experts from the field or experts known to be in sympathy with their cause. Hence, when a dispute arises over spending more money on research versus actual production, we would expect differing answers from outside research consultants and outside production consultants. Most consultants have experienced situations in which their clients fed them information and biases they hoped the consultant would repeat in a meeting.

Bureaucratic Gamesmanship. In some situations, the organizations own policies and procedures provide ammunition for power plays, or **bureaucratic gamesmanship**. For instance, a group may drag its feet on making changes in the workplace by creating red tape, work slowdowns, or "**work to rule**." (Working to rule occurs when employees diligently follow every work rule and policy statement to the letter; this typically results in the organization's grinding to a halt as a result of the many and often conflicting rules and policy statements.) In this way, the group lets it be known that the workflow will continue to slow down until they get their way.

Coalitions and Alliances. The final power tactic to be discussed here is that of **coalitions** and *alliances.* One unit can effectively increase its power by forming an alliance with other groups that share similar interests. This technique is often used when multiple labor unions in the same corporation join forces to gain contract concessions for their workers. It can also be seen in the tendency of corporations within one industry to form trade associations to lobby for their position. Although the various members of a coalition need not agree on everything—indeed, they may be competitors—sufficient agreement on the problem under consideration is necessary as a basis for action.

Although other power tactics could be discussed, these examples serve to illustrate the diversity of techniques available to those interested in acquiring and exercising power in organizational situations. In reviewing the major research carried out on the topic of power, Pfeffer states:

If there is one concluding message, it is that it is probably effective, and it is certainly normal that these managers do behave as politicians. It is even better that some of them are quite effective at it. In situations in which technologies are uncertain, preferences are conflicting, perceptions are selective and biased, and information processing capacities are constrained, the model of an effective politician may be an appropriate one for both the individual and for the organization in the long run.[13]

Symbols of Managerial Power

How do we know when a manager has power in an organizational setting? Harvard professor Rosabeth Moss Kanter has identified several of the more common symbols of managerial power.[14] For example, managers have power to the extent that they can intercede favorably on behalf of someone in trouble with the organization. Have you ever noticed that when several people commit the same mistake, some don't get punished? Perhaps someone is watching over them.

Moreover, managers have power when they can get a desirable placement for a talented subordinate or get approval for expenditures beyond their budget. Other manifestations of power include the ability to secure above-average salary increases for subordinates and the ability to get items on the agenda at policy meetings.

And we can see the extent of managerial power when someone can gain quick access to top decision makers or can get early information about decisions and policy shifts. In other words, who can get through to the boss, and who cannot? Who is "connected," and who is not?

Finally, power is evident when top decision makers seek out the opinions of a particular manager on important questions. Who gets invited to important meetings, and who does not? Who does the boss say "hello" to when he enters the room? Through such actions, the organization sends clear signals concerning who has power and who does not. In this way, the organization reinforces or at least condones the power structure in existence.

The Ethical Use of Power

People are often uncomfortable discussing the topic of power, which implies that somehow they see the exercise of power as unseemly. On the contrary, the question is not whether power tactics are or are not ethical; rather, the question is *which* tactics are appropriate and which are not. The use of power in groups and companies is a fact of organizational life that all employees must accept. In doing so, however, all employees have a right to know that the exercise of power within the organization will be governed by ethical standards that prevent abuse or exploitation.

Several guidelines for the ethical use of power can be identified. These can be arranged according to our previous discussion of the five bases of power, as shown in **Table 13.1**. As will be noted, several techniques are available that accomplish their aims without compromising ethical standards. For example, a manager using reward power can verify subordinate compliance with work directives, ensure that all requests are both feasible and reasonable, make only ethical or proper requests, offer rewards that are valued by employees, and ensure that all rewards for good performance are credible and reasonably attainable.

The Ethical Use of Power	
Basis of Power	Guidelines for Use
Referent power	• Treat subordinates fairly • Defend subordinates' interests • Be sensitive to subordinates' needs, feelings • Select subordinates similar to oneself • Engage in role modeling

Table 13.1 (Attribution: Copyright Rice University, OpenStax, under CC BY-NC-SA 4.0 license)

The Ethical Use of Power	
Basis of Power	**Guidelines for Use**
Expert power	• Promote image of expertise • Maintain credibility • Act confident and decisive • Keep informed • Recognize employee concerns • Avoid threatening subordinates' self-esteem
Legitimate power	• Be cordial and polite • Be confident • Be clear and follow up to verify understanding • Make sure request is appropriate • Explain reasons for request • Follow proper channels • Exercise power regularly • Enforce compliance • Be sensitive to subordinates' concerns
Reward power	• Verify compliance • Make feasible, reasonable requests • Make only ethical, proper requests • Offer rewards desired by subordinates • Offer only credible rewards
Coercive power	• Inform subordinates of rules and penalties • Warn before punishing • Administer punishment consistently and uniformly • Understand the situation before acting • Maintain credibility • Fit punishment to the infraction • Punish in private
Source: Adapted from Gary A. Yukl, *Leadership in Organizations,* 8th edition 2013 (Englewood Cliffs, N.J.; Pearson), pp. 44–58.	

Table 13.1 (Attribution: Copyright Rice University, OpenStax, under CC BY-NC-SA 4.0 license)

Even coercive power can be used without jeopardizing personal integrity. For example, a manager can make sure that all employees know the rules and penalties for rule infractions, provide warnings before punishing, administer punishments fairly and uniformly, and so forth. The point here is that managers have at their disposal numerous tactics that they can employ without crossing over into questionable managerial behavior. In view of the increasing number of lawsuits filed by employees for harmful practices, it seems wise for a manager to consider his behaviors before acting; this will help ensure the highest ethical standards.

ETHICS IN PRACTICE

Investing the Challenger Disaster

The January 1986 explosion of the space shuttle *Challenger,* at a cost of seven lives, has been analyzed from several managerial standpoints: poor decision-making, poor management control, and poor leadership have all been blamed. We can also see in this tragedy an example of the unethical use of organizational power.

It has been determined that the explosion that doomed the space shuttle was caused by poorly designed seals on the booster rockets. The boosters were manufactured by Morton Thiokol, a major defense contractor. When the U.S. Congress initiated its investigation of the causes of the disaster, it found several disturbing facts. To begin with, several Morton Thiokol engineers had warned that the boosters were unsafe early in the design stage, but no one listened. Once the boosters were in production, engineers again warned of possible problems, but to no avail. The company kept the information quiet.

Equally disturbing was the fact that after two company engineers testified in the congressional hearing, they were abruptly transferred to undesirable assignments elsewhere in the company. When asked by Congress whether they thought their transfers were in retaliation for their whistleblowing, both engineers responded yes. One noted, "I feel I was set aside so I would not have contact with the people from NASA." The company had, in effect, used its power to try to isolate those who talked freely with the congressional investigators. In its defense, Morton Thiokol responded that it had *demoted* no one as a result of the investigation. "We've changed a lot of duties . . . because we're reorganizing," a management representative said.

Sources: A. E. Tenbrussel and M. Bazerman, *Blind Spots: Why we Fail to Do What's Right and What to Do About It,*" (Princeton, N.J.: Princeton University Press), © 2012; A. J. McDonald, "Ethics Lessons Learned From the Challenger Disaster," *National Society of Professional Engineers*, July 17, 2015; "Two Critics of Shuttle Perished," *Register-Guard,* May 11, 1986, pp. 1 and 4.

CONCEPT CHECK 

1. How is power used in organizations?
2. How can managers use strategy to counteract the negative use of power in organizations?

13.3 Political Behavior in Organizations

3. How do managers cope effectively with organizational politics?

Closely related to the concept of power is the equally important topic of politics. In any discussion of the exercise of power—particularly in intergroup situations—a knowledge of basic political processes is essential. We will begin our discussion with this in mind. Next, on the basis of this analysis, we will consider political strategies for acquiring, maintaining, and using power in intergroup relations. Finally, we look at ways to limit the impact of political behavior in organizations.

What Is Politics?

Perhaps the earliest definition of politics was offered by Lasswell, who described it as who gets what, when, and how.[15] Even from this simple definition, one can see that politics involves the resolution of differing preferences in conflicts over the allocation of scarce and valued resources. Politics represents one mechanism to solve allocation problems when other mechanisms, such as the introduction of new information or the use of a simple majority rule, fail to apply. For our purposes here, we will adopt Pfeffer's definition of politics as involving "those activities taken within organizations to acquire, develop, and use power and other resources to obtain one's preferred outcomes in a situation in which there is uncertainty or dissensus about choices."[16]

In comparing the concept of politics with the related concept of power, Pfeffer notes:

If power is a force, a store of potential influence through which events can be affected, politics involves those activities or behaviors through which power is developed and used in organizational settings. Power is a property of the system at rest; politics is the study of power in action. An individual, subunit or department may have power within an organizational context at some period of time; politics involves the exercise of power to get something accomplished, as well as those activities which are undertaken to expand the power already possessed or the scope over which it can be exercised.[17]

In other words, from this definition it is clear that political behavior is activity that is initiated for the purpose of overcoming opposition or resistance. In the absence of opposition, there is no need for political activity. Moreover, it should be remembered that political activity need not necessarily be dysfunctional for organization-wide effectiveness. In fact, many managers often believe that their political actions on behalf of their own departments are actually in the best interests of the organization as a whole. Finally, we should note that politics, like power, is not inherently bad. In many instances, the survival of the organization depends on the success of a department or coalition of departments challenging a traditional but outdated policy or objective. That is why an understanding of organizational politics, as well as power, is so essential for managers.

Intensity of Political Behavior

Contemporary organizations are highly political entities. Indeed, much of the goal-related effort produced by an organization is directly attributable to political processes. However, the intensity of political behavior varies, depending upon many factors. For example, in one study, managers were asked to rank several organizational decisions on the basis of the extent to which politics were involved.[18] Results showed that the most political decisions (in rank order) were those involving interdepartmental coordination, promotions and transfers, and the delegation of authority. Such decisions are typically characterized by an absence of established rules and procedures and a reliance on ambiguous and subjective criteria.

On the other hand, the managers in the study ranked as least political such decisions as personnel policies, hiring, and disciplinary procedures. These decisions are typically characterized by clearly established policies, procedures, and objective criteria.

On the basis of findings such as these, it is possible to develop a typology of when political behavior would generally be greatest and least. This model is shown in **Exhibit 13.5**. As can be seen, we would expect the greatest amount of political activity in situations characterized by high uncertainty and complexity and high competition among employees or groups for scarce resources. The least politics would be expected under conditions of low uncertainty and complexity and little competition among employees over resources.

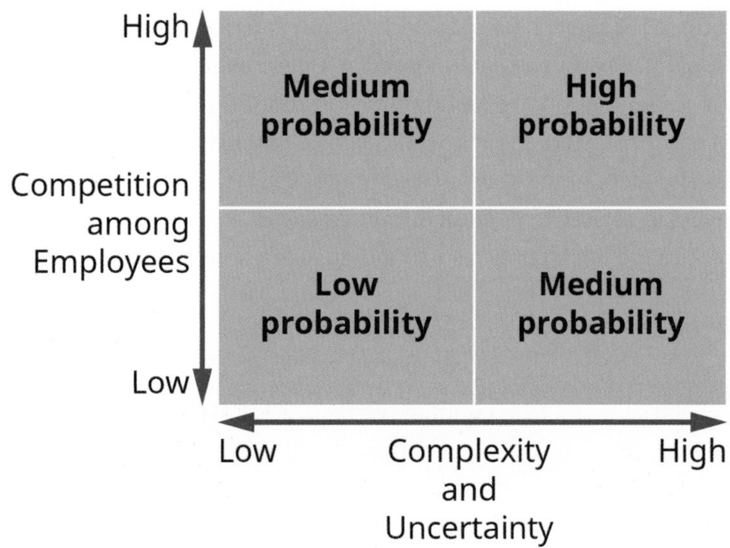

Exhibit 13.5 Probability of Political Behavior in an Organization *Source:* Adapted from "The Use and Abuse of Corporate Politics" by Don R. Beeman and Thomas W. Sharkey. Reprinted from *Business Horizons,* March–April 1987. (Attribution: Copyright Rice University, OpenStax, under CC BY-NC-SA 4.0 license)

Reasons for Political Behavior

Following from the above model, we can identify at least five conditions conducive to political behavior in organizations.[19] These are shown in **Table 13.2**, along with possible resulting behaviors. The conditions include the following:

1. *Ambiguous goals*. When the goals of a department or organization are ambiguous, more room is available for politics. As a result, members may pursue personal gain under the guise of pursuing organizational goals.
2. *Limited resources*. Politics surfaces when resources are scarce and allocation decisions must be made. If resources were ample, there would be no need to use politics to claim one's "share."
3. *Changing technology and environment*. In general, political behavior is increased when the nature of the internal technology is nonroutine and when the external environment is dynamic and complex. Under these conditions, ambiguity and uncertainty are increased, thereby triggering political behavior by groups interested in pursuing certain courses of action.
4. *Nonprogrammed decisions.* A distinction is made between programmed and nonprogrammed decisions. When decisions are not programmed, conditions surrounding the decision problem and the decision process are usually more ambiguous, which leaves room for political maneuvering. Programmed decisions, on the other hand, are typically specified in such detail that little room for maneuvering exists. Hence, we are likely to see more political behavior on major questions, such as long-range strategic planning decisions.
5. *Organizational change.* Periods of organizational change also present opportunities for political rather than rational behavior. Efforts to restructure a particular department, open a new division, introduce a new product line, and so forth, are invitations to all to join the political process as different factions and coalitions fight over territory.

Because most organizations today have scarce resources, ambiguous goals, complex technologies, and sophisticated and unstable external environments, it seems reasonable to conclude that a large proportion of contemporary organizations are highly political in nature.[20] As a result, contemporary managers must be sensitive to political processes as they relate to the acquisition and maintenance of power in organizations. This brings up the question of why we have policies and standard operating procedures (SOPs) in organizations. Actually, such policies are frequently aimed at reducing the extent to which politics influence a particular decision. This effort to encourage more "rational" decisions in organizations was a primary reason behind Max Weber's development of the bureaucratic model. That is, increases in the specification of policy statements often are inversely related to political efforts, as shown in **Exhibit 13.6**. This is true primarily because such actions reduce the uncertainties surrounding a decision and hence the opportunity for political efforts.

Conditions Conducive to Political Behavior	
Prevailing Conditions	**Resulting Political Behaviors**
Ambiguous goals	Attempts to define goals to one's advantage
Limited resources	Fight to maximize one's share of resources
Dynamic technology and environment	Attempts to exploit uncertainty for personal gain
Nonprogrammed decisions	Attempts to make suboptimal decisions that favor personal ends
Organizational change	Attempts to use reorganization as a chance to pursue own interests and goals

Table 13.2 (Attribution: Copyright Rice University, OpenStax, under CC BY-NC-SA 4.0 license)

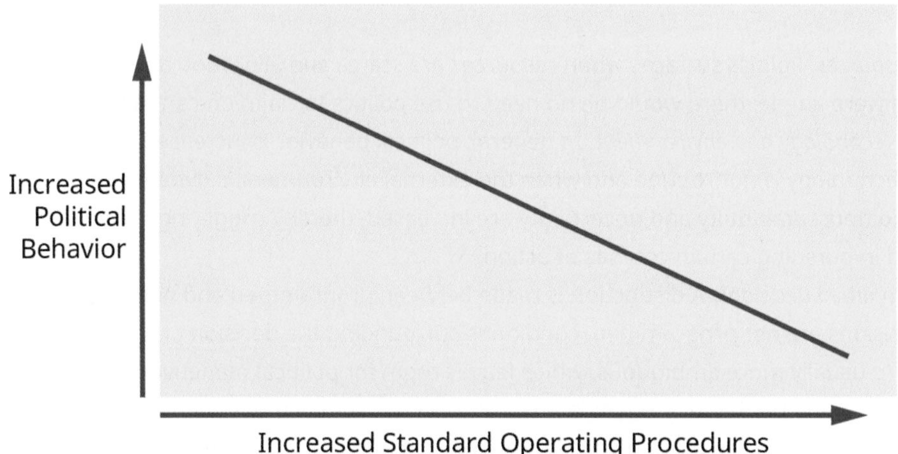

Exhibit 13.6 Relationship Between Company Standard Operating Procedures and Political Behavior (Attribution: Copyright Rice University, OpenStax, under CC BY-NC-SA 4.0 license)

(a) (b)

Exhibit 13.7 Open Office Corner Office Corner offices are considered desirable because they have windows on two exterior walls, as opposed to a typical office with only one window or none at all. They are usually assigned to the head of the organization or division. The open office concept has been around for some time and has evolved as technology has reduced the need to have access to stored paper records of a fixed phone or office computer. Having no walls, no doors, and shared workspaces is designed to achieve increased communication and flow of ideas amongst employees, but there is concern that an open concept decreases employees' job satisfaction and decreases privacy, which also affects productivity. (Attribution; Nic Bastian (Corner office) Loozerboy (Open Concept)/ flickr/ Attribution 2.0 Generic (CC BY 2.0))

MANAGERIAL LEADERSHIP

Technology, Innovation, and Politics in Performance Appraisals

Developing a strategy for a performance appraisal is an important step for any company, and keeping out political bias is a main concern as well. Unfortunately, many times there is no way around bringing some bias into a performance appraisal situation. Managers often think of the impact that their review will have on the employee, how it will affect their relationship, and what it means for their career in the future. There are a lot of games played in the rating process and whether managers admit it or not, they may be guilty of playing them. Many companies, such as Adobe, are looking at ways that they can revamp the process to eliminate potential biases and make evaluations fairer.

In 2012, Adobe transformed its business, changing its product cycle; while undergoing process changes, Adobe understood that there needed to be a cultural shift as well. It announced the "Check-in" review process to allow for faster feedback, as well as an end to their outdated annual review process. With the faster-paced reality of their product cycles and subscription-based model in technology, this made complete sense.

This process established a new way of thinking, allowing for two-way communication to become the norm between managers and employees. They were able to have frequent candid conversations, approaching the tough subjects in order make improvements rather than waiting until an annual review and letting bad performance go unchecked or good performance go unnoticed. Eliminating a once-a-year cycle of review also eliminates the issue of politics creeping into the process. Managers are able to think critically about the performance, working alongside their employees to better the outcome rather than worrying about having a tough conversation and the bad result that may follow—and having to live with the fallout. Employees also are given chances to provide feedback and their own personal evaluation, which then is discussed with the manager. They review the items together, and what is formally submitted is agreed upon, rather than set in stone. The addition of the employee feedback is another great way to reduce the insertion of politics or bias in the review.

In result of this change, Adobe's employees showed higher engagement and satisfaction with their work, consistently improving. They no longer had negative surprises in their annual review and were able to adjust priorities and behaviors to become more effective workers.

Questions:

1. What are important considerations to eliminate potential political bias in a performance review?
2. Why was Adobe successful in the changes that they implemented in their performance review process?
3. What other positive outcomes could be achieved from an ongoing feedback model versus annual performance review?

Sources: D. Morris, "Death of the Performance Review: How Adobe Reinvented Performance Management and Transformed its Business," *World at Work Journal*, Second Quarter, 2016, https://www.adobe.com/content/dam/acom/en/aboutadobe/pdfs/death-to-the-performance-review.pdf; "How Adobe retired performance reviews and inspired great performance," *Adobe* website, accessed January 4, 2019, https://www.adobe.com/check-in.html; K. Duggan, "Six Companies That Are Redefining Performance Management," *Fast Company*, December 15, 2015, https://www.fastcompany.com/3054547/six-companies-that-are-redefining-performance-management.

Political Strategies in Intergroup Relations

Uo this point, we have explained the related concepts of power and politics primarily as they relate to interpersonal behavior. When we shift our focus from the individual or interpersonal to the *intergroup* level of analysis, the picture becomes somewhat more complicated. In developing a portrait of how political strategies are used to attain and maintain power in intergroup relations, we will highlight two major aspects of the topic. The first is the relationship between power and the control of critical resources. The second is the relationship between power and the control of critical resources where the second is the relationship between power and the control of strategic activities. Both will illustrate how subunit control leads to the acquisition of power in organizational settings.

Power and the Control of Critical Resources

On the basis of what has been called the **resource dependence** model, we can analyze intergroup political behavior by examining how critical resources are controlled and shared.[21] That is, when one subunit of an organization (perhaps the purchasing department) controls a scarce resource that is needed by another subunit (for example, the power to decide what to buy and what not to buy), that subunit acquires power. This power may be over other subunits within the same organization or over subunits in other organizations (for example, the marketing units of other companies that are trying to sell to the first company). As such, this unit is in a better position to bargain for the critical resources it needs from its own or other organizations. Hence, although all subunits may contribute something to the organization as a whole, power allocation within the organization will be influenced by the relative importance of the resources contributed by each unit. To quote Salancik and Pfeffer,

Subunit power accrues to those departments that are most instrumental in bringing or in providing resources which are highly valued by the total organization. In turn, this power enables these subunits to obtain more of those scarce and critical resources allocated within the organization.

Stated succinctly, power derived from acquiring resources is used to obtain more resources, which in turn can be employed to produce more power—“the rich get richer.”[22]

To document their case, Salancik and Pfeffer carried out a major study of university budget decisions. The results were clear. The more clout a department had (measured in terms of the department’s ability to secure outside grants and first-rate graduate students, plus its national standing among comparable departments), the easier it was for the department to secure additional university resources. In other words, resources were acquired through political processes, not rational ones.[23]

Power and the Control of Strategic Activities

In addition to the control of critical resources, subunits can also attain power by gaining control over activities that are needed by others to complete their tasks. These critical activities have been called **strategic contingencies**. A contingency is defined by Miles as “a requirement of the activities of one subunit that is affected by the activities of other subunits.”[24] For example, the business office of most universities represents a strategic contingency for the various colleges within the university because it has veto or approval power over financial expenditures of the schools. Its approval of a request to spend money is far from certain. Thus, a contingency represents a source of uncertainty in the decision-making process. A contingency becomes *strategic* when it has the potential to alter the balance of interunit or interdepartmental power in such a way that interdependencies among the various units are changed.

Perhaps the best way to illustrate this is to consider the example of power distribution in various organizations attempting to deal with a major source of uncertainty—the external environment. In a classic study by Lawrence and Lorsch, influence patterns were examined for companies in three divergent industries: container manufacturing, food processing, and plastics. It was found that in *successful* firms, power distribution conformed to the firm’s strategic contingencies. For example, in the container-manufacturing companies, where the critical contingencies were customer delivery and product quality, the major share of power in decision-making resided in the sales and production staffs. In contrast, in the food-processing firms, where the strategic contingencies focused on expertise in marketing and food sciences, major power rested in the sales and research units. In other words, those who held power in the successful organizations were in areas that were of central concern to the firm and its survival at a particular time. The functional areas that were most important for organizational success were under the control of the decision makers. For less-successful firms, this congruence was not found.

The changing nature of strategic contingencies can be seen in the evolution of power distribution in major public utilities. Many years ago, when electric companies were developing and growing, most of the senior officers of the companies were engineers. Technical development was the central issue. More recently, however, as utilities face greater litigation, government regulation, and controversy over nuclear power, lawyers are predominant in the leadership of most companies. This example serves to emphasize that “subunits could inherit and lose power, not necessarily by their own actions, but by the shifting contingencies in the environment confronting the organization.”[25]

To better understand how this process works, consider the model shown in **Exhibit 13.8**. This diagram suggests that three factors influence the ability of one subunit (called *A*) over another (called *B*). Basically, it is argued that subunit power is influenced by (1) *A*’s ability to help *B* cope with uncertainty, (2) the degree to which *A* offers the only source of the required resource for *B*, and (3) the extent to which *A*’s contributions are central to organizational success. Let us consider each of these separately.

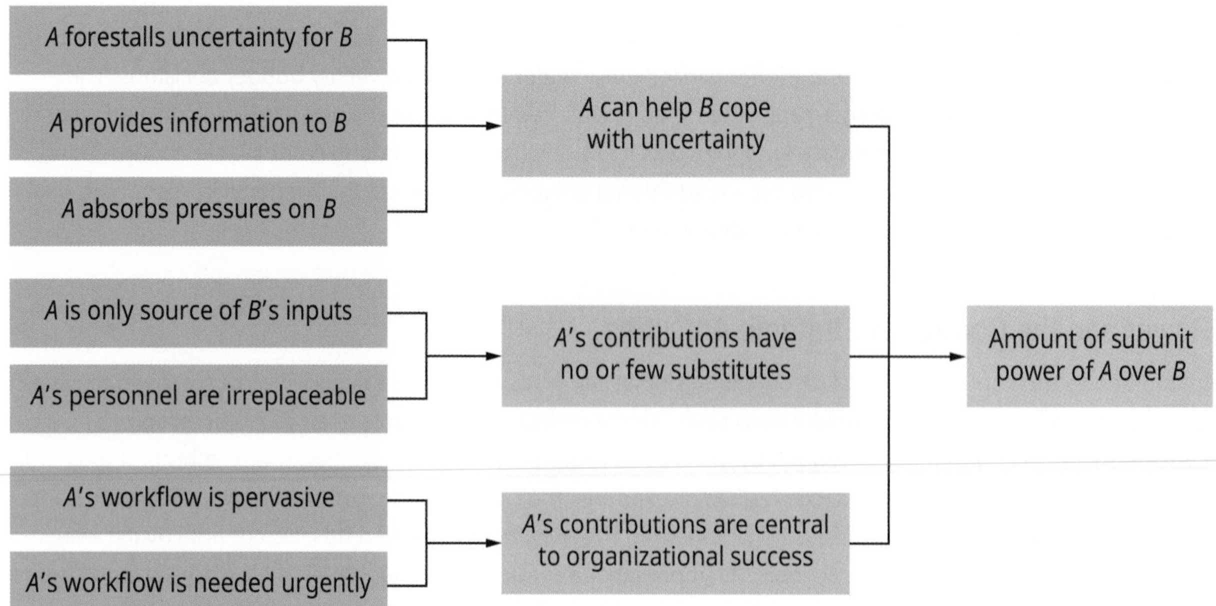

Exhibit 13.8 A Strategic Contingencies Model of Subunit Power (Attribution: Copyright Rice University, OpenStax, under CC BY-NC-SA 4.0 license)

Ability to Cope with Uncertainty. According to advocates of the strategic contingencies model of power, the primary source of subunit power is the unit's ability to help other units cope with uncertainty. In other words, if our group can help your group reduce the uncertainties associated with *your* job, then our group has power over your group. As Hickson and his colleagues put it:

Uncertainty itself does not give power; coping gives power. If organizations allocate to their various subunits task areas that vary in uncertainty, then those subunits that cope most effectively with the most uncertainty should have most power within the organization, since coping by a subunit reduces the impact of uncertainty on other activities in the organization, a shock absorber function.[26]

As shown in **Exhibit 13.8** above, three primary types of coping activity relating to uncertainty reduction can be identified. To begin, some uncertainty can be reduced through steps by one subunit to *prevent or forestall uncertainty* for the other subunit. For example, if the purchasing group can guarantee a continued source of parts for the manufacturing group, it gains some power over manufacturing by forestalling possible uncertainty surrounding production schedules. Second, a subunit's ability to cope with uncertainty is influenced by its capacity to *provide or collect information.* Such information can forewarn of probable disruptions or problems, so corrective action can be taken promptly. Many business firms use various forecasting techniques to predict sales, economic conditions, and so forth. The third mechanism for coping with uncertainty is the unit's *ability to absorb pressures* that actually impact the organization. For instance, if one manufacturing facility runs low on raw materials and a second facility can supply it with needed materials, this second facility effectively reduces some of the uncertainty of the first facility—and in the process gains influence over it.

In short, subunit *A* gains power over *B* subunit if it can help *B* cope with the contingencies and uncertainties facing it. The more dependent *B* is upon *A* to ensure the smooth functioning of the unit, the more power *A* has over *B*.

Nonsubstitutability of Coping Activities. Substitutability is the capacity for one subunit to seek needed resources from alternate sources. Two factors influence the extent to which substitutability is available to a subunit. First, the *availability of alternatives* must be considered. If a subunit can get the job done using different products or processes, it is less susceptible to influence. In the IBM-compatible personal computer market, for example, there are so many vendors that no one can control the market. On the other hand, if a company is committed to a Macintosh and iPad computing environment, only one vendor (Apple Computer) is available, which increases Apple's control over the marketplace.

Second, the *replaceability of personnel* is important. A major reason for the power of staff specialists (personnel managers, purchasing agents, etc.) is that they possess expertise in a specialized area of value to the organization. Consider also a reason for closed-shop union contracts: they effectively reduce the replaceability of workers.

Thus, a second influence on the extent of subunit power is the extent to which subunit *A* provides goods or services to *B* for which there are no (or only a few) substitutes. In this way, *B* needs *A* in order to accomplish subunit objectives.

Centrality of Coping Activities. Finally, one must consider the extent to which a subunit is of central importance to the operations of the enterprise. This is called the subunit's **work centrality**. The more interconnected subunit *A* is with other subunits in the organization, the more "central" it is. This centrality, in turn, is influenced by two factors. The first is **workflow pervasiveness**—the degree to which the actual work of one subunit is connected with the work of the subunits. If subunit *B* cannot complete its own tasks without the help of the work activities of subunit *A*, then *A* has power over *B*. An example of this is an assembly line, where units toward the end of the line are highly dependent upon units at the beginning of the line for inputs.

The second factor, **workflow immediacy**, relates to the speed and severity with which the work of one subunit affects the final outputs of the organization. For instance, companies that prefer to keep low inventories of raw materials (perhaps for tax purposes) are, in effect, giving their outside suppliers greater power than those companies that keep large reserves of raw materials.

When taken as a whole, then, the strategic contingency model of intergroup power suggests that subunit power is influenced when one subunit can help another unit reduce or cope with its uncertainty, the subunit is difficult to replace, or the subunit is central to continued operations. The more these three conditions prevail, the more power will become vested in the subunit. Even so, it should be recognized that the power of one subunit or group can shift over time. As noted by Hickson and his colleagues, "As the goals, outputs, technologies, and markets of organizations change, so, for each subunit, the values of the independent variables [such as coping with uncertainty, nonsubstitutability, and centrality] change, and the patterns of power change."[27] In other words, the strategic contingency model suggested here is a dynamic one that is subject to change over time as various subunits and groups negotiate, bargain, and compromise with one another in an effort to secure a more favorable position in the organizational power structure.

MANAGERIAL LEADERSHIP

The Politics of Innovation

A good example of the strategic contingencies approach to the study of power and politics can be seen in a consideration of organizational innovation. It has long been recognized that it is easier to invent something new from outside an organization than to innovate within an existing company. As a result, a disproportionate share of new products originates from small businesses and entrepreneurs, not the major corporations with all the resources to innovate. Why? Much of the answer can be found in politics.

When a person or group has a new idea for a product or service, it is often met with a barrage of resistance from different sectors of the company. These efforts are motivated by the famous "not-invented-here syndrome," the tendency of competing groups to fight over turf, and the inclination to criticize and destroy any new proposal that threatens to change the status quo. Other groups within the company simply see little reason to be supportive of the idea.

This lack of support—indeed, hostility—occurs largely because within every company there is competition for resources. These resources can include money, power, and opportunities for promotion. As one consultant noted, "One person's innovation is another person's failure." As a result, there is often considerable fear and little incentive for one strategic group within a company to cooperate with another. Because both groups usually need each other for success, nothing happens. To the extent that politics could be removed from such issues, far more energy would be available to capitalize on an innovative idea and get it to market before the competition.

Sources: M. Z. Taylor, The Politics of Innovation, (New York: Oxford University Press), 2017; B. Godin, "*The Politics of Innovation: Why Some Countries Are Better Than Others at Science and Technology* by Mark Zachary Taylor (review)," *Technology and Culture*, April 2018; W. Kiechel, "The Politics of Innovation," *Fortune,* April 11, 1988, p. 131.

CONCEPT CHECK 

1. What is politics and political behavior in organizations?

13.4 Limiting the Influence of Political Behavior

4. How do you recognize and limit inappropriate or unethical political behavior where it occurs?

The final topic we will examine concerns ways in which people and groups can attempt to lessen the impact of political behavior. Clearly, politics in organizations cannot be eliminated. Yet to some extent, the negative aspects of it can be neutralized if managers carefully monitor the work environment and take remedial action where necessary. Part of this issue was discussed above, in the section on counterpower. Beyond this, however, several strategies can be identified that can help manage organizational politics. As shown in **Table 13.3**, four basic strategies can be used.[28]

First, efforts can be made to reduce the uncertainty in the organization through clarifying job responsibilities, bases for evaluations and rewards, and so forth. The less ambiguity in the system, the less room there is for dysfunctional political behavior. Second, managers can try to reduce interpersonal or intergroup competition by using impartial standards for resource allocation and by emphasizing the superordinate goals of the entire organization—toward which all members of the organization should be working. Third, managers can attempt to break up existing political fiefdoms through personnel reassignment or transfer or by changing the reward system to encourage interunit cooperation. Finally, managers can work to prevent the development of future fiefdoms through training programs, selection and promotion, and reward distribution.

To the extent that employees see the organization as a fair place to work and to the extent that clear goals and resource allocation procedures are present, office politics should subside, though not disappear. In organizations where politics prosper, in fact, you are likely to find a reward system that encourages and promotes such behavior. The choice is up to the organization.

Limiting the Effects of Political Behavior
To Reduce System Uncertainty • Make clear what are the bases and processes for evaluation. • Differentiate rewards among high and low performers. • Make sure the rewards are as immediately and directly related to performance as possible.
To Reduce Competition • Try to minimize resource competition among managers. • Replace resource competition with externally oriented goals and objectives.
To Break Existing Political Fiefdoms • Where highly cohesive political empires exist, break them apart by removing or splitting the most dysfunctional subgroups. • If you are an executive, be keenly sensitive to managers whose mode of operation is the personalization of political patronage. First, approach these persons with a directive to "stop the political maneuvering." If it continues, remove them from the positions and preferably from the company.
To Prevent Future Fiefdoms • Make one of the most important criteria for promotion an apolitical attitude that puts organizational ends ahead of personal power ends.
Source: Adapted from "The Use and Abuse of Corporate Politics," by Don R. Beeman and Thomas W. Sharkey. Reprinted from *Business Horizons,* March–April 1987 by the Foundation for the School of Business at Indiana University.

Table 13.3 (Attribution: Copyright Rice University, OpenStax, under CC BY-NC-SA 4.0 license)

CONCEPT CHECK

1. How can managers limit inappropriate and unethical behavior in the organization?

Key Terms

Authority Represents the right to seek compliance by others.

Bases of power The five bases of power are referent, expert, legitimate, reward, and coercive power.

Bureaucratic gamesmanship A situation where the organizations own policies and procedures provide ammunition for power plays.

Coalition A situation where one unit can effectively increase its power by forming an alliance with other groups that share similar interests.

Coercive power Involves forcing someone to comply with one's wishes.

Counterpower Focuses on the extent to which person *B* has other sources of power to buffer the effects of person *A*'s power.

Expert power Occurs when person *A* gains power because *A* has knowledge or expertise relevant to person *B*.

Leadership The ability of one individual to elicit responses from another person that go beyond required or mechanical compliance.

Legitimate power Exists when person *B* submits to person *A* because *B* feels that *A* has a right to exert power in a certain domain.

Normative power Rests on the beliefs of the members in the right of the organization to govern their behavior.

Politics Involves those activities taken within an organization to acquire, develop, and use power and other resources to attain preferred outcomes in a situation in which there is uncertainty and disagreement over choices.

Power The probability that one actor within a social relationship will be in a position to carry out his own will despite resistance.

Power dependencies A state where all people are not subject to (or dependent upon) the same bases of power.

Referent power A state where allegiance is based on interpersonal attraction of one individual for another.

Resource dependence When one subunit of an organization controls a scarce resource that is needed by another subunit, that subunit acquires power.

Reward power Exists when person *A* has power over person *B* because *A* controls rewards that *B* wants. These rewards can cover a wide array of possibilities, including pay raises, promotions, desirable job assignments, more responsibility, new equipment, and so forth.

Strategic contingencies A requirement of the activities of one subunit that is affected by the activities of other subunits.

Utilitarian power Power based on performance-reward contingencies; for example, a person will comply with a supervisor in order to receive a pay raise or promotion.

Work centrality The more interconnected subunit *A* is with other subunits in the organization, the more central it is.

Work to rule Occurs when employees diligently follow every work rule and policy statement to the letter; this typically results in the organization's grinding to a halt as a result of the many and often conflicting rules and policy statements.

Workflow immediacy Relates to the speed and severity with which the work of one subunit affects the final outputs of the organization.

Workflow pervasiveness The degree to which the actual work of one subunit is connected with the work of the subunits.

Summary of Learning Outcomes

13.1 Power in Interpersonal Relations

1. How do power bases work in organizational life?

We might think of power like a car battery and influence as the current that actually gets the starter motor to turn over. There are many potential sources of power such as knowledge, information, and money. But just as the car battery unconnected cannot start an engine, these sources of power do not by themselves cause others to do anything. Actually, influencing others is achieved by possessing, or having others believe you possess, resources that they desire and depend upon and for which substitutes are not easily obtained and then establishing behavioral contingencies in the direction of the behaviors you desire to evoke.

Power is an interpersonal relationship in which one person or group has the ability to cause another person or group to take an action that it would not have taken otherwise.

There are five basic kinds of power: (1) referent, (2) expert, (3) legitimate, (4) reward, and (5) coercive.

Depending upon which kind of power is employed, the recipient of a power effort can respond with commitment, compliance, or resistance.

13.2 Uses of Power

2. How do you recognize and account for the exercise of counterpower and make appropriate use of strategic contingencies in interunit or interorganizational relations?

Power dependency is the extent to which a person or group is susceptible to an influence attempt. Included here is the notion of counterpower, or the ability of the subordinate to exercise some power and buffer the influence attempt of another.

Common power tactics include controlling access to information, controlling access to persons, the selective use of objective criteria, controlling the agenda, using outside experts, bureaucratic gamesmanship, and forming coalitions and alliances.

The resource dependence model suggests that one unit within an organization has power over another unit when the first unit controls scarce and valued resources needed by the second unit.

The strategic contingencies model asserts that one unit has power over another when the first group has the ability to block the second group's goal attainment—that is, when it controls some strategic contingency needed by the second group to complete its task.

13.3 Political Behavior in Organizations

3. How do managers cope effectively with organizational politics?

Politics involves those activities taken within an organization to acquire, develop, and use power and other resources to attain preferred outcomes in a situation in which there is uncertainty and disagreement over choices.

Political behavior is more likely to occur when (1) there are ambiguous goals, (2) there is a scarcity of resources, (3) nonroutine technology and a complex external environment are involved, (4) nonprogrammed decisions are being considered, and (5) organizational change is occurring.

13.4 Limiting the Influence of Political Behavior

4. How do you recognize and limit inappropriate or unethical political behavior where it occurs?

Political behavior can be reduced or minimized in organizations through four techniques: (1) reducing organization uncertainty, (2) reducing interunit competition, (3) breaking up political fiefdoms, and (4) preventing the development of future fiefdoms.

Chapter Review Questions

1. Compare and contrast power, authority, and leadership.
2. Identify five bases of power, and provide an example of each. Which base (or bases) of power do you feel would be most commonly found in organizations?
3. Discuss the concept of power dependencies. What is the relationship between power dependencies and bases of power?
4. What is counterpower? Provide an example of counterpower from your own experience.
5. Why is it important to understand political behavior in organizations?
6. Define politics. How does politics differ from power?
7. Compare and contrast the resource dependence model of power and politics with the strategic contingency model.
8. Identify several specific power tactics in organizations, and provide an example of each.
9. Why is it important that the exercise of power and politics be handled in an ethical fashion? What might happen if employees felt that managers were using power in an unethical fashion?

Management Skills Application Exercises

1. You might find it interesting to look at your own bases of power in an organization you have worked with. To do this, simply think of your present or past job, and complete this self-assessment. When you have finished, refer to **Appendix B** for scoring procedures.

What Are Your Bases of Power?

Instructions: Using a current or former job, answer each of the following items by circling the response that most suits your answer.

	Strongly Disagree			Strongly Agree	
1. I always try to set a good example for other employees.	1	2	3	4	5
2. My coworkers seem to respect me on the job.	1	2	3	4	5
3. Many employees view me as their informal leader at work.	1	2	3	4	5
4. I know my job very well.	1	2	3	4	5
5. My skills and abilities help me a lot on this job.	1	2	3	4	5
6. I continually try to improve the way I do my job.	1	2	3	4	5
7. I have considerable authority in my job.	1	2	3	4	5
8. Decisions made at my level are critical to organizational success.	1	2	3	4	5
9. Employees frequently ask me for guidance.	1	2	3	4	5
10. I am able to reward people at lower levels in the organization.	1	2	3	4	5
11. I am responsible for evaluating those below me.	1	2	3	4	5
12. I have a say in who gets a bonus or pay raise.	1	2	3	4	5
13. I can punish employees at lower levels.	1	2	3	4	5
14. I check the work of lower-level employees.	1	2	3	4	5
15. My diligence helps to reduce the errors of others on the job.	1	2	3	4	5

2. It might be interesting for you to evaluate your own level of political behavior. To do this, complete this self-assessment. When you have finished, score your questionnaire according to the procedure outlined in **Appendix B**.

How Political Are You?

Instructions: To determine your political appreciation and tendencies, please answer the following questions. Select the answer that better represents your behavior or belief, even if that particular behavior or belief is not present all the time.

1. You should make others feel important through an open appreciation of their ideas and work.	____ True ____ False

2. Because people tend to judge you when they first meet you, always try to make a good first impression.	____ True ____ False
3. Try to let others do most of the talking, be sympathetic to their problems, and resist telling people that they are totally wrong.	____ True ____ False
4. Praise the good traits of the people you meet and always give people an opportunity to save face if they are wrong or make a mistake.	____ True ____ False
5. Spreading false rumors, planting misleading information, and backstabbing are necessary, if somewhat unpleasant, methods to deal with your enemies.	____ True ____ False
6. Sometimes it is necessary to make promises that you know you will not or cannot keep.	____ True ____ False
7. It is important to get along with everybody, even with those who are generally recognized as windbags, abrasive, or constant complainers.	____ True ____ False
8. It is vital to do favors for others so that you can call in these IOUs at times when they will do you the most good.	____ True ____ False
9. Be willing to compromise, particularly on issues that are minor to you but important to others.	____ True ____ False
10. On controversial issues, it is important to delay or avoid your involvement if possible.	____ True ____ False
Source: Adapted from Joseph F. Byrnes, "Connecting Organizational Politics and Conflict Resolution," *Personnel Administrator,* June 1986, p.49.	

Managerial Decision Exercises

1. You have recently been promoted to the position of president of the division from your current role as VP of accounting and finance. Many people thought that the VP of sales and marketing would get the position, but you and he had always been friendly, and you thought that things would go smoothly. After about six months in the new position, you notice that he has been fighting you in small and subtle ways. You recognize his value, so you decide to let things play out and even mention other possibilities for promotion within the organization that he could apply for and that you would be supportive. After 11 months, things have not improved, and you are considering letting your colleague go. You are hesitant, however, because your organization needs a strong sales and marketing department. What should you do? If this power struggle continues, how do you think it will affect the larger organization?

Critical Thinking Case

The Ohio Connection

Janey worked as an executive assistant to a product manager at her company: Ohio Connection. Overall, she loved her job; she was happy to work with a company that provided great benefits, and she and found enjoyment in her day-to-day work. She had the same product manager boss for years, but last year, her manager left Ohio Connection and retired. Recently her new manager has been treating her unfairly and showcasing bullying behavior.

Yesterday, Janey came into work, and her boss decided to use their power as her manager and her "superior" to demand that she stay late to cover for him, correct reports that he had made mistakes on, and would not pay her overtime. She was going to be late to pick up her son from soccer practice if she stayed late; she told him this, and he was not happy.

Over subsequent days, her boss consistently would make comments about her performance, even though she had always had good remarks on reviews, and created a very negative work environment. The next time she was asked to stay late, she complied for fear of losing her job or having other negative impacts on her job. Janey's situation was not ideal, but she didn't feel she had a choice.

Questions:

1. What type of power did Janey's boss employ to get her to do the things that he wanted her to do?
2. What negative consequences are apparent in this situation and other situations where power is not balanced in the workplace?
3. What steps should Janey take do to counteract the power struggle that is occurring with her new manager?

Sources: A. Morin, "How to Prevent a Workplace Bully from taking Your Power," *Inc.*, June 25, 2018, https://www.inc.com/amy-morin/how-to-prevent-a-workplace-bully-from-taking-your-power.html; V. Giang, "The 7 Types Of Power That Shape The Workplace," *Business Insider,* July 31, 2013, https://www.businessinsider.com/the-7-types-of-power-that-shape-the-workplace-2013-7; B. Weinstein, "10 Tips for Dealing with a Bully Boss," *CIO*, accessed October 13, 2018, https://www.cio.com.au/article/198499/10_tips_dealing_bully_boss/.

14 Conflict and Negotiations

Exhibit 14.1 (Credit: Charles Edward Miller/ flickr/ Attribution 2.0 Generic (CC BY 2.0))

Introduction

Learning Outcomes

After reading this chapter, you should be able to answer these questions:

1. How do you recognize and resolve short- and long-term conflicts among group members and among groups?
2. How does conflict arise in organizations?
3. When and how do you negotiate, and how do you achieve a mutually advantageous agreement?
4. How do you recognize and respond to cultural differences in negotiation and bargaining strategies?

EXPLORING MANAGERIAL CAREERS

Conflict at Google

Over the past two years at Google, 48 people have been terminated for sexual harassment. There is a firm policy at Google pertaining to this type of misconduct, but when the effects of these types of events cause an uproar based on reports that a former top executive was paid millions of dollars after leaving Google despite misconduct and harassment allegations, it's important to get to the point of conflict and face it head on.

That's exactly why Chief Executive Officer Sundar Pichai did just that. In an attempt to get ahead of the storm, Pichai wrote an email to explaining that none of the individuals that were asked to leave were given severance packages. Despite this, employees are still feeling upset over such claims.

"The culture of stigmatization and silence *enables* the abuse by making it harder to speak up and harder to be believed," Liz Fong-Jones, who is quoted in the *Times*'s story, wrote on Twitter. "It's the abuse of power relationships in situations where there was no consent, or consent was impossible."

After the article came out in the *New York Times* reporting that Google gave Andy Rubin, former Android chief, a $90 million exit package, it was not just employees that were upset; there was external conflict between the company and Rubin. The media was heavily involved, including Bloomberg, and Rubin used social channels as well, making it even more complicated to counteract the negative comments or come to a resolution. Since the reports of Rubin's actions as well as additional reports regarding Google's permissive culture became public, Google has taken actions to update its policy on relationship disclosure.

This stance from the Google executive team is just one step in the right direction to address a culture that suggests a high level of conflict due to the protection of executives over the safety and well-being of the employees, who may be less likely to report incidents of abuse of power.

Sources: A. Barr, "Google CEO Tries to Calm Staff After Executive Misconduct Report," *Bloomberg*, October 25, 2018, https://www.bloomberg.com/news/articles/2018-10-25/google-ceo-tries-to-calm-staff-after-executive-misconduct-report; D. Wakabayashi and K. Benner, "How Google Protected Andy Rubin, the 'Father of Android'," *New York Times*, October 25, 2018, https://www.nytimes.com/2018/10/25/technology/google-sexual-harassment-andy-rubin.html; A. Panchadar, "Alphabet Harassment," New York Times, October 25, 2018, https://www.nytimes.com/reuters/2018/10/25/business/25reuters-alphabet-harassment.html.

In all organizations, including Google, some conflict is inevitable. Simply making a decision to do *A* instead of *B* often alienates the supporters of *B*, despite the soundness of the reasons behind the decision. Moreover, the consequences of conflict (and failed negotiations) can be costly to an organization, whether the conflict is between labor and management, groups, individuals, or nations. In an era of increasing business competition both from abroad and at home, reducing conflict is important. For these reasons, contemporary managers need a firm grasp of the dynamics of intergroup and interorganizational conflict and of negotiation processes.

We begin with a discussion of the conflict process, followed by a look at negotiations both within and between organizations.

14.1 Conflict in Organizations: Basic Considerations

1. How do you recognize and resolve short- and long-term conflicts among group members and among groups?

By any standard of comparison, conflict in organizations represents an important topic for managers. Just how important it is can be seen in the results of a study of how managers spend their time. It was found that approximately 20 percent of top and middle managers' time was spent dealing with some form of conflict.[1] In another study, it was found that managerial skill in handling conflict was a major predictor of managerial success and effectiveness.[2]

A good example of the magnitude of the problems that conflict can cause in an organization is the case of General Concrete, Inc., of Coventry, Rhode Island.[3] Operations at this concrete plant came to a halt for more than three weeks because the plant's one truck driver and sole member of the Teamsters Union began picketing after he was laid off by the company. The company intended to use other drivers from another of their plants. In response to the picketing, not a single employee of General Concrete crossed the picket line, thereby closing the plant and costing the company a considerable amount in lost production and profit. Could this problem have been handled better? We shall see.

In the sections that follow, several aspects of conflict in organizations are considered. First, conflict is defined, and variations of conflict are considered by type and by level. Next, constructive and destructive aspects of conflict are discussed. A basic model of the conflict process is then examined, followed by a look at several of the more prominent antecedents of conflict. Finally, effective and ineffective strategies for conflict resolution are contrasted. Throughout, emphasis is placed on problem identification and problem resolution.

There are many ways to determine conflict as it relates to the workplace. For our purposes here, we will define **conflict** as the process by which individuals or groups react to other entities that have frustrated, or are about to frustrate, their plans, goals, beliefs, or activities. In other words, conflict involves situations in which the expectations or actual goal-directed behaviors of one person or group are blocked—or about to be blocked—by another person or group. Hence, if a sales representative cannot secure enough funds to mount what she considers to be an effective sales campaign, conflict can ensue. Similarly, if *A* gets promoted and *B* doesn't, conflict can emerge. Finally, if a company finds it necessary to lay off valued employees because of difficult financial conditions, conflict can occur. Many such examples can be identified; in each, a situation emerges in which someone or some group cannot do what it wants to do (for whatever reason) and responds by experiencing an inner frustration.

Types of Conflict

If we are to try to understand the roots of conflict, we need to know what type of conflict is present. At least four *types of conflict* can be identified:

1. *Goal conflict.* **Goal conflict** can occur when one person or group desires a different outcome than others do. This is simply a clash over whose goals are going to be pursued.
2. *Cognitive conflict.* **Cognitive conflict** can result when one person or group holds ideas or opinions that are inconsistent with those of others. This type of conflict is evident in political debates.
3. *Affective conflict.* This type of conflict emerges when one person's or group's feelings or emotions (attitudes) are incompatible with those of others. **Affective conflict** is seen in situations where two individuals simply don't get along with each other.
4. *Behavioral conflict.* **Behavioral conflict** exists when one person or group does something (i.e., behaves in a certain way) that is unacceptable to others. Dressing for work in a way that "offends" others and using profane language are examples of behavioral conflict.

Each of these types of conflict is usually triggered by different factors, and each can lead to very different responses by the individual or group.

Levels of Conflict

In addition to different types of conflict, there exist several different *levels* of conflict. *Level* refers to the number of individuals involved in the conflict. That is, is the conflict within just one person, between two people, between two or more groups, or between two or more organizations? Both the causes of a conflict and the most effective means to resolve it can be affected by level. Four such levels can be identified:

1. *Intrapersonal conflict.* **Intrapersonal conflict** is conflict within one person. We often hear about someone who has an approach-avoidance conflict; that is, she is both attracted to and repelled by the same object. Similarly, a person can be attracted to two equally appealing alternatives, such as two good job offers

(approach-approach conflict) or repelled by two equally unpleasant alternatives, such as the threat of being fired if one fails to identify a coworker guilty of breaking plant rules (avoidance-avoidance conflict). In any case, the conflict is within the individual.

2. *Interpersonal conflict.* Conflict can also take form in an **interpersonal conflict**, where two individuals disagree on some matter. For example, you can have an argument with a coworker over an issue of mutual concern. Such conflicts often tend to get highly personal because only two parties are involved and each person embodies the opposing position in the conflict. Hence, it is sometimes difficult to distinguish between the opponent's position and her person.
3. *Intergroup conflict.* Third, conflict can be found between groups. **Intergroup conflict** usually involves disagreements between two opposing forces over goals or the sharing of resources. For example, we often see conflict between the marketing and production units within a corporation as each vies for more resources to accomplish its subgoals. Intergroup conflict is typically the most complicated form of conflict because of the number of individuals involved. Coalitions form within and between groups, and an "us-against-them" mentality develops. Here, too, is an opportunity for groupthink to develop and thrive.
4. *Interorganizational conflict.* Finally, we can see **interorganizational conflict** in disputes between two companies in the same industry (for example, a disagreement between computer manufactures over computer standards), between two companies in different industries or economic sectors (for example, a conflict between real estate interests and environmentalists over land use planning), and even between two or more countries (for example, a trade dispute between the United States and Japan or France). In each case, both parties inevitably feel the pursuit of their goals is being frustrated by the other party.

The Positive and Negative Sides of Conflict

People often assume that all conflict is necessarily bad and should be eliminated. On the contrary, there are some circumstances in which a moderate amount of conflict can be helpful. For instance, conflict can lead to the search for new ideas and new mechanisms as solutions to organizational problems. Conflict can stimulate innovation and change. It can also facilitate employee motivation in cases where employees feel a need to excel and, as a result, push themselves in order to meet performance objectives.

Conflict can at times help individuals and group members grow and develop self-identities. As noted by Coser:

Conflict, which aims at a resolution of tension between antagonists, is likely to have stabilizing and integrative functions for the relationship. By permitting immediate and direct expression of rival claims, such social systems are able to readjust their structures by eliminating their sources of dissatisfaction. The multiple conflicts which they experience may serve to eliminate the causes for dissociation and to reestablish unity. These systems avail themselves, through the toleration and institutionalization of conflict, of an important stabilizing mechanism.[4]

Conflict can, on the other hand, have negative consequences for both individuals and organizations when people divert energies away from performance and goal attainment and direct them toward resolving the conflict. Continued conflict can take a heavy toll in terms of psychological well-being. As we will see in the next chapter, conflict has a major influence on stress and the psychophysical consequences of stress. Finally, continued conflict can also affect the social climate of the group and inhibit group cohesiveness.

Thus, conflict can be either functional or dysfunctional in work situations depending upon the nature of the conflict, its intensity, and its duration. Indeed, both too much and too little conflict can lead to a variety of negative outcomes, as discussed above. This is shown in **Exhibit 14.2**. In such circumstances, a moderate amount of conflict may be the best course of action. The issue for management, therefore, is not how to eliminate conflict but rather how to manage and resolve it when it occurs.

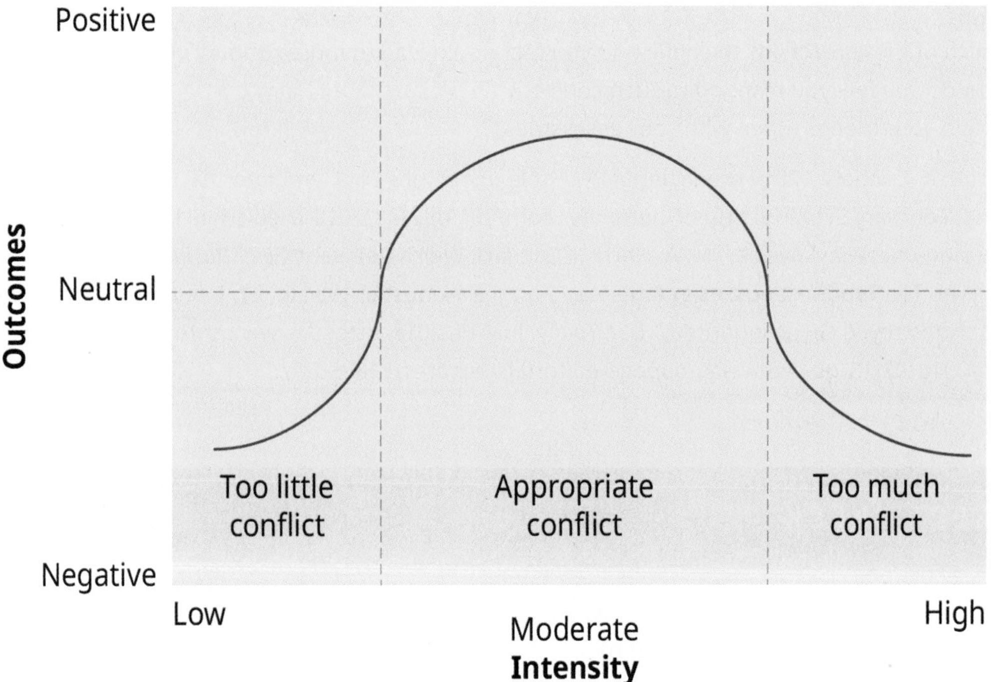

Exhibit 14.2 The Relationship Between Conflict Intensity and Outcomes *Source:* Adapted from L. David Brown, *Managing Conflict at Organizational Interfaces,* 1986 by Addison-Wesley Publishing Co., Inc., Reading, Massachusetts, Figure 1.1, p.8. (Attribution: Copyright Rice University, OpenStax, under CC BY-NC-SA 4.0 license)

MANAGERIAL LEADERSHIP

Executive Conflict Resolution Strategies

A good way to see how conflict can be functional or dysfunctional is to observe the behaviors of many of America's CEOs. Classic examples include the cases of Jack Welch, former chairman of General Electric, and Fred Ackman, former chairman of Superior Oil. Welch enjoyed a good fight and took pleasure in the give-and-take of discussions and negotiations. On one occasion, he engaged a senior vice president in a prolonged and emotional shouting match over the merits of a certain proposal. Several managers who were present were embarrassed by the confrontation. Yet after the argument, Welch thanked the vice president for standing up to him and defending his views. This is what Welch calls "constructive conflict," also termed **constructive confrontation**.

On the other hand, according to one account, Fred Ackman approached conflict quite differently. Ackman has been accused of being autocratic—he often refused even to discuss suggestions or modifications to proposals he presented. Disagreement was seen as disloyalty and was often met with an abusive temper. As one former subordinate said, "He couldn't stand it when someone disagreed with him, even in private. He'd eat you up alive, calling you a dumb S.O.B. . . . It happened all the time."

Many today will suggest that Jack Welch's management approach and the conglomerate approach of GE has led to the company's fiscal problems, while others fault the direction that Jack Welch's successor Jeff Immelt. Others say that leaders at other companies, such as Apple's Tim Cook, are making the same leadership errors as Jack Welch.

Questions:

1. Which of these reactions to conflict do you feel would lead to more productive results?
2. How do you feel you respond to such conflict?
3. Would your friends agree with your assessment?

Sources: R. X. Cringely, "2019 prediction #1 -- Apple under Tim Cook emulates GE under Jack Welch, *BetaNews*, February 27, 2019, https://betanews.com/2019/02/28/2019-prediction-1-apple-under-tim-cook-emulates-ge-under-jack-welch/; M. A. Harris, "Can Jack Welsh Reinvent GE?" *Business Week,* June 30, 1986; S. Flax, "The Ten Toughest Bosses in America," *Fortune,* August 6, 1984, p. 21; J. A. Byrne, "Jack Welch successor destroyed GE he inherited," *USA Today*, July 15, 2018, https://www.usatoday.com/story/opinion/2018/07/15/ge-ceo-welch-oppose-editorials-debates/36895027/.

CONCEPT CHECK 

1. Describe the types and levels of conflict found in organizations.
2. How can the use of power help and harm organizations?

14.2 Causes of Conflict in Organizations

2. How does conflict arise in organizations?

Here we will examine two aspects of the conflict process. First, several factors that have been found to contribute to conflict will be identified. After this, a model of conflict processes in organizations will be reviewed.

Why Organizations Have So Much Conflict

A number of factors are known to facilitate organizational conflict under certain circumstances. In summarizing the literature, Robert Miles points to several specific examples.[5] These are as follows:

Task Interdependencies. The first antecedent can be found in the nature of **task interdependencies**. In essence, the greater the extent of task interdependence among individuals or groups (that is, the more they have to work together or collaborate to accomplish a goal), the greater the likelihood of conflict if different expectations or goals exist among entities, in part because the interdependence makes avoiding the conflict more difficult. This occurs in part because high task interdependency heightens the intensity of relationships. Hence, a small disagreement can very quickly get blown up into a major issue.

Status Inconsistencies. A second factor is **status inconsistencies** among the parties involved. For example, managers in many organizations have the prerogative to take personal time off during workdays to run errands, and so forth, whereas nonmanagerial personnel do not. Consider the effects this can have on the nonmanagers' view of organizational policies and fairness.

Jurisdictional Ambiguities. Conflict can also emerge from **jurisdictional ambiguities**—situations where it is unclear exactly where responsibility for something lies. For example, many organizations use an employee selection procedure in which applicants are evaluated both by the personnel department and by the department in which the applicant would actually work. Because both departments are involved in the hiring process, what happens when one department wants to hire an individual, but the other department does not?

Communication Problems. Suffice it to say that the various *communication problems* or ambiguities in the communication process can facilitate conflict. When one person misunderstands a message or when information is withheld, the person often responds with frustration and anger.

Dependence on Common Resource Pool. Another previously discussed factor that contributes to conflict is *dependence on common resource pools.* Whenever several departments must compete for scarce resources, conflict is almost inevitable. When resources are limited, a zero-sum game exists in which someone wins and, invariably, someone loses.

Lack of Common Performance Standards. Differences in performance criteria and reward systems provide more potential for organizational conflict. This often occurs because of a *lack of common performance standards* among differing groups within the same organization. For example, production personnel are often rewarded for their efficiency, and this efficiency is facilitated by the long-term production of a few products. Sales departments, on the other hand, are rewarded for their short-term response to market changes—often at the expense of long-term production efficiency. In such situations, conflict arises as each unit attempts to meet its own performance criteria.

Individual Differences. Finally, a variety of *individual differences*, such as personal abilities, traits, and skills, can influence in no small way the nature of interpersonal relations. Individual dominance, aggressiveness, authoritarianism, and tolerance for ambiguity all seem to influence how an individual deals with potential conflict. Indeed, such characteristics may determine whether or not conflict is created at all.

A Model of the Conflict Process

Having examined specific factors that are known to facilitate conflict, we can ask how conflict comes about in organizations. The most commonly accepted model of the conflict process was developed by Kenneth Thomas.[6] This model, shown in **Exhibit 14.3**, consists of four stages: (1) frustration, (2) conceptualization, (3) behavior, and (4) outcome.

Stage 1: Frustration. As we have seen, conflict situations originate when an individual or group feels **frustration** in the pursuit of important goals. This frustration may be caused by a wide variety of factors, including disagreement over performance goals, failure to get a promotion or pay raise, a fight over scarce economic resources, new rules or policies, and so forth. In fact, conflict can be traced to frustration over almost anything a group or individual cares about.

Stage 2: Conceptualization. In stage 2, the conceptualization stage of the model, parties to the conflict attempt to understand the nature of the problem, what they themselves want as a resolution, what they think their opponents want as a resolution, and various strategies they feel each side may employ in resolving the conflict. This stage is really the problem-solving and strategy phase. For instance, when management and union negotiate a labor contract, both sides attempt to decide what is most important and what can be bargained away in exchange for these priority needs.

Stage 3: Behavior. The third stage in Thomas's model is actual *behavior*. As a result of the conceptualization process, parties to a conflict attempt to implement their resolution mode by competing or accommodating in the hope of resolving problems. A major task here is determining how best to proceed strategically. That is, what tactics will the party use to attempt to resolve the conflict? Thomas has identified five modes for conflict resolution, as shown in **Exhibit 14.3**. These are (1) competing, (2) collaborating, (3) compromising, (4) avoiding, and (5) accommodating. Also shown in the exhibit are situations that seem most appropriate for each strategy.

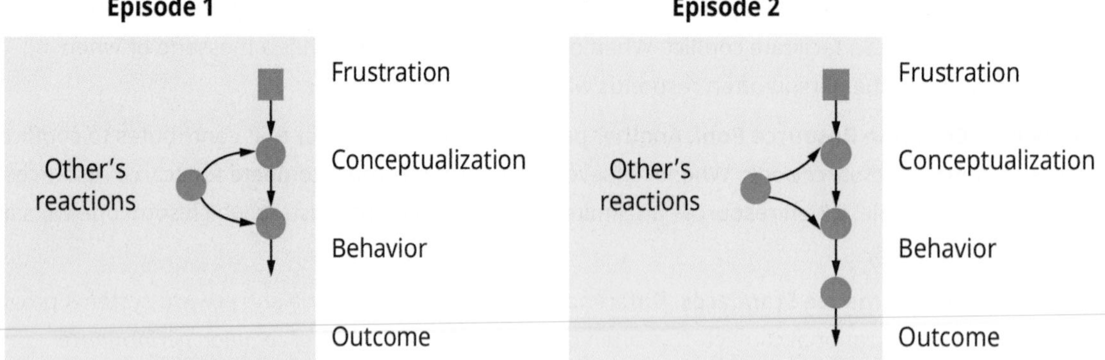

Exhibit 14.3 A Model of the Conflict Process *Source:* Adapted from Kenneth Thomas, "Conflict and Conflict Management," in M. D. Dunnette (ed.), *Handbook of Industrial and Organizational Behavior* (New York: Wiley, 1976), p. 895. (Attribution: Copyright Rice University, OpenStax, under CC BY-NC-SA 4.0 license)

The choice of an appropriate conflict resolution mode depends to a great extent on the situation and the goals of the party. This is shown graphically in **Exhibit 14.4**. According to this model, each party must decide the extent to which it is interested in satisfying its own concerns—called **assertiveness**—and the extent to which it is interested in helping satisfy the opponent's concerns—called **cooperativeness**. Assertiveness can range from assertive to unassertive on one continuum, and cooperativeness can range from uncooperative to cooperative on the other continuum.

Once the parties have determined their desired balance between the two competing concerns—either consciously or unconsciously—the resolution strategy emerges. For example, if a union negotiator feels confident she can win on an issue that is of primary concern to union members (e.g., wages), a direct competition mode may be chosen (see upper left-hand corner of **Exhibit 14.4**). On the other hand, when the union is indifferent to an issue or when it actually supports management's concerns (e.g., plant safety), we would expect an accommodating or collaborating mode (on the right-hand side of the exhibit).

Five Modes of Resolving Conflict	
Conflict-Handling Modes	Appropriate Situations
Competing	1. When quick, decisive action is vital—e.g., emergencies 2. On important issues where unpopular actions need implementing—e.g., cost cutting, enforcing unpopular rules, discipline 3. On issues vital to company welfare when you know you're right 4. Against people who take advantage of noncompetitive behavior

Table 14.1 (Attribution: Copyright Rice University, OpenStax, under CC BY-NC-SA 4.0 license)

Five Modes of Resolving Conflict	
Conflict-Handling Modes	**Appropriate Situations**
Collaborating	1. When trying to find an integrative solution when both sets of concerns are too important to be compromised 2. When your objective is to learn 3. When merging insights from people with different perspectives 4. When gaining commitment by incorporating concerns into a consensus 5. When working through feelings that have interfered with a relationship
Compromising	1. When goals are important but not worth the effort or potential disruption of more assertive modes 2. When opponents with equal power are committed to mutually exclusive goals 3. When attempting to achieve temporary settlements to complex issues 4. When arriving at expedient solutions under time pressure 5. As a backup when collaboration or competition is unsuccessful
Avoiding	1. When an issue is trivial, or when more important issues are pressing 2. When you perceive no chance of satisfying your concerns 3. When potential disruption outweighs the benefits of resolution 4. When letting people cool down and regain perspective 5. When gathering information supersedes immediate decision 6. When others can resolve the conflict more effectively 7. When issues seem tangential or symptomatic of other issues
Accommodating	1. When you find you are wrong—to allow a better position to be heard, to learn, and to show your reasonableness 2. When issues are more important to others than yourself—to satisfy others and maintain cooperation 3. When building social credits for later issues 4. When minimizing loss when you are outmatched and losing 5. When harmony and stability are especially important. 6. When allowing subordinates to develop by learning from mistakes.
Source: Adapted from K. W. Thomas, "Toward Multidimensional Values in Teaching: The Example of Conflict Behaviors," *Academy of Management Review 2* (1977), Table 1, p. 487.	

Table 14.1

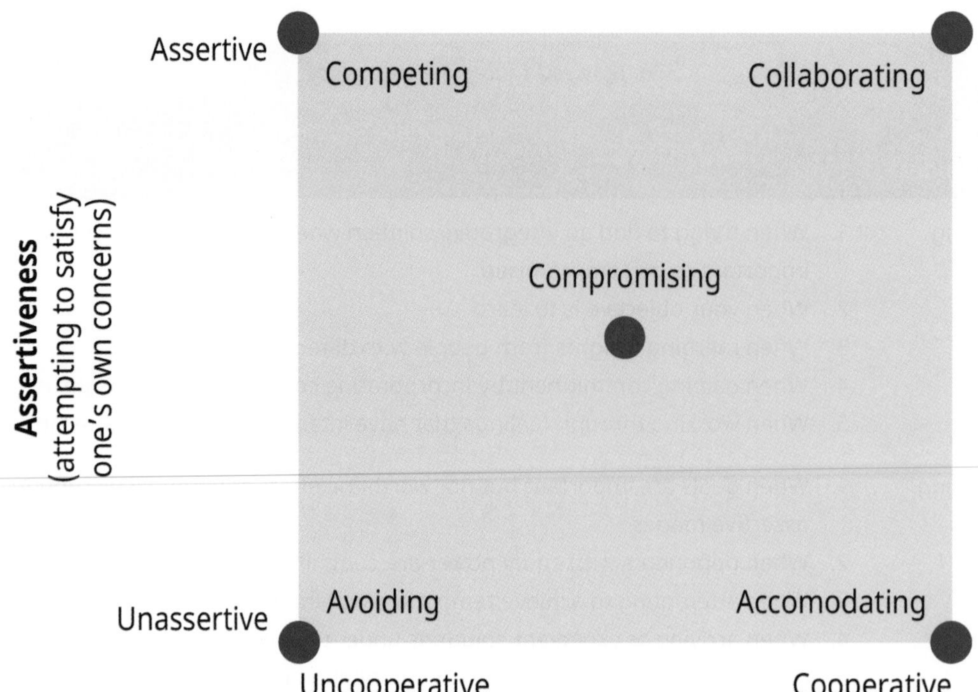

Exhibit 14.4 Approaches to Conflict Resolution *Source:* Adapted from Kenneth Thomas, "Conflict and Conflict Management," in M. D. Dunnette (ed.), *Handbook of Industrial and Organizational Behavior* (New York: Wiley, 1976), p. 900. (Attribution: Copyright Rice University, OpenStax, under CC BY-NC-SA 4.0 license)

What is interesting in this process is the assumptions people make about their own modes compared to their opponents'. For example, in one study of executives, it was found that the executives typically described themselves as using collaboration or compromise to resolve conflict, whereas these same executives typically described their opponents as using a competitive mode almost exclusively.[7] In other words, the executives underestimated their opponents' concern as uncompromising. Simultaneously, the executives had flattering portraits of their own willingness to satisfy both sides in a dispute.

Stage 4: Outcome. Finally, as a result of efforts to resolve the conflict, both sides determine the extent to which a satisfactory resolution or outcome has been achieved. Where one party to the conflict does not feel satisfied or feels only partially satisfied, the seeds of discontent are sown for a later conflict, as shown in the preceding **Exhibit 14.2**. One unresolved conflict episode can easily set the stage for a second episode. Managerial action aimed at achieving quick and satisfactory resolution is vital; failure to initiate such action leaves the possibility (more accurately, the probability) that new conflicts will soon emerge.

CONCEPT CHECK

1. Why do organizations have so much conflict?
2. Describe the process of the conflict model.

14.3 Resolving Conflict in Organizations

3. When and how do you negotiate, and how do you achieve a mutually advantageous agreement?

We have discovered that conflict is pervasive throughout organizations and that some conflict can be good for organizations. People often grow and learn from conflict, as long as the conflict is not dysfunctional. The challenge for managers is to select a resolution strategy appropriate to the situation and individuals involved. A review of past management practice in this regard reveals that managers often make poor strategy choices. As often as not, managers select repressive or ineffective conflict resolution strategies.

Common Strategies that Seldom Work

At leave five conflict resolution techniques commonly found in organizations prove to be ineffective fairly consistently.[8] In fact, not only do such techniques seldom work—in many cases, they actually serve to increase the problem. Nonetheless, they are found with alarming frequency in a wide array of business and public organizations. These five ineffective strategies are often associated with an avoidance approach and are described below.

Nonaction. Perhaps the most common managerial response when conflict emerges is *nonaction*—doing nothing and ignoring the problem. It may be felt that if the problem is ignored, it will go away. Unfortunately, that is not often the case. In fact, ignoring the problem may serve only to increase the frustration and anger of the parties involved.

Administrative Orbiting. In some cases, managers will acknowledge that a problem exists but then take little serious action. Instead, they continually report that a problem is "under study" or that "more information is needed." Telling a person who is experiencing a serious conflict that "these things take time" hardly relieves anyone's anxiety or solves any problems. This ineffective strategy for resolving conflict is aptly named **administrative orbiting**.

Due Process Nonaction. A third ineffective approach to resolving conflict is to set up a recognized procedure for redressing grievances but at the same time to ensure that the procedure is long, complicated, costly, and perhaps even risky. The **due process nonaction** strategy is to wear down the dissatisfied employee while at the same time claiming that resolution procedures are open and available. This technique has been used repeatedly in conflicts involving race and sex discrimination.

Secrecy. Oftentimes, managers will attempt to reduce conflict through *secrecy.* Some feel that by taking secretive actions, controversial decisions can be carried out with a minimum of resistance. One argument for pay secrecy (keeping employee salaries secret) is that such a policy makes it more difficult for employees to feel inequitably treated. Essentially, this is a "what they don't know won't hurt them" strategy. A major problem of this approach is that it leads to distrust of management. When managerial credibility is needed for other issues, it may be found lacking.

Character Assassination. The final ineffective resolution technique to be discussed here is **character assassination**. The person with a conflict, perhaps a woman claiming sex discrimination, is labeled a "troublemaker." Attempts are made to discredit her and distance her from the others in the group. The implicit strategy here is that if the person can be isolated and stigmatized, she will either be silenced by negative group pressures or she will leave. In either case, the problem is "solved."

Strategies for Preventing Conflict

On the more positive side, there are many things managers can do to reduce or actually solve dysfunctional conflict when it occurs. These fall into two categories: actions directed at conflict *prevention* and actions directed at conflict *reduction.* We shall start by examining conflict prevention techniques, because preventing conflict is often easier than reducing it once it begins. These include:

1. *Emphasizing organization-wide goals and effectiveness.* Focusing on organization-wide goals and objectives should prevent goal conflict. If larger goals are emphasized, employees are more likely to see the big picture and work together to achieve corporate goals.
2. *Providing stable, well-structured tasks.* When work activities are clearly defined, understood, and accepted by employees, conflict should be less likely to occur. Conflict is most likely to occur when task uncertainty is high; specifying or structuring jobs minimizes ambiguity.
3. *Facilitating intergroup communication.* Misperception of the abilities, goals, and motivations of others often leads to conflict, so efforts to increase the dialogue among groups and to share information should help eliminate conflict. As groups come to know more about one another, suspicions often diminish, and greater intergroup teamwork becomes possible.
4. *Avoiding win-lose situations.* If win-lose situations are avoided, less potential for conflict exists. When resources are scarce, management can seek some form of resource sharing to achieve organizational effectiveness. Moreover, rewards can be given for contributions to overall corporate objectives; this will foster a climate in which groups seek solutions acceptable to all.

These points bear a close resemblance to descriptions of the so-called Japanese management style. In Japanese firms, considerable effort is invested in preventing conflict. In this way, more energy is available for constructive efforts toward task accomplishment and competition in the marketplace. Another place where considerable destructive conflict is prevented is Intel.

MANAGERIAL LEADERSHIP

Sustainability and Responsible Management: Constructive Conflict that Leads to Championships

Dealing with conflict lies at the heart of managing any business. Confrontation—facing issues about which there is disagreement—is avoided only at a manager's peril. Many issues can be postponed, allowed to fester, or smoothed over; eventually, they must be solved. They are not going to disappear. This philosophy not only applies to business but to sports dynamics as well.

Take two NBA all-stars, Kobe Bryant and Shaquille O'Neal. Although they are world-renowned athletes now, when they first started in the NBA, there was plenty of conflict that could have caused their careers to take a much different path.

In 1992, O'Neal was the first play taken in by the NBA draft, he dominated the court with his size and leadership from day one. Four years later, Kobe Bryant, the youngest player to start in the NBA was brought onto the same team: the Los Angeles Lakers. The two were not fast friends, and the trash talk started as Bryant publicly criticized his teammate—and continued for years.

Ultimately in 1999, Phil Jackson was brought in to coach the LA Lakers, and his creative approach to their conflict changed everything. Instead of seeing this tension and ignoring it, or chastising the players for their feud, he used their skills to develop a new way of playing the game. O'Neal brought power and strength to the court, while Bryant was fast and a great shooter. Jackson developed a way of playing that highlighted both of these talents, and he built a supporting cast around them that brought out the best in everyone. The outcome: three NBA championships in a row.

While many may have just ignored or tried to separate the two superstars, Jackson was innovative in his approach, saw the opportunity in using the conflict to create a new energy, and was able to build a very successful program.

Questions:

1. What was the key to the success for Phil Jackson and his team?
2. How would you have approached the two players (or employees) that were in conflict and causing tension on your team?
3. What strategies would have been important to employ with these two individuals to resolve the conflict?

Sources: J. DeGraff, "3 Legendary Creative Conflicts That Sparked Revolutionary Innovation," *Huffington Post*, September 26, 2017, https://www.huffingtonpost.com/entry/3-legendary-creative-conflicts-that-sparked-revolutionary_us_59c85a9de4b08d66155043d6; K. Soong, "'I owe you an apology': Shaquille O'Neal explains why he loves Kobe Bryant years after feud," *Washington Post*, February, 17, 2017, https://www.washingtonpost.com/news/early-lead/wp/2018/02/17/i-owe-you-an-apology-shaquille-oneal-explains-why-he-loves-kobe-bryant-years-after-feud/?utm_term=.b9cca63b5761; M. Chiari, "Kobe Bryant Discusses Getting into Fist Fight with Shaquille O'Neal," *Bleacher Report*, March 9, 2018, https://bleacherreport.com/articles/2763468-kobe-bryant-discusses-getting-into-fist-fight-with-shaquille-oneal.

Strategies for Reducing Conflict

Where dysfunctional conflict already exists, something must be done, and managers may pursue one of at least two general approaches: they can try to change employee *attitudes,* or they can try to change employee *behaviors*. If they change behavior, open conflict is often reduced, but groups may still dislike one another; the conflict simply becomes less visible as the groups are separated from one another. Changing attitudes, on the other hand, often leads to fundamental changes in the ways that groups get along. However, it also takes considerably longer to accomplish than behavior change because it requires a fundamental change in social perceptions.

Nine conflict reduction strategies are shown in **Exhibit 14.5**. The techniques should be viewed as a continuum, ranging from strategies that focus on changing behaviors near the top of the scale to strategies that focus on changing attitudes near the bottom of the scale.

1. *Physical separation.* The quickest and easiest solution to conflict is physical separation. Separation is useful when conflicting groups are not working on a joint task or do not need a high degree of interaction. Though this approach does not encourage members to change their attitudes, it does provide time to seek a better accommodation.
2. *Use of rules and regulations.* Conflict can also be reduced through the increasing specification of rules, regulations, and procedures. This approach, also known as the bureaucratic method, imposes solutions on groups from above. Again, however, basic attitudes are not modified.
3. *Limiting intergroup interaction.* Another approach to reducing conflict is to limit intergroup interaction to

issues involving common goals. Where groups agree on a goal, cooperation becomes easier. An example of this can be seen in recent efforts by firms in the United States and Canada to work together to "meet the Japanese challenge."

4. *Use of integrators.* Integrators are individuals who are assigned a boundary-spanning role between two groups or departments. To be trusted, integrators must be perceived by both groups as legitimate and knowledgeable. The integrator often takes the "shuttle diplomacy" approach, moving from one group to another, identifying areas of agreement, and attempting to find areas of future cooperation.
5. *Confrontation and negotiation.* In this approach, competing parties are brought together face-to-face to discuss their basic areas of disagreement. The hope is that through open discussion and **negotiation**, means can be found to work out problems. Contract negotiations between union and management represent one such example. If a "win-win" solution can be identified through these negotiations, the chances of an acceptable resolution of the conflict increase. (More will be said about this in the next section of this chapter.)
6. *Third-party consultation.* In some cases, it is helpful to bring in outside consultants for **third-party consultation** who understand human behavior and can facilitate a resolution. A third-party consultant not only serves as a go-between but can speak more directly to the issues, because she is not a member of either group.
7. *Rotation of members.* By rotating from one group to another, individuals come to understand the frames of reference, values, and attitudes of other members; communication is thus increased. When those rotated are accepted by the receiving groups, change in attitudes as well as behavior becomes possible. This is clearly a long-term technique, as it takes time to develop good interpersonal relations and understanding among group members.
8. *Identification of interdependent tasks and superordinate goals.* A further strategy for management is to establish goals that require groups to work together to achieve overall success—for example, when company survival is threatened. The threat of a shutdown often causes long-standing opponents to come together to achieve the common objective of keeping the company going.
9. *Use of intergroup training.* The final technique on the continuum is intergroup training. Outside training experts are retained on a long-term basis to help groups develop relatively permanent mechanisms for working together. Structured workshops and training programs can help forge more favorable intergroup attitudes and, as a result, more constructive intergroup behavior.

Target of Change	Conflict Reduction Strategy
Behavior	
↑	1. Physical separation
	2. Bureaucratic method
	3. Limited interaction
	4. Integrators
	5. Confrontation and negotiation
	6. Third-party consultants
	7. Rotation of members
	8. Interdependent tasks and superordinate goals
↓	9. Intergroup training
Attitudes	

Exhibit 14.5 Conflict Reduction Strategies *Source:* Adapted from concepts in E. H. Neilsen, "Understanding and Managing Conflict," in J. Lorsch and P. Lawrence, eds., *Managing Group and Intergroup Relations* (Homewood, III.: Irwin, 1972). (Attribution: Copyright Rice University, OpenStax, under CC BY-NC-SA 4.0 license)

CONCEPT CHECK 

1. Describe conflict strategies that seldom work.
2. What are the strategies that managers can use that can reduce conflict?

14.4 Negotiation Behavior

4. How do you recognize and respond to cultural differences in negotiation and bargaining strategies?

We have seen the central role conflict plays in organizational processes. Clearly, there are some areas where managers would prefer to solve a problem between two parties before it results in high levels of conflict. This is usually accomplished through negotiation. **Negotiation** is the process by which individuals or groups attempt to realize their goals by bargaining with another party who has at least some control over goal attainment. Throughout the negotiation process, considerable skill in communication, decision-making, and the use of power and politics is required in order to succeed.

We will consider several aspects of negotiation, including stages of negotiation, types of negotiation behavior, and the negotiation process itself. We begin with the reasons why people engage in negotiation and bargaining in the first place.

Stages of Negotiation

In general, negotiation and bargaining are likely to have four stages. Although the length or importance of each stage can vary from situation to situation or from one culture to another, the presence and sequence of these stages are quite common across situations and cultures.[9]

1. *Non-task time.* During the first stage, the participants focus on getting to know and become comfortable with each other and do not focus directly on the task or issue of the negotiation. In cultures such as ours, this stage is often filled with small talk. However, it is usually not very long and is not seen as important as other stages. North Americans use phrases such as "Let's get down to business," "I know you're busy, so let's get right to it," and "Let's not beat around the bush." However, in other cultures such as Mexico or South Korea, the non-task stage is often longer and of more importance because it is during this stage the relationship is established. In these cultures, it is the relationship more than the contract that determines the extent to which each party can trust the other to fulfill its obligations.
2. *Information exchange.* The second stage of negotiations involves the exchange of background and general information. During this stage, participants may, for example, provide overviews of their company and its history. In Japan, this is an important stage because specific proposals or agreements must be considered and decided in the larger context. The information exchanged during the second stage provides this larger context.
3. *Influence and persuasion.* The third stage involves efforts to influence and persuade the other side. Generally, these efforts are designed to get the other party to reduce its demands or desires and to increase its acceptance of your demands or desires. There are a wide variety of influence tactics, including promises, threats, questions, and so on. The use of these tactics as well as their effectiveness is a function of several factors. First, the perceived or real power of one party relative to another is an important factor. For example, if one party is the only available supplier of a critical component, then threatening to go to a new supplier of that component unless the price is reduced is unlikely to be an effective influence tactic. Second, the effectiveness of a particular influence tactic is also a function of accepted industry and cultural norms. For example, if threats are an unacceptable form of influence, then their use could lead to consequences opposite from what is desired by the initiator of such tactics.
4. *Closing.* The final stage of any negotiation is the closing. The closing may result in an acceptable agreement between the parties involved or it may result in failure to reach an agreement. The symbols that represent the close of a negotiation vary across cultures. For example, in the United States, a signed contract is the symbol of a closed negotiation. At that point, "a deal is a deal" and failure to abide by the contents of the document is considered a breach of contract. In China, however, there is not the strong legal history or perspective that exists in the United States, and a signed document is not necessarily a symbol of the close of the negotiations. In fact, to some extent it symbolizes the beginning of the final points of negotiation. The signed document identifies the key issues that still need to be negotiated despite the fact that it may contain specific obligations for the involved parties concerning these issues. Quite simply, even though the document may obligate one party to deliver a product on a certain day and obligate the other party to pay a certain price for delivery, the document itself does not symbolize that the negotiation concerning these specifics is closed.

Each of these four stages and the sequence described above are common across most situations and cultures. However, the length of time devoted to each stage, the importance of each stage, and the specific behaviors associated with each stage can vary by situation and certainly do vary by culture.

Bargaining Strategies

Within the context of these four stages, both parties must select an appropriate strategy that they believe will assist them in the attainment of their objectives. In general, two rather distinct approaches to negotiation can be identified. These are **distributive bargaining** and **integrative bargaining**. A comparison of these two approaches is shown in **Table 14.2.**

Distributive Bargaining. In essence, distributive bargaining is "win-lose" bargaining. That is, the goals of one party are in fundamental and direct conflict with those of the other party. Resources are fixed and limited, and each party wants to maximize her share of these resources. Finally, in most cases, this situation represents a short-term relationship between the two parties. In fact, such parties may not see each other ever again.

A good example of this can be seen in the relationship between the buyer and seller of a house. If the buyer gets the house for less money (that is, she "wins"), the seller also gets less (that is, she "loses"). This win-lose situation can also be seen in classes where the professor insists on grading on a specified curve. If your friends get an A, there are fewer As to go around, and your chances are diminished.

Two Approaches to Bargaining

Bargaining Characteristic	Distributive Bargaining	Integrative Bargaining
Payoff structure	Fixed amount of resources to be divided	Variable amount of resources to be divided
Primary motivation	I win, you lose	Mutual benefit
Primary interests	Opposed to each other	Convergent with each other
Focus of relationships	Short term	Long term

Table 14.2

Under such circumstances, each side will probably adopt a course of action as follows. First, each side to a dispute will attempt to discover just how far the other side is willing to go to reach an accord. This can be done by offering outrageously low (or high) proposals simply to feel out the opponent. For example, in selling a house, the seller will typically ask a higher price than she actually hopes to get (see **Exhibit 14.6**). The buyer, in turn, typically offers far less than she is willing to pay. These two prices are put forth to discover the opponent's resistance price. The **resistance price** is the point beyond which the opponent will not go to reach a settlement. Once the resistance point has been estimated, each party tries to convince the opponent that the offer on the table is the best one the opponent is likely to receive and that the opponent should accept it. As both sides engage in similar tactics, the winner is often determined by who has the best strategic and political skills to convince the other party that this is the best she can get.

Integrative Bargaining. Integrative bargaining is often described as the "win-win" approach. That is, with this technique, both parties try to reach a settlement that benefits both parties. Such an approach is often predicated on the belief that if people mutually try to solve the problem, they can identify some creative solutions that help everyone. A good example can be seen in bilateral trade negotiations between two nations. In such negotiations, participants usually agree that a trade war would hurt both sides; therefore, both sides attempt to achieve a balance of outcomes that are preferable to a trade war for both sides. In doing so, however, the trick is to give away as little as possible to achieve the balance.[10]

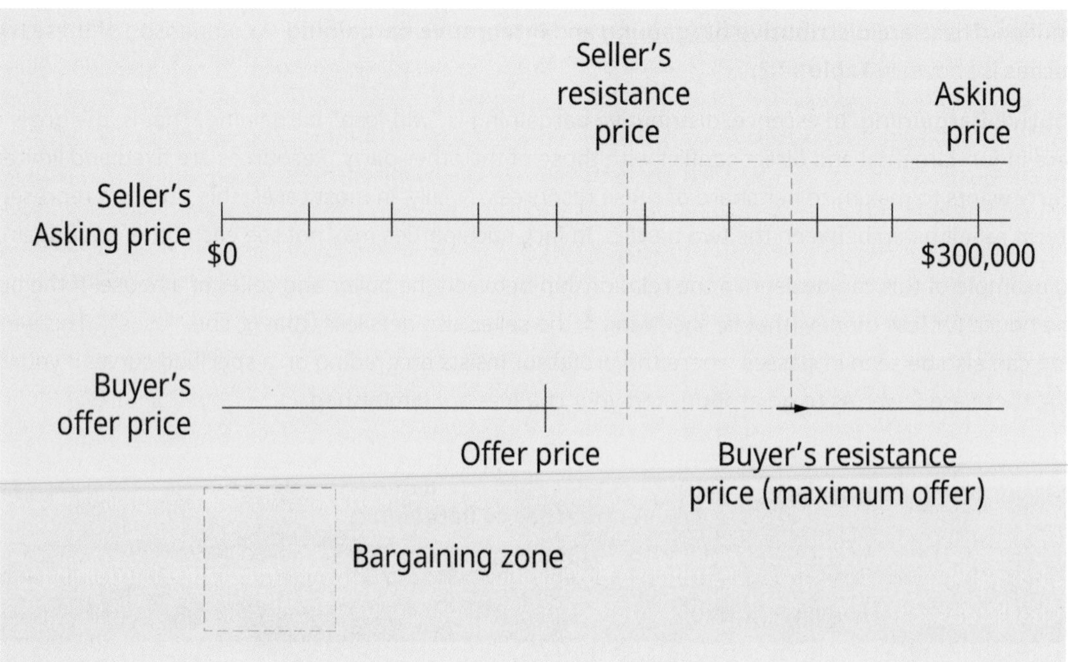

Exhibit 14.6 Distributive Bargaining in Buying a Home (Attribution: Copyright Rice University, OpenStax, under CC BY-NC-SA 4.0 license)

As shown previously in **Table 14.2**, this approach is characterized by the existence of variable resources to be divided, efforts to maximize joint outcomes, and the desire to establish or maintain a long-term relationship. The interests of the two parties may be convergent (noncompetitive, such as preventing a trade war between two countries) or congruent (mutually supportive, as when two countries reach a mutual defense pact).

In both cases, bargaining tactics are quite different from those typically found in distributive bargaining. Here, both sides must be able and willing to understand the viewpoints of the other party. Otherwise, they will not know where possible consensus lies. Moreover, the free flow of information is required. Obviously, some degree of trust is required here too. In discussions, emphasis is placed on identifying communalities between the two parties; the differences are played down. And, finally, the search for a solution focuses on selecting those courses of action that meet the goals and objectives of both sides. This approach requires considerably more time and energy than distributive bargaining, yet, under certain circumstances, it has the potential to lead to far more creative and long-lasting solutions.

The Negotiation Process

The negotiation process consists of identifying one's desired goals—that is, what you are trying to get out of the exchange—and then developing suitable strategies aimed at reaching those goals. A key feature of one's strategy is knowing one's relative position in the bargaining process. That is, depending upon your relative position or strength, you may want to negotiate seriously or you may want to tell your opponent to "take it or leave it." The dynamics of bargaining power can be extrapolated directly from the discussion of power **Table 14.3** and indicate several conditions affecting this choice. For example, you may wish to negotiate when you value the exchange, when you value the relationship, and when commitment to the issue is high. In the opposite situation, you may be indifferent to serious bargaining.

When to Negotiate		
	Bargaining Strategies	
Characteristics of the Situation	Negotiate	"Take It or Leave It"
Value of exchange	High	Low
Commitment to a decision	High	Low
Trust Level	High	Low
Time	Ample	Pressing
Power distribution*	Low or balanced	High
Relationship between two parties	Important	Unimportant
* Indicates relative power distribution between the two parties; "low" indicates that one has little power in the situation, whereas "high" indicates that one has considerable power.		

Table 14.3 (Attribution: Copyright Rice University, OpenStax, under CC BY-NC-SA 4.0 license)

Once goals and objectives have been clearly established and the bargaining strategy is set, time is required to develop a suitable plan of action. Planning for negotiation requires a clear assessment of your own strengths and weaknesses as well as those of your opponents. Roy Lewicki and Joseph Litterer have suggested a format for preparation for negotiation.[11] According to this format, planning for negotiation should proceed through the following phases:

1. Understand the basic nature of the conflict. What are the primary areas of agreement and disagreement?
2. What exactly do you want out of this negotiation? What are your goals?
3. How will you manage the negotiation process? Here, several issues should be recognized:
   a. Identify the primary issues to negotiate.
   b. Prioritize these issues.
   c. Develop a desirable package including these important issues.
   d. Establish an agenda.
4. Do you understand your opponent?
   a. What are your opponent's current resources and needs?
   b. What is the history of your opponent's bargaining behavior? What patterns can you see that can help you predict her moves?

Exhibit 14.7 Negotiating with the Referee Minnesota Gophers coach, Lindsay Whalen talks to a referee during a University of Minnesota Gophers game against Cornell University. Is this negotiation or persuasion? (Attribution: Laurie Schaul/ flickr/ Attribution 2.0 Generic (CC BY 2.0))

Research indicates that following such procedures does, in fact, lead to more successful bargaining. In **Table 14.4**, for example, we can see differences in both the planning approaches and the actual behaviors of successful and average negotiators. Preparation clearly makes a difference, as does interpersonal style during the actual negotiation.

Differences Between Successful and Average Negotiations		
Negotiation Behavior	Skilled Negotiators	Average Negotiators
Before the Negotiation		
Number of options considered per issue	5.1	2.6
Portion of time spent focusing on anticipated areas of agreement instead of conflict	39%	11%
During Negotiation		
Portion of time spent asking questions of opponent	21%	10%

Differences Between Successful and Average Negotiations		
Negotiation Behavior	Skilled Negotiators	Average Negotiators
Portion of time spent in active listening	10%	4%
Portion of time spent attacking opponent	1%	6%
Source: Based on data reported in N. J. Adler and A. Gunderson, *International Dimensions of Organizational Behavior* 5th edition (Mason, OH: Cengage Learning, 2008), pp. 165–181.		

Table 14.4

Cultural Differences in International Negotiations

In view of the increased emphasis on international industrial competitiveness, it is important to understand what happens when the two parties to a negotiation come from different cultures or countries. A knowledge of cultural differences can assist the manager both in understanding the other party's position and in striking the best possible deal given the circumstances.

A good way to start this analysis is by recognizing how different cultures approach the art of persuasion; that is, how do people in different countries try to win you over to their side in a dispute? Although we cannot possibly examine all cultures, consider the results of a study of differences in *persuasion techniques* for North America, the Middle East, and the former Soviet Union.[12] As can be seen in **Table 14.5**, Americans, Arabs, and Russians have significantly different approaches to persuasion. Americans tend to enter into a discussion emphasizing facts and figures, whereas Arabs may focus on emotions. The Russians may talk about ideals.

Moreover, in a negotiation situation, the American is ever-conscious of deadlines, whereas the Arab takes a more casual approach, and the Russian is often unconcerned about time. Americans make small concessions early in the bargaining process to establish a relationship. Arabs, on the other hand, make concessions throughout the bargaining process, and the Russians try not to make any concessions at all. Clearly, this study has only highlighted trends, and exceptions can be easily found. Even so, a knowledge of such differences, however general, can greatly facilitate improved interpersonal relations and bargaining success for both parties.

National Styles of Persuasion			
	North Americans	Arabs	Russians
Primary negotiating style and process	Factual: appeals made to logic	Affective: appeals made to emotions	Axiomatic: appeals made to Ideals

Table 14.5

National Styles of Persuasion			
	North Americans	Arabs	Russians
Conflict: opponent's arguments countered with	Objective facts	Subjective feelings	Asserted ideals
Making concessions	Small concessions made early to establish a relationship	Concessions made throughout as a part of the bargaining process	Few, if any, small concessions made
Response to opponent's concessions	Usually reciprocate opponent's concessions	Almost always reciprocate opponent's concessions	Opponent's concessions viewed as weakness and almost never reciprocated
Relationship	Short-term	Long-term	No continuing relationship
Authority	Broad	Broad	Limited
Initial position	Moderate	Extreme	Extreme
Deadline	Very important	Casual	Ignored
Source: Adapted from J. S. Martin, *Intercultural Business Communication,* (Englewood Cliffs, N.J.: Pearson, 2005).			

Table 14.5

We can also examine the personal characteristics of negotiators from different countries. A study by John Graham focused on the key characteristics of negotiators from different countries, in this case the United States, Japan, Taiwan, and Brazil. Results of the study are shown in **Table 14.6**, which shows the rank order of the defining characteristics.[13] Again, we can see major differences in negotiators from around the world. Each has certain strengths, yet these strengths vary considerably from country to country. Americans are seen as prepared and organized, thinking well under pressure, whereas Japanese are seen as more dedicated and shrewd. Taiwanese negotiators were found in the study to be highly persistent and determined, working hard to win the opponent's respect, and the Brazilians were amazingly similar to the Americans.

Key Individual Characteristics of Negotiators (Rank Order)			
American Managers	Japanese Managers	Chinese Managers (Taiwan)	Brazilian Managers
Preparation and planning skill	Dedication to job	Persistence and determination	Preparation and planning skill

Table 14.6

Key Individual Characteristics of Negotiators (Rank Order)			
American Managers	Japanese Managers	Chinese Managers (Taiwan)	Brazilian Managers
Thinking under pressure	Perceive and exploit power	Win respect and confidence	Thinking under pressure
Judgment and intelligence	Win respect and confidence	Preparation and planning skill	Judgment and intelligence
Verbal expressiveness	Integrity	Product knowledge	Verbal expressiveness
Product knowledge	Listening skill	Interesting	Product knowledge
Perceive and exploit power	Broad perspective	Judgment and intelligence	Perceive and exploit power
Integrity	Verbal expressiveness		Competition
Source: "Key Individual Characteristics of Negotiators" by John Graham, Graduate School of Management, University of California, Irvine.			

Table 14.6 (Attribution: Copyright Rice University, OpenStax, under CC BY-NC-SA 4.0 license)

Finally, we should note that negotiators from different countries differ markedly in their verbal and nonverbal *communication patterns.* In one study (again among Americans, representing North America; Japanese, representing East Asia; and Brazilians, representing South America), observers counted the number of times each negotiator did certain things within a given time limit.[14] The results are shown in **Table 14.7**. As can be seen, these negotiators use both verbal and nonverbal communication in very different ways. Note, for example, that Brazilians on average said "no" 83 times within a 30-minute segment, compared to 5 times for Japanese and 9 times for Americans. On the other hand, Japanese appealed to ideals and societal norms and simply sat in silence more than the others. Such differences affect not only the negotiation process but also, in many cases, the outcomes. That is, if a negotiator from one culture has annoyed or insulted the opponent (intentionally or unintentionally), the opponent may resist doing business with that person or may fail to offer attractive terms. Hence, again we see the value of better understanding cultural variations in negotiations, as in other matters.

Communication Patterns during Negotiations for Three Cultures			
Tactic	Japan	United States	Brazil
Verbal Communication			
Making promises	7	8	3
Making threats	4	4	2

Table 14.7 (Attribution: Copyright Rice University, OpenStax, under CC BY-NC-SA 4.0 license)

Communication Patterns during Negotiations for Three Cultures			
Tactic	Japan	United States	Brazil
Making recommendations	7	4	5
Appealing to ideals and norms	4	2	1
Giving a command	8	6	14
Saying "no"	5	9	83
Making initial concessions	6	7	9
Nonverbal Communication			
Periods of silence	6	3	0
Interrupting opponent	12	10	29
Looking directly into opponent's eyes	1	3	5
Touching opponent	0	0	5
Source: Based on data reported in J. Graham, "The Influence of Culture on Business Negotiations," *Journal of International Business Studies,* Spring 1985, pp. 81–96.			

Table 14.7 (Attribution: Copyright Rice University, OpenStax, under CC BY-NC-SA 4.0 license)

Concluding Thoughts about Conflict and Negotiations

One of the classic negotiations approaches that you might encounter is the book, Getting to Yes. This book expound the authors favored method of conflict resolution, which they term *principled negotiation*. This method attempts to find an objective standard, typically based on existing precedents, for reaching an agreement that will be acceptable to both interested parties. Principled negotiation emphasizes the parties' enduring interests, objectively existing resources, and available alternatives, rather than transient positions that the parties may choose to take during the negotiation. The outcome of a principled negotiation ultimately depends on the relative attractiveness of each party's so-called **BATNA**: the "Best Alternative To a Negotiated Agreement", which can be taken as a measure of the objective strength of a party's bargaining stance. In general, the party with the more attractive BATNA gets the better of the deal. If both parties have attractive BATNAs, the best course of action may be not to reach an agreement at all.[15]

Conflict is most likely to occur when the goals, expectations, and/or behaviors of at least two parties differ and when those differences are difficult to avoid (such as when interdependence among the parties involved is high). Conflict itself is neither good nor bad, productive nor destructive. The key to the outcome of conflict is the manner in which it is managed. Negotiation, as a key means of managing conflict, has four distinct stages. However, the length, importance, and norms for each stage can vary by situation and especially by culture.

EXPANDING AROUND THE GLOBE

Negotiating Styles in Malaysia and America

One of the emerging countries in Southeast Asia is Malaysia, whose natural resources and stable economic growth are allowing it to develop as an important manufacturing center in the region along with Singapore, Indonesia, and Thailand. What happens when American businesspeople visit Malaysia to do business? In the following example, cross-cultural researcher George Renwick describes major differences between the two cultures as they approach a negotiation.

Americans' patterns of negotiation, like all of their patterns, differ somewhat depending upon their context. The negotiating patterns of government officials working out a treaty, for example, are somewhat different from those of a business executive "hammering out" a contract. The pattern portrayed here will be that of the business executive.

The American businessperson usually begins a series of negotiating sessions in a cordial manner, but he is intent on getting things under way. He is very clear as to what he and his company want, when it is wanted, and how he will go about getting it; he has planned his strategy carefully. And he has done what he could to "psyche out" his counterpart, with whom he will be negotiating. From the outset, the American negotiator urges everyone to "dispense with the formalities" and get on with the business at hand. As soon as possible, he expresses his determination, saying something like, "Okay, let's get down to brass tacks."

The American usually states his position (at least his first position) early and definitely. He plans before long to "really get down to the nitty gritty." He wants to "zero in" on the knotty problems and get to the point where "the rubber meets the road" (the point, that is, where "the action" begins). Once the negotiations are "really rolling," the American usually deals directly with obstacles as they come up, tries to clear them away in quick order, and becomes impatient and frustrated if he cannot.

Most of what the American wants to convey, of course, he puts into words—often many of them. His approach is highly verbal and quite visible—and thoroughly planned. He has outlined his alternative ahead of time and prepared his counterproposals, contingencies, backup positions, bluffs, guarantees, and tests of compliance, all carefully calculated, and including, of course, lots of numbers. Toward the end, he sees that some bailout provisions are included, but he usually doesn't worry too much about them; making and meeting business commitments "on schedule" is what his life is all about—he is not too concerned about getting out. If he has to get out, then he has to, and he will find a way when the time comes.

The American experiences real satisfaction when all the problems have been "worked out," especially if he has been able to get provisions very favorable to his company—and to his own reputation as a "tough negotiator." He rests securely when everything is "down in black and white" and the contract is initialed or signed.

Afterward, the American enjoys himself; he relaxes "over some drinks" and carries on some "small talk" and "jokes around" with his team and their counterparts.

Malay patterns of negotiation, as might be expected, differ considerably. When they are buying something, Malays bargain with the merchant, and when they are working, they socialize with their boss and coworkers. Their purpose is to develop some sense of relationship with the other person. The relationship then provides the basis, or context, for the exchange. Malays take the same patterns and preferences into their negotiating sessions. When all is said and done, it is not the piece of paper they trust, it is the person—and their relationship with the person.

A Malay negotiator begins to develop the context for negotiations through the interaction routines appropriate to this and similar occasions. These routines are as complicated and subtle as customary American routines; they are cordial but quite formal. Like Americans and their own routines, Malays understand the Malay routines but are seldom consciously aware of them. Neither Malays nor Americans understand very clearly the routines of the other.

As the preliminary context is formed, it is important to the Malay that the proper forms of address be known beforehand and used and that a variety of topics be talked about that are unrelated to the business to be transacted. This may continue for quite a while. A Malay negotiator wants his counterpart to participate comfortably, patiently, and with interest. As in other interaction, it is not the particular words spoken which are of most importance to the Malay; rather he listens primarily to the attitudes which the words convey—attitudes toward the Malay himself and toward the matter being negotiated. Attitudes are important to the relationship. At this point and throughout the negotiations, the Malay is as much concerned about the quality of the relationship as the quantity of the work accomplished. Motivation is more important to the Malay than momentum.

The Malay negotiator, as in other situations, is also aware of feelings—his own and those of his counterpart, and the effects of the exchanges upon both. He is also aware of, and concerned about, how he looks in the eyes of his team, how his counterpart looks in the eyes of the other team, and how both he and his counterpart will look after the negotiations in the eyes of their respective superiors.

The Malay is alert to style, both his own and that of his counterpart. Displaying manners is more important than scoring points. The way one negotiates is as important as what one negotiates. Grace and finesse show respect for the other and for the matter under consideration. Negotiating, like other interaction, is something of an art form. Balance and restraint are therefore essential.

The agenda that the Malay works through in the course of the negotiation is usually quite flexible. His strategy is usually rather simple. His positions are expressed in more general terms than the American's, but no less strongly held. His proposals are more offered than argued: they are offered to the other party rather than argued with him. Malays do not enjoy sparring. They deeply dislike combat.

In response to a strong assertion, the Malay negotiator usually expresses his respect directly by replying indirectly. The stronger the assertion and the more direct the demands, the more indirect the reply—at least the verbal reply.

The Malay and his team usually formulate their positions gradually and carefully. By the time they present their position, they usually have quite a lot of themselves invested in it. Direct rejection of the position, therefore, is sometimes felt to be a rejection of the person. Negotiating for the Malay is not quite the game that it is for some Americans.

If the Malay and his team have arrived at a position from which they and those whom they represent cannot move, they will not move. If this requires a concession from the counterpart, the Malays will not try to force the concession. If the counterpart sees that a concession from him is necessary, and makes it, the Malays, as gentlemen, recognize the move and respect the man who made it. A concession, therefore, is not usually considered by the Malay team to be a sign that they can press harder and extract further concessions. Instead, a concession by either side is considered as evidence of strength and a basis for subsequent reconciliation and cooperation.

What about getting out a contract? Making and meeting business commitments is *not* what a Malay's life is all about. He has other, often prior, commitments. He therefore enters into contracts cautiously and prefers to have an exit provided.

In addition, Malays are certain of their control over the future (even their control of their own country) than are Americans. Therefore, promising specific kinds of performance in the future by specific dates in a contract, especially in a long-term contract where the stakes are high, is often difficult for Malays. It is even more difficult, of course, if they are not certain whether they can trust the persons to whom they are making the commitment and from whom they are accepting commitments. Malays therefore give a great deal of thought to a contract and to the contracting party before signing it. And they are uneasy if provisions have not been made for a respectable withdrawal should future circumstances make their compliance impossible.

Questions:

1. What are the differences between an American and Malay approach to business relationships?
2. How are the different approaches important to understanding negotiations and cultural differences?

Source: G. Renwick, *Malays and Americans: Definite Differences, Unique Opportunities* (Yarmouth, Maine: Intercultural Press, 1985), pp. 51–54.

CONCEPT CHECK

1. Describe the stages of negotiations.
2. Understand the strategies in bargaining.
3. Understand the role that cultural differences have in the negotiation process.

Key Terms

Administrative orbiting An ineffective strategy for resolving conflict.

Affective conflict Seen in situations where two individuals simply don't get along with each other.

Assertiveness Can range from assertive to unassertive on one continuum.

BATNA An acronym popularised by Roger Fisher and William Ury which stands for 'Best Alternative to a Negotiated Agreement'. BATNA answers the question: 'What would you do if you weren't able to agree a deal with your negotiation counterparty?' Your BATNA is the alternative action you'll take should your proposed agreement fail to materialize.

Behavioral conflict Exists when one person or group does something that is unacceptable to others.

Character assassination An ineffective resolution technique where the person with a conflict attempts to discredit and distance an individual from the others in the group.

Cognitive conflict Can result when one person or group holds ideas or opinions that are inconsistent with those of others.

Conflict The four types of conflict are goal conflict, cognitive conflict, affective conflict, and behavioral conflict.

Constructive confrontation A conflict that leads to a positive result.

Cooperativeness The extent to which someone is interested in helping satisfy the opponent's concerns.

Distributive bargaining Where the goals of one party are in fundamental and direct conflict with those of the other party. Resources are fixed and limited, and each party wants to maximize its share of these resources.

Due process nonaction The strategy of wearing down a dissatisfied employee while at the same time claiming that resolution procedures are open and available. This technique has been used repeatedly in conflicts involving race and sex discrimination.

Frustration May be caused by a wide variety of factors, including disagreement over performance goals, failure to get a promotion or pay raise, a fight over scarce economic resources, new rules or policies, and so forth.

Goal conflict Can occur when one person or group desires a different outcome than others do. This is simply a clash over whose goals are going to be pursued.

Integrative bargaining Essentially "win-lose" bargaining where the goals of one party are in fundamental and direct conflict with those of the other party. Resources are fixed and limited, and each party wants to maximize its share of these resources.

Intergroup conflict Usually involves disagreements between two opposing forces over goals or the sharing of resources.

Interorganizational conflict Disputes between two companies in the same industry, two companies in different industries or economic sectors, or two or more countries.

Interpersonal conflict Where two individuals disagree on some matter.

Intrapersonal conflict A conflict within one person.

Jurisdictional ambiguities Situations where it is unclear exactly where responsibility for something lies.

Negotiation The process by which individuals or groups attempt to realize their goals by bargaining with another party who has at least some control over goal attainment.

Resistance price The point beyond which the opponent will not go to reach a settlement.

Status inconsistencies Situations where some individuals have the opportunity to benefit whereas other employees do not. Consider the effects this can have on the nonmanagers' view of organizational policies and fairness.

Task interdependencies The greater the extent of task interdependence among individuals or groups, the greater the likelihood of conflict if different expectations or goals exist among entities, in part because the interdependence makes avoiding the conflict more difficult.

Third-party consultation An outside consultant that serves as a go-between and can speak more directly to the issues because she is not a member of either group.

Summary of Learning Outcomes

14.1 Conflict in Organizations: Basic Considerations

1. How do you recognize and resolve short- and long-term conflicts among group members and among groups?

Conflict is the process by which a person or group feels frustrated in the pursuit of certain goals, plans, or objectives. Conflict may take one of four forms: (1) goal, (2) cognitive, (3) affective, or (4) behavioral. Conflict may occur on several levels, including intrapersonal, interpersonal, intergroup, and interorganizational.

14.2 Causes of Conflict in Organizations

2. How does conflict arise in organizations?

Conflict in organizations can be caused by task interdependencies, status inconsistencies, jurisdictional ambiguities, communication problems, dependence on common resource pools, lack of common performance standards, and individual differences. A model of the conflict process follows four stages. Conflict originates (stage 1) when an individual or group experiences frustration in the pursuit of important goals. In stage 2, the individual or group attempts to understand the nature of the problem and its causes. In stage 3, efforts are made to change behavioral patterns in such a way that the desired outcome, or stage 4, is achieved.

14.3 Resolving Conflict in Organizations

3. When and how do you negotiate, and how do you achieve a mutually advantageous agreement?

Ineffective conflict resolution strategies include nonaction, administrative orbiting, due process nonaction, secrecy, and character assassination. Strategies for preventing conflict include (1) emphasizing organization-wide goals; (2) providing stable, well-structured tasks; (3) facilitating intergroup communication; and (4) avoiding win-lose situations. Strategies for reducing conflict include (1) physical separation, (2) use of rules and regulations, (3) limiting intergroup interaction, (4) use of integrators, (5) confrontation and negotiation, (6) third-party consultation, (7) rotation of members, (8) identification of interdependent tasks and superordinate goals, and (9) use of intergroup training. Negotiation is the process by which individuals and groups attempt to reach their goals by bargaining with others who can help or hinder goal attainment. Negotiation is helpful in three primary instances: (1) a conflict of interest, (2) the absence of clear rules or procedures, and (3) when there is a desire to avoid a fight. Distributive bargaining attempts to resolve a win-lose conflict in which resources are limited and each party wishes to maximize its share of these resources. Integrative bargaining occurs when both parties attempt to reach a settlement that benefits both sides in a dispute.

14.4 Negotiation Behavior

4. How do you recognize and respond to cultural differences in negotiation and bargaining strategies?

A resistance point is the point beyond which an opponent will not go to reach a settlement. Planning for a negotiation session involves (1) understanding the basic nature of the conflict, (2) knowing what the group wants to achieve in the session, (3) selecting a chief negotiator, and (4) understanding one's opponent. Cultural differences play a major role in the negotiation process and influence such factors as persuasion techniques, the key characteristics of the negotiators, and communication patterns.

Chapter Review Questions

1. Identify the types of conflict commonly found in organizations, and provide examples of each.
2. How can conflict be good for an organization?
3. Identify some reasons for the prevalence of intergroup conflict in organizations.
4. How does intergroup conflict affect behavior within a work group? behavior between two or more groups?
5. Review the basic conflict model discussed in this chapter. What lessons for management follow from this model?
6. Of the various strategies for resolving and preventing conflicts that are presented in this chapter, which ones do you feel will generally be most effective? least effective? Why?
7. What is the difference between distributive and integrative bargaining? When would each be most appropriate?
8. How can cultural differences affect bargaining behavior? If you were negotiating with a Japanese firm, what might you do differently than if you were facing an American firm? Explain.

Management Skills Application Exercises

1. You might find it interesting to see how you approach conflict resolution. To do this, simply complete this self-assessment. When you are done, refer to **Appendix B** for scoring details.

What Is Your Approach to Conflict Resolution?

Instructions: Think of a typical situation in which you have a disagreement with someone. Then answer the following items concerning how you would respond to the conflict. Circle the number that you feel is most appropriate.

	Highly Unlikely			**Highly Likely**	
1. I firmly push for my goals.	1	2	3	4	5
2. I always try to win an argument.	1	2	3	4	5
3. I try to show my opponent the logic of my position.	1	2	3	4	5
4. I like to discuss disagreements openly.	1	2	3	4	5
5. I try to work through our differences.	1	2	3	4	5
6. I try to get all concerns on the table for discussion.	1	2	3	4	5
7. I try to work for a mutually beneficial solution.	1	2	3	4	5

8. I try to compromise with the other person.	1	2	3	4	5
9. I seek a balance of gains and losses on each side.	1	2	3	4	5
10. I don't like talking about disagreements.	1	2	3	4	5
11. I try to avoid unpleasantness for myself.	1	2	3	4	5
12. I avoid taking positions that may incite disagreement.	1	2	3	4	5
13. I try to think of the other person in any disagreement.	1	2	3	4	5
14. I try to preserve relationships in any conflict.	1	2	3	4	5
15. I try not to hurt the other person's feelings.	1	2	3	4	5

Managerial Decision Exercises

1. The president of your company has just told you that an Indian multinational company is interested in purchasing a large amount of the products that you and your group are responsible for. You have been charged with meeting with the team from India, hosting their visit, and negotiating the agreement, including pricing. How do you communicate during the meeting with your colleagues? What are some aspects of the social and business interactions that you will want you and your staff to avoid? What will you report back to the president regarding the meeting, and will you encourage her to take part in the meeting?

Critical Thinking Case

College Corp.

Janice just graduated college, she's ready to head out on her own and get that first job, and she's through her first interviews. She receives an offer of a $28,000 salary, including benefits from COLLEGE CORP, from an entry-level marketing position that seems like a perfect fit. She is thrown off by the salary they are offering and knows that it is lower than what she was hoping for. Instead of panicking, she takes the advice of her mentor and does a little research to know what the market range for the salary is for her area. She feels better after doing this, knowing that she was correct and the offer is low compared to the market rate. After understanding more about the offer and the rates, she goes back to the HR representative and asks for her preferred rate of $32,500, knowing the minimum that she would accept is $30,000. Instead of going in for her lowest amount, she started higher to be open to negotiations with the company. She also sent a note regarding her expertise that warranted why she asked for that salary. To her happy surprise, the company counter offered at $31,000—and she accepted.

Questions:

1. What key points of Janice's negotiation led to her success?

2. What could have Janice done better to get a better outcome for her salary?

Sources: "Good & Bad Salary Negotiations," *Salary.com*, April 19, 2018, https://www.salary.com/articles/good-bad-examples-of-salary-negotiations/; M. Herner, "5 Things HR Wishes You Knew About Salary Negotiation," *Payscale.com*, accessed October 21, 2018, https://www.payscale.com/salary-negotiation-guide/salary-negotiation-tips-from-hr.

15

External and Internal Organizational Environments and Corporate Culture

Exhibit 15.1 (Credit: Free-Photos/ Pixabay/ (CC BY 0)), modified from an original image by Ivan Mlinaric)

Introduction

Learning Outcomes

After reading this chapter, you should be able to understand these statements:

1. Define the external environment of organizations.
2. Identify contemporary external forces pressuring organizations.
3. Identify different types of organizational structures and their strengths and weaknesses.
4. Explain how organizations organize to meet external market threats and opportunities.
5. Identify the fit between organizational cultures and the external environment.
6. Identify environmental trends, demands, and opportunities facing organizations.

EXPLORING MANAGERIAL CAREERS

Jeff Bezos of Amazon

Amazon's market value was estimated at $1 trillion USD dollars in 2018. The company was recognized as the most innovative company in Fast Company's 2017 list, accounting for 44 percent of all U.S. e-commerce that year—approximately 4 percent of the U.S.'s total retail sales. Amazon market value is greater than the sum of the market capitalizations of Walmart, Target, Best Buy, Nordstrom, Kohl's, JCPenney, Sears, and Macy's. Jeff Bezos, founder and leader, has creatively accomplished what most large companies fail at: meshing size, scale, and external opportunities with agility. Sales figures reached $100 billion in 2015 while the stock price climbed over 300% in the past five years. The company plans on creating over 50,000 new jobs starting in 2018. Bezos has blended his strategy of virtually reaching unlimited numbers of online customers while maintaining land-based distribution centers using Prime's $99-per-year—$119 in 2018—membership. Stephenie Landry, an Amazon's vice president, stated that Prime has reached 49 cities in seven countries. Over 100 million people in 2018 subscribe to the Prime service. She noted that the business has only to answer two questions from customers: "Do you have what I want, and can you get it to me when I need it?" The answer seems to be yes, especially with Bezos's strategy of having high-tech robots already working side by side with human employees—resembling a "factory of the future."

Bezos's digital commerce strategy has led the firm to become the leader of retail commerce. Amazon's digital strategy uses Prime memberships that are supplied and supported by land-based distribution centers; Prime takes in reaching about 60% of the total dollar value of all merchandise sold on the site. That accounts for 60 million customers in the United States who use Prime and who spend $2,500 on Amazon annually. A study of 3,000 independent businesses, half of whom were retailers, listed competition from Amazon as their primary concern. Industry after industry is being disrupted, some replaced, by Bezos's strategy. He has said, "Everybody wants fast delivery. Low prices. I'm serious about this. Our job is to provide a great customer experience, and that is something that is universally desired all over the world".

Still, Amazon faces such challenges as high shipping cost (over $11 billion annually), pressures on employees (especially those working in warehouses that have been criticized for poor working conditions), shipping contractors who go on strike demanding higher wages and reduced workloads, and the possibilities of more governmental regulation (especially with regard to adding drones as a delivery method), as well as pressures to pay more taxes. Bezos has countered these arguments by adding more full-time jobs in different cities, promising to improve working conditions, supporting public spaces for the public, and most importantly, contributing to the U.S. economy.

Sources: https://www.bloomberg.com/news/articles/2018-04-26/amazon-eyes-second-biggest-market-cap-surging-past-microsoft. Noah Robischon, (2017). Why Amazon Is The World's Most Innovative Company Of 2017, https://www.fastcompany.com/3067455/why-amazon-is-the-worlds-most-innovative-company-of-2017; L. Thomas, (2018). Amazon grabbed 4 percent of all US retail sales in 2017, new study says, https://www.cnbc.com/2018/01/03/amazon-grabbed-4-percent-of-all-us-retail-sales-in-2017-new-study.html

Organizations and industries are again at a crossroads when confronting new and challenging external environmental demands. Exceptional companies such as Amazon, in the opening case, Apple, Netflix, and Google/Alphabet Inc. exemplify evolving business models that combine strategic innovation, technological prowess, and organizational cultural agility that not only meet external environmental demands, but also shape them.

Many businesses with traditional business models, however, have failed or are not succeeding strategically, operationally, and organizationally by not realizing and/or adapting to changing external environments. Such firms that were once successful but did not anticipate and then adapt to such changes include Blockbuster, Toys R Us, Borders, Sun Microsystems, Motorola, Digital Equipment Corporation, Polaroid, and Kodak, to name only a few. A sample of contemporary external environmental trends and forces that currently challenge organizations' survival and effectiveness includes:

- *Digital technologies and artificial intelligence (AI)*: Extensions of AI help automate a firm's value chain, thus speeding up and increasing efficient operations and service to customers—as Amazon exemplifies. A current survey showed that 59% of organizations are collecting information to develop AI strategies, while others are moving forward in piloting and/or adopting AI solutions to compete faster and at less cost.[1] However, there are also risks that accompany firms that incorporate new digital and online technologies without adequate security measures. For example, some newer online technologies can expose operational systems to cyberattacks and large-scale manipulation. Hacking is now both an illegal and ongoing "profession" for those who are able to paralyze organizations from accessing their data unless they pay a ransom. While hacking is not new, it is more widespread and lethal, to the point of even threatening national security. Emerging evidence from the U.S. presidential election between Donald Trump and Hillary Clinton suggests that international hackers affected online U.S. election processes. Still, the future of most businesses is using some type of digital and AI technologies.

- The advent of *blockchain* technologies that are interrupting new industry practices. Blockchain is not a single technology; it is "an architecture that allows disparate users to make transactions and then creates an unchangeable record of those transactions." It is "a public electronic ledger—similar to a relational database—that can be openly shared among disparate users and that creates an unchangeable record of their transactions, each one time-stamped and linked to the previous one."[2] These technological inventions will continue to affect almost every business process from procurement to legal management. The banking industry is already using it. It increases speed, security, and accuracy of transactions.
- *Sharing-economy cultural and economic value-added business models* that use information technologies to gain competitive advantage. Companies such as Airbnb and Uber have ushered in new business models that have already disrupted real estate, hotel, taxi, and other industries. Taking out the middle layer of management in transactions to increase efficiencies and customer satisfaction while cutting costs through the use of information and social media technologies will continue. This trend has already had both positive and disruptive effects on companies. Many customers are likely benefitted; businesses with outdated and ineffective business models have either failed or struggle to adapt.
- *Shifts in learning and learning credentials*. Identifying, recruiting, and retaining talent is crucial to organizations. An evolving crisis for the current generation—future talent—is the continued rise in higher educational institutions' tuitions, student debt, and the changing nature of jobs. With the advent of online resources, prospective students' inability to pay creates both a crisis and opportunity for traditional higher educational institutions. While bachelor's degrees remain a requirement for many companies hiring needed higher-level talent, online resources such as Khan Academy, Udacity, and Coursera are gaining recognition and legitimacy toward providing financially challenged students opportunities for entry-level jobs. While many higher-skilled students and professionals may not presently be included in this trend, companies seeking to pay lower wages while offering flexible working conditions are attracting students.[3] Again, how higher educational private, not-for-profit, and even for-profit educational institutions adapt, innovate, and manage their external environments is yet to be seen.
- *Ethics, corporate social responsibility (CSR), and sustainability.* Corruption, lying, and fraud have been and continue to be part of the landscape of governments and public- and private-sector corporations. However, public awareness through social and online media has awakened consumers and corporations to the impending dangers and drawbacks of illegal and unethical activities of certain large corporations. And external environmental problems, created in part by humans, such as pollution and climate change pressure companies to be responsible for their share of the costs associated with these problems.

This small sample of powerful external forces illustrates the continuing pressure companies encounter to innovate in their industries. Basic theories, concepts, and principles are presented in this chapter to help explain elements of external environments and how organizations and corporations can organize and are organizing to survive and thrive in the 21st century.

15.1 The Organization's External Environment

1. Define the external environment of organizations.

To succeed and thrive, organizations must adapt, exploit, and fit with the forces in their external environments. Organizations are groups of people deliberately formed together to serve a purpose through structured and coordinated goals and plans. As such, organizations operate in different external environments and are organized and structured internally to meet both external and internal demands and opportunities. Different types of organizations include not-for-profit, for-profit, public, private, government, voluntary, family owned and operated, and publicly traded on stock exchanges. Organizations are commonly referred to as companies, firms, corporations, institutions, agencies, associations, groups, consortiums, and conglomerates.

While the type, size, scope, location, purpose, and mission of an organization all help determine the external environment in which it operates, it still must meet the requirements and contingencies of that environment to survive and prosper. This chapter is primarily concerned with how organizations fit with their external environments and how organizations are structured to meet challenges and opportunities of these environments. Major takeaways for readers of this chapter include the following: 1) Be able to identify elements in any organization's external—and internal—environment that may interest or affect you as an employee, shareholder, family member, or observer. 2) Gain insights into how to develop strategies and tactics that would help you (and your organization) navigate ways to cope with or try to dominate or appeal to elements (e.g., market segments, stakeholders, political/social/economic/technological issues) in the environment.

The big picture of an organization's **external environment**, also referred to as the *general environment*, is an inclusive concept that involves all outside factors and influences that impact the operation of a business that an organization must respond or react to in order to maintain its flow of operations.[4] **Exhibit 15.2** illustrates types of general macro environments and forces that are interrelated and affect organizations: sociocultural, technological, economic, government and political, natural disasters, and human-induced problems that affect industries and organizations. For example, economic environmental forces generally include such elements in the economy as exchange rates and wages, employment statistics, and related factors such as inflation, recessions, and other shocks—negative and positive. Hiring and unemployment, employee benefits, factors affecting organizational operating costs, revenues, and profits are affected by global, national, regional, and local economies. Other factors discussed here that interact with economic forces include politics and governmental policies, international wars, natural disasters, technological inventions, and sociocultural forces. It is important to keep these dimensions in mind when studying organizations since many if not most or all changes that affect organizations originate from one or more of these sources—many of which are interrelated.

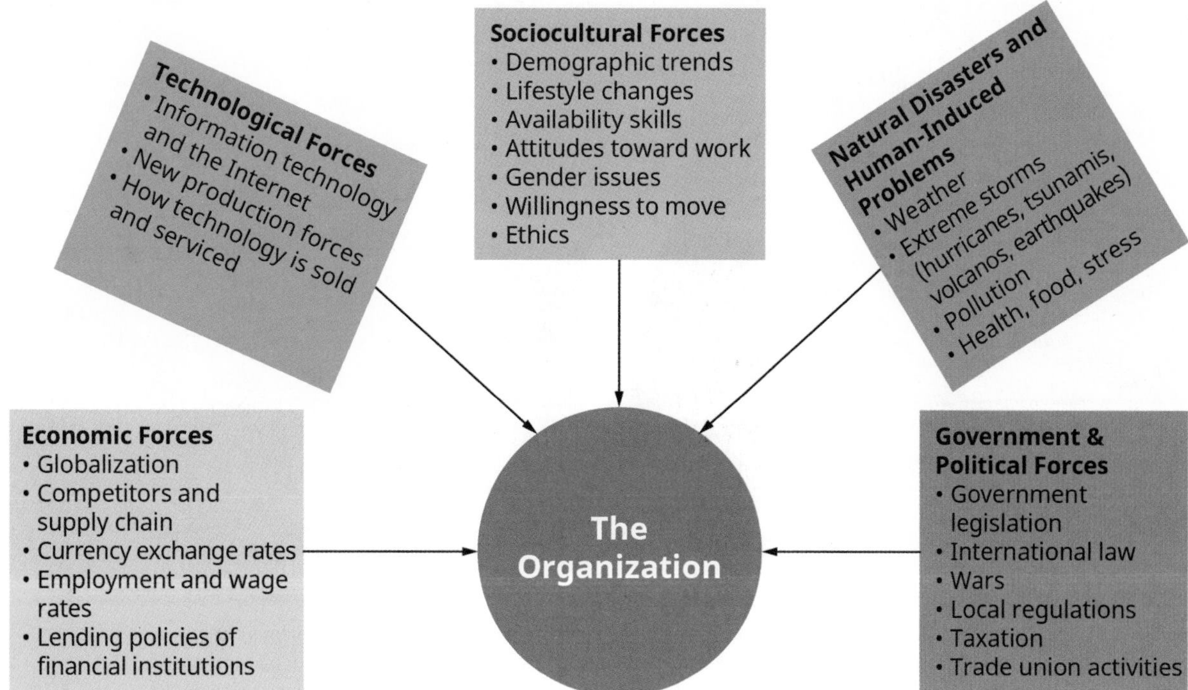

Exhibit 15.2 Macro Forces and Environments (Attribution: Copyright Rice University, OpenStax, under CC-BY 4.0 license)

Globalization is a combination of external forces shaping environments of organizations. Defined as the development of an integrated global economy and characterized by free trade, capital flows, communications, and cheaper foreign labor markets, the processes of globalization underlie the forces in the general international economic environment. This dimension continues to present opportunities and pressures to companies operating locally as well as globally. Globalization continues to affect industries and companies in ways that benefit some and not others. Amazon, for example, is thriving. The firm sells low-end products through its brand AmazonBasics. The company has individual retail websites for the United States, the United Kingdom and Ireland, France, Canada, Germany, Italy, Spain, the Netherlands, Australia, Brazil, Japan, China, India, and Mexico. Uber and Airbnb represent some of the larger sharing-economy companies that operate internationally and have to date prospered in the so-called new but fragmenting global economy.

Exhibit 15.3 Bezos Jeff Bezos' digital commerce strategy has led the firm to become the leader of retail commerce, and forced traditional retailers like Toys R Us to close their operations, and retailers like Walmart, Target, and Sears to reassess their business environment. Amazon's digital strategy uses Prime memberships that are supplied and supported by land-based distribution centers; Prime takes in reaching about 60% of the total dollar value of all merchandise sold on the site. (Credit: Sam Churchill/flickr/ Attribution 2.0 Generic (CC BY 2.0))

In general, countries that have gained from globalization include Japan, South Korea, Taiwan, Malaysia, Singapore, Hong Kong, Thailand, and China. China's markets and growing economic prowess have particularly been noticed. China's GDP (gross domestic product) is estimated at $13.2 trillion in 2018, outpacing the $12.8 trillion combined total of the 19 countries that use the euro.[5] Corporations worldwide, large and small, online and land-based, strive to gain access to sell in China's vast markets. Moreover, China at the beginning of 2018 owns $1.168 trillion of the United States' debt.[6] Japan, in second place, owes $1.07 trillion of this debt. Any instability politically and economically with China could result in increasing inflation and interest rates in the U.S. economy that could, in turn, negatively affect U.S. businesses.

Economic forces

Economically, "The strategic challenge of the next decade is navigating a world that is simultaneously integrating and fragmenting. Stock markets have set new records and economic volatility has fallen to historic lows, while political shocks on a scale unseen for generations have taken place. Seemingly contradictory realities do co-exist."[7] Overall, while economic data indicates that globalization has had a positive effect on the world economy, a dark side also shows that two-thirds of all households in 25 advanced-economy countries had incomes stagnate and/or decline between 2005 and 2014. Moreover, the U.K. and U.S. witnessed falling wages. Wealth distribution in these countries continues to decline. Income inequality globally is also rising. Other trends that also affect the global, regional, and local economies are discussed in this chapter as well as below.

Technological forces are another ubiquitous environmental influence on organizations. Speed, price, service, and quality of products and services are dimensions of organizations' competitive advantage in this era. Information technologies and social media powered by the Internet and used by sharing-economy companies such as Airbnb and Uber have democratized and increased, if not leveled, competition across several industries, such as taxis, real estate rentals, and hospitality services. Companies across industry sectors cannot survive without using the Internet, social media, and sophisticated software in R&D (research and development), operations, marketing, finance, and sales. To manage and use big data in all these functional areas, organizations rely on technology.

Government and political forces also affect industries and organizations. Recent events that have jarred the global economy—and are too early to predict the long-term outcomes of—are the United Kingdom's exit from the European Union, President Trump's nationalistic policies echoed by other presidents in Chile and Argentina,[8] wars in the Middle East, policies that question and disrupt free trade, health-care reform, and immigration—all of which increase uncertainty for businesses while creating opportunities for some industries and instability in others.

Sociocultural forces

Sociocultural environmental forces include different generations' values, beliefs, attitudes, customs and traditions, habits, and lifestyles. More specifically, other aspects of societal cultures are education, language, religion, law, politics, and social organizations. The millennial (ages 20 to 35) workforce, for example, generally seeks work that engages and interests them. Members of this generation are also health conscious and eager to learn. Since this and the newer generation (Generation Z) are adept and accustomed to using technology—social media in particular—organizations must be ready and equipped to provide wellness, interesting, and a variety of learning and work experiences to attract and retain new talent. Millennials are also estimated to be the United States' largest living adult generation in 2019. This generation numbered about 71 million compared with 74 million baby boomers (ages 52 to 70) in 2016. By 2019, an estimated 73 million millennials and 72 million boomers are projected. Because of immigration, millennials are estimated to increase until 2036.[9]

Other general sociocultural trends occurring in the United States and internationally that affect organizations include the following: (1) Sexual harassment at work in the era of #MeToo has pressured organizations to be more transparent about relationships between owners, bosses, and employees. Related to this trend, some surveys show new difficulties for men in workplace interactions and little effect on women's career opportunities taking place in the short term.[10] (2) While fewer immigrants have been entering the United States in recent years, diversity in the U.S. workplace continues. For example, 20 million Asian Americans trace their roots to over 20 countries in East and Southeast Asia and the Indian subcontinent—"each with unique histories, cultures, languages and other characteristics. The 19 largest origin groups together account for 94% of the total Asian population in the U.S."[11] (3) Young adults in the United States are living at home longer. "In 2016, 15% of 25- to 35-year-old Millennials were living in their parents' home. This is 5 percentage points higher than the share of Generation Xers who lived in their parents' home in 2000 when they were the same age (10%), and nearly double the share of the Silent Generation who lived at home in 1964 (8%)."[12] (4) While women have made gains in the workplace, they still comprise a small share of top leadership jobs—across politics and government, academia, the nonprofit sector, and business. Women comprised only about 10% of CEOs (chief executive officers), CFOs (chief financial officers), and the next three highest-paid executives in U.S. companies in 2016–17.[13] A 2018 study by McKinsey & Company "reaffirms the global relevance of the link between diversity—defined as a greater proportion of women and a more mixed ethnic and cultural composition in the leadership of large companies—and company financial outperformance."[14] These and other related sociocultural trends impact organizational cultures and other dimensions involving human talent and diverse workforces.

Natural disasters and human-related problems

Natural disaster and human induced environmental problems are events such as high-impact hurricanes, extreme temperatures and the rise in CO2 emissions as well as 'man-made' environmental disasters such as water and food crises; biodiversity loss and ecosystem collapse; large-scale involuntary migration are a force that affects organizations. The 2018 Global Risks Report identified risks in the environmental category that also affect industries and companies—as well as continents and countries. These risks were ranked higher than average for both likelihood and impact over a 10-year horizon. The report showed that 2017 was characterized by high-impact hurricanes, extreme temperatures, and the first rise in carbon dioxide emissions in four years; "man-made" environmental disasters; water and food crises; biodiversity loss and ecosystem collapse; and large-scale involuntary migration to name a few. Authors of this study noted that "Biodiversity is being lost at mass-extinction rates, agricultural systems are under strain and pollution of the air and sea has become an increasingly pressing threat to human health."[15] Most vulnerable to rising seas are low-lying islands in the Indian and Pacific Oceans. The Republic of the Marshall Islands has more over 1,100 low-lying islands on 29 atolls that include island nations with hundreds of thousands of people. Predictions indicate that rising sea levels could reach 3 feet worldwide by 2300 or sooner. One report stated that in your child's lifetime, Miami, Florida, could be underwater.[16] Large sections of Louisiana's marshes separating the ocean from the coastline are submerging. Oil producers and other related corporations are being sued by that state, claiming that fossil fuel emissions have contributed to natural disasters such as climate change. Many new companies in the United States are already constructing buildings to withstand increasing flooding and predicted rising water levels.

CONCEPT CHECK 

1. Define the components of the internal and the external business environments.
2. What factors within the economic environment affect businesses?
3. Why do demographic shifts and technological developments create both challenges and new opportunities for business?

15.2 External Environments and Industries

2. Identify contemporary external forces pressuring organizations.

Industry and organizational leaders monitor environments to identify, predict, and manage trends, issues, and opportunities that their organizations and industries face. Some corporations, such as Amazon, anticipate and even create trends in their environments. Most, however, must adapt. External environments, as identified in the previous section, can be understood by identifying the uncertainty of the environmental forces. **Exhibit 15.4** illustrates a classic and relevant depiction of how scholars portray environment-industry-organization "fit," that is, how well industries and organizations align with and perform in different types of environments.

Simple + Stable = 1 Low Uncertainty	Complex + Stable = 2 Low to Moderate Uncertainty
1. Small number of external elements, and elements are similar 2. Elements remain the same or change slowly Examples: soft drink bottlers, container manufacturers, food processors	1. Large number of external elements, and elements are dissimilar 2. Elements remain the same or change slowly. Examples: universities, appliance manufacturers, chemical companies, insurance companies
Simple + Unstable = 3 High to Moderate Uncertainty	**Complex + Unstable = 4**
1. Small number of external elements, and elements are similar. 2. Elements change frequently and unpredictably. Examples: e-commerce, fashion clothing, music industry, toy manufacturers	1. Large number of external elements, and elements are dissimilar 2. Elements change frequently and unpredictably Examples: computer firms, aerospace, telecommunications, airlines

Uncertainty →

Exhibit 15.4 Company Industry Fit Adapted from: Duncan, R. (1972). *Characteristics of organizational environments of uncertainty*. American Science Quarterly, 17 *(September), 313-327; Daft, R.* Organizational Theory and Design, 12th edition, p. 151, *Mason, OH, Cengage Learning*.

The two dimensions of this figure represent “environmental complexity” (i.e., the number of elements in the environment, such a competitors, suppliers, and customers), which is characterized as either simple or complex, and “environmental change,” described as stable or unstable. How available monetary and financial resources are to support an organization’s growth is also an important element in this framework.[17] Certain industries—soft drink bottlers, beer distributors, food processors, and container manufacturers—would, hypothetically, fit and align more effectively in a stable (i.e., relative unchanging), simple, and low-uncertainty (i.e., has mostly similar elements) external environment—cell 1 in **Exhibit 15.4**. This is referred to when organizations are in a **simple-stable environment**. Of course unpredicted conditions, such as global and international turmoil, economic downturns, and so on, could affect these industries, but generally, these alignments have served as an ideal type and starting point for understanding the “fit” between environment and industries. In a stable but complex, low- to moderate-uncertainty environment, cell 2 in **Exhibit 15.4**, universities, appliance manufacturers, chemical companies, and insurances companies would generally prosper. This is referred to when organizations are in a **complex-stable environment**. When the external environment has simple but high to moderate uncertainty, cell 3 of **Exhibit 15.4**, e-commerce, music, and fashion clothing industries would operate effectively. This is referred to when organizations are in a **simple-unstable environment**. Whereas in cell 4 of **Exhibit 15.4**, an environment characterized by a high degree of uncertainty with complex and unstable elements, industries and firms such as computer, aerospace, airlines, and telecommunications firms would operate more effectively. This is referred to when organizations are in a **complex-unstable environment**.

Exhibit 15.4 is a starting point for diagnosing the “fit” between types of external environments and industries. As conditions change, industries and organizations must adapt or face consequences. For example, educational institutions that traditionally have been seen to operate best in low- to moderate-uncertainty environments, cell 4 of **Exhibit 15.4**, have during this past decade experienced more high to moderate uncertainty (cell 2)—and even high uncertainty (cell 1). For example, for-profit educational institutions such the University of Phoenix and others—as compared to not-for-profit universities and colleges, such as public state institutions, community colleges, and private nonprofit ones—have undergone more unstable and complex forces in the external environment over the past decade. Under the Obama administration, for-profit universities faced greater scrutiny regarding questionable advertising, graduation rates, and accreditation issues; lawsuits and claims against several of these institutions went forward, and a few of the colleges had to close. The Trump administration has shown signs of alleviating aggressive governmental control and monitoring in this sector. Still, higher educational institutions in general currently face increasingly complex and unstable environments given higher tuition rates, increased competition from less-expensive and online programs, fewer student enrollments, and an overabundance of such institutions. Several private, not-for-profit higher educational institutions have merged and also ceased to exist. Adapting to increasingly rapid external change has become a rallying call for most industries and organizations as the 21st century evolves.

Organizational Complexity

It is important to point out here that external (and internal) organizational complexity is not often as simple as it may seem. It has been defined as "...the amount of complexity derived from the environment where the organisation operates, such as the country, the markets, suppliers, customers and stakeholders; while internal complexity is the amount of complexity that is internal to the organisation itself, i.e. products, technologies, human resources, processes and organisational structure. Therefore, different aspects compose internal and external complexities."[18]

The dilemma that organizational leaders and managers sometimes face is how to deal with external, and internal, complexity? Do you grow and nurture it or reduce it? Some strategies call for reducing and managing it at the local level while nurturing it at the global level—depending on the organization's size, business model, and the nature of the environments. Without going into complicated detail, it is fair to say at the beginning of the chapter that you may want to read through the chapter first, then return here afterward.

In the meantime, here are some simple rules from organizational practitioners De Toni and De Zan to keep in mind for managing high levels of complexity from the external environment, internally, after you have diagnosed the nature of the external complexity—as we discuss throughout in this chapter: first, assemble "...a set of self-managing teams or autonomous business units,[known as modularized units] with an entrepreneurial responsibility to the larger organization." These focused self-organizing teams use creative methods to deal with the diversity to the advantage of the organization. A second method when facing high external environmental complexity when you want to gain value from it is to find and develop "...simple rules to drive out creativity and innovation ... to keep the infrastructure and processes simple, while permitting complex outputs and behaviours." An example offered is found in the rules of the Legos company: "(1) does the proposed product have the Lego look? (2) Will children learn while having fun? (3) Will parents approve? (4) Does the product maintain high quality standards? (5) Does it stimulate creativity?"[19]

A third strategy for dealing with external complexity involves companies' building on their own capabilities manage too much complexity, which otherwise lead to chaos. Some of those strategies include creating open networks internal and outside the organization to promote cooperation and integration and to develop brand and reputation. Also, sharing "...values, vision, strategy, organizational processes and knowledge, through the development of trust and incorporation and promotion of leaders at all levels" can help internal teams exploit external complexity to the organization's advantage. Keep these ideas in mind as you read through the chapter and think about how leaders, managers, employees, and you can learn to read external environmental clues that organizations can use to creatively and proactively use organizational resources to be more competitive, effective, and successful.

CONCEPT CHECK

1. What factors within the economic environment affect businesses?
2. Why do change and shifts and technological developments create both challenges and new opportunities for business?

15.3 Organizational Designs and Structures

3. Identify different types of organizational structures and their strengths and weaknesses.

A 2017 Deloitte source asked, before answering, "Why has organizational design zoomed to the top of the list as the most important trend in the Global Human Capital Trends survey for two years in a row?"[20] The source continued, "The answer is simple: The way high-performing organizations operate today is radically different from how they operated 10 years ago. Yet many other organizations continue to operate according to industrial-age models that are 100 years old or more."[21]

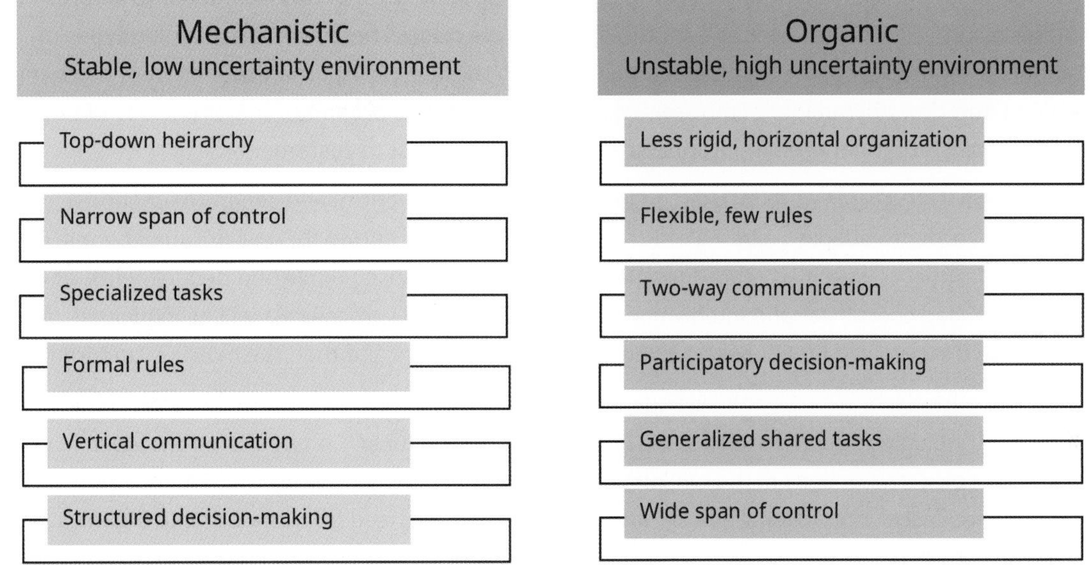

Exhibit 15.5 Mechanistic and Organic Organizations (Attribution: Copyright Rice University, OpenStax, under CC-BY 4.0 license)

Early organizational theorists broadly categorized **organizational structures** and systems as either mechanistic or organic.[22] This broad, generalized characterization of organizations remains relevant. **Mechanistic organizational structures** (Exhibit 15.5) are best suited for environments that range from stable and simple to low-moderate uncertainty (Exhibit 15.4) and are characterized by top-down hierarchies of control that are rule-based. The chain of command is highly centralized and uses formal authority; tasks are clearly defined and differentiated to be executed by specific specialized experts. Bosses and supervisors have fewer people working directly under them (i.e., a narrow span of control), and the organization is governed by rigid departmentalization (i.e., an organization is divided into different departments that perform specialized tasks according to the departments' expertise). This form of organization represents a traditional type of structure that evolved in environments that were, as noted above, stable with low complexity. Historically, the

U.S. Postal Service and other manufacturing types of industries (**Exhibit 15.4**) were mechanistic. Again, this type of organizational design may still be relevant, as **Exhibit 15.4** suggests, in simple, stable, low-uncertainty environments.

Organic organizational structures and systems, however, have opposite characteristics from mechanistic ones. As **Exhibit 15.4** shows, these organizational forms work best in unstable, complex, changing environments. Their structures are flatter, with participatory communication and decision-making flowing in different directions. There is more fluidity and less-rigid ways of performing tasks; there may also be fewer rules. Tasks are more generalized and shared; there is a wider span of control (i.e., more people reporting to managers). **Exhibit 15.5** offers examples of organically structured industries, such as high tech, computer, aerospace, and telecommunications industries, that must deal with change and uncertainty. Contemporary corporations and firms engaged in fast-paced, highly competitive, rapidly changing, and turbulent environments are becoming more organic in different ways, as we will discuss in this chapter. However, not every organization or every part of most organizations may require an organic type of structure. Understanding different organizational designs and structures is important to discern when, where, and under what circumstances a type of mechanistic system or part of an organization would be needed. The following section discusses five types of structures with variations.

Types of Organizational Structures

Within the context of mechanistic versus organic structures, specific types of organizational structures in the United States historically evolved over at least three eras, as we discuss here before explaining types of organizational designs. During the first era, the mid-1800s to the late 1970s, organizations were mechanistic self-contained, top-down pyramids.[23] Emphasis was placed on internal organizational processes of taking in raw materials, transforming those into products, and turning them out to customers.

Early organizational structures were focused on internal hierarchical control and separate functional specializations in order to adapt to external environments. Structures during this era grouped people into functions or departments, specified reporting relationships among those people and departments, and developed systems to coordinate and integrate work horizontally and vertically. As will be explained, the **functional structure** evolved first, followed by the divisional structure and then the matrix structured.

The second era started in the 1980s and extended through the mid-1990s. More-complex environments, markets, and technologies strained mechanistic organizational structures. Competition from Japan in the auto industry and complex transactions in the banking, insurance, and other industries that emphasized customer value, demand and faster interactions, quality, and results issued the need for more organic organizational designs and structures.

Communication and coordination between and among internal organizational units and external customers, suppliers, and other stakeholders required higher levels of integration and speed of informational processing. Personal computers and networks had also entered the scene. In effect, the so-called "horizontal organization" was born, which emphasized "reengineering along workflow processes that link organizational capabilities to customers and suppliers."[24] Ford, Xerox Corp., Lexmark, and Eastman Kodak Company are examples of early adopters of the **horizontal organizational design**, which, unlike the top-down pyramid structures in the first era, brought flattened hierarchical, hybrid structures and cross-functional teams.

The third era started in the mid-1990s and extends to the present. Several factors contributed to the rise of this era: the Internet; global competition—particularly from China and India with low-cost labor; automation of supply chains; and outsourcing of expertise to speed up production and delivery of products and services. The so-called silos and walls of organizations opened up; everything could not be or did not have to be produced within the confines of an organization, especially if corporations were cutting costs and outsourcing different functions of products to save costs. During this period, further extensions of the horizontal and organic types of structures evolved: the divisional, matrix, global geographic, modular, team-based, and virtual structures were created.

In the following discussion, we identify major types of structures mentioned above and discuss the advantages and disadvantages of each, referenced in **Exhibit 15.6**. Note that in many larger national and international corporations, there is a mix and match among different structures used. There are also advantages and disadvantages of each structure. Again, organizational structures are designed to fit with external environments. Depending on the type of environments from our earlier discussion in which a company operates, the structure should facilitate that organization's capability to achieve its vision, mission, and goals. **Exhibit 15.6** offers a profile of different structures that evolved in our discussion above.

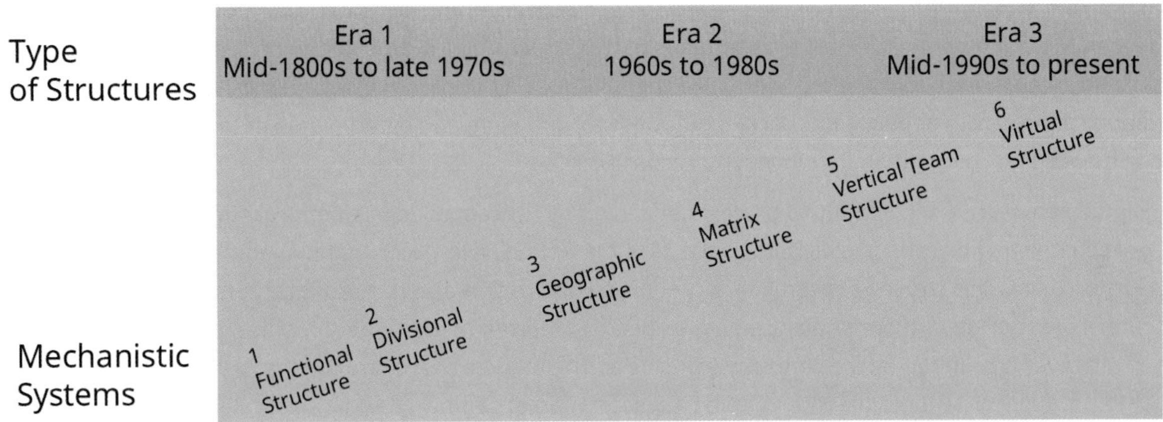

Exhibit 15.6 Evolution of Organizational Structure Adapted from: Daft, R., 2016, Organization Theory and Design, 12th edition, Cengage learning, Chapter 3; Warren, N., "Hitting the Sweet Spot Between Specialization and Integration in Organizational Design", People and Strategy, 34, No. 1, 2012, pp. 24-30.

Note the continuum in **Exhibit 15.6**, showing the earliest form of organizational structure, functional, evolving with more complex environments to divisional, matrix, team-based, and then virtual. This evolution, as discussed above, is presented as a continuum from mechanistic to organic structures—moving from more simple, stable environments to complex, changing ones, as illustrated in **Exhibit 15.6**. The six types of organizational structures discussed here include functional, divisional, geographic, matrix, networked/team, and virtual.[25]

The functional structure, shown in **Exhibit 15.7**, is among the earliest and most used organizational designs. This structure is organized by departments and expertise areas, such as R&D (research & development), production, accounting, and human resources. Functional organizations are referred to as pyramid structures since they are governed as a hierarchical, top-down control system.

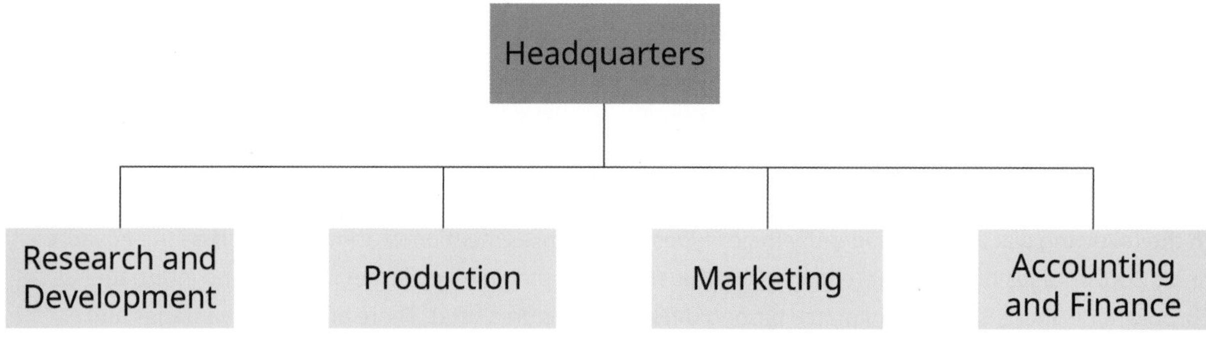

Exhibit 15.7 Functional Structure (Attribution: Copyright Rice University, OpenStax, under CC-BY 4.0 license)

Small companies, start-ups, and organizations working in simple, stable environments use this structure, as do many large government organizations and divisions of large companies for certain tasks.

The functional structure excels in providing for a high degree of specialization and a simple and straightforward reporting system within departments, offers economies of scale, and is not difficult to scale if and when the organization grows. Disadvantages of this structure include isolation of departments from each other since they tend to form "silos," which are characterized by closed mindsets that are not open to communicating across departments, lack of quick decision-making and coordination of tasks across departments, and competition for power and resources.

Divisional structures, see **Exhibit 15.8**, are, in effect, many functional departments grouped under a division head. Each functional group in a division has its own marketing, sales, accounting, manufacturing, and production team. This structure resembles a product structure that also has profit centers. These smaller functional areas or departments can also be grouped by different markets, geographies, products, services, or other whatever is required by the company's business. The market-based structure is ideal for an organization that has products or services that are unique to specific market segments and is particularly effective if that organization has advanced knowledge of those segments.

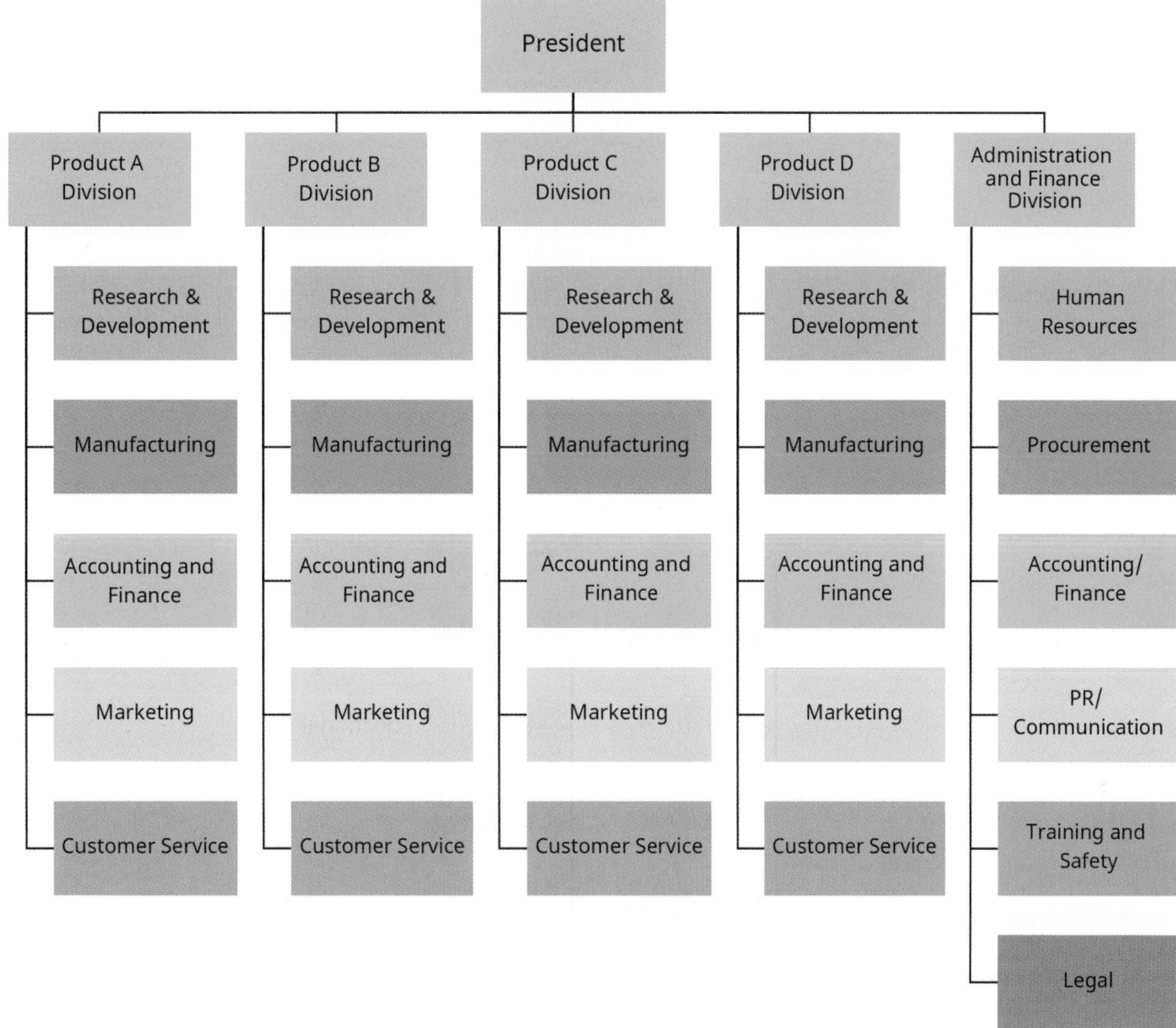

Exhibit 15.8 Divisional Organization Structure (Attribution: Copyright Rice University, OpenStax, under CC-BY 4.0 license)

The advantages of a divisional structure include the following: each specialty area can be more focused on the business segment and budget that it manages; everyone can more easily know their responsibilities and accountability expectations; customer contact and service can be quicker; and coordination within a divisional grouping is easier, since all the functions are accessible. The divisional structure is also helpful for large companies since decentralized decision-making means that headquarters does not have to micromanage all the divisions. The disadvantages of this structure from a headquarters perspective are that divisions can easily become isolated and insular from one another and that different systems, such as accounting, finance, sales, and so on, may suffer from poor and infrequent communication and coordination of enterprise mission, direction, and values. Moreover, incompatibility of systems (technology, accounting, advertising, budgets) can occur, which creates a strain on company strategic goals and objectives.

A **geographic structure**, Exhibit 15.9, is another option aimed at moving from a mechanistic to more organic design to serve customers faster and with relevant products and services; as such, this structure is organized by locations of customers that a company serves. This structure evolved as companies became more national, international, and global. Geographic structures resemble and are extensions of the divisional structure.

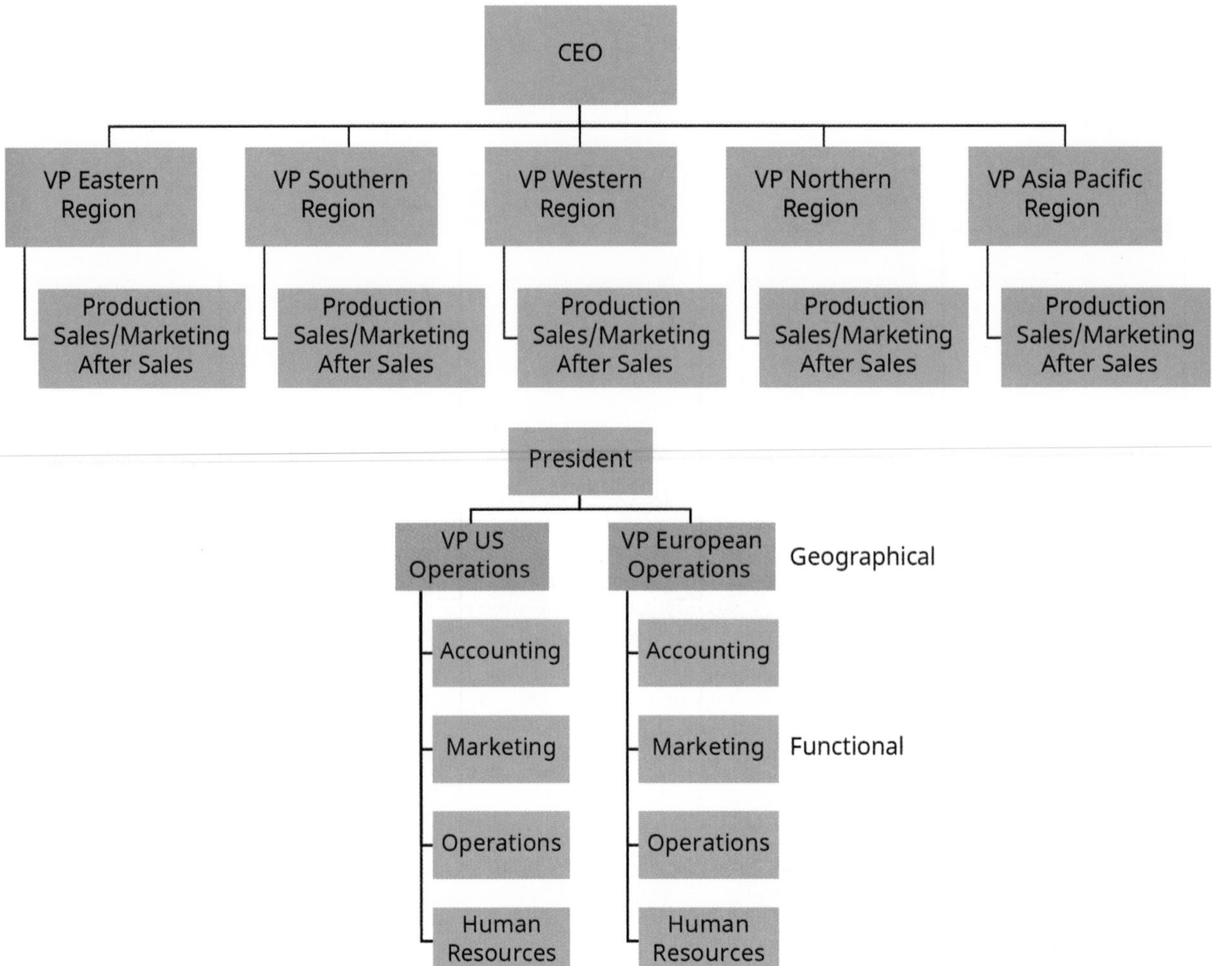

Exhibit 15.9 Geographic Structure (Attribution: Copyright Rice University, OpenStax, under CC-BY 4.0 license)

Organizing geographically enables each geographic organizational unit (like a division) the ability to understand, research, and design products and/or services with the knowledge of customer needs, tastes, and cultural differences. The advantages and disadvantages of the geographic structure are similar to those of the divisional structure. Headquarters must ensure effective coordination and control over each somewhat autonomous geographically self-contained structure.

The main downside of a geographical organizational structure is that it can be easy for decision-making to become decentralized, as geographic divisions (which can be hundreds if not thousands of miles away from corporate headquarters) often have a great deal of autonomy.

Exhibit 15.10 IBM China IBM has chosen a geographic structure which is aimed at moving from a mechanistic to more organic design to serve customers faster and with relevant products and services; as such, this structure is organized by locations of customers that a company serves. This structure evolved as companies became more national, international, and global. Geographic structures resemble and are extensions of the divisional structure. (Credit: Cory Denton/ Flickr/ Attribution 2.0 Generic (CC BY 2.0))

Matrix structures, illustrated in Exhibit 15.6 and depicted in Exhibit 15.11, move closer to organic systems in an attempt to respond to environmental uncertainty, complexity, and instability. The matrix structure actually originated at a time in the 1960s when U.S. aerospace firms contracted with the government. Aerospace firms were required to "develop charts showing the structure of the project management team that would be executing the contract and how this team was related to the overall management structure of the organization." As such, employees would be required to have dual reporting relationships—with the government and the aerospace company.[26] Since that time, this structure has been imitated and used by other industries and companies since it provides flexibility and helps integrate decision-making in functionally organized companies.

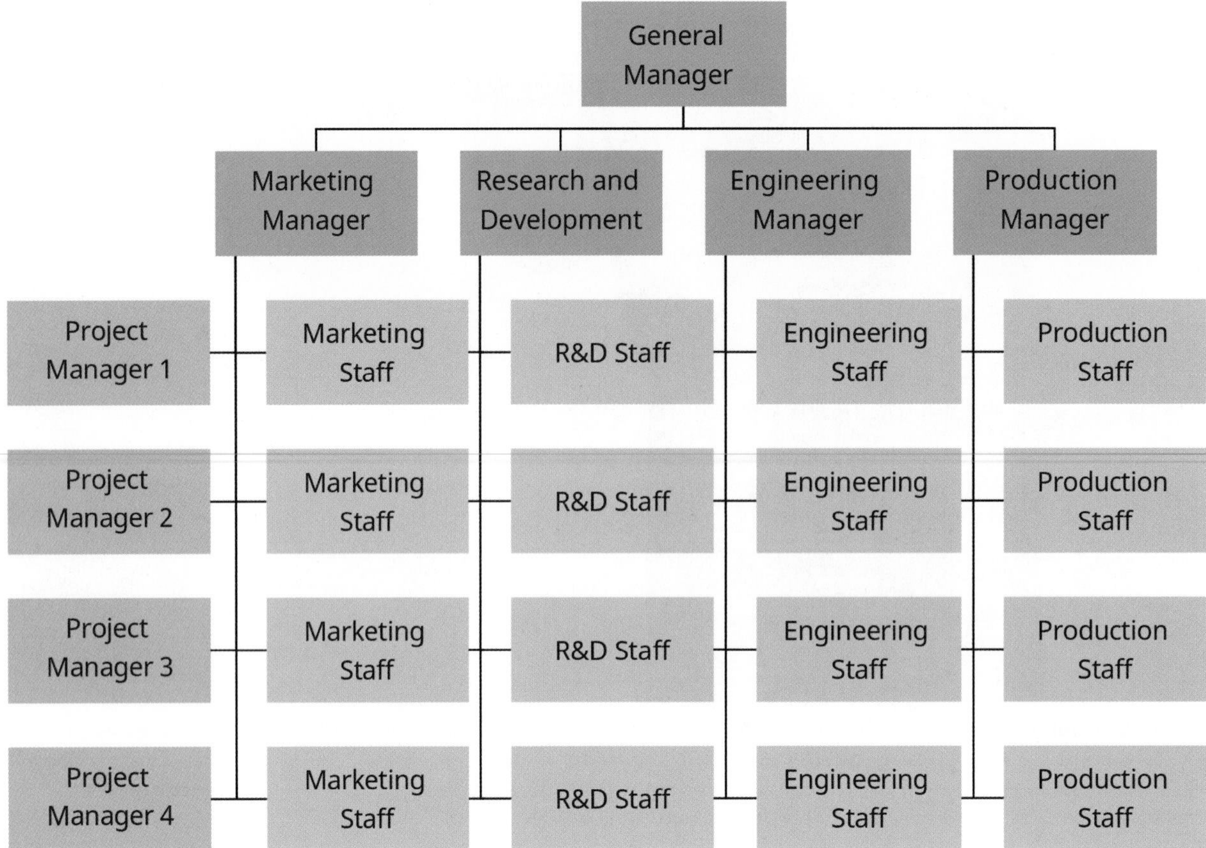

Exhibit 15.11 Matrix Structure (Attribution: Copyright Rice University, OpenStax, under CC-BY 4.0 license)

Matrix designs use teams to combine vertical with horizontal structures. The traditional functional or vertical structure and chain of command maintains control over employees who work on teams that cut across functional areas, creating horizontal coordination that focuses projects that have deadlines and goals to meet within and often times in addition to those of departments. In effect, matrix structures initiated horizontal team-based structures that provided faster information sharing, coordination, and integration between the formal organization and profit-oriented projects and programs.

As **Exhibit 15.11** illustrates, this structure has lines of formal authority along two dimensions: employees report to a functional, departmental boss and simultaneously to a product or project team boss. One of the weaknesses of matrix structures is the confusion and conflicts employees experience in reporting to two bosses. To work effectively, employees (including their bosses and project leaders) who work in dual-authority matrix structures require good interpersonal communication, conflict management, and political skills to manage up and down the organization.

Different types of matrix structures, some resembling virtual team designs, are used in more complex environments.[27] For example, there are cross-functional matrix teams in which team members from other organizational departments report to an "activity leader" who is not their formal supervisor or boss. There are also functional matrix teams where employees from the same department coordinate across another internal matrix team consisting of, for example, HR or other functional area specialists, who come together to develop a limited but focused common short-term goal. There are also global matrix teams consisting of employees from different regions, countries, time zones, and cultures who are assembled to achieve a short-term project goal of a particular customer. Matrix team members have been and are a growing part of horizontal organizations that cut across geographies, time zones, skills, and traditional authority structures to solve customer and even enterprise organizational needs and demands.

As part of the next discussed organizational type of structure, networked teams, organizational members in matrix structures must "learn how to collaborate with colleagues across distance, cultures and other barriers. Matrix team members often suffer from the problem of divided loyalties where they have both team and functional goals that compete for their time and attention, they have multiple bosses and often work on multiple teams at the same time. For some matrix team members this may be the first time they have been given accountability for results that are broader than delivery of their functional goals. Some individuals relish the breath and development that the matrix team offers and others feel exposed and out of control." To succeed in these types of horizontal organizational structures, organizational members "should focus less on the structure and more on behaviors."[28]

Networked team structures are another form of the horizontal organization. Moving beyond the matrix structure, networked teams are more informal and flexible. "[N]etworks have two salient characteristics: clustering and path length. Clustering refers to the degree to which a network is made up of tightly knit groups while path lengths is a measure of distance—the average number of links separating any two nodes in the network."[29] A more technical explanation can be found in this footnote source.[30] For our purposes here, a networked organizational structure is one that naturally forms after being initially assigned. Based on the vision, mission, and needs of a problem or opportunity, team members will find others who can help—if the larger organization and leaders do not prevent or obstruct that process.

There is not one classical depiction of this structure, since different companies initially design teams to solve problems, find opportunities, and discover resources to do so. Stated another way, "The networked organization is one that is connected together by informal networks and the demands of the task, rather than a formal organizational structure. The network organization prioritizes its 'soft structure' of relationships, networks, teams, groups and communities rather than reporting lines."[31] **Exhibit 15.12** is a suggested illustration of this structure.

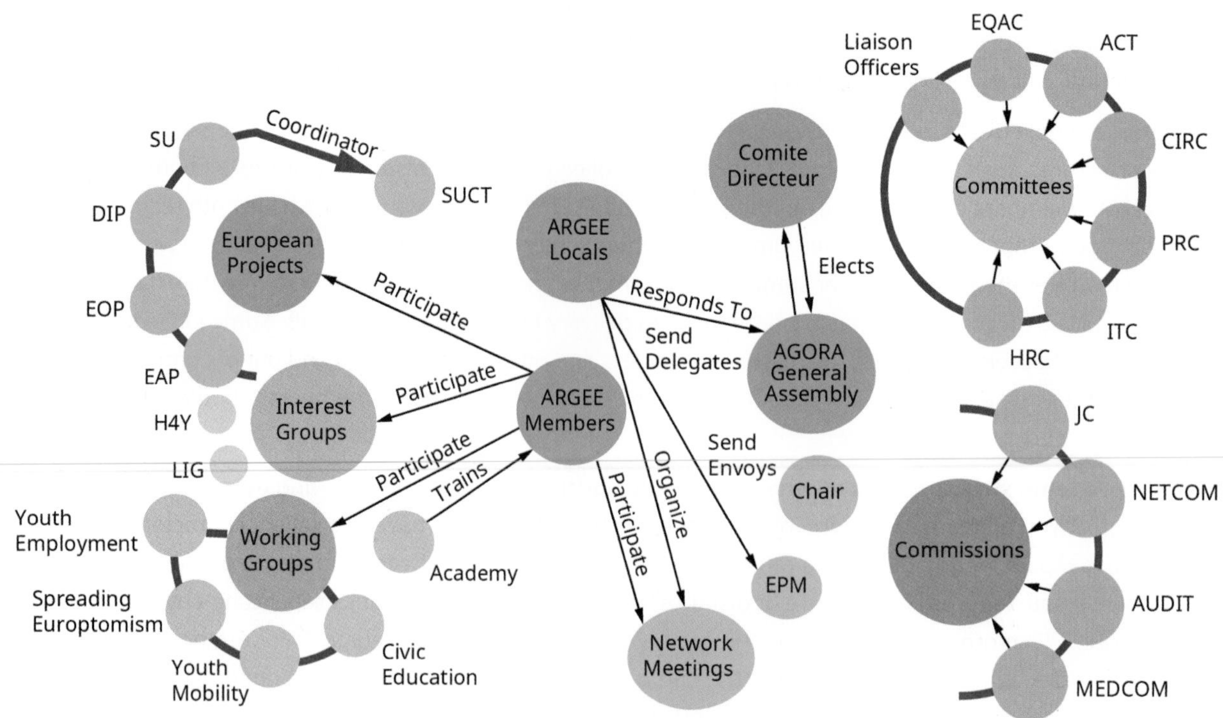

Exhibit 15.12 **Networked Team Structure**

A Deloitte source based on the 2017 Global Human Capital Trend study stated that as organizations continue to transition from vertical structures to more organic ones, networked global designs are being adapted to larger companies that require more reach and scope and quicker response time with customers: "Research shows that we spend two orders of magnitude more time with people near our desk than with those more than 50 meters away. Whatever a hierarchical organization chart says, real, day-to-day work gets done in networks. This is why the organization of the future is a 'network of teams.'"[32]

Advantages of networked organizations are similar to those stated earlier with regard to organic, horizontal, and matrix structures. Weaknesses of the networked structure include the following: (1) Establishing clear lines of communication to produce project assignments and due dates to employees is needed. (2) Dependence on technology—Internet connections and phone lines in particular—is necessary. Delays in communication result from computer crashes, network traffic errors and problems; electronic information sharing across country borders can also be difficult. (3) Not having a central physical location where all employees work, or can assemble occasionally to have face-to-face meetings and check results, can result in errors, strained relationships, and lack of on-time project deliverables.[33]

Virtual structures and organizations emerged in the 1990s as a response to requiring more flexibility, solution-based tasks on demand, fewer geographical constraints, and accessibility to dispersed expertise.[34] Virtual structures are depicted in **Exhibit 15.13**. Related to so-called modular and digital organizations, virtual structures are dependent on information communication technologies (ICTs).

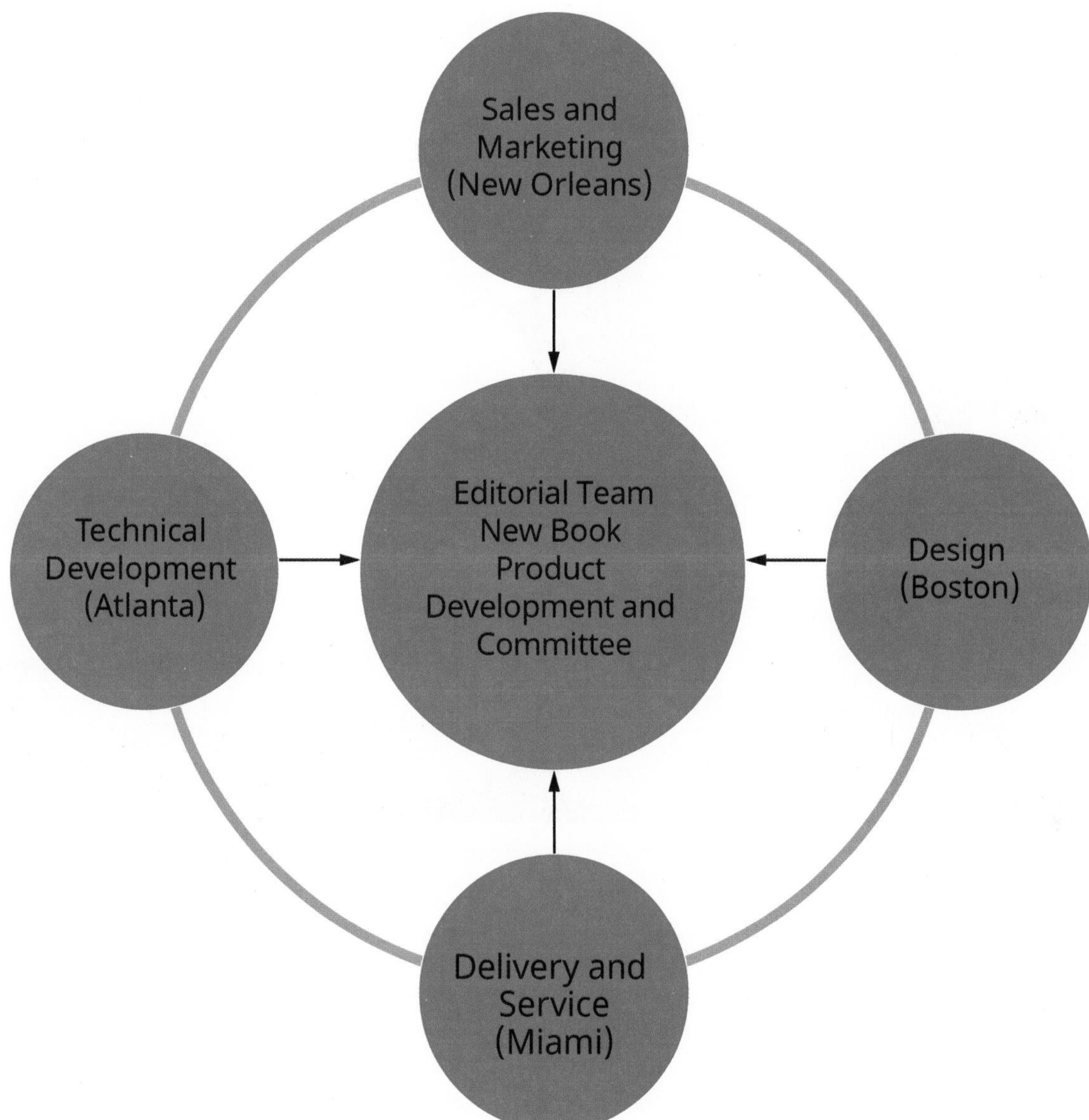

Exhibit 15.13 Virtual Structure (Attribution: Copyright Rice University, OpenStax, under CC-BY 4.0 license)

These organizations move beyond network team structures in that the headquarters or home base may be the only or part of part of a stable organizational base. Otherwise, this is a "boundaryless organization." Examples of organizations that use virtual teams are Uber, Airbnb, Amazon, Reebok, Nike, Puma, and Dell. Increasingly, organizations are using different variations of virtual structures with call centers and other outsourced tasks, positions, and even projects.

Exhibit 15.14 Using Technological Disruption Information technologies and social media powered by the internet and used by sharing economy companies such as Airbnb and Uber have democratized and increased, if not leveled, competition across several industries such taxis, real estate rentals, and hospitality services. (Credit: Grid Engine/ flickr/ Attribution 2.0 Generic (CC BY 2.0))

Advantages of virtual teams and organizations include cost savings, decreased response time to customers, greater access to a diverse labor force not encumbered by 8-hour workdays, and less harmful effects on the environment. "The telecommuting policies of Dell, Aetna, and Xerox cumulatively saved 95,294 metric tons of greenhouse gas emissions last year, which is the equivalent of taking 20,000 passenger vehicles off of the road."[35] Disadvantages are social isolation of employees who work virtually, potential for lack of trust among employees and between the company and employees when communication is limited, and reduced collaboration among separated employees and the organization's officers due to lack of social interaction.

In the following section, we turn to internal organizational dimensions that complement structure and are affected by and affect external environments.

CONCEPT CHECK

1. Why does the matrix structure have a dual chain of command?
2. How does a matrix structure increase power struggles or reduce accountability?
3. What are advantages of a formal committee structure? Disadvantages?

15.4 The Internal Organization and External Environments

4. Explain how organizations organize to meet external market threats and opportunities.

At a basic level of understanding how internal organizations respond to environments, consider the theory of Open Systems, which the organizational theorists Katz and Kahn[36] and Bertalanffy introduced.[37]

Exhibit 15.15 illustrates this theory's view of organizations as open systems that take in resources and raw materials at the "input" phase from the environment in a number of forms, depending on the nature of the organization, industry, and its business. Whatever the input resources are—information, raw materials, students entering a university—to be transformed by the internal processes of the organization. The internal organizational systems then process and transform the input material, which is called "through-put" phase, and move the changed material (resources) to the "outputs" and back into the environment as products, services, graduates, etc.

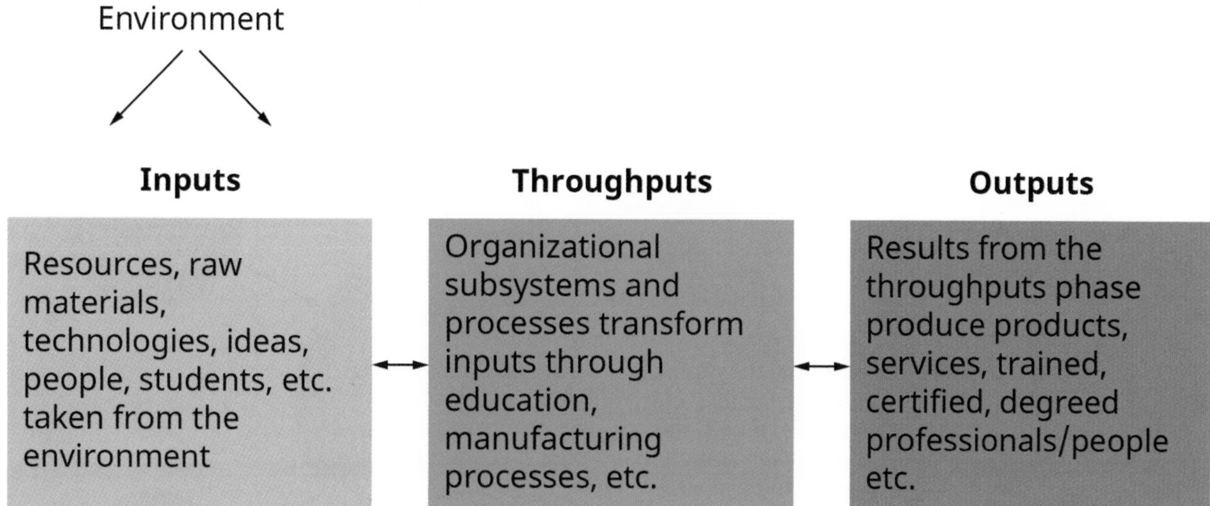

Exhibit 15.15 Open System Model of an Organization (Attribution: Copyright Rice University, OpenStax, under CC-BY 4.0 license)

The open systems model serves as a feedback loop continually taking in resources from the environment, processing and transforming them into outputs that are returned to the environment. This model explains organizational survival that emphasizes long-term goals.

Organizations according to this theory are considered as either Open or Closed systems, (or relatively opened or closed) depending on the organization's sensitivity to the environment. Closed systems are less sensitive to environmental resources and possibilities, and open systems are more responsive and adaptive to environmental changes. For example, during the 1980's the then Big 3 U.S. auto manufacturers (Ford, General Motors and Chrysler) were pressured by Japanese auto manufacturers' successful 4-cylinder car sales that hit the U.S. like a shock wave. The Detroit producers experienced slumping sales, plant closures, and employee lay-offs in response to the Japanese wave of competition. It seemed that the U.S. auto makers had become closed or at least insensitive to changing trends in cars during that time and were unwilling to change manufacturing processes. Similarly, Amazon's business model, discussed earlier, has and continues to pressure retailers to innovate and change processes and practices to compete in this digital era.

Organizations respond to external environments not only through their structures, but also by the domains they choose and the internal dimensions and capabilities they select. An organization defines itself and its niche in an environment by the choice of its **domain**, i.e., what sector or field of the environment it will use its technology, products, and services to compete in and serve. Some of the major sectors of a task environment include marketing, technology, government, financial resources, and human resources.

Presently, several environmental domains that once were considered stable have become more complex and unstable—e.g., toys, public utilities, the U.S. Postal Service, and higher education. And even domains are changing. For example, as referred to earlier, the traditionally stable and somewhat unchanging domain of higher education has become more complex with the entry of for-profit educational institutions, MOOCs (massive open online courses), internal company "universities," and other certification and degree programs outside traditional private institutions. Sharing-economy companies such as Uber and Airbnb have redefined the transportation domain in which taxis operate and the hospitality domain in which hotels and bed and breakfasts serve. New business models that use mobile phones, ICTs (information communication technologies), and apps remove middle management layers in traditional organizations and structures.

With a chosen domain in which to operate, owners and leaders must organize internal dimensions to compete in and serve their markets. For example, hierarchies of authority and chain of command are used by owners and top-level leaders to develop and implement strategic and enterprise decisions; managers are required to provide technologies, training, accounting, legal, and other infrastructure resources; and cultures still count to establish and maintain norms, relationships, legal and ethical practices, and the reputation of organizations.

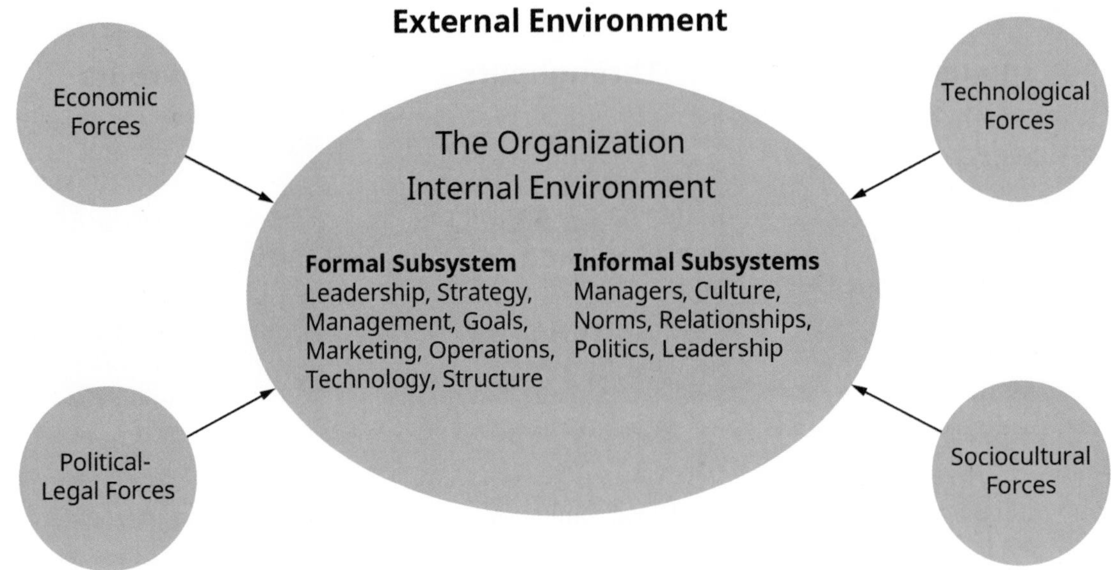

Exhibit 15.16 Internal Organization (Attribution: Copyright Rice University, OpenStax, under CC-BY 4.0 license)

Exhibit 15.16 shows internal organizational dimensions. These dimensions and systems include leadership, strategy, culture, management, goals, marketing, operations, and structure. Relationships, norms, and politics are also included in the informal organization. There are other internal functions not listed here, such as research and development, accounting and finance, production, and human resources. Another popular depiction of internal organizational dimensions is the **McKinsey 7-S model**, shown in **Exhibit 15.17**. Similarly, *strategy, structure, systems, skills, staff*, and style all revolve around and are interconnected with *shared values* (or culture) in an organization.

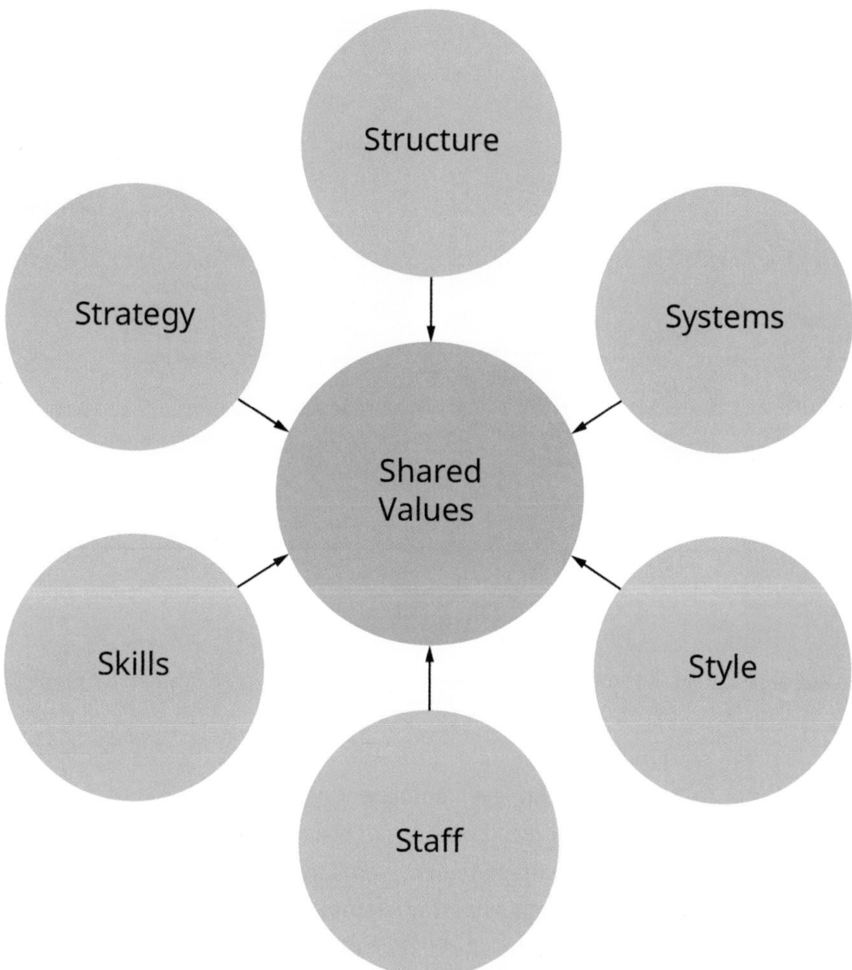

Exhibit 15.17 The McKinsey 7-S Model (Attribution: Copyright Rice University, OpenStax, under CC-BY 4.0 license)

A unifying framework shown in **Exhibit 15.18**, developed by Arie Lewin and Carroll Stephens,[38] illustrates the integration of internal organizational dimensions and how these work in practice to align with the external environment. Note that it is the CEO and other top-level leaders who scan the external environment to identify uncertainties and resources before using a SWOT analysis (identifying strengths, weaknesses, opportunities, and threats) to confirm and update the domain of an organization and then to define the vision, mission, goals, and strategies. Once the enterprise goals and strategies are developed, the organizational culture, structure, and other systems and policies can be established (human resources, technologies, accounting and finance, and so on).

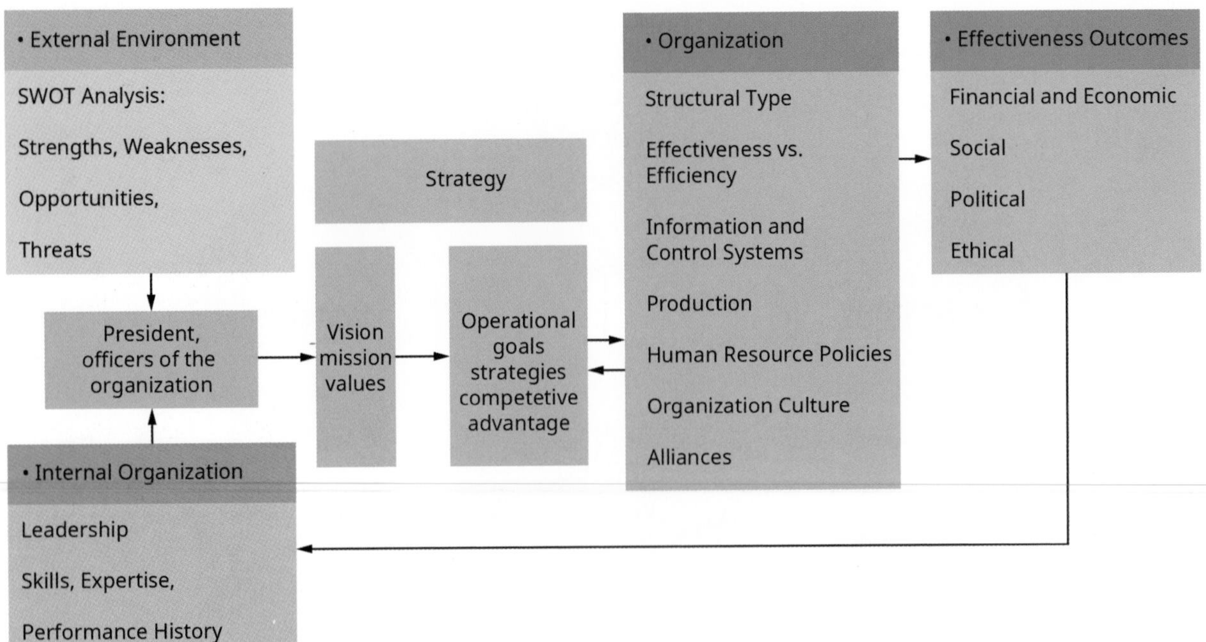

Exhibit 15.18 The Internal Organization and External Environment (Attribution: Copyright Rice University, OpenStax, under CC-BY 4.0 license)

As **Exhibit 15.18** shows, after a CEO and the top-level team identify opportunities and threats in the environment, they then determine the domain and purpose of the organization from which strategies, organizational capabilities, resources, and management systems must be mobilized to support the enterprise's purpose.[39] The company McDonald's has, for example, successfully aligned its enterprise with the global environments it serves, which is "1% of the world's population—more than 70 million customers—every day and in virtually every country across the world." The major operating goal of the firm driving its internal alignment is a "fanatical attention to the design and management of scalable processes, routines, and a working culture by which simple, stand-alone, and standardized products are sold globally at a predictable, and therefore manageable, volume, quality, and cost."[40] A more detailed SWOT analysis of McDonald's operations can be found in endnote.

Exhibit 15.19 McDonald's Processes McDonalds, major operating goal of the firm driving its internal alignment is a "Fanatical attention to the design and management of scalable processes, routines, and a working culture by which simple, stand-alone, and standardized products are sold globally at a predictable, and therefore manageable, volume, quality, and cost." Here employees are reminded of the time that the ingredients should stay on a secondary shelf. (Credit: Walter Lim/ flickr/ Attribution 2.0 Generic (CC BY 2.0))

In practice, no internal organizational alignment with its external environment is perfect or permanent. Quite the opposite. Companies and organizations change leadership and strategies and make structural and systems changes to meet changing competition, market forces, and customers and end users' needs and demands. Even Amazon continues to develop, expand, and change. With a mission statement as bold and broad as Amazon's, change is a constant: "Our vision is to be earth's most customer-centric company; to build a place where people can come to find and discover anything they might want to buy online" (Amazon.com, Apr 15, 2018).

Amazon has a functional organizational structure that focuses on business functions for determining the interactions among the different parts of the company. Amazon's corporate structure is best characterized as global function-based groups (most significant feature), a global hierarchy, and geographic divisions, as **Exhibit 15.20** shows. This structure seems to fit with the size of Amazon's business—43% of 2016 retail sales were in the United States.[41] Seven segments, including information technology, human resources and legal operations, and heads of segments, report to Amazon's CEO. "Senior management team include two CEOs, three Senior Vice Presidents and one Worldwide Controller, who are responsible for various vital aspects of the business reporting directly to Amazon CEO Jeff Bezos." [42] The strategic goal underlying this structure is to facilitate Amazon.com to successfully implement e-commerce operations management throughout the entire organization.[43]

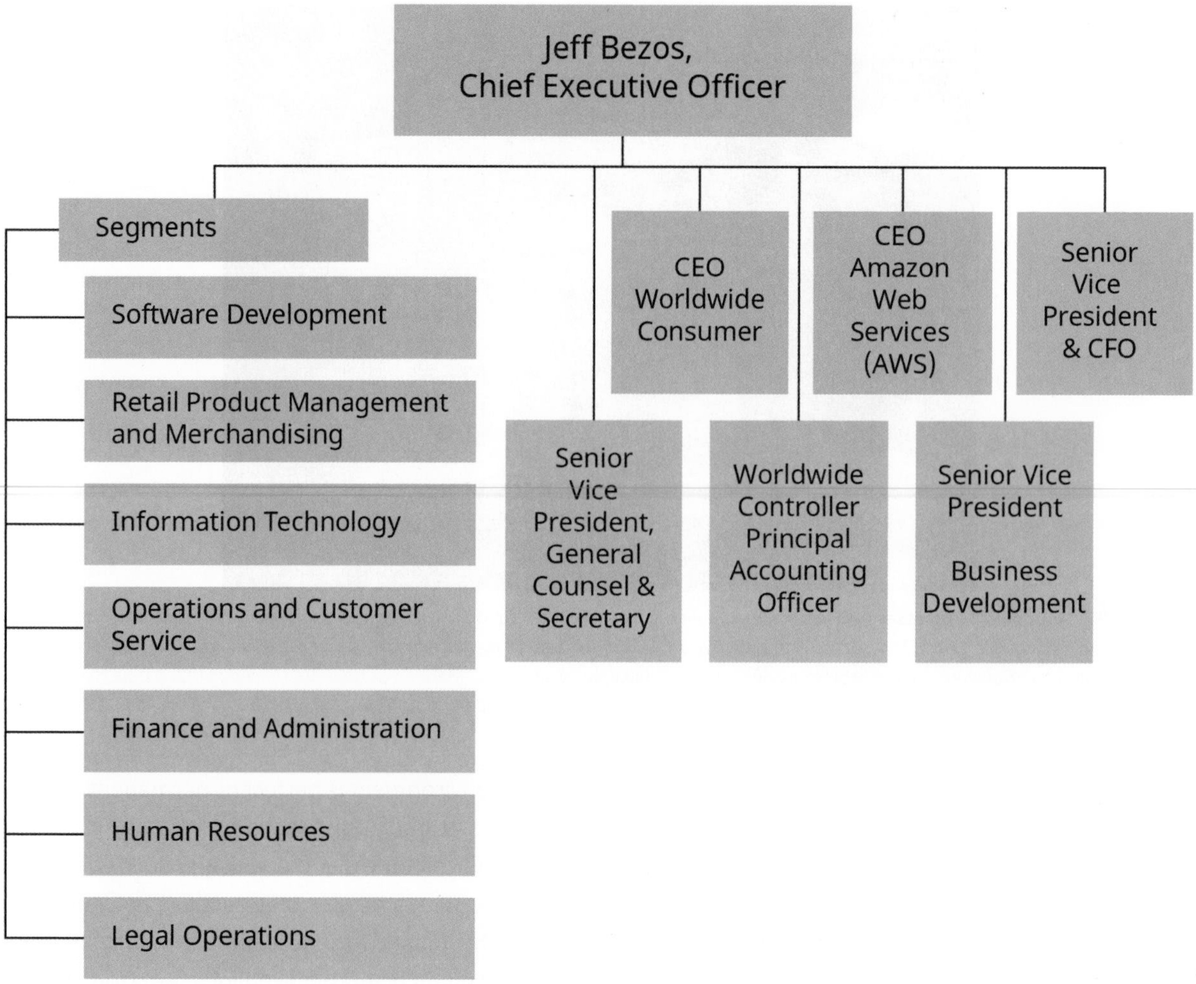

Jeff Bezos, Chief Executive Officer

Segments

- Software Development
- Retail Product Management and Merchandising
- Information Technology
- Operations and Customer Service
- Finance and Administration
- Human Resources
- Legal Operations

CEO Worldwide Consumer

CEO Amazon Web Services (AWS)

Senior Vice President & CFO

Senior Vice President, General Counsel & Secretary

Worldwide Controller Principal Accounting Officer

Senior Vice President Business Development

Exhibit 15.20 Amazon's Corporate Structure (Attribution: Copyright Rice University, OpenStax, under CC-BY 4.0 license)

Despite the company's exponential growth and success to date, as noted earlier in the section on organizational structures, a disadvantage of structures such as Amazon's, and in this case Amazon's, is that it has limited flexibility and responsiveness even with its current growth. "The dominance of the global function-based groups and global hierarchy characteristics reduces the capacity of Amazon to rapidly respond to new issues and problems encountered in the e-commerce business."[44] Still, Amazon's most outstanding success factor remains its CEO, Jeff Bezos—his ingenuity, vision and foresight, and ability to sustain and even extend the company's competitive advantages. Amazon customers value these factors—customer purchase criteria (CPC) that include price, fast delivery, and reliable service. "Consumers choose Amazon because it does better than its competition on these CPC."[45]

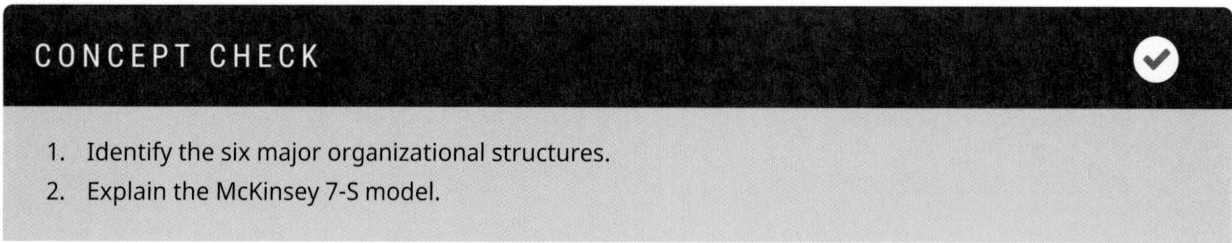

CONCEPT CHECK

1. Identify the six major organizational structures.
2. Explain the McKinsey 7-S model.

15.5 Corporate Cultures

5. Identify the fit between organizational cultures and the external environment

Organizational culture is considered one of the most important **internal dimensions of an organization**'s effectiveness criteria. Peter Drucker, an influential management guru, once stated, "Culture eats strategy for breakfast."[46] He meant that **corporate culture** is more influential than strategy in terms of motivating employees' beliefs, behaviors, relationships, and ways they work since culture is based on values. Strategy and other **internal dimensions of organization** are also very important, but organizational culture serves two crucial purposes: first, culture helps an organization adapt to and integrate with its external environment by adopting the right values to respond to external threats and opportunities; and secondly, culture creates internal unity by bringing members together so they work more cohesively to achieve common goals. [47]ulture is both the personality and glue that binds an organization. It is also important to note that organizational cultures are generally framed and influenced by the top-level leader or founder. This individual's vision, values, and mission set the "tone at the top," which influences both the ethics and legal foundations, modeling how other officers and employees work and behave. A framework used to study how an organization and its culture fit with the environment is offered in the Competing Values Framework.

The **Competing Values Framework** (CVF) is one of the most cited and tested models for diagnosing an organization's cultural effectiveness and examining its fit with its environment. The CVF, shown in **Exhibit 15.21**, has been tested for over 30 years; the effectiveness criteria offered in the framework were discovered to have made a difference in identifying organizational cultures that fit with particular characteristics of external environments.[48]

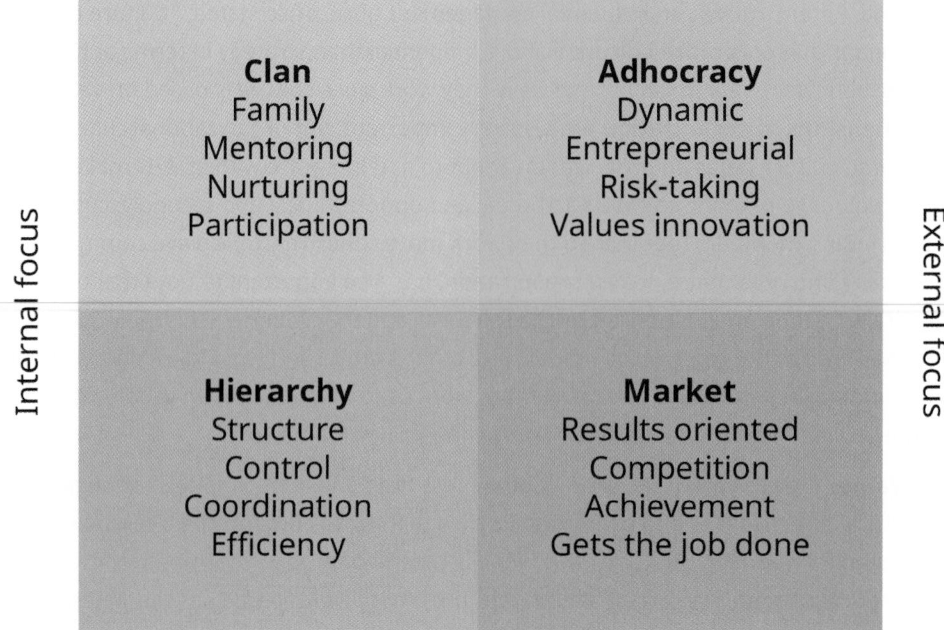

Exhibit 15.21 The Competing Values Framework Source: Adapted from K. Cameron and R. Quinn, 1999. Diagnosing and Changing Organizational Culture, Addison-Wesley, p. 32.

The two axes in the framework, external focus versus internal focus, indicate whether or not the organization's culture is externally or internally oriented. The other two axes, flexibility versus stability and control, determine whether a culture functions better in a stable, controlled environment or a flexible, fast-paced environment. Combining the axes offers four cultural types: (1) the dynamic, entrepreneurial **Adhocracy Culture**—an external focus with a flexibility orientation; (2) the people-oriented, friendly **Clan Culture**—an internal focus with a flexibility orientation; (3) the process-oriented, structured **Hierarchy Culture**—an internal focus with a stability/control orientation; and (4) the results-oriented, competitive **Market Culture**—an external focus with a stability/control orientation.

The orientation of each of these cultural types is summarized as follows. The **Adhocracy Culture** profile of an organization emphasizes creating, innovating, visioning the future, managing change, risk-taking, rule-breaking, experimentation, entrepreneurship, and uncertainty. This profile culture is often found in such fast-paced industries as filming, consulting, space flight, and software development. Facebook and Google's cultures also match these characteristics.[49] It should be noted, however, that larger organizations may have different cultures for different groupings of professionals, even though the larger culture is still dominant. For example, a different subculture may evolve for hourly workers as compared to PhD research scientists in an organization.

The **Clan Culture** type focuses on relationships, team building, commitment, empowering human development, engagement, mentoring, and coaching. Organizations that focus on human development, human resources, team building, and mentoring would fit this profile. This type of culture fits Tom's of Maine, which has strived to form respectful relationships with employees, customers, suppliers, and the physical environment.

The **Hierarchy Culture** emphasizes efficiency, process and cost control, organizational improvement, technical expertise, precision, problem solving, elimination of errors, logical, cautious and conservative, management and operational analysis, and careful decision-making. This profile would suit a company that is bureaucratic and structured, such as the U.S. Postal Service, the military, and other similar types of government agencies.

The **Market Culture** focuses on delivering value, competing, delivering shareholder value, goal achievement, driving and delivering results, speedy decisions, hard driving through barriers, directive, commanding, and getting things done. This profile suits a marketing-and-sales-oriented company that works on planning and forecasting but also getting products and services to market and sold. Oracle under the dominating, hard-charging executive chairman Larry Ellison characterized this cultural fit.

Amazon illustrates a company that can have a mix of cultures and be effective. For example, Amazon blends a high-performance Adhocracy Culture with regard to its external expansion and Bezos's leadership style; at the same time, Amazon resembles a Hierarchy Culture internally with regard to its tight control over employees at lower levels. The company propelled its domain from an "online bookstore" "to selling everything online to being the pioneering in adopting cloud computing with AWS . . . to adopting the latest robotics in its warehouses to improve productivity . . . to thinking and testing disruptive technologies like drones and so on."[50] It has been criticized, at the same time, for its "toxic cut-throat work environment," asserting that Jeff Bezos is overly demanding and sets very high standards for Amazon employees, as well as for himself. This type of culture extends down to the warehouse employees. Amazon employees have complained that "Work came first, life came second, and trying to find the balance came last." This criticism peaked with an alleged suicide attempt in 2017 of a disgruntled employee who requested a transfer to a different department within in the company but was placed on an employee improvement plan—"a step that could result in his termination from Amazon if his performance didn't improve."[51] Amazon has since changed many of its working rules and regulations for warehouse employees.

CONCEPT CHECK 

1. How can employee diversity give a company a competitive advantage?
2. Explain the concept of hiring for fit as it relates to corporate culture.
3. What are some organizational issues that must be addressed when two large firms merge or grow rapidly like Amazon?

15.6 Organizing for Change in the 21st Century

6. Identify environmental trends, demands, and opportunities facing organizations.

The 2018 annual Global Risks Perception Survey (GRPS) predicts the following trends in the external environment: (1) persistent inequality and unfairness, (2) domestic and international political tensions, (3) environmental dangers, and (4) cyber vulnerabilities. With this context, authors in this report suggest that complex organizations approach their futures with the "nine resilience lens"—i.e., the capacity of a company or other organization to adapt and prosper in the face of high-impact, low-probability risks.[52] The nine lenses are grouped into three categories. First, structural resilience considers the systemic dynamics within the organization itself. The author calls for "system modularity," i.e., structures and designs that are "loosely coupled," which is another way of saying that rigid, mechanistic hierarchies will not function as well in these high-impact environments. Secondly, integrative resilience underlines complex interconnections with the external context. Here the author suggests that organizations must be part of and aware of their contexts: geographically and the health of "individuals, families, neighborhoods, cities, provinces, and countries" that are affected. Relatedly, the author notes that organizations must rely on their social cohesion—such as the social capital an organization has to fall back on in times of crisis—which is a strong source of resilience. Third, transformative resilience requires that mitigating some risks requires transformation. Important to organizations here is the need "to proactively change or it will end up being changed by external circumstances." This process requires organizational foresight, not forecasting. Organizations need to apply different search, environmental scanning, and new discovery techniques "to engage with the uncertainty of multiple futures." They do this through innovation and experimentation. In practice, Google, Amazon, Facebook, SpaceX, Tesla, Airbnb, Uber, and the resilience of other industry and organizational pioneering will be required.

Another trend on the horizon is that "[o]rganizations are no longer judged only for their financial performance, or even the quality of their products or services. Rather, they are being evaluated on the basis of their impact on society at large—transforming them from business enterprises into social enterprises."[53] A recent survey showed that 65 percent of CEOs rated "inclusive growth" as a "top-three strategic concern, more than three times greater than the proportion citing 'shareholder value.'"[54] Deloitte researchers noted that "[a] social enterprise is an organization whose mission combines revenue growth and profit-making with the need to respect and support its environment and stakeholder network. This includes listening to, investing in, and actively managing the trends that are shaping today's world. It is an organization that shoulders its responsibility to be a good citizen (both inside and outside the organization), serving as a role model for its peers and promoting a high degree of collaboration at every level of the organization."[55]

Key Terms

Adhocracy culture Creates an environment of innovating, visioning the future, accepting of managing change, and risk taking, rule-breaking, experimentation, entrepreneurship, and uncertainty.

Clan culture Focuses on relationships, team building, commitment, empowering human development, engagement, mentoring, and coaching.

Competing Values Framework Developed by Kim Cameron and Robert Quinn this model is used for diagnosing an organization's cultural effectiveness and examining its fit with its environment.

Complex-Stable environments Environments that have a large number of external elements, and elements are dissimilar and where elements remain the same or change slowly.

Complex-Unstable environments Environments that have a large number of external elements, and elements are dissimilar and where elements change frequently and unpredictably

Corporate culture Defines how motivating employees' beliefs, behaviors, relationships, and ways they work creates a culture that is based on the values the organization believes in.

Divisional structure An organizational structure characterized by functional departments grouped under a division head.

Domain The purpose of the organization from which its strategies, organizational capabilities, resources, and management systems are mobilized to support the enterprise's purpose.

Functional structure The earliest and most used organizational designs.

Geographic structure An Organizational option aimed at moving from a mechanistic to more organic design to serve customers faster and with relevant products and services; as such, this structure is organized by locations of customers that a company serves.

Government and political environment forces The global economy and changing political actions increase uncertainty for businesses, while creating opportunities for some industries and instability in others.

Hierarchy culture Emphasizes efficiency, process and cost control, organizational improvement, technical expertise, precision, problem solving, elimination of errors, logical, cautious and conservative, management and operational analysis, careful decision making.

Horizontal organizational structures A "flatter" organizational structure often found in matrix organizations where individuals relish the breath and development that their team offers.

Internal dimensions of organizations How an organization's culture affects and influences its strategy.

Market culture Focuses on delivering value, competing, delivering shareholder value, goal achievement, driving and delivering results, speedy decisions, hard driving through barriers, directive, commanding, competing and getting things done.

Matrix structure An organizational structure close in approach to organic systems that attempt to respond to environmental uncertainty, complexity, and instability.

McKinsey 7-S model A popular depiction of internal organizational dimensions.

Mechanistic organizational structures Best suited for environments that range from stable and simple to low-moderate uncertainty and have a formal "pyramid' structure.

Natural disaster and human induced environmental problems Events such as high-impact hurricanes, extreme temperatures and the rise in CO2 emissions as well as 'man-made' environmental disasters such as water and food crises; biodiversity loss and ecosystem collapse; large-scale involuntary migration are a force that affects organizations.

Networked-team structure A form of the horizontal organization.

Organic organizational structures The opposite of a functional organizational form that works best in unstable, complex changing environments.

Organizational structures A broad term that covers both mechanistic and organic organizational structures.

Simple-Stable environments Environments that have a small number of external elements, and elements are similar, and the elements remain the same or change slowly.

Simple-Unstable environments Environments that have a small number of external elements, and elements are similar and where elements change frequently and unpredictably.

Socio-cultural environment forces Include different generations' values, beliefs, attitudes and habits, customs and traditions, habits and lifestyles.

Technological forces Environmental influence on organizations where speed, price, service, and quality of products and services are dimensions of organizations' competitive advantage in this era.

Virtual structure A recent organizational structure that has emerged in the 1990's and early 2000's as a response to requiring more flexibility, solution based tasks on demand, less geographical constraints, and accessibility to dispersed expertise.

Summary of Learning Outcomes

15.1 The Organization's External Environment

1. Define the external environment of organizations

Organizations must react and adapt to many forces in their internal and external environments. The context of the firms such as size and geographic location impact how environmental forces affect each organization differently. An understanding of the forces and they currently affecting organizations and pressuring structural change is crucial.

15.2 External Environments and Industries

2. Identify contemporary external forces pressuring organizations

An understanding of the various industries and organizations 'fit' with different types of environment in crucial. There are small and large organizations that face environments that are either stable of unstable and managing the organization by recognizing their environment is a crucial skill.

15.3 Organizational Designs and Structures

3. Identify different types of organizational structures, and their strengths and weaknesses

An understanding of Mechanistic vs Organic Structures and Systems and how they differ and how these major concepts help classify different organizational structures is crucial to recognizing organizational structures. Finally, the issue of organizational complexity and its impact on organizational structure needs to be understood.

You should be able to discuss the evolution of different types of Organizational Structures. You should understand and identify the six types of organizational structures, and the advantages and disadvantages of each: Functional, Divisional, Matrix, Geographic, Networked Team, and Virtual.

15.4 The Internal Organization and External Environments

4. Explain how organizations organize to meet external market threats and opportunities

You should understand and identify the six types of organizational structures, and the advantages and disadvantages of each structure:

- Functional
- Divisional

- Matrix
- Geographic
- Networked Team
- Virtual

You should also understand why the internal dimensions of an organization matter with regard to how it fits with its external environment.

15.5 Corporate Cultures

5. Identify the fit between organizational cultures and the external environment

You should be able to identify and differentiate between the four types of organizational cultures and the fit of each with the external environment and describe the CVF framework. Finally, you can identify the internal dimensions of organizations, the interconnection among the dimensions, and how these affect the 'fit' with external environments.

15.6 Organizing for Change in the 21st Century

6. Identify environmental trends, demands, and opportunities facing organizations.

Among the trends in the external environment: (1) persistent inequality and unfairness, (2) domestic and international political tensions, (3) environmental dangers, and (4) cyber vulnerabilities. Another trend is that organizations will no longer solely be judged only for their financial performance, or even the quality of their products or services. Rather, they will be evaluated on the basis of their impact on society at large—transforming them from business enterprises into social enterprises.

Chapter Review Questions

1. Explain how several current environmental forces are affecting and will affect organizations and organizational structures' effectiveness and efficiency in the near future?
2. What are ways to classify and describe how industries and organizations fit and do not fit with their external environments?
3. What are a few industries and/or organizations that are fitting well with their current environments? What are a few that are not? Why?
4. What are some major differences between organic and mechanistic organizational structures and systems?
5. Which organization would you work best in, an organically or mechanistically structured one, and why?
6. What are some advantages and disadvantages of functional structures?
7. Do you think it's true that every organization has a hidden functional structure in it? Explain your answer.
8. Why have functional structures been criticized for not accommodating new changes in the environment?
9. What are some advantages and disadvantages of divisional structures?
10. How is a product structure one type of a divisional structure? Explain.
11. What are some disadvantages in working in a matrix structure and why?
12. What advantages do matrix structures have compared to functional structures?
13. What advantages do geographic structures have compared to a functional structure?
14. What are issues that working in a networked team structure present?
15. In what ways is a virtual organization and structure different from the other ones discussed in the chapter?
16. What major trends discussed at the end of this chapter are different from previous external environments

and the ways organizations were organized?

17. What purposes does an organization's culture serve when considering the external environment?
18. How does **Exhibit 15.16** facilitate an understanding of how the internal organization functions with external environments?

Management Skills Application Exercises

1. You have just been assigned to lead a functionally structured organization. Explain what types of skills you would need to best perform this function.
2. What types of problems would you expect to have managing a divisionally structured organization? What skills would you need to excel in this undertaking?
3. If you were assigned to work in a matrix team structure, explain the issues and benefits you might expect to experience and why. What skills would help you in this function?
4. .You have just been assigned to work with a strategy team in an organization to predict issues and opportunities that might be expected for the next 2 years. Using this chapter, explain what information you would provide to this team?
5. Use **Exhibit 15.21**, "The Competing Values Framework," to identify the type of organizational culture at IKEA, Home Depot, and Best Buy.

Managerial Decision Exercises

1. You are a manager working in a functionally structured organization. A disgruntled employee is complaining about problems she is having in that structure. Outline a way you would find out more about her complaints with regard to her being in this type of structure and some ways to assist her.
2. You are a manager working in a networked team structured organization. A disgruntled employee is complaining about problems he is having in that structure. Outline a way you would find out more about his complaints with regard to his being in this type of structure and some ways to assist him.
3. You have been selected to lead a team to decide on a different type of structure in your organization to better serve customers who are complaining about poor service that is slow, impersonal, and not meeting their needs to be heard. Presently, the functional structure isn't working well. Outline some information from your knowledge using this chapter that would help the team in its assignment.
4. You witness a senior executive at your firm engaging in overly aggressive methods of pressuring employees to increase their sales quotas beyond reasonable means. You are in a networked team structure that is partly a matrix. You are uncertain about whom to discuss this issue with. What would you do?
5. As a new graduate, you have been hired to help a medium-sized company come into the 21st century. Products need revamping, people aren't sharing information, and customers are gradually leaving. The firm has a traditional top-down managed, vertical hierarchy. It is believed that the firm has very good potential to sell its products, but new markets may be needed. Outline an agenda you would work on to research and make suggestions with regard to this chapter's focus and content.

Critical Thinking Case

Wells Fargo, Crisis and Scandal

The recent widespread scandal at Wells Fargo jolted and shocked the corporate world. How could such internal corrupt and outrageously illegal and unethical activities by professionals have occurred? Wells Fargo is "an American multinational financial services company headquartered in San Francisco, California" with offices nationwide and "the world's second-largest bank by market capitalization and the third largest bank in the U.S. by total assets." In September 2016 it was discovered that the company was continuing to create fake customer accounts to show positive financial activity and gains. 5,000 salespeople had created 2 million fake customer accounts to meet high-pressure internal sales goals, including a monthly report called the "Motivator."

The out-of-control sales leadership pressured sales employees to meet unrealistic, outrageous sales targets. Dramatically unrealistic sales goals propelled by continuous pressure from management coerced employees to open accounts for customers who didn't want or need them. "Some Wells Fargo bankers impersonated their customers and used false email addresses like noname@wellsfargo.com, according to a 2015 lawsuit filed by the city of Los Angeles."

The "abusive sales practices claimed in a lawsuit that Wells Fargo employees probably created 3.5 million bogus accounts" starting in May 2002. Wells Fargo is awaiting final approval to settle that case for $142 million. However, regulators and investigations found that the misconduct was far more "pervasive and persistent" than had been realized. "The bank's culture of misconduct extended well beyond the original revelations." For example, regulators found that the company was (1) "overcharging small businesses for credit card transactions by using a 'deceptive' 63-page contract to confuse them." (2) The company also charged at least 570,000 customers for auto insurance they did not need. (3)The firm admitted that it found 20,000 customers who could have defaulted on their car loans from these bogus actions; (4) The company also had created over 3.5 million fake accounts attributed to customers who had no knowledge of such accounts.

Wells Fargo has had to testify before Congress over these charges, which have amounted to $185 million dollars, and more recently the company has been ordered by regulators to return $3.4 million to brokerage customers who were defrauded. The CEO and management team have been fired and had millions of dollars withheld from their pay.

In the aftermath of the scandal, even though Wells Fargo executives were not imprisoned for the extensive consumer abuses committed by the company, the CFPB (Consumer Financial Protection Bureau) and Office of the Comptroller of the Currency (OCC) imposed a $1 billion fine on Wells Fargo for consumer-related abuses regarding auto loan and mortgage products. The OCC also forced the company to allow regulators the authority to enforce several actions to prevent future abuses, such as and including "imposing business restrictions and making changes to executive officers or members of the bank's board of directors." The new president of the company, Tim Sloan, stated, "What we're trying to do, as we make change in the company and make improvements, is not just fix a problem, but build a better bank, transform the bank for the future."

Sources: https://en.wikipedia.org/wiki/Wells_Fargo; Pasick, Adam, "Warren Buffett Explains the Wells Fargo Scandal," *Quartz*, May 6, 2017. https://qz.com/977778/warren-buffett-explains-the-wells-fargo-scandal/ https://qz.com/977778/warren-buffett-explains-the-wells-fargo-scandal/; Bloomberg, "The Wells Fargo Fake Accounts Scandal Just Got a Lot Worse," *Fortune*, August 21, 2017. http://fortune.com/2017/08/31/wells-fargo-increases-fake-account-estimate/; Horowitz, Julia, "'huge, huge, huge error' in Wells Fargo Handling of Ethics Line Calls, *CNN*, May, 6, 2017. https://money.cnn.com/2017/05/06/investing/buffett-wells-fargo-berkshire-annual-meeting/index.html; http://money.cnn.com/2018/02/05/news/companies/wells-fargo-timeline/index.html; Wattles, Jackie, Grier, Ben, and Egan, Matt, "Wells Fargo's 17 Month Nightmare," *CNN Business*, February 5, 2018. https://money.cnn.com/2018/02/05/news/companies/wells-fargo-timeline/index.html.

Hudson, Caroline, "Wells Fargo Stocks Still Struggling in Wake of Scandal," *Charlotte Business Journal*, April 2, 2018. https://www.bizjournals.com/charlotte/news/2018/04/02/wells-fargo-stocks-still-struggling-in-wake-of.html

Critical Thinking Questions

1. What happened at Wells Fargo with regard to past activities that led to this major scandal?
2. What internal dimensions of the company were part of the problems that occurred?
3. How might the organizational structure of the company have been part of the problems that occurred?
4. . Identify and use relevant concepts from this chapter as well as your own thoughts and analysis to diagnose the scandal at Wells Fargo. How could such a scandal have occurred in the first place? Who and what was at fault?
5. Suggest some solution paths the company might consider, using knowledge from this chapter and your own thoughts/research, to avoid such a scandal from reoccurring.

16 Organizational Structure and Change

Exhibit 16.1 (Credit: GLady/ Pixabay/ (CC BY 0))

Introduction

Learning Outcomes

After reading this chapter, you should be able to answer these questions:

1. What are mechanistic versus organic organizational structures?
2. What are the fundamental dimensions of change?
3. How do managers deal with change?

EXPLORING MANAGERIAL CAREERS

Jackie Smith, CareSource University

Jackie Smith is a human resources, training and organizational development professional with more than 20 years of experience. She has worked in a variety of organizations and industries in both the for-profit and not-for-profit sectors.

Jackie is vice president of CareSource University at CareSource, a Medicaid managed care organization. She oversees CareSource University as well as the company's performance management, succession, and goal-setting processes. In 2017 CSU delivered more than 240,000 learning hours, coached 300 leaders, and onboarded 1,100 new hires. CareSource University has been nationally recognized for seven years as one of *Training* magazine's Top 125 training organizations, ranking in the top 19 for six years. In 2017, CSU was named to the global Learning Elite, ranking 18th among worldwide organizations. Prior to CareSource, Jackie was president of Reflections on Learning, a performance-consulting firm, and worked as a senior organizational development consultant, regional human resources manager, training specialist, and manager in the financial services, retail, and transportation industries.

Jackie's instructional focus has been in the area of leadership development, designing programs including:

- Developing Your Leadership Vision
- Leading through Extraordinary Change
- Transforming Team Performance through Dialogue
- Building Sustainable Strategy with Appreciative Inquiry

Her educational background includes a BS in education from Miami University, Ohio and Luxembourg and an MS in organizational development and leadership from St. Joseph's University in Philadelphia. In addition, she has served as an adjunct faculty member at Antioch McGregor University and is a certified facilitator in a variety of training and development programs, organizational assessments, and Myers-Briggs profiling. She also serves as a team leader facilitating business strategy sessions in countries around the world including Ecuador, Jordan, Guinea, and Senegal.

This chapter will cover several concepts that deal with how leaders develop and shape organizations. An understanding of the concepts in this chapter is essential for leaders who need to pull people together to accomplish the essential work of a business in a consistent process over time. We will address the essential ideas.

16.1 Organizational Structures and Design

1. What are mechanistic versus organic organizational structures?

First, an **organizational structure** is a system for accomplishing and connecting the activities that occur within a work organization. People rely on structures to know what work they should do, how their work supports or relies on other employees, and how these work activities fulfill the purpose of the organization itself.

Second, **organizational design** is the process of setting up organizational structures to address the needs of an organization and account for the complexity involved in accomplishing business objectives.

Next, **organizational change** refers to the constant shifts that occur within an organizational system—for example, as people enter or leave the organization, market conditions shift, supply sources change, or adaptations are introduced in the processes for accomplishing work. Through **managed change**, leaders in an organization can intentionally shape how these shifts occur over time.

Finally, **organizational development (OD)** is the label for a field that specializes in change management. OD specialists draw on social science to guide change processes that simultaneously help a business achieve its objectives while generating well-being for employees and sustainable benefits for society. An understanding of OD practices is essential for leaders who want to maximize the potential of their organizations over a long period of time.

Together, an understanding of these concepts can help managers know how to create and direct organizations that are positioned to successfully accomplish strategic goals and objectives.[1]

To understand the role of organizational structure, consider the experience of Justin, a young manager who worked for a logistics and transportation company. His success at leading change in the United States gave his leaders the confidence that he could handle a challenging assignment: organize a new supply chain and distribution system for a company in Northern Europe. Almost overnight, Justin was responsible for hiring competent people, forming them into a coherent organization, training them, and establishing the needed infrastructure for sustained success in this new market.

If you were given this assignment, what would you do? How would you organize your employees? How would you help them understand the challenge of setting up a new organization and system? These are the kinds of questions that require an understanding of organizational structure, organizational design, organizational change, and organizational development.

One of the first issues Justin will need to address deals with how he will organize the system he will manage. "The decisions about the structure of an organization are all related to the concept of organizational design. There are two fundamental forms of structure to remember when designing an organization.

To address these questions, we need to be familiar with two fundamental ways of building an organization.

The **formal organization** is an officially defined set of relationships, responsibilities, and connections that exist across an organization. The traditional organizational chart, as illustrated in **Exhibit 16.2**, is perhaps the most common way of depicting the formal organization. The typical organization has a hierarchical form with clearly defined roles and responsibilities.

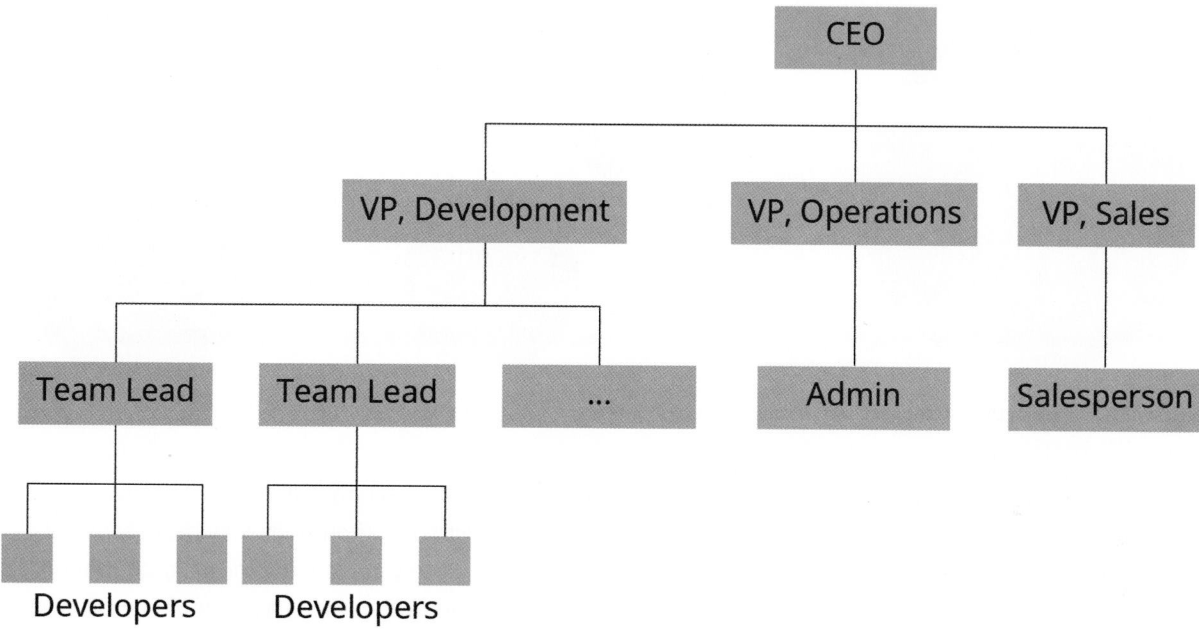

Exhibit 16.2 Formal Organizational Chart (Attribution: Copyright Rice University, OpenStax, under CC-BY 4.0 license)

When Justin sets up his formal organization, he will need to design the administrative responsibilities and communication structures that should function within an organizational system. The formal systems describe how flow of information and resources should occur within an organization. To establish the formal organization, he will identify the essential functions that need to be part of the system, and he will hire people to fill these functions. He will then need to help employees learn their functions and how these functions should relate to one another.

The **informal organization** is sometimes referred to as the invisible network of interpersonal relationships that shape how people actually connect with one another to carry out their activities. The informal organization is emergent, meaning that it is formed through the common conversations and relationships that often naturally occur as people interact with one another in their day-to-day relationships. It is usually complex, impossible to control, and has the potential to significantly influence an organization's success.

As depicted in **Exhibit 16.3**, the informal organization can also be mapped, but it is usually very different than the formal organization. The chart you see in this example is called a network map, because it depicts the relationships that exist between different members of a system. Some members are more central than others, and the strength of relationships may vary between any two pairs or groups of individuals. These relationships are constantly in flux, as people interact with new individuals, current relationships evolve, and the organization itself changes over time.[2]

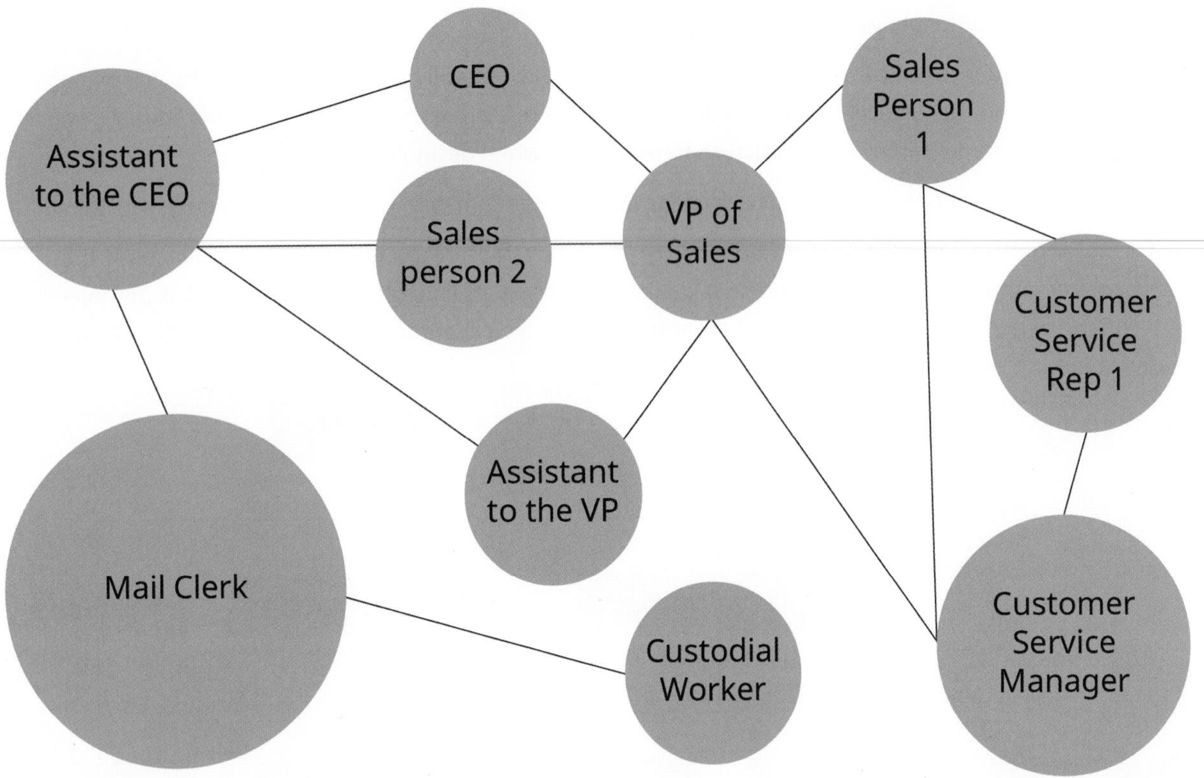

Exhibit 16.3 **Informal Organizational Chart** (Attribution: Copyright Rice University, OpenStax, under CC-BY 4.0 license)

The informal organization in Justin's design will form as people begin interacting with one another to accomplish their work. As this occurs, people will begin connecting with one another as they make sense of their new roles and relationships. Usually, the informal organization closely mirrors the formal organization, but often it is different. People quickly learn who the key influencers are within the system, and they will begin to rely on these individuals to accomplish the work of the organization. The informal organization can either help or hinder an organization's overall success.

In sum, the formal organization explains how an organization *should* function, while the informal organization is how the organizational *actually* functions. Formal organization will come as Justin hires and assigns people to different roles. He can influence the shape of the informal organization by giving people opportunities to build relationships as they work together. Both types of structures shape the patterns of influence, administration, and leadership that may occur through an organizational system.

As we continue our discussion of structure and design, we will next examine different ways of understanding formal structure.

Types of Formal Organizational Structures

Now, Justin will need to choose and implement an administrative system for delegating duties, establishing oversight, and reporting on performance. He will do this by designing a formal structure that defines the responsibilities and accountability that correspond to specific duties throughout an organizational system. In this section, we'll discuss the factors that any manager should consider when designing an organizational structure.

Exhibit 16.4 Smoke coming out of chapel chimney Almost all organizations have established organizational hierarchies and customs. As an older, large organization, the Catholic Church has a tall global structure with the pope in the Vatican at the apex. A process of succession has the cardinals voting on a new pope, and white smoke billowing out of the Sistine Chapel signals that they have chosen the new pope. (Credit: Jeffrey Bruno/ flickr/ Attribution 2.0 Generic (CC BY 2.0))

Bureaucracy

One of the most common frameworks for thinking about these issues is called the **bureaucratic model**. It was developed by Max Weber, a 19th-century sociologist. Weber's central assumption was that organizations will find efficiencies when they divide the duties of labor, allow people to specialize, and create structure for coordinating their differentiated efforts, usually within a hierarchy of responsibility. He proposed five elements of bureaucracy that serve as a foundation for determining an appropriate structure: specialization, command-and-control, span of control, centralization, and formalization.[3]

Specialization

The degree to which people are organized into subunits according to their expertise is referred to as

specialization—for example, human resources, finance, marketing, or manufacturing. It may also include specialization within those functions. For instance, people who work in a manufacturing facility may be well-versed in every part of a manufacturing process, or they may be organized into specialty units that focus on different parts of the manufacturing process, such as procurement, material preparation, assembly, quality control, and the like.

Command-and-Control

The next element to consider is the reporting and oversight structure of the organization. **Command-and-control** refers to the way in which people report to one another or connect to coordinate their efforts in accomplishing the work of the organization.

Span of Control

Another question addresses the scope of the work that any one person in the organization will be accountable for, referred to as **span of control**. For instance, top-level leaders are usually responsible for all of the work of their subordinates, mid-level leaders are responsible for a narrower set of responsibilities, and ground-level employees usually perform very specific tasks. Each manager in a hierarchy works within the span of control of another manager at a level of the organization.

Centralization

The next element to consider is how to manage the flows of resources and information in an organization, or its **centralization**. A highly centralized organization concentrates resources in only one or very few locations, or only a few individuals are authorized to make decisions about the use of resources. In contrast, a diffuse organization distributes resources more broadly throughout an organizational system along with the authority to make decisions about how to use those resources.

Formalization

The last element of bureaucracy, **formalization**, refers to the degree of definition in the roles that exist throughout an organization. A highly formalized system (e.g., the military) has a very defined organization, a tightly structured system, in which all of the jobs, responsibilities, and accountability structures are very clearly understood. In contrast, a loosely structured system (e.g., a small, volunteer nonprofit) relies heavily on the emergent relationships of informal organization.

Mechanistic and Organic Structures

Using the principles of bureaucracy outlined above, managers like Justin have experimented with many different structures as way to shape the formal organization and potentially to capture some of the advantages of the informal organization. Generally, the application of these principles leads to some combination of the two kinds of structures that can be seen as anchors on a continuum (see **Table 16.1**).

Elements of Organizational Structure and Their Relationship to Mechanistic and Organic Forms		
Mechanistic	⟷	Organic
Highly formalized	**Standardization**	Low
High/Narrow	**Specialization**	Low/Broad
Centralized	**Centralization**	Decentralized
Functional	**Departmentalization**	Divisional

Table 16.1

On one end of the continuum is **mechanistic bureaucratic structure**. This is a strongly hierarchical form of organizing that is designed to generate a high degree of standardization and control. Mechanistic organizations are often characterized by a highly **vertical organizational structure**, or a "tall" structure, due to the presence of many levels of management. A mechanistic structure tends to dictate roles and procedure through strong routines and standard operating practices.

In contrast, an **organic bureaucratic structure** relies on the ability of people to self-organize and make decisions without much direction such that they can adapt quickly to changing circumstances. In an organic organization, it is common to see a **horizontal organizational structure**, in which many individuals across the whole system are empowered to make organizational decision. An organization with a horizontal structure is also known as a **flat organization** because it often features only a few levels of organizational hierarchy.

The principles of bureaucracy outlined earlier can be applied in different ways, depending on the context of the organization and the managers' objectives, to create structures that have features of either mechanistic or organic structures.

For example, the degree of specialization required in an organization depends both on the complexity of the activities the organization needs to account for and on the scale of the organization. A more organic organization may encourage employees to be both specialists and generalists so that they are more aware of opportunities for innovation within a system. A mechanistic organization may emphasize a strong degree of specialization so that essential procedures or practices are carried out with consistency and predictable precision. Thus, an organization's overall objectives drive how specialization should be viewed. For example, an organization that produces innovation needs to be more organic, while an organization that seeks reliability needs to be more mechanistic.

Similarly, the need for a strong environment of command-and-control varies by the circumstances of each organization. An organization that has a strong command-and-control system usually requires a vertical, tall organizational administrative structure. Organizations that exist in loosely defined or ambiguous environments need to distribute decision-making authority to employees, and thus will often feature a flat organizational structure.

The span of control assigned to any specific manager is commonly used to encourage either mechanistic or organic bureaucracy. Any manager's ability to attend to responsibilities has limits; indeed, the amount of work anyone can accomplish is finite. A manager in an organic structure usually has a broad span of control, forcing her to rely more on subordinates to make decisions. A manager in a mechanistic structure usually has a narrow span of control so that she can provide more oversight. Thus, increasing span of control for a manager tends to flatten the hierarchy while narrowing span of control tends to reinforce the hierarchy.

Centralization addresses assumptions about how an organization can best achieve efficiencies in its operations. In a mechanistic structure, it is assumed that efficiencies will occur in the system if the resources and decisions flow through in a centralized way. In an organic system, it is assumed that greater efficiencies will be seen by distributing those resources and having the resources sorted by the users of the resources. Either perspective may work, depending on the circumstances.

Finally, managers also have discretion in how tightly they choose to define the formal roles and responsibilities of individuals within an organization. Managers who want to encourage organic bureaucracy will resist the idea of writing out and tightly defining roles and responsibilities. They will encourage and empower employees to self-organize and define for themselves the roles they wish to fill. In contrast, managers who wish to encourage more mechanistic bureaucracy will use tools such as standard operating procedures (SOPs) or written policies to set expectations and exercise clear controls around those expectations for employees.

When a bureaucratic structure works well, an organization achieves an appropriate balance across all of these considerations. Employees specialize in and become highly advanced in their ability to perform specific functions while also attending to broader organizational needs. They receive sufficient guidance from managers to stay aligned with overall organizational goals. The span of control given to any one manager encourages them to provide appropriate oversight while also relying on employees to do their part. The resources and decision-making necessary to accomplish the goals of the organization are efficiently managed. There is an appropriate balance between compliance with formal policy and innovative action.

Functional Structures

Aside from the considerations outlined above, organizations will often set structures according to the functional needs of the organization. A functional need refers to a feature of the organization or its environment that is necessary for organizational success. A functional structure is designed to address these organizational needs. There are two common examples of functional structures illustrated here.

Product structures exist where the business organizes its employees according to product lines or lines of business. For example, employees in a car company might be organized according to the model of the vehicle that they help to support or produce. Employees in a consulting firm might be organized around a particular kind of practice that they work in or support. Where a functional structure exists, employees become highly attuned to their own line of business or their own product.

Geographic structures exist where organizations are set up to deliver a range of products within a geographic area or region. Here, the business is set up based on a territory or region. Managers of a particular unit oversee all of the operations of the business for that geographical area.

In either functional structure, the manager will oversee all the activities that correspond to that function: marketing, manufacturing, delivery, client support systems, and so forth. In some ways, a functional structure is like a smaller version of the larger organization—a smaller version of the bureaucracy that exists within the larger organization.

One common weakness of a bureaucratic structure is that people can become so focused on their own part of the organization that they fail to understand or connect with broader organizational activities. In the extreme, bureaucracy separates and alienates workers from one another. These problems can occur when different parts of an organization fail to communicate effectively with one another.

Some organizations set up a **matrix structure** to minimize the potential for these problems. A matrix structure describes an organization that has multiple reporting lines of authority. For example, an employee who specializes in a particular product might have both the functional reporting line and a geographic reporting line. This employee has accountability in both directions. The functional responsibility has to do with her specialty as it correlates with the strategy of the company as a whole. However, her geographic accountability is to the manager who is responsible for the region or part of the organization in which she is currently working. The challenge is that an employee may be accountable to two or more managers, and this can create conflict if those managers are not aligned. The potential benefit, however, is that employees may be more inclined to pay attention to the needs of multiple parts of the business simultaneously.

CONCEPT CHECK 

1. What is an organizational structure?
2. What are different types of organizational structures?
3. What is organizational design?
4. What concepts should guide decisions about how to design structures?

16.2 Organizational Change

2. What are the fundamental dimensions of change?

Our discussion about organizational structure to this point has focused on the forms that an organization might take and the options that are available to managers as they design structures for their organizations. However, organizations are constantly evolving. One common refrain is that "there is nothing so constant as change." Because of this, there is no one best way to organize in all circumstances. Effective managers need to be aware of the various factors that drive the need for change. There advantages and disadvantages of each the various forms of organizing we have discussed. Managers need to adapt the organization so that it is ideally situated to accomplish current organizational goals. Thus, effective managers need to know how to plan and implement change to achieve organizational success.

We will begin this section by reviewing the types of changes that may occur in an organization. Then we will explore the organizational life cycle model, which explains how the structural needs of an organization evolve over time.[4]

Types of Change

There are many different types of changes in organizations. The first, consistent with what we talked about so far in this chapter, is **structural change**. This has to do with the changes in the overall formal relationships within an organization. Examples of structural change include reorganizing departments or business units, adding employee positions, or revising job roles and assignments. These changes should be made to support broader objectives such as to centralize or decentralize operations, empower employees, or find greater efficiencies.

Another common type of change is **technological change**. Implementation of new technologies is often forced upon an organization as the environment shifts. For example, an industry upgrade in a commonly used software platform may require that employees learn new ways of working. Upgraded machinery or hardware may require employees to learn new procedures or restructure the way that they interact with one another. The advent of web-based cloud technologies is an example from the last decade and an example of ways which new forms of collaboration are becoming more available. Technological change often induces structural change because it requires different ways of connecting across an organizational system.

A third type of organizational change is **culture change**. Organizational culture refers to the common patterns of thinking and behaving within an organization. Culture is rooted in the underlying beliefs and assumptions that people hold of themselves and of the organization. These beliefs and assumptions create mindsets that shape the culture. Culture change is among the most difficult kinds of changes to create within an organizational system. It often involves reshaping and reimagining the core identity of the organization. A typical culture change process, if it is successful, requires many years to achieve.[5]

The Organizational Life Cycle

Most organizations begin as very small systems that feature very loose structures. In a new venture, nearly every employee might contribute to many aspects of an organization's work. As the business grows, the workload increases, and more workers are needed. Naturally, as the organization hires more and more people, employees being to specialize. Over time, these areas of specialization mature through **differentiation**, the process of organizing employees into groups that focus on specific functions in the organization. Usually, differentiated tasks should be organized in a way that makes them complementary, where each employee contributes an essential activity that supports the work and outputs of others in the organization.

The patterns and structures that appear in an organization need to evolve over time as an organization grows or declines, through four predictable phases (see **Exhibit 16.5**). In the **entrepreneurship** phase, the organization is usually very small and agile, focusing on new products and markets. The founders typically focus on a variety of responsibilities, and they often share frequent and informal communication with all employees in the new company. Employees enjoy a very informal relationship, and the work assignments are very flexible. Usually, there is a loose, organic organizational structure in this phase.

	Entrepreneurship	Survival and Early Success	Sustained Success	Renewal (or Decline)
Organization				
Extent of formal systems	Minimal to nonexistent	Minimal	Basic/Developing/ Maturing	Extensive
Key Ideas	• Marshalling of resources • Lots of ideas • Entrepreneurial activities • Little planning and coordination • Formaion of a ''niche'' • "Prime mover" has power	• Informal communication and structure • Sense of collectivity • Long hours spent • Sense of mission • Innovation continues • High commitment	• Formalization of rules • Stable structure • Emphasis on efficiency and maintenance • Conservatism • Institutionalized procedures	• Elaboration (or reduction) of structure • Decentralization (or centralization) • Domain expansion (or reduction) • Adaptation (or stagnation) • Renewal (or decline

Exhibit 16.5 Organizational Life Cycle (Attribution: Copyright Rice University, OpenStax, under CC-BY 4.0 license)

The second phase, *survival and early success*, occurs as an organization begins to scale up and find continuing success. The organization develops more formal structures around more specialized job assignments. Incentives and work standards are adopted. The communication shifts to a more formal tone with the introduction of hierarchy with upper- and lower-level managers. It becomes impossible for every employee to have personal relationships with every other employee in the organization. At this stage, it becomes appropriate for introduce mechanistic structures that support the standardization and formalization required to create effective coordination across the organization.

In a third phase, *sustained success* or *maturity*, the organization expands and the hierarchy deepens, now with multiple levels of employees. Lower-level managers are given greater responsibility, and managers for significant areas of responsibility may be identified. Top executives begin to rely almost exclusively on lower-level leaders to handle administrative issues so that they can focus on strategic decisions that affect the overall organization. At this stage, the mechanistic structures of the organization are strengthened, and functional structures may be introduced. Often, tension emerges over how to find balance in the structure. Most organizations at this stage of development need to have elements of a mechanistic bureaucracy while maintaining an environment that allows for the innovation and flexibility that is a feature of an organic structure.

A transition to the fourth phase, *renewal* or *decline*, occurs when an organization expands to the point that its operations are far-flung and need to operate somewhat autonomously. Functional structures become almost essential, and subunits may begin to operate as independent businesses. Often, the tensions in the company between mechanistic and organic inclinations may be out of balance. To address these issues, the organization has to be reorganized or restructured to achieve higher levels of coordination between and among different groups or subunits. Managers may need to address fundamental questions about the overall direction and administration of the organization.

To summarize, the key insight about the organizational life cycle is that the needs of an organization will evolve over time. Different structures are needed at different stages as an organization develops. The needs of employees will also change. An understanding of the organizational life cycle provides a framework for thinking about changes that may be needed over time.

Dimensions of Change

When considering how to assess the need for change in an organization, it can be helpful to think of three dimensions: the scope of change, the level of change, and the intentionality of change.

The first, the **scope of change** refers to the degree to which the required change will disrupt current patterns and routines. **Incremental change** refers to small refinements in current organizational practices or routines that do not challenge, but rather build on or improve, existing aspects and practices within the organization. Common incremental change practices are LEAN and Six Sigma, which are used to find relatively small changes that can generate greater efficiencies in a process. An organization can improve its product-line efficiencies by identifying small discrepancies in process, then fixing them in a systematic way. Incremental change does not typically challenge people to be at the edge of their comfort zone.[6]

In contrast, **transformational change** refers to significant shifts in an organizational system that may cause significant disruption to some underlying aspect of the organization, its processes, or structures. Transformational change can be invigorating for some employees, but also highly disruptive and stressful for others. Examples of transformational change include large systems changes and organizational restructuring. Culture change often requires transformational change to be successful.[7]

Finally, a **strategic change** is a change, either incremental or transformational, that helps align an organization's operations with its strategic mission and objectives. This kind of change is necessary for an organization to achieve the focus it needs to make needed transfer missions and work it does feel to stay competitive in the current or larger organization, larger market environment, or societal environment.

Exhibit 16.6 Uber Eats on bicycle An example of a small organizational structure is exemplified by jobs in the sharing economy like Uber and Lyft drivers. Here an Uber Eats food delivery driver cycles along a very busy Oxford Road in Manchester, England. (Credit: Shopblocks/ flickr/ Attribution 2.0 Generic (CC BY 2.0))

The **level of change** refers to the breadth of the systems that need to be changed within an organization. **Individual-level change** focuses on how to help employees to improve some active aspect of their performance or the knowledge they need to continue to contribute to the organization in an effective manner. Individual-level change programs include leadership development, training, and performance management. **Group-level change** centers on the relationships between people and usually focuses on helping people to work more effectively together. Team development, or teambuilding, is one of the most common forms of a team change process. **Organization-level change** is a change that affects an entire organizational system or several of its units. Strategic planning and implementation is perhaps the most common type of organization-level change. Higher-level change programs usually require changes at lower levels—an organization-level change may require change at both team and individual levels as well.

Intentionality is the final dimension of change and refers to the degree to which the change is intentionally designed or purposefully implemented. **Planned change** is an intentional activity or set of intentional activities that are designed to create movement toward a specific goal or end. Planned change processes often involve large groups of people and step-by-step or phase-by-phase activities that unfold over a period of time. Usually, effective leaders identify clear objectives for the change, the specific activities that will achieve those objectives, and the indicators of success.

In contrast, **unplanned change** is unintentional and is usually the result of informal organizing. It may or may not serve the aims of the organization as a whole. Unplanned change may be completely spontaneous, occurring simply because employees in some part of an organization want to initiate change. But sometimes it occurs as a byproduct of a planned change process. This is because it is difficult for leaders to anticipate all the consequences of a planned change effort. Employees react in unpredictable ways, technologies don't work as expected, changes in the marketplace don't happen as expected, or other actors may react in unanticipated ways.

As we will discuss below, some change models are designed to take advantage of the potential for spontaneous organizing among employees. Unplanned change can be harnessed as a positive force when employees are invited to be proactive about working toward common organizational goals.

CONCEPT CHECK 

1. What is organizational change?
2. What are the fundamental dimensions of change?

16.3 Managing Change

3. How do managers deal with change?

To this point in the chapter, we have focused on factors that influence the need for change. We have also discussed how to think about the dimensions of change that may be needed. In this section, we will describe different approaches to designing and implementing change.

Change management is the process of designing and implementing change. Most leaders are responsible for some degree of change management. In addition, as indicated in the introduction, **organizational development (OD)** is a specialized field that focuses on how to design and manage change.[8]

An **OD consultant** is someone who has expertise in change management processes. An internal consultant is someone who works as an employee of an organization and focuses on how to create change from within that organization. An external consultant is an OD specialist hired to provide outside expertise for a short period of time, usually for a major change effort. Leaders are more effective in managing change if they understand the common practices for managing change as well as the perspectives and practices used by OD specialists.

Basic Assumptions about Change

There are numerous models of change available to managers, and it can be difficult to discern the differences between them when creating a planned change process. Many approaches and methodologies for developing organizations and managing change have been developed and practiced during the last century. Indeed, it can be daunting and confusing to sort through and understand which models are most appropriate and relevant for a particular situation. Every model of change has its strengths and its limitations, and it is important to understand what these may be. The type of change methodology used in a particular situation should be matched to the needs of that situation.

It may be helpful to use several questions when deciding on the appropriate approach to use in a planned change process.

A first question has to do with the starting place for the change: *Is the organization in a state of deficiency that needs significant fixing, or is it in a state of high performance, where there exists a need for refining and tweaking*?

One common motivation for change is the perception that an organization may be in some state of dysfunction with significant and serious problems, somewhat like a patient in a hospital in need of serious medical attention. A dysfunctional organization may require transformational change, in which the fundamental assumptions, beliefs, and organizing ideas of the organization are thoroughly challenged and altered. This set of perceptions often leads to **deficit-based change**, in which leaders assume that employees will change if they know they will otherwise face negative consequences.

In contrast, leaders may perceive that an organization is highly functional, much like an Olympic athlete or highly accomplished team. A high-performing organization may require incremental change as the organization continues to build on solid fundamentals to refine and add to its capacity for high performance. This set of perceptions often leads to **abundance-based change**, in which leaders assume that employees will change if they can be inspired to aim for greater degrees of excellence in their work.

A second important question addresses the mechanisms of change: *What are our assumptions about how to create change*? This question is crucial, because the answers determine the preferred designs for planned change and the perceptions of the effectiveness of the change.

Top-down change approaches rely on mechanistic assumptions about the nature of an organization. In this approach, a relatively small group of individuals in the organization will design a process and instruct others throughout the organization as to how the process of change should unfold. Most employees in the top-down approach play a passive role during the design process and are generally expected to follow the directions given to them by leaders in the organization. In other words, this approach to change relies on the formal organization to drive the legitimacy of the change.

The opposite of the top-down change approach is the **emergent or bottom-up approach**. This approach relies on the belief that employees will be more invested in change if they play some role in the process of designing the change. **Participatory management**, the inclusion of employees in the deliberations about key business decisions, is a common practice that aligns with the emergent approach to change.

The differences between top-down and bottom-up approaches can be dramatic. For example, following the top-down approach, leaders might determine that the organizational structure needs to be reconfigured to better accommodate a significant shift in its business. They might assume that they can implement the new structure and that employee routines and patterns of behavior will then change in a natural progression.

The bottom-up approach may reverse this logic. Employees might first work together to explore the tasks that are essential to a specific business problem, they might experiment with potential changes, and *then* managers might rearrange structures to match the new, emergent way of doing work. In contrast to the top-down approach, in a bottom-up process a shift in structure may be a last step.

A challenge for many managers in the bottom-up approach is a perception that they cannot directly control planned changes. Rather, they must rely on processes that draw employees together and expect that employees will respond. This requires a leap of faith, trusting that the process of involving people will lead to desirable emergent changes.

In practice, top-down and bottom-up practices often work together. For example, leaders might exercise top-down authority to define and declare what change is necessary. Then, they might design processes that engage and empower employees throughout an organization to design how the change will be brought about. Working toward a generally defined goal, employees at all levels are highly engaged in the change process from beginning to end. This approach has the effect of encourage self-organizing through the informal organization as employees make and implement decisions with minimal direction.

As a general rule of thumb, the more complex the potential change, the greater the need to involve employees in the process of planning and implementing change.

A final question addresses the mindset for change: What are our fundamental beliefs about people and change?

Again, a simplistic dichotomy is helpful for defining the approach that may be employed to create change. In the **conventional mindset**, leaders assume that most people are inclined to resist change and therefore they need to be managed in a way that encourages them to accept change. In this view, people in an organization may be seen as objects, sometimes even as obstacles, that need to be managed or controlled. When leaders use conventional methods, they demonstrate a tendency to assume that their perspectives are more informed sound and logical than the perspectives of employees. They will work hard to convince employees about the correctness of their decisions, relying on logic to prove the point. They may be inclined to use methods that may be seen by employees as manipulative or coercive. Some authors claim that the conventional mindset is the default, or dominant mode of change in most organizations.[9]

In contrast, in the **positive or appreciative mindset**, leaders assume that people are inclined to embrace change when they are respected as individuals with intrinsic worth, agency, and capability. In this view, employees in an organization may be seen as partners, sometimes even as champions of change, who can do significant things. When leaders use appreciative methods, they involve employees through meaningful dialogue and seek to lead with a sense of purpose. They may start the change process by highlighting the values that people may hold in common to establish an environment in which employees develop a strong sense of connection with one another. With a strong social infrastructure, they involve employees through participatory processes that allow them to develop common goals and processes for achieving significant changes.

Exhibit 16.7 IBM building in China IBM is a U.S.-based company with several divisions organized geographically. Pictured here is the "Dragon Building," their China-based headquarters. (Credit: bfishshadow/ flickr/ Attribution 2.0 Generic (CC BY 2.0))

The three questions we have raised here can lead to many variations in the way that leaders design and implement change. For example, it is possible for a change process to be deficit-based, top-down, and conventional, while another change process may be abundance-based, bottom-up, and positive. Other change processes may be mixed in their design and delivery—for example, starting with a deficit-based perspective yet choosing to use an abundance-based design to create transformational change through a bottom-up, participatory, appreciative process. In today's business environment, it is rare to find an approach that purely fits any of these categories.

We will next turn to a discussion of common change models that may be analyzed through the three questions just raised.

SUSTAINABILITY AND RESPONSIBLE MANAGEMENT

Why Is the National Hockey League Interested in Climate Change, and Why Did They Hire Kim Davis?

Because of demographics, with most of their employees coming from northern U.S. states, Canada, and northern European countries, there was probably no organization more racially uniform than the National Hockey League. In these days of increased attention on social issues and changing demographics, the NHL needed a drastic shift in its approach to inclusivity and the social issues it addresses. Two of the best people to usher in change, they decided, were an accomplished executive untouched by old-guard hockey culture and a former player.

Kim Davis knew that she was different from many executives, managers, coaches, and players in the National Hockey League. She welcomed the challenge, and it was a major attraction that led her to accept the position. She looks like no one else holding the position of executive vice president at the NHL, which has primarily been run by (a) men and (b) white men in its over-100-year history. The league signaled a long-overdue shift in thinking when it named Davis, a black woman, as executive vice president of social impact, growth initiatives, and legislative affairs.

In a time when the NHL is trying to adapt and become more welcoming to those who feel they don't belong or haven't been allowed to belong in the sport, the perfect person to initiate change was someone from the outside, someone free of a hockey culture that has become stale by current social standards.

Especially compared to the other major North American pro sports, hockey sometimes unfairly gets accused of being tone-deaf or at least resistant to change. The league is working hard to improve its commitment to inclusivity, with initiatives like the Declaration of Principles and Hockey Is For Everyone, but change doesn't come easy for players, coaches, administrators, and fans of the sport. Davis represents the NHL's attempt to shepherd the game through social change—internally and externally. That's been her area of expertise throughout her professional life. At JPMorgan Chase she endured nine different mergers, and her job was to help her employees prepare for change.

"Most people aren't comfortable with change, and often when they say that, what they really mean is that they are comfortable with change, but they aren't comfortable with change happening to *them*," she said. "It's all about what happens to us, so how as a leader do you help people get through that?

"We may not be able to control that fan and that microcosm of society that is over-indexed in our sport," she said. "Over time it will change as we introduce new fans, and guess what? Even that classic model of our fans, that white male, generationally, their kids, they're not buying into that even if their parents are."

"Find another hockey executive who will touch a topic like that without tapdancing." And that's why Kim Davis is here. She's the outsider turned insider, the voice of those formerly neglected. And she's just getting started.

Regarding climate change, why did the NHL attend the historic climate change conference in Paris? As NHL President Gary Bettman states: "Our game, which is probably unique to most other professional sports, is so tied to the environment. We need cold weather; we need fresh water to play. Therefore, our game is directly impacted by climate change and fresh water scarcity. So, we developed NHL Green, a mandate to promote this type of awareness across all our organizations. Over the course of the last five years, we've done everything from a food recovery initiative, which was taking all the unused food that we prepare in our arenas and donating it to local food banks ... to a water restoration program. All of that culminated in the release of a sustainability report in 2014, which was the first of its kind from any U.S. pro sports league. It's important to us."

The NHL players are also interested. One individual is recently retired player Andrew Ference, who introduced green initiatives like the NHL Players Association Carbon Neutral Challenge. While he was a player with the Stanley Cup champion Boston Bruins, he knew that he wanted a career after retirement from the NHL and decided to attend the Harvard Business School, where he earned a certificate in Corporate Sustainability and Innovation. Since he really prioritized sustainability in his life, it was a natural progression to a second career after his retirement. Ference says, "I've had a lifelong passion for the environment and sustainability issues. But, before leaving the NHL, I wanted to back that up with some formal education. When I signed up for that first class, I knew in my gut it was a big moment."

Commissioner Gary Bettman says that the next stage regarding sustainability is to "...engage more players around this issue because when we put out stuff on our social media platforms, 12 million followers on social media, that definitely gets messaging out to fans. But when you get an Andrew Ference, that's when you get a lot more engagement. We need to educate our athletes on this issue because they grew up on frozen ponds, they get the connection between learning to play outside and environmental issues. They get it."

Sources: Matt Larkin, "Kim Davis is the kind of Leader the NHL Needs in 2018: A Hockey Outsider," *The Hockey News*, April 6, 2018, http://www.thehockeynews.com/news/article/kim-davis-is-the-kind-of-leader-the-nhl-needs-in-2018-a-hockey-outsider; Kevin Blackistone, "Why the NHL is getting involved in climate-change efforts, *'The Chicago Tribune*, January 3, 2016, http://www.chicagotribune.com/sports/hockey/ct-nhl-climate-change-epa-20160103-story.html; Miranda Green, "NHL Report Finds that Climate Change Hurts the Sport," *The Hill*, March 28, 2018, http://thehill.com/policy/energy-environment/380648-national-hockey-league-report-finds-climate-change-hurts-the-sport; "Andrew Ference; Student Spotlight," *Harvard University Extension- Inside Insight*, Accessed March 15, 2018, https://www.extension.harvard.edu/inside-extension/andrew-ference; Amalie Benjamin, "Andrew Ference Excited About New Sustainability Role," *NHL.com*, March 13, 2017, https://www.nhl.com/news/andrew-ference-flourishing-in-role-with-nhl-green/c-287680614.

1. What types of changes that Kim Davis is addressing for the National Hockey League, such as demographics, "hockey culture," and climate change, relate to the concepts in this chapter?
2. How are the roles of Kim Davis, Gary Bettman, and the players regarding change defined in the concepts of this chapter?

Common Change Models

In this section, we will share four common approaches to OD and organizational change. Lewin's model and Kotter's model are common planned change processes that usually rely on the mechanisms of formal organization.[10] The other two models, Cooperrider's Appreciative Inquiry model[11] and the Olson and Eoyang Complex Adaptive Systems model,[12] are designed to promote informal organizing and emergent change.

Lewin's Change Model

Psychologist Kurt Lewin proposed one of the first models of change. **Lewin's change model** shows organizational change occurring in three phases (see **Exhibit 16.8**).

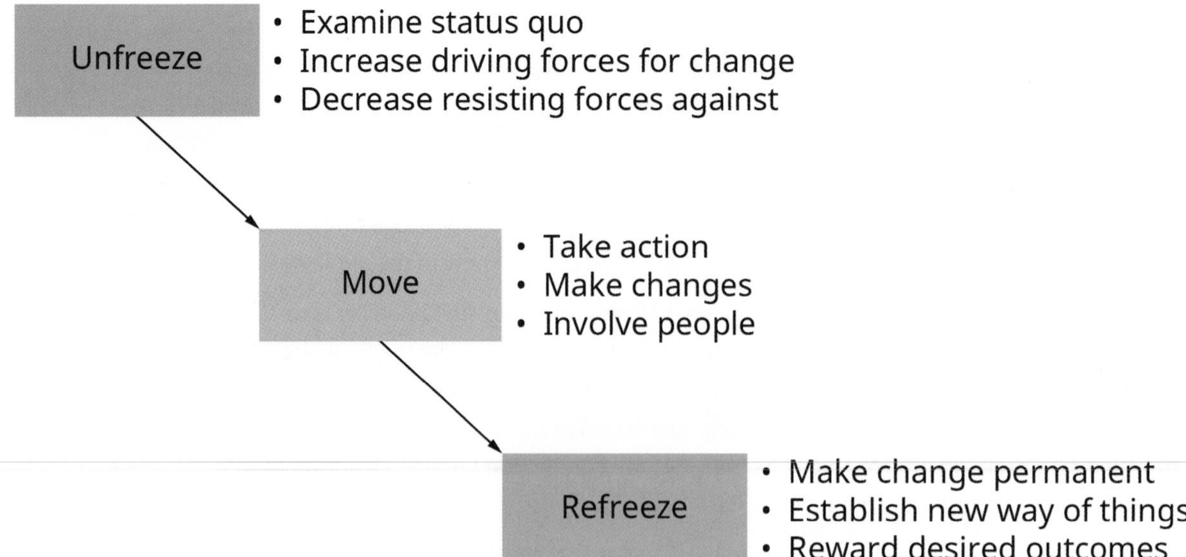

Exhibit 16.8 Summary of Kurt Lewin's Change Model (Attribution: Copyright Rice University, OpenStax, under CC-BY 4.0 license)

First, an organization must be "unfrozen" in that existing norms, routines, and practices need to be disrupted. This can be done in several ways. For example, structural changes that cause a disruption in the system can be introduced to the organization. Similarly, the introduction of a new technology or policy can cause an organization to "unfreeze." Whatever the cause, unfreezing sets the stage for change.

Next, changes are introduced in the organization to shift the system to a new state or reality. Typically, people react to moments of disorder by creating a new form of order. As changes are introduced, managers might provide a number of interventions that help people adjust to the new norms of reality they are facing. For example, they might require employees to go through a training program, or they might hold discussion sessions or town-hall meetings with people talk about the changes and troubleshoot. The intent of this phase is to help people adjust to the expected change.

The final phase is to "refreeze" the organization. That is, leaders of the organization reinforce the new norms or practices that should accompany the change. They might adjust the resources, policies, and routines to fit the new expected norms.

Lewin's model explains a very basic process that accompanies most organizational changes. That is, many people prefer a stable, predictable organization, and they become accustomed to the routines that exist in their organizational environment. For this reason, common routines and behaviors need to be disrupted. When past routines and behaviors are no longer available, people naturally adjust. As they react to a new reality, they establish new routines and patterns of behavior.

However, Lewin's model is most understandable when we assume that an organization is generally stable unless otherwise acted upon. That is, this model seems to fit in organizations in which any change is likely to last for a long period of time. Such a stable organizational context is increasingly rare in contemporary society.

Still, Lewin's model really describes a basic pattern of change that plays out in all organizational systems: stability gives way to instability, something shifts in the system, then stability emerges once again. An understanding of this pattern can be viewed through either deficit-based or abundance-based lenses, and it applies in either top-down or bottom-up approaches.

Kotter's Change Model

Kotter's change model is one of the most widely used in organizations today. Generally, it aligns with mechanistic view of structure and thus it may be especially useful in organizations where there is a strong, hierarchical structure. This is an eight-step model, shown in **Exhibit 16.9**, that relies on a centralized, top-down process for creating planned change.

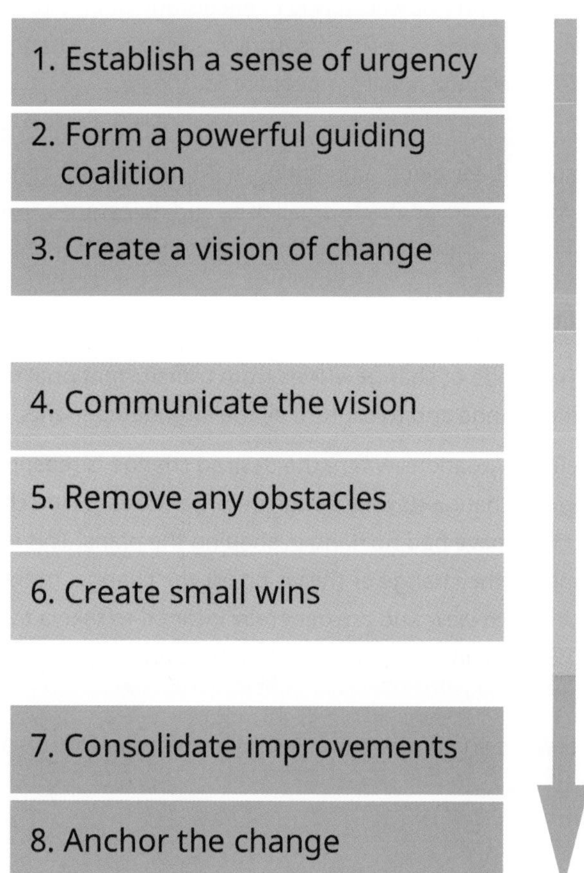

Exhibit 16.9 Summary of John Kotter's Change Model (Attribution: Copyright Rice University, OpenStax, under CC-BY 4.0 license)

In the first step, managers *establish a sense of urgency*. They do this by creating a narrative about why the change is necessary. Top managers often use diagnostic tools to gather data that supports the case for change. They strive to convince key organizational leaders and employees that the change is absolutely necessary. A common metaphor is to "create a burning platform," or to make it clear that the organization cannot survive if it continues doing what it has done.

In the second step, *form a powerful guiding coalition*, managers assemble a group of influential people to help shape the planned change. Ideally, the guiding coalition should represent the areas of an organization that will be affected by the change. The guiding coalition should become ambassadors for the change as it unfolds.

In the third phase, *create a vision of change*, the manager and guiding coalition together create a vision of the expected change. They outline the scope of the change, the reason for the change, and what will be better or different as a result of the change.

The fourth step is to *communicate the vision*—reach out to all members of the organization and communicate the vision for change. Ideally, they connect with all the key areas of the organization that will be affected. They clearly explain why the change is needed and how the change should unfold. If needed, they answer questions and clarify problems.

The fifth step is to *remove any obstacles.* This step is intended to reduce the resistance to change and/or to provide the necessary resources to make the change successful. The success of this step helps to smooth the way for successful implementation.

The sixth step is to *create small wins*. A very powerful way to encourage people to support changes to help them to see the path to success. Short wins signal to the organization that a change is possible and that tangible benefits will come once the change is fully implemented.

The seventh step is to *consolidate improvements*. Small changes build up over time and become big changes. As the organization successfully moves toward implementation, it is important to consolidate and solidify successes. Managers should reinforce and celebrate small wins and milestones. The unfolding success of the change helps to convince all members of the organization that the change is real and will produce its intended benefits.

The last step is to *anchor the changes.* In this step, the new norms and practices that accompany the change are standardized and refined. The mode of change moves from transformational to incremental. Refinements are implemented to fine-tune the change and to capture all the intended benefits.

Kotter's model is especially useful in situations where the desired change is reasonably predictable and where leaders are empowered to drive the change down through an organization. One challenge is that many employees may resist change if they have had no hand in shaping the plans. This is especially true if they do not fully comprehend the urgency of the change or the vision for the change. In this regard, it tends to be used when leaders hold a deficit-based view and are generally inclined to take a top-down approach from a conventional perspective. Still, where leaders need to clearly define and implement a large-scale change, Kotter's model may work very effectively.

A comparison and contrast of Lewin's and Kotter's models is illustrated in **Exhibit 16.10**.

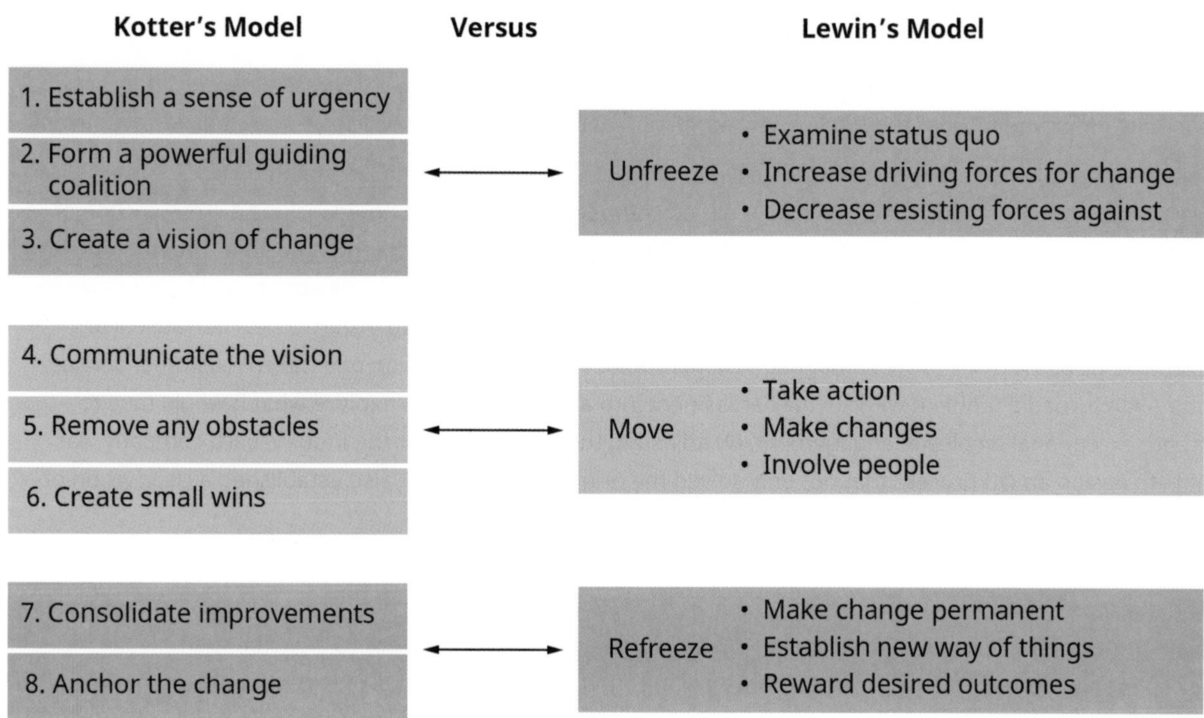

Exhibit 16.10 Kotter's Model versus Lewin's Model (Attribution: Copyright Rice University, OpenStax, under CC-BY 4.0 license)

Appreciative Inquiry

The **Appreciative Inquiry (AI) model** is a model specifically designed as an abundance-based, bottom-up, positive approach. An Appreciative Inquiry, broadly defined, can be any question-focused, participatory approach to change that creates an appreciative effective on people and organizations.[13] That is, the process of asking and discussing questions (inquiry) causes people to appreciate the people around them, the strengths of their organization, and the opportunities before them. Simultaneously, the process of having conversations expands the social capital of the organization, or the ability of people to work effectively together.

Developed in the 1980s by David Cooperrider at Case Western Reserve University, AI relies on the assumption that people continuously create their organizations through an emergent process that occurs in the common conversations of organizational life. These conversations are shaped by "narratives" about the reality of the organization in which people find themselves. For example, a dominant narrative might be that an organization's leaders are corrupt and intent on exploiting employees, or in contrast, that an organization's leaders are compassionate, forward-thinking, and innovative. Whatever the narrative, employees tend to justify actions that align with their views. Over time, a narrative can become a self-reinforcing reality. Based in this understanding of organizations as a socially constructed system, the key to creating change is to change the dominant narratives of an organization.

In AI, group dialogue is the primary mechanism for helping people to create new narratives.[14] Specifically, **appreciative conversations** are intense, positively framed discussions that help people to develop common ground as they work together to co-create a positive vision of an ideal future for their organization. When leaders use appreciative inquiry, they intentionally invite dialogue that generates a narrative for a positive organizational reality. This shift in narrative will inspire a shift in the actions that employees initiate in their daily work. While this approach may sound somewhat ambitious and abstract, in reality it is simply an opportunity for employees to envision the future changes they would like to see, then work together to design how they will make these changes a reality.

OD consultants have developed many different variations of AI practices that address different organizational contexts. However, most of them rely on some version of a 5-D cycle: define, discover, dream, design, destiny.

The first phase is *define*, in which the objective for change and inquiry is established. In this phase, the leaders will create a guiding group, often called a steering committee. This group should include a cross-section of perspectives that represent the different parts of the organization where change is desired. Together, they will decide on a compelling way of describing an objective that invites people to think about ideal possibilities for the organization. In this process, they might turn a problem upside down to inspire a new narrative. For example, British Airlines turned a baggage-claim problem into an exploration of excellent customer service, and Avon turned a problem with sexual harassment into an opportunity to explore what it would take to create exceptional employee engagement. By adjusting the perspective for the inquiry, each company was able to design an OD process that not only solved the original problem but also established a clear vision of what they most wanted as the positive alternative.

The second phase, *discover,* focuses on questions that explore ideal, existing examples of the desired future. The question "who are we when we are at our best?" is commonly used to encourage this exploration through dialogue among employees. For example, British Airways asked its employees to describe examples of exceptional customer service anywhere in its organization. By sharing stories of exceptional customer service, they found examples of exemplary service, even though the dominant narrative was that they had challenges in this area. Finding existing examples of the desired future—no matter how small—causes people to see that a positive alternative is possible. Such examples also provide the data for documenting the strengths of an organization and the factors that make success possible.

The third phase, *dream*, is an exploration of ideal future possibilities for the organization. The strengths and factors revealed in the discovery phase provide a foundation this discussion. Employees are invited to think creatively about what the organization might do if it were to build on its strengths. "What could be?" is a commonly used question to encourage this exploration. Many organizations have used creative techniques to encourage employees to innovate about the future. They might have employees work in groups to design prototypes of a process or write a mock newspaper article about a future successful project. The idea of the dream phase is to encourage employees to think as expansively as possible about the possibilities for change, usually in a fun and inviting way.

The fourth phase, *design*, starts with a process of prioritizing the ideas that have been developed in the dream phase. Employees might work together to brainstorm a list of all the possible areas for action that might help them to accomplish the objective. Then they use a collective process to identify the ideas that have the most promise. Usually senior leaders will add their voice to endorse the ideas that they want to encourage as actual action initiatives. Employees might be invited to join project teams that will carry out specific actions to develop and implement key actions.

The final phase, *destiny*, occurs as employees implement the plans they have developed. Project groups will continue to work on the agreed-upon action steps for a period of time. Typically, they will meet with other employee-based groups to check in, report on progress, and adjust their plans. Some organizations will also create celebrative events to commemorate key successes.

The appreciative inquiry cycle can become an intrinsic part of an organization's culture. Some companies will go through the AI process on an annual basis as an integral part of strategic planning. Other organizations use it only as needed when major transformational changes are desired. Though the examples in this section illustrate appreciative inquiry as used to change organizations as a whole, the model can also be applied at any level of organization—for example, in work with individuals and teams.

Complex Adaptive Systems

The final model we will review builds on the assumption that all organizations are **complex adaptive systems (CAS).**[15] That is, an organization is constantly developing and adapting to its environment, much like a living organism. A CAS approach emphasizes the bottom-up, emergent approach to the design of change, relying on the ability of people to self-manage and adapt to their local circumstances. Before reviewing the CAS model in more depth, perhaps it would be helpful to examine a change process that is grounded in the CAS model.

One common CAS-based approach is Open Space Technology, a technique in which dozens of people may be involved.[16] To set the stage, let's suppose that we want to create a series of innovations to improve the culture of innovation in an organization. The first task would be to invite as many interested stakeholders as possible to participate in a discussion on various topics related to the culture of innovation, perhaps over a two-day period. At the beginning of the first session, a leader in the organization might greet the participants and invite them to be part of an open-ended exploration of ideas and solutions. A facilitator would then distribute a single sheet of paper and a marker to each participant. She would ask each person to propose a topic or question for discussion, explaining that the purpose of this exercise is to attract other people to join a discussion.

Then she will go around the room, giving each person in turn up to 30 seconds to propose a topic or question and describe the significance and urgency of the idea. The go-around continues until a variety of topics are identified. Next, the facilitator works with participants to define a list of topics for discussion. The facilitator then designates times and locations for discussions on those topics. Finally, participants "vote with their feet" to choose groups that they want to join for discussion. Typically, each discussion in an Open Space meeting will include an exploration of key questions, actions related to those questions, and proposals for resolving key questions.

As shown by this example, this approach is similar to AI in that it focuses on creating the conditions for people to self-organize in ways that align with the overall objectives of an organizational system. However, one big difference is that it relies less on step-by-step processes for creating change and more on principles that can be applied in many variations to shape the conditions for change in an organization.

The CAS approach provides a useful perspective on how organic organizational structures emerge and develop through the informal organization. An understanding of CAS, therefore, provides leaders with the key knowledge they need to influence the direction of the informal organization, even if they cannot directly control it.

To use the CAS approach, it is essential to understand a few key features about how self-organizing occurs among employees.[17] To begin, the direction of any organization is emergent and requires involvement from many people. Yet, when people react to change, their exact behaviors may be unknowable, unpredictable, and uncontrollable. Most often, people react to change based on the perceptions of the people in their immediate circle of relationships within the organization. Every person in an organization is both influencing others and being influenced by others. This means that a key locus of change must involve the relationships that people have with one another. From the perspective of CAS, a change in the nature or patterns of interpersonal relationships in an organization will lead to changes in the outcomes of that organization. Leaders, in this regard, should think of themselves as facilitators of relationships and as supporters of employees who are constantly engaged in self-organizing to create needed changes.

So, how can a leader (as a facilitator) influence the way in which self-organizing occurs? For starters, a leader needs to pay attention to the key conditions that allow for informal self-organizing to occur. There are three basic questions to consider.

First, to what degree do people feel empowered to act as **change agents** in the system? Self-organizing originates in the people who comprise the organization. If they view themselves as agents who have discretion to act, they are more likely to take initiative, engaging in nondirected activities that may benefit the organization. Do people feel empowered as agents of the organization? If not, interventions may be designed to help people understand their own capacities and competencies.

Second, *how connected are people to one another* in the organization? Relationships are the building blocks of all informal organizational activities. The more connected people feel to one another, the more likely they are to work with others in self-directed activity. Do people feel like they have high-quality relationships with coworkers? Are people regularly connecting with other individuals that they do not know very well? If the answers to these questions are negative, then interventions can be designed to strengthen the quality and configurations of connections within and across an organization.

Third, to what extent are *flows* of information and energy passing through the connections that exist between people? Both informal and formal feedback loops provide a mechanism whereby people receive information about what is working and or not in their activities. Do people quickly receive information about breakdowns or successes in the system? Is the emotional energy in the system generating a positive dynamic that encourages people to be engaged? Again, if the answers to these questions are negative, then processes or initiatives should be designed that will help people to communicate more effectively across their relationships.

Aside from examining these basic conditions for self-organizing, the CAS approach assumes that every organizational outcome is the product of an indeterminable number of variables. No one cause produces a single outcome. For instance, the accurate delivery of a product to a customer is caused by a whole system of interrelated factors, each influencing the other. Therefore, where broad changes in outcomes are desired, the whole system of interrelated factors needs to be engaged at once. The preferred method of doing this is to engage broad groups of stakeholders simultaneously, using dialogue and conversation to help people develop their sense of agency, their connections with others, and the processes that need to be adjusted to create desired changes in outcomes. Appreciative inquiry is one method that works especially well to accomplish all these impacts.

In addition, leaders may also influence the structures that shape patterns of self-organizing. From a CAS perspective, a structure is anything that causes people to engage in a particular pattern of activity. Structures can be physical, such as the work environment, or they can be assumptions or beliefs that are broadly held, such as the ideas about bureaucracy we discussed earlier in this chapter. To create change, leaders can change the structures that are producing current patterns of organization.

There are three ways in which self-organizing structures can be altered.[18] First, a leader can influence the **boundary conditions** that establish the limits for emergent activity. Boundary conditions define the degree of discretion that is available to employees for self-directed action. Giving employees more responsibility, empowering them to make decisions at the local level, and providing them with more discretion in the work they do are some of the ways that the boundary conditions may be expanded. The more undefined the boundaries, the more self-organizing can be expected.

Second, self-organizing is altered through the introduction of **disturbances** to the system. Sometimes this can be as simple as helping employees learn about the tensions that exist within an organization around existing patterns of self-organizing activity. For example, there are nearly always significant differences in perspective among different subgroups in an organization. Helping employees to have conversations with others who have significantly different perspectives can introduce a positive disturbance that causes people to reorganize their activities to overcome hidden structures. In manufacturing organizations, for instance, it is common for engineering and production departments to be isolated from one another. Dialogue that includes and connects the employees from such groups can help them overcome and change the structural assumptions that may cause them to self-organize in ways that antagonize the other. The conversation itself can be a catalyst for change.

One final suggestion is a reminder to pay particular attention to the flows and connections that exist among employees across an organizational system. It is essential to healthy organizing to regularly create opportunities for transformational connections, in which employees are able to learn about the perspectives of other areas of an organization. As they develop and maintain healthy connections, they will empathize with and consider those perspectives as they engage in their own self-organizing activities.

The CAS approach, as indicated earlier, provides both a perspective and a set of principles that can be used in many ways. Many methodologies build on the assumptions of the CAS approach. These include appreciative inquiry and others such as Open Space Technology, Whole Systems Change, Future Search, and more. In this section, we have barely scratched the surface of the variety of practices that can be used to catalyze change.

Planning a Change Management Process

The perspectives we have reviewed in this section provide a very brief menu of the options that are available to leaders as they consider how to manage change. In reality, many of these can be used together, and they should not be considered as mutually exclusive. For example, Kotter's model can be seen as an overall framework for designing a long-term change process. The Open Space or appreciative inquiry models can be used in certain parts of the Kotter process—for example, in the creation of a guiding coalition or creating a vision for the change.

Moreover, there are many, many practices and methodologies that may align in different ways to the framework of questions provided in this section. These can be used in different combinations to design change processes that meet the needs of a particular context.

CONCEPT CHECK

1. What are organizational development (OD) and change management?
2. What questions may be used to guide OD and change management?
3. What are the common models of OD and change management?

Key Terms

abundance-based change Leaders assume that employees will change if they can be inspired to aim for greater degrees of excellence in their work.

appreciative conversations Intense, positively framed discussions that help people to develop common ground as they work together to cocreate a positive vision of an ideal future for their organization.

Appreciative Inquiry model A model specifically designed as an abundance-based, bottom-up, positive approach.

boundary conditions Define the degree of discretion that is available to employees for self-directed action.

bureaucratic model Max Weber's model that states that organizations will find efficiencies when they divide the duties of labor, allow people to specialize, and create structure for coordinating their differentiated efforts within a hierarchy of responsibility.

centralization The concentration of control of an activity or organization under a single authority.

change agents People in the organization who view themselves as agents who have discretion to act.

change management The process of designing and implementing change.

command-and-control The way in which people report to one another or connect to coordinate their efforts in accomplishing the work of the organization.

Complex Adaptive Systems (CAS) A model that views organizations as constantly developing and adapting to their environment, much like a living organism.

conventional mindset Leaders assume that most people are inclined to resist change and therefore need to be managed in a way that encourages them to accept change.

culture change Involves reshaping and reimagining the core identity of the organization.

deficit-based change Leaders assume that employees will change if they know they will otherwise face negative consequences.

differentiation The process of organizing employees into groups that focus on specific functions in the organization.

disturbances Can cause tension amongst employees, but can also be positive and a catalyst for change.

emergent or bottom-up approach Organizations exist as socially constructed systems in which people are constantly making sense of and enacting an organizational reality as they interact with others in a system.

entrepreneurship The process of designing, launching, and running a new business.

flat organization A horizontal organizational structure in which many individuals across the whole system are empowered to make organizational decisions.

formal organization A fixed set of rules of organizational procedures and structures.

formalization The process of making a status formal for the practice of formal acceptance.

geographic structures Occur when organizations are set up to deliver a range of products within a geographic area or region.

group-level change Centers on the relationships between people and focuses on helping people to work more effectively together.

horizontal organizational structure Flat organizational structure in which many individuals across the whole system are empowered to make organizational decisions.

incremental change Small refinements in current organizational practices or routines that do not challenge, but rather build on or improve, existing aspects and practices within the organization.

individual-level change Focuses on how to help employees to improve some active aspect of their performance or the knowledge they need to continue to contribute to the organization in an effective manner.

informal organization The connecting social structure in organizations that denotes the evolving network of interactions among its employees, unrelated to the firm's formal authority structure.

intentionality The degree to which the change is intentionally designed or purposefully implemented.

Kotter's change model An overall framework for designing a long-term change process.

level of organization The breadth of the systems that need to be changed within an organization.

Lewin's change model Explains a very basic process that accompanies most organizational changes.

managed change How leaders in an organization intentionally shape shifts that occur in the organization when market conditions shift, supply sources change, or adaptations are introduced in the processes for accomplishing work over time.

matrix structure An organizational structure that groups people by function and by product team simultaneously.

mechanistic bureaucratic structure Describes organizations characterized by (1) centralized authority, (2) formalized procedures and practices, and (3) specialized functions. They are usually resistant to change.

OD consultant Someone who has expertise in change management processes.

organic bureaucratic structure Used in organizations that face unstable and dynamic environments and need to quickly adapt to change.

organization development (OD) Techniques and methods that managers can use to increase the adaptability of their organization.

organization-level change A change that affects an entire organizational system or several of its units.

Organizational change The movement that organizations take as they move from one state to a future state.

organizational design The process by which managers define organizational structure and culture so that the organization can achieve its goals.

organizational development (OD) Specialized field that focuses on how to design and manage change.

organizational structure The system of task and reporting relationships that control and motivate colleagues to achieve organizational goals.

participatory management Includes employees in deliberations about key business decisions.

planned change An intentional activity or set of intentional activities that are designed to create movement toward a specific goal or end.

positive or appreciative mindset Leaders assume that people are inclined to embrace change when they are respected as individuals with intrinsic worth, agency, and capability.

product structures Occurs when businesses organize their employees according to product lines or lines of business.

scope of change The degree to which the required change will disrupt current patterns and routines.

span of control The scope of the work that any one person in the organization will be accountable for.

specialization The degree to which people are organized into subunits according to their expertise—for example, human resources, finance, marketing, or manufacturing.

strategic change A change, either incremental or transformational, that helps align an organization's operations with its strategic mission and objectives.

structural change Changes in the overall formal relationships, or the architecture of relationships, within an organization.

technological change Implementation of new technologies often forces organizations to change.

top-down change Relies on mechanistic assumptions about the nature of an organization.

transformational change Significant shifts in an organizational system that may cause significant disruption to some underlying aspect of the organization, its processes, or its structures.

unplanned change An unintentional activity that is usually the result of informal organizing.

vertical organizational structure Organizational structures found in large mechanistic organizations; also called "tall" structures due to the presence of many levels of management.

Summary of Learning Outcomes

16.1 Organizational Structures and Design

1. What are mechanistic versus organic organizational structures?

The organizational structure is designed from both the mechanistic and the organic points of view, and the structure depends upon the extent to which it is rigid or flexible. Flexible structures are also viewed as more humanistic than mechanistic structures. The mechanistic organizational structure is similar to Max Weber's bureaucratic organization. Organic structures are more flexible in order to cope with rapidly changing environments. These structures are more effective if the environment is dynamic, requiring frequent changes within the organization in order to adjust to change. It is also considered to be a better form of organization when employees seek autonomy, openness, change, support for creativity and innovation, and opportunities to try new approaches.

All organizations need structures to accomplish their work, and they need an ability to change in order to sustain and renew themselves over time

16.2 Organizational Change

2. What are the fundamental dimensions of change?

It is often said that the only constant is change. Managers need to have the ability to understand the dimensions of change, know what drives change, and know how to implement changes to meet and exceed organizational goals. The three types of change are structural, technological, and culture changes. Managers need to understand change as organizations evolve and grow over time.

One of the key responsibilities of management is to design organizational structures that will allow an organization to accomplish its primary objectives. The structure should always match the need for coordination. Often, managers cannot tell what form the organization should take until they experience the informal organization that determines how work is actually accomplished. Only then can they understand how to draw on the concepts of bureaucracy to appropriately design a structure that will maximize the likelihood of organizational success.

16.3 Managing Change

3. How do managers deal with change?

As an organization grows and matures, change becomes necessary to its sustained viability. Thus, another key responsibility for most leaders is the task of designing and managing change. We have reviewed several questions that should be considered when designing a change process, and we have explored several approaches that may be used to guide the development of organizational change.

The field of knowledge about how to change and develop organizations is vast and can be somewhat confusing to the novice learner. The material presented in this chapter provides an overview of key ideas, but there is so much more to learn. Should you wish to become an influential leader of change, it is important to learn more about this very important field of research and practice.

Chapter Review Questions

1. What is an organizational structure?

2. What are different types of organizational structures?
3. What is organizational design?
4. What concepts should guide decisions about how to design structures?
5. What is organizational change?
6. What are the fundamental dimensions of change?
7. What are organizational development (OD) and change management?
8. What questions may be used to guide OD and change management?
9. What are the common models of OD and change management?

Management Skills Application Exercises

1. Refer to **Exhibit 16.2**, **Exhibit 16.3**, and **Exhibit 16.5** for this exercise. Pick a business that you are familiar with, and draw their existing organizational chart. You may be able to infer much of the information from their website or through a short interview with someone in their organization. After completing this task, construct an alternative organizational chart and comment on why it may be more effective than the current organizational structure and what risks that new structure may have.
2. You have been assigned the task of working with a company that had a traditional, functional organizational structure with sales, marketing, product development, finance and accounting, and operations teams each reporting to a VP, who then reported to the CEO. The company wants to move to a matrix organization that will retain the efficiencies of the functional organization but also groups employees by product teams. You have been asked to comment on how to manage this change and how to communicate and respond to employee concerns. Specifically, you need to address: What are the desired impacts or benefits of this project on the organization? What are the emotions that your employees may have about this organizational change? How could the employee emotions impact the organization or its operations? How can the organization manage these emotions, or in what ways do you think they should manage these emotions to get desired outcome?

Managerial Decision Exercises

1. Place yourself in the position of a CEO who is contemplating a reorganization of your company and has received conflicting opinions from two of your trusted reports. Presently you are a wholesaler with 45 regional warehouses who acquires products from manufacturers and distributes them to retailers and service establishments. You have over 100,000 SKUs (stock keeping unit) ranging from ACE bandages to Ziploc bags. You have 825 field-based sales representatives who represent all the products within a geographic area.
   One of the ideas that has been brought up by the vice president of marketing is to specialize the salesforce into three groups, fashion retail, general retail, and services. Basically, individual sales representatives would be able to specialize with greater expertise and product knowledge to better serve customers. The vice president of sales fears that many of her salespeople will leave due to the expanded geography that this change would require.
   What process would you take to address the concerns of your managers? How would you implement the plan? What customer considerations would you need to address?
2. You have recently accepted the position of director for a full-service retirement home that has three components. The first component is for retired individuals and married couples who can still manage on

their own but appreciate the amenities such as medical care and having other residents that they interact with through planned activities. The second is for residents who are still relatively healthy but do need assistance for specific tasks such as mobility and the like. The third section is for individuals with chronic health issues and palliative care patients.

You have learned during the interview process that the facility has performance and morale issues and that the previous director had a rigid structure, did not allow workers from different roles to interact, and wanted all decisions to be directed to her. This has led to dramatic staff turnover and a larger number of empty units compared to other facilities.

As the incoming new director, you will need to address the staff, and your new assistant asks whether you would like to address the staff in one large room or in smaller meeting rooms with employees from the different functional units. She also asks how to handle the workers who are from different shifts. Make your communication decisions, and write up an opening statement to make to the employees before you open the meeting to questions.

Critical Thinking Case

Danny Meyer Leads His Company through the Challenges of Eliminating Tips

What happens when your CEO wants to remove the tip structure from your restaurant? Do you complain about the new prices as a customer? Do you worry about your paychecks as a server?

Danny Meyer, CEO of Union Square Hospitality (home to some of the most successful New York restaurants), discovered these answers when he began eliminating the tip structure in most of his restaurants. He had seen firsthand the largest negative impact of a tipping culture: employees stuck in front-line positions with no chance to advance to management without taking significant pay cuts.

Meyer began by first involving the affected employees in town-hall talks. These town halls happened months before any publicity was released. Meyer then hosted town halls with customers to explain the importance of fair wages for all his employees at the restaurant, not just the few who served the food. The transition period for each restaurant to eliminate tips was usually three to six months.

As a result of eliminating the tip structure in most of his restaurants, Meyer has been able to increase the pay structure for cooks at those locations, which enables him to fill more cook positions and address a common industry shortage. Meyer has also been able to hire employees with a purpose to deliver exceptional hospitality. Meyer encourages his employees to take care of each other first, and to then take care of the customer, which creates a virtuous cycle of hospitality.

Meyer constantly uses feedback from his employees even after the tip structure was eliminated. He wants to ensure that each employee feels their voice is heard and understood. Employees continue to have access to town-hall meetings and internal feedback channels to offer honest feedback.

Critical Thinking Questions

1. What type of change is this: transformational or incremental? Why?
2. What level(s) of change is Meyer aiming for in this case?
3. What models are consistent with Meyer's process for designing and implementing change?

Sources: Mark Matousek, Dannu Meyer Banned Tipping at his Restaurants- But Employees Say it has Led to Lower Pay and High Turnover," *Business Insider*, October 20, 2017, http://www.businessinsider.com/danny-meyers-no-tip-policy-struggles-2017-10; Loren Feldman, "Danny Meyer On Eliminating Tipping: "It Takes a

Year to Get The Math Right," *Forbes*, January 14, 2018, https://www.forbes.com/sites/lorenfeldman/2018/01/14/danny-meyer-on-eliminating-tipping-it-takes-a-year-to-get-the-math-right/#189bd5c8431f; Elizabeth Dunn, "The Limitations of American Restaurants' No-Tipping Experience," *The New Yorker*, February 24, 2018, https://www.newyorker.com/culture/annals-of-gastronomy/the-limitations-of-american-restaurants-no-tipping-experiment.

17 Human Resource Management

Exhibit 17.1 (Credit: Ludovic Bertron /flickr / Attribution 2.0 Generic (CC BY 2.0))

Introduction

Learning Outcomes

After reading this chapter, you should be able to answer these questions:

1. What has been the evolution of human resource management over the years, and what is the current value it provides to an organization?
2. How does the human resources compliance role of HR provide value to a company?
3. How do performance management practices impact company performance?
4. How do companies use rewards strategies to influence employee performance and motivation?
5. What is talent acquisition, and how can it create a competitive advantage for a company?
6. What are the benefits of talent development and succession planning?

EXPLORING MANAGERIAL CAREERS

Eva Hartmann, Trellis LLC

Eva Hartmann has nearly 20 years of experience as a strategic, results-driven, innovative leader with significant expertise in human resources strategy, talent and leadership development, and organizational effectiveness. She has worked in a variety of industries, from manufacturing to Fortune 500 consulting. Eva is a transformational change agent who has developed and led strategic human capital programs and talent initiatives in multiple challenging environments globally. Eva is passionate about enhancing both individual and organizational performance.

Eva began her career in one of the large “Big 6” management consulting firms at the time, and she happily returned several years ago to consulting. She is the founder and president of Trellis LLC, a human capital consulting and staffing firm in Richmond, Virginia.

Prior to Trellis, Eva was the global human resources leader for a large global manufacturer of plastic film products and was responsible for the HR strategy and operations of a $600 million global division. In this role, Eva led a global team of HR managers in North and South America, Europe, and Asia to support global HR initiatives to drive business results and build human capital and performance across the division.

Eva has also held a variety of leadership and managerial roles in both human resources and quality functions at several nationally and globally recognized companies, including Wachovia Securities, Genworth Financial, Sun Microsystems, and Andersen Consulting (now Accenture).

Eva holds an MBA from the College of William and Mary in Williamsburg, Virginia, and a BA in anthropology from the University of Virginia in Charlottesville, Virginia. She is also an adjunct faculty member with the University of Richmond Robins School of Business. Eva currently serves on the board of the Society of Human Resource Management (SHRM) of Richmond, Virginia.

Human resource management is an area that has evolved a great deal over the last few decades. From the days of the very tactical "personnel" management to the current and more strategic state of human resources, businesses and HR professionals alike have changed the way they see the function. In the current economy, human capital assets (i.e., people) are the greatest value creators. Companies compete for talent, and they distinguish themselves in their business performance by the talent they have in their ranks. Human resource management, therefore, becomes a key lever companies can utilize to find, recruit, develop, and grow talent for competitive advantage. This chapter discusses the value and benefits that human resource management brings to an organization, as well as the challenges that the function still faces as a strategic partner to the business.

17.1 An Introduction to Human Resource Management

1. What has been the evolution of human resource management (HRM) over the years, and what is the current value it provides to an organization?

Human resource management over the years has served many purposes within an organization. From its earliest inception as a primarily compliance-type function, it has further expanded and evolved into its current state as a key driver of human capital development. In the book *HR From the Outside In* (Ulrich, Younger, Brockbank, Younger, 2012), the authors describe the evolution of HR work in "waves".[1] Wave 1 focused on the administrative work of HR personnel, such as the terms and conditions of work, delivery of HR services, and regulatory compliance. This administrative side still exists in HR today, but it is often accomplished differently via technology and outsourcing solutions. The quality of HR services and HR's credibility came from the ability to run administrative processes and solve administrative issues effectively. Wave 2 focused on the design of innovative HR practice areas such as compensation, learning, communication, and sourcing. The HR professionals in these practice areas began to interact and share with each other to build a consistent approach to human resource management. The HR credibility in Wave 2 came from the delivery of best-practice HR solutions.

Wave 3 HR, over the last 15–20 years or so, has focused on the integration of HR strategy with the overall business strategy. Human resources appropriately began to look at the business strategy to determine what

HR priorities to work on and how to best use resources. HR began to be a true partner to the business, and the credibility of HR was dependent upon HR having a seat at the table when the business was having strategic discussions. In Wave 4, HR continues to be a partner to the business, but has also become a competitive practice for responding to external business conditions. HR looks outside their organizations to customers, investors, and communities to define success—in the form of customer share, investor confidence, and community reputation. HR's credibility is thus defined in terms of its ability to support and drive these external metrics. Although each "wave" of HR's evolution is important and must be managed effectively, it is the "outside in" perspective that allows the human resource management function to shine via the external reputation and successes of the organization.

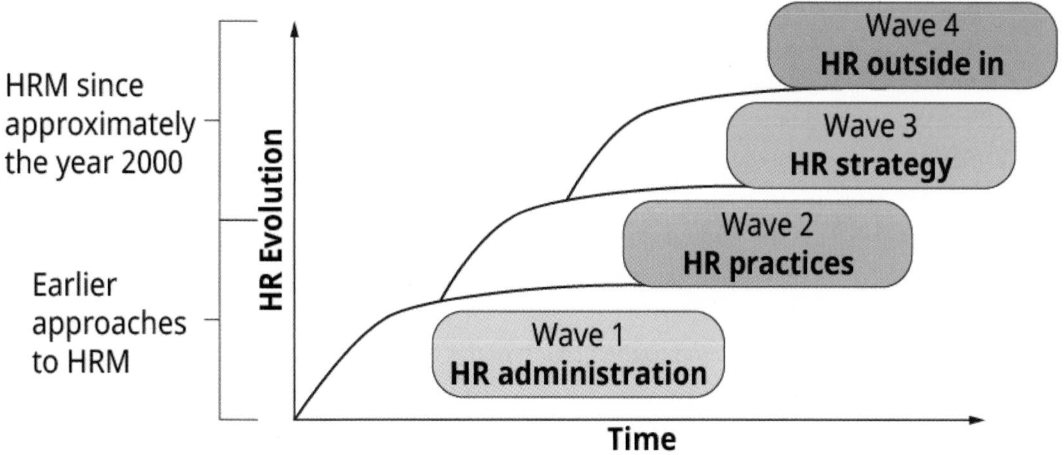

Exhibit 17.2 Evolution of HR Work in Waves (Attribution: Copyright Rice University, OpenStax, under CC-BY 4.0 license)

CATCHING THE ENTREPRENEURIAL SPIRIT

Human Resources Outsourcing—Entrepreneurial Ventures

Human resources is a key function within any company, but not all companies are able to afford or justify full-time HR staff. Over the last decade, HR outsourcing has become a good business decision for many small companies whose current staff doesn't have the bandwidth or expertise to take on the risks of employee relations issues, benefits and payroll, or HR compliance responsibilities. This has led many HR practitioners to try out their entrepreneurial skills in the areas of HR outsourcing and "fractional HR."

Human resources outsourcing is very commonly used by smaller companies (and often large companies too) to cover such tasks as benefits and payroll management. This is an area that has been outsourced to third parties for many years. More recent is the trend to have "fractional HR" resources to help with the daily/weekly/monthly HR compliance, employee relations, and talent management issues that companies need to address. Fractional HR is a growing industry, and it has become the service offering of many entrepreneurial HR ventures. Fractional HR is essentially as it sounds—it is the offering of HR services to a company on a part-time or intermittent basis when the company may not be able to justify the cost of a full-time HR resource. An HR professional can be available onsite for a specified number of hours or days weekly or monthly, depending on the company's needs and budget. The HR professional handles everything from HR compliance issues and training to employee issues support. Also, for companies that are keen on development of employees, the HR resource can drive the talent management processes—such as performance management, succession planning, training, and development—for companies who require more than just basic HR compliance services.

How does a business leader decide whether HR outsourcing is needed? There are generally two factors that drive a leader to consider fractional HR or HR outsourcing—time and risk. If a leader is spending too much time on HR issues and employee relations, he may decide that it is a smart tradeoff to outsource these tasks to a professional. In addition, the risk inherent in some HR issues can be very great, so the threat of having a lawsuit or feeling that the company is exposed can lead the company to seek help from a fractional HR professional.

HR entrepreneurs have taken full advantage of this important trend, which many say will likely continue as small companies grow and large companies decide to off-load HR work to third parties. Some HR companies offer fractional HR as part of their stated HR services, in addition to payroll and benefits support, compensation, and other HR programmatic support. Having a fractional HR resource in place will often illuminate the need for other HR services and program builds, which are generally supported by those same companies. Whether you are an individual HR practitioner or have a small company of HR practitioners and consultants, fractional HR and HR outsourcing can be a very viable and financially rewarding business model. It can also be very personally rewarding, as the HR professional enables smaller companies to grow and thrive, knowing that its HR compliance and processes are covered.

Discussion Questions

1. What do you believe is contributing to the growth of the fractional HR and HR outsourcing trend? Do you expect this trend to continue?
2. At what point should a company consider bringing on a full-time HR resource instead of using a fractional HR resource? What questions should the company ask itself?

Human resource management provides value to an organization, to a large extent, via its management of the overall **employee life cycle** that employees follow—from hiring and onboarding, to performance management and talent development, all the way through to transitions such as job change and promotion, to retirement and exit. **Human capital** is a key competitive advantage to companies, and those who utilize their human resource partners effectively to drive their human capital strategy will reap the benefits.

Human resource management includes the leadership and facilitation of the following key life cycle process areas:

- Human resources compliance
- Employee selection, hiring, and onboarding
- Performance management
- Compensation rewards and benefits
- Talent development and succession planning

Human resources is responsible for driving the strategy and policies in these areas to be in accordance with and in support of the overall business strategy. Each of these areas provides a key benefit to the organization and impacts the organization's value proposition to its employees.

CONCEPT CHECK

1. How has the function of human resource management evolved over the years?
2. In what way do you usually interact with human resources?

17.2 Human Resource Management and Compliance

2. How does the human resources compliance role of HR add value to an organization?

Human resources compliance is an area that traces back to the very origin of the human resources function—to administrative and regulatory functions. Compliance continues to be a very important area that HR manages, and there are numerous regulations and laws that govern the employment relationship. HR professionals must be able to understand and navigate these laws to help their organizations remain compliant and avoid having to pay fines or penalties. The additional threat of reputational harm to the organization is another reason that HR needs to be aware and alert to any potential gaps in compliance.

Some of the most common examples of laws and regulations that govern the **employer-employee relationship** include the following (SHRM.org):

- Age Discrimination in Employment Act (ADEA)
- Americans with Disabilities Act (ADA)
- Fair Labor Standards Act (FLSA)
- Family and Medical Leave Act (FMLA)
- National Labor Relations Act (NLRA)
- Worker Adjustment and Retraining Notification Act (WARN)

The Age Discrimination in Employment Act (ADEA) of 1967 protects individuals who are 40 years of age or older from employment discrimination based on age. These protections apply to both employees and job applicants. It also makes it unlawful to discriminate based on age with respect to any terms of employment, such as hiring, firing, promotion, layoff, compensation, benefits, job assignments, and training.

The Americans with Disabilities Act (ADA) of 1990 prohibits private employers, state and local governments, employment agencies, and labor unions from discriminating against qualified individuals with disabilities. The ADA defines an individual with a disability as a person who: 1) has a mental or physical impairment that substantially limits one or more major life activities, 2) has a record of such impairment, or 3) is regarded as having such impairment. An employer is required to make a reasonable accommodation to the known disability of a qualified applicant or employee if it would not impose an "undue hardship" on the operation of the employer's business.

The Fair Labor Standards Act (FLSA) of 1938 establishes the minimum wage, overtime pay, recordkeeping, and youth employment standards affecting full-time and part-time workers in the private sector and in federal, state, and local governments. Special rules apply to state and local government employment involving fire protection and law enforcement activities, volunteer services, and compensatory time off instead of cash overtime pay.

The Family and Medical Leave Act (FMLA) of 1993 entitles eligible employees to take up to 12 weeks of unpaid, job-protected leave in a 12-month period for specified family and medical reasons. FMLA applies to all public agencies, including state, local, and federal employers, local education agencies (schools), and private-sector employers who employed 50 or more employees in 20 or more workweeks in the current or preceding calendar year, including joint employers and successors of covered employers.

The National Labor Relations Act (NLRA) of 1947 extends rights to many private-sector employees, including the right to organize and bargain with their employer collectively. Employees covered by the act are protected from certain types of employer and union misconduct and have the right to attempt to form a union where none exists.

The Worker Adjustment and Retraining Notification Act (WARN) of 1988 generally covers employers with 100 or more employees, not counting those who have worked less than six months in the last 12 months and those who work an average of less than 20 hours a week. Regular federal, state, and local government entities that provide public services are not covered. WARN protects workers, their families, and communities by requiring employers to provide notification 60 calendar days in advance of plant closings and mass layoffs.

These are just a few of the key regulatory federal statutes, regulations, and guidance that human resources professionals need to understand to confirm organizational compliance. For additional information on HR compliance resources, the **Society of Human Resource Management (SHRM)** at SHRM.org maintains a plethora of resources for the HR professional and the businesses that they support.

To ensure the successful management and oversight of the many compliance rules and regulations, the human resources team must utilize best practices to inform and hold employees accountable to HR compliance practices. Some of these best practices include education and training, documentation, and audit. Each of these is described in greater detail, and will help HR achieve its important goal of maintaining HR compliance for the organization.

Education and training in the areas of compliance and labor law is critical to ensure that all applicable laws and regulations are being followed. These laws can change from year to year, so the HR professionals in the organization need to ensure that they are engaged in ongoing education and training. It is not just imperative for the HR professional to receive training. In many organizations, managers receive training on key rules and regulations (such as FMLA or ADA, to name a few) so that they have a foundation of knowledge when dealing with employee situations and potential risk areas. Human resources and management need to partner to ensure alignment on compliance issues—especially when there is a risk that an employee situation treads into compliance regulation territory. See **Table 17.1** for a partial list of federal labor laws by number of employees, as displayed on the Society for Human Resource Management website.

Refer to **Table 17.1**: Federal Labor Laws by Number of Employees.

Federal Labor Laws by Number of Employees
American Taxpayer Relief Act of 2012
Consumer Credit Protection Act of 1968
Employee Polygraph Protection Act of 1988
Employee Retirement Income Security Act of 1974 (ERISA)
Equal Pay Act of 1963
Fair and Accurate Credit Transaction Act of 2003 (FACT)
Fair Credit Reporting Act of 1969
Fair Labor Standards Act of 1938
Federal Insurance Contributions Act of 1935 (Social Security) (FICA)
Health Insurance Portability and Accountability Act of 1996 (if a company offers benefits) (HIPPA)
Immigration Reform and Control Act of 1986

Table 17.1 (Attribution: Copyright Rice University, OpenStax, under CC-BY 4.0 license)

Federal Labor Laws by Number of Employees
These federal laws cover all employees of all organizations. Several other factors may apply in determining employer coverage, such as whether the employer is public or private, whether the employer offers health insurance, and whether the employer uses a third party to conduct background checks. Source: SHRM website, https://www.shrm.org/, accessed October 20, 2018.

Table 17.1

Documentation of the rules and regulations—in the form of an employee handbook—can be one of the most important resources that HR can provide to the organization to mitigate compliance risk. The handbook should be updated regularly and should detail the organization's policies and procedures and how business is to be conducted. Legal counsel should review any such documentation before it is distributed to ensure that it is up-to-date and appropriate for the audience.

Scheduling HR compliance audits should be part of the company's overall strategy to avoid legal risk. Noncompliance can cause enormous financial and reputational risk to a company, so it is important to have audits that test the organization's controls and preparedness. When the human resources function takes the lead in implementing audits and other best practices, they create real value for the organization.

CONCEPT CHECK 

1. What are some of the key regulations that guide the compliance work of human resource management?
2. What does an employee handbook provide to an organization?

17.3 Performance Management

3. How do performance management practices impact company performance?

Performance management practices and processes are among the most important that human resources manages, yet they are also among the most contentious processes in an organization. Many people view performance management as a human resources role and believe that it is in some parallel path with the business. On the contrary, for the process to be successful, it should not only be human resources that is responsible for driving performance. For the (typically) annual performance management process, human resources and line management should partner on the implementation and ongoing communication of the process. Although HR is responsible for creating and facilitating the performance management processes, it is the organizational managers that need to strongly support the process and communicate the linkage of performance management to overall organizational goals and performance. In my experience, it was helpful when business leadership emphasized that performance management isn't a human resources process—it is a mission-critical business process. If a business manager can't track and drive performance at the individual level, then the overall organization won't know how it's tracking on overall organizational goals. Performance Management Before discussing the state of performance management in the workplace today, it is important to understand the origin of performance management. Performance management began as a simple tool to drive accountability (as it still does) but has evolved more recently into a tool used for employee development.

Performance management can be tracked back to the U.S. military's "merit rating" system, which was created during World War I to identify poor performers for discharge or transfer ("The Performance Management Revolution," Harvard Business Review, October 2016).[2] After World War II, about 60% of all U.S. companies were using a performance appraisal process. (By the 1960s nearly 90% of all U.S. companies were using them.) Although the rules around job seniority determined pay increases and promotions for the unionized worker population, strong performance management scores meant good advancement prospects for managers. In the beginning, the notion of using this type of system to *improve* performance was more of an afterthought, and not the main purpose. By the 1960s or so, when we started to see a shortage of managerial talent, companies began to use performance systems to develop employees into supervisors, and managers into executives.

In 1981, when Jack Welch became CEO of General Electric, he championed the forced-ranking system—another military creation. He did this to deal with the long-standing concern that supervisors failed to label real differences in performance (HBR, The Performance Management Revolution). GE utilized this performance management system to shed the people at the bottom. They equated performance with people's inherent capabilities and ignored their potential to grow. People were categorized as "A" players (to be rewarded), "B" players (to be accommodated), and "C" players (to be dismissed). In the GE system, development was reserved for the "A" players—and those with high potential were chosen to advance to senior positions. Since the days of GE's forced ranking, many companies have implemented a similar forced-ranking system, but many have backed away from the practice. After Jack Welch retired, GE backed away from the practice as well. Companies, GE included, saw that it negatively fostered internal competition and undermined collaboration and teamwork and thus decided to drop forced ranking from their performance management processes.

Most people agree, in theory, that performance management is important. What people may *not* agree on is *how* performance management should be implemented. As the dissatisfaction with performance management processes began to increase, some companies began to change the way they thought about performance. In 2001, an "Agile Manifesto" was developed by software developers and "emphasized principles of collaboration, self-organization, self-direction, and regular reflection on how to work more effectively, with the aim of prototyping more quickly and responding in real-time to customer feedback and changes in requirements." (Performance Management Revolution, HBR). The impact on performance management was clear, and companies started to think about performance management processes that were less cumbersome, incorporated frequent feedback, and delivered performance impacts.

In a recent public survey by Deloitte Services, 58% of executives surveyed believed that their current performance management approach drives neither employee engagement nor high performance. They need something more nimble, real-time, and individualized—and focused on fueling performance in the future rather than assessing it in the past.[3] ("*Reinventing Performance Management*," Harvard Business Review, Buckingham and Goodall, 2015). In light of this study, Deloitte became one of the companies that has recently sought to redesign their performance processes. As part of their "radical redesign," they seek to see performance at the individual level, and thus they ask team leaders about their own future actions and decisions with respect to each individual. They ask leaders what they'd do with their team members, not what they think of them ("Reinventing Performance Management," HBR). The four questions that Deloitte asks of its managers are as follows:

- Given what I know of this person's performance, and if it were my money, I would award this person the highest possible compensation increase and bonus.
- Given what I know of this person's performance, I would always want him or her on my team.
- This person is at risk for low performance.
- This person is ready for promotion today.

Although there has been some discussion over the last several years about some companies wanting to drop performance appraisals completely, most of the research seems to support that the total absence of performance management doesn't help either. A recent global survey by CEB Global reports that more than 9,000 managers and employees think that not having performance evaluations is worse than having them.[4] ("Let's Not Kill Performance Evaluations Yet," HBR, Nov 2016, Goler, Gale, Grant). Their findings indicate that even though every organization has people who are unhappy with their bonuses or disappointed that they weren't promoted, research shows that employees are more willing to accept an undesirable outcome when the process is fair. The key question really becomes: how can HR help the business create a process to fairly evaluate performance and enhance employee development while *not* burdening the business with undue bureaucracy and non-value-added activities?

MANAGING CHANGE

Global versus Local HR

Multinational companies are always challenged to determine the balance between global and local needs when creating a human resource management strategy. Some large companies weigh heavily on the side of centralization, with very few local deviations from the global strategy. Others may allow more localization of processes and decision-making if there are very specific local cultural needs that must be addressed. In either case, companies are well-served by maintaining global standards while also allowing for local market adaptation in the human resources areas where it makes the most sense.

According to the *MIT Sloan Management Review* article "Six Principles of Effective Global Talent Management" (Winter 2012), most multinational companies introduce global performance standards, competency profiles, and performance management tools and processes. These are the human resources areas that are most closely linked to the overall strategies and goals, and thus remain at the global level. Those HR processes that are not perceived as being as closely linked to the strategy and that may need to have local market inputs include processes such as training and compensation. Hiring practices may also need to be locally adapted, due to country-specific labor laws and challenges. One caveat, however, is that a company may limit itself in terms of its global talent management if it has too many country-specific adaptations to hiring, assessment, and development processes for top talent. It is important that the company takes a global approach to talent management so that cross-learning opportunities and cross-cultural development opportunities can take place.

One of the most important aspects of global talent management is that a company can break down silos and pollinate the business with talented employees from around the globe. Some companies even have global leadership programs that bring together high-potential leaders from across the organization to build camaraderie, share knowledge, and engage in learning. Others have created rotational programs for leaders to be able to experience new roles in other cultures in order to build their personal resumes and cultural intelligence. Human resources can have an enormous impact on the company's ability to harness the power of a global talent pool when they create a global network for talent while also balancing this with the requirements of the local market.

Discussion Questions

1. What are the challenges of a company developing a different competency model or performance management process for each of its local offices?
2. Why might compensation programs and hiring practices need to have local adaptation? What would be the risks if these were not adapted to local markets?

As organizations evaluate their options for a performance management system, human resources and business leadership need to consider several challenges that will need to be addressed—no matter what the system.[5] ("*The Performance Management Revolution*," Capelli and Tavis, HBR, pp. 9-11).

The first is the challenge of aligning individual and company goals. Traditionally, the model has been to "cascade" goals down through the organization, and employees are supposed to create goals that reflect and support the direction set at the top. The notion of SMART goals (Specific, Measurable, Achievable, Relevant, Timebound) has made the rounds over the years, but goal setting can still be challenging if business goals are complex or if employee goals seem more relatable to specific project work than to the overall top-line goals. The business and the individual need to be able to respond to goal shifts, which occur very often in response to the rapid rate of change and changing customer needs. This is an ongoing issue that human resources and business leadership will need to reconcile.

The next key challenge to think about when designing a performance management process is rewarding performance. Reward structures are discussed later in this chapter, but reward systems must be rooted in performance management systems. Currently, the companies that are redesigning their performance processes are trying to figure out how their new practices will impact their **pay-for-performance** models. Companies don't appear to be abandoning the concept of rewarding employees based on and driven by their performance, so the linkage between the two will need to be redefined as the systems are changed.

The identification of poor performers is a challenge that has existed since the earliest days of performance management, and even the most formal performance management process doesn't seem to be particularly good at weeding out poor performers. A lot of this is due to the managers who evaluate employees and are reluctant to address the poor performers that they're seeing. Also, the annual performance management process tends to make some managers feel that the poor performance should be overlooked during the year and only addressed (often ineffectively) during a one-per-year review. Whatever new performance management models an organization adopts, they will have to ensure that poor performance is dealt with in real time and is communicated, documented, and managed closely.

Avoiding legal troubles is another ongoing challenge for organizations and is another reason for real-time communication and documentation of performance issues. Human resources supports managers as they deal with employee relations issues, and the thought of not having a formal, numerical ratings system is unfathomable for some people who worry about defending themselves against litigation. However, because even formal performance processes can be subjective and may reveal ratings bias, neither the traditional formal process nor some of the radical new approaches can guarantee that legal troubles will never develop. From my experience, the best strategy for effective and fair performance management is real-time communication and documentation of issues. The employee is told about his or her performance issues (in as close to real time as possible), and the manager has documented the performance issues and conversations objectively and has engaged human resources with any larger or more complex issues.

"Managing the feedback firehose" and keeping conversations, documentation, and feedback in a place where it can be tracked and utilized is an ongoing challenge. The typical annual performance process is not conducive to capturing ongoing feedback and conversations. There have been some new technologies introduced (such as apps) that can be used to capture ongoing conversations between managers and employees. General Electric uses an app called PD@GE (PD = performance development) that allows managers to pull up notes and materials from prior conversations with employees. IBM has a similar app that allows peer-to-peer feedback. Although there are clearly some technology solutions that can be used to help communicate and collect feedback, human resources will need to continue to communicate and reinforce rules around objectivity and appropriate use of the tools.

Performance management processes—traditional and inventive new approaches alike—will face the same challenges over time. Human resource management professionals need to be aware of these challenges and design a performance management system that addresses them in the format and within the context of their culture.

CONCEPT CHECK 

1. Where did the concept of performance management originate?
2. What are some of the key challenges of any performance management process?

17.4 Influencing Employee Performance and Motivation

4. How do companies use rewards strategies to influence employee performance and motivation?

Both performance management and rewards systems are key levers that can be used to motivate and drive individual and group performance ... which leads to overall organizational performance, productivity, and growth. Performance and rewards systems are also "cultural" in that they provide a glimpse into the way a company manages the performance (or nonperformance) of its employees, and to what extent they are willing to differentiate and reward for that performance. There has been a great deal of discussion over the years to identify best practices in the ways we differentiate and reward employees, which will also drive employee performance and motivation.

Before we can talk about best practices and findings in rewards and motivation systems, we must first define the terms. Rewards systems are the framework that an organization (generally via human resources) creates and manages to ensure that employee performance is reciprocated with some sort of reward (e.g., monetary or other extrinsic) that will drive and motivate the employee to continue to perform for the organization. Rewards programs consist primarily of compensation programs and policies, but can also include employee benefits and other extrinsic rewards that fulfill employee needs.

Within human resource management, the primary focus of a rewards program in an organization is to successfully implement a compensation system. Most organizations strive to implement a **pay-for-performance** compensation program that offers competitive pay in the marketplace and allows differentiation of compensation based on employee performance. Pay for performance begins with a philosophy that an organization adopts that states that they seek to reward the best-performing employees to enhance business performance and take care of those who can have the greatest impact.

In the 2011 SHRM article by Stephen Miller, entitled "Study: Pay for Performance Pays Off," Miller says that companies' top four drivers for moving to a pay-for-performance strategy are to:

- Recognize and reward high performers (46.9%)
- Increase the likelihood of achieving corporate goals (32.5%)
- Improve productivity (7.8%)
- Move away from an entitlement culture (7.8%)

The study also showed that the drivers differed depending on whether the company was high performing or lower performing.[6] Almost half of high-performing organizations indicated that recognizing and rewarding top performers was the main driver of their pay-for-performance strategy, making it number one on the list of primary drivers. Lower-performing organizations did not appear to be as sure about the drivers behind their strategy. The number one driver among this group was achieving corporate goals. It appears that those top-performing organizations that implement a pay-for-performance strategy truly believe in the idea of differentiating among different levels of performance.

According to the 2015 World at Work "Compensation Programs and Practices Report," pay for performance continues to thrive with better than 7 in 10 (72%) companies saying that they directly tie pay increases to job performance, and two-thirds (67%) indicating increases for top performers are at least 1.5 times the increase for average performers. In addition, the results of the survey seem to indicate that employees' understanding of the organization's compensation philosophy improves when there is higher differentiation in increases between average and top performers. The greater differentiation of increases is more visible and drives home the point that the company is serious about pay for performance.[7]

A pay-for-performance program may have many components, and the human resources organization has the challenge of designing, analyzing, communicating, and managing the different components to ensure that the philosophy and the practices themselves are being carried out appropriately and legally. Human resource management's role in establishing pay for performance is that HR must engage business leadership to establish the following elements of the framework:

1. Define the organization's pay philosophy. Leadership needs to agree that they will promote a culture that rewards employees for strong performance.
2. Review the financial impacts of creating pay-for-performance changes. How much differentiation of performance will we have? What is the cost of doing this?
3. Identify any gaps that exist in the current processes. If any of the current human resources and compensation policies conflict with pay for performance, they should be reviewed and changed. Examples may lie in the performance management process, the merit increase process, and the short-term and long-term bonus processes. If the performance management process has gaps, these should be corrected before pay for performance is implemented; otherwise this will generate more distrust in the system. The salary structure should also be benchmarked with market data to ensure that the organization is compensating according to where it wishes to be in the marketplace.
4. Update compensation processes with new pay for-performance elements. This includes the design of a **merit matrix** that ties employee annual pay increases to performance. Other areas of focus should be the design of a short-term bonus matrix and a long-term bonus pay-for-performance strategy. In other words, how does performance drive the bonus payouts? What is the differential (or multiplier) for each level?
5. Communicate and train managers and employees on the pay for-performance philosophy and process changes. Explain the changes in the context of the overall culture of the organization. This is a long-term investment in talent and performance.

Human resource management professionals play a key role in the rewards processes, and employee compensation is only one piece (although a key piece!) of the "total rewards" pie. World at Work defines *total rewards* as a "dynamic relationship between employers and employees." World at Work also defines a **total rewards strategy** as the six elements of total rewards that "collectively define an organization's strategy to attract, motivate, retain and engage employees." These six elements include:

- Compensation—Pay provided by an employer to its employees for services rendered (i.e., time, effort, and skill). This includes both fixed and variable pay tied to performance levels.
- Benefits—Programs an employer uses to supplement the cash compensation employees receive. These health, income protection, savings, and retirement programs provide security for employees and their families.
- Work-life effectiveness—A specific set of organizational practices, policies, and programs, plus a philosophy that actively supports efforts to help employees achieve success at both work and home.

- Recognition—Formal or informal programs that acknowledge or give special attention to employee actions, efforts, behavior, or performance and support business strategy by reinforcing behaviors (e.g., extraordinary accomplishments) that contribute to organizational success.
- Performance management—The alignment of organizational, team, and individual efforts toward the achievement of business goals and organizational success. Performance management includes establishing expectations, skill demonstration, assessment, feedback, and continuous improvement.
- Talent development—Provides the opportunity and tools for employees to advance their skills and competencies in both their short- and long-term careers.

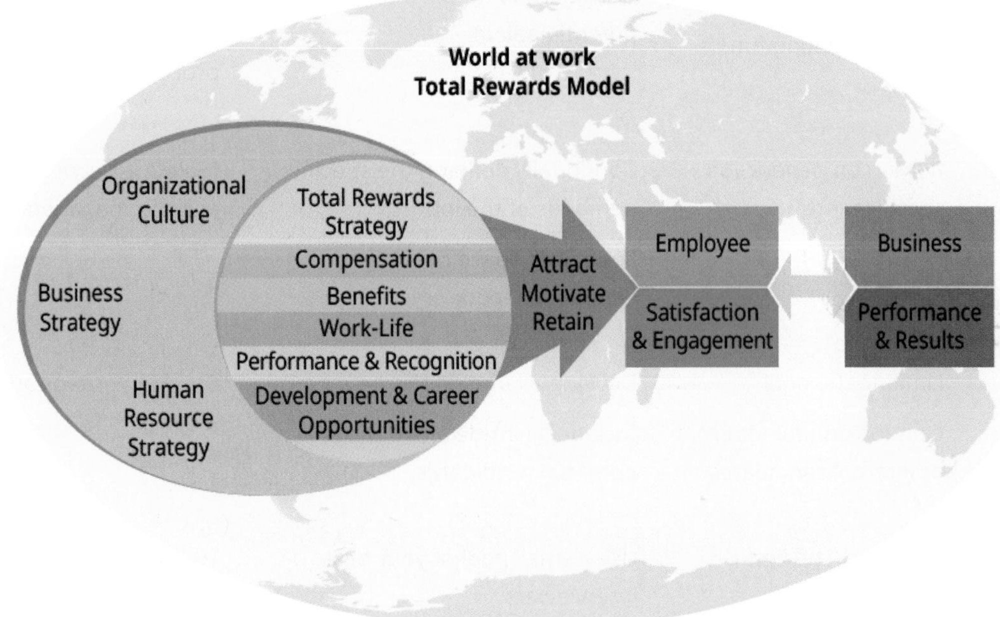

Exhibit 17.3 Total Rewards Model, World at Work

Human resource management is responsible for defining and driving the various elements of an organization's total rewards strategy and ensuring that it is engaging enough to attract and retain good employees. It is easy to see that there are many different types of rewards that can motivate individuals for many different reasons. In the HBR article "Employee Motivation: A Powerful New Model" (Nohria, Groysberg, Lee), August 2008, the authors describe four different drives that underlie motivation. They assert that these are hardwired into our brains and directly affect our emotions and behaviors. These include the drives to acquire, bond, comprehend, and defend. **Table 17.2** illustrates each of these drives, the primary levers found in an organization to address those drives, and the actions that should be taken to support the primary levers.[8]

Hiring Top-Level Executives			
Steps in the Process	Poor Practices	Best Practices	Challenges
Anticipate.	Hiring only when you have an opening Poor succession plan Not anticipating future needs	Conduct ongoing analysis of future needs. Always evaluate the pool of potential talent.	Linking the talent plan to the strategic plan Incorporating HR into the strategic planning process
Specify the job.	Relying on generic job specifications	Continually defining the specific demands of the job Specifying specific skills and experience requirements	Dialogue between HR and top management
Develop a pool.	Limiting the pool Only looking for external or internal candidates	Develop a large pool. Include all inside and outside potential candidates.	Breaking organizational silos
Assess the candidates.	Don't pick the first OK choice. Don't only use your "gut."	Use a small pool of your best interviewers. Conduct robust background checks.	Training senior managers on interviewing techniques
Hire the choice.	Don't assume money is the only issue. Don't only discuss the positives of the job.	Show active support of the candidates' interests. Realistically describe the job. Ensure that offered compensation is fair to other employees.	Getting commitment of top managers Ensuring compensation equity
Integrate the new hire.	Don't assume that the hew hire is a "plug and play."	Use a "top performer" as a mentor. Check in often early in the process even if no problems seem imminent.	Rewarding mentors

Table 17.2 (Attribution: Copyright Rice University, OpenStax, under CC-BY 4.0 license)

Hiring Top-Level Executives			
Steps in the Process	Poor Practices	Best Practices	Challenges
Review the process.	Don't hang on to bad hires.	Remove bad hires early on. Review the recruiting practices. Reward your best interviewers.	Institutionalizing audit and review practices Admitting mistakes and moving on
Adapted from "The Definitive Guide to Recruiting in Good Times and Bad," from article "Hiring Top Executives: A Comprehensive End-to-End Process," Harvard Business Review, May 2009.			

Table 17.2 (Attribution: Copyright Rice University, OpenStax, under CC-BY 4.0 license)

The drive to acquire describes the notion that we are all driven to acquire scarce goods that bolster our sense of well-being. This drive also seems to be relative (we compare ourselves to others in what we have) and insatiable (we always want more). Within an organization, the primary lever to address this drive is the reward system, and the actions are to differentiate levels of performance, link performance to rewards, and pay competitively.

The drive to bond describes the idea that humans extend connections beyond just individuals, to organizations, associations, and nations. In organizations, this drive is fulfilled when employees feel proud to be a part of the company and enjoy being a member of their team. Within an organization, the primary lever to address this drive is culture, and the actions are to foster mutual reliance and friendships, to value collaboration and teamwork, and to encourage best practice sharing.

The drive to comprehend is the concept of all of us wanting to make sense of the world around us and producing different theories and accounts to explain things. People are motivated by the idea of figuring out challenges and making a contribution. In organizations, the primary lever to address this drive is job design, and the actions are to design jobs that have distinct and important roles in the organization, as well as jobs that are meaningful and foster a sense of contribution.

The drive to defend is our instinct to defend ourselves, our families, and our friends, and it describes our defensiveness against external threats. This drive also tells us a lot about our level of resistance to change, and why some employees have especially guarded or emotional reactions. In organizations, the primary levers that address this drive are performance management and resource-allocation processes, and the actions are to increase process transparency and fairness, and to build trust by being just in granting rewards, assignments, and other recognition.

Within human resource management, the area of compensation and reward systems is exceedingly complicated. In organizations, we think primarily of compensation rewards, which are very important drivers and motivators for most people. We need to also remember the other aspects of the total rewards strategy, as well as the drives and levers we can utilize to motivate employees.

CONCEPT CHECK

1. What does a pay-for-performance strategy mean for a company?
2. What is the first step in defining an organization's pay-for-performance strategy?

17.5 Building an Organization for the Future

5. What is talent acquisition, and how can it create a competitive advantage for a company?

We've discussed some of the key focus areas that human resource management professionals need to address to ensure that employees are performing their roles well and are being fairly rewarded for their contributions. We haven't yet addressed how we think about where these employees come from—Whom do we hire? What skills do we need now and in the future? Where will we even look for these employees? What are some best practices? **Talent acquisition** is the area within human resource management that defines the strategy for selection, recruiting, and hiring processes, and helps the organization fight the "**war for talent**" during good times and bad.

Hiring strong talent is a key source of competitive advantage for a company, yet so many companies do it poorly. Often, the recruiting and hiring processes happen reactively—someone leaves the organization and then people scramble to fill the gap. Very few companies take a longer-term, proactive approach and work to create a strategic plan for talent acquisition. In the article "The Definitive Guide to Recruiting in Good Times and Bad" (Fernandez-Araoz, Groysberg, Nohria, HBR, 2009), the authors advocate for a rigorous and strategic recruiting process that includes the following critical actions:

- Anticipate your future leadership needs based on your strategic business plan.
- Identify the specific competencies required in each position you need to fill.
- Develop a sufficiently large candidate pool.

In organizations today, there are often pieces of the talent acquisition process that are outsourced to external recruiters, as opposed to being managed internally by human resources employees.[9] While outsourcing specific searches is not an issue, there must be internal HR/talent acquisition employees responsible for creating the overall strategic plan for the recruiting function. Contract recruiters may then take responsibility for a piece of the overall process by leveraging the strategy and competencies that the HR team puts forth.[10]

Recruiting and hiring of high-level leadership candidates has special risks and rewards associated with it. The risk that a key leadership position is vacant or becoming vacant poses a risk to the organization if it is left open for too long. These high-level positions are often harder to fill, with fewer candidates being available and the selection of the right talent being so critical to the organization's future. The reward, however, is that with due diligence and clear goals and competencies/skills defined for the position, the HR/talent acquisition professional can create a competitive advantage through the recruitment of key high-level talent.

The following best practices illustrate the key steps for effective recruiting of key leadership hires. Both human resources and business leadership should partner to discuss and define each of the elements to ensure alignment and support of the recruiting plan and process (Definitive Guide to Recruiting, HBR, 2009).

Anticipate your needs. Every two to three years there should be a review of high-level leadership requirements based on the strategic plan. Some of the questions to answer here are:

- How many people will we need, and in what positions, in the next few years?
- What will the organizational structure look like?

- What must our leadership pipeline contain today to ensure that we find and develop tomorrow's leaders?

Specify the job. For each leadership position identified, specify competencies needed in each role. For example:

- Job-based: What capabilities will the job require?
- Team-based: Will the applicant need to manage political dynamics?
- Firm-based: What resources (supporting, talent, technology) will the organization need to provide the person who fills this role?

Develop the pool. Cast a wide net for candidates by asking suppliers, customers, board members, professional service provides, and trusted insiders for suggestions. It helps to start this process even before you have a role that you're hiring for. During succession planning and talent discussions internally, it helps to start making of list of internal *and* external contacts and potential candidates before the need arises.

Assess the candidates. Have the hiring manager, the second-level manager, and the top HR manager conduct a "behavioral event interview" with each candidate. Candidates will describe experiences they've had that are like situations they'll face in the organization. Gain an understanding of how the candidate acted and the reasoning behind their actions. Make sure to evaluate a broad range of references to ask about results the candidate achieved.

Exhibit 17.4 The Job Fair A job fair, career fair, or career expo, like this one at the College of DuPage, is an event in which employers, recruiters, and schools give information to potential employees and job seekers attend hoping to make a good impression on potential employers. They also interact with potential coworkers by speaking face-to-face, exchanging résumés, and asking questions in an attempt to get a good feel for the work needed. Likewise, online job fairs give seekers another way to get in contact with probable employers using the Internet. (Credit: Taavi Burns/ flickr/ Attribution 2.0 Generic (CC BY 2.0))

Close the deal. Once you have chosen the final candidate, you can increase the chance that the job offer will be accepted by:

- Sharing passion about the company and role, and showing genuine interest in the candidate
- Acknowledging the opportunities and challenges of the role, differentiating the opportunities at your organization from those of your competitor
- Striking a creative balance between salary, bonuses, and other long-term incentives

Integrate the newcomer. It is important to integrate new hires into the company's culture:

- During the first few months, have the managers and the HR team check in with each new hire.
- Assign a mentor (star employee) to provide ongoing support to each new hire.
- Check in with the new hire to ensure that they are getting enough support, and inquire about what other support might be needed. Ensure that new hires are adequately building new relationships throughout the organization.

Refer to **Table 17.2**: Hiring Top-Level Executives, adapted from "The Definitive Guide to Recruiting in Good Times and Bad," from the article "Hiring Top Executives: A Comprehensive End-to-End Process," *Harvard Business Review*, May 2009.

By following these best practices, human resources and business leadership can ensure that the new hire is integrating well and has the best possible start in the new role. Talent acquisition is a key element of any human resource management program, and the right process can mean the difference between a poor hire and a distinct competitive advantage gained through top talent.

CONCEPT CHECK 

1. What are some best practices for recruiting and hiring leadership candidates?
2. How can we ensure a more successful integration of the new hire?

17.6 Talent Development and Succession Planning

6. What are the benefits of talent development and succession planning?

Talent development and **succession planning** are, in my opinion, two of the most critical human resource management processes within an organization. You can work tirelessly to recruit and hire the right people, and you can spend a lot of time defining and redesigning your performance and rewards programs, but if you can't make decisions that effectively assess and develop the key talent that you have, then everything else feels like a wasted effort. Talent development describes all process and programs that an organization utilizes to assess and develop talent. Succession planning is the process for reviewing key roles and determining the readiness levels of potential internal (and external!) candidates to fill these roles. It is an important process that is a key link between talent development and talent acquisition/recruiting.

The human resources function facilitates talent development activities and processes, but they are also heavily reliant on business inputs and support. Each of the talent development processes that will be discussed require heavy involvement and feedback from the business. Like performance management, talent development is a process that HR owns and facilitates, but it is a true business process that has a fundamental impact on an organization's performance. Talent is a competitive advantage, and in the age of the "war for talent," an organization needs to have a plan for developing its key talent.

One of the key tools that is used in talent development is the talent review. This process generally follows an organization's performance management process (which is primarily focused on *current* employee performance) and is more focused on employee development and potential for the *future*. Talent reviews often employ the use of a **9-box** template, which plots employee performance versus employee potential and provides the reviewer with nine distinct options, or boxes, to categorize where the employee is.

Refer to **Table 17.3:** Performance and Potential Grid.

Performance and Potential Grid				
		Potential		
Performance over time		**Lowest potential rating**	**Middle potential rating**	**Highest potential rating**
	Highest	John Smith Melanie Roper Keegan Flanagan	Chieh Zhang Edgar Orrelana	Rory Collins Aimee Terranova
	Medium	Joseph Campbell Alina Dramon Alex Joiner Lauren Gress	Christina Martin Thomas Weimeister	Richard Collins
	Lowest	Marty Hilton		

Table 17.3

The performance axis ratings are low/medium/high and based on the employee's recent performance management rating. Low = below target, medium = at target, and high = above target. Like the performance rating, this reflects performance against objectives and the skills and competencies required in the employee's current role and function. Performance can change over time (for example, with a promotion or job change). Performance is overall a more objective rating than potential, which leaves the rater to make some assumptions about the future.

Potential is defined as an employee's ability to demonstrate the behaviors necessary to be successful at the next highest level within the company. **Competencies** and behaviors are a good indicator of an employee's potential. Higher-potential employees, no matter what the level, often display the following competencies: business acumen, strategic thinking, leadership skills, people skills, learning agility, and technology skills. Other indicators of potential may include:

- Top performance in current job
- Success in other positions held (within or outside of the company)
- Education/certifications
- Significant accomplishments/events
- Willingness and desire to advance

MANAGING CHANGE

Tech in Human Resources

There has been a boom in HR technology and innovation over the last several years—and it is making some of the traditional HR systems from last decade seem enormously outdated. Some of the trends that are driving this HR tech innovation include mobile technology, social media, data analytics, and learning management. Human resources professionals need to be aware of some of the key technology innovations that have emerged as a result of these trends because there's no sign that they will be going away any time soon.

Josh Bersin of Bersin by Deloitte, Deloitte Consulting LLP, wrote about some of these HR technology innovations in his SHRM.org article "9 HR Tech Trends for 2017" (Jan. 2017). One of these technology innovations is the "performance management revolution" and the new focus on managing performance by team and not just by hierarchy. Performance management technologies have become more agile and real time, with built-in pulse surveys and easy goal tracking. Now, instead of the formal, once-a-year process that brings everything to a halt, these performance management technologies allow ongoing, real-time, and dynamic input and tracking of performance data.

Another HR tech trend named is the "rise of people analytics." Data analytics has become such a huge field, and HR's adoption of it is no exception. Some disruptive technologies in this area are predictive—they allow analysis of job change data and the prediction of successful versus unsuccessful outcomes. Predictive analytics technologies can also analyze patterns of e-mails and communications for good time-management practices, or to predict where a security leak is likely to occur. One other incredible analytics application consists of a badge that monitors employees' voices and predicts when an employee is experiencing stress. That is either really cool or really eerie, if you ask me.

The "maturation of the learning market" is a fascinating trend to me, as an HR professional who grew up in the days of multiple in-class trainings and week-long leadership programs. Learning processes have changed greatly with the advent of some of these innovative HR technologies. Although many larger companies have legacy learning management systems (like Cornerstone, Saba, and SuccessFactors), there are many new and competitive options that focus on scaling video learning to the entire organization. The shift has gone from learning management to learning—with the ability to not only register and track courses online, but to take courses online. Many companies are realizing that these YouTube-like learning applications are a great complement to their existing learning systems, and it is predicted that the demand will continue to grow.

Other trends of note include technologies that manage the contingent workforce, manage wellness, and automate HR processes via artificial intelligence. It is amazing to think about so many interesting and innovative technologies that are being designed for Human Resources. The investment in human capital is one of the most critical investments that a company makes, and it is refreshing to see that this level of innovation is being created to manage, engage, and develop this investment.

Discussion Questions

1. How does real-time performance management compare to the traditional annual performance process? How can a real-time process help an employee be more effective? What are some potential drawbacks?
2. Why do you think learning systems evolved in this way? Is there still a place for group classroom training? What types of learning might require classroom training, and what is better suited for

online and YouTube-style learning?

In the talent review, the potential axis equates to potential for advancement within the organization: low = not ready to advance, medium = close to ready, and high = ready to advance. Potential does *not* equate to the value of an individual within the organization, nor does it state the quality of individual. There are likely many strong performers (top contributors) in every company who prefer to stay in their current role for years and be specialists of their own processes. A specialist or expert may not want to manage people, and thus would be rated as low on potential due to the lack of interest in advancement. Advancement may also mean relocation or lifestyle change that an employee is not willing to make at that time, so the employee would be rated low on potential for that reason. Potential can certainly change over time, given people's individual situations and life circumstances. Potential tends to be the more subjective ratings axis, as it involves some assumptions into what a team member could be capable of based on limited information that is available now.

Exhibit 17.5 This is a flight simulator for a Boeing 737 aircraft. There is a drastic shortage of aircraft pilots, and training future pilots is a critical function with the challenge of limited actual flight training time. Consider how technology helps companies develop skilled workers both on and off the job. (Credit: Michael Coghlan/Flickr/ Attribution 2.0 Generic (CC BY 2.0))

A human resources team member should absolutely facilitate the talent review process and provide leaders with clear session objectives and specific instructions in order maintain the integrity and confidentiality of this important talent process. The book *One Page Talent Management* (Effron and Ort, HBS Press, 2010) describes the talent review meeting as a **talent review calibration process** that "ensures objective performance and potential evaluations, clear development plans, and an understanding of what high potential means in your company. A calibration meeting brings together a manager and her team members to discuss their talent. Each team member presents the performance and potential (PxP) grid that he prepared on direct reports and briefly describes how each person is rated. Other team members contribute their opinions based on their firsthand interactions with that person. The discussion concludes after they have discussed each person, agreed on their final placement, and identified key development steps for them."[11]

After everyone being discussed has been placed in one of the boxes on the 9-box template, the leadership team should discuss key development actions for each employee. (If there isn't time to discuss development activities for each employee, the group should start with the high-potential employees.) After the talent review calibration process is complete, human resources should keep a master list of the documented outcomes, as well as the development activities that were suggested for everyone. HR should follow up with each of the leaders to help with the planning and execution of the development activities as needed. The key outputs of the talent review process include:

- Identification of the "high-potential" employees in the organization
- Definition of development actions/action plans for each employee
- Insight into talent gaps and issues
- Input into the succession planning process

Succession planning generally follows shortly after (if not right after) a talent review because human resources and organizational leadership now have fresh information on the performance and potential of employees in the organization. Succession planning is a key process used to identify the depth of talent on the "bench" and the readiness of that talent to move into new roles. The process can be used to identify gaps or a lack of bench strength at any levels of the organization, but it is usually reserved for leadership roles and other key roles in the organization. In succession planning, human resources will generally sit down with the group leader to discuss succession planning for his group and create a defined list of leadership and other critical roles that will be reviewed for potential successors.

Once the roles for succession planning analysis have been defined, both HR and the business leader will define the following elements for each role:

- Name of incumbent
- Attrition risk of incumbent
- Names of short-term successor candidates (ready in <1 year)
- Names of mid-term successor candidates (ready in 1–3 years)
- Names of long-term successor candidates (ready in 3+ years)
- Optional—9-box rating next to each successor candidate's name

The names of longer-term successor candidates are not as critical, but it is always helpful to understand the depth of the bench. With the information recently collected during the talent review process, HR and management will have a lot of quality information on the internal successor candidates. It is important to include external successor candidates in the succession planning analysis as well. If there are no candidates that are identified as short-, mid-, or long-term successor candidates for a role, then the word "EXTERNAL" should automatically be placed next to that role. Even if there are internal candidates named, any external successor candidates should still be captured in the analysis as appropriate.

Talent reviews and succession planning processes both generate excellent discussions and very insightful information on the state of talent in the organization. Human resources facilitates both processes, in very close partnership with the business, and ultimately keeps the output information from the sessions—i.e., the final succession plan, the final 9-box, and the follow-up development actions and activities as defined in the talent review session. With this information, human resources possesses a level of knowledge that will allow it to drive talent development and coach managers on the follow-up actions that they need to set in motion. Some examples of follow-up development activities that may be appropriate based on the outputs of the succession and 9-box events include **training, stretch assignments, individual assessments,** and **individual development plans**. Training and training plans identify the learning events that an individual would benefit from, either in a classroom or online format. Stretch assignments may be an appropriate development action for an employee who is being tested for or who wants to take on additional responsibility. Individual assessments, such as a **360 assessment** for managers, is a good developmental tool to provide feedback from manager, peers, direct reports, customers, or others who interact with the employee regularly. Finally, an individual development plan is an important document that employees should use to map out their personal development goals and actions, and to track their own status and progress toward those goals.

Talent development is a collection of organization-wide processes that help to evaluate talent strengths and gaps within the organization. Although many of the processes are carried out in a group setting, the output of talent development needs to be very individualized via a collection of development tools and strategies to enhance performance. Human resources is a key resource and partner for these tools and strategies, and thus plays a critical role in the future of talent for the organization.

Conclusion

Human resource management is a complex and often difficult field because of the nature of the key area of focus—people. In working with people, we begin to understand both the expressed and the hidden drives—intentions and emotions that add complexity and additional context to the processes and tasks that we set forth. We also begin to understand that an organization is a group of individuals, and that human resources plays a critical role in ensuring that there are philosophies, structures, and processes in place to guide, teach, and motivate individual employees to perform at their best possible levels.

CONCEPT CHECK

1. What is the difference between the performance and potential categories used in the talent review?
2. What roles should an organization discuss as part of the succession planning process?

Key Terms

360 assessment An evaluation tool that collects feedback from manager, peers, direct reports, and customers.

9-box A matrix tool used to evaluate an organization's talent pool based on performance and potential factors.

Competencies A set of defined behaviors that an organization might utilize to define standards for success.

Employee life cycle The various stages of engagement of an employee—attraction, recruitment, onboarding, development, retention, separation.

Employer-employee relationship The employment relationship; the legal link between employers and employees that exists when a person performs work or services under specific conditions in return for payment.

Human capital The skills, knowledge, and experience of an individual or group, and that value to an organization.

Human resource management The management of people within organizations, focusing on the touchpoints of the employee life cycle.

Human resources compliance The HR role to ensure adherence to laws and regulations that govern the employment relationship.

Merit matrix A calculation table that provides a framework for merit increases based on performance levels.

Pay-for-performance model The process and structure for tying individual performance levels to rewards levels

Performance management The process by which an organization ensures that its overall goals are being met by evaluating the performance of individuals within that organization.

Society for Human Resource Management The world's largest HR professional society, with more than 285,000 members in more than 165 countries. It is a leading provider of resources serving the needs of HR professionals.

Succession planning The process of identifying and developing new leaders and high-potential employees to replace current employees at a future time.

Talent acquisition The process of finding and acquiring skilled candidates for employment within a company; it generally refers to a long-term view of building talent pipelines, rather than short-term recruitment.

Talent development Integrated HR processes that are created to attract, develop, motivate, and retain employees.

Talent review calibration process The meeting in which an organization's 9-box matrix is reviewed and discussed, with input and sharing from organizational leadership.

Total rewards strategy As coined by World at Work, includes compensation, benefits, work-life effectiveness, recognition, performance management, and talent development.

Training, stretch assignments, individual assessments, individual development plans These are tools that may be used in talent development:
Training—a forum for learning in person or online
Stretch assignments—challenge roles for high-potential employees
Individual assessments—personality and work style inventories of employees
Individual development plans—documents that highlight an individual employee's opportunities for growth and path of action

War for talent Coined by McKinsey & Company in 1997, it refers to the increasing competition for recruiting and retaining talented employees.

 Summary of Learning Outcomes

17.1 An Introduction to Human Resource Management

1. What has been the evolution of human resource management over the years, and what is the current value it provides to an organization?

Human resource management began in its first "wave" as a primarily compliance-type function, with the HR staff charged with enforcing compliance of employees and running the ongoing administrative processes. In the second wave, HR became focused on the design of HR practice areas, which could be built upon best-practice models. Wave 3 of HR brought with it the concept that HR should be a true partner to the business and should support the business strategy through its programs and services. Finally, in the fourth wave, HR is still a partner to the business, but it looks outside of the business to customers, investors, and communities to see how it can be competitive in terms of customer share, investor confidence, and community reputation.

Some key areas that HR supports within the employee life cycle process include: human resources compliance, employee selection and hiring, performance management, compensation rewards, and talent development and succession planning.

17.2 Human Resource Management and Compliance

2. How does the human resources compliance role of HR provide value to a company?

Human resources helps protect the company and its employees to ensure that they are adhering to the numerous regulations and laws that govern the employment relationship. The impact of noncompliance can be very costly and can be in the form of financial, legal, or reputational cost. Some of the key legislation that HR manages compliance around includes the Fair Labor Standards Act (FLSA), the Age Discrimination in Employment Act (ADEA), the Americans with Disabilities Act (ADA), and the Family and Medical Leave Act (FMLA), among others.

Some of the best practices for informing and holding employees accountable are to provide education and training to explain the regulations, to provide reference documentation for guidance with the regulations, and to schedule regular compliance audits to ensure that processes are being followed. Scheduling regular internal HR audits help the organization plan and feel comfortable with its level of preparedness and illustrates the value that a strong HR group can bring to the organization.

17.3 Performance Management

3. How do performance management practices impact company performance?

Performance management is a critical business process that the human resources group manages for the business. Performance management aligns the work of individual groups with the overall business objectives and enables the business to work toward its goals. Performance management should also help the company differentiate between different levels of employee performance through the management of feedback and a rewards structure.

Performance management also allows a company to identify its poor performers and provides a consistent process for tracking and managing poor performance in a manner that is fair and consistent with the law. There has been much discussion of best practices for a performance management process beyond a formal, annual process that often feels cumbersome to the business. However formal or informal, human resource management needs to ensure that the process helps to differentiate different levels of performance, manages the flow of feedback, and is consistent and fair for all employees.

17.4 Influencing Employee Performance and Motivation

4. How do companies use rewards strategies to influence employee performance and motivation?

Companies use rewards strategies to influence employee performance and motivation by differentiating between the various levels of performance. This strategy is called pay for performance, and it ties the employee's performance level to a consistent framework of rewards at each level. Research indicates that the primary reason that companies implement pay for performance is to be able to recognize and reward their high performers.

To implement a pay-for-performance structure, HR and the organization first need to define a compensation philosophy, then perform a review of the financial implications of such a system. Gaps in the current system must be identified, and compensation practices should be updated in accordance with the determined pay-for-performance design. Finally, communication and training are key to help employees understand the context and philosophy, as well as the specific methodology.

17.5 Building an Organization for the Future

5. What is talent acquisition, and how can it create a competitive advantage for a company?

Human resource management plays the important role of managing the talent processes for an organization, and it is critical in the process of acquiring talent from the outside. Talent acquisition is the process of determining what roles are still needed in the organization, where to find people, and whom to hire. Hiring top talent is a key source of competitive advantage for a company, and not all organizations are good at doing it.

The impact of hiring is especially magnified when you talk about top leadership talent. The right leadership candidate can make all the difference in an organization's growth, performance, and trajectory over the years. HR should work with the business to assess need and specifics of the job, develop a pool of candidates, and then assess candidates for the right person to bring into the organization.

17.6 Talent Development and Succession Planning

6. What are the benefits of talent development and succession planning?

Talent development and succession planning processes provide organizations with the systems needed to assess and develop employees and to make the appropriate decisions on their internal movement and development. One important talent development process involves a talent review, in which leadership discusses the employees in its groups in terms of their performance and potential. Performance is based on current performance management evaluations on the current role. Potential is based on behavioral indications that would predict future high performance and promotability in an organization. There is then a discussion on the follow-up actions and development plans for the employees, based on where they fall in the performance/potential matrix. The benefit of this process is that the organization gains a better understanding of where the top talent is within the organization and can make plans to manage the development of that talent.

Another key process for managing talent is succession planning. In this process, leadership and HR meet to identify leadership roles and other critical roles in the organization, and then they discuss a potential pipeline of internal and external successor candidates at different levels of readiness for the role. The output of succession planning is that an organization gets to understand the depth of its talent bench and knows the gap areas where it may need to focus on developing or acquiring additional candidates.

Chapter Review Questions

1. What are the four "waves" of the human resource management evolution?
2. What are some of the key regulations that human resources must manage compliance with?
3. What are some of the unintended consequences of a forced ranking system?
4. What are some of the performance management challenges that must be addressed, no matter what the system?
5. Why are many companies interested in moving to a pay-for-performance strategy?
6. What are the main process steps for implementing pay for performance?
7. What are some best practices for recruiting new leadership candidates?
8. Describe the steps of a talent review session.
9. What is the difference between performance and potential?
10. How can you tell if a candidate has potential?

Management Skills Application Exercises

1. How has human resource management's evolution over the years helped to make it a better partner to the business? In what way would you expect HRM to continue to evolve over the years?
2. Do you believe that a formal, annual performance management process is necessary to help an organization reach its goals? Why or why not? What are the minimum process requirements that must be met to successfully evaluate performance?
3. .Is it possible for an organization to reward people fairly without implementing a pay-for-performance process? Why or why not? Do you see any pitfalls to a pay-for-performance process?
4. How does the "war for talent" impact talent acquisition processes? How can HR be more successful working with the business to navigate the competitive talent landscape?
5. What are the benefits of having talent review calibration processes? What is the downside of the process? Should an organization let employees know what their talent review "rating" is? Why or why not?

Managerial Decision Exercises

1. You have been hired as a new Finance VP, and you oversee a team of almost 30 people. Your HR manager has recently informed you that there have been several employee relations in your group in the recent past, and you are concerned about the level of knowledge that your management team has around dealing with these issues. What could you do to close the gap in knowledge and mitigate the risk of issues in your group?
2. Your company has decided to drop their formal, annual performance management process and move to a system based on ongoing feedback and communication with employees. You are concerned because you have always been careful to differentiate your employees by performance level, and you're worried that this will hurt your stronger employees. How can use ensure that your feedback and communication with employees provides performance management, despite the lack of a formal system?
3. Your company has recently implemented a pay-for-performance model for compensation. This worries you because you know that your employees will be even more upset with their performance ratings if they know that they are tied to compensation. What actions can you take to start to prepare for this change?
4. You are the director of an engineering organization and have been fighting the "war for talent" for a while. It seems that whenever you have a role vacancy, you let HR know but it takes forever to find

someone—and the candidate often turns down the job. What are some ways to better partner with HR to get ahead of the curve for the next time?

5. You are the VP of a line of business at an international manufacturing company. You and several of your long-time colleagues will be retiring over the next few years, and you need to start thinking about talent and succession planning. You are going into a talent review discussion next week, and you're realizing that you have a dearth of potential within your organization. What are some actions you (and HR) can take now to ensure that your business unit isn't floundering when you leave for retirement?

Critical Thinking Case

Zappos, Holacracy, and Human Resource Management

In 2013, Zappos was performing well under the leadership of Tony Hsieh and was getting ready to take on a new challenge that would, among other things, push the boundaries of traditional human resource management. Although business was booming, Tony Hsieh was not a man who wanted to be in status quo mode for too long, so he set out to implement an organizational and cultural change called Holacracy. Zappos was the largest and best known of the 300 companies worldwide that had adopted Holacracy—a new form of hierarchy that is a "flexible, self-governing structure, where there are no fixed jobs but simply temporary functional roles."

In a Holacracy, the main unit is called the "circle," which is a distinct yet fluid team. Leadership became similarly fluid with the changing circles. Circles are designed to meet certain goals and are created and disbanded as project needs change. The intent is that people self-select to work on projects that they want to work on and that they have the skills for. Tony also removed all previous titles. The role of manager went away and was replaced with three roles: "lead links" would focus on guiding the work in the circles; "mentors" would work on employee growth and development; and "compensation appraisers" would work on determining employees' salaries. In 2015, he decided to further break down the divisions between many of the functions, changing them all to business-centric circles. There were changes to almost every human resource management structure that you can think of, and there were quite a few growing pains within the organization. Zappos began to look at employee pay, and Holacracy seemed to have a steep learning curve for many people, even though a "constitution" was created to provide guidance. Zappos was also facing 14% attrition, as some of the rapid and excessive changes were wearing on employees. Tony was a visionary, but for a lot of people it was hard to catch up and see the same vision.

From a human resource management perspective, there could be some positive attributes of a Holacracy if it were to succeed—such as building engagement and helping to build talent and skill sets. There were also a few risks that needed to be dealt with carefully. When you create an organization in which people don't have set teams or projects but instead determine what they want to work on, one of the big challenges is going to be determining the level and nature of their role, as well as the compensation for that role. If Holacracy is compared to a consulting organization, in which consultants are brought into different projects with different requirements, it is critical to first determine the level of their consultant role (based on their education, skills, experience, etc.) so that they can properly move from project to project yet maintain a role of a certain level. That level is then tied to a specific pay scale, so the same consultant will receive the same salary no matter which project he is on. If that consultant is "on the bench," or not placed on a project (or self-placed, in the case of Holacracy), then after a certain defined period that consultant may be at risk of termination.

Holacracy is in some ways a challenging concept to think about, and self-management may not be able to work in all environments. A company that is implementing a Holacracy may find that they are able to master the process of self-selection of work in the "circles." The "task" part of the equation may not be much of an issue once people figure out how to navigate the circles. However, the "people" part of the equation may need some work. The greatest challenge may lie in the structures and processes of human resource management that ultimately define the employer-employee relationship.

Critical Thinking Questions

1. What are some of the human resource management processes that might be enhanced by a Holacracy? What processes will be challenged?
2. Do you think that a Holacracy can be compared to a consulting company? How are they similar,s and how are they different? Can you think of work areas or industries in which Holacracy would be very difficult to implement?

Sources: Askin and Petriglieri, *"Tony Hsieh at Zappos: Structure, Culture, and Change"*, INSEAD Business School Press, 2016.

18

Stress and Well Being

Exhibit 18.1 (Credit: Steven Lilley/ flickr/ Attribution 2.0 Generic (CC BY 2.0))

Introduction

Learning Outcomes

After reading this chapter, you should be able to answer these questions:

1. How do you recognize the symptoms of stress in yourself and in others?
2. What are the underlying causes of stress in a particular situation?
3. How do managers and organizations minimize the dysfunctional consequences of stressful behavior?
4. What are the remedies for job-related stress, and how can managers motivate employees to participate actively in health promotion efforts for the benefit of all concerned?

EXPLORING MANAGERIAL CAREERS

Workplace Perks: Are They Worth It?

Often tech companies top the charts as the best places to work, touting fancy benefits and big-time perks. However, recent studies have shown that big tech companies can also be extremely stressful places to work. According to research conducted by PayScale.com, more turnover can be expected at companies like Facebook and Amazon due to employees reporting low levels of job satisfaction and job meaning. Also topping the charts for Amazon are reported levels of stress, higher than the tech average—64 percent compared to 58 percent.

"Amazon will work you to death, either you are gone after two years, or you stay forever because you love working that hard," stated a former employee of Amazon's cloud business.

Adding to the workplace environment is the company culture. Long hours, often times on weekends, and the expectation of staying connected to e-mail 24/7 add to the stressful workplace.

"Amazon is a culture of self-driven workaholics," stated Lydia Leong, research analyst for Gartner covering the company. "There is a culture of frugality, and unlike many recent companies in Silicon Valley, you are not compensated for it with an array of free services."

These conditions may be considered acceptable by many individuals that choose to continue at Amazon and are motivated by the fast-paced environment, but according to the American Institute of Stress, this can cause health risks. Sixty-two percent of individuals studied routinely found that they end the day with work-related neck pain, 44 percent reported stressed-out eyes, 38 percent complained of hurting hands, and 34 percent reported difficulty in sleeping because they were too stressed out.

Work-related stress is one of the most prominent—and costly—issues of today. The World Health Organization reports that physical and mental stress costs businesses $300 billion each year, not to mention the tolls on productivity. However we look at it, stress and stress-related problems have a direct impact on the effective management of organizations, and contemporary managers must be willing to commit the necessary energy and resources to minimize the dysfunctional consequences of such problems if they are to achieve an effective level of operations.

Sources: L. Rao, "Amazon: Working There Will Kills You. But You'll Love It," *New York Times*, August 17, 2015, http://fortune.com/2015/08/17/amazon-new-york-times-workers/; "Tech Industry Salaries," *Payscale*, accessed January 12, 2019, https://www.payscale.com/data/tech-industry-salaries; I. Ivanova, " The Most Stressed-Out Tech Companies," CBS News, July 25, 2017, https://www.cbsnews.com/news/tech-most-stressful-companies/; "Workplace Stress," *Stress.org*, accessed January 12, 2019, https://www.stress.org/workplace-stress/; B. Covert, "Longer Hours, More Stress, No Extra Pay: It's Not Just Amazon, It's the Modern Workplace," *The Motley Fool*, August 26, 2015, https://www.thenation.com/article/longer-hours-more-stress-no-extra-pay-its-not-just-amazon-its-the-modern-workplace/.

In this chapter, we will examine several aspects of job-related stress and consider several ways in which corporations can facilitate employee health and well-being. We begin by looking at problems of work adjustment as a general framework for the study of stress.

18.1 Problems of Work Adjustment

1. How do you recognize the symptoms of stress in yourself and in others?

Failure to adjust to work represents a major problem in industry today. It has been estimated that between 80 and 90 percent of industrial accidents are caused by personal factors.[1] Turnover, absenteeism, drug abuse, alcoholism, and sabotage remain relatively permanent fixtures of most contemporary work organizations. To the extent that individuals are unable to adjust to work, we would expect them to persist in counterproductive behavior.

W. S. Neff has identified five types of people who have problems adjusting to work. He suggests that each of the five types represents a "clinical picture of different varieties of work psychopathology":[2]

- *Type I:* People who lack motivation to work. These individuals have a negative conception of the work role and choose to avoid it.
- *Type II:* People whose predominating response to the demand to be productive is fear or anxiety.
- *Type III:* People who are characterized predominantly by open hostility and aggression.
- *Type IV:* People who are characterized by marked dependency. These people often exhibit the

characteristic of helplessness. They are constantly seeking advice from others and are unable to initiate any action on their own.

- *Type V:* People who display a marked degree of social naïveté. These individuals lack perception when it comes to the needs and feelings of others and may not realize that their behavior elicits reactions from and has an effect on others. Typically, these individuals are socially inept and unaware of appropriate behavior in ordinary social situations.

Several important points follow from this analysis. First, note that failure to adjust to a normal job or work schedule does not automatically imply that an individual is lazy or stupid. Several deeply ingrained psychological problems keep people from making normal adjustments in many cases. Second, note that only one of the five types (Type I) exhibits a motivational problem. Managers must look beyond motivation for answers to the psychopathology of work. One type (Type V) exhibits a form of personality disorder, or at least social immaturity. But the remaining three types—those exhibiting anxiety, aggression, or dependency—all have problems relating not only to personality, but more importantly, to how the nature of the job affects that personality. In fact, anxiety, aggression, and dependency are major factors inherent in stressful jobs in organizations. Hence, it seems that at least three of the five reasons for failure to adjust to work relate to the extent to which the job is experienced as stressful and causes the individual to want to withdraw.

It has been wisely observed that "if, under stress, a man goes all to pieces, he will probably be told to pull himself together. It would be more effective to help him identify the pieces and to understand why they have come apart."[3] This is the role of the contemporary manager in dealing with stress. Managers cannot simply ignore the existence of stress on the job. Instead, they have a responsibility to understand stress and its causes.

We will explore the topic of work-related stress in several stages, first examining major organizational and personal influences on stress, then considering several outcomes of stress, and finally exploring methods for coping with stress on the job. Throughout, emphasis will be placed on how stress and its consequences affect people at work and what role managers can play in attempting to minimize the effects of stress on both the individual and the organization. We will make liberal use of practical examples, and, as usual, you will be given an opportunity to evaluate yourself on several aspects of stress and wellness in organizations.

Work-Related Stress

For our purposes here, **stress** will be defined as a physical and emotional reaction to potentially threatening aspects of the environment. This definition points to a poor fit between individuals and their environments. Either excessive demands are being made, or reasonable demands are being made that individuals are ill-equipped to handle. Under stress, individuals are unable to respond to environmental stimuli without undue psychological and/or physiological damage, such as chronic fatigue, tension, or high blood pressure. This damage resulting from experienced stress is usually referred to as **strain**.

Before we examine the concept of work-related stress in detail, several important points need to be made. First, stress is pervasive in the work environment.[4] Most of us experience stress at some time. For instance, a job may require too much or too little from us. In fact, almost any aspect of the work environment is capable of producing stress. Stress can result from excessive noise, light, or heat; too much or too little responsibility; too much or too little work to accomplish; or too much or too little supervision.

Second, it is important to note that all people do not react in the same way to stressful situations, even in the same occupation. One individual (a high-need achiever) may thrive on a certain amount of job-related tension; this tension may serve to activate the achievement motive. A second individual may respond to this tension by worrying about her inability to cope with the situation. Managers must recognize the central role of individual differences in the determination of experienced stress.

Often the key reason for the different reactions is a function of the different interpretations of a given event that different people make, especially concerning possible or probable consequences associated with the event. For example, the same report is required of student A and student B on the same day. Student A interprets the report in a very stressful way and imagines all the negative consequences of submitting a poor report. Student B interprets the report differently and sees it as an opportunity to demonstrate the things she has learned and imagines the positive consequences of turning in a high-quality report. Although both students face essentially the same event, they interpret and react to it differently.

Third, all stress is not necessarily bad. Although highly stressful situations invariably have dysfunctional consequences, moderate levels of stress often serve useful purposes. A moderate amount of job-related tension not only keeps us alert to environmental stimuli (possible dangers and opportunities), but in addition often provides a useful motivational function. Some experts argue that the best and most satisfying work that employees do is work performed under moderate stress. Some stress may be necessary for psychological growth, creative activities, and the acquisition of new skills. Learning to drive a car or play a piano or run a particular machine typically creates tension that is instrumental in skill development. It is only when the level of stress increases or when stress is prolonged that physical or psychological problems emerge.

General Adaptation Syndrome

The general physiological response to stressful events is believed to follow a fairly consistent pattern known as the **general adaptation syndrome**.[5] General adaptation syndrome consists of three stages (see **Exhibit 18.2**). The first stage, *alarm,* occurs at the first sign of stress. Here the body prepares to fight stress by releasing hormones from the endocrine glands. During this initial stage, heartbeat and respiration increase, blood sugar level rises, muscles tense up, pupils dilate, and digestion slows. At this stage the body prepares basically for a "fight or flight" response. That is, the body prepares to either get away from the threat or to combat it. Following this initial shock, the body moves into the second stage, *resistance.* The body attempts to repair any damage and return to a condition of stability and equilibrium. If successful, physical signs of stress will disappear. If the stress continues long enough, however, the body's capacity for adaptation becomes exhausted. In this third stage, *exhaustion,* defenses wear away, and the individual experiences a variety of stress-related illnesses, including headaches, ulcers, and high blood pressure. This third stage is the most severe and presents the greatest threat both to individuals and to organizations.

Exhibit 18.2 The General Adaptation Syndrome (Attribution: Copyright Rice University, OpenStax, under CC BY-NC-SA 4.0 license)

Types of Stress: Frustration and Anxiety

There are several different ways to categorize stress. However, from a managerial perspective, it is useful to focus on only two forms: frustration and anxiety. **Frustration** refers to a psychological reaction to an obstruction or impediment to goal-oriented behavior. Frustration occurs when an individual wishes to pursue a certain course of action but is prevented from doing so. This obstruction may be externally or internally caused. Examples of people experiencing obstacles that lead to frustration include a salesperson who continually fails to make a sale, a machine operator who cannot keep pace with the machine, or even a person ordering coffee from a machine that fails to return the correct change. The prevalence of frustration in work organizations should be obvious from this and other examples.

Whereas frustration is a reaction to an obstruction in instrumental activities or behavior, **anxiety** is a feeling of inability to deal with anticipated harm. Anxiety occurs when people do not have appropriate responses or plans for coping with anticipated problems. It is characterized by a sense of dread, a foreboding, and a persistent apprehension of the future for reasons that are sometimes unknown to the individual.

What causes anxiety in work organizations? Hamner and Organ suggest several factors:

"Differences in power in organizations which leave people with a feeling of vulnerability to administrative decisions adversely affecting them; frequent changes in organizations, which make existing behavior plans obsolete; competition, which creates the inevitability that some persons lose 'face,' esteem, and status; and job ambiguity (especially when it is coupled with pressure). To these may be added some related factors, such as lack of job feedback, volatility in the organization's economic environment, job insecurity, and high visibility of one's performance (successes as well as failures). Obviously, personal, nonorganizational factors come into play as well, such as physical illness, problems at home, unrealistically high personal goals, and estrangement from one's colleagues or one's peer group."[6]

CONCEPT CHECK 

1. What are the 5 types of people identified by W. S. Neff?
2. What is work related stress?

18.2 Organizational Influences on Stress

2. What are the underlying causes of stress in a particular situation?

We will now consider several factors that have been found to influence both frustration and anxiety; we will present a general model of stress, including its major causes and its outcomes. Following this, we will explore several mechanisms by which employees and their managers cope with or reduce experienced stress in organizations. The model presented here draws heavily on the work of several social psychologists at the Institute for Social Research of the University of Michigan, including John French, Robert Caplan, Robert Kahn, and Daniel Katz. In essence, the proposed model identifies two major sources of stress: organizational sources and individual sources. In addition, the moderating effects of social support and hardiness are considered. These influences are shown in **Exhibit 18.3**.

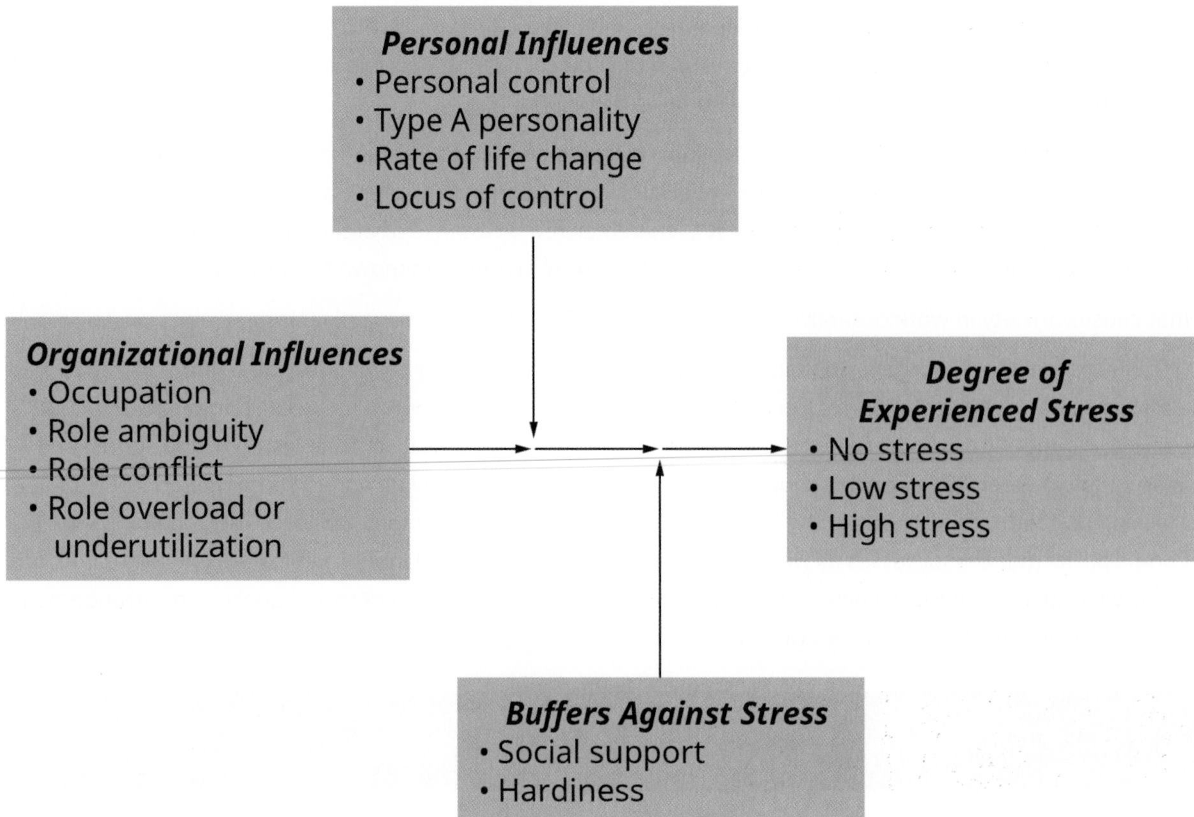

Exhibit 18.3 Major Influences on Job-Related Stress (Attribution: Copyright Rice University, OpenStax, under CC BY-NC-SA 4.0 license)

We begin with organizational influences on stress. Although many factors in the work environment have been found to influence the extent to which people experience stress on the job, four factors have been shown to be particularly strong. These are (1) occupational differences, (2) role ambiguity, (3) role conflict, and (4) role overload and underutilization. We will consider each of these factors in turn.

Occupational Differences

Tension and job stress are prevalent in our contemporary society and can be found in a wide variety of jobs. Consider, for example, the following quotes from interviews with working people. The first is from a bus driver:

"You have your tension. Sometimes you come close to having an accident, that upsets you. You just escape maybe by a hair or so. Sometimes maybe you get a disgruntled passenger on there who starts a big argument. Traffic. You have someone who cuts you off or stops in front of the bus. There's a lot of tension behind that. . . . Most of the time you have to drive for the other drivers, to avoid hitting them. So, you take the tension home with you. Most of the drivers, they'll suffer from hemorrhoids, kidney trouble, and such as that. I had a case of ulcers behind it."[7]

Or consider the plight of a bank teller:

"Some days, when you're aggravated about something, you carry it after you leave the job. Certain people are bad days. (Laughs.) The type of person who will walk in and say, 'My car's double-parked outside. Would you hurry up, lady?' . . . you want to say, 'Hey, why did you double-park your car? So now you're going to blame me if you get a ticket, 'cause you were dumb enough to leave it there?' But you can't. That's the one hassle. You can't say anything back. The customer's always right."[8]

Stress is experienced by workers in many jobs: administrative assistants, assembly-line workers, foremen, waitresses, and managers. In fact, it is difficult to find jobs that are without some degree of stress. We seldom talk about jobs without stress; instead, we talk about the degree or magnitude of the stress.

The work roles that people fill have a substantial influence on the degree to which they experience stress.[9] These differences do *not* follow the traditional blue-collar/white-collar dichotomy, however. In general, available evidence suggests that high-stress occupations are those in which incumbents have little control over their jobs, work under relentless time pressures or threatening physical conditions, or have major responsibilities for either human or financial resources.

A recent study attempted to identify those occupations that were most (and least) stressful.[10] The study results are presented in **Table 18.1**. As shown, high-stress occupations (firefighter, race car driver, and astronaut) are typified by the stress-producing characteristics noted above, whereas low-stress occupations (musical instrument repairperson, medical records technician, and librarian) are not. It can therefore be concluded that a major source of general stress emerges from the occupation at which one is working.

The Most and Least Stressful Jobs	
High-Stress Jobs	**Low-Stress Jobs**
1. Firefighter	1. Musical instrument repairperson
2. Race car driver	2. Industrial machine repairperson
3. Astronaut	3. Medical records technician
4. Surgeon	4. Pharmacist
5. NFL football player	5. Medical assistant
6. City police officer	6. Typist/word processor
7. Osteopath	7. Librarian
8. State police officer	8. Janitor
9. Air traffic controller	9. Bookkeeper
10. Mayor	10. Forklift operator
Source: Adapted from *The Jobs Rated Almanac* by Les Krantz. 1988 Les Krantz.	

Table 18.1 (Attribution: Copyright Rice University, OpenStax, under CC BY-NC-SA 4.0 license)

A second survey, by the American Psychological Association, examined the specific causes of stress.[11] The results of the study showed that the most frequently cited reasons for stress among administrative professionals are unspecified job requirements (38 percent), work interfering with personal time (36 percent), job insecurity (33 percent), and lack of participation in decision-making (33 percent).

Finally, a study among managers found that they, too, are subject to considerable stress arising out of the nature of managerial work.[12] The more common work stressors for managers are shown in **Table 18.2**.

Typical Stressors Faced by Managers	
Stressor	Example
Role ambiguity	Unclear job duties
Role conflict	Manager is both a boss and a subordinate.
Role overload	Too much work, too little time
Unrealistic expectations	Managers are often asked to do the impossible.
Difficult decisions	Managers have to make decisions that adversely affect subordinates.
Managerial failure	Manager fails to achieve expected results.
Subordinate failure	Subordinates let the boss down.
Source: Adapted from D. Zauderer and J. Fox, "Resiliency in the Face of Stress," *Management Solutions*, November 1987, pp. 32–33.	

Table 18.2 (Attribution: Copyright Rice University, OpenStax, under CC BY-NC-SA 4.0 license)

These stressors range from task ambiguity and role conflict to overwork and the possibility of failure. Indeed, responsibility for others may be the greatest stressor of all for managers. Studies in the United States and abroad indicate that managers and supervisors consistently have more ulcers and experience more hypertension than the people they supervise. Responsibility for people was found to be a greater influence on stress than responsibility for nonpersonal factors such as budgets, projects, equipment, and other property. As noted by French and Caplan:

"If there is any truth to the adage that 'man's greatest enemy is himself,' it can be found in these data—it is the responsibility which organizational members have for other organizational members, rather than the responsibility for impersonal aspects of the organization, which constitutes the more significant organizational stress."[13]

Thus, a person's occupation or profession represents a major cause of stress-related problems at work. In addition to occupation, however, and indeed closely related to it, is the problem of one's role expectations in the organization. Three interrelated role processes will be examined as they relate to experienced stress: role ambiguity, role conflict, and role overload or underutilization.

Role Ambiguity

The first role process variable to be discussed here is **role ambiguity**. When individuals have inadequate information concerning their roles, they experience role ambiguity. Uncertainty over job definition takes many forms, including not knowing expectations for performance, not knowing how to meet those expectations, and not knowing the consequences of job behavior. Role ambiguity is particularly strong among managerial jobs, where role definitions and task specification lack clarity (refer to **Table 18.2**). For example, the manager of accounts payable may not be sure of the quantity and quality standards for her department. The uncertainty of the absolute level of these two performance standards or their relative importance to each other makes predicting outcomes such as performance evaluation, salary increases, or promotion opportunities equally difficult. All of this contributes to increased stress for the manager. Role ambiguity can also occur among nonmanagerial employees—for example, those whose supervisors fail to make sufficient time to clarify role expectations, thus leaving them unsure of how best to contribute to departmental and organizational goals.

How prevalent is role ambiguity at work? In two independent surveys of employees, it was found that 35 percent of one sample (a national random sample of male employees) and 60 percent of the other sample (primarily scientists and engineers) reported some form of role ambiguity.[14] Hence, ambiguity of job role is not an isolated event.

Role ambiguity has been found to lead to several negative stress-related outcomes. French and Caplan summarized their study findings as follows:

"In summary, role ambiguity, which appears to be widespread, (1) produces psychological strain and dissatisfaction; (2) leads to underutilization of human resources; and (3) leads to feelings of futility on how to cope with the organizational environment."[15]

In other words, role ambiguity has far-reaching consequences beyond experienced stress, including employee turnover and absenteeism, poor coordination and utilization of human resources, and increased operating costs because of inefficiency.

It should be noted, however, that not everyone responds in the same way to role ambiguity. Studies have shown that some people have a higher **tolerance for ambiguity** and are less affected by role ambiguity (in terms of stress, reduced performance, or propensity to leave) than those with a low tolerance for ambiguity.[16] Thus, again we can see the role of individual differences in moderating the effects of environmental stimuli on individual behavior and performance.

Role Conflict

The second role-related factor in stress is **role conflict**. This may be defined as the simultaneous occurrence of two (or more) sets of pressures or expectations; compliance with one would make it difficult to comply with the other. In other words, role conflict occurs when an employee is placed in a situation where contradictory demands are placed upon her. For instance, a factory worker may find himself in a situation where the supervisor is demanding greater output, yet the work group is demanding a restriction of output. Similarly, a secretary who reports to several supervisors may face a conflict over whose work to do first.

One of the best-known studies of role conflict and stress was carried out by Robert Kahn and his colleagues at the University of Michigan. Kahn studied 53 managers and their subordinates (a total of 381 people), examining the nature of each person's role and how it affected subsequent behavior. As a result of the investigation, the following conclusions emerged:

Contradictory role expectations give rise to opposing role pressures (role conflict), which generally have the following effects on the emotional experience of the focal person: intensified internal conflicts, increased tension associated with various aspects of the job, reduced satisfaction with the job and its various components, and decreased confidence in superiors and in the organization as a whole. The strain experienced by those in conflict situations leads to various coping responses, social and psychological withdrawal (reduction in communication and attributed influence) among them.

Finally, the presence of conflict in one's role tends to undermine her reactions with her role senders and to produce weaker bonds of trust, respect, and attraction. It is quite clear that role conflicts are costly for the person in emotional and interpersonal terms. They may be costly to the organization, which depends on effective coordination and collaboration within and among its parts.[17]

Other studies have found similar results concerning the serious side effects of role conflict both for individuals and organizations.[18] It should again be recognized, however, that personality differences may serve to moderate the impact of role conflict on stress. In particular, it has been found that introverts and people who lack flexibility respond more negatively to role conflict than do others.[19] In any event, managers must be aware of the problem of role conflict and look for ways to avert negative consequences. One way this can be accomplished is by ensuring that their subordinates are not placed in contradictory positions within the organization; that is, subordinates should have a clear idea of what the manager's job expectations are and should not be placed in "win-lose" situations.

Role Overload and Underutilization

Finally, in addition to role ambiguity and conflict, a third aspect of role processes has also been found to represent an important influence on experienced stress—namely, the extent to which employees feel either overloaded or underutilized in their job responsibilities. **Role overload** is a condition in which individuals feel they are being asked to do more than time or ability permits. Individuals often experience role overload as a conflict between quantity and quality of performance. *Quantitative* overload consists of having more work than can be done in a given time period, such as a clerk expected to process 1,000 applications per day when only 850 are possible. Overload can be visualized as a continuum ranging from too little to do to too much to do. *Qualitative* role overload, on the other hand, consists of being taxed beyond one's skills, abilities, and knowledge. It can be seen as a continuum ranging from too-easy work to too-difficult work. For example, a manager who is expected to increase sales but has little idea of why sales are down or what to do to get sales up can experience qualitative role overload. It is important to note that *either* extreme represents a bad fit between the abilities of the employee and the demands of the work environment. A good fit occurs at that point on both scales of workload where the abilities of the individual are relatively consistent with the demands of the job.

There is evidence that both quantitative and qualitative role overload are prevalent in our society. A review of findings suggests that between 44 and 73 percent of white-collar workers experience a form of role overload.[20] What induces this overload? As a result of a series of studies, French and Caplan concluded that a major factor influencing overload is the high achievement needs of many managers. Need for achievement correlated very highly both with the number of hours worked per week and with a questionnaire measure of role overload.[21] In other words, much role overload is apparently self-induced.

Similarly, the concept of **role underutilization** should also be acknowledged as a source of experienced stress. Role underutilization occurs when employees are allowed to use only a few of their skills and abilities, even though they are required to make heavy use of them. The most prevalent characteristic of role underutilization is monotony, where the worker performs the same routine task (or set of tasks) over and over. Other situations that make for underutilization include total dependence on machines for determining work pace and sustained positional or postural constraint. Several studies have found that underutilization often leads to low self-esteem, low life satisfaction, and increased frequency of nervous complaints and symptoms.[22]

Both role overload and role underutilization have been shown to influence psychological and physiological reactions to the job. The inverted U-shaped relationship between the extent of role utilization and stress is shown in **Exhibit 18.5**. As shown, the least stress is experienced at that point where an employee's abilities and skills are in balance with the requirements of the job. This is where performance should be highest.

Employees should be highly motivated and should have high energy levels, sharp perception, and calmness. (Recall that many of the current efforts to redesign jobs and improve the quality of work are aimed at minimizing overload or underutilization in the workplace and achieving a more suitable balance between abilities possessed and skills used on the job.) When employees experience underutilization, boredom, decreased motivation, apathy, and absenteeism will be more likely. Role overload can lead to such symptoms as insomnia, irritability, increased errors, and indecisiveness.

Taken together, occupation and role processes represent a sizable influence on whether or not an employee experiences high stress levels. One job where the profession and its required roles almost guarantee significant stress is air traffic control. Consider for a moment whether you would want to have this job.

EXPANDING AROUND THE GLOBE

Are the Japanese Working Themselves to Death?

Karoshi literally means death from overwork, and unofficial estimates are that as many people die each year from *karoshi* as from traffic accidents in Japan—approximately 10,000. In 2016, the legal claims of karoshi rose to a record high of 1,456 according to government figures. Additionally, just under 2,000 suicides linked to work-related causes were reported. In October 2017, the latest employee death that shook the media was 31-year-old journalist Miwa Sado, and before that 24-year-old Matsui Takahashi, an employee working at Dentsu advertising agency, leapt from the roof on Christmas Day 2015.

These incidents are just two of many that occur more frequently in Japan due to the culture of overtime and stress within the work environment. Each of these women logged over 100 hours of overtime over the course of one month. Often the causes of death include heart failure, stroke, and suicide due to the stress, lack of sleep, and sleep deprivation that is caused by being overworked. Takahashi posted on Twitter, "It's 4 a.m. My body's trembling, I'm going to die. I'm so tired." Soon after her death, the president of Dentsu resigned from his post.

Many reports suggest that performance reviews are marked negatively for those that don't work lots of overtime, while others suggest employees must strive to make good impressions on their bosses, and staying late or working extra is perceived as loyalty to their jobs and companies.

The Japanese government has taken strides since the two incidents to implement policies to help to combat karoshi for good. One attempt implemented in 2016 is A Premium Friday plan, where Japanese workers are allowed the chance to leave at 3 p.m. on the last Friday of each month. This has only made some employees busier because some companies have organized their monthly finances to hit sales goals before the end of the month. Little success has been seen from this initiative. One Tokyo-best IT Service company forced employees to wear purple capes on the third Wednesday of the month if they worked late, which was a very bold and visual tactic to showcase the "working late is not cool" vibe. This shaming tactic worked, decreasing the overtime worked by 50 percent. Some companies have implemented individual changes such as breakfast offerings and allowing time off as needed.

Changing the Japanese work culture will take time. Although these small changes have not made a large impact yet, the discussion is widening, and workplaces are becoming more aware of the need for drastic changes in policy to counteract the growing issue of stress in the workplace.

Questions:

1. What measures can a manager take in order to counteract the stress-related issues within the work environment?
2. What considerations should a manager take before implementing changes to a work environment and policies when managing a global team?
3. What environmental and cultural factors can affect an employee's work ethic and their level of stress in their workday?

Sources: C. Weller, "Japan is facing a 'death by overwork' problem — here's what it's all about," *Business Insider*, October 8, 2017, https://www.businessinsider.com/what-is-karoshi-japanese-word-for-death-by-overwork-2017-10?r=UK&IR=T; E. Warnock, "Japan by the Numbers: 'Karoshi'," *Tokyo Review*, October 12, 2017, http://www.tokyoreview.net/2017/10/japan-numbers-karoshi-overwork/; (Why Japanese Workers Keep Working Themselves to Death," *CBS News*, October 20, 2017, https://www.cbsnews.com/news/karoshi-japan-deaths-persist-japanese-overwork/; D. Demetriou, "Death for Overworking Claims Hit Record High in Japan," *The Telegraph*, April 4, 2016, https://www.telegraph.co.uk/news/2016/04/04/death-from-overworking-claims-hit-record-high-in-japan/; D. Hurst, "First step in changing Japan's workaholic culture: less overtime," *NBC News*, January 8, 2018, https://www.nbcnews.com/news/world/first-step-changing-japan-s-workaholic-culture-less-overtime-n833051.

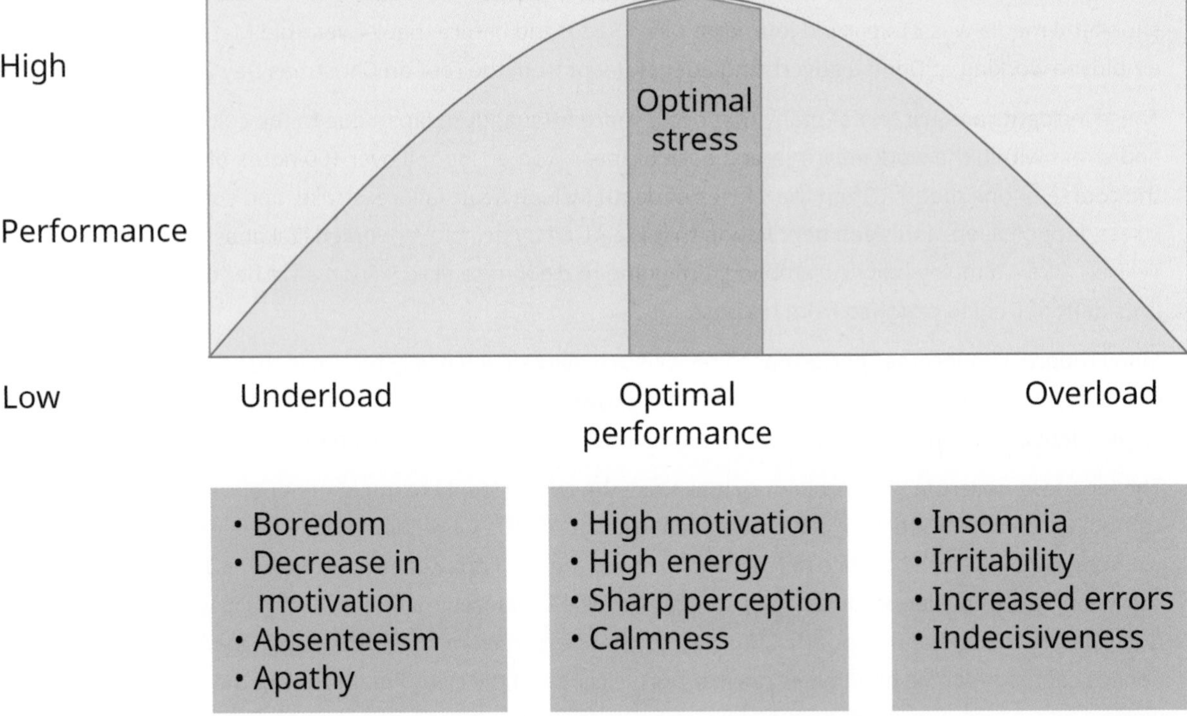

Exhibit 18.4 The Underload-Overload Continuum Source: Adapted from *Organizations: Behavior, Structure, Processes* 14th edition by James L. Gibson, John M. Ivancevich, and Robert Konopaske, McGraw Hill, 2013. (Attribution: Copyright Rice University, OpenStax, under CC BY-NC-SA 4.0 license)

Personal Influences on Stress

The second major influence on job-related stress can be found in the employees themselves. As such, we will examine three individual-difference factors as they influence stress at work: (1) personal control, (2) Type A personality, and (3) rate of life change.

Personal Control

To begin with, we should acknowledge the importance of **personal control** as a factor in stress. Personal control represents the extent to which an employee actually has control over factors affecting effective job performance. If an employee is assigned a responsibility for something (landing an airplane, completing a report, meeting a deadline) but is not given an adequate opportunity to perform (because of too many planes, insufficient information, insufficient time), the employee loses personal control over the job and can experience increased stress. Personal control seems to work through the process of employee participation. That is, the more employees are allowed to participate in job-related matters, the more control they feel for project completion. On the other hand, if employees' opinions, knowledge, and wishes are excluded from organizational operations, the resulting lack of participation can lead not only to increased stress and strain, but also to reduced productivity.

The importance of employee participation in enhancing personal control and reducing stress is reflected in the French and Caplan study discussed earlier. After a major effort to uncover the antecedents of job-related stress, these investigators concluded:

"Since participation is also significantly correlated with low role ambiguity, good relations with others, and low overload, it is conceivable that its effects are widespread, and that all the relationships between these other stresses and psychological strain can be accounted for in terms of how much the person participates. This, in fact, appears to be the case. When we control or hold constant, through statistical analysis techniques, the amount of participation a person reports, then the correlations between all the above stresses and job satisfaction and job-related threat drop quite noticeably. This suggests that low participation generates these related stresses, and that increasing participation is an efficient way of reducing many other stresses which also lead to psychological strain."[23]

On the bases of this and related studies, we can conclude that increased participation and personal control over one's job is often associated with several positive outcomes, including lower psychological strain, increased skill utilization, improved working relations, and more-positive attitudes. These factors, in turn, contribute toward higher productivity. These results are shown in **Exhibit 18.5**.[24]

Related to the issue of personal control—indeed, moderating its impact—is the concept of **locus of control**. It will be remembered that some people have an *internal* locus of control, feeling that much of what happens in their life is under their own control. Others have an *external* locus of control, feeling that many of life's events are beyond their control. This concept has implications for how people respond to the amount of personal control in the work environment. That is, internals are more likely to be upset by threats to the personal control of surrounding events than are externals. Recent evidence indicates that internals react to situations over which they have little or no control with aggression—presumably in an attempt to reassert control over ongoing events.[25] On the other hand, externals tend to be more resigned to external control, are much less involved in or upset by a constrained work environment, and do not react as emotionally to organizational stress factors. Hence, locus of control must be recognized as a potential moderator of the effects of personal control as it relates to experienced stress.

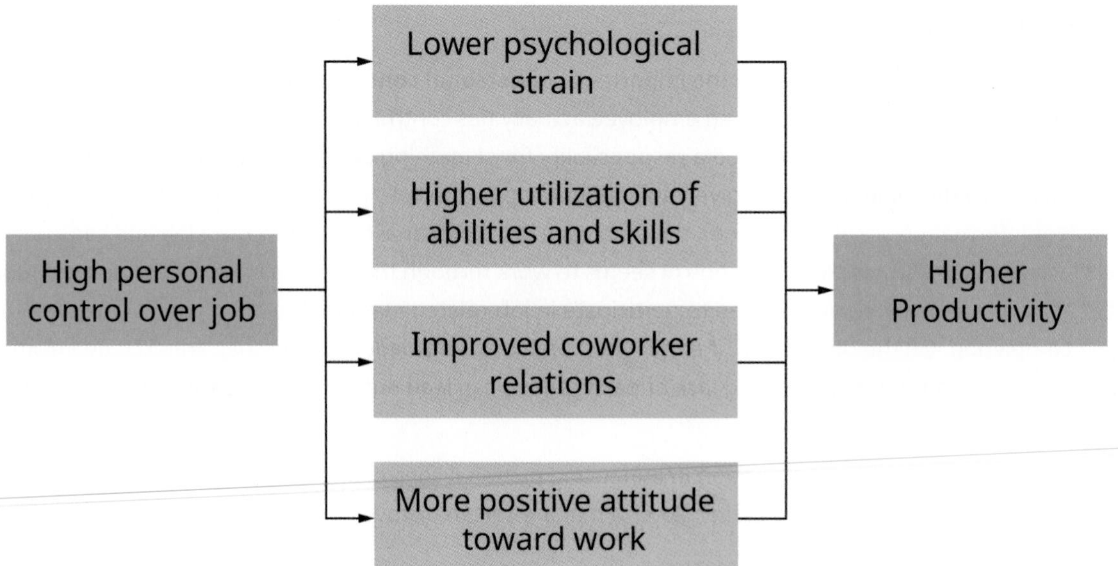

Exhibit 18.5 Consequences of High Personal Control (Attribution: Copyright Rice University, OpenStax, under CC BY-NC-SA 4.0 license)

Type A Personality

Research has focused on what is perhaps the single most dangerous personal influence on experienced stress and subsequent physical harm. This characteristic was first introduced by Friedman and Rosenman and is called **Type A personality.**[26] Type A and Type B personalities are felt to be relatively stable personal characteristics exhibited by individuals. Type A personality is characterized by impatience, restlessness, aggressiveness, competitiveness, polyphasic activities (having many "irons in the fire" at one time), and being under considerable time pressure. Work activities are particularly important to Type A individuals, and they tend to freely invest long hours on the job to meet pressing (and recurring) deadlines. Type B people, on the other hand, experience fewer pressing deadlines or conflicts, are relatively free of any sense of time urgency or hostility, and are generally less competitive on the job. These differences are summarized in **Table 18.3**.

Profiles of Type A and Type B Personalities	
Type A	Type B
Highly competitive	Lacks intense competitiveness
"Workaholic"	Work only one of many interests
Intense sense of urgency	More deliberate time orientation
Polyphasic behavior	Does one activity at a time
Strong goal-directedness	More moderate goal-directedness

Table 18.3 (Attribution: Copyright Rice University, OpenStax, under CC BY-NC-SA 4.0 license)

Type A personality is frequently found in managers. Indeed, one study found that 60 percent of managers were clearly identified as Type A, whereas only 12 percent were clearly identified as Type B.[27] It has been suggested that Type A personality is most useful in helping someone rise through the ranks of an organization.

The role of Type A personality in producing stress is exemplified by the relationship between this behavior and heart disease. Rosenman and Friedman studied 3,500 men over an 8 1/2-year period and found Type A individuals to be twice as prone to heart disease, five times as prone to a second heart attack, and twice as prone to fatal heart attacks when compared to Type B individuals.[28] Similarly, Jenkins studied over 3,000 men and found that of 133 coronary heart disease sufferers, 94 were clearly identified as Type A in early test scores.[29] The rapid rise of women in managerial positions suggests that they, too, may be subject to this same problem. Hence, Type A behavior very clearly leads to one of the most severe outcomes of experienced stress.

One irony of Type A is that although this behavior is helpful in securing rapid promotion to the top of an organization, it may be detrimental once the individual has arrived. That is, although Type A employees make successful managers (and salespeople), the most successful *top* executives tend to be Type B. They exhibit patience and a broad concern for the ramifications of decisions. As Dr. Elmer Green, a Menninger Foundation psychologist who works with executives, notes, "This fellow—the driving A—can't relax enough to do a really first-rate job, at the office or at home. He gets to a level that dogged work can achieve, but not often to the pinnacle of his business or profession, which requires sober, quiet, balanced reasoning."[30] The key is to know how to shift from Type A behavior to Type B.

How does a manager accomplish this? The obvious answer is to slow down and relax. However, many Type A managers refuse to acknowledge either the problem or the need for change, because they feel it may be viewed as a sign of weakness. In these cases, several small steps can be taken, including scheduling specified times every day to exercise, delegating more significant work to subordinates, and eliminating optional activities from the daily calendar. Some companies have begun experimenting with retreats, where managers are removed from the work environment and engage in group psychotherapy over the problems associated with Type A personality. Initial results from these programs appear promising.[31] Even so, more needs to be done if we are to reduce job-related stress and its serious health implications.

Rate of Life Change

A third personal influence on experienced stress is the degree to which lives are stable or turbulent. A long-term research project by Holmes and Rahe has attempted to document the extent to which **rate of life change** generates stress in individuals and leads to the onset of disease or illness.[32] As a result of their research, a variety of life events were identified and assigned points based upon the extent to which each event is related to stress and illness.

The death of a spouse was seen as the most stressful change and was assigned 100 points. Other events were scaled proportionately in terms of their impact on stress and illness. It was found that the higher the point total of recent events, the more likely it is that the individual will become ill. Apparently, the influence of life changes on stress and illness is brought about by the endocrine system. This system provides the energy needed to cope with new or unusual situations. When the rate of change surpasses a given level, the system experiences overload and malfunctions. The result is a lowered defense against viruses and disease.

CONCEPT CHECK

1. What are the major influences of work related stress?

2. What impact do different occupations have of the stress levels of workers in those jobs?
3. What impact do role ambiguity, job overload or underutilization have on stress levels?
4. What are Type A and Type B personalities and how does stress affect each personality type

18.3 Buffering Effects of Work related Stress

3. How do managers and organizations minimize the dysfunctional consequences of stressful behavior?

We have seen in the previous discussion how a variety of organizational and personal factors influence the extent to which individuals experience stress on the job. Although many factors, or stressors, have been identified, their effect on psychological and behavioral outcomes is not always as strong as we might expect. This lack of a direct stressor-outcome relationship suggests the existence of potential moderator variables that buffer the effects of potential stressors on individuals. Recent research has identified two such buffers: the degree of social support the individual receives and the individual's general degree of what is called hardiness. Both are noted in **Exhibit 18.2**.

Social Support

First, let us consider social support. **Social support** is simply the extent to which organization members feel their peers can be trusted, are interested in one another's welfare, respect one another, and have a genuine positive regard for one another. When social support is present, individuals feel that they are not alone as they face the more prevalent stressors. The feeling that those around you really care about what happens to you and are willing to help blunts the severity of potential stressors and leads to less-painful side effects. For example, family support can serve as a buffer for executives on assignment in a foreign country and can reduce the stress associated with cross-cultural adjustment.

Much of the more rigorous research on the buffering effects of social support on stress comes from the field of medicine, but it has relevance for organizational behavior. In a series of medical studies, it was consistently found that high peer support reduced negative outcomes of potentially stressful events (surgery, job loss, hospitalization) and increased positive outcomes.[33] These results clearly point to the importance of social support to individual well-being. These results also indicate that managers should be aware of the importance of building cohesive, supportive work groups—particularly among individuals who are most subject to stress.

MANAGERIAL LEADERSHIP

Disconnecting from the "Always On" Work Culture

It is very rare that you are farther than an arm's length away from your smartphone. You get anxious when there is no Wi-Fi in a hotel room, and if your battery is running low, the stress skyrockets through the roof just imagining what you could miss out on. All of these stresses, combined with an increasing demand for being reachable for your work, can relate to high stress and other negative health effects.

Many workplaces, such as medical professionals, have a high importance to the response rate they employ. Others, such sales teams, may require certain response times to e-mails, calls, or texts, with explanation of why they were not achieved. According to the recent study by the Academy of Management, "employees tally an average of 8 hours a week answering work-related emails after leaving the office." This also could include regularly taking work home or working while on scheduled time off and vacation, and all can cause stress and lack of sleep and greatly reduce focus and engagement during office hours.

In the UK, surveys have uncovered the impact of technology, with 72.4 percent of respondents admitting that they were performing work tasks outside of regular work hours (https://businessadvice.co.uk/hr/employment-law/always-on-culture-affecting-employees/). Increasing the stress and potential negative affects is when the smartphones are being accessed: mainly before bed and right when they wake up. Feeling groggy in the morning and not getting a good night's sleep could be due to the exposure to cell phones, computers, and TVs during the two hours before bed. Further studies have also shown that the blue light from devices can disrupt circadian rhythms and the internal clock the helps determine when to sleep and when to wake. (https://www.sciencenewsforstudents.org/article/evening-screen-time-can-sabotage-sleep)

Other countries outside of the U.S. have changed their ways and implemented policies to counteract the "always on" cultural norm that pervades the modern workplace. As of January 1, 2017, French employees now have a new law with the "right to disconnect." This law allows employees to walk away from their smartphone technology and does not allow employers to fire individuals that do not respond to work-related inquiries while out of office.

Questions:

1. What are some ways as a new manager that you can help positively impact your new team to counteract the "always on" mentality?
2. What are some negative workplace behaviors that could arise from promoting an "always on" work culture?

Sources: S. Caldwell, "Revealed: How Britain's always-on culture is really affecting employees," *Business Advice*, May 15, 2018, https://businessadvice.co.uk/hr/employment-law/always-on-culture-affecting-employees/; J. M. O'Connor, "The Always on Smartphone Culture, Turn it Off," *Forbes*, September 8, 2017, https://www.forbes.com/sites/forbescoachescouncil/2017/09/08/the-always-on-smartphone-culture-turn-it-down/#236c2e7521c0; M. Kitchen, "How to Disconnect From 'Always On' Work Culture," *The Wall Street Journal*, October 5, 2018, https://www.wsj.com/articles/how-to-disconnect-from-always-on-work-culture-1538740171?mod=searchresults&page=1&pos=2; M. Wall, "Smartphone stress: Are you a victim of 'always on' culture?," *BBC*, August 14, 2014, https://www.bbc.com/news/business-28686235.

Hardiness

The second moderator of stress is hardiness. **Hardiness** represents a collection of personality characteristics that involve one's ability to perceptually or behaviorally transform negative stressors into positive challenges. These characteristics include a sense of commitment to the importance of what one is doing, an internal locus of control (as noted above), and a sense of life challenge. In other words, people characterized by hardiness have a clear sense of where they are going and are not easily deterred by hurdles. The pressure of goal frustration does not deter them, because they invest themselves in the situation and push ahead. Simply put, these are people who refuse to give up.[34]

Several studies of hardiness support the importance of this variable as a stress moderator. One study among managers found that those characterized by hardiness were far less susceptible to illness following prolonged stress. And a study among undergraduates found hardiness to be positively related to perceptions that potential stressors were actually challenges to be met. Thus, factors such as individual hardiness and the degree of social support must be considered in any model of the stress process.

Consequenses of Work Related Stress

In exploring major influences on stress, it was pointed out that the intensity with which a person experiences stress is a function of organizational factors and personal factors, moderated by the degree of social support in the work environment and by hardiness. We come now to an examination of major *consequences* of work-related stress. Here we will attempt to answer the "so what?" question. Why should managers be interested in stress and resulting strain?

As a guide for examining the topic, we recognize three intensity levels of stress—no stress, low stress, and high stress—and will study the outcomes of each level. These outcomes are shown schematically in **Exhibit 18.6**. Four major categories of outcome will be considered: (1) stress and health, (2) stress and counterproductive behavior, (3) stress and job performance, and (4) stress and burnout.

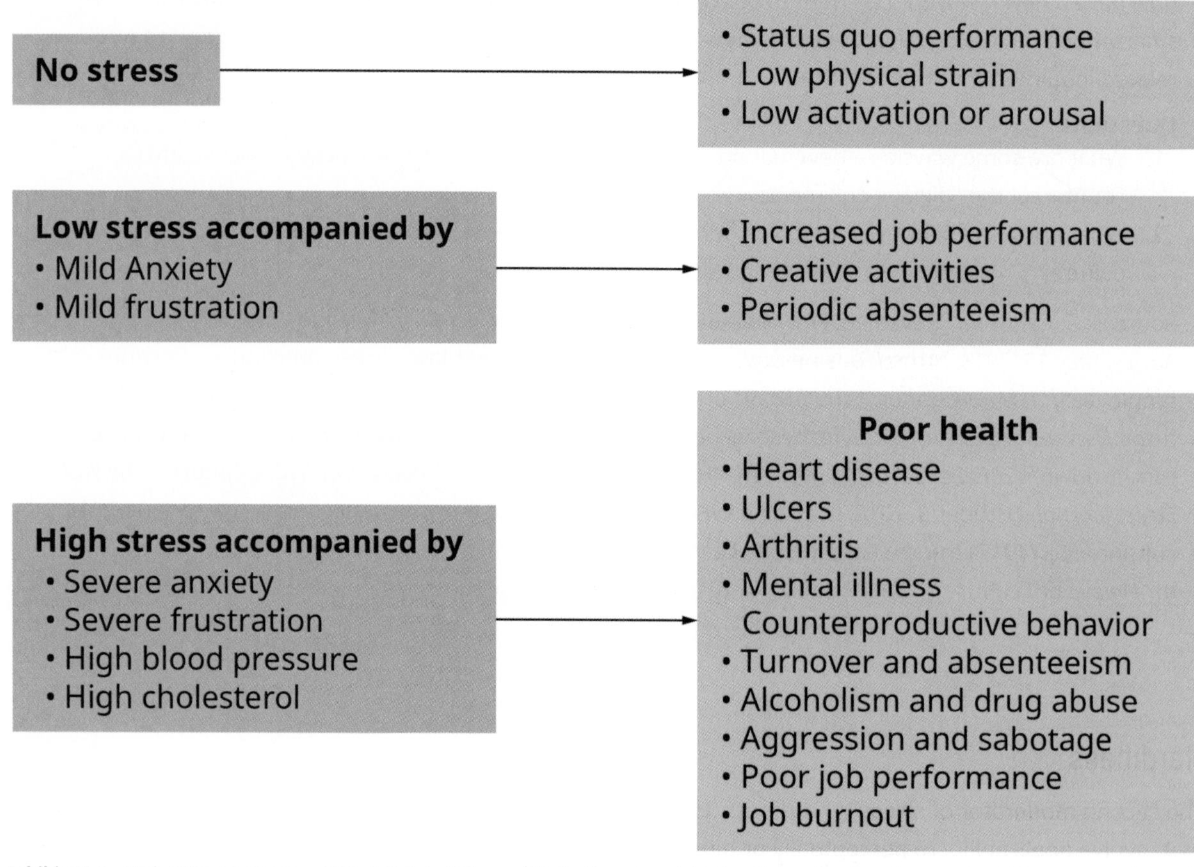

Exhibit 18.6 Major Consequences of Work-Related Stress (Attribution: Copyright Rice University, OpenStax, under CC BY-NC-SA 4.0 license)

Stress and Health

High degrees of stress are typically accompanied by severe anxiety and/or frustration, high blood pressure, and high cholesterol levels. These psychological and physiological changes contribute to the impairment of health in several different ways. Most important, high stress contributes to heart disease.[35] The relationship between high job stress and heart disease is well established. In view of the fact that well over a half-million people die of heart disease every year, the impact of stress is important.[36]

High job stress also contributes to a variety of other ailments, including peptic ulcers, arthritis, and several forms of mental illness. In a study by Cobb and Kasl, for example, it was found that individuals with high educational achievement but low job status exhibited abnormally high levels of anger, irritation, anxiety, tiredness, depression, and low self-esteem.[37] In another study, Slote examined the effects of a plant closing in Detroit on stress and stress outcomes. Although factory closings are fairly common, the effects of these closings on individuals have seldom been examined. Slote found that the plant closing led to "an alarming rise in anxiety and illness," with at least half the employees suffering from ulcers, arthritis, serious hypertension, alcoholism, clinical depression, and even hair loss.[38] Clearly, this life change event took its toll on the mental and physical well-being of the workforce.

Finally, in a classic study of mental health of industrial workers, Kornhauser studied a sample of automobile assembly-line workers. Of the employees studied, he found that 40 percent had symptoms of mental health problems. His main findings may be summarized as follows:

- Job satisfaction varied consistently with employee skill levels. Blue-collar workers holding high-level jobs exhibited better mental health than those holding low-level jobs.
- Job dissatisfaction, stress, and absenteeism were all related directly to the characteristics of the job. Dull, repetitious, unchallenging jobs were associated with the poorest mental health.
- Feelings of helplessness, withdrawal, alienation, and pessimism were widespread throughout the plant. As an example, Kornhauser noted that 50 percent of the assembly-line workers felt they had little influence over the future course of their lives; this compares to only 17 percent for nonfactory workers.
- Employees with the lowest mental health also tended to be more passive in their nonwork activities; typically, they did not vote or take part in community activities.[39]

In conclusion, Kornhauser noted:

"Poor mental health occurs whenever conditions of work and life lead to continuing frustration by failing to offer means for perceived progress toward attainment of strongly desired goals which have become indispensable elements of the individual's self-esteem and dissatisfaction with life, often accompanied by anxieties, social alienation and withdrawal, a narrowing of goals and curtailing of aspirations—in short . . . poor mental health."[40]

Managers need to be concerned about the problems of physical and mental health because of their severe consequences both for the individual and for the organization. Health is often related to performance, and to the extent that health suffers, so too do a variety of performance-related factors. Given the importance of performance for organizational effectiveness, we will now examine how it is affected by stress.

Stress and Counterproductive Behavior

It is useful from a managerial standpoint to consider several forms of counterproductive behavior that are known to result from prolonged stress. These counterproductive behaviors include turnover and absenteeism, alcoholism and drug abuse, and aggression and sabotage.

Turnover and Absenteeism. Turnover and absenteeism represent convenient forms of withdrawal from a highly stressful job. Results of several studies have indicated a fairly consistent, if modest, relationship between stress and subsequent turnover and absenteeism.[41] In many ways, withdrawal represents one of the easiest ways employees have of handling a stressful work environment, at least in the short run. Indeed, turnover and absenteeism may represent two of the less undesirable consequences of stress, particularly when compared to alternative choices such as alcoholism, drug abuse, or aggression. Although high turnover and absenteeism may inhibit productivity, at least they do little physical harm to the individual or coworkers. Even so, there are many occasions when employees are not able to leave because of family or financial obligations, a lack of alternative employment, and so forth. In these situations, it is not unusual to see more dysfunctional behavior.

Alcoholism and Drug Abuse. It has long been known that stress is linked to alcoholism and drug abuse among employees at all levels in the organizational hierarchy. These two forms of withdrawal offer a temporary respite from severe anxiety and severe frustration. One study by the Department of Health, Education, and Welfare reported, "Our interviews with blue-collar workers in heavy industry revealed a number who found it necessary to drink large quantities of alcohol during lunch to enable them to withstand the pressure or overwhelming boredom of their tasks."[42] A study in New York revealed a surprising amount of drug abuse by young employees on blue-collar jobs—especially among assembly-line employees and long-haul truck drivers. A third study of a UAW local involving 3,400 workers found 15 percent of the workforce addicted to heroin. And, finally, there is an alarming increase of drug and substance abuse among managers.[43]

Both alcohol and drugs are used by a significant proportion of employees to escape from the rigors of a routine or stressful job. Although many companies have begun in-house programs aimed at rehabilitating chronic cases, these forms of withdrawal seem to continue to be on the increase, presenting another serious problem for modern managers. One answer to this dilemma involves reducing stress on the job that is creating the need for withdrawal from organizational activities.

Aggression and Sabotage. Severe frustration can also lead to overt hostility in the form of aggression toward other people and toward inanimate objects. Aggression occurs when individuals feel frustrated and can find no acceptable, legitimate remedies for the frustration. For instance, a busy secretary may be asked to type a stack of letters, only to be told later that the boss changed his mind and no longer needs the letters typed. The frustrated secretary may react by covert verbal abuse or an intentional slowdown on subsequent work. A more extreme example of aggression can be seen in the periodic reports in newspapers about a worker who "goes berserk" (usually after a reprimand or punishment) and attacks fellow employees.

One common form of aggressive behavior on the job is sabotage. As one study found:

"The roots of sabotage, a frequent aspect of industrial violence, are illustrated by this comment of a steelworker. 'Sometimes, out of pure meanness, when I make something, I put a little dent in it. I like to do something to make it really unique. Hit it with a hammer deliberately to see if it'll get by, just so I can say I did it.' In a product world where everything is alike, sabotage may be a distortion of the guild craftsman's signature, a way of asserting individuality in a homogeneous world—the only way for a worker to say, 'That's mine.' It may also be a way of striking back against the hostile, inanimate objects that control the worker's time, muscles, and brain. Breaking a machine in order to get some rest may be a sane thing to do."[44]

The extent to which frustration leads to aggressive behavior is influenced by several factors, often under the control of managers. Aggression tends to be subdued when employees anticipate that it will be punished, the peer group disapproves, or it has not been reinforced in the past (that is, when aggressive behavior failed to lead to positive outcomes). Thus, it is incumbent upon managers to avoid reinforcing undesired behavior and, at the same time, to provide constructive outlets for frustration. In this regard, some companies have provided official channels for the discharge of aggressive tendencies. For example, many companies have experimented with *ombudsmen,* whose task it is to be impartial mediators of employee disputes. Results have proved positive. These procedures or outlets are particularly important for nonunion personnel, who do not have contractual grievance procedures.

Stress and Job Performance

A major concern of management is the effects of stress on job performance. The relationship is not as simple as might be supposed. The stress-performance relationship resembles an inverted J-curve, as shown in **Exhibit 18.7**. At very low or *no-stress* levels, individuals maintain their current levels of performance. Under these conditions, individuals are not activated, do not experience any stress-related physical strain, and probably see no reason to change their performance levels. Note that this performance level may be high or low. In any event, an absence of stress probably would not cause any change.

On the other hand, studies indicate that under conditions of *low stress,* people are activated sufficiently to motivate them to increase performance. For instance, salespeople and many managers perform best when they are experiencing mild anxiety or frustration. Stress in modest amounts, as when a manager has a tough problem to solve, acts as a stimulus for the individual. The toughness of a problem often pushes managers to their performance limits. Similarly, mild stress can also be responsible for creative activities in individuals as they try to solve difficult (stressful) problems.

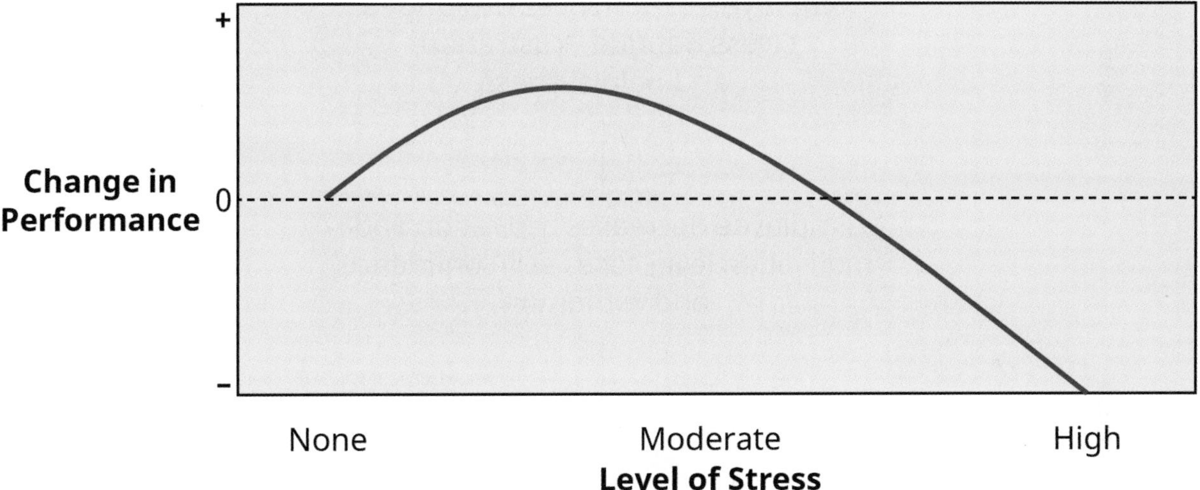

Exhibit 18.7 The Relationship Between Stress and Job Performance (Attribution: Copyright Rice University, OpenStax, under CC BY-NC-SA 4.0 license)

Finally, under conditions of *high stress,* individual performance drops markedly. Here, the severity of the stress consumes attention and energies, and individuals focus considerable effort on attempting to reduce the stress (often employing a variety of counterproductive behaviors as noted below). Little energy is left to devote to job performance, with obvious results.

Stress and Burnout

When job-related stress is prolonged, poor job performance such as that described above often moves into a more critical phase, known as burnout. **Burnout** is a general feeling of exhaustion that can develop when a person simultaneously experiences too much pressure to perform and too few sources of satisfaction.[45]

Candidates for job burnout seem to exhibit similar characteristics. That is, many such individuals are idealistic and self-motivated achievers, often seek unattainable goals, and have few buffers against stress. As a result, these people demand a great deal from themselves, and, because their goals are so high, they often fail to reach them. Because they do not have adequate buffers, stressors affect them rather directly. This is shown in **Exhibit 18.8**. As a result of experienced stress, burnout victims develop a variety of negative and often hostile attitudes toward the organization and themselves, including fatalism, boredom, discontent, cynicism, and feelings of personal inadequacy. As a result, the person decreases his or her aspiration levels, loses confidence, and attempts to withdraw from the situation.

Research indicates that burnout is widespread among employees, including managers, researchers, and engineers, that are often hardest to replace by organizations. As a result, it is estimated that 70 percent of the largest U. S. companies have some form of antiburnout/stress reduction training.[46]

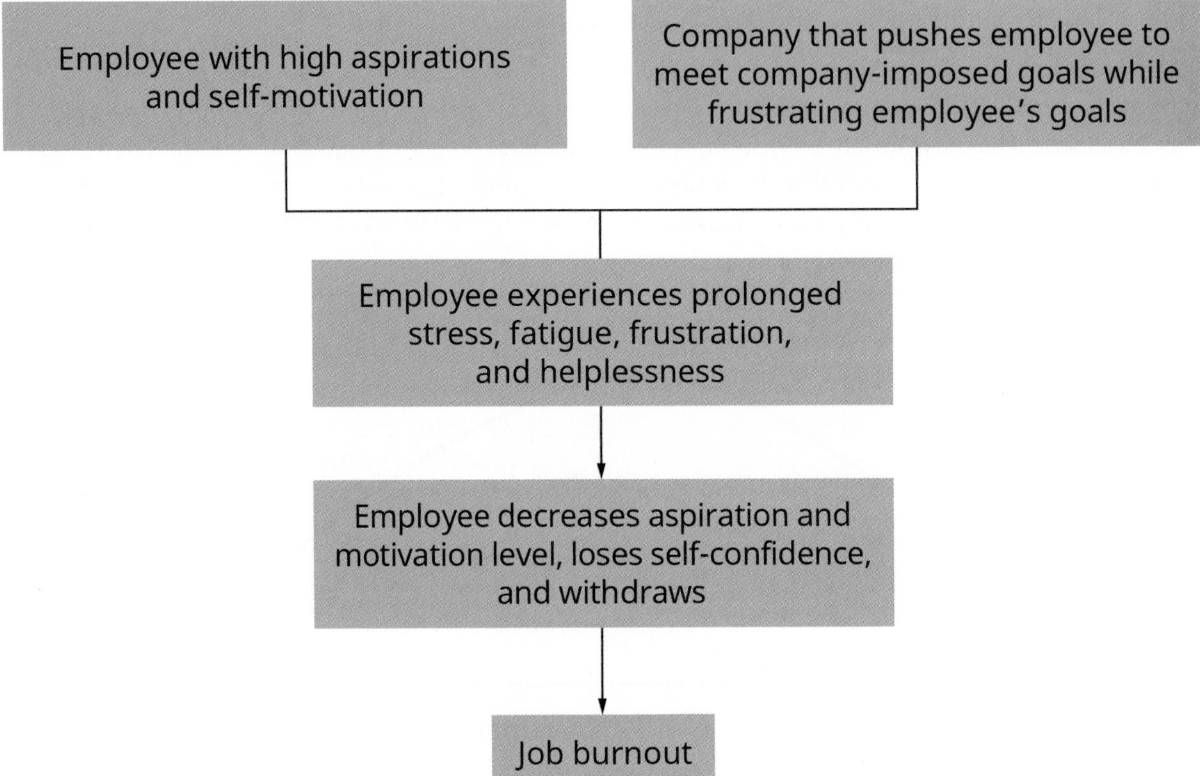

Exhibit 18.8 Influences Leading to Job Burnout (Attribution: Copyright Rice University, OpenStax, under CC BY-NC-SA 4.0 license)

CONCEPT CHECK

1. What role does health, social support and hardiness have on the level of stress?
2. What can managers do ro reduce stress levels in employees that can harm productivity and can lead to counterproductive behavior in the workplace, absenteeism, as well as alcoholism and drug abuse.

18.4 Coping with Work related Stress

4. What are the remedies for job-related stress, and how can managers motivate employees to participate actively in health promotion efforts for the benefit of all concerned?

We come now to the most important question from a managerial standpoint: What can be done to reduce job-related stress? Many suggestions for coping with stress are implicit in the previous discussions. However, it is possible to summarize several important actions employees and managers can take in order to provide a more desirable work environment and improve employee adjustment to work.

Individual Strategies

There are many things people can do to help eliminate the level of experienced stress or, at the very least, to help cope with continuing high stress. Consider the following:

Developing Self-Awareness. Individuals can increase awareness of how they behave on the job. They can learn to know their own limits and recognize signs of potential trouble. Employees should know when to withdraw from a situation (known to some as a "mental health day" instead of absenteeism) and when to seek help from others on the job in an attempt to relieve the situation.

Developing Outside Interests. In addition, individuals can develop outside interests to take their minds off work. This solution is particularly important for Type A people, whose physical health depends on toning down their drive for success. Employees can ensure that they get regular physical exercise to relieve pent-up stress. Many companies sponsor athletic activities, and some have built athletic facilities on company premises to encourage employee activity.

Leaving the Organization. Sometimes an employee may be unable to improve her situation and, as a result, may find it necessary (i.e., healthful) simply to leave the organization and find alternative employment. Although this is clearly a difficult decision to make, there are times when turnover is the only answer.

Finding a Personal or Unique Solution. Another means individuals can use to cope with stress is through a variety of personal or unique solutions. For instance, here is how one manager described his reaction to a stressful situation: "If someone finally bugs me, I politely hang up the phone and then pound the hell out of my typewriter, saying all the things on paper I wanted to say to that person on the phone. It works every time. Then, I rip up the paper and throw it into the trash can."[47] If an employee cannot leave a stressful situation, this may be a good temporary way out of it.

Physical Exercise. Because part of the cause of the fatigue resulting from stress is the body's physical reaction, exercise can be an effective means of enabling the body to more effective deal with the physical components of stress. Regular exercise can be an important and effective individual strategy.

Cognitive Perspective. Finally, because stress is in part a function of how events are perceived and interpreted, controlling one's cognitive perspective of events can also be an effective strategy. Although one would not want to go so far as framing a truck speeding toward you as an opportunity rather than a threat, positively framing situations as well as distinguishing factors that are within as well as outside your control and influence can be effective means of reducing stress.

Organizational Strategies

Because managers usually have more control over the working environment than do subordinates, it seems only natural that they have more opportunity to contribute to a reduction of work-related stress. Among their activities, managers may include the following eight strategies.

Personnel Selection and Placement. First, managers can pay more attention in the selection and placement process to the fit between job applicants, the job, and the work environment. Current selection and placement procedures are devoted almost exclusively to preventing qualitative role overload by ensuring that people have the required education, ability, experience, and training for the job. Managers could extend these selection criteria to include a consideration of the extent to which job applicants have a tolerance for ambiguity and can handle role conflict. In other words, managers could be alert in the job interview and subsequent placement process to potential stress-related problems and the ability of the applicant to deal successfully with them.

Skills Training. Second, stress can be reduced in some cases through better job-related skills training procedures, where employees are taught how to do their jobs more effectively with less stress and strain. For instance, an employee might be taught how to reduce overload by taking shortcuts or by using new or expanded skills. These techniques would only be successful, however, if management did not follow this increased effectiveness by raising work quotas. Along with this could go greater effort by managers to specify and clarify job duties to reduce ambiguity and conflict. Employees could also be trained in human relations skills in order to improve their interpersonal abilities so that they might encounter less interpersonal and intergroup conflict.

Job Redesign. Third, managers can change certain aspects of jobs or the ways people perform these jobs. Much has been written about the benefits of job redesign. Enriching a job may lead to improved task significance, autonomy, responsibility, and feedback. For many people, these jobs will present a welcome challenge, which will improve the job-person fit and reduce experienced stress. It should be noted, however, that all people do not necessarily want an enriched job. Enriching the job of a person with a very low need for achievement or external locus of control may only increase anxiety and fear of failure. Care must be taken in job enrichment to match these efforts to employee needs and desires.

In addition to job enrichment, a related technique aimed at reducing stress is *job rotation.* Job rotation is basically a way of spreading stress among employees and providing a respite—albeit temporary—from particularly stressful jobs. Job rotation is particularly popular in Japan as a means of allocating the more tedious or boring tasks among a large set of employees so prolonged stress is reduced. Japan is also finally working toward a reduced workweek as a means of reducing job-related stress.[48]

Company-Sponsored Counseling Programs. Several companies have begun experimenting with counseling programs, the fourth strategy suggested here. For instance, Stanford University's executive program includes a module on coping with stress, and the Menninger Foundation conducts a one-week anti-stress seminar in Topeka. In one experiment among police officers, the value of a stress management program was examined.[49] In the program, which consisted of six two-hour sessions, officers were told about the nature and causes of stress, were shown useful relaxation exercises, and were put through several simulated stressful situations—such as role playing the handling of an arrest. Throughout, emphasis was placed on reinforcing the officers' confidence that they could, in fact, successfully cope with on-the-job stress. The results of the program showed that those officers who went through the program performed better, exhibited greater self-control, and experienced less stress than officers in comparable positions who did not go through the program. Similar findings have emerged in a variety of business organizations. Once again, much work-related stress can be reduced simply by encouraging managers to be more supportive and to provide the necessary tools for people to cope with stress.

Increased Participation and Personal Control. Fifth, managers can allow employees greater participation and personal control in decisions affecting their work. As noted above, participation increases job involvement and simultaneously reduces stress by relieving ambiguity and conflict. However, although the benefits of increased participation are many, it should be noted that being more participative is no easy task for some supervisors. One study, for example, found significant differences in the extent to which different supervisors would allow their subordinates to participation in decision-making.[50] Females were found to allow more participation than males. Supervisors with high achievement needs, high levels of confidence in the abilities of their subordinates, and low feelings of being threatened by others allowed more subordinate participation. The issue of participation does not appear to be whether subordinates desire it; instead, it appears to be whether superiors will allow it.

Exhibit 18.9 Stress Ball Stress balls have been used for centuries, particularly in Chinese culture, to help relieve anxiety and improve hand coordination. These days, people still turn to stress balls for reliable anxiety relief. (Attribution: Katy Warner/ Flickr/ Attribution 2.0 Generic (CC BY 2.0))

Work Group Cohesiveness. Sixth, managers can attempt to build work group cohesiveness. Team-building efforts are common in industry today. These efforts focus on developing groups that will be both more productive and mutually supportive. A critical ingredient in the extent to which stress is experienced is the amount of social support employees receive. Team building represents one way to achieve this support.

Improved Communication. Managers can open communication channels so employees are more informed about what is happening in the organization. With greater knowledge, role ambiguity and conflict are reduced. Managers must be aware, however, that communication is a two-way street; they should allow and be receptive to communication from subordinates. To the extent that subordinates feel their problems and complaints are being heard, they experience less stress and are less inclined to engage in counterproductive behavior.

Health Promotion Programs. Finally, many companies have recently embarked on a more systematic and comprehensive approach to stress reduction and wellness in the workplace. These programs are usually referred to as **health promotion programs**, and they represent a combination of diagnostic, educational, and behavior modification activities that are aimed at attaining and preserving good health.[51] A typical program includes risk assessment, educational and instructional classes, and counseling and referrals. Health promotion programs tackle a wide array of health-related concerns, including physical fitness, weight control, dietary and nutritional counseling, smoking cessation, blood pressure monitoring, alcohol and substance abuse problems, and general lifestyle modification.

Companies involved in such programs usually feel that the costs invested to run them are more than returned through higher levels of productivity and reduced absenteeism and stress-related illness.[52] Moreover, many companies have found that providing such services serves as an attractive incentive when recruiting employees in a tight job market.

Stress is a function of the objective environment but also of individuals' subjective interpretation of events and their consequences. Both body and mind are involved the process. It is important for both firms and individuals to take preventive measures before the cumulative effects of stress manifest themselves in ways that cost both the individual and the company.

Eustress is a term that signifies beneficial stress, either psychological, physical. The term was coined by using the Greek prefix "eu", meaning "good", and stress, literally meaning "good stress". Eustress was originally explored in a stress model by Richard Lazarus. It is the positive cognitive response to stress that is healthy, or gives one a feeling of fulfilment or other positive feelings.[53]

CONCEPT CHECK

1. What are some things that managers can do ro reduce stress in the organization?

Key Terms

anxiety A feeling of inability to deal with anticipated harm.

burnout A general feeling of exhaustion that can develop when a person simultaneously experiences too much pressure to perform and too few sources of satisfaction.

Eustress Beneficial stress.

frustration Refers to a psychological reaction to an obstruction or impediment to goal-oriented behavior.

general adaptation syndrome Consists of three stages: the first stage, alarm; the second stage of resistance; and the third stage, exhaustion.

hardiness Represents a collection of personality characteristics that involve one's ability to perceptually or behaviorally transform negative stressors into positive challenges.

health promotion programs Represent a combination of diagnostic, educational, and behavior modification activities that are aimed at attaining and preserving good health.

locus of control The concept that much of what happens in one's life is either under or outside of their own control.

personal control Represents the extent to which an employee actually has control over factors affecting effective job performance.

rate of life change The variety of life events were identified and assigned points based upon the extent to which each event is related to stress and illness.

role ambiguity Occurs when individuals have inadequate information concerning their roles.

role conflict The simultaneous occurrence of two (or more) sets of pressures or expectations; compliance with one would make it difficult to comply with the other.

role overload A condition in which individuals feel they are being asked to do more than time or ability permits.

role underutilization Occurs when employees are allowed to use only a few of their skills and abilities, even though they are required to make heavy use of them.

social support The extent to which organization members feel their peers can be trusted, are interested in one another's welfare, respect one another, and have a genuine positive regard for one another.

strain The damage resulting from experiencing stress.

stress A physical and emotional reaction to potentially threatening aspects of the environment.

tolerance for ambiguity Individuals measure and affect by role ambiguity (in terms of stress, reduced performance, or propensity to leave) than others with a low tolerance for ambiguity.

Type A personality Type A personality is characterized by impatience, restlessness, aggressiveness, competitiveness, polyphasic activities, and being under considerable time pressure.

Summary of Learning Outcomes

18.1 Problems of Work Adjustment

1. How do you recognize the symptoms of stress in yourself and in others?

Stress is a physical and emotional reaction to potentially threatening aspects of the environment. The damage resulting from stress is called strain. The general adaptation syndrome is the common pattern of events that characterizes someone who experiences stress. The three stages of the syndrome are alarm, resistance, and exhaustion. Two primary types of stress can be identified: frustration and anxiety.

18.2 Organizational Influences on Stress

2. What are the underlying causes of stress in a particular situation?

Four organization influences on stress can be identified: (1) occupational differences, (2) role ambiguity, (3) role conflict, and (4) role overload or underutilization. Three personal influences on stress are (1) personal control, or the desire to have some degree of control over one's environment; (2) rate of life change; and (3) Type A personality. Type A personality refers to individuals characterized by impatience, restlessness, aggressiveness, competitiveness, and polyphasic activities (that is, attempting to do several activities at the same time).

18.3 Buffering Effects of Work related Stress

3. How do managers and organizations minimize the dysfunctional consequences of stressful behavior?

The effects of potential stress can be buffered by two factors: (1) social support from one's coworkers or friends and (2) hardiness, or the ability to perceptually and behaviorally transform negative stressors into positive challenges. Sustained stress can lead to (1) health problems; (2) counterproductive behavior, such as turnover, absenteeism, drug abuse, and sabotage; (3) poor job performance; and (4) burnout.

18.4 Coping with Work related Stress

4. What are the remedies for job-related stress, and how can managers motivate employees to participate actively in health promotion efforts for the benefit of all concerned?

Burnout is defined as a general feeling of exhaustion that can develop when a person simultaneously experiences too much pressure to perform and too few sources of satisfaction. Individual strategies to reduce stress include (1) developing one's self-awareness about how to behave on the job, (2) developing outside interests, (3) leaving the organization, and (4) finding a unique solution. Organizational strategies to reduce stress include (1) improved personnel selection and job placement, (2) skills training, (3) job redesign, (4) company-sponsored counseling programs, (5) increased employee participation and personal control, (6) enhanced work group cohesiveness, (7) improved communication, and (8) health promotion programs.

Chapter Review Questions

1. Discuss the five types of problems related to employee work adjustment.
2. Define stress. How does it differ from strain?
3. Describe the general adaptation syndrome.
4. Contrast frustration with anxiety.
5. Identify the major categories of variables that have been found to influence stress. What role does social support play in the process? What role does hardiness play?
6. In the chapter, the plight of assembly-line workers was discussed. What realistic suggestions would you make to relieve the tension and stress of this job?
7. Compare and contrast role conflict and role ambiguity.
8. How does a manager achieve a useful balance in a person-job fit so neither role overload nor role underutilization occurs?
9. How should a manager deal with a subordinate who is clearly a Type A personality? How should a manager who is a Type A personality handle her own stress?
10. Of what utility is the rate-of-life-change concept?
11. In organizations with which you are familiar, which of the many suggestions for coping with stress would be most applicable? Are the strategies you selected individual or organizational strategies?

 Management Skills Application Exercises

1. You may wish to see if you have experienced stress in your present (or previous) part- or full-time job. To do so, simply complete this self-assessment. When you have finished, refer to the scoring procedures in **Appendix B**.

How Stressful Is Your Job?

Instructions: This instrument focuses on the stress level of your current (or previous) job. Think of your job, and answer the following items as frankly and honestly as possible.

	Strongly Disagree			Strongly Agree	
1. I am often irritable with my coworkers.	1	2	3	4	5
2. At work, I constantly feel rushed or behind schedule.	1	2	3	4	5
3. I often dread going to work.	1	2	3	4	5
4. I often experience headaches, stomachaches, or backaches at work.	1	2	3	4	5
5. I often lose my temper over minor problems.	1	2	3	4	5
6. Everything I do seems to drain my energy level.	1	2	3	4	5
7. I often interpret questions or comments from others as a criticism of my work.	1	2	3	4	5
8. Time is my enemy.	1	2	3	4	5
9. I often have time for only a quick lunch (or no lunch) at work.	1	2	3	4	5
10. I spend considerable time at home worrying about problems at work.	1	2	3	4	5

2. Are you interested in determining whether you are a Type A or Type B? If so, simply complete this self-assessment. When you have finished, score your results as shown in **Appendix B**.

Are You a Type A?

Instructions: Choose from the following responses to answer the questions below:

a. Almost always true
b. Usually trued.
c. Seldom true
d. Never true

Answer each question according to what is generally true for you:

———	1. I do not like to wait for other people to complete their work before I can proceed with my own.
———	2. I hate to wait in most lines.
———	3. People tell me that I tend to get irritated too easily.
———	4. Whenever possible I try to make activities competitive.
———	5. I have a tendency to rush into work that needs to be done before knowing the procedure I will use to complete the job.
———	6. Even when I go on vacation, I usually take some work along.
———	7. When I make a mistake, it is usually due to the fact that I have rushed into the job before completely planning it through.
———	8. I feel guilty for taking time off from work.
———	9. People tell me I have a bad temper when it comes to competitive situations.
———	10. I tend to lose my temper when I am under a lot of pressure at work.
———	11. Whenever possible, I will attempt to complete two or more tasks at once.
———	12. I tend to race against the clock.
———	13. I have no patience for lateness.
———	14. I catch myself rushing when there is no need.
Source: Adapted from "Are You a Type A?" *The Stress Mess Solution: The Causes and Cures of Stress on the Job,* by G. S. Everly and D. A. Girdano. Reprinted by permission of the authors.	

3. The Holmes and Rahe "Schedule of Recent Experiences" is shown here in this self-assessment. You are encouraged to complete this scale by checking all those events that have occurred to you within the past year. Next, follow the scoring procedures described in **Appendix B**.

How Stable Is Your Life?

Instructions: Place a check mark next to each event you experienced within the past year. Then add the scores associated with the various events to derive your total life stress score.

Life Event	Scale Value
——— Death of spouse	100
——— Divorce	73
——— Marital separation	65
——— Jail term	63
——— Death of a close family member	63
——— Major personal injury or illness	53
——— Marriage	50
——— Fired from work	47
——— Marital reconciliation	45
——— Retirement	45
——— Major change in health of family member	44
——— Pregnancy	40
——— Sex difficulties	39
——— Gain of a new family member	39
——— Business readjustment	39
——— Change in financial state	38
——— Death of a close friend	37
——— Change to a different line of work	36
——— Change in number of arguments with spouse	35
——— Mortgage or loan for big purchase (home, etc.)	31
——— Foreclosure of mortgage or loan	30
——— Change in responsibilities at work	29
——— Son or daughter leaving home	29
——— Trouble with in-laws	29

——— Outstanding personal achievement	28
——— Spouse begins or stops work	26
——— Begin or end school	26
——— Change in living conditions	25
——— Revision of personal habits	24
——— Trouble with boss	23
——— Change in work hours or conditions	20
——— Change in residence	20
——— Change in schools	20
——— Change in recreation	19
——— Change in church activities	19
——— Change in social activities	18
——— Mortgage or loan for lesser purchase (car, etc.)	17
——— Change in sleeping habits	16
——— Change in number of family get-togethers	15
——— Change in eating habits	15
——— Vacation	13
——— Christmas	12
——— Minor violations of the law	11
Total Score = ———	
Source: Adapted from "Scaling of Life Change: Comparison of Direct and Indirect Methods" by L. O. Ruch and T. H. Holmes, *Journal of Psychosomatic Research* 15 (1971): 224, 1971.	

4. If you are interested in your own potential for burnout, you may wish to complete this self-assessment. Simply answer the ten questions as honestly as you can. When you have finished, follow the scoring instructions shown in Appendix B.

Are You Suffering from Burnout?

Instructions: Check whether each item is "mostly true" or "mostly untrue" for you. Answer as honestly as you can. When you have finished, add up the number of checks for "mostly true."

	Mostly True	Mostly Untrue
1. I usually go around feeling tired.	———	———
2. I think I am working harder but accomplishing less.	———	———
3. My job depresses me.	———	———
4. My temper is shorter than it used to be.	———	———
5. I have little enthusiasm for life.	———	———
6. I snap at people fairly often.	———	———
7. My job is a dead end for me.	———	———
8. Helping others seems like a losing battle.	———	———
9. I don't like what I have become.	———	———
10. I am very unhappy with my job.	———	———

Critical Thinking Case

Managerial Leadership, Sustainability, and Responsible Management: Mindfulness at Google Inc.

Even though the outside appearance of Google headquarters may be filled with stereotypical visions of nap pods and scenes from "The Internship," there is still a lot of work that is accomplished by those working there. With work, there can come stress, and job-related stress is a huge issue, with studies by the Behavioral Science and Policy Association stating that working long hours has been shown to increase mortality by 20 percent. No matter how many cushy perks you can get, they won't make everyone happy, and Google is combating this with creativity. They attempt to counteract the stress-related issues by offering specific classes—for example Meditation 101 and Mindfulness-Based Stress Reduction. They also encourage their employees to join their online and in-person community called gPause. This specific group helps support and encourage meditation practice. The key to this stress-reducing revolution at Google is that they have a company culture that supports the behavior. The company also promotes day meditation retreats at a handful of their locations. This type of creativity is sure to take hold at other companies across the globe.

Questions:

1. Google is one of the leading tech companies in the world. What do you think of their approach to handling stress within the workplace? Do you think that this approach will be effective? Why or why not?
2. A company culture that supports stress reduction is key to the success of any program within the company. What are some obstacles that can arise when handling stress within a workplace? What are some methods that you would employ as manager to counteract these obstacles and implement stress-reduction programs within your workplace?

Sources: J. Goh, J. Pfeffer, S. A. Zenios, "Workplace stressors & health outcomes: Health policy for the workplace," *Behavioral Science and Policy Association*, February 15, 2017, https://behavioralpolicy.org/articles/workplace-stressors-health-outcomes-health-policy-for-the-workplace/; J. Porter, "How Google And Others Help Employees Burn Off Stress In Unique Ways," *Fast Company*, November 16, 2015, https://www.fastcompany.com/3053048/how-google-and-other-companies-help-employees-burn-off-stress-in-unique-ways.

19 Entrepreneurship

Exhibit 19.1 (Credit: Marco Verch /flickr / Attribution 2.0 Generic (CC BY 2.0))

Introduction

Learning Outcomes

After reading this chapter, you should be able to answer these questions:

1. What are some different types of entrepreneurship?
2. What characteristics lead individuals to become entrepreneurs?
3. How can the business model canvas help us to describe and assess a business model?
4. How do entrepreneurs finance their new business ideas?
5. How can entrepreneurs leverage design thinking to solve complex problems and navigate uncertain environments?
6. How can government support entrepreneurship?

EXPLORING MANAGERIAL CAREERS

Maria Rose Belding, MEANS Database

One day while volunteering at her local food shelter in Iowa, middle school student Maria Rose Belding was forced to throw out hundreds of boxes of expired macaroni and cheese. While Maria carried the boxes to the trash, she walked past hungry families waiting for food, and she considered the sheer size of the world's hunger problem. In the United States alone, over 133 billion pounds of food is thrown out annually, and there are over 45 million Americans who do not have enough to eat. Belding's experience led her to create MEANS (Matching Excess and Need for Stability) Database, a nonprofit organization that creates an online network for food pantries and shelters to communicate with anyone that may have extra food, such as restaurants, grocery stores, and caterers. Through MEANS's app and website, excess food that would be discarded is instead sent to a shelter or food pantry.

Belding knew that she needed to create a platform to connect food pantries to food surpluses, but she did not know how. Grant Nelson, a law student at George Washington University, cofounded MEANS with Belding. Nelson led the data science and technology components and built the cloud infrastructure that MEANS needed to be successful in Belding's goal of connecting people or organizations with extra food to those who need it. MEANS Database uses cloud-based software and e-mail-based communications to match food pantries with surplus food.

Many people donate food to shelters with good intentions, but it often is not the right type of food for a certain shelter. For example, some shelters predominantly serve senior citizens with health issues such as hypertension, mandating a low-sodium diet. When a food pantry receives a ramen noodle donation, the staff should not give it to the elderly, and might instead throw the ramen away. MEANS allows pantry staff to post the unwanted food so that another pantry can claim the donation. For both food recipients and donors, the process is straightforward, and it is free to create an account with MEANS. The shelter provides its location, needs, and distance willing to travel for a food dimension. On the donation end, a shelter, restaurant, or any other potential donor of extra food can report the type and amount of food they are trying to give away, and MEANS e-mails the local pantries looking for that type of food. The MEANS technology enables the transactions in which both parties must agree for the food to be transferred.

Belding continued to build MEANS Database during her high school studies and later as a premedical undergraduate student at American University. She received several honors for her efforts, including L'Oréal Women of Worth and one of CNN's top ten recipients of "Hero of the Week" of 2018. Belding plans to pass daily management of MEANS to her staff and remain on the board during her medical school studies. MEANS Database has moved over two million pounds of food across 48 states and is exploring international possibilities.

Sources: Maria Belding, "Math matters (but actually): We Can Solve Hunger With Numbers," December 02, 2015, https://www.huffingtonpost.com/maria-rose-belding/math-matters-but-actually_b_8698146.html; Ykaie Du, "Feeding the Hungry with Data Science - The Possibility Report," 2017, https://www.theatlantic.com/sponsored/vmware-2017/hungry-data-science/1796/; Nancy Dunham, "How a Once-Bullied Student Created a Network to Feed Thousands: 'We Want to Get Wasted Food to People Who Need It,'" March 17, 2016, http://people.com/human-interest/maria-rose-belding-bullied-student-created-a-network-to-feed-thousands/ Ron Fournier, "Fighting Hunger the Millennial Way," December 22, 2015, Retrieved from https://www.theatlantic.com/politics/archive/2015/12/fighting-hunger-the-millennial-way/461856/ Terrence McCoy, "The revolutionary technology helping to fight food waste," December 6, 2015, https://www.washingtonpost.com/local/social-issues/the-revolutionary-technology-thats-helping-end-americas-chronic-food-waste/2015/12/06/0a491cb8-9a9c-11e5-8917-653b65c809eb_story.html?noredirect=on&utm_term=.d4f9663f5cfc MEANS Database - a nonprofit food rescue platform, 2019, https://www.meansdatabase.com/

Maria Rose Belding is one of millions of the world's entrepreneurs—that is, individuals who recognize and pursue opportunities, take on risk, and convert these opportunities into value-added ventures that can survive in a competitive marketplace. Entrepreneurs hail from many backgrounds and age groups—with Belding representing young middle school, high school, and college entrepreneurs. Entrepreneurs have in common a drive to achieve and grow and a willingness to take initiative and personal responsibility. Entrepreneurs frequently require other resources such as cofounders and teams, and then must build a large network of customers, suppliers, and other stakeholders. While MEANS Database is a registered nonprofit, MEANS has many for-profit competitors and partners.

19.1 Overview of Entrepreneurship

1. What are some different types of entrepreneurship?

Entrepreneurship is a global phenomenon, with individuals all over the world at various stages of the process. While there are many definitions of **entrepreneurs** and **entrepreneurship**, we consider the scholarly field as defined by Shane and Venkataraman[1] that seeks to understand how opportunities are discovered, created, and exploited; by whom; and with what consequences. When most people think of entrepreneurship, they may think of individuals such as Maria Rose Belding, as well as Jeff Bezos (Amazon) and Elon Musk (Tesla and SpaceX). However, there are many other types of entrepreneurship that we will explore in this chapter. MEANS Database is an example of **social entrepreneurship**—that is, creating innovative solutions to immediate social and/or environment problems and mobilizing resources to achieve social transformation. MEANS Database illustrates how social entrepreneurs often solve problems more effectively than the government. Entrepreneurs can also operate inside existing organizations: **corporate entrepreneurship** involves the creation of new products, processes, and ventures within large organizations. Another prevalent type is **family entrepreneurship**—that is, when a business is owned and managed by multiple family members, usually for more than one generation. **Serial or habitual entrepreneurship** refers to individuals who start several businesses, simultaneously or one after another. Entrepreneurship can also be classified according to the desired goals—for example, individuals who pursue **lifestyle entrepreneurship** typically create a venture to suit a personal lifestyle and not for the sole purpose of making profits. **High-technology entrepreneurship** involves ventures in the information, communication, and technology space, which typically have high expectations for revenue growth. Entrepreneurs can also be classified according to the stage of their venture development, as outlined in the Global Entrepreneurship Monitor (GEM) research program in the next section.

Global Entrepreneurship Prevalence

Each year, the Global Entrepreneurship Monitor (GEM)[2] study gathers data from 60+ countries to determine how many individuals are engaged in various phases of entrepreneurship. The first phase captures **potential entrepreneurs** who believe that they have the capacity and knowledge to start a venture and don't fear failure. If you are reading this book and believe that you are developing the skills necessary to someday start your own company, and you believe that the risk-reward payoff is promising, then you fit this definition of a potential entrepreneur. The next GEM category is **nascent entrepreneurs** who have set up or are in the process of setting up a venture that they will own/co-own that is less than three months old and has not yet generated wages/salaries. **New business owners** operate a business for over three months but less than three years. And finally, **established business owners** actively run a business that is over three and a half years old. GEM researchers calculate a Total Entrepreneurial Activity (TEA) rate, which is the percentage of the adult population (ages 18–64) who are either nascent entrepreneurs or owner-managers of a new business. **Exhibit 19.2** provides an overview of the GEM model to measure entrepreneurial activity in a given economy. As shown, GEM data captures attributes of the individual entrepreneur, industry sector, and expected impact in terms of potential business growth, use of innovation, and share of international customers. **Exhibit 19.3** shows the most recently available rates of entrepreneurial activities across geographic regions. These regions are classified by their development status, with factor-driven countries the least developed; these countries subsist primarily on agriculture and extraction businesses, and rely heavily on unskilled labor and natural resources. Efficiency-driven economies are more competitive and utilize more advanced and efficient production processes to provide better-quality products and services. Innovation-driven economies are the most developed, typically relying on knowledge-intensive industries and an expanded service sector. As shown, entrepreneurial activity rates range from nearly 20 percent of the adult population in Ecuador to lows of less than 5 percent in several countries such as Bulgaria, Bosnia & Herzegovina, Italy, and Japan. Entrepreneurship rates can be extremely high in factor-driven countries as there are fewer traditional businesses and entrepreneurship may be the only good opportunity in the labor market. Among innovation-driven economies, the U.S. has one of the highest TEA levels, perhaps due to the American culture of individualism and the many organizations that support entrepreneurship. Another key factor is societal value, which we review in the next section.

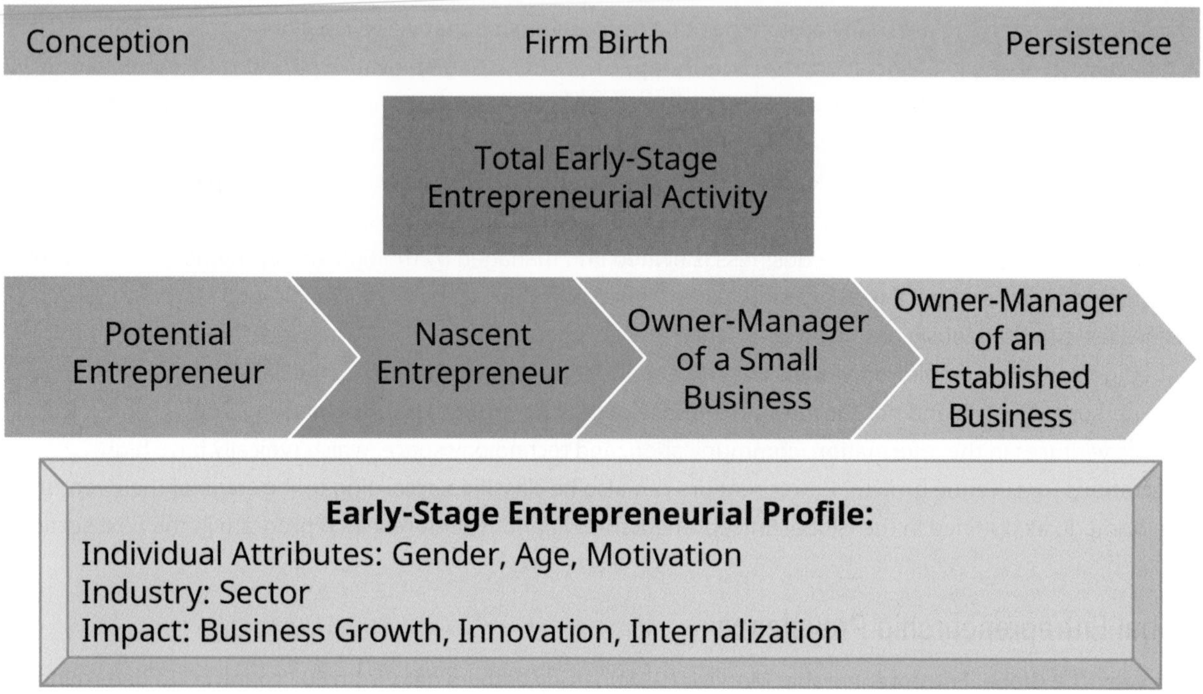

Exhibit 19.2 Model and Measures of Entrepreneurial Activity Source: Adapted from *Global Entrepreneurship Monitor* 2017/2018 report, page 22 (Attribution: Copyright Rice University, OpenStax, under CC BY-NC-SA 4.0 license)

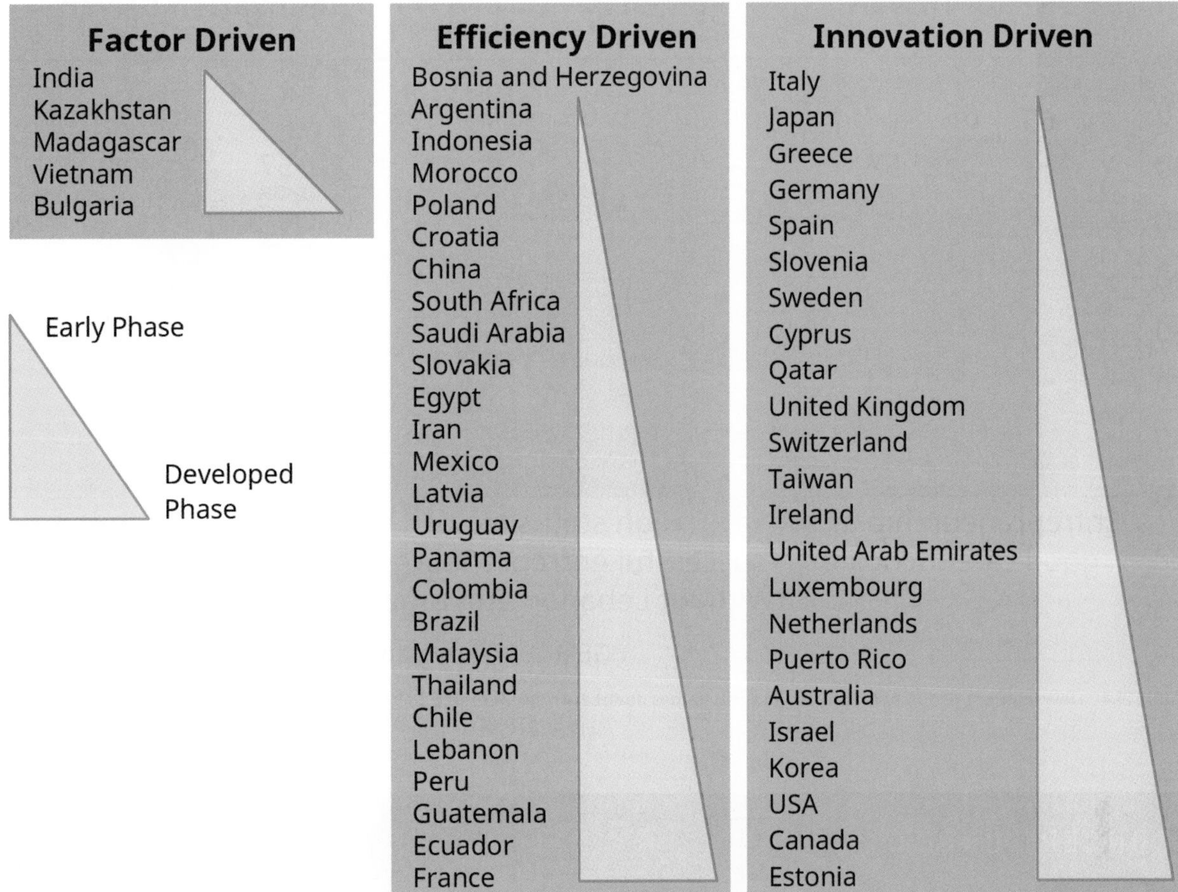

Exhibit 19.3 Entrepreneurial Activity in 2017/2018 Source: Global Entrepreneurship Monitor 2017/2018 report, pages 34-35 (Attribution: Copyright Rice University, OpenStax, under CC BY-NC-SA 4.0 license)

Societal Value for Global Entrepreneurship

The GEM research project also examines societal values for entrepreneurship, which can help drive an abundance or lack of entrepreneurs. In the 2017/2018 report, across 52 economies, there was strong support for entrepreneurship as a good career choice. The lowest levels were reported in innovation-driven economies, perhaps because there are many good corporate career options. GEM researchers identified that almost 70 percent of the adult population believes that entrepreneurs enjoy high status within their societies. There are slight differences, with factor-driven countries reporting higher status levels as compared to innovation- and efficiency-driven countries. Moreover, across 52 economies, about 61 percent of adults believe that entrepreneurs garner substantial media attention, with the higher levels in increasingly developed economies. This data suggests that when entrepreneurs are portrayed favorably in the media, individuals will be more likely to consider entrepreneurship as a career.

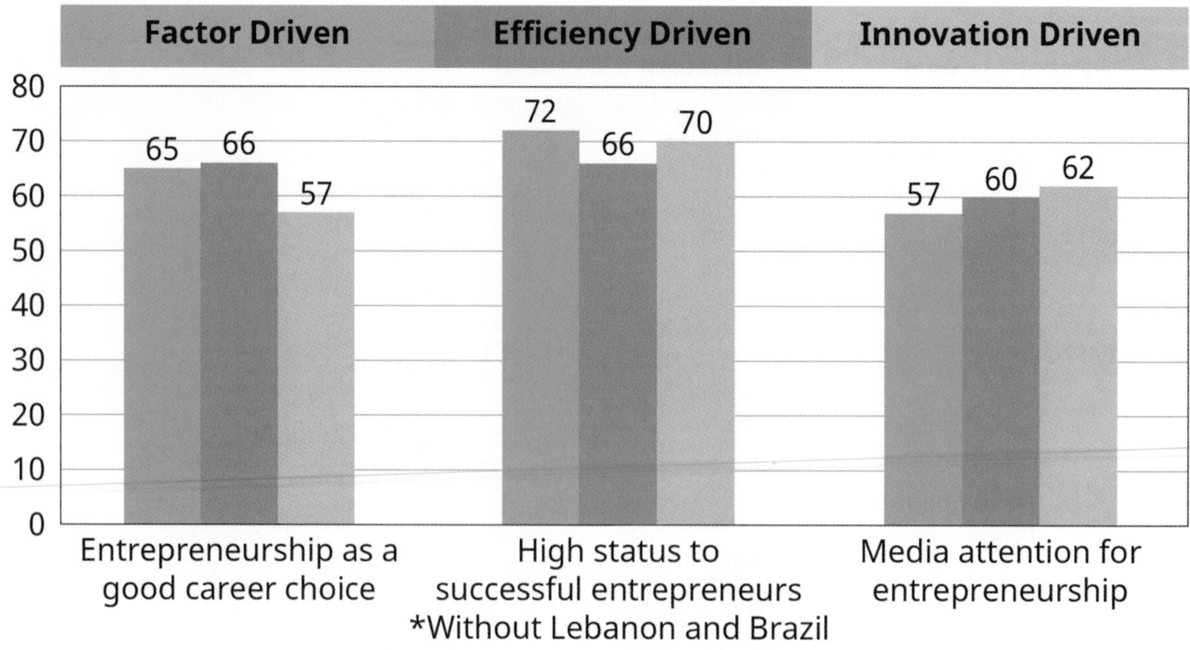

Exhibit 19.4 Development Group Averages for Societal Values about Entrepreneurship in 52 Economies Source: Adapted from Global Entrepreneurship Monitor 2017/2018 report, page 27 (Attribution: Copyright Rice University, OpenStax, under CC BY-NC-SA 4.0 license)

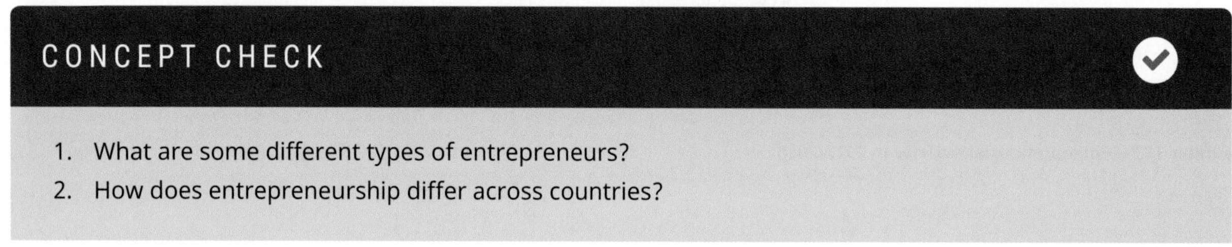

CONCEPT CHECK

1. What are some different types of entrepreneurs?
2. How does entrepreneurship differ across countries?

19.2 Characteristics of Successful Entrepreneurs

2. What characteristics lead individuals to become entrepreneurs?

Will you join the millions of entrepreneurs operating around the world? Wanting to be an entrepreneur is not enough—an individual must be able to develop and refine a new business opportunity, and it also requires a special personality as well as key skills.

Entrepreneurial Personality

Studies of the entrepreneurial personality find that entrepreneurs share certain key traits. Most entrepreneurs are:

- *Ambitious*—competitive, with a high need for achievement
- *Independent*—individualists and self-starters who prefer to lead rather than follow
- *Self-confident*—understand the challenges of starting and operating a business and are decisive and confident in their ability to solve problems

- *Risk takers*—willing to accept a moderate (and sometimes large) degree of risk relative to potential returns
- *Visionary*—spot trends and act on them
- *Creative*—offer innovative solutions and approach functions such as creative product designs and bold marketing strategies
- *Energetic*—offer high energy levels and perseverance, often working a full-time job while starting a venture
- *Passionate*—love their ideas and are delighted to bring them to the market, sometimes turning a hobby into a venture
- *Committed*—willing to make personal sacrifices to achieve their goals

ETHICS IN PRACTICE

Ethical Choices Transform Family Business into International Brand

Even as a young girl growing up in Paris, Apollonia always knew what she wanted to do when she grew up: take over the family business. But she didn't anticipate how quickly this would happen. When her father, Lionel Poilâne, and mother died in a helicopter crash in 2002, France lost its most celebrated baker, and Apollonia stepped into the role. She was just 18 years old at the time with plans to matriculate to Harvard in the fall, but the moment her parents had prepared her for had come. As her Harvard admissions essay said, "The work of several generations is at stake."

With organization and determination, Apollonia managed one of the best French bakeries in the world, based in Paris—from her apartment in Cambridge, Massachusetts. She would usually wake up an extra two hours before classes to make sure she could make all the phone calls for work. "After classes I check on any business regarding the company and then do my homework," she says. "Before I go to bed I call my production manager in Paris to check the quality of the bread." Because the name Poilâne has earned a place with a very small group of prestige bakers, the 18-year-old was determined to continue the tradition of customer satisfaction and quality her grandfather established in 1932. When her grandfather suffered a stroke in 1973, his 28-year-old son, Lionel, poured his heart into the business and made the family bread into the global brand it is today. Lionel opened two more bakeries in Paris and another in London. He developed and nurtured a worldwide network of retailers and celebrities where bread is shipped daily via FedEx to upscale restaurants and wealthy clients around the world.

Experimenting with sourdough is what distinguished Poilâne's products from bread produced by Paris's other bakers, and it has remained the company's signature product. It is baked with a "P" carved into the crust, a throwback to the days when the use of communal ovens forced bakers to identify their loaves, and it also ensures that the loaf doesn't burst while it's baking. Today, Poilâne also sells croissants, pastries, and a few specialty breads, but the company's signature item is still the four-pound *miche*, a wheel of sourdough, a country bread, *pain Poilâne*.

"Apollonia is definitely passionate about her job," says Juliette Sarrazin, manager of the successful Poilâne Bakery in London. "She really believes in the work of her father and the company, and she is looking at the future, which is very good."

Apollonia's work ethic and passion fueled her drive even when she was a student. Each day presented a juggling act of new problems to solve in Paris while other Harvard students slept. As Apollonia told a student reporter from *The Harvard Crimson*, "The one or two hours you spend procrastinating I spend working. It's nothing demanding at all. It was always my dream to run the company."

Her dedication paid off, and Apollonia retained control of important decisions, strategy, and business goals, describing herself as the "commander of the ship," determining the company's overall direction. Today, Poilâne is an $18 million business that employs 160 people. Poilâne runs three restaurants called Cuisine de Bar in Paris and in London, serving casual meals such as soups, salads, and open-faced *tartines*. The company ships more than 200,000 loaves a year to clients in 20 countries, including the United States, Japan, and Saudi Arabia. "More people understand what makes the quality of the bread, what my father spent years studying, so I am thrilled about that," says Apollonia.

Critical Thinking Questions

1. What type of entrepreneur is Apollonia Poilâne?
2. What personal ethics drove Apollonia's decision to take over the family business?

Sources: "About Us," https://www.poilane.com, accessed February 1, 2018; Meg Bortin, "Apollonia Poilâne Builds on Her Family's Legacy," *The New York Times,* https://www.nytimes.com, accessed February 1, 2018; Lauren Collins, "Bread Winner: A Daughter Upholds the Traditions of France's Premier Baking Dynasty," *The New Yorker,* https://www.newyorker.com, December 3, 2012; Gregory Katz, "Her Daily Bread," *American Way* magazine, July 15, 2005, p. 34; Clarel Antoine, "No Time to Loaf Around," *Harvard Crimson,* http://www.thecrimson.com, October 16, 2003.

Most entrepreneurs combine many of the above characteristics. Sarah Levy, 23, loved her job as a restaurant pastry chef but not the low pay, high stress, and long hours of a commercial kitchen. So, she found a new one—in her parents' home—and launched Sarah's Pastries and Candies. Part-time staffers help her fill pastry and candy orders to the soothing sounds of music videos playing in the background. Cornell University graduate Conor McDonough started his own web design firm, OffThePathMedia.com, after becoming disillusioned with the rigid structure of his job. "There wasn't enough room for my own expression," he says. "Freelancing keeps me on my toes," says busy graphic artist Ana Sanchez. "It forces me to do my best work because I know my next job depends on my performance."[3]

Managerial Ability and Technical Knowledge

A person with all the characteristics of an entrepreneur might still lack the necessary business skills to run a successful company. Entrepreneurs need the technical knowledge to carry out their ideas and the managerial ability to organize a company, develop operating strategies, obtain financing, and supervise day-to-day activities. Jim Crane, who built Eagle Global Logistics from a start-up into a $250 million company, addressed a group at a meeting, saying, "I have never run a $250 million company before, so you guys are going to have to start running this business."[4]

Good interpersonal and communication skills are important in dealing with employees, customers, and other business associates such as bankers, accountants, and attorneys. As we will discuss later in the chapter, entrepreneurs believe they can learn these much-needed skills. When Jim Steiner started his toner cartridge remanufacturing business, Quality Imaging Products, his initial investment was $400. He spent $200 on a consultant to teach him the business and $200 on materials to rebuild his first printer cartridges. He made sales calls from 8.00 a.m. to noon and made deliveries to customers from noon until 5:00 p.m. After a quick dinner, he moved to the garage, where he filled copier cartridges until midnight, when he collapsed into bed, sometimes covered with carbon soot. And this was not something he did for a couple of months until he got the business off the ground—this was his life for 18 months.[5] But entrepreneurs usually soon learn that they can't do it all themselves. Often they choose to focus on what they do best and hire others to do the rest.

CONCEPT CHECK

1. Describe the personality traits and skills characteristic of successful entrepreneurs.
2. What does it mean when we say that an entrepreneur should work on the business, not in it?

19.3 Business Model Canvas

3. How can the business model canvas help us to describe and assess a business model?

A **business model** describes the rationale of how an organization creates, delivers, and captures value. Entrepreneurs need to develop and refine a business model for themselves as they seek clarity about what they are doing, and also for discussing with colleagues, partners, and other stakeholders. Moreover, this business model will help them to identify opportunities in their internal and external environment. Originally developed by Alex Osterwalder and colleagues,[6] the **business model canvas** covers the four main areas of any venture: customers, offering, infrastructure, and financial viability. There are nine building blocks that describe and assess a business model: customer segments, value propositions, channels, customer relationships, revenue streams, key resources, key activities, key partnerships, and cost structure. **Table 19.1** depicts the business model canvas.

Business Model Canvas				
Key Partnerships • Who are our key partners and suppliers? • Which key resources are from which partner? • What key activities are done by partners?	**Key Activities** • What key activities do our value proposition, channels, customer relationships, and revenue streams require?	**Value Proposition** • What do we provide our customers? • What problem are we solving? • What are we offering to each customer segment?	**Customer Relationships** • What type of relationship does each customer segment want? • How costly are the relationships? • How do we integrate them with the rest of our business model?	**Customer Segments** • Who are our customers? • From whom are we creating value?
	Key Resources • What key resources do our value proposition, channels, customer relationships, and revenue streams require?		**Channels** • How will we reach our customer segments? • How are our channels integrated? • Which channels are the most efficient?	
Cost Structure • What are the most important costs in our business model? • Which key activities and key resources are the most expensive?			**Revenue Streams** • What are customers willing to pay? • What and how do they currently pay? • How much does each revenue stream contribute to overall revenue?	

Table 19.1 (Attribution: Copyright Rice University, OpenStax, under CC BY-NC-SA 4.0 license)

Nine Building Blocks of the Business Model Canvas

Customer segments: Without customers, businesses cannot survive. Businesses must identify and understand their customers, and they can group these customers into segments with common characteristics.

Value propositions: A company creates value, or benefits, for customers by solving a problem or satisfying a need. The value proposition is the reason that customers choose one option over another when deciding what to buy. Although certainly not an exhaustive list, customers may value: newness, performance, customization, design, brand, price, cost reduction, risk reduction, accessibility, and convenience.

Channels: Channels bring the value proposition to the customers through communication, distribution, and sales. Companies can reach their customer segments through a mix of channels, both direct (e.g., through sales force and web sales) and indirect (e.g., through own stores, partner stores, and wholesalers), to raise awareness, allow for purchase and delivery, provide customer support, and support other important functions of the business.

Customer relationships: Companies need to maintain relationships with their customers to acquire and retain customers and boost sales. Strong customer relationships can significantly impact overall customer experience. There are many categories of customer relationships including personal assistance, self-service, automated service, user communities, and cocreation.

Revenue streams: There are two types of revenue stream: revenues from one-time customers and revenues from ongoing payments. Revenue pricing mechanisms vary from fixed (e.g., predefined prices based on static variables) to dynamic (e.g., price changes based on market conditions). Revenue streams can be generated through asset sales (e.g., selling a physical product), usage fees, subscription fees, licensing, brokerage fees, advertising, and temporarily selling the use of a particular asset (e.g., lending, renting, or leasing).

Key resources: Any business needs resources—physical, financial, intellectual, and/or human—to function. These resources enable the company to provide their products or services to their customers.

Key activities: Key activities are the critical tasks that a company does to succeed and operate successfully. Different companies focus on different activities in categories such as production, problem-solving, and platform/network.

Key partnerships: Companies build partnerships to optimize their business, reduce risk, or gain resources. There are four main types of partnerships: strategic alliances between noncompetitors, coopetition—strategic alliances between competitors, joint ventures, and buyer-supplier relationships.

Cost structure: All businesses incur costs through operation, whether fixed or variable. They may also face economies of scale and scope. Companies consider their cost structures in two strategies—cost-driven, where all costs are reduced wherever possible, and value-driven, where the focus is on greater value creation. Cost structures will often consider fixed costs, variable costs, economies of scale, and economies of scope.

Business Model Canvas Application: Apple

To best illustrate the business model canvas, we can take a look at Apple illustrated in **Table 19.2**.

Customer segments: Apple's main consumer segment is the mass market, and Apple sells globally to customers all over the world. These customers tend to have similar needs and problems that can be addressed through globally standardized offerings such as the iPhone and iPad (hardware) as well as iTunes (software).

Value proposition: In a competitive marketplace, Apple must offer a bundle of products and services that cater to the customer segment. As one illustration, Apple iTunes offers a seamless music experience where customers can easily find, purchase, and download music all in one place.

Channels: Customers are able to interact with Apple in person through retail stores and Apple stores as well as online through the iTunes store and Apple's company website.

Customer relationships: Apple's customers are dedicated to the brand and often have many Apple products, such as iPhones, iPads, and MacBooks. The Apple lovemark has become a status symbol.

Revenue streams: Apple earns most of its revenues from selling products such as iPods, and the iTunes store protects them from competition with similar features.

Key resources: Apple's key resources include its name brand, hardware and software, and content.

Key activities: Apple products have outstanding marketing and hardware design.

Key partnerships: Through negotiations and contracts, Apple's iTunes store is one of the world's largest online music libraries.

Cost structure: Most of Apple's costs come through manufacturing and marketing, including employee salaries.

<table>
<tr><th colspan="5">Business Model Canvas for Apple</th></tr>
<tr>
<td rowspan="2">Key Partnerships<ul><li>Record companies</li><li>OEMs</li><li>People</li><li>Content & agreements</li></ul></td>
<td>Key Activities<ul><li>Marketing</li><li>Hardware design</li></ul></td>
<td rowspan="2">Value Proposition<ul><li>Seamless music experience</li></ul></td>
<td>Customer Relationships<ul><li>Lovemark</li><li>Switching costs</li></ul></td>
<td rowspan="2">Customer Segments<ul><li>Mass market</li></ul></td>
</tr>
<tr>
<td>Key Resources<ul><li>Apple brand</li><li>iPad hardware</li><li>iTunes software</li><li>Content & agreements</li></ul></td>
<td>Channels<ul><li>Retail stores</li><li>Apple stores</li><li>Apple.com</li><li>iTunes store</li></ul></td>
</tr>
<tr>
<td colspan="3">Cost Structure<ul><li>People</li><li>Manufacturing</li><li>Marketing/sales</li></ul></td>
<td colspan="2">Revenue Streams<ul><li>iTunes store</li><li>Large hardware revenues</li><li>Some music revenues</li></ul></td>
</tr>
</table>

Table 19.2 (Attribution: Copyright Rice University, OpenStax, under CC BY-NC-SA 4.0 license)

The business model canvas can be used to determine how to compete, as either an initial entrant or a fast follower. An entrepreneurial organization is often a **first mover** by introducing a new product or service category that can potentially define an innovation's characteristics in the minds of buyers, gaining valuable name recognition and brand loyalty. First movers can also lock in key resources (such as certain distribution channels) and set a technology standard. **Second movers** have the potential advantage of learning from and improving on the first mover's efforts. For example, second movers can take advantage of existing customers and optimize the first mover's product to add new features, especially when customers are willing to switch. Research on the battle between first and second movers indicates that they are equally likely to win the market.[7] One illustration of first and second movers is in China's competitive mobile payment industry.

EXPANDING AROUND THE GLOBE

The War of Two "Horses": First and Second Movers in China's Mobile Payment Industry

Over the last decade, Chinese people have been rapidly and systematically utilizing mobile payment—that is, payment services performed through a mobile device. This trend kicked off with China's first e-commerce wholesale platform Alibaba, founded by Jack Ma from his humble apartment in Hangzhou, China, in 1999. Responding to eBay's growing presence in China a few years later, Jack Ma launched taobao.com, a consumer-to-consumer (C2C) and business-to-consumer (B2C) online marketplace. To support taobao.com's transactions, Jack Ma released Alipay later that year as a "third-party online payment platform." Mobile payment became a reality in China when Alipay released its mobile app in 2008, which can be used to pay water, electricity, and gas bills as well as mobile phone fees. After 2011, when the first third-party payment license was issued to Alipay, more Chinese consumers replaced their credit cards and debit cards with Alipay. By 2013, Alipay overtook PayPal as the world's largest mobile payment platform. Alipay dominated 69.6 percent of China's mobile payment market. Jack Ma was the "only horse" (the surname Ma means "horse" in Chinese) in the field and a clear first mover, but faced a solid rival in second mover IT giant Tencent.

Ma Huateng founded Tencent Inc. in 1998, and its early years focused on the iconic product of QQ, China's first instant messaging software product. Tencent expanded into other Internet fields such as games, music, microblogging, and online shopping. By 2011, Tencent's QQ was China's most successful instant messaging software with over 700 million active users, and the company released WeChat, another instant messaging software product. Tencent's two software products competed in the same space, with QQ primarily PC-based with "online" and "offline" status, and WeChat smartphone-based without "offline" status. WeChat soon acquired over 300 million users. Tencent is often described as a successful "second mover," imitating a promising business model introduced by innovative first-mover firms and then surpassing these firms.

The two IT giants faced off in 2013 when each invested in a taxi booking app: Didi (by Tencent) and Kuaidi (by Alibaba). In an August 2013 5.0 version update of WeChat, users were surprised to find a "wallet" function added to the app, but most did not know how to use it. However, for Jack Ma and Ma Huateng, all had become clear: the two "horses" were going to war.

Tencent offered and then linked three seemingly unrelated apps: smartphone-based WeChat, taxi-booking app Didi, and a new wallet function. In January 2014, WeChat wallet was linked to Didi as the payment method. Passengers using WeChat to pay the taxi fare received a generous subsidy from Tencent, making taxi fare lower than bus fare. Alipay and the Kuaidi app responded in a similar way.

While widely welcomed by white-collar workers, the money-burning campaign cost each side approximately 1.5 billion RMB (US$244 million). For Ma Huateng, the campaign is not just about occupying the newly born taxi-booking app market in China, but also about penetrating Jack Ma's precious share of the mobile payment market by "teaching" WeChat users how to use make mobile payments. Weeks later, Ma Huateng continued his "teaching" in the virtual red envelope campaign during Chinese Spring Festival. The virtual red envelope is modeled after the Chinese tradition of exchanging packets of money among friends and family members during holidays. WeChat introduced the "red envelope shake" to the Chinese Spring Festival Gala, during which users were invited to shake their smartphones for a chance to win red envelopes, and eight million WeChat users participated in this promotion campaign. WeChat users can save the money won to their WeChat "wallet" and then send it to others with their own red envelope. WeChat sent 1.2 billion red envelopes worth over half a billion RMB (US$82 million) during the promotion. However, to use the money from the red envelope, WeChat users needed to add their bank card to their WeChat account and thus fully activate the WeChat payment function. Retrospectively, Jack Ma regarded the WeChat red envelope promotion as a "Pearl Harbor attack" on his territory.

After the Chinese Spring Festival, the money-burning war game between first mover Alipay and second mover WeChat continued. Both sides heavily subsidized taxi passengers on their taxi-booking apps through 2014. In the third quarter of 2014, Alipay's market share reached a peak of 82.6 percent, but WeChat's increasing presence the in mobile payment market was unstoppable. Both sides engaged in a new red envelope campaign during the next Spring Festival holiday. While Alipay fought hard to defend its market share, WeChat's social nature smoothly transformed users into payers.

By the end of 2016, both sides saw continuous growth in user population; however, Alipay's market share dropped to 54.10 percent, and Tencent and WeChat's market share rose to 37.02 percent. In that year, consumers spent 157.55 trillion RMB (US$23.72 trillion) on mobile devices in China, and QR codes and POS machines supporting both Alipay and WeChat could be found at street food vendors, supermarkets, department stores, and online markets.

Discussion Questions:

1. What tactics did Tencent use to encroach on Alibaba's share of the mobile payment market?
2. What key resources did WeChat use to compete with Alipay?
3. Does WeChat's presence in the mobile payment market always negatively affect Alipay?
4. Would you rather be a first mover or a second mover in a new technology market?

Sources: Sophia Yan, "6 things you never knew about Alibaba", CNN, May 12, 2015, http://money.cnn.com/2015/05/12/technology/alibaba-surprising-facts/index.html; Paul Mozur, "In Urban China, Cash Is Rapidly Becoming Obsolete", New York Times, July 16, 2017, https://www.nytimes.com/2017/07/16/business/china-cash-smartphone-payments.html; Eva Xiao, "How WeChat Pay became Alipay's largest rival", Tech in Asia, April 20, 2017, https://www.techinasia.com/wechat-pay-vs-alipay; Anonymous Author, "WeChat", Wikipedia, October 2 2017, https://en.wikipedia.org/wiki/WeChat#WeChat_Pay_payment_services; Anonymous Author, "WeChat red envelope", Wikipedia, September 19, 2017, https://en.wikipedia.org/wiki/WeChat_red_envelope; Anonymous Author, "Alipay", Wikipedia; September 8, 2017, https://en.wikipedia.org/wiki/Alipay; Nie Chenjing, "Mobile Payment Report: Alipay Shares Occupy Half of the Country", Xinhuanet, March 31, 2017; http://news.xinhuanet.com/fortune/2017-03/31/c_1120732899.htm; Li Yanxia, "Central Bank Report: China Mobile's payment amount increased by nearly 50% year-on-year in 2016, March 16, 2017, http://it.people.com.cn/n1/2017/0316/c1009-29150183.html.

CONCEPT CHECK

1. What are the key components of the business model canvas?
2. What are the advantages and disadvantages of being a first mover?

19.4 New Venture Financing

4. How do entrepreneurs finance their new business ideas?

Many entrepreneurs don't start a business because they believe that starting a venture will require substantial sums of funding, and they personally do not possess these reserves. The most common means of starting new ventures is by **bootstrapping**—that is, attempting to found and build a company from personal finances or from the operating revenues of the new company. This term comes from the expression "pull yourself up by your bootstraps" (the fingerholds on boots). Bootstrapping can complement traditional finance sources, helping entrepreneurs to reduce their reliance on them or eliminate these sources entirely. **Table 19.3** depicts seven bootstrapping strategies.

Bootstrapping Strategies	
Strategy	Example
1. Stick to a business domain you know and love.	Two recent Florida Atlantic University alumni transformed their love of surfing and the ocean into 4ocean, which sells bracelets and other products. The sales pay local fishermen to clean up plastic and trash in waterways.
2. Find team members to work for equity rather than cash.	In 2005, Sean Parker, founding president of Facebook, asked artist David Choe to take stock instead of cash for painting the Facebook office walls. That stock was eventually worth $200 million.
3. Build a plan around your budget rather than your wishes.	Cam Ross started Celise, a biodegradable goods supplier, in college. Strapped for financing, Cameron planned around his available budget, which depended on current sales and wins in business plan competitions.

Table 19.3

Bootstrapping Strategies	
Strategy	Example
4. Defer your urge to have office space until you have customers.	In July 2014, Amazon founder Jeff Bezos started the company from the garage of a home he rented in Bellevue, Washington.
5. Ask for advances on royalties and vendor-deferred payments.	In the music industry, many songwriters have sought advances against future royalties from their songs.
6. Negotiate inventory management with suppliers and distributors.	Pet food delivery start-up Petcircle is one of Australia's fastest-growing companies. They attribute their early success to bootstrapping via managing supplier terms carefully.
7. Choose a business model to optimize your revenue flow and timing.	Chicago-based restaurant Alinea creates themes and sells out seats month in advance, allowing them to buy in bulk with cash from customers. As payments are upfront and all sales are final, revenue is fixed prior to delivering the meals. This business model eliminates many of the downsides of traditional restaurants' business models.
Source: Adapted from Martin Zwilling,"7 Ways to Bootstrap Your Business," Entrepreneur Magazine, December 25, 2015, https://www.entrepreneur.com/article/254217; https://business.fau.edu/centers/adams-center/ace-success-stories/ ; Lucy England, "The artist who painted Facebook's 1st office took stock instead of cash — and now he is worth $200 million," *Business Insider*, June 9, 2015, https://www.businessinsider.com/graffiti-artist-painted-facebooks-first-office-now-worth-200-million-2015-6; Todd Bishop, "Amazon at 20 years: From garage startup to global technology powerhouse," *GeekWire*, July 9, 2014, https://www.geekwire.com/2014/amazon-20-years-garage-startup-global-powerhouse/.	

Table 19.3 (Attribution: Copyright Rice University, OpenStax, under CC BY-NC-SA 4.0 license)

Types of Capital

There are two main types of capital for entrepreneurs. Entrepreneurs can access **debt capital**, which is borrowed money that must be repaid at some agreed-upon future date (e.g., from banks, credit cards, or finance companies), and **equity capital**, which is the owner's investment in the company and does not have a specific date for repayment (e.g., angel investors, venture capital).

Debt financing is available to most entrepreneurs and can involve loans of various lengths. Short-term loans typically require repayment in less than 1 year and are often credit-created or bank loans. Immediate-term loans must be repaid in between 1 and 10 years, usually in periods. They are useful for small and moderate-sized companies. Long-term loans last over 10 years. Businesses must be operating for a long period of time to be approved for these loans to show stability and reliability to repay their debt. Equity capital does not require a business to promise to repay any debt. Equity capital is an investment in the business, frequently from selling common stock.

Sources of Capital

Entrepreneurs can utilize capital from several sources. The most common type of capital is personal savings. By using personal savings, the venture eliminates the expectation of repayment on a loan, and the entrepreneur does not face as much financial backlash when profits do not meet expectations. Friends and relatives can often be a fast way to gain capital. However, financial issues may create tension in these relationships. **Angel investors** are individual investors or groups of experienced investors who provide venture financing from their own funds. **Venture capital** is financing obtained from venture capitalists, investment firms that specialize in financing small, high-growth companies and receive an ownership interest and a voice in management in return for their investment. Internal funds are retained earnings within a firm that can be reinvested into the business.

Banks offer many types of loan services, including lines of credit, straight commercial loans, term loans, accounts-receivable loans, warehouse-receipt loans, and collateral loans. A line of credit is an informal agreement between the bank and the borrower (the business). Straight commercial loans are based on the borrower's financial statements and are typically made for 30–90 days. Term loans mature in 1 to 10 years. Accounts-receivable loans are made against a borrower's receivables, and once collected, the bank is repaid. Warehouse-receipt loans use inventory as collateral for a loan, and as the inventory is sold, the loan is paid off. Collateral loans use real estate mortgages, life insurance policies, stocks, and bonds as security to ensure loan repayment.

Crowdfunding is the process of raising new venture funds from a large "crowd" audience, typically virtually from the Internet. Crowdfunding is rapidly becoming a popular way to fund new ventures, with over $1.04 billion in 2018 for U.S. businesses alone. Crowdfunding comes in three main forms: (1) reward-based, in which backers receive an early version of the product or another reward, (2) equity, through which individual investors receive a company share, and (3) debt, which allows the backer to earn interest. The world's largest crowdfunding platform is Kickstarter, which has received over $4 billion in pledges from 15.5 million backers for 25,700 projects.[8] The average crowdfunding campaign raises $818[9]; however, some companies raise millions of dollars. Typically, each crowdfunding project sets a goal for a specific time period, and entrepreneurs publish web pages to depict their product services.

CATCHING THE ENTREPRENEURIAL SPIRIT

Making a Heavenly Deal

You need financing for your start-up business. How do you get angels interested in investing in your business venture?

- Show them something they understand, ideally a business from an industry they've been associated with.
- Know your business details: potential investors want to know about annual sales, gross profit, profit margin, and expenses.
- Be able to describe your business—what it does and who it sells to—in less than a minute. Limit PowerPoint presentations to 10 slides.
- Angels can always leave their money in the bank or invest in another promising ventures, so an investment is often in a sector that interests them. Timing is also important—knowing when to reach out to an angel can make a huge difference.
- Present a competent management team with a strong, experienced leader who can explain the business and answer questions from potential investors with specifics, and can quickly earn potential investors' trust and respect.
- Angels prefer something they can bring added value to and may want to be involved with your company—for example, with a seat on your board of directors.
- Emphasize the likely exits for investors and know who the competition is, why your solution is better, and how you are going to gain market share with an infusion of cash.

Sources: Guy Kawasaki, "The Art of Raising Angel Capital," https://guykawasaki.com, accessed February 2, 2018; Murray Newlands, "How to Raise an Angel Funding Round," *Forbes,* https://www.forbes.com, March 16, 2017; Melinda Emerson, "5 Tips for Attracting Angel Investors," *Small Business Trends,* https://smallbiztrends.com, July 26, 2016; Nicole Fallon, "5 Tips for Attracting Angel Investors," *Business News Daily,* https://www.businessnewsdaily.com, January 2, 2014; Stacy Zhao, "9 Tips for Winning over Angels," *Inc.,* https://www.inc.com, June 15, 2005; Rhonda Abrams, "What Does It Take to Impress an Angel Investor?" *Inc.,* https://www.inc.com, March 29, 2001.

CONCEPT CHECK

1. What sources of capital are available to entrepreneurs?
2. What are the associated risks for various sources of capital?

19.5 Design Thinking

5. How can entrepreneurs leverage design thinking to solve complex problems and navigate uncertain environments?

Design thinking is a process commonly used by designers to find the solution to complex issues, navigate new or uncertain environments, and create a new product for the world. Design thinking uses core elements and skills of play, empathy, reflection, creation, and experimentation to collaborate, create, and build upon findings. In design thinking, failure is not a threat, but an avenue to further learning. Through observation, synthesis, alternatives, critical thinking, feedback, visual representation, creativity, problem-solving, and value creation, entrepreneurs can use design thinking to identify unique venture opportunities.

Design thinkers welcome difficulties and constraints, as these pave the way to innovative ideas and solutions. It is important, however, that these ideas are feasible, viable, and desired by people.

Exhibit 19.5 Ideo To demonstrate the process for innovation for a 1999 episode of ABC's late-night news show *Nightline*, IDEO created a new shopping cart concept, considering issues such as maneuverability, shopping behavior, child safety, and maintenance cost. The show concentrated on IDEO's design process, recording as a multidisciplinary team brainstormed, researched, prototyped, and gathered user feedback on a design that went from idea to a working appearance model in four days. (Credit: David Armano/ flickr/ Attribution 2.0 Generic (CC BY 2.0))

There are three main phases of design thinking: inspiration, ideation, and implementation. The problem, or design challenge, is the inspiration. Ideation is a creative process of solving the design challenge based on observations. Ideas are turned into actions in the implementation phase. Possible solutions are tested through experiments to create the best version of the product. In all of these phases, there are two main types of thinking: convergent and divergent. Convergent thinking moves from broad thoughts to concrete understanding, where the thoughts from divergent thinking can be narrowed down to the most promising ideas and solutions. Divergent thinking uses the imagination to open the mind to new possibilities and solutions, and ultimately become more innovative.

Stanford Design Thinking

IDEO 6 Tips

1. **Always say yes to an offer.** Whether the other person offers you a glass of water, snacks, or even a tour of their home, you should always accept. This small gesture allows you to transition from a researcher to a guest in their home. It's always important to spend time building rapport, even if your initial conversation feels completely off topic. Later, when you actually dive into your research questions, the conversation will flow more freely.
2. **Wear generic clothing.** Oftentimes, clothing can communicate social status or reflect personal taste that others may disagree with. It's better to make yourself as neutral as possible so that you can fit in with people of all backgrounds. Try to avoid wearing logos or looking too fancy.
3. **Treat people like partners in research.** The people you interview aren't just research subjects or data points. Instead, you should be transparent with them and show that you value their input. Their stories and feedback play a huge role in what we end up designing, so it's great to let them know why they are a fundamental part of our project.
4. **Leave comfortable silences.** When it seems like the other person is finished speaking, most people feel the need to immediately move on to the next question. Instead, you should create some space by just nodding and writing things down—it gives the other person room to continue speaking beyond the parameters of the previous question and to perhaps reveal information about themselves that you wouldn't learn otherwise.
5. **Take the spotlight off the other person.** As part of our design process, we like to bring provocations into research sessions. This means that we sketch out rough concepts to show the other person, and we ask them for feedback. By shifting our attention from the person to another object, we can remove any pressure they're feeling. These outside objects also allow participants to communicate in a nonverbal way—the way they interact with them can reveal tacit attitudes or behaviors. As a side bonus, you get to bring home some tangible artifacts that you can refer back to during the design process.
6. **Try very intentionally to fall in love with each person** (even if it's just a little bit). Even if you don't naturally click with someone, you can always find something you truly appreciate about them, whether it's their voice or their passion for the topic at hand. When you want to fall in love with someone, everything changes—your curiosity about their life story, your body language, and your empathy toward their situation. These small shifts will show your interviewee that they don't have to perform or show the "best" parts of themselves, because they can tell that you're deeply on their side. Even after the interview, you'll find yourself coming up with better ideas because it's much easier to design for someone that you love.

Source: Maggie Zhao. 6 Tips from IDEO designers on how to unlock insightful conversation. https://www.ideou.com/blogs/inspiration/6-tips-from-ideo-designers-on-how-to-unlock-insightful-conversation; https://dschool.stanford.edu/resources.

CONCEPT CHECK

1. What is design thinking?
2. What are some advantages of design thinking?

19.6 Optimal Support for Entrepreneurship

6. How can government support entrepreneurship?

Governments generally want to support entrepreneurship because successful businesses create value among the population. This value permits companies to provide jobs, pay corporate taxes, and enable workers to pay taxes. Governments also get political credit for policies that increase commerce, wealth creation, and job creation. In general, government sets and changes the institutional conditions that encourage or discourage entrepreneurs from either innovating or seeking profit by other means. Government can support entrepreneurship by reducing negative incentives or by increasing positive ones. In particular, government can:

- Reduce barriers to entrepreneurship erected by previous governments or in society.
- Protect intellectual property and capital through the patent system and the rule of law.
- Provide businesses with technology ready for commercialization.
- Increase incentives for entrepreneurship, which comes at a cost to other priorities.
- Provide special benefits to favored industries, businesses, or regions, although such **cronyism** can come at a political and economic cost by distorting markets and playing favorites.

Less Discouragement: Reducing Barriers

Regulations, like laws, set rules that help entrepreneurs predict what will happen if they take certain risks. For this reason, regulations should be clear and should not change quickly or merely when a new political majority takes power. In general, a regulation is a restriction, and any restriction tends to reduce innovation by limiting options. For this reason, reducing regulations tends to unleash innovation. This is not always the case. For example, zoning restrictions might push similar businesses to be near one another, leading to increased cross-fertilization of ideas. Also, when government enforces property rights including intellectual property, preventing others from using that property, entrepreneurs feel more secure in employing their capital. Similarly, entrepreneurs feel more secure when their government refrains from appropriating property via eminent domain or socialist takeovers.

Laws and regulations often reflect the values of a particular political and economic moment, and they become outdated because of the speed of innovation. Technology changes faster than bureaucrats can keep up. For example, two different companies had similar revolutionary technology: Skype and Free World Dialup (FWD). Both were able to provide free "telephone calls" over the Internet worldwide. In the United States, FWD had to wait 18 months for regulators to determine that FWD was exempt from traditional U.S. telecommunication regulations. Meanwhile, abroad, free from this process, Skype had years to develop its user base. FWD could not compete and went out of business, leaving Skype the undisputed champion.[10]

Regulations also tend to favor larger, established businesses that innovate less, and they tend to disfavor smaller, entrepreneurial ventures. International trade barriers such as tariffs often protect a country's existing businesses and make it relatively difficult for new businesses from other countries to compete. Bureaucracy also can make it difficult, costly, and time consuming to start a business. In countries with high levels of corruption, proprietors may have to pay extra fees to bureaucrats to get their paperwork to the top of the pile.

Taxation also reduces the profit from an enterprise, so taxation reduces the likelihood that entrepreneurs will risk their capital. Progressive taxation, unlike a flat tax, penalizes businesses at higher rates for making more money, which also can discourage entrepreneurship. Reducing taxes and regulation can encourage entrepreneurship, although these changes also can increase the competitiveness of established businesses, which entrepreneurs will take into account. Also, providing tax exemption for nonprofit enterprises and social entrepreneurship encourages a wide variety of value-creating services in civil society.

In addition to government barriers to entrepreneurship, there often are cultural barriers. For example, in some countries, discrimination on the basis of sex, race, or religion prevents many would-be entrepreneurs from getting equal access to the resources they would need to thrive. Government can step in to outlaw such discrimination and protect equal rights. Government also can address culturally discriminatory attitudes that are not illegal by means of education campaigns. Government also can subsidize external constraints on growing a business, such as by subsidizing childcare so that entrepreneurs can spend more time on their work at lower cost.

More Discouragement: Increasing Positive Incentives

Government can reduce the cost of technological innovation by simply giving government-produced technology to the private sector so that the technology can be commercialized. Government also can change the rules of financing to reduce the transaction cost or the actual cost of acquiring funds. For instance, government can make it easier or less costly for businesses to receive government loans, can subsidize lending, or can subsidize borrowing. All of these efforts come at a cost either directly, at the cost of the subsidy, or indirectly, by providing cheaper funds to riskier ventures than the private loan market would otherwise provide.

Government also can provide venture capital to attract new ventures, especially in areas where the private sector cannot afford to take expensive risks or has little experience with this kind of funding. This capital, however, can prop up lower-quality businesses that ultimately will not succeed. The private sector, risking its own capital instead of taxpayers' money, generally may not have supported such less-investible businesses. Furthermore, by focusing on potential high-growth firms, government can shortchange other kinds of firms. Finally, research suggests that high-quality projects are what attract dollars, rather than extra dollars attracting investible projects.[11]

Government also can subsidize other elements of innovation and building businesses, such as direct subsidies for research and technology development or for building facilities. This kind of support easily slides into cronyism where, for a variety of reasons, particular industries or regions receive special treatment even when they are not the best-positioned options from an economic perspective. For example, government might limit its business contracts to only certain kinds of small businesses, even though a larger business might provide better service per dollar.

Government also can put resources into training programs, which can include formal entrepreneurship and business courses at institutions of higher education, "incubators" that provide business advice, or informal networking events in local communities.

Longer-term projects, closer to the beginning of the entrepreneur pipeline, include public financing of education in financial literacy, comfort with risk taking, historical exemplars of entrepreneurship, and leadership to develop a culture of entrepreneurial thinking that can start as early as elementary school.

The local government can market the value of social entrepreneurship and small businesses for the community, providing moral support for volunteerism, low-profit and nonprofit service ventures, and structures such as a local chamber of commerce. In thriving economies where many people have leisure to pursue low-profit and nonprofit ventures, there is room for more social entrepreneurship. Therefore, to maximize social entrepreneurship, pro-growth policies that support entrepreneurship in general may be the best policies in the long run.

Finally, the government can also support entrepreneurship by making technology developed in federal labs available for commercialization, as illustrated by The Right Stuff case.

Exhibit 19.6 The Right Stuff Rather than use traditional advertising methods like magazine, newspaper, and television advertising, many entrepreneurs use social media to connect to existing and future customers. Posting information about products and services is the obvious use. Twitter also gives entrepreneurs a two-way channel for listening to and finding out more about their customers—what they like or dislike about their products and services, how they feel about the brand, and what suggestions they have for improvement. (Credit: David Belaga/ Attribution 2.0 Generic (CC BY 2.0))

MANAGING CHANGE

Technology and Innovation: *The Right Stuff*

David Belaga enjoyed a successful corporate career of over 25 years at Pepsi, Wyeth, Hallmark, and other leading companies, and was keen to start his own technology-based venture. Although Belaga possessed an undergraduate degree in psychology, he sought to take advantage of technology from federal labs across the United States. While searching the National Aeronautics and Space Administration (NASA) database of available patents to license, Belaga discovered NASA scientist Dr. John Greenleaf's patent to rehydrate astronauts who suffer from severe dehydration when reentering Earth's atmosphere. Greenleaf et al.'s research suggested that the formula would also be ideal for athletes facing dehydration due to exertion, sun exposure, or altitude, which could then result in headaches, muscle cramps, dizziness or light-headedness, and other side effects. Key ingredients are: filtered water, sodium citrate (to protect against gastrointestinal upset), sea salt or sodium chloride (key components of sweat), all-natural flavors, citric acid (to cut saltiness), high-intensity sweetener, natural flavors, and preservatives. The liquid concentrate ensures quick absorption by the body, and the formula does not contain any World Anti-Doping Agency (WADA)-listed banned substances, heavy metals, or other adulterants.

NASA's Technology Partnership Division has the mission of developing partnerships between NASA enterprises and nonaerospace U.S. industrial firms to commercialize innovative technologies. NASA's Technology Partnership Division offers space, licensing, software, and other small business agreements, and NASA benefits from division license agreements that help fund vital research and development for future products. NASA prioritizes "small business" partnerships, classified by the U.S. Small Business Administration as ". . . firms that are independently owned and operated, organized for profit, and not dominant in the field." Belaga liked that the formula was used by astronauts, and thought to himself, "The reality is that in less time than it takes to read this paragraph, Coke (Powerade) and Pepsi (Gatorade) could do a work-around formula, but it wouldn't be the one supported by all the science." Belaga named the formula "The Right Stuff," reflecting the book and movie linked to the NASA program and due to the formula's superior efficacy. Following the submission of a 150-page business plan for The Right Stuff's commercialization and a 60-day public comment period on the *Federal Register*, Belaga negotiated final approval and exclusive rights to the technology with a share of royalties for NASA and a guarantee of production in the U.S.

Belaga started his venture with $300,000 in personal funds and $325,000 in "friends and family" investment, and developed a network of contracts with suppliers for supply chain management, manufacturing, and marketing activities. Prior to the launch, Belaga empaneled a set of endurance athletes to create the preferred flavor profiles. He later learned that power athletes (e.g., football, baseball, hockey, and basketball) prefer a sweeter and fruitier taste than do endurance athletes.

Although initial consumer market research suggested the possibility for use by individual endurance athletes (e.g., runners) and first responders (e.g., military, fire, and police), Belaga focused on the institutional market of professional athletic teams, universities, sports clubs, and high schools. Today The Right Stuff is used by most professional North American sports teams (MLB, NBA, NFL, NHL, MLS, etc.) and hundreds of universities across the U.S.

Discussion Questions

1. What benefits do David Belaga and The Right Stuff accrue from the affiliation with NASA technology?
2. What are the societal benefits of the government making technology available for commercialization licensing?

Sources: Siri Terjesen. 2015. The Right Stuff. Entrepreneurship Theory & Practice.

CONCEPT CHECK

1. How can governments reduce barriers to entrepreneurship?
2. How can governments increase positive incentives for entrepreneurship?

Key Terms

angel investors Individual investors or groups of experienced investors who provide venture financing from their own funds.

business model Rationale of how an organization creates, delivers, and captures value.

business model canvas A tool to describe and assess a business model, encompassing nine components: customer segments, value propositions, channels, customer relationships, revenue streams, key resources, key activities, key partnerships, and cost structure.

corporate entrepreneurship The creation of new products, processes, and ventures within large organizations.

crowdfunding Process of raising new venture funds from a large "crowd" audience, typically virtually from the Internet.

debt capital Borrowed money that must be repaid at some agreed-upon future date.

design thinking Processes used by designers and entrepreneurs to find the solution to complex issues, navigate new or uncertain environments, and create a new product for the world.

entrepreneurs Individuals who recognize and pursue opportunities, take on risk, and convert these opportunities into value-added ventures that can survive in a competitive marketplace.

equity capital Owner's investment in the company; does not have a specific date for repayment.

established business owners Individuals who are still active in a business that is more than three and a half years old.

family entrepreneurship A business is owned and managed by multiple family members, usually for more than one generation.

first mover Introducing a new product or service category first can potentially define an innovation's characteristics in the minds of buyers, gaining valuable name recognition and brand loyalty.

high-technology entrepreneurship Ventures in the information, communication, and technology space; typically have high growth expectations.

lifestyle entrepreneurship Creating a venture to suit a personal lifestyle and not for the sole purpose of making profits.

nascent entrepreneurs Individuals who have set up a business they will own or co-own that is less than three months old and has not yet generated wages or salaries for the owners.

new business owners Former nascent entrepreneurs who are actively involved in a business for more than three months but less than three and a half years.

potential entrepreneurs Individuals who believe that they possess the capacity and knowledge to start a business.

second movers Second-to-market organization that can learn from and improve on the first mover's efforts.

serial or habitual entrepreneurship Individuals who start several businesses, simultaneously or one after another.

social entrepreneurship Creating innovative solutions to immediate social and/or environment problems and mobilizing resources to achieve social transformation.

venture capital Financing obtained from venture capitalists, investment firms that specialize in financing small, high-growth companies and receive an ownership interest and a voice in management in return for their investment.

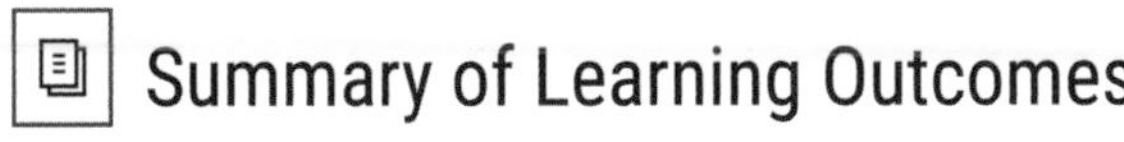

Summary of Learning Outcomes

19.1 Overview of Entrepreneurship

1. What are some different types of entrepreneurship?

Entrepreneurship is the creation of something valuable. Social entrepreneurship involves creating innovative solutions to immediate social and/or environmental problems and mobilizing resources to achieve social transformation. Corporate entrepreneurship involves the creation of new products, processes, and ventures within existing large organizations. Family entrepreneurship involves a business that is owned and managed by multiple family members, usually for more than one generation. Serial or habitual entrepreneurship refers to individuals who start several businesses, simultaneously or one after another. Lifestyle entrepreneurship involves a venture to suit a personal *lifestyle* and not for the sole purpose of making profit. High-technology entrepreneurship involves ventures in the information, communication, and technology space.

19.2 Characteristics of Successful Entrepreneurs

2. What characteristics lead individuals to become entrepreneurs?

Most entrepreneurs are ambitious, independent, self-confident, risk-taking, visionary, creative, energetic, passionate, and committed. Entrepreneurial individuals are often competitive, with a need to achieve, and are self-starters who prefer to lead. Compared to the average population, entrepreneurs are more decisive and confident in their abilities, and they choose moderate risk where they can affect outcomes. Entrepreneurs spot and act on trends, often producing innovative product designs, marketing strategies, and managerial solutions. Entrepreneurs are able and willing to work hard, and are attached to the work and the outcomes, so much that they are willing to make personal sacrifices to achieve their goals.

19.3 Business Model Canvas

3. How can the business model canvas help us to describe and assess a business model?

A business model provides an explanation of how an organization creates, delivers, and captures value. The business model canvas achieves this goal by describing four main areas of any venture—customers, offering, infrastructure, and financial viability—through nine building blocks that describe and assess a business model. Customer segments are categories of customers that have common characteristics. The value proposition is the reason that customers choose one option over another when deciding what to buy. Channels bring the value proposition to the customers through communication, distribution, and sales. Companies need to maintain relationships with their customers to acquire and retain customers and boost sales. There are two general types of revenue stream: revenues from one-time customers and revenues from ongoing payments. Any business needs resources—physical, financial, intellectual, and/or human—to function and provide their products or services to their customers. Key activities are the critical tasks that a company does to succeed and operate successfully. Companies build partnerships to optimize their business, reduce risk, or gain resources. All businesses incur costs through operation, whether fixed or variable.

19.4 New Venture Financing

4. How do entrepreneurs finance their new business ideas?

Bootstrapping is attempting to found and build a company from personal finances or from the operating revenues of the new company. Entrepreneurs can access debt capital, which is borrowed money that must be repaid by a future date, and equity capital, which is the owner's investment in the company and does not have a specific date for repayment. Crowdfunding is the process of raising new venture funds from a large "crowd" audience, typically virtually from the Internet.

19.5 Design Thinking

5. How can entrepreneurs leverage design thinking to solve complex problems and navigate uncertain

environments?

Design thinking uses core elements and skills of play, empathy, reflection, creation, and experimentation to collaborate, create, and build upon findings. Through observation, synthesis, alternatives, critical thinking, feedback, visual representation, creativity, problem-solving, and value creation, entrepreneurs can use design thinking to identify unique venture opportunities. There are three main phases of design thinking: inspiration, ideation, and implementation. The problem, or design challenge, is the inspiration. Ideation is a creative process of solving the design challenge based on observations. Ideas are turned into actions in the implementation phase. Possible solutions are tested through experiments to create the best version of the product. In all of these phases, there are two main types of thinking: convergent and divergent. Convergent thinking moves from broad thoughts to concrete understanding, while the thoughts from divergent thinking can be narrowed down to the most promising ideas and solutions. Divergent thinking uses the imagination to open the mind to new possibilities and solutions, and ultimately to become more innovative.

19.6 Optimal Support for Entrepreneurship

6. How can government support entrepreneurship?

Government can support entrepreneurship by reducing negative incentives or by increasing positive ones. In particular, government can:

- Reduce barriers to entrepreneurship erected by previous governments or in society.
- Protect intellectual property and capital through the patent system and the rule of law.
- Provide businesses with technology ready for commercialization.
- Increase incentives for entrepreneurship, which comes at a cost to other priorities.
- Provide special benefits to favored industries, businesses, or regions, although such cronyism can come at a political and economic cost by distorting markets and playing favorites.

Chapter Review Questions

1. What are the differences between classic entrepreneurs, multipreneurs (entrepreneurs with many start ups), and intrapreneurs (Entrepreneurs in traditional businesses)?
2. What differentiates an entrepreneur from a small-business owner?
3. What are some major factors that motivate entrepreneurs to start businesses?
4. How can potential business owners find new business ideas?
5. Why is it important to develop a business plan? What should such a plan include?
6. What financing options do small-business owners have? What risks do they face?
7. How do the small-business owner's and entrepreneur's roles change over time?
8. What are the benefits to small firms of doing business internationally, and what steps can small businesses take to explore their options?
9. Describe the financial and management assistance programs offered by the SBA.
10. What significant trends are occurring in the small-business arena?
11. How is entrepreneurial diversity impacting small business and the economy?
12. How do ethics impact decision-making with small-business owners?

Management Skills Application Exercises

1. After working in software development with a major food company for 12 years, you are becoming

impatient with corporate "red tape" (regulations and routines). You have an idea for a new snack product for nutrition-conscious consumers and are thinking of starting your own company. What entrepreneurial characteristics do you need to succeed? What other factors should you consider before quitting your job? Working with a partner, choose one to be the entrepreneurial employee and one to play the role of his current boss. Develop notes for a script. The employee will focus on why this is a good idea—reasons he will succeed—and the employer will play devil's advocate to convince him that staying on at the large company is a better idea. Then switch roles and repeat the discussion.

2. What does it really take to become an entrepreneur? Find out by interviewing a local entrepreneur or researching an entrepreneur you've read about in this chapter or in the business press. Get answers to the following questions, as well as any others you'd like to ask:
   - How did you research the feasibility of your idea?
   - How did you develop your vision for the company?
   - How long did it take you to prepare your business plan?
   - Where did you obtain financing for the company?
   - Where did you learn the business skills you needed to run and grow the company?
   - What are the most important entrepreneurial characteristics that helped you succeed?
   - What were the biggest challenges you had to overcome?
   - What are the most important lessons you learned by starting this company?
   - What advice do you have for would-be entrepreneurs?
3. Your class decides to participate in a local business plan competition. Divide the class into small groups, and choose one of the following ideas:
   - A new computer game based on the stock market
   - A company with an innovative design for a skateboard
   - Travel services for college and high school students

   Prepare a detailed outline for the business plan, including the objectives for the business and the types of information you would need to develop product, marketing, and financing strategies. Each group will then present its outline for the class to critique.

Managerial Decision Exercises

1. A small catering business in your city is for sale for $250,000. The company specializes in business luncheons and small social events. The owner has been running the business for four years from her home but is expecting her first child and wants to sell. You will need outside investors to help you purchase the business. Develop questions to ask the owner about the business and its prospects, as well as a list of documents you want to see. What other types of information would you need before making a decision to buy this company? Summarize your findings in a memo to a potential investor that explains the appeal of the business for you and how you plan to investigate the feasibility of the purchase.
2. As the owner of a small factory that makes plastic sheeting, you are constantly seeking ways to increase profits. As the new year begins, one of your goals is to find additional funds to offer annual productivity and/or merit bonuses to your loyal, hardworking employees. Then a letter from a large national manufacturer of shower curtains seems to provide an answer. As part of a new "supplier diversity" program it is putting in place, the manufacturer is offering substantial purchase contracts to minority-owned suppliers. Even though the letter clearly states that the business must be minority owned to qualify for the program, you convince yourself to apply for it based on the fact that all your employees are Latino. You justify your decision by deciding they will benefit from the increased revenue a larger contract

will bring, some of which you plan to pass on to them in the form of bonuses later in the year. Using a web search tool, locate articles about this topic, and then write responses to the following question. Be sure to support your arguments and cite your sources.

a. Is it wrong for this business owner to apply for this program even though it will end up benefiting his employees as well as his business?

Critical Thinking Case

Fostering Entrepreneurship in Unlikely Places

Vic Ahmed is no stranger to business start-ups; he's been involved in at least 15 or 20. But his latest venture is a start-up . . . for start-ups. Ahmed founded Innovation Pavilion (IP), a business incubator in Centennial, Colorado (Denver's tech center), in 2011. A typical business incubator provides start-up companies with workspace, mentoring, training, and sometimes a path to funding, but Innovation Pavilion goes further.

Innovation Pavilion is an 80,000-square-foot "entrepreneurial ecosystem," housing dozens of start-ups and renting out desks, office space, and event space. But it also hosts meetups, educational workshops, and a Toastmasters group designed specifically for entrepreneurs. It contains a makerspace (a workspace providing shared tools and manufacturing equipment for prototyping products) and encourages the growth of niche entrepreneurial communities based on specific industries. For example, IP has a space for IoT (the Internet of Things), one for health care, and another for aerospace. These communities bring together people in an industry to learn from and collaborate with each other.

While IP has a traditional incubator program, with companies housed within the IP campus, it also has a semivirtual hypergrowth accelerator program for more mature firms that is open to companies around the country. It also seeks out educational partnerships, working with the Highlands Ranch STEM program, for instance, and has its own educational spin-off, Xuno Innovative Learning, designed to help companies train their staff and find new employees with the skills they need. IP operates its own streaming TV service, filming educational events and interviews with entrepreneurs. Innovation Pavilion has national expansion plans—and several signed agreements with specific cities—targeting not the giant metropolitan areas but also second-tier and "ring" cities across the country, such as Joliet, Illinois, and Olathe, Kansas, smaller cities that don't get the attention of the larger cities yet have plenty of educated and creative people. IP is in discussions with 20 cities around the nation, with the goal of building 200,000-square-foot campuses providing incubator services, office space, makerspace, education and training, outreach to young entrepreneurs, conference centers, retail space, and even housing. Entrepreneurs will be able to live and work in a space with everything they need, providing a complete entrepreneurial ecosystem in smaller cities across the nation. Steve Case, the cofounder of America Online (AOL), shares Vic Ahmed's vision for entrepreneurship in mid- America. His "Rise of the Rest" bus tour has traveled 8,000 miles over the last three years, investing in local start-ups in 33 cities across the country. Case hosts a pitch competition with the best start-ups in each city, and one lucky winner receives a $100,000 investment from Case. Media attention has focused on the entrepreneurial engines of America's coastal cities, but Ahmed and Case have a more expansive entrepreneurial vision, in which smaller cities throughout the nation rise up alongside larger start-up hot spots.

Sources: Innovation Pavilion website http://www.innovationpavilion.com/ accessed February, 13, 2018; Tamara Chuang, Centennial incubator plans coworking office expansion to Illinois, complete with STEM school, housing," *Denver Post,* August 1, 2017, https://www.denverpost.com/2017/08/01/innovation-pavilion-illinois-expansion/; Jan Wondra, Innovation Pavilion Expands Base," *The Villager*, November 29, 2017, https://villagerpublishing.com/innovation-pavilion-expands-geographic-base/.

 Scientific Method in Organizational Research

Students of management often complain about "theoretical" or "abstract" approaches to a subject; they argue instead in favor of "relevant" and "applied" approaches. The feeling is that there usually exist two distinct ways to study a topic, and from a managerial standpoint, a focus on application is the preferred way. Serious reflection about this problem may suggest a somewhat different approach, however. Consider the following situation.

As a personnel manager for a medium-sized firm, you have been asked to discover why employee turnover in your firm is so high. Your boss has told you that it is your responsibility to assess this problem and then to offer suggestions aimed at reducing turnover. What will you do? Several possible strategies come to mind:

Talk with those who have quit the organization.
Talk with those who remain.
Talk to the employees' supervisors.
Consult with personnel managers in other companies.
Measure job satisfaction.
Examine company policies and practices.
Examine the jobs where most turnover occurs.

None of these actions will likely be very successful in helping you arrive at sound conclusions, however. Talking with those who have left usually yields a variety of biased responses by those who either want to "get back at" the company or who fear that criticism will negatively affect their chances for future recommendations. Talking with those still employed has similar problems: why *should* they be candid and jeopardize their jobs? Talking with supervisors will not help if they themselves are the problem. Asking other personnel managers, while comforting, ignores major differences between organizations. Measuring job satisfaction, examining company policies, or examining the jobs themselves may help if one is fortunate enough to hit upon the right problem, but the probability of doing so is minimal. In short, many of the most obvious ways a manager can choose to solve a problem may yield biased results at best, and possibly no results at all.

A more viable approach would be to view the situation from a research standpoint and to use accepted methods of scientific inquiry to arrive at a solution that minimizes biased results. Most of what we know about organizational behavior results from efforts to apply such methods in solving organizational problems (e.g., How do we motivate employees? How do we develop effective leaders? How do we reduce stress at work?). An awareness of the nature of scientific inquiry is useful for understanding how we learned what we know about organizations as well as in facilitating efforts to solve behavioral problems at work.

Theory Building in Organizations

Briefly stated, a *theory* is a set of statements that serves to explain the manner in which certain concepts or variables are related. These statements result both from our present level of knowledge on the topic and from our assumptions about the variables themselves. The theory allows us to deduce logical propositions, or hypotheses, that can be tested in the field or laboratory. In short, a theory is a technique that helps us understand how variables fit together. Their use in research and in management is invaluable.

Uses of a Theory

Why do we have theories in the study of organizational behavior? First, theories help us *organize* knowledge about a given subject into a pattern of relationships that lends meaning to a series of observed events. They provide a structure for understanding. For instance, rather than struggling with a lengthy list of factors found to relate to employee turnover, a theory of turnover might suggest how such factors fit together and are related.

Second, theories help us to *summarize* diverse findings so that we can focus on major relationships and not get bogged down in details. A theory "permits us to handle large amounts of empirical data with relatively few propositions." [M. E. Shaw and P. R. Costanzo, *Theories of Social Psychology* (New York: McGraw-Hill, 1970), p. 9.]

Finally, theories are useful in that they *point the way* to future research efforts. They raise new questions and suggest answers. In this sense, they serve a useful heuristic value in helping to differentiate between important and trivial questions for future research. Theories are useful both for the study and for the management of organizations. As Kurt Lewin said, "There is nothing so practical as a good theory."

What Is a Good Theory?

Abraham Kaplan discusses in detail the criteria for evaluating the utility or soundness of a theory. [A. Kaplan, *The Conduct of Inquiry* (San Francisco: Chandler, 1964).] At least five such criteria can be mentioned:

1. *Internal consistency.* Are the propositions central to the theory free from contradiction? Are they logical?
2. *External consistency.* Are the propositions of a theory consistent with observations from real life?
3. *Scientific parsimony.* Does the theory contain only those concepts that are necessary to account for findings or to explain relationships? Simplicity of presentation is preferable unless added complexity furthers understanding or clarifies additional research findings.
4. *Generalizability.* In order for a theory to have much utility, it must apply to a wide range of situations or organizations. A theory of employee motivation that applies only to one company hardly helps us understand motivational processes or apply such knowledge elsewhere.
5. *Verification.* A good theory presents propositions that can be tested. Without an ability to operationalize the variables and subject the theory to field or laboratory testing, we are unable to determine its accuracy or utility.

To the extent that a theory satisfies these requirements, its usefulness both to researchers and to managers is enhanced. However, a theory is only a starting point. On the basis of theory, researchers and problem solvers can proceed to design studies aimed at verifying and refining the theories themselves. These studies must proceed according to commonly accepted principles of the scientific method.

Scientific Method in Organizational Behavior Research

Cohen and Nagel suggested that there are four basic "ways of knowing." [M. Cohen and E. Nagel, *An Introduction to Logic and Scientific Inquiry* (New York: Harcourt, Brace and Company, 1943). See also E. Lawler, A. Mohrman, S. Mohrman, G. Ledford, and T. Cummings, *Doing Research That Is Useful for Theory and Practice* (San Francisco: Jossey-Bass, 1985).] Managers and researchers use all four of these techniques: tenacity, intuition, authority, and science. When managers form a belief (e.g., a happy worker is a productive worker) and continue to hold that belief out of habit and often in spite of contradictory information, they are using *tenacity.* They use *intuition* when they feel the answer is self-evident or when they have a hunch about how to solve a problem. They use *authority* when they seek an answer to a problem from an expert or consultant who supposedly has experience in the area. Finally, they use *science*—perhaps too seldom—when they are convinced that the three previous methods allow for too much subjectivity in interpretation.

In contrast to tenacity, intuition, and authority, the scientific method of inquiry "aims at knowledge that is *objective* in the sense of being intrasubjectively certifiable, independent of individual opinion or preference, on the basis of data obtainable by suitable experiments or observations." [C. G. Hempel, *Aspects of Scientific Explanation* (New York: The Free Press, 1965), p. 141.] In other words, the scientific approach to problem-solving sets some fairly rigorous standards in an attempt to substitute objectivity for subjectivity.

The scientific method in organizational behavior consists of four stages: (1) observation of the phenomena (facts) in the real world, (2) formulation of explanations for such phenomena using the inductive process, (3) generation of predictions or hypotheses about the phenomena using the deductive process, and (4) verification of the predictions or hypotheses using systematic, controlled observation. This process is shown in **Figure A.1**. When this rather abstract description of the steps of scientific inquiry is shown within the framework of an actual research study, the process becomes much clearer. A basic research paradigm is shown in **Figure A.2**. In essence, a scientific approach to research requires that the investigator or manager first recognize clearly what research questions are being posed. To paraphrase Lewis Carroll, if you don't know where you're going, any road will take you there. Many managers identify what they think is a problem (e.g., turnover) only to discover later that their "problem" turnover rate is much lower than that in comparable industries. Other managers look at poor employee morale or performance and ignore what may be the real problem (e.g., poor leadership).

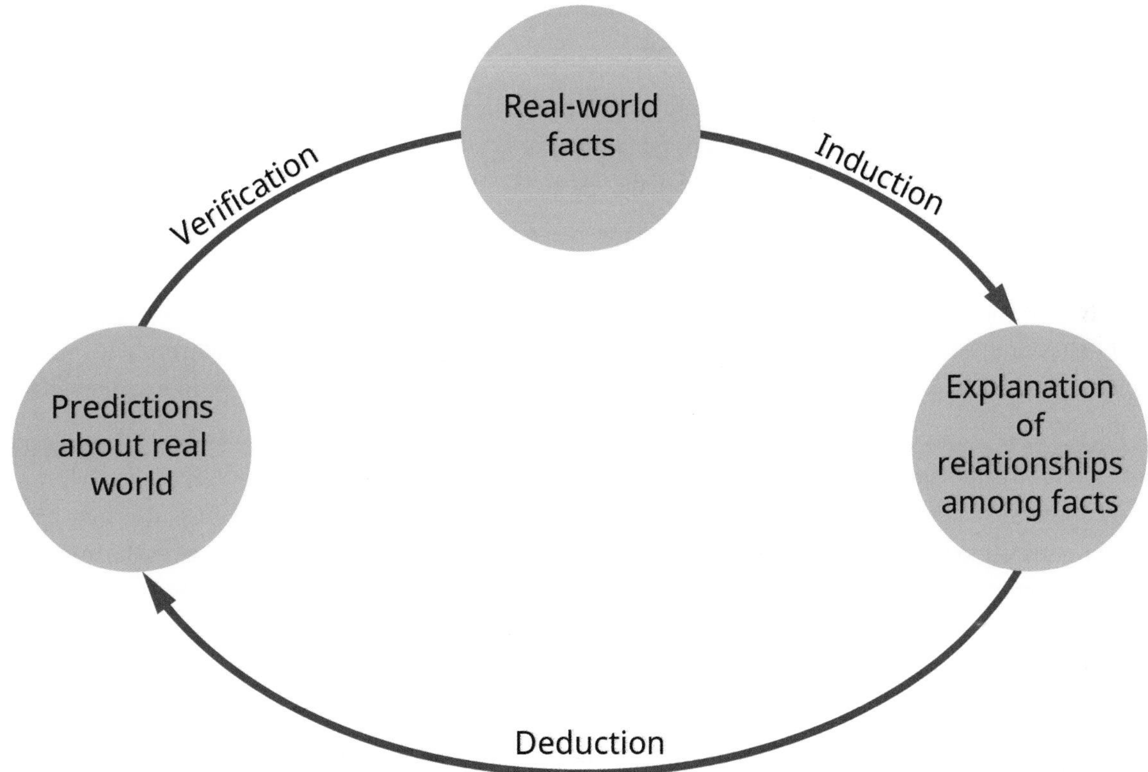

Exhibit A1 A Model Depicting the Scientific Method *Source:* Adapted from E. F. Stone, *Research Methods in Organizational Behavior* (Glenview, Ill.: Scott, Foresman and Company, 1978), p. 8. (Attribution: Copyright Rice University, OpenStax, under CC BY-NC-SA 4.0 license)

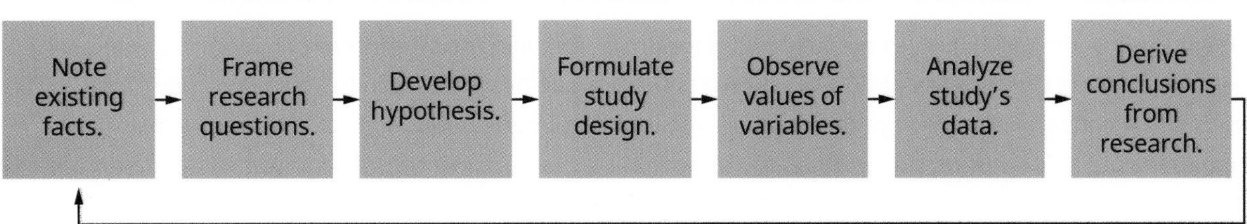

Exhibit A2 A Model of the Empirical Research Process *Source:* Adapted from E. F. Stone, *Research Methods in Organizational Behavior* (Glenview, Ill.: Scott, Foresman and Company, 1978), p. 17. (Attribution: Copyright Rice University, OpenStax, under CC BY-NC-SA 4.0 license)

On the basis of the research questions, specific hypotheses are identified. These hypotheses represent best guesses about what we expect to find. We set forth hypotheses to determine if we can predict the right answer so we can select a study design that allows for suitable testing. On the basis of the study design (to be discussed shortly), we observe the variables under study, analyze the data we collect, and draw relevant conclusions and management implications. When we follow this process, the risks of being guided by our own opinions or prejudices are minimized, and we arrive at useful answers to our original research questions.

Basic Research Designs

Although a detailed discussion of the various research designs is beyond the scope of this Appendix, we can review several common research designs that have been used to collect data in the study of people at work. Specifically, we will examine five different research designs that are frequently used to study behavior at work: (1) naturalistic observation, (2) survey research, (3) field study, (4) field experiment, and (5) laboratory experiment. In general, the level of rigor of the design increases as we move from naturalistic observation toward laboratory study. Unfortunately, so do the costs, in many cases.

Criteria for Evaluating Research Designs

Before examining the five designs, it will be helpful to consider how a researcher selects from among the various designs. Clearly, no one strategy or design is superior in all cases. Each has its place, depending upon the research goals and the constraints placed on the research.

However, when choosing among the potential designs, researchers generally must consider several things. For example, does the design require that you *specify hypotheses* a priori? If you specify appropriate hypotheses and are able to confirm them, then you can predict behavior in organizations. As a manager, being able to predict behavior in advance allows you to intervene and make necessary changes to remedy problem situations. The ability to accurately predict behavior is clearly superior to simply being able to explain behavior after the fact.

Other factors to examine are the *method of measurement* and the *degree of control* to be used. Does the method of measurement use qualitative or quantitative measures? Although qualitative measures may be useful for generating future hypotheses, quantitative measures add more perceived rigor to results. Also, if you are interested in demonstrating casual relationships, it is necessary to have a high degree of control over the study variables. You must be able to manipulate the primary study variable to determine the results of this manipulation while at the same time keeping other potentially contaminating variables constant so they do not interfere in the results.

In addition, a researcher must know to what extent he or she can generalize the results from the study to apply to other organizations or situations. Results that are situation-specific are of little use to managers. *External validity* is of key importance. And, of course, in practical terms, how much is it going to cost to carry out the study and discover a solution? *Cost* can be measured in many ways, including time and money.

The analysis of the previous five criteria provides insight concerning the *overall level of rigor* of the research design. The more rigorous the design, the more confidence one has in the results. This is because more rigorous designs typically employ more accurate measures or interventions and attempt to control for contaminating influences on study results. With this in mind, we can now consider various research designs.

Naturalistic Observation

Naturalistic observations represent the most primitive (least rigorous) method of research in organizations. Simply put, *naturalistic observations* represent conclusions drawn from observing events. At least two forms of such research can be identified: (1) authoritative opinions and (2) case studies.

Authoritative opinions are the opinions of experts in the field. When Henri Fayol wrote his early works on management, for example, he was offering his advice as a former industrial manager. On the basis of experience in real work situations, Fayol and others suggest that what they have learned can be applied to a variety of work organizations with relative ease. Other examples of authoritative opinions can be found in Barnard's *The Functions of the Executive,* Sloan's *My Years with General Motors,* and Peters and Waterman's *In Search of Excellence.* Throughout their works, these writers attempt to draw lessons from their own practical experience that can help other managers assess their problems.

The second use of naturalistic observation can be seen in the *case study.* Case studies attempt to take one situation in one organization and to analyze it in detail with regard to the interpersonal dynamics among the various members. For instance, we may have a case of one middle manager who appears to have burned out on the job; his performance seems to have reached a plateau. The case would then review the cast of characters in the situation and how each one related to this manager's problem. Moreover, the case would review any actions that were taken to remedy the problem. Throughout, emphasis would be placed on what managers could learn from this one real-life problem that can possibly relate to other situations.

Survey Research

Many times, managers wish to know something about the extent to which employees are satisfied with their jobs, are loyal to the organization, or experience stress on the job. In such cases, the managers (or the researchers) are interested mainly in considering quantitative values of the responses. Questionnaires designed to measure such variables are examples of *survey research.* Here we are not attempting to relate results to subsequent events. We simply wish to assess the general feelings and attitudes of employees.

Surveys are particularly popular with managers today as a method of assessing relative job attitudes. Hence, we may make an annual attitude survey and track changes in attitudes over time. If attitudes begin to decline, management is alerted to the problem and can take steps to remedy the situation.

Field Study

In a *field study,* the researcher is interested in the relationship between a *predictor* variable (e.g., job satisfaction) and a subsequent *criterion* variable (e.g., employee turnover or performance). Measures of each variable are taken (satisfaction, perhaps through a questionnaire, and turnover, from company records) and are compared to determine the extent of correlation. No attempt is made to intervene in the system or to manipulate any of the variables, as is the case with experimental approaches.

To continue the simple example we began with, a manager may have a hypothesis that says that satisfaction is a primary indicator of employee turnover. After measuring both, it is found that there is a moderate relationship between the two variables. Hence, the manager may conclude that the two are probably related. Even so, because of the moderate nature of the relationship, it is clear that other factors also influence turnover; otherwise, there would be a much stronger relationship. The manager concludes that, although efforts to improve job satisfaction may help solve the problem, other influences on turnover must also be looked at, such as salary level and supervisory style.

Field Experiment

A *field experiment* is much like a field study, with one important exception. Instead of simply measuring job satisfaction, the manager or researcher makes efforts to actually change satisfaction levels. In an experiment, we attempt to manipulate the predictor variable. This is most often done by dividing the sample into two groups: an experimental group and a control group. In the experimental group, we intervene and introduce a major change. Perhaps we alter the compensation program or give supervisors some human relations training. The control group receives no such treatment. After a time, we compare turnover rates in the two groups. If we have identified the correct treatment (that is, a true influence on turnover), turnover rates would be reduced in the experimental group but not in the control group.

In other words, in a field experiment, as opposed to a field study, we intentionally change one aspect of the work environment in the experimental group and compare the impact of the change with the untreated control group. Thus, we can be relatively assured that the solution we have identified is, in fact, a true predictor variable and is of use to management.

Laboratory Experiment

Up to this point, we have considered a variety of research designs that all make use of the actual work environment, the *field.* In this last design, *laboratory experiments,* we employ the same level of rigor as that of the field experiment and actually manipulate the predictor variable, but we do so in an artificial environment instead of a real one.

We might, for instance, wish to study the effects of various compensation programs (hourly rate versus piece rate) on performance. To do this, we might employ two groups of business students and have both groups work on a simulated work exercise. In doing so, we are simulating a real work situation. Each group would then be paid differently. After the experiment, an assessment would be made of the impact of the two compensation plans on productivity.

Comparing Research Designs

Now that we have reviewed various research designs, we might wonder which designs are best. This is not an easy call. All designs have been used by managers and researchers in studying problems of people at work. Perhaps the question can best be answered by considering the relative strengths and weaknesses of each, on the basis of our earlier discussion of the criteria for evaluating research designs (see **Table A1**). We should then have a better idea of which design or designs would be appropriate for a particular problem or situation.

Specification of Hypotheses in Advance. It was noted earlier that the ability to specify a priori hypotheses adds rigor to the study. In general, hypotheses are not given for naturalistic observations or survey research. These two techniques are used commonly for exploratory analyses and for identifying pertinent research questions for more rigorous future study. On the other hand, the remaining three designs (field study, field experiment, and laboratory experiment) do allow explicitly for a priori hypotheses. Hence, they are superior in this sense.

A Comparison of Various Research Designs

Research Design	A Priori Hypotheses	Qualitative vs. Quantitative Measures	Control	External Validity	Cost	Overall Level of Rigor
Naturalistic observation	No	Qualitative	Low	Low	Low	Low
Survey research	No	Qualitative and quantitative	Low	High	Low	Medium

Table A1 (Attribution: Copyright Rice University, OpenStax, under CC BY-NC-SA 4.0 license)

A Comparison of Various Research Designs						
Research Design	A Priori Hypotheses	Qualitative vs. Quantitative Measures	Control	External Validity	Cost	Overall Level of Rigor
Field study	Yes	Quantitative	Medium	High	Medium	Medium
Field experiment	Yes	Quantitative	High	High	High	High
Laboratory experiment	Yes	Quantitative	High	Low	High	High
Note: This table represents general trends; exceptions can clearly be identified.						

Table A1 (Attribution: Copyright Rice University, OpenStax, under CC BY-NC-SA 4.0 license)

Qualitative versus Quantitative Measures. Naturalistic observations typically involve qualitative data, whereas field studies and both forms of experiment typically involve quantitative data. Survey research most often provides for both. Hence, if it is important to collect hard data concerning a problem (e.g., what is the magnitude of the relationship between satisfaction and turnover?), quantitative designs are to be preferred. On the other hand, if one is more concerned about identifying major reasons for turnover and little prior knowledge about the problem exists, qualitative data may be preferred, and survey research may be a better research strategy. The selection of an appropriate design hinges in part on the intended uses for the information.

Control. As noted earlier, control represents the extent to which potentially contaminating influences can be minimized in a study. Clearly, experimental procedures allow for better control than do nonexperimental ones. The researcher or manager can systematically structure the desired work environment and minimize irrelevant or contaminating influences. As a result, conclusions concerning causal relations between variables can be made with some degree of certainty. Where it is not possible to secure such high control, however—perhaps because the organization does not wish to make a major structural change simply for purposes of an experiment—a field study represents a compromise design. It allows for some degree of control but does not require changing the organization.

External Validity. The question of external validity is crucial to any study. If the results of a study in one setting cannot be applied with confidence to other settings, the utility of the results for managers is limited. In this regard, survey research, field studies, and field experiments have higher levels of external validity than naturalistic observations or laboratory experiments. Naturalistic observations are typically based on nonrandom samples, and such samples often exhibit characteristics that may not allow for transfers of learning from one organization to another. A clear example can be seen in the case of a small company in which the president implemented a unique compensation plan that proved successful. It would be impossible to predict whether such a plan would work in a major corporation, because of the different nature of the organizations. Similarly, there is some question about how realistic a work environment is actually created in a laboratory situation. If managers are to learn from the lessons of other organizations, they should first learn the extent to which the findings from one kind of organization are applicable elsewhere.

Cost. As one would expect, the quality of information and its price covary. The more rigorous the design (and thus the more accurate the information), the higher the cost. Costs can be incurred in a variety of ways and include actual out-of-pocket expenses, time invested, and residue costs. The organization is left with the aftermath of an experiment, which could mean raised employee expectations and anxieties, as well as the possibility of disillusionment if the experiment fails. It should be noted that, in survey research, a large amount of general information can be gathered quickly and cheaply.

Overall Level of Rigor. In summary, then, the real answer to the question concerning which strategy is best lies in the degrees of freedom a manager has in selecting the design. If an experiment is clearly out of the question (perhaps because one's superior doesn't want anything altered), a field study may be the best possible strategy, given the constraints. In fact, field studies are often considered a good compromise strategy in that they have a medium amount of rigor but are also fairly quick and inexpensive. On the other hand, if one simply wishes to take an attitude survey, survey research is clearly in order. If one is not allowed to do anything, authoritative opinions from others may be the only information available. However, if constraints are not severe, experimental methods are clearly superior in that they allow for greater certainty concerning major influences on the criterion variable and on the problem itself.

B Scoring Keys for Self-Assessment Exercises

Chapter 2

1. **What Is Your Locus of Control?**
   This assessment measures your locus of control. After completing the instrument, score it by assigning a zero (0) to any *A* you assigned and a one (1) to any *B*. Add up your total score, and compare it to the following norms:
   1–3 = an external locus of control
   4–5 = a balanced locus of control
   6–7 = an internal locus of control
2. **What Values Are Most Important to You?**
   This instrument is intended as an informal measure of instrumental and terminal values. There are no right or wrong answers here. This is simply a way for you to see what your value structure looks like. Simply examine the pattern of responses you made for both sets of values. What did you learn about yourself? Which values are most important to you?

Chapter 3

1. **Can You Understand This Passage?**
   The appropriate frame of reference for reading the passage in this self-assessment is *washing clothes*.
2. **How Do You Feel about Women Executives?**
   This questionnaire asks 10 questions concerning people's attitudes toward women in managerial positions. To score this instrument, total up your score and compare your results to this national sample.
   10–21 = an unfavorable attitude toward women as managers
   22–38 = a neutral attitude toward women as managers
   39–50 = a favorable attitude toward women as managers
   What did you learn about yourself on the basis of this exercise?
3. **Are You Satisfied with Your Job?**
   Two scales are used here, one for satisfaction with the level of personal recognition you receive and one for your satisfaction with pay of salary. To score this, add up your responses for questions 1–5 and 6–10. Items 1–5 refer to your satisfaction with the level of personal recognition you receive, and items 6–10 refer to your satisfaction with compensation. For both factors, scoring norms are as follows:
   5–10 = low satisfaction
   11–19 = moderate satisfaction
   20–25 = high satisfaction

   How did you do on each factor? If you were a manager and saw these results, what would you do to improve the scores of your coworkers?

Chapter 4

1. **Designing Your Own Behavioral Self-Management Program**
   The key to this exercise is to see if you can put the concepts of behavioral self-management into practice. Were you able to identify a specific problem that lends itself to the BSM approach? Does your own BSM program follow the procedures outlined in the chapter? What were the major problems you encountered

when you tried to apply the procedures to your program? Did the program work? What did you learn about yourself from this exercise?

Chapter 8

1. **How Would You Rate Your Supervisor?**
   There are no right or wrong answers to this exercise. You are asked to evaluate the performance of a current or past supervisor. Because it is typically the supervisor who evaluates the subordinate, this is usually an interesting experience. When you are done, share your evaluation with another student in your class and explain or defend your evaluation. Are there any rating biases in your evaluation? Is this a fair appraisal? How would your coworkers evaluate this supervisor/boss?
2. **How Much Feedback Are You Getting from Your Job?**
   This exercise gives you the opportunity to analyze feedback patterns for your current or previous job. Add up your four scores according to the four types of job-related feedback.

Corrective feedback	(add up items 1–3)
Positive supervisory feedback	(add up items 4–6)
Positive coworker feedback	(add up items 7–9)
Self-administered feedback	(add up items 10–12)

   When finished, examine and study the results. Where did you get the most feedback? Where did you get the least feedback?

Chapter 9

1. **How Do You Behave in a Group?**
   This questionnaire asks you to describe your own behavior within a group setting. To score the instrument, add up your scores as follows for the three categories of behavior.

Task-oriented behavior	(add up items 1–4)
Relations-oriented behavior	(add up items 5–8)
Self-oriented behavior	(add up items 9–12)

   Examine the resulting pattern in your answers. As usual, there are no correct or incorrect answers. Instead, this is an opportunity to view how you describe your own role-related activities in a group. What did you learn about yourself? How does your role in a group differ from those of other individuals?
2. **How Effective Is Your Work Group?**
   This instrument measures the relative effectiveness of a group to which you belong. Count the number of times that you answered "mostly yes." The larger the number, the more productive and satisfied the group members should be. There are no norms for this exercise, so you might wish to create your own norms by comparing scores amongst others in your class who have completed this instrument for the

groups that they belong to. Look at the range of scores, and then describe the characteristics of each group. Are there any common characteristics that distinguish the groups with the highest scores? The lowest scores? Why do these differences occur?
You could also use this questionnaire to compare groups to which you belong. If you were the leader of one of these groups, what would you do to make the group more effective? Why hasn't this been done already?

Chapter 13

1. **What Are Your Bases of Power?**
This instrument examines the five bases of power. When you have finished the questionnaire, add up your score for each scale as follows:

Referent power	(add up items 1–3)
Expert power	(add up items 4–6)
Legitimate power	(add up items 7–9)
Reward power	(add up items 10–12)
Coercive power	(add up items 13–15)

To interpret the scores, consider the following:
A score of 3–6 points indicates a weak power base on a particular scale.
A score of 7–11 points indicates a moderate power base on a particular scale.
A score of 12–15 points indicates a strong power base on a particular scale.

On the basis of all of this, what does your power profile look like? Does this seem to be an accurate reflection of your actual situation? If you wished to change your power bases, which would you change? How would you try to change these bases?

2. **How Political Are You?**
This questionnaire is designed to measure your political behavior. You have been asked to answer "true" or "false" to 10 questions. When you have finished, consider the following. If you answered true to almost all of the questions, you should consider yourself a confirmed politician. (This is meant to be a compliment!) If you answered false to questions 5 and 6, which deal with deliberate lies and uncharitable behavior, you have shown yourself to be someone with high ethical standards. Finally, if you answered false to almost all of the questions, you are most definitely not a politician; rather, you are a person who rejects manipulation, incomplete disclosure, and self-serving behavior. On the basis of this instrument, how political are you? How political are your friends? On the basis of your answers to these questions, what have you learned about political behavior in organizations? What implications follow from these results concerning your future management style?

Chapter 14

1. **What Is Your Approach to Conflict Resolution?**
In this exercise there are no right or wrong answers. Instead, you are simply asked to describe your own approach to conflict resolution. To do this, score the instrument as follows:

Competition	(add up items 1–3)
Collaboration	(add up items 3–6)
Compromise	(add up items 7–9)
Avoidance	(add up items 10–12)
Accommodation	(add up items 13–15)

Compare the relative strengths of your preferences in each of the five conflict-resolution modes. The higher your score on any of the scales, the more you favor this mode of resolution. What pattern do you see in this analysis? How will this inform you in future negotiations?

Chapter 18

1. **How Stressful Is Your Job?**
   To score this instrument, first add up your score:
   If you scored 1–18 points, you see yourself as having a normal amount of stress.
   If you scored 19–38 points, you feel that stress is becoming a problem.
   If you scored 39–50 points, you feel that stress is a serious problem.

   Where did you score on this instrument? Does this seem like an accurate description of the real situation? On the job you described, what could you do to reduce stress levels?
2. **Are You a Type A?**
   This instrument is somewhat complicated to score. Follow these instructions carefully:
   Time urgency: Time urgency reflects one's race against the clock, even on items when there is little reason to hurry. It is measured by the following items 1, 2, 8, 12, 14. For each *A* or *B* answer you gave on these questions, give yourself 1 point. Put the total number on the line on the left.
   Inappropriate aggression and hostility: This dimension reflects excessively competitive behavior and frequent displays of hostility. It is measured by items 3, 4, 9, and 10. For each *A* or *B* answer you gave on these questions, give yourself 1 point. Put the total number on the line on the left.
   Polyphasic behavior: This is the tendency to undertake several activities simultaneously at inappropriate times. As a result, individuals often end up wasting time instead of saving it, which leads to wasted energy. It is measured by items 6 and 11. For each *A* or *B* answer you gave on these questions, give yourself 1 point. Put the total number on the line on the left.
   Goal directedness without proper planning: This is the tendency to rush into work without knowing how to accomplish the desired result. Consequently, incomplete work or errors are likely to occur. It is measured by items 5 and 7. For each *A* or *B* answer you gave on these questions, give yourself 1 point. Put the total number on the line on the left.

   Now add up your total score.
   If you received a total of 5 or greater, you may possess some of the attributes of a Type A personality. How did you do? If you received a high score, what are some things that you can do to reduce your stress level?
3. **How Stable Is Your Life?**
   This instrument attempts to assess your rate of life change—that is, how much activity and change do you have that may cause stress? To score this instrument, add up the score or units assigned to the various

life units assigned to the events listed in the past year.

If your total score is less than 150, this suggests that you should remain generally healthy during the next year.

If your total score is 150 to 300, this suggests that there is a 50 percent chance that you will experience illness during the coming year.

If your total score is over 300, this suggests that there is a 70 percent chance of impending illness during the coming year.

Remember that when evaluating your result, a high score does not automatically mean an illness is imminent. Rather, it means that statistically speaking an illness is more likely for you than for those with lower scores. Where did you score? Is this a reasonable description of your current situation? If so, what actions could you undertake to reduce your score?

4. **Are You Suffering from Burnout?**
   This instrument measures your self-perceptions regarding burnout. To score it, add up the number of times you answered "mostly true." If you answered mostly true seven or more times, you may be suffering from burnout. If you received a high score, consider what actions you can undertake to reduce the level of burnout.

References

The Nature of Work

1. S. Terkel, *Working* (New York: Pantheon, 1974).

2. S. Freud, Lecture XXXIII, *New Introductory Lectures on Psychoanalysis* (New York: Norton, 1933), p. 34.

The Changing Workplace

3. Michael E. Porter and Jan V. Rivkin, *The Looming Challenge to U.S. Competitiveness,* Harvard Business Review, March 2012.

4. World Economic Outlook Database, *International Monetary Fund.* Retrieved 2018-07-15.

5. "The Future of Computing," *The Economist,* March 12, 2015, https://www.economist.com/leaders/2016/03/12/the-future-of-computing.

6. Bureau of labor Statistics, "Labor Force Characteristics by Race and Ethnicity, 2016," October 2017, https://www.bls.gov/opub/reports/race-and-ethnicity/2016/home.htm.

7. Elaine Pofeldt, "This Crime in the Workplace is Costing US Business $50 Billion a Year," *CNBC*, September 12, 2017, https://www.cnbc.com/2017/09/12/workplace-crime-costs-us-businesses-50-billion-a-year.html; and "Shoplifting, other Fraud Cost US Retailers $44 Billion in 2014: Survey," CNBC, June 24, 2015, https://www.cnbc.com/2015/06/24/shoplifting-other-fraud-cost-us-retailers-44-billion-in-2014-survey.html.

The Nature of Management

8. R. Katz, "Skills of an Effective Administrator," *Harvard Business Review,* September-October 1974, pp. 34–56.

9. J. Lindzon, "Five Skills That You'll Need to Lead the Company of the Future," Fast Company, May 18, 2017, https://www.fastcompany.com/40420957/five-skills-youll-need-to-lead-the-company-of-the-future; A. Bennett, "Going Global: The Chief Executives in the Year 2000 Are Likely to Have Had Much Foreign Experience," *Wall Street Journal,* February 27, 1989, p. A–4.

10. Jacob Morgan, "5 Qualities of the Modern Manager," *Forbes,* July 23, 2013, https://www.forbes.com/sites/jacobmorgan/2013/07/23/5-must-have-qualities-of-the-modern-manager/#644a2b6a3a0b.

A Model of Organizational Behavior and Management

11. D. Nadler and M. Tushman, "A Model for Diagnosing Organizational Behavior," *Organizational Dynamics,* 1980, p. 35.

12. Ibid.

Individual and Cultural Factors in Employee Performance

1. V.H. Vroom, *Work and Motivation* (New York: Wiley, 1964).

Employee Abilities and Skills

2. R.J. Ebert and T.R. Mitchell, *Organization Decision Processes: Concepts and Analysis* (New York: Crane, Russak, 1975), p. 81.

3. Ibid.

4. T.R. Mitchell, "Cognitive Complexity and Leadership Style," *Journal of Personality and Social Psychology,* 1970, *16,* pp. 166–174.

5. H. M. Schroder, M. H. Driver, and S. Streufert, *Human Information Processing* (New York: Holt, Rinehart and Winston, 1967).

6. E. J. McCormick and J. Tiffin, *Industrial Psychology* (Englewood Cliffs, N.J.: Prentice-Hall, 1976).

7. Dale Feuer & Chris Lee. 1988. The Kaizen Connection: How Companies Pick Tomorrow's Workers. Training. May, 23–35.

Personality: An Introduction

8. S.R. Maddi, *Personality Theories: A Comparative Analysis* (Homewood, III.: Dorsey, 1980), p. 10.

9. C. Kluckhohn and H. Murray, *Personality in Society and Nature,* (New York: Knopf, 1953).

10. P.H. Mussen, *The Psychological Development of the Child* (Englewood Cliffs, N.J.: Prentice-Hall, 1963).

11. Ibid.

12. J. C. Abegglen, "Personality Factors in Social Mobility: A Study of Occupationally Mobile Businessmen," *Genetic Psychology Monographs,* August 1958, pp. 101–159.

Personality and Work Behavior

13. G.W. Allport, *Pattern and Growth in Personality* (New York: Holt, Rinehart and Winston, 1961).

14. R. A. Ellis and M. S. Taylor, "Role of Self-Esteem within the Job Search Process," *Journal of Applied Psychology,* 1983, *68,* pp. 632–640.

15. P. Spector, "Behavior in Organizations as a Function of Locus of Control," *Psychological Bulletin,* May 1982, pp. 482–497; P. Nystrom, "Managers' Salaries and Their Beliefs About Reinforcement Control," *Journal of Social Psychology,* August 1983, pp. 291–292.

16. L. R. Morris, *Extroversion and Introversion: An Interactional Perspective* (New York: Hemisphere, 1979), p.8.

17. T. W. Adorno, E. Frenkel-Brunswik, and D. J. Levinson, *The Authoritarian Personality* (New York: Harper & Row, 1950).

18. V. H. Vroom, *Some Personality Determinants of the Effects of Participation* (Englewood Cliffs, N.J.: Prentice-Hall, 1960).

19. M. Rokeach, *The Open and Closed Mind* (New York: Basic Books, 1960).

20. R. N. Taylor and M. D. Dunnette, "Influence of Dogmatism, Risk-Taking Propensity, and Intelligence on Decision-Making Strategies for a Sample of Industrial Managers," *Journal of Applied Psychology,* 1974, *59,* pp. 420–423.

21. R. Stogdill, "Personal Factors Associated with Leadership: A Survey of the Literature," *Journal of Psychology,* 1948, *25,* pp. 35–71; F. L. Greer, *Small Group Effectiveness* (Philadelphia: Institute for Research on Human Relations, 1955).

Personality and Organization: A Basic Conflict?

22. C. Argyris, "Personality and Organization Theory Revisited," *Administrative Science Quarterly,* 1973, *18,* pp. 141–167.

Personal Values and Ethics

23. M. Rokeach, *The Nature of Human Values* (New York: Free Press, 1973), p. 5.

24. Ibid.

25. Paul R. Sackett, Laura R. Burris, and Christine Callahan. 1989. Integrity Testing for Personnel Selection. Personnel Psychology, *42,* 491–529.

26. R. M. Steers, Y. K. Shin, and G. R. Ungson, *The Chaebol: Korea's New Industrial Might* (New York: Harper & Row, 1989), p. 96.

27. L. Smith, "Cracks in the Japanese Work Ethic," *Fortune,* May 14, 1984, pp. 162–168; K. Van Wolferen, *The Enigma of Japanese Power* (New York: Knopf, 1989).

Cultural Differences

28. G. Hofstede, *Culture's Consequence,* (Beverly Hills, Calif.: Sage, 1980), p. 25.

29. Ibid.

30. A. Laurent, "The Cultural Diversity of Western Conceptions of Management," *International Studies of Management and Organization,* XII, 1–2, Spring-Summer 1983, pp. 75–96.

31. F. Kluckhohn and F. Strodtbeck, *Variations in Value Orientations* (Evanston, III.: Row, Peterson, 1961).

32. T. Cox, et al., "Effects of Ethnic Group Cultural Differences on Cooperative and Competitive Behavior on a Group Task," Academy of Management J., *34,* pp. 827–847; and S. Gruman, cited in N. Adler, *International Dimensions of Organizational Behavior* (Boston: PWS/Kent, 1986), pp. 13–14.

The Perceptual Process

1. M. W. Levine and J. M. Shefner, *Fundamentals of Selection and Perception* (Reading, Mass.: Addison-Wesley, 1981).

2. D. Kretch, R. S. Crutchfield, and E. L. Ballachey, *Individual in Society* (New York: McGraw-Hill, 1962).

3. F. L. Ruch, *Psychology and life* (Glenview: Scott, Foresman, 1983).

4. J. S. Bruner and L. Postman, "On the Perception of Incongruity: A Paradigm," *Journal of Personality*, 1949, 18, pp. 206–223.

5. S. T. Fiske and S. E. Taylor, *Social Cognition* (Reading, Mass.: Addison-Wesley, 1984).

6. D. J. Mason, "Judgements of Leadership Based on Physiognomic Cues," *Journal of Abnormal and Social Psychology*, 1957, *54,* pp. 273–274.

7. P. F. Secord, "The Role of Facial Features in Interpersonal Perception," in R. Tagiuri and L. Petrullo, eds., *Person Perception and Interpersonal Behavior* (Palo Alto: Stanford University Press, 1958), pp. 300–315.

8. J. W. Thibaut and H. W. Riecker, "Authoritarianism, Status, and the Communication of Aggression," *Human Relations*, 1955, *8,* pp. 95–120.

9. D. C. Dearborn and H. A. Simon, "Selective Perception: A Note on Departmental Identification of Executives," *Sociometry,* 1958, *21*, p. 142.

10. R. Likert, *New Patterns of Management* (New York: McGraw-Hill, 1961).

11. Levine and Shefner, op. cit.

12. Ibid.

13. K. J. Frauenfelder, "A Cognitive Determinant of Favorability of Impression," *Journal of Social Psychology,* 1974, 94, pp. 71–81.

Barriers to Accurate Social Perception

14. R. Jain, H. C. Triandis, and C. W. Weick, *Managing Research, Development and Innovation: Managing the Unmanageable, 3rd Edition* (New York: Wiley, 2010).

15. C. von Hippel, et al, "Age-based stereotype threat and work outcomes: Stress appraisals and ruminations as mediators," *Psychology and Aging,* February 2019, pp. 68-84.

16. Dearborn and Simon, op. cit.

17. J. B. Miner, *Organizational Behavior 2: Essentials Theories of Process and Structure* (Routledge, 2015).

18. Levine and Shefner, op. cit.

19. M. Haire and W. Grunes, "Perceptual Defenses: Processes Protecting an Organized Perception of Another's Personality," *Human Relations,* 1950, *3*, pp. 403–412.

20. Ibid., p. 409.

Attributions: Interpreting the Causes of Behavior

21. H. H. Kelley, "The Process of Causal Attributions," *American Psychologist*, February 1973, pp. 107–128; F. Forsterling, "Attributional Retraining: A Review," *Psychological Bulletin,* November 1985, pp. 495–512; B. Weiner, *Human Motivation* (New York: Holt, Rinehart and Winston, 1980).

22. Kelley, op. cit., p. 193.

23. Ibid.

24. Ibid.

Attitudes and Behavior

25. Based on G. W. Allport, "Attitudes," in C. Murchison, ed., *Handbook of Social Psychology* (Worcester: Clark University Press, 1935).

26. Jain, Triandis, and Weick op. cit.

27. B. M. Staw and J. Ross, "Stability in the Midst of Change: A Dispositional Approach to Job Attitudes," *Journal of Applied Psychology*, 1985, 70, pp. 469–480.

28. G. Salancik and J. Pfeffer, "A Social Information Processing Approach to Job Attitudes and Task Design,"

Administrative Science Quarterly, 1978, 23, pp. 224–253.
29. L. Festinger, *A Theory of Cognitive Dissonance* (Palo Alto: Stanford University Press, 1957).

Work-Related Attitudes

30. T. Lodahl and M. Kejner, "The Definition and Measurement of Job Involvement," *Journal of Applied Psychology*, 1965, *49*, pp. 24–33.
31. R. T. Mowday, L. W. Porter, and R. M. Steers, *Employee-Organization Linkages: The Psychology of Employee Commitment, Absenteeism and Turnover* (New York: Academic Press, 1982).
32. E. A. Locke, "The Nature and Causes of Job Satisfaction," in M. D. Dunnette, ed., *Handbook of Industrial and Organizational Psychology* (Chicago: Rand McNally, 1976).
33. L. W. Porter and R. M. Steers, "Organizational, Work, and Personal Factors in Employee Turnover and Absenteeism," *Psychological Bulletin,* 1973, *80,* pp. 151–176.
34. B. M. Staw, *Intrinsic and Extrinsic Motivation* (Morristown, N. J.: General Learning Press, 1976).

Basic Models of Learning

1. Rose E. Spielman, Kathryn Dumper, William Jenkins, Arlene Lacombe, Marilyn Lovett, and Marion Perlmutter, *Psychology* (Houston: OpenStax, 2015).
2. J. M. Ivancevich, A. D. Szilagyi, and M. Wallace, *Organizational Behavior and Performance* (Glenview, Ill.: Scott, Foresman, 1977), p. 80.
3. B. F. Skinner, "Operant Behavior," *American Psychologist,* 1963, 18, pp. 503–515.
4. J. B. Watson, Behavior: An *Introduction to Comparative Psychology* (New York: Holt, Rinehart and Winston, 1914).
5. E. L. Thorndike, *Animal Intelligence* (New York: Macmillan, 1911), p. 244.
6. F. Luthans, et. al., *Organizational Behavior* 13th Edition (Charlotte: *Information Age Publishing,* 2016).
7. A. Bandura, *Social Learning Theory* (Englewood Cliffs, N.J.: Prentice-Hall, 1977).
8. A. Filley, R. J. House, and S. Kerr, *Managerial Process and Organizational Behavior* (Glenview, III.: Scott, Foresman, 1975).
9. E. J. McCormick and D. Illgen, *Industrial Psychology* 8th edition (Englewood Cliffs, N.J.: Prentice-Hall, 1984).
10. B. M. Bass and J. Vaughn, *Training in Industry: The Management of Learning* (Belmont, Ca.: Wadsworth, 1966); G. Wexley and G. P. Latham, *Developing and Training Human Resources in Organizations*, Third Edition (Pearson: 2002); and G. P. Latham, "Human Resource Training and Development," in M. Rosenzweig and L. W. Porter, eds., *Annual Review of Psychology* (Palo Alto: Annual Reviews, 1988), pp. 545–581.

Reinforcement and Behavioral Change

11. B. F. Skinner, *Science and Human Behavior* (New York: Macmillan, 1953), p. 73.
12. W. C. Hamner, "Reinforcement Theory," in H. L. Tosi and W. C. Hamner, eds., *Organizational Behavior and Management: A Contingency Approach* (Chicago: St. Clair, 1977), p. 98.
13. T. W. Costello and S. S. Zalkind, *Psychology in Administration: A Research Orientation* (Englewood Cliffs, N. J.: Prentice-Hall, 1963), p. 193.
14. Hamner, op. cit., p. 105.
15. David Kolb, *Experiential Learning*, 2nd Edition, (Pearson FT Press: New York, 2015) and Mel Silberman, Elaine Beich and Carol Auerbach, *Active Training*, (Wiley: New York, 2016).

Behavior Modification in Organizations

16. B. F. Skinner, *Beyond Freedom and Dignity* (New York: Knopf, 1971).
17. F. Luthans and R. Kreitner, *Organizational Behavior Modification and Beyond* (Glenview, III.: Scott, Foresman, 1985), pp. 150–159.

Behavioral Self-Management

18. F. Luthans and R. Davis, "Behavioral Self-Management—The Missing Link in Managerial Effectiveness,"

Organizational Dynamics, Summer 1979, p. 43; F. Luthans and R. Kreitner, *Organizational Behavior Modification and Beyond: An Operant and Social Learning Approach* (Glenview, III.: Scott, Foresman, 1985).
19. F. H. Kanfer and A. P. Goldstein, *Helping People Change: A Textbook of Methods* (New York: Pergamon Press, 1980).
20. C. C. Neck and C. P. Manz, Mastering Self Leadership 6th edition, (Pearson, 2013).
21. A. Bandura, "Self-Reinforcement: Theoretical and Methodological Considerations," *Behaviorism,* Fall 1976, pp. 135–155; Luthans and Kreitner, *Organizational Behavior Modification and Beyond.*
22. G. Latham and C. Fayne, "Self-Management Training for Increasing Job Attendance," *Journal of Applied Psychology,* 1989, pp. 411–416.

An Introduction to Workplace Diversity

1. McGrath, J. E., Berdahl, J.L., & Arrow, H. (1995). Traits, expectations, culture, and clout: The dynamics of diversity in work groups. In S.E. Jackson & M.N. Ruderman (Eds.), Diversity in Work Teams, 17-45. Washington, D.C.: American Psychological Association.
2. Thomas, R. R. 1991. Beyond race and gender. New York, NY: AMACOM.
3. Cox, Taylor H., and Stacy Blake. "Managing cultural diversity: Implications for organizational competitiveness." The Executive (1991): 45-56.
4. Pelled, L. H., Ledford, G. E., Jr., & Mohrman, S. A. (1999). Demographic dissimilarity and workplace inclusion. Journal of Management Studies, 36, 1013-1031.
5. Lambert, J.R., & Bell, M.P. (2013). Diverse forms of difference. In Q. Roberson (Ed.) Oxford Handbook of Diversity and Work (pp. 13 – 31). New York: Oxford University Press.
6. Harrison, D.A., Price, K.H., & Bell, M.P. (1998). Beyond relational demography: time and the effects of surface- and deep-level diversity on work group cohesion. Academy of Management Journal, 41(1), 96-107.
7. Lambert, J.R., & Bell, M.P. (2013). Diverse forms of difference. In Q. Roberson (Ed.) Oxford Handbook of Diversity and Work (pp. 13 – 31). New York: Oxford University Press.
8. Clair, J.A., Beatty, J.E., & Maclean, T.L. (2005). Out of sight but not out of mind: Managing invisible social identities in the workplace. Academy of Management Review, 30 (1), 78-95.
9. Philips, K.W., Rothbard, N.P., & Dumas, T.L. (2009). To disclose or not to disclose? Status distance and self-disclosure in diverse environments. Academy of Management Review, 34(4), 710-732.

Diversity and the Workforce

10. Judy, R.W., D'Amico, C., & Geipel, G.L.(1997). Workforce 2020: Work and Workers in the 21st Century. Indianapolis, Ind: Hudson Institute.
11. U.S. Bureau of Labor Statistics. (2017). Labor force characteristics by race and ethnicity, 2016. Retrieved from https://www.bls.gov/opub/reports/race-and-ethnicity/2016/home.htm
12. U.S. Department of Labor, Bureau of Labor Statistics. (2017). Table A-1. Employment status of the civilian population by sex and age. Retrieved from https://www.bls.gov/news.release/empsit.t01.htm; DeWolf, M. (Mar 1 2017). 12 stats about working women. Retrieved from https://blog.dol.gov/2017/03/01/12-stats-about-working-women
13. Toosi, Mitra,"Labor force projections to 2024: the labor force is growing, but slowly," Monthly Labor Review, U.S. Bureau of Labor Statistics, December 2015, https://doi.org/10.21916/mlr.2015.48.
14. U.S. Bureau of Labor Statistics. (2017). Labor force characteristics by race and ethnicity, 2016. Retrieved from https://www.bls.gov/opub/reports/race-and-ethnicity/2016/home.htm
15. U.S. Department of Labor, Bureau of Labor Statistics. (2017). Table 2: Employment status of the civilian noninstitutional population 16 years and over by sex, 1977 to date 11. Retrieved from https://www.bls.gov/cps/cpsaat02.pdf.
16. Toosi, Mitra,"Labor force projections to 2024: the labor force is growing, but slowly," Monthly Labor Review, U.S. Bureau of Labor Statistics, December 2015, https://doi.org/10.21916/mlr.2015.48.

17. U.S. Department of Labor, Bureau of Labor Statistics. (2017). Table 2: Employment status of the civilian noninstitutional population 16 years and over by sex, 1977 to date 11. Retrieved from https://www.bls.gov/cps/cpsaat02.pdf.

18. DeWolf, M. (2017). 12 stats about working women. U.S. Department of Labor Blog.

19. Eagly, A.H., & Karau, S.J.(2002). Role congruity theory of prejudice toward female leaders. Psychological Review, 109 (3): 573-598.

20. EEOC, "Facts About Sexual Harassment." Retrieved from https://www.eeoc.gov/eeoc/publications/fs-sex.cfm

21. Ibid.

22. EEOC, "Sexual Harassment." Retrieved from https://www.eeoc.gov/laws/types/sexual_harassment.cfm

23. Feldblum, C.R., & Lipnic, V.A. (2016).Report of the Co-Chairs of the EEOC Select Task Force on the Study of Harassment in the Workplace. Retrieved from https://www.eeoc.gov/eeoc/task_force/harassment/report.cfm

24. Hernandez, T.K. (2000). Sexual Harassment and Racial Disparity: The Mutual Construction of Gender and Race. Gender, Race and Justice (4J): 183 -224. Retrieved from http://ir.lawnet.fordham.edu/faculty_scholarship/12

25. Fitzgerald, L.F., Drasgow, R., Hulin, C.L., Gelfand, M.J., & Magley, V.J. (1997). Antecedents and consequences of sexual harassment in organizations: A test of an integrated model. Journal of Applied Psychology, 82: 578-589; Shaffer, M.A., Joplin, J.R.W., Bell, M.P., Lau, T., & Oguz, C. (2000). Gender discrimination and job-related outcomes: A cross-cultural comparison of working women in the United States and China. Journal of Vocational Behavior, 57(4): 395-427.

26. Toosi, Mitra,"Labor force projections to 2024: the labor force is growing, but slowly," Monthly Labor Review, U.S. Bureau of Labor Statistics, December 2015, https://doi.org/10.21916/mlr.2015.48.

27. Ibid.

28. Ibid.

29. U.S. Equal Employment Opportunity Commission. African-Americans in the American Workforce. Retrieved from https://www1.eeoc.gov/eeoc/statistics/reports/american_experiences/african_americans.cfm?renderforprint=1

30. Quilian, L., Pager, D., Midtboen, A.H., & Hexel, O. (Oct 2017). Hiring discrimination against Black Americans hasn't declined in 25 years. Harvard Business Review.

31. https://www.theguardian.com/technology/2016/sep/08/airbnb-discrimination-policy-changes-racial-discrimination

32. U.S. Department of Labor, Bureau of Labor Statistics. (2017). Table 11: Employed persons by detailed occupation, sex, race, and Hispanic or Latino ethnicity. Retrieved from https://www.bls.gov/cps/tables.htm#charemp.

33. Ibid

34. Adams, S. (June 2014). White high school drop-outs are as likely to land jobs as black college students. Forbes. Retrieved from https://www.forbes.com/sites/susanadams/2014/06/27/white-high-school-drop-outs-are-as-likely-to-land-jobs-as-black-college-students/#51715c547b8f

35. Pager, D. (2003). The mark of a criminal record. *American Journal of Sociology, 108* (5): 937-975.

36. Bertrand, M. & Mullainathan, S. (2004). Are Emily and Greg more employable than Lakisha and Jamal? A field experiment on labor market discrimination. *American Economic Review, 94* (4): 991-1013

37. Robinson, C. L., Taylor, T., Tomaskovic-Devey, D., Zimmer, C. & Irwin Jr., M.W. (2005). "Studying race or ethnic and sex segregation at the establishment level: Methodological issues and substantive opportunities using EEO-1 reports." *Work and Occupations 32*(1): 5–38.

38. Kraiger, K., & Ford, J. K. (1985). A Meta-Analysis of Ratee Race Effects in Performance Ratings. *Journal of Applied Psychology, 70*(1), 56-65.

39. Mays, V. M., Coleman, L. M., & Jackson, J. S. (1996). Perceived Race-Based Discrimination, Employment

Status, and Job Stress in a National Sample of Black Women: Implications for Health Outcomes. Journal of Occupational Health Psychology, 1(3), 319–329.
40. Lopez, G., Ruiz, N.G., & Patten, E. (2017). Key facts about Asian Americans, a diverse and growing population. Pew Research Center. Retrieved from http://www.pewresearch.org/fact-tank/2017/09/08/key-facts-about-asian-americans/; Flores, A. (Sep 18 2017). How the U.S. Hispanic population is changing. Pew Research Center. Retrieved from http://www.pewresearch.org/fact-tank/2017/09/18/how-the-u-s-hispanic-population-is-changing/ft_17-09-18_hispanics_ushispanicpop/
41. U.S. Bureau of Labor Statistics. (2017). Labor force characteristics by race and ethnicity, 2016. Retrieved from https://www.bls.gov/opub/reports/race-and-ethnicity/2016/home.htm
42. Tafoya, S. (2004). Shades of belonging. Pew Hispanic Center. Retrieved from http://www.pewhispanic.org/2004/12/06/shades-of-belonging/
43. Ibid.
44. Hispanics in the U.S. fast facts. (Mar 31 2017). CNN. Retrieved from https://www.cnn.com/2013/09/20/us/hispanics-in-the-u-s-/index.html
45. Ibid.
46. Liu, E. (May 30 2014). Why are Hispanics identifying as white? CNN.
47. Ibid.
48. Tafoya, S. (2004). Shades of Belonging. Washington D.C.: Pew Hispanic Center. Retrieved from http://pewhispanic.org/files/reports/35.pdf.
49. Taylor, P., Lopex, M.H., Martinez, J., & Velasco. G. (2012). When labels don't fit: Hispanics and their views of identity. Retrieved from http://www.pewhispanic.org/2012/04/04/when-labels-dont-fit-hispanics-and-their-views-of-identity/
50. Flores, A. (Sep 18 2017). How the U.S. Hispanic population is changing. Pew Research Center. Retrieved from http://www.pewresearch.org/fact-tank/2017/09/18/how-the-u-s-hispanic-population-is-changing/ft_17-09-18_hispanics_ushispanicpop/
51. Avery, D.R., McKay, P.F., Wilson, D.C., Tonidandel, S. (2007). Unequal attendance: The relationships between race, organizational diversity cues, and absenteeism. Personnel Psychology, 60: 875-902.
52. Lopez, G., Ruiz, N.G., & Patten, E. (2017). Key facts about Asian Americans, a diverse and growing population. Pew Research Center. Retrieved from http://www.pewresearch.org/fact-tank/2017/09/08/key-facts-about-asian-americans/
53. Ibid.
54. Ibid.
55. Ono, K. A., & Pham, V. N. (2009). Asian Americans and the Media. Cambridge, England: Polity.; Paek, H.J., & Shah, H. (2003). Racial ideology, model minorities, and the 'not so silent partner:" Stereotyping of Asian Americans in U.S. magazine advertising. Howard Journal of Communications, 14(4): 225-244.
56. Hernandez, T.K. (2000). Sexual Harassment and Racial Disparity: The Mutual Construction of Gender and Race. Gender, Race and Justice (4J): 183 -224. Retrieved from http://ir.lawnet.fordham.edu/faculty_scholarship/12
57. Ibid.
58. Committee of 100: American attitudes toward Chinese Americans and Asian Americans. (2004, Summer). The Diversity Factor, 12(3): 38-44. Retrieved from http://www.committee100.org/publications/survey/C100survey.pdf
59. Hernandez, T.K. (2000). Sexual Harassment and Racial Disparity: The Mutual Construction of Gender and Race. Gender, Race and Justice (4J): 183 -224. Retrieved from http://ir.lawnet.fordham.edu/faculty_scholarship/12
60. Committee of 100: American attitudes toward Chinese Americans and Asian Americans. (2004, Summer). The Diversity Factor, 12(3): 38-44. Retrieved from http://www.committee100.org/publications/survey/

C100survey.pdf

61. Multiracial in America. (June 11 2015) Pew Research Center. Retrieved from http://www.pewsocialtrends.org/2015/06/11/multiracial-in-america/

62. Ibid.

63. Ibid.

64. U.S. Bureau of Labor Statistics. (2017). Labor force characteristics by race and ethnicity, 2016. Retrieved from https://www.bls.gov/opub/reports/race-and-ethnicity/2016/home.htm

65. Ibid.

66. Ibid.

67. Philips, K.W., Rothbard, N.P., & Dumas, T.L. (2009). To disclose or not to disclose? Status distance and self-disclosure in diverse environments. Academy of Management Review, 34(4), 710-732.

68. U.S. Bureau of Labor Statistics. (2017). Labor force characteristics by race and ethnicity, 2016. Retrieved from https://www.bls.gov/opub/reports/race-and-ethnicity/2016/home.htm

69. Alley, D., & Crimmins, E. 2007. The demography of aging and work. In K. S. Shultz & G. A. Adams (Eds.), Aging and work in the 21st century: 7-23. New York: Psychology Press.

70. Cuddy, A. J. C., & Fiske, S. T. (2002). Doddering but dear: Process, content, and function in stereotyping of older persons. In T. D. Nelson (Ed.), Ageism: Stereotyping and prejudice against older persons (pp. 3–26). Cambridge, MA: MIT Press.; Cuddy, A. J. C., Norton, M. I., & Fiske, S. T. (2005). This old stereotype: The pervasiveness and persistence of the elderly stereotype. Journal of Social Issues, 61, 267–285.

71. Desmette, D., & Gaillard, M. (2008). When a "worker" becomes an "older worker": The effects of age-related social identity on attitudes towards retirement and work. Career Development International, 13, 168–185.

72. Ng, T. W., & Feldman, D. C. (2008). The relationship of age to ten dimensions of job performance. Journal of Applied Psychology, 93, 392–423.

73. Bell, M.P., Ozbilgin, M.F., Beauregard, T.A. and Surgevil, O. (2011), "Voice, silence, and diversity in 21st century organizations: strategies for inclusion of gay, lesbian, bisexual, and transgender employees", Human Resource Management, Vol. 50 No. 1, pp. 131-146.

74. Human Rights Campaign. (2018). State maps of laws and policies. Retrieved from http://www.hrc.org/state-maps/employment

75. Ragins, B.R., Cornwell, J.M. and Miller, J.S. (2003), "Heterosexism in the workplace: do race and gender matter?", Group & Organization Management, Vol. 28, pp. 45-74.

76. Button, S.B. (2001), "Organizational efforts to affirm sexual diversity: a cross-level examination", Journal of Applied Psychology, Vol. 86 No. 1, pp. 17-28.

77. Human Rights Campaign Foundation (2018), "Corporate equality index 2018 ", available at:https://assets2.hrc.org/files/assets/resources/CEI-2018-FullReport.pdf?_ga=2.120762824.1791108882.1521675202-2105331900.1521675202

78. GLAAD media reference guide (10th ed.). 2016. Los Angeles, CA: Gay and Lesbian Alliance Against Defamation. Retrieved from http://www.glaad.org/sites/default/files/GLAAD-Media-Reference-Guide-Tenth-Edition.pdf

79. Lamber, J. (2015). The impact of gay-friendly recruitment statements and due process employment on a firm's attractiveness as an employer. Equality, Diversity, and Inclusion: An International Journal, 34 (6): 510-526.

80. Black, D., Gates, G., Sanders, S., & Taylor, L. 2000. Demographics of the gay and lesbian population in the United States: Evidence from available systematic data sources. Demography, 37(2): 139-154.

81. Ragins, B.R., Cornwell, J.M., & Miller, J.S. 2003. Heterosexism in the workplace: Do race and gender matter? Group & Organization Management, 28: 45-74.;Tilcsik, A. (2011), "Pride and prejudice: employment discrimination against openly gay men in the United States", American Journal of Sociology, Vol. 117 No. 2, pp.

586-626.
82. Clair, J.A., Beatty, J.E., & Maclean, T.L. (2005). Out of sight but not out of mind: Managing invisible social identities in the workplace. Academy of Management Review, 30 (1), 78-95.
83. Ibid.
84. Barron, G.L. and Hebl, M. (2013), "The force of law: The effects of sexual orientation anti-discrimination legislation on interpersonal discrimination in employment", Psychology, Public Policy, and Law, Vol. 19 No. 2, pp. 191-205.
85. Button, S.B. (2001), "Organizational efforts to affirm sexual diversity: a cross-level examination", Journal of Applied Psychology, Vol. 86 No. 1, pp. 17-28.
86. Trautwein, C. Apr 7 2017. H-1B Visa applications just hit their limit for the year in less than a week. Time. Retrieved 4/21/2017 from http://time.com/4731665/h1b-visa-application-cap/; U.S. Citizenship and Immigration Services. (2017, Apr 7). USCIS reaches FY 2018 H-1B Cap. Retrieved on 4/21/2017 at https://www.uscis.gov/news/news-releases/uscis-reaches-fy-2018-h-1b-cap
87. U.S. Citizenship and Immigration Services. (2013). Working in the U.S. Retrieved from http://www.uscis.gov/working-united-states/working-us; U.S. Department of State, Bureau of Consular Affairs. (2014). Directory of Visa Categories. Retrieved from http://travel.state.gov/content/visas/english/general/all-visa-categories.html#iv
88. Bureau of Labor Statistics, U.S. Department of Labor. (2016, May 19). Labor force characteristics of foreign-born workers summary. Economic News Release. Retrieved online at https://www.bls.gov/news.release/forbrn.nr0.htm
89. Kandel, W. A. (2011). The US foreign-born population: Trends and selected characteristics. Congressional Research Service Report. Retrieved from http://www.fas.org/sgp/crs/misc/R41592.pdf
90. Bound, J., Demirci, M., Khanna, G., & Turner, S. (2014). Finishing degrees and finding jobs: U.S. higher education and the flow of foreign IT workers (NBER Working Paper No. 20505). Retrieved January 4, 2015, from http://www.nber.org/papers/w20505
91. Avery, D. R., Tonidandel, S., Volpone, S. D., & Raghuram, A. (2010). Overworked in America?: How work hours, immigrant status, and interpersonal justice affect perceived work overload. Journal of Managerial Psychology, 25(2), 133–147.; Bloomekatz, R. (2007). Rethinking immigration status discrimination and exploitation in the low-wage workplace. UCLA Law Review, 54, 1963-2010.
92. Lambert, J.R., Basuil, D.A., Bell, M.P., & Marquardt, D. (2017).Coming to America: Work Visas, International Diversity, and Organizational Attractiveness among Highly Skilled Asian Immigrants. International Journal of Human Resource Management, 1-27.
93. Jamieson, D. (2011). Student guest workers at Hershey plant allege exploitative conditions.Huffington Post. Retrieved from http://www.huffingtonpost.com/2011/08/17/student-guestworkers-at-hershey-plant_n_930014.html.
94. Wigglesworth, V. (2013). Tech giant Infosys settles allegation of visa fraud in Plano office for $34 million. Dallas News. Retrieved from http://www.dallasnews.com/news/community-news/plano/headlines/20131030-tech-giant-infosys-settles-allegations-of-visa-fraud-in-plano-office-for-34-million.ece?nclick_check=1
95. U.S. Department of Labor. (2012). Key points on Disability and Occupational Projections Tables. Retrieved from https://www.dol.gov/odep/pdf/20141022-KeyPoints.pdf
96. Ibid.
97. U.S. Census Bureau. (2008). Table 75. Self-Described Religious Identification of Adult Population: 1990, 2001 and 2008. Retrieved from https://www2.census.gov/library/publications/2010/compendia/statab/130ed/tables/11s0075.pdf

Diversity and Its Impact on Companies

98. Cox, T.H. & Blake, S. (1991). Managing cultural diversity: Implications for organizational competitiveness.

Academy of Management Executive, 5(3): 45-56.
99. Williams, K., & O'Reilly, CA. 1998. Demography and diversity: A review of 40 years of research.In B. Staw and R. Sutton (Eds.), Research in organizational behavior, 20: 77-140. Greenwich, CT: JAI Press.
100. Tsui, A.S., Egan, T. D., & O'Reilly, C.A. 1992. Being different: relational demography and organizational attachment. Administrative Science Quarterly, 37: 549-579.
101. Kim, S.S. & Gelfand, M. J. (2003).The influence of ethnic identity on perceptions of organizational recruitment. Journal of Vocational Behavior, 63: 396- 416.
102. Perkins, L. A., Thomas, K. M., & Taylor, G. A. 2000. Advertising and recruitment: Marketing tominorities. Psychology and Marketing, 17: 235-255.; Thomas, K.M., & Wise, P.G. 1999. Organizational attractiveness and individual differences: Are diverse applicants attracted by different factors? Journal of Business and Psychology,13: 375-390.
103. Janis, I.L. (1972). Victims of groupthink: A psychological study of foreign policy decisions and fiascoes. Boston: Houghton Mifflin Company.
104. Richard, O.C., Barnett, T., Dwyer, S., Chadwick, K. (2004). Cultural diversity in management, firmperformance, and the moderating role of entrepreneurial orientation dimensions. Academy of Management Journal, 47 (2): 255-266.
105. McMahan, G.C., Bell, M.P., & Virick, M. (1998). Strategic human resource management: Employee involvement, diversity, and international issues. Human Resource Management Review, 8 (3): 193-214.
106. Barney, J. (1991). Firm resources and sustained competitive advantage. Journal of Management, 17(1): 99-120.
107. Kauflin, J. (Jan 23 2018). America's best employers for diversity. Forbes. Retrieved from https://www.forbes.com/sites/jeffkauflin/2018/01/23/americas-best-employers-for-diversity/#84f151c71647
108. Graduate Management Admission Council. (Oct 6 2016Where are women in graduate business school? Retrieved from https://www.gmac.com/market-intelligence-and-research/research-insights/application-trends/where-are-women-in-graduate-business-school.aspx
109. Cox, T. H., Lobel, S. A., & McLeod, P. L. (1991). Effects of ethnic group cultural differences on cooperative and competitive behavior on a group task. Academy of management journal, 34(4), 827-847.
110. Richard, O.C., Barnett, T., Dwyer, S., Chadwick, K. (2004). Cultural diversity in management, firm performance, and the moderating role of entrepreneurial orientation dimensions. Academy of Management Journal, 47 (2): 255-266.
111. Dezso, C.L., & Ross, D.G. (2012). Does female representation in top management improve firm performance? A panel data investigation. Strategic Management Journal, 33: 1072-1089.

Challenges of Diversity

112. Tsui, A.S., Egan, T. D., & O'Reilly, C.A. 1992. Being different: relational demography and organizational attachment. Administrative Science Quarterly, 37: 549-579.
113. New York Times. (March 31, 1995). Reverse discrimination complaints rare, labor study reports. Retrieved from https://www.nytimes.com/1995/03/31/us/reverse-discrimination-complaints-rare-labor-study-reports.html
114. Mosbergen, D. (Oct 25 2017). Majority of White Americans believe White people face discrimination. Huff Post. Retrieved from https://www.huffingtonpost.com/entry/white-americans-discrimination-poll-npr_us_59f03071e4b04917c594209a
115. U.S. Equal Employment Opportunity Commission. (2018). About EEOC. Retrieved from https://www.eeoc.gov/eeoc/
116. Discrimination by Type. https://www.eeoc.gov/laws/types/index.cfm (Accessed February 15, 2018); Equal Pay and Compensation Discrimination. https://www.eeoc.gov/laws/types/equalcompensation.cfm (Accessed February 15, 2018)

117. Institute for Women's Policy Research. https://www.iwpr.org (Accessed February 22, 2018)
118. U.S. Equal Employment Opportunity Commission. https://www.eeoc.gov (Accessed February 22, 2018)
119. Harassment. https://www.eeoc.gov/laws/types/harassment.cfm (Accessed February 22, 2018)
120. Age Discrimination. https://www.eeoc.gov/laws/types/age.cfm(Accessed February 22, 2018)
121. ADA at 25. The Law. https://www.eeoc.gov/eeoc/history/ada25th/thelaw.cfm (Accessed November 26, 2017).
122. Disability Discrimination. https://www.eeoc.gov/laws/types/disability.cfm (Accessed February 27, 2018)
123. National Origin Discrimination. https://www.eeoc.gov/laws/types/nationalorigin.cfm (Accessed February 27, 2018)
124. Pregnancy Discrimination. https://www.eeoc.gov/laws/types/pregnancy.cfm (Accessed February 27, 2018)
125. Race/Color Discrimination. https://www.eeoc.gov/laws/types/race_color.cfm (Accessed February 27, 2018)
126. Religious Discrimination. https://www.eeoc.gov/laws/types/religion.cfm (Accessed February 27, 2018)
127. Sex-Based Discrimination. https://www.eeoc.gov/laws/types/sex.cfm (Accessed February 27, 2018)
128. Bell, Myrtle P. Diversity in organizations. Cengage Learning, 2011.
129. King, Eden B., et al. "The stigma of obesity in customer service: A mechanism for remediation and bottom-line consequences of interpersonal discrimination." Journal of Applied Psychology 91.3 (2006): 579.

Key Diversity Theories

130. Miller, C. C., Burke, L. M., & Glick,W. H. 1998. Cognitive diversity among upper-echelon executives: Implications for strategic decision processes. Strategic Management Journal, 19: 39-58.
131. Horwitz, S.K., & Horwitz, I.B. (2007). The effects of team diversity on team outcomes: A meta-analytic review of team demography. Journal of Management, 33 (6): 987-1015.
132. Watson, W.E., Kumar, K., & Michaelsen, L.K. (1993). Cultural diversity's impact on interaction process and performance: Comparing homogeneous and diverse task groups. Academy of Management Journal, 36(3): 590-602.
133. Tsui, A.S., Egan, T. D., & O'Reilly, C.A. 1992. Being different: relational demography and organizational attachment. Administrative Science Quarterly, 37: 549-579.
134. Byrne, D. (1971). The attraction paradigm. New York: Academic Press.
135. Perkins, L. A., Thomas, K. M., & Taylor, G. A. 2000. Advertising and recruitment: Marketing to minorities. Psychology and Marketing, 17: 235-255.; Thomas, K.M., & Wise, P.G. 1999. Organizational attractiveness and individual differences: Are diverse applicants attracted by different factors? Journal of Business and Psychology, 13: 375-390.
136. Lambert, J. R. (2015). The impact of gay-friendly recruitment statements and due process employment on a firm's attractiveness as an employer. Equality, Diversity and Inclusion: An International Journal, 34, 510–526.
137. Lambert, J.R., Basuil, D.A., Bell, M.P., & Marquardt, D. J. (2017). Coming to America: Work visas, international diversity, and organizational attractiveness among highly skilled Asian immigrants. The International Journal of Human Resource Management, 0, 1-27.
138. Bertrand, Marianne, and Sendhil Mullainathan. "Are Emily and Greg more employable than Lakisha and Jamal? A field experiment on labor market discrimination." *The American Economic Review* 94, no. 4 (2004): 991-1013.
139. Tajfel, H. 1974. Social identity and intergroup behavior. Social Science Information, 15: 1010-118.; Tajfel H, Turner JC. (1985). The social identity theory of intergroup behavior. In S. Worchel, and W.G. Austin (Eds.), Psychology of Intergroup Relations (2nd ed., pp. 7–24). Chicago:Nelson-Hall.
140. Goldberg, Caren B. "Relational demography and similarity-attraction in interview assessments and subsequent offer decisions: are we missing something?." *Group & Organization Management* 30, no. 6 (2005):

597-624.

141. Fiske ST, Taylor SE. (1991). Social cognition (2nd ed.). New York: McGraw-Hill.

142. Crandall, Christian S., and Amy Eshleman. "A justification-suppression model of the expression and experience of prejudice." Psychological bulletin 129.3 (2003): 414.

Benefits and Challenges of Workplace Diversity

143. Ely, Robin J., and David A. Thomas. "Cultural diversity at work: The effects of diversity perspectives on work group processes and outcomes." Administrative science quarterly. 46.2 (2001): 229-273.

144. Ely, Robin J., and David A. Thomas. "Cultural diversity at work: The effects of diversity perspectives on work group processes and outcomes." *Administrative science quarterly.* 46.2 (2001): 229-273.

145. Ely, Robin J., and David A. Thomas. "Cultural diversity at work: The effects of diversity perspectives on work group processes and outcomes." *Administrative science quarterly.* 46.2 (2001): 229-273.

Recommendations for Managing Diversity

146. McCarthy, J.M, Van Iddekinge, C.H., & Campion, M.(2010). Are highly structured job interviews resistant to demographic similarity effects?: *Personnel Psychology, 63*: 325-359.

147. McCarthy, J.M, Van Iddekinge, C.H., & Campion, M.(2010). Are highly structured job interviews resistant to demographic similarity effects?: *Personnel Psychology, 63*: 325-359, p.333.; Campion M.A., Palmer D.K., Campion J.E. (1997). A review of structure in the selection interview. *Personnel Psychology, 50*, 655–702.

148. Young, Cheri A., Badiah Haffejee, and David L. Corsun. "Developing Cultural Intelligence and Empathy Through Diversified Mentoring Relationships." *Journal of Management Education* (2017): 1052562917710687.

149. Thoms, D.A., & Ely, R.J. (Sep 1996). Making differences matter: A new paradigm for managing diversity. Harvard Business Review.

Overview of Managerial Decision-Making

1. Lynn Stout. 2012. The Shareholder Value Myth: How Putting Shareholders First Harms Investors, Corporations, and the Public. San Francisco, CA: Berrett-Koehler Publishers.

How the Brain Processes Information to Make Decisions: Reflective and Reactive Systems

2. Peter A. Facione & Noreen C. Facione. 2007. Thinking and Reasoning in Human Decision Making: The Method of Argument and Heuristic Analysis, Millbrae, CA: The California Academic Press.

3. Matthew D. Lieberman. 2003. "Reflexive and reflective judgment processes: A social cognitive neuroscience approach." In (Eds.) Joseph P. Forgas, Kipling D. Williams, & William von Hippel's: Social judgments: Implicit and explicit processes, 44-67. Cambridge, UK: Cambridge University Press.

4. Adam L. Darlow & Steven A. Sloman. 2010. "Two systems of reasoning: Architecture and relation to emotion," *WIREs Cognitive Science*, 1: 382-392.

5. Malcolm Gladwell. 2005. Blink: The Power of Thinking Without Thinking. New York: Back Bay Books.

6. Jennifer M. George. 2000. "Emotions and leadership: The role of emotional intelligence." *Human Relations*, 53, 1027-1055.

Barriers to Effective Decision-Making

7. Christopher L. Aberson, Michael Healy, & Victoria Romero. 2000. Ingroup Bias and Self-Esteem: A Meta-Analysis. *Personality and Social Psychology Review*, 4: 157-173.

8. Elizabeth Kolbert. 2017. Why Facts Don't Change our Minds. *The New Yorker*, February 27, 2017.

9. Karen A. Jehn & Elizabeth A. Mannix. 2001. The Dynamic Nature of Conflict: A Longitudinal Study of Intragroup Conflict and Group Performance. *Academy of Management Journal*, 44: 238-251.

Improving the Quality of Decision-Making

10. Linda K. Trevino & Michael E. Brown. 2004. Managing to be ethical: Debunking five business ethics myths. *Academy of Management Executive*, 18: 69-81.

11. James R. Rest. 1986. *Moral development: Advances in research and theory*. Praeger Publishers.

Motivation: Direction and Intensity

1. J.E. Hunter & R.E. Hunter. 1984. Validity and utility of alternative predictors of job performance. *Psychological Bulletin* 96: 72–98.
2. Statistics on the prevalence of this choice are available. "Calling in Well: A Look at leave Time Tracking Trends," *actiTIME* website, June 2016, https://www.actitime.com/human-resources/leave-time-tracking-trends.php.

Content Theories of Motivation

3. H. A. Murray. 1938. *Explorations in personality.* New York: Oxford University Press.
4. Murray also hypothesized that people would differ in the degree to which they felt these needs. His list of secondary needs became a basis for his theory of personality.
5. Representative references include J.W. Atkinson & D.C. McClelland. 1948. The projective expression of needs. II. The effect of different intensities of the hunger drive on thematic apperception. *Journal of Experimental Psychology* 38:643–658; D.C. McClelland, J.W. Atkinson, R.A. Clark, & E.L. Lowell. 1953. *The achievement motive.* New York: Appleton-Century-Crofts; R.C. DeCharms. 1957. Affiliation motivation and productivity in small groups. *Journal of Abnormal Psychology* 55:222– 276; D.C. McClelland. 1961. *The achieving society.* Princeton, NJ: Van Nostrand; and D.C. McClelland. 1975. *Power: The inner experience.* New York: Irvington.
6. In fact, McClelland argued that the success of entire societies is dependent on its achievement needs.
7. D. C. McClelland. 1970. The two faces of power. *Journal of International Affairs* 24:29–47.
8. A.H. Maslow. 1943. A theory of human motivation. *Psychological Bulletin* 50:370–396; A.H. Maslow. 1954. *Motivation and personality.* New York: Harper & Row; A. H. Maslow. 1965. *Eupsychian management.* Homewood, IL: Irwin.
9. D. McGregor. 1960. *The human side of enterprise.* New York: McGraw-Hill; D. McGregor. 1967. *The professional manager.* New York: McGraw-Hill.
10. Maslow, 1943, 382.
11. C.P. Alderfer. 1972. *Existence, relatedness, and growth: Human needs in organizational settings.* New York: Free Press.
12. D.T. Hall & K.E. Nougaim. 1968. An examination of Maslow's need hierarchy in an organizational setting. *Organizational Behavior and Human Performance* 3:12–35; E.E. Lawler, III & J.L. Suttle. 1972. A causal correlational test of the need hierarchy concept. *Organizational Behavior and Human Performance* 7:265–287; M.A. Wahba & L.G. Bridwell. 1973. Maslow reconsidered: A review of research on the need hierarchy theory. *Proceedings of the thirty-third annual meeting of the Academy of Management,* 514–520.
13. C.P. Alderfer. 1972. *Existence, relatedness, and growth: Human needs and organizational settings.* New York: Free Press.
14. Note that Herzberg's theory has often been labeled the "two-factor theory" because it focuses on two continua. This name, however, implies that only two factors are involved, which is not correct. Herzberg prefers not to use the term "two-factor theory" because his two *sets* of needs identify a much larger *number* of needs.
15. F. Herzberg, B. Mausner, & B. Snyderman. 1959. *The motivation to work.* New York: Wiley; F. Herzberg. 1966. *Work and the nature of man.* New York: Crowell; F. Herzberg. 1968. One more time: How do you motivate employees? *Harvard Business Review* 46:54–62.
16. R.B. Dunham, J.L. Pierce, & J.W. Newstrom. 1983. Job context and job content: A conceptual perspective. *Journal of Management* 9:187–202.
17. R.M. Ryan & E.L. Deci. 2000. Self-determination theory and the facilitation of intrinsic motivation, social development, and well-being. *American Psychologist* 55:68–78.

Process Theories of Motivation

18. B.F. Skinner. 1953. *Science and human behavior.* New York: Free Press; B.F. Skinner. 1969. *Contingencies of reinforcement.* East Norwalk, CT: Appleton Century-Crofts; B.F. Skinner. 1971. *Beyond freedom and dignity.* New York: Bantam Books.

19. Ibid.

20. R. W. Kempen & R. V. Hall. 1977. Reduction of industrial absenteeism: Results of a behavioral approach. *Journal of Organizational Behavior Management* 20:1-21.

21. J.S. Adams. 1965. Inequity in social exchange. In L. Berkowitz (ed.), *Advances in experimental social psychology* (Vol. 2). New York: Academic Press; G.C. Homans. 1961. *Social behavior: Its elementary forms.* New York: Harcourt, Brace, & World.

22. Ibid.

23. J. Kane & E.E. Lawler, III. 1979. Performance appraisal effectiveness. In B. Staw (ed.), *Research in organizational behavior* (Vol. 1). Greenwood, CT: JAI Press.

24. E.E. Lawler, III. 1972. Secrecy and the need to know. In M. Dunnette, R. House, & H. Tosi (eds.), *Readings in managerial motivation and compensation.* East Lansing: Michigan State University Press.

25. I.R. Andrews. 1967. Wage inequity and job performance: An experimental study. *Journal of Applied Psychology* 51:39–45; J.S. Adams. 1963a. Towards an understanding of inequity. *Journal of Abnormal Social Psychology* 67:422–436; J.S. Adams. 1963b. Wage inequities, productivity and work quality. *Industrial Relations* 3:9–16.

26. R.C. Huseman., J.D. Hatfield, & E.W. Miles. 1987. A new perspective on equity theory: The equity sensitivity construct. *Academy of Management Review* 12:222–234; E.W. Miles, J.D. Hatfield, & R.C. Huseman. 1989. The equity sensitivity construct: Potential implications for worker performance. *Journal of Management* 15:581–588.

27. R.J. Bies. 1987. The predicament of justice: The management of moral outrage. In B.M. Staw & L.L. Cummings (eds.), *Research in organizational behavior* (Vol. 9). Greenwich, CT: JAI Press, 289–319; J. Greenberg. 1987. A taxonomy of organizational justice theories. *Academy of Management Review* 12:9–22.

28. E.L. Locke. 1978. The ubiquity of the technique of goal setting in theories of and approaches to employee motivation. *Academy of Management Review* 3:594–601; F.W. Taylor. 1911. *The principles of scientific management.* New York: Norton; K. Lewin. 1935. *A dynamic theory of personality.* New York: McGraw-Hill; K. Lewin. 1938. *The conceptual representation and the measurement of psychological forces.* Durham, NC: Duke University Press; K. Lewin, T. Dembo, L. Festinger, & P.S. Sears. 1944. Level of aspiration. In J. McVicker Hunt (ed.), *Personality and behavior disorders.* New York: Ronald Press, 333–378; P. Drucker. 1954. *The practice of management.* New York: Wiley; D. McGregor. 1957. An uneasy look at performance appraisal. *Harvard Business Review* 35:89–94; E.A. Locke. 1968. Toward a theory of task motivation and incentives. *Organizational Behavior and Human Performance* 3:157–189; E.A. Locke, K.N. Shaw, L.M. Saari, & G.P. Latham. 1981. Goal setting and task performance: 1969- 1980. *Psychological Bulletin* 90:125–152; G. P. Latham & E.A. Locke. 1984. *Goal setting: A motivational technique that works!* Englewood Cliffs, NJ: Prentice Hall.

29. C.C. Pinder. 1984. *Work motivation: Theory, issues, and applications.* Glenview, IL: Scott, Foresman.

30. Locke, 1979.

31. T.R. Mitchell & W.S. Silver. 1990. Individual and group goals when workers are interdependent: Effects on task strategies and performance. *Journal of Applied Psychology* 75:185–193.

32. A. Bandura. 1977. Self-efficacy: Toward a unifying theory of behavioral change. *Psychological Review* 84:191–215; A. Bandura. 1986b. The explanatory and predictive scope of self- efficacy theory. *Journal of Social and Clinical Psychology* 4:359– 373; A. Bandura. 1997. *Self-efficacy: The exercise of control.* New York: Freeman.

33. D.G. Gardner & J.L. Pierce. 1998. Self-esteem and self-efficacy within the organizational context: An empirical comparison. *Group and Organization Management* 23:48–70.

34. Locke, 1978.

Recent Research on Motivation Theories

35. M.L. Ambrose & C.T. Kulik. 1999. Old friends, new faces: Motivation research in the 1990s. *Journal of Management* 25: 231–292.

36. Chad H. Iddekinge, Herman Aguinis, Jeremy D. Mackey, Philip S. DeOrtentiis, "A Meta-Analysis of the Interactive, additive, and Relative Effects of Cognitive Ability and Motivation on Performance," *Journal of Management*, Vol. 44, No. 1, January, 2018.

Performance Appraisal Systems

1. S. Johnson, "Tips on Evaluating your Boss," *Chron,* July 1, 2018, https://work.chron.com/tips-evaluating-boss-7179.html.

2. C. J. Fombrum and R. L. Laud, "Strategic Issues in Performance Appraisal Theory and Practice," *Personnel,* 601 (6), pp. 23–31.

3. S. Maier, "5 unconscious factors impacting your performance appraisals," *The Business Journals*, January 25, 2019, https://www.bizjournals.com/bizjournals/how-to/human-resources/2019/01/5-unconscious-factors-impacting-your-performance.html.

4. R. L. Mathis, J. H. Jackson, and S. R. Valentine, *Human Resource Management,* 14th ed. (Stamford, CT: Cengage Learning, 2014), p. 357.

Techniques of Performance Appraisal

5. J. Smither and M. London, *Performance Management Putting Research Into Action*, (San Francisco: Jossey Bass, 2008), pp. 187–328.

6. L. Slavenski, "Matching People to Jobs," *Training and Development Journal,* August 1986, pp. 54–57.

7. F. D. Frank, D. W. Bracken, and M. R. Smith, "Beyond Assessment Centers," *Training and Development Journal,* March 1988, pp. 65–67.

Feedback

8. M. S. Taylor, C. D. Fisher, and D. R. Ilgen, "Individuals' Reactions to Performance Feedback in Organizations: A Control Theory Perspective," in K. M. Rowland and G. R. Ferris, eds., *Research in Personnel and Human Resources Management,* Vol. 2, (Greenwich, CT: JAI Press, 1984), pp. 81–124.

Reward Systems in Organizations

9. R. T. Mowday, L. W. Porter, and R. M. Steers, *Employee-Organization Linkages: The Psychology of Employee Commitment, Absenteeism, and Turnover,* (New York: Academic Press, 1982).

10. E. E. Lawler, "New Approaches to Pay Administration," *Personnel* Vol. 5, 1976, pp. 11–23.

11. Cited in *Eugene Register-Guard,* July 15, 1980, p. B1.

12. Stephen J. Sauer, Matthew S. Rodgers, William J. Becker, "The Effects of Goals and Pay Structure on Managerial Reporting Dishonesty," *Journal of Accounting, Ethics & Public Policy*, 2018.

13. R. L. Opsahl and M. D. Dunnette, "The Role of Financial Compensation in Industrial Motivation," *Psychological Bulletin* Vol. 66, 1966, pp. 94–96.

14. E. E. Lawler, *Rewarding Excellence,* (San Francisco: Jossey Bass, 2001).

15. L. W. Porter, G. Bigley, and R. M. Steers, *Motivation and Work Behavior,* 7th ed., (New York: McGraw-Hill, 2003).

16. E. E. Lawler, *Rewarding Excellence,* op. cit.

17. Ibid., p. 136.

Individual and Group Incentive Plans

18. Lawler, *Rewarding Excellence,* op. cit.

19. M. Wallace, cited in N. Perry, "Here Come Richer, Riskier Pay Plans," *Fortune,* December 19, 1988, pp. 50–58.

20. Perry, op. cit.

21. E. E. Lawler, "The Design of Effective Reward Systems," Technical Report, University of Southern California, April 1983.

Work Groups: Basic Considerations

1. J. Hackman and C. Morris, "Group Tasks, Group Interaction Process, and Group Performance Effectiveness," in L. Berkowitz, ed., *Advances in Experimental Social Psychology,* vol. 8 (New York: Academic Press, 1975), p. 49.
2. J. McDavid and M. Harari, *Social Psychology: Individuals, Groups, and Societies* (New York: Harper & Row, 1968), p. 237.
3. B. Bass. *Leadership, Psychology, and Organizational Behavior* (New York: Harper & Row, 1960), p. 39.
4. G. Homans, *Social Behavior* (New York: Harcourt, Brace and World, 1950).
5. B. Tuckman and M. Jensen, "Stages of Small Group Development Revisited," *Groups and Organizational Studies,* 1977, *2,* pp. 419–442.

Work Group Structure

6. L. Hoffman, "Applying Experimental Research on Group Problem Solving to Organizations," *Journal of Applied Behavioral Science,* 1979, 15, pp. 375–391.
7. A. Hare, "Group Size," *American Behavioral Scientist,* 1981, *24,* pp. 695–708.
8. R. Bales and E. Borgatta, "Size of Group as a Factor in the Interaction Profile," In A. Hare, E. Borgatta, and R. Bales, eds., *Small Groups* (New York: Knopf, 1956).
9. L. Cummings and C. Berger, "Organization Structure: How Does It Influence Attitudes and Performance?" *Organizational Dynamics,* 1976, 5, pp. 34–49.
10. S. Rhodes and R. Steers, *Managing Employee Absenteeism* (Reading, Mass.: Addison-Wesley, 1990).
11. L. Porter and R. Steers, "Organizational, Work, and Personal Factors in Employee Turnover and Absenteeism," *Psychological Bulletin,* 1973, *80,* pp. 151–176.
12. Cummings and Berger, op. cit.
13. T. Mitchell, *People in Organizations* (New York: McGraw-Hill, 1978), p. 188.
14. B. Latane, K. Williams, and S. Harkins, "Many Hands Make Light the Work: The Causes and Consequences of Social Loafing," *Journal of Personality and Social Psychology,* June 1979, pp. 822–832; J. Jackson and S. Harkins, "Equity in Effort: An Explanation of the Social Loafing Effect," *Journal of Personality and Social Psychology,* November 1985, pp. 1199–1206.
15. J. Hackman, "Group Influences on Individuals," in M. D. Dunnette, ed., *Handbook of Industrial and Organizational Psychology* 2nd Edition (Chicago: Nicholas Brealey Publishing , 1996).
16. D. Feldman, "The Development and Enforcement of Group Norms," *Academy of Management Review,* January 1984, pp. 47–53.
17. S. Asch, "Studies of Independence and Conformity: A Minority of One Against a Unanimous Majority," *Psychological Monographs,* 1955, *20,* Whole No. 416.
18. H. Reitman and M. Shaw, "Group Membership, Sex Composition of the Group, and Conformity Behavior," *Journal of Social Psychology,* 1964, 64, pp. 45–51.
19. S. Schachter, "Deviation, Rejection, and Communication," *Journal of Abnormal and Social Psychology,*1951, *46,* pp. 190–207.
20. I. Janis, *Victims of Groupthink* (Boston: Houghton Mifflin, 1972), p. 32.
21. R. L. Daft, *Organization Theory & Design* 12th edition (Boston, Ma.: Cengage Learning, 2016).
22. J. Dean, *Blind Ambition* (New York: Simon & Schuster, 1976).
23. A. Fluker, "Orlando firm tests the boundaries of cool in office space," *Orlando Business Journal,* February 28, 2019, https://www.bizjournals.com/orlando/news/2019/02/28/orlando-firm-tests-the-boundaries-of-cool-in.html.
24. M. Shaw, *Group Dynamics* (New York: McGraw-Hill, 1981), p. 197.
25. D. Cartwright and A. Zander, *Group Dynamics: Research and Theory* (New York: Harper & Row, 1968); M.

Shaw, op. cit.

Managing Effective Work Groups

26. J. R. Hackman, "The Design of Work Teams," in J. Lorsch, ed., *Handbook of Organizational Behavior* (Englewood Cliffs, N.J.: Prentice-Hall, 1987), pp. 300–345.

Intergroup Behavior and Performance

27. J. M. George and G. R. Jones, *Understanding and Managing Organizational Behavior* 6th edition, (Englewood Cliffs, N.J., Pearson, 2012).

28. J. Pfeffer, *Organizations and Organization Theory* (Boston: Pittman, 1982).

Teamwork in the Workplace

1. Katzenbach and Smith, *"The Discipline of Teams", Harvard Business Review, July 2005.*

2. Gratton and Erickson, "*Eight Ways to Build Collaborative Teams*", Harvard Business Review, Nov 2007.

Team Development Over Time

3. Bruce Tuckman, "Development Sequence in Small Groups", 1965.

Things to Consider When Managing Teams

4. J.J. Gabarro, The Dynamics of Taking Charge, Harvard Business School Press, 1987, pp. 85-87.

5. Linda A. Hill, "Managing Your Team", Harvard Business Review, 1995.

6. Linda A. Hill, "Exercising Influence", Harvard Business Review, 1994.

Opportunities and Challenges to Team Building

7. Patrick Lencioni, The Five Dysfunctions of a Team, *2002, p. 188.*

8. Capobianco, Davis and Kraus, Managing Conflict Dynamics: A Practical Approach, (2005)

Team Diversity

9. David Rock and Heidi Grant, "*Why Diverse Teams are Smarter*", Harvard Business Review, Nov 2016.

10. Ibid.

11. Lorenzo, Yoigt, Schetelig, Zawadzki, Welpe, Brosi, "The Mix that Matters: Innovation Through Diversity", Boston Consulting Group, April 2017.

Multicultural Teams

12. Brett, Behfar, Kern, "*Managing Multicultural Teams*", Harvard Business Review, 2007.

13. Li and Liao, "*Cultural Competence: Why it Matters and How You Can Acquire It*", IESE Insight, 2015.

14. Earley and Mosakowski, "*Cultural Intelligence*", Harvard Business Review article 2004.

The Process of Managerial Communication

1. C. Shannon and W. Weaver, *The Mathematical Theory of Communication*, University of Illinois Press, 1948.

2. R. E. Quinn, S. R. Faerman, M. P. Thompson, M.R. McGrath, and D. S. Bright, *Becoming a Master Manager*, Sixth edition, Wiley, 2015, Page 48.

Types of Communications in Organizations

3. F. M. Jablin and Linda L. Putnam, *The New Handbook of Organizational Communication*, Sage, 2005.

4. D. L. Worthington and G. D. Bodie, *The Sourcebook of Listening Research: Methodology and Measures*, Wiley, 2018.

Factors Affecting Communications and the Roles of Managers

5. Mintzberg, H. (1973). *The Nature of Managerial Work*. New York: Harper & Row, p. 31.

6. Ibid, p. 166-167.

7. Ibid, p. 167.

8. McGregor, J. (2008). "Bezos: How Frugality Drives Innovation," *BusinessWeek*, April 28, 2008, pp. 64–66.

9. Mintzberg, H. (1990). “The Manager’s Job: Folklore and Fact.” *Harvard Business Review*, March–April 1990, pp. 166–167.

10. Ibid.

11. Ibid

12. H. Mintzberg, *Mintzberg on Management: Inside our Strange World of Organizations*, Free Press, 2007.

13. Mintzberg, H. (1990). “The Manager’s Job: Folklore and Fact.” *Harvard Business Review*, March–April 1990, pp. 166–167.

Managerial Communication and Corporate Reputation

14. Drucker, P. F. (1954). *The Practice of Management*. New York: Harper & Row.

15. Eccles, R. G. & Noria, N. (1992). *Beyond the Hype: Rediscovering the Essence of Management*. Boston: The Harvard Business School Press, p. 205.

16. Ibid, p. 211.

17. Ibid, p. 209.

The Major Channels of Management Communication Are Talking, Listening, Reading, and Writing

18. Ziegler, B. (1994). “Video Conference Calls Change Business,” *Wall Street Journal*, October 13, 1994, pp. B1, B12.

19. Rankin, P. T. (1952). *The Measurement of the Ability to Understand Spoken Language.* (unpublished Ph.D. dissertation, University of Michigan, 1926). Dissertation Abstracts 12, No. 6 (1952), pp. 847–848; Nichols, R. G. & Stevens, L. (1957). *Are You Listening?* New York: McGraw-Hill; and Wolvin, A. D. & Coakley, C. G. (1982). *Listening*. Dubuque, IA: Wm. C. Brown and Co.; and Werner, E. K. (1975). *A Study of Communication Time.* (M.S. thesis, University of Maryland, College Park)

20. Kotter, J. P. (1999). “What Effective General Managers Really Do,” *Harvard Business Review*, March–April 1999, pp. 145–159

21. Berger, P. L. & Luckmann, T. (1966). *The Social Construction of Reality*. New York: Doubleday; and Searle, J. R. (1967). *The Construction of Social Reality*. New York: The Free Press, 1995.

22. Larkin, T. J. & Larkin, S. (1994). *Communicating Change: Winning Employee Support for New Business Goals*. New York: McGraw-Hill.

23. Ibid.

Introduction

1. Louise Axon, Elisa Friedman, and Kathy Jordan. 2015 (July). Leading Now: Critical Capabilities for a Complex World. *Harvard Business Publishing,* (Accessed July 25, 2017) http://www.harvardbusiness.org/leading-now-critical-capabilities-complex-world.

2. K. Labich. 1988 (Oct. 24). The seven keys to business leadership. *Fortune,* 58.

3. W. Bennis. 1989. *Why leaders can’t lead.* San Francisco: Jossey-Bass.

The Nature of Leadership

4. B.M. Bass. 1990. *Bass & Stogdill’s handbook of leadership: Theory, research, and managerial applications.* New York: The Free Press.

5. W. Bennis. 1989. *Why leaders can’t lead.* San Francisco: Jossey-Bass; W. Bennis, & B. Nanus. 1985. *Leaders: The strategies for taking charge.* New York: Harper & Row.

6. T.B. Pickens, Jr. 1992 (Fall/Winter). Pickens on leadership. *Hyatt Magazine,* 21.

7. E.P. Hollander & J.W. Julian. 1969. Contemporary trends in the analysis of leadership process. *Psychological Bulletin* 7(5): 387–397.

8. E.P. Hollander. 1964. Emergent leadership and social influence. In E.P. Hollander (ed.), *Leaders, groups, & influence.* New York: Oxford University Press.

9. F.E. Fiedler. 1996. Research on leadership selection and training: One view of the future. *Administrative*

Science Quarterly 41:241–250.

The Leadership Process

10. Hollander & Julian, 1969.

11. R.M. Stogdill. 1948. Personal factors associated with leadership: A survey of the literature. *Journal of Psychology* 28: 35–71.

12. A.J. Murphy. 1941. A study of the leadership process. *American Sociological Review* 6:674–687.

13. Hollander, 1964.

14. R.J. House & T.R. Mitchell. 1974 (Autumn). Path-goal theory of leadership. *Journal of Contemporary Business* 81–97.

15. G. Yukl. 1971. Toward a behavioral theory of leadership. *Organizational Behavior and Human Performance* 6:414–440.

16. D.G. Gardner & J.L. Pierce. 1998. Self-esteem and self-efficacy within the organizational context. *Group & Organization Management* 23(1):48–70.

17. P. Hersey & K.H. Blanchard. 1988. *Management of organizational behavior utilizing human resources.* Englewood Cliffs, NJ: Prentice-Hall.

18. C.N. Greene. 1975. The reciprocal nature of influence between leader and subordinate. *Journal of Applied Psychology* 60: 187–193.

19. Hollander & Julian, 1969.

20. B.B. Graen & M. Wakabayashi. 1994. Cross-cultural leadership-making: Bridging American and Japanese diversity for team advantage. In M. D. Dunnette (ed.), *Handbook of industrial and organizational psychology,* 4 (2nd ed.): 415–446. Palo Alto: Consulting Psychologists Press.

21. C.A. Schriesheim, S.L. Castro, & F.J. Yammarino. 2000. Investigating contingencies: An examination of the impact of span of supervision and upward controlling on leader-member exchange using traditional and multivariate within- and between-entities analysis. *Journal of Applied Psychology* 85:659–677; A.S. Phillips & A.G. Bedeian. 1994. Leader-follower exchange quality: The role of personality and interpersonal attributes. *Academy of Management Journal* 37:990–1001.

Leader Emergence

22. J.A. Conger. 1993. The brave new world of leadership training. *Organizational Dynamics* 21(3):46–59.

23. Pickens, 1992, 21.

24. G.R. Salancik & J. Pfeffer. 1977 (Winter). Who gets power and how they hold on to it: A strategic contingency model of power. *Organizational Dynamics,* 3–21.

25. A.J. Murphy. 1941. A study of the leadership process. *American Sociological Review* 6:674–687.

26. L. Smircich & G. Morgan. 1982. Leadership: The management of meaning. *Journal of Applied Behavioral Science* 18(3): 257–273; Stogdill, 1948.

27. Hollander, 1964.

28. J. R. P. French, Jr. & B. Raven. 1959. The bases of social power. In D. Cartwright (ed.), *Studies in social power.* Ann Arbor, MI: Institute for Social Research, University of Michigan, 150- 167.

29. A. Etzioni. 1961. *A comparative analysis of complex organizations, on power, involvement, and their correlates.* New York: Free Press of Glenco; H. C. Kelman. 1958. Compliance, identification, and internalization: Three processes of attitude change. *Journal of Conflict Resolution*, 51–61.

30. G. Yukl & J. B. Tracey. 1992. Consequences of influence tactics used with subordinates, peers, and the boss. *Journal of Applied Psychology* 77:525–535; T.R. Hinkin & CA. Schriesheim. 1990. Relationships between subordinate perceptions of supervisor influence tactics and attributed bases of supervisory power. *Human Relations* 43:221–237; P.M. Podsakoff & C.A. Schriesheim. 1985. Field studies of French and Raven's bases of power: Critique, reanalysis, and suggestions for future research. *Psychological Bulletin* 97:398–411.

31. T.R. Hinkin & C.A. Schriesheim. 1990. Relationships between subordinate perceptions of supervisor

influence tactics and attributed based of supervisory power. *Human Relations* 43:221–237.
32. Bennis, 1989.
33. L. Smircich & G. Morgan. 1982. Leadership: The management of meaning. *Journal of Applied Behavioral Sciences* 18(3): 257–273.
34. R. Tannenbaum & W.H. Schmidt. 1958 (Mar.–Apr.). How to choose a leadership pattern. *Harvard Business Review,* 95–101; R. Tannenbaum & W.H. Schmidt. 1973 (May–June). How to choose a leadership pattern. *Harvard Business Review,* 162–175.
35. K. Davis & J.W. Newstrom. 1985. *Human behavior at work: Organization behavior.* New York: McGraw-Hill.
36. D. McGregor. 1957. The human side of enterprise, *Management Review* 46:22–28, 88–92; D. McGregor. 1960. *The human side of enterprise.* New York: McGraw-Hill.
37. M. Haire, E.E. Ghiselli, & L.W. Porter. 1966. *Managerial thinking: An international study.* New York: Wiley.
38. R.E. Miles. 1975. *Theories of management: Implications for organizational behavior and development.* New York: McGraw-Hill.
39. J.P. Muczyk & B.C. Reimann. 1987. The case for directive leadership. *The Academy of Management Executive* 1:301–311.
40. W. A. Pasmore. 1988. *Designing effective organizations: The sociotechnical systems perspective.* New York: Wiley; T. J. Peters & R.H. Waterman, Jr. 1982. *In search of excellence: Lessons from America's best-run companies.* New York: Harper & Row.

The Trait Approach to Leadership

41. F. A. Kramer. 1992 (Summer). Perspectives on leadership from Homer's Odyssey. *Business and the Contemporary World* 168–173.
42. K. Labich. 1988 (Oct. 24). The seven keys to business leadership. *Fortune,* 58.
43. Stogdill, 1948; R. M. Stogdill. 1974. *Handbook of leadership: A survey of theory and research.* New York: Free Press.
44. Ibid., 81. See also Stogdill, 1948.
45. S.A. Kirkpatrick & E.A. Locke. 1991. Leadership: Do traits matter? *The Executive* 5(2):48–60. E.A. Locke, S. Kirkpatrick, J.K. Wheeler, J. Schneider, K. Niles, H. Goldstein, K. Welsh, & D.-O. Chad. 1991. *The essence of leadership: The four keys to leading successfully.* New York: Lexington.
46. Kirkpatrick & Locke. 1991. The best managers: What it takes. 2000 (Jan. 10). *Business Week,* 158.
47. Locke et al., 1991; T.A. Stewart. 1999 (Oct. 11). Have you got what it takes? *Fortune* 140(7):318–322.
48. W. Mischel. 1973. Toward a cognitive social learning reconceptualization of personality. *Psychological Review* 80:252– 283.
49. R.J. House & R.N. Aditya. 1997. The social scientific study of leadership: Quo vadis? *Journal of Management* 23:409– 473; T.J. Bouchard, Jr., D.T. Lykken, M. McGue, N.L. Segal, & A. Tellegen. 1990. Sources of human psychological differences: The Minnesota study of twins reared apart. *Science* 250:223–228.
50. S. Helgesen. 1990. *The female advantage.* New York: Doubleday/Currency; J. Fierman. 1990 (Dec. 17). Do women manage differently? *Fortune* 122:115–120; J.B. Rosener. 1990 (Nov.–Dec.). Ways women lead. *Harvard Business Review* 68(6): 119–125.
51. J.B. Chapman. 1975. Comparison of male and female leadership styles. *Academy of Management Journal* 18:645–650; E.A. Fagenson 1990. Perceived masculine and feminine attributes examined as a function of individual's sex and level in the organizational power hierarchy: A test of four theoretical perspectives. *Journal of Applied Psychology* 75:204–211.
52. R.L. Kent & S.E. Moss. 1994. Effects of sex and gender role on leader emergence. *Academy of Management Journal* 37: 1335–1346.
53. Ibid.
54. A.H. Early & B.T. Johnson. 1990. Gender and leadership style: A meta-analysis. *Psychological Bulletin*

108:233–256.
55. G.H. Dobbins, W.S. Long, E. Dedrick, & T.C. Clemons. 1990. The role of self-monitoring and gender on leader emergence: A laboratory and field study. *Journal of Management* 16:609–618.
56. B.M. Staw & S.G. Barsade. 1993. Affect and managerial performance: A test of the sadder-but-wiser vs happier-and-smarter hypothesis. *Administrative Science Quarterly* 38:304–331.
57. J.M. George & K. Bellenhausen. 1990. Understanding prosocial behavior, sales performance, and turnover: A group-level analysis in a service context. *Journal of Applied Psychology* 75:698–709.
58. Dobbins et al., 1990.

Behavioral Approaches to Leadership

59. K. Labich, 1988, 58–66.
60. C. Williams. 2017 (June 23). Leadership: Coaching has a Role to Play in Business. *Central Penn Business Journal*. http://www.cpbj.com/article/20170623/CPBJ01/170629935/leadership-coaching-has-role-to-play-in-business
61. J. Anthony. 2017. *This Much We Know.* (Accessed August 4, 2017). https://thismuchweknow.net/2016/09/21/10-ideas-and-concepts-that-describe-me-really-well/
62. E.A. Fleishman. 1953. The description of supervisory behavior. *Personnel Psychology* 37:1–6; E.A. Fleishman & E.F. Harris. 1962. Patterns of leadership behavior related to employee grievances and turnover. *Personnel Psychology* 15:43–56; A. W. Halpin & B. J. Winer. 1957. A factorial study of the leader behavior descriptions. In R.M. Stogdill & A.C. Coons (eds.), *Leader behavior: Its description and measurement.* Columbus: Bureau of Business Research, Ohio State University; J.K. Hemphill & A.E. Coons. 1975. Development of the leader behavior description questionnaire. In R. M. Stogdill & A. E. Coons (eds.), *Leader behavior*; S. Kerr & C. Schriesheim. 1974. Consideration, initiating structure, and organizational criteria—an update of Korman's 1966 review. *Personnel Psychology* 27:555–568.
63. D. Katz & R.L. Kahn. 1952. Some recent findings in human relations research. In E. Swanson, T. Newcomb, & E. Hartley (eds.), *Readings in social psychology,* New York: Holt, Rinehart, & Winston; D. Katz, N. Macoby, & N. Morse. 1950. *Productivity, supervision, and morale in an office situation,* Ann Arbor, MI: Institute for Social Research; F.C. Mann & J. Dent. 1954. The supervisor: Member of two organizational families. *Harvard Business Review* 32:103–112.
64. D. G. Bowers & S. C. Seashore. 1966. Pretesting organizational effectiveness with a four-factor theory of leadership. *Administrative Science Quarterly* 11:238–262; Yukl, 1971; D.A. Nadler, G.D. Jenkins, Jr., C. Cammonn, and E.E. Lawler, III. 1975. *The Michigan organizational assessment package progress report.* Ann Arbor: Institute for Social Research, University of Michigan.
65. Bowers & Seashore, 1966.
66. R.R. Blake & J.S. Mouton. 1964. *The managerial grid.* Houston: Gulf; R.R. Blake & J.S. Mouton. 1981. *The versatile manager: A grid profile,* Homewood, IL: Dow Jones-Irwin; R.R. Blake & J.S. Mouton. 1984. *The new managerial grid III.* Houston: Gulf.
67. R.R. Blake & J.S. Mouton. 1981. Management by grid® principles or situationalism: Which? *Group and Organization Studies* 6:439–455.
68. L. L. Larson, J. G. Hunt, & R. N. Osborn. 1976. The great hi-hi leader behavior myth: A lesson from Occam's razor. *Academy of Management Journal* 19:628–641.
69. D. Tjosvold. 1984. Effects of warmth and directiveness on subordinate performance on a subsequent task. *Journal of Applied Psychology* 69:422–427; A.W. Halpin. 1957. The leader behavior and effectiveness of aircraft commanders. In R.M. Stogdill & A. E. Coons (eds.). *Leader Behavior: Its description and measurement.* Columbus, OH: The Ohio State University, Bureau of Business Research.; E.A. Fleishman & J. Simmons. 1970. Relationship between leadership patterns and effectiveness ratings among Israeli foremen. *Personnel Psychology* 23:169–172.

Situational (Contingency) Approaches to Leadership

70. Stogdill, 1948, 63.

71. House & Aditya, 1997.

72. F.E. Fiedler & M.M. Chemers. 1974. *Leadership and effective management.* Glenview, IL: Scott, Foresman.

73. F.E. Fiedler. 1976. The leadership game: Matching the men to the situation. *Organizational Dynamics,* 4, 9.

74. Personal conversation between Robert J. House and Fred Fiedler in September 1996, as reported in House & Aditya, 1997.

75. F.E. Fiedler. Sept.–Oct. 1965. Engineering the job to fit the manager. *Harvard Business Review,* 115–122.

76. See, for example, the supporting results of M.M. Chemers & G.J. Skrzypek. 1972. Experimental test of the contingency model of leadership effectiveness. *Journal of Personality and Social Psychology* 24:172–177; and the contradictory results of R.P. Vecchio. 1977. An empirical examination of the validity of Fiedler's model of leadership effectiveness. *Organizational Behavior and Human Performance* 19:180–206.

77. R.B. Dunham. 1984. [Interview with Fred E. Fiedler.] *Organizational behavior: People and processes in management.* Homewood, IL: Irwin, 368; J. L. Kennedy, Jr. 1982. Middle LPC leaders and the contingency model of leadership effectiveness. *Organizational Behavior and Human Performance* 30:1–14.

78. Chemens & Skrzpek, 1972; Vecchio, 1977.

79. House & Aditya. 1997; L.H. Peters, D.D. Hartke, & J.T. Pohlman. 1985. Fiedler's contingency model of leadership: An application of the meta-analysis procedure of Schmidt and Hunter. *Psychological Bulletin* 97:274–285.

80. R.J. House. 1971. A path goal theory of leader effectiveness. *Administrative Science Quarterly* 16:324.

81. R. Hoojiberg. 1996. A multidimensional approach toward leadership: An extension of the concept of behavioral complexity. *Human Relations* 49(7):917–946.

82. R.J. House & T.R. Mitchell. 1974 (Autumn). Path-goal theory of leadership, *Journal of Contemporary Business,* 86; R.J. House & G. Dessler. 1974. The path-goal theory of leadership: Some post hoc and a priori tests. In J. Hunt & L. Larson (eds.). *Contingency approaches to leadership.* Carbondale, IL: Southern Illinois University Press.

83. House & Mitchell, 1974; House & Dessler, 1974; R.T. Keller. 1989. A test of the path-goal theory of leadership with need for clarity as a moderator in research and development organizations. *Journal of Applied Psychology* 74:208–212.

84. G. Bristol. 2016. Why Diversity in the Workplace is Imperrative. *Entrepreneur,* March 25. (Accessed august 4, 2017) https://www.entrepreneur.com/article/270110

85. J.R. Meindl, S.B. Ehrlich, & J.M. Dukerich. 1985. The romance of leadership. *Administrative Science Quarterly* 30:78–102.

86. C. Robert, T. M. Probst, J. J. Martocchion, F. Drasgow, & J. J. Lawler. 2000. Empowerment and continuous improvement in the United States, Mexico, Poland, and India: Predicting fit on the basis of the dimensions of power distance and individualism. *Journal of Applied Psychology* 85:643–658.

87. P.W. Dorfman & S. Roonen. 1991. *The universality of leadership theories: Challenges and paradoxes.* Paper presented at the Academy of Management Meetings, Miami.

88. P.W. Dorfman, J.P. Howell, S. Hiblino, J.K. Lee, U. Tate, & A. Bautista. 1997. Leadership in Western and Asian countries: Commonalities and differences in effective leadership processes across cultures. *Leadership Quarterly* 8(3):233–274.

Substitutes for and Neutralizers of Leadership

89. P.M. Podsakoff, B.P. Niehoff, S.B. MacKenzie, & M.L. Williams. 1993. Do substitutes for leadership really substitute for leadership: An empirical examination of Kerr and Jermier's situational leadership model. *Organizational Behavior and Human Decision Processes* 54:1–44; S. Kerr. 1977. Substitutes for leadership: Some implications for organizational design. *Organization and Administrative Sciences* 8:135–146; S. Kerr & J.M.

Jermier. 1978. Substitutes for leadership: Their meaning and measurement. *Organizational Behavior and Human Performance* 22:375– 403; J. P. Howell & P. W. Dorfman. 1981. Substitutes for leadership: Test of a construct. *Academy of Management Journal* 24:714– 728; J.L. Pierce, R.B. Dunham, & L.L. Cummings. 1984. Sources of environmental structuring and participant responses. *Organizational Behavior and Human Performance* 33:214–242.

90. D.G. Gardner, R.B. Dunham, L.L. Cummings, & J.L. Pierce. 1989. Focus of attention at work: Construct definition and empirical validation. *Journal of Occupational Psychology* 62:61–77.

91. D.G. Gardner, R.B. Dunham, L.L. Cummings, & J.L. Pierce. 1987. Focus of attention at work and leader-follower relationships. *Journal of Occupational Behaviour* 8:277–294.

Transformational, Visionary, and Charismatic Leadership

92. G.A. Yukl. 1981. *Leadership in organizations.* Englewood Cliffs, NJ: Prentice-Hall.

93. B. Kellerman. 1984. *Leadership: Multidisciplinary perspectives.* Englewood Cliffs, NJ: Prentice-Hall; F. L. Landy. 1985. *Psychology of work behavior.* Homewood, IL: Dorsey Press.

94. J.M. Burns. 1978. *Leadership.* New York: Harper & Row; B. M. Bass. 1985. *Leadership and performance beyond expectations.* New York: Free Press.

95. R.L. Daft. 2018. *The Leadership Experience* 7th edition. Mason, OH: Cengage Learning.

96. J. R. Baum, E. A. Locke, & S. A. Kirkpatrick. 1998. A longitudinal study of the relation of vision and vision communication to venture growth in entrepreneurial firms. *Journal of Applied Psychology* 83:43–54; J.M. Howell & P.J. Frost. 1989. A laboratory study of charismatic leadership. *Organizational Behavior and Human Decision Processes* 43:243–269.

97. Bennis, 1989.

98. T. A. Judge & J.E. Bono. 2000. Five-factor model of personality and transformational leadership. *Journal of Applied Psychology* 85:751–765.

99. R. Pillai, C.A. Schriesheim, & E.S. Williams. 1999. Fairness perceptions and trust as mediators for transformational and transactional leadership: A two-sample study. *Journal of Management* 25:897–933.

100. C.C. Manz & H.P. Sims, Jr. 1987. Leading workers to lead themselves: The external leadership of self-managed work teams. *Administrative Science Quarterly* 32:106–129.

101. Pillai, Schriesheim, & Williams, 1999.

102. Ibid., 901.

103. S.N. Eisenstadt. 1968. *Max Weber: On charisma and institution building.* Chicago: University of Chicago Press, 46.

104. J.A. Conger & R.N. Kanungo. 1987. Toward a behavioral theory of charismatic leadership in organizational settings. *Academy of Management Review* 12:637–647; Howell & Frost, 1989.

105. R.J. House & M.L. Baetz. 1979. Leadership: Some empirical generalizations and new research directions. *Research in Organizational Behavior* 1:341–423; Conger and Kanungo, 1987.

106. Howell & Frost, 1989.

107. R. J. House. 1977. A 1976 theory of charismatic leadership. In J. G. Hunt & L. L. Larson (eds.). *Leadership: The cutting edge.* Carbondale, IL: Southern Illinois University Press.

108. A. R. Willner. 1984. *The spellbinders: Charismatic political leadership.* New Haven, CT: Yale University Press.

Leadership Needs in the 21st Century

109. Conger, 1993.

110. Ibid.

111. House & Aditya, 1997.

Power in Interpersonal Relations

1. Cited in A. Henderson and T. Parsons, *Max Weber: The Theory of Social and Economic Organization.* (New York:

The Free Press, 1947), p. 152.

2. R. Emerson, "Power Dependence Relations," *American Sociological Review,* 1962, *27*, p. 32.

3. H. Mintzberg, *Power in and Around Organizations* (Englewood Cliffs, N.J.: Prentice Hall, 1983); R. J. House, "Power and Personality in Complex Organizations," in B. M. Staw and L. L. Cummings, eds., *Research in Organizational Behavior* (Greenwich, Conn.: JAI Press, 1988), pp. 307–357.

4. A. Grimes, "Authority, Power, Influence, and Social Control: A Theoretical Synthesis," *Academy of Management Review,* October 1978, p. 726.

5. A. Etzioni, *Modern Organizations* (Englewood Cliffs, N.J.: Prentice-Hall, 1964).

6. J. French and B. Raven, "The Bases of Social Power," in D. Cartwright and A. Zander, eds., *Group Dynamics* (New York: Harper & Row, 1968); P. Podsakoff and C. Schriesheim, "Field Studies of French and Raven's Bases of Power: Critique, Reanalysis, and Suggestions for Future Research," *Psychological Bulletin,* May 1985, pp. 376–398.

7. D. Tjosvold, "Power and Social Context in the Superior-Subordinate Interaction," *Organizational Behavior and Human Decision Processes,* June 1985, pp. 281–293.

8. Y. Shetty, "Managerial Power and Organizational Effectiveness: A Contingency Analysis," *Journal of Management Studies,* 1978, *15*, pp. 178–181.

9. D. Kipnis, *The Powerholders* (Chicago: University of Chicago Press, 1976), p. 77.

10. Ibid.

11. T. R. Mitchell and J. Larson, *People in Organizations* (New York: McGraw-Hill, 1988).

Uses of Power

12. J. Pfeffer, *Power: Why Some People Have it and Others Don't* (New York: Harper Business, 2011).

13. Ibid., p. 370.

14. R. Kanter, *On the Frontiers of Management,* (Boston: Harvard Business Review Books) 2004.

Political Behavior in Organizations

15. H. D. Lasswell, *Politics: Who Gets What, When, How* (New York: McGraw-Hill, 1936).

16. Pfeffer, op. cit., p. 8.

17. Ibid.

18. J. Gandz and V. Murray, "The Experience of Workplace Politics," *Academy of Management Journal,* 1980, *23*, pp. 237–251.

19. R. Miles, *Macro Organizational Behavior* (Glenview, III.: Scott, Foresman, 1980); C. Leana, "Power Relinquishment versus Power Sharing: Theoretical Clarification and Empirical Comparison of Delegation and Participation," *Journal of Applied Psychology,* 1987, *72*, pp. 228–233.

20. D. Madison, R. Allen, L. Porter, P. Renwick, and B. Mays, "Organizational Politics: An Exploration of Manager's Perceptions," *Human Relations,* February 1980, pp. 79–100.

21. J. Pfeffer and G. Salancik, *The External Control of Organizations* (New York: Harper & Row, 1978).

22. Ibid., p. 470.

23. Ibid.

24. Miles, op. cit., p. 170.

25. Ibid., p. 169.

26. D. Hickson, C. Hinings, C. Lee, R. Schneck, and J. Pennings, "A Strategic Contingencies Theory of Intraorganizational Power," *Administrative Science Quarterly,* 1971, *14*, pp. 219–220.

27. Ibid., p. 227.

Limiting the Influence of Political Behavior

28. D. Beeman and T. Sharkey, "The Uses and Abuses of Corporate Politics," *Business Horizons,* March-April 1987, pp. 25–35.

Conflict in Organizations: Basic Considerations

1. K. Thomas and W. Schmidt, "A Survey of Managerial Interests with Respect to Conflict," *Academy of Management Journal,* 1976, pp. 315–318.

2. J. Graves, "Successful Management and Organizational Mugging," in J. Paap ed., *New Directions in Human Resource Management* (Englewood Cliffs, N.J.: Prentice-Hall, 1978); M. Rahim, "A Measure of Styles of Handling Interpersonal Conflict," *Academy of Management Journal,* 1983, pp. 368–376.

3. Cited in the *Register-Guard,* October 31, 1981, p. 23.

4. L. Coser, *The Functions of Social Conflict* (New York: Free Press, 1956). p. 154.

Causes of Conflict in Organizations

5. R. Miles, *Macro Organizational Behavior* (Glenview, Ill.: Scott, Foresman, 1980).

6. K. Thomas, "Conflict and Conflict Management," In M. D. Dunnette, ed., *Handbook of Industrial and Organizational Psychology* (Chicago: Rand McNally, 1976).

7. K. Thomas and L. Pondy, "Toward and Intent Model of Conflict Management Among Principal Parties," *Human Relations,* 1967, *30,* pp. 1089–1102.

Resolving Conflict in Organizations

8. Miles, op. cit.

Negotiation Behavior

9. J. Graham, "The Influence of Culture on Business Negotiations," *Journal of International Business Studies,* Spring 1985, pp. 81–96.

10. Ibid.

11. Ibid.; R. J. Lewicki, B. Barry, and D. M. Saunders, *Essentials of Negotiation*, (New York, N.Y., McGraw Hill, 2016), M. Baserman, "Why Negotiations Go Wrong," *Psychology Today,* June 1986, pp. 54–58; J. Graham and Y. Sano, Smart Bargaining (New York: Harper & Row, 1989).

12. E. Glenn, D. Witmeyer, and K. Stevenson, "Cultural Styles of Persuasion," *International Journal of Intercultural Relations,* Fall 1977, pp. 62–66.

13. Data supplied by John Graham, Graduate School of Management, University of California, Irvine. Cited in N. J. Adler and A. Gunderson, *International Dimensions of Organizational Behavior* 5th edition (Mason, OH: Cengage Learning, 2008), p. 167.

14. J. Graham, "The Influence of Culture on Business Negotiations," *Journal of International Business Studies,* Spring 1985, pp. 81–96.

15. Roger Fisher,William L. Ury and Bruce Patton, *Getting to Yes*, (New York: Penguin; 2012); Douglas D. Edwards, *De Dicto*, March 18, 2013, http://is.gd/ys8Hny.

Introduction

1. Panetta, Kasey, "Gartner Top 10 Strategic Technology Trends for 2018", *Gartner*, October 3, 2017. https://www.gartner.com/smarterwithgartner/gartner-top-10-strategic-technology-trends-for-2018/

2. Mearian, Lucas, "What is blockchain? The most disruptive technology in decades", *Computerworld*, May 31, 2018. https://www.computerworld.com/article/3191077/security/what-is-blockchain-the-most-disruptive-tech-in-decades.html; https://www.forbes.com/sites/theyec/2018/01/10/23-trends-that-will-shake-the-business-world-in-2018/#6b6c3524583f

3. Young Entrepreneurship Council, "23 Trends That Will Shake the Business World in 2018", *Forbes*, January 10, 2018. https://www.forbes.com/sites/theyec/2018/01/10/23-trends-that-will-shake-the-business-world-in-2018/#6b6c3524583f

The Organization's External Environment

4. This is a broad definition which has been used in different forms. The source here is "What is an External Environment in Business" Chapter 5, *study.com*, Accessed October 15, 2018. https://study.com/academy/

lesson/what-is-an-external-environment-in-business-definition-types-factors.html
5. Jamrisko, Michelle, "China's Economy to Overtake Euro Zone This Year", *Bloomberg*, March 6, 2018. https://www.bloomberg.com/news/articles/2018-03-06/china-s-economy-is-set-to-overtake-combined-euro-area-this-year
6. China Owns US Debt, but How Much? | *Investopedia*, April 6, 2018. https://www.investopedia.com/articles/investing/080615/china-owns-us-debt-how-much.asp#ixzz5DcHG4d7k
7. Rawlinson, Paul, "A prediction for globalization in 2018", *World Economic Forum*, January 22, 2018. https://www.weforum.org/agenda/2018/01/prediction-globalization-2018/
8. Bersin, Josh and Mazor, Art, "Culture Engagement and Beyond", *Deloitte Insights*, February 28, 2017. https://www2.deloitte.com/insights/us/en/focus/human-capital-trends/2017/improving-the-employee-experience-culture-engagement.html?id=us:2ps:3gl:confidence:eng:cons:::na:LIxmKVLK:1079836504:244787795449:b:RLSA_Human_Capital
9. Cilluffo, Anthony and Cohen, D'Vera, "10 demographic trends shaping the U. S. and the World in 2017", *Pew Research Center*, April 27, 2017. http://www.pewresearch.org/fact-tank/2017/04/27/10-demographic-trends-shaping-the-u-s-and-the-world-in-2017/
10. Graf, Nikki, Sexual Harassment at work in the Era of #MeToo", *Pew Research Center*, April 4, 2018. http://www.pewsocialtrends.org/2018/04/04/sexual-harassment-at-work-in-the-era-of-metoo/
11. The Global Risks Report 2018 13th Edition. (2018). *The World Economic Forum*, http://www3.weforum.org/docs/WEF_GRR18_Report.pdf, p. 6. Also see http://reports.weforum.org/global-risks-2018/global-risks-landscape-2018/
12. Fry, Richard, "It's becoming more common for young adults to live at home for longer stretches", *Pew Research Center*, May 5, 2017. http://www.pewresearch.org/fact-tank/2017/05/05/its-becoming-more-common-for-young-adults-to-live-at-home-and-for-longer-stretches/
13. DeSilver, Drew, "Women scarce at the top of U.S. business- and in the job that lead there", *Pew Research Center*, April 30, 2018. http://www.pewresearch.org/fact-tank/2018/04/30/women-scarce-at-top-of-u-s-business-and-in-the-jobs-that-lead-there/
14. Hunt, Vivian et al, "Delivering Through Diversity", *McKinsey*, January 2018. https://www.mckinsey.com/~/media/McKinsey/Business%20Functions/Organization/Our%20Insights/Delivering%20through%20diversity/Delivering-through-diversity_full-report.ashx
15. The Global Economic Report, 13th Edition, *World Economic Forum*, 2018. http://www3.weforum.org/docs/WEF_GRR18_Report.pdf
16. Rice, Doyle, "Thousands of low-lying islands may become 'uninhabitable' within decades as seas rise", *USA Today*, April 25, 2018. https://www.usatoday.com/story/news/world/2018/04/25/thousands-low-lying-islands-may-become-uninhabitable-within-decades-seas-rise/550659002/

External Environments and Industries

17. Felice De Toni, A. and G. De Zan. (2016), The complexity dilemma, Three tips for dealing with complexity in organizations, *Practitioner*, Dec. 31, https://journal.emergentpublications.com/article/the-complexity-dilemma/
18. Eisenhardt, K. M., & Sull, D. N. (2001). "Strategy as simple rules", *Harvard Business Review*, 79(1): 106-119
19. Ibid.

Organizational Designs and Structures

20. Bersin, Josh, et al, "2017 Global Human Capital trends", *Deloitte Insights*, February 28, 2017. https://www2.deloitte.com/insights/us/en/focus/human-capital-trends/2017/organization-of-the-future.html
21. Ibid.
22. Burns, T. & Stalker, G. M. (1961), The Management of Innovation, Tavistock, London; Mintzberg, H. 1979. The structuring of organizations. Englewood Cliffs, NJ: *Prentice-Hall*; Emery, Fred E. and Eric L. Trist, (1965), "The

Causal Texture of Organizational Environments", pp 21-32 in *Human Relations*, February 1965

23. Anand, N. and R. Daft. (2007). What is the Right Organization Design? *Organizational Dynamics*, Vol. 36, No. 4, pp. 329–344.

24. Ibid.

25. This section draws on a number of scholarly and practitioner sources, including the following: R. Daft. (2016). Organization Theory & Design, 12th ed. *Cengage Learning*, Boston, MA; https://blog.hubspot.com/marketing/team-structure-diagrams; Burton and Obel. (2018). *Journal of Organization Design* Vol. 7, Issue 5, Devaney, Erik, "7 types of organizational Structure & Whom They're Suited For [Diagrams], *Hubspot*, accessed November 18, 2018. https://doi.org/10.1186/s41469-018-0029-2; "Matrix Teams", *Global Integration*, accessed November 18, 2018. http://www.global-integration.com/glossary/matrix-teams/; and Bersin, josh, "The organization of the Future: Arriving Now', 2017 Global Human Capital Trends, *Deloitte Insights*, February 28, 2017. https://www2.deloitte.com/insights/us/en/focus/human-capital-trends/2017/organization-of-the-future.html

26. Brent Durbin. Matrix organization, *Encyclopedia Britannica*, https://www.britannica.com/topic/matrix-organization

27. "Matrix Teams", *Global Integration*, accessed November 18, 2018. http://www.global-integration.com/glossary/matrix-teams/

28. ibid.

29. G. Satell. (June 8, 2015). What Makes an Organization "Networked", *Harvard Business Review*, https://hbr.org/2015/06/what-makes-an-organization-networked

30. Satell, Greg, "The Story of Networks", *Digital Tonto*, September 26, 2010. https://www.digitaltonto.com/2010/the-story-of-networks/; and "Networked Organizations", *Global Integration*, accessed November 18, 2018. http://www.global-integration.com/glossary/matrix-teams/ http://www.global-integration.com/glossary/networked-organization/

31. J. Bersin, T. McDowell, A. Rahnema, and Yves Van Durme. (February 28, 2017), "The organization of the future: Arriving now, 2017" Global Human Capital Trends, *Deloitte*. https://www2.deloitte.com/insights/us/en/focus/human-capital-trends/2017/organization-of-the-future.html

32. Lister, Jonathan, "The Disadvantages of Network-based organizational Structure", *Chron*, accessed November 18, 2018. http://smallbusiness.chron.com/disadvantages-networkbased-organization-structure-35988.html

33. Sources in this section include the following: C. Handy. (May–June 1995). Trust and the Virtual Organization, *Harvard Business Review*, https://hbr.org/1995/05/trust-and-the-virtual-organization; M. Ahuja and K. Carley. (1999), Network Structure in Virtual Organizations, *Organization Science*, Volume 10, Issue 6, June, pp. 741 - 757; http://www.yourarticlelibrary.com/organization/what-is-virtual-organisation-definition-characteristics-and-types/35533

34. D. Onley. (Apr 29, 2015), *Environment*, https://www.shrm.org/ResourcesAndTools/hr-topics/technology/Pages/How-Telecommuting-Helps-the-Environment.aspx

35. I. McCarthy, T. Lawrence, B. Wixted, and B. Gordon. (2010). A Multidimensional Conceptualization of Environmental Velocity, *Academy of Management Review* 34, no. 4, pp. 604-626

The Internal Organization and External Environments

36. Katz, D. & Kahn R. L. (1966). The social psychology of organizations, *John Wiley*, New York, N.Y.

37. Bertalanffy, L. (1968). General System Theory, *George Braziller*, publisher, New York.

38. Adapted from Arie Y. Lewin and Carroll U. Stephens, "CEO Attributes as Determinants of Organization Design: An integrated Model," *Organization Studies* 15, no. 2 (1994): 183-212

39. J. Trevor and B. Varcoe. (2017). How Aligned Is Your Organization? Harvard Business Review, February, https://hbr.org/2017/02/how-aligned-is-your-organization

40. Dalavagas, Iason, "McDonald's Corp: A Short SWOT Analysis, *Value line*, May 11, 2015. http://www.valueline.com/Stocks/Highlights/McDonalds_Corp__A_Short_SWOT_Analysis.aspx#.WyqOj1VKiig
41. "Amazon accounts for 43% of US online retail sales" *Business Insider*, February 3, 2017. http://www.businessinsider.com/amazon-accounts-for-43-of-us-online-retail-sales-2017-2
42. Dudovskiy, John, "Amazon Organizational Structure", *Research Methodology*, August 1, 2018 https://research-methodology.net/amazon-organizational-structure-2/
43. Meyer, Pauline, "Amazon.com Inc.'s Organizational Structure Characteristics (An Analysis)", *Panmore Institute*, September 8, 2018 http://panmore.com/amazon-com-inc-organizational-structure-characteristics-analysis
44. Ibid.
45. Cohan, Peter, "3 Reasons Amazon Is the World's Best Business", *Forbes*, February 2, 2018. https://www.forbes.com/sites/petercohan/2018/02/02/3-reasons-amazon-is-the-worlds-best-business/#563e86e63565

Corporate Cultures

46. Hyken, Shep, "Drucker said Culture Eats Strategy for Breakfast", *Forbes*, December 5, 2015. https://www.forbes.com/sites/shephyken/2015/12/05/drucker-said-culture-eats-strategy-for-breakfast-and-enterprise-rent-a-car-proves-it/#7a7572822749
47. Ed Schein. (2010). Organizational Culture and Leadership, 4th ed., San Francisco, CA: *Jossey-Bass*; J.W. Weiss. (2014). An Introduction to Leadership, 2nd ed., Bridgepoint Education, Inc.C
48. This discussion of the CVF is based on these sources: K. Cameron, R. Quinn, J. Degraff, and A. Thakor, (2014). Competing Values Leadership, 2nd ed., *New Horizons in Management*, Northampton, MA; K. Cameron and R. Quinn (2006). Diagnosing and Changing Organizational Culture: Based on the Competing Values Framework, San Francisco, CA: *Jossey-Bass*; and https://www.ocai-online.com/blog/2016/09/Organizational-culture-Create-Collaborate-Control-Compete
49. T. Yu and N. Wu. (2009). "A Review of Study on the Competing Values Framework", *International Journal of Business Management*, Vol.4, No. 7, July, pp. 47-42.
50. Nocera, Joe, "Jeff Bezos and The Amazon way", *The New York Times*, August 21, 2015. https://www.nytimes.com/2015/08/22/opinion/joe-nocera-jeff-bezos-and-the-amazon-way.html
51. Farber, Madeline, "Amazon Employee Attempts Suicide After Sending Email to Colleagues", *Fortune*, November 29, 2016. http://fortune.com/2016/11/29/amazon-employee-suicide-attempt/

Organizing for Change in the 21st Century

52. The Global Economic Report, 13th Edition, *World Economic Forum*, 2018. http://www3.weforum.org/docs/WEF_GRR18_Report.pdf, p. 8 and pp. 54-57.
53. Agarwal, Dimple, "Introduction: The Rise of the Social Enterprise", *Deloitte Insights*, March 28, 2018.? https://www2.deloitte.com/insights/us/en/focus/human-capital-trends/2018/introduction.html
54. Ibid.
55. Ibid.

Organizational Structures and Design

1. For an in-depth exploration of the field of organizational development and change, see Cummings, Thomas G. and Worley, Christopher G., *Organization Development and Change*, 11th edition, Cengage Learning, 2019.
2. Katz, D. and Kahn, R. L., *The Social Psychology of Organizations*, 2nd edition, John Wiley and Sons, 1978; and Schein, Edgar, *Organizational Psychology*, 3rd edition, Prentice Hall, 1980.
3. Weber, Max, *From Max Weber: Essays in Sociology*, Oxford University Press, 1958.

Organizational Change

4. Brown, K. and Eisenhardt, M., "The Art of Continuous Change: Linking Complexity Theory and Time-Paced

Evolution in Relentlessly Shifting Organizations", *Administrative Science Quarterly*, 42, 1997, pp 1-34.
5. Kotter, J. and Schlesinger, L., "Choosing Strategies for Change", *Harvard Business Review*, 57, 1979, pp. 106-114.
6. Setter, Craig Joseph and The Council for Six Sigma Certification, *Six Sigma: A Complete Step-by-Step Guide*, The Council for Six Sigma Certification, 2018.
7. Eisenbach, R., Watson, K., and Pillai, R., "Transformational Leadership in the Context of Organizational Change", *Journal of Organizational Change Management*, 12, 1999, pp. 80-89.

Managing Change

8. Cummings, Thomas G. and Worley, Christopher G., *Organization Development and Change*, 11th edition, Cengage Learning, 2019.
9. Quinn, R. E. (2015). *The Positive Organization: Breaking Free from Conventional Cultures, Constraints, and Beliefs* (1 edition). Oakland: Berrett-Koehler Publishers.
10. Lewin, K., *Field Theory in Social Science*, Harper & Row, 1951; and Kotter, J., *Leading Change*, Harvard Business School Press, 2012.
11. Cooperrider, David L., *The Appreciative Inquiry Handbook: For Leaders of Change*, Berrett-Kohler, 2008.
12. Olson, Edwin E. and Eoyang, Glenda H., *Facilitating Organizational Change: Lessons from Complexity Science*, Pfeiffer, 2001.
13. Bright, D. S. (2009). Appreciative Inquiry and Positive Organizational Scholarship: A Philosophy of Practice for Turbulent Times. *OD Practitioner, 41*(3), 2–7.
14. Whitney, D., & Trosten-Bloom, A. (2010). *The Power of Appreciative Inquiry: A Practical Guide to Positive Change* (Second Edition). Berrett-Koehler Publishers.
15. Burnes, B. (2005). Complexity theories and organizational change. *International Journal of Management Reviews, 7*(2), 73–90.
16. Owen, H. (2008). *Open Space Technology: A User's Guide* (Third Edition). Berrett-Koehler Publishers.
17. Olson, E. E., & Eoyang, G. H. (2001). *Facilitating Organization Change: Lessons From Complexity Science* (1st ed.). Pfeiffer.
18. ibid.

An Introduction to Human Resource Management

1. Ulrich, Younger, Brockbank, Younger, HR From the Outside In, 2012. SHRM.org

Performance Management

2. "The Performance Management Revolution", Harvard Business Review, October 2016).
3. Buckingham and Goodall, "Reinventing Performance Management", Harvard Business Review, 2015.
4. Goler, Gale and Grant, "Let's Not Kill Performance Evaluations Yet", Harvard Business Review, Nov 2016.
5. Capelli and Tavis, "The Performance Management Revolution", Harvard Business Review, 2016, p. 9-11.

Influencing Employee Performance and Motivation

6. Stephen Miller, "Study: Pay for Performance Pays Off", Society for Human Resource Management, 2011.
7. 2015 World at Work "Compensation Programs and Practices Report"
8. Nohria, Groysberg, Lee, "Employee, Motivation: A Powerful New Model" Harvard Business Review, August 2008.

Building an Organization for the Future

9. Fernandez-Araoz, Groysberg, Nohria, "The Definitive Guide to Recruiting in Good Times and Bad", Harvard Business Review, 2009.
10. Ibid.

Talent Development and Succession Planning

11. Effron and Ort, One Page Talent Management, Harvard Business School Press, 2010.

Problems of Work Adjustment

1. S. Yolles, "Mental Health at Work," in A. McLean, ed., *To Work Is Human* (New York: Macmillan, 1967); R. Poe, "Does Your Job Make You Sick?" *Across the Board,* January 1987, pp. 34–43.

2. W. S. Neff, *Work and Human Behavior* (New York: Atherton, 1968), p. 208.

3. R. Ruddock, *Six Approaches to the Person* (London: Routledge and Kegan Paul, 1972), p. 94.

4. J. McGrath, "Stress and Behavior in Organizations," in M. D. Dunnette, ed., *Handbook of Industrial and Organizational Psychology* (Chicago: Rand McNally, 1976).

5. H. Selye, *The Stress of Life* (New York: McGraw-Hill, 1956).

6. W. C. Hamner and D. Organ, *Organizational Behavior* (Dallas: BPI, 1978), p. 202.

Organizational Influences on Stress

7. S. Terkel, *Working* (New York: Avon, 1972), p. 275.

8. Ibid., p. 348.

9. C. Cooper and R. Payne, *Stress at Work* (London: Wiley, 1978); K. Hall and L. Savery, "Tight Rein, More Stress," *Harvard Business Review,* January-February 1986, pp. 160–162, 164.

10. L. Krantz, *The Jobs Rated Almanac* (New York: Pharos Books, 1988).

11. Stress in the Workplace, *American Psychological Association*, March, 2011.

12. D. Zauderer and J. Fox, "Resiliency in the Face of Stress," *Management Solutions*, November 1987, pp. 32–33.

13. J. French and R. Caplan, "Organizational Stress and Individual Strain," in A. Marrow, ed., *The Failure of Success* (New York: Amacom, 1972), p. 48.

14. Ibid.

15. Ibid., p. 36.

16. Cooper and Payne, op. cit.

17. R. Kahn, D. Wolfe, R. Quinn, J. Snoek, and R. Rosenthal, *Organizational Stress: Studies in Role Conflict and Ambiguity* (New York: Wiley, 1964), pp. 70–71.

18. J. Quick and J. Quick, *Organizational Stress and Preventive Management* (New York: McGraw-Hill, 1984); R. Sutton and A. Rafaeli, "Characteristics of Work Stations as Potential Occupational Stressors," *Academy of Management Journal,* June 1987, pp. 260–276.

19. French and Caplan, op. cit.

20. Ibid.

21. Ibid.

22. G. Gardell, *Arbetsinnehall och Livskvalitet* (Stockholm: Prisma, 1976).

23. French and Caplan, op. cit., p. 51.

24. R. Schuler and S. Jackson, "Managing Stress Through P/HRM Practices," in K. Rowland and G. Ferris, eds., *Research in Personnel and Human Resource Management* (Greenwich, Conn.: JAI Press, 1986), pp. 183–224.

25. C. Carver and D. Glass, "Coronary Prone Behavior Pattern and Interpersonal Aggression," *Journal of Personality and Social Psychology,* 1978, pp. 361–366; M. Fusilier, D. Ganster, and B. Mayes, "The Social Support and Health Relationship: Is There a Gender Difference?" *Journal of Occupational Psychology,* June 1986, pp. 145–153.

26. M. Friedman and R. Rosenman, *Type A Behavior and your Heart* (New York: Knopf, 1974).

27. J. Howard, D. Cunningham, and P. Rechnitzer, "Health Patterns Associated with Type A Behavior: A Managerial Population," *Journal of Human Stress,* 1976, pp. 24–31.

28. Friedman and Rosenman, op. cit.

29. C. Jenkins, "Psychologic Disease and Social Prevention of Coronary Disease," *New England Journal of Medicine,* 1971, 284, pp. 244–255; T. Beehr and R. Bhagat, *Human Stress and Cognition in Organizations: An*

Integrated Perspective (New York: Wiley, 1985).

30. *Business Week*, October 17, 1977, p. 137.

31. Ibid.

32. T. H. Holmes and R. H. Rahe, "The Social Readjustment Rating Scale," *Journal of Psychosomatic Research,* August 1967, pp. 213–218. See also O. Behling and A. Darrow, "Managing Work-Related Stress," in J. Rosenzweig and F. Kast, eds., Modules in Management (Chicago: SRA, 1984).

Buffering Effects of Work related Stress

33. S. Cohen and T. Wills, "Stress, Social Support, and the Buffering Hypothesis," *Psychological Bulletin,* September 1985, pp. 310–357.

34. S. Kobasa, S. Maddi, and S. Kahn, "Hardiness and Health: A Prospective Study," *Journal of Personality and Social Psychology,* January 1982, pp. 168–177; J. Hull, R. VanTreuren, and S. Virnelli, "Hardiness and Health: A Critique and Alternative Approach," *Journal of Personality and social Psychology,* September 1987, pp. 518–530.

35. Cooper and Payne, op. cit.

36. D. Glass, "Stress, Competition, and Heart Attacks," *Psychology Today,* July 1976, pp. 55–57.

37. S. Cobb and S. Kasl, "Blood Pressure Changes in Men Undergoing Job Loss: A Preliminary Report," *Psychosomatic Medicine,* January-February 1970.

38. A. Slote, *Termination: The Closing of Baker Plant* (Ann Arbor: Institute for Social Research, University of Michigan, 1977).

39. A. Kornhauser, *Mental Health and the Industrial Worker* (New York: Wiley, 1965).

40. Ibid., p. 342.

41. D. Allen and P. Bryant, *Managing Employee Turnover: Dispelling Myths and Fostering Evidence-Based Retention Strategies*, (Chicago: Business Expert Press, 2013); W. Mobley, *Managing Employee Turnover* (Reading, Mass.: Addison-Wesley, 1982); S. Rhodes and R. Steers, *Managing Employee Absenteeism* (Reading, Mass.: Addison-Wesley, 1990).

42. U. S. Department of Health, Education, and Welfare, *Work in America,* 1973. p. 85.

43. T. Rosen, "Identification of Substance Abuse in the Workplace," *Public Personnel Management,* Fall 1987, pp. 197–207; S. Flax, "The Executive Addict," *Fortune,* June 24, 1985, pp. 24–31.

44. U. S. Department of Health, Education, and Welfare, op. cit.

45. S. Jackson, R. Schwab, and R. Schuler, "Toward an Understanding of the Burnout Phenomenon," *Journal of Applied Psychology*, November 1986, pp. 630–640.

46. B. Dumaine, "Cool Cures for Burnout," *Fortune,* June 20, 1988, pp. 78–84.

Coping with Work related Stress

47. Cited in *U. S. News & World Report,* March 13, 1978, p. 81.

48. C. Smith, "Labor: Working on a Change," Far *Eastern Economic Review,* April 14, 1988, pp. 62–63.

49. I. Sarason, J. Johnson, J. Berberich, and J. Siegel, *Helping Police Officers Cope with Stress: A Cognitive-Behavioral Approach,* Technical Report, University of Washington, February 1978.

50. R. M. Steers, "Individual Differences in Participative Decision Making," *Human Relations,* 1977, *30*, pp. 837–847.

51. M. Matteson and J. Ivancevich, "Health Promotion at Work," in C. Cooper and I. Robertson, eds., *International Review of Industrial and Organizational Psychology* (London: Wiley, pp. 279–306).

52. M. Roberts and T. Harris, "Wellness at Work," *Psychology Today,* May 1989, pp. 54–58.

53. D. L. Nelson; B. L. Simmons. P. L. Perrewé; D. C. Ganster, eds. *Eustress: An Elusive Construct an Engaging Pursuit,* 1st edition (Oxford, UK: Elsevier Jai., 2004); *and Lazarus, R. S. Psychological Stress and the Coping Process.* (New York: McGraw-Hill Book Co. 1966).

Overview of Entrepreneurship

1. Scott Shane, and Sankara Venkataraman, S. 2000. The promise of entrepreneurship as a field of research. Academy of Management Review, 25(1), 217-226.

2. Global Entrepreneurship Monitor. 2018. GEM 2017/2018 Global Report. https://gemconsortium.org/report/50012

Characteristics of Successful Entrepreneurs

3. Martha Irvine, "More 20-Somethings Are Blazing Own Paths in Business," San Diego Union-Tribune, November 22, 2004, p. C6.

4. Keith McFarland, "What Makes Them Tick," Inc. 500, October 19, 2005, http://www.inc.com.

5. Ibid.

Business Model Canvas

6. Alexander Osterwalder, Yves Pigneur, Alan Smith, and 470 practitioners from 45 countries. 2010. Business model generation. Wiley.

7. Lieberman, M.B. and Montgomery, D.B., 1988. First-mover advantages. Strategic Management Journal, 9(S1), pp.41-58.

New Venture Financing

8. Kickstarter. 2019. Kickstart stats. https://www.kickstarter.com/help/stats

9. Statista. 2019. Crowdfunding worldwide. https://www.statista.com/outlook/335/100/crowdfunding/worldwide#market-users

Optimal Support for Entrepreneurship

10. Adam Thierer, Permissionless Innovation, 109-10.

11. Steve Kreft, and Russell Sobel, "Public Policy, Entrepreneurship, and Economic Freedom," Cato Journal 25:3 (2005).

Index

R

S